Child Care and Early Education

Series List

Related books

Understanding Child Development Jennie Lindon

Working Together for Young Children Jennie Lindon and Lance Lindon

Caring for the Under-8s Jennie Lindon and Lance Lindon

Playwork: Play and Care for Children 5–15 Annie Davy

Can Do Play Activity Series Annie Davy (editor)

Familiar Things (Birth–3) Sally Thomas

Whatever the Weather (4–9) Jane Gallagher

Eco-Ventures (4–9) Kids' Club Network

Serious Fun: Games for 4–9s Dynamix

Cool Creations (10–14) Kids' Club Network

Sticks and Stones (10–14) Sharon Crockett

Serious Fun: Games for 10–14s Dynamix

Child Care and Early Education

Good practice to support young children and their familes

Jennie Lindon

THOMSON

Australia • Canada • Mexico • Singapore • Spain • United Kingdom • United States

THOMSON

Child Care and Early Years Education:
Good practice to support young children and their families

For more information, contact Thomson Learning, High Holborn House, 50–51 Bedford Row, London WC1R 4LR or visit us on the World Wide Web at:
http://www.thomsonlearning.co.uk

British Library Cataloguing-in-Publication Data
A catalogue record for this book is available from the British Library

---

ISBN 1-86152-722-5

Typeset by Saxon Graphics Ltd, Derby
Printed in Croatia by Zrinski

To Lance, Drew and Tanith – with my love and appreciation of the many ways in which you have all helped me

Contents

Acknowledgements

I very much appreciate all that I have learned over the years from early years practitioners in the different types of early years settings, out of school care and home based care by nannies and childminders. It would be a huge list if I tried to name everyone, so I will simply say a heartfelt thank you.

I am grateful to many people for their help as I checked on information for this book and for conversations in recent years on issues about early years practice and student support. Thank you especially to Jacqui Cousins (Early Years Consultant), Joyce Dale, Rose Drury and Prue Ruback (University of Hertfordshire), Annie Davy (Early Years Education Officer, Oxford), Judy Denziloe (Action for Leisure), Collette Drifte (Early Years/SEN Consultant), Peter Elfer (University of Surrey at Roehampton), Eva Lloyd (National Early Years Network), Marjorie Ouvry (Early Years Consultant), Penny Tassoni (Early Years Consultant), Pat Worcester and Julie McLaughlin (Soho Family Centre). Many thanks to my son Drew and daughter Tanith for their help as temporary assistants updating and organising my information resources.

I am grateful to the following people for helping me to make some sense of the variation between the different countries that comprise the UK. I take the usual responsibility for any outstanding mistakes. With many thanks to Natalie Branosky (Scottish Child Law Centre), Pat Davies (Head of the Early Childhood Unit, Children in Wales), Douglas Hamilton (Children in Scotland), Kevin Kelman (Deputy Head, Glasgow), Alice Sharp (Early Years Executive SINA) and several team members from NIPPA, Childcare Northern Ireland and Disability Action.

The photographs in this book were taken in the following settings:

Abacus Nursery, Balham Family Centre, Balham Nursery School, Bishops House Early Years Centre, Eveline Day Nursery Schools, New River Green Early Years Centre and Family Project, Newtec Day Nursery, Ravenstone Primary School, Rydevale Community Nursery, Saplings Nursery, St Mary's Pre-School, St Peter's Eaton Square CE Primary School Nursery Class, Staffordshire University Day Nursery and The Grove Nursery School.

I would like to thank all the children, staff and parents from these settings for their help and friendly cooperation. The photographs were taken either by myself or by Lance Lindon. Many thanks to Shailesh Patel for his care with our negatives and for doing the enlargements.

Introduction

Good practice in working with young children

In the last decade of the twentieth century, the early years field has experienced considerable change. There have been many new initiatives since childcare and early education finally became of central political interest. Yet the core of what is regarded as good practice with children and families has remained relatively stable.

Some level of change will always be part of good professional practice and it would be naïve to believe that early years practice is now fixed. Any profession, but especially one that shares the responsibility for our youngest citizens, should be willing to learn and to modify practice in the light of new information and ideas.

Using this book

Early years practitioners can potentially work in a range of different early years settings, in primary schools, out of school care and home based as a nanny or a childminder. Over your career you are likely to experience more than one type of work. This book will support you in any of these working situations and you will find a wealth of information, practical suggestions to apply and ideas to provoke your own thoughts.

Many readers of this book will be undertaking an early years qualification. Some readers will be at the very beginning of their career, whereas others will have gained experience in a job and are now gaining a qualification. The content of this book covers the main modules and units of the major early years qualifications but for flexibility is not locked into any single qualification. You can use Appendix 1 to identify the links to specific early years qualifications and to the Key Skills (Core Skills in Scotland).

You can use this book on your own to extend your own knowledge and examine your practice. But if you are studying for one of the early years qualifications, then your supervisor, college tutor or NVQ assessor will advise you on how to use the chapters of the book to support the current topics studied on your course. You will also find some advice in this book about building your portfolio (page 663), learning to use resources (page 664) and continued professional development (page 32).

Many of the activities, as well as the ideas within the book, will be that much more useful to you if you take opportunities to discuss the issues with your tutor, supervisor, colleagues and, where appropriate, with parents and other users of your service.

The features of this book have been developed to help readers to explore ideas and to support their application to your practice. You will find the following features in highlighted boxes close to the text to which they relate:

- **Activity:** a suggestion for something you can do to explore or apply an idea or find out useful information.

- **Activity (observation):** a suggestion for something to do that includes a brief for an observation.
- **To think about:** taking an idea further and suggesting ways you could consider and discuss it.
- **Scenario:** a description of practice in fictional settings, with questions to consider and relate to your own practice.
- **Tips for practice:** the practical application of what you would do as you apply an idea or suggestion in your days with children and families.
- **Progress check:** questions at the end of each chapter, for you to check your understanding of the content.

Many of these boxed features are cross referenced to some of the Key/Core Skills. Your tutor will help you in planning any work that would form evidence of your skills. It is possible for that work to be more or less challenging.

Terms used in the book

Different traditions within early years services have created a varied terminology applied to settings that serve children and their families. To avoid complicated 'either–or' sentences, I have used the following general words and phrases:

- **Colleagues** is used to mean the people with whom you work or study. An activity or think about box may suggest you discuss with your colleagues. This could be other practitioners who are part of the team where you work or fellow students on a full or part time course.
- **Early years practitioner**, or just practitioner, is used as a general term to cover any person who is working in an early years setting. If I wish to specify a particular qualification or experience background, I will make that clear.
- **Early years setting**, or just setting, is used for any of the different kinds of establishment that offer a service to young children and their families.
- **Manager** is used for the person who is in charge of the early years setting on a daily basis.
- The term **parent** is used to mean any adult who is taking parental responsibility for a child and forming a relationship with early years practitioners. So 'parent' effectively covers the phrase 'parent or other carer'. The term covers children's birth parents, foster or adoptive parents and other relatives or carers who are taking parental responsibility.

Practitioners, parents or children can, of course, be female or male. In order to avoid repetition of phrases like 'he or she', I have usually used the plural. Specific examples include male and female and it will be obvious in any section of the book when the sex of individuals is an important part of the discussion.

Use of scenarios

A range of early years settings and other services for children appear as examples throughout the book to illustrate points and to help you consider the practical application of ideas. In these scenarios, the places and people, both adults and children, are fictitious. However, I have developed the incidents and dilemmas from real experiences of early years practitioners, parents and children. So, however familiar a scenario may be, you cannot know this setting or people. But I will have encountered, and changed the details, of something very similar. Scenarios are provided from six different group settings, a childminding network and the working situation of two nannies. These are named:

- Sunningdale Day Nursery
- Greenholt Pre-school
- Dresden Road Nursery School
- The Dale Parent and Toddler drop-in group
- St Jude's Primary School, with the nursery class and after school club
- Baker Street Children and Family Centre
- Wessex childminding network
- Two nannies, Nancy and Kimberley

The aim of the scenarios is to give you material to work on, either on your own or in discussion with colleagues.

- Readers who are not currently in post will find it useful to consider and discuss some realistic issues and dilemmas linked with a particular kind of early years practice.
- The scenarios also provide an opportunity to think through practice in work settings of which you have limited or no experience as yet.
- The advantage of using scenarios is that you can also discuss practice in detail, without the sensitive complications that can arise when the real person is part of the discussion.
- However, the scenarios give you the scope then to apply a range of ideas to your own practice.

The dedicated website for this book is
www.thomsonlearning.co.uk/childcare/lindon

Using the website will give you access to further material linked to each chapter and suitable for students and college tutors. You will find:

- Additional ideas for a selection of scenarios, 'to think about' and 'tips for practice' boxes
- Pointers to help with the progress checks at the end of each chapter
- Further resources for some of the topics covered
- The websites given in the book by chapter, with direct links to the sites
- Updates on important issues of practice, changes in legislation or the qualification structure
- An opportunity to email your views, ideas and questions

1

The early years of childhood

After reading this chapter you should be able to:

- identify general features of the experience of childhood
- understand the broad areas of child development and theories about development
- describe the early childhood services in the UK
- explain the main features of the legal framework for such services
- understand key principles and values in working with children
- understand the positive framework of anti-discriminatory practice.

Introduction

Childhood is a time of change for children, their families and also for the early years practitioners who care for children. This chapter provides a broad framework of how children change over their first eight years and the range of explanations for that development. Young children live within a society that has organised a range of early years services for them and their families. You will find a description of the range of services, the legislation that mainly affects those settings in which you work and a summary of what are regarded as the most important values to underpin work with young children.

Links to early years qualifications

This chapter especially supports the following units:

Diploma in Child Care and Education: 4, 8, 9, 10 ,11

National Vocational Qualification in Early Years Care and Education

Level 2: CU10

Level 3: M6

BTEC National Early Years Diploma: 1, 4, 7, 12, 21

The experience of childhood

Around the world traditions vary as to how children should be raised. Even within an apparently single culture or social group, you will still find a great deal of diversity. Parents and other adults will not hold identical views about how to raise children, nor behave in the same way day by day. The experience of children varies considerably, both in terms of their daily experiences and the environment in which they live and learn. Despite the variety, there are some general themes that all children share and it is valuable for you to bear these in mind within your work as an early years practitioner.

Childhood is a time of change

It is inevitable that children themselves change as time passes. Even if the rest of a child's world remains fairly static, the child will change. Children grow physically and their abilities extend; this development in turn opens other possibilities for them. The consequence for adults is that you need to adjust as well. Even if you are responsible for a child for a relatively short period of time, there will still be change and, for the well being of the child, you will need to be flexible and sensitive to how the child's world has extended.

Children in their turn react, more or less positively, to changes in their social world. During the early years of childhood, young children are faced with a range of adjustments. Some changes will seem major to the children, even though the events are within normal family life, such as the arrival of a new baby or moving home. Some children deal with even more disruptive life changes, such as the breakdown of their family, the loss of a loved relative through death or a sudden move from one country to another as a refugee.

As childhood progresses, children in UK society have to deal sooner or later with becoming accustomed to non-family group settings such as nurseries. In contrast with the generations raised in the 1950s and 1960s, children of the late twentieth and early twenty-first century are most likely to experience some group setting before formal school.

Experiences affect children

What happens to children changes them one way or another; they learn from their experiences. Sometimes that learning will be wholly positive for their future development, sometimes it may be highly negative and often it will be some blend of the two. Learning from experience may be as simple as the realisation that it hurts when fingers get shut in a door or drawer. Other events may be more complex and it is unwise for adults, even with a great deal of experience, to become over-confident about predicting a child's reaction. For instance, some children are angry over the arrival of a new baby, some are happy and excited, others are perplexed.

Distressing events can create long-term emotional and psychological problems for children but much seems to depend on how a child is supported by people who are close. On balance children seem to be more seriously disturbed by continued stress than single events. Each experience gains meaning for children through how important adults in their lives explain, or fail to explain, what has happened.

Events like divorce are only a word until children can understand what it means for their life and relationships. What matters most is how adults behave towards children, including what they say. Children need to be helped to understand what is likely to happen as a consequence of any change in family life and to be reassured about the stability of their own daily life.

Adults responsible for children often seek a greater level of certainty than is realistic. It might seem attractive to be able to say this experience or event causes this consequence, or that this way of behaving towards children will ensure positive outcomes. But life does not work like that, as a limited amount of adult reflection will confirm. H. Rudolph Schaffer undertook a careful review of research studies on a range of significant life events for children and concluded that,

> care needs to be taken about making sweeping generalisations and advancing global solutions. 'It all depends' may be an annoying phrase and it does not make good headlines, but it accurately reflects reality.
> (Schaffer, *Making Decisions about Children*, Basil Blackwell, 1990: 235)

Children in twenty-first-century society

Successive generations of children within the same society may share many similar experiences and there is no basis for assuming that children themselves have changed. They still appreciate time, attention and affection from their parents and other key carers. Despite a bewildering array of commercially produced toys, twenty-first-century babies still want to play peep-bo with Mum or Dad or do crawling-chasing on the floor. This generation of children is equally happy with dressing-up clothes, cardboard boxes that become anything they want and with the music of saucepans and a wooden spoon.

Activity

Over about a month collect evidence of the different images of children in our society. You can look at, copy if possible and make notes on:

- advertisements that feature babies and children
- newspaper headlines and leading news stories
- the front covers of magazines in a newsagents
- leaflets that are freely available in health clinics, pharmacies or high street stores.

What are the main images or contrasting themes? Are children promoted as:

- young consumers, agents of 'pester power' to get parents to buy particular food, clothes or toys?
- couch potatoes with eyes stuck to a television or computer screen?
- brave little tots who have overcome illness or accident?
- a highly vulnerable group who have to be protected at all costs?
- a source of trouble, bad behaviour or disruption?

Consider the range that you have collected and share your ideas with colleagues. You could:

- write up your findings with images

- present your ideas to the group on the different images of a 'normal' child and of childhood in our current society
- contribute to a discussion with your colleagues to explore how your own images and assumptions may be shaped.

Key skills link: C2/3.1a–3, depending on the level of challenge introduced into this activity.

Children have not changed but the society in which the current young generation in the UK is growing up has changed.

- One highly visible shift is the significant level of everyday technology.
- Young children can become adept at handling television controls, videos and computers. The availability of such equipment, combined with increased adult concern about safety has raised a genuine problem about whether children get enough physical exercise.
- A strongly consumer society also raises the problems of financial pressure on children and their families and the fact that children themselves are increasingly targeted as direct consumers or indirectly through their ability to nag parents.
- The other significant change for many children in contrast with previous generations, especially now their grandparents, is that so many children attend some kind of early years setting before they go to primary school.
- Some families need childcare because one or both parents have paid work. But it has become very usual for two, three and four years olds to attend nursery, pre-school or playgroup for some sessions in each week as a form of pre-school experience.

Figure 1.1

Children nowadays still enjoy peep-bo!

Activity

Advice to parents and carers can change over time, even within the same cultural group. Children themselves have not changed, so one could reasonably ask what is happening. In some cases new research may overturn previous received wisdom, but not always.

Gather some examples of advice given over the last 30–40 years. You could gather this on your own or with colleagues by:

- Asking your own parents, if possible, whether they used any books to help raise you and are they still on the shelf?
- Look out for older books at jumble sales or second hand bookshops.
- Look through *Perfect parents*, a book written by social historian Christina Hardyment (1995 Oxford University Press). The book describes the conflicting advice given to UK parents over a couple of centuries and the fact that some views return in a circling manner.

Questions

1. What differences can you identify in what was or is considered normal for babies and young children in feeding, weaning or toilet training?
2. What about views on behaviour and how best to develop appropriate habits in children?
3. What could your findings warn you about current assumptions and the need to be ready to check and continue to learn as a responsible adult?
4. Write up and present to your colleagues.
5. Contribute to a discussion about patterns of advice. Do avoid any temptation to believe that anyone offering what reads like odd advice in the past was just wrongheaded, because the current generation of adults has finally found the correct way to raise children!

Key skills link: C2/3.1a–3, depending on the level of challenge introduced into this activity.

Changing families

Children need to be cared for in their early years and the usual way that this is managed world wide is that children are raised within their own family. There are, however, many variations in how families appear.

Who is in the family?

In twenty-first-century UK most children still live with two parents, although increasingly these may not both be the child's **birth parents** (the man and woman who conceived the child). Marriage is still popular, so often children's parents are married to each other but not always.

About 20 per cent of families in the UK are headed by one parent living with dependent children. **Lone parent** families are most often led by mothers but about 10 per cent of lone parents are fathers. Children in lone parent families may have regular contact with the other parent. But sometimes contact is intermittent or conflict between the parents makes a close relationship difficult.

Key terms

Birth parents
the biological mother and father of a child

Lone parents
mothers or fathers who are raising their children on their own

Key terms

Stepfamilies
families formed when one or both adults bring their children from a previous relationship into the new relationship. Stepparents will not be the biological parent of all the children in their family

Foster carers
people who take temporary responsibility for children when their own family is unable to care for them

Respite care
a service offering temporary care of children to families in order to give the parents a break from stressful childcare

Adoptive families
when one or two adults take legal responsibility for children whose own families cannot care for them and commit to raise the children

Looked after children
a description for the status of children and young people who have become the responsibility of the local authority because their own families cannot take care of them on a temporary or permanent basis. The local authority assumes parental responsibility

Stepfamilies are formed when adults set up home together with children from previous partnerships. Neither stepfamilies nor lone parent families are a new form of family life. However, in previous decades, especially earlier than the mid-twentieth century, they were likely to be formed as a result of widowhood. Divorce and women choosing to have babies without a permanent partner are now more common.

Although many children will continue to live with their two birth parents, many will experience changes in their family arrangements over the years of childhood. Children who experience their parents' separation will spend some time in a lone parent family or shared custody arrangements and may later become part of a stepfamily. If current trends continue, it is estimated that:

- more than a third of new marriages will end within 20 years and 4 out of 10 will end in divorce
- more than 1 in 4 children will experience the divorce of their parents by their 16th birthday
- 1 in 4 children will spend some time in a lone parent family (most likely with their mother)
- 1 in 8 children will spend some time in a stepfamily.

There are other possibilities for those children who are not raised within their birth family.

- Children who cannot be raised by their parents for some reason may spend time with **foster carers**, who take responsibility for the children within their own family home. Some foster care arrangements are relatively short but some last for years. Sometimes the plan is to prepare children for adoption. Foster parents are usually part of the family support services of local authorities. Private fostering arrangements made between birth parents and another carer remain legal in the UK, although there are moves to introduce regulation for the protection of children.
- Some children stay with a foster family for many years and form strong attachments, others may be with the family for only a short while.
- Some foster families offer **respite care**, a service for parents who need a break from their children for reasons of family stress, illness or the child's' severe disability. Respite care is also sometimes offered within residential units for children with disabilities.
- Some children are cared for through **adoption,** a legal process that means they are by law the responsibility of their adoptive parents. Many adoptive parents are not related to the children but in some cases a stepparent legally adopts the child of his or her partner.
- Some children whose families cannot take care of them become the responsibility of the local authority and are **looked after children**. The children or teenagers may be with foster parents or in a residential home for children.

Most parents are heterosexual but there is a growing, although small, group of families led by gay or lesbian parents. Some parents have children from heterosexual partnerships before they accepted their sexual orientation. Others are formed by a child from this partnership, through artificial insemination from an unknown donor or cooperative parenting between gay and lesbian friends. There are some gay or lesbian foster parents.

Tips for practice

Since family situations vary it can be useful to get into the habit of using non-specific terms to avoid making assumptions about family structure:

- it is straightforward to refer to 'your partner' rather than 'husband' or 'wife'.
- some children are mainly cared for by relatives other than the parents, so many early years settings use the phrase 'parents and carers' in written communication.

Extended families?

Increased mobility in many parts of our society has meant that many young people move away from where they were born and raise their own children at some distance from their extended family. Within some cultural and social groups the **extended family** structure is still fairly usual and some families live in households with grandparents or other relatives. In parts of the west country in England, for example, and in parts of Wales it is still the case that children raise their own families in the neighbourhood where they were born.

Who is the primary carer?

In many families women are still the **primary carer** (the person who spends most hours on childcare and organising the household). However, an increasing number of families have the father as primary carer or, over the years of childhood, the parents alternate, depending on other factors like employment.

Changes in social attitudes are more supportive of fathers' involvement in the upbringing of their children and it is certainly far more common to see fathers on the street pushing buggies or with babies strapped to their chest. Mothers are still mainly the primary carer and fathers can find themselves ill at ease in very female environments such as a nursery or drop-in (see chapter 21 on 'Partnership with parents').

Key terms

Extended family the relatives in a family beyond the mother and father

Primary carer the parent who undertakes most of the daily care and responsibility for children

Activity

What are the varied patterns in your current early years setting on the types of family patterns represented?

- You need to undertake this activity with sensitivity and the suggestion is that you use information that you already have from partnership with parents. You are *not* being asked to quiz families.
- Make a simple chart of the kinds of families (look back over this section) and the variety that is normal for your setting.
- Discuss your findings with colleagues on your course but maintain confidentiality about individual families.

Key skills links: N2.3 C3.1 a and b

Activity

Many of our own ideas about children and childcare are shaped by our own childhood. It can be useful to reflect on your life as a child. For instance:

1 Did you attend a nursery or pre-school?
2 Where did you play as a child?
3 What do you remember as your favourite games: playing on your own or with friends?
4 How did you travel to school?
5 How often did you watch television (for instance, every day, with or without time limits)? What were your favourite programmes?
6 Did you have access to a computer: at home? at school?
7 How old were you when you were allowed to make short local trips on your own or with another child? For instance, to the local shop, or walking to school?
8 What kind of diet did you eat? What were your favourite meals?

Write up briefly and then discuss some of the highlights with your colleagues. Your aim is to remember what was important to you as a child and perhaps some contrasts with the children for whom you are now responsible. You could all consider:

- Was your childhood very different in some ways from the childhood you see around you now? Different does not necessarily mean better or worse.
- Compare and contrast different experiences with your colleagues. Be sensitive to the variety and that perhaps the childhood of some people was unhappy or disrupted.
- Use the opportunity to explore diversity if you can share experiences with colleagues who were raised in a very different area from yourself: urban or rural, different countries around the world.

Key skills link: C2/3.3 C2/3.1a

Children in poverty

For all the apparent wealth of some parts of society in the UK, there is also serious poverty and deprivation in certain areas. The UK is one of the European countries with the starkest difference between the 'have's' and the 'have not's' in economic terms and the record on children living in poverty is very unfavourable. The most widely used definition of poverty is a household income that is less than half the national average. By this definition one-sixth of UK children are living in poverty – a total of 4.4 million.

Poverty is often linked with lack of employment for adults and areas of the UK where there has been long-term unemployment with little prospect of any improvement. Lack of work for parents is another way of looking at likely poverty for children. In 2000 the Joseph Rowntree Foundation reported that 2.2 million children in the UK (almost one-sixth of the child population) were living in households where no adult had any paid work.

The picture varies considerably across the UK. For instance the south of England is on balance more affluent than the north but there are definite areas of deprivation in the south. There can be a whole area of a city or town that is blighted. On the other hand, there can be quite small disadvantaged pockets in an area that is otherwise reasonably affluent. Scotland has significant levels of deprivation with 41 per cent of under fives living in poverty. Wales and Northern Ireland have serious pockets of poverty and long-term unemployment. Wales is one of the poorest regions in Western Europe – only Spain, Portugal, Greece and the former East Germany have a lower standard of living. In some areas of the UK particular minority ethnic groups or refugee families are living in especially deprived circumstances, but poverty is a condition that is experienced by families from many different ethnic groups.

Rural poverty

The extent of rural poverty is often underestimated and isolation and lack of neighbourhood facilities can make life considerably more difficult for families who may live in what look like very attractive countryside areas. The Forum for Rural Children and Young People (*www.ncb.org.uk/rural.htm*), in June 2001, estimated that rural children form about one-quarter of the children judged to be living in poverty in England. Lack of public transport can be a serious issue when families cannot afford a car or the car is the only way for the family breadwinner to get to work each day.

What does poverty mean for children?

There are significant consequences for children whose families are living in poverty and early years settings can play an important role in supporting families and offsetting some of the problems:

- Babies of families living in poverty are more likely to have a low birth weight and to experience more ill health and accidents within childhood.
- Limited family income often means restrictions to a healthy diet (see page 83) and therefore possible health and developmental effects.
- In many families, parents give up things themselves in order that their children may be better cared for. Parents may eat less so there is more for the children or go without warm clothes so that children can have a winter coat.
- Family stresses can increase the likelihood of lower attainment in school, especially where continued poor family prospects mean there are low expectations of achievement.
- Although families may be eligible for financial support, they may not know about or wish to claim some benefits. Children themselves may not wish to stand out at school by accepting free school meals.
- Families in poverty often also live in neighbourhoods with fewer facilities, including play facilities for the children. The local area may be realistically more dangerous for children than other parts of the same town or city.
- Some of the initiatives in early years services have been developed to support children living in poverty or deprived conditions, for instance Sure Start projects that target under fours and Neighbourhood Nurseries initiatives.

To think about

Young children usually assume that what they experience in early childhood is normal, that is that other children have very similar experiences.

- In what ways can you imagine that children who live in poverty could begin to realise that not all families are so financially restricted?
- How might children feel when they realise that some of their peers, perhaps children they know well, are in much more comfortable family circumstances?

Discuss your ideas with your colleagues.

Key skills link: C2/3.1a

Making sense of child development

It is sobering for you to think for a moment about just how much children learn and change over the first eight years of their young lives. The breadth of change can seem ordinary to people who spend time with children, perhaps because you are focused on current events for much of your time. However, useful adults need to step back in order to appreciate what children manage in the normal course of events and to understand that it is not surprising if children sometimes go through periods of confusion and struggle. If somebody offered to set you an equivalent set of learning goals to achieve over the same number of years, you would probably think twice before agreeing. Young children, of course, do not realise what is ahead; they take one day at a time and they are also primed to be curious and keen learners.

What happens in children's development?

As an involved and interested adult, you can observe what happens within the development of children. Your knowledge of child development, and a willingness to continue to learn, will be a vital part of your own professional development as an early years practitioner. Detailed descriptions of what happens in development are usually grounded within a particular cultural and social group. However, many theories are also products of a particular time and place. The majority of theoretical perspectives that have influenced early years practice are European or North American in origin.

It is well worth thinking a bit about the different kinds of influences on how children can develop. Babies have much in common when they are born, they are after all the young of our species. But from day one their development is shaped by the circumstances in which they are raised, including adults' beliefs about what is right and proper to do with children (see Figure 1.2).

You have to develop your own good practice in a particular place and time. So you need some blend of flexibility within boundaries about what you do and why. A major part of the framework has to be developmentally appropriate expectations of children. You will find many descriptions throughout the book of what usually happens in the development of children at different ages. There are undoubtedly potential problems in laying out information that attempts to give a 'normal range', but there are even more problems in store for early years practitioners if you do not have some developmental framework to which you can refer.

Tips for practice

- You need a balanced approach to using information about norms in development or developmental milestones.
- Such information can be a valuable guide. So long as you remember that individual children can vary considerably and still grow and learn within the bounds of healthy development.
- Recall that children with disabilities will develop along some different paths. But they have some experiences and patterns in common with children who have no identified disability or health condition.
- You need to recall that children develop within a social and cultural context. Different cultural traditions can have diverse views of childhood as a time, the priorities within the early years and how children should be treated.

Learning in childhood

A **whole child** or **holistic** view of development stresses the importance of treating children as entire individuals. Children continue to change in all areas of their development. It is more manageable sometimes, especially in a book like this, to address one area of development at time. When you make observations of children, you may for the moment focus on one area of their learning. But it is important to recall that children do not develop in separate compartments.

Key term

Whole child or **holistic approach** a perspective on children's development stressing that children should not be viewed from just one part of their development and learning; they should be treated as entire individuals

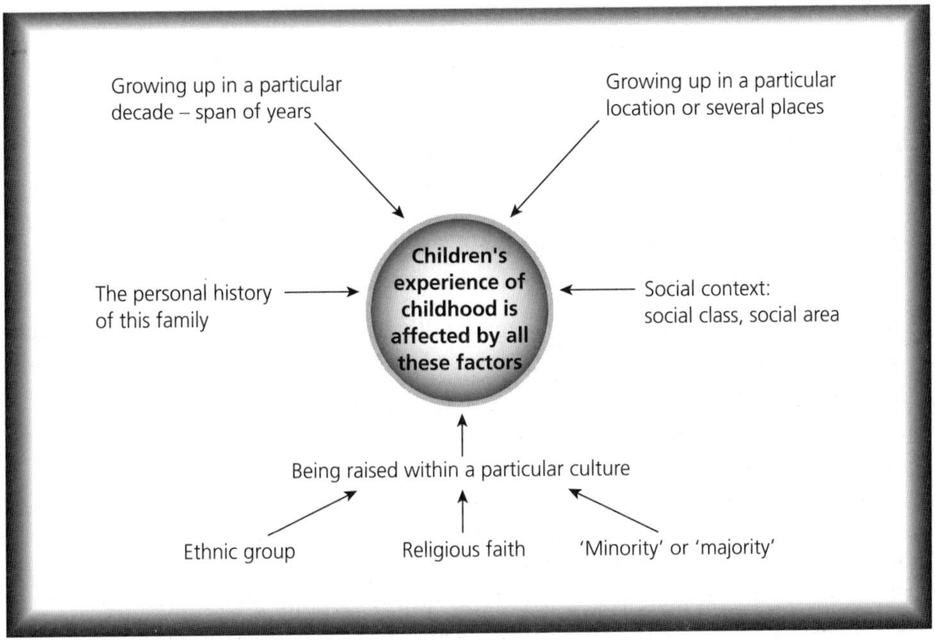

Figure 1.2 Childhood in context: influences on childhood experiences

Different areas of child development

The broad areas of development include the following.

- *Physical development* as babies and children gain control over their bodies and develop skills in fine and large scale movements. They learn to recognise and coordinate the evidence of their senses, to make choices about movement and the use of fine skills.
- Children also change over the years of childhood as they grow physically, changing shape and growing stronger. *Physical growth* and development is dependent on diet and overall health, as well as emotional well being.
- Children develop in the ability to share their own care as they grasp the skills of **self reliance**. Children become more able to make choices and organise themselves, although full independence is still many years away.
- The development of *communication* starts from the earliest use of looking and touching. Children develop in the skills of expressing their own communication and understanding that of others. Spoken language follows, including more than one language in many communities.
- *Intellectual development*, also called **cognitive development**, includes all the skills of thinking, making connections between experiences, recall and reasoning. Even very young children show evidence of the development of ideas and intellectual development is closely linked with communication skills.
- *Social development* unfolds as children develop close attachments and friendships. Children come to understand themselves as part of a social community as well as being an individual. They learn the **social skills** of interaction and other ways of behaving.
- *Personal and emotional development* underpins all other areas of development, since feelings of confidence or anxiety can shape any of a child's efforts. Children develop a sense of personal identity and self worth. Children become more able to recognise, understand and express feelings, their own and those of familiar children or adults.
- *Moral and spiritual development* is usually taken to mean a child's understanding of values and of choices about right and wrong. Spirituality may be linked with a family faith but can be a more general appreciation of experiences that are felt rather than touched or talked about.

Close links between areas of development

You will find many examples and diagrams throughout the book that highlight connections between different areas of a child's development day by day. Here are two examples to show the links now.

Imagine the task required for a child to become literate: to learn to read and write.

- At first sight, this may seem like an intellectual task and so part of cognitive development. Children certainly do need to grasp ideas and use their powers of recognition and recall.
- But learning to read is also part of communication, relating to written rather than spoken language.
- Literacy is also part of a child's social development as they recognise that writing is all around them and directs some aspects of social life.
- Learning to read and write also needs physical skills of coordination and of eye–hand movements. There is greater understanding now that active physical play and movement is crucial for these skills to develop.

Figure 1.3

Any activity can support children's learning in different aspects of their development

There will be further discussion of literacy starting on page 324.

Children can grow in creativity in the early years and this development links with many of the other broad areas of learning:

- Creativity requires imagination and flights of fancy and possibility, so cognitive development is involved.
- Children will want to express their creative ideas in a tangible form, so physical skills can also be important to them.
- Some creative projects involve learning from others, children or adults, so social relations and communication are important.
- An appreciation of possibilities as well as what has been created is an experience of feelings, so emotional and sometimes spiritual development is intertwined as well.

There will be more about creativity starting on page 412.

To think about

Consider the following examples of how a child could learn and change in a way that is observable to alert adults. Look at each example in turn and decide what areas of development could be involved in this achievement. Make brief notes and discuss with colleagues.

- 8 month old Darcus is a keen crawler and looks towards his older sister before he starts. Darcus likes his sister to chase him on all fours.
- Two year old Sara likes to wipe the table after lunchtime in her nursery. She gets the cloth and wrings it out afterwards.
- A group of three year olds play Mums and Dads in the home corner of their nursery.

- Four year old Anthony recognises his own name on his label at playgroup and the names of several stores up and down the high street and on carrier bags.
- Six year old Carrie takes part in a discussion in her after school club about what she likes about the club and what she would like to change.

Key skills link: C2/3.1a

Why and how does development unfold?

Study of the development of young children partly covers efforts to describe the details of *what* happens as babies and children grow. However, the other side is an attempt to explain *why* and *how* development unfolds. This understanding through explanation is often explored by **theories of child development**.

Key term

Theories of child development attempt to explain how and why the events of child development unfold. People who propose a particular theory try to go beyond a description of what happens in child development to a prediction of what might happen under certain conditions

What is a theory?

Theories are distinctive approaches to a topic and are usually a blend of:

- abstract ideas and beliefs about what is most important in this area: as a starting point to an explanation or a way of organising priorities
- information to support the theory and its explanations and predictions
- some theories are developed from a basis of research, either experimental or observational or from clinical practice with children or adults with problems
- other theories start more from a belief or philosophical stance and may gather information to support the theory along the way
- some theories are developed deliberately so as to make predictions about what will happen under certain circumstances. These predictions form a hypothesis based on theory and are tested in some way through research.

Early years practitioners form a very practical professional group and although theories of child development may seem far removed from everyday actions, the ideas of the main theoretical approaches have made their way into childcare advice, for parents as well as professionals. Therefore, it is useful to recognise the source of some ideas and practice.

Theories about child development

Key terms

Nature the part of children's development that is shaped by heredity, what is inherited through the child's genes

Nurture everything that happens to influence child development after birth

One of the broad differences between types of theory has tended to be how each one handles the relative balance of the impact of nature and nurture in child development.

- **Nature** refers to that part of children's development that is shaped by heredity, that which is inherited through the genes passed on by parents.
- **Nurture** refers to everything that happens to shape development after birth and represents the impact of environment.

The so-called nature–nurture (or heredity–environment) debate has not really been an either–or argument for most people for many years. Even those theorists who place more weight in one direction do not usually claim that the other side of the balance is completely irrelevant. The most recent research on the development of the brain has also made the debate, or any sense of argument over nature and nurture, fairly pointless (see page 243).

Biological theories

Biological theorists do not usually claim that biology is everything and that the environment has no part to play. A **biological approach** tends to focus on genetic programming as a pattern that shapes development unless powerful environmental forces knock it off course.

Arnold Gesell and his colleagues, working during the 1920s and 1930s, gathered a substantial amount of material about what children were able to manage by certain ages. This team believed that the sequence of development for babies and children was controlled by a biologically determined process of **maturation**. Gesell's ideas were influential in gaining acceptance for the ideas of 'milestones' and 'developmental norms' and that certain behaviours were phases through which children passed.

Learning theories

Learning theorists focus on what children or adults can learn through experience and the consequences of their behaviour. Humans are seen as having vast potential, bounded by the biological limits. Human behaviour is understood to change following patterns of reward and punishment. The approach is also called **behaviourism.**

The principles of *learning theory* were first explored in work with animals but application to understanding child development gained a social context, recognising that humans imitate out of choice, are motivated by feelings as well as tangible rewards and have a tendency to think as well as act.

Psychoanalytic theories

The **psychoanalytic tradition** (sometimes called psychodynamic) started with Sigmund Freud but has diversified significantly since his first ideas. This theoretical approach focuses on the impact of personality and conflicts on children's development. The approach allows for instinctive drives, that is the impact of biology, but the major influence is then childhood experience. The psychoanalytic group of theories proposes that children's development unfolds in definite stages that everyone shares within childhood. The theory proposes that behaviour is influenced by unconscious thoughts and feelings as well as conscious thought.

Cognitive theories

This theoretical approach focuses on how children think and make sense of their world. Jean Piaget, who was in the forefront of the cognitive emphasis in developmental theories, gave far less attention to the emotional or social aspects of children's development. This focus contrasts with the psychoanalytic theorists who were relatively uninterested in the cognitive aspects. Further exploration within **cognitive developmental theory** has extended into the more social context as well as modifying the firm developmental stages originally laid out by Piaget.

Social constructivism

The social constructivism model developed from the ideas of Piaget and of Lev Vygotsky who emphasised the social context in which children learn. The approach recognises that children make sense of their world and are not simply passive receivers of information and direction from adults. The **social constructivist approach** highlights the importance of alert and sensitive adults who are prepared to observe and consider their own role in any situation relevant to children's learning or behaviour.

Key terms

Biological approach
theories that focus on the importance of genetic programming to explain child development or adult behaviour

Maturation
a biologically determined pattern for the sequence of development for babies and children

Behaviourism
a theoretical approach that emphasises how human behaviour responds to patterns of reward and punishment. The approach is also called *learning theory. Social learning theory* recognises the importance of feelings and thinking on actions

Psychoanalytic tradition
theories that focus on how early conflicts and unconscious thoughts shape personality

Cognitive (or cognitive developmental) theory
theories that focus on how children think and make sense of their world

Social constructivist approach
emphasises how children and adults make sense and meaning of situations

Figure 1.4

Any theory has to make sense of real children

The ecological approach

Theorists in the first half of the twentieth century tended to take up rather isolated positions and often studied children as if it were irrelevant where and how they lived. Within the last decades of the century some theorists from all the different traditions have acknowledged the social or cultural context in which children learn. Urie Bronfenbrenner has directly addressed children's development within their social environment. In his **ecological approach**, Bronfenbrenner describes the impact of different aspects of children's environment on individual children.

Key term

Ecological approach theory that focuses on children's development within their social environment

Early childhood services in the UK

The full name of the UK is the United Kingdom of Great Britain and Northern Ireland, but the shorthand of UK is regularly used and will be followed in this book. The UK comprises four countries: England, Wales, Scotland and Northern Ireland.

The central government based in London still makes some decisions that affect all four countries and some legislation remains UK-wide. However, in the last years of the twentieth century many aspects of government became devolved to the National Assembly of Wales, the Northern Ireland Assembly and the Scottish Parliament. The National Assembly in Wales can decide how funds from central government or the European Union are spent. But the assembly does not have the power to make laws, unlike the situation in Scotland and Northern Ireland. The relevant departments in Wales determine guidance, for instance on the early years curriculum (see page 407).

In particular, the legislation and guidance that shapes public services for children and families have become the responsibility of each individual country.

These are the services that especially affect readers of this book: early years services, statutory education, child protection and social services. The principles underlying these services and what is regarded as good practice have a great deal in common between the four countries of the UK. However, the laws and organisation of service can be rather different. Throughout this book it will be made clear when there are national differences of which you need to be aware.

Services relevant to children and families

There are a range of services and professions that are directly relevant to the well being of children and their families. This section describes the most relevant services but you need to be aware that the availability of a service and exactly what it is called can vary between regions.

Educational services

It is a legal obligation that children are given an education from the age of five years in England, Wales and Scotland and four years of age in Northern Ireland. For most children, education means attending school, either a state or independent school. A minority of children are educated by their parents at home. Such families need to reassure local education authorities that they have clear plans to support their children's learning. This pattern is sometimes called **home schooling.**

Local educational services include not only the schools and their staff team but also a number of advisory services.

- *Advisory teachers* support schools or early years settings, may advise on individual children and support the professional development of early years teams.
- *Educational psychologists* offer assessment and advice for children whose educational experience is proving difficult in some way. Some educational psychologists may be able to offer general support to teams.
- *Support services for children with disabilities* (CWD) may include different professionals, some of whom may specialise in early years. The special educational needs coordinator (**SENCO**) will be responsible for supporting children and their families and organising assessment as appropriate (see page 528).

Key term

Home schooling
when families educate their children within the family for part or all of their childhood

Community health services

A range of services are available to families within the general framework of community health care. The primary health care team sometimes works together in a health centre serving a defined local community. In other areas professionals may be based separately in a doctor's surgery and child health clinic. The primary health care team aims to keep children healthy and generally promote health in the population as a whole. The team includes general practitioners and health visitors. Community midwives visit women at home in the ten days after birth (see page 154) and community nurses visit adults who need nursing care or support at home. This section focuses on services for children.

- *General practitioners* (GPs) are doctors who have taken additional training in general practice to serve the health needs of adults and children. When children are ill, parents will take the child to their own GP or telephone for a home visit if a child is too sick to move. The GP may make a referral to other specialised services.

- *Health visitors* have a nursing qualification and further training to enable them to support families in their home. They are responsible for supporting local families with babies and young children. Health visitors will visit families, especially when babies are young, and they organise the baby health clinics that offer regular developmental checks and advice to parents. Health visitors will offer advice about immunisations and these will be given by a doctor at the local clinic (see page 185).
- The *school health service* includes doctors and nurses who visit schools to carry out developmental checks to which parents are invited. The school health service also carries out those immunisations that can be given in school to older children. School nurses are usually responsible for several schools in an area and sometimes become involved in health education for children or teenagers.
- The *community dental service* supports good care of teeth as well as dealing with the results of decay or when children's teeth need corrective work (*orthodontics*). They are usually pleased to see young children for simple checks, so that the children get used to going to the dental surgery. The community dental service may have practitioners who would visit early years settings for information sessions.
- *Opticians* undertake thorough checks of the eyes and assess when children need glasses or corrective work to improve their sight.

Additional support and therapy

Health services offer a range of other professionals to whom a family could be referred when it becomes clear that additional support is needed. These professionals may sometimes be based at the local hospital but can also be part of the team in a large community health clinic. In rural areas there may be considerable distances for families to travel to other services.

The main objectives of therapeutic support are to:

- make an assessment of a child that will be a firm basis for further work
- on the basis of the assessment, develop activities, exercises or a therapeutic programme that will support the child
- share ideas and exercises with parents and other carers so that support for the child can extend beyond appointments with this professional.

Tips for practice

- As an early years practitioner you need to know about these different kinds of services and be able to explain to parents what could be offered.
- However, you would not consult such services about children without reference to parents.
- It will be parents' responsibility to seek further help and take their child to any other professional.
- Your aim is to develop good communication with parents in partnership so that it is easy for you to make suggestions and for parents to share ideas with you.

Activity

- Gather basic information about what is available in your local area.
- Your setting may have a folder or notice board that will help you start your own file.
- Organise your material into types of service and include any useful leaflets to explain what is offered by different clinics or therapists.

Key skills link: LP1/2.2

- *Child and family guidance clinics* offer a service to families who have difficulties of some kind with their children. Examples could include children whose fears dominate their life or who have refused consistently to attend school. Children would not usually be referred to the clinic until a range of support strategies had been tried in the family.
- Children and families are likely to be seen by a *clinical psychologist*, who has a degree in psychology and a further qualification that enables her or him to offer assessment and advice for a wide range of emotional or behavioural problems in childhood or adulthood. A *family therapist* will work with the whole family to identify and support how family dynamics may have affected one or more children. A *child psychiatrist* is a medical doctor who has taken a further qualification related to children with emotional or behavioural difficulties.
- *Paediatric care* is health care that focuses on children. In hospital a *paediatric nurse* will have specialised in working with children and a *paediatrician* is a doctor who has special training and expertise to assess and treat children's health. The prefix *paed* comes from the Greek word meaning child.
- *Speech* and *language therapists* assess children who are significantly delayed in any aspect of their language development or who are having difficulties in talking. They can then offer specialised support to the children and explain exercises or practice to parents and carers.
- *Physiotherapists* help children with physical difficulties or chronic ill health through appropriate exercise or by providing specialist equipment.
- *Occupational therapists* (OT) advise about appropriate aids for disabled children to enable them to become more mobile or cope with the skills of self reliance.
- *Play therapists* support children who have serious emotional distress for whatever cause. The therapist uses the medium of play to enable children to express and deal with what troubles them.
- *Music*, *art* or *drama therapists* will have qualifications in their subject but with further experience in using this medium to support children. Such therapists may be employed by the health services but could also be part of an educational or social services team.

Activity

Choose a practitioner or service from the possibilities described in this section and which is available locally. Make arrangements to visit and prepare some questions before you go. You might like to ask:

- How are children or families referred to this practitioner or service?
- How often and for how long is the child usually seen?
- What are the main ways in which this practitioner seeks to help a child?
- In what ways does the practitioner involve parents or share ideas with them to do at home?

Write up your notes of the visit and make a short presentation to your colleagues. It would be useful if they could have made visits to other kinds of practitioners and then you will learn from each other.

Key skills link: LP1/2.2 C1/2.3 C2.1b

Social services

Social workers support families who are under stress and where children are judged to be in need. Families will be assigned a social worker if there is concern about children's well being and certainly if child protection issues have been raised. Social workers may also be involved in the support of families with children who have severe disability, in order to help organise access to services and respite care. Children who become the responsibility of the local authority (looked after children) should have their own social worker.

Multi-disciplinary teams

The professionals described above will not always operate within one area of service. Sometimes, community health, education or social services bring together different professions on a permanent basis to work as a team.

'Care' and 'education' in the UK system

In common with some other European countries, the UK has a division between services that are known as 'care' and those categorised as 'early education'. This division has a very long history and has not been changed despite the many innovatory developments at the end of the twentieth century and beginning of the twenty-first. The two broad types of service are:

- *Childcare services:* for parents who are in work or are students. The hours fit a working day or one of study and parents pay the necessary fees or part of them. A childcare place can be offered from the early months of babyhood through to the school years, when the service becomes known as out of school care.
- *Early educational provision:* for children, usually, from about three years through to their entry into primary school. This kind of provision is normally offered on a sessional basis and follows school terms and holidays. The service cannot meet parents' childcare needs without some additional form of provision.

There is no proper developmental basis to support this persistent division and many early years professionals have argued long and hard for a coherent early years service. The care–education split also tends to create a divide between provision for the under- and over-threes. There are, of course, significant differences between children when they are still very young and as they grow physically and develop. However, differences properly focused on the children do not justify the firmly separate traditions of 'care' and 'education' and you will notice that the other chapters in this book regularly blend children's needs and learning within 'care' and 'education'.

Some Scandinavian countries have reorganised the entire system to form a coherent early years service with recognised early years practitioners and Spain has also developed a system to overcome the care–education division. Denmark, Finland and Sweden have successfully created settings for children and a qualification structure that is genuinely for the early years.

Who runs early years provision?

The system of early years provision that you know well can seem like an obvious way to organise services for children and their families. However, many national systems in Europe, including the UK, have not been developed in a logical way. On the contrary, they have emerged in a piecemeal fashion, shaped by the current views of children, parents and families and by economic considerations.

Early years provision in the UK is funded in different ways and falls broadly into three categories: statutory, voluntary and private provision.

Statutory provision is organised and offered by the state: whether by local or national government. Families are unlikely to have to pay for this service, as it will be offered as part of the educational service or as social services to families in need.

Figure 1.5

Many pre-schools have to share space – like this one, which is in a church hall

Provision within the *voluntary sector* covers the very broad range of services run by voluntary organisations. The word 'voluntary' is rather confusing because it does not mean that everyone involved in the organisation gives their time as a volunteer, although some may. Voluntary organisations are independent of local or national government and often have charitable status.

Some voluntary organisations work exclusively in early years, for instance the Pre-School Learning Alliance. Others have a broad area of interest, of which early years provision or special units are a part. For example, NCH Action for Children is a national children's charity that undertakes the promotion of children's interests, a wide range of projects and has some family and neighbourhood centres.

Private early years provision has expanded in recent years both in terms of childcare and early educational provision. Group settings are run as part of a business and families pay directly for the service.

Home based care through childminding, although regulated as a service, is still an arrangement made between families and self-employed childminders who are paid for their work. Nannies are employed directly by a family and so far have not had to be registered. The exception is a nanny share involving more than two families, because the nanny is judged then to be working like a childminder.

These broad distinctions can be blurred in practice, especially with the complex pattern of funding and new initiatives to expand provision within the Childcare Strategy. For instance:

- Private day nurseries may be registered to offer free early educational places, so that part of an otherwise non-statutory service is free to families. Some nurseries have agreements with the local authority to take an agreed number of children whose fees will be paid for by the authority to support families in need.
- Childminders usually have a business relationship with the parents of the children for whom they take responsibility. But in some areas there are sponsored childminders paid by the local authority to take care of children 'in need' because of family stress or because the child is disabled.
- Voluntary organisations may be involved in collaborative ventures with statutory provision of local authorities.

Useful websites

www.pre-school.org.uk
www.nch.org.uk
www.cache.org.uk

The range of early years provision

The system in the UK is highly diverse. We have many different kinds of early years settings, although all the possibilities are definitely not represented in every neighbourhood. All the different kinds of provision are developing and changing. In 2001 CACHE (Council for Awards in Children's Care and Education) estimated that there were about 600,000 adults working with children in all the different kinds of early years and out of school provision in the UK. Over your career you will probably work in a number of different settings so it is important to have a full perspective on the range.

State (maintained) nursery schools and *classes* are part of the state education system but are run for younger children than school age, specifically for three and four year olds. Some nurseries are now taking children as young as two and half years of age. Nursery schools are located in separate buildings, whereas nursery classes are part of a primary school site.

Independent (private) nursery schools are part of the independent educational system, sometimes called private schools. These schools may be separate establishments or part of an independent school that takes school age children.

Pre-schools and *playgroups* emerged from a large network of groups developed in the 1960s to give children the opportunity to learn through play activities when nursery schools and classes were less widespread.

Figure 1.6

Many nurseries are in purpose-built environments

Those groups affiliated to the Pre-School Learning Alliance are now called pre-schools. Other groups, some of whom are affiliated to the Playgroup Network, have chosen to continue to be known as playgroups. This kind of setting usually takes three and four year olds, although some groups accept children as young as two and a half years.

Wales, Scotland and Northern Ireland have playgroup movements that have promoted the national language, either as bilingual playgroups or as Welsh-medium or Gallic-medium groups.

Scenario

Dresden Road Nursery School has developed a wide range of services over the last five years. In response to local community needs, the nursery team has developed a range of services for families and works hard to make links with the local community.

- Many of the local families are bilingual and some are recent arrivals to the UK. As well as their existing commitment to partnership with all parents, Dresden Road has organised English as an additional language sessions for parents. Some moves have been made to gain accreditation for the course.
- A drop-in parent and toddler club started one afternoon a week as a way to ease the entry of children to the nursery. A link made with a community arts project has been extended to the whole nursery.
- The nursery is exploring the possibility of a breakfast club and after school care to meet the needs of children who go on to the local primary school.

- There is a possibility that the new childminding network for the area may meet in the nursery's activity room.

Dresden Road aims to develop appropriate services around the core service of nursery education. The team has learned a great deal about developing additional services: researching a genuine need, planning, reviewing and making suitable changes.

Questions

1 What might be the reasons for an early years setting to extend the services offered to children and parents?

2 You could make contact with local nurseries and find out in what ways they have built onto the core service of early education.

3 Write up and present to your colleagues.

Key skills links: C2.3 C2.1b

Combined early years centres within the UK have worked very hard to merge the service of childcare with opportunities for children to learn. There have been different kinds of combined settings.

- Combined nursery centres in the 1970s and 1980s were an attempt to blend the two traditions.
- Different kinds of children's centres and early childhood centres have been set up with the specific aim of bridging the care–education divide for children and for parents.
- In the 1990s the idea of early excellence centres was launched, again with the aim of a coherent service for children and families.
- The idea of neighbourhood nurseries, launched in 2001, combines the concept of bringing together care and education with other family services. In order to qualify for the funding, a neighbourhood nursery must be able to serve one of the 20 per cent of wards in the UK that have high social deprivation.

Day nurseries and *daycare centres* offer different types of childcare:

- Private day nurseries offer a childcare service for employed parents and students. These settings offer up to full day childcare places for children from the early months to school age and some also offer out of school care. There are now a considerable number of private nurseries, some of which are part of larger nursery chains.
- Local authority day nurseries and family centres offer a service to families who are under stress. These nurseries do not provide childcare for local working parents. Day nurseries may be called children's centres and those that undertake supportive work with parents will probably be called family centres.
- Community and workplace nurseries offer childcare for families in a local catchment area, to employees of specific companies or to students of a local college.

Mobile provision was pioneered by the playbus movement, taking play experience to children whose play opportunities were limited. Mobile projects often work with school age children but some are dedicated to early years and making contact with children who are unlikely to attend a nursery or playgroup. Children may live on run down estates with no early years setting or drop-in group. Playbuses have been a way to make contact with traveller families and their children. Some playbuses visit rural areas on a predictable schedule for families who would have great difficulty travelling to their nearest setting.

There are two types of *home based provision* of childcare based in a family home rather than a special early years setting.

- Nannies look after children in the child's own home and are employed by the parents.
- Childminders look after children in the minder's own home and run their own business as a carer. There is a new development of childminding networks, supported by a local authority advisor.

Informal groups run as *drop-in centres* and *crèches*. Drop-in services are often for children younger than three years and parents or carers have to stay with the children. Such provision may be called a parent and toddler group or a one o'clock club (because it runs from that time into the afternoon). Sometimes a day or community nursery offers a regular drop-in session for local families. Crèches are informal settings, often linked with a facility like a shopping mall or leisure centre, or set up to support a conference.

Out of school care services cover the parts of a primary school day that do not match an adult's working or student day. This provision can include:

- breakfast clubs before the beginning of the school day
- after school sessions run in primary schools or as separate clubs; playschemes may then be run in school half-terms and holidays
- some private day nurseries as well as state nursery schools have extended their provision to offer a before and after school service, sometimes called wrap around care.

Activity

Find out all the types of early years provision that are available in your neighbourhood, say within a five mile radius if you live in a large town or city.

- As well as your existing local knowledge, you can find out about provision by accessing your local Children's Information Service in England.
- List the types of provision: what is available, what is in short supply, what is missing?
- Compare your list with colleagues who live far enough away to have researched a different neighbourhood.
- Look for possibilities to link up with colleges in other parts of the UK. If you can establish an email link, then you could exchange information on the local profiles.

Key skills link: C2/3.1b IT2.1C

Free early education places

Throughout the UK, children have free state education from five years of age in England, Scotland and Wales and from four years in Northern Ireland. Each national government has made commitments to offer a free early educational place to children in the year before they start statutory schooling, and increasingly for the year before that.

These places can be offered in any of the kinds of group provision described so far. Childminding networks can be registered, so long as the provision meets the standards of the required inspection. Some mobile facilities also have been registered. The free early educational places are sessional and do not meet parent's childcare needs unless combined with further hours in a nursery or with other forms of provision.

Religious affiliation

Some early years provision, like some schools, are affiliated to a particular religious faith. Within England, Scotland and Wales most settings have no specific religious affiliation. The situation is reversed in Northern Ireland, where the whole early years and educational system has to be understood against the backdrop of the great significance of religion in the Province. Most early years settings are specifically Protestant or Catholic. Settings that aim to be non-sectarian are set up as community provision.

The legal framework for services

All early years services and the practitioners who work in them have to operate within the law. Several significant pieces of legislation are relevant for early years practitioners because these laws affect good practice in the welfare of children and their rights as young citizens, equality legislation, education including the curriculum and health and safety.

Of these areas of law, the equality legislation is UK-wide. Legislation on children with disabilities is set for the whole UK but those parts that are put into practice through early years and educational services operate within the different systems of the four countries.

Why do you need to know about laws?

As an early years practitioner, you are expected to know and understand the practical implications of legislation for your work. You are not expected to read original law documents, nor understand every single detail.

The laws described briefly in this section are what are called **primary legislation**. Laws are written in a precise way and do not usually show readily how practitioners would need to behave on a day by day basis in order to follow the legal requirements. Many laws have associated written volumes of **guidance** issued by the relevant government department. This guidance is expressed in more ordinary language and forms a basis for what practitioners must do within the services for children. For example:

- The Children Act 1989 has several volumes of detailed guidance. Volume 2 is the most relevant to early years settings and is entitled *Family support, day care and educational provision for young children*.

Key terms

Primary legislation laws that have been passed and have to be obeyed as a legal obligation

Guidance government guidelines that are issued to explain how the details of laws should work in practice

- Some guidance is shorter, perhaps in booklet form. For example, the Health and Safety Executive has published a guide for employers on *Violence at work*. It is not compulsory for employers to follow this guidance. But by doing so employers could be confident that they were complying with the relevant health and safety legislation.

Good practice in early years is not always tightly related to legislation. Sometimes what practitioners regard as good practice is established before there is any legal requirement. For instance, it has long been regarded as unacceptable in nurseries and pre-schools to hit children as a way of dealing with their behaviour. Although it became illegal to hit children in state schools as long ago as 1986, this requirement was only extended to early educational settings in 1998. (See also page 511.)

The welfare of children and their rights as young citizens

In the UK there are several key pieces of legislation that affect children's overall welfare. The laws provide the framework for child protection, family matters and services for children judged to be 'in need'. These are:

- The Children Act 1989 for England and Wales
- The Children (Scotland) Act 1995
- The Children (Northern Ireland) Order 1995

These laws have similarities but are not identical and, of course, operate within the social welfare and early years services of the different countries of the UK. In Scotland there was an active attempt to build a greater recognition of children's rights to be heard from the UN Convention (see page 28).

Some key principles are common between these laws, for example:

- The welfare of children must be the primary concern of services, practitioners and parents. The child's own views and preferences must be sought and considered in any decision.
- Parents have responsibilities towards their children, rather than rights over them.
- Services are required to work in partnership with parents and to ensure that as far as possible children are enabled to stay within their family.
- In the provision of services, local authorities must actively take into account the child and family's racial origin, religious persuasion and cultural and linguistic background.
- For the first time, children with disabilities were defined within the law as children in need and it was stated that services should be provided for them and their family.

These laws are of direct relevance to early years practitioners because they:

- establish a system of regulation for the early years settings, other than those in the educational system
- determine a framework for child protection, an area important for your practice and covered in greater detail in Chapter 19.

Registration and inspection

All the different types of provision are regulated through a process of registration and inspection. The main framework for the regulation of services has been set either by educational legislation for provision within the state education system or by the legislation for child welfare within the UK. The system works slightly differently throughout the UK but still reflects the care–education split in how provision is viewed.

During 2001–2 the responsibility for the regulation of childcare provision in England, Wales and Scotland passed from the local authorities (social services) to newly established national bodies. National childcare standards have been set to replace the previous system in which local authorities set their standards following the guidance of the main Children Act legislation.

England

The Early Years Directorate (a division of the schools inspectorate, Ofsted) has taken responsibility for the regulation of provision for children under eight years. The aim is that eventually the same visit will cover the childcare standards and the inspection required for government funding of free early educational places to three and four year olds. For the near future, the 'care' and 'education' inspections will remain separate.

Nursery schools and classes that are part of the state education system are still inspected under educational legislation. Nursery provision in independent schools was left exempt from meeting the childcare standards, but proposals being discussed at the end of 2001 mean that these facilities may have to meet the requirements in the future.

Wales

The Care Standards Inspectorate has taken over the regulation of childcare and will apply the new national standards. The Welsh regulation and inspection procedures are similar but not identical to those in England. The aim is that the new Inspectorate and Schools Inspectorate work together.

Scotland

The Scottish Commission for the Regulation of Care has taken responsibility for the regulation of early years childcare settings. HM Inspectorate of Education will continue to carry out separate educational inspections and no change is foreseen in this split at the moment. The aim is that HM Inspectorate will work collaboratively with the Commission.

Northern Ireland

The social services inspects the non-school childcare settings for children under 12 years of age and the Department of Education covers the educational settings.

The UN Convention on the Rights of the Child 1989

The Convention was the first international agreement in which the rights of children world wide were detailed in one document. The UK signed the Convention in 1991 and this means that the central government, and the national assemblies, have to ensure that the laws and practice regarding children meet the standards established in the Convention. This Convention is important because it has, to a greater or lesser extent, influenced the drafting of some legislation and the focus on children's rights has shaped the move to consult with children about their everyday lives and changes.

The UN Convention is organised in a series of statements called articles, that describe the rights of children and young people up to the age of eighteen years.

The articles cover different issues within children's right to be well cared for, safe, free from cruelty and exploitation and to exercise some say over their own lives. The right to be free of all kinds of discrimination is applied to children and the right to practise their own culture and religion, whether raised within their own family or in alternative care. The Convention also states children's right to play and recreation.

Equality legislation

These laws apply to the whole UK and determine many aspects of what is acceptable or unacceptable in the everyday treatment of other people, especially with regard to possible discrimination on the basis of sex, race or disability.

The Sex Discrimination Acts 1975 and 1986 made it illegal to discriminate against people on the grounds of their sex, either as a woman or a man. So, for instance, no early years setting could decide not to employ men, no more than a business organisation can decide it does not want female employees. Exceptions can be only be made if the sex of a worker can be justified as a genuine occupational qualification. Treating someone less favourably just because of their sex is classed as a form of **direct discrimination** and therefore illegal. The law has not been used with reference to children.

The Race Relations Act 1976 aimed to define racial discrimination and make such behaviour illegal. The Act made it unlawful to discriminate on racial grounds, including skin colour, race, ethnic or national origins. Discriminatory behaviour was defined and is applicable to the treatment of children and adults. The Race Relations (Northern Ireland) Order 1996 covers similar ground. This legislation covers both direct discrimination, and **indirect discrimination**, that is when the consequences of an action are discriminatory, although that may not have been the intention. An example of direct racial discrimination in early years would be if children were offered or refused a place in a setting because of their ethnic identity. An example of indirect discrimination would be if conditions were linked with the offer of a place that could not be met by families from some ethnic groups. (See page 589 for further discussion of these issues.)

The 2000 Amendment to the Race Relations Act strengthened some of the requirements of the earlier legislation and made it an active duty for public bodies, which would include early years settings and schools, to work towards racial equality. In practice, this will mean that any organisation must be alert to how it promotes the service, recruits staff and makes the service genuinely accessible to all.

Religious affiliation is not included in the definitions of the Race Relations Act. In Northern Ireland, where religious affiliation can be the basis for discrimination, the Fair Employment (Northern Ireland) Act 1989 requires organisations to monitor job applicants and acceptance by religious affiliation. At the time of writing (2001) a Single Equality Bill is being developed in the Province that aims to take account of developments in the rest of the UK, European Union directives and the particular need to address civil rights and religious liberties in Northern Ireland.

The Disability Discrimination Act 1995 made broad requirements relating to discrimination against people with disabilities but, at that time, excluded education from these legal requirements. The Special Educational Needs (SEN) and Disability Bill 2001 removed this exception and made it unlawful for educational providers to treat a child less favourably on the grounds of disability. This change means that inclusion of disabled children in mainstream provision is now more

Key terms

Discrimination when any kind of behaviour is more or less favourable to other people on the basis of their group identity. **Direct discrimination** is when somebody deliberately acts so as to favour or disadvantage members of given groups. **Indirect discrimination** occurs when the actions of a person or organisation result in more or less favourable treatment by group identity, even if this consequence was not deliberately intended likely. This issue for practice and other legislation relating to special educational needs is also discussed within Chapter 18.

Education including the curriculum

A series of laws have shaped the educational system and the development of a national curriculum within the UK. There are differences between countries in the UK on the organisation of state schooling and the details of both the curriculum for children of school age and those in early years settings. These details are covered in Chapter 14.

Health and Safety

There are a number of laws that relate to health and safety at work. Many of the requirements relate to your safety as an employee. Other requirements mean that employers must offer good standards of health and safety to protect members of the public. Within an early years setting that means the children, their parents, other carers, students or volunteers. The broad requirements of health and safety legislation are that any employer must:

- display the most up to date version of the poster *Health and safety law – what you should know*
- prepare a written safety policy statement appropriate to the organisation
- make suitable assessments of the risks to the health and safety of employees and everyone else who visits this setting
- communicate emergency and evacuation procedures to everyone
- report the more serious accidents or diseases in the setting

Figure 1.7
Early years practitioners bring the curriculum alive for children

- consult with employees before making decisions that could affect their health and safety
- keep records of accidents and any first aid treatment given
- exchange information on hazards or risks with any other employers who share the premises.

These legal requirements fit into what is regarded as good practice for early years provision, schools and out of school care. They emphasise clear communication, consultation, good record keeping and an awareness of risks that leads to sensible precautions. There are responsibilities for employers but the legislation also assumes that employees, in your case early years practitioners, will behave in a responsible and sensible way by using the health and safety equipment provided and reporting any problems.

Principles and values in working with children

The view of what makes up good practice in early years is not fixed and professional discussion should always allow for exploring new ideas and taking a fresh look at areas of practice and perspectives. A considered view of what is good practice tends to be a blend of:

- The experience and accumulated wisdom of people who work with children and their families or who advise and consult in this area.
- The application of new theoretical and research findings about children and what these imply for practice.
- The requirements of the law and associated guidance for early years practitioners. The details of this source are in turn influenced by the two first points through the process of consultation and working committees when changes are proposed to laws and guidance.

The main principles underlying good practice are explored in much more detail throughout this book, so this section offers only a brief summary. The main issues are as follows.

A child-centred approach

Responsible and caring adults should:

- enable children to enjoy their childhood
- care for and care about children, showing respect and active consideration for the child as an individual
- ensure the welfare and safety of each child without making children anxious about their well being or oppressed by over protection
- enable young children to learn without pressure and to move towards their full potential
- use the full range of learning opportunities in order to support children's full development
- use their adult skills, such as observation, to offer appropriate help to children and to appreciate what children can manage and are learning
- behave as a responsible grown up towards children: willing to tune into the perspective of children and to create boundaries where necessary

Key term

Child-centred (or **child-oriented**) **approach** a perspective that aims to make children's interests and focus central to all aspects of child care and learning

- avoid using adult strength of words or action inappropriately or in a way that is oppressive of children.

Partnership with families

Key term

Partnership with parents
the value and practice of working together with parents for the care and learning of their children, acknowledging the continuing importance of parents in the lives of their children

Early years practitioners share the care of children with their parents or other key carers, who are the children's first and continuing carer and educator. Practitioners should:

- work in **partnership with parents**, or other key family carers, as the continuity in children's lives
- respect parents as people with unique knowledge and expertise on their own children
- respect the customs, values and spiritual beliefs of the child and family
- respect and protect the confidentiality and privacy of a child or family, unless disclosure is required for the safety of the child.

There are examples of partnership throughout the book and Chapter 21 covers the main aspects important to good practice.

Continued professional development

Key term

Reflective practitioner
an outlook for early years, and other professionals, in which you are ready to think as well as to act and to be open to new ideas and approaches

Initial training is important but early years professionals need to continue to learn and be open to new ideas and approaches. A positive approach is summed up by the idea of the **reflective practitioner.**

Effective early years practitioners need to be closely involved with the children; there needs to be activity and doing. However, good practice includes reflection as well as action. Being a reflective practitioner means being willing and able to:

- Think over what has happened as well as become closely involved in activities with children.
- Think about issues from more than one perspective, be open-minded and willing to continue to learn.
- Acknowledge and recognise feelings: your own, those of the children and of other adults (colleagues and parents).

Figure 1.8
Parents provide the essential continuity in their children's lives

- Accept that feelings shape events and can affect the sense that you are prepared to make of a situation.
- Be actively involved, enthusiastic about the practice of being a practitioner.
- Take an active part with children, which should bring in other aspects, like sharing feelings (excitement, puzzlement or disappointment when an activity does not go well) and thinking about issues.
- Plan ahead, whilst being flexible for the possibilities of the moment and children's interests. Useful plans all depend on applied adult thinking skills: what will the children learn, how will you recognise it?
- Review activities and approaches – how has it gone, what have you learned, what do the children think and feel? Finding scope for improvement is not necessarily a criticism of what has gone before.

You will find many examples within the book of being a reflective practitioner in action. Figure 1.9 summarises the main strands.

Activity

Look at the diagram of the reflective practitioner (Figure 1.9)

- Take each circle one at a time and note an example of how you have worked as a thoughtful adult in that way.
- Discuss what you have considered with colleagues. Are some aspects of being a reflective practitioner harder than others? Do you have any ideas about why?
- Make some specific plans about ways in which you could improve your own practice.

Key skills link: C3.1a LP3.1–3

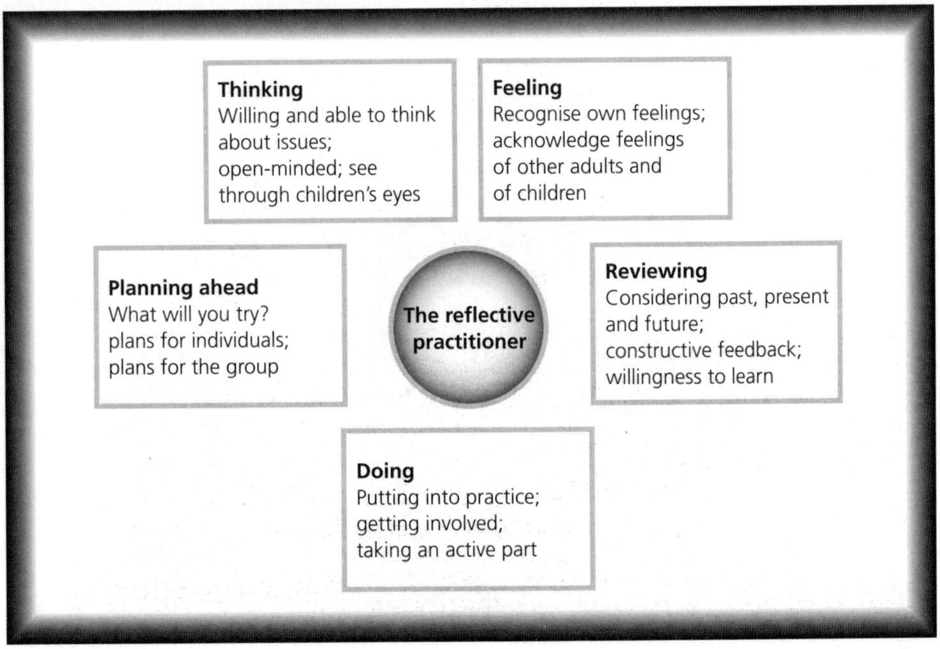

Figure 1.9 Ways of being a reflective practitioner to support children

Sources of learning for adults

If you are currently working towards an early years qualification, then you may focus on that experience as if it is your only source of learning. But many experiences contribute to knowledge and understanding of children. Figure 1.10 suggests some of main sources.

Activity

Look at the diagram in Figure 1.10.

- Take at least 3–4 of the different sources and note down what you feel you have learned from these sources that supports you as an early years practitioner.
- Compare your ideas with colleagues.
- Together discuss what could be the downside of depending too much on one or two of the sources, for instance raising your own children or information from television programmes.
- Consider ways that you could improve your own practice.

Key skills link: C3.1a LP3.1–3

The contribution of your own childhood

As an early years practitioner you will gain professional experience but your own personal experience is also relevant.

- Everyone is shaped by their own childhood and in some ways your experience and memories will support you in offering good quality experiences to children.
- In other ways your own childhood might misdirect, confuse or block your current practice now as a grown up.

Figure 1.10

Possible sources of our own knowledge and understanding about children

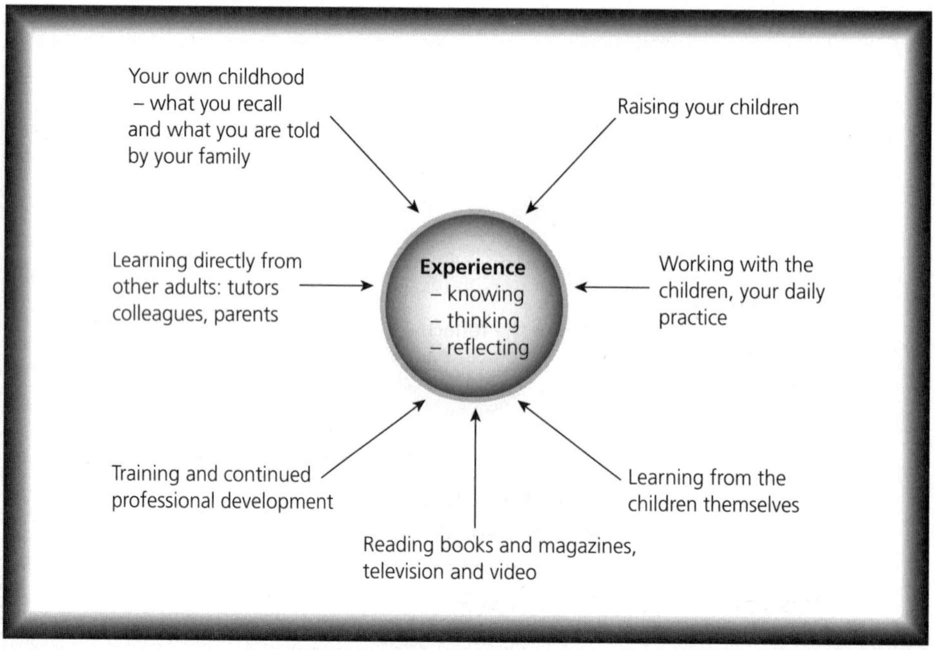

- The child that you once were is still inside you and, released as a happy playmate for children, can be a positive force.
- But you will not help children day by day if there is any chance that your own family experience leads you to be very restricted in your view of what is the right or wrong way to raise children.

Activity

This activity has similarities to the one earlier in the chapter on page 8. You may not wish to do both, but if you do this activity then focus on the sources of your learning that influence you as an early years practitioner.

Reflect back on what was normal behaviour in your own family in your childhood. Look at your memories now with a more adult eye. You could consider and make some brief notes on any of the following issues:

- What was the pattern at mealtimes? Did you have meals together as a family? How did the adults deal with table manners, talking over mealtimes or eating habits?
- Who did the household tasks? Were children expected to help out and in what way?
- Did you go to an early years setting and what do you recall of your own experience from that time? What did you like the best and what did you not like much?
- In your family, what kind of behaviour brought you smiles and praise from the adults? What kind of behaviour got you into trouble and how was that handled?
- What are the family phrases that still go through your mind and probably pop out of your mouth? Clichés like 'Courtesy costs nothing' or 'Who's "she" – the cat's mother?'
- Perhaps you were not raised in a family home for at least part of your childhood. If you spent time in foster or residential care, then in what ways do you feel you have built a picture of family life?

Questions

Without sharing more personal information than you wish, discuss some of the issues and insights with colleagues or fellow students.

1. What variety can you see in a group, even those from apparently similar ethnic and cultural backgrounds?
2. If you have diversity in your discussion group, then what may be explained by different cultural traditions? But what is still down to individual family styles or your parents deliberately being different parents to your grandparents?
3. What do you bring to your work with children as an early years practitioner. Be honest – what works well and what may be a hindrance?
4. How might you deal with those issues that can be a block for you? Make some specific plans for your own practice.

Key skills link: C3.1 PS2/3.1 LP3.1–3

Anti-discriminatory practice

A key value in good early years practice is that you apply anti-discriminatory practice in all aspects of your work. This area of good practice is often misunderstood, so this section describes the main ideas and ways in which principles can be put into daily practice. There are further examples in every chapter of the book.

What is anti-discriminatory practice?

The key issues in good practice are that early years teams:

- actively seek to promote equal opportunities for all children and families with whom they work and come into contact
- work to equalise opportunities for those children and families whose situation or group identity may place them at a disadvantage
- promote respect and mutual understanding between children and families who see themselves as different from each other.

Of course, you and your colleagues can only address those issues that arise within your setting and your direct experience with children and families. However, this framework gives you substantial scope for positive anti-discriminatory practice. You are not responsible for what has happened in the past or elsewhere in the country or your neighbourhood. You are responsible, together with the children, for what happens within and directly around your setting.

Words matter, but it does not usually help good practice in this area if practitioners become too enmeshed in the 'correct' terms or phrases. In this book the phrase **anti-discriminatory practice** is used to mean the active attempt to promote positive attitudes and behaviour and to challenge and change negative outlooks and actions. The phrase **equal opportunities** is very similar in meaning. It is used to mean the daily practice of ensuring that all children are enabled to have positive experiences in an early years setting, to use the resources to the full and ensure that active steps are taken if, for some reason, children's opportunities are being blocked.

Key terms

Anti-discriminatory practice
an active attempt to promote positive attitudes and behaviour and to challenge and change negative outlooks and actions, on the basis of any group identity

Equal opportunities
the daily practice to ensure that all children are enabled to have positive experiences, to use the resources of a setting fully and see that action is taken if children's opportunities are blocked

Sources of diversity

Anti-discriminatory practice refers to all aspects of diversity and group identity; the principles do not only apply to ethnic group diversity.

Good early years practice is sensitive to diversity of all kinds and practitioners need to be aware of diversity issues for children and adults in the areas of:

- gender: boys and girls, men and women
- ethnic group and culture
- linguistic background
- social class and family background, including different ways of running family life, for instance travelling communities
- religious faith and other family beliefs
- disability and continuing health conditions.

Anti-discriminatory practice needs to be an integral part of all aspects of good practice in early years settings and services for children and their families. For this reason, apart from the explanatory section you are reading now, further discussion and examples of anti-discriminatory practice form part of all the other chapters in this book, rather than being a separate chapter.

Anti-discriminatory practice applies to everyone; we all have a responsibility to consider our adult assumptions, extend our knowledge and promote equal opportunities. It is no more acceptable that girls are offensive to boys on the basis of sex than the other way around. Children who have experienced offensive racial name calling deserve support and action on their behalf. But their experiences do not make it alright, or less important, if they in their turn are deeply offensive, on racial or other grounds. The rules apply to everyone.

Children are in the process of learning, so you can make a difference and support them to learn positive attitudes towards others and help them to want to learn more about life experiences different from their own. You offer this effective support through what is sometimes called an **anti-bias curriculum**, in which you offer play materials and experiences from a wide range of sources, some of which are not to be seen in your local neighbourhood. You extend children's horizons beyond their own backyard. Anti-discriminatory practice within an early years curriculum also seeks to remove and replace materials that may strengthen inaccurate assumptions or stereotypes about particular groups of people.

Stereotypes are simple, strongly held beliefs about the characteristics shared by individuals in an identified group, of any kind. Some stereotypes are clearly negative and can be identified easily as restrictive and offensive. But apparent compliments are not really positive, if they limit individuality, for instance, children with chronic illness are not all 'brave' and children with Down's syndrome do not all have a 'sunny, loveable' disposition.

Good practice needs to recognise that there is great diversity within groups as well as between. All the major world faiths have different sects, some of which have major disagreements. Families whom Europeans may class together as

Key terms

Anti-bias curriculum a framework of activities, play materials and experiences that avoid stereotypes and actively promote understanding and knowledge of all the groups within society

Stereotypes simple, strongly held beliefs (positive or negative) about the characteristics shared by individuals in an identified group

Figure 1.11 Adults' assumptions may be voiced without thought

'Asian' vary considerably in ethnic background, language and faith. Even what may seem a basic matter of description by words is not always simple. For instance, some families who choose a travelling life like to be known as travellers but some definitely prefer the term gypsies.

Good practice with children and families

The broad themes in your good practice should be to:

- Treat all children with equal concern and attention to individuality. It is not good practice to claim to treat children 'all the same'. They are not the same and this approach denies children sources of their identity in some way.
- Avoid and remove discriminatory or unfair practice, even if the result was not intentional.
- Actively promote equality, understanding and personal identity along all the diversity issues.
- Be willing to address and constructively challenge assumptions, in a way that is likely to help you, the children and other adults to change and learn.
- Be willing to extend your own knowledge as well as share with others, respecting your colleagues' wishes to understand rather than criticising misunderstanding and lack of knowledge.

You will address good practice in many ways, for example, in:

- all aspects of the care and well being of the children, including food, clothes, hygiene and ideas of courtesy
- your understanding of the impact of disability and continuing ill health
- your treatment of boys and girls – consider carefully the meaning of equal opportunities on gender for adults and children
- your partnership with parents through continued and equal communication
- how you plan the early years curriculum, the play materials and experiences you offer
- how you show support for bilingual children, different languages and forms of literacy
- respecting family diversity yet holding true to children's rights to be protected in childhood
- your careful but active approach in dealing with offensive behaviour and name calling between children.

Further resources

Greig, Liz (2001) *Supporting Development and Learning 3–5* Learning and Teaching Scotland.

Lindon, Jennie (1998) *Equal Opportunities in Practice* Hodder and Stoughton.

Lindon, Jennie (1998) *Understanding Children's Development: Knowledge, theory and practice* Thomson Learning.

Lindon, Jennie (2000) *Child Care and Education in Europe* Hodder and Stoughton.

Progress check

1 Describe two ways in which the daily lives of young children now differ from those of their parents or grandparents.

2 Describe three ways in which family organisation might differ between children of a similar age.

3 List the main broad areas of child development.

4 What are the main kinds of early years provision for children younger than school age?

5 Give three examples of why early years practitioners need to have a practical grasp of the law.

6 Describe three sources of learning that can contribute to your good practice with children and families, in addition to studying for an early years qualification.

7 Give three examples of how anti-discriminatory practice might be shown in an early years setting.

2

Caring for children – caring about children

After reading this chapter you should be able to:

- understand and appreciate the central importance of care and caring for children
- promote children's self reliance as they share in their own care and daily routines
- follow appropriate practice in hygiene for an early years setting
- organise appropriate routines to support children's sleep and rest
- support children in their toilet training.

Introduction

Good quality care is essential for babies, toddlers and children. Their health and well being needs to be supported and protected. But good care of children is an effective support of their all round development. Care routines can be a valuable time for supporting children's sense of self worth and their understanding of how their world works. The role of an early years practitioner is not only to offer good quality care to children but to support them as they learn to take care of themselves, growing in the skills of self reliance. This chapter, together with Chapters 3 and 4, will help you to understand your role in this important area.

Links to early years qualifications

This chapter especially supports the following units:

Diploma in Child Care and Education: 2, 3, 5, 10

National Vocational Qualification in Early Years Care and Education

Level 2: C1, E1, E2, P1, C13

Level 3: C2, E3, P2, M8

BTEC National Early Years Diploma: 3, 5, 6

The central importance of care and caring

An integral part of caring for children's development is caring about them as individuals. It is vital that children should feel confident that the key adults in their lives care about them and what happens to them. This vital and positive message is communicated to children through the care routines of a day or session in early years settings or in your work as a nanny in a family home, or a childminder in your own home.

'Care' and 'education' are equally important

Unfortunately, the development of the early years services in the UK occurred within a split system that has undervalued 'care' in favour of 'education' (see page 2). The consequence has been that many commentators feel able to talk in a dismissive way about services or early years practitioners who 'just care' for children. Such settings are contrasted with 'educational' settings or 'educational' activities as the more valuable sources of learning. I have yet to hear anybody talk about 'just education'. The many exciting developments in early years services have not addressed that basic division to create a coherent early years system.

Of course, the care–education split makes no sense whatsoever when children's development and well being are considered as a whole. Children certainly do not distinguish between 'educational' and 'care' activities as a source of learning. You will find many examples in this chapter and others to highlight how children are ready and keen to learn from all sources.

Any early years setting, whatever its name, should combine a positive outlook on and good quality in care routines with a wide range of opportunities for children to learn, some of which will be in the form of 'educational' activities. Children need to be and feel cared for, which creates a healthy state and positive psychological frame of mind to allow them to benefit from all the opportunities to learn within their day.

To think about

Consider how a child may appear who is cared for and feels that people care about him or her.

1 How might the child look?
2 How might he or she behave?
3 How might a child appear who feels that nobody really cares or notices them in any positive way?

- Discuss your ideas with your colleagues and raise any views you have absorbed from other people that could lead you to downgrade the care in your practice.
- How can you bring care and caring to the fore and really value what you give to children?
- Attitudes based in 'just care' and 'only caring' create problems for children. Make some specific plans for how you can challenge such attitudes and resolve problems in your own practice.

Key skills link: C3.1a PS3.1 LP3.1–3

Why care matters so much

Figure 2.1
Sometimes children appreciate a helping hand

Caring for children's health and well being is just as important as providing specific activities that stretch them in other areas of their development such as communication or the growth of ideas. You support children's emotional and social development as well as creating opportunities to learn through meaningful routines:

- Respectful, physical care through which you treat a baby, toddler or child as an individual, shows children that they are welcome to your time and skills in caring for them.
- Caring supports children's whole development when it is part of your personal relationship with a child. Children can feel affirmed as an individual. They should never feel like baby number three in a routine of changing, nor child number five at the meal table.
- You can show your pleasure as children grow in the skills of self reliance and begin to share in their own care.
- You show through your words and actions that you value the caring time. You are not rushing through a nappy change or a meal because you or your colleagues regard this as 'lost time'.
- An enjoyable conversation over lunch or tea or an unhurried and affectionate nappy changing time can support children's skills of communication.
- Involvement in tidying up or laying the table not only boosts children's sense of self worth but can be an ideal opportunity to add to their powers of memory, of understanding a sequence or practical early number work.

Scenario

The team at Sunningdale Day Nursery have made significant changes in practice since Erin took over as manager two years ago. The previous manager had put pressure on the staff to introduce a wide range of what were called educational activities but without valuing the necessary care routines for the children, especially the under twos. Erin identified problems that arose because:

- some staff pressed children to eat meals at a swift pace in order to get through what was seen as wasted time
- staff in the baby and toddler room had focused on an efficient changing time rather than one that was personal for the babies and toddlers
- a large group of three year olds had to sit still on the mat for a long story time with one practitioner while the other practitioner tidied up, because it was easier not to involve the children in tidying.

Erin worked steadily to help the staff to broaden their view of what was learning for young children and potential sources for their learning. It has taken time, but most rooms are now more relaxed and the staff are less stressed, since they see the whole day as valuable.

Questions

1 What would you anticipate happened to the children in each of the three practice problem areas mentioned above?

2 In what ways can a felt time pressure and an attitude of 'we must do all these educational activities' undermine the creation of a relaxed atmosphere for children to learn?
3 Discuss with your colleagues and suggest some strategies that Erin may have used to address the problems.

Key skills links: C3.1a PS3.1

Children need touch

Babies and children need physical contact. It is a vital channel for warm communication and is also reassuring when children are upset, scared or ill. Close physical contact is essential while children need help with the routines of physical care and some disabled children will need help well into middle childhood or beyond.

There are differences between families in the amount and kind of physical affection shown to children. Some of these differences may be about this particular family and the way that the parents were raised. Sometimes, there may be a broader cultural tradition about appropriate personal space (how close you sit or stand to another person) and touch. Early years practitioners need to be sensitive to what children have learned so far in their family. But young children usually like to be close, to make physical contact and be able to access such contact when they want.

Children should of course be treated with respect and not used as comfort objects, either by adults or by older children. You may need to step in if some children are treating a younger or much smaller child like a doll or a prop in a game. Equally, it is not acceptable for practitioners responsible for rather exhausting older groups to appear in the baby room for a bit of peace and a baby to cuddle because it makes them feel better as adults.

Tips for practice

- Be alert to a child's feelings and do not show hurt just because he does not feel like a cuddle at the moment.
- Babies, toddlers and young children will show you when and how they appreciate close physical contact by being close, touching you and taking your hand or snuggling up close.
- Children who do not want to sit on a lap may like to lean against you or be close enough to reach out when they wish.
- Do not stop showing affection or using appropriate touch to older children. Adults often withdraw, especially from boys, and it is hard for children to avoid a message that contact is less welcome or not for 'big' children.
- Six and seven year olds often appreciate a friendly hand touch or will want to sit very close if they are sad.

Sources of concerns about physical contact

An increased awareness of child protection issues has confused good practice over touch. See Chapter 19 for a thorough coverage of this topic.

Concern about the minority (and most people do *not* abuse children) has sometimes led to restrictive rules about contact and witnessing procedures in care routines (when two practitioners must be present). Some of these rules, including 'no-touch' practices are unworkable for younger children and give some very bizarre messages to slightly older ones.

An excessive concern about 'what might people think' will lead to poor practice in which early years practitioners behave in a distant way to children. Far from solving child protection concerns, this approach can be emotionally cold to children, who wonder what they have done that is so wrong that adults do not want them close.

Learning about appropriate touch

Young children are in the process of learning about gentle and appropriate physical contact. They cannot experience respectful contact if early years practitioners keep their distance. In fact the children could be put at risk because they have a less strong foundation for judging intrusive or inappropriate contact. If children have been deprived of safe and happy closeness, then they are even more at risk because they are desperate for affection from anyone who offers.

Early years settings and schools are usually even more sensitive or uneasy about practice for male practitioners. Again, the problem has arisen with an excessive concern about the prevalence of child abuse and also a myth that men are more likely to be abusers than women. Most identified sex abusers are men but most men are not abusers of any kind. So, this perspective is not only untrue but also raises serious equal opportunities issues. It is important that children have positive and affectionate male role models for the healthy development of girls as well as boys.

Within a friendly early years setting you can help children learn about appropriate touch, for instance:

- One child feels squashed by another and wants some more space.
- Another child likes to be asked to hold hands and does not want her hand simply grabbed by her friend.
- Male and female practitioners can set a good example of friendly and respectful physical contact and give children direct experience of how a safe adult behaves.
- Female practitioners often find that a very young child may pat a breast or slip a hand down the front of a blouse. Just remove the hand gently and place it somewhere less intimate.

It would be a matter for concern if children persist in intimate touching once you have said a kind 'No'. Also you need to be alert to possible problems, if a child seems unnerved by physical closeness. Be aware that it may be the result of a bad experience. These issues are addressed in Chapter 19.

Activity (observation)

Keep a simple log over at least a week of all the occasions when you touch a child and children touch you. You can group the examples by broad types, for instance, touch as part of:

- welcoming and greeting
- offering reassurance or comfort
- showing pleasure, encouragement, a message of 'well done!'
- supporting children to boost their confidence to get involved
- physical care routines
- guiding a child's hand or body to manage a task.

Look over your findings and identify any common patterns.

- Make a simple chart to show the pattern.
- What can you learn about the expressed needs of the children who initiated touch with you?
- What would be the likely consequences if you had withdrawn from their touch?
- Discuss your findings with colleagues or prepare and make a short presentation.
- Use your findings and discussion to plan improvements in your own practice.

Key skills links: C3.1a LP2/3.1–3 N2.3

Promoting self reliance through routines and sharing care

The value of care routines

Predictable routines in the day can be a source of security to children; they start to understand what happens when and how one event follows another. Predictable routines do not have to be inflexible and certainly the routine should never feel more important than the children themselves. A regular pattern creates a rhythm to the day that can be very reassuring to young children who have little understanding yet of time in an adult framework. Babies, toddlers and young children do come to understand mealtime, clean up time, rest or quiet time and lively play time.

Good practice for the physical care of children

Within predictable routines, with some flexibility, you can offer children respectful and appropriate physical care, that is part of friendly communication and a warm personal relationship with a child.

These are the key themes of good practice in every early years setting:

- Let a child know that you are about to start a care routine.

- It is disrespectful to children, and sometimes makes them scared or uneasy, if you appear without warning, start to move them about and do not give them time to adjust.
- Adults need to be alert to children's preferences for their personal care and these wishes may be expressed through words, facial expressions or a child's whole body language.
- Wherever possible you should follow or at least be flexible to the child's wishes.
- All children should be enabled to partake in their own care as much as possible and you need to be alert to promoting children's skills of self reliance.
- Care routines should not be rushed and children should be treated as individuals who deserve time and attention.
- Good practice in physical care routines helps children to understand respectful touch. They are then more likely to treat others with care and to be wary if someone treats them roughly or with disrespect.
- Early years practitioners need to work in partnership with children's parents, so that children are not handled in very different ways. Some families will also have cultural or religious reasons for preferring particular ways of meeting children's physical needs.

Activity

- Even young children have a sense of bodily dignity and some soon show that they want some privacy during care routines.
- Note at least five or six ways in which you could show respect for a child and promote their sense of dignity through physical care.
- Discuss your ideas with colleagues and consider what may block good practice from adults in this area (in general).
- Make some specific plans that could improve your own practice.

Key skills links: C2/3.1a LP2/3.1–3 WO2/3.1–3

Sharing their care with children

Part of growing up is that children steadily learn to take care of themselves. They are able to help in and then take responsibility for physical care routines such as feeding, dressing and toileting themselves. Children also learn broad life skills over a period of time. All these skills of self reliance support their move towards independence. A range of the skills of self reliance will be covered in this chapter and in Chapters 3 and 4. This section highlights the general issues that shape your good practice.

Supporting and encouraging children

Very young children, especially babies, need a great deal of physical care because they cannot look after themselves (see Chapter 6). But if you observe babies and toddlers, you will realise that even babies want to use their physical skills. Young

Figure 2.2
This toddler can see his friend needs some help

children are keen to feel competent and they often show by gestures and phrases like 'me do it' that they want to feel active and not passive in a care routine. Children who are continually discouraged, prevented from taking part or criticised for their failings will give up in the end, probably only to be further criticised by thoughtless adults for being 'lazy'.

In this area of children's learning, the word **independence** can be misleading if it is used to mean that children should manage without help or encouragement on acquiring this skill. During childhood the move towards independence is a steady process, as children become able to take on their own care and make their own decisions. Young children can be relatively independent in some areas of their care and still very dependent in others.

An alternative is to understand and observe how young children practise the skills of **self reliance** within daily routines and become able to share in their own care.

By the time children reach their third birthday they can take an active part in much of their own physical care. They can usually:

- manage a great deal of their own toileting and hygiene
- feed themselves, handle drinks and make choices about food
- dress and undress, sometimes with help, and express preferences about what they will wear
- take appropriate responsibility, so long as adults allow, for instance in tidying up, serving out food and running simple messages
- make choices about activities and plan a bit ahead with the support of a patient adult.

Adult attention to children's skills of self reliance can be an effective way to promote other areas of their development, for instance:

- Children can be a trusted and enthusiastic helper in an early years setting or their own family home. Feeling of value and importance boosts their sense of self worth.

Key terms

Independence
the move in childhood toward children's being able to take responsibility for their own care and decisions

Self reliance
an area of children's skills in which they become more able to use their own resources and knowledge to undertake their own care and make choices

- Ordinary daily routines offer children practice in recalling steps in a simple sequence or to notice that something has been forgotten. Thinking skills, communication and making choices can be involved.
- When adults value children's growing self reliance, the children are supported in a positive disposition to learn (see also page 393). They have direct experience that they can learn ('I can do it') and if they forget or become confused, they can ask for help.

Young children need to feel positive about being more self reliant and adult behaviour is key.

- Children are motivated to persevere and practise when you are generous with your encouragement or thanks. For instance, 'well done, you got your mittens on' or 'you've found the book, thank you!'
- Be patient and give children time. It is better for a child who wants to button up her coat to be allowed to do it, rather than an adult insisting on 'helping'. You can step in if you really are pressed for time, but often this will not be the case.
- Be flexible in your standards and do not re-do something unless really necessary. A child who is proud that she has buttoned up her coat does not really need it re-done because she did not line up the buttons.
- In a friendly atmosphere adults and children help each other out. Sometimes a child is able to do something but for the moment would like you to do it, so he feels cared for by you. You are physically capable of fetching the tissue box or pouring yourself some more juice, but you ask for help because a child is nearby and because she likes to help.
- Children need to practise in order to hone their skills of self reliance, just like any other area of learning. They are more likely to keep trying when their resistance or difficulties are met with patience, good humour and help from adults.
- Children are discouraged by ungracious adults who take the line of 'you're four years old, you ought to be able to …'. If children are behaving in a hopeless-helpless way, then being rude to them or making them feel silly will not improve matters.
- Children's successes should be met with pleasure and a 'well done' from adults; never with any sense of 'so what, you should be doing that anyway', which is most discouraging for anyone of any age.

Everyday skills can seem ordinary but this does not mean that they are easy skills to learn. Young children can be motivated to learn skills of self care but they need caring adults to show them how and support them. You learned physical skills such as cutting your food or tying up shoelaces a long time ago. Do you recall how difficult these tasks seemed to you as a child?

For example, suppose that a three year old is learning how to pour herself a drink from a jug. She has to look carefully at the jug, pick it up and hold it steady as she moves it to her cup or mug. She has to concentrate on holding the jug and looking at the cup as she starts to pour. She has to stop before the drink goes over the top of her cup. Then she has to straighten the jug and look carefully as she moves it back and places it down on the table.

Activity

Take one daily care routine.

- For instance, when children can manage some of their own dressing and undressing or have understood to wash their hands after going to the toilet or before a cooking activity.
- In what ways could this achievement be linked with their learning in the other areas of their development (see page 12 for a summary)?
- Draw a simple chart to show how such learning could be linked.
- Make a short presentation to your colleagues and explore how you can keep such connections fresh in your mind in your day by day practice.

Key skills links: C2/3.1b LP2/3.1–3

Scenario

Nancy works as a full time daily nanny with 18 month old Annmarie and four year old Jerome. Nancy had previously worked in a day nursery and is having to make some adjustments to how children can learn at home. Nancy had been used to a very structured day working with three and four year olds in the nursery's pre-school group. Annmarie and Jerome are used to a family life in which they have a role in family routines like bringing in the post, shopping in the local market and simple cooking. Jerome has always liked being the helper with Annmarie's physical care and is unhappy when Nancy's first reaction is to do all the care herself.

Questions

1. In what important ways is family life unlike nursery life?
2. In what ways could Nancy draw on the advantages of family life for the children's learning?
3. In what ways could Nancy bring in her experience of the nursery but adjusted for her job as a nanny?
4. Discuss your ideas with colleagues.

Key skills links: C2/3.1a

Activity (observation)

If you are under a lot of pressure, you may be tempted to expect young children to feed and dress themselves without much help or encouragement. But this is expecting too much of many three and four year olds and certainly of two year olds.

Within the last few weeks what have you expected the children to manage largely without any help from adults?

- Going to the toilet?

- Putting on outdoor clothes before playing outside?
- Eating a meal?

Looking back over this section of the book with your own notes.

- Are you expecting too much?
- Or perhaps your expectations are realistic for the children's age, yet you have forgotten to say 'Well done', to appreciate and encourage.
- Bear in mind as well that sometimes children just like some help. It may be their way of asking for some personal attention in a rushed and impersonal atmosphere. You can lose a friendly balance in a family home as a nanny or in an early years setting.

Discuss your observations and thoughts with your colleagues. Be pleased about examples of good practice in your own work and make some specific plans for any improvements in your practice, however minor.

Key skills link: C3.1a LP2/3.1–3 WO2/3.1–3

Activity (observation)

- Look carefully at all that is involved in some other very ordinary activities that young children are learning. Think about the physical skills and the importance of concentration and not being distracted.
- Take one or two of the following ideas, perhaps in discussion with colleagues, and list the separate steps that children have to manage and the skills involved.

Here are some examples from which to choose:

- cutting up a piece of chicken or meat
- turning an inside out sweatshirt or jumper the right way around
- buttoning up a shirt, blouse or coat
- doing up an open-ended zip on a coat or jacket
- tying shoelaces.

What can you learn about your positive help for children?

- What could be difficult, how can you show and encourage?
- Look at the possibility of using photos to show the steps in a self care routine.
- Discuss with your colleagues. Be pleased about the ways that you currently help children and make some specific plans for improvements to practice, even if minor.

Key skills links: C2/3.1a LP2/3.1–3 WO2/3.1–3

The impact of disability

Some features of good quality care are especially relevant when children are very young. However, the need for such an approach continues into later childhood when children have disabilities.

- A child with learning disabilities may take longer than her peers to understand and be able to take over her own care.
- A child with physical disabilities may know what has to be done but cannot manage some part of the physical coordination or balance.
- Alternatively, disabled children may need much more time, and therefore adult patience, and perhaps some special equipment to enable them to take over their own care.

Tips for practice

You do need to be sensitive to children's feelings, when physical disability may limit their current ability to take on their own care like their peers. Disabled four and five years olds may be uncomfortably aware that their friends need less help with dressing or going to the toilet. You can help when you:

- Work for a respectful balance between helping and letting the child do as much as she can.
- Ask if a child would like help, rather than swooping in without asking.
- Treat the child in a manner appropriate for her age and ensure that, just because she needs to be changed, she does not feel like a baby.
- Talk with the child's parents and take advantage of any special equipment, for example modified cutlery, that could help this child.
- Be alert to any changes you could make in your routine that would enable a disabled child to be more of a full member of your group. Such a change might mean that a routine takes longer but it would be time well spent if a child feels more competent and involved.
- Children can sometimes help each other and you can look for opportunities for a fully-abled child to help a disabled peer. Ideally look for a way that the disabled child can then help in her turn.

Children as partners in helping out

Young children are keen to learn everyday skills and are enthusiastic about having a trusted part in the daily routine of home or early years setting. Unfortunately they will give up if their offers are regularly refused. Children also stop offering if adults set such exacting standards that the children inevitably fail.

Helping out in the daily routines

You can find many opportunities for children to help and learn:

- Young children enjoy learning some of the simpler tasks of everyday life. Tasks that seem dull or very routine to you can be refreshing to children and also intriguing because they are part of the adult social world.

Figure 2.3

Children can help with the tidying up

- An 18 month old can be delighted to hand you items you need. Your words and expression tell him that the book or tissue he brought over is just what you needed.
- Young children can learn skills while they help you sort out cupboards or track down the missing pieces of jigsaw. They often like this time for conversation. You chat together while you share the activity.
- Children are flattered that you ask and let them take simple messages from one room to another.
- Children like to be involved in the care of children younger than themselves. Three and four year olds are often fascinated by baby care and basic child development.
- Of course, you must remain responsible for a baby's safety, yet children can hand you a clean nappy or the tub of cream. They could choose clean clothes for the baby. Children are also often adept at amusing a baby while you do the changing.

Tidying up

It is valuable that children learn about tidying up.

- Give children a simple count down that tidying up will be soon. They can then prepare themselves.
- Give enough time so that children are not rushed. They will not want to be involved if tidying up means being nagged and criticised.
- Have a system that makes it easy for children to know where items go: a written label, a picture or a shape board for tools.
- Encourage children to put equipment like a posting box back together and encourage them to be good spotters of missing jigsaw pieces.

- Show the children that you value tidying up time as a routine of learning. It is not wasted time, so be encouraging and say 'thanks' or 'well done'.

Watch out for any sense that everything must be tidied up and put away if that means that a child's work in progress is demolished. Some settings have great difficulties because they share premises, such as pre-school and playgroups that use church halls. However, some settings that do not experience these pressures nevertheless can get into thoughtless habits.

- If children are in the middle of a large construction, a painting or piece of craft or woodwork, do look for places to put it safely, so that they can come back to it.
- Use cameras to record work in progress or take a permanent record of something that took children a lot of time and of which they are proud: a den in the garden, a substantial sand or earthwork that will not survive the next rain.

Scenarios

- The children in St Jude's after school club are keen on rotas at the moment. Pam and Naomi had been puzzled about the request for a 'proper grown up rota'. Then they worked out that washing up the crockery and cutlery from tea is of particular importance because the helper gets the undivided attention of the adult who is also washing up today.
- Tyrone in Baker Street Children and Family Centre has an enthusiastic 'team and delegation' approach that the current group of children clearly relish. Tidying up time starts with a 'team meeting' and agreement about who will tidy up what today. The children scatter and Tyrone moves around to offer help and a humorous chivvying to keep children on track. Tyrone realises that this approach will not necessarily work with all children, but it suits the dynamics of the current group.
- Dresden Road Nursery School has learning spaces with some materials that can only be stacked away in one or two ways. Rosemary recently undertook a project with children in which they took photos of ways to stack their big items like foam or the large wooden blocks. Rosemary fully involved the children in doing this task and explained she believed it would help everyone to have a picture to check. The photos are now enlarged and fixed in the relevant learning spaces.
- Sunningdale Day Nursery has some children who are not used to being involved in tidying up. Penny has developed an approach of asking children, especially the less keen ones, which bit of tidying they would like to do and then offer, 'Shall I come and help?' Penny has found this strategy works better than making the decision and asking children to join her. When she and the child or children have completed one task, she asks what they would like to tidy next.

Questions

1 There are different ways to encourage children to be involved in tidying up and much of the strategy depends on positive adult attitudes and behaviour.

2 Your own approach needs to fit with your temperament and that of the children. So these scenarios are examples, not a template for what you 'ought' to do.

3 Discuss with your colleagues and make some specific plans to improve or vary practice.

Key skills links: LP2/3.1–3 WO2/3.1–3

Step by step learning

You can help children by understanding the step by step process of learning ordinary tasks. Make everyday tasks simpler if necessary or find a part of a task that the children can do. Keep to realistic standards for how long a task will take and how well it is done. Ordinary daily routines in a nursery can take a little longer; maybe you can finish off the task discreetly later and then children feel encouraged and ready to have a go another time.

Remember that the process does not have to be all or nothing. Look at it as several stages:

- You are totally responsible – you judge that babies or children cannot manage something or it is not yet safe for them to try, however much they want to try. They may watch you but do not actually join in.
- You encourage them to join in – you enable children to help you out a bit, though you are still basically in charge.
- Children take responsibility but you watch over them – you can say, 'Go on, you try it' and you stay close to help if they need it
- Children are wholly responsible – you allow children to take responsibility for the task with little or no supervision. You may check on the task afterwards and give encouragement and any helpful feedback.

Activity

Make a list of at least 10–15 tasks that have to be undertaken in your early years settings or in a family home as a nanny or childminder. You might include some of the following as your starter ideas for the list:

- choosing the menu for next week
- taking a message to someone in another room
- cleaning up when the baby has been sick
- cleaning out the rabbit
- answering the telephone, taking telephone messages
- reorganising the book corner or shelf.

Now look at each task and link up with the basic steps of learning in this section.

- To what extent are the children involved?

- Could they be involved if you took more time or adjusted the task a bit?
- Plan and make a short presentation of how you could adjust, or have adjusted, a daily routine so that children can have a helpful, active role.

Key skills link: LP2.1–3 C2.1b

Cleanliness and personal hygiene

Once a nursery, pre-school or home environment is clean enough there is no advantage, and some disadvantages to greater attention to cleanliness. Over attention to cleaning and tidying means that your time is diverted from the children. There is also some suggestion that an obsessive concern with cleaning and 'zapping' germs mean that children's bodies do not encounter the range of ordinary germs that enable their bodies to build up immunities. Basically, children and their surroundings need to be clean but not sterile (see Care and development of babies, Chapter 6.)

In the play area

A safe environment for babies and children is free from threats to their physical well being and health. The environment should be clean, some areas, like toilets and kitchens, need to be kept within a good standard of hygiene. The whole play area needs to be tidy enough for people to be able to move around and not trip

Figure 2.4 Children like helping out and they learn

over objects. However, children need to spread out with their play materials if they are to enjoy and learn.

An appropriate standard of cleanliness allows for enjoyable play:

- Children will get grubby on occasion and happy outdoor play will involve natural substances that mark hands and clothes.
- Children clean up very well and soon become active participants in the cleaning up and tidying process.
- Children who are expected to remain unnaturally clean cannot help out properly in the daily routines, cannot play with their friends and cannot learn.
- Younger children are unlikely to make it through the day in the same set of clothes.
- Older children may be fine apart from the odd accident, so long as they get into the habit of using aprons or overalls for art, craft and cooking activities.
- Play materials need to be clean but, unless children have health conditions that make them especially vulnerable, you do not need to be forever scrubbing and polishing.
- Your storage systems should keep play materials as free from dust as possible.

You will need to pay close attention to the hygiene needs of babies and young toddlers.

- Babies and toddlers suck and chew their play materials, so it is particularly important that their toys are regularly washed in hot soapy water, rinsed and left to drip dry.
- Rattles and similar baby toys should not ideally pass from baby to baby without being cleaned.

Kitchens and bathrooms

Strict standards of hygiene are needed in the kitchen and bathroom. Infections, especially those causing stomach upsets, can pass like wildfire around a group of children and adults who spend their days in close proximity.

- In an early years setting you will be responsible for cleaning up after children but there will be cleaning staff on the team who do the regular cleaning.
- If you work as a nanny then you may share some of the cleaning responsibility with parents – as it affects the children – but you should not be expected to do household cleaning as such.
- As a childminder you will be responsible for your own household tasks and cleaning. But you should ensure that cleaning does not impose on generous time and attention given to the children.

Hygiene procedures

You should wash your hands with soap, or an alternative if you are allergic to soap:

- before and after changing a child
- before cleaning cuts or grazes

- after you have been to the toilet
- before you handle food or prepare a baby's bottle.

You should cover any cuts or grazes on your hands with a plaster.

Adults in an early years setting need to follow a consistent procedure to avoid cross infection between children and adults. Contact with body fluids and body products can be a very efficient way of passing on minor and major infections.

- You should wear a fresh pair of disposable gloves each time you change a child or deal with any accident in which a child's skin is broken.
- After use the gloves should be placed in a sealed bag in the same careful way as a disposable nappy, used dressings and bandages.
- Precautions such as wearing a light apron and using disposable gloves became more usual in nurseries in response to conditions such as HIV/AIDS and hepatitis. You will not necessarily know if children are infected and, even if you do, it would be thoughtless to treat that child noticeably differently from his or her peers.

You might still choose to use disposable gloves if you work as a nanny or child-minder, but the risks of cross infection are less.

Tips for practice

You can be caring in word and action while you are following hygienic procedures.

- Children should never be made to feel unclean or that there is something the matter with them that makes you wear plastic gloves.
- You should talk to and smile at a baby you are changing.
- You can reassure a child who is scraped and comfort one who is bleeding.
- Explain simply to any child or adult who asks what the reasons are for wearing plastic gloves: that you could otherwise pass on germs between people without realising it.
- However, since you will use gloves with any child under given circumstances, they may not ask. What you are doing simply looks normal; it is what adults do in your setting.

Sharing the care on hygiene

You can set a good example in hygiene that will promote health without making children over-anxious about bugs and germs.

- Show and remind children so that they learn hand washing after going to the toilet and before handling food or eating their meal.
- In a group setting they also need to understand about using only their own towel, flannel or toothbrush. Children can be helped to follow hygiene when they have an individual peg with the child's name and a photo or picture to help them recognise their own items.
- You can explain simply about germs passing when you sneeze or cough and that is why everyone should put their hand in front of their mouth and use a handkerchief or tissue.

- Younger children need guidance and redirection to understand that sand and earth are not for eating and you may need to clean up their hands more often than those of older children. Children with learning disabilities will take longer to learn and you may need to offer this care and support into middle childhood.
- Children are often very interested in the care of others and like to watch you change or clean a baby. Use these opportunities to explain and answer questions.
- Special care and explanations need to be given about hygiene if you have a pet in the setting or you visit a children's farm. The main dangers come from children touching an animal and then putting their fingers into their mouth.

Activity

- Draft a short description of the main ways to ensure hygiene when children have contact with animals.
- Plan ways that you could communicate this message to children and remind them in ways that do not feel like nagging, nor make them over-anxious.
- Look for ways to use photos and children's drawings.
- Make a short presentation to colleagues.

Key skills links: C2/3.1b LP2/3.1–3

Skin care

Generally you will only need to ensure that children keep clean enough and that you deal with any scrapes or bruises. You may need to use cream on a child if her skin has a tendency to become dry and cracked. This is a normal part of daily care for many dark skinned children and should be discussed with their parents. However, some lighter skinned children have sensitive skin and also need some personal attention. (See page 131 about eczema.) You will probably find a cream that is appropriate for all children who need this extra help. You may not need to put cream on some children unless they have a long day with you or you take the group swimming. Some four and five year olds will be ready to help with their own skin care.

Care in the sun

All children need protection against the sun when they are playing outside in hot weather. Children's skin is especially sensitive and later problems with skin cancer can arise from sunburn in childhood. Light skinned children will be the first to burn but dark skinned children will also get sunburn and heatstroke if you do not take care of them. Children do not understand this risk, although they can comprehend getting hot and sticky. It is the adults' responsibility to keep children safe:

- Children should not be kept inside during hot weather. They need to get out, but equipped with a suitable sun hat and sun cream.
- Discuss with parents the need for sun protection creams and ask them to send in a hat that their child is prepared to wear.

- The best kind of sun hats are the kind with a neck flap as well as the hat part – the legionnaire style.
- You will need to put the sun cream on younger children but you can start the process of encouraging them to rub in the dabs of cream that you put on exposed limbs and their face.
- In a long hot spell, you will need to limit children's time in the direct sun and ensure that everyone has water easily available for drinking.
- You also need some shade in a garden or outdoor area. If you do not have natural shady areas in your garden then you need to create some shade with an awning or an impromptu tent or tepee. Children will like these kind of facilities and play in them even when the sun is not that hot.

Children need sunlight

It is good practice to help children protect themselves from overheating and sunburn. However, children need to get out in the air and they need sunlight; it is a vital and free source of vitamin D. This vitamin is also available from some foods (see page 84), but since the vitamin is stored by our bodies, summer is a good time to build up children's reserves.

Scenario

The team at St Jude's Primary School was aware that sun care and reminders for children should continue into their school years. The nursery practitioners had been putting sun cream on the children and monitoring that they wore hats. The nursery team set a good example by wearing a sunhat themselves. A significant hot spell brought home to staff the fact that the primary school playground has few shady areas and that children have become overheated and close to getting sunburned.

In a recent full team meeting, the primary school staff expressed concerns about the possibility of some children being allergic to certain sun creams and whether anyone should risk the physical contact necessary to put the cream onto children. The playground supervisory assistants are anxious about the contact issues but pointed out that sun protection is too important to be overlooked. They also raised the problems of children getting enough to drink in a hot spell. The nursery team pointed out that they have always worked in partnership with parents to ensure that children come with hats and suitable cream in hot weather, and suggested that a way be found to extend that good practice into the school years.

Questions

1. Consider and discuss with colleagues the scope of the problem faced by St Jude's. What are the main issues and what are the priorities?
2. Suggest some ways to resolve this problem.

Key skills links: C3.1a PS3.1.

Hair care

Children can learn to brush or comb their hair, although they have to learn how to approach tangles with care. You will need a different kind of comb if children have a head of thick, curly hair. Parents will sometimes have specific concerns about hair and you may be unaware of these if you do not share the same cultural background.

- Boys from Rastafarian families will probably have their hair in dreadlocks and these must not be combed. They wear a tam (hat).
- Young Sikh boys have a small cloth covering their hair, which will have been wound up neatly on the top of their head.
- Some families will require their daughters to keep their hair covered. In Hindu families, this may be a loose scarf; Muslim families will send their daughters in a close fitting head covering the style of which varies. Girls from Rastafarian families will also be expected to keep their hair covered, probably with a scarf.

None of these head coverings should be removed. If you are from a different ethnic group the coverings may seem optional, but they are not. If a child's head covering creates a safety issue, perhaps if the scarf is loose, then talk with parents about acceptable ways to secure the scarf.

Afro-Caribbean girls sometimes have their hair in intricate plaits and it may also be oiled. Boys also sometimes have plaiting. Parents will be cross if they find sand or earth in their children's hair. It is impossible to get it out without abandoning the whole style, and some will have taken hours to do. Talk with parents about a scarf or other head covering that their child is willing to wear when playing with sand or other fine, natural materials.

Tips for practice

- If you are in any doubt, it is always better to talk with parents. It is wiser to admit to being unsure than to offend out of avoidable ignorance.
- You cannot be expected to know everything. Even in a culturally diverse area, you may not have had contact with families from some ethnic groups until now.
- If you work with school age children, they will be far more able than younger ones to tell you and explain themselves.
- Build up your knowledge but be careful about over-generalising. There is great variety within ethnic groups as well as between groups.

Clothes and dressing

Choice of clothes

Ideally children should be wearing clothes in which they can have a relaxed and enjoyable day. From the perspective of an early years setting this tends to mean comfortable clothes that are not too fussy and that parents will tolerate getting a bit grubby or dotted with paint.

Some parents will put their children in clothes that are good for play and be fairly calm about the evidence on clothes of a good day for children. However, some parents want their children well turned out all the time and may spend a lot of money on fashionable clothes for even very young children. Your preferences for clothes may not be those of parents and in different ways you do need to reach some compromise. For instance:

- Talk with parenıs before children join your setting about the activities that they will enjoy.
- Offer overalls, aprons or even a change of clothing for art, craft and gardening activities.
- Do your very best to protect children's clothes but not to the point of restricting their play and playful exploration.
- Offer practical advice to parents about how to remove paint or glue. Some paint has to be washed out with cold water; hot water sets it like a dye. Some glue comes off more easily if the item is cooled in the fridge or freezer first of all.
- Understand that for some parents there will be issues about modesty and girls.
- Muslim parents in particular will not be happy for their daughters to strip down to underwear for games or possibly to go swimming. See what compromises can be reached.

Scenario

Baker Street Children and Family Centre has faced several awkward situations recently over children's clothes. The centre team feels strongly about not imposing on parent's choices about how they dress their children. However, they feel they do need to address the problems with two families:

- Four year old Tanya wears slip on shoes and she regularly falls over when she runs. Tanya's key worker wants to suggest that Tanya's father buy her some shoes that will fasten securely or agree to some system of fixing her shoes so they will not trip her.
- Three year old Wesley's parents like to dress him in very smart clothes and get irritated when he has spilt paint or glue. His mother has asked that Wesley does not do any more painting or sticking but, quite apart from the fact that this activity is regularly available, Wesley is very keen on arts and crafts.

Questions

1. How could the Baker Street team talk with parents?
2. Form pairs to create a role play in which you explore diplomatic ways to approach the problem about a child's clothes. One person takes the role of the early years practitioner and one of the parent in these two situations.
3. Explore in group discussion what the main problems and priorities are.

Key skills links: PS2/3.1

Growing self reliance

Very young babies cannot help in their physical care, indeed their waving arms and legs can make simple dressing quite a marathon. Within a few months however they start to join in.

- A baby or toddler will push his arm into a sleeve if you hold it out for him. From the baby's perspective it may be just as interesting to take his arm out again.
- Toddlers who gain the skills required to take their hats on and off sometimes continue this action for the sheer pleasure of doing it successfully.
- Toddlers who are in the mood may cooperate in dressing, so long as they are not rushed and the dressing is not taking them away from a more interesting activity. They aim their arms and legs into clothing that you hold out.
- Two and three year olds learn to manage the simpler parts of dressing: pull on or pull up clothes, slip on shoes.
- They will find some fastenings difficult and it is not unusual to see them tug hard and hope for the best.
- Children also find the sequence of dressing complicated at the outset. Without your help, they may put on pants over the top of trousers, so line up their clothes so they can follow a sequence and say out loud when you dress them.
- Three, four and five year olds learn to tackle the more common ways of fastening clothes and many garments for children are made easier with elasticated waists or velcro to fasten shoes.
- Children of this age need to see what they are doing and you may be able to direct their attention to how the task is progressing.
- Children will have more difficulty if fastenings are at the back or their clothes are tight fitting.
- You can help children by being patient as they learn and helping them sometimes. Children appreciate a helping hand and not just because they have failed and ought to be able do up their buttons.

Scenario

In the Wessex childminding network the group of childminders has explored issues about time and children learning the skills of self reliance. Sophie shared an experience that had made her think recently.

Sophie had heard herself pressing Alison to let her do the child's coat up with, 'Why not let me help, then you go out to play sooner'. But Sophie then realised that Alison, as much as she loved going out in the garden, was not interested in speed and wanted to do up her coat, every button, herself. Sophie realised that it was unwise to press Alison on the grounds that help would be quicker. There was no real time pressure and Alison could then gain the satisfaction of 'doing it myself'.

Questions

1 Do you find yourself pressing children when there is no real time pressure?

2 How can you ensure that you relax and be appreciative of what children have accomplished?
3 Recognise your current good practice and make some specific plans for improvements, even minor ones.

Key skills links: LP2/3.1–3

Activity

Children benefit from a chance to practise tricky fastenings when there is no pressure of time. List ways that you could help, for instance:

- You could make a fastenings hanging or cloth book in which there is a selection of buttons and button holes, poppers, zips and laces.
- Doing up shoe laces is especially challenging and it can be sobering as an adult to try to explain in words exactly what you do to tie up shoelaces. This verbal task can remind you that it is a complex task.
- Do you have a doll or teddy with clothes that fasten? Can children practise in this way?
- Try one or two approaches with children. Write up the activity and use photos or children's drawings, if they would like to be involved.

Key skills links: C2.3

Rest and activity

Children need a healthy combination of varied activity, quiet and restful periods and actual sleep. Babies, toddlers and children vary in terms of how much sleep they need in total and how they gain this amount. It is in everyone's interests, adults as well as children, that children get enough sleep and that in the end they do their sleeping in the night time.

Children who do not get enough sleep can have dark rings under their eyes or nod off regularly during the day. But they can also be irritable and more likely to squabble with their peers and you may not immediately explain this behaviour by insufficient sleep. Young children do not know that they are lacking enough sleep and they may, of course, be very resistant to going to bed and staying there in the evening at home. It is an adult responsibility to help children develop healthy sleeping habits and that needs a bedtime routine.

Sleeping patterns

Babies sleep for a large amount in total of the 24 hour day but they do this sleeping in bursts of 3–4 hours, waking for feeding throughout the day and night. A lot of babies do seem to reach a more settled pattern, with longer night sleeps by about three months or earlier. But this is not an absolute and some apparently

Figure 2.5
Children need a quiet sleeping area

settled babies start a wakeful pattern later on. At some point during the first year of life many, but certainly not all, babies sleep for the longest period through the night. Their parents, or a nanny with sole charge, will then get a decent night's sleep, although possibly with a prompt start to the day.

Older babies and toddlers will have one or two daytime naps. But some children up to three and four years of age may still need a short daytime nap, probably after lunch, or at least a quiet period. Some children attend an early years setting for full childcare because their parents work or study. The full day can then be long and children are likely to need a quiet, peaceful time to recoup their energy, even if they do not actually fall asleep.

Rest and quiet in the day

An early years setting needs comfortable areas where children can rest or nap in comfort. Sleepers need to be undisturbed by other children who are awake, but close enough that someone can be with them swiftly as they move back into wakefulness.

All children need a set of bedding for nap time that is not shared with others and is laundered regularly. If bedding like sleeping bags have to be dry cleaned, then they must be aired thoroughly before they are used for sleeping, in order to remove any residue of the cleaning chemicals.

Tips for practice

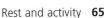

- Babies should be allowed to take naps when they want and not pushed into a nursery routine.
- By 18 months or so, toddlers will be more able to take naps at the same time as their peers, probably after lunch. But you still need to be flexible about the toddler or young child who needs a longer nap.
- Young children appreciate physical contact such as a cuddle or stroke as they drift into sleep and they often feel better if they have a gentle return to wakefulness.
- By your considerate behaviour and words you can help children learn about and recognise their own feelings.
- What does it feel like to be tired and ready for a nap or rest, or pleasantly tired after a good physical game? What does it feel like to be rested and keen to get back into play?

Activity (observation)

Children benefit from a blend of energetic and more peaceful occupations. Gather ideas for what children could do, and what you observe they enjoy, for a quiet time in the day.

Questions

1. Do children enjoy browsing through books and how can you make a welcoming corner or choice of books for children who are less keen?
2. Can you use quiet music to communicate that this is a peaceful time of the day?
3. Are there some quiet, yet intellectually challenging activities that older children enjoy because they have your undivided attention?
4. How do you create a useful routine that runs into quiet time and avoids simply telling children they must be quiet now? How do you behave and set a good example?

- Write up your observations with photos and children's drawings, if they would like to contribute.
- Discuss your ideas with colleagues and add any more that they have encountered.
- Plan some changes or improvements to your current practice.

Key skills links: C2.1a C2.3 LP2/3.1–3 WO2/3.1–3

Bedtime routines and night waking

By no means all very young children sleep all through the night, every night. Readers, who are not themselves parents, need to be aware that night-time waking and general sleep disruptions in the family are the most commonly reported problems for which parents would like advice, especially for children aged 12–18 months. Studies of sleep and waking patterns show that children,

Figure 2.6

Sometimes children just need to rest

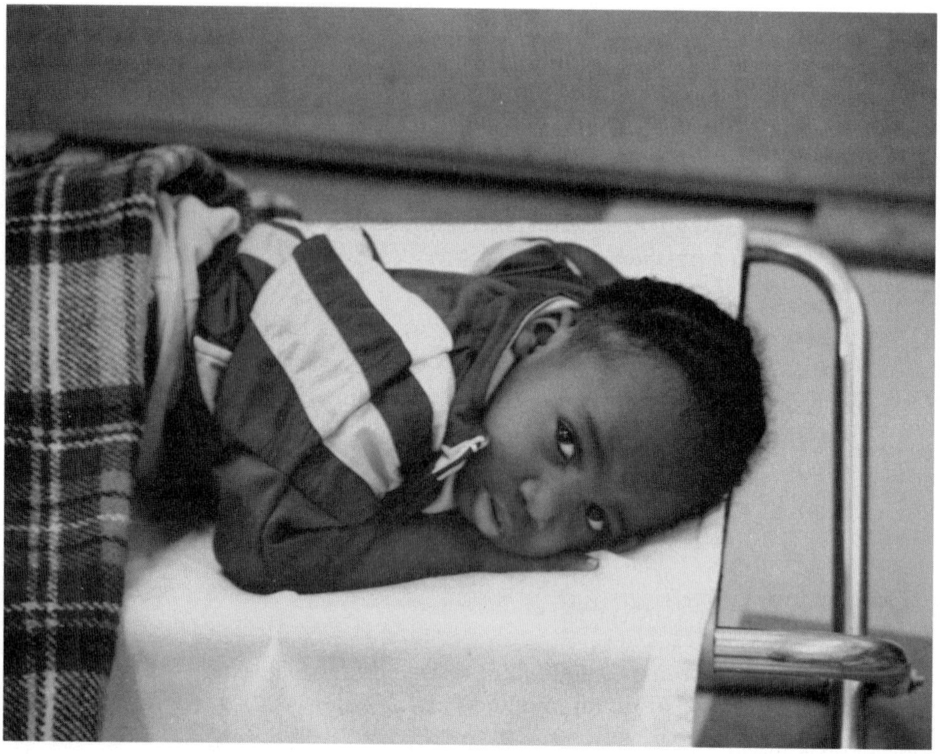

just like adults, vary a great deal in how long they sleep in total, how restless their sleep is, how deep their sleep is and how much they move about. Young children wake a great deal but some drift back into sleep and do not call for their parents.

You may directly face the issue of night waking because you work as a nanny with some night-time responsibility. Alternatively if you work in an early years setting, parents may ask your advice about night waking.

Tips for practice

If parents ask your advice, there are no certain solutions but some positive guidelines can accompany the ideas in this section about what to do:

- First of all, acknowledge parents' exhaustion and show sympathy for what they are going through. If you have not experienced broken nights, recognise that sleep deprivation is a very effective form of psychological torture!
- Ask open ended questions and listen to what parents say: what is going on with the child and in the family? Is the problem one of very early starts to the day or regular waking in the middle of the night? A child who wakes screaming from nightmares is different from one who wakes wanting a drink and a play.
- Sometimes it helps to keep a sleep diary, so that a nanny or parents can look for any patterns.
- Sometimes there may be a relatively straightforward suggestion to make, such as a last night feed for hungry baby, a night light for a scared toddler or shorter daytime naps for an older child.

The current generation of children has later bedtimes than previous generations and sometimes working parents enjoy a longer evening to spend time with their children. Even with some flexibility, a regular bedtime and bedtime routine is important to help children to settle and to get enough sleep so that they enjoy their days to the full.

- Establish a regular bedtime routine that creates a different feel to the end of the day.
- A wash or bath can be followed by putting on night-time clothes and reading a bedtime story.
- For a younger child, the light is then put out or turned low. Some children of five or six years of age may need a quiet time in bed with books because they genuinely are not ready to sleep yet.
- After settle time, calls from a child or appearances in the living room are dealt with calmly but the child is tucked back in or taken back up and told it's bedtime now. Adults, a nanny or parents, need to be patient and be prepared to return the child again and again.

Three main themes run through the most useful advice about dealing with night waking. It helps if:

- toddlers and children are settled to rest and not to sleep
- adults cut back on lengthy settling rituals that do not help
- children are reassured briefly and then left for short periods of time (the checking procedure).

Many of the lengthier bedtime rituals (at official bedtime and during the night) come from trying to find a way to send young children to sleep. Children are nursed, rocked, sung to sleep, all sorts of patterns, rather than settled to rest. You want to get babies and toddlers into the habit of settling themselves and being content to lie awake and look at a mobile, chat to themselves or hug a teddy. Apparently older babies and toddlers wake quite a lot, the problem comes when they cry and wake everyone else.

A friendly checking procedure is different from the old style of letting children 'cry it out' for ages. The pattern for a nanny in sole charge or for parents whom you advise is as follows:

- Don't go in at the first whimper, see if the young child will settle.
- If not, then go in, say comforting words, settle the child briefly and tuck him in with a comforter.
- Go out of the room or well out of sight and wait it out through a short crying period of only a few minutes.
- If the child continues to cry, then go back in and follow the same short comforting approach.
- Keep going in this way and stay calm. You can gradually extend the time you wait but do not leave a child to cry for more than five minutes in total.
- This approach is not a magical one-night solution but it will work because a young child gradually learns that the situation has changed. Parents or the family nanny are available for brief comfort but not for lengthy contact or night-time play.
- Consistency and support is key between all the adult members of the household. You all need patience and a willingness to have bad nights, maybe even worse until it gets better.

It is a different situation when toddlers and children are ill or frightened, but undoubtedly you have to beware giving more comfort and attention for illness than a child usually experiences.

If children still wake at night, then parents may ask you to restrict their daytime naps or ensure they do not doze off after a certain time in the day at the nursery. Discuss this issue with parents and, if need be, offer some practical advice on settling children and dealing with night waking. But also give what practical help you can, by ensuring that children do not sleep through large amounts of the day.

Self reliance with toileting

Becoming toilet trained is a major issue in early childhood and will take some time, although not always a very long period. Children need to become reliably trained for day and night time and to be confident about dealing with their needs at the toilet, which also includes being able to handle their own dressing and undressing.

When are children ready?

There is no point in trying to toilet train children before they are ready. Being over prompt only means frustration and many wet pants. Talk with a child's parents about their own view and ensure that the toilet training is done in partnership. It is not helpful if parents leave it all up to the nursery; toilet training needs to be a joint enterprise.

The signs of readiness are only partly physical:

- Young children need to have reached the point where they recognise that they have wet or filled their nappy; something has happened.
- This physical awareness is unlikely before 18–24 months of age and some children are really not ready until after their second birthday. Girls on average are ready a little earlier than boys, but you will see a great deal of variety between individual children.
- Children also need to be able to understand simple requests. The new idea of 'Let's sit you on your pot' has to make some sense, so that children start to sit themselves, rather than your doing it all. Nearly all two year olds have also started playing simple pretend and this shows you that they can imagine and think ahead a little.

Some young children will not be ready by two years because their overall development has been slowed for some reason. Perhaps this child was born very premature or has a health condition or disability that means that toilet training is less straightforward. In consultation with the child's parents, you need to be guided by what children can manage and understand, not just their age in years and months.

Be supportive and realistic with parents. If a new baby is on the way, it can seem very attractive to parents to get the older one toilet trained before the new baby arrives. But if the older child is not ready, then everyone's efforts will bring little change and even reliably toilet trained children sometimes slip back when a new sibling arrives.

Helping children to become toilet trained

Children vary a great deal and some get the hang of toilet training in a matter of weeks, some steadily learn over a period of months. Some toileting accidents are usual for children who are toilet trained. Children are absorbed in play or try to hold on too long.

In a nursery there may be several children at one time in the process of getting toilet trained, so they have company and perhaps some idea of what happens. If you are a nanny working in a family home, then only one child may be working at this developmental task at any one time. A sensible way forward is as follows:

- When it looks as if a child is ready, then encourage him or her to try out sitting on a pot in the bathroom for short periods of time.
- Although little boys will eventually learn to urinate standing up, they start by sitting down.
- Many children start with pots, but some children like to sit on the toilet from the very beginning. In a nursery there will be low, child-sized toilet seats. In a family home, you will need a child seat to set within the ordinary toilet seat and a safe step for them to get up.
- It is an adult responsibility to ensure that a pot or the toilet seat is wiped clean after use. In an early years setting there may be a pot for each child or parents may bring in the child's own pot from home.
- Initially, the aim is to encourage a young child to sit on the pot, or the toilet, several times a day, but only for short periods of time.
- If children are lucky and get something in the pot, then say encouraging words like 'well done' and smile. If not, then maybe next time.
- It does not help to put pressure on children to sit until they have done something.
- In a nursery, there may be times when you encourage all the children to go to the toilet, perhaps before going out into the garden. Try to avoid an institutionalised routine and allow for personal toileting patterns.

Your aim is that the child's parent is following a similar pattern during their time with their child. Keep talking with the parent and compare how the process is coming along. If, after a couple of weeks, a child is really not keen, then stop. You will achieve nothing if toilet training becomes a battleground. It will be wiser to try again in a few weeks' time.

Tips for practice

- An early years team will probably have some agreement about what to call the pot productions. Most children themselves tend to use some version of 'pee' and 'poo'.
- If you are working as a nanny, then be guided by the words that parents would like to use.
- However, do alert parents, if they have not considered it, that their young child will then use the family words at top volume. Robust adult language to describe going to the toilet will be less welcome when broadcast across the local supermarket or bank.

With practice over the weeks, young children start to recognise not just that they've done a pee or a poo, but that they are about to do something. Then they may be able to speak up and say they want to go or simply take themselves to the toilet.

When children are happy to cooperate with going on the pot or toilet and have far fewer wet or soiled nappies, then you can take the next step of trying a child with pants and no nappy. Talk with parents and see if they feel their child is ready.

- Once children are minus their nappy, they do need regular reminders (every couple of hours) to sit on the pot or toilet. They also need continued encouragement by word and expression from adults. They are managing a tough developmental task and there should be no sense of 'about time too!'
- It is important to keep calm about the inevitable accidents and explain how normal this situation is to parents who have their first child. Explain to children that they need to have their pants changed, but avoid looking or sounding cross, because this is an accident.

Nowadays disposable trainer pants offer a halfway house option, but children need to make the move into proper, unpadded pants to be fully toilet trained. Padded pants may be useful on the odd occasion but, despite the enthusiastic advertising hype, are not evidence that children have managed this task.

Activity

- Plan for the toilet training of an individual child who appears ready. Consider what you will do and how.
- Track the progress of the child in toilet training. Write up the work.
- Ideally compare, with discretion and confidentiality, the pattern for several children. Toilet training can be very varied.

Key skills links: C2.3

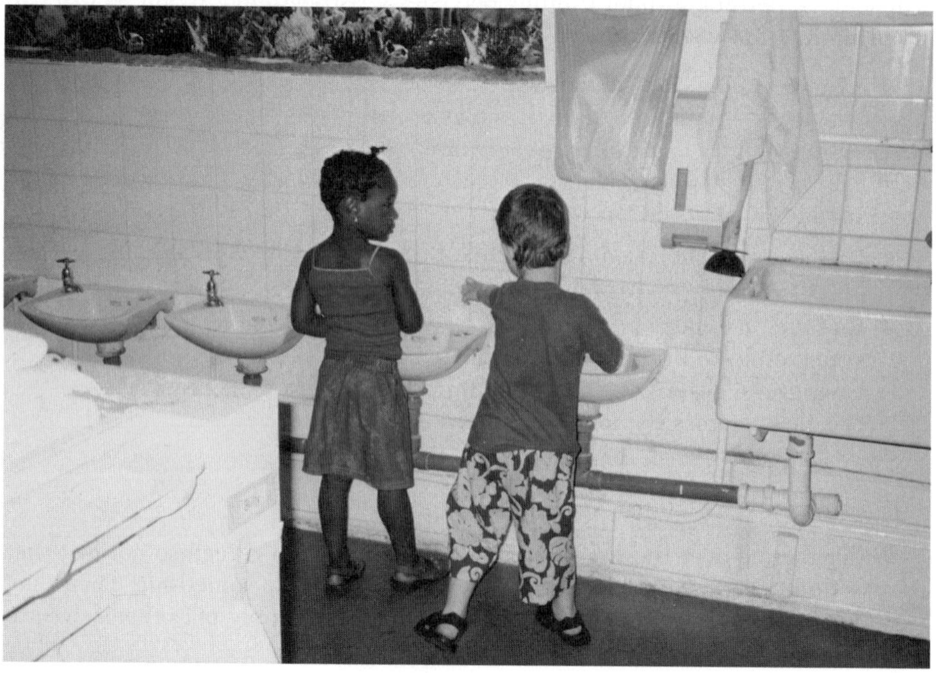

Figure 2.7
Children learn bathroom hygiene with your help

Self reliance in the bathroom

It is very usual that even children who are toilet trained have some accidents or have a period where they are less reliable. It is important to continue to be encouraging and to offer friendly reminders to go to the toilet.

- Three and four year olds, who are absorbed in their play, may ignore the physical sensations that tell them they should head for the toilet.
- Young children have much better muscle control than when they were younger but they cannot hold for very long.
- Tight clothing or difficult fastenings can defeat a child's fingers and they start to go before their pants are down fully.

Tips for practice

When children are toilet trained, it is time to help them share some of the responsibility for hygiene.

- Children need help with wiping their bottom until at least three or four years old.
- Be ready to hand over the task when they are ready.
- Show children how to wipe and explain to little girls that they should wipe from front to back (otherwise they risk vaginal infections such as thrush). Encourage all children in the habit of hand washing after using the toilet.

Boys need to learn to stand up for what they may call a 'big boy pee'.

- Talk with parents about what they would like, but there is no real point until a boy is tall enough to position his penis over the toilet.
- At home, with a full size toilet, he may need the help of a suitable step. Boys will probably be at least three and maybe four years old before standing up to urinate is a realistic possibility.
- Chatty boys also need to be encouraged to focus on what they are doing, or else there can be a wide splash zone.

Privacy

Children deserve privacy and attention to their dignity in the bathroom. If you pay attention to children's words and expressions, then it will be clear if they want to go to the toilet with the door shut. Some are less concerned and like the door open so they can chat. They may need to understand that their friend or adults prefer some privacy. An early years setting should be designed so that privacy is consistent with safety. For instance, if the toilet doors have latches, it should be possible for an adult to lean over and release the catch if a child has locked herself into the toilet.

When children are in school

Many four year olds are in school in England, Wales and Scotland and children start at this age in Northern Ireland.

- It is unreasonable to expect four, five or even six year olds to wait for break times to go to the toilet. They should be allowed to go when they need; they will manage to hold on soon.

- Young children in school will have some toileting accidents. A run of wet pants for a child could mean that she is uneasy or very unhappy about the new setting.
- Primary school will bring the new experience of separate toilets for boys and girls. Explain this situation to the children since they will not know and may wander into the 'wrong' one without any intention of misbehaving.

Tips for practice

- It is very important that school toilets are kept clean and well stocked with toilet paper and paper towels.
- It is unreasonable to expect children to manage if the toilets are unpleasant places. Be a champion for children if the toilets in your school are poorly maintained.
- Children who are repelled by school toilets will try to hold on and this strategy can be bad for their health, either because they risk constipation or they do not drink enough.
- Also listen to the children if they indicate that the school toilets are a trouble zone. Toilets are sometimes a focus for bullying behaviour or disruptive and distressing patterns like children banging on doors, barging in or looking over the top of cubicles. It is an adult responsibility to resolve such problems.

Possible problems

Constipation

Children vary considerably in how often they need to pass stools. A child who usually goes once or twice a day could be constipated when he has not passed a stool for two days. Yet his friend who usually goes every two days would not be having any trouble at this point.

The signs of constipation are:

- A child has pain on trying to pass stools. This pain can make a child resistant to going and the holding back makes matters worse.
- Children show signs of straining and complaining that they cannot 'go'.
- Sometimes a child experiences 'overflow' when more liquid stools leak out around a hard mass that cannot be expelled. Without careful observation, adults may assume wrongly that the problem is diarrhoea.

Constipation is rare in breast fed babies but can occur when bottle fed babies need water between feeds. Children can get constipated because their diet is low on fresh fruit, vegetables and enough liquids. Children also need enough fibre in their diet because the cellulose in fibre holds water in the stools and makes them easier to pass. But children should not have too much fibre (see page 82).

When children are constipated you need to take action, in partnership with their parents:

- Conversation between adults can be important to establish what is happening. For a while everyone may assume the child is passing stools when going to the toilet elsewhere.
- Make this a discreet conversation since children usually do not appreciate their toileting habits being discussed in open conversation.

You can also have a private conversation with a child.

- Constipation sometimes develops because a child has become very anxious over toilet training. The child may be able to express something of her worries.
- Older children in school will sometimes tell you about problems with the toilets. They may be reluctant to use the facility because toilets are poorly cleaned or smelly. Toilets are also sometimes the location for bullying or maybe other children barge in and disturb their peers.

You need to tackle any problems with the environment or other children as well as a specific problem for this child.

- Make any sensible adjustments to a child's diet now and for later. Encourage the child to drink regularly: water, milk or fruit juice. Fresh and pureed fruit, like grapes, apricots or prunes, can help.
- Express sympathy for the child's predicament and encourage taking time on the toilet.
- In a group setting, ensure that other practitioners do not nag the child.
- Discourage straining and pushing, since this can cause anal fissures, tiny splits that can become infected and sore.
- Sometimes it helps if children rock on the toilet as they push, but gently. Breathing out as they push can also help, if children can manage this technique. None of these suggestions should be pursued too vigorously by a child.
- Reassure children that they and you can take steps to help avoid constipation returning.

It is unwise to give a child laxatives as a first step and certainly not as a regular solution. Children's bowels become dependent on the laxative. If children have repeated problems with constipation, then their parents should take them to see their doctor.

Diarrhoea

The consistency of children's stools will depend on their diet: food and drink intake. Sometimes children have a bout of diarrhoea as a direct consequence of over indulgence in a food or as a reaction to a new food.

However, diarrhoea should be taken seriously and regarded as a symptom to watch if you cannot explain it by the child having taken a large amount of fruit juice or fresh fruit.

- Diarrhoea can be a symptom of specific illnesses (see page 135).
- It should be treated since children, especially babies and toddlers, can become dehydrated quickly.
- Give children plenty of fluid and watch out for any other symptoms.
- Be sympathetic to children who are toilet trained and have had an accident as a result of their condition. They will be upset and embarrassed. Talk discreetly with their parents about what has happened.

Low urine

Again children vary as to how much they drink and that will affect their urine. However, children's urine should be pale yellow and should not smell unpleasant when fresh. Dark coloured urine, a smell or very infrequent passing of urine could be a sign of illness, including dehydration.

Getting dry at night

If you work in an early years setting, getting children to be dry at night will not be a task you cover, except in terms of advice if parents ask. If you work as a nanny, you may be involved in this second part to toilet training.

There is no point in trying for dry nights until children are fully reliable in the daytime. Then, if a child has a series of dry nappies at night, it is probably time to try without the night-time nappy. Alternatively, if the months are passing, you may take the chance and remove her nappy.

- It is important to talk with children about what happens next and that you should be ready for some wet beds. Much like daytime training, getting dry at night varies considerably between children, even in the same family.
- Adults need to be consistently encouraging: to be pleased with children about dry beds and do not look irritated about wet ones.
- Some children will have dry beds because they wake and use a pot in their room or wake an adult to take them to the toilet.
- Some children manage but only if their parent or other carer 'lifts' them and takes them to the toilet before adult bedtime. Every couple of months, you need to stop the lifting and see what happens.

Many children manage to become dry at night between three and five years old, some with the support of 'lifting' for a matter of months. However, there is a substantial minority of children of school age who have not yet managed this task. You may need to reassure parents of a five, six or seven year old that many other children are still not dry at night at this age and specialists do not regard children as late developers over bed wetting until seven or eight years of age.

Activity

The Enuresis Resource and Information Centre (ERIC) has experience in offering practical advice including leaflets written for children as well as their parents. ERIC can be contacted at 34 Old School House, Britannia Road, Kingswood, Bristol BS15 8DB tel: 0117 960 3060 email: *info@eric.org.uk* website: *www.eric.org.uk* The website has sections that are accessible for children and teenagers.

- Use the website and any other information that you follow up to build your understanding of how children can be helped when toilet training has been especially difficult or children have regressed, perhaps because of emotional distress.
- Write up your findings and make a short presentation to colleagues.

Key skills links: IT2.1–3

Older disabled children

Some children will have physical disabilities that mean it will be much harder for them to become toilet trained. For a number of children their disability means that, with the best will in the world, their body is never going to manage this kind of physical control. If continence continues to be an issue with older children, then they need respectful support and consideration for their dignity.

- When children cannot become toilet trained, they will need proper continence pads. They will not want these items called 'nappies', because young children have those.
- You will need an area where older children can be changed with privacy and attention to their personal dignity.
- Make sure that any toiletries, decorations to the room or changing mats are appropriate for an older child. Where possible, involve the child in making choices about illustrations or styles of equipment.

Progress check

1 Give four reasons why early years practitioners need to value care routines and caring for children.

2 What are the risks if practitioners hold back on close contact with and touching children?

3 Use one daily routine to explain how children's involvement supports other areas of their learning.

4 Explain three ways in which you might need to adjust help with self reliance for disabled children.

5 Describe the ways in which children of three or four years could share in their own care.

6 Give two examples of how children might need extra attention for their skin care.

7 What are the main signs that suggest a child could be ready for toilet training?

3

Promoting health and well being through food and mealtimes

After reading this chapter you should be able to:

- plan a well balanced diet for children and help to establish healthy eating habits
- understand and support diversity in diet for children from a range of different cultural backgrounds
- help children learn through mealtimes and food preparation
- support children in good care of their teeth.

Introduction

Food matters to children and happy mealtimes can promote their physical health but also their sense of involvement with the daily routines and warm communication with adults and other children. A balanced diet for food and drink is essential for the health of babies, toddlers and children and it is also the opportunity to establish good habits for later life and protect children's teeth. Adults carry most of the responsibility for offering and encouraging a good diet but children can be enthusiastic partners in food appreciation and preparation.

Your role as an early years practitioner is to provide good quality care to children but you can also promote their learning and sense of personal satisfaction in the skills of self reliance. This chapter, together with Chapters 2 and 4, will help you to understand your role in this important area.

Links to early years qualifications

This chapter especially supports the following units:

Diploma in Child Care and Education: 3, 10

National Vocational Qualification in Early Years Care and Education

Level 2: C1, C8

Level 3: C2, M8

BTEC National Early Years Diploma: 6

A well balanced diet for children

As a responsible adult, it is up to you to organise children's food and drink intake so that over the days the children have a well balanced diet. You are also responsible for helping children to develop healthy eating habits.

Why is food important?

Food matters because:

- A well balanced diet is essential for good health, energy levels and to fuel all the growing that children have to do.
- Diet also affects children's teeth.
- If children do not have enough food or a very poor diet, they can be tired, lethargic and unable to enjoy the day.
- Good diet supports children in resisting illness and recovering more swiftly after being ill.

Childhood is the best time to establish good eating habits in terms of what and how children eat.

- An enthusiasm for good food is likely to last, as are habits of eating plenty of fruit and vegetables.
- Children can learn about feeling hungry, feeling full and enjoying their food. Some of the later problems for children who are overweight seem to arise from constant snacking rather than proper meals.
- Children can enjoy what they eat and learn to savour taste, texture and smell. You can share these sensations with children, at the actual mealtime and smelling the food as it is about to arrive.
- Mealtimes are also a good opportunity for children to learn social skills: enjoying a relaxed conversation as well as eating, helping others with dishing up and using physical and intellectual skills applied to laying the table and clearing up afterwards.
- Food and enjoyable mealtimes are important to children. Several consultation projects have shown that children spontaneously mention 'nice food' as part of what they like at nursery and they recall special mealtimes like picnics with affection.
- Food and eating are part of a child's identity within the family. When children eat home-cooked food, meals are part of the cultural tradition for any family. In some families, special meals are part of the family faith or shared traditions of this individual family.

Activity

Explore ways to demonstrate the importance of food and mealtimes for children.

- Make a visual display with illustrations and photos to share the ideas in this section with colleagues and parents.
- Add children's drawings if they would like to contribute.
- Add some simple written captions to show the possibilities.
- Share your idea with colleagues.

Key skills link: C2.3 C2.1a

You will find it difficult, if not impossible, to balance a child's overall diet unless you have clear meal and snack times. Children need an intake of food and drink spread throughout their day. The usual pattern is three meals: at the beginning of the day, around midday and towards late afternoon or early evening. Children will vary in how much they eat and some also welcome a drink or a small snack at mid-morning and mid-afternoon. Your setting needs some sit-down mealtimes but there can be flexibility about drink and snack times (see the example on page 97).

A well balanced diet works together with healthy physical exercise of children (see Chapter 10). Children who eat well have the energy they need to dash about as well as concentrate on their play. The enjoyable physical activity burns up the calories, as well as strengthening bone and muscles, and leaves children hungry for the next meal.

To think about

With a group of colleagues or fellow students exchange memories about food and mealtimes from your own childhood. This discussion may need to be sensitive if anyone has unhappy memories.

- What were your favourite meals at home and at school (not everybody hates school dinners)?
- What do you recall about mealtimes: did you have sit-down meals with your family, were you expected to finish everything on your plate, how important were table manners?
- Did you help with food shopping, meal preparation or laying the table?

Consider the range of experiences in the group and what you therefore bring to your time with the children.

- For instance, if money was short in your family, it may be hard for you now to tolerate children who appear 'fussy' about good food.
- On the other hand, you may be keen that you never turn into the fearsome dinner lady who made you eat that disgusting liver stew.
- Pull out the main points to guide your good practice now that you are the adult at the meal table.

- How could you resolve your firm feelings about food and promote happy mealtimes within your work?

Key skills links: C2/3.1a Ps2/3.1

A healthy diet

Food is an area where there is no shortage of advice from the media and advertising industry. Newspapers and magazines regularly seem to pronounce new rules about diet or challenge previous guidelines. The advertising and packaging of convenience foods and drinks is also aimed at making consumers accept that this food is ideal for healthy eating or better at delivering necessary nutrients than a rival food.

Despite all the media headlines on diet, in reality, the basic issues are much as they have been for a long time:

- Are children eating an adequate amount of food and drinking enough liquid in total – not too much and not too little?
- Are children eating and drinking a healthy balance between different kinds of food and drink?

Figure 3.1
Mealtimes can be enjoyable, social occasions

To think about

It is important that the messages you give to children are balanced, like their diet.

- There are few, if any, foods that are absolutely good or bad. The problems arise from unbalanced diets and using too much processed and convenience foods, rather than cooking from fresh ingredients.
- For example, carrots are a nutritious food, but you will be ill if you eat them in ludicrous quantities and instead of other foods.
- Chips are not 'bad' or 'unhealthy' as a food. Crisp and tasty chips are enjoyable for children (and adults!) to eat from time to time. But chips should not be eaten every day, nor be the only way children experience that nutritionally useful vegetable, the potato.
- Consider with colleagues the words that you use to help children understand about healthy eating. Do you need to change some of your phrases?

Key skills link: C2/3.1a PS2/3.1

Do you go organic?

Some early years settings and family homes will use organic produce. As an early years practitioner you will fit in with the established pattern. This chapter is not recommending that children should all be fed organic food, because the quality varies depending on the source of food. Some of the marketing claims about 'better taste' or 'free of chemicals' have been very misleading. 'Organic' produce has now also spread into snack food but organic popcorn should no more form a major part of a child's diet than non-organic!

Hygiene and food preparation

A healthy diet is promoted when, over the days, children's food intake includes enough from all the different food groups (see page 81). A well balanced diet is also promoted through good practice in the preparation and cooking of food. If you work in a group setting, then the cook may take responsibility for meal preparation. However, you will ideally do some food preparation and cooking with the children. If you work as a nanny or childminder, you will do the meal planning and cooking.

- Use fresh ingredients as often as you can. Healthy diets have freshly cooked food in preference to processed convenience foods.
- Children, and adults, benefit from eating fresh fruit, salad and some vegetables in their raw state, not always cooked.

Most incidents of food poisoning are caused by people breaking basic rules of kitchen hygiene and food handling.

- Cooked food that has not all been used needs to be allowed to cool swiftly and then placed in the fridge or freezer as appropriate.
- Food needs to be stored with care and used before the 'use by' date.
- Only store cooked food that is left untouched in the cooking or serving dish. Do not store leftover meals from plates or bowls, because once saliva has mixed with food it starts the digestive process.

- Defrost food properly when it is then taken out of the freezer.
- Re-warm only once and then ensure that food is thoroughly heated to 'piping hot'. If necessary, let it cool a little before the children start.
- Defrosted or partially defrosted food should now be used, not re-frozen.

Supermarkets promote a range of anti-bacterial products for supporting hygiene in the kitchen. You need good standards of cleanliness in the kitchen, but using anti-bacterial products will not correct the situation when basic rules are broken.

- Wash your hands before cooking and food preparation. Wash your hands again if you stop to go to the toilet yourself or to change a child.
- Use a different knife and cutting board for raw meat and poultry than for other foods. Or else wash the items thoroughly before re-use.
- In a fridge, raw meat or poultry should be covered and placed on the lowest shelf, never allowed to drip over other foods.
- In a family home with pets you should have separate bowls and spoons for dealing with the animals' food. If you store part-used tins of pet food in the fridge, keep them well covered and away from the family food.

Balanced drink and food

Drinks

Children need liquid from different sources:

- *Water*: tap or filtered, depending on what you use in the setting or family home. Spring and bottled waters may have too much sodium (salt) for babies or very young children.
- *Milk*: once babies are a year old they can drink cow's milk or soya if children cannot have dairy produce. Children need the nutrients from whole milk. They should certainly drink this until they are at least two years old. They can move onto semi-skimmed if they prefer the taste. But in a well balanced diet there is no reason why children should not continue to drink whole milk if that is what they enjoy. Skimmed milk is not suitable for children.
- Water and milk can be supplemented by *fruit* or *vegetable juices*. Dilute the drinks for younger children. However, do not overdo the fruit juice, since teeth do not distinguish between natural sugars in juice and added sugar in squashes.

Children do not need squashes, fortified fruit drinks, carbonated drinks or colas. An occasional drink of squash or cola will not unbalance a healthy diet but their teeth are under threat when these drinks form much of their liquid intake. Sugary drinks are especially risky when they are put into bottles for very young children or when young children have cartons with straws and they swish the drink around in their mouth for some time.

Food groups

Menus should include foods each day from each of the four basic food groups. Children, like adults, need variety in their diet, so it is wise to draw from all the possibilities within each group. Some foods, like cheese or beans, fit into more than one group because of the blend of nutrients they contain.

Carbohydrates form a food group that occurs as sugars and starches. Some foods are also a useful source of fibre – but see the comment below about children and fibre. Children gain carbohydrates from:

- all the different kinds of leavened bread and rolls (bread that has yeast to

make it rise). Children can become enthusiastic about the taste of proper bread when they experience more than the pre-sliced variety
- different kinds of unleavened bread (that remains flat), like chapatis, puris or pitta bread
- cereals, beans and lentils
- dishes made from maize, millet and cornmeal
- the many different kinds of pasta and noodles
- plantains and green bananas
- potatoes – that can be served in so many different ways
- rice
- sweet potatoes.

Children should not be given extra fibre and the high-fibre diets promoted for adults are unhealthy for children. Young children's digestive systems are not yet well equipped to process fibre and any excess fibre can also interfere with their body's absorption of zinc and iron.

Children need the sugar sources of carbohydrates and their diet is unbalanced if adults try to remove this food entirely. The problem in unbalanced diets, for adults as well as children, is when this source of carbohydrate is too dominant.

- Sugar is present naturally in many fruits, both fresh and dried. Sugar, or other sources like honey, is an ingredient in puddings and cakes.
- The problems arise when sweet foods dominate the menu or have unbalanced a child's diet because of excessive consumption of confectionery and biscuits, perhaps as regular 'treats' or filling up between meals.
- Children do not need the added sugars that are in ready made juice and carbonated drinks or in many shop-bought biscuits and cakes. Some convenience foods claim to be reduced or low sugar, but they often have artificial sweetener, otherwise the product has no taste.

Children need *protein* and this food group can be found in two broad types. Some foods provide protein in a form that can be fully used by the body even when the food is eaten by itself. These are called 'complete proteins' and sometimes 'first class proteins'. These foods include:

- milk and cheese
- eggs
- fish
- meat
- poultry.

With the exception of soya beans, the plant proteins are 'incomplete proteins'. They are sometimes called 'second class proteins', but this term can be misleading and causes non-vegetarians to claim that children must have meat in order to be healthy. The plant proteins just need to be eaten in combination to provide the completeness within each meal. Choose from:

- cereals
- chickpeas
- lentils
- nuts – cut up very finely for nut roast or rissoles, do not give them loose to young children, especially the under threes (see also page 96)
- beans.

These foods work in combinations that make ordinary meals. Baked beans on toast is a good example in which the cereal in the bread and the beans combine to give a complete protein. Some grated and melted cheese on top makes a very nutritious child meal or adult snack. Other examples include breakfast cereals with milk, millet milk pudding, rice mixed with lentils (and obviously other ingredients like vegetables if you wish), bread with cheese or hummus (made with chickpeas and sesame seeds).

You can try textured vegetable proteins, such as Quorn, as an alternative to meat. But children from vegetarian families may not find this food palatable, especially if it is made to look like a meat or poultry dish.

The food group of *fats* is equally necessary. Children need this source of nutrition. The fats that are necessary for a balanced diet have been confused with excessive use of fat in cooking or being 'too fat'. There is nothing 'bad' about fats as a nutrient and this food group is as important as the other three groups. Children can get the fats they need from:

- lean meat and poultry
- dairy produce including cheese, milk, yoghurt and fromage frais
- nuts (but not loose for children)
- fats like butter and margarine as ingredients in cakes, biscuits and pastries.

Of course, children's diets can become unbalanced if any of these foods come to dominate their diet, for instance, if children are allowed to fill up on biscuits or cakes between meals and then have little appetite for the other foods. Do not use low- or no-fat products for children, they need the nutrients. Also the very low-fat products often have very little taste and will make it harder for you to encourage young children to enjoy their food. Obviously, you do not load them up foolishly with fats:

- cut the excess fat from meat
- use yoghurt or fromage frais for toppings rather than cream
- use vegetable oils for cooking rather than animal fats like lard and this will mean your menus are suitable for vegetarian children too
- watch out for the hidden fats that enter a child's diet with the regular eating of crisps and biscuits.

Some of the advice over the last 10–15 years about adult diet will be very inappropriate if applied to children. Unlike fully grown adults, children's diet has to fuel their growing as well as maintain their general health. Babies and children need three to four times as many calories per day in proportion to their body size, in comparison with adults. Children also have different nutritional requirements from adults because their bodies work differently.

The low-fat diets generally promoted for adult are unhealthy for children because they need the fat content, for instance from full and not skimmed milk. Children can be missing vital nutrients and be malnourished amidst plenty of food. Children's bodies also seem to be designed to use fat more efficiently than adults are. See page 89 for what to do if children are overweight.

There are a wide range of *vitamins* and *minerals* that children need in their diet, often in small amounts. They will get a balanced diet if they eat a range of fruit, vegetables and salads. Children can enjoy a wide range when they are introduced to different foods and these are presented in an attractive way. Children will get the best from these foods when they eat as much as possible in its raw state (a few foods have to be cooked). Fruit, carrots, peas, salad vegetables, white cabbage, cauliflower and broccoli can all be eaten raw.

Figure 3.2

The nursery cook is an important member of your team

When you cook fruit or vegetables many of the vitamins and minerals are reduced or end up in the cooking water. It is therefore best to cook lightly by steaming or microwaving, so that minimum liquid is needed and wherever possible use the water as juice or to make a sauce or gravy. Go easy on added salt or sugar and avoid practices like adding bicarbonate of soda to keep the colour of vegetables because it destroys the vitamin C.

Activity

- Draft a sample menu for a week to suit a group of two to five year olds. Look at your draft and identify the sources of the four food groups in the meals and snacks you have chosen.
- Make any adjustments to balance the diet over a week.
- Now double check whether you would need to make some further adjustments if some of the children were vegetarian (see page 93).
- Finalise your menu.
- Discuss other draft menus with your colleagues and gather some ideas about how you would make the meals and snacks attractive and appetising to the children.

Key skills link: C2.3 C2.1a

Consequences of dietary deficiencies

If children eat a well balanced diet of raw and freshly cooked food, they should not have nutritional deficiencies. Problems can arise when children:

- are fed a diet heavy in processed and convenience meals
- have become very restricted in what they are prepared to eat
- have allergies or a health condition that seriously limits their range of possible foods
- share a family diet that has removed many kinds of foods. A vegan diet needs very careful balancing for children (see page 94).

You should talk with parents, if you are concerned about a child's health linked with their diet. Some possibilities include:

- Children may develop iron-deficiency anaemia, or be borderline, if their diet does not include sufficient sources of iron. Children may be tired and listless, get out of breath easily and have a lowered resistance to infection. If children eat meat, then good sources of iron include the red meats, liver and kidney. Non-meat sources of iron are egg yolks, peas, pulses, chocolate, bran and wheatgerm, parsley, some dried fruits and shellfish. Watch out for an excessive milk intake by children, because milk is low in iron and a quantity of drink before food makes children feel full.
- Calcium deficiency can lead to reduced growth, badly formed teeth and rickets (a disease in which children's bones do not harden properly). Vitamin D deficiency also puts children at risk from rickets because this vitamin helps the absorption of calcium. Children obtain calcium from milk, cheese, sardines and bread. Vitamin D is available from dairy products and oily fish and the effects of sunlight on the oils in our skin (see page 59).

- Vitamin C deficiency can lead to depression, low resistance to infection, poor skin and slow healing of cuts and scrapes. Our bodies cannot store vitamin C, so children need a daily intake from fruit and vegetables: fresh and ideally eaten raw when appropriate. Some vitamin C is lost as soon as you cut the food and more is lost in the heat of cooking.

Of course children who are tired or prone to infection are not necessarily having an unbalanced diet. Anaemia, for instance, can be a warning sign of leukaemia or sickle cell anaemia (see page 520).

Vitamin supplements

Manufacturers try every trick in the book to persuade parents and carers that their drink or food product has crucial added vitamins or that a sugary drink is somehow 'good' for the development of children's teeth.

- If children have a well balanced diet, they will get all their vitamins from meals. They do not need 'vitamin-enriched' drink or food.
- If children have nutritional deficiencies (see above), then these need to be addressed directly through meals that provide the missing vitamins or minerals.
- There is some concern now from the United States that children can experience a potential overdose of some nutrients because of the ploy of adding them to non-essential products in order to persuade parents or carers to purchase.

There are many vitamin supplements on the market but as a general rule vitamins are best absorbed through meals. The process is not entirely understood, but vitamin pills do not seem to offer an equivalent level of nutrition as the same vitamins eaten as food.

- You should not give a child any supplement without consultation with their parents.
- Some babies or children may take a supplement but as they get older a balanced diet should offer what they need. Vitamins are a supplement, an addition, to a healthy diet; they do not solve the problems of an unbalanced diet for children.
- If children do have vitamin or mineral supplements, you must always use products that are suitable for their age, follow the instructions and never exceed the suggested dose.
- It is possible to overdose on some vitamins or minerals, for example vitamins A and D, that are stored in the body. Excessive amounts of some nutrients can interfere with the effective digestion of other important food groups.
- A well balanced diet is key. It is not the case that, because something is healthy in small amounts, it must be even healthier in larger amounts!

When children are ill

As you will be aware yourself, one consequence of illness can be a reduced interest in food. Healthy children are more likely to relish their food when it is attractively presented and mealtimes are happy occasions (see page 97). When a child feels ill or is recovering, it is doubly important that their interest is encouraged:

- Offer small helpings of what you know the child likes, from a range of nutritional foods.

- Present it attractively and help the child to eat and drink if they need this support.
- If children find it hard to chew or to swallow, then choose more mushy or liquid foods or cut up food very small.
- Talk with children about what they would like. For instance, home made soups can be very nutritious and are an easy way to get food in when you feel ill.
- Consult with parents, who will in turn talk with the family GP, about whether this is an occasion when children would benefit from a vitamin and mineral supplement.

Do you need to provide 'children's food'?

At different times over the past decades the prevailing advice has been that children need very different food to adults. Some of their nutritional requirements are different from adults (see page 83) but not so dramatically that children require completely different meals.

The idea of 'traditional children's food' that now prevails has been created by fast food outlets and convenience food manufacturers. Non-vegetarian children can learn to relish fish or chicken in different meals; it does not have to be fish fingers and chicken nuggets all the time, if at all. Children develop an enthusiasm for pasta, mixed with different other ingredients. It does not have to come in 'fun' shapes or lurid colours.

The best approach is to give young children experience of the kind of food eaten by adults, in smaller portions as appropriate and cut up smaller if necessary. Food should be presented in an attractive way and children encouraged to dish up for themselves, at least sometimes. If they are not keen on a food, then try again another time but do not insist if children's opinion does not change.

Partnership with parents

A conversation with parents about what their children like to eat, any known allergies and details of the family diet should be part of your early information gathering about a family whose child is about to join your setting. In some cases you may need to have a further conversation about a child's diet, perhaps because you are unsure what parents would prefer. If you work with slightly older children, in primary school, a breakfast or after school club, you will be able to talk over the details with the children themselves.

Scenario

The nursery and reception class team of St Jude's Primary School have been planning a topic for the children around healthy eating and wish to work in partnership with parents about promoting good habits for the future.

The team has found a draft policy and letter for parents that was used by another local school. But, within a team discussion, Pam and Maryam start to question what the other school has written. For instance, the food policy has a sentence that reads, 'We provide a mixture of traditional children's fare such as fish fingers, chips and beans and exotic Caribbean chicken with rice and peas'. As Pam points out, why are fish fingers described as traditional and Caribbean chicken and peas is no more exotic than fish and chips, if it is part of the family's usual diet.

Questions

1. Discuss with colleagues the reasons that the policy statement is unhelpful. How might the St Jude's team rework the ideas to show how they promote a range of foods.
2. In what ways have you encountered views about what is 'normal' food and 'exotic' or what is suitable food for children?
3. Be pleased about good practice in your setting and make some specific plans for improvements, even minor.

Key skills link: C2/3.1a LP2/3.1–3 WO2/3.1–3

There will be always be some variety in the diet of children in a group. Children have likes and dislikes in food. It is good practice to encourage them to try new foods and extend their eating habits but would never be appropriate to insist. However, you may be working in an area that is ethnically very diverse and this variety will be reflected in family diets. There are some general guidelines on page 95 but some broader issues can arise whatever the mix of your local area:

- If the children come from a variety of ethnic backgrounds (see page 103), it can be complex to find menus that will suit everyone. It is possible to build in some variations but, if there are many different meat preferences, it can often be easier to offer interesting menus built around fish and vegetarian meals.
- If a family diet is unusual to you or the nursery cook, then ask parents for some recipes and perhaps to visit the nursery and demonstrate some cooking. Bear in mind that every ethnic group includes good and bad or unenthusiastic cooks. So do not assume that a less familiar cuisine is unpalatable. You may just be unlucky that this parent cannot cook!
- A genuinely strict diet or firm guidelines about food preparation may be hard to organise. So talk with parents and see if they would be willing to send their child's food in to the nursery. For instance, it simply is not possible to prepare and cook proper kosher food in a non-kosher kitchen. Children from Jewish families who follow strict dietary rules will probably go to a Jewish nursery, but this is not always an option.
- If children have allergies to relatively common ingredients, such as gluten in flour, then parents will usually be happy to send in special biscuits or cakes.

To think about

Some nurseries have a healthy eating policy and part of the written document can be suggestions for what parents can send in for special occasions such as birthdays or leaving parties.

Parents should then be left with some choice about what to bring into the setting. For instance, if you are hoping for a range of foods from families of different ethnic groups, there should be no expectation that Teja's Mum has to send in some samosas because they are an Indian family. Perhaps Teja's Mum would rather bake a cake.

- Discuss with your colleagues in what ways working to involve parents could be restrictive.

- What assumptions may need to be aired if parents are to have a proper choice?
- If Teja's Mum is asked to bring in 'traditional Indian food' why is Gareth's Dad not asked to bring in some 'traditional English food' and what is this?
- Suggest some improvements for practice in your own setting.

Key skills link: C2/3.1a PS2/3.1 WO2/3.1–3

Scenario

Greenholt Pre-school have recently extended their service so that some children stay for the whole day and have lunch at the pre-school. Now that children have a meal rather than snacks and a drink, it has become even more important that the pre-school team communicates clearly about different family eating patterns and any allergies. They have therefore developed their child records to keep more information about food and drink and made simple reminder sheets that go on the board.

Marjorie and Trisha summarise any conversation with a child's parent by written notes in the child's personal file. For example, they have written:

- Lottie is allergic to cow's milk. No cheese, yoghurt, milk puddings or custard. Mrs Pierce will bring in Lottie's soya milk.
- Michael and his family do not eat any pork.
- They have also drafted brief reminders for the board of 'no pork for Michael', 'give Lottie her soya milk' or 'Angela has her special biscuits'.

Questions

1. Good practice is to be aware of ingredients in meals. For instance, Michael does not eat pork, so what foods will you need to check for him and what alternatives could you offer?
2. What ways can you identify that you could alert Michael not to eat without making him feel left out?
3. Discuss possibilities with your colleagues – identifying good and less good practice in what could be said and how.
4. Make some suggestions for improvements in your own practice.

Key skills link: C2/3.1a LP2/3.1–3 WO2/3.1–3

Tips for practice

You can help young children to develop good eating habits and enjoyment of food in an early years setting or family home.

- Children should eat most of their food at mealtimes.
- Avoid regular use of fill-up snacks or letting children graze on anything throughout the day.
- Mealtimes should be focused yet social. It is a time for everyone to eat but the meal can still be friendly.
- Set a good example about eating.
- Set boundaries about eating without getting unduly fierce. You can walk a firm but friendly middle course between letting children eat what and when they want and turning yourself into the food ogre.
- Help children, especially younger ones to focus on food and avoid distractions.

Children who are overweight

It is unlikely that children will get overweight if they develop good habits about what they eat and drink, as outlined in this chapter and if they are allowed to run about as children normally wish. Food and exercise work in a healthy partnership.

Toddlers are naturally rounded and some are quite chubby but they grow into a more child like shape. Health practitioners can judge whether a child is overweight

Figure 3.3 Children watch your face as well as listening to your words

by the growth charts but a child who is genuinely overweight can be judged by looking at her or him. Children should not normally have rolls of fat, especially around the thighs and abdomen, nor should they have to have clothes that are two or three age sizes larger because the items will not do up around their waist or wrists.

There is an increasing problem with obesity in children in the western world, including especially the United States. Obesity is defined as weighing at least 20 per cent heavier than the recommended body weight for height. The problem seems to have two closely related causes:

- Children are allowed to develop poor eating habits, with an excessive use of convenience foods, snacks like different kinds of crisps, high sugar drinks and sweets.
- Poor diet is often then combined with a severe lack of physical exercise and far too many hours of passive activity watching television or playing computer games.

Obesity in childhood is a serious issue, not only because obese children grow into obese adults, with the related health risks. Children who are very overweight are often also unhappy about their size and shape and may be bullied by other children. Serious obesity and the often related lack of physical exercise also brings the risk of health problems that are more usually associated with middle age: lack of muscle and bone strength, respiratory problems and the appearance of type 2 diabetes that usually affects adults over 50 years of age (see page 520).

Tips for practice

Unless advised by their doctor, you would not usually put children who are overweight on a slimming diet to lose weight.

- The best approach is steadily to change children's eating habits and increase their level of enjoyable physical activity.
- Children have plenty of growing to do. If you focus on mealtimes, cut out snacks and severely limit sweets and sweetened drinks, they will move into a more appropriate weight for their height.
- There needs to be full cooperation between the family and an early years practitioner, whether you are working as a nanny with the family or children attend your nursery.
- You are less likely to be successful if the good eating habits that you encourage are undermined by parents, or grandparents, who let the children eat sweets and drink cola.

A rare condition, Prader-Willi syndrome, can affect children's eating patterns. The syndrome is a genetic disorder that, amongst other symptoms, causes a chronic feeling of hunger, so that children will continue to eat, unless firmly guided by adults. The syndrome is unusual, but it is worth considering if children eat excessively and there is no other likely explanation, such as eating as a source of emotional comfort or a family pattern of substantial eating.

Scenario

Dresden Road Nursery School has developed a range of services (see the scenario on page 23) and has positive partnership with parents. Recently they have worked with two families whose children were significantly overweight for their age. This work has made the team think about their more general approach to food and weight, for adults as well as children.

- The two children who were genuinely overweight had become aware that they had a 'problem'. The team and the children's parents needed to boost the children's confidence since they did feel low, as well as address eating habits and exercise.
- The team was also provoked to think about setting a good example in their own eating patterns and in obvious enjoyment of physical activity.
- Jessica pointed out that children will probably be confused if they hear adults (parents or early years practitioners) talking at length about being 'fat' (the adults) and needing to diet. This situation has arisen in the parents' group and once or twice with staff.
- The team discussed how they might shift to talking in front of the children in more positive ways related to developing good eating habits. For example that 'I'd like another piece of fruit' rather than 'I'd better not have a helping of steamed pudding'.

Questions

1 Consider some practical applications to your own work, both for support of children and adult behaviour and conversation.

Key skills links: LP2.1

Refusal to eat and faltering growth

Sometimes the problem is one of children not eating enough. Understandably, adults can become anxious about this situation and the efforts to get children to eat, or to eat more than they wish, can worsen the situation. If children's limited eating goes on for some time, then they can become tired or recover less well from illness or ordinary childhood scrapes. If they fail to put on weight, the children may be said to have **faltering growth**, the term now used instead of 'failure to thrive'.

The majority of children with faltering growth are in caring family homes; they are not being neglected (see page 568). What has usually happened is that a baby, toddler or child has for some reason become hard to feed or resistant to eating much at mealtimes. There is sometimes a related, temporary health or family problem that may seem to explain what has happened, but often there is not.

More usually, the parents, or other carers, have become anxious or have been told by the health visitor or clinic that they must get more calories into the child. Sometimes this direction by medical professionals is accompanied by some sensible advice, but sometimes there are no helpful hints, only a sense of pressure. The continued weighing of the child raises anxieties even further and parents resort to tactics that make food and mealtimes even more stressful. A vicious circle has then been established.

Key term

Faltering growth when babies and children do not put on weight and may also appear in poor health, for no obvious reason. The condition used to be called failure to thrive

A positive way forward for you as carer, or to advise to parents is as follows:

- Establish proper mealtimes if the child has been grazing. Anxious parents sometimes keep offering food or leaving meals around in the hope that the child will eat. Children then get confused between mealtime and playtime and adults have little idea of what children have actually eaten in total.
- A discrete food diary may sometimes help and be a way of tracking improvement.
- Sit with children and make mealtimes a social occasion but not extraordinarily drawn out. Ensure that all the food and drink offered is nutritious and ideally take at least some meals with the child.
- Give young children, or let older ones, serve themselves a small helping. Support them in eating if they need. They can have a second helping if they want.
- Avoid complex rituals to try to persuade a child to eat but offer sensible flexibility. For instance, sandwiches can taste nicer with the crusts off or children really may like their apple peeled and sliced.
- Avoid giving attention for refusal to eat or pushing food around on the plate. Keep calm and avoid nagging – not easy for parents or carers who have become worried!
- Give simple encouragement when a child has eaten – mainly at the end of the mealtime, not for every spoonful. Say something like, 'Would you like some more fish pie? (When the child has indicated they would.) Yes, I thought that was tasty as well.' Alternatively, if you are the cook, perhaps, 'It's better with more cheese on top, isn't it?' You could also simply comment, 'Well done, you had a good lunch' or 'Looks like you enjoyed the chicken and rice.'
- If children do not eat much, then after a reasonable mealtime, call a halt. Say something like, 'Are you finished then? Alright, the next meal is teatime'. If children complain later, 'I'm hungry', say simply, 'I'm sorry you weren't in the mood for food at lunch. There will be plenty at tea'. Avoid the temptation to let them fill up in between mealtimes.
- As a child becomes more enthusiastic or cooperative about food, then involve them in plans for meals and choices.

Finding out more

The Children's Society has published a free booklet *My child still won't eat* that offers advice to parents. Download from *www.the-childrens-society.org.uk* or call 0845 600 4400 to request a copy. *When feeding fails* by Angela Underdown can be purchased from the Children's Society.

Supporting diversity in diet

All around the world a family's diet is influenced by cultural tradition and any religious considerations, as well as by what food is easily available locally. Your own view of a 'normal' diet will have been influenced by your own upbringing.

- Part of your professional development is to become more aware of the variety in different social and ethnic groups: both in your local area and in the UK as a whole.
- You certainly should not talk about 'restricted' diets when you actually mean that a child or family does not eat the same foods as you do. A genuinely restricted diet is when a child, for reasons of allergy or ill health, cannot follow the family pattern of eating.
- Also it is better to avoid the weird phrase 'ethnic food'. Everybody belongs to an ethnic group, so the phrase has to apply to every possible world cuisine. Fish and chips or steak and kidney pie is therefore 'ethnic food' just as much as tandoori chicken or couscous. The phrase is used inappropriately to apply to food other than the diet that the speaker regards as normal.

To think about

You will bring expectations about a 'normal' diet and mealtime behaviour from your own childhood as well as your current eating habits. To be a responsible early years practitioner, you need to learn about the variety in diet for families in the UK and to address any firm assumptions that you still hold. For instance:

- If you happily eat meat, then you may wonder at first how to achieve a healthy vegetarian diet.
- If your family is Muslim or Jewish, you will find it hard to grasp how anyone could eat meat from pigs.
- If you are a vegetarian, you will have trouble understanding how people can eat dead animals at all.

You need to show respect to the family diets of the children with whom you work, and it is also fair to expect your workplace to provide food that you are able to eat as well.

Discuss the practice issues with your colleagues and plan any changes that could improve your own work.

Key skills links: C3.1a LP2/31–3 WO2/31–3

People who confidently announce, 'But I eat anything!' rarely do eat absolutely anything. Families who eat meat as part of their diet do not usually eat happily every possible kind of animal or fish. Some families, of course, avoid particular animals for religious reasons or require that animals be killed in a particular way (see page 95). However, families who have no religious reservations often draw the line at some animals. For instance, English families will probably be outraged at the suggestion that they eat horse, yet this is an item on the menus in parts of mainland Europe. In contrast, some European countries think it very odd to eat lamb: a traditional meat in the UK and Greece.

A vegetarian diet

Strictly speaking, vegetarians will not eat any food that requires the killing of animals, poultry or fish. If you are planning menus for children who are vegetarian, then you need to get into the habit of checking the ingredients on convenience foods. For instance, some cheaper ice cream contains animal fat and some ready made desserts are set by gelatine, an animal product. You should also use vegetarian cheese, since some cheeses are made with rennet, derived from animals. The use of 'suitable for vegetarian' symbols has made buying easier.

Some families who describe themselves as vegetarians nevertheless eat fish or are not that concerned about hidden ingredients in convenience foods. As with any other practical care issue, you need to check with parents so that you understand what they would like for their child.

A vegan diet

Vegans go further than vegetarians in that they will not eat any animal products, even those that do not require killing the animal. So a vegan family will avoid all dairy produce, eggs and some vegans will not eat honey. A balanced vegan diet needs careful attention, especially if you are not used to menu planning for vegans. For example:

- Vitamin B12 is largely found in animal products. Vegans can get traces of B12 in sea vegetables (edible seaweeds) but children will need a supplement.
- Calcium can be a problem with the loss of dairy produce. Babies and young children who are not yet on a very mixed diet, may need a calcium supplement. Soya bean milk is sometimes fortified with calcium.
- Fat is only present in traces in fruit and vegetables, so vegans need to ensure they get enough fat from other sources, such as all kinds of nuts and soya flour.

Talk with children's parents about how they balance their child's diet. You certainly should not give children nutritional supplements without discussion with the family.

Finding out more

The tremendous array of cookery books include some on vegetarian and vegan cooking. A cookbook may be useful if you work as a nanny or if your early years setting has not really adjusted to diversity in diets. You can also contact:

- The Vegetarian Society, Parkdale, Dunham Road, Altrincham, Cheshire WA14 4QG tel: 0161 925 2000 website: *www.vegsoc.org* They have produced a helpful free booklet *Growing up: preschool vegetarian catering.*
- The Vegan Society tel: 01424 427393 website: *www.vegansociety.com*

Religious beliefs and diet

All of the major world faiths have some rules about food or food preparation. Every faith includes different sects and families may also vary in how strictly they follow the rules. So, it is not accurate to follow predictions like, 'Surely all Hindus ...'. Also some parents may no longer practise their faith but are more comfortable following the dietary rules in which they were raised. A good guideline for early years practitioners is, 'if in doubt – ask' on a child's diet as with any other aspect of their care. What follows is a general guide.

- Buddhists are sometimes vegetarian, but not always. Some Buddhist sects believe strongly that diet is a personal decision.
- Most Christians do not follow particular rules for their diet, although some make a case against vegetarianism by quoting the Bible. However, a few Christian groups do avoid certain foods, for instance Catholics may avoid meat on Fridays (the day of the death of Christ) and some give up one or two foods for Lent (the forty days leading up to Easter). Families from the Orthodox Church may avoid meat, eggs and milk products for Lent.
- Jehovah's Witnesses require that meat has been bled in the method of slaughter and avoid foods like black pudding because of the blood.
- Mormons avoid black pudding and caffeine in any form, so children should not have cola drinks.
- Some Rastafarians follow a vegetarian diet which is close to vegan – avoiding dairy products. If families eat meat, they will probably avoid pork and shellfish. (The Rastafarian faith is a blend of Biblical teachings and African cultural traditions.)
- Some Hindus are vegetarian, but those who eat meat will avoid any beef and beef products, since cows are regarded as sacred.
- Orthodox Jewish families follow the laws of Kashrut that determine the permitted foods (kosher, meaning allowed) and the method of slaughter. Additionally, meat and dairy products have to be kept completely separate at all stages of food preparation, eating and washing up afterwards. Less strict Jewish families will ask that their children are not given pork in any form, nor shellfish.
- Muslim families avoid pork in any form. As with meals for Jewish children, you have to watch out for unexpected pork products in processed foods. Any meat or poultry must be Halal (meaning lawful) which is produced by the method of slaughter that allows a body to bleed. If you cannot get Halal meat, then children from Muslim families will have to have fish and vegetarian meals.
- Some Sikhs are vegetarian, but those who eat meat will probably avoid beef and pork. Families will want meat from a butcher that has *not* been bled in the Halal or Kosher method.

Fasting

Giving up foods at particular times or fasting for periods is part of religious practice in some faiths. However, you are most likely to encounter fasting if you work with children from Muslim families, who will fast throughout the daylight hours during the weeks of Ramadan. The Islamic year is based on the lunar calendar and so the exact date moves 'earlier' each year in terms of the western calendar. At the time of writing (2002) Ramadan falls from mid-November to mid-December, but it will make its way back to the summer months.

Families are careful about bringing children into the tradition slowly and younger children are not expected to fast. However, if you work in a primary school or after school club, then be aware that children may join the fast for some days or for a few hours within the day.

Food allergies

Some children need to avoid certain foods in order to stay well. You need to talk with parents at the beginning of your working relationship and understand what this means for the child's diet. Some **food allergies** are life threatening, so take seriously what parents say.

Food allergies are caused by an over reaction of the body's immune system. When a child or adult eats a food to which they are allergic, they will become ill quickly. The food, even small traces, may cause skin rashes, very serious stomach upsets or even life threatening reactions. Some children are allergic to egg, wheat, cow's milk, nuts or fish. Milk and egg allergies sometimes pass when children get older, but many allergies last a lifetime.

It was advised on page 82 that younger children, especially the under threes, should not be given whole nuts. Young children do not chew the nuts properly into smaller bits and the nut can get stuck in their throat. However, some children have an extremely serious reaction to nuts, especially peanuts, and some other foods. The term to describe a severe allergic reaction is **anaphylaxis**. An injection of adrenaline can be essential to reverse the reaction and a family should obviously alert you if this is the case. As with any medicines, you would need to know exactly what to do.

Some adverse reactions to food are less obvious and can be difficult for parents to track and demonstrate. Some children seem to have an intolerance of milk, wheat, caffeine, citrus fruits, chocolate, dairy products and food additives including some colourings. The impact includes rashes, stomach upsets, migraine and some behavioural changes such as hyperactivity and aggression.

Early years practitioners should follow parents' requests where possible and be honest if you are struggling.

- If you have difficulty in maintaining a balanced diet for a child, then ask for advice from parents. In an early years setting you could ask parents to send food in with their child.
- A well balanced diet of fresh, non-processed food will deal with many of the food additive issues.

Key terms

Food allergies
when a child or adult becomes ill after eating particular foods or ingredients. The consequences of a food allergy may be mild through to very severe

Anaphylaxis
a severe and sudden allergic reaction to foods or other substances, that can be fatal without a swift injection of adrenaline or other appropriate medication

Scenario

The team of Greenholt Pre-school (see also the scenario on page 88) have discussed what is a sensible approach to family diet and children's allergies. They are aware that the local primary school has responded to the problem of nut allergies by removing, or trying to remove, all traces of nuts from school meals. The pre-school team has also listened to irritated parents, whose older children are at the school, and who received a letter from the head insisting that there must be no nut products whatsoever in children's packed lunches.

The Greenholt Pre-school team consider that the primary school has over-reacted but still wonder should they take this route.

Questions

Obviously any team has to take sensible steps to protect children who have food allergies. Discuss this dilemma with colleagues.

1. Weigh up what the scope of this problem is.
2. What are possible options for good practice?
3. What are the likely consequences of the different options, including the school approach of a total ban?

4 Overall, what do you judge is the best balanced approach?
5 Write up this option as a brief set of guidance notes.

Key skills links: C3.1a C3.3 PS3.1

Learning around food and mealtimes

Food is an important part of the day for children and they look forward to meals when the experience is pleasant. There are plenty of opportunities for learning as a natural part of this routine, when children are involved in social and friendly mealtimes.

Being appreciative about food

Part of helping children to enjoy their food can be expressing appreciation. A number of world faiths have some tradition of giving thanks for food – either at most mealtimes or on specific occasions. Unless your setting has a specific religious affiliation, it will be appropriate to find general ways of expressing thanks. Certainly, there is no justification for insisting on a specifically Christian 'saying grace'.

It can be pleasant for the nursery cook to be thanked on occasion, not everyday as a habit because that soon does not sound genuine. Children will have favourite meals or puddings or be appreciative that the cook has completed their own cooking of a cake. Encourage the children to say 'thank you' or communicate that today's apple tart was the best ever.

Activity

- Return to the sample menu plan that you developed for the activity on page 84.
- Describe ways in which the children could be involved in making a large wall menu or menu board.
- Take one or two meals from your week's plan and describe ways in which the children could be involved in the food preparation or serving.
- Write up your project and present to colleagues.

Key skills links: C2/3.1b

Encouraging good eating habits

You can support children towards healthy eating by a positive approach to mealtimes, creating a friendly atmosphere in which the main task is still to eat and drink.

- Mealtimes need to be relaxed. Taking your time at meals can mean that children are able to chat as well as eat and can come back for seconds if they wish. Mealtimes are more relaxed when you value them as times of learning and not just as routines to get done.

- By all means remind children courteously to keep eating or to eat up as far as possible. But definitely avoid nagging and any situation in which a child is told by different adults in succession to 'hurry up' or 'finish your meal'. Help children with cutting up or spooning in the food as necessary.
- It is worth having food in dishes or on serving plates that enable children to help themselves and their friends. Children can then see and choose the proportions of food they would prefer and add any sauces or savoury additions such as chutney, custard or yoghurt if they wish.
- Sometimes there may be pressure from other staff, perhaps the cook. If you cannot easily resolve the issue with the other person, then it will be important that the manager of your centre addresses what is getting in the way of a relaxed mealtime.
- You need a comfortable seating arrangement for everyone, including yourself. Adults will not be comfortable if perched on a child sized seat.
- You should sit down with the children and ideally eat with them, although you may not want to eat at every meal or snack time. This habit will model good eating habits and helps you to pay full attention and not be tempted to rush children.
- Some children may not be used to a sit-down mealtime when they join your centre. Try to be flexible and understand that the child is not being awkward, she may genuinely have no idea how to sit and eat because her family lets her pick food and move about. With your patience and an attractive social mealtime, she will join you all soon.
- Children also bring different experiences of how to eat. Using a knife and fork in the English way is far from a universal way of eating and some English families may live mainly on take-away and finger food.
- It is a useful social skill for children to learn to use cutlery as well as other ways of eating. But you need to be aware that some families will use other utensils, such as chopsticks or regularly use different kinds of breads as a form of utensil.
- Eating with the fingers is a perfectly hygienic way to eat so long as children have washed their hands before a meal. You can help children in good habits of personal hygiene for meals and when they are involved in food preparation and cooking activities.

To think about

Some early years settings have developed the idea of the self service snack bar for three year olds and older. The mid-session drinks and snacks are put on a table and children are welcome to take their snack when they wish. Children can indicate that they have had their drink by moving their name card from one open container on the table to another 'done' container or into a wall hanging. Practitioners can then easily see which children still need their drink.

- Discuss with colleagues the advantages, and any possible drawbacks, of the self service system.
- Write up the pros and cons and consider whether self service would be a positive change in your own early years setting.

Key skills link: C2/3.3 WO2/3.1

Social skills and table manners

Your own childhood will have influenced your beliefs about the importance or not of table manners and what this idea means in practice. You will want to encourage the children towards courteous behaviour at mealtimes but do be careful that you do not claim a rule is universal when in fact it is the tradition only of the culture with which you are most familiar.

There may be some basics that all children can learn:

- Give other eaters space and don't crowd them.
- You eat what is on your plate rather than sneaking other people's food.
- You say you have had enough rather than dumping your unwanted bits.

Children can learn courtesy at the meal table so long as adults set a good example and are patient in helping children to learn. Some of the practical issues include using courtesy words such as 'please', 'thank you' and 'would you like ...?' Be flexible and recognise that there are more ways to say 'thank you' than the actual words. A nod and an enthusiastic smile is fine.

Learning about food and bodies

Children can learn about healthy eating and develop an interest in how food fuels their energy and growing bodies.

- Friendly communication extends children's vocabulary with the names for different foods and meals. Step by step they also learn the words to express enthusiasm and preferences over taste, smell and texture.
- You can extend the food experience of children and the staff by offering some foods for tasters at snack time and some meals that are outside their daily experience (see page 100).

Figure 3.4
Young children are able to clean up their own spills

- Children will have their own likes and dislikes about food that is unusual to them. It is fair to have a ground rule that children can say they do not like a particular food, but not that it is 'disgusting' or 'muck', especially when this is the family food of a child who is present at the table.

Children can become interested in how their bodies work to digest food and in different kinds of food. You may introduce some of these resources as part of a themed topic (see page 435) but there is no need to wait if children express curiosity now.

Here are some useful books to make available as a resource. These books are written primarily for five and six year olds, but remember that children who cannot yet read the text can be very interested in looking at good illustrations and will ask you for more information:

- The *Look at your body* series from Franklin Watts with titles including digestion, reproduction and growing up, brains and nerves and senses.
- The *How our bodies work* series written by Carol Ballard and published by Hodder Wayland, with titles including *How do we taste and smell?*, *How do our ears move?*, *How do we move?* and others.
- Books can also be a resource about different kinds of food. Try the *Exploring food in Britain* series published by Mantra Publishing and *Food and drink*, a series published by Wayland.

Activity

- Look at one or two of the suggested books and plan how you could use the material with three or four year olds.
- Which illustrations could be useful and how would you link them to children's current knowledge?
- Write up and present to colleagues.

Key skills links: C2/3.1b C1/2.3 C2.2.

Practice for physical skills

Meals and snack times can be good opportunities for children to learn and to practise fine physical skills within a meaningful context.

- Children coordinate sight, feel and movement when they feed themselves.
- As well as feeling helpful, children also apply fine physical skills when they hand round the plate of sandwiches or hold a yoghurt carton steady for a friend to spoon it out onto her fruit.
- Physical skills as well as understanding a sequence are needed to help to lay the table, wipe up spills and clear away at the end of the meal.
- In an early years setting, children are keen to take turns to push the trolley back to the kitchen. A rota for this or other helpful activities can also be a practical way for children to recognise their name label and that of friends, as they come round for their turn.

Abstract ideas in a meaningful context

Children experience a considerable number of meal and snack times. They can learn many things from the routine.

- A sense of pleasant predictability and what follows what in a sequence. Children who are slightly confused by the day or who miss their parents can be reassured by explanations like, 'First we have tea, then we'll do some singing and then your Daddy will be here.'
- Anticipating a meal, including the use of your sense of smell can help children to imagine, think ahead and make connections between information.
- Some days you could lead a discussion around, 'I wonder what we've got for lunch. Now I saw Esme (the cook) with a lot of potatoes, she had the grater out and I smelt fish. What might that be?' (perhaps fish pie with cheese topping, a favourite in the group).
- Laying the table and helping with snack time is often a very practical way to introduce number work (see the tips box).
- You can lay the lunch or tea with name cards for each child (perhaps with a photo) and children learn to recognise letters and look carefully within a meaningful routine important to the group.

Tips for practice

Helping out with mealtimes is an ideal application of an early understanding of number. Rising threes are often ready for an active part in this routine and four and five year olds can be very adept.

- You can involve children who wish in the daily routines with 'How many people have we got for tea?'
- With younger children or those who are not sure of their numbers, count by saying the names and showing the numbers on your fingers.
- You can answer as appropriate, 'That's 6 of us. So we need 6 plates. ... Let's count them as we lay the table. ... Now we need 6 spoons, one for each plate.'
- You can sometimes make a deliberate mistake such as, 'Who hasn't got a plate? I haven't, we didn't count me!'
- Children who have practised this kind of practical number work can often take full responsibility for the task. It is then your role to thank them and express appreciation for their skills.

Choice and planning

It would be unwieldy to give children total choice about food and they would probably find it rather wearing. However, some level of choice and being asked for your opinion is attractive to children.

- Children can be involved in menu planning and displaying the menus for the week ahead.
- A decorated menu board could be made with slots or see-through pockets into which the day's or week's menus are placed with words and an illustration. The board can be a useful form of communication with parents

in an early years setting. As the responsible adult, you need to check all the spellings of foods or meals.

- This kind of activity can work just as well in a family home, if children are interested to discuss, cut out pictures and organise a display.
- Children can be asked for their views on regular meals and kinds of food. They can cut out pictures or sort photos of meals into piles that could become a display. You can use a set of three faces: smiley turned up face, straight face and turned down face to cover the options of 'I like it', 'it's alright' and 'I don't like it'. Four, five and six years olds could do some simple number work on adding up the views of the group on different meals.

Activity

- Take any of the ideas in this section about how children can learn through mealtimes, food preparation and choices.
- Draw a diagram to show the different sources of learning.
- Then plan an activity to explore one of the areas that you have identified.
- Make a short presentation to your colleagues.

Key skills link: C2/3.3 C2/3.1b

Young cooks

Children are very interested in becoming involved in food preparation and cooking. Although a responsible adult needs to keep children safe, there are plenty of opportunities for them to learn. Cooking and food preparation are important because:

- Children learn and apply practical physical skills such as use of tools and techniques like mixing and measuring.
- Keen cooks will learn the safe use of tools or caution around heat.
- Children gain immense satisfaction in making something that can then be eaten by themselves, friends and admiring adults.
- Children are also learning skills useful for later life and they can make sense of your simple messages about healthy eating.
- Cooking and food preparation brings in the skills of planning ahead, understanding a sequence, recall of techniques and 'what we did last time'.
- Children can learn to understand and follow a recipe (see the activity box below).
- Cooking brings in basic science, as it is a kind of chemistry. Children learn about changes as they add liquid, mix and bake.
- Cooking builds children's creative development since they can make choices about decoration and laying out food for a meal in an attractive pattern.
- They gain useful experience in early mathematics: counting, measuring, working out the size of bowl they will need, calculating cooking times and when something will be ready.

Enthusiastic cooks also take their experience into their pretend play and this can be another positive consequence of the cooking activity. However, the real cooking is a source of learning on its own; it does not have to become part of play to be most valuable.

Preparation for cooking

Look also for the possibility of building a shopping trip into the activity. Children can then see the whole process through from purchase all the way to eating the final product. Shopping in a market or local shop can also be the way for children to understand how foods start before they are turned into a meal. There can also be meaningful, practical opportunities to learn about money through the purchase of ingredients.

If you work as a nanny such outings can be part of your week. If you work in an early years setting, you may need more organisation to ensure you can get out with enough adults to keep the children safe. It is important that you make the effort, otherwise children who spend many hours in group childcare can risk losing opportunities to understand how daily life works.

Diversity in cooking

Meal planning and cooking activities are a natural way to include different diets that reflect the families whose children attend your setting.

- It is also a valuable way to explore foods and meals that are not everyday experiences for anyone.
- You can gather your own experience and learn from parents, some of whom may be happy to join you in a shopping or cooking activity.
- Build up experience of different recipes and foods with the children.
- For instance, there are many different kinds of bread to explore or everyone can try a fruit that you discovered on the market trip.
- Basic techniques like learning how to make batter can then be used for different meals.
- Use the correct words for any foods or meals. Avoid, in conversation or written material, the odd phrase 'ethnic food' (see page 93) and the equally odd 'multicultural recipes'. You can draw on recipes from different cultures but no recipe is in itself 'multicultural', any more than the word can be applied to toys or books.

Activity

- Make up a recipe book or set of large recipe cards with the children.
- Look at ways to combine simple written instructions with a picture (sketch or photo) for each stage of the process.
- Do a draft and try out the recipes with children. What do they think, are the instructions straightforward to follow?
- Make any final changes, laminate the cards or use transparent punched pockets in a ring binder.

Tips for practice

Cooking works well as an activity so long as you give children the opportunity to do the work and make some choices. Cooking is not enjoyable for children if they have to wait forever for their turn, are nagged about technique or made to decorate to a set pattern.

- Try to keep cooking as a fairly small group activity and ensure that every child has some materials to work with or gets a go on a longer project.
- Pick recipes that children can manage, so no complicated creaming. Cakes and biscuit mixes are easier to stir if you use the Welsh method of melting the butter or margarine.
- Use materials that are robust. Yeast-based doughs (buns and pizza bases) like to be handled whereas pastry gets tough.
- Pick recipes with choices for decoration: gingerbread people and currants or different cutters for shapes.
- Avoid taking over the work unless it is genuinely too difficult for children. Watch, be ready to help if necessary and encourage children's efforts.
- You need to be aware if children have any allergies, since handling a food can sometimes be enough to trigger a reaction.

If you work as a nanny, then you need to find safe ways to help children develop their cooking skills in the family kitchen. In early years settings there has been considerable reluctance to allow children into the kitchen and some settings work with a total ban, for health and safety reasons. If children spend a full day with you from a very young age, they need to learn about safe behaviour in the kitchen and to do some proper cooking.

You need the cooperation of the cook in an early years setting, but if you work together it should be possible to:

- Organise times when children can have access to the kitchen with an adult.
- Children will learn and understand that they do not simply wander into the kitchen and a gate with a clear illustration will give the message when it is a very busy time in this room.
- If you work with the cook, then you can time cooking activities so that food that needs baking can go in the oven and be ready to be eaten at a suitable time.
- Look for any possibilities for food preparation that does not involve cooking, such as buttering bread and making sandwiches or laying fruit and vegetable slices in an attractive pattern on the plate.

Figure 3.5
Cooking can be a most enjoyable activity

Scenario

The Dale Parent and Toddler group has faced a serious disagreement within the team and between some of the parents. Some people feel strongly that food should be on the meal table and should never be used as a play resource. The difference of opinion arose when Vicky came back from a workshop with the idea of letting the toddlers play in a large container of soft jelly or softly cooked pasta. The group leader, Annie, is very uncomfortable about this activity as she feels that food is in short supply in some parts of the world and it gives the wrong message to let children play with it. One of the fathers on the group management committee agrees and says that he has never been very happy about pasta pictures.

Questions

1. Discuss with your colleagues the two different perspectives represented within the Dale Parent and Toddler group.
2. In turn make the case for each opinion: that it is fine to use food as a play material and why, then the view that food should stay on the meal table and the reasons.
3. Consider what could be a way forward for this group. Can they find a compromise?

Key skills links: C2/3.1a PS2/3.1

Helping children with tooth care

Children's teeth develop during early childhood and good habits can be established from the early years. Healthy eating and drinking habits are one of the most important parts of the care of teeth.

Development of teeth

The first teeth appear in babyhood:

- The first tooth is not usually much earlier than 6 months: incisors come first, with the two central top and two central bottom teeth.
- At about 8 months: two more incisors to make a set of four top and bottom teeth.
- 10–14 months: the first molars, these are the double teeth for efficient chewing.
- 18 months: the canines, at the side of the front incisors.
- Two to two and a half years: the second molars at the back of the mouth.
- In total children have 20 milk teeth and these usually last until about six years of age when the second set start to push out the milk teeth one by one until children have close to a full set of second teeth.
- By the time they are 12–14 years old children will have 28 permanent teeth. The last four of a full set of 32 are the wisdom teeth, right at the back of the

mouth and these do not always emerge until late adolescence or early adulthood.

Ways to prevent tooth decay

Dental decay is a serious problem for many young children in the UK and is largely preventable. The main ways to support good dental health for children are:

- A balanced diet with limited sugar from confectionery and sweetened fizzy drinks (see page 8).
- Regular brushing of teeth with fluoride toothpaste. It used to be said that children should brush their teeth after every meal. But dentists expressed concern that over brushing can damage the tooth enamel and no more than twice a day is now recommended.
- Regular visits to the dentist so that children can have their teeth checked and become familiar with the routine.

Caring for children's teeth is primarily the responsibility of parents. As an early years practitioner you make an important contribution but should not take over that responsibility:

- In an early years setting or family home your role is to organise and promote a healthy diet for the children.
- You will find opportunities to help children learn about teeth as part of their body, through conversation, books or project work.
- If you work as a nanny, then you may help with tooth brushing and may sometimes take the children to their dental appointments.

Figure 3.6

Drinks are as important as food – for teeth and nutrition

Poor diet, with excessive confectionery and sweet, fizzy drinks can cause cavities in the milk teeth, sometimes so bad that children have to have teeth extracted. Worse still, for some children their second set of teeth actually rots in the gums. This level of dental decay is completely avoidable and definitely an adult responsibility.

In partnership with parents you can promote healthy eating and explain how you use different methods of encouragement (see page 485) rather than rewarding children with sweets or biscuits. It would not be appropriate to ban all sweet foods from your early years setting. A birthday cake or special sweetmeats for some religious celebrations can be a change. You can, however, make suggestions to parents about a range of foods that would be welcome for parties and other celebrations, so that sweets are not the main contribution.

Useful resources

Usborne First Experience series *Going to the Dentist* by Anne Civardi and Stephen Cartwight.

Further resources

Whiting, Mary (2001) *Managing Nursery Food: A practical guide for early years professionals* TSL Education/Nursery World.

Progress check

1 Give three reasons why food and mealtimes are important for children's health and learning.

2 Name the four main food groups and give three examples of foods that would provide nutrition for each group.

3 Describe three ways in which you could work in partnership with parents over food and mealtimes.

4 Explain the food traditions or rules of three major world faiths, including the faith that has most influenced your own cultural background.

5 Describe four ways in which positive experiences of food and mealtimes can support other aspects of children's development.

4

Keeping children well and healthy

After reading this chapter you should be able to:

- organise and maintain a safe setting so that children learn about safety and risks
- deal with accidents safely and in a way that promotes children's learning
- recognise the main signs of common illnesses or health problems in children
- take care of your own health and well being as an early years practitioner.

Introduction

Children need to be kept safe and as healthy as possible but in a way that involves them steadily in their own care. Children can learn about their own bodies and health and about other children who differ from themselves. In partnership with parents, early years practitioners can help children to feel cared for when they are ill as well as beginning to understand health and illness.

Keeping children safe

When children are young, they need adults to ensure that their usual environment is safe enough that children can explore, play and learn without undue problems.

Links to early years qualifications

This chapter especially supports the following units:

Diploma in Child Care and Education: 3, 5

National Vocational Qualification in Early Years Care and Education

Level 2: C1, E2, M1

Level 3: C2, E3, C14, M8

BTEC National Early Years Diploma: 3, 5, 6, 10

Checks for safety

Play materials should only be bought from reputable companies and should conform to British safety standards, whenever these apply. Even if your setting is very short of money, it is unacceptable to buy second hand or accept donated equipment that does not meet safety requirements.

You need to check play materials and equipment on a regular basis. If something needs mending, for example torn dressing-up clothes or a screw that needs tightening, then make the repair promptly. Children can be part of this safety procedure to the extent that they may point out that something needs mending and will be flattered to hear, 'Well spotted, I'll see about that this morning'. Check with a senior if any equipment looks as if it needs specialist attention or is beyond safe repair.

It is good practice to check your setting for obvious hazards and any problems that arise because of the inconsiderate behaviour of neighbours. Some settings have no choice but to check the garden for rubbish or dog excrement before letting children go out to play.

Tips for practice

Beyond sensible checks you will keep children safe by your involved and caring supervision. A supportive early years team needs to be positive:

- Explore the ways in which you can do some real gardening with the children rather than thinking 'We can't do that – what about the dirt';
- Children like to help with pets. Think about how you can give them a safe role in a family home or early years setting, rather than taking over because of hygiene concerns or because you can do the task more quickly.
- Children' s play often gets noisy and lively. Respect their play and consider with the children themselves how to make the monster and rescue game less intrusive on other activities. Avoid the knee jerk reaction of 'You're knocking into people. Stop it right now!'

A learning environment that is safe enough

Normal childhood includes an array of bumps, bruises and scrapes. If adults try to make an environment 100 per cent risk-free, they will not only set themselves an impossible task, they risk creating a boring environment in which children cannot learn.

An equally important point is that children need to learn steadily to keep themselves safe and to assess ordinary everyday risk.

- Early years practitioners make a real contribution to ways in which children learn about taking care of themselves.
- Children become physically more able to take on some of this responsibility.
- However, their understanding of the world also extends so that they can better anticipate what may happen.
- They may grasp why you are sometimes concerned when they are not, although they will still often think you are fussing.

Disabled children still need this support for learning and they do not benefit from over protection:

- Children with physical disabilities may need more support and direct help.

- If children have learning disabilities, then you need to adjust your expectations since the children's understanding may be more like that of a younger child.
- Otherwise the sign of a good day for a disabled child in your setting will mean some mess and the odd bump or scrape.

Supporting children's learning

As an early years practitioner, you are responsible for other people's children. So it is easy, especially in a setting where the team has become anxious, to be too afraid 'what may happen if …' and of being blamed for any accident. But you cannot run a good day for children in which they will learn, if you mainly think about what can go wrong or abandon valuable activities because of a small level of risk that could be resolved.

Your setting's policy on health and safety should set a framework. But in the end it is attentive and supportive adults who keep children safe enough without harassing them or making the children unduly anxious.

- Young children cannot learn to anticipate and weigh up the very ordinary risks of everyday life, unless they have experienced different situations and been guided by supportive adults.
- Parents as well as early years practitioners are often most sensitive to physical risks, but part of childhood is that children need to handle emotional and intellectual risks.
- They need to experience that mistakes are not all disasters and that some practical problems can be overcome.

Figure 4.1
Lively physical activity helps keep children healthy

- They also need to learn practical life skills, such as how to handle ordinary tools, simple cooking and how to move around their neighbourhood, including road safety (see page 117).
- Early childhood is an excellent time to help children learn since they are keen and still willing, at least sometimes, to pay attention to caring adults.

Scenario

St Jude's nursery and reception team have thought carefully about safety and helping children learn about everyday risks. They offer a well equipped woodwork table that the children greatly enjoy and there has never been an accident with the tools. This term a family has joined St Jude's that appears to be highly anxious about the well being of their children, aged four and six years. Both parents have expressed concern about the wood-work table in the nursery class and the climbing frame and large tyres in the school playground.

Pam and Maryam have spoken with the parents explaining how children are kept safe and still enabled to have an enjoyable day in which they can learn. The head of school, Alastair, is still concerned about the parents who are outspoken in their concerns about 'what may happen if ...'

Questions

1 Discuss with your colleagues the main issues that the St Jude's team face.

2 What are their learning priorities and how can these be reconciled with partnership with parents?

3 Draft some options for how the team could resolve this problem. You could consider the options of further conversation with the parents, bringing in other parents who are not anxious, use of displays as information, and inviting the parents into the setting.

4 What are the likely consequences if St Jude's responds to the anxiety of this family and removes the woodwork table or the climbing equipment?

Key skills links: C3.1a C3.3 PS3.1

Step by step

It is important to recall that children's learning stretches over all the years of childhood. Useful skills are learned a bit at a time and rarely in a single activity or conversation. You are not responsible for passing on everything about safe use of tools or personal and road safety (see page 116) in your relatively short period with children in a nursery or playgroup. Children start the process in the early years, ideally within a partnership between home and early years settings. They continue to learn and extend their skills throughout childhood. Children like to help out and this can be an ideal opportunity for practising skills (see page 116).

Children learn some realities of safety the hard way with a bump or a bruise. You cannot prevent them entirely from having accidents, but you should, of course, keep a wary eye and ear and babies or toddlers should not be out of your sight. Early years settings will usually be adjusted for the height of young children and access to rooms like kitchens will be restricted. The environment may give fewer daily risks than an ordinary home. But poor practice in a setting can develop if practitioners are inattentive to children or ignore basic procedures of hygiene (see page 56).

Tips for practice

Although some under twos have learned a few basic cautionary lessons, the excitement of the moment can push them to the back of a toddler's mind. Helping children learn is a steady process.

- Two and three year olds will learn to follow some basic warnings that relate to their familiar environment.
- Four year olds and older will begin to grasp your reasons for saying, 'Don't touch', 'Watch out' or 'remember what I said about dogs'.
- However you do need to be ready to repeat reminders, warnings and simple reasons.
- Children learn bit by bit about more general safety rules. Helpful adults never forget that this area of learning is closely linked to other aspects of children's development, including their intellectual understanding.
- Children can be very literal when they are young. They may listen carefully to you about standing back a little from the local pond that you visit, but not take this warning to apply to any stretch of water.

A safe setting

Your role in keeping children safe covers a range of actions, checks and your skills of observation. Children do not want to be tracked and watched all the time but attentive early years practitioners can keep an eye and ear without the children feeling oppressed.

- Make sure that children have enough space to move about. Some games may need a bit of organisation or an agreement that they are outdoor activities.
- Do you have some areas that are out of bounds to children? Remember from your own childhood that such a ban is only likely to make children want to go there. See if you can avoid completely no-go areas and enable visits to rooms that do not have unrestricted access, like the office or kitchen, in a setting.
- Adults need to be in sight and earshot of children who are playing. There should always be a practitioner in the garden if the children are playing outside. Your setting will need to be flexible about ratios if adults are not to move abruptly just because the children have moved.
- You do need to have a suitable ratio when you take trips out, and it is worth the effort because children can learn a great deal from trips out and about in your local neighbourhood (see page 426).
- Children must be safe and secure in your setting, so that they cannot wander out of your building and so that people with no legitimate business to visit cannot simply wander in through the front gate or door.
- Attentive adults offer the best protection for children, but secure gates and doors, with a check on visitors, are an important part of safety.
- Unless your setting is situated in a genuinely high-risk neighbourhood, then close circuit television (CCTV) is probably unnecessary.

Scenario

The Dale Parent and Toddler drop-in group operate in a large building where they use different rooms for different kinds of activity. The building itself is kept secure by an entry phone.

A review of safety led to a decision to count the children each time they moved in and out of rooms. This procedure was also influenced by the concern of one of the practitioners, Liz, whose young daughter had been distressed by being left behind in her nursery toilet when the whole group had gone to see a video elsewhere in the school building.

The counting procedure has been followed now for two months and the team decides to review it. They are uncertain about whether it is a wise or necessary way to ensure safety. Two of the children have become anxious, saying, 'Are there bad people here? Is that why you count us?' and one father asked, only half joking, 'How many children have you actually lost?'

Questions

1. Discuss with your colleagues the issues that the Dale team need to weigh up.
2. They need to keep the children safe but is the counting procedure necessary for safety? Are there other less obvious ways to keep check? What are the possible downsides to this regular counting?
3. It was poor practice for Liz's daughter to be left in the toilet of her nursery but what should that team have been doing to avoid such a distressing incident?

Key skills links: C3.1a PS2.1

Tips for practice

- You should know how to get yourself and the children out of the building in the event of an emergency or other kind of crisis.
- In many areas, the emergency is most likely to be a fire. However, there are places in the UK where the emergency could be a bomb.
- Settings should have regular practice drills that enable you and the children to practise a safe exit.
- Adults should be familiar with the location of fire alarms, extinguishers and possible alternative exit routes.
- If you are working as a nanny, you should have equipment such as a fire blanket or extinguisher in the kitchen, but you will be dependent on the family as to whether they have chosen to buy these.

Who is responsible for children?

It must always be clear who is responsible for the children. If you are called away or are taking a break, you must explicitly pass responsibility for your group to another practitioner. You cannot just assume someone will keep an eye on the children. In a family home the responsible person will continue to be you.

Figure 4.2

Responsible adults are there to help when necessary

Handing over responsibility

Transition times can be confusing for children and adults. For instance, it needs to be clear when the children pass into your responsibility from their parent or other carer at the beginning of the day and the point at which the responsibility has passed back at the end of the day. You can sort this out between the adults, without it being heavy-handed. You may need a quiet conversation with a parent if the child appears to be playing you off against each other, or if the parent is unreasonably extending the time when you are responsible.

Trips out

Children benefit from simple local trips as well as journeys to venues further afield. Any trip needs enough adults to ensure children are safe and adults are not required to keep a close eye on too many children. But enough adults are also important to enable children to be sure of attention and replies to their questions.

If you do not know the venue of a trip it is wise for somebody to make a visit prior to taking the children. A thorough check of a venue or an activity is called a **risk assessment**.

Key term

Risk assessment the process of checking the likely risks involved in an activity or an outing and sensible ways to address the risks

- This procedure can be useful to check for any possible issues relevant to this group or individual children and to find ways to resolve any problems.
- Adults should not use risk assessments to become anxious about everything that could go wrong.
- Useful information will be whether the venue is accessible for any disabled children or adults.
- Will it be interesting for the younger children? Are there some parts of the visit that will require more adults and practical issues like the location of the toilets?

Activity

Do a risk assessment on a local facility such as the library or visiting the market.

- Check out any practical issues that need to be resolved, without becoming unduly anxious about unlikely things that can go wrong. Your objective is to problem solve, not to get frightened.
- How will you keep children safe on the route to and from the facility and within the building or area?
- What could they learn from this trip? Collect photos or leaflets to show the potential from this outing.
- Discuss your assessment with colleagues and explore whether there are general themes within the different examples.

Key skills link: C3.1a C3.1b

On trips out with the children, everyone needs to be clear about who is responsible for which children. This check can be especially important for larger group outings and when parents join you as well. If you are the practitioner in overall charge of the trip, then make sure that every adult understands who is in their small group, tell the children as well, and where you will all meet up if you are dividing within the day. Parents and other volunteers need to understand that the outing is a form of work, They are responsible for the named children and the trip is not a free ride.

Tips for practice

- Ensure that all adults know exactly the children for whom they are responsible.
- It can also help to have a chat with children. An experienced nursery teacher explained to me how she evokes children's sense of responsibility. She tells the children that they need to keep close to (named adult) on this trip, because adults do wander sometimes and children need to ensure that they can get the adult's hand.
- Children who are prone to wandering or dashing off will need to be in a more favourable ratio or with more experienced adults.
- A child with very challenging behaviour will need to be one-to-one with his or her key person or the practitioner who has most experience with the child.
- Count all children carefully when you leave any part of an outside trip or move on within a large area that you have visited. But do not count for limited internal travels in your own building (see the scenario on page 113).
- Similar care should be taken if you take a group of children from one part of a large school building to another.
- You can count discretely and five and six years olds can start to work a buddy system in which everyone ensures that their 'buddy' is present.

Skills sharing

No child learns about safe behaviour, like how to hold a hammer safely or how to clean a cut, because they have passed a certain birthday. Children learn because adults have taken the trouble to share their own skills through a process of tell–show–do. You:

- Tell children about what you do in an activity or routine. You can highlight safety without becoming boring.
- Show them how to hold the hammer or needle and demonstrate through your actions and good example how to be calm when there is an accident or gentle with the baby.
- Give children plenty of opportunities to do the tasks, to practise and to ask for more help as and when they want.

Using conversations

In an ordinary day as well as organised opportunities, perhaps in circle time, you can use words and actions to highlight the practical safety guidelines.

- Ask individual children or a small group before they start a gardening or needlework activity to recount what they will do or the best sequence. Give an encouraging 'well done' for what they remember and remind the children of anything else that is important.
- Circle time can be an opportunity to review the day's or session's activities. Children can also be invited to remind their peers about 'what do we do first of all at the woodwork table?' (put on our special goggles) or 'who uses the big sharp scissors?' (only an adult).
- You can share useful tips and techniques in how to do a practical activity.
- Be encouraging when a child brings something to your attention or has a good idea. You might say, 'You're right, I should watch my fingers with the knife'.
- Support children's learning and be friendly about mistakes. See also page 393 about developing a positive disposition to learn.

Personal safety

Part of children's growing self reliance is to be aware of their own personal safety. You can begin to share some basic rules with four year olds but you would not cover personal safety in one telling, nor should you depend upon one source of communication, like a single story book.

Remember that you are not trying to do it all – children learn about personal safety issues over time and they add on ideas and understanding as the months and years pass. Useful learning for children includes the rights over their own body and understanding about their private areas and experiencing respectful touch (see page 43).

You can share and show children's rights to personal safety:

- The right to say 'No' – a child's body belongs to her. She has the right to say 'No' to any adult or child who touches her in a way that she does not want.
- The right to tell – if anybody refuses to take notice when a child says 'No', then he can tell on that person.
- The right not to keep secrets – children need to be encouraged not to keep a secret that does not feel right.

- The right not to be bound by social rules – reassure children that if adults do not behave properly, then the usual politeness rules do not apply.

It is misleading to place too much emphasis on adults who are unknown to children: the so-called 'stranger danger'. Most strangers who kill or seriously injure children are behind the wheel of a vehicle. Children are statistically far more at risk of abusive harm from people they know: family and friends and people who have access to children through their work or voluntary activities (see Chapter 19). Furthermore, good safety rules also support children who face bullying.

Communicate with parents about what you do in a low key way, so that they understand what you explain and can support their children at home. You can use incidents that arise and explain simply to children, for instance, why you took the group away from the market because somebody was shouting and appeared to be drunk. You can show children practical safety rules like what to do if you get lost on a school outing.

The aim of supportive safety guidelines for children is to help them to make judgements at the time, to empower them. It is important to avoid leaving children with the feeling that they hold the whole responsibility for keeping themselves safe from harm.

- Adults have the responsibility to behave properly and not impose on children or ask them to do something that makes the child uneasy.
- Adults who do not behave well, do not deserve courtesy.
- Children need to feel sure they have permission to shout, run away and tell on adults or other children who threaten them.
- However, some bullies or abusers may be too strong or it is very hard to tell. Children must not be left feeling that the situation is their fault.

Finding out more

Kidscape has published a range of books and leaflets on personal safety for children. Contact them at 2 Grosvenor Gardens, London SW1W 0DH tel: 020 7730 3300 *www.kidscape.org.uk*

Road safety

You ensure the safety of babies and young children by having them safe in buggies or holding your hand. But you can help children to learn about road safety as part of your normal conversation and local excursions with them.

- Books, role play and play with dolls can support an understanding but effective support of children has to include regular kerb side practice. Otherwise children do not make the link between play and real road safety and they do not get the guided practice that is essential for them to learn.
- Road safety takes time, it is a step by step learning process that can be started when they are young but continues beyond the age when children will leave you.
- Use local trips to show children what you do to ensure their safety by saying out loud what you are doing: looking up and down the road, listening for traffic, finding a safe place to cross or waiting for the 'green person' at a lighted crossing.

- Children learn best through regular safe practice with responsible adults. Do not expect even six or seven year olds to be reliable.

Activity

- Plan for how you can support your current group of children towards road safety.
- What will be appropriate experiences given their age?
- Write up and present to your colleagues.

Key skills links: C2.3 C2.1a

Dealing with accidents

Children will get hurt on occasion, however safe your setting and careful you are. Indeed if you try to make your setting free of any risks, it will be so boring that the children will either become passive and physically inactive, with all the risks that this entails, or else they find excitement and challenge despite your restrictions.

If you follow good practice in care and friendly supervision of children then you will prevent those accidents that can be avoided. Good maintenance of play materials and equipment will reduce the risks even more. However, unless you restrict children in ways that will seriously limit their learning, you will never reduce accidents to zero.

Figure 4.3

There will be minor accidents in any interesting early years setting

Tips for practice

- You can comfort and support a child at the same time that you give whatever care is needed.
- Children actually do feel better for having a plaster and a kind word.
- Sometimes children are more shaken up than actually hurt. Sometimes they may expect you to be angry, since they have been careless or broken one of the rules in your setting.
- You can reassure them kindly and deal with any hurt, as well as emphasise kindly that this was why you warned about, 'Look before you jump'.
- It will not help children to learn if you are angry or nag them. Ensure that your feelings do not blur the main message. You might, for instance, be frightened for what could have happened, frustrated because you warned the child or concerned about what the parents will say.
- It will be disrespectful to deny children's feelings with, 'That doesn't hurt' or 'You're making a big fuss'. Even if you believe that a child is making rather a fuss, given the injury, accept her feelings as she expresses them.
- Look for an opportunity to be encouraging when she takes a braver outlook or is prompter in rejoining the play.
- Do not expect a boy to be more able to hold back tears than a girl of the same age.

Coping with injuries

You need to know what to do in response to common accidents that can happen with young children. This section covers only the most basic points for first aid and cannot substitute for a proper first aid course.

Activity

- Check on the contents of the first aid box in your setting.
- What common accidents can be dealt with by using this equipment?
- Does your setting use any antiseptic on cuts and if not do parents know that they will need to disinfect a cut or scrape when they take their child home?
- Compare your findings in different settings through discussion with colleagues on your course.

Key skills link: C2.1a

Nosebleeds

Children sometimes get nosebleeds because they have crashed into something or someone. But sometimes there is no obvious reason and children just get apparently spontaneous nose bleeds. The treatment is to:

- Sit the child down leaning forward and pinch the nose firmly between finger and thumb just below the hard part of the nose. An older child will probably be able to do this action himself but you will need to help a younger one. A flannel soaked in cold water and then wrung out can be placed on the bridge of the nose.
- This treatment will usually work. Explain to the child not to blow their nose for at least a couple of hours.
- Tell the parents when they pick up the child or come home.
- If the nosebleed does not stop in ten minutes then the child should be taken to the Accident and Emergency (A&E) department of the local hospital.

Bumps and bruises

Small cuts and grazes can be cleaned with water and cotton wool and protected with a mild antiseptic cream. Use the contents of the first aid box to clean cuts and grazes and to cover them if necessary.

Slight bleeding will be stopped by gentle cleaning. More persistent bleeding may need you to lay a clean cloth over the wound and press firmly. Raise a limb slightly and this will help to stop the bleeding.

Activity

Consider any of the possible accidents described in this section.

- Imagine a child falling or getting a nosebleed in your setting.
- Make brief notes about how you would handle the situation.
- Consider also what to do with other children who are close to the accident and watch as you deal with the incident.
- Discuss the possibilities with colleagues and explore whether some settings vary in the more likely accident areas.

Key skills link: PS3.1 C3.1a

Falls

Help the child up and let her sit quietly while she recovers. Children need to be taken to hospital if they are drowsy after the fall, lose consciousness, are limp or very pale, also if they vomit.

If children are very drowsy, they should be put in the recovery position and then get the child to hospital. If you are uncertain what is wrong or the child seems to have a serious injury, then call an ambulance.

Choking

Unless you can reach and hook out an object very easily, then do not persist, you will only push it further. Hold a toddler or young child upside down by the legs and slap him smartly between the shoulder blades with the heel of your hand. If the object does not shoot out, do it again. An older or bigger child should be laid over your knees, face down. Use the same movement.

If you try this several times without success, as a last resort you can give the baby or child's stomach a short, sharp squeeze which should push the object out

1 Place the child's head to the side and tilt her chin to clear the airway.
2 Tuck the arm closest to you under her bottom, palm upwards. Then bring her other arm over her body.
3 Hold onto her shoulder and waist. Cross the child's legs with the leg furthest away on top.
4 Gently roll her towards you. Bend the knee of her top leg so it supports her body. Place her top arm palm downwards and release her lower arm. It is important that you straighten her airway once more.

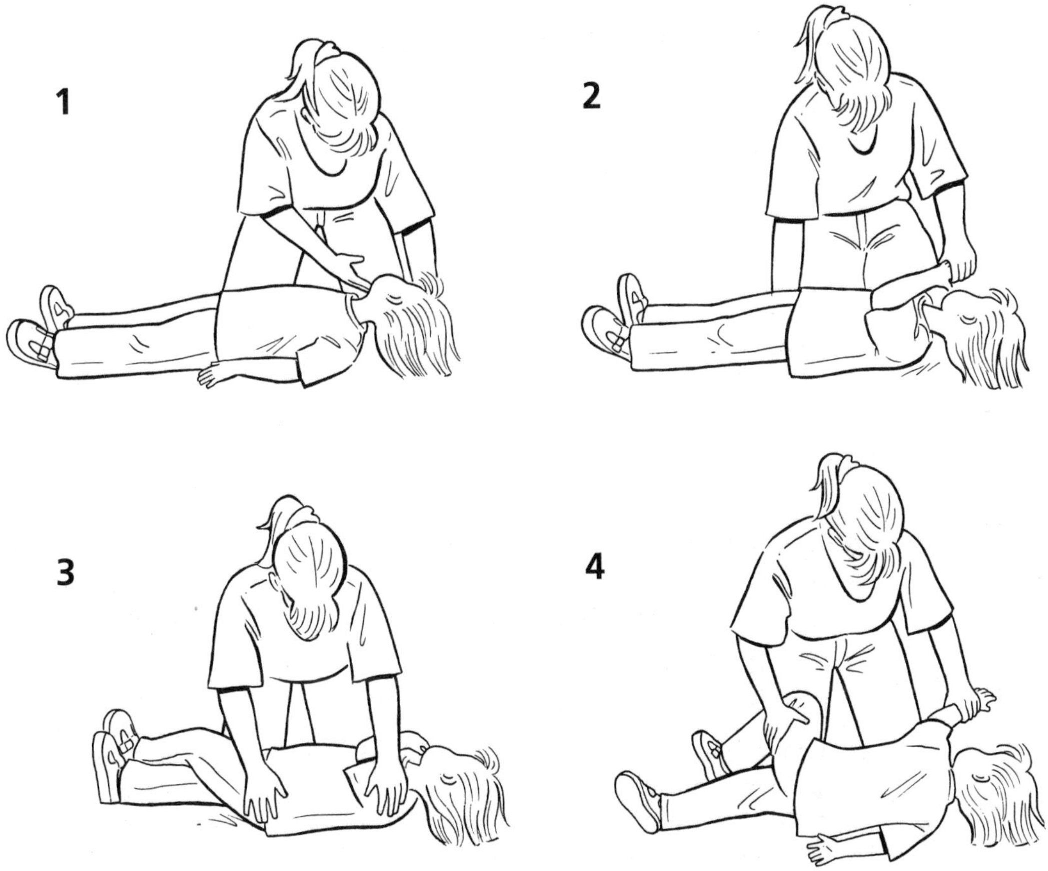

Figure 4.4 Placing a child in the recovery position

of the windpipe. If all else fails then take the child to the closest medical assistance and get someone to phone in advance.

Burns and scalds

- Carry the child to the nearest tap and run cold water over the burned or scalded area immediately. Comfort the child and hold her close but keep the water running for ten minutes. This action reduces the heat in the skin and the risk of scarring.
- Remove clothing that is not stuck to the skin, otherwise leave it. Take off jewellery or belts since burned skin can swell.
- Cover the burn or scald with a clean, non-fluffy cloth soaked in cold water.
- Take a child to hospital for anything more than a very small burn or scald.
- Do not put any cream or ointment on the skin and do not prick any blisters.

The accident book

All settings should have an accident book in which the details and time of any accident are recorded. You should make brief notes of a descriptive kind that follow general good practice in writing records (see page 461).

If you work as a nanny or childminder, you would not use a formal accident book. But it would be good practice to have a working notebook that guides you in a conversation with parents at the end of the day. You would not only talk about what has gone wrong but an accident should be mentioned.

Activity

Look at the accident book in your setting.

- What details are written down each time?
- Are there any very minor incidents that would not be entered?

Communication with parents

You should tell parents when they pick up their child that she has had an accident with a scrape or a bruise that will probably come out later.

- Most parents are understanding about everyday bumps and scrapes, *so long as they are told promptly*. The most cooperative parents will get angry if they find unexplained bruises later.
- Parents will also react unfavourably if the setting policy is to ask them about bruises, for reasons of child protection, and yet the team reacts frostily if parents ask for an explanation of a bruise obtained in the setting. The relationship will seem very unequal to parents and their perception is accurate; this way of working is not a partnership. (See Chapter 19 and the scenario on page 564).
- Parents will also want to know what is being done about the situation, for example if another child was the cause of the accident, by shoving or biting. You would not name the other child but it is fair for parents to want to be reassured that you have the problem in hand.
- Does your setting have rules about what, if anything, is put on a cut or graze? If so, then tell parents, or else they will reasonably assume that you have used antiseptic or other simple first aid measure as they would do at home.

Accidents, near misses and problem areas

Caring adults do not want children to be hurt or frightened, but our own feelings sometimes blur the message. Be honest about your own feelings and ready to apologise if your concern has made you speak sharply to a child. You may need to admit, 'I was frightened you would hurt yourself.'

Good practice in an early years or school team would be some discussion following an accident or a problem area in the setting. However, some teams respond with an absolute ban on an activity, pretend play theme or temporary craze. Imposed bans by adults are disruptive of children's learning and a lost opportunity for children's problem solving schemes in a meaningful context. It is also worth noting that adults tend to ban activities that children like, but that adults do not value, such as playing superhero games or lively football. Problems that arise during activities that adults believe to be educational are far more often addressed as an issue about behaviour.

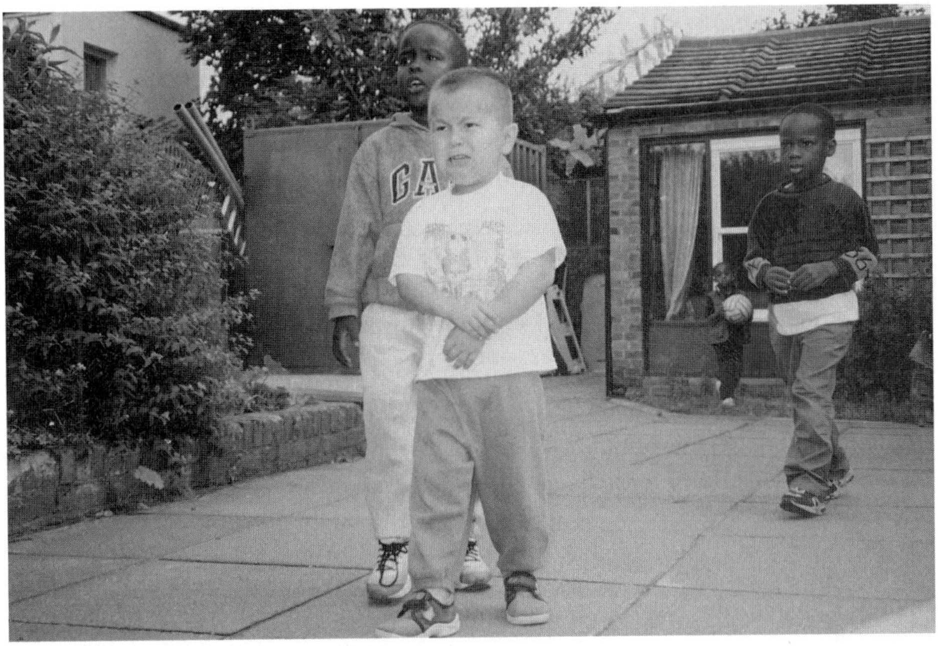

Figure 4.5

Sometimes there are lessons to be learned – but sometimes it's just an accident

Tips for practice

If necessary, you can review after an accident, but do not get drawn into knee-jerk reactions of 'this must never happen again' and removing legitimate play materials. There may be sensible steps to take:

- Do the children need a reminder about safe behaviour in the garden? Choose your timing and words with care, so that the child who was hurt does not feel embarrassed or that his accident has caused trouble for the group.
- Were adults inattentive? If so, what needs to be discussed and changed in how you work together?
- It the problem seems to have arisen from the layout of the setting, then the team needs to talk about the issue.
- If faulty or broken equipment was a factor, then it needs to be mended or removed.

Activity

- Gather information about any outright bans on activities in your setting or other local settings.
- Why was the ban imposed and were the children involved in any meaningful discussion?
- What did the children feel?
- Can you identify other ways through which the problem might have been resolved? Discuss with your colleagues.

Key skills links: C3.1a PS3.1

Learning problem solving skills

Children feel more respected and can learn when adults enable an open discussion about a problem area in an early years setting, school or out of school facility. The basic steps in effective problem solving are as follows:

- Step one: a full discussion about the problem

You need to explore what, who, when, where and perhaps why? Listen to the children: their perspectives and priorities are important too. Be honest when it is you as an adult who feel this is a problem (the children may not think so). Be ready to listen when children tell you, to your surprise perhaps, that there is a problem they want to resolve.

- Step two: generate a range of possible solutions

You want to explore options to resolve the problem, rather than jumping at the first proposal. Children often have good ideas and one suggestion may piggyback onto another.

- Step three: decide on the best solution

Which is overall the best option of those discussed. Talk through how this solution will work in this setting and with the problem you face. Both children and adults have to be committed; it will not work if adults impose the solution.

- Step four: put the proposed solution into action

You need to try out the preferred option for long enough to see how it works. Give it time and remind the children if necessary of what was agreed.

- Step five: review

You need to monitor and evaluate the situation and discuss again as necessary. Be pleased with the children, alert them to the fact that, 'You had great ideas' or 'We've solved it, haven't we?'

This approach to problem solving works well and children become more able to use the skills themselves, even at four and five years of age. The steps work so long as adults give their time and attention and genuinely listen to children. Even children younger than school age soon observe if adults (practitioners or parents) pretend to invite children's views, but then press on regardless with their preferred adult solution. Similar principles apply in the skills of conflict resolution (see page 208).

Activity

- Apply the steps of problem solving to an issue that you currently face in your setting or home.
- Take your time and hold proper conversations with the children. Listen as well as talk.
- Write up what you have done, including the children's views, and present to colleagues.

Key skills links: PS2/31–3

Going to hospital

After more serious accidents, children may well need to visit the accident and emergency department of the local hospital or may stay in overnight for observation. Children and their families need information and support under these circumstances. You will find more in Chapter 18, especially from page 542, about children who have longer or more regular hospital stays.

The children in the group may all be affected by an accident, not only the child who was actually hurt. Children may feel better to play out their concerns and they often like to play doctors at home or in a role play area in an early years setting. You can provide simple outfits and some pretend medical equipment. Sensitive involvement and observation of their play will help you to judge if one or more children need reassurance. You can offer this support in partnership with their parents.

Finding out more

The organisation Action for Sick Children promotes child-friendly hospital practices and changes in organisation that support children and families. Contact them at 300 Kingston Road, London SW20 8LX tel: 020 8542 4848
email: *enquiries@actionforsickchildren.org*
website: *www.actionforsickchildren.org*

Activity

- The Child Accident Prevention Trust (CAPT) aims to raise awareness of risks to children and to reduce the level of preventable accidents at home and elsewhere in the daily life of children.
- CAPT produced a very useful set of leaflets for supporting children after accidents. You could obtain the leaflet for supporting young children and use the material to plan sensible steps in your setting if you needed to offer emotional support to a child.
- Contact them at Clerks Courts, 18–20 Farringdon Lane, London EC1R 3HA tel: 020 7608 3828 website: *www.capt.org.uk*

Key skills links: IT2/3.1–3 C3.2.

Health and illness

This section covers minor and some more major infectious illnesses. You will find out more about illness in the first year of life in Chapter 6 and details about continuing health conditions and chronic illness in Chapter 18.

Talking with parents about illness

Obviously you will have to contact individual parents if children are sufficiently ill that they need to be picked up before the end of the usual day or session. Any early years setting or individuals such as childminders or nannies should have a contact number (landline or mobile) to get them swiftly in contact with a parent. If you do need to call in the day then explain your reasons, perhaps saying that the child has a high temperature or that she has already vomited twice.

It is practical and courteous to tell parents if you have an outbreak of an infectious illness. You would not usually name the children involved. You would say, or put up a notice explaining that 'we have two cases of mumps in the pre-school' or 'there has been a case of head lice, all parents are advised to check their child's head tonight'.

Children often feel very ill with some of the common childhood infections. An illness like chicken pox may seem ordinary but it is still unpleasant to have. Adults often feel even more ill with the so-called childhood diseases and some illnesses pose a particular threat. Although there have been extensive vaccination programmes, mumps and rubella (German measles) are still around. Rubella can cause very serious damage to a fetus in the early months of pregnancy so pregnant women – parents or practitioners – who have not been vaccinated need to know. Mumps carry the slight risk to men of inflammation of the testicles and subsequent sterility.

Judging when children are ill

Of course you aim, in partnership with children's parents, to keep them as healthy as possible, but they will get ill sometimes, it is inevitable. Some children will experience more ill health than their peers. When a child in your care seems to be ill, you have the difficult task of deciding, in consultation with colleagues or seniors:

- What is the matter?
- How serious is it? And therefore …
- Do you need to contact the child's parent before the end of the day?

Very young children cannot say much to guide you when they are ill or sickening for something. You will also depend a great deal on your knowledge of this child as an individual.

- Is she behaving in a different way from normal: more lethargic, prone to tears or whining?
- An underused sense is that of smell. Children who are ill may smell different, not unpleasant, just different from how they do normally.
- Four and five year olds may be more able to tell you what is wrong when they feel ill. Children, however, much like adults, can be subjective in answering 'How much does it hurt?'
- Children may also be vague or confused about names for parts of the body, so do ask, 'Show me where it hurts' and not just 'Tell me'.

When you share the care of very young children with parents it is especially important that you communicate at transition times: when you pass over responsibility at the beginning and end of the day. If a baby or child is poorly, you both need to have accurate information on the symptoms and how long they have lasted. Vomiting and diarrhoea can be particularly dangerous for babies and toddlers, who swiftly become very ill and dehydrated.

Activity

Find out about the medication policy and practice in your setting.

- What is seen as medication, in contrast with ordinary first aid measures?
- How is medication stored and what are the safety procedures for dealing with the medication needs of individual children?
- What kind of records are kept? Write up the general policy.
- With the parents' permission, write up a short description of the medication needs of one child in the setting.
- See also the section about regular medication on page 525.

Key skills links: C2/3.3

Activity

- Check with your setting and explore any guidelines on when mildly ill children could be accepted for the day or when you would wait until a parent or carer came to pick up the child.
- What kind of symptoms would lead to prompt contact with a parent?
- What are the guidelines about when a child can return after common childhood infections such as chicken pox? Write up your findings.
- Discuss with colleagues in different settings whether the guidelines vary at all.

Key skills links: C2.1a C2.3

Raised temperature

A child's temperature should usually be 37°C (98.6°F). It is normal for the temperature to vary a little but a rise in a child's temperature is a sign of illness. Fever is reached with a temperature of 38°C (100.4°F) and a child is at risk of high temperature convulsions if it reaches 41°C (106°F).

- You can check a child's temperature with a standard mercury thermometer or a digital thermometer. These are placed under the arm of a child younger than five years.
- Older children can have the thermometer in their mouth, since they will understand not to bite on it.
- It takes 4–5 minutes for the thermometer to register the temperature under the arm and about 2 minutes in the mouth.
- A plastic strip or a fever scan is less accurate but better than a guess, if a child finds it impossible to keep still.

A high temperature should be treated by:

- keeping a child cool
- giving plenty of liquids to avoid dehydration
- a paracetamol liquid suitable for the child's age.
- aspirin should not be given to children younger than 12 years because of the danger of the complication of Reye's syndrome if the child has chicken pox.

Stomach ache

Children quite often complain of stomach or tummy ache. Usually this symptom is not a sign of something serious, but it is important to respond to children and to track their complaints. (See also page 169 about apparent stomach pains and colic in babies.)

- Listen to the child and suggest she sits quiet for a while. If she soon gets bored and starts playing again then she is probably not ill.
- If a child looks to be in pain and clutches or rocks holding their stomach, they probably are in pain. Pain can travel and be felt in the stomach when the problem is elsewhere, because the nerves in the abdomen are linked to the spinal cord.
- Young children are not yet sure of the names for all the parts of their body. 'My tummy hurts' can be a description applying to almost anything on the front of their body from the throat to the lower trunk. You need to ask 'show me where it hurts' to get a better idea.
- Aches combined with a temperature of more than 38°C could mean an infection. So you would need to tell the child's parent and suggest that a trip to the doctor might be wise.
- When children's bodies are fighting infection their immune system is working hard. A lot of the lymphoid tissue that is part of this system is in the lower abdomen, so children's stomachs can feel tender or swell.

Some children have frequent stomach aches. In these cases it is worth looking for a pattern using your own informal observation and some simple questions of the child:

- Are they hungry? Sometimes children have not yet worked out that hunger can make the stomach ache as well as rumble.
- Have they got indigestion because they eat their food very fast, perhaps not chewing well? Try for a more relaxed mealtime. Consider also if this child gets so hungry that she or he bolts the food. Can you produce a meal earlier (as a nanny) or organise a nutritional snack to keep the child going?
- Have they got constipation? Apart from making it painful to go to the toilet and pass stools, constipation can give children stomach and lower back ache. Have a discreet chat with the child and see what is happening or not happening (see page 72).
- The onset of a stomach upset or diarrhoea can give a child pain. You would need to watch out for any other symptoms as well as treating the diarrhoea (see page 73).
- Are they lifting heavy objects in play? Children can strain themselves and you may need to explain how to lift and carry something properly and that it is wise to get help.
- Pain over the loins could mean a kidney problem.

Severe abdominal pain may indicate *appendicitis*, although this more usually affects children older than five years.

- In this case the pain typically starts in the bottom right hand side of the abdomen and may then spread.
- It persists over a couple of hours and is often associated with a slightly raised temperature and vomiting.
- The child's abdomen feels hard to the touch.
- You or the parent should contact a doctor urgently if the stomach ache takes on these features.

Illness and emotional distress

Children may use stomach aches or generally feeling ill as a way of gaining attention or to communicate that they are worried:

- You should find ways to meet this emotional need without criticising the child as attention-seeking or as a hypochondriac (see also page 129 about not labelling children by their behaviour).
- Check that nothing serious is wrong, then pay limited attention to the child's complaints about feeling ill. Ensure that you and your colleagues pay friendly and positive attention to the child at other times. Look for ways to notice what she has done and alert her to what she has learned recently.
- Children sometimes say they are ill as a way of communicating that they are troubled or to get out of going somewhere that makes them very unhappy.
- If there is a pattern that means children avoid going to nursery or school, then you need to open up the conversation with 'Is something the matter?', 'Are you having troubles at playgroup?' or 'Did the teachers sort out that problem in the school toilets?'.

Children who complain of feeling ill when there seems to be nothing physically wrong may genuinely feel that they are at risk.

- One possibility is that the child's parents are so concerned that they have given the child the impression that germs are everywhere. You may need to give the child a more realistic view of ordinary life.
- Another possibility is that the child has experienced bereavement and is scared of serious illness and death. This situation is more likely when parents and other adults have scarcely talked with the child about the family loss. The child needs to be able to express her fears and distress (see page 224).
- In any of these situations you will need to talk with parents to share what you have noticed and suggest that they may wish to talk with their child.

Rashes

You may notice signs of rashes or swellings and there may be more obvious events such as vomiting or diarrhoea. Illnesses that produce rashes will look different on individual children depending on their skin colour and many books still only give photos of light skinned children.

- If children are light skinned, then spots or an unusual flush will show up as red against the skin.
- When they run a temperature, children will look unnaturally flushed or, if very ill, children's colour may drain.

- The darker a child's skin colour, the more the spots or a rash will show as raised areas.
- You may notice a different shading of skin colour around the spots.
- As soon as children start scratching, the spots will show redder and any blistering will be more obvious.
- Darker skinned children may also drain of colour, in contrast with how they look when they are healthy.

Some common illnesses have a rash as one of the symptoms but this is not always the first sign. A few common illnesses are now described. Even though some of these are covered by the immunisation programme, not all children are immunised. In addition, some who have been immunised will still get the illness. As you read the following section, you will notice that children usually become infectious before the first symptoms appear. The most caring parents cannot help the fact that their children may have passed on the illness. Once the symptoms appear, children would need to be cared for at home and remain away from an early years setting, not only for reasons of infection but also because children will feel ill.

Chicken pox

Children with chicken pox have a mild fever and they feel unwell. Small, itchy, dark red spots appear over a period of 3–4 days. Some children have quantities of spots and some only have a few. The spots then blister and crust over. Children are infectious from two days before the rash appears until the last blister has scabbed. The illness is unpleasant but not usually dangerous unless the child's immune system is already compromised for some reason. Children need to be treated for any fever and calamine lotion helps relieve the itching. Discourage them from scratching (and recognise that this is very hard!), otherwise the spots may get infected or leave scars.

German measles (rubella)

Children with German measles may not feel ill enough for anyone to realise. There may be a mild fever, cough or sore throat and sometimes swollen glands. The rash is of pink, slightly raised spots. Children are infectious from one week before until four days after the rash has appeared. The greatest risk is to pregnant women in their first trimester (see page 522).

Measles

Measles is a miserable illness to experience and can bring dangerous complications. The symptoms at the outset are similar to a heavy cold with a cough and a high fever. There may be a rash of small white spots inside the mouth. Then after 3–4 days of the apparent cold, a rash of brownish-pink spots will start, often from behind the ears. The rash spreads across the body sometimes joining to form blotches. Children may have swollen glands and be very sensitive to light. Children are infectious from a few days before the rash appears until five days after it has gone.

You should call the doctor once the illness looks like measles. Children may need antibiotics for a secondary infection and you must be ready for complications that can affect a minority of children. All children need to be kept quiet and given home nursing care, including treating any fever. About 1 in 15 children develop a serious ear infection, pneumonia, bronchitis, convulsions or encephalitis.

Mumps

The first sign of mumps is usually a swelling in one or both of the salivary glands below the ear or in front of the jaw. Children are in pain and they may have earache or difficulty in swallowing. These symptoms can disturb their sleep. Children are infectious for six days before the swelling until it has gone.

Children need care and comfort if they are unhappy. Soft food and plenty of drinks can ease the problems of swallowing. There is no need to call a doctor unless the child is more ill or develops a rash.

Activity

Take one of the illnesses covered in this section.

- Make a brief plan for how you would care for children while they are ill.
- How would you keep them entertained when children are better enough to be bored, but not well enough return to nursery or playgroup?
- Present your ideas to colleagues.

Key skills link: C2.3 C2.1a

Allergic conditions

There are a number of conditions that are triggered by allergies and which children may experience in differing levels of severity.

Hay fever

The term hay fever is used to cover a wide range of allergies to different tree and plant pollens and other common substances such as house dust. The symptoms are like those of a heavy cold: runny nose, sneezing and coughing. Additionally the eyes become itchy and sore, so that they may be red and swollen. Hay fever seems to run in families and is often linked to asthma or other allergies.

Tests can sometimes establish exactly which substances trigger the allergic reaction, although many people do not know exactly what sets off their allergy. Tree or plant pollens may only be around at certain times of the year whereas an allergy to house dust (literally the dead house mites in the dust) is a continuing problem.

Depending on the severity of a child's reaction, there are a number of practical steps:

- A range of medication is now available that deals with the allergy without making a child or adult sleepy. You would need to be guided by parents and their GP, since not all preparations are suitable for young children.
- Children who have an allergy to house dust may need an especially clean environment.
- Allergies to food are covered on page 95.

Eczema

Eczema is a miserable condition for a child, even in a mild version. Children can become very irritated by itchy skin and will be in pain if their skin cracks and

Figure 4.6

Hygiene is important but some children will be allergic to soaps

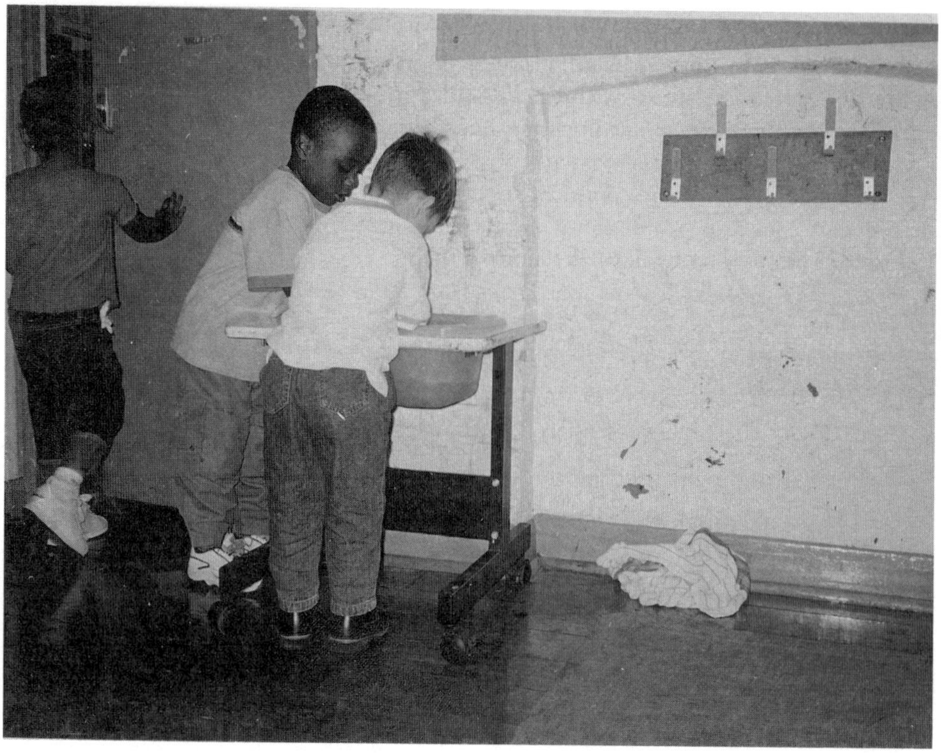

bleeds. Pain and severe discomfort can keep them awake at night and their parents with them.

Atopic eczema is the most common kind of eczema and is found among babies and young children. Atopic means a family or hereditary tendency to allergic conditions such as asthma, eczema and hay fever. Over the last three decades there has been a significant increase in atopic eczema and it is estimated that the condition now affects about 10 per cent of children. The reason for the increase seems to be environmental change in that many homes now have central heating and fitted carpets. This shift has increased children's exposure to allergens like house dust mites. Some children develop other allergic conditions such as asthma (see page 520).

The symptoms of eczema can vary:

- In babies it can begin with patches of dry and itchy skin on the face.
- The skin behind the knees and ears, the neck, elbow and wrist skin folds are often affected.
- In severe cases the rash can cover a baby or child's whole body.
- The skin irritation can lead to redness and inflammation, tiny blisters that can weep.
- With severe itching the skin may scale and, in chronic eczema, the skin may actually thicken (lichenification) as a self-protective mechanism.
- In severe cases there may be swelling (oedema).
- A child with severe eczema is also more vulnerable to infections because the skin has broken.

Most children seem to outgrow the condition, at least to an extent, but about 10 per cent will continue to have to cope with eczema throughout their lives. A child's parents and their GP will need to decide on treatment and to review its effectiveness on a regular basis.

Eczema is a dry skin condition, so the most important approach is to keep children's skin soft and moist. You will need to follow the pattern established by the family.

- Emollients in liquid form are added to a child's bath and emollient creams can be applied to her skin, smoothed on in downward strokes. Emollients are mild and part of the daily care for a child with eczema.
- Topical steroid creams reduce inflammation and help to heal damaged skin. They are medicines and should be used according to the instructions and only for short periods of time.
- Steroid creams have the side effect of thinning the skin over time. So you should wash your hands thoroughly after using such cream on a child.
- You will do the skin care for a younger child, although children will learn to take over their own skin care as they grow.

You need to avoid any food or toiletries that parents have discovered makes the skin condition worse. In a family home, the products should all be suitable anyway. If you work in an early years setting, then you will need to be alert over foods. It is good practice to use non-perfumed toiletries with young children in general, but some children may have extra sensitive skin. Children with eczema are best dressed in cotton clothing and they may need to avoid contact with some materials in the dressing up box or within some sensory activities.

For more information

The National Eczema Society has information packs (send an sae) and offers advice over their telephone helpline. Contact them at Hill House, Highgate Hill, London N19 5NA help and information line 0870 241 3604 website: *www.eczema.org.uk*.

Parasites

Most children will experience at least one visitation from the common parasites – head lice, threadworms and roundworms. Children are not ill but they can be in a lot of discomfort and will be tired if their sleep is disturbed. The other issue to bear in mind is that children may be embarrassed if their parents or other carers have reacted as if lice or threadworms are something to be ashamed about.

Tips for practice

If you work on a daily basis with children you are unlikely to treat the children yourself for these conditions. Your role will be to:

- Inform parents discreetly if you see signs of worms or lice. This will not be the most enjoyable conversation of your life, especially if it is the parents' first encounter with the problem.
- Make the conversation private, calm and practical.
- Have some general information available in your setting and show this to parents at the time. You will often find leaflets in a local child health clinic or at the counter of a high street chemist.

Head lice

The first sign of head lice may be that a child keeps scratching part of her head, although sometimes the lice get well established before this reaction. You may see the lice themselves, but they are small and move swiftly. Alternatively you may spot their eggs, called nits. These are small white or greyish specks that can look like dandruff. Lice are unpleasant and need to be cleared but they do not carry any diseases.

Special anti-lice shampoos are available from the local chemists and parents and carers need to use whatever is currently recommended. Ordinary shampoos do not kill lice. The lice eggs then need to be removed by combing the child's hair with a special fine toothed nit comb. Some shampoos provide the comb in the packet. You would not use the shampoo on a baby.

Do be ready to reassure parents that lice do not mean their child's hair is dirty. It is, however, a myth that lice prefer clean hair; the truth is that they are happy to jump into any available head. Some parents react with horror to the first outbreak of lice and cut their children's hair very short. There is no need to do this and a child who has taken ages to grow her hair will be very distressed.

It is unwise to wash children's hair in anti-lice shampoos as a preventative. The chemicals that kill lice are strong and, like any other medication, the shampoo should not used in an indiscriminate way. You may find that your local advice is to use gentler remedies like tea tree shampoo. Whichever lotion is used, the best (and preventative) action against head lice is to comb children's hair thoroughly morning and evening. This clears the hair of eggs and dead lice and breaks the legs of any live ones – their days are then numbered. If regular combing is not possible, for religious reasons or because a child's hair is plaited, an adult will just have to check the child's head with great care.

Head lice usually jump from one head to another and this is an easy task in an early years setting, since children and adults often sit very close. Lice occasionally survive for a short while on combs or brushes. So it is wise to wash them thoroughly and not to share the same comb.

Threadworms

These are tiny white worms that easily get onto children's hands (or adults') from contaminated food or just as easily from the toilets or from playing outside. Children put their hands to their mouths and the eggs enter their body. These eggs hatch in the intestine and about two weeks later the female threadworm lays eggs around the child's anus, usually at night. This causes a most uncomfortable itching, children scratch themselves and may break the skin.

Parents or carers need to get the recommended medicine from a pharmacy. It works by giving children mild diarrhoea and this action flushes out the threadworms. The diarrhoea is not usually hard to handle, but if a child is worried about a toileting accident, or has a delicate digestion, it may be better to give the medicine on a day when they can stay at home. Mixtures vary but children are in agreement that they usually taste pretty bad. Until the worms have gone, it can help to cut children's finger nails and have them wear close fitting pyjamas or pants at night, so that they do not make themselves sore with scratching.

Again do reassure parents that it is very easy to pick up threadworms; it is not a sign of a dirty household. Bedding and night clothes can be thoroughly washed but there is no need to start boiling or throwing household items in the dustbin.

The practical steps for reducing the incidence of threadworms are part of good hygiene:

- Show and remind children to wash their hands after playing in the garden and going to the toilet and before mealtimes or cooking activities.

- Make sure that toilets and washbasins are well cleaned and disinfected. They should not run out of soap, clean towels or toilet paper. Children should not share the same towels or flannels.

Activity

- Collect information leaflets about the current advice for dealing with head lice or threadworms. You will find material at your local health clinic or pharmacy.
- Prepare yourself for a friendly conversation with a parent whose child has shown the signs of lice or threadworms.
- Explore a role play with a colleague who plays the parent as distressed or angry ('my child must have picked those up here!') Consider strategies to deal with this situation.

Key skills link: PS2.1

Meningitis

Meningitis causes an inflammation of the meninges, the linings surrounding the brain. There are two kinds of meningitis:

- Bacterial meningitis is more dangerous, needs swift treatment with antibiotics and can be fatal. The serious risk is of meningococcal septicaemia: blood poisoning caused by bacteria entering the bloodstream and multiplying in an uncontrollable way. Most children recover completely but some can be left with serious complications like deafness or learning disabilities. There are different strands of this version of the disease and the immunisations (see page 185) only cover some kinds.
- Viral meningitis is more common than the bacterial version, has similar symptoms but is less severe. Children need good nursing care but antibiotics have no effect with a viral infection. Children recover without complications, although headaches and lack of energy can be an issue.

Meningitis is rare compared with other illnesses but the seriousness means that you need to be aware of the warning signs. Children are particularly vulnerable because they have not yet built up an immunity. Also they tend to play close together and are easily infected by the coughing and sneezing that passes on the infection.

- In babies or children (or adults) you should watch out for a high temperature, possibly with cold hands and feet. There may be convulsions.
- Babies refuse feeds or are sick. Children may have vomiting or diarrhoea.
- Babies give a high pitched moaning or whimpering cry. They may have a blank and staring expression. The fontanelle (soft spot on the head) may be tense or bulging.
- Babies may be floppy, fretful or dislike being handled. Children and babies may be drowsy and difficult to wake.
- Children may complain of a severe headache, neck stiffness (unable to touch the chin to the chest), joint or muscle pains and dislike of bright lights.

- Light skinned babies and children may be pale and blotchy.
- A septicaemic rash is very serious and means that the child should be taken immediately to hospital. This symptom starts as a cluster of tiny blood spots which join to look like a fresh bruise. If you press a clear drinking glass onto the rash, it does not fade. You can see the rash on dark skinned children, although less easily – look on any paler areas of skin, like the palms or the soles of the feet.

Children will not show all of these symptoms and some, like vomiting, could of course be due to another cause. Be attentive and do not assume that some of these symptoms are 'flu. Call a child's parent if you are concerned but, if you cannot get in contact swiftly, do not delay but call your closest heath clinic. If the baby or child is getting worse then take her to the nearest hospital and do this straight away if she has a rash.

Finding out more

The Meningitis Trust offers information, advice and posters. Contact them at Fern House, Bath Road, Stroud, Gloucestershire GL5 3TJ tel: 01453 768000 helpline: 0845 6000 800 email: *info@meningitis-trust.org.uk* website: *www.meningitis-trust.org.uk*

Tuberculosis

This disease is an example of a serious illness that many people believe no longer poses a health risk in the UK. In fact there are now more people in the UK with tuberculosis (TB) than catch measles. TB never went away and is a disease that continues to be a serious problem in many parts of the world. TB can flourish when families live in poverty. An outbreak in a south London nursery in May 2001 was a reminder that nobody should be complacent. Without close contact TB is not highly infectious, but some children were infected in this nursery because the practitioner had TB for six months before being diagnosed.

TB usually affects the lungs but can affect other parts of the body such as the lymph nodes. The symptoms are fever and night sweats, a cough, weight loss and blood in the phlegm. The disease is passed through the droplets in coughs and sneezes. There is a good chance of recovery when the disease is diagnosed and a full course of antibiotics is taken.

TB should be taken seriously and your local public health authority notified if you have reason to believe that a child or adult is infected. Some city areas of the UK have populations that are at higher risk. Families who come to the UK from very deprived conditions, especially refugee and asylum seeker families, are at great risk of TB. You will need to address the health issues with consideration, because the families may be very uneasy about official intervention. You will need to involve your local advisor for refugee families as well.

Finding out more

You can find more information about TB or any illness by phoning the service NHS Direct on 0845 4647 or by checking their website: *www.nhsdirect.nhs.uk*

AIDS/HIV

Acquired Immune Deficiency Syndrome (AIDS) is a condition in which the body's immune system is seriously weakened. It appears to be caused by a virus named the Human Immunodeficiency Virus (HIV). When individuals are infected, they show as HIV-positive on the appropriate test. They can then pass on the condition to others, although they may be outwardly healthy for months or even years. When individuals become unwell, then they are said to have developed AIDS itself.

Children with this condition are likely to have contracted it in the womb from their mothers, who may not have known that they were themselves HIV-positive. The baby can become infected during delivery and through breast feeding. Children can also contract HIV if they have been given medical treatment such as injections or blood transfusions under conditions of very poor hygiene.

Finding out more

Children with AIDS Charity, Lion House, 3 Plough Yard London EC2A 3LP tel: 020 7247 9115 website: *www.cwac.org*

This organisation publishes a booklet on *Talking with Children about Illness and HIV*. The booklet has sensible general advice on talking with children about serious illness, their own or that of a loved parent.

In the time since the condition was identified in the 1980s, there has been considerable research and development of drug regimes that enable affected children and adults to remain relatively healthy for longer. Currently AIDS is still ultimately a terminal condition, but there has been significant progress in delaying the disease's pattern and helping individuals to make the most of their periods of health.

It is preferable that parents tell you if their child is HIV-positive, but there has been such negative media coverage over the years that parents may remain silent. Unlike some other serious health conditions (such as scarlet fever), there is no legal obligation to notify the authorities. If families come to trust you, they may tell you and it is certainly preferable that at least one person knows and keeps the fact confidential, since you can then protect the child's health.

Consistent medical advice is that children who are HIV-positive cannot infect practitioners or other children through the normal daily contact of early years settings. Your standard hygiene procedures for changing nappies, dealing with toileting or caring for children who have hurt themselves will be an effective protection (see page 56).

Children who are HIV-positive pose a very low risk to others, but can be at risk from their peers. Infections like measles or chicken pox can be dangerous to children with a compromised immune system. Children have also been put at risk when their HIV status has become known and they have been bullied.

Supporting children's learning about their bodies and health

Children are interested to learn about bodies and health and they can gain in confidence and awareness of their own bodies. You do not want children to

Figure 4.7
Children will learn about cleaning up after enjoyable outdoor play

become anxious that 'bugs' are everywhere. But you can explain simply how germs can enter our bodies by:

- *being swallowed* – why we do not suck objects other than food and why we wash our hands
- *being breathed in* – why we do not cough and sneeze over other people
- *entering our body by a cut* – why we clean cuts and grazes.

You can help children through conversation, role play and the use of suitable books and stories:

- Children can learn about the words and feelings needed to express themselves about feeling ill, feeling well and energetic.
- Children whose health means they are very tired can sometimes be the best judge of whether they will sit down with a book or are ready for the climbing frame.
- Children can understand a bit at time about health conditions that they may not experience directly.
- They can link health and a healthy diet (see page 81).
- Books can help them understand about growing, how their bodies work and simple explanations of what happens when they are ill.

Children can learn through your guidance what to do for themselves and a sense of how to help others.

- The best opportunities will be when you explain why you take these steps when Henry has a nose bleed or why it is important to clear up vomit quickly.
- You will need to reassure a child and her friends. It can be scary the first time that a child is sick or blood pours from their nose.
- Children can also learn about what illnesses are infectious and those which are not – an important understanding when a child attends your setting with a condition that is visible but not catching (see page 538).

Activity

- Take two or three of the bullet points in the text and plan how you could take the opportunity to extend a child's understanding as well as deal with any emotional distress.
- Write up any real incidents that you handle, with a view to improving your practice.

Key skills links: C2/3.3 LP2/3.1–3

Taking care of yourself

The work of an early years practitioner requires a lot of physical activity, but also emotional energy and commitment. Young children require that you are able to do several things at the same time and readjust swiftly from one child or activity to another. You need to cultivate the skills of being able to change direction, tolerate interruptions and keep track of several children and events at the same time. For example:

- You change a toddler's nappy while chatting with an older child who is interested in what you are doing.
- You need to hold onto what one child has said to you whilst you, 'Excuse me', deal with a child who had your attention first, then turn back to the second one.

The importance of a positive outlook

Focus on what you have achieved – a supportive practitioner encourages children and alerts them to what they have learned, seeing mistakes as something positive and not as disasters. You need to offer the same kindness and 'half full bottle' approach to yourself. Your colleagues and seniors should support you by pointing out how you have helped and cared for the children, at those times when you are tempted to dwell gloomily on what you have not managed or what has not gone as well as you hoped. You could also look at page 120 for a positive outlook on working with babies and very young children.

Let annoyances go – young children tend to focus on the present and let the past go and adults can usefully learn from them. Your work will not go smoothly all the time and a bad day will only get worse if you chew over frustrations and dwell on imagined slights. By all means, talk about problems and take what action is possible, then start afresh. In a supportive team your colleagues and seniors should help with ways to carry on after an argument with a parent or ways to start afresh with a child whom you do not find at all easy.

Keep healthy

Many of the sections in Chapter 3 focus of course on how you help children to keep healthy and to learn healthy habits in their young life. Do try to apply some of this good advice to yourself. You also need enough rest and good food.

You will inevitably come into close contact with many children and adults. You are therefore liable to catch illnesses, especially in your first years of working with young children. Some practitioners find that they get more robust. Good standards of hygiene will help to safeguard you as well as the children.

Watch your back

You need to watch your back, as straining and wrenching the back is a common occupational hazard for people working with children.

- It is important to get into the habit of bending at the knees, rather than at the waist, to pick up children or shift equipment.
- Ensure that there are two of you if equipment is heavy or unwieldy.
- Facilities for changing babies and toddlers should be at a comfortable height so that you do have to bend over children. It is surprising how quickly you will feel an ache in your back if you have to bend over to a low angle.
- When you talk and play with young children, they need you at their eye level for good communication. So, get down comfortably – sitting or kneeling – rather than bending over them.
- When babies are very young you may carry them in front baby carriers. Make sure that the carrier is well placed for you as well as the baby. The carrier should support the baby's head and hold him snugly close to you, with his bottom about level with your waist.
- When babies are ready for a back carrier (probably no younger than about 7–8 months), make sure that this type of carrier is also of a good quality and sits comfortably on your shoulders and back.

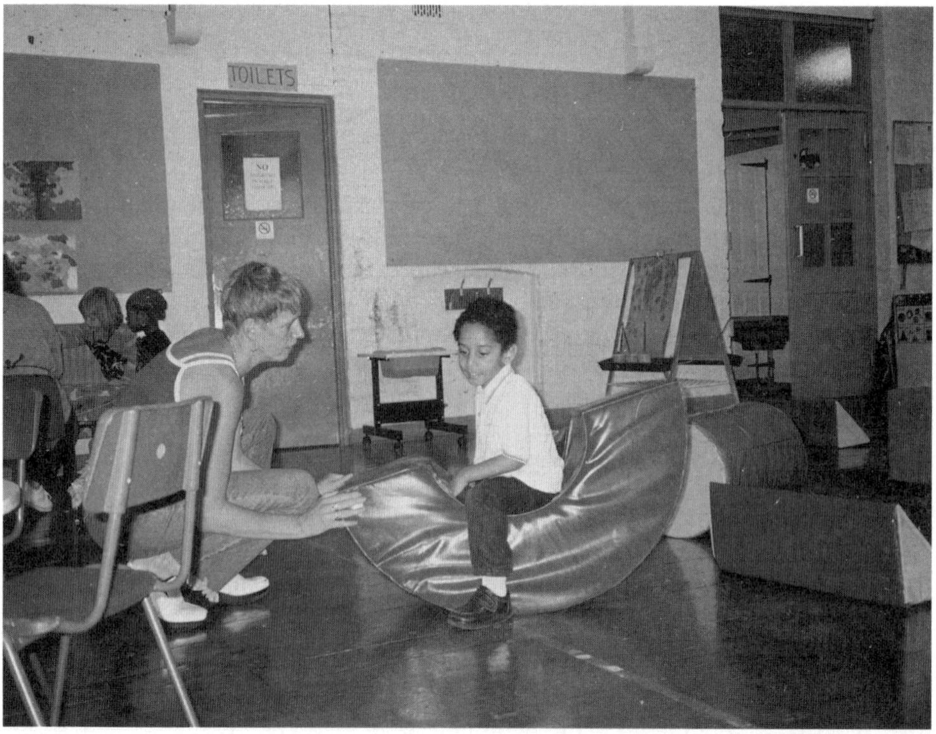

Figure 4.8
Bending at the knees protects your back and brings you to the child's eye level

Activity

Build up some ideas for how to protect your back in working with young children.

- As well as the ideas in this section you can contact BackCare (the National Organisation for Healthy Backs), 16 Elmtree Road, Teddington, Middlesex TW11 8ST tel: 020 8977 5474 website: *www.backpain.org*
- Develop a short presentation with some visuals if possible to show colleagues and fellow students how you can all avoid preventable back injuries.

Key skills link: C3.1b

Pregnancy

The early years workforce is overwhelmingly female, so pregnancy is a likelihood within any team. If you are pregnant, then discuss with your senior and colleagues how your pattern of work should be adjusted. You will still be able to complete most of your job. But it would be wise to let a colleague carry heavier equipment or join in the more vigorous games with children.

You do not want to view yourself as a walking project, but the children will be very interested in what is happening to you and your body. So be ready to explain at an appropriate time in your pregnancy that you are expecting a baby and follow through conversations that the children wish to have.

Leave your work behind

When days with the children have gone very well, you will feel a glow of satisfaction. On those days when the children, or the adults, have strained your patience to the limits you may feel as if your reserves are drained.

You do need to leave your work behind at the end of the day and enjoy a personal life. You may find this harder to do if the children with whom you work have unhappy or deprived lives. As hard as it may feel, you need to focus on what you contribute to make their lives better and recognise that worrying outside the job will not make a single difference – except that it may prevent you coming back fresh to them on the next day.

Activity

- What helps you personally to relax at the end of a working day?
- Make a list of simple and cheap ideas or activities that help you unwind.

Sadness when children move on

Part of caring for children as individuals is a sense of loss when they move on, as they inevitably will, even those children who attend your setting for a matter of years. You may be excited for the children as they approach a new stage of their life and still a little sad at their going. Of course, the exit of some children, who have been a serious handful, may be more of a relief. Early years professionals have feelings and in a supportive team it should be possible to talk about how you feel. (See also the section on attachment on page 000.)

Further resources

Lindon, Jennie (1999) *Too Safe for their own Good? Helping children learn about risk and lifeskills* National Early Years Network.

Miller, Judy (1997) *Never Too Young: How young children can take responsibility and make decisions* National Early Years Network and Save the Children.

Shabde, Neela (1999) *The A–Z of Child Health* Step Forward Publishing (tel: 01926 420046).

Troyna, Alexandra (1998) *Providing Emotional support to children and their Families after an Accident: Guidelines for professionals* Child Accident Prevention Trust.

Vine, Penny and Todd, Teresa (n.d.) *Ring of Confidence: A quality circle time programme to support personal safety for the foundation stage* Positive Press.

Many local health authorities have their own websites, on which they post information directly relevant to local health issues.

Progress check

1 List and describe the main ways in which you would check an early years setting or family home for safety.
2 Explain the drawbacks of trying to achieve zero risk in any setting.
3 Describe two ways in which you could help young children start to learn about personal safety.
4 Identify two signs that mean a child needs to be taken to hospital after an incident.
5 Briefly describe two illnesses for which a rash could be a warning symptom.
6 Identify two sources of risk to the backs of early years practitioners and how you might protect yourself.

5

Conception and birth

After reading this chapter you should be able to:

- understand the details of conception and development prior to birth
- understand and support the aims of antenatal care
- understand the process of childbirth
- be able to support in the postnatal care of babies and mothers.

Introduction

In this chapter you will learn about the usual events of the development of babies prior to birth and how antenatal care can support and protect the health of mothers. The role of early years practitioners is to understand what happens in order to be able to support through conversation and information sharing. Practitioners who work in hospitals may have a more direct role. Sharing the care of babies and offering support to families after birth is covered in Chapter 6.

From conception to birth

The development of a human baby is a long process starting before birth. This section describes some of the main events and what the problems or risks can be for the mother or baby. It is important to bear in mind that most pregnancies are without serious complications.

Development before birth

Conception occurs when the sperm from a male penetrates the cell wall of an egg from the female. The development of the resulting baby lasts about 40 weeks and is divided into three phases:

- The germinal period lasts from the moment of conception until the fertilised

Links to early years qualifications
This chapter especially supports the following unit: Diploma in Child Care and Education: 7

egg is implanted in the wall of the uterus. The process of travelling from the fallopian tubes and implantation takes 10–14 days.

- The embryonic period lasts from week 2 to week 8 after conception. The **embryo** at this time develops all the major organs of the human body.
- The fetal period is from week 8 until the baby is born. The **fetus**, now about 2.5 centimetres in length, develops in size. The organs mature and gradually take on some of their functions. By week 20, the mother can usually feel the fetus move (now about 20 centimetres long). By week 32 the fetus can normally breathe, suck and swallow and by week 36 shows a response to light and sound waves.

Key terms

Embryo
the term used to describe a baby in the first 8 weeks after conception

Fetus
the term used to describe a baby from 8 weeks after conception to birth

Gestation
the development of the embryo and fetus over the months of a pregnancy

Full term babies
when babies are born close to the usual gestation period of about 40 weeks

Premature babies
when babies are born earlier than the usual gestation period, usually less than 37 weeks

Miscarriage
the loss of a fetus before 24 weeks gestation within the pregnancy

Stillbirth
the loss of a fetus after 24 weeks of gestation within a pregnancy

The usual **gestation** time for the development of human babies is roughly nine months from the time of conception. This period is an average and healthy pregnancies can last slightly less or more than 40 weeks. A **full term baby** has spent most of the usual 40 week gestation period before being born. A **premature** baby has arrived earlier than the estimated 40 weeks – usually if they arrive before 37 weeks of pregnancy. Being premature is not necessarily a major problem for newborns, so long as they are not very early (see page 157). It is also sometimes the case that women are uncertain about the likely date of conception, especially if their periods follow an irregular pattern and therefore their baby may not be premature at all.

Miscarriage

It is estimated that about one in six of all pregnancies are lost through miscarriage, sometimes at such an early stage that the woman is unaware or uncertain that she is pregnant. The term **miscarriage** refers to a fetus delivered dead before the 24th week of gestation. A baby born dead after this time is referred to as a **stillbirth.** Legally the fetus is regarded as viable, able to live, after the 24th week. The boundary used to be the 28th week but medical advances (see page 157) have meant that very premature babies now have a chance of survival.

Parents can be distressed by miscarriage and wonder if they have done something wrong to cause the loss of their baby. In fact, there is usually no obvious reason for miscarriage and some pregnancies go to full term despite very adverse conditions. It is thought that a frequent reason for early miscarriage is that the fetus has a genetic abnormality. Another possibility is that the mother's womb does not expand to allow the fetus space, sometimes because of undetected fibroids. Women are not usually offered a medical investigation for the cause until they have had three miscarriages.

Full term babies

Full term or close to full term human babies are born at a stage when their bodies are mature enough to survive an independent life outside the womb. However, if their brain were more developed and therefore larger, normal vaginal delivery would not be possible, because the head would be too big. The brain of a full term infant weighs about 350 grams at birth. This weight trebles over the next twelve months to reach about 1000 grams. Brain development continues so that the brain weighs about 1300 grams at puberty and 1500 grams in adulthood.

Antenatal care

Pregnant women are encouraged to attend an antenatal clinic, either at the hospital where they are booked to give birth or with their midwife or GP. The usual pattern of attendance is once a month up to 32 weeks, then fortnightly and

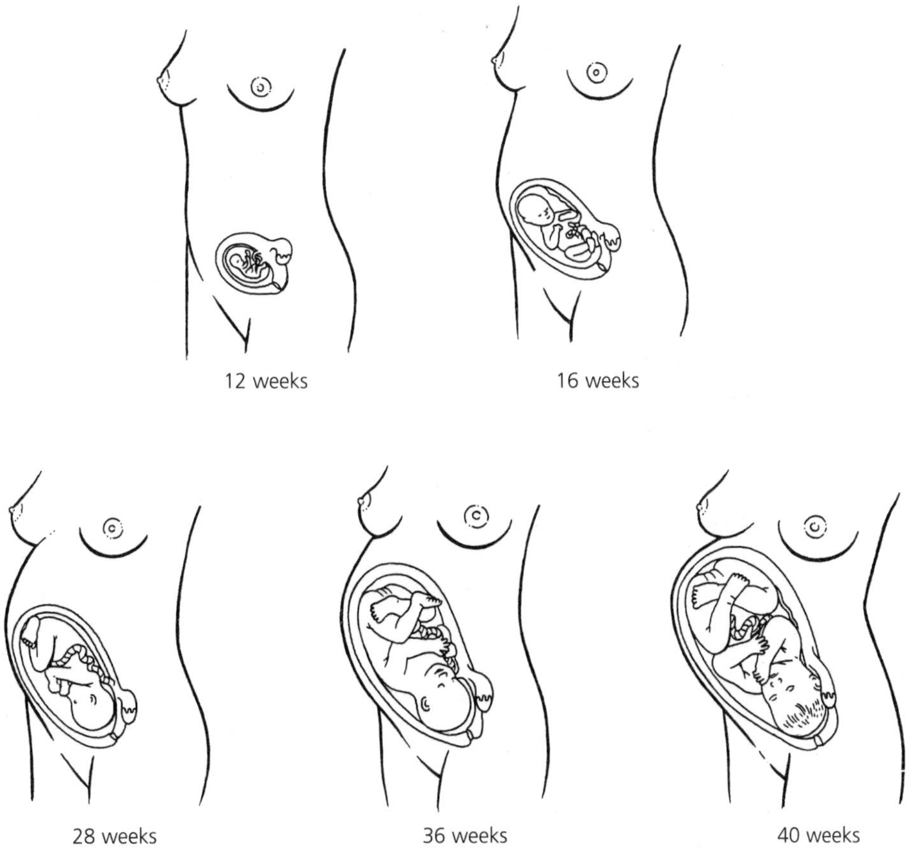

Figure 5.1 The development of the fetus from 12 to 40 weeks

then once a week in the final month of pregnancy. Regular health checks throughout the pregnancy aim to:

- ensure the continued health of the mother and baby
- identify any problems with the pregnancy
- offer advice as required on diet, continued activity and any of the normal physical problems of being pregnant.

Generally speaking, women are advised to continue with the physical activity that is part of their normal life, unless their leisure pursuits pose a risk, for instance, swimming is good exercise but diving is not recommended. A woman should inform any health practitioner that she is pregnant since some medication and procedures, such as X-rays, can harm the fetus.

Normal health changes in pregnancy

The most usual pattern is that women have a pregnancy that is free of serious concerns. However, simple checks at the antenatal clinic can identify conditions that can be serious if allowed to continue. There are a number of normal physical problems during pregnancy. It would be an unlucky woman who experienced more than a few from the possible list:

- feeling nauseous or actually being sick for the first trimester (three months) of the pregnancy and sometimes longer

- increasing tiredness and backache
- constipation, indigestion and incontinence (need to pass urine more frequently and with some urgency)
- fainting and palpitations
- bleeding gums and nosebleeds
- cramps
- swelling of the legs, feet or hands
- varicose veins and piles
- skin stretch marks or itchy skin.

To think about

Many pregnant women will have partners. Fathers in waiting can feel uninvolved or uncertain how to support their partners.

- List five ways in which men could support a woman through her pregnancy in ways that are helpful to her and could help the man to feel involved. Explain briefly why male partners might feel left out or uncertain what to do.
- Discuss your ideas with colleagues.
- Extend the discussion to include ways in which early years practitioners could help, through contact at an early years setting or working as a nanny.

Key skills links: C2.2 C2/3.1a

Health checks

At each antenatal visit, there are a number of standard checks:

- *The mother's weight*: it is inadvisable to put on a great deal of weight, but slow weight gain is usually a concern because it may mean that the baby is not growing steadily.
- *A urine test*: checks for sugar levels (possible diabetes), protein traces (possible pre-eclampsia), ketones (a by-product of when fats are broken down – possible problems with the kidneys).
- *Blood pressure*: high blood pressure can be another sign of pre-eclampsia.

Pre-eclampsia is taken seriously because the placenta may grow poorly so that the baby is ill nourished. The condition is treated with bed rest and possibly tablets to bring the blood pressure down. Women will be carefully monitored since eclampsia is dangerous and can lead to convulsions, threatening the lives of mother and baby.

Women are given a blood test at the first antenatal clinic visit. This test will usually:

- Confirm the woman's blood group out of the four possible different blood groups
- Identify whether she is Rhesus positive or negative. Most people are Rh-positive, which means their blood has an antigen that stimulates the

formation of antibodies to fight disease. Problems arise if the mother is Rh-negative and the baby is Rh-positive. The first baby is usually fine but in subsequent pregnancies the mother's body reacts to the 'foreign' blood cells of the fetus to form antibodies that attack the fetus' blood cells. Once the condition is known there are steps which can be taken to protect the fetus.

- The blood is also screened for diseases that can damage the fetus: syphilis, viral hepatitis and blood disorders such as sickle cell disease (see page 520). Some hospitals offer AIDS/HIV screening to women who are in high risk groups. This test does not identify the AIDS virus itself but shows whether antibodies to the virus are in the bloodstream, in which case that person has been infected.

Blood tests on later antenatal visits are to check the level of haemoglobin to advise if women need to take iron supplements.

Ultrasound scans

Ultrasound scans are usually offered at about 18–20 weeks and sometimes towards the end of pregnancy. These scans work by bouncing very high frequency sound waves off solid objects, in this case the woman's body with the fetus inside. Scans may be done for several reasons.

- To confirm a pregnancy if there is some doubt and identify whether this is a multiple birth. From the end of the second month it is possible to see the fetus kicking.
- To gain an estimated date for delivery from the size and maturity of the fetus.
- To detect certain defects (then called an anomaly scan) such as congenital heart defects, spina bifida and gastrointestinal and kidney malfunctions.
- In the later stages of pregnancy it is also possible to confirm that the placenta is clear of the outlet of the uterus. A low lying placenta causes problems during the birth since the baby cannot be born and the mother may haemorrhage.

Activity

It will be valuable to familiarise yourself with the usual procedures in antenatal clinics. Some ways to do this include the following:

- Make contact with your closest health clinic. Can you talk with a community midwife to help you understand the common checks that are offered to pregnant women?
- It is also important to understand the different experiences of pregnant women. What makes a positive experience of antenatal care and what can be unhelpful or distressing? You could make contact with pregnant women or those who have not long had their baby through the clinic or a local branch of the National Childbirth Trust.
- Write up your findings, ensuring that any personal experiences are presented in a way that remains anonymous.
- Make a short presentation to your colleagues, highlighting the factors that can make antenatal care a positive experience.

Key skills links: C2/3.3 C2/3.1a

Additional tests

Some further checks may be offered depending on the age and health of the woman and the policy of the hospital. Such checks are usually to identify if the fetus will be born with a disability or serious health condition. Women are not obliged to undergo these tests, nor to accept a termination of the pregnancy if a problem is confirmed. Some families will opt for termination, but some want the information in order to prepare themselves for life with a disabled child.

- A chorion biopsy can be done at 10–11 weeks when cells are checked for inherited diseases such as cystic fibrosis, Duchenne muscular dystrophy, haemophilia and thalassaemia.
- Amniocentesis is a procedure done at 15–16 weeks in which a small amount of the amniotic fluid is drawn off and the fetus' cells checked for the chromosomal abnormality that causes Down's syndrome (see page 518).

Since both these procedures bring a small risk of miscarriage, they would not be offered unless the family history included these conditions or, in the case of Down's syndrome, women were older than 37 years old, since the risk is greater with older mothers.

Antenatal classes

The antenatal clinic offers support for health and well being during pregnancy. Antenatal classes offer women a preparation for the birth and very early days with a baby. The main aims of an antenatal class should be to help women to understand what will happen in the birth process, without making them anxious about everything that could go wrong. Realistic expectations can be based on information, whilst allowing for the fact that birth is a very personal experience.

The content of classes varies considerably and not surprisingly women differ in how useful they found their class. Classes run within a hospital usually give women an opportunity to see the labour ward and talk about hospital policy and options during the birth. Some preparation for parenthood is usually offered within classes, although first time mothers are understandably more focused on the impending birth.

Classes run by the National Childbirth Trust (NCT) focus on explaining how the birth process works and the value of specific breathing techniques at the different stages of labour. Successful use of these techniques can help women to feel more in control of what is happening, and manage the contractions as they become more frequent and painful. Breathing techniques can enable women to postpone the use of pain relief (see page 151) and sometimes to manage without it completely, so-called **natural childbirth**. Breathing techniques do not make labour pain free! The involvement of a birth partner, usually the baby's father, can offer support and practical help such as back massage.

NCT classes are organised through a local branch and many also offer post-birth support by linking new mothers with other local women and offering advice services such as a breastfeeding counsellor. Friendships and baby-sitting circles are often formed as a result of NCT classes and this contact can be especially useful for women whose work has hindered their making many local friends.

The **active birth movement**, led by Janet Balaskas, gained influence in the 1980s as part of a reaction against rigid hospital procedures that insisted women in labour should remain on their backs on a bed. In fact, labour is easier to manage and less painful if women can move about and different positions are possible for actually giving birth. Research has now fully supported the idea that

Key terms

Natural childbirth
labour without medical intervention in which women manage the process by breathing techniques and movement

Active birth movement
an approach emphasising that women in labour should be enabled to move and to take up different positions for managing contractions and the birth itself

labour is more straightforward, on average shorter and women need less pain relief if they can move around and take up a position that feels right to them in order to manage painful contractions.

Sheila Kitzinger has also been an outspoken critic of treating pregnant women and those giving birth as if they were ill and should therefore cooperate as 'patients'. Although the approach of community health services varies considerably, the work of Kitzinger and the National Childbirth Trust has been effective in challenging traditional medical attitudes towards women who are pregnant and giving birth.

Finding out more

The National Childbirth Trust was established in 1957, inspired by the work of Dr Grantly Dick-Read who pioneered the use of relaxation and breathing techniques in the UK.

You can contact them for leaflets or specific information at Alexandra House, Oldham Terrace, London W3 6NH tel: 0870 444 8707
email: *enquiries@national-childbirth-trust.co.uk*
website: *www.nctpregnancyandbabycare.com*

In collaboration with Harper Collins, the NCT publish a wide range of practical books on baby care.

Labour and birth

Labour itself can begin with three signs but the order of these, like the whole experience of labour and birth, can follow different patterns as well as a varied duration in total:

- During pregnancy the neck of the womb or cervix has been sealed with a mucus plug, which now comes away as the cervix is dilated. The resulting bloodstained mucus is called a 'show', but this may happen a couple of days before full labour.
- At some stage in labour, but not always at the beginning, the pressure of the baby's head breaks the membrane of the amniotic fluid and it flows out in a trickle or a rush, called the 'waters breaking'.
- The woman starts to feel muscle contractions, although Braxton Hicks (practice contractions) can be felt in the days before labour and trigger false alarms.

The process of labour is described in terms of three stages.

First stage

Strangely it is still not entirely understood what starts labour, the process by which the baby moves down the birth canal and is then born through the mother's vaginal opening. It is thought that a chemical or hormonal message may be passed from the baby across the placenta into the mother's blood stream. Something stimulates the production of chemicals called prostaglandins and the hormone oxytocin from the pituitary gland. These together cause the cervix to soften and the uterus to contract, which pulls the side of the uterus upwards and dilates the cervix.

Contractions in labour usually start as a low level ache, sometimes as backache, then, over the hours, they build into more frequent, longer and more painful contractions. The cervix opens to allow the baby to pass through and when the cervix is 10 centimetres dilated, the first stage of labour is complete. This stage is the longest and is unlikely to last less than 10–12 hours in a first pregnancy. Some first births are shorter and some are much longer.

Second stage

The contractions now work to push the baby out of the uterus to be born. The tissues of the vaginal opening stretch to enable the baby's head to emerge, followed by the shoulders and the rest of the body. The second stage is complete with the birth of the baby. If there is no cause for concern, then the baby can be lifted to rest on the mother's stomach and the parents can greet their baby. The midwife cuts the umbilical cord that has joined the baby to the mother through the placenta.

The most straightforward birth presentation is head first. Some babies have not turned in late pregnancy and are feet first (breech delivery). It is possible to have a vaginal delivery with a breech birth but it would be watched very carefully.

This second stage is sometimes fast, but can take longer. If the woman is tiring and certainly if there are signs that the baby is in distress, then assistance will be given by helping the baby out with forceps or suction (ventouse).

Third stage

It is essential that the placenta, or afterbirth, is also expelled from the womb in its entirety. Without intervention this usually takes about 20 minutes but it is more usual for the midwife to give an injection which promotes contractions and speeds up this third stage. The advantage is that a swift delivery of the placenta reduces the risk of bleeding.

The experience of labour

A description of the stages of labour can only be a very general indicator. The pattern varies considerably between women and so does the personal experience of giving birth. Different kinds of support are helpful:

- Personal support from a midwife who stays with the woman and who preferably is already known to her.
- Support from the woman's partner or a friend, who will understand and encourage the use of controlled breathing techniques.

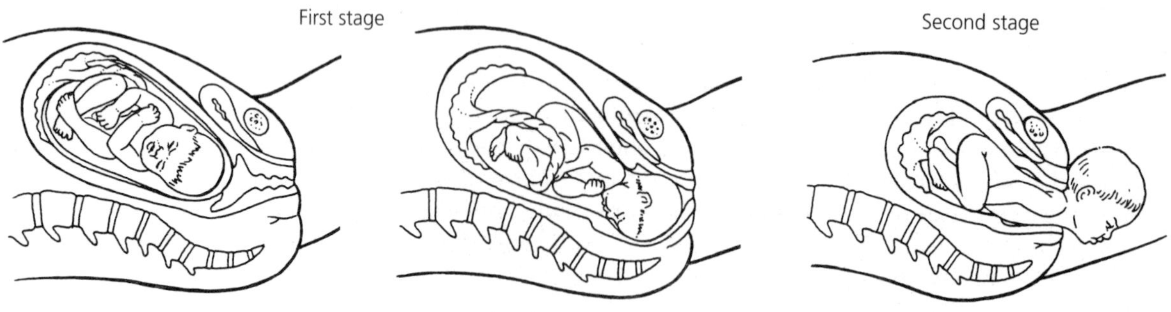

Figure 5.2 The process of childbirth: first and second stages

Pain relief is available but certainly should never be pushed upon a woman. The main options include:

- Entonox (known as gas and air) – a mix of oxygen and a painkiller breathed in through a mask.
- Pethidine that is injected and creates a drowsy state.
- An epidural anaesthetic that is injected into the spine. It either blocks the pain-carrying nerves or can remove all sensation below the waist.
- A small mobile unit can deliver transcutaneous nerve stimulation (TNS) though pads fixed either side of the spine. The system uses electrical impulses to dull the sensation of pain and is controlled by the woman in labour.
- Less frequently women may find midwives or other health practitioners who help the control of pain by acupuncture, aromatherapy or hypnosis.

Caesarean delivery

Normal childbirth is through vaginal delivery. Babies can be delivered surgically by caesarean section, in which an incision is made in the woman's abdomen and the baby is lifted out. The term derives from the belief that this method was how Julius Caesar was born in ancient Rome.

- In some cases this form of delivery is planned – an elective caesarean. This option would normally be taken because the health of the mother or the baby is known to be at risk. The woman might have a very narrow pelvis and measurements suggest that the baby's head will not be able to pass. Some health conditions, such as AIDS/HIV or genital herpes can be passed to the child during vaginal delivery.
- Unplanned or emergency caesareans are undertaken when a woman has begun a vaginal delivery and an unexpected emergency arises.

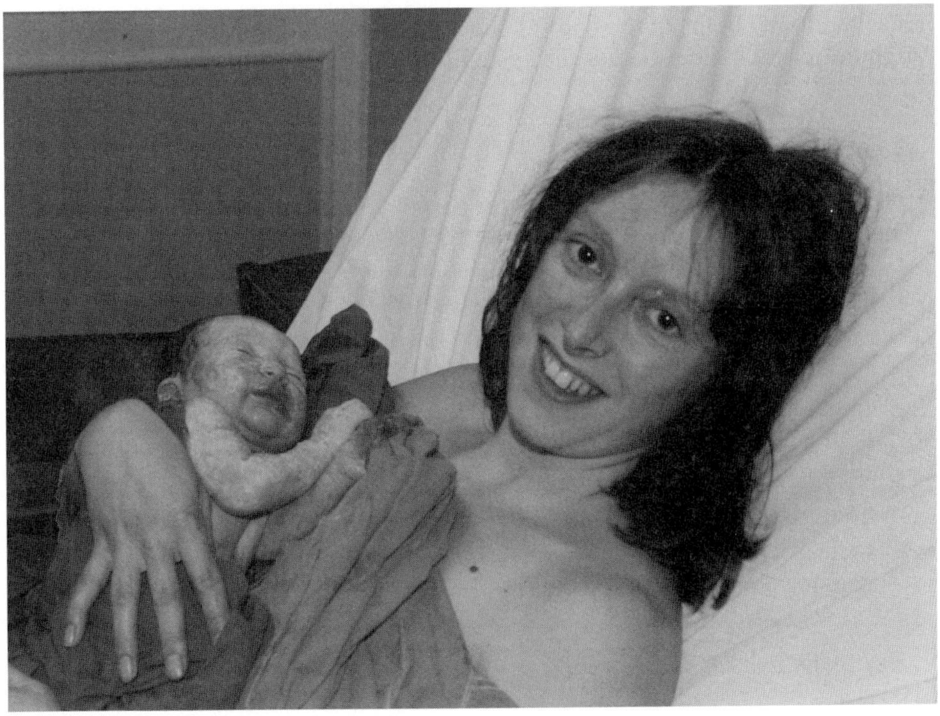

Figure 5.3

The first minutes of life outside the womb

- Caesareans can be undertaken with a full anaesthetic. However, if the woman wishes, an epidural anaesthetic is sufficient and the baby can be delivered into her arms.

The proportion of caesarean deliveries varies between hospitals and parts of the UK. When the proportion is higher than average there is some concern that surgical intervention in birth is encouraged for the convenience of the medical team.

Postnatal care

Care of babies after birth

There is no need to clean up newborn babies immediately. So long as there is no reason for concern, the usual practice is that they are given to the mother and father to hold close to their body. The midwife will check that the baby is breathing unsupported and gently clean the airway if there is any obstruction. Babies do not need to cry in order to breathe and some do not cry at all at birth, rather they fix their parents with a steady stare.

Newborn babies can be rather wrinkled, may have traces of blood (the mother's not usually the baby's) and their genitals, especially those of little boys, can look alarmingly large. First time parents, and early years practitioners who work in hospitals, can be misled by the fact that most allegedly new babies who feature in fictional television programmes or films are not newborns at all; most are at least several weeks old! Genuine newborns also have some vermix, a white creamy substance that is absorbed into their skin in the last weeks of gestation. This substance is far from unpleasant and, as some parents will tell you, newborn babies smell wonderful. This unique smell seems to support the first attachment between parents and baby.

Health checks

The overall well being of the baby is checked by the Apgar score, named after Dr Virginia Apgar who developed the system. At one minute after birth and then at

To think about

Hospital practice used to be to clean babies and do checks before giving the baby to the mother. It also used to be normal routine to put babies in a nursery rather than in a cot beside the mother's bed. These procedures have now been changed.

- Why is it so important that babies are given to their mother and father to hold as soon as possible after birth? What can be gained by this approach?
- Why is it better for babies to be beside their mother rather than taken away and placed in a nursery with all the other babies?
- Discuss your ideas with colleagues and, if at all possible, with women who have had babies in hospital.

Key skills links: C2/3.1

five minutes the midwife or doctor checks the newborn's heartbeat, breathing, muscle tone, reflexes and colour. Each of these are given a score of 0, 1 or 2 and the total is the Apgar score. A score of 10 is the best but a score over 7 is a normal baby. A newborn with score of 5–7 may need a little help but babies who score less than 5 may need oxygen to help their breathing.

Midwives also record the time of birth, the baby's weight and the circumference of the head. A baby is classified as low birth weight if less than 2500 grams (5½ pounds) and as a large baby if more than 4000 grams (10 pounds). The importance of head circumference is that an unusually large head circumference for the size of baby may indicate hydrocephalus, in which fluid accumulates in the brain. An unusually small circumference may indicate serious learning disability. All these measures also form a baseline to compare the baby against as the months pass. Many hospitals routinely give newborns vitamin K by injection as this protects against a kind of spontaneous bleeding in the newborn period.

Babies are then given a full check after about 24 hours by a paediatrician or nurse practitioner. This check will cover all parts of the baby's body with a gentle physical examination. Babies are observed to check that they can breathe well and that the remains of the umbilical cord is drying. A degree of jaundice is fairly common and more likely in premature babies, but this usually clears by itself.

The first full check will also observe babies' **reflex reactions**, the automatic responses that are normal in a healthy newborn.

- These include the reflex to suck and to blink in response to light or sound.
- Healthy newborns also have a grasping reflex, closing a palm around an adult finger.
- The Moro reflex is an automatic reaction when the baby's head or bottom is allowed to droop or the baby is startled by a sound. The baby flings his arms sideways with fingers spread and then brings them in again close.
- Babies also have a walking reflex. If they are held upright and their soles press onto a firm surface they lift their feet and put them down as if walking.

Key term

Reflex reactions physical movement of newborn babies that are inborn; the reflexes are instinctive reactions and are not learned

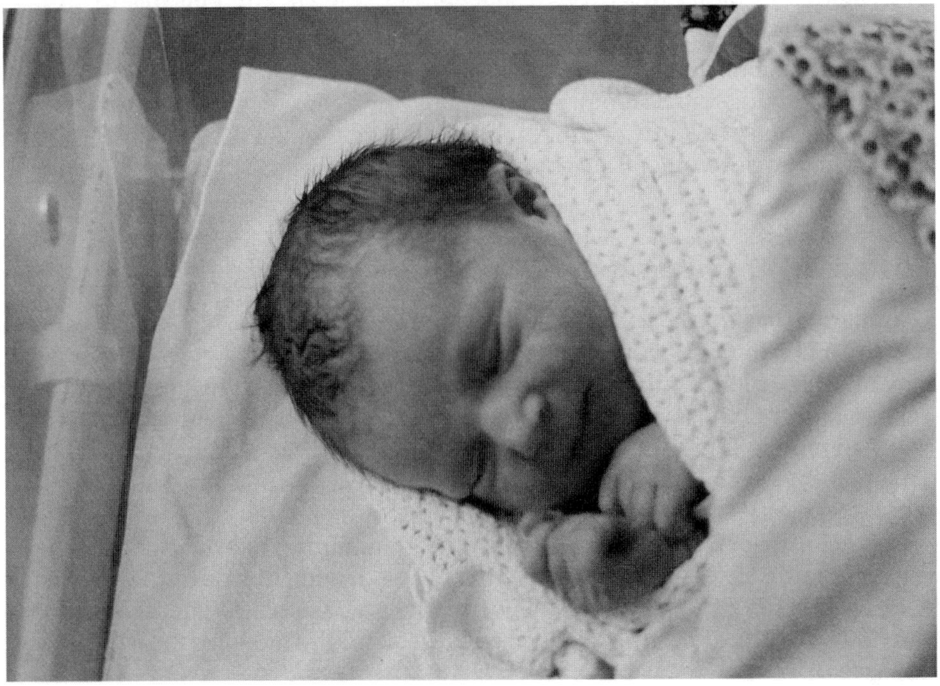

Figure 5.4 Newborns take a while to 'uncurl'

Babies are given the Guthrie test on about the sixth day after birth. This simple blood test checks for a rare but dangerous condition called phenylketonuria (PKU). If babies are affected then a careful diet can limit the effects of PKU that otherwise causes brain damage. The Guthrie test is also a check that the baby's thyroid gland is working properly. Detection of such problems means that treatment can ensure that the baby develops normally.

From Spring 2001 a pilot programme was started for routine screening of newborns for hearing loss. The plan is that national screening will mean that hearing loss will be detected early and very young children can then be offered appropriate support for communication and learning.

Until now, the hearing of babies has been tested by a simple distraction test when they are eight or nine months old. A health visitor or GP makes noises at different angles to babies, including some out of sight, to check whether they turn in the direction of the noise. This test has proved an unreliable way to test hearing, since nine month old babies can be distracted by many events.

Now newborns of a few hours old will be checked by the minute long Oto-Acoustic Emission (OAE) test that establishes whether sounds are echoed back from the eardrum. In any doubt, a further more detailed test can then be undertaken. There are also plans to start universal screening for cystic fibrosis in 2002.

Tips for practice

Some early years practitioners work in the labour and maternity wards of a hospital. Your role can be supportive of parents of new babies:

- Ensure that you understand the procedures of the ward, including the various medical checks on newborn babies.
- Find ways to explain what is done and why in straightforward language, so that you can answer and anticipate the questions that new parents are likely to ask.
- Of course, with some questions it will be appropriate to refer the mother or father to a nurse or doctor. But you will often be able to give information or reassurance.
- Good practice is to recall that parents deserve courtesy as people. Medical practice has improved in many ways, but be wary of any suggestion on your ward that mothers are 'just patients' who ought to follow advice without question or comment.

Postnatal care of mothers

Community health care services will support families with new babies. Unless there is a health problem with mother or baby, it is not usual now for women to stay in hospital longer than a couple of days. Some women with support at home stay no longer than is needed to recover from the birth. The community midwife will visit mother and baby at home and carry out any outstanding health checks on either and offer any advice. Ten days after the birth the community midwife will be replaced by the health visitor assigned to the family.

As well as health checks on the baby, the community midwife will also check on the health of the mother: that stitches are healing and the recovery of a woman who has had a caesarean delivery. The six week check up of the baby at the hospital or local health clinic is also a check on the mother's health and well being.

Women are advised about postnatal exercises that help them regain muscle tone and get their figure back after the expansion of pregnancy. Specific exercises are important to strengthen the pelvic floor muscles and avoid the risk of mild incontinence.

Becoming a parent

First time parents – fathers as well as mothers – can lack confidence in their ability to take care of such a vulnerable little person. Parents can feel very confident in the rest of their lives but a successful job or social network does not prepare you for parenthood. Additionally parents, especially mothers who are more likely to be the ones getting up in the night, can be seriously tired. Fathers can be uncertain about how or whether to become involved in baby care, but in fact men can undertake any of the care routines, with affection and closeness to their baby, except breast feeding.

Baby blues and depression

Uncertainty about their skills, exhaustion and sleep deprivation can be enough to make anyone distressed. Many women feel close to tears in the early days after birth and this state has been called the **baby blues**. With support and help women feel more able to face the challenge and daily practice with their baby boosts mothers' confidence.

Some women experience **postnatal depression**, a state far beyond feeling tired and stunned by the hard work of looking after a baby. Postnatal depression can affect any woman and is characterised by great anxiety and feelings of being unable to cope. Women may feel that they cannot love their baby and are unable to take care of him or her. The baby blues will lift as first time mothers feel more competent and second and third time mothers recall that it will get better. Postnatal depression does not lift without help and families should contact their GP. This condition does not only affect women having their first baby. Postnatal depression may arise with second or third births.

Key terms

Baby blues
the term describing a temporary low state for mothers in the first few days after birth

Postnatal depression
a more serious and longer lasting condition when women feel unable to cope with their baby, are highly anxious and sometimes reject the baby

Tips for practice

As an early years practitioner you may work as a nanny in a family with a new baby, either the first or subsequent births. You will be able to help through:

- Your knowledge and support, for instance on breast feeding or encouraging women to make time for their postnatal exercises.
- Communication with parents about what you do and what they do, sharing the care and in what way.
- Being aware of the importance of not taking over. You can share your expertise, showing that confidence takes time and practice.
- Organising a day that enables mothers and fathers to spend time with their babies for close attachments to develop.

Scenario

A husband and wife team, Marilyn and James, are registered childminders with the Wessex childminding network. One of the children in their care has a new baby at home. Brief recent contact with the mother has made Marilyn concerned that Mum is possibly depressed. She discusses her reasons for concern with James and, since it is mainly Dad who currently brings three year old Callum, they wonder if it would be better if James has the conversation.

Questions

1 Look back through this section and check the kind of signs that might have alerted Marilyn to be concerned.

2 Consider and discuss with your colleagues what might be said to Callum's father. What would be the possible advantage of James having this conversation?

3 In what ways might Callum be affected if his Mum does have postnatal depression?

4 Consider what you might need to do as a nanny with a family or an early years practitioner who feels this kind of concern.

5 In what ways might you have to weigh up confidentiality with concern for the baby and other child as well as the mother's well being?

Key skills links: C3.1a

Babies who need special care

Some newborns need extra care because of health needs identified soon after birth, for example low birth weight or the potential complications of premature birth. Multiple births with twins, triplets or more babies tend to need additional care because the babies are more likely to be of low birth weight and to be delivered prematurely.

Activity

The availability of fertility treatment has increased the rate of multiple births. A family with twins or more babies has a great deal of hard work ahead and may also have concerns for the well being of one or more of the babies.

Find out more about family life with more than one new baby. You could:

- Talk with the health visitor at your local clinic and perhaps make contact with families who have experienced multiple births.
- Contact the Twins and Multiple Births Association. TAMBA provides information and support networks for families. They can be contacted at Harnott House, 309 Chester Road, Little Sutton, Ellesmere Port, CH66 1QQ tel: 0151 348 0020 helpline (the Twinline) on 01732 868000 and website: *www.tamba.org.uk*
- Write up what you have found out from these different sources of information. Make a short presentation to colleagues.

Key skills links: IT2/3.1 C3.3 C31.b

Premature babies

Technically speaking, premature babies are those who are born before 37 weeks gestation, although the term is sometimes used to apply to any babies who arrive before their due date.

If babies are a couple of weeks earlier than the estimated 40 weeks, then they may just be smaller than average but perfectly well. The seventh month is usually the earliest age at which a premature baby can survive without medical assistance. Babies are born and survive younger than this maturity, but their outlook is more fragile. With modern technology it is possible for a baby to survive outside the womb from about 23 weeks gestation, although such immature babies do not always survive and have a high rate of disability. Once babies have reached 26 weeks gestation they have about an 80 per cent chance of survival in a special care baby unit. With each further week of gestation the baby's prospects improve.

The difficulty for very premature babies is that their major organs, such as their lungs, cannot yet function independently. There is a high risk of brain damage, with resulting physical and learning disabilities. Some problems do not become apparent until a child struggles to reach the developmental milestones that peers have managed.

Special care on the wards

Nowadays many babies who would previously have been placed in a special unit are given the additional medical help they need while staying with their mothers. Babies with mild jaundice or who needed a little help to start breathing can be observed easily or screening undertaken. Babies may have conditions that are not life threatening, such as cleft palate or Down's syndrome. Parents will need support and information but there is no need to place the baby in a special unit. Medical practice has recognised that unless more significant medical intervention is needed, babies thrive better with their mothers than separated from them.

Special care and intensive care

About five babies out of every hundred will need caring for in a Special Care Baby Unit (SCBU). Modern technology can now enable sick or premature babies to:

- breathe when their own lungs are too immature to do this work
- take in nourishment before the babies are able to suck, swallow or digest
- be safe because the technology monitors temperature, heartbeat, breathing and the level of oxygen in the blood.

Neonatal intensive care units are necessary for the sickest and most fragile babies. The medical distinction between special care and intensive care for babies is whether the baby can breathe unaided. Apart from special help to keep babies healthy, the unit enables very premature babies to continue the growing that they would otherwise have done in the womb before birth. Very premature babies will often stay in hospital until what would have been their time of birth if they had gone to full term. As they improve, the babies will move towards care in an ordinary cot and being looked after in the same way as a healthy baby.

Babies who need intensive care will often need to be in hospital for weeks, perhaps months in some cases. This experience is a significant strain on families and unit teams work hard to involve and make parents welcome in the units. Research has established that babies thrive better if they have physical contact. Incubators are designed so that parents can put a hand into the cot and hold a baby's hand or gently stroke him. Whenever possible parents are encouraged to hold their baby for regular periods and to talk with him or her. This contact is as important for the parents as the baby since it enables parents to start the process of attachment to their baby (see page 189). Units usually welcome siblings as well and it will be important for them to be able to see their baby brother or sister.

Scenario

Kimberley works in a nanny share with two families. One family has just had a premature baby girl who is currently in intensive care, but whose prospects are good. Kimberley is supporting the family, including the father who is finding it hard to understand why his wife wants to sit by the incubator and hold the baby's hand. Kimberley is also dealing with questions from children of the second family in the nanny share who are distressed that the much-awaited new baby is 'too little and sick'.

Questions

1. Consider and practise ways that Kimberley could explain considerately to the baby's father why touch and sound will be so important for this sick premature baby.
2. Kimberley is caring for a three year old from the first family and four year old twins in the second family. Discuss with colleagues and practise some appropriate ways for her to talk with the three year old whose baby sister has not come home yet and the other children who had been so excited in preparing for the baby.

Key skills links: C3.1a PS2/3.1

For some families there is the anxiety about whether the baby will live. Parents need honest information as well as support. Families need to make decisions themselves about how they cope with this strain. However, on balance it is better that the parents and siblings make a relationship with the baby as an individual. If the baby does not survive then the family can grieve for the loss of a real person who was part of their life, if only for a short while, and remains in their memories and of whom they have photographs.

Development of babies who had special care

The age of babies is always calculated from their actual birth. But the growth and development of very premature babies will follow more closely the pattern that would have occurred if they had gone to full term. The difference between the babies' chronological age in months and their developmental age will be most marked in the early years. Parents may need support to bear in mind that significant developmental milestones like sitting up, crawling or the first words may be on time, if they count the months from when their baby should have been born.

You may offer this reassurance as a nanny working with the family or as an early years practitioner in a nursery. Of course, you would not continue to give reassurance if other features of the baby or toddler's development gave cause for concern. Babies should usually have their immunisations at the usual chronological age in months, unless the family doctor advises otherwise.

Further resources

- Hilton, Tessa with Messenger, Maire (1997) *The Great Ormond Street New Baby and Childcare Book: The essential guide for parents of children aged 0–5* Vermilion.
- Kitzinger, Sheila (1997) *The New Pregnancy and Childbirth* Penguin.
- Leach, Penelope (1997) *Your Baby and Child: The essential guide for every parent* Penguin.

Progress check

1. Describe three routine checks on pregnant women within antenatal care.
2. In what ways could antenatal classes help women with the experience of birth?
3. Suggest three ways in which an early years practitioner might support mothers and families through pregnancy and childbirth.
4. Describe two reflex actions that should be observed in newborn babies.
5. Describe three reasons why premature babies may need special care.

6

Care and development of babies

After reading this chapter you should be able to:

- understand and organise to meet babies' needs for physical care in a personal way
- work in partnership with parents as you share the care of babies
- support the health and well being of babies
- recognise when babies are ill and understand what you should do.

Introduction

In this chapter you will learn about good practice in the care of babies up to about one year of age. The role of early years practitioners is a combination of support for parents, especially mothers with very young babies, and responsibility in sharing the actual care of those babies.

Early years practitioners have to meet the physical needs of babies, whilst being very aware of the emotional and social development of such very young children. A warm and affectionate approach to babies is part of good quality care. Early years practitioners need to learn how best to care for children physically but the knowledge and skills described in this chapter are more than technical competence. Babies need caring adults who use care routines in a positive way and are very aware that babies are already learning.

Links to early years qualifications

This chapter especially supports the following units:

Diploma in Child Care and Education: 3, 7, 11

National Vocational Qualification in Early Years Care and Education

Level 2: C12, C13

Level 3: C14

BTEC National Early Years Diploma: 6, 8

Meeting the needs for physical care

Babies need a great deal of physical care for them to remain well and healthy. So their care routines are a major feature of their day – and night as well when your responsibility covers 24 hours. You will share the care of babies and very young toddlers with their parents, either as a nanny or as an early years practitioner in a nursery. You will find out more about this important relationship on page 631.

Good practice in care routines

Early years practitioners need to gain confidence in meeting the needs of babies and toddlers. But it is equally important that you value the times of physical care with babies. You gain expertise in:

- Understanding what babies and toddlers need in terms of their physical care.
- How you give this care in a way that ensures the baby's health and well being.
- How to ensure babies' emotional well being by placing them central to the care routines, giving them personal attention and behaving towards babies as if this time of care is as important as any other part of their day.

Activity

- Look at the diagram on page 162 about making care of babies a personal experience.
- Draft a similar diagram for toddlers of 12–24 months of age.
- Look at your own practice and consider how you already use some of these ideas.
- What else could you do to improve your practice, even minor changes? Discuss your ideas with your colleagues.

Key skills links: LP2/3.1–3 WO2/3.1–3

Becoming competent

Of course it takes time to learn the steps in caring for babies: how do you bath a baby safely or change a nappy? Confidence comes with practice as well as relevant knowledge. The value of your becoming confident in your skills is that you can then focus on the baby or toddler.

- Your skills with feeding or changing become a natural part of how you relate to babies; it seems the obvious thing to do.
- So, for instance, you do not have to keep thinking, 'I must support the baby's head because she hasn't got the muscle strength to do it herself'. Your hand and arms move deliberately to pick up a baby with care and support her head. You no longer have to think through your actions in advance.
- You then have some spare energy and attention to give to the baby, to make the routines of physical care a supportive and personal time.
- Poor practice with babies and toddlers develops if practitioners use this additional energy to ignore the baby, rush the routines or chat with colleagues rather than the baby.

Figure 6.1

Ways to make care of babies a personal and individual experience

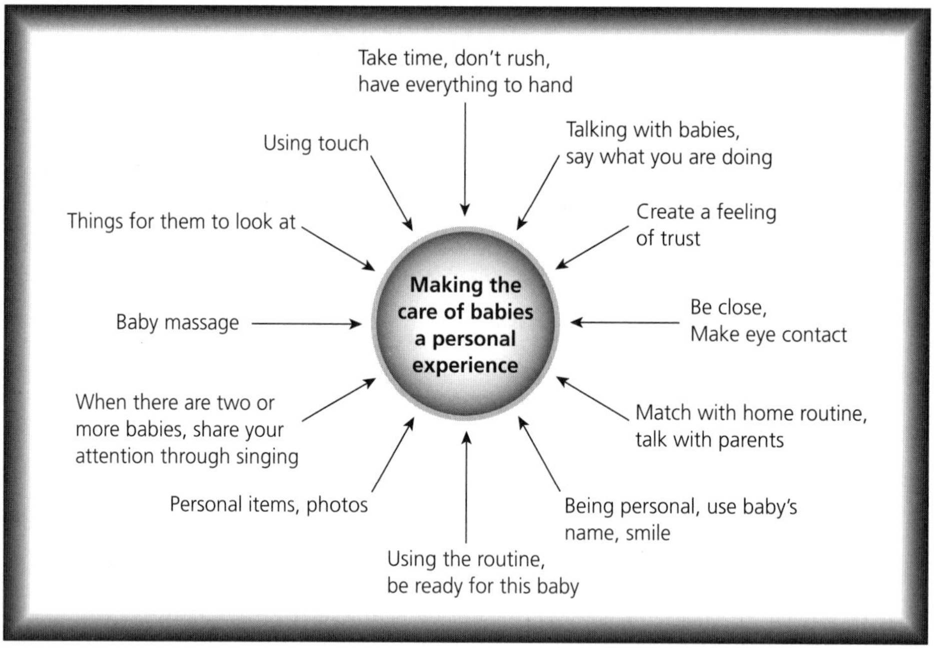

Scenario

When Erin became manager of Sunningdale Day Nursery she took responsibility for a team that had some very different views about baby care. There is a strong difference of opinion in the baby and toddler room with Christopher and Tamar feeling that care routines should be relaxed. They spend time talking with the children as they deal with their physical needs. In contrast Donna insists on what she calls an efficient approach to changing and feeding. She says that the previous manager introduced a more 'educational' early years curriculum and routines just need to be completed swiftly so everyone can get on to the more valuable activities. Erin calls a team meeting to resolve the conflict in the room and to explain clearly what she regards as good practice now that she is the manager.

Questions

1 What is likely to be the impact of Donna's 'efficient' approach with care routines? How are the babies and toddlers likely to feel and react?

2 What key ideas need to be aired in the team meeting? Look back at the section in Chapter 2 about caring (from page 41) and use some of those ideas to shape what Erin, Christopher or Tamar may say.

3 Donna has seriously misunderstood good practice and early learning. How do you think this could have happened?

Key skills links: C3.3. C3.1a

Warmth and affection

Babies need an affectionate and caring environment, because their brains need emotional support and not just intellectual stimulation.

- Caring adults need to give babies time, attention and affection. You need to relish all the early signs that babies are taking notice and are learning: their smiles, waves and that steady stare showing interest.
- Babies and toddlers learn best at their own pace and by following their absorbing current interests. There is plenty of time for them to explore, find out, practise and learn.
- They learn through everyday experiences, the daily moments of interest and by building on what they already know, understand and can do.
- Children need touch and affectionate communication. Physical closeness, singing and cuddling all send strong and positive messages to babies, that actually stimulate the growth of neural connections.
- Warm social relationships enable learning through the security of a safe base and a predictable, familiar daily life.

These general guidelines are applicable whatever the situation where you work with babies: in a nursery or centre, in the baby's own home as a nanny or your own home as a childminder. You will find more about appropriate learning activities with babies in other chapters, especially the section about early learning from page 267.

Crying and comfort

All babies cry, although some are much noisier than others. Some are undoubtedly also easier to comfort. There are a number of different possible reasons and even very familiar carers do not necessarily know the reason. Considerate carers explore the possibilities:

- Babies cry if they are hungry, starting with a low level cry but definitely building up if their needs are not met.

Figure 6.2
Babies grow fond of their siblings

- Babies may cry because they have wet or soiled their nappy. This condition does not necessarily lead to crying, since feeling rather damp or squishy is a regular experience for babies. Feeling cold or sore from nappy rash, however, is likely to make a baby or toddler cry.
- Discomfort and pain makes babies cry and the type and volume of their cry will tell you something about their pain. Babies sometimes get stomach pains from trapped wind or colic (see page 169). They are also often distressed if they have a cold and cannot breathe easily.
- They may also cry because they are chilled or too hot, either because it is high summer or because they are wrapped up too warmly.
- Babies who are too young to turn themselves over may also cry because they are uncomfortable.
- Babies can be startled or frightened by sudden noises or unexpected sights. They may cry at this experience and need to be comforted. Avoid creating fierce startle reactions in babies.
- Babies can simply cry for company; they want to be cuddled, walked around and entertained. Babies who cry are not always tired and need to have a nap, sometimes they are communicating, 'I'm bored, please entertain me!'

Comfort and cuddlies

Babies need sources of comfort, some of which will be from the comfort offered by caring adults. But they are also able to comfort themselves sometimes by sucking:

- Babies may use their own fingers and thumbs to suck for comfort and some babies learn how to manage this by about 3–4 months.
- For some reason some babies do not suck a finger or thumb, or else are dissuaded by adults. An alternative is that a baby has a soother (sometimes called a dummy).

Adults – parents and early years professionals – sometimes express strong views about different ways that babies and toddlers can comfort themselves. It has been claimed that sucking a thumb or fingers causes teeth to stick out and that dummies are unhygienic. There seems to be no reliable evidence that says thumb sucking causes children's teeth to slope outwards. The possible exception is if children have an unusual thumb-sucking style in which they push hard against their teeth and continue to do so through early childhood. Soothers are only unhygienic if adults fail to keep them clean or allow them to be passed around from one baby to another.

Babies and young toddlers need to be able to comfort themselves and removing all their options will make them very distressed. So long as their thumb or finger is reasonably clean and soothers are kept clean (soothers can also be sterilised), then there is no cause for concern. Genuine risks for health arise if babies and toddlers are permitted to suck on bottles or mini-drink soothers filled with sweet drinks. The consequence of this practice is serious dental decay for babies' first teeth.

It is also wise gently to discourage thumbs and soothers as a full time support when a toddler starts to talk. You can request, not demand, that a thumb or soother comes out of a toddler's mouth, so you can understand what is said.

Other sources of comfort to a baby or toddler will be something that he or she has chosen to cuddle. Such comfort objects may be a soft toy, a baby blanket, bits of cloth, almost anything that feels comforting to this child. These comfort objects should be respected and you should help a child take care of them. Conversation with parents will let you know what is important to a baby or very young child.

Activity

Build up information on babies you know and talk with parents.

- What are the different sources of comfort for individual babies and very young children?
- How do you think that babies 'decide' on their source of comfort?
- How can you ensure their comfort objects are kept clean enough but not scrubbed or washed so thoroughly that the comforting and familiar smell is destroyed.
- Compare your findings with colleagues and build up a short presentation of how babies and very young children comfort themselves.

Key skills links: C2/3.1

Feeding

For the first four months of life babies are completely fed on milk, either breast or bottle fed or some combination of both options. The baby's full nutritional needs are met by milk in these early months and their digestive system is not ready to manage anything else.

Routines of feeding

Young babies need to be fed on a regular basis over the 24 hour period. Newborn babies feed every 3–4 hours day and night and many will continue to need night or evening feeds for months.

Advice about how to organise feeds for babies has varied over the years. Mothers in the 1950s and 1960s were told very firmly that they should follow an uncompromising four hourly schedule or else they would spoil their babies. By the 1980s mothers were told that feeding on demand, that is whenever a baby cried, was necessary for good care.

Some middle ground is probably the best way forward.

- A fierce timed schedule does not allow for the fact that some babies are hungry more often than every four hours. If babies are made to wait because it is 'too soon' for a feed, they can be in serious distress by the time they are offered milk.
- On the other hand an uncompromising demand schedule can overlook the fact that after a couple of months some babies cry because they want comfort and entertainment, not because they are hungry.
- An often overlooked problem with inflexible rules about demand feeding is that very young babies need food every 3–4 hours and premature or very sleepy babies may not wake and demand milk. They will then get weak through lack of nutrition and be even less likely to demand a feed.

In the early weeks the most workable routine is that babies are fed and then changed. When they wake they want food and will become very distressed if you make them wait while you change them. A practical point is also that the action of sucking and feeding seems to stimulate the digestive system in general and lead to activity at the other end. Then you will only have to change them again.

Feeding should be an affectionate and calm event. Babies should be held close and the ideal position for breast or bottle feeding is also a young baby's ideal focusing distance. The mealtime is a time of close communication and supports the growing attachment. When you share the care of a baby it is important to follow the personal routines that have been established in the family: babies are fed because they are hungry, not because every baby is fed at this time.

Supporting breast feeding

Human babies are designed for breast milk and it contains all the nutrients they need in the first four months of life.

- The milk emerges at the right temperature, the right consistency and nothing needs sterilising afterwards.
- Breast milk transmits immunities to the baby through the mother's antibodies in the milk and these protect babies from illnesses in the early months.
- Breast feeding is very practical when babies move about with their mothers, because breast milk is ready and available; there is no need to travel with bottles and sterilising equipment. That said, of course breast feeding requires the mother to be available.

Breast feeding needs to be started at birth when a woman's body is ready to give milk. It will be progressively more difficult to breast feed as the days pass by. In the UK it is estimated that about two-thirds of women at least try breast feeding but that many give up, so that less than half the babies are being breast fed at six weeks of age (the lowest rate in Europe). Women obviously stop for many reasons but lack of support, especially if breast feeding is less than straightforward, seems to be a major reason.

You may be involved in encouraging mothers to breast feed at least for some time, perhaps because you work on a maternity ward or as a nanny in a family home when a new baby arrives. For something that is so natural, establishing breast feeding can sometime require perseverance. It does not help women who have become mothers, especially first time mothers, to imply that breast feeding is always easy. The most useful support for mothers is to help them to continue breast feeding if there are problems that can be overcome, for instance:

- Some babies have difficulty latching on to the breast and mothers appreciate help in positioning themselves and the baby.
- Slightly premature babies may be sleepy and need to be woken so that they get enough food until they are strong enough to wake and yell – possibly only a few days.
- Babies produce a strong suck and nipples need to toughen up a bit. Some women develop sore nipples or blocked milk ducts and need support to get through the discomfort and occasionally the pain.

Most problems can be resolved with support within the family, from the health visitor or from a professional skilled in this support, such as the National Childbirth Trust network of breastfeeding counsellors. New mothers also need to rest as much as possible, eat a healthy diet and drink six to eight cups of fluid a day.

Activity

Organise a talk with a breast feeding counsellor from the National Childbirth Trust (see page 149 for contact details). Make notes on issues such as:

- What are the main reasons why women stop breast feeding in the early weeks? What difficulties do they face?
- What are the best ways to offer support and advice?
- Write up your notes to offer a guide on the best ways to support a woman who is breast feeding: if you are working in a hospital, as a nanny or as an early years practitioner.

Key skills links: C2/3.3

There are few circumstances in which women would be actively dissuaded from breast feeding. Some rare viruses can pass to the baby through breast milk, so women would be told not to breast feed if they had AIDS/HIV or Hepatitis B.

The obvious disadvantage of full breast feeding is that other carers and the baby's father cannot feed the baby. If women know they will need to return to work in the baby's early months when the baby is still wholly or mainly milk fed, then it can be wise to get the baby used to a bottle, as a supplement to the breast. Otherwise, a fully breast fed baby can be deeply unimpressed by being given a bottle out of the blue at around three or four months. They may not mind but some show in no uncertain terms that breast is best.

Women who return to work when their babies are very young can sometimes express milk and store it in bottles to be given by a nanny, childminder or early years practitioner in a nursery. Nurseries can also be helpful by welcoming mothers who are close enough to the nursery to come in during the day and breast feed. Of course, that option is not always realistic. Shared care arrangements can involve breast feeding by the mother when she is with the baby and bottle feeding when another carer is in charge.

Bottle feeding

Cow's milk is actually designed for calves. So the formula milk that is produced for human babies has to be modified in a number of crucial ways. Bottle feeding with formula milk provides all the nutrients needed by babies and is safe and hygienic, so long as the exact instructions for making up feeds and sterilising all the bottle feeding equipment are followed. Even with the modifications, some babies are allergic to cows milk and adverse reactions may mean that an alternative will have to be found, probably soya milk.

You must follow the instructions for mixing formula milk. Babies who are hungry after a feed should be given more milk, made up correctly. By four months this further demand is a sign that the baby is ready to start some solid foods as well as milk (see page 170).

Tips for practice

Feeding a baby is a time of close contact and affectionate warmth as well as meeting the baby's feeding needs. When you bottle feed a baby you need to:

- Sit comfortably so that you hold the baby in your arms and at an angle so that he or she can feed easily (see Figure 6.3 on this page).
- You need to be comfortable as well as the baby, since feeding can take 15–20 minutes depending on the baby. This time is long enough to get cramp or to be so uncomfortable that you make the baby restless.
- You always hold a baby for feeding and never, ever prop them with a bottle. Apart from the danger of them slipping and choking, propping shows such an uncaring approach towards babies. It says to them that they do not matter enough to be cuddled.
- While you are feeding, make eye contact and have gentle communication with the baby. Babies need to concentrate on sucking but, once the most pressing needs of hunger are satisfied, they are reassured and warmed by looks and soft words.
- You can feed babies in a room with other babies or toddlers. They like to be part of daily life. If there are older children around – in a family home or nursery – let them stay peaceably. There is no need to shoo them away and they will be interested.

Bacteria multiply fast in milk and saliva starts the digestive process of the breakdown of milk or food. So any milk left in a baby's bottle after he has completed the feed must be thrown away and not kept for the next feed. Bottles and teats must also be sterilised according to the instructions on the products you use. Ordinary washing is not enough to remove traces of milk. The choices are:

- sterilisation by heat in a steam steriliser
- by heat in a container and bottles that can go into the microwave

Figure 6.3
Bottle feeding a young baby

- by cold water and sterilising tablets or liquid in a container designed for that purpose.

Whatever method you use, you must read and follow the instructions carefully. Ensure that anything you put into the microwave is safe for that way of sterilising.

Winding babies after feeding

Parents of previous generations were given the impression that problems of wind (air swallowed along with the milk) were a frequent difficulty for babies and they were advised always to 'wind' babies after a feed. The problem of wind was overstated, but some babies do need to burp or clear a bout of hiccups and some experience painful colic (see below).

If you hold a baby resting over your shoulder after a feed (Figure 6.4) any wind will come up if necessary, probably over you, so a clean cloth or muslin over your shoulder will protect your clothes a bit. This position is an enjoyable cuddle for a baby as you settle her back to sleep, so nothing is lost if she does not have any wind.

Dealing with colic

Some babies cry a considerable amount and draw their knees up over their stomach as if they are in pain. Normally digestion operates with smooth rhythmic movements but in colic the food is moved along in painful spasms. Babies with colic are otherwise healthy, although it is wise to check with the GP if the babies' pains seem severe and definitely if the baby has any other symptoms such as diarrhoea.

The condition is often called three month colic because it happens when babies are aged between two to four months. The only medication for colic is gripe water or a mild antacid suitable for babies, both of which can be bought without prescription at a chemists' shop. Your local pharmacist can offer advice, as can the health visitor. Otherwise families have to find ways to share the care of a screaming baby and this is very wearing. Some babies may be calmed a little

Wind is not always a problem, although bottle fed babies sometimes swallow quite a lot of air with their milk. Put a cloth or muslin square close to where he is likely to bring up any milk with the wind.

1 Hold him against your shoulder, supporting his head when he is still very young. Gently rub his back.
2 Or lie him across your lap and gently rub his back.
3 Not for a newborn, but when he is able to sit more upright, you can cuddle him on your lap and gently rub his back.

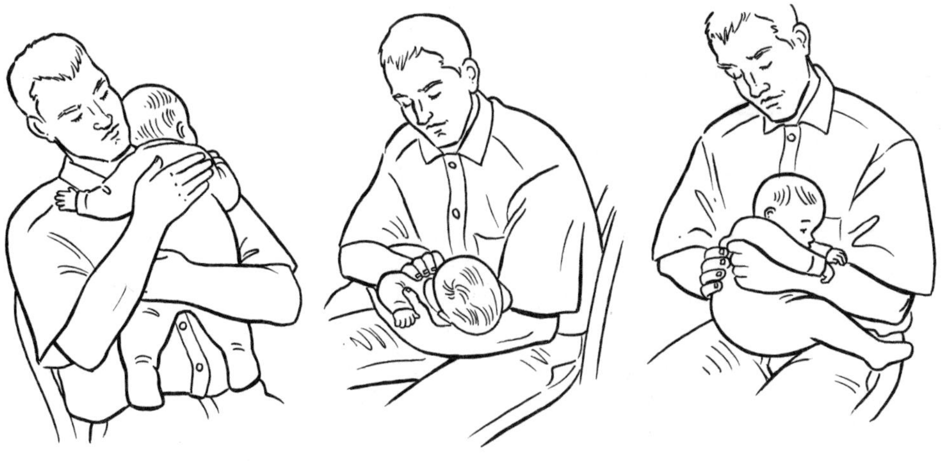

Figure 6.4 Three ways to help a baby bring up trapped wind

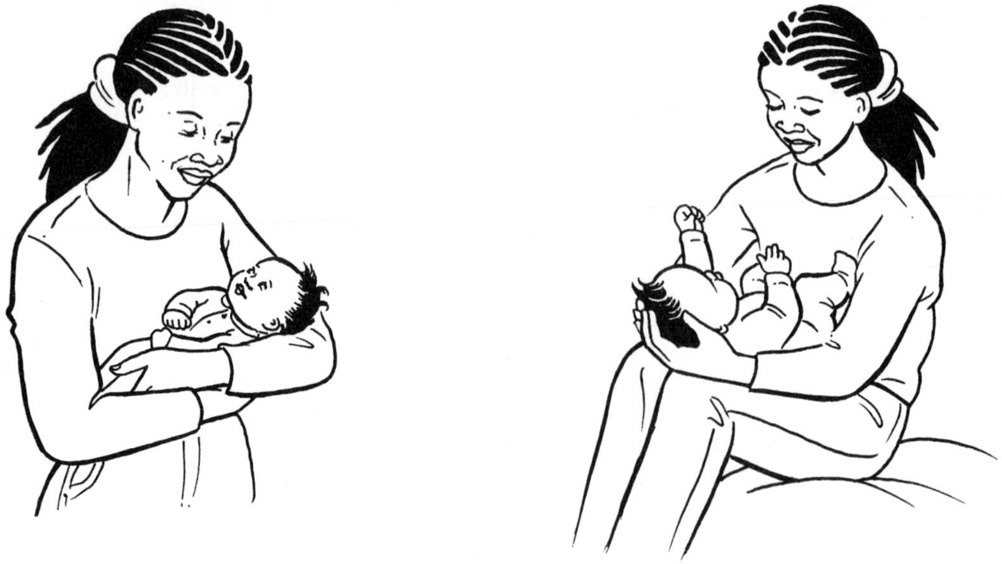

Figure 6.5 The importance of supporting a baby's head

by sucking, being walked around or rocked. Colic often seems to be worse in the evening and in some families that may mean there is more than one person to take turns. If you are a nanny, you may help the family out in the evening, or sometimes have responsibility so the parents can get out together and have a break from the crying.

Weaning

Babies should be totally milk fed until about 16 weeks (four months) of age, when many babies will start to show that they are still hungry after their usual feeds. You can then start **weaning**, also called **mixed feeding**.

Key term

Weaning
when babies are introduced to first foods in addition to their milk diet, also sometimes called mixed feeding

First foods

The first foods are extras, not desperately needed meals, so be relaxed and let the baby become familiar with this new experience. Babies are getting used to foods as first tasters and milk is their main source of nutrition for some time yet. The usual advice is to start babies on baby rice cereal and then steadily introduce foods one at a time. The best way is to give babies freshly prepared food, then you will know exactly what has gone into a baby's meal if you, or the nursery cook, has made it.

Commercially produced baby foods can be useful and convenient when you are on the move or if a baby is still hungry and you have fed him all the food you have freshly pureed. Good quality brands are nutritious but most have combinations of ingredients, so you cannot control the introduction of one food at a time to babies.

Baby rice cereal should be mixed with the baby's usual milk (formula or expressed breast milk) or boiled and cooled water to a runny consistency. You do not want too much difference between this first food and the milk with which the baby is familiar. Babies may take to rice cereal but some are unimpressed. Baby rice is not very exciting in taste and babies can distinguish tastes. Persevere with this simple cereal but also look to introduce other basic foods.

Wheat based baby cereals are not recommended until about 6 months because they are harder for babies to digest. You should never add rice or wheat based cereals to a baby's bottle (some people do). Such a practice can force a baby to take in more cereal than he needs in order to drink the amount of milk that he does need.

From four to six months you can introduce babies to their first fruit and vegetable purees: ripe apples or pears, root vegetables like potato or carrot. These foods can be cooked until soft, pureed (in a blender or a sieve) with no added sugar or salt. You can steam, microwave or lightly boil fruit or vegetables in a small amount of water. Do not add butter or any other fats. Some fruits, like banana, can be mashed.

Tips for practice

- You feed babies small amounts of food on a proper plastic baby spoon.
- Take your time; if a baby feels rushed she often refuses food or spits it back out. The baby is getting used to the spoon as well as the food.
- Try one food at a time, then you can combine, when you are sure that the baby can digest all the foods you are combining.
- Babies do not like all tastes the first time, so it is worth trying more than once.
- But if the baby still does not seem to like the taste and certainly if any food seems to give him an upset stomach, then leave that out of his diet.
- You should be concerned about reactions such as vomiting, diarrhoea and blotchy rashes, since these could mean the baby is intolerant of these foods.
- It will be important to talk with the baby's parents on a regular basis so that you can effectively share this aspect of the baby's care and the parents can alert you to whether there are any allergies in the family.

Figure 6.6
Babies can enjoy their food

From five to six months you can introduce other fruits that mash or puree easily:

- Examples are mango, peach, melon and vegetables like cauliflower, spinach or tomato.
- You can cook pulses like lentils to a soft mush and perhaps mix in a vegetable that you know the baby likes.
- Avoid citrus fruits like oranges since they can cause diarrhoea.
- From 6 months onwards, depending on the family diet, you could try small amounts of mild cheese, very finely grated or mixed in with pureed vegetables.
- Yoghurt introduces a pleasant texture and flavours.
- Wheat based cereals or rusks produced for babies make an enjoyable change. It is important to use proper baby cereals, since cereals for older children and adults, even if they are mushy like porridge, do not have enough nutrition for babies at this stage of development.
- You can introduce chicken, finely minced, and white fish broken into fine flakes and carefully checked for bones. You would obviously avoid these foods if the family is vegetarian.
- From about 8 months, you can introduce a range of finger foods and finely grated cheese, carrot or apple and then an older baby can enjoy feeding herself.
- Fruit and vegetable sticks can be raw or gently cooked to be soft but not floppy.
- Increasingly you can puree or mash up part of a freshly cooked meal that is also served for toddlers or children, or a family meal in a household. The main point is to avoid added salt or sugar and any highly spiced or seasoned food.
- Current advice is to avoid eggs until children are 12 months old and then to cook them very thoroughly.

Tips for practice

Steadily you can move babies towards being part of social mealtimes. But you need to remain relaxed about food as babies will make a mess.

- They may spit out food, blow raspberries or spoon flick. You can gently discourage these actions and try very hard not to laugh at food spraying, although it can be funny the first time.
- Babies steadily learn to feed themselves, with fingers and using a spoon for them and a spoon for you.
- By six to nine months babies can put a hand to a bottle or be able to manage a feeder cup well.
- Never leave a baby alone with food or drink. She may choke but that is not the only point. As with the rule of never propping a baby with a bottle, it is an uncaring action, the message is 'I have more interesting things to do than sit and keep you company'.

Key term

Projectile vomiting when a baby brings up milk or food with force – a sign of possible serious digestive problems needing medical attention

It is not unusual for babies to spit food back out or even to vomit up small amounts that have not progressed far down their throat. However, it is *not* usual for babies to vomit a great deal, nor to be sick in such a way that the food hurtles out at speed, called **projectile vomiting**. You should speak with a parent about either of these situations. Projectile vomiting can be sign of digestive problems that need medical attention.

Babies and toddlers absolutely do not need high fibre or low fat diets (see page 83). They need foods with plenty of calories and nutrients in appropriate amounts, such as eggs, dairy produce, meat, fish and poultry (depending on the family diet). Too much fibre can be bulky and it fills them up before they have been able to eat enough to provide the nutrients. Too much fibre also can reduce young children's absorption of essential minerals like calcium and iron. In terms of fibre, toddlers will be fine with some fingers or squares of wholemeal bread or a small amount of wholewheat cereal. See the section about children's diets on page 81.

Drinks

Babies who are fully breast or bottle fed will not need water unless the weather is very hot. Ask the advice of your nursery manager or a health visitor under these circumstances. Babies who are moving onto mixed feeding will still be taking in most of their nutrition from breast or formula milk. Bottle feeding would normally fade away as an older baby becomes able to take her drinks in a cup.

Breast feeding can continue until the baby or mother wishes to stop, usually by 12 months or not long into the second year of life. There is no need to stop because a baby has developed his first teeth, which can be as early as four to six months. A firm yet kind 'No' and a look can stop a baby biting at the breast. Some mothers do continue to breast feed longer, even until a child is three or four years old. Such a choice is for comfort; the child does not need the milk. Later breast feeding is a family decision, but can lead to socially embarrassing situations in which competent toddlers or young children help themselves in public.

Formula milk can continue until twelve months, when babies can move onto full cream cow's milk, so long as there is no reason to suppose that they may be allergic. You would not give cow's milk as the baby's source of milk before this age because it does not contain all the nutrients the baby needs. A small amount will not hurt in pureed vegetables or in a mashed portion of food that the older children or family are eating. You do not need to use the so-called follow-on milks that are marketed as an interim step between formula or breast and cow's milk. Nor do babies need the flavoured versions of these.

By 14–15 months, toddlers need no more than one pint of full fat milk per day and two small cups of watered pure fruit juice (not squash or squash-type drinks). Older babies and toddlers can drink straight water – from the tap or filtered, whatever you drink. Avoid bottled or spring water for babies and young children, some of it has far too much sodium (salt) for their well being. In a family home, you also need to check whether water softeners have been fixed to the system, since they change the water chemically in ways that are not good for babies.

Babies' needs for drink will be met by these options. They do not need any of the bewildering array of so-called 'baby juice' drinks on the market. None of these are essential for the health of babies or toddlers, whatever the packet claims. Some are bad for health, especially the teeth, if they are used with any regularity. Early years practitioners and parents need to develop a healthy scepticism about marketing claims on commercially produced food and drink, much as with toys.

You should continue to sterilise bottles as long as a toddler is using one and it is also wise to sterilise the lid of a teacher beaker. Cups can be thoroughly washed and milk cannot get trapped in the same way.

Added vitamins

Totally bottle fed babies should not be given vitamin drops since formula milk has vitamins added. Drops may be advised for breast fed babies after 6 months but you should never give babies, or children, vitamins without consultation with their parents. It is the parents' choice and also you must avoid the situation where two carers, who fail to talk to each other, both give a baby vitamin drops. It is possible to overdose on some vitamins, as a child and adult as well as a baby. Once a baby is weaned, vitamin drops (containing A, D and C and formulated for children) are usually recommended up to about five years of age.

Care of teeth

A baby's first set of teeth forms in the gums before birth. Many babies begin to cut their first teeth, known as milk teeth, at about six months, but this is very variable and some babies still have none at their first birthday. When babies are relatively late cutting teeth, you can face a situation in which a 10–12 month old's enthusiasm for more chunky food is not matched by her ability to chew it. You may need to continue with mashing and cutting food up into small pieces while the baby has only hard gums to work with.

The most usual pattern for cutting teeth is as follows:

- *6 months*: incisors, with the two central top and two central bottom teeth
- *8 months*: two more incisors to make a set of four top and bottom teeth
- *10–14 months*: the first molars, that are the double teeth for efficient chewing. Other teeth follow later (see page 105).

It is important to take care of the milk teeth of babies and children. Teeth should be cleaned as soon as they appear. Adults initially do this task for babies by wiping the teeth with a clean flannel and then in the second year with a gentle toothbrush and small amount of toothpaste. Fluoride drops may be recommended from

Figure 6.7
Meals can become a social occasion

about six months if there is no fluoride added to the local water. But this decision is for parents to make and you should never give babies or children drops without consulting parents. Too much fluoride causes discoloration of the teeth.

A healthy diet and good tooth care can ensure that toddlers and young children do not get any cavities and therefore have to endure fillings (see page 106.)

Teething

Cutting teeth does not always cause great distress, but babies and toddlers can be in discomfort. They are more likely to be in pain when the molars start to appear, if they cut several teeth at once or if their teeth are relatively late in appearing and have to cut through tough gums.

Babies who have trouble with their teething need patience and comfort. Previous generations were encouraged to put all sorts of symptoms down to teething. You need to be very wary about ignoring symptoms of ill health, that would usually concern you, just because a baby is teething. The process of teething produces teeth and some discomfort. It does not cause diarrhoea, fever or vomiting.

Tips for practice

- Babies who are teething often feel better if they can press their gums against something hard and cool.
- Teething rings and safe teething toys can be a comfort.
- Some teethers can be placed in the fridge to cool them and then sucking on the teether can be a comfort to sore gums.
- Teethers should *never* be put in the freezer. Teethers may not survive the temperature. But also there is a risk, if they do not warm up enough, that a semi-frozen teether could stick to a child's mouth or lips.
- Older babies may like to gnaw on a carrot stick or a rusk. You would obviously only give them this kind of hard food if you remain with them; they would not take it into their cot like a toy.
- Teething babies sometimes dribble more and may need your attention to pat their chin dry, so that they do not get sore.

Clothes and dressing

Parents will choose how they dress their babies, toddlers and children. You can make suggestions if asked or volunteer a comment if a child's clothes are seriously hampering their chance to play. Otherwise it is a family decision and clothing will of course reflect the family cultural background.

It is preferable that clothing for babies is:

- easy for carers to undo and do up again in order to change a child
- composed of layers, so that it is easy to add another layer in the winter if a baby is not warm enough, yet similarly easy to keep a baby cool in warm weather
- without ties or loose fastenings that could entangle a baby
- suited to easy physical movement – once babies start crawling and later walking, they can do so more easily in all-in-one outfits like babygros and dungarees. Baby girls can become snarled up in little frocks, especially when

they are crawling or climbing – although it will be their parents' choice about clothing

- easy to launder because baby clothes and those of toddlers will get covered in milk, leakage from nappies and interesting play materials.

Self care

Very young babies cannot help with their dressing and undressing. As they start to gain control of their limbs, their energetic physical movements can make life more complicated, as two legs go down one leg space. From 6 to 9 months, babies may start to join in the dressing process, pushing an arm into a sleeve that you line up. But this is a playful activity, so do not be surprised if the baby takes the arm back out again. Toddlers who are given the time and encouragement will start to pull elasticated trousers up or down and pull down the last part of a t-shirt. It is well worth showing appreciation for toddlers' efforts and allowing them time when they want to try, since this is the beginning of the skills of self reliance (see page 47).

Cleaning and toileting

If you work in a nursery, then you will clean babies and change their nappy, but it is likely that parents will do the bathing and hair washing at home. If you work as a nanny, then you are far more likely to be involved in the whole routine.

Unlike mobile toddlers, babies do not get grubby from interesting play and exploration. Babies need gentle cleaning to ensure that their bottoms do not get nappy rash and their mouths do not get sore from dribble or milk.

Any bath products for babies should be fragrance free, with no lanolin (babies are often allergic to this ingredient) and suitable for baby skins. Ask parents if they like any particular products used for their baby or whether the baby has any sensitivities or allergies. Parents can also tell you whether they cream their baby's or toddler's skin. Creaming is usually part of normal skin care for children with dark skin.

Babies often like bathtime and it can be a playful part of their daily routine, regardless of the fact that they do not need that much cleaning. Babies are not all enthusiastic at the outset. Some show a panic reaction when first put into a baby bath. It usually helps to hold them with their feet against the end of the baby bath. This contact seems to reassure them that there is a boundary to their world. Babies who continue to be very unhappy about bathtime can be cleaned perfectly well on a changing mat by 'topping and tailing'. This method simply means uncovering one half of the baby and gently cleaning and drying her and then doing the other half.

Tips for practice

Like changing time, you need a comfortable and warm (not hot) environment where you have everything you need close to hand: a warm towel, baby soap or lotion and any toy the baby likes in the bath.

- Babies should be bathed in a warm atmosphere, free of draughts. They need water that is warm, not hot. Test it with your elbow; your hands will be used to hotter water from domestic tasks.
- Let the baby enjoy the water by kicking or by dribbling it over him. Let him splash.

- Gently clean the baby with whatever products you use, holding a baby who cannot yet sit up firmly under the shoulders. Be ready to support a sitting baby.
- Babies who can sit up will be ready to go in the main bath. Use a non-slip mat for them to sit on.
- *Never, ever* leave the bathroom when a baby, toddler or young child is in the bath. It only takes a moment for a baby to slip and they drown in small amounts of water.

Babies do not need hair washing as such until they have a head of hair. You can wipe their head over gently. Use baby shampoo once they have hair. Most babies and toddlers are deeply unimpressed with hair washing. You can try one of the products that keeps the shampoo from running down their face but some are still unhappy and you just have to be as swift as you can.

Young babies sometimes develop cradle cap, which is a minor skin problem on the scalp. Cradle cap usually shows as non-itchy yellow scales and can be softened and removed by gentle washing or brushing. It does not usually cause discomfort to babies unless it spreads down the face and becomes itchy and red. Cradle cap that has been neglected may need more care to remove and special lotions – ask your manager or a pharmacist.

Activity

- Write up the care routine of bathing a baby and highlight how you would help a baby to feel safe and comfortable.
- What steps might you try for additional comfort with a baby who is not at all keen on being bathed?
- How will you make bathtime a happy and communicative experience?
- Share your ideas with colleagues or make a short presentation to a group.

Key skills links: C2.3 C2.1b

Changing nappies

Over the first couple of years of life a baby and then toddler will get through a considerable number of nappies until they are reliably toilet trained for day and night. The youngest that a child is likely to be ready to start toilet training will be 18–24 months. Any pressure to try to get a child out of nappies much younger will simply lead to frustration and upset all round and masses of wet knickers. Toilet training is covered in Chapter 2, from page 68.

What kind of nappy?

There are two main options: towelling or disposable nappies. Previous generations used terry towelling nappies that are folded to shape and then pinned securely on the baby or toddler, probably with plastic pants over the top. Ready shaped towelling nappies are also now available. All towelling nappies need to be cleaned with care: first placed in an appropriate sterilising solution in a large container and then washed at a high temperature. The nappy bucket and washing machine is part of the routine unless a nappy laundering service is used.

Over the last couple of decades there has been a great increase in the use of disposable nappies, in which the padding to soak up waste products and the plastic outing coating are part of the same shaped nappy. Most families and nurseries choose this option, since disposables do not require washing; you simply use and then discard with care.

Disposable nappies are often sold in boy and girl versions. They vary in terms of where the thickest padding is provided. The urine of boys tends to go in the front part of the nappy, where his penis is, whereas the urine of girls tends to flow more towards the back. If you use towelling nappies, you can fold them to achieve the same effect.

In recent years there has been more awareness of the environmental impact of disposable nappies. Each baby uses about one tonne of disposable nappies over their early years before they are toilet trained. This creates 800,000 tonnes of nappy waste each year in the UK. It is estimated that disposable nappies now form about 4 per cent of all household waste in the UK and about 50 per cent of the waste in a household with one baby. Most of this ends up in the landfills where local councils put rubbish that cannot be recycled. Disposable nappies are hopeless for any form of recycling; they do not break down over time. The first disposable nappies have yet to degrade – in whatever landfill they are lurking.

As an early years practitioner you will probably have to work with whatever system is in place in the family home where you work as a nanny or in a day nursery. However, it is worth considering the environmental impact of disposables.

A friendly and safe changing time

Hygiene is important for babies but the changing area and your routine can still be warm and personal:

- If you work as a nanny in a family home you can ensure with the parents that the changing area is safe, easy to keep clean and at a level to protect adult backs.
- In a nursery the changing area will be for more than one baby, so it is good practice to have a personal toiletries box or little basket for each child. This contains any special cream that they need, a toy or book they like to hold, any personal wipes and a clear note about any health needs that relate to changing.
- From the baby's point of view changing time is a good time for happy contact and playful communication. You and the baby have many changing routines to get through and it is in everyone's interest to make this a pleasant time.
- Young babies may stare at you with interest. You can smile back, chat with them using infant directed speech (see page 306) or sing.
- Babies of three to four months may like something to hold, like a rattle and this option can be useful if little fingers tend to get in the way.
- Talk with babies or toddlers and tell them what you are doing. Your voice will be reassuring and you develop a good habit of sharing care with the baby or toddler – a matter of courtesy and personal dignity.
- Older children can watch, chat and help with care, either in a family home or in a nursery that has recognised the value of bringing the ages together.

Activity

- Write up the care routine for changing the nappy of a baby.
- Explain what you would have ready before you start.
- How would you help a baby to feel that changing time was personal, a time that you enjoy sharing with him or her?
- How could you organise and decorate a nappy changing area in a family home or in a nursery?
- Share your ideas with colleagues or make a short presentation to a group.

Key skills links: C2.3 C2.1b

Practical hygiene and safety

The changing mat and area needs to be clean and hygienic. But there is no need to be so lavish with disinfectant that the changing area smells.

- Have everything ready easily to hand. Never take your eyes off the child and never move away from them. A moment has been enough for older babies to lever themselves off a changing mat. Babies' physical skills develop swiftly. One day they lie fairly still, but by the next they have achieved a full roll over.
- A natural hazard with baby boys is that, once their penis is uncovered, they sometimes pass urine. It can travel some distance, including upwards and then inevitably downwards. A practical step is to place a tissue or clean muslin over a baby boy's penis. If baby girls pass urine, it simply trickles onto the changing mat.

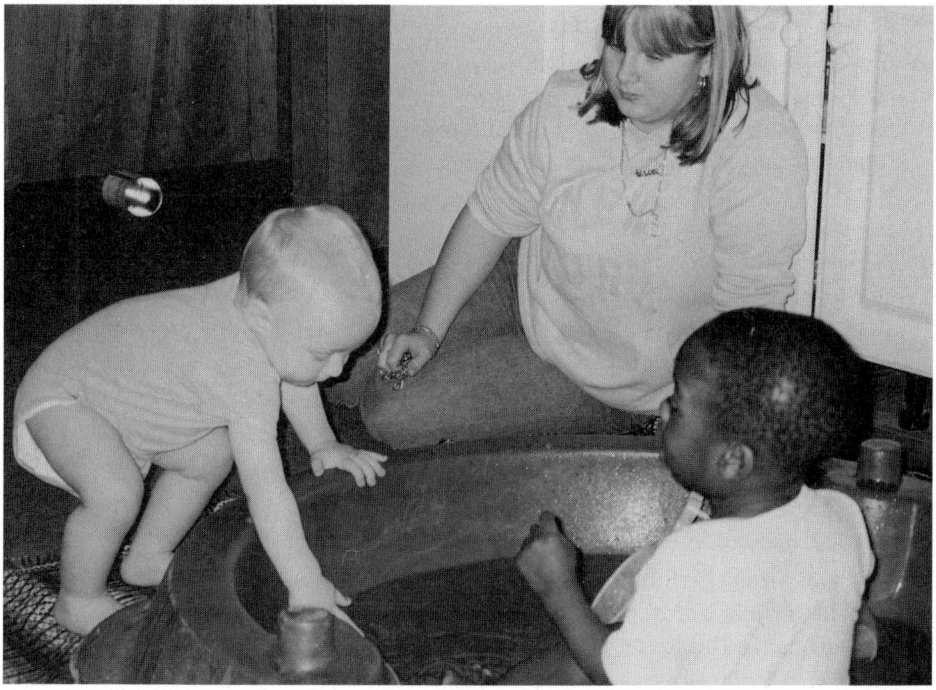

Figure 6.8
Your friendly presence helps keep babies safe in play

- In a nursery, you will probably wear thin disposable gloves and an apron because you may change more than one child. These items offer hygienic protection for babies as well as for you. In a family home, you would probably not use this equipment, in which case you must wash your hands carefully before and after changing a baby.

The health of the baby

Changing time can be an opportunity to check on the well being of the baby, whilst of course being gentle and communicative as you do it. Look carefully to see that babies are free of nappy rash or sore skin, especially in the folds of their arms or legs.

Make a note of scratches or bruises and if you can guess how the baby came by minor bumps then remember to tell the parents. If you do not know how the baby or toddler gained slight injuries, or the injuries are not slight, then talk with your manager about whether and how you will raise the question with the baby's parents. (See Chapter 19 for when there can be child protection concerns.)

The contents of a baby's nappy will tell you something about her general well being. The stools of a breast fed baby have a milder, milky smell in comparison with a bottle fed baby and both tend to be soft. Once babies move into mixed feeding, then their stools become firmer, although they should not have problems in passing them. Constipated babies and toddlers can be in pain and the first step will be to ensure that they are drinking enough liquid (see page 72).

Rest and sleep

Very young babies will sleep many hours in the day, when they are not being fed and changed.

- Some babies have wakeful periods from the early weeks but all babies will move towards having wakeful times and will not go straight back to sleep after a feed.
- From two to three months onwards babies will want to be entertained and have playful company.
- By six to nine months many babies will have established a fairly regular pattern of naps during the day.
- It is important that nursery staff respect the pattern of a baby and fit in with the personal schedule when babies join a nursery. As the months pass, it is possible to encourage a group of toddlers to take a nap at about the same time, but you still should not insist.

Tips for practice

- Babies and toddlers need a safe and comfortable place to sleep. This will be a cot for the babies.
- Babies and toddlers should all have their own personal bedding and place to sleep.
- If you work in a family, then you will notice that babies and young children can fall asleep anywhere they feel safe and comfortable: in the buggy, on your lap or in their car seat.
- Make sure that older babies or toddlers in a buggy do not get chilled if you are outside.
- If you bring them back indoors asleep in a buggy, then ease off any hats or outer garments. Otherwise they could get too warm and overheat in the home.

Activity

Those readers who have their own children will know from experience that full time care of a baby or toddler is very absorbing and tiring, especially since the care is round the clock. It is valuable for practitioners, who are not also parents, to have an insight into these demands.

One option is to interview several parents of very young children and ask them friendly questions about their experiences in the early months.

- You could ask about their own tiredness and how they managed night waking.
- What had they anticipated in life with a new baby and what was unexpected?
- Write up your findings.

Another option, offered by some colleges, is the 'virtual baby' or 'simulator doll'. Students have full 24 hour responsibility for the doll over a period of about a week. The doll looks and operates like a real baby in that it needs to be supported and is programmed to cry at regular intervals, on an easy, normal or cranky pattern. The locked electronics box in the baby's back provides a readout that shows how the baby has been treated over a period of time.

The advantage of the living doll is that early years practitioners can gain an insight, and it only lasts a week, into how tiring it can be to care full time for a young baby. Even if you never have full responsibility as a nanny, the experience will help you understand the stresses on parents, as a daytime nanny or a sympathetic early years practitioner.

Source: 'Cry babies' a feature about the simulator dolls used in Evesham and Hertford College, *Nursery World*, 21 June 2001.

Key skills links: C2/3.3

Safety in sleep

Some babies in the early months of life die in their sleep for no apparent reason. This loss is called **sudden infant death syndrome** (SIDS) and sometimes cot death. Babies who die unexpectedly are normally aged between 1–12 months and more usually between 3–6 months of age. There is often no explanation other than that the baby has stopped breathing, but nobody knows why.

Research in the 1990s established that babies are safest if put to sleep on their backs. Unexplained rises in infant death were linked with firm advice to parents in the 1980s that they should put their babies to sleep on their stomachs and that babies risked choking if laid on their backs. The change in direction is a timely reminder that childcare advice does change over time, in the light of new or more reliable information. The current advice is as follows:

- Put babies to sleep lying on their back and in a position with their feet towards the end of the cot.
- The problem is that young babies cannot move themselves if their mouth and nose is covered. Once they are agile enough to shift from the position in which you lay them, they will be able to move if their nose is temporarily into the mattress.

Key term

Sudden infant death syndrome (SIDS) the term that describes the unexpected death of a baby, that cannot be easily explained by specific illness or accident; also known as cot death

- Babies under 12 months old should lie on a suitable mattress with sheet and blanket bedding. They should not have a pillow, because a young baby can be smothered if she turns into the depth of the pillow.
- Breathing becomes more difficult in a smoky atmosphere and can be doubly hard if a baby or child has a cold. Nobody should be smoking around babies and children and this will be a clear-cut rule if you work in a nursery. If you work in a family home and are a smoker, it is undoubtedly good practice that you never smoke in the presence of the children.
- Babies can get too cold and should not be left to sleep outside for long periods. This habit is far less usual nowadays. Certainly a good rule of thumb is that neither babies nor children should be having a sleep outside, unless the weather is comfortable enough for you to sit out close by them as well.
- With the increase in central heating and very warm baby clothes, it has become clear that babies are at risk from being too hot, and not only from becoming chilled. Overheating appears to be a factor in the unexplained death of some babies.
- Young babies need to be warmly dressed until they get better at keeping themselves warm. However, by a couple of months of age, babies do not usually need more layers of clothing indoors than the adults who care for them.
- It is also advised that babies should not have duvets or sleep in baby nests. They need to be in a room without draughts but not hot: a suitable temperature is 18°C (65°F). The cot should not be placed next to direct sources of heat like a radiator.
- Babies taken out in the pram or buggy for a local trip need more clothing than walking adults but hats and extra layers need to be removed when you return to the warm indoor atmosphere, even if babies are sleeping.
- Babies should not usually sweat, nor feel hot to your touch, nor should they get heat rashes in cold weather. You can check whether they are comfortably warm by slipping your hand inside their clothes. Their stomach should feel warm but not hot.
- Sick babies can get hot and run a temperature. Feverish babies need less clothes and bedding, not more. (See page 184 about when babies are ill.)

Activity

- Use the information in this section and supplement it with material from the Foundation for the Study of Infant Deaths (FSID). You can contact them at Artillery House, 11–19 Artillery Row, London SW1P 1RT tel: 020 7222 8001 for general inquiries, the helpline is on 020 7233 2090 email: *fsid@sids.org.uk* and website: *www.sids.org.uk/fsid*
- Make a short presentation to colleagues about safe practices to reduce the possibility of cot death.

Key skills link: C3.2 C3.1b

Health and well being of babies and toddlers

Figure 6.9
Activity and interest are also important for the health of babies and toddlers

Health checks

Following the newborn checks (see page 152), parents are invited to take their baby for developmental checks at about six weeks, 8–9 months, 18 months, at about three and a half and before they start school. At each check the health visitor or doctor will ask about feeding and sleeping patterns and health.

- At six weeks they will check babies for alertness, ability to follow objects with the eye and ability to support their own head. They will listen to the baby's heart and check that the hip joint fits properly into the socket (a problem that can be corrected if identified early).
- At eight months the baby will be checked for physical abilities appropriate to her age and also that babies have been checked for hearing, as universal checks for hearing are planned for newborns (see page 154).
- Subsequent checks are to see whether the child is reaching the main developmental milestones and is in good health.

Parents are also welcome to bring their babies to the baby clinic sessions at their local health clinic on a regular basis for the baby to be weighed and for any questions to be answered. Parents, especially with first babies, can be reassured by this contact.

The growth of babies

Newborn babies lose weight, about 5–10 per cent of their birth weight in the first few days of life. They then regain the weight and continue to grow. Babies usually put on weight at about 150–200 grams a week (5–6 ounces) but the pattern is variable.

In the first year babies' growth is measured by their weight. Babies are measured for length as well but this is not a very easy task, as babies tend to curl up rather than straighten out. At the health clinic the health visitor or doctor compare the baby's weight against average growth charts and check the baby against the *centile growth curve*. The baby's continued growth is then plotted to monitor whether this individual seems to be putting on about enough weight, not enough or too much.

Some babies will need special attention but most are fine. For example, if the baby was on the second centile, it means that of 100 babies of this age, 98 would be larger than this baby and 2 would be smaller. So this is a light baby, compared with the average and there is not necessarily a problem so long as she continues to put on weight and is healthy. See page 245 for more on growth and the ways in which children's bodies change.

Care in the heat

It is important to keep babies warm enough in the winter but equally important for their well being to protect them in hot weather and against strong sunshine.

- Babies should not be allowed to lie out or play in direct hot sunshine.
- Their skin is especially vulnerable and this care, as with older children, should be taken whatever the child's skin colour and tone.
- In summer hot spells you can keep babies in the shade. You can go out, but keep out of the direct sunlight.

- Mobile toddlers need sunhats and suncream and you should talk with their parents about both these practical steps (See page 58).
- Make sure everyone has enough to drink, with drinks that are cool but not cold, throughout a hot day.

When babies are ill

Babies are in some ways tough little beings and they are designed to cry if they do not feel fine. However, they cannot tell you what is wrong and they can become ill very quickly. In this section you will find useful information, but you will need to be ready to continue to learn: in general and from what parents tell you about their own baby or toddler.

Fevers

Babies can overheat and run a high temperature. You need to know how to take a baby's temperature under their armpit. If this proves difficult, you could use a fever scan strip. This method gives a less accurate reading in terms of degrees, but will show if the baby is running a high temperature.

If babies have a fever, they need to be kept cool and not wrapped up. You also need to be aware of signs of possible dehydration as this is dangerous for babies. The signs include:

- a sunken fontanelle, the soft spot on top of a baby's head
- reduced urine output from what is normal for this baby
- a dry mouth or tongue, increased thirst
- sunken eyes
- failure of the skin to go back quickly when pinched (skin elasticity).

These may all be signs that a baby is dehydrated and needs fluids. Some of these signs would also apply to toddlers and young children.

Judging if a baby is ill

You make a judgement about illness in babies from your knowledge of this individual as well as your general knowledge about babies:

- You get to know a baby – is her cry different, does she seem less interested in her surroundings than usual?
- Is she less alert, more floppy or sleepy?
- What does the baby's skin usually look like? Does a light skinned baby look very drained of colour?
- You even get to know how an individual baby smells when she is well. Sick babies often smell different – not unpleasant, just unwell.

There are some symptoms that should raise your concerns for any baby or toddler:

- If babies have taken much less fluid than they usually do – they could be getting dehydrated, and this is dangerous for babies. Likewise it would be concerning if babies had passed much less urine that is usual for them.
- Healthy babies bring some of their feed back up quite often. Vomiting up noticeable amounts over more than one feed could be a cause for concern.
- Green vomit is a cause for concern (unless you know the baby has just eaten vegetables that are green). Otherwise, green vomit will be bile from below the stomach and is a possible sign of an obstruction in the intestine.

- Large amounts of blood in a baby's nappy, not small flecks, could be the result of a blockage or damage to the bowel.
- Healthy babies breathe easily. A bit of wheezing or snuffling may be down to a cold but should still be watched. Babies who are having serious difficulty in breathing, pull in their lower chest and upper stomach with each breath, so that there is a significant dip. This is called 'indrawing' and is a cause for concern. (It occurs in well babies when they have the hiccups or cry very hard.)
- Healthy babies' fingernails are usually pink, they should not go blue in tone.
- A higher temperature than 38.3°C (100.8°F) is higher than normal and a cause for concern.

Under most of these individual circumstances, you might let a parent know the situation when she or he comes home if you are a nanny or picks the baby up from nursery. Parents will decide what to do next, but in partnership with parents, it would be appropriate for you to offer advice or to say that the baby is too unwell to come back to nursery for the next day or so. When more than one circumstance is present or the symptoms are severe, then you need to consult swiftly with your senior and probably contact the parent. The system called Baby Check is a straightforward way of assessing the severity of a illness in babies younger than six months (see the resources box for details).

Conditions that require immediate medical help include if the baby:

- stops breathing, goes blue or has a fit
- cannot be woken
- is unresponsive and not aware of what is going on
- has glazed eyes and is not focusing on anything
- has been badly or seriously injured.

You need to get immediate help under these circumstances. Call the doctor, or an ambulance if you cannot get through (and say it is a baby who is ill) or take the baby to hospital. Do not wait to call the parent before you take action. Call emergency action, then call the parents and explain the situation.

Useful resources

If you are seriously concerned about a baby in your care you would usually contact the parents or the family doctor if you are a nanny. These other resources can be useful if you want more information or guidance.

- NHS Direct is a national helpline for anyone with concerns about health. Tel: 0845 4647 website: *www.nhsdirect.nhs.uk*
- I also recommend that you send for a copy of *Baby Check: Is your baby really ill?* This valuable booklet gives guidance for assessing the degree of illness in a baby of up to six months of age. Contact Baby Check at PO Box 324, Wroxham, Norwich NR12 8EQ or telephone on 01603 784400.

Immunisations

The UK has a comprehensive, free system of immunisations for babies and children as part of the health programme to prevent serious and life threatening illnesses. The aim of an immunisation programme is that the vast majority of babies or children in the target group do receive their full set of immunisations. This result then ensures that the disease remains under control.

The recommended pattern of immunisations is:

- Between 2–4 months of age, babies are immunised against polio, diptheria, tetanus, meningitis C and the type of meningitis called Hib (Haemophilus influenza type b).
- Most babies should also be immunised against whooping cough. Parents used to be advised against this immunisation if there was a family history of epilepsy. GPs will now tend to recommend the immunisation so long as a child's epilepsy is under control.
- At the age of 12–15 months, children are given the measles, mumps and rubella (MMR) vaccine.
- At 3–5 years children are given a booster immunisation of diphtheria, tetanus and polio and the second dose of MMR.
- The last immunisations are usually given in the early teenage years: BCG (against tuberculosis) and a booster against tetanus and polio. The BCG programme in schools was suspended in 2000, although the reappearance of tuberculosis may led to a rethink (see page 136).

Reactions to immunisations

It is not unusual for babies to have a slightly raised temperature after immunisations. You would usually give a child paracetemol to keep down the temperature. This preventative step can avoid the situation where some babies and children suffer a febrile convulsion brought on by a suddenly rising temperature.

There has been concern about an increased risk of autism following the MMR vaccine, because of the use of mercury in the vaccine. This link looks unlikely but parents are not necessarily reassured by government pronouncements, given the range of health scares in the last couple of decades. It is the parents' choice whether to accept immunisations for their babies and later for their children. Parents cannot be forced into having their babies immunised (it is not compulsory in the UK) and all parents have a right to reliable information about any health prevention programme.

Tips for practice

- You can gather useful leaflets for information about immunisation and the seriousness of the diseases against which babies and children are immunised. Measles, for example, for all its reputation as a 'childhood illness' is very unpleasant and complications include serious damage to vision and a brain disease called SSPE.
- Nurseries can offer information sessions to which you invite parents to hear a health visitor or GP.
- As a nanny you can share information and listen to parents if they wish to weigh up their decision.
- But do not give reassurance that immunisations are completely safe when you cannot be 100 per cent certain. Parents have to make this decision.

Emily her ability to have such a thing within her reach, even if it was Harmony Cottage she was considering.

She was just about to ask Emily about her job when Dylan appeared around the corner.

"Mam? Can I go over to Tim's for a while?"

"It's a bit late, Dylan. You'll see him at school tomorrow anyway."

Sandra wasn't sure where her son's burgeoning friendship with Tim Kelleher was going, in light of the vast differences in their financial status. Jennie and Vincent Kelleher lived in Rathmollin Woods, the village's most desirable residential location, unfortunately too close to Dylan's grandparents' house for Sandra's liking. It wasn't that she had anything against Tim – he was great – but the fact that he had everything she couldn't afford for Dylan bothered her enough to wish he hadn't picked him for a best friend.

"I'll only go for a few minutes." He was pleading now, mad to get over to his friend's PlayStation for an hour before bedtime.

"He'll be getting ready for bed by now. We'll be going home soon anyway. Go on in and get your things together while I'm talking to Emily." Sandra glanced at Emily and winked as Dylan skulked off in the direction of the house, disappointed that his great idea was out of the question.

"He's a lovely little fellow," Emily commented and Sandra had to admit with a smile that she was right.

"He's great, to be honest. Even when he was a baby he was easy to manage." Again, she had the feeling that she was so much older than Emily, who looked much the same as she had as a teenager. She was as slim as ever while Sandra was still threatening to lose her "baby weight" eight years on.

"I'd better keep going and let you get back inside," said Emily. "You never know – your mam and dad might have a neighbour yet!"

"They'd be delighted if it was you, you know. There was talk of a housing development going up in the field behind them and the cottage being knocked to make an entrance. The last thing they need is a load of houses overlooking the back garden."

"That'd be desperate all right. Hopefully this whole property boom thing will slow down a bit soon or I'll never be able to afford anything."

After Emily left, something like dismay set in for Sandra at the thought of the property boom. It all seemed so far removed from her own life – a million miles if the truth be told. It occurred to her that even with a degree in Social Work under her belt and a good job, Emily was talking about house prices being prohibitive. In that case, she wondered, where did that leave *her* in the grand scheme of things?

It was just as well that Sandra had decided against letting Dylan call over to Rathmollin Woods to play with Tim Kelleher. By the time Emily had satisfied herself that Harmony Cottage was a true reproduction of the picturesque image on the property page and Sandra had gathered up as many of Dylan's toys as possible from her parents' sitting-room, Jennie Kelleher was on her way to the A&E Department with Tim and his younger sister bundled into the back of the car.

It was typical, Jennie fretted as she waited impatiently for the painfully slow parting of the electronic gates, that Vincent would be out of the country for this latest episode in their children's lives. And it was unfortunate that Lucy should come out in an inexplicable rash on a Sunday evening when both her father *and* the baby-sitter were out of bounds. Tim, therefore, had to be brought along for the expedition to the A&E.

There had been no sign of the rash that morning when Jennie was helping Lucy get dressed. It was only when she'd hopped the pair of them into the bath after supper that she'd noticed the rash covering her daughter's tummy and chest.

"Are you itchy, love?" Her voice was casual but she could hardly believe that Lucy hadn't been unwell at all during the day with such a profusion of spots covering her torso. She had complained about being too hot when she and Tim were trying to see who could bounce the highest on the trampoline but Jennie had merely whipped off the five-year old's light cotton cardigan and thought no more about it.

"No. They're funny," Lucy giggled, examining the rash now that her mother had drawn attention to it.

Tim too studied the small clusters of spots. "Pocahontas died of measles!" He was ecstatic at the thought of his sister having the same disease as the exotic heroine. "Maybe they're measles!"

Lucy's face fell at the idea of a possible untimely death

and her lip started to wobble. "Mum! Is it true?" she asked tearfully.

Her older brother looked on with some satisfaction, the prospect of their bedtime being delayed by an interesting diversion uppermost in his mind. At eight, he was allowed to stay up a full half hour later than his sister but any small extension would be a bonus.

Jennie had to diffuse the drama. "No, no, no," she said. "Anyway, it can't be measles – you both got an injection against measles when you were small."

Lucy looked relieved, Tim disappointed. Jennie lifted her daughter out of the bath and began to dry her efficiently, checking surreptitiously under her arms and in the creases of her legs for any more spots, as the meningitis leaflets often advised. Or maybe it wasn't the meningitis leaflets that said it.

Light was the thing – children couldn't tolerate bright light if they had meningitis. How bright was bright, she wondered as the children continued to chatter away about Lucy's fascinating spots. If only Vincent was here to talk it out with.

Without letting the fear that was in her chest come out in her voice, Jennie lifted Lucy onto her hip and carried her to the walk-in closet in the spare room, leaving Tim to dry himself. It was the only place in the house that didn't have a window. Before her daughter could start complaining about not being allowed to dry herself, Jennie flicked on the fluorescent light in the poky little room, flooding it with brightness and praying that Lucy wouldn't react.

"I'm not sleeping in here," Lucy whined, wriggling to

get out of Jennie's arms. "All my things are in my own room!" She ran off naked towards the small pink room at the front of the house lest there be any question of her missing out on her books before bedtime.

At least she doesn't have photophobia. The ominous-sounding word came back to her now that some slight relief had set in.

Jennie remained in the pale blue and beige guest room for a few minutes, her mind frantic as she tried to plot her next move. The pair of them, for once, were in their pyjamas before she had to threaten a withdrawal of all toys and DVDs. For Lucy's sake she needed to act normally but she still wasn't satisfied about the rash.

"Okay – downstairs now and you can watch *Toy Story* for a while."

"Two! Two! I want *Toy Story 2!*" Lucy was yelling her head off in her anxiety to get her demand in ahead of Tim's.

They had a rule that whoever said something first got the choice. Tim, defeated on account of not being quick enough with the shouting, resigned himself to foregoing the original film and followed his sister. *Toy Story* was a bit babyish for him but Tim was a diplomat and knew he'd be able to get a bit of *Spiderman* in as soon as Lucy was packed off to bed.

Their mother, meantime, collected the sodden towels from the bathroom floor in a bid to allow herself thinking space.

There was a test with a glass that she'd read about in the GP's surgery a few times but she couldn't remember what exactly was supposed to happen when you pressed the glass against the skin. Was it more dangerous if the spots disappeared or if they *didn't* disappear? She couldn't remember and vowed now to watch the meningitis adverts on television from here on in if Lucy was spared the terrible disease.

It was pointless phoning Vincent in Dubai for advice. For one, he probably wouldn't know any more than she did about meningitis. And whether he did or he didn't, it would be horrendous to alert him to the fact that one of the children was sick when he was so far away and unable to actually do anything.

Jennie's mother or her older sister Molly were the only other people she could ask, but she couldn't bear the thought of them criticising her afterwards if it was a false alarm. Vincent's mother Elsie, efficient as ever, would probably have a definitive answer, but Jennie hadn't actually rung her even once in all the years she'd been married to her son and she wasn't about to start now. Even Maxine, her best friend, was away tonight at some sort of gardening thing with her husband. Jennie was on her own and she'd just have to deal with it herself.

The children had settled themselves in front of the television by the time she'd selected a plain water glass with a flat base from the kitchen cabinet.

"Show me the rash again and I'll do a trick!" Maybe the correct procedure would come back to her if she placed the glass on the skin.

Lucy, delighted with all the attention, pulled up her pyjama top and stretched straight out on the couch, as self-important as if she were being examined at a high-profile medical conference.

"Can I do the trick as well?" Poor Tim was feeling left out.

"Course you can, love. We'll see if it's different on boys than on girls."

Lucy let out a yelp as soon as the bottom of the glass was planted on her bare tummy and Jennie's heart froze. She almost got weak with relief when the children started to giggle with Lucy shrieking her head off, "That's freezing!"

Her tummy was wobbling now with all the laughing and Jennie was finding it difficult to tell if the spots were disappearing or not.

"Stay still, Lucy, or I won't be able to see it."

Lucy immediately stiffened out like a board, causing Jennie to look up in alarm.

"Can you see now?" Lucy asked obligingly, holding her tummy as rigid as she could. Jennie had thought she was about to get some sort of seizure and tried to calm herself enough to look at the glass. The skin of Lucy's abdomen was pale where the glass pressed into it but the small spots were still faintly visible. Defeated, Jennie removed it, still as wise as ever regarding the seriousness of the rash.

"Next we'll have to take your temperature," she announced officiously, the way she did when they played "Doctors" and the children were the unfortunate patients.

"You never checked *my* tummy!"

Tim's plaintive whine made Jennie smile to herself – despite being three years older than Lucy, he seemed younger in many ways than the sassy Lucy.

Less meticulous this time, she did the glass test on Tim

and sped off to the kitchen for the ear thermometer while Lucy made room for Tim on the sofa and they got themselves ready for their examination.

She did Tim's first this time, hoping to get some sort of baseline to compare Lucy's to.

"Very normal, 37 degrees. Next, please."

Lucy tilted her head this time, anxious to see if her temperature was as normal as her brother's, notwithstanding her spotty tummy. To her mother's relief, the thermometer again rested at 37 degrees.

For the millionth time, she wished that Vincent was at home. He might not know what to do next either but at least they could decide together. The Nurseline that the health insurance company provided was the only other option open to her. Leaving the children to continue watching *Toy Story*, she made her way to the kitchen so that they wouldn't hear her making the phone call. All the literature that she'd ever read said to look at the child and see if they were off form or listless, neither of which Lucy was. Yet she couldn't ignore such a rash, even if the temperature was normal. And she still didn't know the significance of the glass thing.

The voice at the other end of the phone was calm and reassuring but as soon as she mentioned that the rash hadn't disappeared when pressed under a glass, her worst fears were confirmed.

"You really need to take Lucy to your GP or to the nearest A&E."

"But could it be meningitis?" Jennie had phoned so that she could hear out loud that she was worrying unnecessarily

– instead she was being told that her child needed to see a doctor immediately.

"It's a possibility, along with normal childhood illnesses or even a simple viral infection. She needs to be examined by a doctor to rule it out."

"Thank you, I'll get her seen straight away." Shocked, she sat for a moment on one of the kitchen chairs, trying to decide what was best to do. If Lucy really did have meningitis, then the time lost waiting for the GP could be crucial, particularly if he was out on a call miles away.

The A&E would be better, especially if there was any sudden deterioration in her condition. She'd seen parents on television telling their story and recounting how their child was a lively infant one minute but hooked up to tubes and wires in the ICU the next. She couldn't let that happen to Lucy.

A new sense of urgency came over her suddenly and she headed straight for the playroom, car keys in hand, her mind already plotting the route to St Angela's. She'd already lost precious minutes with all her checking for signs and symptoms.

"Come on, you two. We're going on an adventure to get rid of Lucy's spots."

The question came as one voice, incredulous. "In our pyjamas?"

"Yes, in your pyjamas."

Jack hammered away at the bottom of an old fish-pond that had been closed off even as far back as his own schooldays, oblivious to the fact that it was practically dark. He'd switched on the light at the gable of the school so that he could finish the job that he'd started three hours ago but the beam was poor and he was working almost on instinct at this stage.

The base of the old pond had been filled with concrete, a far cry from the PVC pond liners available today and he repeatedly cursed the original craftsman's primitive efforts.

Despite the fact that any normal person had more to be doing on a Sunday evening than hacking out a ton of concrete, he ignored the painful ache that was starting in his shoulder muscles and kept going. If he didn't, then the load of topsoil that he needed to have removed from the Sycamore Drive site further up the street would have to go elsewhere, meaning that the reality of the school having its own herb garden would be yet another unfulfilled dream for the Parents' Council.

The only available site for the educational garden was the spot he was now working on, a spot that was mercifully almost clear now of the solid layer of concrete that had covered it a few hours ago. He straightened to admire his handiwork – although it was now almost too dark to appreciate it. The evening air was still fresh and crisp and he felt the coolness of it kick in as he stood there.

Moving the discarded shards of uprooted concrete was going to be another job but that could be tackled later in the week when the long-suffering parents had levelled out the topsoil to their liking. Jack had decided that he'd just barrow it to one side to make room for the excavator that would land the topsoil in the designated area

Minutes later, having collected his tools and switched

off the outside light, he was done. The village was quiet as he walked the short distance to the solid two-storey house that he'd inherited from his parents. He was fantasising about a hot shower even before he opened the door. His personal rule about working on the weekends was rarely broken but, on this occasion, he'd actually got satisfaction out of the strenuous physical labour.

It was a long time since he'd felt the need to burn off excess energy like that but all that day the events of the previous evening had glowed in his brain with an annoyance that he could never have imagined Heather igniting in him.

It wasn't the loss of her that bothered him, as much as the manner of it. Even almost twenty-four hours later, it still surprised him just how little he'd actually known her. As far as he'd been concerned, after six months their relationship had passed the early stage of merely getting to know someone, although it was still nowhere near the stage of talking about the future or how they really felt about each other.

It was Heather who'd suggested they stay in on Saturday night instead of going out for a meal in town the way they usually did. It had suited Jack at the time, considering it was the first Saturday he'd worked past lunch-time in years. He'd decided to cook dinner for them, knowing that Heather would be staying over as she had on most of their recent Saturday nights, her smart navy Saab parked discreetly near the back door to avoid the gossip that the inhabitants of most small villages seemed to thrive on.

"I have a reputation to protect," she was fond of saying and Jack had appreciated that this was indeed true. The classic green and gold frontage of the Sutherland & Lucas office was very much an institution of Rathmollin's main street and the personal life of one of its senior solicitors would be considered juicy gossip, especially in terms of where she'd spent the night and with whom. On the other hand, it was probably well known that he and Heather were in a relationship but as far as Heather was concerned, discretion had to be observed at all costs.

And as she was always so keen to point out, with Aggie Lenihan prowling around the village first thing every Sunday morning, there was nothing that didn't get logged on the gossip register. Now, after what had happened the previous evening, Jack was beginning to wonder about the real reason that she'd insisted on theirs being such a discreet liaison.

While he liked to cook, Jack was a man with a limited repertoire and had expected to see Heather roll her eyes in amusement at the two steaks sitting beside the grill pan awaiting her arrival. Gratin potatoes were already bubbling in the oven and his usual accompaniment of steamed vegetables, onions and mushrooms were just reaching culmination in various pots and pans around the hob.

In place of amusement, he immediately saw the reserve in her eyes and sensed that their evening wasn't about to go as he'd planned it. Food, he reasoned, wasn't a priority, but it was certainly a distraction so he went on with preparing the meal, somehow doubtful as to whether it would be eaten at all.

He was right, as it transpired. Heather had started to talk almost straight away, as if she needed to get it out as quickly as possible.

Gerard, she told him, was someone that she'd been very close to in college and for a few years afterwards. He'd moved to London, ostensibly to gain experience in family law in the context of the new divorce legislation in Ireland, but more so to spread his wings and put some space in what he'd described at the time as a "prematurely mature" relationship with Heather.

The relationship had fizzled out but now it seemed that Gerard was back and conveniently installed in Sutherland & Lucas in an office adjoining her own. The last few weeks had been cathartic for them, she told Jack, and there was a chance that they could restore their former bond. It occurred to Jack that things with Gerard hadn't been so life-shattering that she hadn't been able to share Jack's bed and make love to him in the intervening weeks, but he imagined it would have been less than gentlemanly to say this out loud to her over the kitchen table. Instead, he just sat and listened while she tried to make him understand that it was all for the best anyway.

"And it's not as if *we* were going anywhere anyway, is it?"

"Sorry?" Jack wasn't sure what she meant but wasn't about to make the deception of the past few weeks easier for her, if that was what she wanted.

Reddening just a little, she spread her hands expansively in an attempt to explain. "Well, you know what I mean, Jack. It was never going to work out really. I mean, we're so different – our lifestyles and everything . . ."

Here she trailed off, leaving Jack in no doubt as to

what she meant. She'd obviously considered him to be some kind of "bit of rough".

"I see," he'd said evenly. Why prove her right and act like the boor that she seemed to have him down for? "Heathcliff Syndrome." He hated sounding so cynical but the reality was that, despite his wealth, Heather wanted someone more educated with a fine-tuned accent to settle down with.

She'd blushed at that – to know she'd treated him appallingly was one thing but to know that he was wise to it was another. *And* the fact that he'd made her aware that he might not be as well educated as Gerard but that he wasn't exactly as thick as a plank either.

"I'm not saying . . ."

She was blustering all of a sudden and Jack had actually felt sorry for her. It was a solicitor or someone she considered to be of equal status that Heather wanted, he realised. Not necessarily Gerard, who had already treated her dreadfully by her own account, but definitely not Jack. Notwithstanding his wealth being significant by anyone's standards, the fact that he was a mere builder was obviously not on. He wondered, with a slight tinge of bitter amusement, if perhaps he should start describing himself as a property developer.

He'd felt a little sorry for her then. "I know what you're saying. Really I do, Heather. I wish you and Gerard the best of luck." There was no point in expending his energy on a relationship that had no chance of survival.

She'd left shortly afterwards and Jack had spent the night tossing and turning, alternating between indignation at his now-ex-girlfriend's elitist attitude and curiosity as to why she had wasted her time in a relationship that she had no value on and a man she clearly had no respect for.

Now, almost twenty-four hours and a session of hard labour later, he was feeling more resigned to the situation. He was only twenty-eight, he consoled himself. There was plenty of time to meet someone who would actually accept him for who he was.

Chapter 2

It was half ten on Monday morning and Jennie had just put the finishing touches to her make-up. In spite of her sleepless night, she had to admit that she didn't look too bad – thanks to the smear of Touché Éclat that she'd swept under her eyes.

Their family outing to the A&E the previous evening had turned out to be the antithesis of the experiences that people outlined angrily on the daytime radio shows. Lucy had been assessed straight away and a battery of tests performed, all of them ruling out anything more serious than a mild viral infection. Jennie had almost cried with relief when the all-clear was given but poor Lucy had been wholly disappointed, having set herself up for having an appendix out at the very least.

By midnight, the children had been tucked up in bed with Lucy insisting on being woken for school the next day. The very least she could do was show off her rash. And they had the school concert to look forward to. Jennie said nothing but wondered if it would be wiser to keep Lucy at home.

The relief of the doctor in A&E telling her that her daughter did not have meningitis wore off as soon as the poor little mite was soundly asleep. Straight away, Jennie started to wonder whether he was right or not. What if the symptoms hadn't developed properly yet? What if Lucy got worse during the night and didn't wake up enough to call out for her?

In the end, she'd rooted out the Baby-Talk that she'd had when they were babies and set it up in Lucy's room. Even at that, she'd spent the night half-awake, terrified that she'd miss something.

By morning, however, Lucy's rash had all but faded – to Lucy's disappointment and Jennie's immense relief – and so Lucy had gone to school.

At least Vincent would be home for tonight and she was already relishing the fact that she could relax, knowing that he'd be there if Lucy's rash returned.

She stood back in front of the mirror now to take in her outfit. The dark blue Armani jeans with their slightly flared legs fitted her to perfection and the pale-pink shirt looked fresh and crisp against her honey-blonde hair.

Feeling decidedly optimistic about the afternoon ahead, she plucked her slim Raymond Weil watch from her jewellery box and settled on a pair of cultured pearl earrings and a matching necklace to complete her look.

She knew that it gave Vincent a certain proprietary pride to see her looking cool and elegant in the arrivals hall and Jennie had to admit that she did get a heady sense of satisfaction from it every time. Even during her pregnancies, she'd managed to look good, despite the crippling pelvic pain and swollen ankles that had plagued her each time.

The phone was ringing downstairs as she sprayed herself liberally with Burberry Weekend, a scent that she didn't particularly like but felt that she ought to wear seeing as it had been one of Vincent's gifts from the last trip. Ignoring the phone, she checked her handbag to see if she had her purse and a lipstick, but immediately she opened it her mobile started chiming with the Laughing Baby ring tone that Tim had insisted was the latest in cool.

Jennie's heart sank when she saw the foreign-looking number displayed. He hadn't even left Dubai and here *she* was ready to leave for the airport.

"Vincent?" she said cautiously by way of a greeting, trying to sound somewhere between disbelief that he was not actually on a plane and concern in case there was a very genuine reason for his not being on a flight that would land in Cork airport in forty-five minutes.

"Hiya, babe. All okay there?"

"Grand. Just leaving the house now actually," Jennie answered coolly, hurt oozing through her like molten lava at the impending let-down.

"That's the thing, Jen, I won't be able to make it home today. The whole thing went into freefall yesterday evening because John Williams started picking and poking at the contract. We were sure it was a done deal but now it looks like we'll have to stay on until tomorrow at least."

When she'd phoned him the previous night after the

expedition to the hospital, he'd been in the middle of a late dinner, finalising a contract with their foreign associates.

"What about the kids? They're expecting you at the concert."

"You'll have to tell them I got held up – they'll understand. I'll bring them something nice."

"It's just a pity that you didn't tell them yesterday. They'll be expecting to see you in the audience."

"I didn't know yesterday, Jen."

As far as Tim and Lucy were concerned, both of their parents would be there to cheer them on – now it would be up to Jennie to turn up alone and explain to them once again that Dad's flight had been delayed. The thought of them shooting the messenger as usual made her blood boil.

"So it's up to me to explain your absence and fill in the gaps?"

"Ah, for God's sake Jennie, I haven't time to think about school concerts out here!" Vincent snapped back, clearly exasperated at having to get into a confrontation. "What's it for anyway?"

"The Chernobyl Children's Project. They're hoping to raise €500 tonight."

"Can't you give a donation or something? Look, I'll be home tomorrow and we can make out a cheque together and they can post it off to Bono. That'll give them a kick."

"Bono? Why would they post it to Bono?" Jennie was livid now at his thoughtlessness and she wasn't letting him get away with it the way she usually did for a quiet life.

"He's tied up with all that crack, isn't he? Look, I have

to go – I'll give a bell later to let you know how it goes, okay?"

Annoyed that her husband didn't know that it was Bono's *wife* who was involved in the Chernobyl Project and that he didn't care less anyway, Jennie muttered a resentful "Fine" and hung up. She didn't care one way or another how his latest land deal went and couldn't imagine that she'd be in the humour to talk to him after putting up with two disappointed children for the evening.

Jennie knew exactly how the evening would play out. She, as usual, would turn up as planned at the after-school concert and clap her heart out. She'd bring the queen cakes and Rice Krispie buns that she'd made this morning as soon as she'd dropped the kids off at the school gates. She'd pour endless cups of tea with the other mothers, all the while waiting until either Tim or Lucy got the opportunity to tackle her about their father's absence.

"But you *said* he'd come," Tim would whine plaintively.

"You *told* us," Lucy would state in the accusatory way that was becoming all too familiar of late.

As always, it would be Jennie's fault for promising.

Catching sight of herself in the long mirror, she marvelled that she still looked the same as she had before Vincent's phone call. She still looked elegant – a glamorous yummy mummy in her designer gear and cultured pearls. Pearls, she realised now, that he'd brought her back after last year's failed anniversary weekend. That had been all about a problem in Dubai too, if she remembered rightly.

Practically everything I own is as a result of a let-down by Vincent, she thought bitterly, grabbing her Prada bag off the bed and hammering it savagely against the duvet a few times in rage.

The offending bag was one that she'd splashed out on in defiance a few months previously when Vincent had phoned one Friday evening to tell her that he was staying in Cork with his business partner, Bob Ferris, after a particularly arduous meeting about some parcel of land in Bahrain that they were trying to acquire. They'd had a few drinks after the clients had left and he wasn't happy to drive home. Jennie had lain awake for most of the night, teetering between anger at him not caring whether he saw the children before they went to bed and a much darker feeling of terror at the thought that he might not be tucked up in the Ferrises' opulent guest room in Montenotte at all. She'd woken up the following morning with bags under her eyes and packed the kids off to a birthday party they'd been invited to. At a loose end, with no sign of Vincent returning, she'd hit Brown Thomas like a hurricane, determined to be compensated for the hour's worth of "Where's Dad?" and "Why wasn't he home last night?" that she'd had to endure over breakfast.

Smoothing out the bed cover after her manic handbag attack, Jennie wondered what exactly she would do with her morning now that her trip to the airport and the cosy lunch that she'd booked at Jacobs on the Mall was cancelled.

Maxine, she knew, would be packing for her week away in Kerry. Her five-year-old daughter, Sasha, was Lucy's best friend and the two women had become close since first meeting at the school gates. Now that both families lived in Rathmollin Woods, they saw more of each other than ever, with Lucy and Sasha demanding "playdates" almost every weekend.

It would have been lovely to phone Maxine and go out somewhere for a coffee but it would have meant explaining the aborted airport trip and Vincent's non-attendance at the concert. Besides, Maxine was determined to be packed and ready so that they could leave for their holiday home in Kerry as soon as the concert was over. Needless to say, her husband Seán would be cheering Sasha from the front row, his weather-beaten face alight with excitement.

Now that she was dressed and ready, Jennie knew her only option was to go into Cork and have a look around the shops. She could always pack the cakes for the concert into the boot in case she got waylaid and didn't get home in time to collect them for half three.

By half past two, Jennie was whacked. One thing had led to another and, apart from half an hour sipping a vanilla-flavoured latte in Gloria Jean's on Patrick Street, she hadn't drawn breath.

It had started with a navy silk wrap dress in BT's, something that she knew would serve her well for evenings when they had Vincent's business associates over for dinner. The fact that it was €600 was immaterial considering that, on those same evenings, she had to cook *and* look elegant because Vincent thought it was pretentious-looking to get caterers in if it was for only five or six people.

It really riled Jennie that while Vincent seemed to

think that they were running an effortlessly elegant home, it was she who'd be slaving away in the kitchen trying to produce an exquisitely presented and delicious meal. Meanwhile, *he* would be holding court in the sitting-room offering all sorts of aperitifs that they mightn't even have the ingredients for.

Thinking on it had made her realise that the dress was a small price to pay for the stress she endured with the dinner parties. Dainty, round-toed navy shoes had followed at a cost of €250, the heels high enough to be glamorous but not so high that she'd trip and land a bowl of chilled gazpacho in Bob Ferris's fat lap.

Passing through the new Quin and Donnelly collection on her way to the service desk, she'd spotted a tweed trouser suit in a heathery hue that would be great for lunches out in the autumn. She immediately diverted into one of the spacious dressing-rooms to try it on, although she was fairly sure that the size 10 would be perfect.

I deserve this, she thought later as she closed her eyes and let the Yves Saint Laurent girl demonstrate the new season's colours, after being dropped like a lead balloon by my husband with barely an hour's notice. The thought of explaining it to the kids enraged her enough to add almost everything that the make-up assistant recommended to her existing purchases, despite the fact that she already had a shed-load of cosmetics in the drawers of the dressing-table at home, most of them unopened.

So bloody what, she thought defiantly as she gathered her bags together and made her way through the revolving door of the department store and out onto

Patrick Street. The thought of Vincent silently raising his eyebrows at her credit-card receipts during his monthly trawl of their household bills enraged her now. It was true that she was useless with money and that she was happy to leave it all to him to sort out but, at times like this when a small spree went well above the €1000 mark, she wished it were she who did the accounts. It's *my* money too, she reasoned, mentally adding up the hours of child-minding duties she carried out in Vincent's absence. I'm the one who'll take Tim and Lucy home after the concert today, give them their tea and put them to bed. And the one who'll be watching late-night television alone while my husband is up to God knows what in Dubai. A finger of fear crept through her as this last thought played its way into her consciousness. What would Vincent be doing once the day's business was concluded?

The fresh April air hit her as she stepped out into Patrick Street and turned in the direction of the car park. Jennie shook herself mentally, pushing away the thoughts before she had time to consider the possibilities.

Chapter 3

Emily swung her legs off the bed as soon as she heard the "ding" of the microwave coming from the kitchen. Her mother considered the microwave to be the greatest modern convenience on earth when she'd discovered that she could warm the plates in it instead of having to rinse them in boiling water the way she'd always done before the new invention had come into the house. Any minute now, she'd be calling out to Emily and Tom to say that the tea was ready.

Emily looked around the bedroom that she'd grown up in and wondered what it would be like to decorate a bedroom from scratch – a bedroom of her own this time, she thought with a pang. The brochure that she'd collected earlier at the auctioneer's office was still in her hand and she now took one more look at it – as if she didn't know it off by heart already.

She'd spotted the advertisement for Harmony Cottage in the property section of *The Examiner* on Saturday and had been attracted to it immediately. It looked different in the brochure than it did in reality, making her aware that she'd barely looked twice at it in all the years that she'd lived in Rathmollin. The fact that it might well be within her price range made it even more attractive, considering that she'd practically walked the soles off her shoes going around to new developments looking at apartments and townhouses that she couldn't afford in a million years.

"Emily – tea's ready!" her mother called out.

The waft of sausages had already wended its way down the hall and Emily realised that she was ravenous. She'd skipped her lunch earlier so that she could call in to The Property People office to collect the brochure for Harmony Cottage.

"This is a great set-up," her father teased as soon as she arrived into the kitchen.

Her mother, making a pot of tea at the range, sighed and rolled her eyes at Emily, knowing full well what her husband was on about.

"What is, Dad?" Emily decided to humour him, although she too knew that he was making a point about the sausages.

"Three years it is since a sausage was allowed inside the door of this house and now we're having them morning, noon and night. Look, I even got a rasher!"

"It'll be another bypass operation you'll be getting if you're not careful," Jacinta cautioned, a small smile playing at the corners of her lips.

"Everything in moderation," Tom said, winking at Emily, still delighted that she was back at home.

"Enjoy it while you can, Dad. As soon as the novelty

of me being back wears off it'll be back to the brown bread again."

Since the evening that her husband had developed a severe pain in his chest three years previously, Jacinta had been adamant about the whole family adhering to a low-fat diet. Tom's subsequent triple bypass had effectively put paid to him ever eating a fried tea again until Emily had opted to leave Dublin behind and move home to Rathmollin a few months ago. Now, knowing it was her daughter's favourite, Jacinta seemed to be allowing a cautious weekly treat again.

"What kind of a day did you have at work, love?"

Jacinta was always interested in the goings-on that her daughter encountered in the course of her working day, although she could never understand how people got themselves into debt in the first place. In her day, she was fond of telling Emily, they didn't buy anything that they couldn't afford and indeed there was no such thing as all the credit cards that were available nowadays. She and Tom had simply done without until they put the money together to buy things.

"The usual," Emily told her, tucking into the delicious meal before her. "First Communion is coming up so people have loans out that they can't repay. It's desperate the amount people need for Communion and Confirmation now."

Emily's job with the Voluntary Budgeting Agency had been an eye-opener in the few months that she'd been there. Although the agency itself was a voluntary one, all of the facilitators worked closely with statutory bodies such as the council to help resolve the debt that their clients incurred through poor management of their finances.

"It's no wonder people are running up huge bills if they're getting bouncy castles and marquees for every occasion. We had the aunts and uncles back for tea and that was that. The children entertained themselves out the front with a picnic."

Now that she saw the level of stress that parents encountered after the events on which they'd spent outrageous amounts of money, Emily was inclined to agree with her mother. On the other hand, though, she could see that many of her clients felt that they were doing their best for their children and in that she had to commend them. The fact that they ended up depriving them of essentials such as schoolbooks to pay everything back was secondary in most cases.

"Things have changed," Tom interjected. "Kids would be hopping mad now if they didn't have a bouncy castle."

"That's it exactly. It's all about trying to keep up with what other kids are getting. It's really hard for parents to say no."

"You only have to look over the wall to see that." Jacinta nodded sagely at her daughter while giving her husband a warning look out of the corner of her eye on account of the thick layer of butter he was spreading on the thin slice of soda bread that she'd left on his side plate.

"Over the wall" was a phrase that had always been used in the Gordon household to describe St Ciaran's primary school next door. Jacinta considered the school a barometer of Rathmollin's progress down the years and measured everything from affluence to the growth in the village population by it.

"I can't believe they have three prefabs there now," Emily commented. "I hear there are twenty children in most of the classes now. Imagine! There were only four of us the year I started. Oh, by the way, I met Sandra Coyne when I was out walking last night."

"How was Sandra? Her mother's very bothered over her, you know."

Emily spread some of her mother's delicious raspberry jam onto a slice of wholemeal bread and realised just how much she'd missed this evening chat when she was living in Dublin.

"She seemed to be in good form. What's her mother bothered about?"

Rathmollin, despite a plethora of housing developments, was still a small village where everyone knew everything about everyone and Emily could almost guess why Rose Coyne was worried about her daughter.

"She's back with that Delaney fellow again. He was nothing but trouble before and they were delighted when he took off. He's back from England now and Sandra has him staying."

"I hope he's good to the little fellow."

When Emily had met Sandra the previous evening, she'd said nothing about whether she had a partner or boyfriend. Emily had noticed how tired Sandra looked and how she appeared to be much older than her twenty-eight years. She now knew why.

"That's the problem, I think. He's a bit of a drinker by all accounts. Rose doesn't like the idea of him coming and going in a state in front of Dylan."

"Dylan seems happy enough – he was out running around when I met them. There was no sign of the boyfriend though."

"Probably down in The Stone's," Tom sighed. "Dan says he's there day and night."

Tom had been friendly with Sandra's father for years but this was the first time that he'd mentioned any discussion with him about his daughter since her surprise pregnancy had been discovered all those years ago. Emily had been in college in Dublin then and the whole thing had gone over her head.

The Stone's Throw was Rathmollin's one and only pub and the hub of all gossip. If Sandra's boyfriend was spending most of his time there, then her parents were bound to be aware of it.

"It's desperate altogether," Jacinta concluded, topping up her husband's teacup. "She's a lovely girl and it's a shame she got in with that fellow in the first place." Jacinta paused to consider the extent of such waste, the teapot suspended in mid-air.

"I never told you what I was looking at when I went up the village last evening," Emily said, filling the gap that her mother had left.

"Looking at?" Tom's interest was piqued immediately.

Jacinta came out of her reverie the moment she thought there was something of note in the village that she didn't already know about.

"I saw an ad in *The Examiner* for Ina Harrington's cottage so I went up to have a look at it." She wondered what they'd think of this.

"Would you think of buying it?" Tom looked more surprised than Emily had imagined he would, although it was probably because she'd been traipsing around new developments for the past few months.

"I'll look at it at least. I know it's probably small but the site is huge. I could build on to it later if I wanted. What do you think?"

"We'd have to look at it first and see how much renovation it'd need. But it's in a nice spot – I'm surprised it hasn't been snapped up already."

"Jack Rooney will have it levelled before you even get a look at it," Jacinta commented, obviously tuned in to the development potential of the little cottage.

"That's the thing," Emily agreed. "I rang the auctioneer earlier and made an appointment for tomorrow afternoon. There will probably be a queue outside it before the weekend."

"How much are they looking for?"

Emily's budget had been settled for her the day that she'd decided to resign her permanent post with the Health Service Executive in Dublin and Jacinta was terrified that her daughter would have to get a 100 per cent mortgage and be at the mercy of the bank until she was pension age.

"Two hundred thousand."

When it was said out loud, it seemed enormous to Emily's ears, yet at this juncture in Irish life, Harmony Cottage was well below the asking price of anything else that she'd looked at.

Tom nodded thoughtfully while Jacinta breathed a sigh of relief. Emily remembered The Property People brochure that she was sitting on and took it out from under her to show her parents.

"It's in good enough nick. I remember Dan Coyne putting in a new septic tank for Ina and Minnie a few years back so the sewerage side of things will be fine anyway. You'll have to see if there's an engineer's report going with it."

Tom was knowledgeable on things like sewerage since his days with the County Council and was prone to judging houses on the speed of the toilet flush before anything else came into the equation.

"There's a lovely little garden too," said Jacinta. "Ina and Minnie always had the place nice. Will we come with you tomorrow?"

"Maybe I'll have a sconce at it first. It might be desperate for all I know – there's no point in us all traipsing up."

To date, Emily had spent most of her weekends since Christmas roaming around show-houses to no avail and was only too aware that Harmony Cottage might be yet another dead end. Although she had a good feeling about it somehow.

Tom and Jacinta studied the colour photographs of this latest offering while Emily made another pot of tea.

"It's on a fine big site," Tom commented. "One-third of an acre, it says. Your mother's right, you know. Jack Rooney will have a line of townhouses up on it if someone doesn't snap it up soon."

Suddenly Emily felt fiercely protective about her little cottage, almost as if she owned it already. Although she hadn't set eyes on him in years, she was sick of hearing what Jack Rooney was building here, there and everywhere. He was only her own age, yet he seemed to have a finger in every pie around Rathmollin. Well, on this occasion, she decided stubbornly, he could feck off and build on some other little patch. This little patch, she felt, was going to be hers.

Chapter 4

From the time she'd got out of bed this morning, Sandra had felt unsettled. Now, a full twenty-four hours had passed since Emily Gordon had stopped to talk to her and the feeling was showing no sign of going away.

"Mam, when are we having the tea?"

"Soon," she told him for the third time. "Go on back in and I'll call you."

"Ah, Ma . . ."

Dylan began to complain but Sandra wasn't in the humour for him.

"I *said* go back into the sitting-room. It'll be ready in a minute."

Her head was bursting but the look that her son threw in her direction as he left the kitchen again wasn't lost on Sandra. Lately, she seemed to be letting him down all the time – or that was how it felt when she saw the wounded, hangdog look that he responded with every time she lost her temper. And losing her temper was something that she'd been doing with increasing regularity these days.

"Here, have a bar to keep you going," she placated him, following him into the sitting-room with a Twix.

The television was blaring – Dylan's way of letting her know that he was annoyed with her. A grunt was all she got when he stuck out his hand and grabbed the chocolate bar from her.

"What about 'Thanks'?"

Another grunt.

Sighing, Sandra left him to it, shutting the door to drown out the television before making her way back to the kitchen. The bolognese sauce that she'd made at six o'clock had thickened considerably in the hour that it had been sitting on the gas ring and had started to stick to the bottom of the pot.

She glanced at the clock again, wishing that Paul would at least ring. The thought of Dylan munching on the Twix annoyed her. At any other time, she would have been absolutely adamant about him having his dinner before a treat could even be mentioned. Now here she was stuffing him on purpose so that he'd wait a bit longer.

She jumped when she heard the small timber gate at the side of the house rattling, a sure sign that Paul had arrived at last. Knowing full well that he'd be grumbling if there wasn't a plate in front of him in five seconds, she blasted up the heat under the pasta saucepan that had been simmering for what seemed like hours.

Swiftly she opened the top oven of the cooker and removed the large, white pasta bowls that she'd collected on a promotional offer at the grocery the previous summer. Straightening, it occurred to her that Paul hadn't actually materialised around the corner of the house. Disgusted, she glanced up to see if Sparky Lenihan, the hound from next door, was the culprit at the side gate. Unbelievably, all she could see was a toe-capped boot, skewed at an angle between the gate and the fence.

"Jesus Almighty!" was the first thing that came to mind as annoyance turned to alarm. Careful not to alert Dylan to the unfolding drama, Sandra exited through the kitchen door at a rate of knots, the lid of the pasta saucepan forgotten as it started to rattle violently over the flame. Her boyfriend, she could now see, was lying face down in a heap on the concrete footpath that ran around the small council cottage.

"Paul! Here – turn over! What happened to you?"

In her panic, she shook him violently, her strength coming from nowhere as she held onto his plaid work shirt and attempted to heave him over onto his side. She could smell the drink off him and was terrified that he'd stopped breathing.

"For fuck's Sandra, would you ever leave me alone?"

Sandra jumped back when she heard the aggressive growl, relief mingling with fear in a bizarre combination of emotions. The thought of Dylan seeing him like this made her press on, although she was doubtful of how successful she might be at covering this one up. For a start it was ten past seven on a Monday evening – half the village had probably seen Paul taking the two sides of the road between The Stone's and the cottage.

"Come on, Paul," she urged, "you'll have to get up out

of here. Your dinner's ready, for a start." Maybe the thought of a feed would get him moving.

"Shut the fuck up, you stupid bitch! And don't start on about the dinner again!" His voice was thick and slurred but surprisingly strong considering that his eyes were half closed from the amount of alcohol he'd obviously consumed.

Her stomach felt sick from the smell of him. "I'm not," she placated him, her mind on Dylan. Please let him still have the television turned up to the hilt! "You'll perish out here. Give me your arm and I'll get you up."

"I'll get up if I want to. I'm not going to be led and said by you." All the same, he lunged up suddenly, his head hitting the metal attachment that Sandra's father had screwed to the wall to keep the gate closed when Dylan was smaller. "What the fuck?" he yelled as he fell back on the footpath again.

Sandra jumped back in fright as he made another lunge, this time flailing his fists around as if to get a swipe at whoever had hit him on the head. He was too drunk to even be aware that he'd hit his head off an inanimate object.

"It's grand," she soothed. "Here, go on."

Grunting, she half pushed, half pulled him into a standing position. He towered above her, his six-foot bulk a dead weight where his elbow dug heavily into the delicate area between her shoulder and her neck. Sick at the thought of Aggie Lenihan knowing that Paul was causing a racket again, Sandra guided him as best she could towards the back door and prayed that Dylan wouldn't arrive out with another request for his dinner.

"Fucking step!" Paul stumbled away from her as his foot caught in the bottom edge of the uPVC doorframe.

"Jesus, the saucepan!" Sandra shrieked, panicking when she saw the steam and boiling water spitting out from under the lid. She grabbed the handle, abandoning Paul.

It was like being in the middle of a nightmare, was all she could think as she burned her hand on the handle and had to drop the saucepan back down onto the ring. Boiling water splashed onto her wrist, the pain hitting her like a wave of white light. Another yelp escaped her and suddenly Paul was shoving her away from the cooker, his voice raised angrily.

"Will you shut the fuck up yelling, you thick wagon you! I can't fucking hear myself think!"

Pain seared through her hip as it connected with the corner of the table but this time she kept her mouth shut. It was to no avail though as she watched in slow motion her three precious pasta dishes sliding off the table before she could grab them. Shards of white shattered to the four corners of the small kitchen and her boyfriend's face was like thunder.

"Stupid bitch!" It was almost as if he himself had bought the two-packs of pasta sauce every week for six weeks in order to collect a full set of six bowls.

"Mam?"

Despite the bedlam, Sandra could hear her son's voice as if it had been somehow magnified tenfold. His face was white, highlighting the dimples that he'd inherited from his father, the same father that he was now staring at in open-mouthed horror.

"Dylan – I told you to stay in the sitting-room!" She hated herself for the admonishment but just wanted her son away from the scene in the kitchen.

"But, Ma . . ."

Dylan was staring at the floor, littered with the remains of the broken bowls. Paul, however, was having none of his son's objections.

"Did you not hear, you little pup? Get back inside!" His face was an ugly mask of anger and condescension and spit flew out of his mouth as he snarled his orders at poor Dylan.

Backing away towards the door in order to get as far away from his father as possible, Dylan reversed into the stainless-steel saucepan rack that stood tidily in the corner between the door and the fridge. Mercifully, despite a precarious rattle, it remained standing.

"Sss–orry," Dylan stuttered, the speech impediment that Sandra had thought resolved returning out of nowhere.

"Go on, Dylan," Sandra encouraged, trying to keep her voice light and comforting. "Watch your programme and I'll bring the dinner in to you." Her son, she could see, was barely capable of moving. "Go on now," she insisted, urgency entering her tone as Paul seemed about to intervene belligerently.

"Fucking typical – no wonder he's such a little Nancy. It's a bloody servant he wants."

"Leave him, Paul," Sandra pleaded. "Go on, Dylan, or the programme will be over by now – I'll be in there in a minute."

Slowly and somewhat reluctantly, Dylan made a timid exit from the kitchen as Paul, suddenly losing interest in his son, started to kick at the broken crockery strewn all over the tiles.

"Bloody kip!"

For once, his girlfriend had to agree with him. The place was indeed a kip at that moment. Paul seemed to have sobered up considerably since she'd pulled him up off the path outside and was now lurching towards the cooker.

"You sit down and I'll get up the dinner!" she said quickly.

It was far too dangerous to allow him near a pan of boiling water in this state. Things were bad enough without him roaring like a bull and having to be brought to the A&E.

Flopping down onto one of the kitchen chairs that Sandra's parents had bought with the matching table when she'd first moved into the house, Paul propped his head up in his hands. It was amazing, Sandra thought as she quietly slipped three old plates from one of the presses and started to dish up the now overcooked pasta, how much Dylan looked like his father. It was only now that she noticed the same funny cow's lick at the back of Paul's head that had annoyed hairdressers as long as she'd been bringing her son to get his hair cut.

Paul's eyes shot open as she slid the plate in front of him. Sandra hadn't even noticed him dozing off.

"Dried-up shite," was his immediate announcement although he followed it up by shovelling the pasta sauce into his mouth as if he hadn't had a bite in weeks.

Sandra glanced at him in disgust as she put a smaller portion on Dylan's plate. At least he was occupied for a while, she thought as she opened the adjoining door and carried out her son's dinner and the glass of milk that she insisted on every evening.

"There you go, love." She was aware that she was

speaking in a whisper and was immediately ashamed of it, especially when Dylan whispered a meek "Thanks" with his head down.

"When you eat that you can go up to Granny's for a while if you like. I'll come up for you later on."

"I can go on my own?" Dylan was astounded at this unprecedented development. Normally, going outside the front gate without permission was a cardinal sin and now his mother was telling him he could go the whole way up the main street unsupervised.

"On the path," Sandra instructed as severely as she could. "And no bike – you have to stay on the path."

She just wanted him out of the house before Paul caused any more of a ruction though she was terrified of what might happen to her son in the short distance between her own house and that of her parents. Children could be abducted from their own front gardens. A car could mount the footpath with a drunk driver at the wheel. Right at that moment though, she was sensible enough to realise that the greatest threat to her little boy was here under their own roof.

"Cool."

At least he sounded more like himself now. She dreaded to think what her father would think when he saw Dylan arriving at the back door. He'd already arrived down for a serious talk a few days ago about Paul's fondness for the pub and his daughter had assured him that there would be no question of there being any carry-on with Dylan in the house. Now here she was sending him up the street on his own.

Her mind was whirling – if she rang her father and mother to say that she was sending Dylan up for a few hours, one of them would insist on walking down to get him. There was no way she could let them see Paul in this state and anyway he'd go mad if he heard her phoning them. She had no choice, it seemed, but to let Dylan off on his own.

"You can ring me on Granny's phone when you get there, okay?"

Dylan knew his own and his grandparents' numbers off by heart. It was something that Sandra had taught him at an early age as a safeguard in case he ever wandered out of the schoolyard or away from her in a shop.

"Okay," he agreed. He started to shovel his dinner rapidly into his mouth, in a hurry now that an adventure was on the cards.

It shocked Sandra when it crossed her mind that he might be cute enough to leave for his grandparents' house via the front door instead of coming through the kitchen as he usually did. She blinked to stop the tears that threatened to find their way to her eyes and ruffled his hair.

"See you later then."

There it was – her silent warning to her son that there was no need to venture into the kitchen to say that he was leaving. Stifling the sigh that she needed badly to emit, Sandra made her way back to the scene of destruction that her boyfriend was presiding over.

Paul's plate was pushed to one side and balanced precariously on the edge of the table. His arms were spread out in front of him with his head resting between them and thankfully, gloriously, he was sound asleep.

Far from being disgusted at the slobber of pasta sauce all over his face and the fact that the small room reeked of alcohol and sweat, she actually felt relief. If he dozed there for a bit while she tidied up, it might be easier to get him up the stairs and into bed when he did wake. Silently she opened the press under the sink and took out the dustpan and brush.

She hated herself for thinking that the sooner Dylan was gone the better. Was this, she wondered, all that her great reunion with his father had brought her to?

Chapter 5

By four o'clock on Tuesday Emily was hopping impatiently from one foot to the other on the shallow limestone doorstep of Harmony Cottage while Dermot Leahy, the estate agent, fiddled with the key. Her heart was beating a little faster than was strictly normal with the anticipation of seeing the place that she felt might become her home.

"It's very good value this, for €200,000. Lots of original features *and* in a prime location. Ideal starter property."

She'd had a full day to ponder over the brochure and plan her future while the secretary at The Property People made a song and dance about organising a viewing. At this stage, Emily felt as if she knew the cottage off by heart already. The entrance hall had antique cream paintwork above pale blue wainscoting and a pitch pine floor. Opening off to the left would be the one and only bedroom, while the door to the right would lead into the living area. As far as she could make out from her intense study of the estate agent's specification, the living area ran straight through to the kitchen-cum-dining-room, which took up the full width of the back of the little house.

"South-facing as well." Dermot, the auctioneer, kept up a running commentary as he produced another set of keys and restarted his efforts at the antique-looking lock.

The door, Emily noticed, was in need of a coat of paint as were the two sash windows either side of it. A deep red, it was peeling at the edges and the brass knocker looked as if it hadn't seen a rub of Brasso in many a long year. Finally, after another few minutes of jangling keys, the auctioneer mastered the lock and swung open the object of her study to reveal the interior.

"Entrance hall," he announced, stating the obvious. "Pitch pine flooring – original."

It was original all right, Emily observed. Almost black with years of grime and footfalls, it was crying out for a sander and a dose of varnish. Hoping that the rest of the house was less in need of elbow grease, she stoically pushed her auburn curls behind her ears and stepped over the threshold.

Proudly, Dermot led the way, swinging open the painted cream door on the left.

"Master bedroom with an original fireplace and coving."

The man was a walking buzz word. Emily studied the interior, which was much larger than she'd imagined. Trying to visualise it with a bed, wardrobe and chest of drawers in place, she concluded that she'd still have room to swing the proverbial cat if she went for a queen-sized bed instead of the luxurious king-sized one that she imagined herself in.

Lost in thought, she barely noticed Dermot, his burly frame lodged in the doorway, watching her expectantly. At any other time, Emily would have been amused at the fact that he fitted her idea of a typical auctioneer, his sales pitch tripping off his tongue like honey out of a beehive. He only looked about twenty, she'd noticed when he stepped out of a brand new Avensis outside the cottage earlier. His hair was gelled up in trendy spikes at the front and his suit was typically slick and clean-cut.

"Close proximity to all the amenities," he interjected now, obviously terrified of letting a silence develop in case he lost the momentum of a sale.

Emily wished he would be quiet and let her think. The young auctioneer, unaware that she'd spent most of her life in Rathmollin, kept up his patter, trying to convince his client that the post office and Curly Locks hairdressing salon could be classed as amenities – the pub, "aptly named The Stone's Throw", was a few minutes' walk up the street from Harmony Cottage – Connolly's Master Butcher and Gleeson's Grocery, on the opposite side of the street, "made up the heart of the village when coupled with the adjoining funeral home".

"Now, what's next?" Dermot smiled expansively as if he couldn't possibly remember what room might be next.

Tearing herself away from the bedroom and her vision of natural Hessian curtains, Emily followed her guide back into the hall.

"This is the bathroom. In need of some modernisation, mind you."

Almost ready to congratulate him on the understatement of the year, she now realised why the glossy brochure had failed to feature this particular room. She stared in awe and wondered who on earth had thought that the pink bathroom suite surrounded ceiling to floor with a chequered sequence of pink and black tiles was attractive.

"Easily remedied by a person with a good eye for interior design," Dermot commented ingratiatingly. "Structurally, the place is as sound as a pound."

"Is there an engineer's report available?" Gina at work had hammered this point into Emily's head as soon as she heard that she was considering a cottage that was almost a hundred years old.

"Absolutely," he confirmed expansively. "Full service record, so to speak."

Once again mustering her powers of visualisation, Emily tried to imagine a simple white suite with fresh white and turquoise tiles. She already had a mirror with a tiled turquoise border and a selection of matching bath and hand towels that she'd picked up in the January sales for just such an occasion. She'd have to price a bathroom suite before she made any commitment, she decided.

"Now for the *pièce de résistance*!"

Across the narrow hall, Dermot swung open the door of the living-room, pausing for effect on the threshold.

"Well?" he prompted.

Emily's heart, having slowed to its normal speed after the experience of viewing the bathroom, revved up considerably as she took in the sight before her.

The size of the master bedroom and bathroom combined, the room was all she could have hoped for. Admittedly, the pine flooring needed a sand and varnish – or maybe even a carpet – and the paintwork needed to be freshened up to remove the existing hideous green. It was the light, however, that flooded in through the bare window that made her gasp with barely concealed anticipation. Her imagination went into overdrive immediately and she could almost feel herself lounging on a large comfy sofa in front of a blazing fire, the oriental rug that she'd bought in Turkey soft under her bare feet.

"More original features," Dermot persisted, breaking in on her thoughts. "Coving, dado rail and of course the cast-iron fireplace. Plenty of room for a couple of two-seaters either side of it."

Emily's gaze travelled now through an open archway to what she imagined was the dining-room. On cue, Dermot struck forth, extolling the virtues of the empty space like it was the Sistine Chapel.

"Very spacious – open plan to make the most of it."

Emily was about to agree with him but stopped in case she sounded too gullible. Gina had warned her about that too. As soon as she glanced to her left, she began to appreciate her friend's wisdom.

"Kitchen. In need of freshening up, admittedly. But all in good working order."

To prove this, Dermot opened and closed a few of the pine doors, all of which were stained a grotesque shade that might have been an attempt at teak or mahogany but which resembled something that had survived extensive fire damage.

"It's all a bit dark," Emily ventured now, recalling

Gina's caution about sounding too enthusiastic. In the back of her mind though, she could see the tidy kitchen units painted a deep cream, coupled with terracotta tiles and a warm terracotta on the walls that would carry through to the dining-room. A simple cream table and chairs and some painted shelving would complete the look, especially when she resurrected the Stephen Pearse lamps that she and Richard had been given as an engagement present. He'd hated them on sight, considering them too "countrified" for the kind of décor he envisaged for their stylish home. Emily, therefore, had inherited the pair of terracotta lamps that she actually loved from the wreckage of their relationship.

"Mmm . . ." Emily switched off the thoughts of Richard and tried to make her mumble sound as disinterested and noncommittal as possible, all the while thinking that the little house was as near to perfect as she'd ever imagined.

"The garden, of course, is the major selling point of this property," Dermot continued, blithely ignoring Emily's attempt at dampening his spirits.

Immediately apprehensive about what she would find beyond the frosted glass door of the kitchen, Emily followed Dermot once again, her feet sticking to the dreadful brown lino that covered the floor.

For once, the reality lived up to Dermot's sales pitch. Ignoring the fact that the place was ferociously overgrown, Emily let her powers of visualisation take over and tried to imagine the garden as she would have it as soon as she was able to buy a lawnmower and a pair of shears.

When she'd read in the brochure that Harmony Cottage stood on one-third of an acre, Emily hadn't had a clue of what that might mean in terms of size or maintenance. Now, glancing around what she considered to be its vast proportions, she thought of all the semi-detached houses she'd visited and wondered if maybe their postage stamp squares of grass mightn't be more suitable to someone like herself.

Nothing, however, about living in a housing estate had appealed to her. Not the endless rows of identical, brick-fronted dwellings, not the lines of cobble-locked driveways and certainly not the fact that she'd never again forget to turn on the television in time for *Coronation Street* because she would always be able to hear the theme tune starting next door through the cardboard walls.

No – Harmony Cottage was exactly what she wanted and with an asking price safely within her paltry limits she might even have enough money to remove the offensive kitchen door and stretch to something that would let in some light and expose the wonderful garden that she would create in no time at all.

As it stood, what she now gazed out on resembled a scene out of *Jurassic Park*. Dermot, conscious no doubt of his highly polished shoes, was gesturing at the various points of interest while avoiding having to wander too far into the wilderness.

"The elevated aspect is just the thing – brilliant for a raised patio."

In this again, he was correct. Immediately outside the back door was an expanse of gravel that was littered with leaves and twigs. Beyond this was the "elevated aspect" to which he had just referred. Treading carefully across the gravel, Emily ascended the six narrow brick steps that led to the upper level of the garden.

The site on which Harmony Cottage stood was wedge-shaped, widening at the back. Right next door was Dan and Rose Coyne's neat bungalow, although the two houses were well separated by the Coyne's side garden.

The long grass in which Emily now stood was rough underfoot but she could immediately see the long-term potential. Flooded with afternoon sunlight, she could visualise how it might look with an area of raised decking to one side and the remainder neatly mowed. Large pots of the vibrant bedding plants that her mother was so fond of would adorn her little garden, with a lavender bed surrounding the decking. Enrapt with this fantasy garden, Emily could almost smell the heady fragrance of the lavender as she reclined on one of her imaginary garden chairs on her imaginary decking.

Dermot, meanwhile, was hopping from foot to foot at the back door, very obviously anxious to get back into the house and complete his sales pitch.

"Lovely and sheltered!" he called out from his position below her, indicating the twenty-foot escallonia hedge that surrounded the site.

The hedge will have to go, Emily decided, her mind now set on Harmony Cottage. Remembering that she wasn't supposed to look too eager, she made her way carefully down the steps again, already thinking about replacing the gravel outside the back door with patio slabs.

"Overall, it's an excellent opportunity to get onto the property ladder."

"Do you have a copy of the engineer's report?"

Now that she'd made up her mind, it was killing her to have to hold back a bit.

"It's right here," Dermot assured her, extracting a document from the leather folder that he'd had wedged under his arm since he got out of the car.

"I'll have to get this looked at over the next few days," she told him in as noncommittal voice as she could muster. "Has there been much interest in it?"

"It only went on the market this week. It belonged to an elderly lady for years so obviously the décor is a bit dated. The garden hadn't been attended to in a while either. It's her nephew that's selling it and he seems to be anxious for a quick sale."

Gina at work had warned her about this too. The idea that a house might be snapped up by someone else was often enough to make a buyer rush into something that they might otherwise have had time to reconsider.

On the other hand, Emily thought that the story might actually be true. Ina Harrington who'd lived in Harmony Cottage her whole life had never been seen to have a visitor and had barely left the house since the death of her sister, which Emily remembered as being about ten years ago. The idea of her having a nephew waiting in the wings to claim the decrepit little cottage seemed all too plausible.

"Well, I'll let you know over the next few days if I need a second viewing," she told Dermot evasively.

"Here's my card. I can be available any evening after six by arrangement if it's a thing that you're working."

Ingratiating was certainly the word that sprang to mind in relation to Dermot. Emily smiled to herself as she took one last look around the living-room. He was right about one other thing though. The décor did leave a lot to be desired but then Ina Harrington had probably had no interest in updating the house once Minnie had passed on.

If the structural report was in good order, Emily figured that she could talk to the bank about a mortgage almost straight away. If the money, along with her own deposit, was forthcoming then she might be able to make an offer. And perhaps the sooner she did it the better, just in case another bidder came on the scene.

Her heart lifted as she turned to look at the outside of the cottage one more time. In all the years that she'd lived in the village, she'd barely noticed it. Now, there was a very real possibility that Harmony Cottage might become her first home. Well, her first proper home, she amended, thinking of the aborted plans for the "superior five-bed residence" in Blanchardstown that she'd *thought* would be her home with Richard.

Sighing, she pushed aside the thoughts of that other house. As a priority now, she had to get someone to take a look at the engineer's report as well as pricing the necessities like a bathroom suite, tiles and furniture.

Who knows, she thought happily as she bade goodbye to Dermot – maybe I'll be a proper resident of Rathmollin before the summer is out.

Chapter 6

Tuesday evening hadn't come a moment too soon for Jennie. The kids were like demons and had moaned for Ireland when she'd told them that Vincent hadn't been able to leave Dubai as planned.

"Why can't he have a job like Sasha's dad?" Lucy had demanded after the concert the previous evening. "He's always at home."

"I know he is, Lucy, but it's just the way it works." Jennie was sick to the back teeth of defending Vincent's absence to her children.

As if to rile her further, Tim chipped in that his friend Rex from school was going on a camping trip with *his* dad. "In the summer. For a whole week. They'll be in a tent at night and everything." This was said in such a wistful tone that Jennie smiled to herself despite her annoyance. Tim was such a little drama queen about everything and always knew when to spin out a sob story.

"And what about summer holidays? Are they going anywhere sunny?"

She knew only too well that the Brady were much less well off than themselves and that it was unlikely they'd be going on a foreign holiday. Tim, on the other hand, had a week in Euro Disney to look forward to.

"I dunno," he mumbled, suddenly aware of what side his bread was buttered on. A camping trip was far less appealing than the excitement of the plane journey and the subsequent adventures in the world-renowned amusement park.

Congratulating herself on the efficacy of her distraction ploy, Jennie reminded her offspring that their baby-sitter would be arriving any minute.

"Right so. If you're in your PJs before Donna comes, you can watch a video before bed."

Bullets out of a gun was the only way to describe the speed at which Tim and Lucy skidded out of the room and raced up the stairs. Normally a series of protests would ensue with a treat being demanded in exchange for the hardship of having to don their pyjamas.

Donna, however, was the key to their speedy response this evening, something Jennie was glad of as she prepared once again for her trip to the airport. Lucy and Tim thought that Donna was actually a real live princess on account of the sheath of white-blonde hair that fell halfway down her back and the peachy skin and large blue eyes that accompanied it.

Lucy thought she was Snow White whereas Tim was more inclined to believe that she was the embodiment of Rapunzel and Donna, to her credit, made a great production of plaiting her hair to humour him. She'd been their baby-sitter since they'd moved into Rathmollin woods three years previously and was still happy to oblige as often as she could even though she was now in her first year at college. Jennie, for her part, was always happy to leave the children with the reliable nineteen-year-old and paid her above the odds to make it worth her while.

The doorbell rang just as the pair of them shot down the stairs.

Through the frosted glass panels, Jennie could see Donna sticking her thumbs in her ears and wiggling her fingers to amuse the kids as they waited for their mother to open the door.

"Donna, Donna," Lucy shouted before Tim got his spoke in, "Tim gave Pocahontas the measles! Wait until I show you the state of her!"

The baby-sitter looked at Jennie, amazed that she hadn't heard before now that one of them had had measles.

"Only a few," Tim corrected as Jennie rolled her eyes at Donna.

Donna decided to seek clarification. "So where is she now?"

"Dead." This was Tim's succinct answer, one that he imagined might rile his younger sister as a payback for telling on him earlier when he'd attempted to climb the eucalyptus tree in the back yard unknown to Jennie.

He pulled Donna into the lounge now and resurrected Pocahontas from behind the sofa. His face doleful, he proffered the doll with its now-speckled face to her.

"You can't die of measles," Lucy insisted. "And anyway, I'm cutting her hair with Donna – I don't care if she's dead."

"She really did die from the measles, didn't she, Mum?"

The two adults could now see where he was coming from.

"She did," Jennie agreed, "but that was years ago – you can't die of measles now."

Lucy was triumphant. "Told you so, told you so!"

Donna, seeing that a bickering match was about to break out, distracted the pair by holding up her handbag. As usual, she had a small treat in store.

"Kisses for your mam first," she insisted as Jennie returned with her jacket on.

No wonder she's worth her weight in gold, Jennie thought as her offspring pecked her on the lips obligingly. If it wasn't for Donna's strategies, she'd be there all night. As it stood, she was already leaving five minutes later than she'd planned.

Finally, after another round of kisses, she gave Donna all the usual instructions and left the house with a clear head. Vincent's flight would be in at seven and hopefully they'd be at their table in Nouvelle by nine. After almost a week without the benefit of adult company, she was looking forward to a catch-up with her husband over a delicious meal.

Tonight, Jennie wore a patterned silk knee-length wrap dress in black and white with sheer stockings and the elegant heels that she spotted in Shularie in Midleton a few weeks previously. She'd had her hair professionally straightened earlier in the day, despite Maxine's insistence that her own efforts with the GHD were always perfect.

There was a slight chill in the air when she stepped out

of the car in the short-term car park. As always, she thanked God for the fact that Cork airport was small enough for people to park practically in front of the main entrance without having to trek halfway around the world.

The breeze barely lifted her hair as she prayed that there would be no delay with the flight, although she imagined that Vincent would have phoned her if there was. She'd already cancelled their table in Jacobs on the Mall yesterday and was damned if her night out in Nouvelle was going to fail.

The arrivals board heartened her. Vincent would be striding through the gates within the next few minutes as long as his luggage didn't go astray. The first trickle of people had started to emerge and Jennie was reminded of the way she used to feel in the early years of their marriage when her husband was returning home from a trip. In those days, she used to fling herself into his arms unselfconsciously, much like the girl next to her now was doing.

Jennie had always been a people-watcher and she now surreptitiously studied the interaction between the young couple. The husband, about her own age, was dressed in a business suit and carried a smart briefcase, obviously just off the Heathrow flight. His wife, around the same age, was dressed casually in linen drawstring trousers and a denim jacket. As Jennie watched their reunion she was struck by two things. Firstly at how comfortable and confident the girl looked with her broad smile as she turned her face up for a kiss. Secondly, Jennie noticed how much at ease she looked as her husband introduced her proudly to the two older men who'd accompanied him through the arrivals gate.

Something like envy hit Jennie then. She herself was always conscious of how she looked to others, especially where Vincent's business associates were concerned. The one occasion that she'd turned up at the airport unprepared had been a lesson to her and was something that stuck out in her mind to this day.

It had been the day that she'd completed the final exam of her secretarial course and she and Vincent had agreed to celebrate later in the evening. Planning to shower and doll herself up after she'd met his flight, she'd arrived at the airport straight from college with her hair lank and her eyes black-ringed from a long night of studying. She'd been horrified when she found that a few of Vincent's London contacts had been on the flight and that he'd been roped into going for an early dinner with them. They'd insisted on Jennie coming as well and despite her mortification at being caught without a scrap of make-up she'd had to go along with them. Even now, she could vividly recall how exposed and uncomfortable she'd felt in her jeans and simple cotton top compared to the group of men in their smart casuals. The fact that Vincent had proposed to her later that evening only served to implant the memory of the whole experience in her consciousness for good and all.

She jumped in fright when her husband appeared in front of her suddenly. She'd been so caught up in the other couple that her eyes had strayed away from the arrivals gate for a few minutes.

"Dreaming?"

He looked tired although he grinned at her as he kissed her and wrapped his free arm around her shoulder. His luggage trolley contained the large suitcase she'd watched him pack almost a week ago as well as his briefcase and laptop.

She kissed him back and somehow didn't feel the sense of anticipation that she usually did. As they walked towards the exit together, she wondered whether anyone was looking at them with envy or whether they looked like a couple jaded from too much time spent apart.

"How was the flight?" She asked this automatically and it struck her that it was the type of thing that people said to fill a gap in conversation. She and Vincent had been apart for days – surely they should have more to talk about than the flight.

"Grand. I missed you." He glanced down at her and squeezed her shoulder. "And the kids. All okay with them?"

"Fine – squabbling over Donna!" She could tell him about the events of Sunday night as soon as they were settled in the restaurant.

"As usual!"

"I warned them they could watch *Shrek 2* as long as they gave Donna no trouble. I told her they could stay up for a bit."

"I'm dying to see them. I was disgusted about missing the concert but nothing went right."

"They'll probably be asleep by the time we get home – I thought we could have something to eat in Nouvelle."

"God, Jen, I'm wrecked. Could we just have a

sandwich for one night?" He ran his free hand through his hair, now rumpled attractively from the long flight.

Stunned at his thoughtlessness, Jennie just looked at him. How typical of Vincent to deny her a quiet night out after a week of bedlam chasing around after the kids.

"My head is melted from talking for the last few days." He stopped next to the car and drew her into his arms. "All I want to do is sit back with a Bud and hear what's been going on here."

Resentment surged through Jennie. She wasn't going to give in like a good little wife when he hadn't even noticed that she'd dressed up. She'd already told Donna that they wouldn't be in until midnight or thereabouts and would feel like a right fool landing back before nine.

"I've booked it," she told him, her voice displaying the irritation she felt at his lack of consideration. She stabbed violently at the remote central-locking device on her key-ring and Vincent's face was lit up momentarily by the flash of the Audi's lights. He *did* look tired but now that she'd started to make a stand it was too late to back down.

"Jesus, Jennie, I was up at six this morning for the flight. I've been on the go since last Wednesday, for God's sake!" He sounded irritated as he threw the enormous suitcase easily into the boot.

"Why does it always have to be about you, Vincent? Answer me that." She was seeing red now and tears were close but she was damned if she was going to cry. She flung herself into the driving seat, seething inside.

"It's not about me. It's just tonight isn't great, that's all. I've been working all week non stop and –"

"And I haven't been, is that it?" She gripped the steering wheel like a lifebuoy and raised her chin defiantly. Let him get out of that one.

"I didn't say that. I know it's not easy having to do everything yourself, especially for a whole week, but I'll be at home for a few weeks now. Maybe we could go somewhere at the weekend?"

He treated her like a child, Jennie realised. Bargaining the way she herself did with Tim and Lucy. *We can't eat out tonight but I promise I'll bring you somewhere nice at the weekend, if you're good.*

"Fine."

She was heading for the Airport Roundabout now and there was a tight, hard lump in her throat that threatened to choke her. Grappling for her phone in the small compartment between their seats, she exited for the N25 and tried to concentrate on the road as she dialled the number of her favourite restaurant.

"Jennie, be careful," Vincent cautioned.

He was always at her for using the phone while she was driving.

Stubbornly, she ignored him. "I'd like to cancel a booking please. Kelleher for 9 pm." Her voice was clipped and Vincent sighed beside her in the darkness of the car.

"Jennie, I'm sorry . . ." he began as soon as she'd made her excuses to the restaurant.

"Forget it." She knew her voice was hard and angry and was glad.

Vincent sighed again, a deep, long sigh that suggested he was at the very end of his tether with exhaustion.

Seething, Jennie stared straight ahead, her face a tight, rigid mask. It was obvious that the last thing he wanted was to spend time with her, even after a week apart. Surely that wasn't normal, unless he'd had his fill of female entertainment and now needed a break, she thought cattily.

Vincent closed his eyes and made no further attempt at conversation, not even to placate her. The journey home was made in silence, with Jennie's mind working overtime all the way. It hadn't always been like this and she was shocked to think that she couldn't even pinpoint when this emotional gap between them had come to be. She couldn't honestly say that it was all the foreign trips – lately Vincent had become vague and distracted about all sorts of things, even when he was at home.

By the time they reached the entrance to Rathmollin Woods, she'd begun to wonder if he'd lost interest in his wife and family to the point where he didn't actually care what they'd been up to for the past week. Maybe her husband's interest lay elsewhere. And maybe she'd been conveniently blaming all the travelling when it was possible that something closer to home was occupying his thoughts. What about all the evenings that he didn't make it home from business meetings in time to see Tim and Lucy before bed? What about the night last week that he'd turned away from her in bed, "too tired" after a long day at work?

Vincent opened his eyes as soon as they pulled up outside the house and Jennie could barely look at him. She needed to calm her mind down before the children came bounding out to the door, wide-eyed that their father was back so early in the evening. She needed to think but now was not the time to do it – especially now that a world of horrible possibilities had opened up to her.

Jennie predicted that as soon as he got in the door, Vincent would be all sunshine and light with the children, the homecoming hero with a suitcase full of the foreign sweets that they loved to show off in school.

Maybe it's just *me* that he has no interest in, she thought bleakly. Slamming the door of the Audi 4 x 4 that he'd arrived home with on New Year's Day as a surprise, she strode towards the front door while her husband lifted his bags out of the boot. The thought of having to make an excuse to Donna angered her almost as much as the fact that her husband couldn't be bothered to spend an evening in her company after being away from her for almost a week. Again, she wondered whether he'd been at a loss for female company on his trip abroad.

"Mom, Mom, did you bring Dad?" Tim was the first to hurtle towards her as soon as she opened the door. So much for Mom!

"Did he not come?" Lucy, on the other hand, was suspicious.

Jennie hated it that Vincent's constant let-downs had created an edge of doubt in her five-year-old mind.

"He's just getting the bags," she said. "Go back inside or you'll get cold."

Lucy wasn't to be fobbed off and skirted around her to check for herself.

"It's all right, Timmy, he *is* there," she squealed as

Vincent arrived into the hall and dropped the bags so that he could grab the two of them at once.

"Of course I'm here. Now what have you two been up to? I hear you've been allowed up late!" Laughing, he made his way into the lounge with the children clinging to him. Their adulation annoyed Jennie and she made her way to the playroom where she knew Donna would have been presiding over *Shrek*.

"Home early?" the baby-sitter greeted her.

Jennie kept her voice light. No point in letting Donna see the chinks that were fast appearing in her marriage. "Vincent was wrecked so we decided to forget about going out. We'll chill out with a bottle of wine instead."

"And I can get away without the kids making me put in the plaits! They still haven't tired of the Rapunzel thing."

"Well, thanks for coming anyway, Donna. The pair of them would have been hyper waiting for the flight to come in." Jennie opened her purse and paid her the same amount that she would have if she'd stayed until midnight although Donna protested sincerely at this. "You're worth it," Jennie laughed, mimicking the L'Oréal advert. Donna shook her head in defeat as they made their way towards the lounge where the noise level had risen significantly.

"Donna's just heading off now." Jennie felt an ache at her temples that she thought must have arisen from the effort of behaving as if her nerves weren't as taut as a drum.

Extricating themselves from their father, Lucy and Tim flung themselves at Donna for a kiss and a hug which she obligingly bestowed while greeting Vincent.

"Hi, Vincent, welcome back." Donna, as always, was smiling and friendly.

"Thanks, Donna. How's the study going?"

The way that Vincent was interested in everyone and anything was one of the things that had attracted Jennie to him in the first place. Now, as her baby-sitter rolled her eyes and explained that accountancy was more boring than she could ever have imagined, she took in the girl's slim figure and pert high breasts and wondered if he wasn't just a little too interested. With a pang, she could see that her husband's eyes were glued to the sliver of taut, tanned abdomen that was exposed between her low-cut jeans and fitted white T-shirt.

"It won't be half as boring when you're earning buckets of money and driving a swizzy little car," Vincent retorted, his eyes twinkling.

A huge hollow opened up inside Jennie as she watched the interaction. It was such a long time since her husband's eyes had crinkled up like that at something *she* said.

"I suppose you're right. Although I'm a long way from the fancy car bit."

Donna was only in her first year and was finding the study for her upcoming exams tedious.

Jennie was glad when she finally left after a bit more conversation with Vincent, although she was dreading the evening ahead once Tim and Lucy were in bed.

Deciding that it would be in her own interest to allow them one late night, she returned to the security of the playroom and started to tidy up. Pocahontas, as well as being dead, was now bald. She sank down onto one of the small chairs that littered the colourful room and stared at the doll's pale, measly face and the random tufts of plastic hair that remained on her crown.

"I'm fecked as well, Poco," she admitted.

Maybe it was madness to talk to a mutilated toy but Jennie knew that her options were limited. The giggles and squeals coming from the lounge made her feel more alone than she could ever have imagined. She knew it was on the verge of paranoia to think that there could be anything between Vincent and Donna but the way they'd been smiling into each other's eyes made her wonder seriously about it. How many unwitting women wrote off their feelings as paranoia only to discover the truth when it was too late?

Sighing deeply, she straightened the last of the toys and replaced the books on their shelves. If she were the type of person who had a friend to confide in, now would be the time to leave Vincent and the children to their own devices and take off for a quiet drink and a cry. As it stood, there was only Maxine who would think that Jennie was bonkers if she landed on her doorstep at half past eight when Vincent was only just in the door. If she suggested an early night, her husband might think she was issuing an invitation for sex, something that she couldn't countenance after the debacle that the evening had become.

"I'll open a bottle of wine!" she called through the hall as she made her way into the spacious kitchen that had been her pride and joy when they'd first moved into the house. Jack Rooney had made an enormous effort to source the deep hardwood worktop that ran around the cream units and covered the central island. She'd been surprised that her old school friend had such exquisite taste at a time when most people were looking for a natural wood finish on their kitchen units.

"It's a bit Americanised all right," he'd laughed when he'd first suggested the painted look.

Jack, she remembered then, had worked in construction in the States since he'd left school and had only recently returned to Rathmollin.

"I like it," she had decided impulsively, despite the fact that she'd already convinced Vincent that maple was what she wanted, notwithstanding the cost.

Automatically she pulled lettuce, ham, tomatoes and cheese out of the Smeg fridge, more for something to be doing rather than any desire to make the sandwich that Vincent seemed to prefer to a delicious meal in the city.

"It's all right, I'll do that," he said now, coming up behind her.

Her shoulders tensed immediately and she moved away in the direction of the wine rack. She hated the thought that he might touch her, knowing how good it would feel as soon as he kissed her and the way that all her savage thoughts would wash out of her head if his arms went around her.

"Will you have wine or a beer?" she asked.

He'd taken up where she'd left off and was carefully slicing a tomato, neat and precise as always.

"Wine is good." He placed his sandwich on the plate and carried it through to the lounge where the children were playing with a long metallic snake that lit up and vibrated depending on which part of it they touched.

His originality needled Jennie who only ever bought Tim and Lucy the things that they demanded from Smyth's Toys. She never got the opportunity to arrive home with new and exciting gadgets that the kids in school wouldn't have seen.

"God, that's lovely. It's great to have a drink in peace without having to haggle over contracts. Did I tell you that Bob and Noeleen are having an anniversary do at the weekend?" His feet were stretched out on the leopardskin footstool that matched the cushions on the sofa. Tim and Lucy, for once, were quiet, obsessed as they were with the electronic snake.

"What anniversary is it for them?" She wondered if she was being paranoid or did Vincent's comment about the trip being all about business seem a bit staged.

"Thirty. It's on in Montenotte. Dinner first and then music. We must ask Donna if she's free on Saturday night."

It hit Jennie that it was easier for him to get revved up for his partner's anniversary party than it was to go out for a meal with his wife but before she had time to answer, Tim piped up that Donna was going to let them try on her make-up the next night she was minding them. Vincent looked at her, clearly alarmed at his son's obvious interest. Remembering Pocahontas and her new hair-do, Jennie wondered if her son needed to spend more time in male company.

"I must try and cut down on the trips." Vincent, for the first time that evening, was on the same wavelength as her.

Jennie relaxed a little, although she was still annoyed at

the way Bob and Noeleen's anniversary had to be prioritised. Especially as Vincent had shot down the idea of the restaurant tonight with the promise of a night out at the weekend that would clearly not materialise.

"Not a bad idea," Jennie answered him dryly. "What time is the dinner? I'll give Donna a ring in the morning."

"Around eight. Should we buy a present or something?"

Jennie wondered if it was just her or if Vincent too felt the tension that had entered their relationship. When they were first married, she couldn't wait to hear how the business side of his foreign trips had gone. Now, she was afraid to ask for fear of hearing some little discrepancy that might substantiate the doubts that seemed to be eating away at her.

"The deeds of the land in Dubai finally got transferred over to us." It was almost as if he could read her thoughts and wanted to assure her that the week in Dubai had been productive.

"That's great." Jennie knew she sounded vague and disinterested. Her wine-glass was almost empty but so far it hadn't helped to ease the tension that had entered her muscles in the short-term car park when he'd refused to go to Nouvelle for the evening.

"The plans have been ready for ages so it's only a matter of finalising things with the builders."

As well as their main auctioneering business, Bob Ferris and Vincent had used the substantial cash flow that had come their way with the Irish property boom to expand their horizons abroad. Now that they'd acquired the parcel of land in Dubai that they'd been chasing for months, they could start on the three blocks of luxury seafront apartments that they knew would sell like hot cakes. Each block would house twenty high-end units with a private swimming pool, gym and sauna attached. Dubai was hot property now according to Vincent. It seemed the Alicante days were long gone for wealthy Irish property hunters.

"When will the building start?" Despite herself, Jennie was interested.

"In the next month or so. These guys are like machines once they get going – they have a big enough share of the construction work over there. Bob is happier to be working with Irish contractors as well, especially when we know Jack."

"He has a finger in plenty of pies, doesn't he?" Jennie curled her legs under her in the enormous leather chair. Vincent seemed to be in the form for talking, even though he still looked a bit tired and puffy around the eyes.

The kids had dragged their snake off to the playroom and by the sound of it, were wrecking the place again. She was tempted to threaten them with bed but desisted on account of enjoying this rare moment of simple conversation. It was what she had hoped to achieve, she realised, when she'd booked the table at Nouvelle earlier.

"He was well set up coming back from the States. And he's good at what he does – no bullshit."

Jennie had to admit that what her husband said about Jack Rooney was true. Rathmollin Woods had been his first development on his return to his home village and even now it stood out among the many other exclusive developments that littered the county. On the outskirts of the village, the ten houses nestled in what many of the property pages described as a clearing in the woods. The timber balconies and open wrap-around porches, some of which boasted authentic swinging seats, were certainly a departure from the lines of semis with their tiny gardens of the more mediocre estates.

At the time, the idea of open-plan gardens at the front caused a swell of incredulity in the village. How would anyone know where one property ended and the next began? Territorial as ever about their boundaries, the majority of the villagers thought it would surely come to a bad end. It was only the advent of *Desperate Housewives* that started to make any sense of it at all. Once Wisteria Lane became known to people, the concept of a neighbourhood without walls and hedges began to sink in.

The electronic entrance gates had been another bone of contention. Why would anyone need security gates in Rathmollin? To this day, Jennie couldn't really answer her father on that one. To explain to him about preserving an air of exclusivity to justify the extortionate price tag would be like a red rag to a bull. Jennie's father was very much anti-snobbery.

"Mom, can we go to bed now?" Lucy, as usual, was the spokesperson.

"This is a first." Vincent was grinning as he lifted his daughter onto his lap. "I thought you said you were going to stay up all night? Until the morning?"

This was one of Lucy's favourite ambitions, one that she constantly complained was thwarted by her mother.

"I was. But I thought it would be different." She sounded sulky.

"How do you mean?" Vincent was clearly anxious to hear her logic on late nights.

"It's the same as daytime. You and Mom are only talking about ordinary stuff and all the toys are the same. I thought they might be alive."

"Alive?"

"Like in *Toy Story*. Woody can talk at night in the DVD but our Woody is just sitting there."

Jennie had bought the *Toy Story* characters for the children when they'd been laid up with chickenpox two years earlier. Vincent probably didn't have a clue who Woody was.

"What about Buzz? Did he do anything?" he asked and Jennie found that she was almost disappointed at how tuned in he was.

"Not a thing," Tim reported, his tone disparaging. "We might as well go to bed."

Jennie had heard him explaining to Lucy before that the *Toy Story* characters were unlikely to come to life but Lucy had her own opinion on it.

"I think," Vincent said now, "that they probably do come alive during the night – if there is nobody watching. They probably can't if people are there."

"But that's no good!" Lucy was very much ahead of her years in some ways and Jennie often wondered how long it would be before she started to get suspicious of Santa.

"We'll have to get evidence," said Vincent. "You know, catch them out."

Tim looked on, bored with the whole idea.

"How?" Lucy was still belligerent about it.

"We'll set them up exactly right and see if they've moved by the morning. We'll do it now and then you can go to bed." Vincent's face was alight at his great idea.

Jennie agreed that this was the only way to tell and scooted them all off to the playroom while she refilled the wine-glasses. His interaction with the kids had thawed her a little and she knew now that she and Vincent would make love later. Somehow the idea didn't seem anathema to the same degree as it had earlier in the kitchen.

Feeling more mellow than she had all week, she wondered whether it was because of the wine or because of having had her husband to herself for the past half hour. It reminded her of the way they used to sit up talking until the early hours before they were parents, nibbling bits of cheese with their wine when they eventually got peckish. She seemed to be thinking a lot tonight about the way things used to be between them and it alarmed her a bit. It was almost as if she were seeing them in the past tense.

Shaking herself out of such a terrifying thought, Jennie tiptoed to the kitchen lest her offspring decide that nothing but cereal – a frequent ploy – would help them to sleep. Rummaging among the bottles of Ribena and Petit Filous she pulled out a quarter wheel of Edam and started to chop cubes of it onto a plate. She added a handful of grapes and made her way silently back to the lounge. The playroom was quiet and she could hear Vincent instructing the children to go to the toilet before getting into bed.

Jennie settled back on the sofa and sipped her wine,

content to let him take over the storytelling for one night. She was glad now that they'd ended up not going out. She was also glad that she'd showered and smothered herself in the gorgeous Clarins body cream that made her feel sensual and sexy. Suddenly, she was looking forward to the children being asleep and really having Vincent to herself.

Because no matter how irritated she got at being alone for days on end and no matter how much she hated his business trips, the one thing that hadn't changed was the chemistry between them. Smiling dreamily to herself, Jennie slipped off her shoes and curled up contentedly on the sofa, waiting for Vincent.

Chapter 7

By Wednesday, Sandra had got over the worst of her annoyance at Paul for the racket that he'd caused on Monday evening. He'd slept like a log once she'd managed to get him up the stairs, allowing her to make her way sheepishly down the street to her parents' house where Dylan was potting annuals in brightly coloured tubs with her father.

"I'll say nothing." Dan's voice was quiet lest Dylan pick up the tone of disappointment and warning in it.

Sandra wondered what Dylan had said when he arrived, whether he'd mentioned anything about the shouting or the mess of the kitchen – she hoped he might have been wise enough not to.

Paul had gone to work on Tuesday with a massive hangover and she'd been terrified that he would think of going to the pub afterwards to "clear his head" as he tended to put it himself. He didn't and they spent the evening watching television, with their son playing quietly with his Power Rangers.

This was what she'd expected when she'd agreed to have Paul living with them again. She really believed that her son had a right to know his father and was heartened to see Paul actually chatting to Dylan about school when she came back into the sitting-room at one point with three mugs of hot chocolate.

Later, when Dylan was sound asleep, she and Paul had watched *Desperate Housewives* and ended up making love on the cramped sofa before sneaking up the stairs and curling up together in the queen-sized bed that she'd thought was huge the day she'd bought it. With Paul's huge bulk, it was like being in a sardine tin but the feeling of closeness after so many years on her own made it worth it.

To Sandra, packing Dylan off to school and Paul off to work on Wednesday morning had seemed like the height of normality. Apart from the loss of her three pasta bowls – and she wondered if she might have been a tad petty about them – the kitchen was back to its usual homely state and she'd set about making a beef casserole for dinner that evening. If only Paul could stay away from the pub, the three of them could have a great life together. The rent on the cottage was cheap and they could always apply to the council to be transferred to a bigger place if one came up in the area.

Sandra spent the better part of the afternoon plotting a future for them, oblivious to the drama that was unfolding on the building site at the far end of the village.

It was after four when Paul arrived home and she'd just let Dylan out the back to play for a bit. Throwing himself down on one of the kitchen chairs, he rested his elbows on the Formica tabletop and glowered until she'd placed a mug of tea in front of him. Her heart had sunk at the familiar smell of drink the moment he'd walked through the door, telling her that he'd already been to the pub. She listened as he started to rant.

He was pissed off, he kept saying, and Sandra did her best to keep up with the story. It was just as well that Dylan was out watering the tubs of flowers in the backyard with the little green watering can that his grandfather had given him or he'd have been upset by all the loud talk.

It wasn't that her boyfriend was annoyed at her or Dylan – it was his job that was bothering him and now it seemed that he'd resigned in some sort of protest over his rights to a proper lunch break.

Having moved back from London three months ago, he'd been lucky to get the job so close to home. Conveniently, he'd met Sandra in The Stone's Throw that first weekend and had been pleased to hear that she'd been given a council house since he'd last seen her.

The fact that they had an eight-year-old child in common was good enough grounds for him to move in with her, although his contact with Dylan up to then had been limited, sending whatever he could afford to her parents' house every Christmas.

"That Jack Rooney is a prick anyway," he concluded eventually, after regaling Sandra with a diatribe about his boss for fifteen minutes.

"What will you do now?" It was one thing to have Paul coming in drunk a few evenings a week but it was quite another to have him unemployed and under her feet all day now that he'd told Jack Rooney to "go fuck himself".

"He'll be back after me in no time. There's no way they'll be able to finish that development if they're short on labour," Paul said confidently.

The story that he'd told Sandra of the day's events had centred around the fact that Paul and one of the other labourers had decided to go to The Stone's for their lunch instead of having it in the on-site canteen like everyone else. As it happened, the foreman had been called away to a problem on another job and Jack Rooney had arrived on the site. He'd been livid to find Paul and the other fellow arriving back "a bit late" and had tackled them on it, resulting in the walkout that had Paul arriving home at four o'clock.

Filling in the blanks, Sandra wondered exactly how late "a bit" was and whether Paul and his buddy had smelled of drink. The timescale of events was somewhat vague and he certainly reeked of alcohol now. Either he had been like this on the site or he'd returned to the pub *after* his walkout as well.

Either way, Sandra wasn't sure she could manage to subsidise Paul on the Lone Parent's Allowance that barely supported herself and Dylan. The sooner Jack Rooney, whom Sandra had known since childhood, arrived to beseech Paul to come back to work the better.

"That'd be great. The money's good and it's local." She needed to make him see that it was okay for him to go back to work if Jack approached him, that he wouldn't be losing face.

"I'll see. I'll sign on tomorrow or Friday anyway."

Sandra didn't like the sound of this. If Paul was intent on signing on for social welfare it implied that he had no real intention of going back to work. Not that it mattered one way or another – he hadn't given her so much as a penny since he'd moved in with her.

With that, he removed himself to the sitting-room and turned on the television, leaving Sandra in the kitchen wondering if the idyllic future that she'd been planning might be less of a reality than she'd imagined.

The future was something that she thought about a lot, to the point a few months ago when she was planning to restart the four-year hairdressing course that she'd been halfway through when she'd found herself pregnant with Dylan. Meeting Paul again had put the kibosh on it, especially when he'd reminded her that she would lose all her entitlements and maybe even her council house if she was earning a significant wage at Curly Locks.

Meeting Emily Gordon the other night had made her think about what things might have been like if she'd finished the hairdressing course and had been able to set up her own business. Emily was in the process of looking for a house to *buy* while here she was thinking that getting up the council list was an achievement. She'd envied Emily on Sunday evening, with her ability to consider buying her own house.

They'd sat next to each other in primary school and had been the best of friends. Jack Rooney and Jennie McCarthy had sat directly behind them in another double desk, poking Sandra and Emily when the teacher wasn't watching. Their paths had diverged however after primary school, with Emily and Jennie going to a convent school in the city while Sandra and Jack went to the vocational school, considered then to be the choice of those less academically inclined.

Somehow, the other three had made a success of themselves while Sandra seemed to lurch from one disaster to the next – not that she'd consider Dylan a disaster for anything. Emily had gone straight to college with an excellent Leaving Cert. Jennie, stunningly beautiful, had excelled at her secretarial course and landed Vincent Kelleher almost straightaway. Jack, despite hating every minute of school, had taken off to New York and arrived back the success story of the century.

Taking Paul back again had been Sandra's way of trying to make a success of herself too. She didn't want to be just another single mother for the rest of her life – she wanted the kind of cosy family life that Jennie had, even if she didn't have a career like Emily or Jack's money.

But now, listening to the blare of the television over Paul's snoring and her son playing out in the yard to avoid encountering his father, she could see that for all her trying, she wasn't even able to achieve that much.

Chapter 8

Racing along Patrick Street at high speed, Emily made her way towards the offices of the Electricity Board. She knew it was going to be difficult to persuade the debts officer that Maggie Harvey would eventually repay the enormous bill that she'd run up but Emily was confident that once she explained the situation on her client's behalf, they might be able to reach some agreement.

Knowing how important it was not to antagonise the debts officer, she let out a sigh of relief when she finally reached the building on time and made her way towards the familiar office on the second floor.

After sitting patiently in the impersonal, minimalist waiting room in a shiny plastic bucket seat for twenty minutes, she was finally called to the inner sanctum. Emily had presented herself at this same office on many occasions in the past few months and had developed a mutually respectful relationship with Derry Cronin, who'd recently retired. She was anxious now to see whether she could reach the same accommodating arrangement with his replacement.

"Miss Gordon, please sit down. You're here to represent Mrs Harvey, I believe?"

Talk about getting straight down to business. Emily studied the serious-looking young man in front of her and figured that he could only be twenty-five at the very most. She almost smiled as she observed his earnest face and smooth brow, something that it wouldn't take long to alter once he was working in the area of debt retrieval for a while. A small black and white sign on his desk announced him as Michael Moran.

"Yes, indeed. Mrs Harvey, as I've outlined in my letter, has had some personal difficulties of late and has got behind in her repayments on account of it."

"Going through the records here, I notice that there has been no repayment at all in the past seven months or indeed no contact from the client regarding any difficulties."

Mentally cursing the poor hapless Maggie for not calling to the agency before the situation had really got out of hand, Emily drew on all her reserves to convince this young paper-pusher that the mother of six should be given a chance to redeem herself before her supply was cut off.

"Mrs Harvey's husband had an unfortunate accident around that time, which resulted in the loss of both of his legs and subsequently his income. Naturally, with six children to care for, my client lost her sense of organisation and neglected many of her household duties," Emily said piously.

What she chose to gloss over was the fact that Ned Harvey had fallen down a railway embankment after a night's drinking and had caused the derailment of a grain-supply train as the driver tried in vain to stop. She also neglected to mention that four of Maggie's children were adults who no longer lived at home.

"Non-payment of bills and failure to respond to correspondence regarding this can lead to a court appearance and indeed a custodial sentence in some cases, Miss Gordon," the young Mr Moran pointed out gravely.

"While I'm very much aware of this, Mr Moran, I'd like to think that a compromise could be reached whereby the Electricity Board could recoup the debt, albeit in a protracted manner and that the distraught lady in question could retain her supply and maintain regular ongoing payments. Surely this would be to everyone's benefit?"

"Perhaps," the debts officer conceded, "although Mrs Harvey would need to supply a guarantor in this case, in the event that a larger bill would accumulate at any stage in the future." He looked at Emily enquiringly.

"I'm sure that can be arranged, if you could allow the customer a few days to organise this. I can liaise with my client and contact you here on Monday if that's acceptable."

"There is the matter of the amount of the repayments. You had suggested in your correspondence a sum of €10 per week for the arrears. I would be more inclined to think that €20 per week would be appropriate."

Emily had anticipated this, which was why she had suggested such a meagre figure in the first place. If she had mentioned €20 at the outset, she imagined that the debts officer would have wanted to increase it to €30, a sum that Maggie could ill afford with her penchant for a glass or two of Beamish almost every night of the week.

"I'm sure my client would attempt to rise to €20 per week along with her regular repayments. She's very committed to regaining her status as a reliable customer," Emily told him seriously, now that it seemed the deal was hammered out.

"I'm sure," Michael Moran murmured in the non-committal tone of one not to be soft-soaped until the offending customer had proved her commitment in a material sense.

Five minutes later, Emily was back out on Patrick Street, relieved that Maggie was off the hook momentarily but aware of the difficulty she would encounter to secure an acceptable guarantor. There was also the matter of Maggie's other arrears to attend to, most notably the €500 that had built up with the local council from non-payment of rent. There was also a mobile phone bill that Emily felt was impossible to repay at this stage. It was her hope that she could negotiate with the phone company to strike it off altogether and that she could organise a "pay as you go" system in Ned's name.

Satisfied that she'd made at least some progress at untangling the web of debt that was strangling the Harveys, Emily ducked into a small coffee shop she liked on Academy Street to regroup her thoughts and catch up on the lunch that she'd missed when a white-faced young mother had tapped urgently at the VBA's frosted window at five to one. As Emily's parents were always pointing out, she never could resist a person in trouble, which was exactly why her job in the Voluntary Budgeting Agency suited her perfectly.

Now, as she sat in a quiet corner eating her sandwich, she was able to appreciate the part of her job that gave her the most satisfaction. Helping people had always been something that made her feel good, back as far as primary school when she'd been the one who helped the smaller ones out with their laces after the "exercise" sessions on Friday mornings.

It sometimes baffled her that she was so good at sorting out other people's lives when in fact her own was far from sorted. Moving home to Rathmollin had made her realise just how much other people of her age had achieved and here she was with precious little to show for herself, except a failed engagement to a rat of the highest order.

Her mother was always talking about who was married with kids and whose husband did what for a living, making Emily realise she'd achieved almost nothing in her twenty-eight years. Although if her dad's friend thought the structural report on Harmony Cottage was as good as it sounded, she might at least have her own home at last.

She'd already been to the bank and it seemed there would be no trouble at all with getting a mortgage that would include enough to do some minor renovations to the cottage. This evening would be the deciding factor when her father's friend, an engineer with the council, would let her know the exact status of Harmony Cottage.

He'd even obligingly agreed to visit it himself if there was anything in the report that he needed to query.

Emily sighed into her coffee. Maybe everyone reached a certain point in their life where they compared themselves to other people and came up short. If that was the case, she thought that perhaps she'd just about reached that point. She'd always imagined herself as a married career woman with a brood of children by the time she was thirty, yet that milestone was fast approaching and she hadn't even made a start on most of it.

She was just completing another deep sigh when she was interrupted by a polite cough right next to her.

"Er, do you mind if I sit here? The place seems to be full to the rafters today."

Glancing up distractedly, Emily realised that the man who'd spoken was waiting patiently for an answer rather than just sequestering the spare chair as if the request was entirely arbitrary.

"Sure, no problem."

Hurriedly, Emily gathered up her work notebook and phone, conscious that he was balancing a laden tray and a briefcase, as well as blocking up the small corridor between her table and the adjoining booth.

He was familiar-looking and attractive in a rugged sort of way, kind of outdoorsy and tanned. Probably one of the elite sailing crowd that were so prominent on the Cork social scene, Emily decided, a quick glance taking in the silver streaks in his light blond hair that must have come from years of crewing the family yacht. Definitely sailing, she decided as he slotted himself in opposite her leaving his legs at an angle to the tiny table. The expensive suit was another giveaway. She definitely thought he looked a bit familiar, probably from seeing his face in glossy magazines like *Cork Now* and *RSVP*.

Emily concentrated on the remaining few items on her list of "things to do", glad that she had the Electricity Board debts officer out of the way.

She jumped when her neighbour's mobile rang out shrilly from the far side of the table. It really annoyed Emily the way that people had to have louder and more brash ring-tones these days. Her own was on silent most of the time, with only the vibration to let her know that a call was coming in.

As well as having an obnoxious ring-tone, the man across the table from her seemed to have a matching personality, answering with an abrupt "Yeah?" and proceeding to yell in monosyllables that could probably be heard on the Grand Parade.

"What?" he shouted, his voice rising an octave. "Tell me this is a joke, Tony!"

Emily remembered that it was the first of April – Fool's Day. She was mesmerised by this display of conversational finesse and stared at him in fascination as his dark-blue eyes narrowed and a frown appeared across his superbly tanned forehead.

"Where?" was the next utterance. "Get them out of there. I'll be over straight away. Just get them out."

He snapped his phone shut at that, leaving Emily in no doubt that whatever minion had displeased him would be well and truly taken care of.

Jesus, take the whole table with you, why don't you, Emily fumed as he swiped up a stack of papers he'd been studying and sent the pepper and salt skidding in her direction. Oblivious, he stuffed the wad of pages back into his briefcase and strode away from the table as if he hadn't just disrupted the quiet lunch that she'd planned for herself. Ignorant git, Emily shouted mentally, wishing that she had the nerve to actually say it out loud to his retreating back.

Well and truly disturbed, she decided to abandon the remainder of her sandwich and head back to the tiny office she occupied in Friar Street, confident that she could at least have a cup of tea in peace there.

She was still fuming over her aborted lunch as she tore past Brown Thomas.

"Emily?"

She swung around, wondering who it could be. She had so few friends in Cork at this stage.

"Hi, Emily, it *is* you!"

Jennie McCarthy, or Kelleher as she was called now, was smiling at her. As ever, her old school friend looked like something out of a fashion shoot, even though she was only wearing jeans. Not the kind of jeans that Emily herself wore, mind, but the kind that looked well with the lime-green Lacoste sweater that they were teamed with. Emily felt like a small mousey animal that had just come out of hibernation by comparison.

"Hi, Jennie, it's great to see you."

Jacinta Gordon was always talking about how well Jennie had done for herself and Emily could see why by the hank of shopping bags that she was clinging onto. "How're things?"

"The usual. Chasing around after the kids." She grinned at Emily and indicated the bags. "The only chance I have to get anything done is when they're in school."

Emily would have loved to see what exactly was in them – by the look of it, there was at least a couple of hundred euros' worth of clothes. Anything from Quin and Donnelly cost an arm and a leg, not to mind the fact that there seemed to be a smaller cardboard-type bag stuffed with Benefit stuff. There was a big, square Louise Kennedy bag as well, probably full of expensive glassware for all the entertaining she did. Emily felt a pang of regret for the heavy Galway crystal glasses she'd left behind in Dublin, not that she needed them now that her days of endless entertaining were over.

Even the waft of perfume was glorious. Emily recognised it as a Chanel one that she'd had a tester of a couple of months before, although she couldn't imagine that Jennie would actually use the testers that came as samples with her make-up purchases.

"I can imagine," she responded now. "I met Sandra the other day and she's up to her ears with Dylan so your two must be twice the work."

"Tell me about it! Are you working in Cork now, Emily?"

Emily could feel the blush rising up along her throat. Of course Jennie would have heard about her cancelled wedding – bloody Aggie Lenihan had dined out on it for weeks so that the whole of Rathmollin knew every detail that she'd been able to prise from Emily's mother. Putting on her brightest face, she filled Jennie in on her job, deciding that the whole engagement debacle was her own business.

"I'm with a voluntary group called the VBA. Voluntary Budgeting Agency. People come to us if they get into debt or need help with bills and saving. We liaise with people like the banks, Electricity Board or whoever to get them sorted."

"Sounds interesting. Even though there probably isn't too much business for you these days. What with the boom and everything." Like most middle-class people, Jennie thought that the economic boom being experienced in Ireland at the moment meant that there were no "poor" people left.

"You must be joking! There's so much money about at the moment that the people who have it are living well and the people who don't have it expect to lead the same kind of lifestyle. People borrow too much and then can't pay it back."

Jennie looked as if she had no concept of poverty whatsoever. Her sunglasses alone, with their Armani logo, could probably have settled Maggie Harvey's bills in one fell swoop. "I never thought of it like that, Emily. I saw this documentary the other night about moneylenders. I didn't think they even existed in this day and age."

"They're very much in existence," Emily assured her with a grin. "How's Vincent? The last time I met you he was in Croatia selling apartments."

"Same thing – different country." Jennie looked as if

this was a trial and tribulation although it was obviously working out financially for them. "He's away a lot but I suppose that's the nature of the job."

"I suppose so." Although Emily wasn't convinced.

"I'd better go and pick the pair up from school," Jennie said now, glancing at her watch.

"And I'd better get back and earn another few bob." It was well into the afternoon and she still had calls to make before she left for home. On impulse, she suggested that they meet for coffee or lunch the next time Jennie was in town. After all, she'd vowed to make a new life and new friends in Cork and it was Jennie who'd greeted *her* earlier and seemed pleased to see her.

"That'd be great, Emily. I'm in town at least once a week. I'll put your number in my phone and give you a bell."

The phone that Jennie produced from the depths of her handbag was a slim, state-of-the-art one, unlike Emily's plain VBA-issue model.

"There," Jennie said when they'd finished keying in the numbers. "I'll definitely call you. Bye for now, Emily."

"Bye, Jennie. See you soon." Emily turned in the direction of Friar Street as Jennie headed for her car with long elegant strides. They were worlds apart, she knew, but it would be nice to meet someone for lunch now and again. She'd left everything behind when she'd left Dublin but there was no reason why she couldn't start again.

By the time she'd finally made her way back to the office, the uncharacteristic warmth of the early April sun had seeped into her and restored her good form.

"A Mrs Harvey called while you were out – wondering whether you'd sorted out her electricity bill . . ." Gina greeted her from the reception desk.

"That's grand, Gina. I'll give Mrs Harvey a ring later. Right now I need a cuppa."

"I'll follow you as soon as Orla comes back. That phone has my head done in – I'm sure I'll get some kind of brain shrinkage from it yet."

Emily grinned and wondered that Gina had any brain at all left at that rate. When she wasn't answering calls from the general public and patching them through to the various facilitators, she was taking personal calls from a variety of different men or phoning her friends to tell them the details of the suitors' calls.

Emily made her way to the homely kitchen at the back of the building and put the kettle on for herself and Gina, aware that the receptionist must have another conquest to discuss if she was in such a rush for a coffee break.

Twenty minutes later, Emily was in the throes of Gina's drama, her feet restless under the table in her anxiety to get back to work. She still had loads of calls to make but it was proving almost impossible to break into Gina's flow about some fella she'd met in Redz at the weekend.

"He's practically single, only that his girlfriend can't accept that it's all over between them," she explained, her enormous, brown doe-eyes pleading with Emily to agree that this Romeo was a good prospect for the future.

"He has your phone number," Emily said finally, having been down this particular road with Gina on more than one occasion in the past few months. "Let him know that he's welcome to ring you as soon as he has his affairs sorted out."

"I suppose you're right," Gina conceded, her fluffy blonde curls swinging around her face dejectedly. "Why do I always meet the wasters?"

"At least you meet men," Emily reminded her as she washed her cup. "Be they good, bad or indifferent, I don't even get in with a shout."

"They're not going to line up outside the door in an orderly queue, you know. You'll have come out on the town with myself and Orla some night."

Orla was the VBA's other secretary/receptionist and doubled by night as Gina's going-out partner. The thought of tripping around the city's hot-spots in their company filled Emily with horror – just the thought of what she'd have to wear to fit in with them made her weak. On the few occasions that she seen them leaving directly from work for a night out, she'd wondered how on earth their clothes could even be hung on a conventional hanger, there was so little of them.

"Thanks, Gina," Emily mumbled, escaping to her office before her colleague would actually attempt to inveigle her out, seeing as it happened to be Thursday.

Maybe that's my problem, Emily thought as she pulled out various files and her precious list of contact numbers. I spend all day giving everybody else advice, yet here I am with my own life far from sorted.

Somehow, she'd always thought that meeting someone would happen naturally, without all the contrived dressing-up and batting of eyelashes at men she knew she had nothing in common with. And it had, she realised when she thought about her first meeting with Richard Carmody in the library at UCD. But now that the debacle that was her first long-term relationship had reached a very conclusive end, she wasn't so sure that anything of merit was likely to happen in the near future.

Aware that she was sighing deeply for the umpteenth time that day, she picked up the phone to tell Maggie Harvey the good news about her electricity bill, wishing the hours away until six o'clock when she would find out whether Harmony Cottage was a runner or not.

Chapter 9

Even though the fire appeared to be under control now, Jack Rooney could still feel the heat radiating from it warming his face. The pounding of his heart had slowed as soon as one of the foremen had phoned him to say that the last of the occupants had been safely taken out by the firemen. He'd actually run the whole way from the coffee shop on Academy Street to Linen Street, leaving his car in the Paul Street multi-storey.

"Look, Mr Rooney, there's nothing more you can do here for the moment." The chief fire officer was serious as he advised Jack on the impending procedures. "The building should be pretty safe but I'd recommend that you stay out of it until a full investigation is carried out into the cause of the fire."

"Have you any idea how it started?"

"Cooking by the sound of it – but we'll know more over the next few days. One of the occupants said that she was heating a pan of oil but that she left it for a moment when one of the children ran out into the road. It must have ignited."

"I had no idea that there were so many people in there," Jack told the fire officer, his distress evident.

"It happens all the time. People think that fire regulations are the government's way of penalising them rather than seeing them as safety procedures."

"There were two smoke alarms," Jack observed, wondering if they'd been of any benefit at all when the fire broke out.

"Just as well or there would have been more casualties."

Two of the occupants of Number 5, The Grove, had been taken to hospital by ambulance. One was a small child who'd been asleep in a cot upstairs; the other was the woman who'd apparently been running a small child-care concern without Jack's knowledge. Neither of them, to his relief, had been seriously injured.

"Thanks again for everything," he said now as the fire officer prepared to leave, his job done now that the fire had been extinguished and the ambulances had departed the scene.

Jack's next step this afternoon would have to be sorting out alternative accommodation for the two Eastern European families who were now suddenly homeless.

He'd bought the city centre property two years previously with the express purpose of using it to house the workers that he contracted from Poland until they organised their own living arrangements. The large two-storey had been easily converted into two spacious apartments and the arrangement had worked out more than satisfactorily until now.

Most of the new arrivals tended to arrive in the country alone, sending for wives and children as soon as they'd established a base, so Number 5 had been an ideal stepping-stone. Recently, a few of the newcomers had brought their families from the outset and Jack didn't have a problem with this so long as there was no overcrowding.

A cold sweat came out all over him again at the thought of the eight children who'd been inside when the alarm had been raised. As far as he could gather, Monika Malisa, married to one of the plasterers, had been taking care of some of the other workers' children while their wives took on cleaning jobs around the city. Hence the advent of the crèche in Apartment 2.

In all honesty, Jack found it hard to be angry with the families who arrived in Ireland with the dream of a better lifestyle and the endless opportunities to be had on the back of the famous Celtic Tiger. The reality of course was that they were met with extortionate rental costs, a prohibitively high cost of living and a crippling taxation system. No wonder so many of them got involved in tax-free earning schemes to keep afloat.

"Okay," he addressed the small group who remained now that the drama was over and the neighbours and assorted on-lookers had dispersed. "First things first. As soon as we can, we'll get the house sorted out but in the meantime, we need to decide where everyone's going to stay tonight."

The house, as far as he could gather from the fire

officers, wasn't too badly damaged. Certainly nothing that couldn't be remedied in a matter of a week if he put everyone on overtime for a few evenings. He could see the relief on the faces of his now homeless employees and their families that he was taking charge of the situation.

Ten minutes later, he was en route to the nearby hospital, having successfully secured temporary board for both of the families after a succession of phone calls. Stan Kovaciwycz sat ashen-faced next to him in the front, his wife Sibile already gone to St Angela's with their son in the ambulance. In the back, Greg Malisa stared silently ahead, terrified that his wife, Monika, might be seriously injured.

Jack, normally accustomed to being on familiar terms with all the newcomers, was embarrassed that he barely knew the Malisa family. Stan Kovaciwycz, living in Ireland for some time now, would translate for them when they reached the hospital.

His head was bursting with the shock he'd had when Tony Callaghan had phoned to say that Number 5 was on fire and that the fire service were in the process of evacuating it. In the back of his mind however was an overriding sense of relief that nobody had been seriously injured. Everything else, he figured, could be sorted out.

Emily could hardly contain herself when she heard Leonard Horan say that the little cottage was indeed as sound as a pound, as the auctioneer had told her on her first visit. Now, as far as she was concerned, it was all systems go.

First thing in the morning, she was going to phone Dermot Leahy at The Property People and make an offer. If all went well, she could be the owner of Harmony Cottage in a matter of weeks.

There was plenty of work to be done, she knew, like getting the bathroom suite sorted out. Her dad would help her to find a plumber or whoever might be needed to install everything. Bathroom tiles would be another investment. There was no way that she'd be able to live with the pink and black checks.

"The work will take time," her mother warned, "but at least you'll be near enough to keep an eye on things."

"As long as there aren't any other offers in."

Now that she'd made her mind up she was starting to get nervous about it being pushed beyond her price range.

"Don't worry, love – what's for you won't pass you by." Her father, as always, was reassuring.

"I hope you're right."

Tomorrow would be a big day for her and she didn't want anything to go wrong.

After tea she lay on her bed, plotting her future and thinking about the way that things had turned out for her so far. Leaving Dublin had been a wrench but she knew it was something that had to be done when she'd realised she was never going to be able to afford her own house there, now that she was suddenly single. She'd resented giving up her job as a senior social worker but in the end she'd made up her mind that she couldn't start paying extortionate rent alone as well as saving *and* she needed a change from the stress of bumping into friends when she couldn't decide whether they were more entitled to be hers or Richard's.

Getting an equally senior job in Cork hadn't been as easy as she might have expected, leaving her in the unenviable position of accepting the post in the VBA for a much smaller salary than she was used to. Now, although house prices were considerably lower in Cork than they were in Dublin, she had less money than ever to play around with.

Harmony Cottage was her best bet – but only if nobody else had spotted it yet.

Chapter 10

It was five to eight on Thursday evening and Jennie was watching the clock and wondering where Vincent was. Since his return from Dubai on Tuesday night, he'd been back to work with a vengeance, straightening out everything that had piled up in his absence. He'd phoned in the morning to say that it'd be a long day and to have dinner without him but she hadn't expected him to be this late.

If she had, she wouldn't have asked Maxine to call over with Seán for a drink when they'd met at the school gates earlier. Now she was putting the finishing touches to the delicious bites she planned to serve with the drinks while Tim and Lucy watched *Cars* in the playroom.

Jennie grinned as the doorbell pealed just as the hands of the clock reached eight. She always checked the time when Maxine arrived and she had yet to be disappointed by her friend's punctuality.

"Hi, Jennie – I presume Vincent has the beers lined up in front of the telly for the City match?" Seán was an avid

Cork City supporter and Jennie merely rolled her eyes in response.

"He's not even home yet. Come on in and we'll see what we can do."

"Don't even think about entertaining him on that one, Jen – it was hard enough to get him out the door in the first place." Maxine kissed her lightly on the cheek and handed her a huge bunch of scented white lilac tied with a hessian bow.

Seán, predictably, made a beeline for the lounge and the large plasma screen.

"Maxine, it's gorgeous – the scent is just divine. Come on in and I'll get a vase."

Maxine followed Jennie through to the utility room off the kitchen and kept up a steady stream of conversation while the lilac was arranged in a heavy Galway crystal vase.

"I still can't believe you grew this from a slip!" said Jennie.

Maxine grinned proudly when Jennie reminded her of the day she'd nicked the switch of lilac from the garden of a hotel as they were packing their things into the car after a relaxing spa weekend a few years previously.

"I'm telling you – gardening is the new sex."

"I thought you said cooking was the new sex!"

"I did – but that was last year. Move on, girl!"

Jennie was laughing as she opened a bottle of wine and plucked two glasses from one of the pristine kitchen units. Maxine rooted in the fridge until she resurrected a bottle of Miller for Seán. The sound of the soccer match was already revving up in the lounge.

"He's turning that off straight away," Maxine stated firmly as they made their way to the lounge. "I came over here to get a break from it."

"No point. Vincent will be home any minute and it'll be turned right back on again. I can always depend on him coming home on time if there's a match – otherwise he'd stay in the office all night."

"Surely he's not that bad?" Maxine handed Seán his beer, then settled herself in a deep recliner and stretched her legs out as far as they'd go. Almost purring in the comfort, she raised an eyebrow at Jennie.

Seán glanced over – he didn't know his luck to find the television still on.

"He was in Dubai last week and all over the weekend," Jenny answered Maxine. "He's been in the office since he came back. I might as well be single."

She said this jokingly but Maxine, always perceptive, picked up the slight tinge of bitterness in her friend's voice.

"That's what you get for your Louboutin shoes," she retorted lightly, reminding Jennie that she led the lifestyle she did simply because Vincent was working all hours.

"I have to have something to compensate." Jennie saw herself as a victim of circumstance whereby she had nothing to do but spend when her husband was away so much. She might as well make the most of it rather than mope around the house.

"Did you think any more about getting a weekend place here in Ireland?" Maxine and Seán had a small cottage in Kenmare that they'd renovated over the years.

"Vincent's going to keep one of the units in Dubai, I think."

The two women lapsed into silence as Seán started to shout, his tone and volume rising in a manner not unlike Meg Ryan's orgasm scene, as Colin O'Brien approached the opposition's goal mouth in an impressive solo run. The scene on the plasma screen unfolded as if in slow motion until the ball was in the back of the net and Seán fell back on the sofa, sated.

Maxine, secretly a football fan herself, was drawn to the replay like a moth to a flame and Jennie sat back with her wine, reflecting on the idea of having a summer home in Dubai.

For the past few years, their existing apartment in Croatia had been rented out through a local letting agent because they hadn't been able to find the time to take off together as a family. Vincent didn't understand why Jennie and the kids couldn't go out there during the school holidays and have him join them at weekends. Jennie didn't see the point of dragging two small children off to a foreign country, isolating them from their friends for the whole summer. Not to mention the fact that it would be she who'd be in charge of everything, with no support, in a country whose language she didn't speak.

It was fine for Vincent to think he could show up for the weekends and expect everything to be running smoothly. Jennie couldn't see that having a home in Dubai would be any different from having one in Croatia if it was impractical to get to and unmanageable and isolating for her and the children. She'd loved Croatia the few times that she and

Vincent had gone there together and had wanted him to keep it free for the odd week that he was able to get away. He was adamant, though, about not having a property just lying there and had engaged the letting agent to deal with it rather than have it idle.

"It's all the flights that'd bother me," Maxine said now, having torn herself away from the match to resume their conversation.

Jennie shook herself out of her reverie. "True. But it's the sun as well. It's hard to depend on getting good weather here. At least Dubai will have guaranteed sun."

She and Maxine chatted away until it was half-time.

Then Seán, grinning, suddenly remembered his manners when Jennie handed him another beer and he apologised to her for hogging the television.

"I just get a bit carried away," he admitted sheepishly. "Where's Vincent, anyway?"

"Held up, as usual. I'll give him a quick buzz in a minute in case you have to celebrate on your own." Cork were still 1-0 up and she knew Seán would be on a high if they beat Derry City.

"What did you make of the concert?" he asked now, referring to the school concert that the Tim, Lucy and Sasha had starred in.

Seán, Maxine and Sasha had been heading off to Kenmare directly after the concert so Jennie hadn't had a chance to dissect the performance with them.

"Sasha was brilliant," said Jennie. "With that hair she'll be playing Annie until she's twenty-one!"

"She told us that Annie had to wear a wig every other

year. There was one in the costume box but Sash had her own hair so she didn't need it." Seán laughed uproariously as he said this and patted his own carroty curls.

Maxine smiled proudly, her eyes meeting those of her husband, and Jennie was struck by how much the production of *Annie* seemed to mean to them. Sasha was an only child, conceived after five attempts at IVF.

"Oh, that must be Vincent." Jennie swivelled around in her seat when she heard her husband's key in the door.

"Hi, lads, sorry I'm late." He glanced apologetically at Jennie, who rose to get him a beer, and kissed Maxine on the cheek.

Seán was loud in his welcome, cutting straight to the topic of soccer. "You *should* be sorry – O'Brien got a cracker after twenty minutes. If they can hold them off . . ."

Vincent quickly sat down. "Woods is back," he commented absently as the team came out for the second half.

It didn't take him long to focus on his beloved Cork City, Jennie noted sourly to herself when she handed him the chilled can of Budweiser.

She took in his appearance as Maxine started to rant about the number of parents who had failed to contribute to the catering effort after the concert and suddenly a frisson of alarm shot through her like an arrow.

Vincent's hair was wet. Not fully wet, as if he'd just come out of the shower, but around the edges and at the back – as if he'd allowed it to dry a bit before coming home.

A feeling of weakness started up inside her, flooding

her chest and stomach like a large spreading puddle. His face was flushed too, almost ruddy compared to Seán who had a high colour at the best of times due to working outdoors so much.

She tried to tune back in to Maxine as she outlined exactly what each parent had contributed.

"It's not that you'd expect everyone to bring the same amount but there's Sandra Coyne who's on her own with the small fellow to bring up and yet she arrived with three rhubarb tarts. That Nuala Crawford wouldn't give you the itch, never mind bring a few cakes to a kid's party!"

Maxine was venomous on the subject of Nuala, who was prone to swanning in and partaking of whatever was going and almost expecting to be served by the other mothers. A family law solicitor, she was considered to be among the upper echelon in terms of Rathmollin society. It didn't suit Jennie and Maxine at all that she lived in Rathmollin Woods with her husband, a pale-faced accountant, and Rufus, a timid seven-year-old with thin, spindly legs and soft, fair hair that Tim, Lucy and Sasha referred to as "girl's hair".

"Typical," Jennie agreed, trying to keep up while still studying Vincent for any other telltale signs that it wasn't work that had held him up.

"It's always the 'usual suspects' who produce the goods."

Maxine was chairperson of the Parents' Council and always had a finger on the pulse. Her blunt-cut glossy hair swung in around her face now in a jet-black curtain as she became more annoyed at the parents who behaved like dead wood at the school events.

Jennie couldn't have cared less if Nuala Crawford and her cronies did a pole dance at *Annie*. She topped up her friend's wine carefully, her hands visibly shaking at the thought that her husband had been somewhere that he ought not to have been and most probably with *someone* that he ought not to have been with. His tie had been loosened when he came in as well, something that she hardly ever saw until now.

"Desperate," she said now. Maxine only needed the occasional riposte to keep her going when she was in mid-tirade.

Vincent was standing again now with the two empty cans in his hand. It was unlike him to leave the television during play, even to pick up another beer. He was pulling at his tie, almost in agitation.

"God, Jen, it's like a sauna in here. That's the worst about the under-floor heating – we'll have to turn it down a bit."

"Leave the door open for a bit and it'll cool down."

Seán, she noticed, was still wearing a denim shirt over his Simpson's T-shirt and didn't look remotely uncomfortable. No wonder Vincent was under pressure and overheated if he'd had to rush home from some rendezvous, she fumed. She'd only texted him at seven to say that she'd invited their neighbours over for a drink.

I need to get near him to see if he smells of anything different – a shower gel, maybe, or even a perfume.

"I'll just nip to the kitchen for a few nibbles, Max. Have to keep Seán fed for the duration of the match."

Seán grinned up at her as she left the room while

Maxine commented that he'd be looking for refreshments during every match, now that he knew the service Vincent got.

Vincent followed her into the kitchen and put the empty cans in the sink.

"Sorry I was so late," he said. "The time differences are a nuisance."

He was behind her now as she arranged the goodies on the worktop and it surprised her that he didn't seem to feel the tension that she imagined was radiating visibly from her.

This was often his excuse for being home late – having to stay on to deal with contacts in different time zones. She wondered if Noeleen Ferris suffered as much at the hands of the time zones as she did and made a mental note to drop it into conversation at the party on Saturday night.

"I thought you'd like a bit of social contact seeing as you're so busy at work. And Maxine was dying to see the guest room."

"So what did she think of it?"

Jennie had redecorated the already pristine guest room during one of Vincent's recent absences but hadn't had an opportunity to show it off to Maxine in the meantime. One wall of the stark white bedroom had been covered in rich black and white flocked wallpaper, with deep red curtains picking up the touches of crimson trim on the snowy bed linen. A heavy brocade coverlet and matching cushions in the same flocked pattern adorned the bed, completing the look perfectly.

"I haven't got around to showing her yet – I'll bring her up later. Are you getting straightened out at work at all?"

"Pretty much. I've to meet Jack Rooney in the morning to finalise the finishes for the units in Dubai so that'll be sorted for a while. There's a new girl in the office covering for Melissa and she's a bit slow off the mark."

"Where's Melissa?"

The secretary had been there since Vincent had joined Bob Ferris in The Property People and was now more of a PA since the business had grown so much in the last few years. Melissa had sprung into her mind for a moment earlier when she'd noticed Vincent's wet hair but she'd dismissed the thought as ludicrous when she'd mentally pictured the girl's plump figure and plain, mousey hairstyle.

"Her mother's not well so she's taken a few months off. Unpaid leave."

Jennie had taken some of the plates she'd prepared out of the fridge and was adding various little garnishes to them. Vincent, as was his habit, was picking bits off the various plates and commenting on them. Taking her opportunity, she leaned across him to pick up a little china jug of maple syrup, taking a deep breath as she did so to see if she could detect any foreign scents that might be lingering in his clothes. Almost immediately, Vincent sprang away from her towards the back door.

"Jesus, the heat is something shocking in here!" The back door was open now and he stepped outside. "That's better – I'll leave it open for a bit to cool the place down."

Stunned, Jennie kept her eyes firmly fixed on the bowl of fresh raspberries in front of her. She already had the chocolate sauce that Vincent liked warming in the ceramic fondue bowl. She hadn't been able to decide if there was any evidence of another woman's perfume clinging to him or not.

"I'll take these inside for you." Picking up a warmed platter of prawns in filo pastry and their accompaniment of a sweet chilli dip, he disappeared back to the lounge.

He was definitely behaving erratically. Dawdling in the kitchen in the middle of a match was unheard of and probably born out of some level of guilt. Plus, he'd actually come to the kitchen for drinks for himself and Seán and had been too distracted to remember them.

Just as Jennie reached into the fridge, he appeared back.

"Beer?" she said.

He was grinning sheepishly but Jennie could only muster a small, tight excuse of a smile.

"I got carried away when I saw the prawns. Seán has them nearly gone already."

At any other time, she'd have taken his enthusiasm for the food as a compliment but now she could only see it as sweet-talk.

She looked at the man that had agreed to love and honour her almost nine years ago and wondered what had happened to them in the meantime. Vincent was still the same powerful build, with the same thick, dark hair and the same soft brown eyes that she'd fallen in love with during her work experience at The Property People office all those years ago. She wondered if she too looked the same on the outside.

It took a few minutes for her to rearrange her facial features and rejoin the others in the lounge. Maxine had brought her recliner upright and was leaning forward to see what Jennie had on the other plates that she was carrying.

"Salmon roulade! I'll have to really push the boat out the next time. Give it here, girl!"

It had become something of a game to the two women to see who could come up with the tastiest snacks at the occasional evenings the two couples spent together. Traditionally, Maxine would host the next soirée. Jennie loved the relaxed nature of their friendship and considered now whether she could confide in Maxine about the fears that were becoming more and more real to her with every day that passed.

She dismissed the thought almost immediately as a non-runner. If she was wrong about Vincent, she'd feel like a paranoid fool. If she was right, well then, it'd almost be worse. She'd hate the thought of Maxine and Seán knowing what a failure she was, unable to keep her husband from straying.

She almost jumped out of her skin when a blood-curdling shout came from the far side of the room.

"*Go on, ya good thing, go oooonnnnn!*" Seán was on his feet, hollering at Colin O'Brien again.

"Bloody hell, keep it down or we'll have Sasha awake over the road as well as Tim and Lucy!" Maxine was well used to Seán yelling at the television in their own house but drew the line at him raising the roof in someone else's.

"Hard luck, boy."

"Nice try."

These solemn statements came from Vincent and Seán as they sank back into their seats defeated, without having noticed the disturbance the near-goal had caused.

"Every time his mother hears me complaining about the soccer she tells me he could be at something worse – down the pub or off somewhere with a dolly-bird," Maxine giggled. "Mostly I think she's right but sometimes the shouting and roaring makes me wonder."

Startled at how close to the bone her friend was, it was all Jennie could do to answer her. She wondered what her own mother-in-law would think if she knew the suspicions that Jennie had about her precious son. If Vincent was Osama Bin Laden in disguise, Elsie would still think he was the best thing on wheels, a fact that made Jennie keep her at a very definite arm's length since the first day they'd met. She could just picture her mother-in-law's all-knowing look if she knew what was going on in Jennie's head right now. She'd probably think that Vincent was right to have an affair seeing as Jennie hadn't been good enough for him from the start. Not that Elsie had ever criticised her openly – Jennie hadn't dared to give her an opportunity to – but it always seemed to be there just waiting.

"It's harmless enough, I suppose," Jennie said now in response to Maxine's comment about the soccer. Vincent, while a big City fan, wasn't inclined to actually go to any of the games in Turner's Cross. Seán on the other hand, would go almost every week, taking Sasha with him.

"So, tell me about this do on Saturday night. Where's

it on?" Maxine refilled their wine-glasses and settled back into her luxurious recliner again.

"Their house." She rolled her eyes at Maxine in such a way that Vincent couldn't see her doing it. "It's Bob and Noeleen's thirtieth wedding anniversary."

"What are you getting them? It's always hard buying for these people who have everything."

"I was thinking the same. I called into Brown Thomas earlier and got a set of Louise Kennedy champagne flutes. Vincent can pick up a bottle of bubbly to go with them tomorrow."

"Will you wear the black and white dress?"

Jennie hadn't told her friend about the cancelled meal in Nouvelle on Tuesday evening so could hardly tell her now that she'd gone off the silk monochrome dress already. But she *had* after the aborted night out and couldn't bear to put it on again.

"I got a navy silk wrap dress a while back – I think I'll wear that." It wasn't even a week since her last big shopping spree in BT's, not to mind the things she'd bought earlier, but she hated letting Maxine know when her friend already thought she spent far too much on clothes as it was. Emily Gordon, too, had looked at her armful of shopping bags with interest, making Jennie feel slightly guilty. Especially when Emily had spoken about her work with the poorer people of Cork city.

"Nice. What shoes?"

"I have navy ones somewhere." Again she was reluctant to admit how much she'd spent last Friday. "I'll pull them out and see if they match."

"Did you book Donna in time? I forgot the last night we were going out and Seán had to drive poor old Sasha the whole way to Kinsale to Mum's."

"I rang her yesterday and she's okay for Saturday night but I imagine we won't have her for much longer. She's bound to have a hectic social life as soon as the exams are over."

There, it was said. Jennie had spent the past two days wondering if she was one of those stupid women whose husband runs off with the baby-sitter. She teetered between this and the idea that maybe there was someone in Dubai or even one of the team at The Property People office, confusing even herself with the erratic nature of her thoughts. All the same, in terms of baby-sitting, she had promised herself that she'd start looking for a younger model who would have nothing to chat to Vincent about. Just to be on the safe side.

"I thought that too – we've been very lucky with her."

On the nights that both couples wanted to go out together, Donna obliged by minding Lucy, Tim and Sasha in one of the houses, incorporating a sleep-over for the children.

"I suppose we'll have to start looking further afield soon. There's nobody in here old enough yet." Both of them referred to the enclosed haven of Rathmollin Woods as "in here".

"One of the kiddies in the crèche has an older sister that I was thinking of sussing out. Suzy was a late lamb, according to her mother. The older girl is fifteen, I think."

"Sounds good. Where are they living?" There was no

point in having a baby-sitter that had to be driven miles or taxied home after a night out.

"Only in Carraun, out on the main road. I'll talk to her mother and see if she's interested."

Maxine, as usual, had her finger on the pulse of every situation. As well as being a super-mum and the head beetler on the Parents' Council, she also ran a busy crèche and pre-school in the village. Busy Kidz catered for eight pre-school children and, at the moment, six older ones who arrived at three o'clock when the primary school closed.

"Would it be okay to share her if it works out?" Jennie didn't want to take advantage, even though it was a chance to cut down on Donna sooner rather than later. She felt guilty even thinking like this, especially when she knew how much Tim and Lucy loved Donna.

"No bother. Only bring out the raspberries and chocolate while I think about it properly!"

"Nothing for nothing around here," Jennie teased, making her way to the kitchen again, ashamed at how relieved she was to be getting rid of Donna. Hopefully Suzy's big sister would be an overweight frump.

"Do you want a hand, Jen?"

The match was over and Vincent was suddenly solicitous now that his team were still top of the league. Yet she had that same feeling that it was a cover-up for wherever it was that he'd been earlier. Glancing over her shoulder, she watched him entering the kitchen and felt only fear. The strain of entertaining and keeping up the chat with Maxine was exhausting and she hoped it didn't show in her face. Maxine and Seán were lovely – great neighbours and great to Tim and Lucy as well.

"Just get out the prongs for the raspberries – I have everything else."

"Give me some of those or you'll drop the lot." He was too close to her now and she suddenly had a flashback of their lovemaking on Tuesday night. She'd felt warm and mellow then, once she'd got over the disappointment of cancelling the meal. Now she was back to feeling tense and angry again.

"I'm fine," she hissed under her breath, her voice catching with emotion.

"Jesus, Jen, what's wrong? I said I was sorry for being late." His face was quizzical and again she observed the sudden high colour. He was definitely hiding something.

"Just leave it, Vincent." She sounded weary, even to her own ears. Another deep breath and she was back in the lounge. Vincent trailed after her carrying the stainless steel two-pronged forks with which to spear the plump raspberries.

They devoured the delicious fruit and rich, dark chocolate between them and chatted comfortably until midnight. As usual, their children featured heavily in the conversation and it saddened Jennie to see how much more au fait Seán was with the goings-on in St Ciaran's primary school than Vincent was.

"The garden will be great for them when it's finished," he commented.

"When is it supposed to be finished?" Vincent was always interested in new developments but wasn't a member of the outdoor part of the Parents' Council as Seán was.

"It's almost ready now. There's just the grass to be laid but to be honest it's too late in the year now to let the kids use it. We'll need to wait till September really to give it a chance to come on a bit." Seán was a landscape gardener and gave a considerable amount of time to projects at the primary school.

"Fair play – it's a great achievement." Vincent, as ever, was warm in his praise.

Jennie thought bitchily that it would be fitter for him to actually *do* something instead of just contributing money every year.

"We're sorting out the beds for the herb garden at the moment too, if you want to do a bit of hard labour. Jack Rooney dropped in a load of top-soil that needs levelling."

"No problem. Let me know and I'll drop down for a few hours some evening."

This surprised her – it wasn't like Vincent to make time for anything outside of work these days. Unless of course he had tracks to cover that he hadn't had up to now.

For the rest of the evening, Jennie felt almost detached from the conversation that was going on around her and was glad when their neighbours finally stood to leave.

"You go on up," she told him after they'd waved Seán and Maxine off at the door. She was hoping that he'd be asleep by the time she'd loaded the dishwasher and switched off the lights downstairs.

"I will so. I'm wrecked, to be honest. It must be delayed jet-lag or something."

Jennie murmured a reply and headed for the kitchen. It shocked her to be reminded just how typical her life had become when it entered her head to remember to check his pockets when she got a chance. Surely she wouldn't find anything but it was certainly not something she could neglect to do either.

This is the start of it, she reflected, her heart heavy. Watching his every move, reading into everything he says, maybe even starting to follow his car at a safe distance. Getting rid of a too-pretty baby-sitter was surely the action of a paranoid woman but Jennie wasn't going to be made a fool of in her own home.

Maybe she was wrong to even be thinking like this but she wasn't going to take that chance. If there was something to be found out, then it was going to be found out sooner rather than later.

Chapter 11

Sandra reached out to switch off the alarm clock before it started its annoying beeping. She could do without Paul grumbling about being up at the crack of dawn when he had no call to be. Thursday had passed without Jack Rooney or the foreman coming with entreaties that he return to work and Sandra had her doubts now as to whether they would at all.

Dylan was up as soon as he heard her pottering about downstairs.

"Hi, sleepyhead!"

He scowled at her, too old now for teasing. He glanced hopefully at the large box of Honey Crunchers when Sandra opened the cupboard that housed the cereals. Paul had started to insist on her getting "decent cereal" in her weekly shop, "decent cereal" meaning sugar or chocolate-coated.

"Weetabix or porridge?" Damn Paul and his Honey Crunchers.

Dylan sighed and mumbled something about the

Famine. Sandra took it to mean that he was having the porridge and grinned to herself as she poured milk over the oats and popped the bowl into the microwave. The Famine was something that Mrs Grace had mentioned to her pupils in recent weeks and Dylan seemed to use the mention of it to signify just how miserable his mother was in relation to treats and general refusals.

"Don't forget to bring the seeds in," she reminded him.

The First Class teacher was encouraging her charges to watch their seeds sprout on damp wads of cotton wool so that they'd know that food didn't come directly out of cans and jars. Sandra still couldn't get to the bottom of exactly what kind of plant was emerging in spindly green shoots from the bed of cotton wool but was as excited as Dylan when she saw them appearing. Paul thought it was dopey, having young fellows growing flowers.

"Tim Kelleher says his never came out at all because he forgot to water them but his mam took half of Lucy's and put them in another can."

The wads of cotton wool were housed in miniature bean cans. Sandra thought it unlikely that Jennie Kelleher's kids had to eat things like canned beans. She'd been in the same class as Sandra in primary school but had fared considerably better over the years and certainly wouldn't have to be watching her grocery budget.

"Handy having a sister at times like that. Is he going to tell Mrs Grace what happened?"

"No. And Lucy made him give her €5 so that she won't tell her either."

Sandra smiled at this, having noticed that Lucy was

streetwise enough to buy and sell her more innocent brother.

"It won't be the end of the world if she does find out," she advised, knowing full well that Dylan was as innocent as Tim and that one of them would probably let it slip.

"What about Rufus? Did his seeds grow all right?" The last time she'd been on lollipop duty Sandra had noticed that Rufus Crawford was a little apart from the rest of the children in the playground.

"Dunno. Probably." Dylan shovelled the porridge into his mouth in much the same way as Paul did. He had no interest in Rufus. "He never tells you anything but he always has everything right."

Sandra had thought as much. Poor Rufus seemed to be the first to be dropped off at the school, with Nuala hopping him out and disappearing in her Lexus as soon as whoever was on lollipop duty arrived at the gate. Nuala Crawford was what could be described as "highly motivated" and Sandra suspected that she expected the same from Rufus. The poor little devil had been landed into school at the earliest possible moment, meaning that he was a full year younger than most of the others in his class.

"Maybe he's shy, Dylan," she explained now. "Ask him about things and I bet he'll tell you."

"Suppose."

Dylan didn't sound convinced but Sandra had at least planted the idea in his head. She hated to see poor Rufus kicking at his schoolbag while the others bombed around the yard. Rufus was always the first to head for the door when the bell rang to call them in.

Dylan's porridge wasn't yet finished, probably because he'd been distracted with their chat. She heard Paul shifting around upstairs and was glad that Dylan wouldn't have to see him laying into a bowl of sugary cereal.

"Will I look out and see if the lads are there yet?" This was the benefit of living directly opposite the school. If Tim and Rex Brady were in the yard, Dylan would scoot over even though it was still fifteen minutes before the bell.

Sandra went through to the sitting-room while Dylan rinsed his bowl and spoon at the sink, another good habit he'd had a notion of abandoning when he discovered that Paul just left his plate on the worktop. A word in his dad's ear had rectified the situation although the word "nag" was sometimes mumbled under Paul's breath on the occasions that he forgot and had to be reminded with a glance.

Sure enough, Dylan's two best friends were kicking a ball around the schoolyard, watched by Jennie and Laura Brady. Most mornings, Sandra would walk over with her son but one look at Jennie's snow-white, tight jeans and the smart suit that Laura was obviously going to work in put paid to that.

Her own jeans, comfort-fit Levis, were washed to within an inch of their lives and even in their heyday hadn't fitted her the way Jennie's did. Her hair, washed the evening before, had dried during the night and was now sticking out at angles all over the place. Jennie and Laura both looked as if they'd come straight from Curly Locks.

Laura worked with the Health Service Executive and would need to look smart all day but Sandra wondered why Jennie was always so done up first thing in the morning.

Or maybe the fact that she made such an effort with herself was the reason that she was living in Rathmollin Woods and Sandra was installed in her two-bedroomed council cottage, clapped up next to the oddball Lenihans.

She waved at the two women now as she shooed Dylan off. Maxine Daly was on lollipop duty and ruffled his hair as she ushered him across the road. It was Sandra's turn next week and she made a mental note to tidy herself up a bit over the weekend, maybe put a colour in her hair if she could afford one. Otherwise she'd be there like a fluorescent blob in her bulky Hi-Viz jacket.

The building site, further along the street from the school, was a hive of activity, she noticed. According to Paul, it had been going to grind to a standstill without him.

He was in the kitchen now, his bare feet pale against the shiny, ceramic floor tiles. His hair needed a cut, she noticed. It amazed her that he and Dylan were so alike with their bushy dark-brown mops – Dylan's needed cutting almost every other week to keep it under control. The fact that father and son were so much alike heartened Sandra – especially when Paul's mother had been in a habit of raising subtle little queries about Sandra's morals after she'd "trapped" her son with her unexpected pregnancy.

Paul had been in a foul humour the evening before when there had been no show from the site manager to offer him his job back and today he would either have to head out and look for something else or go to Cork and sign on for social welfare. Sandra was loath to bring up the subject but neither could she afford to subsidise him much longer. It was Dylan's birthday soon and he'd been talking about the PlayStation 3 since it was released. The way she was going, there wouldn't be enough for a decent cake never mind a PlayStation.

"No sign of Jack?" This she said mildly as a means of opening a conversation.

"Prick. He can go screw himself if he thinks I'll work for him after this."

Paul was shovelling Honey Crunchers into his mouth and had the box beside him on the table for his refill.

Sandra filled the kettle for tea and wondered out loud if there was any other work about the place.

"There's nothing around here that Rooney isn't tied up in. I'll see what's nearer Cork, maybe."

Heartened, Sandra made him a cup of tea and put some toast on for both of them. It was true that Jack Rooney was involved in most of the building and development work around Rathmollin and there was no way that Paul would kowtow to him now. If things were right, which they weren't, she and Paul and Dylan could have managed very well on what Paul had been earning. Anyone around the village who worked for Jack agreed that he was more than fair although Sandra had no real idea. She hadn't seen much of her boyfriend's earnings since he'd moved into the cottage although he was generous on their nights out in The Stone's.

"Good idea. Where will you head for?" Now that he was open to looking for work, she'd need to motivate him to do it today rather than putting it off indefinitely, as had happened before.

Just after Dylan had been born, they'd been renting a flat over the butcher's and Paul had been out of work for months. Eventually, Sandra and Dylan had had to move back in with her parents. It didn't take long after that for their relationship to dissolve and Paul to take off to London. There had been promises of course but nothing concrete in the line of regular maintenance for Dylan.

"What's with all the questions?"

This was her cue to shut up and mind her own business. But the fact that he had no job *was* her business, now that she had Dylan's ever-increasing needs to consider. It was all right going to her parents when she was stuck years ago but she'd started getting back on her feet this last while and didn't want to have to take a retrograde step just because Paul couldn't keep out of the pub.

"It'd save you signing on if you got something fairly quickly, that's all." The edge of suspicion in his voice unnerved her and she was getting to a stage where she was almost watching every word that came out of her mouth.

"Well, I'll see." Paul never was one to admit that something she said made sense so he just drained his cup and went back upstairs.

Sandra didn't know if this meant he was going to leave the house in search of work or whether he'd simply gone back to bed as he had yesterday. His breakfast things, of course, he'd left to her.

Sandra bumped into Jack Rooney almost as soon as she left the house.

"Hiya, Sandra, how's it going?"

He always appeared so laid back that she used to wonder how he managed to keep on top of the enormous amount of work he had on, even in the Middle East according to Jennie Kelleher.

"Grand, kept busy chasing after Dylan."

Even in his working clothes, Jack was gorgeous, his fair hair almost silver from being outdoors. He was almost as tall as Paul but leaner and the creases at the edges of his eyes were deep from being in the sun so much. He looked like someone who was on a permanent holiday but Sandra knew the tan was more associated with hard outdoor work than lying on a beach.

"I saw him out in the school yard a few minutes ago. He's going to be tall."

This was her cue to bring up the subject of Paul. "In the genes, I suppose," she grinned, referring to the fact that Dylan's dad was over six feet in height.

"How *is* Paul, anyway? Has he started anywhere else yet?"

"Nothing yet."

They'd been friends since childhood and she was mortified that she didn't know exactly what had gone on between himself and Paul on Wednesday. Paul's version of the story had Jack down as the baddie but where the pub was involved, who knew?

"The job's still there, you know – if he wants it."

For a moment Sandra was almost ecstatic but it was a short moment when it occurred to her that Paul would probably have to actually approach Jack about it. And there was no way he'd do that.

"That'd be great. He's inside if you want to come in for a quick cuppa." Sandra had been on her way to the grocery but that could wait. She'd be mortified if Paul was back in bed but at least there was some sign of hope on the horizon.

He glanced at his watch and then down the street towards the huge sign that advertised the Sycamore Drive development that Paul should have been working on at this very moment. "Better not – I told a fellow I'd meet him at half nine. Look, tell Paul to come up later on. I'll be there until lunchtime."

She knew this was as good as she could expect but she also knew enough about Paul's stupid, misplaced pride to know what he'd say to this.

"Can I tell him he'll be starting work straight away?" She knew she sounded desperate but if Paul could just walk back in without losing face then so much the better.

"Do, Sandra, tell him that." His voice was quiet and his deep blue eyes studied her face intently. Did she imagine it or was there a hint of pity in his tone?

Dismissing the thought, she took a deep breath and mentally started to formulate the spin she would give Paul on her meeting with his boss. She watched Jack now, gratefully, as he walked along the street towards the soon-to-be Sycamore Drive, looking every bit as if he wasn't actually a millionaire times over.

Chapter 12

It never ceased to amaze Jack that a nice girl like Sandra Coyne could have anything to do with a waster like Paul Delaney. He knew that it was probably a mistake to take him back when he'd been nothing but trouble from the word go but he hated to think of Sandra having to deal with such a layabout around the house.

It was the drinking that he found hard to tolerate about fellows like Paul. The incident had been just typical and he wondered what would have happened if he hadn't turned up on the site when he did.

Not having been in Rathmollin for weeks, Jack hadn't noticed that Paul Delaney and Ronan Costello were absent from the Portacabin that was kitted out as a canteen when he arrived at lunch-time. He did notice, however, when he saw the pair of them strolling back at five past three, obviously having taken full advantage of the fact that Tony Callaghan, the foreman, had been called to a site in Cork that morning.

"Well, lads," he'd greeted them amiably. Both of them had a reputation as drinkers but he found it hard to believe that either of them would even think about operating machinery or climbing scaffolding with drink taken. He'd stepped right up to them as they approached, wanting to know for sure if they were just late or both late *and* drunk.

Paul looked belligerent straight away while Ronan was sheepish in the face of his boss turning up unexpectedly. Jack had seen immediately who the ringleader was.

"What time did ye head off at?" Neither of them had been on the site when he'd arrived at one o'clock.

Paul was facing up to him, his face red. The smell of alcohol was overpowering, even out in the open.

The rest of the crew had disappeared, evidence that they were indeed expecting trouble.

"What's this, the Spanish fucking Inquisition?"

Delaney hadn't even been smart enough to keep his mouth shut and Jack's voice immediately became dangerously quiet.

"Well, lads, it's as simple as this. We're all here to work. If you two want to be above in The Stone's instead of here where you should be, then maybe it's the place for you."

"What? Are you going to fire us now? We're entitled to a lunch break – wherever we went."

"That's grand, Paul. What you're not entitled to is to endanger anyone else on the site. Have either of you had a drink today?"

Ronan, younger than Paul by four or five years, was almost quaking and said nothing. Paul, of course, had kept digging an even bigger hole for himself.

"What the fuck business is it of yours?"

Jack was stunned at the stupidity of the man but decided to keep his cool.

"It's my business when I'm in charge of a site and I suspect that two of the workers may have drink taken."

"We had our lunch in The Stone's. That doesn't mean we were drinking." Paul had become the spokesperson for the two of them.

"Then in that case you'll have no objection to giving a urine or blood sample to Dr Carragher. Otherwise, there's no question of returning to the site." Dr Carragher was the official company doctor and his practice was only a few miles away. Either he could come to the site or Jack would drive the two offenders over to him.

Caught between a rock and a hard place, Paul had become aggressive in the extreme and started to shape up to Jack who, though slightly smaller, wasn't in the least intimidated. His would-be opponent was full of drink, for a start.

"You know what, Rooney, you can go fuck yourself," he blustered. "And shove your poxy job!"

"You're resigning? Grand so, if that's the way you want it. I'll get the girls in Wages to send on what you're owed."

Now that they'd come this far, Jack had wanted to finalise matters. No doubt the rest of the crew were listening to the exchange and he needed to be seen to be in control of the situation. And make it clear that slacking was definitely unacceptable.

"Ronan?"

Now that Paul had stormed off, his younger counterpart could be tackled.

"Look, Jack, we did have a few pints. I'm sorry about that. I wouldn't have been driving or anything."

"Last warning – and I mean that. You're better off going home now and starting fresh tomorrow." That was all he needed to say and he knew it. There would be no more trouble out of Ronan Costello. And with the lads listening, he knew he had to be fair to someone who could admit he'd done wrong.

The site had settled down after that but he'd decided to maintain a presence there for the rest of the week. If Paul Delaney did return to work, and Jack wasn't sure that he would, then Tony Callaghan would be keeping a good eye on him in the future.

Paul had all the signs of being a waster and it was desperate to see Sandra and the small fellow having to put up with him but there was no accounting for taste. He'd be giving him a second chance on Sandra's account only but he wasn't Vincent de Paul either. Another strike and he was definitely out.

Chapter 13

By ten o'clock on Friday morning Emily was shaking in her shoes. She'd phoned Dermot, the auctioneer, at half nine to make her offer on Harmony Cottage and was now waiting to hear whether it would be accepted or not.

"I'll let Mr Harrington know straight away. He did mention a quick sale so I hope to be back to you soon with good news."

"So there have been no other offers?" She was almost afraid of what she'd hear but had to ask.

"Plenty of interest but nothing else concrete as yet. Unless of course there are any further developments today." Dermot, commission in mind, was hedging his bets.

"And you'll call me one way or another before five o'clock?" she asked.

"Absolutely. I have your mobile number here in front of me." As if Emily was the most special customer ever.

After she'd hung up, it was impossible to settle at her

desk and she headed for the kitchen to see if a coffee would rev her up enough to complete her day's work enthusiastically.

Gina, as usual, was installed in the kitchen. This time, it was Paddy Lane's head she was melting about the gorgeous man who was *almost* single.

"I told Emily about it," she informed the middle-aged facilitator, "and she thought I should put him on the back burner until he's actually free but I'd like your opinion, Paddy. I mean, you have daughters around my age. What do you think?"

This was Gina's usual ploy. If she didn't hear what she wanted to hear from one of her colleagues, then she simply moved on to the next. And then the next until she found someone who was willing to tell her what she wanted to hear – in this case that Romeo was a sure thing as husband material.

Paddy considered his thoughts on the subject carefully before giving his valued opinion. "He sounds like a nice fellow all right, Gina. And I'm sure he wouldn't want to put you in any kind of an awkward position. I'd give him a chance to sort himself out first, put him on the back burner, like Emily said."

"Oh." Gina had thought at the outset that Paddy was going to give her the green light. Resigned, she drained her cup and left, no longer interested in the opinions of the two straight-laced facilitators.

"Where does she find them, in the name of God?" Paddy had enough to deal with in keeping control of his own trio of teenage girls, not to mind trying to sort out

Gina's affairs. Although, on occasion, he'd been grateful for the tit-bits of information gleaned about the Cork social scene that might ultimately benefit him where his daughters were concerned.

Emily grinned in response as she made her coffee. "You needn't be smirking. Gina was talking earlier about organising a night out in town tomorrow night – and you're included, to the best of my knowledge."

"I suppose you didn't do anything to discourage it?"

Emily was terrified at the thought of going out on the town with Gina and Orla but supposed that she'd be better off making some effort than sitting at home vegetating. The chances of Richard sitting at home pining were miniscule, she imagined, especially seeing as he'd had a head-start with the exotic Lorena on New Year's Eve.

"You never know, Paddy," she grinned now, "I might just get a taste for it. I'll wait and see what Gina has on offer." Taking her coffee with her, she left Paddy in the kitchen and headed back to her office. She needed the day to fly by until her anticipated phone call from Dermot happened.

On Friday mornings, Emily normally held an open "clinic" so that people could simply drop in if they needed to see a facilitator about any financial problems they were experiencing. Invariably, the drop-in clinics were hectic and today's was no exception.

Moneylenders had a big influence on her job, with people taking out small loans to tide them over for Christmas or an occasion and then finding that the level of interest outweighed the value of the loan many times over. Mostly, it was only when the loan-sharks were banging at the door that the terrified recipients approached the VBA for help.

Mostly, Emily or one of the other facilitators would approach a credit institution to agree to a loan that would cover the outstanding debt and that would have reasonable repayment terms. As soon as the heavies were off their backs, it was easier for people to reorganise their finances to avoid the same problem in the future.

Once a client had formed a relationship with the VBA, they tended to return time and time again but with less complex issues. This, for Emily, was the most satisfying part of her job – the ability to teach a person to manage their finances rather than just sorting the problem for them.

It was one o'clock before she even had time to think about Dermot and whether he'd made contact with the owner of Harmony Cottage to relay her offer.

"C'mon, Emily, we're going down to O'Brien's for a sandwich. A bit of fresh air will do you good. *And* stop you fretting about the gorgeous Dermot."

Emily *was* fretting about Dermot, although she wasn't sure that she'd have described him as gorgeous. He was probably just up Gina's street, though.

"Go on then." Grabbing her bag, she made a move towards the door that Orla was holding open for her, only to be arrested by the appearance of a slim, worried-looking girl with her hair scraped back into an unruly pony-tail.

"Am I too late for the clinic? Only I had to leave my young fella off at my ma's before I came over. He wasn't out of playschool until half twelve." She looked anxiously from Emily to Gina to Orla, not quite knowing to whom she should be making her pitch.

Orla glanced pointedly at the clock, unwilling to lose a minute of her precious lunch break over someone so disorganised.

Gina smiled encouragingly at the girl and grinned knowingly at Emily. "BLT, I suppose?"

Nodding gratefully at Gina, Emily put her handbag back in the drawer.

It had taken almost an hour to get to the bottom of it and as on so many occasions, alcohol abuse was the principal cause of Anita Daly's hardship. At only twenty-three, she was the mother of two small children, both under the age of five. Her partner, Martin, had been an alcoholic even when she'd met him but Anita had refused to heed the warnings of her parents and brothers until his drinking had become so out of control that he'd insisted on bathing the children after a six-hour pub marathon the previous Sunday evening. Luckily, Anita told Emily, she'd arrived home from work in time. The kids screaming and Martin lurching drunkenly around the bathroom looking for towels and bubble bath was the last straw.

Her parents had taken the children for the night while her brothers dispatched Martin back to his parents' house and changed the locks on Anita's front and back doors.

"It was all very fine me putting up with him but to do that to the kids, I couldn't bear it. He didn't mean to put them in danger but he hadn't a clue what he was doing he was so drunk."

"You've done the right thing," Emily encouraged, the social worker part of her coming to the fore. "But how are you fixed financially now?"

"That's the thing," the girl explained, more relaxed now that she'd got her tale of woe off her chest. "Even though Martin never actually worked, he was always there to look after the kids. A neighbour used to bring Ryle home from school if I was working."

"How are you going to manage work now that you're on your own?"

This was often a problem that Emily encountered. An abusive partner was often better that no partner at all from a financial perspective and it was all too easy to go back into a bad relationship if the proper supports weren't put in place.

"I think I'll have to give up the job for the minute because it's mainly mornings that they need someone for. I suppose I'll have to go back on social welfare. I'm terrified of falling behind with the bills but I don't know where to start."

"Look, Anita," Emily counselled, "at least you've taken the first step – the most important one actually. You can apply for the Lone Parent's Allowance for a start. There's a lot that your local Community Welfare Officer can do as well so we'll get in touch with him or her about things like a Medical Card and Back to School allowance for Ryle. And there's the Family Support Supplement."

"To be honest, it's the flat I'm most worried about. Martin's parents used to give us a bit towards the rent. I think they felt guilty about the drinking and the kids being short of things. I'm afraid that I won't be able to afford to keep it on but I don't want to disrupt the kids either."

Amazed that such a lovely young girl had ended up in such bother, Emily explained to her about applying for rent allowance and the other benefits to which she was entitled now that she would be unemployed. Armed with a plethora of forms and contacts, Anita Daly had left the VBA office after assuring Emily of her strengthened resolve to keep her ex-partner at arm's length.

By the time she'd eaten her now soggy BLT it was after three and Dermot still hadn't rung. Emily was beginning to get nervous now. If the nephew was so mad for a quick sale, surely he'd have agreed to the offer by now. And she would have thought that Dermot would have been keen to get his commission pinned down as quickly and efficiently as possible.

Gina had been into her office no less than three times, between checking whether the auctioneer had rung and persuading Emily to accompany her and Orla to the opening of a new wine bar the following evening.

But now that there was no sign of a call from Dermot, Emily was taking it as bad news and wondered if she'd be in the form for a night out at all.

She nearly jumped out of her skin when the phone rang, even though it was probably work-related like the last few times.

"Emily? Dermot Leahy here."

The perky introduction gave her a smidgen of confidence and she cut straight to the chase, forgetting her manners for once. "Good or bad?"

She couldn't believe the way her heart was hammering. When she and Richard had been bidding on the house in Maple Woods in Blanchardstown, it had all seemed very civilised, maybe because her then-fiancé had been involved in the design phase of the development and had the inside track on things.

"Well . . ."

Her heart sank at the hesitancy and was justified in doing so.

"There has been another offer in the meantime." He paused for effect. "Is it a thing that you would increase your offer, perhaps even by, say, €5000?"

This was something that had been discussed at length in the Gordon household the night before, in anticipation of there being another offer. Generously, Tom and Jacinta had offered to add a little to their daughter's budget if she really wanted the cottage. Emily had declined, even when her father mentioned hesitantly that the money was there for her, now that it wasn't going to be used for the wedding.

This had earned him a good kick from her mother and a kiss from Emily, who reassured him that she'd be needing her wedding budget at some stage, if not now the way she'd planned.

No, she was going to stand on her own two feet from now on, even if it meant letting Harmony Cottage go.

"I'm afraid not," she answered Dermot squarely, tears of disappointment already forming at the back of her eyes. She'd almost felt she was actually living there.

"I . . . see . . ." Dermot drew out his words as if it were

he who was considering letting his future home go down the drain. "The other offer, while higher than yours, would be subject to some planning regulations. I can certainly keep your offer on the table in case it doesn't come to fruition."

Dermot certainly knew how to keep all the balls in the air, she thought bitterly.

"Do that."

It was soul-destroying but she knew the price would just keep going up and up, even if she availed of her parents' generous offer. All there was to do now was to tell everyone that the whole thing was off. She'd had to do that once already so it wouldn't be too hard when it was only a house.

In fairness to them, her colleagues were as distraught as she was. Paddy and Gina headed straight to the kitchen to make more tea while Orla scooted out to get proper biscuits. Something as upsetting as this required more than the Mariettas and Polos that were provided by their employers. A Chocolate Kimberly at the very least, Orla had insisted.

It was just as well that she and Paddy tended to leave Friday afternoons free to catch up with the paperwork that their clients generated during the week – otherwise there would have been a queue of people out the door as they sat and discussed the appalling state of affairs that was the Irish property market.

Orla and Gina were of the opinion that they were unlikely to ever find their way onto the property ladder, the way things were going. Emily, now, was doomed to join them. Paddy, whose dormer bungalow overlooked the sea in East Cork, agreed that if it weren't for the fact that he'd been installed there since the early 80s, he certainly couldn't afford to live there now.

Depressed, Emily left work early. There was nothing for it only to start again another day.

By nine o'clock the following evening she was starting to come around a little. Her father, disappointed at this latest blow and unsure of what to do, had trotted out his well-used catchphrase: "What's for you won't pass you by." Her mother had stuffed her with food as if it were a proper crisis akin to a funeral or a broken engagement.

Deciding that she'd already spent enough of the year moping, she knew it was time to get out and about and start again. Emily knew all too well that this burst of positive energy might only last for a few hours before she was reminded that she was no further on now than when she left school ten years ago, or college six years ago, but it was as well to make the most of it while it lasted. Especially when Gina and Orla were revving up for a night on the town in less than an hour's time.

Looking at herself in the mirror, she didn't think she looked too bad. Her fitted black top had a deep vee that showed off her newly lifted cleavage, thanks to a Wonderbra purchased in haste earlier in the day. Her skirt, featuring white and red tulips on a black background, was short and silky, in keeping with Gina's guidelines. Her spiky black sandals were new as well and she hoped she'd be able to manage a full night in them, considering that Gina and Orla didn't *do* sitting down. In terms of reeling in men, they insisted that it was much more beneficial to stand up where they could be seen and admired rather than hiding away in a corner.

This was territory that Emily was dreading to revisit. After so many years in the security of a long-term relationship, it was alien to be back on the market again. But Gina was right, she concluded firmly as she dusted her pale brown freckles with Benefit's Get Even. There was no orderly queue forming on her parents' doorstep.

Goosebumps appeared on her arms as soon as she stepped out the front door and she started to question whether Gina had been serious about not bringing a coat.

"Whatever you do, don't bring a jacket that we'll have to be minding all night," she'd warned. "There's nothing worse."

"Can't I put it in the cloakroom or something?" Emily had always been a cold creature and it was still only April.

The two girls had looked at Emily as if she was crazy. "It's a wine bar, for God's sake!"

Now here she was shivering while the taxi-man who'd insisted on her being outside waiting, on account of him being so busy on a Saturday night, was nowhere to be seen. She'd just reached an executive decision about going back inside and waiting for him to beep when she saw the blue plate glowing further up the street. Wobbling precariously on her high heels, Emily started to wave frantically, terrified that he'd miss her. Missing a taxi was one thing – facing the wrath of Gina and Orla over it on Monday morning was quite another.

Much later, Emily would remember the neon taxi

plate coming towards her in slow motion. And eventually she would remember the feeling of being almost weightless and the way she flew through the air like a leaf, her too-short skirt blowing up around her thighs. But all of that would be a long, long way down the line.

Chapter 14

Jennie and Vincent were on their way to Bob and Noeleen's anniversary do in Montenotte when they passed the chaotic-looking scene outside Tom and Jacinta Gordon's house.

"I hope it's not Tom," Jennie commented. An ambulance was always bad news, especially for someone like Tom who'd already had heart surgery.

"He's had a bypass before, hasn't he?" Vincent too remembered Tom Gordon's surgery. "God, would you look at all the gawkers!"

"People are desperate," Jennie agreed, taking in the battered Corolla that was parked skew-ways on the kerb and the taxi that had obviously joined the action.

Sandra Coyne was out on the street as well, Jennie noticed – probably because she lived opposite the Gordons and had heard the commotion.

"I hope he's all right." Vincent looked concerned, even though he didn't know Tom all that well.

"At least the ambulance has arrived anyway – sometimes people can be hours waiting. You should have seen the A&E the night Lucy was in there – it was bedlam. The sooner these private A&Es are opened the better."

"Imagine what the health insurance premiums will be like then! Bob and Noeleen have gone up a level and he says it's pure extortion."

"Well, he's not too badly off, to be fair." The Property People had been a well-established auctioneering firm long before Vincent had become a partner there. And with the property boom of the past ten years, he was certainly far from short of a bob.

Vincent was studying the traffic carefully as he negotiated the slip road onto the dual carriageway. "He's working hard for it, though. Noeleen seems to be at him a lot lately about slowing down. He's not as keen on all the travelling either."

Pity about him, Jennie thought sarcastically. As well as their very grandiose Georgian mansion in Montenotte and a holiday home in West Cork that boasted its own marina, Bob and Noeleen had recently invested in a property in central Paris.

She looked at her husband sharply. "He's still only in his fifties – it's a bit early to be talking about slowing down, isn't it?" A finger of fear had started to wend its way around her heart. Was this Vincent's way of revving up to having to take over all the foreign trips from Bob? An excuse for being in Dubai and Bahrain even more than he was already?

"He's been at it since he was sixteen. He left school after the Inter Cert and went into his father's business but he hated it. His brother took over eventually and Bob started up the property office. He'll soon be forty years at it!"

"What age are the kids now?" Jennie was anxious to change the subject before her throat constricted completely. If Bob genuinely *was* slowing down then Vincent would be away more than ever, either legitimately or otherwise.

"Robert is twenty-five now – he's the fellow who went into medicine. I'd say Bob had an idea that he'd be following him into the business. He brings it up a lot, not having any of his own to take over from him. Carol must be around twenty-three now."

"Is she the one who does the painting?" Jennie knew that one of Bob's daughters had graduated from the Crawford but honestly couldn't remember which one. Nor could she remember the other daughter's name despite being told every time they were going out to meet Bob and Noeleen.

"No, that's Eva. Carol's a physio – remember she was home from Glasgow for the barbecue last summer?"

Jennie vaguely remembered talking to a smiling blonde girl who she thought might have been Carol Ferris. As for Eva, she couldn't seem to put a face to her at all.

"Who else will be here tonight?" Jennie hated the thought of having to make small-talk to the hordes of business contacts of Bob and Vincent's who inevitably graced such events.

"I imagine John Williams and Carmel will be there. Carmel's always a good chat."

Yeah, Jennie thought bitchily, if you're into organic baby food and eco nappies and what to do with nettles in the autumn. She'd already spent one tedious evening listening to Carmel harping on about making blackberry jam.

She sighed as Vincent took the turn-off at the Silver Springs Hotel and tried to drum up some enthusiasm for the evening ahead. The dinner would be fine, with Vincent for company next to her even if she got someone who was hard work on her other side.

It was the after-dinner party that she usually found to be most difficult. Vincent generally felt that he had an obligation to circulate, citing the fact that it was a bit bald to expect to have a good business relationship with people that he might have ignored at a social gathering at some point. Jennie, in that case, would usually be left to her own devices. Occasionally, she hooked up with some like-minded pseudo-widow but otherwise would have to make small-talk with the other abandoned wives.

Soon they were approaching the ostentatious pillars at the end of the Ferrises' driveway and for once, Jennie's husband surprised her.

"Will we try and get away fairly early if we can? Sometimes these things can go on a bit."

This was a new departure and her already over-active imagination immediately sprang into overdrive. "Grand – if that's what you want. You're usually mad to stay until the last post." She glanced over at him but his expression was unreadable as he slotted the car neatly into place between another BMW and a low, silver Mercedes convertible. Did he really have no interest in her company any more? Or maybe there was someone on the guest list that he didn't feel comfortable meeting in the public domain?

"The flights are still catching up on me, I think." His voice was light but she sensed somehow that this wasn't what he really meant.

"Hopefully Lucy will sleep on in the morning and you can get a proper lie-in." Jennie knew she sounded a bit automatic but lately her conversations with her husband seemed to be taking place along parallel lines.

"We should be able to get away by twelve at least – unless Faith Rowney starts the singing again."

Jennie shuddered at the thought. The Williams' Christmas drinks party had gone on until dawn on account of John having had the bad sense to load the normally austere engineer with Bucks Fizz to thaw her out. The ploy had had a dynamic effect, with Faith commandeering a feather boa from one of the guest rooms as a prop to her theatrics. And now that Vincent had mentioned her, Jennie recalled that the sporty silver Merc parked next to them belonged to Faith.

"Is that definitely her car?" Jennie's heels sank into the gravel and she stood on tiptoe to avoid scuffing them as she negotiated her way out of the car.

"I'm afraid so. We'd better make sure not to land next to her."

"And if she starts singing, we'll make our exit before anyone else has the same idea! We were the only fools polite enough to listen on the last time."

They were actually laughing as they mounted the broad

limestone steps and were greeted by a "butler", presumably part of the catering company. Vincent discreetly handed over the gold-and-cream wrapped gift while Jennie divested herself of her pale pink silk wrap and followed him into the room.

"Jennie – welcome!" Bob had his arms outstretched in greeting and Jennie kissed him lightly on the cheek.

"It's good to see you, Bob – and happy anniversary."

"I'm a bit long in the tooth to be broadcasting how long it is since my heyday but I suppose it's a good excuse for a get-together."

"It's not like you to need an excuse, Bob," Vincent countered before launching into a chat about the reputed takeover of Homes of Distinction, their main rivals.

Jennie looked around to see who was present among the glamorous, perfumed guests and immediately spotted the dreaded Carmel Williams wiggling her fingers in greeting from across the room. She wiggled back as enthusiastically as she could muster and grabbed a margarita from the first waitress to approach her. If she was going to have a lesson on Going Green, then her brain was going to have to be well lubricated first.

"Jennie – how lovely to see you!" It was Noeleen Ferris, her rotund frame hurtling towards Jennie like a whirlwind. "How can you manage to look so fabulous all the time? Look at her, Carmel, doesn't she look fabulous?"

Carmel, drab in an olive green skirt that swished around her ankles and a white peasant blouse that did nothing for her willowy figure, approached from stage left and joined in the general admiration.

"You do indeed, Jennie. It's great to see a familiar face among the crowd."

"Lovely to see you too, Carmel," she lied, her evening now laid out before her. She kissed both of the women on the cheek and wondered if her social life was coming near to the air-kissing stage. "You too, Noeleen. The house looks really lovely."

The vast entrance hall did indeed look elegant with its restored tile floor and all the original cornicing intact.

"Keeps me busy, I can tell you that for nothing! It'll have to be re-roofed soon. Dry rot."

"No!"

Carmel looked devastated that the roof should have to be replaced on such a magnificent specimen of architecture and Jennie felt a part of her brain shutting down. She was sorry she'd mentioned the house, Noeleen's hobby, in the first place. Vincent was no use to her, engrossed as he was in his conversation with Bob.

"And what about you, Jennie?"

She came out of her reverie and stared at Carmel Williams blankly.

"Any plans for the summer?" Noeleen prompted.

"Oh – just off to Eurodisney for a week but other than that, nothing too exciting." Jennie accepted another margarita from a passing tray and deposited her empty glass.

"Carmel has the kids enrolled in one of those Sustainable World summer camps. How about that?" Noeleen seemed to think this was a great idea and Carmel was beaming under her approval.

"Really?" Jennie couldn't think what else to say.

Carmel, perhaps expecting more in the line of interest, lost her glow for a moment and Jennie sensed that Noeleen Ferris was somehow disappointed in her. Jolted a little, she rowed back and asked whether it was for all age groups.

"Mine are around the same age as yours, I think, Carmel." She hoped this was true but she thought she remembered a conversation about breast-feeding that didn't seem all that long ago.

"That's right. Eunan is five now – same as Lucy – and Iseult will be seven at Christmas. Tim must be nearly eight now?"

Jennie was embarrassed that Carmel had remembered the children's names and ages while she herself hardly knew whether the Williams children were boys or girls.

"That's right. They're both doing the Samba Soccer in August and there's a swimming camp that Vincent wants them to go to. The Green camp sounds good."

"Some of our friends sent their children the last couple of years but ours weren't old enough up to now. Eight is ideal, really."

Noeleen was looking a bit more pleased now that the conversation she'd initiated was taking off. "Carmel was telling me earlier that they come home with all sorts of ideas. What was that about cutting down on the water?"

Enthused again, Carmel started to explain to Jennie about filling a two-litre bottle and putting it in the toilet-cistern to reduce the amount of water the cistern would hold.

"My friend's little fellow says it saves two litres of water every time you flush – imagine the amount a family would save in a lifetime!"

Jennie supposed it wouldn't be the sustainable thing to suggest simply ripping out the too-large cistern and replacing it with a smaller one altogether and instead decided that a repetition of "Imagine!" would suffice by way of an answer. Better that than getting an earful on the terrors of landfill sites.

"If you ever want the details of it for Tim and Lucy just get Vincent to ask John. He booked it for them."

"The rest of us should be more like you pair, Carmel," Noeleen commended. "Our Eva's fairly good as well. She's always giving out to her father about not having a composter in the garden. There you are, sweetheart, just talking about you!"

A small waif of a girl, presumably Eva Ferris, was now drawn into the conversation. Smiling at Carmel and Jennie, she commented that while her father liked the outdoor life, she had to admit that he seemed to be creating more much carbon dioxide than he was reducing with all his plants.

"That humongous lawnmower for a start – it's pumping out noxious fumes at a rate of knots."

"We'll have to get Carmel here to tackle him about it. Excuse me a moment, ladies, I see Faith is empty. I'll just pop over and see that she gets a drink."

Noeleen disappeared in a bustle of silvery grey brocade that fitted snugly around her ample bottom and bust, leaving Jennie to contend with Carmel and Eva, the latter listening intently to her companion much as her mother had done moments before. She studied them, the ethereal

Eva with her soft, fair hair swept up in a loose knot and her turquoise and red Matthew Williamson dress sweeping the floor, looking like an exotic peacock compared to Carmel's brown mouse approach to style.

"All right, love?" At last Vincent had relieved himself of Bob and had come to rescue her.

"Grand. Lovely margarita."

Vincent too was sipping one. "Mmmm. I'll just have this one so I can drive."

Jennie had forgotten about which of them was going to drive home and had almost finished her second drink. Too late now to offer to drive.

"I'll drive the next time," she promised.

"I'll remember that," he grinned, turning a little to greet Eva and Carmel.

"You'll have to quit all this eco warrior stuff, Carmel," he teased, "or we'll be seeing Eunan and Iseult being dragged out of trees by the Gardaí soon!"

Carmel was practically incandescent from the good-natured banter and riposted that perhaps it was time that Vincent tried it. Jennie suddenly felt like an outsider as Eva chimed in that he could send Tim and Lucy to the Sustainable World camp as envoys first. It was all so insular, she thought sourly, all this back-scratching and pumping up of each other.

She was relieved when dinner was announced by the tinkling of a small metal triangle and she trooped ahead of Vincent into the imposing dining-room. All she needed now was to be sitting next to Carmel for the duration of a long meal.

As it transpired, she was planted at the very end of one side of the lengthy table, with Noeleen, at the head, on one side and Vincent on the other. It was unfortunate though, that her husband was stuck next to Faith Rowney who seemed to be doing her best to engage his attention to the exclusion of all else.

Noeleen tucked into her smoked salmon starter as soon as she'd ensured that all her guests had been served.

"So, Jennie, the complex in Dubai seems to be coming to fruition at last."

"So it seems. Although it'd want to be coming to something at this stage – Vincent seems to spend more time in Dubai than he does in Rathmollin."

"It's hard on them, all right," Noeleen answered sympathetically, obviously under the impression that Jennie was bothered about how difficult it was for Vincent to be away all the time. "Bob's the same. It takes him almost a week to recover from the time difference and all the flights."

Jennie was at a loss as to how to answer this. Vincent was still caught up with Faith Rowney.

"Desperate," she offered eventually.

"I'm at Bob all the time to slow down, you know. He's not getting any younger and there's no point in having all this," she waved her hand around to indicate their obvious wealth, "if he gets into bad health."

"He's not over the hill yet, Noeleen. And he does seem to thrive on it." Both of them looked down the length of the table towards Bob, who appeared to be in the thick of a lively argument with John Williams and a short man with an alarmingly red face that Jennie had noticed earlier.

"That's my point exactly – he loves it all. I worry about all the travelling though but I suppose that's women for you." Noeleen's face relaxed a little as she glanced again in her husband's direction. This time, Bob noticed her and gave the tiniest of winks at which Noeleen's smile broadened, making Jennie the smallest bit jealous.

Irritated at herself, she dug into the succulent smoked salmon that she'd ignored up to now. One minute she was watching her husband like a hawk and wondering if he was having some sort of sordid affair with God knows who. The next, she was wishing that the kind of easy, intimate communication she'd just witnessed between Bob and Noeleen was a part of her own marriage again. But how could it be if Vincent was happier spending more and more time away from his family and if she'd lost the sense of trust that she'd thought would always be there between them?

As soon as their plates were swept discreetly away, Noeleen returned to the subject of their husbands' business abroad, having spoken briefly to the lady on her other side, another solid matron in brocade.

"I wasn't so sure about that Bahrain thing, although I've been proved wrong. I was convinced that they were paying far too much for that land."

Jennie was astounded that Noeleen was so tuned in to The Property People's business affairs. She herself knew about the development of waterfront duplexes but certainly wasn't up to speed on what had been paid for the land.

"It seems to have worked out well." She was non-committal in her answer and hoped that Noeleen wouldn't realise how ignorant she was.

"It was the fact that it was reclaimed land that made me concerned," Noeleen confided, lowering her voice, "even though Jack Rooney had a site engineer check it all out. Anyway, it hardly matters now, considering the way it turned out in the end."

"Mmmm, I suppose," Jennie hedged. Were the duplexes actually built yet? Or were they even sold by now? She wasn't sure and made a mental note to listen a bit more when Vincent spoke about work.

"That Al Saeed fellow must have a ton of money. Imagine buying up thirty duplexes, just like that? Apparently he brings the whole extended family on holiday there now – four mother-in-laws included!"

Noeleen laughed out loud at the idea of it and proceeded to relate the story of the wealthy Arab to the mature lady on her opposite side. She introduced Jennie then and went on to tell her guest about the evening that Mr Al Saeed had approached Bob and Vincent in a Bahrain restaurant before the complex was even finished.

"Honestly, Phil, poor Bob hasn't recovered from it yet. Says it was the easiest deal they ever struck. Didn't even have to bargain with him. And I don't know about your husband, Jennie, but Bob loves to bargain with fellows. He was almost disappointed when the Sheik agreed to the first price they mentioned."

Jennie listened and smiled as if she too knew the story of the Sheik off by heart. All *she* could remember of it was the evening that Vincent had started telling her about some rich Arab looking to practically buy them out but she'd been so annoyed the same evening that she'd cut him short on the phone.

It had been an evening that she'd been looking forward to him being home and he'd called at the last minute to tell her that an offer had been made for the duplexes, an offer that couldn't be refused. As far as she'd been concerned, Vincent always seemed to have an offer that couldn't be refused or a deal that just had to be struck.

Now Noeleen and Phil were looking at her as if she might have something to contribute to the story.

"Unbelievable," was all she could manage, only aware of the full details of the story from listening to Noeleen just now.

"Like I was telling you, Jennie, that's the kind of thing that Bob thrives on. I'm trying to get him to slow down, Phil," she added for her friend's benefit.

Phil, sitting next to an older-looking man with a pale face and thinning hair, nodded her agreement.

"You're right, Noeleen. No point in making money if we don't live to enjoy it. Maurice learnt his lesson the hard way." She indicated her husband, who was picking at the delicious filet mignon that had just been placed in front of him.

"Burst ulcer," Noeleen interjected under her breath to Jennie while Phil continued.

"He's just out of hospital. Insisted on coming tonight to see everyone. But at least he's taken early retirement."

Jennie thought that Maurice looked every bit of

sixty-five but supposed that he must be a bit younger if his wife was talking of early retirement.

"And is he well now, Phil?" Noeleen had an interest in everyone's goings on and Jennie listened absently as the two women talked on about medication and the special diet that Maurice now had to adhere to. Obviously, it must be a middle-aged thing to sit at dinner parties worrying about your husbands' health and discussing it to death, but right now, Jennie had more important things to think about. While Noeleen and Phil were bothered about their husbands' lives being at the slowing-down stage, Jennie was more concerned that Vincent's life was going in quite the opposite direction. *And* with someone other than herself.

She sank her serrated knife into the succulent steak before her and admired the selection of colourful seasonal vegetables although she had no interest in either. As far as she could determine, there were forty people seated along the impressive antique table and, to her mind, all of them seemed to be engaged in the sort of lively conversation that precluded there being anything as worrying as a straying spouse to bother them.

She hoped that Vincent hadn't changed his mind about driving home when she noticed the sheen of perspiration on his brow as he leaned forward to listen to something the girl across from him was saying. If he had decided to abandon the car and take a taxi, they'd be there all night waiting for one to arrive. Taxis were like hens' teeth in Cork city on a Saturday night.

The girl he was talking to, she noted, was speaking animatedly and Vincent was enraptured. She watched him as he started to laugh at whatever she was telling him, his eyes alight with amusement. She was pretty, the girl across the table, and Jennie suddenly wondered if she could be the one that had Vincent late home every evening.

Even thinking this shocked her and her heart tightened in her chest. It was one thing to suspect the worst but it was quite another to be faced with the reality of her husband carrying on with someone in their own social circle. Somehow, in her tortured imaginings, Jennie had only envisaged an anonymous, faceless harlot, not this elegant creature with the silvery-blond hair and child-like smile.

"She has to go back to Glasgow first thing in the morning, poor thing. Her flight is at eight."

Jennie almost leapt out of her skin when Noeleen's voice broke in on her thoughts and she reddened guiltily at the thought that she'd been spotted studying Carol Ferris. What would Noeleen think if she knew the avenues that Jennie's thoughts had been travelling down?

"Carol's a physio, isn't she?" So far tonight, she'd been found wanting in the great competition to know the names of everyone else's offspring but at least she could draw on the little information that Vincent had imparted in the car on this occasion.

"That's right," Noeleen confirmed with evident pride.

Did Jennie imagine it or did Noeleen actually look impressed at her knowledge? "Very demanding job," Noeleen continued. "She's hoping to go into private practice here as soon as she gets enough experience under her belt."

"I'm sure it would be great to have her nearer to home." Jennie tore her eyes away from her husband and commented with an effort at interest. Vincent was back in conversation with Faith Rowney anyway. The main course had been removed by now and she sipped on her red wine while Noeleen extolled the virtues of her elder daughter.

"It would be lovely if she met someone nice and settled down here," she concluded eventually, to Jennie's relief.

She wondered if she herself would ever bore people at dinner parties with her children's achievements.

"Oh, this looks just divine," she gushed gratefully as a melt-in-the-mouth chocolate confection was placed in front of her. She normally refused dessert but on this occasion it was a welcome distraction that delayed the inevitable after-dinner socialising.

"Chocolate and Cointreau – always good together. Nothing like a good match, I say. I've known Bob almost thirty-five years now and we get on as well as we ever did."

"That's marvellous, Noeleen." Now she was going to have to listen to Bob's virtues as well.

"Taking an interest, that's the secret. A wife should know what's going on in her husband's life. No surprises then, you see."

Jennie looked up sharply from her chocolate pudding and tried to hide her alarm. A small crease had appeared between the older woman's brow and she was looking at Jennie a bit too intently. Was it some kind of warning, a warning to keep an eye on her husband before someone else did?

She mentally pulled herself together and dismissed the thought as ludicrous. Surely this was paranoia of the highest degree, if she was imagining signs and signals in the most ordinary of conversations. She and Noeleen weren't even close so why would she of all people feel the need to tip her off if there *was* something to know?

"Well, it's work, work, work with Vincent at the moment so it's easy to keep track of him," Jennie answered lightly. For all her suspicion, she found that the opening up of an opportunity didn't necessarily mean she was able to follow the lead to a conclusion. At least not yet.

"It's important for men – work, I mean." Noeleen seemed to want to persist with her line of conversation. "Most of them love the competition but they need the support too."

Jennie had no idea where the thread of dialogue was going – all she could think of was getting out of it before Noeleen disclosed something that she wasn't ready to hear. She was perspiring now and the navy silk dress was clinging to her underarms. She looked around wildly and wished that Phil and Maurice hadn't just departed the table to join the smokers on the terrace. Although if there was something to know, then they probably knew it already. The Cork social scene was like the proverbial ever-decreasing-circle.

"They do, I suppose . . ."

"No suppose about it – you only have to look at Maurice and Phil. She almost lost him, you know. All the family were called in. Stressed out of his brains, he said to me afterwards, only he didn't realise it. It's up to Phil now to make him slow down and take it easy."

Jennie sat and listened and wondered if she was actually

going mad. All this talk of keeping an eye on things and the reining in of husbands was beginning to overwhelm her. Was she imagining the warning or was Noeleen just waffling on the way she did with everyone? Like she had with Carmel Williams earlier about the Green camp?

"He looks well now, thank God." She was barely keeping pace and was glad when Carol Ferris excused herself and came to sit beside her mother.

"I love this bit," she smiled at Jennie and Noeleen, "when the formalities are over and we can relax a bit!"

It was true what she said. Now that the main body of the meal was over, people had started to disperse somewhat, swapping seats with others so that they could catch up properly. The table buzzed with lively banter and Jennie realised that it was this laissez-faire approach that made the Ferrises' dinner parties such a recurring success.

"Don't even think about taking off your shoes," Carol's mother chided, eliciting a flash of spectacular white teeth from her daughter, accompanied by a hearty laugh.

"I'm not a great one for partying, Jennie," said Carol, "especially with an early morning flight ahead of me. Vincent tells me he's still jet-lagged from earlier in the week."

"That's right – the trips abroad seem to be more frequent lately. It's harder to recover, I suppose." It appeared that she was the only one not concerned about poor Vincent and his jet-lag.

"I've noticed that in Dad too. He's still grumpy a week later!" Carol's smile was open and affectionate as she glanced across the room to where her father was standing with Maurice and Phil.

Jennie was astounded that she'd had this charming and lovely girl down as her husband's mistress only a few moments earlier. She'd never imagined that her own thinking could be this bitter and twisted but there it was – and she hadn't even reached her thirtieth birthday yet. She felt bewildered inside, not to mention a little drunk.

"I think I'll just pop to the Ladies, if you'll excuse me?" She needed to be alone for a bit to get her head straight. But first things first. Wilfully steadying herself, she made her way across the floor, the noise of her heels on the polished hardwood drowned out by the buzz of conversation around her. The kitchen was at the back of the house and she badly needed a glass of water.

The corridors were cool and airy after the noise and heat of loud alcohol-fuelled conversation and expensive cloying perfumes and Jennie was glad of the few moments of real tranquillity. Going by instinct rather than any genuine recollection of where the kitchen was, she made her way through a pair of oak and glass doors at the end of a carpeted hallway and hoped that she was heading in the right direction. Another door confronted her, this time with two small, glass panels at head height – definitely the kitchen.

Relieved that her glass of water was within reach, she tentatively pushed the left-hand panel, hoping that there wasn't someone coming the opposite way with a tray of coffee. Thankfully, there wasn't and she landed into the enormous industrial-type kitchen unscathed. The place was a hive of activity, with catering assistants buzzing from left to right like a colony of ants, some covering food while others stacked items into the oversized dishwasher or stowed crockery into sturdy cardboard boxes.

It wasn't like going into Maxine's kitchen where she could pluck a glass out of one of the cupboards and pour herself a glass of tap water. She was barely noticed as she looked around to see where exactly the glasses might be stocked.

"Can I help you at all, Ma'am?" This was from a perky girl of about eighteen, maybe on a weekend job from college.

"Just looking for a glass of water. Where would I find a glass?"

"I'll get one for you, Ma'am. Would you like still or sparkling?"

The girl had clearly been well-trained for her role in this very professional catering outfit. The work ethic of the staff was evident, leaving Jennie in no doubt as to where much of the success of the Ferrises' dinner party had originated. If the catering ran smoothly, then everything else would fall into place. Noeleen had advised her of that once, at another dinner party where things had gone awry and the guests had had to leave without coffee.

"Still would be great, a large glass if you have one." She looked around now while the young girl scooted off efficiently. Large double doors opened out into what she'd often heard Noeleen describe as the kitchen garden. Jennie had imagined it as a tiny space with a series of herb plots but this area was much larger than she'd expected. Moving closer to the French doors to get a better view, something in the corner of the spacious walled-in garden caught her eye. She felt herself go pale.

"There you go, Ma'am. Would you like a seat?"

Jennie didn't hear her, so focused was she on the scene in front of her. Moving slightly to the left, she watched mesmerised.

"Ma'am?"

"Oh! Thanks." Jennie took the glass from her and was grateful for the icy coldness of it against her palm. Just for a moment, it neutralised the shock of seeing her husband sitting on a timber bench with his elbows propped on his knees and his head resting in his hands.

It was the woman sitting next to him that her eyes were riveted on now and Jennie was startled to find that she was looking at her to see what it was that she possessed that could make Vincent want to forget about the wife he'd promised to love and adore until death parted them.

Even though the garden was flood-lit, the bench was shrouded in shadows thrown from an overhanging tree. She was dark-haired, that much she *could* see but the woman was facing Vincent so that Jennie could only see her back. Her French roll was severe-looking from behind and it looked like she was wearing black, although it could equally have been navy or any number of dark colours.

Suddenly conscious of the noise around her, she sipped her water lest the girl who brought it would think she was a nutcase. She was standing in the middle of the kitchen after all, with the caterers whizzing around her as if she were a monument in the middle of a city roundabout.

Were they arguing? Vincent still had his head in his hands, the way he sometimes did in the study at home in the evenings when something was troubling him at work.

The girl was sitting bolt upright with a glass in her hand. Jennie couldn't recall seeing her at the reception or the dining-table earlier but then she'd been preoccupied with socialising dutifully as she was expected to do at these things. Was it possible that Vincent had kept a safe distance between himself and his *amour* while Jennie was in the main arena and then sneaked away for a rendezvous with her when his wife was well and truly occupied with Noeleen and her cronies? Light-headed, she wondered if all of them were in on it, that she was purposely being entertained while her husband was free to roam the house with his mistress.

Just as a vision of Vincent and the girl in the black dress making passionate love in one of the Ferrises' sumptuous period guest rooms began to rise before her, the girl rose from her position on the bench and started to make her way back towards the house. Vincent straightened but made no attempt to move, something that compounded Jennie's suspicions. If there was nothing to hide, then why not walk back to the house with another guest that he'd simply met in the garden? If there was nothing to hide, then why hadn't he mentioned to Jennie that he was going out for some fresh air? And if it was really fresh air that he wanted, then why not go out onto the picturesque terrace like everyone else?

Definitely not ready for a confrontation yet, Jennie gulped down her water and swung around. This time, she really did need to escape to the rest-room.

Chapter 15

Unbelievably, despite everything that had happened in the past hour, Dylan hadn't actually woken up. And now that both Emily Gordon *and* Paul had been removed from the scene, Sandra had no option but to go back into the house and watch over her son until she could get her head in order. Her parents would come down straight away as soon as she rang them, she knew that. They'd probably heard the ambulance sirens anyway and wondered who it was in the village that needed such a dramatic exit and for what. And if she didn't phone them soon, no doubt Aggie Lenihan would do it for her. Sandra had hated the disgusted gleam in her next-door neighbour's eyes as she'd monitored the situation, loath to leave the scene in case she missed anything yet eager to get going on what would be one of the better scandals of the year. Sandra didn't know how poor Joe put up with Aggie.

It was having to tell them about Paul's part in the accident that made her wince inside. She knew that her father would look at her and shake his head in much the same way that he'd been doing for the last few months since Paul had moved in with her and Dylan. Her mother would try to make the best of things, advising on practical things like a change of clothes for Paul and the possibility of contacting his mother as soon as she knew more. Sandra knew that her mother had exactly the same thoughts on Paul as her father did – it was just that she was a little better at masking her exasperation than her husband.

Sandra looked around the kitchen now and marvelled that only an hour ago she had been admiring her big clean-up. Paul going back to work had given her energy levels a great boost and she'd decided to give the whole house a face-lift, starting with the kitchen. An hour ago, she'd been so proud of herself, with the grout between the tiles scrubbed white again, the cooker scoured and all the presses washed out and tidied. Out-of-date jars, although there weren't many, had been thrown out with the remains of any opened ones that had gone off. Now though, the pride that she'd felt in herself had evaporated, leaving her with a shameful feeling that she was as responsible for Emily Gordon's gruesome accident every bit as much as her drunken boyfriend was.

The noise had been horrendous, so loud that Sandra's first instinct was one of annoyance. She'd spent ages trying to persuade Dylan that he couldn't just turn up at Tim's to play, even though Tim had promised that the baby-sitter wouldn't mind a bit. Eventually, he'd skulked off to bed after watching a DVD that she'd picked up earlier in Xtravision. Now, all of a sudden, someone was making enough noise to wake the dead, never mind a small child.

As soon as she'd ascertained that there was no sound of small feet hitting the carpeted floor upstairs, she ran to the sitting-room window, more curious now than annoyed. It never even occurred to her that the scene before her would have anything to do with herself.

"Jesus!"

The shock of seeing the two cars lumped up against the Gordons' front wall was enough to have the adrenaline shooting through her, even before she recognised Paul's ancient Corolla lodged on the verge where the footpath joined the main road. Leaving the door on the latch lest she find herself locked out when the drama was over, Sandra shot across the road to see if she could help.

Jacinta Gordon's face was the first thing that registered in her mind. That and Tom's voice shouting at her to call an ambulance. Jacinta looked as if she were physically stuck to the doorstep, her hands frozen at her mouth.

Paul had appeared out of nowhere and was leaning over the wall with his head in his hands. Baffled, Sandra started to make her way towards him, wondering stupidly if it was he who'd been hit by a car. Maybe that was the reason why Tom Gordon was still shouting for someone to call an ambulance, even though his wife had by now disappeared from the doorstep.

It was then that Sandra had started to absorb the details of the scene before her. Paul's car on the road's edge with a taxi wedged between it and the wall. Tom Gordon hemmed in between the taxi and the wall, frantically urging someone to stay awake. It was then that Sandra saw the strappy sandals and thin, pale ankles sticking out from under the taxi. Unable to piece it all together, she looked around in shock. Surely there was someone to help. There was no sign of the ambulance yet, just Jacinta Gordon tearing out of the house to join her husband on hands and knees under their front wall.

"Come on, Emily!" she'd cried, her voice shaky. "Listen to your father. You have to stay awake, whatever you do. Listen to me, Emily, love! You can't go asleep. Your father says you have to stay awake. The ambulance is on its way now. Just stay awake until it comes – that's all you have to do, Emily."

On and on it went, leaving Sandra in no doubt as to who exactly was trapped and injured under the taxi. Angered and helpless, she swung around and made her way towards Paul, glad it wasn't he who was pinned underneath a car. And the taxi driver – where was he in all this?

"Paul, what happened? Are you all right?" The low groan he emitted alarmed her, making her wonder if he too was injured. His car was there, yet he looked fine, although he was still leaning heavily on the low wall, his large frame bent almost double.

"Jesus, Sandra. It was only up the road . . ."

"Paul, turn around. Are you hurt? What are you talking about?" She knew it wasn't right to be asking all these questions in the middle of a crisis but she couldn't seem to control herself. She could hear an ambulance siren wailing in the background and saw Jack Rooney jumping out of a pick-up truck further down the street.

Paul turned to face her, his eyes bloodshot and

desperate. Roughly he took hold of her shoulders, almost shaking her. "I have to go before the Guards come. I'm fucked if I'm breathalysed."

The smell assailed her then and Sandra realised that he hadn't been leaning over the wall in pain or shock. He'd been drunkenly propping himself up after wreaking havoc on the street outside the Gordons' house. And somehow, Emily had been in the wrong place just at the wrong time.

Horror coursed through her in the same way that the waves of pain had when she was in labour with Dylan. Paul had been drunk that day too. Well, more hung over than drunk but it had been all the same to Sandra and the young midwife who'd had to put up with the stench of stale drink for twelve hours.

"Oh God, Paul. You weren't driving? Jesus, Paul . . ."

"Get me to fuck out of here, will you? I can't stay . . ." Paul made a sudden dive towards the house.

Sandra remembered a conversation with a few of his friends in The Stone's where they were saying that you couldn't be breathalysed if you were at home. Surely he wasn't going to leave with Emily still under the car?

"No, Paul, you'll have to . . ."

Suddenly Jack Rooney was standing over them, his face like concrete.

"Don't even think about it, Delaney."

Sandra stood stock still, her mind barely registering the ambulance crew as they ministered to Emily in the confined space in which she was trapped. More sirens wailed in the distance and it occurred to Sandra that it might take the fire brigade to free her from the twist of metal above her.

"Who the fuck . . ." As usual, Paul was getting stroppy, even now with the blue lights of an ambulance casting a surreal and erratic light over the scene of carnage that he'd created. No regret, no remorse – just an instinct to walk away from trouble as soon as he'd caused it.

Sickened, Sandra squared her shoulders. If he thought she was going to help him get out of this one then he was very much mistaken.

Jack, too, was having none of it. "What – thought you'd scarper into the house and sober up a bit, did you? You've mowed down two people and you'd fuck off and leave them for dead?"

Two people? Sandra looked around wildly, her eves searching for a second pair of legs under the car. Then it hit her. Only one of the paramedics was attending to Emily Gordon, assisted by Dr Lawlor, a GP living in Rathmollin Woods. The other one had opened the passenger door of the taxi and had placed an oxygen mask over the face of a man in the driver's seat. Sandra almost fainted.

Jack was still gripping Paul by the shoulder, his face a mask of suppressed anger. More blue lights appeared, this time in convoy. Sandra counted another ambulance, two fire brigades and, to her relief, a Garda car. It wouldn't be up to herself and Jack Rooney to restrain Paul indefinitely.

"Christ, Sandra, what about Dylan?" Paul was trying to lunge away from Jack but with little success.

"What about him?" Maybe distracting him with conversation would keep him quiet until a Garda arrived on the scene. And surely Paul wasn't suggesting that she help him into the house out of some misguided attempt at protecting Dylan? That would be too outrageous, even for Paul.

"I can't go to jail . . ."

This really took the biscuit and Sandra could see the pitying expression on Jack's face. She'd been a right fool and now she'd landed Dylan with a criminal for a father on top of everything else.

"What? You're worried about me and Dylan having to fend for ourselves? You should have been worrying about that when you were handing your wages over the counter to Danny Stone."

"For God's sake . . ."

Paul was just revving up for a proper dispute, oblivious to the fact that one of the Gardaí had alighted from the squad car and was approaching them along the footpath.

"I believe one of you gentlemen is the owner of the white Corolla?" His face was set in the usual inscrutable lines that meant business.

Jack had let go of Paul and now remained silent, as did Sandra. Paul emitted a grunt of acknowledgement, which prompted the Garda to commence a line of questioning that Paul didn't want to hear.

At that moment, Sandra saw her life for what it was and promised herself that this time she'd pull herself together and get back on track. She'd taken the easy option when Paul had arrived back on the scene, convincing herself that she was doing it all for Dylan, instead of admitting that she was too spineless to stand on her own two feet. It was the end of the road for Paul this time, that was for sure.

Jack had moved away now and Sandra could see him

standing next to Tom Gordon as one of the firemen began reversing Paul's car from where it was compressing the taxi against the wall while another fireman and a Garda directed him. The remainder of the firemen were using cutting equipment to remove the roof of the taxi cab, probably in order to get the driver out safely. A paramedic was still leaning awkwardly through the passenger door, tending to the injured man.

Next to her, the Garda was instructing Paul to blow into a bag and to continue blowing until advised to stop. For once, he was co-operative.

"I'm afraid, sir, that I will have to ask you to accompany me to the Garda Station."

Sandra felt weak again as the swirling lights flashed around her. It was all only a matter of minutes from when she heard the noise outside and so many lives had changed. Emily Gordon, still and pale on the cold footpath with a red blanket over her; the taxi driver, whose wife would soon have two guards arriving at her door; Dylan, asleep in bed, who would surely hear the full story of his father's crime in the schoolyard, no matter what edited version Sandra spun him.

Suddenly, Paul was being advised to make his way towards the Garda car. Another one had arrived by now to supervise the traffic and the main street was like a scene out of *Miami Vice*.

"I'll come later," was all she said as he was being led away. He was still Dylan's father, after all.

Thinking of Dylan, Sandra slipped quietly back across the road to check on him, her innocent son who would wake up in the morning to be told God only knew what by his mother. Would Emily Gordon be dead or just badly injured? Would the taxi driver's death be announced on the early morning news? She felt that she'd aged ten years in less than an hour but was heartened to see Dylan thrown across the bed with his Spiderman duvet kicked to the floor as usual. At least something in her world was still the same.

The Corolla had been winched onto a Garda transporter by the time Sandra went back out onto the street. One of the ambulances had departed in a blare of sirens, leaving the taxi cab strangely denuded on the footpath. All hands were now concentrating on moving it carefully away from the Gordons' front wall, directed from beneath by the paramedics. Chains were applied, an almost painstaking use of precious time as the Gordons huddled together, their faces white with fear.

Sandra stood immobilised as the shell of the taxi was lifted away, hoping to see some sign of life in Emily. A movement of her limbs or even a groan to reassure her that she was alive. But she saw nothing as the paramedics descended on the inert form en masse. Emily had always been thin and frail-looking, not robust and inclined towards extra weight the way Sandra was. She wondered fearfully if this would go against Emily now, if she had no resources to draw on.

It was like a slow-motion replay to see the stretcher being lifted eventually and the lifeless body being wheeled towards the waiting ambulance. One of the paramedics held a clear inflatable bag that he squeezed rhythmically as the others pushed the trolley carefully along the path. People stood back to allow them to pass while Jack Rooney guided Tom and Jacinta towards his Range Rover. There was no way they'd be able to drive to the hospital.

Guilt tore at Sandra and she couldn't even raise her eyes as they passed her.

"Go on inside, Sandra." Jack's hand was warm where it touched her shoulder through the thin cotton of her top. "I'll phone you later to let you know how things are."

Tears sprang to her eyes at his kindness but it didn't assuage the feeling of shame that she had brought this on the Gordons. She was the reason Paul Delaney was in Rathmollin in the first place. She was part of this now, whether she liked it or not.

Chapter 16

Light filtered through her eyelids from somewhere and Emily had that bewildered feeling of waking up disoriented in a strange place. Her immediate thought was one of panic. She'd been waiting for the taxi but she had a very bad feeling that she hadn't turned up at the wine bar to meet Gina and Orla. Her eyes shot open – Gina would go mental on Monday.

"Tom, look – she's waking up! Get the nurse!"

Emily could hear the urgency in her mother's voice as she ordered her husband to do something but couldn't make out what it was she was saying. She gagged as something hard and inflexible stuck in her throat.

"Nurse, quickly – I think she's choking!"

Jacinta sounded as panicked as Emily felt when she tried to swallow and found that she couldn't do so. Involuntarily, her abdominal muscles contracted and the upper half of her body rose a little, as if she was going to sit up. Suddenly, though, everything disappeared again with the cold feeling creeping slowly up her arm and she fell back against the pillows, her mother's voice echoing strangely in her head.

"Will she come out of it again? Did she know us, do you think?" Jacinta was asking forty questions at once while Tom just stood there with his eyes full of tears. Moira Naughton, the nurse who'd admitted Emily to the Intensive Care Unit on Saturday night was back on duty, to their relief.

"It's too early to say if she knows you just yet but yes, she will come around again. We're reducing the level of sedation gradually to allow her to wake up."

"But when will that be?"

"As soon as she starts doing more breathing on her own. She *is* taking some breaths but not enough to keep going without the ventilator, I'm afraid. I've given her a little more sedation so she should be settled for a few hours at least."

Now it was Tom's turn to ask a question. "How will we know when she's taking enough breaths of her own?" A practical man, Tom had been watching the ventilator pumping air into his daughter's lungs for almost a week now and was only coping by knowing exactly what was going on at all times.

"The ventilator will pick it up. As she improves, the ventilator will have to give her fewer breaths but will kick in, just in case, if she misses any." Moira looked at them sympathetically now, aware of the shock that they'd just had. "Why don't you two go down and have a cup of coffee? I have the mobile number if I need to call you."

Reluctantly, Tom and Jacinta backed away from the mass of wires that surrounded Emily and made their way carefully through the ICU. They'd been warned from the outset that Emily was in there for what might be a long haul and that exhausting and starving themselves wouldn't do her any good. By now, having met some of the families who'd been sitting by bedsides for months on end, they understood where the staff were coming from and obeyed the orders to have their meals and a proper rest while Emily was stable.

"Niall will be back in a few minutes, anyway," Tom reassured his wife, whose anxious face was still gazing back at the figure of Emily in the raised bed. "I told him to leave the immersion on altogether, in case we get home for a shower later."

Their son, having flown from Sydney earlier in the week, had taken a short break to shower and change as soon as his parents had arrived to sit with Emily. It was now Friday and they'd been carrying on this same rotation system day after day so that Emily, if she came around, would have a familiar face beside her and someone to hold her hand. It was all they could do now, having been given no guarantees at the outset as to whether she would even recognise them after the large skull fracture that she'd sustained.

"Do you think she knew you?" Tom asked anxiously as they walked the now-familiar corridor towards the hospital canteen. It was raining outside but neither of them even noticed the rivulets coursing down the large glass panes that lined the hallway.

Jacinta wanted to tell him that of course Emily had recognised her, that there had been something very definite in her eyes that had focused directly on her. But all she could remember was the bewildered, childlike expression and the look of blind panic when Emily had started to choke on the breathing tube inserted in her throat.

"I'm not sure. She looked at me but I couldn't tell if she recognised me or not. The nurse had the sedation into the drip straight away and she relaxed as soon as she got it."

Jacinta's auburn hair, so like Emily's, was in disarray, having missed its usual Friday morning wash and set in Curly Locks.

"We'll just have to wait and see. Will I get you a muffin?"

This was another new routine that had been developed in the past week: Jacinta securing a seat for them in the busy canteen while Tom loaded the tray with tea and sandwiches, adding scones or muffins depending on what was left after the staff lunches.

"Do, so." Jacinta was already making a beeline for a small table just vacated by two medical students.

She sat now with her head in her hands, waiting for Tom to return with yet another round of unwanted tea. It was like they were all the time stocking up, just in case Emily had a turn for the worst and they had to stay by her side indefinitely. So far, everything had gone to plan, just as the consultant had outlined to them in the early hours of Sunday morning. It was the best they could expect now, she supposed – that nothing would jeopardise the tentative recovery their daughter was making.

Every single time she sat still or was alone for a moment, the memories of Saturday evening flooded in on top of Jacinta. *Why didn't I insist on Emily waiting inside for the taxi? We could have watched out for it from the front window.*

"Here you go, love." Tom unloaded the tray, placing cups, saucers, teapot and muffins carefully on the small formica table top.

"He did say there was no bleeding to the brain." Jacinta said this as a statement of fact, knowing instinctively that Tom would follow the line her thoughts were taking.

Mr Creedon, the neurosurgeon, had explained to them in the A&E that as well as a ruptured liver that would need surgical repair almost immediately, Emily had suffered what was known as a depressed skull fracture.

It would have occurred, he informed them, following impact with something flat, possibly the wall, and Emily's skull had been compressed inwards putting pressure on her brain. If that pressure wasn't relieved as a matter of urgency, then damage to the brain tissue would most probably occur.

Jacinta remembered herself asking if he could tell from the scans how bad it was.

"I'm afraid not, but there is some swelling of the brain there already. We'll need your permission to operate immediately. I think that Dr Khan would like to speak to you as well about Emily's other injuries."

They'd signed the consent form in a daze, already terrified of what this Dr Khan would have to say.

Jacinta still remembered the strength she felt as Mr Creedon shook her hand firmly and promised that he'd do his best for their daughter.

Suddenly, Dr Khan was in front of them talking about a rupture of Emily's liver and something called a haematoma in one of her legs. And the fact that she'd already lost a lot of blood.

"The blood appears to be collecting in an area behind the liver so we'll need to repair the damage and drain this haematoma that has formed. She also has swelling in her right thigh, although the X-rays show that there are no bones broken. I suspect that there is a collection of blood there, another haematoma, and that your daughter will need a number of blood transfusions to get her through this surgery."

Jacinta remembered being horrified that Emily would have to have a blood transfusion. There was so much controversy about Hepatitis and HIV these days. What would happen if Emily survived this only to be told she had AIDS or something equally dreadful?

"I'm afraid she definitely will not survive without a transfusion. Your daughter's haemoglobin level is less than 5 at the moment and she is still bleeding. The blood has been ordered and is on its way here now."

"What should it be?" Jacinta needed to know exactly how bad Emily really was.

"A normal healthy young lady should have a haemoglobin level of between 12 and 14, Mrs Gordon. So you can see how ill your daughter is at the moment."

"Then don't lose a moment," Jacinta had stated firmly

as she watched Tom reaching for the form. "Give her whatever she needs to keep her alive."

She reverted back to the present now as Tom handed her the cup of pale hospital tea and took up the thread of conversation that she'd started a moment ago.

"I know he said there was no bleeding but it's the swelling he was worried about." Jacinta knew he was trying to keep an open mind on Emily's prognosis rather than be deliberately pessimistic but she couldn't help hoping that the outcome would be good.

Both Mr Creedon and Dr Khan had come to the waiting-room to speak with them as soon as Emily had been removed from theatre to the ICU. The injury to the liver and to Emily's leg had been repaired, the general surgeon advised them, but a total of ten units of blood had been needed in the process. Her bleeding was under control, he'd told them, but the next forty-eight hours were crucial.

From Dr Creedon's perspective, the large depressed skull fracture had been successfully lifted out to relieve the pressure on Emily's brain. She would need to remain sedated for a number of days to allow the swelling to go down and it was only then they would be able to assess the damage that might have been caused to the brain. The good news was that the fragments of crushed skull had miraculously failed to cause any bleeding on the surface of the brain.

"We'll just have to wait and see," Jacinta conceded. For the past six days, the need to "wait and see" had been at the conclusion of almost every conversation.

They'd phoned Niall in Sydney as soon as the surgery had been completed, relieved to be able to tell him the positive fact that his sister had survived the surgery after imparting the shock news of her accident. As they'd expected, he'd promised to book the first available flight and had arrived bleary-eyed via Bangkok and London on Wednesday morning.

"Imagine we used to worry about Niall being so far away." As usual, Tom's thoughts reflected her own.

"I know. I never thought something could happen to Emily, especially on our own doorstep. She's been through enough this year as it is."

"I suppose someone will tell that Richard fellow at some stage," Tom commented sourly. Richard Carmody had been treated like one of their own for the best part of ten years and Tom refused to find it in his heart to forgive him the upset he'd caused Emily.

"I suppose he'll hear about it some way." Jacinta certainly wasn't going to have anything more to do with Richard either. He was a cad as far as she was concerned, stringing Emily along all that time.

"It's the least of her worries now." Tom rose from the cramped confines of the plastic chair and stretched. "Maybe we should go back up and see if Niall is there yet. They might know more about how her breathing is going."

"We'll have to decide about staying as well. Niall really should get a proper sleep or he'll collapse."

"Maybe I'll stay tonight if you want to go home with him and get him something proper to eat. He'll think it's China he's in otherwise!"

Jacinta responded with the ghost of a smile. Poor Niall had eaten nothing but Chinese take-aways since he'd arrived on Irish soil.

Niall, his foxy hair still wet from the shower, was reading quietly to Emily from the collected poems of Patrick Kavanagh when they returned to the ICU.

"She's been really settled since I arrived. Moira said she woke up a bit earlier?"

Jacinta filled him in and told him about the plan she and Tom had made for the night, insisting on him getting a proper sleep despite his protestations.

"There'll be plenty more nights for you to stay," she reminded him. "And Emily needs all of us in good order. Let your dad stay tonight for a change."

Niall turned away and started to read again but not before Jacinta had seen the tears that sprang to his eyes at the mention of the days and nights ahead of them.

Moira Naughton arrived back to the bedside then to check on Emily.

"Emily's own breathing had been pretty steady so far today," she told them. "All going well, we're thinking of reducing the sedation a bit more overnight and maybe extubating her in the morning. What do you think?"

She looked around the little gathering; Niall clutching the book and Jacinta clutching Tom's hand.

"Does that mean she'll wake up?" Niall was the one to ask the question on each of their lips.

"We hope so," Moira answered gently. "We really do hope so."

Chapter 17

It was a week since the party at Bob and Noeleen's house and the sense of disquiet churning in Jennie's insides was increasing if anything. She and Vincent had left early by their usual standards and were in bed by one on Saturday night, unheard of after the Montenotte parties.

Donna had stayed the night, having been warned that it could be all hours before they returned – a relief to Jennie who used the baby-sitter's presence in the guest-room as an excuse for not making love when Vincent slid over to her side of the bed and started to nuzzle her neck seductively.

Her mind was still whirring with all the little hints, either real or imagined, that Noeleen had been giving, as well as the margaritas and the red wine that she'd consumed.

Seeing Vincent in the kitchen garden of the Ferrises' house had been shocking but not as shocking as the way he'd been able to cover his tracks when they'd met up again a few minutes later in the drawing-room. He'd been all about her suddenly, suggesting an early night and finishing up conversations with a few more people as if he couldn't get her home fast enough. A sure sign that he wanted the night in Montenotte to be over so that he could conveniently separate his home life from his illicit one before any dangerous repercussions arose.

She'd been almost relieved when he moaned about the enormous workload he had on for the week as he was leaving the house on Monday morning. She could hardly bear to look at him now, knowing that her suspicions had been right all along. The vision of the girl in the black dress and her hair in a French roll assaulted her every waking moment, so much so that she'd spent the week rushing around to get the image out of her head.

She was exhausted now after a week of it and her eyes were raw and grainy from lack of sleep as she studied the piece of paper in front of her. She wondered if she was being petty – imagining things that weren't happening at all.

Her mother, if it was a thing that Jennie could actually approach her with a problem, would probably dismiss her fears and say that she had too much time on her hands. Vincent's mother, to whom she would hate to ever have to admit defeat, wouldn't hear a word against her son and would tell her smartly that it was too well off she was.

Wearily Jennie fingered the piece of paper again. Maybe she was too well off with her nice home and two lovely children. Emily Gordon, for instance, was lying at death's door in St Angela's. Jennie still felt guilty about not stopping the car last Saturday night when they'd passed the accident outside the Gordons' house. She and Emily had been good friends at school but somehow they'd lost touch when Emily had left for college in Dublin.

Jennie, of course, had had Vincent and the secretarial course. She wondered now if she'd become totally tied up in her own life, to the detriment of her friendships. If she didn't have Maxine in her life, then who *would* she be able to call a friend? She'd promised last week to phone Emily and make a lunch date but it was too late now. If Emily came through this, then Jennie would pick up the threads of their relationship again – she knew now that she'd be needing all the friends she could get if the course of action she was about to embark on came to anything.

She uncurled the small piece of paper from the tiny ball that she'd squeezed it into and studied it for the hundredth time. *Securicode PI.* The name itself was emblazoned on her memory at this stage and the piece of paper was almost ready to fall apart with all the studying that she'd done of it since she printed it off last Monday.

She'd been burning to look up private investigators since the moment that her husband had fallen into a deep sleep beside her the previous Saturday night but had had to wait until Monday morning before she could do anything about it. There was no way she could risk Vincent finding evidence of her search on their own computer so an Internet café was her only other option.

Even the fact that she'd found herself huddling in the midst of a line of students at an outdated PC at half past ten in the morning was weird. Typing in Private Investigator had been another momentous step, almost an admission of her conviction that Vincent was definitely guilty of adultery.

Adultery was the word used by all the private security companies to describe what Jennie's husband was doing. After ten minutes of trawling through the various websites she was au fait with the services on offer. Discreet surveillance. Within the confines of the law, of course. Photographic evidence. A written report. Evidence that would stand up in court.

A divorce court – that was what it was all about really. And now that she'd gone as far as actually picking out a firm and writing down the phone number, Jennie wasn't quite sure what exactly she would do with the photographic evidence and written report that she might receive if she went ahead with her phone call.

A seven-day service, the ad had promised. The weekend somehow seemed a bit of a strange time to be engaging in such a dangerous business but now that Vincent was out of the house on his Saturday morning trip to their grandmother with Tim and Lucy, she had her new mobile at the ready. Not the landline – that was too fixed an entity to involve in the sordid adventure she was about to embark on. The anonymous pay-per-go mobile that she'd purchased after her stint at the Internet café could get lost at a moment's notice if the need arose.

Why am I doing this? This was the question she kept asking herself but the only answers she came up with were straight off the PI websites that she'd scrolled through earlier in the week. To confirm that he's faithful. To rule out adultery. Despite her suspicions she didn't want to think of the other promises about improving divorce settlements and getting sole custody of the children.

It was perverse, she told herself as she crumpled the piece of paper into a small ball yet again. She wanted to find out, yet she was afraid of what she'd hear and see if she did engage a private detective. Did she really want to disrupt her own life *and* Tim and Lucy's lives? Okay, they didn't see as much of Vincent as perhaps they should but how was it going to benefit them if he was gone altogether? And for herself – did she really want to be rattling around in Rathmollin Woods with sole custody of the children? She asked herself now if she hated her husband and strangely it was actually a sense of fear that she felt. All the same, she told herself firmly in the next breath, I can't allow myself to be made a fool of. She thought of the woman with the black dress and the severe French roll again and carefully unfurled the ball of paper.

"Ron Green."

The voice that came at her across the line was abrupt and almost flippant. Surely it required some sort of gravitas to collect the kind of evidence that could collapse a marriage in an instant?

"Hello." Jennie cleared her throat and tried again. "Hello, I want to enquire about, er, surveillance?"

"Personal surveillance or company surveillance?" Ron Green was businesslike in his approach but Jennie suspected that he knew the answer already. What company would be phoning a private investigator at half eleven on a Saturday morning?

"Personal. My husband." Jennie felt that she should at least give him some information to go on.

"Okay, Mrs . . . just give me an initial for now . . . we can talk details later."

Jennie was flummoxed for a moment – an initial what? Then it dawned on her – an initial from her name to address her by. The website *had* promised the strictest confidentiality.

"Mrs K." She felt like a character in *Murder, She Wrote*.

"Right, Mrs K, I'll outline our services and you can call back with a decision later if you feel you want to go ahead with it. Concerns about an extra-marital affair, I presume?"

At least he hadn't mentioned adultery. "Yes," she confirmed, trying to be as businesslike as the man on the other end of the phone. She imagined him sitting with his feet propped on the desk of a very untidy office. He'd definitely have a cigarette dangling from his lips. And a beer gut. Probably divorced, which was how he got into the PI scene in the first place.

". . . as well as video evidence and access to things like copies of restaurant receipts, hotel slips and other relevant documents . . ."

Jennie realised that she'd missed half of his pitch by allowing herself to dream about the kind of man who broke up marriages for a living. She couldn't exactly backtrack with a load of questions so she tuned in and listened intently to the remainder of Securicode's services. He started to outline hourly rates and the kind of things that might be described as "extras".

"Foreign trips, for example. Although a few shots of an airport farewell are often enough. We wouldn't go down the line of expensive foreign trips unless we hadn't picked up anything else."

It occurred to Jennie that, before the scene in the kitchen garden on Saturday night, she might have been considering a surveillance operation in Dubai as part of the deal but right now she was confident that all the evidence she needed was here in Cork.

"I see," Jennie said slowly, her voice unsure even to her own ears. "I'll ring you back when I've made a decision."

Ron Green had hung up before she'd even finished speaking. He was very obviously a busy man and one who didn't exactly have to tout for business, by the look of it.

Jennie recalled from her trawl through the PI websites that something like 60 per cent of marital surveillance yielded confirmation of an extra-marital affair and wondered if she would be one of the lucky 40 per cent. If so, what did it say about her relationship with Vincent, the fact that she might be investigating the activities of a perfectly innocent man?

The scene in the garden rose before her again and her resolve strengthened. She couldn't go on like this or she'd be admitted to a psychiatric hospital for paranoia. She thought for a moment about Ron Green's hourly rates and decided that they weren't all that exorbitant – as long as she didn't have to shell out for the overseas surveillance that he'd mentioned.

"Mr Green? This is Mrs K here again." Her hand was slippery with sweat on the plastic casing of the mobile phone. "I'd like to engage you for that surveillance job, if you're free, that is." She sounded firmer this time, more confident.

"I'm free all right, Mrs K," he confirmed, the hint of a grin in his voice. "Can you be at my office on Monday at two? I'm sure you have the address."

"Monday?" Surely the man had a waiting list?

"The sooner the better, eh? And bring some recent photographs of your husband as well as car registration details and his workplace address. And photos of any other key players, if that's relevant."

"Key players?" This was suddenly moving a bit too fast for Jennie. What did he mean by key players?

"You know – other parties. Sometimes people have a suspicion about a sister or a close friend in these cases."

"There's nothing like that." Jennie was horrified at the thought and almost put the phone down. How sordid could this turn out to be?

"Two o'clock on Monday it is then."

She couldn't back out now that she'd come this far.

"Okay – two o'clock," she whispered hoarsely.

"Righty-oh then," Ron confirmed, his voice suddenly almost cheery. As abruptly as before, he hung up, leaving Jennie clutching her newly acquired phone. Her hands were wet with perspiration and her forehead was clammy.

What in God's name was she about to do?

Chapter 18

If it wasn't for Dylan, Sandra reckoned that she would have cracked up entirely. As it was, she was barely keeping going. Her mother had promised to phone her straight away if there was any news of Emily, seeing as Sandra herself was too ashamed to even make contact with the Gordons. It was half three on Saturday evening and she was terrified of the thought of going to evening Mass and having to face people.

She'd visited Paul in the Garda station on the Saturday night of the accident, a week ago now – ostensibly to bring him a change of clothes but mainly to tell him that he was on his own from here on in. She'd phoned his mother for him as well, seeing as he was only just managing to stay awake at the time of her visit.

Whatever amount of alcohol he'd had in The Stone's that evening, it was really only kicking in when he'd been arrested. He'd had a blood sample taken as soon as he'd arrived at the station. Typical of Paul, he was convinced that he mightn't actually be over the limit at all.

As it happened, he'd been three times over the legal limit for driving. He'd told her over the phone that his solicitor was concerned about this going against him later in court, especially if either Emily or the taxi driver failed to survive. Sandra hadn't been to see him at his mother's house in Mallow. He'd been released on bail with the condition that he sign on at the Garda station every day and surrender his passport, measures that Sandra felt were more than necessary, considering Paul's penchant for refusing to accept any level of blame for anything. It was only too likely that he'd try to abscond to England if he got half a chance, something Sandra knew from bitter experience could well happen when the pressure was on him.

She couldn't bear to look at him and certainly didn't need convincing of how useless and ultimately disruptive his presence was to Dylan, father or no father. But Paul kept phoning her – on the mobile one minute and on the landline the next – so that he could moan about the injustice of it all, while Emily Gordon lay in a coma in St Angela's.

It was all down to Sandra again, according to Muriel. Her son hadn't been a moment's trouble until he met up with the Brazen Hussy from Rathmollin, her honorary title for Sandra. Not for the first time, she mentioned this to Sandra on the phone when she'd rang to tell her about Paul's "accident".

It was no accident, Muriel had fumed, that Paul was in a spot of bother again. If Sandra hadn't set her cap at him and saddled him with that young scut Dylan, her Paul could have made a lot more of himself.

It fascinated Sandra that Muriel Delaney could be so blind to the faults of her precious son. According to her, poor Paul had been doing well for himself in London until he bumped into Sandra again. Now here he was in more trouble, thanks to Sandra's undoubtedly giddy neighbour being all over the road and Paul getting the flack for it when she got mowed down. Not a word about Emily unconscious in the intensive care unit or the taxi driver who had been airlifted to Beaumont hospital in Dublin. Not to mention the small matter of Paul being over the limit.

As usual, Dan and Rose were staunchly behind Sandra and Dylan. They'd arrived as soon as she'd phoned them on Saturday evening, having waited until all the emergency vehicles and bystanders had vacated the street and the glass had been swept up by Aggie Lenihan who seemed to have the run of the Gordons' house all of a sudden. They'd minded Dylan that night while she'd made her surreal journey to the Garda station and had rarely left her side since.

"The only thing you can do now is put it all behind you," Dan advised repeatedly. By "it", he meant Paul and the whole sorry episode of their "fresh start".

"Would you go back to the hairdressing, do you think?" Rose was all for the idea of Sandra getting a career, something that would give her back a bit of the self-confidence that she seemed to have lost in direct proportion to the number of days she spent in Paul Delaney's company.

"I'd have to see about Dylan – with school and everything . . ." Sandra didn't know what to think. She *had* been thinking about going back to it but Paul had kept on at her about all the allowances and entitlements she'd lose if she were earning again.

She'd mentioned this to her mother during the week, to see what she thought of the wisdom of giving up her social welfare payments.

"It'll be for the long-term good," Rose told her firmly. "You have to speculate to accumulate."

This was always one of her great sayings, of which she had many. Rose had a phrase to suit every occasion and, despite the fact that she knew most of them off by heart at this stage, Sandra was finally starting to see the wisdom in them.

She jumped now as the phone rang. The caller ID button displayed a private number and she was unsure as to whether to answer it in case it might be Paul. She was sick of having to shoo Dylan out of the room every time the phone rang, not wanting him to hear the inevitable altercation, but at least he was safely out the back digging on this occasion.

"Hello?" Even to her own ears, her voice sounded sheepish and timid.

"Well, you're sounding cool enough!" Muriel's trill filled her ears and she wondered exactly what she'd done wrong this time.

"Muriel." It was a statement rather than a greeting but Sandra was beyond politeness after all the abuse she'd suffered at the hands of both Muriel *and* her son of late.

"Not a word out of you. Not even a phone call and Paul as good as on house arrest on account of you."

Muriel's line of reasoning was that Sandra was

responsible for any events that happened in Rathmollin seeing as it was *her* hometown and that poor Paul had been inadvertently caught up in the dodgy dealings of the small village. Sandra knew it was useless to argue the point.

"Anyway –"

Sandra could hear the deep breath that Paul's mother took before continuing.

"Lara Cagney – that's Paul's solicitor – says that Dylan could be very valuable in all this."

"What?" Sandra was bewildered. Muriel rarely mentioned her grandson's name unless she preceded it with brat, scut or the like.

"You know," she snapped, as if Sandra was thick as well as troublesome, "she'll want to include him in the defence. The fact that Paul has a small child would go in his favour if there was any question of him having to serve time."

"Serve time?" This was a new one on Sandra, a genteel way to avoid stating the fact that her precious son might end up in jail. And now she was hoping to drag Dylan into it, implying that Paul was the kind of father that couldn't possibly be done without. At this Sandra drew the line.

"You know," Muriel repeated tersely, "a custodial sentence."

"And what were you hoping for? That I'd be able to vouch for Paul's record as an exemplary father? To say that he's been involved in a 'hands on' capacity these last eight years?"

"Well . . ."

Muriel was spluttering angrily now but Sandra wasn't going to be cowed this time.

"Maybe I could say that he's been more than generous with maintenance payments over the years?"

"Well, really . . ."

"Or we could put Dylan on the stand, maybe?"

"Actually, Lara *did* suggest that . . ."

"Did she now? Well, Muriel, whatever else you think is going to happen, that's one thing that certainly isn't!" For once, Sandra was firm with her son's grandmother. Muriel, however, was well prepared.

"It's not all about *you*, Miss," she snapped smartly. "Paul *is* the child's father."

Sandra didn't know where she got the strength for what she said next but Dylan had been through enough already. A memory of her son cowering in the kitchen during one of his father's many drunken episodes assailed her.

"If anything of this kind is ever mentioned again, I'll have a barring order against Paul so quick his head will be spinning off his shoulders. We'll see how that'll go down with his friend Lara." Triumphant, she waited to see what Muriel would have to say to this.

"In all my born days, I never met such a brazen, bold little madam! A barring order! Who in the name of God would give you a barring order?"

"We'll have to see about that, won't we? But I wouldn't put it to the test, Muriel. Bad publicity is all he needs now."

Sandra knew that this would be the final straw for Muriel Delaney. If getting her precious Paul out of trouble was her number one priority, keeping the whole affair under wraps was following close on its heels. Reputation was everything, something that Sandra had discovered as soon as she'd "forced" Paul into being an unwilling father eight years ago. Muriel had been furious then and Sandra had taken the brunt of it ever since.

"I've nothing more to say to you, Madam. He's as well off without the likes of you."

The dull hum of the line told Sandra in no uncertain terms that the old tyrant had hung up. Shaking, she pressed the button on the electric kettle. At least a cup of tea wasn't beyond her capabilities.

The sharp ring of the phone blasted out again but this time she was relieved to see her parents' number on the display panel.

"Well?" The fact that she didn't even greet Rose in her anxiety went unnoticed. Emily Gordon's welfare was first right now.

"They were to take her off the life-support machine earlier today. Aggie Lenihan met Niall coming out of the house at lunch-time and he told her. I didn't hear anything since though."

"I never thought I'd say it but thank God for Aggie and her reporting." Sandra gave a shaky little laugh, relieved that there might be some positive news on the horizon. Emily was obviously improving if they were thinking of taking her off the life-support machine.

"I know," Rose sighed.

Aggie had been in and out of every house in Rathmollin like a yo-yo over the past week, her head bobbing at a rate of knots as she gathered and dispensed news of Emily Gordon's condition.

"Joe Lenihan must be living like a bachelor because Aggie is on the road full-time. She might know more by Mass time though. Are you going to go?"

Rose knew that evening Mass in Rathmollin would be a big ordeal for her daughter and wondered about the wisdom of putting herself through it.

"I'm not sure."

"Maybe you could go to the ten o'clock in St Jude's in the morning."

"I could, I suppose." St Jude's church in the city was large and impersonal, just the place for someone who wanted to remain anonymous for a bit.

"I might hear a bit more this evening – whether she's woken up, maybe." Rose knew that her daughter was terrified that Emily might die or be left brain-damaged after her accident, something that Aggie and her cronies were already beginning to suggest on account of the brain surgery she'd had a week ago.

"Will you ring me if you hear anything?" Sandra was almost as much a fugitive as Paul was.

"Of course I will, love. None of this is your fault, you know. Why don't you go down to Connolly's and get something nice for the tea? We'll call in on our way to Mass."

Sandra knew that this was her mother's way of making her feel useful as well as providing a distraction. She played along, grateful for her kindness.

"I'll get some of those Chicken Kievs that Dad likes."

"Do, love, and we'll see you around six."

"Bye, Mum."

As soon as she'd hung up, Sandra sat with her head in her hands and wondered where it had all gone wrong. It wasn't her upbringing – that was for sure. It was time now to pull her socks up and stand on her own two feet. Support was one thing but her parents couldn't be expected to drag her along forever.

Chapter 19

"Emily? Can you hear me?"

There was something funny about the voice. It was definitely her mother's voice but it sounded child-like and afraid, fading in and out as if Jacinta was speaking down the length of one of those didgeridoos that Niall had shipped from Australia for Emily's birthday.

"Open your eyes, Emily."

This time it was her father, ordering her to open her eyes, yet not speaking authoritatively the way he would if he was ordering a neighbour's dog out of the garden but more as if he was terrified that she wouldn't obey him.

With a fright, it dawned on Emily that she must be late for work. Through her dreamlike state, she couldn't recollect what day it was. But it must be a weekday if *both* her parents were calling her. Shocked that she'd slept it out, her body shot forward. She had appointments with people, people who were in debt and needed help and couldn't be just stood up.

"It's okay, Emily, we're here," her mother was saying now and hands were pressing against her shoulders, holding her in place.

Panicking, Emily lunged forward again. She had to get up for work, although she was aching all over and the movement had jarred her, causing a splitting pain to shoot through the crown of her head. Something else was holding her too, something on her wrist and something tight on her upper arm. Frustrated, she shook them away.

"Open your eyes, Emily." A different voice now – one that was familiar yet unrecognisable all at once. "Just relax back and open your eyes."

It was like her eyelids were stuck together but she made every effort to respond to the quiet authority in the strange voice. It was an order, albeit a gentle one.

"Oh, God, Emily . . ."

Her mother's face swam before her, blurred and out of focus.

"Emily, we're here. We're here, Emily, you're all right." Her father, telling her it was all right about work. Had he phoned the VBA to say that she would be late?

"Don't try to sit up, Emily. Just lie back and let yourself wake up." It was the strange voice again, although not strange enough for it to be completely new to her. Letting go of her panic, Emily closed her eyes again and lay back on the pillows, feeling exhausted despite having overslept.

They were talking about her but she hadn't the energy to open her eyes again. Unfamiliar words drifted around her. *Sedation. Weaning. Assessment.*

Sleep came again but Emily didn't care. Her father had phoned work and it was all right.

Jacinta sat back in the plastic chair, a feeling of defeat washing over her. They'd waited all afternoon for Emily to open her eyes, yet when she'd done so it had only been for a matter of seconds and she hadn't shown any signs of recognition. Niall had only gone out to the toilet and it had all been over by the time he came back. Emily was lying just as he'd last seen her, deeply asleep with her IV and blood-pressure cuff still attached to her arm.

"It'll take time, Jacinta," Moira Naughton explained for the umpteenth time that day. "It's only a few hours since she was extubated and there is still a certain amount of sedation in her system. Over the next few hours it'll wear off and we'll be able to do a proper assessment. The good news is that she's breathing independently and that her oxygen saturation is remaining above ninety-five per cent."

Jacinta looked across Emily at the bed next to her and the inert form of Tony Collins, whose family they'd come to know in the past week. His mother greeted Jacinta's forlorn look with one of encouragement and determination and Jacinta had to look away. Gretta had been sitting in the ICU for three months.

"All we can do then is wait," Jacinta said staunchly and took Emily's weightless hand again. To her surprise, she felt the slightest of pressure matching her own gentle squeeze. A quiet anticipation coursed through her but she said nothing to the others – the ICU wasn't a place for false hope or unfounded celebration.

"We're not leaving this bed until she wakes up," Niall declared as soon as the nurse had left the bedside.

He was upset, Jacinta could see, that he'd missed the few precious moments of Emily opening her eyes.

"We have to look at the good things. She's breathing on her own, for one." Tom, as usual, was spelling out the good things. He glanced at the flickering blue read-out that hovered between 97 per cent and 100 per cent. "And her oxygen levels are steady."

"I'm sure she can hear us," Jacinta said. "Maybe we should keep talking to her, to get her to remember us."

"You're probably sick of listening to us, Em," Niall said, grinning in his sister's direction.

It was true that they'd been talking to Emily incessantly for the week that she'd been unconscious. Each of them had moments where they'd wondered if it was fruitless but mostly they needed to feel that there was some small chance of comforting or getting through to her.

Silence descended for a few moments. They'd been sitting anxiously by the bed since Dr Khan had removed the breathing tube from Emily's throat at half twelve. It was now half four and the hours seemed like an eternity.

"She's moving," Jacinta whispered urgently, stating the obvious to Tom and Niall who were watching Emily's hand, their eyes wide in their faces.

"Emily!" It was Niall's turn to call his sister and neither of his parents interrupted. Maybe she would respond to *him*.

"Em," Niall persisted, "open your eyes, just for a minute."

Amazingly, she obeyed, her expression both puzzled

and frightened. Unable to speak, Jacinta stroked her daughter's face and took deep breaths. Out of the corner of her eye she could see Gretta Collins watching the scene from her son's bedside.

"What . . .?" It was a croaky whisper but it was a word. Hope surged through Jacinta.

"You're in the hospital, Em," said Niall. "We're all here. It's okay." His voice started to break and Tom took over.

"You got hurt, Emily, but you're all right now. You're getting better."

Emily was focusing on Tom now. "Dad?"

This one word was enough for Jacinta. She recognised Tom. Tears flowed down her face as she stroked her daughter's cheek. Maybe she wouldn't be brain-damaged, left without a voice of her own as Jacinta had feared.

"I'm here, love," Tom reassured her.

Emily's eyes closed wearily again, only to fly open suddenly in alarm.

"Eenaa . . ." It was clear that Emily was trying to say something but the word came out as a dry groan.

"It's okay, Emily," Jacinta soothed. "Don't try too hard."

A fit of shallow coughs followed, drawing Moira Naughton over from where she'd been monitoring the situation from the nurse's station.

"It's fine. Your throat is dry from the tube, Emily. Just rest for a moment and try again."

Emily closed her eyes briefly and took a deep, steadying breath.

"Gina," she said again, this time more clearly.

"The night out, Tom!"

Niall looked confused, having missed the night of the accident.

Jacinta filled her daughter in a little. "We rang Gina – she says there will be plenty of nights to go out once you get better. She didn't mind about the wine bar." It was typical of Emily to worry about letting someone down.

"Mam – Niall?" She was looking around at each of them now, obviously confused as to what was going on.

"You're in hospital," Niall explained again. "I came home to see you – even gave up a shitty job on a building site." He grinned and, amazingly, the ghost of a smile appeared on his sister's face before she lapsed into sleep again.

"It'll be like this for the evening, I imagine," the nurse explained. "Even though we've been reducing her sedation gradually, it'll take a while to wear off fully. And she's still getting a certain amount of pain relief. We can reduce that a bit more over the next few days if she's coping well."

"Should we be trying to get her to wake up?" Niall needed to know from the nurse exactly what to do to help Emily.

"Not necessarily. She'll come around gradually. It's best to answer her questions but not to exhaust her by asking things. It'll become clear after a while how much she's aware of. Just give her time."

"Thanks, Moira," they chorused in unison as the nurse left the bedside.

It had been explained to them before that Emily's other injuries would need to heal as well. The large abdominal wound through which her liver had been repaired was healing well but she still had the horrendous curve of metal clips on the side of her head where her scalp had been opened to repair the skull fracture. Her right thigh, too, had a line of clips where the large pool of blood compressing her muscles had been drained away. It was amazing, most of the ICU staff had said at one time or another, that she hadn't had more injuries considering the way she'd been pinned against the wall.

Jacinta smoothed Emily's auburn ringlets over the bald patch now and noticed how dry her lips were. She reached for the small tub of Vaseline and gently slicked a thin layer of it over her daughter's lips, one of the small jobs she'd been able to do this last week to alleviate the feelings of uselessness that threatened to smother her otherwise.

"Sleep now, Emily, and we'll be here when you wake up. It's only a matter of time now, before we have you home in Rathmollin. Then we'll be able to mind you properly." Jacinta felt again the tiniest answering pressure in her hand and knew, somehow, that all would be well.

Chapter 20

Jennie checked herself in the mirror again, all the while keeping an ear out for Tim and Lucy. She could hear Vincent settling them into the car and instructing them about their seat belts. She looked well, she decided, taking in the fitted white linen trousers and cerise wraparound cardigan under which she wore a lacy white vest. Cerise mules with a trendy wedge heel completed her outfit, making her look like any young wife attending evening Mass with her husband and children. It was amazing how clothes and make-up could disguise what was going on inside.

"Come on, Jen, or we won't get a seat together!" Vincent yelled up the stairs.

He'd been an exemplary husband all day, taking the children to the park after the trip to his mother's to let her have a proper morning to herself – precious time that she'd spent phoning a private detective to stalk him. He'd even brought lunch home so that they could have a "picnic" out in the back garden, a treat that Tim and Lucy loved even more than barbecues.

Jennie didn't know what to think when he spent the whole afternoon out in the garden playing, leaving her with a few hours to go shopping in town by herself. He'd even had them showered and ready for Mass when she got home, something that he'd never done in his life.

Was there no affair at all? Did he really love them or was he just building up some kind of brownie points that could be ticked off in a divorce court? Or maybe all this devotion was just a cover-up to lead Jennie off the path of copping on to an adulterous husband. Was he planning to leave her soon for the girl he'd been with in the Ferrises' garden?

Pushing her visit to Ron Green to the furthest recesses of her mind, she raced downstairs and slammed the front door behind her. She might feel like a ghost inside but she had to perform on the outside until she knew for sure what was going on.

The churchyard was crowded so Vincent dropped Jennie and the children off first and went to park further up the road. The first person they encountered was Dylan Delaney who raced up to Tim with some kind of Power Ranger, followed closely by his grandmother, Rose Coyne.

"Hi, Rose," Jennie greeted her. The older lady looked a bit worn, as if she'd missed a night's sleep. She wondered if Dylan knew the part his father had played in Emily Gordon's accident and if that was what had Rose so stressed looking.

"Hello, Jennie. And Lucy – how are you? No Power Rangers?"

"Power Rangers are only for boys. They're stupid!"

"Lucy!" Jennie admonished, rolling her eyes at Rose. Lucy always felt left out when Dylan arrived.

"What about a lollipop then? To have after Mass?" Rose looked at Jennie for permission before producing a lollipop from her handbag.

Lucy's eyes lit up, more to do with having something that Tim and Dylan *didn't* have than the actual lollipop itself.

"Wow – thanks!" Lucy was into Americanisms and "Wow" was her latest buzz word.

"You're welcome, pet." Rose watched Lucy tearing off to boast about the lollipop to her brother and his friend, before she turned back to Jennie. "Did you hear that Emily Gordon has woken up?"

"That's fantastic. Is she able to talk?" The whole village knew about Emily's accident and even the schoolchildren had held a special prayer service for her on account of her being a past pupil.

"A little, I think. Aggie Lenihan phoned young Niall at half five to see how she was and he said that she'd come around and had even said a few words to them. It's a great relief."

"It is indeed," Jennie agreed as the sacristy bell rang out. She felt sorry for Rose, who must indeed be relieved that the father of her grandchild wouldn't be charged with manslaughter, whatever else he'd be charged with. She and Dan had put up with a lot of worry over the years on account of Sandra and Jennie wondered now if even this latest debacle would make her straighten out and get shot of Paul Delaney.

"Come on, gang!" Jennie called out as the "five-minute-bell" continued its monotonous toll. She hoped that Tim and Lucy hadn't got into devilment with Dylan when there was no sign of an immediate appearance. Then she saw them approaching with Vincent in tow, Lucy explaining to him about the lollipop while the boys looked on enviously.

"We'll see," Vincent was saying, a sure sign that Tim had been demanding a treat now that Lucy had one stuffed into the pocket of her pinafore.

"See you later, Rose," Jennie said kindly, mindful of the second-hand burden of guilt that the Coyne family must be carrying. "I must give Sandra a bell some morning to come over for a cup of coffee. She's probably at a loose end like myself once she has Dylan out the door in the mornings."

The smile of relief that Rose gave her was exactly what Jennie had hoped for. Sandra wasn't to be considered a pariah after all if she could be invited for coffee to Rathmollin Woods and, because of that, Rose would have some of her load lifted.

"I'm sure she'd love that, Jennie." Rose walked alongside her towards the side door of the church, Vincent trailing behind with the children. "She's talking about going back to the hairdressing, you know."

"Good for her," Jennie whispered encouragingly as they made their way into the side aisle together and allowed the silence and the smell of incense to envelope them.

Jennie's mind started flitting from one thing to another as soon as Father Reidy started to intone the Mass in the American twang he'd developed during a two-year sabbatical in the Bronx. All of a sudden the idea of a private investigator didn't seem such a good one and her worries seemed to have shrunk in relation to the worries of Jacinta and Tom Gordon and even those of Sandra and her parents. *Maybe I'm being paranoid because I have too much time on my hands or something,* Jennie thought now as Lucy fidgeted beside her. *Maybe I should be doing like Sandra and considering going back to work.*

The Mass and Communion flew by in a blur and she barely noticed Vincent having to separate Tim and Lucy to stop them whispering. It felt like minutes and they were back out in the churchyard, this time in the company of Aggie Lenihan, chief informer regarding Emily's status. Rose had excused herself hurriedly as soon as she spotted Jennie and Vincent approaching, obviously glad to escape the official spokesperson that Aggie considered herself to be.

"Did you hear that Emily Gordon has come around?" she announced to Vincent and Jennie.

"Rose told us. It's great news, thank God."

Aggie had always been the village gossip and, to Jennie's amusement, still seemed to have the knack of instigating an immediate alliance with whatever family was going through a divorce, bereavement or illness so that she could have the inside track first hand. This time it was Emily's family and, to a degree, Rose Coyne.

"She's been through a lot, that girl has, in the last year –

oh, hello Jack – we're just saying that Emily Gordon has been through a lot in the last year." Aggie's head, always known to bob excitedly when there was news to be relayed, was bobbing in earnest now that Jack Rooney had joined their small group at the church door.

"She's coming around, though, I hear."

Jennie sensed the faint shadow of a wry grin from Jack as he greeted her and Vincent, as if to acknowledge the fact that Aggie Lenihan was still going strong after all the years that had passed since she'd reported him and Jennie to the headmaster when she'd spotted them picking blackcurrants in old Dr Heavey's garden one lunch-time.

They'd been six at the time and neither of them had forgotten the sting of the bamboo cane across their palms and the shame of getting "six of the best" in front of the rest of the High Infants.

"Well, she's had a lot of stress in the last while." Aggie was obviously dying to get her say in and now had an audience of three to be entertained. "That Richard fellow, for one thing. And now the whole thing about the house."

This was Aggie's usual *modus operandi* – a mysterious mention of some hitherto unknown going-on in the hope that one of her audience would ask her to elaborate. It was Jennie's belief that Aggie then convinced herself that she wasn't actually spreading gossip – not when someone had *asked*.

On this occasion, none of the three of them took the opportunity to ask her to elaborate so it was up to Aggie to forge ahead herself.

"She was mad for it – Harmony Cottage, you know. Had the deposit sorted out and all but she was bamboozled at the last minute."

"Bamboozled?" Jennie was interested now.

"You know – someone offered more money and the whole thing was off. She had it as good as bought." Aggie's bubble perm had finally stopped bobbing and her chin was now tucked into her chest as she waited for a reaction from the others. She reminded Jennie of a hen in a farmyard watching her chickens.

"You mean gazumped," Jennie corrected, finally getting the picture.

Vincent, only barely interested in Aggie Lenihan's brand of gossip up to now, was suddenly alert.

"That doesn't seem right. Had she made an agreement?" His voice was businesslike and Aggie immediately picked up on his interest.

Jennie knew where Vincent's radar was going on this and sensed that he was on the point of asking more. If the house was being dealt with by The Property People, then it was one of his own auctioneers who might be involved in Emily being gazumped.

"Did she actually pay a deposit?" Jack too was putting his oar in, even before Aggie had got around to answering Vincent.

"Well, not an agreement exactly." Her head swivelled from one man to the other, her antennae up now that she'd piqued their curiosity. "But as good as. She was ready to put the money down when some high-flier bumped up the price on her. She was very upset the evening she had the accident. Jacinta is sorry she ever encouraged her to go out that evening but she thought it'd do her good, the poor girl."

Jennie could almost feel the tension easing out of her husband, while Jack continued to look perplexed, a deep frown creasing the tanned skin between his eyebrows. To his credit, Vincent had a sense of ethics that had always gone beyond the strict legalities of the property business. Fair play was everything and the dubious practice of abandoning an initial agreement in the face of a better offer was anathema to him. And to Bob Ferris, Jennie had to acknowledge.

"That's a shame." Jennie was sympathetic to Emily's plight, having heard on the grapevine that she'd been left high and dry when her engagement had broken up. No wonder she wanted a place of her own to start again.

Jack, silent on the subject of Emily Gordon's additional misfortune, now changed the subject abruptly.

"Actually, Vincent, I was meaning to call around to you this evening at home."

Vincent looked surprised at this. It was unusual, Jennie knew, for Jack to carry business over into the weekend.

"Not to worry, Vincent, it's not work-related," Jack amended, smiling at Vincent's reaction. "I was only going to nab you for some manpower. Seán Daly said you might be interested in helping out with the playground."

"More like Maxine said it! I can tell you now that I'd be useless at growing herbs so you'll have to get me something easier to do."

"Easier? It's literally breaking stones! There's a low wall running around the back of the school and we can't get in at it with machinery, more's the pity. We'll have to go at it with a Kanga hammer and a few crow-bars on Monday evening, if you're interested."

"Monday evening?" Vincent was running his fingers through his hair, sounding almost nervous to Jennie's ears all of a sudden. Something clicked in her psyche at the tone of his voice, something fearful and bleak. Before he actually said it, she knew that Monday evening would mysteriously be out of the question.

"Around seven, if you're home. Seán will be there as well and some of the Parents' Council members."

"God, Jack, I'd love to but I have a meeting with some of the Bahrain consortium. They're in Cork for a conference so it's not something I can cancel."

Funnily, the lie didn't seem to trip easily off his lips and Jennie could sense that he wasn't happy to have to make excuses to Jack Rooney, especially with Aggie Lenihan looking on. This was the first that Jennie had heard about an evening meeting and she hoped that she'd been able to keep her composure in the face of the village ferret's scrutiny. The last thing she needed was Aggie and her cronies diagnosing the problem before she herself did.

"No bother. I'll be like Schwarzenegger by the time that playground is finished. Whoever did the last bit of landscaping must have expected it to last until the next millennium! It's murder."

"Sorry, Jack. Do give me a shout if there's anything else . . ."

"Something that's not backbreaking?" Jack laughed good-naturedly at Vincent's distress while Aggie tutted at

Jennie and started on about all the money that was being "wasted" on the playground.

"It's not as if they'll have a bit of appreciation for it. Kids nowadays couldn't care less what kind of a playground they have. All they want is computer games and the like." Aggie was like a nodding dog now that she'd got going on another choice topic.

"I think it'll be great for them" Jennie said pointedly, suddenly annoyed at the old biddy and her scavenging instincts. And the fact that she'd been giving out about "the youth of today" since Jennie was a toddler. "People are always giving out about kids hanging around and getting into trouble but there has to be something for them to do instead. Fair play to the people who are actually *doing* something instead of giving out."

Aggie's eyebrows shot up and too late Jennie realised the error of this last comment. Aggie looked from Jennie to Vincent and then, more pointedly, at Jack. Vincent immediately reddened at this perceived dig from his wife about his refusal to do something for the playground and at the fact that Aggie was there to witness it. Jack looked uncomfortable in the silence that developed, especially when Aggie eventually sighed and uttered a long-drawn-out "Well . . ."

Mortified, Jennie tried to backtrack. "It'll be fabulous when it's finished. Vincent has to take the kids to Douglas on Saturdays for the playground there so it'll be great to have one on our doorstep." Great – happy families. Jennie couldn't bear to have Aggie gossiping about her to all the patrons of Curly Locks on a Friday morning.

"Well, it won't be long now," Jack said kindly, coming to her rescue.

"Hmmm . . ." Aggie was still looking at them suspiciously but thankfully Tim and Lucy arrived as if on cue, bored now that Dylan had left.

"Are we getting a DVD, Dad? Mum said we could have Krispie buns and stay up late."

More happy family stuff, Jennie thought with relief, as she patted Lucy's head gratefully. "You can have anything you want sweetheart, so long as it's not too scary. We can't have a repeat of last week." Jennie smiled at Vincent, purposely conspiratorial for Aggie's benefit.

Lucy and Tim nodded vehemently in agreement.

"Definitely no more monsters," Vincent laughed, catching Tim's left hand and Lucy's right one simultaneously. "We'd better go or it'll be bedtime. Give me a ring, Jack, if there's anything I can do during the week. Bye, Aggie. Give our best wishes to Emily, if you're in to see her."

"Grand so. Bye, lads." Jack winked at the children and smiled at Jennie, before taking off down the steep tarmacked churchyard, his stride long and purposeful.

Taking this parting of the ways as the end of anything further for her news bulletin, Aggie Lenihan said her goodbyes and hurried off, no doubt to tell the rest of the village that she had it on good authority from Vincent Kelleher of The Property People that it wasn't right at all that Emily Gordon had been "gazumped". And that the same Vincent wouldn't do a hand's turn for the school that his children were, after all, attending. Not to mention the fact that his wife was clearly very annoyed with him over it.

Jennie watched Jack stride off towards his own house and wondered if there was anyone special in his life or whether he was going home now to get ready for a night out. She'd always half-fancied Jack as a teenager but he'd disappeared to New York before she'd had time to chase him properly. She wondered grimly if she'd have been in the position she was in right now if she married Jack Rooney instead of Vincent. Would *he* be the type to carry on behind her back? Sighing, Jennie followed her husband and children out of the churchyard. The sooner she found out the truth the better or she'd literally kill herself wondering.

Chapter 21

Sandra was awake before the alarm clock went off. The sense of purpose with which she'd fallen asleep the night before hadn't deserted her.

Sunday had come and gone and, to her immense relief, the news about Emily was getting better with every report. Aggie had accosted Sandra over the low fence that separated their houses to tell her primly that Emily had woken again a few times on Sunday morning and had definitely recognised her family, even saying their names. Sandra's mother had called to invite her and Dylan for Sunday lunch and *she'd* heard from Aggie later in the morning that Emily had even asked for a drink.

Sandra's relief was enormous, however, when she met Jack Rooney on the way home from her parents' house on Sunday evening and he stopped to tell her that he'd met Tom Gordon at the Statoil and he'd been thrilled to hear that Emily had been asking about work and whether her friends were cross over their aborted night out. She had appointments to cancel at work, something that her family were delighted over. If she could remember all the names and times in her work schedule, then surely she wasn't brain-damaged.

If Jack was thrilled to hear of Emily's well-being, Sandra was over the moon. She liked Emily and the thought of having her death on her hands was too much to think about. Now, at least, she seemed to be out of the woods.

Sometime in the early part of the night when Dylan's gentle snores had eased him into a deep sleep, she'd lain awake and resolved to approach Chrissie Kennedy about returning to her apprenticeship as a hairdresser. She'd been rolling it around in her mind for a while before Paul had come back into her life and had put it on hold with the mirage of a supportive partner on the horizon. The mirage had been just that.

Even though she met Chrissie almost every other day, going to the salon as a prospective employee was somewhat different than bumping into her in the grocery or the post office. Slipping quietly out of the confines of the bed that was all her own again, she made her way to the bathroom to shower and consider her options.

There was no point in donning a suit and proper "interview" regalia. Firstly she didn't have an interview and secondly, she didn't have a suit. In view of these obvious impediments, she settled on wearing her good black trousers and the black, red and cream top that made her bust look smaller and her face less pale.

Her hair was the most important thing. If there was

one thing she remembered from the two years she'd worked in Curly Locks, it was Chrissie's insistence on all the stylists being an advertisement for the quality of the service she offered. It was just as well that she'd invested in the Garnier Nutrisse colour earlier in the week. Sandra's hair, traditionally a mousey brown, was glowing with a healthy, chestnut vitality. Its natural thickness – "good hair" her mother called it – made the cut that she'd had in Curly Locks almost a month ago look as good as the day she'd visited the salon.

Her make-up would have to be discreet – Chrissie hated "plastery-looking" young girls who she reckoned frightened off many older customers. The older women, she used to advise them, were the backbone of a country hairdressing salon. The older woman would always want her set and colour on a Friday in a regular hairdresser's whereas the young ones would chop and change from one trendy salon to another.

With a shock, Sandra realised that her mind had raced ahead and that she was already imagining herself in the small back room with Chrissie covering the theory all over again.

Looking at herself in the mirrored door of the shabby wardrobe, Sandra didn't think she looked too bad. Not considering the week she'd put down, worrying about Emily Gordon all night and watching the front gate all day in case Paul decided to turn up now that she'd stopped answering his increasingly desperate phone calls.

The black trousers fitted well, now that she'd lost half a stone from stress, and the satiny top settled below her still-wide bottom. Thank God for straighteners, she thought gratefully as she ran her imitation GHD through her hair. Dylan would be up soon, waiting for his breakfast.

"Where are you going, Mam?"

Sandra jumped at the sound of his half-sleepy voice behind her.

"You're all dressed up."

Dylan had always been an observant child. He was up and dressed now, his school tie askew even though it was one of the elasticated ones.

"Nowhere. Did you make your bed?" Changing the subject was the key.

"Yeah."

She followed him down the stairs and put Weetabix in two bowls. Dylan raised his eyebrows.

"What?" she said. Although she knew exactly what he was looking for – the sugary, air-filled nonsense that his dad classed as "decent cereal". She'd spent years encouraging her son to eat a proper breakfast and, to be fair, he'd never objected to his Weetabix until now. But with Paul eating bowls of chocolatey rice and honey-covered popsicles morning and night it was hardly surprising that the poor child wanted some now. This was yet another unsatisfactory reminder of Paul's short duration in her little family.

"Nothing," he retorted sulkily, knowing full well what her answer would be.

She made a mental note to throw out the rest of the tooth-wrecking cereal as soon as she'd returned from her mission to Curly Locks. It had been desperately unfair to expect Dylan to live by one rule when his father was living by another and Sandra was sorry that she'd allowed the situation to go on for so long. Besides, the cost of these latest additions to her shopping had eaten into her already tight budget with detrimental effects to date.

"Don't forget your lunch," she called after him now as he exited the table, the unsatisfactory Weetabix eaten reluctantly. "Wait at the gate – I'll just get my jacket." It was her turn as lollipop lady this week so she pulled out the Hi-Viz jacket that she kept for the job and pulled it on over her outfit, disguising the fact that she was a bit over-dressed for the school gates.

Dylan ran ahead of her to the edge of the footpath, too impatient to wait. She supposed it was a sign that he was growing up little by little, yet she missed the closeness that they'd shared when he was small and depended on her for everything.

There were a few "smallies" waiting for her already, their mothers propped up against the wall in order to allow their offspring to learn the correct procedure for the lollipop lady. Rufus Crawford was the only one on the other side of the road, standing alone outside the gate where his mother had dropped him off.

"Okay, gang, into a line!" Sandra called out.

She guided her charges across the road as soon as the flow of traffic ceased and herded them towards the gate.

"You too, Rufus," she said smiling. Poor Rufus was as quiet as a mouse, as usual.

For the next five minutes, she ferried three lots of children safely across the road until the bell finally rang. Her next step would be to deposit the Hi-Viz jacket back at the house and set out on her mission to Curly Locks. Turning to make her way back across the road, a small movement as someone disappeared around the corner at the side of the now-empty schoolyard caught the edge of her eye. She hoped it wasn't Dylan messing about and headed off across the yard to investigate. She could hear the belligerence in the voice before she rounded the corner to the gable end of the school.

"Hand it over, Crawford!"

Sandra didn't recognise the voice but thanked God it wasn't Dylan's.

The next thing she heard was Rufus Crawford's piping little voice, sounding a bit braver than Sandra imagined he felt.

"N-n-n- o," he stammered.

She rounded the corner swiftly to find poor Rufus wedged up against the wall clutching his schoolbag while Billy Rafter and two other fellows from Second Class pulled roughly at it, trying to separate it from its owner.

"What's going on here?" Sandra demanded authoritatively. The lollipop lady was a figure to be respected.

"Nothing," Billy Rafter spat back stubbornly.

His father, Will, had been the school bully in Sandra's time. It seemed that the trait had been inherited.

"Grand so," she told him mildly. "If there's nothing going on then Mr O'Connor won't have anything to give out about. I'll just knock at his window and call him out." Sandra made as if to go towards the headmaster's classroom window.

"Sorry, Miss." Billy was quick to back down.

Rufus was shaking in his shoes.

She addressed Billy's co-conspirators who were all timidity now that their victim had a protector. "What about you two? What are your names?"

"Kyle Reddy, Miss."

"Patrick O'Driscoll, Miss."

Sandra put on her most grave tone of voice for effect. "Well now, boys. This is very serious and it'll have to be reported to the headmaster."

Rufus was whiter than the other three and Sandra realised that he thought he was in trouble too.

"Now, Rufus, you were very brave to hold on to your schoolbag – go on inside and sit down. You'll have no more trouble from these boys."

Smiling gratefully, Rufus scuttled off clutching his schoolbag containing, Sandra imagined, the Nintendo games that the boys were after.

"As for you three – you could be up for stealing if you're not careful. Now I'll give you one chance but if I hear even one more episode of anyone – anyone – going near Rufus, I'll be reporting it. In fact I'll be expecting you all to be very nice to him and to stick up for him if there's anyone else going near him. Is that understood?" She looked at the three white faces nodding in front of her and felt sorry for them. "Now off ye go."

Sandra *would* mention the episode to Mr O'Connor over the next few days so that he could keep an eye out for bullying. She wondered if Rufus would mention it to his parents but somehow thought not. Nuala Crawford and her high-flying husband were probably too busy to know what was going on with Rufus but Sandra found it hard to be too critical. After all, she thought guiltily, her own house wasn't exactly in order.

Pushing the self-doubts out of her head, Sandra took a deep breath and headed for home before she got cold feet about her next mission. Or before her mother rang to see if she needed anything from the shops. Better to wait and see what Chrissie had to say first before she told the world about her plans.

She was nervous as she set off up the village a few minutes later. The few steps as far as Curly Locks would help her clear her head. It would be great, she reflected, if Chrissie was good enough to take her on again. She could drop Dylan to school on her way to work and he could go to her parents' house in the evenings and do his homework until the salon closed.

She reached the black and gold shop front at a quarter past nine and found a skinny young girl with a mop of golden ringlets cleaning the front window. Chrissie was a stickler for hygiene and order and Sandra wondered if the ineffective-looking circular swipes that she was employing would be up to her boss's standards. No doubt Chrissie would be in some nook or cranny observing her performance.

"Morning!" The waif's chirpy little voice surprised Sandra who'd been just about to push open the familiar glass door. "We're not open until half nine but I can make an appointment for you if you like." Taking initiative was another of Chrissie's mantras.

"I'm just popping in to have a word with Chrissie." Although if this little sprite was the type of staff that Curly Locks were keeping nowadays, maybe it was time for a quick U-turn. Sandra was virtually prehistoric in comparison.

"She's in the back – just call out!" Again the helpful little chirp.

"Thanks." Sandra had forgotten that she'd be encountering some of the staff members and now wondered who might be in the small cubbyhole at the back getting a demonstration on the art of mixing colours from Chrissie. She almost turned on her heel to escape but couldn't face passing the little window-cleaning fairy without completing her mission.

"Sandra!" Chrissie was folding towels by the row of sinks and spotted her as soon as she came in the door. Her own hair, groomed to perfection, surrounded her face like a wavy blonde halo.

Now that she was here, Sandra's nerves began to get the better of her and it occurred to her that she might just be about to make a complete fool of herself. She was twenty-eight, for God's sake, not exactly a spring chicken when she considered what she'd been like starting out in Curly Locks the last time around.

"So what brings you here this hour of the morning?" Chrissie got to the point as soon as their greetings were out of the way, something that Sandra was immediately grateful for.

"Hi, Chrissie, I was just wondering if you'd have time for a word. I can come back if it's a bad time."

She saw her former boss eyeing her ensemble and was

convinced that she already knew why Sandra was here.

"Now is good – you can help me fold these while we're talking." Chrissie indicated the pile of black towels and continued her own neat folding. Sandra was inordinately grateful for the occupation and pulled one of the fluffy towels from the heap, still warm from the dryer.

"Thanks, Chrissie." Her heart was hammering now but she tried to continue confidently. "I was hoping to talk to you about work – to see if there was any chance I could start an apprenticeship again, if you're in need of a junior. Or even continue where I left off, if it were possible."

Chrissie frowned, as she did whenever she was considering something. "I have Nicola on trial at the moment," she nodded towards the front where the sprite was now spraying the mirrors, "so I'm not looking for anyone. But I'd certainly consider it if there was a vacancy down the line. You were very promising at the time, Sandra."

"I loved it, to be honest. I'm just sorry that I made such a mess of things. If Mam hadn't been working at the time I might have been able to continue. But Dylan's getting big now and I'd really love to go back to it."

"Has everything else settled down?" Characteristically, Chrissie wanted to know what else was going on in Sandra's life. There would be no point in taking her on as an apprentice hairdresser if it meant that Paul Delaney had to be part of the equation.

"It has, thank God. Mam and Dad would be helping me out with child-minding after school and I'd have plenty of time to study when there's only Dylan and myself in the house."

This, Sandra knew, was what Chrissie was really asking her. And considering it had been Paul who'd disrupted her career before, she could imagine Chrissie's misgivings if he were still in the picture, especially since the whole town knew about his part in Emily Gordon's accident.

"Right."

The towels were now in four neat piles in front of them and Sandra automatically placed them tidily on the chrome trolley by the steriliser, comforted by the fact that little had changed in the salon in the intervening years. At least she'd be in familiar surroundings if she did get a second chance.

"Thanks, Sandra. Have you approached any other salon?"

"No. And I'm not sure if I will, with Dylan to consider. I'd probably get something in the city but transport would be an issue, for a start."

"I see your point. Look, I'll see how things go with Nicola, whether she works out or not. In the meantime, it'd be no harm to get on to the Training Board to see whether you'd have to go back to scratch or not. And if I hear of anything going elsewhere, I'll let you know. Maybe it's a thing that Paul would be able to help out with Dylan?" Chrissie was making really sure that Paul was out of the picture.

"I'm afraid not, Chrissie," Sandra answered firmly, letting the older woman know in no uncertain terms that Paul was well and truly a thing of the past. She'd get nowhere with Chrissie with him in tow, that she knew for definite.

"Grand so. We'll see what happens."

Sandra knew that their discussion was at a close and that Chrissie would genuinely do her best. She prayed that Nicola would turn out to be a walking disaster but wasn't convinced as she watched the junior guiding an elderly lady smartly towards a styling unit, the customer's heavy shopping bag in her hand.

Sandra said her goodbyes to Chrissie with a brave smile and a heavy heart and watched Nicola stow the customer's shopping carefully behind the counter before chirping "Two sugars and a little milk! Coming up!"

Chapter 22

The fear that she'd been staving off while her parents and Niall were in the room caught up with Emily as soon as the door closed behind them. Alone, she suddenly felt the enormity of her situation hit home. Maybe it was something to do with the massive injuries that everyone said she'd suffered to her head or maybe it was the move from the ICU to her private room on the surgical ward – either way, she felt as if she were on the moon instead of safely tucked up in the security of the hospital that was responsible for saving her life.

Feeling like a big baby as she started to shake in terror, she looked around for the call bell in a panic. It was nowhere to be seen and she remembered her father moving it out of the way after he'd accidentally set it off earlier in the day. He'd been mortified when all the nurses had come running but Emily wished now for the luxury of the team bursting into the room as they had an hour ago.

What would I tell them? She asked herself this as sweat broke out on her back in tiny pinpricks. Straining until she could see the green and white hospital bell resting on the leather armchair, she felt a flood of relief that was short-lived when she realised that she couldn't actually reach it.

The sudden movement had caused her catheter to pull against the wall of her bladder and she lurched back onto the pillows, jerking the IV cannula in her right arm as she did so. Tears pricked her eyes and this time she let them come. Terrified of moving lest she disturb something else, she lay there silently with her cheeks wet and no tissue within reach.

The hopelessness of her situation washed over her again. She was supposed to be resting but it wasn't possible to ignore the fact that her life as she knew it was in ruins. A few short months ago, she'd had everything to look forward to, now she couldn't even see the point in getting better.

From what the doctors had told her this morning, she was lucky to be alive and would not be able to consider returning to work for the foreseeable future. What that meant in terms of the security of her temporary job with the VBA she had no idea. And even if it became available now, there was no way that she'd be able to consider buying Harmony Cottage. Not when her earning ability was so severely compromised.

Despite their protestations, Emily couldn't help thinking of the amount of upset and worry that she'd caused her parents this last few months. First the breaking off of her engagement to Richard with the anxiety over the selling of their unfinished house and the worry about whether she'd see a penny of what she'd put into it. Her hunt for a new job and the move back to Rathmollin had been another palaver, although she knew that her parents were thrilled to have her under their roof again.

Now it was the fact that both of them seemed to have aged by ten years since she'd waved them goodbye and headed out the gate to wait for her taxi to town. Even Niall had been discommoded, his dream trip to Australia cut short on her account.

Feeling like a complete failure, Emily cried harder, her abdominal muscles aching and straining under the padded dressing that covered her surgical wound. Some rest!

Thinking of Richard filled her with something that felt like sadness but even now she couldn't block out the humiliation that seared her. She'd rarely allowed herself to think about him in anything other than practical terms since she'd left Dublin but right now the thought of him intensified her loneliness.

She supposed she should be glad to be alive – her family certainly were – yet she couldn't seem to muster the ecstatic enthusiasm that she'd felt from Niall as he set up the small CD player in her new room or the quiet gratitude of her mother and father as they watched the two nurses and the attendant sliding her gently off the ICU bed onto the trolley for her transfer to the surgical ward. Grateful – that's what she should have felt. But Emily could find no call for gratitude, alone as she was in the small clinical room with a plethora of wires and tubes attached to her.

She couldn't even go to the toilet herself, she railed angrily, cursing as she turned a little to wipe her face on the floral duvet cover and accidentally tugged her catheter again. Exhausted now from crying and with her earlier panic dispersed somewhere in the rain of tears, she sniffled bravely and wished for a paper tissue.

Closing her eyes, she wondered how she'd call the nurses if she had a real emergency and vowed to make sure that the alarm bell was near her from now on. Her face was sticky now and she knew she'd have to wait until her parents came back after lunch before she could get a wet facecloth to wash it.

Resigned to her enforced rest and feeling somewhat better after her protracted crying session, she was just about to let her thoughts drift into calmer waters when she heard the plastic Venetian blind on the outside of the small pane of glass in her door rattle. Startled, Emily watched as the slats parted and a pair of eyes appeared between them, followed closely by the apparition of Aggie Lenihan around the door.

"Emily!" Aggie was hissing, a stage whisper designed to wake Emily up if there was any chance of her being asleep. "Are you awake properly? Will I come in?"

The fact that Aggie was actually installed with the door closed was beside the point.

"Hi, Aggie. How are you keeping?" Emily made an effort to smile and wished that she'd had an opportunity to tidy herself up before her gossipy neighbour had arrived, knowing full well that Aggie would be only too delighted to describe her as a total wreck. Which she probably was, seeing as she hadn't looked in a mirror in over a week.

"It's great to see you, Emily. We were in an awful state over you." For Aggie "we" generally meant the whole village. "I rang the ICU earlier and they said you were moved to the ward, so I just had to come and see you for myself."

Emily felt like a tourist attraction – the Pyramids of Giza or Tutankhamen's tomb. "I'm surprised they even let you in. They said no when Mam asked about the aunts and uncles visiting."

At this, Aggie had the good grace to look slightly shamefaced. "Well, I asked at the front desk and they said 3A Surgical so I just popped along to see if I could find you. Your name is on a thing outside the door. So how are you, anyway?"

Amused at Aggie Lenihan's ability to brazenly brush over her cheeky arrival, Emily decided that the best thing to do was to give her as little fodder as possible.

"Powerful. I should be home before long, I imagine." Her throat was still sore from the tube of the ventilator but she was determined to sound strong.

"But what about all those things? What's that for?" She was pointing now at the 24-hour urine monitor in its plastic casing.

"All routine, I'm told," Emily said breezily.

"But you still have a drip up! They couldn't send you home." Aggie sank down into the leather bedside chair, her brown raisin eyes taking in all the accoutrements that surrounded Emily.

"That's only water – until I'm drinking properly."

Emily glanced up at the large bag of saline as if it could be seen hanging over her head any day in Rathmollin if only Aggie took the time to look.

"But are you able to walk and everything?" It would be of great benefit to Aggie's story if Emily had the misfortune to be paralysed.

"There's not a thing wrong with my legs, thank God." Although the truth was that it might be days before she was strong enough to even bear weight on her legs, especially the right one with its little train-track of metal clips snaking along the thigh. She'd had to be lifted into the bed earlier.

"Well . . ."

Emily had forgotten just how flummoxed Aggie became when a dire story failed to materialise. She tucked her chin into her chest now, something Emily had noticed her doing whenever she arrived to fill Jacinta in on some bit of useless gossip.

"Any news around Rathmollin?" A new subject might just distract her attention for a bit.

"Well, now that you ask. Although, mind you, I wasn't inclined to say anything when I thought you were so bad. But you're improved a lot, thank God, now."

It must be something very exciting or relevant if it was liable to cause alarm to an ill patient like herself.

"Thank God," Emily repeated, a small smirk threatening to break at the corners of her mouth. At least Aggie was a tonic for her maudlin thoughts earlier.

"Your mother told me about Harmony Cottage during the week. It was desperate altogether the way you missed out on it."

Annoyed that the whole town now knew about yet another failure on her part, Emily kept a smile nailed to her face.

"Ah, well, these things happen," she replied, "and there're plenty of houses going around Rathmollin at the moment." *Except I can't afford them.*

"Well, I think it's a disgrace." Aggie's head was nodding up and down now, something that Sandra Coyne used to imitate really well in primary school, Emily remembered. "These big developers buying up everything that stands still long enough and then putting a bulldozer through it."

Emily didn't know where this was going and was damned if she was going to ask. She was tired suddenly and wished that Aggie would shut her trap.

"I'm telling you, Emily, that Jack Rooney wants to own the whole village as far as I can see. I went into the planning office in the County Hall this morning to see if I could get to the bottom of it and there it was. A planning application for twenty houses in Doyles' Field."

Emily still didn't know what Aggie was on about. The Doyles had died within months of each other a couple of years previously and she knew that Kieran and Aaron, both living abroad, had sold their parents' small farm on the outskirts of Rathmollin. But what this had to do with Aggie's long-winded tale about Jack Rooney and indeed Harmony Cottage was beyond her.

"On the Cork Road?" She wished that a nurse would come to check on her and evict Aggie.

"No, Emily," Aggie hissed impatiently, as if Emily was really stupid. "The field behind Ina Harrington's cottage was theirs as well. That's where Jack's looking to build the houses. And he'll need to knock the cottage to make an entrance."

"What?"

"I'm telling you – I saw the plans myself. And there was no cottage on the drawing, just an entrance at the village side of Dan Coyne's house. So now so!"

So it was to be knocked down. As easy as that, a house that Emily had thought valuable enough to make her home was just an impediment in the way of someone like Jack Rooney. Her mother had warned her about snapping up the cottage before Jack got his hands on it but Emily had thought he might buy it to renovate and sell on. This, somehow, was more insulting. And she was damned if she was going to let Aggie know how put out she was about it.

"Well, you never know, I might be able to buy into the new development when it materialises. It seems to be well on track if the cottage is ready to be knocked."

"He hasn't actually *got* the go-ahead for the planning permission yet," Aggie announced primly, as if she personally might just refuse it. "There's a month left for objections if anyone wanted to make one." She watched Emily carefully, aware that news of a crucial nature could be forthcoming.

Talk about David and Goliath, Emily thought bitterly, knowing exactly where Aggie's train of thought was going. As if she didn't have enough on her plate without drawing yet another drama on herself. She'd been on the verge of a legal debacle earlier this year already and she wasn't about to get embroiled in another to feed Aggie Lenihan's expectations.

"I don't imagine that anyone will. It's only a cottage – not exactly a listed building."

There, she'd said it and it was true. There would be other houses, although the light in the little sitting-room came back to her now and she let go of it with a sense of regret.

Aggie was silent now, at a loss as to what subject to tackle next. Neither Emily's supposedly horrific injuries nor the to-do about the cottage had yielded any new information.

"What about your job? Will it be waiting for you when you get back on your feet?"

"Definitely. I imagine they have a temp in at the moment."

"So it's a permanent job then?"

"Permanent and pensionable," Emily declared confidently, all the while thinking of her six-month probation period which was nowhere near up yet. She hadn't factored in illness or injury as being a likely scenario.

"Well . . ."

Emily was starting to wonder what the next topic would be when the door opened and a student nurse arrived in, a mobile blood-pressure apparatus in tow. She literally ground to a halt when she spotted Aggie at the far side of Emily's bed. Emily looked at her helplessly and rolled her eyes as discreetly as she could. The nurse cottoned on immediately.

"I'm afraid you'll have to leave straight away," she announced, to Aggie's disappointment. "It's not visiting time and this patient is not actually allowed visitors at the moment." She glanced at Emily for confirmation and received a grateful nod in response.

Aggie, having hoped to hear that Emily, at the very least, had a bit of high or even low blood pressure, rose from her chair reluctantly.

"I'll call another day, Emily," she snipped brazenly for the nurse's benefit.

"Lovely, Aggie. Make sure to tell everyone I'm on the mend."

Poor Aggie, disgusted that she actually *was* on the mend, left with precious little in the way of news, although she had actually *seen* Emily which was more than anyone else in Rathmollin had done.

"Thanks be to God you arrived," Emily grinned as she held out her arm to the nurse. She remembered the pretty blonde girl introducing herself as Fidelma when she'd welcomed her to the ward earlier in the morning.

Fidelma smiled back as she folded the cuff around Emily's biceps. "You should have rung the bell and said you needed painkillers or something. I'm brilliant at evictions."

"So I see!" The cuff tightened on her arm.

"120 over 80. Perfect. Do you have any pain at the moment?"

"Not a bit. Apart from in my head from listening to Aggie there!"

"It's a bit early for visitors all right."

"She sneaked in to see how disfigured I was. She'll probably sell my story to one of the tabloids. I wasn't half bad enough for her."

Emily often wondered what kind of relationship Aggie and Joe Lenihan had. Aggie was on the road the whole time, tearing up and down the village on her bike looking for news when she wasn't "visiting" people at home or in hospital. Joe was like a lap-dog, looking over the wall but never seeming to actually go anywhere or have any interests.

"You *are* doing great. We might be able to take out the catheter in the morning so I'll take it off the hourly monitoring and give you a smaller bag for the moment." Swiftly she pulled on gloves and removed the large complicated apparatus and replaced it with a smaller one.

"Another bit of baggage gone," Emily commented.

"The drip will be next. How much have you drunk since you woke up this morning?"

Emily recounted her two glasses of water, a small bottle of Lucozade and one of the strawberry-flavoured nutritional supplements that she was advised to have twice a day to build her up.

"Almost a litre in all," Fidelma calculated. "I'll slow the drip down a bit for now and we'll see how much you're managing on your own. We'll plan for stopping it at six, okay?"

"Brilliant. I'll be able to do a bit more for myself without pulling one of my limbs off!"

"And you might feel up to having a shower in the morning when the clips in your scalp and leg come out. You're day 10 tomorrow." She pressed an aural thermometer into her patient's ear as she said this and waited for the beep that Emily had become accustomed to in the ICU.

"I can hardly believe it." Emily looked at Fidelma's

neat pony-tail and wondered what her own frizzy mess looked like. "Will it be too soon to wash my hair?" she asked hopefully. If the whole of Rathmollin was going to descend on her as soon as Aggie came back with a good report, she'd better be prepared.

"We'll manage a minor wash, just with baby shampoo. No GHD, mind."

Fidelma was writing up her notes now and Emily admired her confidence and composure. She couldn't be more than twenty.

"Anything's a bonus at this stage. What about getting out of the bed to walk?"

"The physio's going to come in the morning to see you as soon as all your tubes and wires are out. She's hoping to walk you to the bathroom for your shower. I'll be there as well and you can sit in the shower, just in case you're feeling weak."

"I'm like a big baby. Or a geriatric patient."

"Only temporarily. When Gertrude gets at you – she's the physio – you'll be dying for your bed!"

"So I'd better make the most of my last day in bed, is that what you're telling me?"

"Something like that!" The nurse, without Emily having to ask, replaced the call bell next to her by tying it around the metal bedpost. "Call me if you get any more unexpected visitors."

Emily watched the door close gently behind the nurse and this time she *was* grateful. Tomorrow would be a new day, with lots of progress to be made. Reaching for the small plastic bottle of nutritional supplement, optimistically entitled Pineapple Zip, that Fidelma had thoughtfully opened and left on her bed table, she started to sip. Determinedly. Okay, so she might be almost unemployed, heading towards glorious spinsterhood and Jack Rooney might be about to demolish her little cottage – but she wasn't beaten yet.

Chapter 23

Jennie's two o'clock deadline was branded onto her brain as if it had been stamped there by Ron Green himself. She had the €1000 deposit carefully stashed in the small zipped pocket in the depths of her Fendi handbag. Extortionate as it was for what might only amount to a few days' work, she'd had to think carefully lest a large cash withdrawal might catch Vincent's attention during his monthly totting up of their accounts.

Now as she sat in the shaded interior of an obscure little coffee shop on Baltimore Street sipping a skinny latte, she was something akin to triumphant at her resourcefulness in securing the deposit without it having to appear suspicious on any of her bank statements. Maybe this is how Vincent feels, she mused bitterly, this feeling of getting away with something when he returns from an illicit meeting with the French roll lady.

The apple-green bridesmaid's dress had been hideous

but it was the only one that came in at exactly €1000 in the racks of frothy creations in Brides 'R' Beautiful. She'd tried it on for show, along with a few other equally hideous ones, and then made a production of deciding whether to buy it or not.

"I'm the only bridesmaid so she's letting me choose whatever I want – within reason, of course," she tinkled at the enthusiastic sales assistant. "I'll be able to return it if she really doesn't like it, won't I?" Jennie already knew the answer, having phoned the shop from her new mobile as soon as she'd dropped the children off outside the school.

"Of course. There's no problem as long as it's within seven days and it still has the labels on."

"Maybe I'll pop around to her at work, then," she lied thoughtfully, proffering her credit card. "She's very definite in her views, so I'll have it back by lunchtime if it's not her thing." Another tinkly giggle.

"It *is* hard to get it right," the sales girl agreed, "although it's so much more difficult when there are four or five people to suit."

"True," Jennie agreed, signing her slip. She could always tell Vincent that she'd bought an evening dress for the Chamber of Commerce Summer Ball if he noticed that she'd been shopping in a bridal boutique. The fact that she'd already bought something to wear for that would have gone over his head as usual.

Two hours later, Jennie had arrived back at Brides 'R' Beautiful, disappointed with her mythical sister's opinion.

"Too pale," she explained dolefully to the cool redhead behind the counter. "She wants something more definite.

Can you credit it back to my card, please? I'll just have to go back to the drawing board on it."

"That's no problem."

As Jennie had expected, the card wouldn't swipe and the sales girl held it up to reveal a deep scratch across the all-important bar on the back. "I'm afraid it won't work if it's damaged," she informed her customer regretfully.

Jennie studied the scratch she'd made in the car only a few minutes before she'd entered the shop. "I'm so sorry, this is terrible. It must have been the machine at the supermarket – there was a huge queue and the poor girl was addled. What should I do?"

"Well, I can refund it in cash, if you're happy with that. Or you can certainly come back in when you get a replacement card, if you'd rather."

Jennie felt guilty at the helpfulness and professionalism of the sales assistant as she stood by the till and pretended to think about it.

"I'm away next week on business so I might be better off taking the cash. Otherwise it'll be ages before I get in to town without the kids in tow. And I wouldn't dare let them loose in here!" She hated using the kids in such duplicity but it was Vincent's fault that she was driven to this in the first place.

"I know what you mean – you wouldn't have a moment's peace. My fellow's only eighteen months but the damage he can do from the buggy is unbelievable." To Jennie's relief, she started to count out the €50 notes.

"Try a pair of them!"

"One is plenty, thanks! There you go – €1000. Come

back another day if you want to try anything else. We'll have summer stock coming in over the next week or so."

"Will do – and sorry about all the inconvenience. I'd better get home and order a new card pronto."

Jennie felt terribly guilty now as she sipped her coffee and relived the episode in the bridal boutique. But at least she had her cash for Ron Green's deposit. She hadn't eaten at all and even though her tummy was rumbling, she couldn't bear the thought of food until she had the sordid business with the private investigator out of the way. Glancing at her watch yet again, she realised it was eight minutes to two – enough time to get to Ron Green's office without having to hang around outside waiting. She was terrified of meeting someone she knew and had dreamed up a story about tracing an elderly relation in case she did encounter a person who knew her.

She'd expected something seedy and well tucked away but was surprised to find that Ron Green's premises was located in the same building as that of a firm of well-renowned solicitors. A discreet brass plate announced his business, the script ornate in keeping with that of *Doheny & Doheny Solicitors* and *Baily-Riordan, Auditors*.

She entered via the impressive Georgian door that stood open to reveal a plush hallway and a series of painted timber doors, solid and reliable looking. Studying the smaller plaques to the side of each one, she knocked quietly on the glossy black door next to the sign that said simply, *Ron Green Services*.

Responding to the muffled yet authoritative "Come

in", Jennie felt as if she were going to make a will or carry out some equally sombre business.

"Mrs K? Please come in." The man stretching his hand out towards her was nothing like Jennie had expected. And she'd completely forgotten that he didn't actually have a name for her yet.

Neither tall nor small, his compact athletic body looked completely at one with the smart, dark grey business suit. His hair, thick and dark, was well cut, neither shorn nor overly long. And even though he was far from nondescript, Jennie could see how Ron Green could make himself blend into a crowd.

"Jennie. Jennie Kelleher."

His handshake was firm, as she'd expected, and he motioned her to sit in one of the deep leather armchairs that stood either side of the tall window that looked onto the street. Jennie sat, noting the fine gauze curtain that sequestered those inside from the world outside, while allowing a full view of everything happening on the street.

Ron sat opposite her, his elbows on his knees as he leaned towards her, his eyes interested and all-encompassing. She could smell the soft hint of his aftershave – Armani, she recalled from somewhere at the back of her mind. She wondered now if Ron Green was his name at all.

"So, Mrs Kelleher, tell me what you'd like me to do for you."

"Jennie – please call me Jennie. I think my husband is having an affair. I don't have much to go on but I would like you to find out if I'm right."

Jennie closed her eyes briefly, feeling almost weak. She was reminded suddenly of a charity night out that she and Vincent had gone to at the greyhound track – the way the dogs sprang out as soon as the trap was opened. And once they were out, there was no way back. Until, of course, a conclusion had been reached.

"Tell me as much as you can, then. And I presume you've brought photos and details of his car and workplace. I'd normally like to spend about two weeks gathering evidence and if you can tell me some of the meetings or events he's supposed to attend, it would be helpful."

Jennie felt overwhelmed by it all but tried to recall if Vincent had mentioned any meetings recently. There were no foreign trips on the cards, to the best of her knowledge.

"Is tonight too soon? Only he did mention a meeting with a group from the Middle East who are visiting here. I'm not sure where it's supposed to be though. Or the time."

"We can try to make a start on it then. Will he be leaving from home or directly from his office?" Ron was already flicking through the snapshots of Vincent that she'd brought – some were just him – others, from a Christmas night out, included Bob Ferris and their PA, Melissa, who was supposedly on extended leave to look after her mother. There was also an image of The Property People's main office and a photo of Vincent's car.

"I'm not sure. He's been pretty vague lately." Jennie thought now of Vincent's irrational behaviour outside the church on Saturday evening when Jack had asked for help with the playground and was sure that there was something suspicious about the meeting. He could, for instance, have offered to help out either before or after the meeting but he'd chosen not to divulge too much information about the time.

"Well, we can case out both places to get a handle on things, to begin with. We'll take it from there. And if anything crops up over the next few weeks, just leave a voice message at this number." He slid a slip of paper across the low, oak coffee-table that stood between then. "No need to say your own name – just refer to Mr K2 and we'll follow up the lead."

It was obvious to Jennie that there must be another Mr K on Ron Green's books if Vincent was to be referred to as K2. There were plenty more foolish wives out there, just like her, tracking errant husbands. It was a comforting thought, somehow.

"Okay, so." Jennie tucked the paper into her wallet, noticing that there was no name, just the number on a plain white Post-it.

"I'll leave it to you to contact me in two weeks' time to arrange another meeting. In most cases, we have the information needed at that stage."

It was clear that Ron Green had no more to say and that their brief meeting was now over. Silently, she slid the plain white envelope across the table to him, struck by the fact that she was becoming adept in the use of all things non-identifiable.

Just as silently, Ron passed back a receipt for the €1000, the letterhead stating only a company registration and the innocuous Ron Green Services. Nothing about a private investigator for Vincent to find – if it was a thing that he went through her pockets the way she had his. *She'd* found nothing incriminating on her searches – how ironic if it were Vincent who was to come across a suspicious receipt for €1000!

Thanking Ron for his time, as she would any professional for their services, Jennie left the building. The crumpled white receipt would go into the first litter bin she passed.

Chapter 24

It was Friday morning and Sandra was full of good resolutions. Now that she'd taken the step of asking Chrissie about recommencing her apprenticeship, all she could do was wait to see if anything would come of it. In the meantime, however, she could start planning the rest of her and Dylan's lives.

For starters, she was going to lose weight and get herself back into shape – just in case a place did come up for her in Curly Locks. She was always admiring the career-women when they dropped their children off to school on the way to work, slim and elegant in suits or casual day-wear. Well, there was no reason for her to go around like a slob, just because she was a housewife on a budget. Jennie Kelleher had no job to go to and her hair was always done and her make-up perfect.

And just because she couldn't afford to join a gym didn't mean that she couldn't go for a brisk walk every evening as soon as Dylan's homework was done – he could even come along on his bike to keep up the pace for her.

Affordable housing was the next thing on her list to find out about. Jack had mentioned it to her the night of the accident and it had been on her mind since. She'd told him that night that her relationship with Paul was finally over and that she was determined to pull herself together once and for all. The council, he'd told her, demanded that a certain percentage of all new housing developments be allocated for social and affordable housing these days and he wondered if Sandra would be interested in the scheme, considering the new development he was about to start in Rathmollin. Sandra was thinking now that maybe her next step would be to phone the council and see what she would need to make her eligible for an affordable house.

Now that she'd been on to the hairdressing board, she was satisfied that she might be able to re-start in second year if her employer was happy with that. She should have been going into third year but it was much better than starting from scratch again. Uncharitably, she kept praying that poor Nicola, Chrissie's apprentice, wouldn't make the grade.

Of all Sandra's resolutions, the decision to visit Emily in hospital and apologise for the terrible thing that Paul had done to her was the most important. It was also the most difficult, not knowing how Emily would receive her.

She'd been getting updates all week from her mother and it seemed that Emily was now up and about a little. Aggie Lenihan had reported that she was getting physio every morning and evening and that she was eating well with all her drips and drains removed. Perhaps it was time to pay her a visit – if she didn't do it soon, she'd be discharged home and Sandra didn't want to invade the Gordons at home, certain that the whole neighbourhood would be on top of them for visits.

Sandra thought carefully about this as she washed the breakfast dishes. Dylan had left for school and she had the whole day ahead of her. Perhaps she'd get ready and take the bus into town. The walk from the bus station to St Angela's would be the first step in her new exercise regime.

By half eleven, Sandra was sitting in the foyer of the large general hospital, her hands wrapped around a Styrofoam cup of coffee as she tried to muster up the courage to get into the lift. She'd popped into Lidl on the way and bought a bunch of fresh purple freesias and a cream aluminium jug, predicting that there might not be a vase on the ward to display them in. Now all she had to do was gather them together and make her way to the third floor. The receptionist had said that visiting was at eleven thirty and she prayed now that someone like Aggie Lenihan wouldn't have arrived first to witness her apology to Emily.

The corridor was quiet as she exited the lift and made her way towards the solid door that said *3A Surgical* on the outside. Taking a deep breath and remembering her earlier resolution to be brave and get on with things, she pushed the door open slowly, anticipating a long enquiry with the ward sister before she located the patient.

Instead, the first person she saw was Emily, pale and

ethereal, coming towards her in cream silk pyjamas. She was propped up on a Zimmer frame, the same type of one that Sandra's granny had had to use after her stroke. Shocked, Sandra just stared. Emily, struggling to lift the metal frame with every step, grinned happily as soon as she looked up and spotted Sandra frozen by the door.

"Hi, Sandra!" Panting heavily, she kept going, painfully filling the few steps between them. "At least I know what life will be like when I'm eighty!"

Sandra was at a loss, having expected there to be some awkwardness between them at the outset, at least. "Emily, it's great to see you up. Is it hard to manage the frame?" She knew it sounded foolish but Sandra didn't know what else to say to a twenty-eight-year-old on a Zimmer frame.

"Murder. It's the co-ordination and lifting your legs at the right time. Will we go back to the room? I can't stand still for long."

Sandra moved out of Emily's way as she did a laborious 360-degree turn and started back in the opposite direction.

"It's amazing what you take for granted," Emily continued. "I only have to go as far as Room 5 and it might as well be a million miles away."

Sandra gripped the freesias and felt guilty to the bottom of her heart. Imagine having to learn to walk again!

Eventually, they neared Room 5 and Sandra made herself useful by holding open the door for Emily. The bulky Zimmer caught on the doorframe, causing Emily to curse. Again, a shot of guilt flew through Sandra.

"Thank goodness!" After manoeuvring herself around

the bed, Emily flopped down in a large leather chair and rested back against the headrest.

"How many times a day do you have to do that?" Sandra handed Emily the flowers as she spoke.

"These are fantastic," she enthused, enjoying a long sniff of their exotic scent. "I'm supposed to do two or three walks a day but I've been trying to do more so that I won't seize up altogether. The sooner I can walk, the sooner I'll be out of here. I'll have to get a vase from one of the attendants when the tea comes around," she added, still admiring the flowers.

"I brought this, just in case they didn't have one." Sandra produced the elegant cream jug.

"That's really lovely, Sandra. Will you fill it for me in the bathroom? *I'd* be all day and anyway I can't carry anything because I need my two hands for the frame!"

Emily might look well enough but she still had a lot to deal with, Sandra thought as she filled the jug in the small en suite bathroom.

"Sandra, they're just gorgeous." Emily arranged the flowers to her satisfaction. "How's Dylan doing?"

"Grand, Emily. Giving out about school half the time but still wanting to go in, even when he's sick."

"Sounds typical!"

"Emily . . ." Sandra began, wanting to talk to her about Paul before someone else arrived. If she didn't, the moment would be lost and it would be too late then. "I really wanted to say sorry to you about the accident. Paul and everything . . ." she trailed off as Emily looked at her quizzically.

"Sandra, it wasn't your fault, if that's what you're thinking."

"I knew he drank and drove every now and then – I was always on at him about it but he wouldn't listen. It was never far, just between The Stone's and the house, so I didn't do anything about it. I never thought he would cause an accident on the main street. I'm so sorry, Emily, that you have so much to cope with now on account of it. You could have been killed."

"Well, I wasn't. Okay, it *is* a bit of a drag but I'll be all right. How is Paul getting on?"

"He was arrested and charged with being over the limit but I haven't seen him since. He's back home with his mother at the moment." She wanted Emily to know that Paul was no longer a resident of Rathmollin.

"Oh," was all that Emily said.

"I should have done it sooner. I don't know why I let it go on for so long."

"And is it definitely over?"

"Definitely." Sandra was firm on this.

"What about Dylan? Does he miss him at all?"

"Not really. I think he's glad, to be honest. Paul drank a lot and he wasn't always nice with it. I know it'll sound awful to you, Emily, but I think now that Dylan was afraid of him."

"Really? And are *you* glad it's over, Sandra?"

Emily sounded a bit like a social worker but Sandra knew that it was her own sense of guilt that made her feel defensive.

"I am, really. I kept trying to convince myself that

Dylan was entitled to know his father but it didn't mean I had to move him back in. It was an easy option, that's all. I'll be standing on my own two feet from now on, I can tell you that!"

"All the same – it can't be easy bringing Dylan up on your own."

"Mam and Dad are very good. I'm even thinking of trying to start the hairdressing course again, if Chrissie ever has a vacancy."

"That'd be a great step, Sandra. There's nothing like being independent to give you confidence. Do you think it'll work out?"

Sandra couldn't believe that her visit to Emily was turning out to be a chat about her own future rather than the maelstrom she'd imagined it might be. She did need to get her confidence back.

"I've spoken to Chrissie and she says she'll keep me in mind. I'll have to look into the allowances and that to make sure it'd be viable, though."

"Sandra, there are loads of incentives for getting back to work now. You might be able to get subsidised after-school care for Dylan for a start. Maxine Daly is involved in that kind of thing with her childcare facility – you should chat to her about it. And, depending on what you'd be earning, your rent mightn't be affected at all."

"God, Emily, you're a mine of information – I should have asked you all this ages ago. Jack mentioned something about affordable housing too. He's building a new development in the village – where Doyles' Field is now – and he said I should look into it."

"Are there definitely houses going in there?" Emily asked the question carefully and Sandra wondered if she too was thinking of buying in there, although it mightn't be on the affordable scheme like Sandra.

"He seemed definite when I spoke to him. I think 20 per cent of the houses have to be allocated to social and affordable housing."The more she said it, the more Sandra had started to focus on owning her own house, even if she did have to go the long way about it.

Emily looked a bit exhausted all of a sudden and Sandra felt bad that she'd been airing all her own affairs.

"Do you have a lot of pain?" she asked now, wondering if her visit had been too much for Emily.

"None actually. I got the clips out of my scalp and leg earlier in the week and it was desperate because the hair had started to grow back a bit. But other than that, I'm fine."

"Did they shave much off?" Sandra couldn't see much wrong with her hair at all except that Emily's corkscrew curls were now a bit bushy where they were tied back in a navy velvet scrunchie.

"Did they what! Look!" With that, she turned her head a little to the side and pulled out the scrunchie. Lifting the heavy mane of auburn ringlets, she revealed a shorn, stubbly patch the size of a small saucer with the perfect arc of a surgical wound running through it. Sandra was shocked. She could even see the small dots on either side of the suture line where the metal stitches had been.

"Is it dire? I can't get a good look at it in the bathroom mirror."

"It's not too bad," Sandra lied hesitantly. To think that she'd shared her home and her son with the kind of person who could be responsible for something like this. "It's coming back already – you're lucky they left the growth on top to cover it while it grows."

"Nice of them! I'm half thinking of trimming it a bit so it'll be more manageable. You wouldn't do it for me, would you?"

"Jesus, Emily, I'm not fit to be let loose on anyone!"

"It'd only be trimming it. It'll be ages before I get out of here and it's driving me crazy. Would you come in some other day and take a small bit off?"

"What if I make a mess of it? You have enough to contend with as it is."

"The permanent Bad Hair Day is worse than anything. Aggie Lenihan came in on Monday and I'm sure she reported to the whole village that I was alive but looked like a witch. One of the nurses helped me to wash some of it on Tuesday but she couldn't get the scalp wet because the clips had just come out. Infection and all that."

"I could go out to one of the shopping centres and get scissors now, I suppose. Proper ones, I mean. Are you sure the nurses won't mind you cutting it?"

"They'd be delighted – doing the dressing was a nightmare for them. Have you time to do it now?" Emily looked really excited and Sandra got a burst of enthusiasm. She couldn't do too much damage and if it gave Emily a boost it would be worth it.

"I've loads of time. Dylan won't be out until three. Will I take off and get scissors, so?"

"I hope it's not too much bother. I'm such a plague to everyone at the moment." She looked momentarily doubtful and Sandra was quick to reassure her.

"It's no bother. And maybe it's a good omen for my future hairdressing career. Why don't you rest for a bit while I'm gone?"

"Grand so." Emily settled back against the headrest again, her hair like a halo around her head.

The Maplegrove shopping centre was directly across from the hospital and Sandra had located a hairdressing salon in minutes. As soon as she'd explained her mission, the head stylist produced a pair of professional scissors at cost price, happy to help Sandra improve her friend's quality of life while in hospital. By the time she arrived back on the ward, there was a nurse with Emily, taking her blood pressure.

"This is Sandra," Emily introduced. "She's going to give my hair a trim so it won't look like a whin bush."

Fidelma, her favourite of all the nurses, laughed. "It's not that bad. Are you going to wash it as well?" She addressed Sandra, who looked blank at the suggestion. How on earth would she manage that, although it *would* be better to cut it wet rather than dry.

"There's a portable shower-head there, if you like. That's if you feel up to leaning over the sink, Emily?"

"I'd hang out the window if I thought I'd get my hair washed and cut! Have you time, Sandra?"

"Of course I've time." Now that the nurse had okayed it, she felt more confident. "Let's get started then. What about a hairdryer?"

"Mam brought mine in, just in case. It's a professional one but it mightn't be what you're used to."

"If only you knew! You'll be telling me you have the GHD here as well soon."

Emily and Fidelma started to laugh.

"She actually has," Fidelma announced, "and I was almost persuaded to use it on Tuesday."

"Almost but not quite," Emily retorted, getting out of the chair slowly.

Fidelma, meanwhile, moved the plastic shower chair out in front of the sink for Emily to sit on.

"I'll leave you to it," she smiled at Sandra.

"God, Emily, I hope this is a good idea." Regardless of Sandra's nerves, Emily was positioned in front of the sink, her face obliterated by the sea of ringlets thrown upside down into it.

"Of course it's a good idea."

As gently as she could, Sandra massaged the shampoo and conditioner into Emily's hair, taking care to avoid the angry red scar. It was with relief that she wrapped the rough hospital towel around Emily's head and guided her client back to the bedroom.

"You'll have to sit on the shower chair," she instructed, after realising that the high-backed leather chair was useless for hairstyling. Emily was on for anything and waited patiently while the cumbersome plastic chair was dragged out of the tiny bathroom and placed by the bed. Another towel as a makeshift cape and Emily was ready.

"What if your mother comes in? She'll think you're after losing your marbles to let me at your hair."

"She's so delighted that I'm alive, she wouldn't care if I was bald! Anyway, I've sent them all home to get a rest – they've been here constantly since the night of the accident."

Emily's curls had already started to fall to the ground, although Sandra was erring on the cautious side of the customer's instructions.

"Are you angry about it all?" she asked.

"The accident? I was a bit, on Monday. Although it was more feeling sorry for myself than anger. I had a good cry and then Aggie came in to melt my head about Jack Rooney knocking down the cottage. I was well pissed off about that, I can tell you. Where's he getting the money for all this development?"

"I think he was pretty well set up when he came home from the States and I suppose it was just being in the right place at the right time after that. Did you really want the cottage?" Sandra still couldn't believe that Emily would want to take on the hassle of doing up a house as decrepit as Ina Harrington's.

"You probably heard about me and Richard splitting up?"

As far as Sandra knew, this was the first time that Emily had mentioned her ex-fiancé's name to anyone in Rathmollin since the news of her broken engagement came out.

"Mmmm . . ." Sandra was non-committal, not wanting Emily to think that the whole village had been talking about it.

"We'd bought a house in Dublin but it wasn't finished or anything. Then it all went pear-shaped and we decided that Richard would buy me out. It was terrible – there was even talk of court at one stage. I'd actually put most of the money into the house because he'd just bought into a firm of architects."

"That must have cost a lot," Sandra commented. Emily was such a nice, ordinary person that it was hard to believe she'd been embroiled in a messy separation. These things usually only happened to people like herself.

"It was supposed to be an investment for both our futures," Emily continued bitterly. "He would fund the practice and I'd fund the house until we got established. But of course when the house was valued, it was all split half and half, so I got much less than I'd put in. Hence the fact that I can't afford another house."

"But what about the practice?"

"Anything he'd invested was in his own name so that remained unchanged. The house was bought jointly so it was technically equal." Emily emitted a deep sigh as she said this.

"But *he* knew!" Sandra protested. "Surely he had the decency to pay you more than half."

"I'm afraid not, Sandra. I found out fairly fast that decency is all very fine until there's money involved. I felt like such an eejit."

The last of Sandra's handiwork hit the floor and she stood back in the confined space to let Emily off the chair. "How's that?" she enquired, hoping that the poor girl wouldn't be horrified when she looked in the mirror.

Holding onto the wall and then the doorframe, Emily made her way to the bathroom to examine her new haircut.

"Brilliant. Did you thin it out a bit? It feels way lighter." Her hair was now shoulder length with a few layers cut in to take the weight out of it.

"Is it okay?" Sandra was nervous now and wondered if she'd taken liberties with the layers.

"It's great. I have a bit of anti-frizz serum in the locker. Will you be able to get it out for me?"

It was then that Sandra realised how poor Emily's mobility still was. She looked fine – a little pale and thin – but she walked like an old woman and still couldn't even bend to get something out of the locker.

"The leg wound really tightened up when the clips came out," Emily explained now.

Eventually they got settled again, Sandra armed with the hairdryer and the GHD plugged in, just in case it was needed. Listening to her traumatic story, she was determined to give Emily a fabulous hairdo – it was only a small thing but at least she might feel some bit better.

"Is that why you left Dublin?" Sandra, securing Emily's hair with a pen for want of a section clip, continued their conversation about Richard. She still didn't know why the relationship had turned so sour in the first place and was loath to ask directly.

"More or less." Emily paused. "There was a lot more to it, though. Because I'd been going out with him so long, all our friends were the same and I didn't feel I could trust a lot of them any more. Richard had been going out with someone else for ages – someone at work. Afterwards, it seemed that loads of people knew about it."

It was almost as if she was talking to herself at this stage and Sandra was afraid to break the mood at first. Eventually though, she realised that Emily was expecting some kind of comment.

"Did *nobody* say anything?"

"Not one. 'Didn't want to get involved' was the theme of the day last January." Again the bitterness, something that Emily seemed to hide well when she was talking about other things, even the accident.

"How did you find out in the end?"

"The hard way! We were at a New Year's Eve party at this house in Foxrock. One of the other partners in the firm puts it on every year – fireworks and all."

"Wow!" Sandra was impressed. Although, glamorous Foxrock parties were a far cry from a small cottage in Rathmollin. No wonder Emily was so bitter.

"Anyway, it was the fireworks brought it all out into the open, in the end. Richard had epilepsy as a child and he was always paranoid about those strobe lights in nightclubs and things that could set off seizures. I was chatting to one of the partner's wife and I didn't miss him for a while. Then the fireworks display started and I got it into my head that they'd given him a headache or something. I was really worried so I went off to look for him and found him in one of the guest rooms with this girl from the office."

"Jesus, Emily, the little shit!"

"I know." Emily shook her head, as if in disbelief that she could have been so blind to his type. "He even tried to deny it – and there he was in a bed with this Lorena one!"

"Fucking hell!" Sandra was flabbergasted at the fact that someone other than herself had such poor judgement with men. No wonder Emily wasn't holding her responsible for Paul's actions. "What did you do?" The soft hum of the hairdryer was like a buffer between them and Sandra wondered if Emily would have had this conversation at all if they weren't distracted by the hairdo.

"I wasn't drinking that night, thank God, so I just left and went back to the apartment that we were renting at the time. He arrived home about twelve the next day, hung over. Eventually he said they'd been seeing each other for about six months but he didn't want to hurt me. Have you ever heard the beat of that?"

"Do you think he would have kept going – with you, I mean? Got married, even?"

"I asked him that but he couldn't answer me. He still had no plans to finish up with her though. I think it was about money, to be honest."

"What? That you were paying for the house? You can't be serious!"

"I know it sounds terrible but I can't see why he didn't just finish with me altogether. The practice meant a lot to him – being a partner and all that. He wanted the big house as well, though. I'd paid the deposit and the first few stage payments. I don't know, maybe he was going to break it off and buy me out when he was settled at work and making big money. I really don't know, Sandra."

"He could have treated you better at the end. Okay, you might excuse him falling in love with someone else, if that's what he says it was, but to screw someone financially as well. That beats all."

"Thanks for the outrage on my behalf! At the time, I didn't know who to talk to or who was in on it. That's why I had to get away from the whole scene. It meant giving up my job but I knew I'd get something in Cork. The job in the VBA is fine but it doesn't pay nearly as much as I was earning in Dublin."

"He really messed up everything for you. Almost as bad as Paul. There, you look the spit of Nicole Kidman."

Emily smiled at the comparison and lumbered up again to go to the bathroom mirror. "Short of mowing someone down, he *is* as bad."

"Well?"

"Oh Sandra, it's fabulous!" Emily seemed to be thrilled with her new shorter, straightened look. She did look like Nicole Kidman – all pale and ethereal, if only she had a bit of make-up on and her freckles covered up.

"Have you your make-up in with you?" Sandra, it seemed, was thinking exactly the same thing. "We could go the whole hog, if you like."

"It's in the side compartment of the locker – bring it over and I'll put on a bit. They gave me a load of blood transfusions but I'm still like one of those alabaster statues – a freckled one."

Sandra rooted in the locker and arrived back with a small Burberry bag.

"Is this it?"

"I know it's tiny but I was never a big fan of make-up. Gina at work says I'm never going to get off the shelf if I don't improve a bit. Maybe that's why Richard was so mad to stray off with Lorena – *she* was like a work of art!"

Emily was smiling wryly at her in the mirror as she

rubbed foundation into her cheeks but Sandra thought there was an element of genuine self-doubt in what she had said.

"Well, if that's what he's into, then let him feck off. She probably won't age well."

"I'll bear that in mind." Emily was dabbing a pressed powder over her foundation, giving her face a translucent look that Sandra envied.

"Paul hadn't a bit of interest in how I looked," Sandra confessed now, "which was just as well, considering I still haven't lost my baby weight."

"You look great, Sandra. We should go out some night soon and try to find men who actually deserve us." Emily was laughing, the first time she had since Sandra arrived.

"I'd love to – but are you sure they're out there? We could be wasting our time."

"Stop it, will you," Emily giggled, her shoulders shaking as she tried valiantly to apply mascara. "Feck this, I've enough on. What about this?" She held up a burnt orange lipstick for Sandra to examine.

"Perfect. That Richard's a mug."

"I'm well shot," Emily agreed.

They both burst out laughing at this, their eyes meeting in the mirror.

"Come on, you'd better sit down and have a rest. Fidelma will have a fit if you get a setback."

"We'll have a tea-break to celebrate my makeover." Emily was elated, her eyes shining in a way they hadn't been when they'd met in the corridor only a short while ago.

"I'll go down to the canteen so . . ."

"No – there's a Thermos under the bed in a little rucksack. The tea is desperate here so Mam fills a flask for me at home. I think there's a second cup in there as well."

"You're well set up in here – personal hairdresser, Teasmade, the lot." Sandra pulled out the bag, conscious again of just how debilitated Emily really was. The little blind on the door rattled as she poured the tea into two small plastic cups.

"It's only the nurses checking on me." A pair of eyes appeared between the slats and disappeared just as quickly. "There should be some biscuits and chocolates in the locker. They're encouraging me to put on weight."

"God, there's no chance that I'd have to be encouraged! I started a big diet this morning so I'll stick to the tea, thanks."

Emily started to examine the contents of a large box of Butler's. "They keep telling *me* I'm underweight – people are never satisfied, are they?"

They sipped their tea companionably, Sandra thinking that she hadn't felt so good about herself in a long time. The past two weeks had been terrible, what with the accident and Paul behaving like a complete scumbag. But even before that, the way he'd been treating her and Dylan had been soul-destroying and humiliating. The upset that her parents must have felt couldn't be measured, yet they still supported her in everything and looked after Dylan as if he were their own child. It was time for her to stand on her own two feet all right and the past few hours had proved to her that maybe she wasn't a terrible person at all.

Draining her teacup, she went to the bathroom to rinse and dry it. "I'd better go for the bus or I'll miss Dylan getting out of school. Thanks a million for trusting me with the hair, Emily. It's given me a great boost."

"I can't believe *you're* thanking *me.* I haven't felt this good since I got ready to go out two weeks ago! I can't wait for Mam, Dad and Niall to come in and see me."

"Can I come and see you again some day next week?" She was delighted when Emily nodded. "And we will go out on the town some night when you're well enough."

"Definitely. I feel up to going out this minute but the only place to go is the physio department."

"It won't be long," Sandra promised, leaving 3A Surgical a million times happier than when she'd arrived.

Chapter 25

"3A surgical . . . 3A surgical . . ."

Jack ran his fingers through his silvery blond hair as he trawled through the list of wards and departments on the enormous whiteboard in the foyer of St Angela's. If it wasn't for meeting Aggie Lenihan outside the grocery earlier, he mightn't have known where to begin but as usual Aggie had the inside track.

Saturday evening had been a revelation to him – in more ways than one. He'd been aware that Harmony Cottage would be coming on the market and had been quick to approach The Property People as soon as the little house had appeared on their books. True, Dermot Leahy had advised him that there was another offer on the scene, no more than he'd expected considering the location of the property. An extra €500 had secured the deal, a fact that Jack had taken to mean that the other potential bidder hadn't been too serious about it. No further offer had been made so Jack had secured the cottage with a deposit, pending permission from the council for the twenty-house development that he had planned for the site behind it.

Now, according to Aggie, the other bidder *had* been serious.

He finally located the directions to 3A Surgical and made his way to the lift, nervous somehow about approaching Emily Gordon. The last time he'd seen her, his view had been limited to the sight of her long, slim legs protruding incongruously from beneath the taxi cab the evening she'd been knocked down. The rest of her had been obscured by the wreckage and he wondered now whether she'd been disfigured by the accident and if his calling would be an imposition. He hadn't spoken to her in years and now here he was barging into her hospital room to talk business, of all things.

"Jack!"

He started, snapped out of his worrying train of thought by Sandra Coyne.

"Hi, Sandra. You weren't visiting Emily by any chance?"

"I was actually. She's in great form."

"Would it be okay to visit her, do you think? I was going to ask the nurses, just in case."

"No need – she's bored out of her tree. And you can't wear her out any more than Aggie Lenihan did. She said it was like an interview!"

"I can imagine." Encountering Aggie in the full of one's health was challenging, never mind meeting her after a serious head injury. "Is there anyone with her now?"

"No, I just left and there was no one else there. Don't worry, I'll distract Aggie if I spot her approaching."

The crowds in the busy hospital corridor swarmed around them as they talked and, not for the first time, Jack noticed how attractive Sandra was. It amazed him that she'd got mixed up with the likes of Paul Delaney, considering that she was such a decent person and a good mother to Dylan. Jack had noticed him up at the school, playing soccer in the yard with his friends and had observed how mannerly he was, even in the height of a furious match. He certainly hadn't learned his manners from Paul, that was for sure.

"How are things with Paul these days? Or should I not ask?" Sandra was too good for him but there was no accounting for attraction.

"Same old, same old." She sighed deeply, obviously sick of the whole saga. "He's under the impression that if a judge sees what a good father he is, he'll get off the hook. His solicitor seems to think it's his only hope of avoiding jail."

"I presume you want to keep Dylan out of it all?" Jack couldn't imagine Sandra allowing her son to be traumatised in a courtroom, however beneficial it might be for his father.

"Too right. He hasn't even asked about Paul, would you believe? I think he's just glad that things have gone back to normal."

"That's the main thing. He's a good little fellow."

"He has his moments," Sandra laughed, secretly proud that Jack might think she was doing something right. "Did you hear any more about the planning permission for the new development?"

"Nothing yet – and there's still plenty of time for objections. It may be a thing that I'll have to rethink it."

"Because of knocking the cottage? Isn't there any other place you could make an entrance?" Sandra looked almost upset and he wondered if she'd taken it seriously when he'd mentioned the affordable housing to her. Maybe she'd set her heart on it, because of the fact that she'd be near her parents and only down the street from Dylan's school.

"It's not just that – although it is a factor. The council might object to more houses in a small village. We'll see."

"Surely twenty houses wouldn't be a problem?"

"It depends on who's objecting! I might have to revise it a bit, that's all."

"But you'd still be building *some* houses there?"

Sandra *was* interested, Jack realised, although he couldn't imagine how she'd manage even the affordable scheme on social welfare. Maybe she was thinking of applying for a transfer to one of those that would be bought up by the council. Perhaps she just needed a change from living next door to Aggie Lenihan, especially now that Aggie was holding poor Sandra almost responsible for the catastrophe that Paul had caused.

"Definitely," he reassured her, glad to see a sparkle back in her eyes after the few weeks of worry she'd had. "I'd better head up to the ward soon – I haven't seen Emily in years so I hope she won't mind me calling."

Jack hadn't been able to get the accident out of his

mind. His anger at Paul Delaney had been fuelled by the sight of Emily's legs protruding from under the car that night and the idea that he himself was in some way responsible hadn't escaped him.

What if he hadn't given Paul back his job after the defiant walk-out that he'd made? Would he have left the village with his tail between his legs? Maybe if he had, Emily might not be lying in a hospital bed now. And maybe he hadn't actually done Sandra and Dylan a favour at all – for all that it was his reasoning for giving Paul his job back at the time. Now Dylan had a criminal father and Sandra was the talk of the village.

"She's actually fine, Jack. A long way to go with walking but well able to talk and everything," Sandra reassured him. "Getting back to work will be a problem for her, I imagine – it wasn't a permanent job so she doesn't know where she stands yet."

Now his guilt was compounded even further. Aggie Lenihan had hinted at the reasons for Emily's broken engagement and now, as well as the accident, she might be out of a job – and because of Jack, she thought Harmony Cottage was out of the picture too.

"Don't look so miserable, Jack." Sandra had obviously noted his frown. "Come on. I'll buy you a cup of horrible, cold coffee in the canteen, if you like. You can go up to Emily afterwards."

Jack took in her radiant smile and wondered for the umpteenth time what she'd seen in Paul Delaney.

"You're on," he grinned. A coffee would fortify him for his meeting with Emily. And a normal, non-work-related conversation where he wasn't giving orders wouldn't go astray either.

Emily grinned when she heard the slatted blind on the door of her room rattle again and the handle start to turn.

"I was wondering when you'd miss it," she started, reaching for the small hairdressing scissors that Sandra had left on the bedside locker.

"Emily?"

The shock of hearing the voice was enough for her, even before she lifted her eyes. The scissors dropped to the floor with a clatter as Emily stared, gobsmacked and silent.

"Emily? It's me – Richard?"

As if she was a moron! "I can see that," she answered smartly, irked by his tone. She'd had enough of being treated like an imbecile by Richard Carmody.

"Can I come in?"

She considered reminding him that he already *was* in but decided quickly that it sounded too bitter. His strawberry blond hair was brushed back from his forehead and, if possible, Richard was thinner than ever. She studied him, having decided that she was entitled to take her time.

"Emily?" He spoke louder this time and she wondered who'd told him that she was in hospital and if maybe they'd mentioned that she was deaf and blind as well as everything else.

"I can hear you, Richard." She waved towards the chair that Sandra had so recently vacated, glad that she looked better than she had a few hours ago. She needed all of her resources to face Richard. "How did you know I was here?"

He looked nervous, almost boyish as he folded his lanky frame into the leather chair. Surely her parents hadn't phoned him. They rarely spoke about Richard and even when they did, neither of them called him by name. There was no way that they'd have phoned him, of that she was convinced.

"I rang your work and a girl there – Gina – told me you'd had an accident. I wanted to come and see you straight away."

"Why were you ringing work?" As far as she was concerned, Richard hadn't known where she worked. They'd had precious little contact since she'd left Dublin and all of that had been concerned with the house and him buying her out. Typical of Gina to blab everything out instead of just saying that she wasn't available.

"Look, Emily, can we not fight? I just want to know that you're all right."

This was a new departure and one that Emily wasn't at all comfortable with. "I'm fine, as you can see." Suspicion crept into her voice. She'd been burned by Richard one time too many. "Why are you here, Richard?"

"As I said, I just wanted to see how you were."

"Getting a fit of the guilts, were you?" It must have been the haircut and the skim of make-up but she was feeling stronger than she had in a long time and well able for Richard. Whatever he was here for, she wasn't buying into it and she certainly wasn't going to tell him that he was forgiven for the appalling way that he'd behaved.

"No, I just . . ." He trailed off miserably, to her satisfaction, and sat there dismally. She wondered how he'd react if either one of her parents arrived. She waited now, to see what he'd come out with. It seemed incongruous now that she'd ever shared a bed with him, made plans with him. He was like someone that she didn't know at all.

"I've been thinking a lot . . . about everything . . . all that happened. I wanted to say I was sorry." His face was a mass of freckles, much like her own. To think that they'd laughed about how their children might look and whether "the ginger gene" might be inherited.

"You've decided to reconsider the house money?" She'd soon see how sorry he was.

"Emily, does it have to be about money again? It's not all . . ."

"It's not all about money? Give me a break, Richard." Did he think she was thick?

He lapsed into silence, his face almost morose. This was all she needed.

"What exactly are you sorry about then?"

"The whole Lorena thing, for a start."

"The whole Lorena thing? She'd hardly like to hear her partner describe her like that!"

"She's not actually my partner. Any more." The sheepish look on his face was enough to tell her that he wasn't lying. Had he dumped her too or had Lorena had more sense than Emily?

"Right."

"Emily, please don't be like that. I just want to make amends." He looked so contrite. Almost contrite enough to be forgiven if she hadn't been so badly stung by him and her trust so badly broken.

"Richard, we were engaged to be married. We bought a house together. You had an affair and defrauded me. What exactly do you want me to say?"

"I just want to put it all behind me."

"Do you now? This is so typical of you, Richard. *You* want to put it all behind you, as if all this wasn't something that you'd actually caused yourself."

Emily was livid – with herself for living with and actually loving such a spineless wimp for so long. When she'd left Dublin, she'd thought her life was over, that she'd never meet anyone else. Now looking at Richard and his whining, she was *glad* that everything had happened as it had. What if she hadn't found out and had gone ahead and married him? She would have discovered sooner or later the kind of man he was. What would she have done then, especially if there were children involved?

"Look, Emily, I'm not saying that I wasn't to blame. I'm just saying that we should try and put it behind us."

"Richard." She could hardly believe he was for real and sitting here looking at her with his white, anxious face. "I've already put this behind me. And I can't see why you need *me* involved for you to put it out of your head as well."

He was silent then, perhaps even a bit shocked that Emily had been able to move on so readily without him. She *hadn't,* in reality, up to now. It was just that the accident had put things into perspective for her and expedited the whole process. If he'd landed in Rathmollin a few weeks ago, he might have met a different, more shaky Emily.

"I've been thinking a lot over the last while and I know I really messed things up. To say the least." At this he gave a weak smile, somewhere between wry and self-deprecating. "I just can't help thinking that we gave up a lot very easily. Maybe we should have tried to make it work."

Emily looked at him in disbelief. The familiar cord trousers and tweed jacket struck her now as affected and dandified. Imagine she used to actually like his academic-looking persona. His use of the word "we" was really beyond the beyonds. As for trying to make it work, she really couldn't fathom what he was talking about. At the time, he'd given no real indication that he was going to give up his relationship with Lorena.

"I really don't know what you're talking about, Richard, but I can tell you here and now that there is absolutely no future for us as a couple." Emily tossed her head, enjoying the feel of the silky hair against the back of her neck. She was glad to hear herself sounding as firm and clear as she meant to and liked the fact that her hair was straightened, thinking that it reflected the new Emily who was no longer all about frizzy curls and freckles.

"But Emily, we should talk about this . . ."

"It wasn't easy to find you in bed with someone else," she continued, sarcasm suddenly entering her voice when she saw how taken aback he was that she was no longer a push-over. She was on a roll now. "Nor were you easy to deal with over the house. So if you want me to absolve you or something – you can forget about it. My conscience is clear. I'm sure you'll be able to find absolution when your own is clear."

She knew she sounded prissy and pious but he really was the last word. She still hadn't figured out where his sudden change of heart had come from but had a feeling that it wasn't for love of her at all.

"I can't believe you've become so bitter, Emily."

He looked a bit shocked, something that she saw through immediately. His tone was almost paternalistic, an emotional ploy to make Emily feel like a bold child who might be persuaded to behave a little better.

"It's not bitterness, Richard. Just disbelief at the cheek of you. You're a cad, that's what you are. A philanderer and a fraudster." Too much Jane Austen, she realised with something like amusement.

"You can't go around saying things like that," he started to bluster. "My reputation . . ."

Emily interrupted with a snort of disgust. "Your reputation? Is that what this is about? You think I'm bad-mouthing you all over the place?"

"I didn't say that." He was sulky looking now and she wondered how he'd managed to hide so many facets of his personality from her in the years that she'd known him. "I'm just saying that we need to put the bad bits behind us. Resolve it, as you put it," he finished lamely.

"Look, Richard, I still don't know why you came here. It certainly wasn't to cheer me up in my sick-bed." It hadn't escaped her that he'd arrived with one arm as long as the other. No chocolates. No flowers. "But whatever it was you wanted, you won't be getting it. I've moved on and you should too. There's no reason for us to have anything more to do with each other."

His face was anxious as he struggled to continue. "It's just that everything changed after you left, Emily . . ."

"Changed? How so, Richard?" She knew that sarcasm was the lowest form of wit but in all fairness, it was warranted at this stage.

"Our whole circle broke up . . . I know they all blamed me." The forlorn look came over his face again, as if this whole thing had somehow just *happened*. "We should have tried to work through it. We were such a good couple – Marcus Deering is always saying what an asset you were."

Emily wondered if the senior partner knew the full story of the scene that Richard's "asset" had come across in the guest bedroom of his Foxrock mansion last New Year's Eve but didn't lower herself to ask, despite how interested she was in the answer. Marcus Deering was a gentleman, one of the few movers on Richard's social climbing ladder that Emily had actually liked. She couldn't imagine Marcus discussing the loss of Emily with Richard if he knew the full story of what he and Lorena had been up to.

"Really?" was all she could say now by way of an answer. It was interesting to hear that their old "circle", as Richard seemed to be calling their friends, had broken up. Perhaps some of them had been less comfortable with his deception than she'd given them credit for. Ostracism wouldn't sit well with Richard, fond as he was of his cosy little group of back-patters.

Richard sighed and looked up at her through his eyelashes. "It's just . . . I don't know . . . I just think it'd be nice if we were able to get back to normal, that's all."

"Normal?" Surely he wasn't suggesting that they get back together?

"Well, why not, Emily? If we can put this behind us. Marcus is always on about family values in the firm, that kind of thing."

So this was what it was all about. Marcus Deering expected Richard to be settling down, to project some kind of wholesome image and he perhaps hadn't been able to find anyone as suitable for the role as Emily. Lorena, it seemed, hadn't passed muster. Emily wondered again which of them had ended the relationship.

"Let me get this right, Richard. After all that's happened, you want to resume where we left off – maybe even get married?"

He sat up, look a bit more hopeful than he had a few minutes ago. "If that's what you'd like . . ."

"Richard, it is very definitely *not* what I'd like. I couldn't even consider it. I can't believe you'd even come looking for me after all these months – just to say that it suited your boss that we get back together and settle down."

"It's not just Marcus – I was only saying that he liked you a lot – it's me too. I do miss you, Emily. You were always better than me at parties and things . . ."

This really defied belief. "Richard, are you all right in the head? Is that all you think about – getting on at work? What about that I don't trust you any more? That you deceived me for months? That I found you in bed with someone else at a party, for God's sake?"

She was livid now that she was getting an opportunity to say all the things that she hadn't got to say in January.

He only wanted her back because she could somehow further his career by licking up to Marcus Deering who happened to like and admire her. Before, this whole scenario would have made her feel like a worthless accessory but now it actually made her look at Richard with pity. It was *his* self-worth that had a problem if he thought he needed a prop to further his career. He clearly didn't believe that he would be able to do it without a wife that his boss approved of.

"Why do you keep rehashing it all, Emily? The house is still there – it's not as if it's not. And I'd never do anything like that again – Lorena, I mean."

There it was again, the dismissive way he spoke about Lorena as if she wasn't worth talking about. And even though Emily didn't have much admiration for the other woman's principles, it was interesting to see that Richard had as little respect for her as he did for Emily. She'd heard enough.

"Look, Richard. You're right. We do need to put this behind us. I'm finished with you, once and for all. You need to know that this is the end of it." Firm yet not too hard, she told herself.

It surprised her how crestfallen he looked and it saddened her to think that it was the failure of a career plan that he was disappointed about rather than the conclusion of their relationship.

"I see," was all he said.

"Well then . . ." She'd had enough of him and hoped he wasn't going to stay for a long-winded analysis of the situation.

"I suppose I'd better go and let you get some rest . . ." He wanted an out now, she could see that. He wasn't too bothered about her rest up to this point.

"Yes, you'd better," she remarked dryly.

"Okay then, so." He stood awkwardly, unsure, she could see, as to whether to extend his hand or not.

"Bye, then," she cut in, interrupting any gesture he might make.

She watched as he sidled around the bed in the tight confines of the small room, eager to make his escape. Hopefully it would be the last she'd see of Richard Carmody.

Emily leaned back against the pillows and closed her eyes briefly as she listened to the door closing behind Richard. She could hear him apologising as he bumped into someone in the process but she decided not to investigate, knowing it was probably one of the nurses attempting to turf out the visitors before the afternoon tea arrived.

"Emily?" The voice was so soft that she almost didn't hear it but her eyes shot open immediately at the thought of another unexpected visitor.

"Yes?" The man standing hesitantly in the doorway, his hand on the frame, looked familiar but she couldn't place where she knew him from.

"It's Jack. Jack Rooney?"

Just as he said the name, Emily realised where she'd seen him before, the silvery blond hair and glorious tan coming back to her. He'd sat opposite her at a table in a café on Academy Street only a few weeks ago and had left her in bad form after spending the whole time shouting orders into his mobile, disrupting her quiet lunch. He'd seemed familiar that day but she'd assumed it was because she'd seen him in some magazine or other. With a shock, she knew now why he'd looked as if she'd seen him somewhere before.

"Jack?" God, I sound dumb, she berated herself. No wonder he was such a hotshot these days. He certainly looked a lot more polished than the Jack Rooney she'd known in primary school.

He looked embarrassed now at not being recognised. "Can I come in?"

His voice today certainly belied the shouting he'd been doing that day in the café. And at least he'd asked to come in before he was ensconced with the door closed, unlike Richard.

"Of course." It was weird sitting up on the bed greeting people in her night clothes, although she was well covered up in the silk pyjamas that her mother had bought to cheer her up after her stint in the ICU paper gown. "Do you want to sit down?"

"Thanks." Like most people, he sounded a bit unsure of himself in the hospital environment. The expensive Gant shirt, though, reminded her that Jack Rooney was far from unsure of himself ordinarily.

As with Richard's sudden appearance, she couldn't imagine why he was here and she wondered if he was about to apologise for treading on her dreams by mowing down Harmony Cottage. She felt like a priest hearing confessions and it was getting almost tedious at this stage. Sandra's visit, too, had started out as an apology and Emily was beginning to feel as if the whole village must think of her as a pity. She sat up straighter and tossed her hair back, although slightly less defiantly than she had in Richard's presence.

"How are you feeling?"

This she was taken aback at. He actually looked as if he was sincere but, after Richard's visit, Emily was well aware that her judgement of people was probably seriously impaired.

"Great. I should be getting home soon." When I can manage to put one foot in front of the other independently, she thought wryly. She was sure that Aggie Lenihan had told the whole village her business but she was damned if she was going to be pitied any further. "How are you keeping, Jack?"

"Fine." He looked a bit stuck for words. "It's just . . . I was there the night of the accident so I couldn't help worrying about you. I didn't know when you'd be well enough for visitors but Aggie thought you might be up to it by now."

She hated the thought that so many people had been looking at her lying there unconscious and suddenly she felt horribly exposed. Paralysed, she stared at him. What if her skirt had been up around her waist or if her top had been torn or even removed by the paramedics in front of everyone? What if she'd been half-naked in front of everyone?

She'd asked about her clothes and her mother had told her they'd been ruined but exactly *how* hadn't occurred to her until now. Colour flew up her neck and into her face at the thought of someone like Jack Rooney standing over her inert body. Mortified, she looked away from him. He probably knew everything about her catheter and her head being shaved as well, knowing Aggie and her motor-mouth. Her arms automatically tightened around her body, as if she were defending herself from something.

It was Jack who broke the uncomfortable silence. "You're probably tired from people visiting, Emily. Maybe I'll call over some day when you're home?"

"No, I'm fine." Her voice came out in a strangled croak and she knew she looked like an eejit with her arms tucked up to cover the red rash of heat that had appeared on her chest and neck. Her face was probably puce under the make-up she'd applied earlier.

"I should have rung first – I'm sorry for just landing in."

He was standing now and she felt even more foolish with him towering over her. He looked as he was dying to escape from the tiny room and she felt like a complete freak. He'd probably tell Aggie that she was on the verge of a nervous breakdown. Tears sprang to her eyes at the injustice of it – she was actually feeling fine and had been determined *not* to look like an object of pity. Now, it had all gone pear-shaped in front of Jack Rooney. She clenched her teeth together in an attempt to hold back the gush of tears that were almost certain to escape. The last thing she needed was Aggie Lenihan coming back to investigate a report of hysteria if she broke down now in front of Jack Bloody Rooney.

"That's okay. I was just going down to physio anyway,"

she lied bravely, trying to pull herself together before he thought she was a complete basket-case.

"Take care, Emily. I'll see you when you get home."

His voice was surprisingly gentle, making her feel even worse. He probably thought she was about to lose the plot altogether. The door closed behind him and once again, Emily threw herself back against the pillows and cried. Maybe she *was* turning into a head-case.

Jack made it back to the Range Rover, his head pounding. He could hardly believe that he'd barged in on Emily after her horrific accident without thinking she mightn't be able for it. The other visitor, the man who he'd bumped into almost in the doorway of her hospital room, had left her lying serenely against the pillows. Yet she'd been almost in tears by the time *he'd* left. He'd seen the way that Emily had been gritting her teeth and how close she was to breaking down. Maybe Heather had been right when she'd implied that he was more rough than diamond.

Chapter 26

"You're not forgetting tomorrow night?"

Jennie came back to earth with a jolt at the sound of Vincent's voice. She'd been thinking about Ron Green and whether she should phone him a few days early or not. The last two weeks had dragged by and she was anxious now to get to the bottom of whatever it was that was going on. But Ron Green had specified two weeks – next Monday – and Jennie was finding the waiting torturous.

"Polly Lucas is coming over later to try out," she told him by way of an answer. Maxine had finally commandeered the new baby-sitter and she was calling at three to spend the afternoon getting to know Lucy and Tim in anticipation of the Chamber of Commerce Summer Ball the following evening. Donna, thankfully, was in the throes of study for her summer exams and had, to Jennie's relief, regretfully declined to baby-sit.

"Pity about Donna," Vincent commented, barely

looking up from the paper. "Though I suppose she hardly wants to spend her Saturday nights watching *Cars* at this stage of her life."

Too right, it's a pity about her, Jennie thought bitterly, visualising the teenager's lithe body and sexy through-the-fringe grin. Vincent was lingering over breakfast due to a meeting being delayed until ten and Jennie wondered if Ron Green or one of his "associates" was waiting impatiently somewhere along the road for him to materialise. She'd been surprised when he'd offered to make breakfast for them while she dropped the children to school. And even more surprised to come home and find the table laden with two bowls of muesli as well as a selection of chopped strawberries, pineapple and blueberries that were normally reserved for the children.

"No bagels?" Normally Vincent's idea of a late breakfast included croissants, pastries and the home-made jam that Jennie picked up at the Farmer's Market in Midleton.

"Noeleen has Bob on a healthy eating routine since Maurice O'Grady got that perforated ulcer. It must be rubbing off on me."

He continued spooning blueberries over the oat cereal, oblivious to the shock on his wife's face. How stupid did he think she was? Or maybe he was right to think her stupid. This was the oldest one in the book of affairs – the husband suddenly starting to take an interest in himself. Now that she looked at him properly, Jennie realised that Vincent had lost a bit of weight.

"No harm." The words, bitchy-sounding and horrible, were out of her mouth before she could stop them.

Ashamed, she spooned honey carefully out of its glass jar and avoided her husband's eyes.

"No harm in looking after yourself," he said quietly, his tone defensive, as she might have expected.

"I suppose not." Her voice, equally quiet, bristled with sarcasm. Was this how it was going to be? Suppressed anger from her and blithe indifference to the effect that his affair would surely have on their children from him?

"Jennie, I need to tell –"

"I have to get going." She couldn't bear to hear what he was about to say, terrified that he was going to tell her something that she'd somehow rather hear in the anonymity of Ron Green's office. Or even over the phone. She stood up abruptly, her chair screeching noisily across the tiled floor.

"At least finish your breakfast. It's not good to be rushing around so much."

The sudden fake solicitousness was now back in place as soon as she looked as if she was copping on – didn't he know how typical he sounded?

"Where are you off to anyway?"

At least he was looking up from *The Examiner.*

"Grocery shopping. I want to get organised before Polly comes. And I'll be busy tomorrow with the ball."

"Are you wearing the navy dress again? That was lovely the last time."

She sat down again and stared at the bowl of muesli that she'd barely touched. This was a new departure. Vincent always said she looked lovely – as soon as she was dressed and ready – in a perfunctory sort of way. But up to now, he'd never referred to a particular dress or outfit.

Another time she would have been pleased that he liked something – now she was looking for ulterior motives left, right and centre.

"No, I've a blue dress. It's a bit more formal, I think."

"Another one?" He was frowning now and she got the feeling that she was in for a lecture, something that had never happened before. "Jennie, we'll have to . . ."

This time she stood up in earnest.

How many times had she read about this? And Vincent didn't even realise that he was displaying all the classic signs. Cutting back on spending so that he could wine and dine another woman? No wonder he was so fond of travelling to the Middle East.

Perhaps that was what Noeleen Ferris had been warning her about at the party – letting her know, woman to woman, that her husband's mistress was accompanying him on expensive foreign trips that wouldn't be covered by the company.

She needed to set out very clearly, right now, that she and the children wouldn't be left short on account of him having to impress some little tart. She stood to her full height, her chest out and her voice firm.

"I needed something in evening wear, Vincent. And yes, it was expensive. But what do you expect when we do so much socialising? Now I really have to go or I won't be back in time for Polly. You'll tidy up here?"

Vincent stared at her open-mouthed. "Jesus, Jennie, where did that come from? I was only saying –"

"And *I'm* only saying that I spend all my time here with the children while you're away. It's the least –"

"Jennie." His voice had risen now and his face had flushed a dull angry colour. "Do you think I like being away, is that it? How would you like to eat shitty airline food and spend hours staring at the four walls in hotels that could be anywhere?" He was shouting now. "Okay, it's not too bad when Bob's around but mostly it's just endless travelling to look at bits of land in the desert and trying to make myself understood with interpreters who can speak neither English nor Arabic properly!"

"Vincent, don't shout at me!" She'd never seen him react like this before, with sweat out on his forehead and his hands clenched tightly as if he were just about holding back from punching the table. Or her.

"I'm sorry for shouting." He took a deep, ragged breath and closed his eyes briefly. When he spoke again, his voice was quiet. "Sorry. It's just that you think I'm having a ball when I'm out there killing myself. We wouldn't have this lifestyle if I didn't, Jennie."

They stood there staring at each other and Jennie felt like bursting into tears at the man her husband had turned into. He was lying to her, carrying on behind her back as she'd so plainly seen at the Ferrises' dinner-party and yet he was defending himself vehemently as if she were at fault somehow. Deflecting the guilt back on to her so that she felt almost beholden to him.

She turned away abruptly and left the kitchen so that he wouldn't see her face crumbling. Three more days was all she had to wait. Surely Ron Green would give her something to go on, something to strengthen her position in the face of this sudden, controlled anger of Vincent's.

Then she'd be able to return the guilt to its rightful owner.

Vincent spent most of Friday evening in the playroom, retiring to his office as soon as Tim and Lucy had departed to bed. Jennie for her part, went to bed early, preferring to feign sleep when Vincent came up rather than have to endure the façade of kissing him goodnight, however brief the kiss might be.

It was his turn to disappear on Saturday morning. Jennie had fallen into a deep sleep in the early hours of the morning and didn't miss Vincent from the bed until she heard the hiss of the shower at seven.

"I'll be back around ten, if you need to get anything done for tonight," he told her gruffly. He was rubbing his hair vigorously with a soft, navy *His* towel that Donna had given him for Christmas, along with matching ones for Jennie, Tim and Lucy. "Getting anything done" meant hair, make-up or nails and she actually did have an appointment at eleven.

"Fine, I'll leave something out for the lunch. And they have the birthday party in Busy Kidz at two." As well as her crèche and after-school facility, Maxine catered for birthday parties of up to ten children with face-painting and a magician in addition to the food, drinks and "party bags".

"Whose is it?"

It irked Jennie that he didn't know whose party it was, never mind knowing what the kids were wearing as fancy dress or what present they were bringing.

"Rufus Crawford. Lucy's Princess Fiona dress is out on the bed. Tim wants to go as Woody so he can wear his cowboy outfit."

"I can't believe Maxine agreed to do a party for Nuala." Vincent grinned, amused at the thought of their friend having to be polite to the pretentious solicitor for two full hours.

For a moment, Jennie forgot her coolness. "She got caught badly. Nuala's PA phoned to make the booking and she'd committed before she knew it was for poor Rufus. She didn't even get a chance to add an extra ten per cent!"

She could hear the low rumble of Vincent's laugh from the dressing-room and the familiar sounds of him getting dressed. Why couldn't he always be like this, easy and relaxed with no foreign trips and no chance to become embroiled in an affair?

"I'll leave the presents out as well," she said now, sitting up in bed and straightening her hair with her fingers. "Rufus told Tim that he should be getting two presents off our two! He used to be such a quiet little thing but he's certainly finding his feet. He'll be as bad as Nuala yet!"

"I suppose the acorn doesn't fall too far from the tree," Vincent commented, emerging from the dressing-room. He was well aware of Nuala's reputed meanness.

Dressed now in jeans and a well-worn navy sweater, his face unshaven, he looked younger somehow. He would shave tonight, before going out.

"I'll see you around ten, okay?" He didn't kiss her as he left the bedroom, she noticed, just touched her shoulder lightly in a gesture that hinted at the truce they seemed to have arrived at. He didn't, however, say where he was off to so early on a Saturday morning, something that, despite the dissolution of some of the tension between them, opened another bleak chamber in her heart.

Something about the vibrant blues and pinks in the short, silk Matthew Williamson dress made Jennie feel strong and defiant as soon as she looked at herself in the mirror. When she'd spent almost €2000 on it a few months ago, she'd been in a fit of rage at another of Vincent's let-downs and had later deemed it a mistake of a buy. Now, in her present frame of mind, it seemed perfect.

The fitted bodice with its thin embroidered straps moulded her breasts to perfection, allowing her to go braless, while the hemline, floating well above her knees, set off her long, slim legs. The high silver sandals encrusted with tiny turquoise stones were perfect, as was the classy chignon that Denise had created earlier that day.

Dangerously sexy was how she felt as soon as the gossamer folds of the delicious dress swirled around her legs and it occurred to her that maybe Vincent had wanted her to play it safe in the navy silk dress that she'd worn a few weeks ago. Maybe the mysterious lady with the severe French roll would be there again tonight. This time, however, Jennie was going to be noticed instead of cowering away in the kitchen like she had at the Ferrises' party.

The idea that maybe it was excitement her husband was after had come to her as she sat in front of the mirror, staring at her own image while the hairdresser teased the long, blonde tresses into a work of art. She knew it wasn't that she was lacking in the looks department – she'd always made sure that she kept her figure and was never less than perfectly groomed.

She'd always imagined that it was overweight wives in tracksuits who found their husbands straying, never thinking that it could happen to someone like herself who took such care to stay attractive, despite the demands of the children and running the house.

Now, she was of the mind that she hadn't been exciting enough. Thinking back, it was always Tim and Lucy that they talked about over the phone when he was away – and at that it was mostly her giving out about what he was missing and him promising ineffectually to be there for the next thing.

Sex, when she thought about it, had even become a little predictable. They always ended up making love the night he came home from a trip and more often than not on Saturday nights, particularly if they'd been out. When had they last made frantic love on the sofa? Vincent never undressed her anymore – it was always when the lights were out that they came together these days. Maybe it was her fault – she'd become so preoccupied with the routine of managing Tim and Lucy on her own.

She'd left the hairdresser's chair today with hardly a word passing between herself and Denise as she tried to figure out what exactly it was she was going to do with Ron Green's information. Pauline, the manicurist, had also remained in blessed silence as Jennie came to the conclusion that she did not want to disrupt the life she had built up, in spite of what the PI might think she was about to do.

Why should I upend everything and drive Vincent out of Rathmollin Woods and straight into his mistress's apartment? How convenient that would be for her – Vincent being freed up without her ever having to force him into a choice. A plan had finally formulated, compounded when Pauline asked her to choose her nail colour for the evening.

"Pearl or Silver Shimmer?"

"Silver's good," she stated firmly, her chin rising ever so slightly, having just realised that perhaps her pearls and twin-set image hadn't done her much good to date.

Now, she was just gathering up her silver beaded purse when Vincent poked his head in the bedroom door to see if she was ready.

"Wow!" His face was a picture of stunned surprise at the transformation in his wife. Jennie knew that she always looked well going out. This time, however, she knew the look was straight off the catwalk.

"Nice?" Slightly flirty was what she sounded as she turned back towards the dressing-table and picked up a bottle of *Allure*. Her dress swirled away from her legs, brushing sexily around her thighs.

"More than nice. You look stunning."

Stunning. Definitely a good start. "We'd better go. I'll say goodbye to the kids." That's it, she thought as she crossed the landing to where Tim and Lucy were reading on Lucy's bed, don't hang around. Take the compliment and move on.

By the time she'd said the last round of bed-time prayers and reminded Polly again of Lucy's toileting arrangements for later, Vincent was waiting for her in the hall, keys in hand.

"What do you say we get a taxi home?" she suggested. If she was going to win her husband back at fairly short notice, she knew there would have to be a certain amount of alcohol involved at the outset to loosen then both up.

"I don't mind driving," he began.

"Not tonight. Why don't we just relax and enjoy ourselves for once? We can ask reception to book a cab later."

"Why not? It's nice to have a glass with the meal." At last he was starting to look some way enthusiastic about the night ahead at the Mount Vernon.

"Why not indeed," Jennie agreed, swishing past him in a cloud of *Allure*, her mind already on the swing band that the tickets had promised.

Chapter 27

Jack checked his bow-tie in the bathroom mirror and wished for the umpteenth time that the Chamber of Commerce would ease up on the whole black tie thing. It wasn't that he was against formal wear – it was just that it seemed a bit incongruous to be dressing up to this extent to meet people that he dealt with every single day, in one way or another.

Struggling, he pulled the tie off and started again. It was a mess, already crumpled from this third attempt and for a nano-second he wished that Heather was still on his radar, if only to fix the blasted tie. Sighing, he knotted it carefully and finally got it right. If that's all he needed Heather in his life for, then he was probably better off without her.

He wondered now who he'd be sitting next to at the Mount Vernon. Thankfully, his stint on the committee had ended so at least he didn't have to entertain Declan Houlihan for the evening as he got progressively more drunk.

The obese President had an unfortunate penchant for

brandy, to the annoyance of those who served on the committee. It was generally accepted that Declan's drink problem was far outweighed by his contacts and business acumen, his weight in every sense of the word being a valuable asset to the Chamber. It was also generally accepted that getting Declan safely off the premises and back to his own home discreetly was part and parcel of the duties of the other committee members.

The idea of avoiding the inevitable 3 a.m. showdown with Declan preoccupied him. John Williams and his wife Carmel would be there, their focus firmly set on the fund-raising aspect of the evening rather than on the networking side of things. Jack admired the couple, especially Carmel and the ease with which she managed John's extensive property portfolio. On the outside, she behaved like a typical flower-child – a fact which Jack teased her about mercilessly whenever they met at functions. A passionate eco warrior, Carmel was as happy campaigning against incinerators as she was chasing land-registration problems and long-lost deeds and was always entertaining company. It would be nice to be seated next to the Williamses, especially if Declan Houlihan got embroiled in the usual series of long-winded speeches over coffee.

With a start, Jack realised that it was already half seven, high time he was on the move. The meal was for eight and as usual there would be the round of mingling beforehand, something that Heather, to give her her due, had been super at.

As soon as Jack pulled up at the hotel, Vincent Kelleher's navy BMW pulled in behind him.

"Jack – good to see you. You'll have to keep me occupied so that Declan doesn't commandeer me as his chauffeur like he did at New Year." Vincent punched Jack playfully on the shoulder as he went around to open Jennie's door.

Jack's breath caught in his throat when he saw the long, tanned length of her legs emerging from the car. Jennie had always been fabulous-looking but tonight she looked like a model in a vibrant blue and pink silk dress that was shorter than anything he'd seen her in before.

"Jack," she greeted him warmly.

"Hi, Jennie. You look great." He meant it. The whole look was like a shimmering mirage – even her eye-shadow was silver to match the beading on the dress. Jack rarely noticed such things but Jennie Kelleher was positively glowing.

"Thanks, Jack. I'm in good company." Vincent had taken her arm and she now held out the other one for Jack.

Smiling up at him, she looked as young as she had in secondary school, but somehow more approachable. Normally, Jennie was reserved with a cool elegance that reminded him of old black and white photos of Grace Kelly.

"The school playground is looking good," Vincent commented as they made the short walk towards the main entrance of the plush hotel. "I had a look when I dropped the kids off yesterday," he added when Jennie looked at him with a slight frown. For a moment, Jack was reminded of the tension between the couple outside the church a few weeks previously.

"It'll be great next year when the grass has had a chance

to come on," he said easily. "Seán Daly has the herb garden planned – vegetables and all. Apparently they're going to have a wormery now as well!"

"Well, that's one project I'll be staying away from," Jennie laughed, wrinkling her nose. She smiled up at Vincent now, her eyes twinkling, all traces of her fleeting frown gone.

Jack wondered if he was getting as bad as Aggie Lenihan for speculating.

The three of them passed through the plate-glass doors and accepted the offering of champagne from an attentive waiter.

"This is gorgeous," Jennie announced, closing her eyes briefly as she sipped from the delicate crystal flute. She spun around suddenly to greet Carmel Williams, her silky dress lifting a little with the movement.

Jack tore his eyes away from the sight of her smooth thighs and slim waist.

"Carmel! You look lovely!" Jennie complimented effusively, kissing Carmel enthusiastically on both cheeks.

Jack hadn't realised that the two women were so friendly.

"So," Vincent began as soon as his wife was engrossed in conversation, "what's the story with the Doyles' field development? Any news on the planning permission yet?" All of Jack's development properties to date had been sold through The Property People so Vincent had more than just a passing interest.

"Nearly there – just a few weeks to wait out the objectors but nothing has come in so far. Normally, they're lining up!"

"Tell me about it. We've turned into a nation of professional objectors, as far as I can see. Sometimes I think people just object for the sake of it."

Jack laughed, appreciating what Vincent meant. A small bite of guilt ate away at him when he thought of Emily Gordon but he really couldn't see any way around the entrance issues for the new development without knocking Ina Harrington's cottage. Plus the fact that he'd already placed a substantial deposit on it pending the planning permission.

Pushing it out of his mind, he tuned back into what Vincent was saying about holiday villas in Zagreb. Almost immediately, the dinner was announced and they followed Jennie and Carmel into the dining-room.

To his relief, the seating arrangements were exactly what he'd hoped for – a round table of six comprising Jennie and Vincent, John and Carmel and the inevitable female pairing for his benefit in the form of Faith Rowney, a robust civil engineer from West Cork. Like Declan Houlihan, Faith was known for her lack of moderation when it came to alcohol, although its effects on her were more pleasant than its effect on the President. Faith, to be fair, would sing a song or two before being led sedately to a waiting taxi by one of the ladies, usually Carmel Williams or Noeleen Ferris. Noeleen and Bob were missing tonight on account of a planned trip to their daughter in Glasgow.

"The Mount Vernon's reputation for excellent food certainly isn't unwarranted," Jack commented to Vincent as he tucked into a succulent fillet of seared beef.

"I'm doing my best to be healthy," Vincent grinned, indicating the salmon that he'd chosen.

"You'll be going to the gym next," Jack laughed.

Jennie, obviously overhearing, looked up distractedly from her conversation with Faith.

Vincent waved away a second round of gratin potatoes and riposted that Tim and Lucy were enough exercise for anyone.

"I can give you a lift home if you want to leave the car, by the way," said Jack. "I have a match in the morning so I'd better stay sober."

"We might take you up on it if the taxis are scarce later. Still playing at your age, are you?"

"I'm just about at the end of my career in soccer, such as it is. Just as well I'm in goal!" Of late, Jack's old football injuries seemed to be catching up with him, making him feel older than his twenty-eight years.

"Golf is all I'm fit for – and even at that I don't have the time. Are you on for a round anytime next week?"

Jack thought about it. "What about Wednesday around five? I could knock off a bit early. God, this is sinful!" His delicious crème brûlée was already half finished in two bites.

"It's not stopping you from laying into it, Jack Rooney," Faith quipped.

Jack laughed and nodded towards Faith's dessert plate, already empty. The waiter arrived with more red wine, which both Faith and Jennie readily accepted. Carmel tipped her glass of non-alcoholic fruit juice and joked that they were very much a table of two halves, with her, Jack and Vincent abstaining from the hard liquor.

John smirked and sniffed his brandy, reminding that it wasn't every night he had the run of a free bar. "Have to make the most of it."

Jack, having seen John Williams in action at business meetings on numerous occasions, knew that it was only at very sociable events that John drank at all. Jennie, on the other hand, was a surprise.

Her face was flushed and animated and she looked as if she was really enjoying herself. He'd often noticed her at functions looking bored and wondered what was different about tonight. Normally she looked as if she was barely hiding her disinterest, as if the whole business of socialising was a strain that had to be tolerated for the sake of Vincent's business contacts.

She turned towards Jack now and brought up the subject of the school wormery again.

"I was just telling Carmel about it – although I'm not sure how it works exactly."

Carmel, ever interested in what was going on in other people's lives, was intrigued as Jack repeated what Seán Daly had explained to him.

"That's fantastic," Carmel enthused. "Would they have room for reed beds there at all? That's another project some schools are getting into."

"It's the future, I suppose," Jennie commented. "They really need to know about recycling and composting and things like that from an early age. Tim and Lucy are actually teaching me! I was mortified the other day in the shopping centre when Lucy made me take a Diet Coke bottle out of a bin."

"She did not!" Carmel and Jack laughed at the idea of the precocious Lucy giving orders.

"No bother to her. It was the only bin in the shopping centre but that wasn't good enough. I had to put it in my handbag and take it home to the recycling bin!"

"I can only imagine the stink in the handbag," Carmel laughed and turned to respond to the waiter who'd appeared at her elbow. "Coffee, please."

"Coffee as well, please," Jennie added, nodding when the waiter indicated her empty wine-glass.

Jack also accepted a coffee and asked for a fresh glass and some of the fruit juice that Carmel was having.

"The herb garden will be great as well," Jennie continued, picking up their earlier conversation. "Tim started on about processed food the other day when I was using dried sage in the stuffing so I'll really have to pull my socks up."

"It's the same in our house – Iseult's obsessed with not leaving the tap running because of all the water getting wasted," Carmel commiserated, referring to her seven-year-old daughter. "But enough of that or we'll put Jack off marriage for life."

Carmel was always thoughtful about not monopolising the conversation with talk of children, especially when Faith was present.

"I was just coming around to thinking that," he admitted. "You'd want a degree in psychology to get parenting right."

"Don't let it put you off, Jack," Vincent interjected. "You're used to having to learn on the job – that's how I do it!"

Jennie laughed. "Good parenting is very easy when it's done from abroad over the phone." She was smiling but there was a slight edge to her voice that suggested she was half joking, whole in earnest. Jack wondered if she was slightly drunk but again recalled the implied criticism he'd heard outside the church. She hadn't had any drink taken that evening. Vincent looked away, his face and neck reddening quickly.

"Virtual parenting," Carmel put in quickly. "My mother reared ten of us and she says now that she should have been getting a 'single mother's allowance' all along! My father only saw us for Mass on a Sunday when we were all dressed up and well-behaved."

"You should take a leaf out of my book, Jack. Just don't go there." Faith, a staunch and confirmed spinster, made no bones about the fact that she considered most children to be annoying little time-wasters. She too seemed to have noticed the tension that had suddenly developed at the table.

"I must admit, if my good wife wasn't present, I might be able to make a case for the virtual style of parenting," said John, "especially if it meant I didn't have to get rid of ghosts at half two in the morning. But she *is* present, so I'd better shut up." He grinned over at Carmel and rolled his eyes.

"Okay, I've heard enough. I'll stick with Faith and have the good sense to stay single." Vincent still hadn't spoken so Jack addressed him now. "I'll concentrate on my handicap instead."

Vincent recovered a little at the change of conversation

and smiled tightly, loosening his collar a bit at the same time. "Faith can advise you on that score as well!"

The outdoorsy civil engineer was renowned for her astonishing handicap and now launched into a plethora of advice for Jack, up to now a half-hearted golfer.

"No half measures, Jack. You'll have to practise. Get a few more tips from the pro out there in Glenconner or wherever it is you play."

"I'll have plenty of time when I give up the soccer," Jack admitted dolefully. A second round of coffee was offered at this point and he accepted a top-up, knowing it was going to be a late night. The noise from Declan Houlihan's table had risen significantly now and the band was setting up on the small raised platform at the opposite end of the room to the bar.

"That's the thing about the hill-walking," John commented. "No need to get involved with all these rules and honing of skills. As long as you close the gates behind you and pick up your rubbish, you're away on a hack."

Jack was inclined to agree with him. Although he played a certain amount of golf, the fanaticism and attention to detail of people like Faith just hadn't grabbed him yet. He was more of a "doer", a bit like John Williams in many ways.

"That's my husband – a perfectionist to the core." Carmel and John had an easy, intimate way with each other that Jack envied a little.

"Aren't you blessed with me? Imagine if you had Declan there to contend with!" Declan Houlihan, clearly inebriated, was trying to pull a reluctant Chamber of

Commerce clerical assistant towards the dance floor. Jack felt sorry for the poor girl, Violet Corcoran, when she eventually had to give in and endure a mauling to the strains of "Come Fly With Me".

"It's all very fine," Vincent said to John with a sigh, "but it'll be us having to drag him into a taxi later. Maurice O'Grady will never manage him."

Maurice and his wife Phil were looking on helplessly as the President lunged around the floor, occasionally pounding into poor Violet and the other dancers.

"True. We'd better keep an eye on him or poor Maurice will burst another ulcer. He's looking well, all the same."

The band had moved on now to "Something Stupid" and the hapless Violet made a polite but ineffectual attempt to escape the dance floor. They watched in fascination as Maurice and Phil joined the fray, probably to lend support to Violet as she was gripped by Declan and swung dangerously in swift pirouette that ended, inevitably, in an undignified stumble.

"He's worse than ever." Jack had supervised Declan's exit on more than one occasion and was glad that Vincent was now Assistant Treasurer and John the Assistant PRO.

"Come on, let's dance," Jennie suggested suddenly. "We can't sit here monitoring Declan all night." She'd been quiet enough since her barbed comment to Vincent earlier but now pulled at his arm impatiently.

"We might as well – it's going to be a long night!" He led Jennie off towards the dancing area and Jack turned to Faith, offering her his arm.

"Definitely not. I don't do dancing. Never did – even in my heyday. Take Carmel, why don't you? She's good at that sort of thing."

Carmel laughed and took Jack's arm, not in the least offended by Faith's abrupt diagnosis of her skills. The older lady's copious consumption of wine during the meal was beginning to tell and only served to make Faith more entertaining than her usual eccentric self.

"I wish someone *would* fly Declan to the moon," Jack grinned as the President bowled past them with Phil O'Grady in tow, entirely out of step with the beat of the classic Frank Sinatra number. The Kellehers were next to himself and Carmel on the dance floor, with Jennie swaying seductively in front of Vincent.

Carmel giggled and shook her head. She'd been down this road many times before and wasn't looking forward to the scene her husband would have to put up with before the evening was out. "God, he's targeting Jennie now."

Jack looked around and saw Vincent being edged out of the way. Phil, it seemed, was to be abandoned mid-dance now that Declan had spotted the much younger and much sexier Jennie. Vincent gave his wife an apologetic look and gallantly took the older lady's elbow to commence dancing at a more sedate and infinitely less exhausting pace than she'd endured for the last few minutes.

This was vintage Declan and Jack was surprised to see Jennie joining him enthusiastically, unlike the other women he'd been pestering.

It was another half hour before the band decided to

take a short break, by which time Declan had marauded over the feet of almost every lady in the room as well as causing extensive bruising to most of the male dancers from bumping into them.

"This is terrible." Carmel had endured a full three minutes on the floor with Declan roaring the words of "The Lady Is A Tramp" at her. It was almost midnight and if previous occasions were anything to go by, the President was only warming up. "Isn't it a wonder he doesn't just fall down?"

"Too used to it. He'll just keep going until he falls down permanently," Faith confirmed, wriggling her bare feet. Despite refusing all offers to dance as usual, she'd been forced into action just before the interval when Declan's insistence had been loud enough to draw the attention of a very young-looking hotel manager. It had taken assurances from Jack, Vincent and John regarding an escort home to calm the situation and prevent Declan being ejected ignominiously from the Mount Vernon.

"I'm off to the Ladies," Jennie announced. She wobbled suddenly as she tried to retrieve her handbag from under the table and Carmel was at her side immediately.

"I'll come too," she decided.

Vincent had risen from his seat but now sat back almost gratefully. It was clear to Jack that he'd be contending with his wife *and* Declan if Jennie continued to down the red wine at the rate she was going. The two women proceeded unsteadily across the parquet floor with Carmel holding Jennie's elbow firmly.

"Right, lads, 'said John'. "And you, Faith."

John sounded deadly serious and Jack and Vincent leaned in to see what solution there was for Declan's predicament. They would make some sort of plan together, Jack imagined, and then one of them, probably John, would cross discreetly to the other table to clear it with Maurice and the others.

"How about if I take him home in a taxi? I'm not taking him in the car after the last time." In that almost-fatal debacle, Declan had tried forcibly to make John turn the car around to go back to the function that they'd just left. They'd ended up in a ditch with John's Saab worse for wear. Declan had been quick to compensate him for the repairs and more than apologetic the following day but it was the fact that the incident could have left Eunan and Iseult without a father that had John wary on this occasion.

"He's impossible to deal with these days," said Vincent. "He was trying to urinate out the window of the cab the last time we took him – poor Jennie was in an awful state about it. Maybe I should come as well."

"I can drop Jennie home," said Jack. "No point in putting her through that again. And you, Faith." He was shocked at just how badly Declan was disintegrating before them. Perhaps it was time they stopped the damage limitation and talked to him about treatment instead.

"That's great, Jack," said Vincent gratefully. "There's no way she'd cope with Declan a second time."

"Carmel will be taking the car home anyway so maybe you could travel with her for company, Faith?" said John.

Faith nodded though without much enthusiasm.

John was a born diplomat and Jack grinned to himself

at his foresight. This plan would sort out Faith's exit fairly neatly if she was three sheets to the wind later on.

"That's settled then," said John. "Will we go over and see if Maurice is happy enough with that?"

They all followed his gaze towards Declan's table. As well as Maurice and Phil O'Grady, there was Peter Connolly, now in his eighties and still proprietor of Connolly's Master Butcher and his old friend Mac Gleeson who ran the grocery with his son, Michael. There was no way that any of the three elderly men could manage Declan in his present condition. Plus there was the fact that each of them was accompanied by their equally senior wives. Phil O'Grady, in her mid-sixties, was probably the youngest of them.

"Grand so," Jack said stoically, standing up with John. "I'll keep Declan occupied while you talk to Maurice."

"I'll get the drinks in, in that case." Vincent excused himself and headed off to the bar.

Faith sighed and massaged her bruised ankles under the table.

Jack didn't have too much work on his hands to distract Declan. Almost as soon as he and John reached the other table the band had struck up again, this time with "Mack The Knife".

Declan was on his feet immediately, brushing Jack aside in favour of Mona Connolly. Peter looked on anxiously as his wife took to the floor with her boisterous partner.

"Desperate altogether," he commented to Jack. "We're going to have to have a word with him soon." Peter looked as if he didn't relish the thought of it for a minute.

"I think so too." Jack was glad that someone else thought that Declan Houlihan's drinking was out of control. "Is there any family who might get involved?" They watched the obese figure dragging Mona Connolly around the dance floor, her silk shawl swinging off her left shoulder.

"I'm afraid not, Jack. Sorry now but I'll cut in, I think." Peter went off to rescue his wife and Jack joined the others, all of whom were in agreement about the fact that Declan was in serious trouble.

"Peter and Mac know him as long as I do," Maurice was saying. "We'll call around some night and talk it out with him. We'll try to get him in somewhere, if he'll go."

"We'll sort him out for tonight then," John promised. "I do think he'll take the treatment idea better from you, to be fair."

"Well, we go back a long way with him," Maurice said, nodding hard and allowing Mac Gleeson to continue.

"I was there before the doctor arrived the night Peg and the baby died. He was never the same since. He started to drink that night."

Jack listened in amazement as Mac told of the way Declan had gone through the funeral of his wife and child in a daze.

"We were the only undertakers in the area so I was there all night. I remember Danny Stone, he was only a young fellow at the time, bringing up a few crates of stout and the bottles of whiskey and brandy to the house for the callers. Declan started in on them and we could hardly get him into the suit the next day."

"I never realised he was married." John too was stunned at the story.

"Less than a year." Dottie Gleeson was clearly affected by her husband's reminiscence. "She was like a film star in her day, Peg was. She was delighted about the baby from the beginning but she never lived to see him. He was only a few pounds in weight. He lasted no time, a few minutes, I think."

Jack looked across at Declan and understood for the first time why the others on the Chamber committee allowed him so much leeway. He wondered if the older men realised that Declan was trying, systematically, to follow his wife and child to the grave.

He watched as Declan and Peter arrived back at the table while Mona headed off to the Ladies, probably to recover from her strenuous ordeal.

John greeted Declan amiably and chatted for a few minutes. Declan though, was sweating heavily and couldn't seem to focus at all on the conversation. Eventually, John and Jack headed back to their own table, the relieved nods of the other men reminding them that they'd be doing the right thing by taking Declan home as soon as possible.

"He'll have to be a bit further gone, I think, before he'll co-operate." John had also been through the routine many times.

"Well, hopefully there won't be much more of it if Mac and the lads get him sorted out," said Jack.

There was no sign of Carmel and Jennie when they arrived back at the table.

"They've probably sneaked off home to avoid the scene with Declan," John joked.

"Can't blame them," said Vincent. "They're going to be abandoned anyway while we take care of him." Too many evenings had been brought to an abrupt end by Declan Houlihan, he thought.

"We'll finish this drink and get things underway," said John. "I'll go out to reception and order a cab." He saw the urgency of the situation as Declan now was wobbling around singing "Ain't That A Kick In The Teeth".

The lead singer in the band was beginning to look annoyed. A table near him, skimmed by Declan, shook precariously but miraculously stayed upright. The drinks resting on it, however, didn't and the sound of shattering glass made almost everyone in the room wince visibly. Things were starting to get out of control.

"Right." Vincent stood up. "I'll go over and see if I can cajole him a bit."

The frazzled young manager was descending again, this time with two suited gentlemen in tow.

Jennie and Carmel were approaching the table as their husbands left in opposite directions. Jennie was sashaying confidently, albeit with a very distinct wobble. Carmel was looking a little pale and anxious but still held on to Jennie's arm valiantly.

"Good old Declan. Always the party animal." Jennie sounded completely plastered. Jack could see a dark red rim around her lips, stained from too much red wine. He wondered if Vincent realised how drunk she'd become and whether she'd come home as planned with him when Declan had been dispatched with Vincent and John. She was pulling Carmel out to dance, despite the fact that

Declan had cleared the floor. The band was still playing though and she seemed to see nothing untoward about the scene unfolding at Declan's table.

"Don't be dry, Carmel," she giggled when Carmel planted herself firmly in her seat and refused to budge. "Okay so – you'll dance, won't you, Jack?" She pouted at him like a 1920s starlet, all red lips and big doe eyes.

"I'm useless, Jennie, you know that. Here, let me get you a drink." Jack pulled out a chair but Jennie was having none of it. What a night this was turning out to be . . .

"No way, Jack Rooney!" Her voice was high-pitched and flirty.

Jack glanced over at the tableau by Declan's table, wondering if Vincent could hear.

"You're definitely going to dance. Definitely." Jennie was on her feet. She swayed, grabbed onto the back of the chair and blinked as if to clear her head. "Whooops-a-daisy. Now, *come on,* Jack!"

Carmel tried to intervene, reminding her that she still had a drink to get through.

"Feck the drink – it's someone to dance with that *I* want. I said *come on,* Jack!"

He looked at Carmel helplessly, knowing they'd have another scene on their hands if he continued to refuse.

"One dance and then we're out of here," he said, trying to sound gracious and firm at the same time.

"Oooh, Jack, you're soooo masterful!" Swaying, she walked out onto the floor with Jack following uncertainly.

Jennie and Carmel had been away from the table for ages, he thought. She must have had more to drink out in the lounge. Reluctantly, he began to dance, still keeping an eye on the situation back at Declan's table. He saw Maurice O'Grady placing a comforting arm around the drunken President as he and John escorted him towards the door. Vincent, looking about, spotted Jennie on the dance floor and made his way towards her.

Jack stood by as he told her that he had to leave with Declan and John.

"Jack says he'll drop you home. Here – you take the house keys – I imagine it'll take a while to settle Declan."

Jack thought it might take him a while to settle Jennie as well but decided the less said the better. "I'll be leaving in a few minutes, Vincent," he said. "I'll just see that Carmel and Faith are sorted first."

Vincent leaned down and kissed Jennie on the cheek. "See you later."

"Good luck!" Jack grinned as Declan reappeared in the doorway. Vincent departed rapidly. "Right so, Jennie, we'll make tracks."

"No way! It's early yet." She continued to dance, her movements becoming more provocative. Perhaps she thought it was still Vincent she was dancing with. Gently, he took her arm and led her back to the table where Faith and Carmel were gathering up their handbags and wraps.

"He's *such* a spoilsport. Dragging me home when it's only getting going."

"We're all taking off now, Jennie. And you'll have Tim and Lucy banging at the door at eight o'clock, if it's anything like my house."

Jack smiled at Carmel gratefully. Faith harrumphed

loudly, a disapproving sound that he feared might be directed at him.

It was a full ten minutes before he got Jennie settled in the car. There was a lot of giggling and shrieking as Carmel tried to tie her seat-belt while Faith tugged at the short blue dress in an attempt to cover Jennie's ever more exposed thighs. Jack imagined that his face had paled visibly at the thought of the journey ahead – it certainly felt like it had.

Eventually, they were on the road, Jack wishing the miles away as Jennie started to doze beside him. He was grateful for the dearth of traffic and for the fact that his passenger seemed to have settled better than he'd expected. Soon the electronic gates of Rathmollin Woods were in front of them and Jack reluctantly disturbed Jennie.

"Jennie, I need the remote. Wake up."

"Remote what?" Her speech was slurred.

"For the gates. The remote control. It's in your bag." He knew this because Carmel had drawn his attention to the fact before they left the Mount Vernon.

"In the bag . . . somewhere . . . I don't know . . ."

Frustrated and a bit annoyed, Jack took the small purse from her lap and rummaged through the lipsticks and other cosmetics. The keys, of course, were right at the bottom.

The wrought-iron gates slid open silently and Jack made his way towards Jennie and Vincent's house. As he'd expected, it was in darkness. He held onto the keys, knowing that Jennie wouldn't be able to manage the door in the state she was in.

"Jennie, you're home, wake up."

A groan was all he got for a response.

He took off his own seat belt and loosened hers. Now he shook her gently, hoping that she'd wake up when the cold air hit her.

He was right. As soon as he went around and opened the passenger door, Jennie's eyes shot open.

"Are we home? God, it's freezing." She shuddered in the cool May air, her light shawl nowhere to be seen. Jack wondered if it had slid off her shoulders in the car park of the Mount Vernon. No doubt it was expensive.

"Come on, Jennie. Let's get you inside before you perish."

Gingerly she started to get her legs out but didn't seem to be able to rise any further and flopped back onto the seat sideways. Jack caught her hands and gave a gentle pull to get her moving. Once out, she swayed unsteadily on her high heels and flopped against the car as he tried to close the door.

"Hold on, Jennie. Don't try to walk." She really was plastered and Jack hoped that her neighbours weren't watching as he slid his arm around her waist and supported her as far as the door.

"Oh, God – the keys!" Jennie was suddenly alert, as if she'd come out of a dream and realised that she was outside her own front door.

"It's all right – I have them." He let go of her briefly to try to get the glossy black front door open. At that, Jennie slumped against the doorframe and started to cry. "It's okay, Jennie. You're home. You can sleep now. Shush for a moment or you'll wake the kids." This is all I need, Jack groaned inwardly, wishing that Vincent would arrive to take over. Crying women were no problem, so long as they weren't married to someone else.

"Why can't Vincent be like you, Jack?" She slumped against him, tears pouring down her face.

Jack was mortified. "Shhhh, Jennie. Come on. Just for a minute until we get you inside." Having built the house and attended many social occasions here, Jack knew his way to the spacious sitting-room at the front of the house. "In here, Jennie. Here, sit down and I'll make coffee."

"It's so typical! He's always the same!" Jennie was on her own planet, sobbing and ranting about Vincent.

Jack settled her on one of the leather sofas and started to pull the curtains.

"Here I am having to find my own way home and he's off God knows where!" she sobbed.

Jack declined to remind her that Vincent had seen to it that she was escorted safely home before he left the Mount Vernon. "He's only gone as far as Declan's house. He'll be home soon. Don't worry." He was whispering, afraid of waking Tim and Lucy. Jennie didn't seem to be aware of her sleeping children.

"Don't make excuses for him, Jack." She was cross now, her face blotchy and tear-stained. "I don't know where he is half the time. Or who he's with."

"Now, Jennie, you've had a lot to drink." Jack really didn't want her to say things she might be embarrassed about in the morning.

"Don't tell me I'm drunk, Jack. I *know* that. I also know what he's up to, even if you all think I'm stupid." She broke into more self-pitying tears, sobbing loudly again. Was she saying that Vincent was having an affair? Jack didn't think this was true – the man hardly had time to bless himself. And he was always talking about Jennie and the kids.

"No one thinks you're stupid, Jennie. And there's nothing going on." Jack hoped he was right in saying this. "Here, lie down and put your feet up for a bit. You can put the rug over you and I'll make coffee."

She was crying silently now at least and for that Jack was grateful. The last thing he needed was two small kids and a baby-sitter appearing. Defeated-looking, Jennie curled up on her side on the voluminous sofa and closed her eyes. Her legs were exposed and the straps of her dress had fallen off her shoulders. One of her sandals was hanging off her foot. Relieved that she seemed to be asleep again, Jack took a fleecy, leopardskin rug from one of the armchairs and started to tuck it around her.

Like a flash, Jennie's arms were around his neck, her lips nuzzling his jaw. "You smell gorgeous, Jack," she mumbled.

"Jesus, Jennie, give over . . . let go . ."

"Why, Jack?" She held on tightly. "Why should I when he's at this all the time?" Her nails raked the back of his neck lightly.

Jack was glad he was sober. Wrenching her arms away, he stood up, putting distance between them. "Jennie for God's sake, cop on!" He was whispering loudly now. "You're completely drunk. This is all in your head, you know – about Vincent. I'll make coffee and then I'm going."

"Jack, don't go . . . nobody would know . . ." She was looking at him seductively through her eyelashes, her shoulders bare where the thin straps had fallen off.

"Jennie," he hissed. "This is madness. *I'd* know! I'm not doing this, Jennie. Whatever is going on with you and Vincent, it's your own business." Shaking, he turned again and made his escape.

Her voice trailed after him, a whimper now, but he was already half way out of the room and heading for the blessed sanctuary of the kitchen.

He stood among the pristine units that he'd had specially built for Jennie and Vincent, shaking. Was she just drunk and paranoid as he thought or was Vincent really having an affair? What if someone had come in just now? Talk about compromising! He waited for the kettle to boil and searched the cupboards for instant coffee. There was a built-in coffee maker, he knew that, but instant would have to do for now.

Minutes later he was back in the sitting-room. Jennie was snoring loudly, her hair fallen across her face obscuring it completely. In all the years he'd known her, Jack had never seen Jennie Kelleher drunk. Controlled was how he would have described her, if anything. And maybe a bit spoilt if the truth be known. She'd certainly never wanted for anything, not on Vincent's account.

As far as Jack could see, the man worked all hours and hated the times when he was away from home. Maybe he was being too harsh, but it seemed to him that Jennie had everything she wanted in terms of material things but still wasn't happy that Vincent had to be away a lot to provide for that.

On the other hand, maybe Vincent Kelleher *was* playing away – he was certainly out of the country enough to get away with it, although Jack wasn't convinced.

"Jennie, coffee. Sit up a bit." This time, Jack was careful to issue instructions from afar rather than risk the same thing happening again. To his relief, she heard him and struggled into a sitting position, knocking three or four cushions off the sofa. "Here you go, Jennie," he whispered. It was hard to be cross with her when she looked such a pathetic mess compared to the vibrant beauty that had emerged from Vincent's car outside the Mount Vernon only a few hours ago.

"Jack, I don't know what to say . . . I can't believe . . ." She looked like a panda with huge smudged eyes in a pale face. Tears hovered on her eyelashes and Jack wondered if he might have been better off leaving her asleep.

"It's all right, Jennie. Drink the coffee, you'll be fine."

"It's just . . ." Her eyes had filled up again.

"Jennie, forget it. Now drink." He smiled encouragingly at her, hoping to head off the tears.

Finally she picked up the mug from where he'd placed it on the coffee-table and took a tentative sip. "Thanks." Another sip and she looked at him from under her eyelashes. Her gaze was direct and suddenly clear and she reminded him of an Indian squaw, sitting cross-legged with the woolly rug tucked around her. "I'm not raving, you know."

"Jennie . . ." He really didn't want to hear this.

All of a sudden her eyes flashed with anger. "Don't patronise me, Jack! I've seen all the signs. Don't tell me you haven't noticed his health drive – no drinking, no dessert – what's that all about?" she sneered.

"I'm not the one you should be asking –"

"Typical," she interrupted. "The big male cover-up, is that it?"

"I'm not covering up for anyone, Jennie. Get that into your head for a start." Jack was livid. It was one thing to accuse her husband of having an affair – it was quite another to accuse *him* of covering it up. "And it's a bit dangerous to go around thinking that Vincent's having an affair when you obviously haven't any evidence of it. What's the story, Jennie? What have you seen or heard?" Jennie, as he'd expected, was silent. "Nothing? Maybe it's just that you feel you're not getting enough attention?" For some reason, Jack was annoyed on Vincent's behalf. He knew how hard he worked – had seen him in action – and wasn't prepared to listen to his spoilt, silly wife ranting and raving any longer. He'd never thought of Jennie as being silly before but tonight he really did wonder. What if he'd had a bit more to drink and had succumbed to her advances? Where would that have left her? Or him, for that matter?

Suddenly, as if he'd wished for it specifically at this moment, a beam of light flashed across the closed curtains. "Vincent's taxi," he announced, cutting off her answer.

"I'm leaving now, Jennie." He felt sorry for her suddenly with her pale, frightened face and her smudged make-up. "I won't be talking about this after tonight. But you need to sort things out properly with Vincent."

"Jack . . ."

He spoke more gently this time, regretting his gruffness. "I mean it, Jennie. This kind of thing isn't helpful, you know."

A few moments' silence ensued as they listened to the engine and then the car door slamming.

"I'll get the door – he gave you the keys, remember?" Jack picked up his own keys from the coffee table.

"Jack . . .?"

She was sobering up now, he reckoned, at the sound of Vincent's footfalls on the paving.

"Let's forget tonight, okay?" He smiled weakly, imagining her hangover. "Sleep well."

"Thanks, Jack," Jennie whispered, her eyes closing.

"No problem," Jack sighed and closed the door behind him.

Chapter 28

Sandra nearly jumped out of her skin when the phone rang. It was only nine o'clock and the first morning in ages that she didn't have to get up with Dylan. He'd insisted Sunday evening on having a sleep-over with his grandparents who hosted a DVD and popcorn evening every now and then. Sandra suspected that they were trying to distract him from the trauma of Paul's disappearance, which Sandra had told him about in the briefest of terms lest he hear it from someone else in school.

She grabbed the phone on the second ring, worried that something might have happened to him on the way to school. She knew all too well the kind of people that were on the roads these days.

"Sandra. Chrissie here." Succinct as always.

Sandra sat up straight in the bed, embarrassed at being caught lying in. Then she realised that Chrissie couldn't actually see her.

"Chrissie, good morning," she said brightly, needing to make a brisk and business-like impression.

As usual, her former boss got straight to the point. "I rang to say that your luck is in, Sandra. Nicola has decided that hairdressing isn't for her – she's going to Australia for a year with her friends instead. So there's a place here for an apprentice if you'd like it."

"Oh, my God, Chrissie, I'd be delighted! When would you like me to start?" Sandra thought her heart would burst out of her chest. She knew she'd have to make arrangements for Dylan but she could sort that out later in the day. Her first priority was to accept Chrissie's offer.

"Would next Monday be too soon?"

"Absolutely not. I'll be outside the door before you arrive."

Chrissie laughed her seasoned smoker's laugh at Sandra's enthusiasm. "I hope you'll still be this excited after late-night closing on Saturdays."

"Chrissie, I'm so grateful that you considered me – I know I left you in the lurch the last time. It certainly won't happen again."

"I know that, Sandra." Chrissie, to be fair, had never held a grudge against Sandra and had come up trumps now for her.

"Do you need me to call in for paperwork or anything? I'll be free all day so it's no problem."

"I'll sort everything out from this end. You just turn up at nine next Monday."

Sandra could sense that Chrissie was enjoying this benevolence and smiled.

"Thanks so much, Chrissie. I won't let you down. See you next Monday, nine sharp."

"And Sandra? I forgot to say you'll be starting as a second-year apprentice. If that's all right with you?"

Sandra was stunned. This was unbelievable. "Chrissie – I don't know what to say. Only thank you, really and truly."

"Monday," was all Chrissie said in response, her voice holding a hint of a smile before she hung up.

Sandra put the phone down and didn't know what way to turn. She was really going to make the most of this second chance, get her qualification and have a career that she could rely on to pay the bills and give Dylan everything he deserved.

Granted, it was only the first step and maybe she'd be down a little financially if she lost some of her social welfare entitlements on account of getting a job. But as her mother kept saying, "You have to speculate to accumulate" and on this occasion, the words of wisdom rang true.

Her first trip today would be to the offices of the Voluntary Budgeting Agency as Emily had advised. Paddy Lane, Emily's friend, would advise her on what to do next. First though, she would have to phone Maxine Daly to see what was available in the line of subsidised after-school care for Dylan. If she could manage without placing an additional burden on her parents, all the better.

But first – before all the other "firsts" – she had to phone her parents. For the first time in a long time, Sandra would be making a phone call with pride in her voice.

Chapter 29

Emily had been awake from the time the drug round started at the far end of the ward. Her first few days on 3A Surgical she'd wondered what the trundling noise was and why it had to start on the dot of six. Eventually, she'd found out that it was the night nurses pushing the medication trolley out of the Treatment Room for the first course of antibiotics and tablets of the day.

It was now almost ten o'clock and neither the neurosurgeon, Mr Creedon, nor the general surgeon, Dr Khan, had arrived to discharge her officially. The house officer had left her discharge letter by the bedside on Sunday evening and the ward sister had dropped in another letter that she was to give to the public health nurse when she came to visit. She didn't even need a prescription for medication so there was no need for any further delay.

Now that she was fairly mobile, Emily was impatient to leave St Angela's. Gertrude, the physio, had been in contact with the community physio who would visit Emily at home to continue her therapy so there was really no reason why she couldn't be in Rathmollin instead of taking up a valuable hospital bed.

The familiar sound of the small blind on the door indicated that someone was approaching and she looked up expectantly. It was Niall's head that peeked around the door instead of the consultant that she expected to see.

"Why the puss?" her brother teased when he saw the disappointed look on her face. "It's not like they're going to detain you indefinitely! Anyway, the doctor's rounds are starting up at the desk so you should be out of here soon."

"Brilliant. I've everything ready."

Niall looked in awe at the arrangement of bags, the CD player and all the other accoutrements that were piled neatly at the end of the bed. "Jesus, Em, you really got settled, to be fair to you. I'll start bringing these down and come back for you in a minute. Should I ask for a wheelchair, do you think?"

"You will not! I haven't been pulling and pushing down in physio to be carted out in a wheelchair. I'm well able to walk."

Niall put his hands up defensively. "Only asking!"

Emily laughed as her brother departed with an armful of bags and sat back down impatiently to await the consultants. It was great to be sitting there dressed in her own clothes for a change, especially seeing as they actually fitted her. The nutritional supplements that she'd forced herself to take three times a day had definitely helped her to regain the weight she'd lost during her stint in ICU and it felt normal to be wearing jeans and the fitted black Next top.

A soft knock preceded the next visitor.

"I can see I'll have trouble persuading you to stay, Emily," Mr Creedon smiled.

"That's why I got dressed so early. No stopping me." She was grinning from ear to ear at the thought of getting back to normal life.

"Can I persuade you to come back to the Out-patients in eight weeks for a check-up?"

"No problem." She bent her head to one side as the consultant examined her wound. The hair had grown back considerably in the short space of time.

"Very well healed – you should have no problems there. As soon as the hair grows fully, there won't be a trace of it." The neurosurgeon turned to wash his hands.

"Thanks for everything. I really mean it – my parents told me how bad I was coming in. I really appreciate all that everyone's done for me."

"Our pleasure. And the very best of luck to you in getting back to work. See you in the OPD."

One down, one to go. As soon as Dr Khan appeared, it would be home-time.

Niall arrived back just as the general surgeon appeared. Again, her wounds were checked, this time her abdominal and thigh ones. And again Emily thanked the team for their care and expertise. She'd already asked Niall to leave a crate of wine at the desk for the staff to enjoy.

"Just take it easy," said Dr Khan. "We'll send you an appointment for the OPD to have your liver function and blood count checked in one month. After that, you should be able to go back to work."

"Brilliant." Emily was thrilled even though her parents and Niall had prohibited any phone calls to the VBA during her hospital stay so she really didn't know where she stood with work. Gina, Orla and Paddy had all visited her on the ward but she really needed to contact her manager in head office to confirm that she would be going back and what effect her sick leave would have on her probation period.

By eleven o'clock Emily was installed in her father's car with Niall driving. It felt strange to be out. The world seemed very bright after being closeted indoors for so long but she was thrilled to be on the way.

Arriving in the door at home felt almost as weird as it had felt when she'd arrived home after her split with Richard. Her father was hovering around, unsure of what to do and her mother was bustling as if there were twenty people coming for lunch instead of just herself and Niall.

"Calm down, it's only me," Emily teased as Jacinta tried to top up her teacup for the third time.

"Yeah," Niall added. "What about making a fuss of *me* for a change. Another sausage, perhaps, Mother?"

"You'll get one when you do something to deserve it. Fill the kettle again and I'll see what I can do."

Tom didn't know his luck to be given a full Irish breakfast at twelve o'clock on a Monday. Emily, on Jacinta's insistence, had been made to order her home-coming meal. Knowing how much her father missed a fry-up since his bypass and bearing in mind the amount of complaining that Niall did about the dearth of Denny sausages in Australia, she'd decided that ordering an Irish breakfast would keep everyone happy.

"You'll have to lie down for a bit as soon as we have this eaten!" said Jacinta. "They did say you have to take it easy."

"No more bed though," Emily specified. "I'll rest in the sitting-room and watch a bit of telly. I have to watch out for clots."

It had been drummed into her by the nurses that even someone as young as herself was at risk of deep vein thrombosis after such prolonged surgery, even in the weeks following her hospital stay. Mobility and constant leg and foot exercises were the only answers and Emily was very conscious of avoiding such a set-back.

"All the same, you're not to overdo it." Jacinta was terrified of a relapse. Her job now, as she saw it, was to ensure a full recovery for her daughter. She'd spoken to the dietician about the fact that Emily had lost so much blood and was all geared up for a high-iron diet. Red meat had been well down on her agenda since Tom's bypass but it was now going to be re-introduced on a temporary basis until Emily's haemoglobin reached normal levels.

"Take the sympathy while it's going, love," Tom advised. "It won't last for long." He winked at her, remembering the weeks after his surgery when he'd been pampered to within an inch of his life.

"It's all right, Mam, I won't let Emily turn into an old softie the way Dad did." Niall grinned at his father who rolled his eyes at the memory.

"Sandra Coyne rang earlier to say that she'd drop down later to see you," Jacinta said now. "She said she'll do your hair again any day you want."

"Great – she did a brilliant job the last time."

Emily still hadn't had the opportunity to tell Sandra about Richard arriving on the ward and how much the make-over had helped her. It would be good to tell someone about it, considering that she still hadn't told her parents or Niall about the visit. Nor did she plan to, knowing how much it would upset them all. It was over now as far as she was concerned – she was just grateful to have been able to face him from a position of strength, albeit from a hospital bed.

"I met Rose down at the grocery and she told me in confidence that Sandra will be starting back with Chrissie Kennedy next week," said Jacinta. "She got a phone call this morning, Rose said."

"That's fantastic. She really wants to make a go of things again." Emily was delighted.

"What about the boyfriend?" Niall had heard enough about Paul Delaney to last him a lifetime and suspected that his parents and sister didn't know the half of it. Or Sandra, for that matter. Since he'd arrived back in the village, every second person seemed to be telling him something new about Paul.

Denis Harkin, a fellow Niall had been in school with, told him that this wasn't the first time Paul had been caught for drink-driving – hence his snappy departure from London.

Jack Rooney said he blamed himself for facilitating his

drinking by giving him his job back after he'd absconded to the pub on his lunch break and arrived back on the site drunk. At the time, Jack had thought he was doing Sandra a favour.

Another school-friend had told Niall that it was probably more than drink that had Paul so off his head the night of the accident – apparently he wasn't beyond pill-popping either when he had the money.

"He's definitely off the scene for good," Emily told her assembled family now. "Sandra told me so herself the day she came to visit."

"High time." Tom knew that Dan and Rose had been heartbroken over Sandra and Dylan since Paul Delaney had come back into their lives. "She might be able to pull herself together a bit now. Dan said she blamed herself for the accident, the poor girl."

Emily confirmed this. "It's hard to believe that she thought it was her fault. I'm delighted that Chrissie has a place for her."

The phone rang just then and Niall hopped up to answer it.

"This is the start of it," Jacinta predicted as Niall beckoned to Emily. "Don't exhaust yourself now."

"It's probably Gina – she said she'd ring today." She took the handset from Niall.

"Hello?" Her face creased into a frown at the unfamiliar voice on the other end. "Yes, it is," she confirmed.

Emily listened in delight as he lady at the other end introduced herself as Betty Lee, Personnel Officer with the Department of Health.

"We received your CV a number of months ago and I'd like to confirm whether you're still interested in a social work post with us. Or perhaps you're in other employment?"

"I do have a temporary job so I am still interested in a Community Social Work post." Emily knew she was winging it. There was always the possibility that Dr Khan mightn't agree to her taking in a job that would require so much driving.

"Well, that's why I'm ringing as opposed to writing with an interview date. We don't have a Community post to offer at the moment but there is a hospital social-work post vacant at St Angela's. We're advising all suitable candidates in case they'd like to attend for interview."

Emily nearly whooped with excitement. A hospital social work job would be much less physically demanding that a Community post. And the money would be miles better than what she was earning in the VBA.

"I'm very interested," she told Betty Lee emphatically.

She could see her mother's frown, her father's concerned expression and Niall's excited one. They all knew how badly she wanted to get back into social work, despite how much she enjoyed the work in the VBA.

"Excellent. I have your email address so I'll forward the appropriate form. As soon as I receive that, we can arrange an interview date over the next couple of weeks. Thank you for taking the call, Emily."

"Thank *you*. I'll return the form straight away."

Emily pressed the "off" button and faced the combined expressions of Tom, Jacinta and Niall, all of whom started to speak at the same time.

"Don't tell me you've agreed to an interview –" Jacinta was very firm on this.

"Fantastic!" As usual, Niall was enthusiastic.

"Make sure and tell them about the accident," Tom cautioned.

Emily started to laugh at the incongruity of it. "A social-work post at St Angela's – can you believe that? I'm only just out of the place!"

"Niall . . ."

"I know, Mam – the kettle." Obediently he made his way to the kitchen.

Jacinta was in a state of high anxiety over this latest development. "Would they let you do part-time for a while, do you think . . .?"

"I haven't even been for the interview yet," Emily reminded her. "I mightn't get it."

Her mother wasn't convinced. "She wouldn't have phoned if you weren't suitable."

"Definitely!" Niall shouted from the kitchen.

Tom, as always the voice of calm, interrupted. "We have plenty of time. Fill the form, Emily, and we'll see what happens."

"You're right – nothing is going to happen in the immediate sense. I sent the CV in January and look how long it's taken before they made contact."

Jacinta looked someway pacified at this. The idea of Emily starting a taxing new job terrified her but perhaps it would take a while to materialise.

"Tea's up," Niall announced.

Again, everyone spoke at once.

"Tea cosy," Jacinta instructed.

"Any chance of a biscuit?" Tom thought he might get away with it in the midst of the excitement.

"Raspberry jam . . .?" Emily held up a thick slice of buttered soda bread.

"It's a slave that's needed here!" Niall seemed to be falling in for all the jobs.

Emily grinned at him, contented. It was great to be home.

Chapter 30

It was one o'clock on Monday and Jennie was still sick after the shambles she'd made of the dinner dance on Saturday night. All day Sunday had been spent in bed, save for the occasional trips to the bathroom to be sick. Vincent, to his credit, had taken the children off to his mother's house and had even told Elsie that Jennie was knocked out with a migraine.

Although the vomiting and retching had stopped and she'd eaten some tea and toast for her breakfast, she still felt raw and miserable. And guilty about having spent all Sunday in bed with a hangover. She'd even missed the short run to the school with the kids this morning, making her feel more guilty than ever.

Despite her delicate stomach, she was determined to have a decent dinner ready for Tim and Lucy when they came in. She was now chopping onions and garlic for the home-made lasagne that they loved. She had two baguettes out as well to make garlic bread, their favourite.

Vincent, too, liked the lasagne and she planned to heat some later with a salad.

Knowing it was bizarre to be planning a dinner for her husband when she had a private investigator tailing him at this very moment, Jennie closed her eyes and let the enormity of what she'd done on Saturday night wash over her.

First of all, she should have known better than to start any evening with two glasses of champagne on an empty stomach. Inevitably, it had gone downhill from there. She could barely remember what she'd said to Carmel Williams in the Ladies' Room, she'd been so drunk. She recalled a long bout of crying and a long-winded tale about Vincent having no interest in her any more. What she couldn't pin down was whether she mentioned the fact that he was having an affair. That in itself made her feel like a fool to have been caught out like countless other hapless women, a stupid little wife minding the children when her husband was cavorting elsewhere. Carmel, she imagined, would never let that happen. Oh no, Carmel's advice, not unlike Noeleen Ferris's, was all about getting involved in Vincent's life and supporting him. And asking him for support in return instead of just holding it all in and being angry and upset.

It was real 1940s Housewife stuff and Jennie felt that the other woman was looking at her as if she was a bit stupid not to have copped on to this. Carmel herself knew every bar of what John was up to and was totally enmeshed in the day-to-day running of his business. Partners, she kept saying – marriage was about partnership.

Jennie didn't think that she'd mentioned Ron Green – or rather she hoped she hadn't. Vincent's business reputation and the effect that such allegations might have on it was now troubling her. It took very little, Vincent had often said, to tarnish a reputation and precious little could be done about it afterwards. Businesses had often failed on account of the loss of trust with colleagues and customers alike. Jennie kept telling herself that it wasn't so much her husband's reputation she was worried about – that would be his own responsibility if he'd been foolish enough to cheat on his wife and young children. It was the resultant backlash in terms of any loss of business that bothered her. What if they did end up in a separation situation? How would she keep the house and two children if Vincent didn't have the means to provide for them? Jennie had been praying non-stop since Sunday morning that Carmel Williams would be discreet about whatever she'd disclosed in her drunken state. She knew that Carmel would tell John – they were that sort of couple. It was what John would think of the information that she wondered about, considering that so much of his business was tied up with The Property Partners.

As for Jack Rooney, Jennie could barely allow her mind to even go there. She'd looked like a wretched hag when she'd looked at herself in the bathroom mirror on Sunday morning. Her face had been deathly pale, almost green, and her eye make-up was smudged down to her cheek-bones as if she was wearing a Halloween mask. The tell-tale rim of caked red wine ringed her lips and the smell of stale alcohol was disgusting, even to herself. The thought of herself making a pass at Jack, and in that condition, sickened her.

She didn't know if it was the chopped onions or the humiliation of throwing herself at Jack, a business associate of Vincent's as well as a family friend, that made her cry now. Tears came silently and she felt helpless and vulnerable. Before the weekend, she'd been all psyched up to hear what Ron Green had found out – now she was terrified. The thought of having to cope on her own petrified her, yet how could she continue to live a lie with a man who had no respect for her? Yes, she'd planned to fight, to make it difficult for his mistress to get him but all that seemed pathetic now that she'd made such a fool of herself.

She could imagine Jack and the Williamses commiserating with her but all the while thinking it was no wonder Vincent had an affair if this was what he'd been dealing with at home. Somehow, it had all flipped over. Jennie would now be the guilty one, a drunken, ungrateful wife who'd tried it on with Jack Rooney and God only knew who else.

She'd been putting it off all morning but now she knew it was time to contact Ron Green and find out exactly what she was dealing with. Who was this woman? Were there others? As soon as the lasagne was in the oven, she'd phone him. Then she'd go and pick Tim and Lucy up from school. The incongruity of fitting such a covert activity into normal family life wasn't lost on her. But needs must, she decided, continuing with her cooking.

It was almost two before she made her way to the

bedroom to retrieve her new mobile phone from its hiding-place in one of her lesser-used handbags in the dressing-room. She waited impatiently now as it booted up. Ron Green's number was the only one keyed into the "Contacts" section and even then she'd been cautious enough to label it Max so that Vincent would think it was Maxine's number if he ever did come across it.

She sat on the end of the bed with a cup of tea in hand for comfort and pressed the small green "call" button. What she was about to hear could alter the course of her life – if she let it. Or maybe Ron would need to look further afield. Either way, Jennie needed to know.

"Ron? This is Jennie Kelleher. I said I'd ring today?" If it was possible to feel pale inside, then that's what she felt at that moment. Pale and bleak and empty with her heart hammering and the surface of the tea rippling from the tremor in her hands.

"Good. You're keeping well?"

Pleasantries were the last thing she'd expected and she brushed the question aside impatiently. "Fine. Do you have anything for me?"

"Well, I'm not sure whether you'll consider it good news or not – but so far we've come up blank."

"You haven't seen anything?" Jennie was stunned. "What about the first evening? The meeting with the Arabs?" Jennie revised this, thinking he might consider it a racist comment. "Saudis, I mean."

"They met in the restaurant of the Mount Vernon, a hotel in the city. There was Vincent and Mr Ferris and three foreign gentlemen. Dinner lasted until 9.45 and he came straight home. Vincent had consommé, the chef's salad and mineral water. No dessert. Bob Ferris paid for the full meal on a business account they have with the hotel."

Jennie was shocked at the detail, even of what Vincent had eaten. The thought of someone watching or maybe even taking photos of her in a changing room or picking up the children made her feel sicker than she already was. What if Vincent put *her* under surveillance? And Ron was right – he had come straight home. Jennie remembered noting the time was ten past ten and the fact that he'd smelled of food that night. She'd checked his pockets the next morning and hadn't found any receipts or anything else extraordinary.

"Last Saturday morning? He left here sometime after seven and was back before eleven. He said he was going to the office."

"That's right. He arrived at the main offices of The Property Partners at 7.25 and left at 10.25. He was alone in the building all the time. He made three calls to Riyadh – as you know the 'weekend' in the Middle East is on Thursday and Friday so Saturday is the start of the week for business."

Jennie hadn't known that.

"He also did some computer work and sorted out files which he took home," Ron continued as if reading from a list. Jennie now remembered Vincent coming home with a stuffed briefcase on Saturday morning as she was leaving to have her hair and nails done in town.

"The bulk of the two weeks of surveillance have been taken up with work and business meetings, to be honest.

The only thing I need to confirm with you is your own birthday, Jennie."

"My birthday? The 21st of June. Why?"

"That makes sense then. The only extraordinary trip he made was to Midleton last Friday morning. He stopped into a craft jeweller and asked about a custom-made necklace. Platinum with black pearls. Our agent was waiting for assistance behind him. He said it would need to be ready in time for his wife's birthday on June 21st. He's arranged to pick it up on the 19th. I *can* tell you the cost . . ."

"No." Jennie cut him off abruptly, baffled now that there was nothing to know except that he planned to surprise her with pearls, which he knew she loved. "What else?"

"Let me see . . . he dropped the children off to school a few mornings . . . went to a funeral on the Thursday of the first week, a Mrs Macintyre in Ballincollig. She's the mother of the PA, Melissa."

Jennie remembered him talking about Melissa's mother being ill but hadn't realised she was dying until Vincent told her on the Tuesday evening. She'd felt bad at the time about not attending the funeral but she'd booked highlights with Denise and knew it could be a week or more before she got another appointment.

"There were drinks in a small hotel in Ballincollig after the funeral. Vincent, Bob and Noeleen had lunch there, three chicken salad wraps. They stayed for an hour and left with another man who we've found out is a Jack Rooney, also from Rathmollin. You may know him already?"

"Yes." The syllable came out as a croak and Jennie was at a loss as to what to say next.

"There are photos and audio tapes to back up everything I've told you plus a full list of Vincent's exact movements. You may like to go through them in more detail here at the office in case there are any names or even comments that you think are unusual."

"Did he say anything much about the children?" Jennie needed to hear more before she could decide whether to listen to the tapes or not. Listening in on conversations and phone calls seemed just too invasive – unless of course there was a need to.

"Just general things . . .okay . . . about the wormery that they're planning at the school – he told a few people about that. Lucy apparently said that they could make money by selling the worms to fishermen. He reckons that she'll make a great businesswoman. Some stuff about Tim as well. He misses the old baby-sitter apparently – Donna – because she used to let him try out her make-up. Vincent thinks he'll turn into Danny La Rue. He talks about them a lot actually."

"And me?"

"Also a lot. One of his clients, a Mrs Donnelly who has rental properties in Croatia, said the children had beautiful manners and Vincent said it was all down to you, considering he's away so much. Apparently she bumped into you recently."

Jennie remembered meeting Bernie Donnelly in Brown Thomas one Saturday and, for a change, Tim and Lucy had been on best behaviour. Normally, they'd be tugging at her coat saying they were bored but on that occasion she'd promised them a treat from Smyth's Toys if they stayed quiet while she picked out something from the Yves Saint Laurent counter. It was shocking, really, the way the most innocuous of situations could be interpreted.

"He spoke to Bob Ferris about your career as well and the fact that you gave it up to rear the children."

"He did?" Jennie was interested that Vincent thought of the secretarial course as a career when she'd only worked a few months at The Property Partners before their wedding.

"He's concerned that you might be regretting that decision now. That perhaps you might be frustrated at home all day when you have so much ability."

Jennie didn't know that Vincent noticed what she did all day.

"Apparently you were excellent at your job for the short while you worked at The Property Partners. Bob agreed, by the way."

Jennie hadn't thought that her brief sojourn as a secretary had made any impression on Bob at all. Vincent, obviously, had had other ideas about her that had nothing to do with her typing speeds. "Oh," was all she said in response to Ron.

"What else now . . ." Ron, continuing with his list, was clearly very professional in his approach and had left no stone unturned. He'd obviously managed to track Vincent very closely, to the point of tuning in to things like Jennie's previous working life. She hadn't told him that.

"Oh, yes. Seán Daly. He's a landscape gardener? Married to Maxine Daly, your friend, if I'm right?"

"Yes?" Jennie hoped he wasn't going to say something that she didn't need to hear.

"Apparently they have a holiday home in Co Kerry and one on the same road has come up for sale. Vincent asked Seán Daly to look into it as a holiday home for the family and it seems it's in pretty good order. He mentioned a surprise day trip to Kerry – it was to be yesterday, actually – to see what you thought. He asked Seán to mention nothing if he bumped into you."

If she'd felt sick already, Jennie thought she was going to revert to throwing up now. Vincent had been planning a day out in Kerry to look at a holiday home for them but had to postpone it because she was puking up her guts in the en suite all day after making a pass at Jack Rooney and telling the wife of a business associate that he was having an affair. And that was only what she remembered.

"How did you find out all this? Is his phone tapped?"

"Mobile phones, in particular, are notoriously easy to tune into with the right technology. And we had his number to hand, remember?"

"Of course." Jennie was brisk now, suddenly seeing the need to pull herself together.

"Now you *did* mention the possibility of foreign surveillance?" he said.

"I really don't think . . ." She wanted to put an end to this before it got any more out of control. Before *she* got any more out of control. She recalled Jack saying that it was all in her head.

"Absolutely no need, as far as I'm concerned," said Ron. "All of the foreign phone calls were business-related, both mobile and landline. There was nothing to suggest an affair abroad – no flowers being sent, for instance. No visitors from afar being put up in hotels as we sometimes see. I feel it would be an unnecessary waste of money at the present time."

"I see."

"Now of course, you can always contact us again if you need to go back to the drawing-board, so to speak. But for now . . ."

Jennie felt that he was giving her an out and she decided to take it. Ron Green was fully paid up for his two weeks' work.

"Yes, it's fine for now. Please destroy everything – I don't need to know any more."

"That can be done straight away. And best of luck, Mrs Kelleher."

"Thank you for everything." Just how much, he would probably never know.

Jenny looked at the small carriage clock on Vincent's side of the bed. Half two. She could smell the spicy aroma of the lasagne emanating for the kitchen below, a reminder of the family that she needed to keep together. She had twenty minutes before the school pick-up to start to put things right – to phone Carmel Williams and Jack with her apologies. First though, she had something more important to deal with.

She picked up the mobile again and brought up Ron Green's number. Very firmly, she placed her finger on the "delete" button.

Chapter 31

Before his father died, Jack remembered his telling him to "think laterally" about some problem he was having at work. At the time, the phrase had seemed too modern and snappy coming from an elderly man but he'd always recalled it as being good advice. Nothing was straightforward and there was always more than one way to tackle a problem.

Jack knew this from the days when his aunts had decided that it would be impossible for a man to bring up a small child on his own. And with a six-year-old boy on his hands and his wife dead, it would have been easy for Bill Rooney to agree.

He hadn't agreed, as it happened, and Jack had been dropped off in the timber lorry every morning outside the school and picked up again at half three. After that, he'd have his two sandwiches and a small flask of tea in the cab before setting off on the last round of deliveries with his father.

The routine had lasted all the way through primary school, with lessons done at the kitchen table after the supper and a bath for both of them before bedtime when the coal fire had warmed the back-boiler.

Secondary school was better again, with Jack now independent and the aunts finally off their backs, after years of waiting for a catastrophe that never happened. They meant well, on both sides of the family, but Bill had known that his wife would never have countenanced somebody other than him rearing her only child. She'd never specified what it was that she'd wanted, according to Bill. All the while she was sick she kept saying that Bill would know what to do when the time came.

"It gave me great confidence," Bill had once told Jack. "The fact that she trusted me. That she knew I'd do what was right."

"And you did, Dad," Jack had reminded him, just to make sure that he knew it. They rarely talked about Sheila. Instead, the two of them had just got on with the business of living, both conscious of not slipping up and being accused of not managing. Not that anyone ever spelled out what would happen if they didn't cope. Jack had always harboured ideas about being sent to a home but later he knew it would be more in the line of having to share a room with a horde of cousins while his father contributed money to support him. At home, he had his own room and everything he wanted. From an early age, he realised that it wouldn't benefit him to misbehave.

He didn't know why these kind of memories were coming back to him now – perhaps it was his father's concept of lateral thinking. He'd done it now, what he'd come to do at the planning office in the County Council. And while the plan wasn't as straightforward as his original idea, he knew he'd feel better about it.

The money he'd lose with the change of entrance for the Doyles' field development would be almost nothing. He'd effectively be giving away one of the houses for free but it was a small price to pay when he took into account the cost of Ina Harrington's cottage, demolition and the removal of the resulting waste material. The change of tack would slow things down a bit as well but that was nothing new these days. Sometimes the planning process took more than a year to get through – on this occasion it would be more like months.

The important step, of course, would be to talk to Dan Coyne. He didn't foresee too much in the line of an objection but all the same, it didn't do to be too confident about the response he might get. Best to tackle it head on when the time came, hopefully no later than a week or so.

First though, he needed to go back to the drawing-board – quite literally.

Chapter 32

The phone was answered on the third ring and despite being heartened after her brief conversation with Carmel Williams, Jennie was still unprepared for the sound of Jack's voice on the other end of the line.

"Jack." She cleared her throat and sat up straighter on the bed to make herself feel more in control. "It's Jennie Kelleher."

"Jennie." Jack was a man of few words and didn't sound either surprised or uncomfortable to hear from her.

She took a breath and continued as briskly as she could. To waver now would make him think of her as even more pathetic than she'd acted on Saturday night. "I wanted to apologise for the way I behaved on Saturday night. It was really good of you to make sure I got home – I'm just sorry I'd had so much to drink. I was appalling and I'm very ashamed of that." She paused for breath, hoping that he'd say something to make it easier but knowing that she didn't deserve it.

"We've all had too much to drink at one time or another, Jennie. Let's just forget about it, okay?"

Jack would probably have preferred if she hadn't rung at all but Jennie persisted. She needed to let him know that whatever it was she might have said, none of it had any basis in fact. It was, as she vaguely recalled Jack saying, all in her head.

"I really am sorry, Jack. I know it must have been terrible – I was talking complete nonsense . . ."

"Look, Jennie, don't feel that you have to explain. But for what it's worth, I think you're wrong about Vincent."

Jennie could have cried with relief at this opportunity to explain her mortifying fall from grace. "I *know* I was wrong, Jack. I don't know what came over me. I was just feeling a bit emotional – and the red wine didn't help. I can't believe I said . . ." She let the sentence trail off, not quite sure of what it was that she *had* said.

"I know it's hard with him being away so much but from what I hear from Vincent, he hates the travelling. He's often talked about it but I suppose he doesn't have much choice."

Jennie sighed, glad to be able to explain her irrational and frankly mad behaviour. "I just wish he'd cut back a bit, that's all. And I think it came to a head the other night. I'm mad about the kids but they can be a bit of a handful 24-7!"

There was the slightest of pauses before Jack spoke again and Jennie sensed that he was trying to tell her something. "It isn't easy, I suppose, to cut back once you get used to a certain lifestyle. I know *I'd* find it hard."

Jennie was shocked to hear Jack come out with this. Carmel Williams had said almost the same thing a few minutes earlier.

"It's not about lifestyle, Jack. It's just about getting the balance right, I suppose," she said firmly. Did everyone think it was *her* choice that Vincent worked around the clock? "I wanted to say I was sorry, that's all. And I'd hate Vincent to think that I didn't appreciate . . ." She needed to know whether he'd already discussed her antics with Vincent.

"Jennie, forget it. I mean it! I'd forgotten about it the next morning and so should you. Just buy me a drink the next time we're out."

She smiled a little, relieved that things might get back to normal without too much damage having been done. And somehow, she didn't think now that Jack would be telling Vincent about the shameful carry-on on Saturday night.

"Thanks, Jack. Bye." Another step forward, yet, despite her feelings of catharsis after the two phone calls, the idea that she was some way partially responsible for Vincent's hectic schedule had lodged at the back of her brain.

It was true that they led a fairly extravagant lifestyle in terms of holidays, and the issue of never having to scrimp or save was something that she'd taken for granted for a long time. The fact that they had a holiday home in Croatia that they rarely used was something that most people, her parents and sister included, would be astounded at if they knew about it. That Vincent had been looking into a home in Kerry was as a result of her mooting it in the first place – Maxine had convinced her of the benefits of an Irish holiday home being accessible and devoid of the language barrier that she found so stressful.

Was she a demanding and selfish person? With a pang, Jennie thought of her duplicity in garnering the money to pay Ron Green only a few weeks ago. It had barely occurred to her that Vincent would take any notice of her spending €1000 in a bridal wear shop. Why? Because she'd been doing it so long that she hardly noticed the price of things any more.

Maxine, she knew, was frequently shocked at the amount of money that Jennie spent on clothes. Not in a bad way – as far as Maxine was concerned it was Jennie's own business how much she spent. But she'd noticed all the same.

Now that she thought about it, Jennie realised that she didn't even know how much her weekly groceries cost. It was just a matter of whipping out one of her many cards and stabbing in the PIN. She had no idea how much a loaf of bread cost, never mind things like wine and the delicious cheeses that she and Vincent loved and took very much for granted.

She drove as far as the school in a daze, sharply aware of the fact that not everyone had been as lucky as she'd been over the past few years. She saw Maxine ordering Dylan Delaney and a horde of other children into a line, some just crossing the road and others for the march to Busy Kidz. *I bet Sandra Coyne could tell me the price of her weekly groceries.*

In the few minutes that it took for Tim and Lucy to disengage themselves from their friends and hurtle into the back of the SUV, Jennie resolved to pull herself together. Carmel had been right earlier on when she quoted a line from the *Forest Gump* movie. "*We only need so much money*," she'd reminded Jennie, "*All the rest is just for showing off.*"

Jennie thought now of the money she'd spent on the daftest of things – handbags upon handbags, redecorating spare bedrooms that were rarely slept in, changing the car because she'd grown to hate the upholstery. Even the children's clothes were bought in Brown Thomas, something that Maxine thought was outrageous. The fact that she hid so much about her daily lifestyle from her sister now stood out like a flashing beacon in Jennie's mind. Molly, if she knew the half of it, would be utterly horrified. The shopping for dresses that had never been worn. The marble hall tiles that had been imported on her insistence, that she'd hated on sight because they were darker in such a large expanse than she'd imagined they'd be. Now the said tiles were gracing the kitchen of Maxine and Seán's holiday home in Kerry.

Is this what Vincent was working for? A vicious circle where he chased his tail day and night to fund a lifestyle that she'd taken for granted this last ten years? So much so that she'd resented him for all the time that he wasn't there, yet still demanded the things his money bought?

Things had almost got out of hand and Jennie was overwhelmingly grateful to have been given this second chance. She'd almost ended their marriage. Vincent would never know about Ron Green and the lengths that she'd gone to in her spoilt and childish paranoia. Nor, hopefully, would he ever know the depths of her self-pity that led to an almost fatal mistake with Jack.

Just how near she'd come to losing everything washed over her like a flood of cold water. From now on it would be different. *She* would be different.

Chapter 33

"That's lovely now, Aggie," Sandra commented as she handed Aggie Lenihan her handbag and the paisley scarf that she'd been wearing as long as Sandra knew her. She'd almost completed her first week in Curly Locks and was in buoyant humour, even with Aggie.

Aggie patted her hair, pleased that Chrissie had touched up the roots so well. "Are you back for good? Only the last time you were gone like a bullet out of a gun."

Sandra could see Chrissie watching the interaction. "I am indeed, for good and all," she answered pleasantly. "Don't forget your shopping, Aggie." She picked up the two small Connolly's Master Butcher bags and handed them to her annoying neighbour, biting down the urge to clock her one. Aggie knew well that Sandra had re-started her apprenticeship – Sandra had told her over the fence two week ago – yet she had to try and rise her in front of Chrissie.

"Well now." Aggie had started her nodding again.

Sandra looked around, aware that Aggie didn't get excited over just anything. Jennie Kelleher, in pristine white jeans and a navy Lacoste sweater had just arrived in. As far as Sandra knew, Jennie wasn't a regular. In fact, Sandra would have gone as far as to say that she might never have set foot in Curly Locks before now.

"Many thanks, Aggie," Sandra said diplomatically, leading her customer towards the door. "I'll be with you in one moment, Jennie."

"No problem." Jennie smiled and nodded at Aggie, seemingly oblivious to her blatant stare. She waited as Aggie was escorted off the premises.

This was part of Sandra's job, greeting customers and manning the desk when Chrissie and Eileen, the other stylist, were busy as well as keeping the place in order, making tea and washing hair when it was needed.

"Hi, Jennie, how are you keeping?" Sandra greeted. A "good manner" was one of Chrissie's top priorities.

"Great, Sandra. Dylan told me you were back to work. How is it going?"

"Marvellous, Jennie, I'm thrilled. Now, what can I do for you?" Chrissie also stressed that there was a fine line between offering a pleasant greeting and being a "gas-bag".

"I know it's short notice but I thought I'd try anyway, in case you had a cancellation. Would you have any appointment for a wash and blow-dry this afternoon?"

It *was* short notice at one o'clock on a Friday but Chrissie had rules about such things. Never turn away a new customer unless it was completely unavoidable. If accommodated on their first outing, then many would return again by appointment.

"I'll have a word with Chrissie and see if she can fit you in. Take a seat there for a minute, Jennie." She indicated the black leather two-seater by the window.

Sandra felt a million dollars in her black trousers and the black wraparound cardigan that her mother had bought her as a gift for starting her new job. Her black faux-suede boots had a wedge heel that gave her a bit of height. Normally, she'd have felt intimidated by Jennie's glamour and poise but the last two weeks had given her an enormous boost.

"Around a quarter past two," Chrissie suggested. "You can wash and condition and I can take over as soon as I have your mother's rollers in." Rose had come in for a wash and set every Friday for as long as Sandra could remember.

"Would quarter past two suit? We'll have you out well before the bell goes." Sandra presumed that Jennie would be picking the kids up from school at three.

"That'd be great, Sandra – thanks a million. I'll see you later."

"Bye for now, Jennie." Sandra would have loved to have found out for definite if this was Jennie's first time in the salon but knew she daren't ask. Chrissie despised gossip. Somehow, though, she had imagined that Jennie would be more used to one of the big city salons than Curly Locks.

Taking the water spray from beneath the desk, Sandra made her way to the seat that Aggie Lenihan had vacated and started the cleaning process. After wiping down the seat, shelf and mirror, she washed the brushes and comb and placed them in the steriliser. Then she shook out the cape and removed the damp towels to the linen hamper before sweeping the area thoroughly. For good measure, she swept around the rest of the salon discreetly to save Chrissie and Eileen from standing in any hair that they'd just cut.

"Would you like another cuppa while you're waiting, Barbara?" Sandra had already given Barbara Carter two cups of coffee while she waited for her highlights to develop but she still had over thirty minutes to go.

"I'd love one. I was on nights last night so I had very little sleep. And I'm supposed to be going out tonight." Barbara was a paediatric nurse at St Angela's.

"Good and strong then!"

Sandra refilled the kettle and started to fold the bundle of fresh towels that she'd placed in the drier earlier. Most large salons sent out their towels to a laundry company but Curly Locks had its own industrial-type washer/dryer. Sandra was now effectively in charge of this and was responsible for the efficient turn-around of towels.

Minutes later, she handed Barbara her coffee.

"Enjoy it," she smiled.

Next, she would top up the shampoo and conditioner dispensers. They were more than half-full but Chrissie had no belief in idleness and felt that a junior should be able to see what was to be done *before* they were asked.

"Are you ready for lunch now, Sandra?" her boss murmured discreetly. "Barbara will be just ready for washing through when you come back."

"No problem." Sandra made her way into the small

kitchenette at the back of the salon and unwrapped her pitta bread sandwich. She brought her own lunch so that she could maintain the diet that she'd started a few weeks ago. A cup of tea and a diet yogurt would keep her going until later. She checked her phone to make sure that everything was okay with Dylan. It was habit more than anything but she liked to be available in case he needed her, considering she'd always been at home up to now.

A text from her mother told her that dinner would be ready for her and Dylan at half six. Since she'd started back to work, Rose had complained that she and Dan didn't see half as much of Dylan as they used to. Sandra knew that this was Rose's way of telling her that they were there any time. She replied to the text, delighted not to have to cook for one evening.

It was lovely to know that Rose and Dan would have looked after Dylan in the evenings for her but even nicer to know that she could do it on her own steam. Emily had been marvellous, telling her about the subsidised after-school service that Maxine Daly ran. Sandra had thought that Busy Kidz was a totally private facility and would have been mortified to ask about her prices.

Dylan was thrilled to join the others, especially his new and altogether more confident friend Rufus Crawford, for the homework club and the sandwich and juice. They were a "gang" now apparently – Dylan, Tim, Rex and Rufus. It also meant that he wasn't starving by the time that Sandra had the dinner on.

Emily had been brilliant about everything – she knew all the incentive schemes for mothers getting back to work and had even phoned Paddy in the VBA office about a few extra forms that had been really useful. Overall, Sandra's finances were pretty much the same as before, only this time she was actually going somewhere. There were her third and fourth year increases ahead of her, even though all that was a long way away.

She'd called to see Emily that first evening to tell her the good news and they'd even gone for a walk a few evenings since then, with Emily propped up between Sandra and a sturdy crutch. Her gait was much better now and she was determined to go to her interview today without the crutch. Sandra really hoped that she'd get the job and planned to phone her in the evening to see how the morning had gone for her. Emily had mentioned the accident in the application form and hoped it wouldn't go against her at the interview, especially if she arrived with a crutch. Despite what many organisations spouted about equal opportunities for disabled people, Emily said that the VBA had a stream of clients with disabilities who'd found it difficult to get work.

Sandra was watching the clock carefully as she sipped her tea and reflected on the changes in her life. Chrissie was a stickler for time and insisted on taking proper breaks in the morning and afternoon. It was no good rushing around and not eating properly, she reasoned, as it only ended up with people getting ratty by mid-afternoon.

By two o'clock, she was back on the floor washing out Barbara's highlights. Two cuts followed, so that meant tea and tidying up for Sandra, then there was Rose and Jennie for their appointments.

"Don't forget the dinner this evening," Rose reminded her. "Dad and I have something to chat to you about." She winked to let her daughter know it wasn't anything serious and left smiling.

Sandra wondered if they were going to take a well-earned holiday at last.

By six o'clock, Sandra's ankles felt as swollen as they had when she was pregnant with Dylan and she made a mental note to start putting money by for a pair of MBT's. Barbara Carter had mentioned earlier to Chrissie that all the nurses wore them now on account of standing so much at work.

"You can get going, Sandra," Chrissie instructed as the Angelus struck. "I'll just give Eileen a quick blow-dry."

"Off out tonight?" Sandra asked her.

Eileen was in her fifties and worked part-time in Curly Locks, mainly on Friday and Saturday when the salon was at its busiest.

"My daughter's 21st. We're having a meal first and then a few drinks in the hotel. The young gang can head off into town after that."

"Well, enjoy it," said Sandra. "And I'll see you both in the morning."

Staff relations were very important in Chrissie's book.

"So, what's the big news?"

Sandra and Dylan were tucking into roast pork and apple sauce.

Dan put down his knife and fork and looked at Rose for confirmation. "Now it's not exactly news – yet. So don't get too excited."

"More of a proposal," Rose added. "Your father's right. Better not to get too carried away in case it doesn't work out."

"In case *what* doesn't work out?" Sandra was impatient now and baffled as to what this proposal could be. They were acting a bit cautious and she hoped it had nothing to do with Paul.

"What, Gran?" Dylan too was bursting to know what this news was.

"We had an offer today," Dan started.

"Jack Rooney called."

This was typical of how her parents discussed something big and Sandra's head swivelled from one to the other.

"Go on."

"He asked about the garden," her father explained. He was taking his time and Sandra knew it was useless to rush it. "You know he was going to buy Ina's cottage and knock it? Well, now he thinks it'd be better to leave the cottage where it is and go straight in through our side garden."

"He wants to buy half the garden?"

Sandra supposed that it'd be cheaper and easier than buying a house to knock it down. And the side garden, almost as wide as the narrow site that Harmony Cottage stood on, was right next to the cottage so the entrance to the housing estate would really only be moving a few yards.

"Not buying it exactly," Rose chimed in. She looked at Dan again.

"He wants it for free?" This was unlike the Jack that Sandra knew.

"No, here's the thing," said Dan. "I think you might have mentioned to him that you'd be interested in the Affordable Housing scheme or something. Well, Jack thinks we might be able to come to some agreement."

"How do you mean?" Sandra didn't know where all this was going and wondered if her parents might have to give up their house in exchange for a new one in the estate. Maybe he intended to knock down their house.

"Instead of paying us for the land," Dan continued, "he'd give us one of the houses at cost price. It'd be a three-bedroomed bungalow. With the price of the garden out of it, the difference would be very small if you put it over twenty-five or thirty years."

"Like a mortgage?" Sandra stared from Rose to Dan and back again. Dylan was the quietest she'd ever seen him. Sandra couldn't believe that her parents were thinking of taking on a mortgage at their age.

"It'd be a great opportunity, love. I rang the bank to see what the repayments would be. I have it all written down." Rose produced a sheet of paper, not unlike her weekly shopping list. She slid it over to her daughter and suddenly Sandra started to see what they were on about. It would be *her* mortgage, not theirs.

"See, that's how much it'd be every week with a twenty-five year mortgage. And that's over thirty years." Sandra's eyes blurred as she looked at the figures. Even the twenty-five year figures were manageable.

"It'd be easier over thirty years and you could increase the payments after a while when you're qualified." Dan's faith in her was unstinting, as ever.

"But the garden. What about the clothes-line? And the rockery?"

"For goodness sake, girl, don't let the clothes-line stop you! And your father is sick of having to cut all that grass. We were talking about buying a ride-on mower last week."

"We'd be delighted to get rid of some of it, to be honest. We have more than enough space out the back. Your mother's right – all the gardening *is* getting a bit much. It's nearly a full day every week in the summer to keep on top of it."

"It'd be brill not to have Mrs Lenihan complaining. And no Sparky barking all night!" Dylan looked ecstatic at the thought of it and the others burst out laughing.

"Well, it's true," he argued defensively. Then he too started to giggle.

"What do you think, Sandra?" Rose was clearly excited about it. "He showed us the plans, love. We said we'd think it over for the weekend and tell him on Monday. He'd have to put it in for planning permission but he's already discussed it with the council and they can't see a problem with the entrance if we're happy to sell the land."

"It sounds good." Sandra was almost scared to think it would be possible. "And did the bank think I'd be able to get a mortgage?"

"You're a working girl now, don't forget. And we'd be able to help with the deposit."

"No way! You'd be doing enough. I have a little bit in the Credit Union for an emergency. And I suppose this could be classed as one."

"So what do we think? Dylan?" Dan always liked to round things up properly.

"Cool! No more Sparky Lenihan."

"Rose?" Dan asked, even though he already knew his wife's decision.

"Check!" Rose called out, as if she was at her weekly Bingo game.

"Sandra?" Dan looked at his daughter and grinned.

Sandra just burst into tears.

Chapter 34

By Monday morning, Emily was like a hen on a hot griddle.

"What are you doing up?" Her mother still thought she should behave like a genuine invalid and stay in bed properly until eleven or twelve at the very least.

"They might ring – I don't want to be half dopey if they do."

"They're hardly going to phone you at half seven! Here, drink this." Jacinta handed her the cup of tea that she'd just poured out for herself. "Go and put on your dressing-gown first, though. You'll catch a cold after being in the hospital so long."

Emily wandered back down to her bedroom, cup in hand. The interview panel had said that she would receive a phone call on Monday morning to say whether she'd got the job or not. They were anxious to fill it as soon as possible as the permanent person had gone out on maternity leave but had now resigned her post altogether.

Emily had asked what "as soon as possible" meant and explained that it would be another two weeks before she'd be allowed back to work.

"That sounds reasonable." The large Head of Recruitment interviewer had nodded thoughtfully. Emily couldn't remember his name now but he'd sounded encouraging enough.

She imagined it would be at least nine, if not later, before the Personnel Officer rang but she'd been awake half the night thinking about it and saw no point in dawdling in the bed all morning fretting. A walk might be the thing, once she'd had her breakfast. It would punch in some time until nine, especially as she might miss her usual treks around the village on account of sitting by the phone all day. They mightn't phone until five.

Since she'd come home, her mobility had come on in leaps and bounds. She no longer needed the stick around the house but brought it on the longer walks in case she got tired. Having gone all the way to Cork for her interview yesterday without it, she now wondered if she should leave it behind this morning.

"I can't wait to see what your iron level is like when you get the blood taken. I'm sure it must be at least 10 at this stage." Jacinta pushed a small plate containing two sausages and a fried egg towards Emily. Her iron tablet and glass of orange juice was beside it. Jacinta was on a personal mission to have Emily's haemoglobin up to at least 12 by the time she went for her Out-patient appointment.

"Mam, it'll be like Uncle Mike's if you're not careful!"

Tom's brother suffered from a disorder called

Haemochromatosis where his haemoglobin level was so high that he actually had to have blood *taken* from him every two months.

"I was thinking that the night you got knocked down, you know. If you'd inherited that gene you mightn't have been in so much trouble." Secretly, Jacinta was still worried about all the blood transfusions that her daughter had received although she'd never expressed this to Emily.

"I don't need a Haemochromatosis gene if you're going to be stuffing me with steak and baked beans all day," Emily laughed. She had more energy now and was sleeping well so she supposed her haemoglobin must be rising towards normal levels.

By eight o'clock, she was dressed in jeans and her green puffa jacket. The last few times they'd gone out walking in the evening, Sandra had admired Emily's slim figure in the bulky jacket.

"If I wore one of those I'd be like an immersion tank in a lagging-jacket!"

Emily had giggled at her turn of phrase but reminded her that her diet was starting to show great effects.

Walking as briskly as she could without her stick, Emily left the house, even more intent on getting her mobility back now that there was a possibility of a new job with more money on the horizon. She'd accepted that Harmony Cottage was no longer an option but at least she'd be able to start saving again. All the economists on RTE seemed to be predicting a slump in house prices – maybe it would happen just when she had a deposit saved again and she'd be able to snap up a cheap house, she thought wishfully.

The school next door was in repose as she passed and Emily wondered now if she could go in and look at the playground and the new site for the herb garden that her mother kept talking about. Jacinta had been heavily involved in the Parents' Council when her own two were in primary school and had never really given it up. She still baked for the Sale of Work and manned the stalls for the annual jumble sale and Christmas concert.

Pushing aside the stile gate that had been there for as long as she could remember, she made her way through and up along the yard. The herb garden was supposed to be in the same place as the old wire-covered fish-pond had been.

Emily grinned. Her very first day at school had been marred by Jennie and Sandra picking a hole in the protective chicken wire so that they could "paddle". Emily and Jack Rooney, the two remaining Baby Infants, had taken off their socks and shoes and joined in only to be caught by the headmaster and lined up against the *cófra*, the large mahogany cupboard that housed everything from catechism books to new boxes of chalk and plasticine. One slap on their outstretched hands and the four culprits had been released back to their desks. The lunch-break had been over for everyone until the hole in the netting had been repaired. After Christmas, they'd returned from their holidays to find the small pond drained and the three fish gone for good. Health and Safety regulations weren't even in existence then, Emily imagined.

Things had changed a lot for all four of them since that first day in Baby Infants.

Of all of them, Jennie seemed to have fallen on her feet. Emily remembered bumping into her one Friday afternoon in Cork and Jennie had been laden down with bags – shiny expensive ones that were far from Emily's reach now that she was earning a pittance. Jennie had looked so together – the picture of a successful wife and mother in comparison to Emily with her Next suit and her hair pulled back into a simple pony-tail. Jennie's husband was some big-wig in property, often appearing in the Property Section of *The Examiner* in connection with the acquisition of large parcels of development land both at home and abroad. No wonder Jennie could afford to be laden down with glossy shopping bags despite the fact that she hadn't worked since she'd become engaged to Vincent.

As far as Emily could remember, the receptionist's job at The Property People was the only job that Jennie had ever had, one she'd snapped up almost as soon as she'd finished the secretarial course at Cork Commercial College. Things had always seemed to work out for Jennie, even in secondary school where she'd got a brilliant Leaving Cert with very little in the line of hard work. The two of them had been friendly during their years at the Little Flower Convent but had lost touch almost as soon as they'd completed their exams. According to Sandra, Jennie was much nicer than the aloof front she presented would suggest and was a great mother to Tim and Lucy who were in the same class as Dylan.

Sandra, like Emily, had had her own ups and downs over the years but unlike Emily, she had Dylan to show for it. Sandra was a great mother to him, firm and sensible and a bit of crack as well. It was just a shame that it was Paul Delaney that she'd fallen for at the time instead of some decent fellow who might have been a good father to Dylan. Still, it seemed to be coming right for her now. Her job was important to her, a means of independence and a level of security for herself and Dylan.

Jack, it seemed to Emily, was still as tough as ever. As a small boy he'd been totally independent, with his own opinions on everything. He never said much but always did his own thing. When they'd started school first, Jack couldn't understand why he wasn't allowed to eat his sandwiches when he was hungry instead of having to wait for everyone else and had spent a few weeks persisting until the teacher had to ask the headmaster to have a word with his father.

Not much had changed, Emily thought wryly, thinking of the snappy shouting match that she'd overheard him having on the phone in the café on Academy Street ages ago. She hadn't recognised him then, until he'd arrived to visit her in hospital. She still didn't know why he came in – probably to warn her off from putting in an objection to knocking Harmony Cottage, thanks to Aggie Lenihan broadcasting that she'd wanted to buy it.

Emily was still mortified about how wobbly she'd been during the few minutes he'd been in the hospital room – the after-effects of Richard probably. She hated him thinking that she was some wimpy little thing that he could walk over but she had neither the money nor the energy to get into a battle with him over the cottage.

Something else would come up, as her father kept telling her.

She looked at her watch now. It was already quarter past eight with all her dawdling, and the full length of the village and back would probably take until nine at the rate she was going. Time to buck up.

Chapter 35

Emily didn't bother jumping the third time the phone rang. The first time, it had been Aggie Lenihan to say that there was something in *The Examiner* about a fellow up on a drunk-driving charge and grievous bodily harm of two people. She was wondering if it was Paul Delaney and if Jacinta or Tom knew anything. Then Sandra had rung to say that she was on her half-day and could she call over for a chat. She had something to tell Emily that might be of interest to her. Emily presumed that it must be about Paul and told Sandra not to worry, they'd chat properly when she called.

This time, Jacinta answered the phone. "It's for you, Emily." She frowned and whispered "A man!" behind her hand. Emily had told her the Personnel Officer was a woman.

"Emily – Dermot here from The Property People."

Emily was completely flummoxed. The last person she expected to hear from was the expansive Dermot – talk about a blast from the past. "Hello, Dermot."

"I think I mentioned that I'd come back to you if there were any further developments with Harmony Cottage. The one-bed in Rathmollin?"

"That's right." Emily was cautious, having been bitten once before by high hopes.

"You were very interested at the time, as I recall. Well, it's come on the market again so I thought I should let you know. Same price tag, by the way."

Emily had to admire Dermot's pizzazz – it was as if he was doing her a personal favour by letting her know that the cottage was for sale again.

"I'm not sure – I'd have to think about it . . ." She wasn't being cagey. If she got the job, then maybe it would be possible. If not, she'd have to look at things very carefully. She'd been on sick pay since the accident so her saving ability had diminished considerably and she'd still have a few weeks to go before she was earning properly again. Plus, she still wasn't certain about her probation period with the VBA.

"That's no problem – I just wanted to put you in the picture from the outset."

"Thank you for that, Dermot. What happened to the other offer, by the way?" She was curious to know why Jack Rooney had dropped the idea of knocking the cottage.

"The developer's plan changed and he no longer needed the cottage. It may be a stroke of luck from your perspective." Fair play to Dermot – he was well able to chase his commission. As for Jack, wouldn't it be great to be like him with enough money to chop and change at random, she thought with a small hint of bitterness. But

Dermot was right, maybe it would turn out to be a stroke of luck.

"Well, thanks for the call, Dermot. I'll give you a ring when I have time to think about it."

She could just visualise his cheesy face as he rang off. "You have my card, Emily."

All the while she'd been on the phone, Tom and Jacinta had been watching her closely.

Emily put up her hand before either of them had a chance to speak. "We'll have to see will I get the job first," she reminded them, already anticipating their excitement.

"I just want to say, Emily," her father began seriously, "there's money there and this time we're going to use it to help you with the house. We should have the last time."

"It mightn't have made a difference, Dad," she reassured him, "Jack Rooney would probably have kept pushing it up and up."

"We should have tried," Jacinta insisted. "The money wouldn't have been much good to us if you were gone." It was the first time that any of them had voiced the fact that Emily really could have died.

"This time," Tom promised, "we'll go for it if we get the chance."

"Thanks. But we'll wait and see about the job first, okay?" Emily was adamant about not buying something that she couldn't afford to pay for into the future.

"I suppose we might as well make more tea." Jacinta was impatient now and would burst a blood-vessel if they didn't hear news of the job soon.

Nothing had happened by the time Sandra arrived

with a large carrot cake for the Gordons and a bar of Turkish Delight for herself.

"Eileen at work is an expert on weight loss and she says Turkish Delight is the best thing for a treat – that and dark chocolate. And it'll stop me delving into the carrot cake."

"Go on into the sitting room, you two, and I'll bring in the tea." Jacinta knew that Sandra had something to tell Emily, probably a repeat of what Aggie had deduced about Paul Delaney.

"Only one slice of carrot cake for Emily, Jacinta," Sandra warned. "Temptation is an awful thing."

"Being sick is the best excuse ever for stuffing yourself," Emily commented. She'd already gained half a stone since getting out of the hospital.

"I've been tempted since the day I was born," Sandra sighed. She flung herself back into one of the squishy upholstered armchairs and yawned. "Sorry. Chrissie seems to be of the opinion that if I stay up all night doing the physiology of hair follicles I'll stay out of trouble. Chance would be a fine thing!"

"I thought we were going to remain positive about men and not get bitter and twisted over our bad experiences?" Emily grinned as she said this and for once she didn't actually feel like raining a silent curse on Richard's head. It was all in the past now, as far as she was concerned.

"I suppose." Sandra looked doubtful but then brightened up and asked Emily if she'd heard anything about the job yet. Emily had told her they were to make contact on Monday.

"Nothing yet. It'll probably be five o'clock before they phone. Anyway, what about this news of yours? Good or bad?"

The last thing Emily wanted to hear about was Paul Delaney but she could appreciate that Sandra needed to get it off her chest.

"Good – I think. If it all goes ahead, that is."

"Actually, I might have news too but I'll tell you that in a minute. Tell me yours first, though."

Sandra waited a moment as Jacinta arrived in with the tea-tray. Emily reached for the carrot cake straight away, to the delight of her mother who thought that gaining weight in anticipation of a serious accident was now the way to go. Sandra reached for her bar of Turkish Delight.

"Don't lose too much weight now, Sandra," Jacinta cautioned. "Emily had very little in the line of resources when she got sick."

Sandra grinned and rolled her eyes. Emily knew that her friend was determined to lose her two stone, regardless of any impending illnesses that she might require the extra "resources" for. As soon as Jacinta had left the room, she bit into her low-fat bar.

"Now, you're not going to believe this," she said then, her mouth full "but I might actually be getting my own house at last!"

"You applied to the council?"

Sandra had been talking about the affordable housing scheme in which she and the council would buy equal parts in a new house. Down the line, when she'd paid for her own half, she could then buy the other half from the council and achieve full ownership. To date, it had only been a dream.

"No actually! You're not going to believe how it came about." Her eyes were shining, something that Emily hadn't seen in Sandra since their schooldays.

"Go on, will you," Emily urged. Whatever it was, Sandra was ecstatic about it.

"Friday morning Jack called in to Mam and Dad with a proposal about the new estate he's building in Doyles' field."

Emily couldn't help thinking that Jack Rooney seemed to be stuck in everything these days.

"Anyway, you know he was going to make the entrance where Ina's cottage was – you'll love this, Emily – well, now he's going to leave the cottage where it is and make the entrance through Mam and Dad's side garden."

"What?" Now she knew why the cottage was no longer needed for Jack's grand plan.

"I know – it's mad. The entrance will be in between their house and the cottage now. But instead of paying them for the garden he's going to give us a house at cost price. I'm going to get a mortgage, Emily!"

"Oh my God, Sandra, that's fantastic!" Emily jumped up from the recliner to give her friend a hug. To anyone else, the idea of having a mortgage was considered one of life's inevitable burdens but to Sandra, who'd never imagined a chance at buying a house the straightforward way, it was a gift.

"It won't be much, Emily. Mam has it all figured out but I'll have to go to the bank on my day off to find out the exact details. I made an appointment this morning."

"Sandra, that's unreal. What kind of a house will it be, do you know?" Emily knew that what Sandra really wanted was a garden for Dylan to play in with his friends instead of being out on the road all the time.

"A three-bedroomed bungalow. They all have stonework on the front and a garden at the back with a block-built wall. Dylan's delighted – he's looking for a dog already."

"That's brilliant." Emily was genuinely delighted for Sandra and Dylan. She just hoped that Paul wouldn't arrive back into their lives now when everything was starting to go their way. "And you'll get mortgage relief now that you're working."

"That's the thing, Emily – I haven't a clue about all this. I always thought I'd be doing it through the council so I never looked into a proper mortgage."

"Well, *I* have," Emily reminded her. "I have all the forms and everything. I'll get them in a minute and explain it to you so at least you won't be boggled when you go to the bank."

"Thanks, Emily. I was dying to tell you over the weekend but I wasn't sure until I rang Jack this morning. He's sending someone down to measure out the garden later in the week to make sure that Mam and Dad have enough room to get around the back of the house. He'll be building a new wall and gate for them as well."

Sandra was talking about Jack Rooney as if he was the tooth fairy instead of an astute property developer who'd obviously spotted a cheaper way of going about his business than demolishing a cottage that he'd have to buy first. And while she was thrilled that his new plan would benefit Sandra and Dylan, she wasn't naïve enough to think that he'd done all this out of the goodness of his heart.

Sandra, though, couldn't see beyond him for benevolence. "He's going to drop over tonight with the actual plans of the house. Imagine. Me looking at house plans!"

"It'll be so exciting. You'll be in it before you know it at the speed houses go up these days. And everyone says Jack is great at what he does." Emily had to be fair in this regard. Whatever she thought of his *modus operandi*, everyone that spoke about him said the quality of Jack's work was second to none, with Rathmollin Woods a case in point. Sandra would have a wonderful home.

"I know – even Paul used to say that. I was thinking of going over to the show-house in Sycamore Drive at the weekend to see what kind of kitchens and bathrooms he puts in. Will you come?"

Sycamore Drive was just opposite Harmony Cottage and the Coynes' house and seemed to be finished apart from a few houses at the front facing the road. The first phase, a crescent of dormer bungalows, had been too far out of Emily's reach when she'd picked up the brochures in The Property People's office in the early days of her house-hunting. Nonetheless, it would be interesting to see if the houses lived up to the impressive specifications described in the promotional material that she'd studied.

"I'd love to see them. And you might get ideas for colour schemes and things for your own house. Show-houses are always brilliant for that."

"Emily, I've never been in a show-house in my life. It

was never on the cards up to now." This had opened up a whole new world to Sandra.

"I've been in buckets of them," Emily laughed. "Before we bought the house in Dublin, we'd been looking at show-houses for a year! And since I came home, I've looked at nearly every one in Cork."

"I wonder will Ina's cottage come back on the market now?" Sandra speculated.

"Dermot, your man from The Property People, rang me this morning," Emily filled her in. "It's back on the market at the same price but I'm not sure if I'd be able to afford it now. With being out of work and everything."

"But if you got the new job? Would you be able to afford it then?" Sandra, now that she had a chance of getting on the property ladder, really understood Emily's need to have her own home too.

"*If* I got the job, maybe. Probably. But it's a big if – they'd have contacted me straight away if they had good news, I imagine."

"Look, wait and see. The fact that they contacted you in the first place is positive."

"That was before they knew I was a crock," she reminded Sandra. "Anyway, we'll see." There was no point in speculating until she knew for definite. And today was one of the most important days of Sandra's life, not to be marred with Emily's concerns. "Will I go up and get the things about life assurance and we can go through them? I'm telling you, I'm an expert!"

"Go on then!" Sandra was like a child on Christmas morning.

Emily grinned and made her way into the hall but was halted by the phone. Sandra picked up the handset from where Jacinta had left it on the coffee table and handed it silently to Emily, crossing the fingers of her other hand as she did so. Emily rolled her eyes dubiously as she answered it. It was probably Niall wondering what time the dinner was at.

"Yes, this is Emily."

Sandra was wide-eyed in anticipation beside her.

"Yes, of course I would." Emily's face still had its cautious expression until she heard what the caller had to say. "That would be great."

Sandra was on the edge of her chair now and Jacinta had appeared quietly at the door, having heard the phone ringing in the kitchen. Her eyebrows were nearly in her hairline and Sandra could only shrug in answer.

"Well, thanks very much, I'm delighted. Two weeks would be perfect."

Jacinta's hands were at her throat but she looked as if she were terrified to get excited until she had full confirmation from Emily. She and Sandra listened silently as the telephone conversation came to a conclusion.

"The first it is then," Emily was saying. "Thanks so much for the call. Bye for now."

She'd hardly pressed the "End" button on the handset before the whoops of delight started from Sandra and Jacinta.

Tom, appearing at the door, was grinning from ear to ear. "I suppose you'll be wanting the kettle on?" he said.

Emily could see the glint of tears in his eyes as he

disappeared again. To see her getting back on her feet again mattered a lot to her father.

"The first – that's not *even* two weeks away." Jacinta was in a flutter now that it looked like her daughter was going to be gone from under her wing again so suddenly.

"I'll have to get my head back in order pronto." Emily was brisk at the thought of the challenges ahead and although the VBA had been a fantastic place to work, what she really loved was the stimulation of a proper social-work environment. She'd have to give them notice, for a start.

"Your head *is* in order," Sandra told her vehemently. "You've been advising me for weeks now. You'll have no bother getting back into it. And we can do more walking in the evenings to get you going properly, if that'll help."

"You're right. I'll have to be in better shape, even for walking up and down the corridors in St Angela's."

Jacinta looked thoughtful. "Maybe a few more sessions of physio . . ."

"No way, Mam." Emily had had enough of the professionals. "I'll have Sandra with me and we can go a bit further every night. I'm nearly there anyway."

"What about the house? Do you think you'll go for it?" Sandra wanted the best for Emily, especially as it was Paul who'd put such a spanner in the works with the accident.

Emily was just about to open her mouth when Jacinta cut in.

"I'll tell you what I've been thinking about the house. Pick up that phone this minute and explain to that Dermot about the accident. Tell him your circumstances have changed but you can offer him €10,000 less than the asking price. If they're so mad for a sale after being held up this long they might just take it."

Jacinta had her determined face on. Sandra's eyes were as round as saucers.

"They'd never . . ."

"I think they might, Emily." Tom had just arrived back with a laden tea tray. "By all accounts, that nephew of Ina's is only looking for drinking money. He never did a hand's turn for herself or Minnie when they were alive." Emily's father had strong principles about looking after elderly relatives and was disgusted at what he'd been hearing about Eamonn Harrington.

Emily looked around, unsure as to what to do.

"They're right," Sandra urged. "Make the offer – it's up to them whether they accept it or not."

"You can tell him you'll have the deposit down this evening if the offer is accepted," Tom stressed.

Emily's heart started to beat a little faster as she reached for the phone again. She knew Dermot's number off by heart at this stage.

"Hello Dermot." She tried to match the auctioneer's up-beat manner. "Emily Gordon here. Just getting back to you about Harmony Cottage." As her mother had instructed, she explained the way her circumstances had been reduced on account of the accident but that she was still interested in the cottage, even though the asking price was now a little beyond her means. Her deposit, though, was ready and waiting, she told him. And a quick sale was what she wanted – she was too unwell for protracted bargaining at this point.

"There, it's done now." She threw the phone down and faced her assembled audience. "He says he'll put it to the vendor straight away. They want the sale completed as quickly as possible too."

"I'll bet," Tom said cynically. He started to pour the tea as Emily filled her parents in about Sandra's good news.

"Fair play to Jack," Jacinta commended, biting into her second slice of carrot cake of the day. "It's a great opportunity for you, Sandra."

"It's been great all round. Now, hopefully, Emily will be sorted as well."

"Don't get too excited," Emily warned. "The offer mightn't be accepted at all." She'd been down this road before with Harmony Cottage and it had ended in disappointment.

"I have a really good feeling about this, Emily. And I'm not leaving here until Dermot pones back." Sandra settled herself on the sofa, fully determined that Emily's fortunes would soon match her own.

Chapter 36

Time, Jennie realised, was what measured out people's lives into good bits and bad bits. The past month had taught her that, as had the months preceding it when she'd been able to think of nothing but herself. Now, in the wake of Ron Green's revelations about Vincent's non-existent affair and the knowledge that she, in part, might be to blame for her husband's relentless work schedule, Jennie's priorities had changed.

In the way that other women were accused of "letting themselves go" in a physical sense, Jennie was aware that she'd let herself go intellectually. For her, it wasn't about getting into a rut, gaining weight and slopping around in a tracksuit with straggly hair that needed the roots touched up. In her case, it was about losing sight of the important things in life, neglecting her relationship with Vincent by blaming everything on his work schedule. She'd lost interest in him as a person, never listening to what it was that worried him or what made him excited any more. She'd abdicated all responsibility for their financial affairs too and simply expected the money to be there for whatever it was that she wanted next. Not *needed* – wanted.

She didn't like spending time at their property in Croatia because it was too much hard work for her, yet she'd been insistent on them keeping it – just in case. She didn't even know how much it cost!

The last four weeks had been a revelation. She'd sorted out the cards in her wallet, shocked that she'd simply been flashing them without a thought for where the money came from.

It was like waking up from a dream and seeing an entirely different person. Instead of sitting down with Vincent to work out a different way of life, she'd compensated by excessive spending, inadvertently fuelling their problems even further. To her shame, it had taken Jack Rooney to tell her that.

Most of the cards were gone from her wallet now, secreted under the expensive underwear in their bedroom. Instead, she'd started to take out cash from the machine like everyone else, needing to know how much things cost. The last few weeks in the supermarket, she'd been shocked at the price differences in similar items and had now started to choose certain products instead of just flinging things in at random. At last, she actually knew what her grocery shop cost and, better still, that cost had been lower today than it had been the last two Thursdays. Growing up was what she was doing now.

The best thing about her new-found frugality was the fact that she probably wouldn't have to buy clothes for at least three years. There were things in the closet of the spare room that she'd never actually tried on, never mind worn. Well, they were going to be worn from here on in, she'd decided. Her Brown Thomas days were over if it meant that Vincent felt secure in cutting back on work a little.

She hadn't talked to him about her plans yet, terrified that he'd ask what had brought all this on. As well as that, Jennie needed to know that she'd be able to keep her side of the bargain, that she'd be able to curtail her spending and live a life that wasn't dependent on Prada bags and a new car every year.

So far, she'd amazed herself. She had enough perfume and make-up lying around to last a lifetime and the amount of money she spent on things like hair and nails would fund a small mortgage. Having her hair washed and blow-dried in Curly Locks had really brought the extent of her former extravagance home to Jennie. €25 compared to the usual €50 for exactly the same job! There was no need to neglect herself at all – simply being sensible would be enough.

Somehow, she felt more in charge of her life than she had in years. And while she didn't deny that she'd worked hard with the children and the house, especially when Vincent was away, there had been no call at all for the way she'd been carrying on. Acting like a spoilt child by calling in a private detective – a private detective that had charged an arm and a leg to tell her what was under her nose already.

She was ashamed now of the devious lengths she'd

gone to. Sneaking around Internet cafés, the buying of the phone and the subterfuge in the bridal wear shop seemed like the acts of a crazy woman now and she shuddered at the thought of Vincent ever finding out. All trust between them would be lost, she knew, maybe causing a rift that could never be fixed.

Of all the new leaves that she'd turned over in the past month, her decision to go back to work had been the best of all. Not that Vincent knew about it yet. This evening she'd tell him about it and how it could be the best thing that ever happened to both of them. Maybe he could talk to Bob about it tomorrow so that he'd have the weekend to mull it over and make a decision.

It fitted perfectly, with Melissa taking a well-deserved leave of absence at exactly the right time. She had to admit that the intensive six-week refresher course was costly but her spending embargo of the past few weeks had almost paid for the course already. Maxine was tuned in to taking Tim and Lucy into the after-school group for the six weeks so that she wouldn't have to be in a panic rushing home. Now all she had to do was convince Vincent that she'd be the ideal replacement as his PA when Melissa left The Property People in two months' time.

He'd be home soon and now that she'd done all her research, she was dying to see what he thought of the idea. The children had eaten as soon as they came in from school and were now fighting heatedly over a jig-saw in the playroom while Jennie cooked dinner for herself and Vincent. She'd even got back into cooking these past few weeks.

Vincent had noticed her renewed interest on Monday evening when she'd produced a leek and bacon quiche that she used to make in the early days of their marriage but had dropped by the wayside in favour of the delicious ones they made in the Fine Food Emporium in the city which were so much handier. Making the 12-inch quiche had even come as a bit of a jolt to Jennie – a bit of pastry, a few eggs and the bacon and leeks for the filling had cost bugger all, yet she'd been handing out €15 each for ones that were about half the size. Shock therapy was what she was enduring now on a daily basis as regards her spending habits. It wouldn't be a bit of harm to actually be earning for a change.

This evening, she'd made a simple pasta dish with bacon, cream and some blue cheese that she'd bought ages ago. She was serving it with the remains of yesterday's bread, which she planned to fry gently in garlic butter as soon as Vincent arrived in. It was a challenge now for her to stay away from the expensive delicatessen meals that she often picked up in the city and stored in the freezer for convenience.

The phone rang beside her and she knew it was Vincent before she picked it up. He used to do this when they were married first, phoning her from the office to tell her he was on the way home. Since she'd started cooking again, he'd reignited the habit so that she had time to put on the rice or pasta. Jennie had forgotten how much she'd loved the intimacy of it and felt something like sadness that she hadn't even missed him doing it the last few years.

"Hi, Jen. All okay there?"

Jennie grinned at the noise that was coming from the playroom. "They're fighting like mad over that jig-saw.

Lucy's allowing Tim two pieces to every three that she gets in!"

"He's well able to stand up for himself – I heard him calling her a 'wagon' under his breath last night, wherever he heard that. I'll call order when I get in."

He was still laughing at the idea of Lucy controlling the jig-saw.

Jennie laughed too. Lucy wasn't one to respond well to being called to order. "What was the day like? Mad busy, I suppose?"

"Not too bad. Bob had a head cold so he went home at lunch-time and I ended up going to Ballincollig for a meeting that he had set up."

It was years, she realised, since she'd actually listened to the minutiae of Vincent's day, yet she had been well able to moan about everything she had to do from the time he left in the morning until he came home in the evening. She never actually asked for help or told him properly about the things that bothered her, just stored it all up resentfully until it came out as a sulk or a jibe.

"Was the traffic desperate?" He would have had to cross the city to get to Ballincollig unless he skirted around it on the new bypass.

"I took the bypass so it was fine. I was hoping to get home a bit earlier but that held me up until now. Then there was a crash in the Tunnel so I was stuck there until now. I'll see you in a few minutes, okay?"

"Grand so. Dinner will be ready, Your Majesty."

He rang off laughing. It was ages too since she'd called him that.

She checked on Tim and Lucy to see if the dispute was any closer to being resolved but was sent away with a flea in her ear for butting in. They wanted to finish the jigsaw before Vincent got home in the hope that he might bring them to the Power House on Saturday morning so that they could check out the new climbing wall that Sasha had told them about. The warehouse-size indoor play area was designated for special occasions only and their birthday was ages away yet.

Jennie was just draining the pasta when Vincent arrived in.

"Smells nice," he commented as he kissed her. "Mmmm . . ."

"Hands off," she instructed, guarding the pile of crumbled gorgonzola that she was ready to sprinkle through the pasta. Vincent, like her, was a cheese-lover.

"Cream too?"

"Butt out and take the garlic bread out of the oven," she grinned, shooing him away. He made his way towards the oven, pulling off his tie as he went. "God, it's boiling in here."

His face was flushed, the same kind of look that had made her so suspicious only a few weeks ago. And like before, his hair was damp at the edges. *Cop on, Jennie, enough is enough. He probably had the heat on too high in the car on the way home.*

"It's the oven. Close it again or it'll be like global warming in here." She took the platter of crispy garlic bread off him with an oven glove and transferred the slices to two smaller plates. "Will you have a beer instead of wine?"

"I'll just have water, I think." Vincent reached for one of the Galway crystal tumblers at the same time as Jennie placed the two laden pasta plates on the slate table mats.

If the plain white Wedgwood plates hadn't already been safely set down, Jennie would have dropped them in fright when the glass fell from Vincent's hand and shattered against the marble floor tiles.

"God, that –"

The noise of the glass crashing against the tiles was nothing compared to the fright that Jennie got when she turned and saw the colour of Vincent's face. Ashen was the only way she could have described it, a greenish-grey that she'd never before seen. Vincent's face was a mask of shock, as if he was stuck in motion, his right arm wrapped across his chest as if he was trying to hold his left shoulder in place.

"Jen . . ." The word was barely squeezed out before his knees buckled in slow motion and he sank slowly to the ground, his back sliding down one of the kitchen presses.

"Vincent!" Jennie, immobilised for a moment, sprang into action now. "What is it?" A small shake of his head was all she got and his face contorted with even that slight movement.

"Is it your chest? A pain in your chest?" Somehow, she knew this already but she also knew that the 999 people would need to know for definite. "Stay there. Don't try to move, okay? I'll call an ambulance." From the moment she'd seen the pallor of his face and the grimace of pain, she'd known that something dreadful was happening to her husband.

"Kids . . ."

It was barely a groan but Jennie knew what Vincent, pale and sweating, was trying to tell her. Tim and Lucy, safe for now in the playroom, mustn't witness this.

"It's okay, Vincent," she promised him. "Just hold on." Swiftly she crossed and grabbed the portable phone, returning quickly to hunker down beside him. She dialled the number with shaking hands and her calmness amazed her as she gave the details and urged them to hurry. She'd have to clear up the glass before they arrived, she realised. "Just come as fast as you can," she finished urgently. All the while her eyes were on Vincent and her hand stroked his face as he huddled quietly in the corner between the sink and the dishwasher with his chin slumped on his chest.

As soon as the emergency service had allowed her to hang up, Jennie dialled Maxine's number. She knew her friend wouldn't let her down.

"Max, it's me. Something's happened and I had to call an ambulance for Vincent. Will you take the kids before it comes?"

To Maxine's credit, she didn't even ask what the problem was. "Send them across the green and I'll come to meet them. They can stay the night so don't worry about them, whatever happens. I'll come out straight away."

Jennie hung up again. "I'm going to leave you for a minute, Vincent. I'll only be a minute. As soon as Max has Tim and Lucy I'll be back, okay?"

Vincent squeezed his eyes tight and gave another small nod in answer. She could see, momentarily, the relief in his eyes that Tim and Lucy would be taken care of. Jennie kissed his forehead before she left him and knew the memory of the damp, cold taste of his skin would be with her forever. She begged God for the ambulance not to be delayed.

She turned back then for a moment and touched his face. "I love you," she told him in a whisper, just in case he didn't know how much.

The scene in the playroom was tense and, for once, quiet as the last few pieces of the jig-saw awaited their placement.

"Tim, Lucy, listen to me."

"Mam . . ."

"Listen, Lucy, please."

Now they both looked up, finally catching the urgency in her voice.

"A pipe is after bursting in the kitchen. Your dad's trying to fix it and the whole place is flooded so the two of you will have to go over to Maxine's straight away."

Tim's eyes were round in his face. "Can I go in and see?"

Jennie was already catching both her children by the arms and was practically dragging them out into the hall.

"Maaaam!" Lucy started to wail. To have a drama and not be allowed into the middle of it was outrageous.

"Now, the pair of you, do what you're told. Dad says you're brilliant and he'll bring you to the climbing wall soon if you're good tonight." Any kind of a bribe that would get them across to Maxine's house was to be implemented at this moment.

Pulling them after her, Jennie opened the hall door and raced across the paving as fast as she could. Maxine, she could see, was already racing towards her from the far side of the large green space that separated the houses.

"There's Maxine. Now be good and you can stay the night." She could see that they were stunned at this impromptu sleep-over. Neither of them had pyjamas and there was a vast selection of gear that could have been packed for the occasion. Lucy started to complain about Barbie dolls.

"Bye now. I love you to bits." She kissed them swiftly, conscious only of Vincent in pain and alone.

Maxine was nearer now and Jennie made eye contact, her right hand pressing silently to her chest to let her friend know the story. She registered the shock that passed across Maxine's face as she turned and ran back to the house. The last thing she heard was Tim's voice, high with excitement, shouting to Maxine about the flood in the kitchen. The front door was miles away and the fear that Vincent would be dead before she reached him was nauseating.

The siren started as she reached the kitchen. Vincent was sweating profusely now, his hair wet and glossy. His breathing was laboured too, something that had started since she'd left the kitchen.

"Vincent, the ambulance is here. You'll be all right now. I'm so sorry for leaving you,"

"'s okay," he croaked.

She knew now that this had been building for months. The high colour, the sweating. The stress of work.

Everything came to her in an instant as she wrapped her arms around him and closed her eyes. *I thought he was having an affair. Please, God, don't let him die.* Quickly she grabbed a tea-towel and swept the shattered glass into a corner so that the paramedics would be able to get to Vincent properly.

"Vincent Kelleher." The paramedic spoke clearly and concisely, checking to see if they were definitely in the right place.

"Here. He can't talk – he's in too much pain." Jennie jumped up to allow the ambulance crew nearer.

"Vincent, my name's Mike and this is Taylor. We're here to help you. Just nod if you can't speak."

Jennie hovered over them as Taylor lowered a metal trolley to the ground. Mike was already pulling an oxygen mask from a small black rucksack and placing it over Vincent's face.

"Is the pain in your chest?"

Vincent gave the faintest of nods as Mike opened his shirt and started to stick a number of tiny round pads all over his chest. Jennie nearly got weak as Taylor connected the attached leads to a small blue and white machine. Surely they weren't going to give him the kind of shocks that she saw on ER before they knew what was wrong?

"Mrs Kelleher, does your husband have any history of heart disease?"

Jennie shook her head in disbelief. Vincent was only thirty-six.

"Is he on any medication for blood pressure or angina?"

Again she shook her head. Vincent groaned as if he

was trying to speak but Jennie squeezed his hand to let him know that she'd do the talking for him.

"Nothing like that. Is it a heart attack?" She was surprised at how clear her voice sounded as she answered their questions. The kitchen was quiet for a moment as both of the paramedics watched the tracings on the small screen of the machine.

"It could be, Mrs Kelleher," Mike answered cautiously, still studying the tracing intently. "Vincent, Taylor here is going to give you an injection. It'll take the pain away. Have you ever had an allergic reaction to morphine?"

Vincent gave a strangled shake of his head as Jennie answered no for him. The veins were standing out on his neck as Taylor wrapped a tourniquet around his arm and inserted a needle. Vincent didn't wince and Jennie knew then that the pain in his chest was so intense that he didn't even feel the sting of the needle.

"This will take a few minutes to work, Vincent, but you should get relief soon. I want you to open your mouth now so that I can spray some medication on your tongue to assist your heart."

Taylor had an American accent and the whole thing felt surreal to Jennie. Vincent obliged and Taylor sprayed something from a small red bottle into his mouth.

Quietly and efficiently, the two men placed a red blanket over the metal stretcher and lifted Vincent onto it.

"Can I come with you? I don't want to leave him." Jennie was holding onto Vincent's hand as Taylor wrapped the blanket over his patient and tied three straps across him.

"Of course, Mrs Kelleher. Vincent? Any better?"

Mike adjusted the oxygen mask and Vincent opened his eyes for a moment. Silently he nodded and relief swept over Jennie. He was going to be all right, he had to be. Lucy and Tim were only babies. They couldn't lose their father like this without any warning. They just couldn't.

"Tim and Lucy think they're going to the climbing wall next week," she whispered as the paramedics lifted the stretcher up onto its legs. "I told them so. You're going to be fine, Vincent, I promise. Going to the Power House with the two of them. It might be a while but you will, I promise."

His eyes were closed now but somehow it seemed important to remind him of all the wonderful things he still had to do in life. His hand was crushing hers and she didn't know if it was the pain or if he was trying to tell her that he was hearing her. She climbed the two steps of the ambulance without letting go. Mike slammed the doors shut behind them.

"Nearly there, Vincent." Taylor was settling the stretcher into place in the back of the ambulance while Mike had gone up front. The engine was running in readiness. "We're heading for St Angela's. We won't be long."

"We're leaving now, Vincent," Jennie reiterated.

"Open your eyes a moment, Vincent," Taylor instructed. Vincent obliged. "I'm going to ask you a question so try to answer as best you can. If the pain was ten out of ten before the injection, what is it now?"

Jennie understood what he was asking and hoped that

Vincent did too. He whispered an answer that she couldn't hear.

"Seven? That's fine, Vincent. You've had five milligrams of morphine. I'm going to give you another two point five." Vincent nodded gratefully. "And I need you to take this – it's an aspirin tablet to clear any clots that may have formed in the blood vessels of the heart."

The paramedic helped Vincent up a little so that he could take the small white tablet, then proceeded immediately with the morphine. This time Taylor inserted a plastic needle into the vein and secured it there with tape. He injected the morphine through it. The procedure reminded Jennie of the way the midwives had given her drugs to speed up her labour before the babies arrived. Only that time she and Vincent had been there together, anticipating the start of brand-new lives. This time, she felt so alone and terrified, her heart convulsing at the thought that Vincent would lose his life here and now.

The next hour was among the most surreal of Jennie's life to date. The shuddering of the ambulance as it rattled over every pebble in the road between Rathmollin and St Angela's. Her own pain as she felt every bit of what the journey must be doing to Vincent. Taylor questioning her about Vincent's medical history as Vincent himself lapsed into what she hoped was a deep sleep due to the morphine. The brightly lit ambulance bay at St Angela's and the speed at which things took off as soon as Mike swung open the doors of the ambulance.

"Please wait out here, Mrs Kelleher," a nurse instructed as soon as they neared a set of double doors marked *Resus*.

"But . . ." She couldn't leave him now. Vincent's hand was still locked tightly in her own, so much so that the tips of her fingers were white and numb. She couldn't let go now.

"Please, Mrs Kelleher. Your husband needs our full attention. I'll call you as soon as we can get him stabilised," she was told firmly.

She released her fingers with difficulty as the trolley was pulled away from her. Vincent opened his eyes briefly as their hands parted, his eyes locking onto hers.

"I'm sorry, Vincent . . ." She needed to let him know that she would have come with him if the choice had been hers.

"I'll call you soon," the nurse promised as the trolley was pushed through the doors. Then Jennie was alone in the busy corridor as staff and relatives rushed past in pursuit of their own concerns. Shell-shocked, she let the human traffic flow around her. What if she never saw Vincent again? What if he was already dead? What if the red-haired nurse came back out to tell her that Vincent was already gone?

She jumped when she felt a hand touch her shoulder.

"Come with us, Jennie, and we'll see if we can find a decent cup of tea for you." It was Taylor and Mike, their trolley already tidied for the next emergency.

"Is he all right?" Jennie was frantic now. She'd felt secure somehow when the paramedics were with him.

"He's here, Jennie, and that's the important thing." She looked at Mike questioningly. What did he mean by that? Here – as in the hospital? Or here – as in *alive*?

"Many people don't get to hospital in time," Taylor explained. His face was full of concern. "Come on – in here." He led her into a small room opposite the Resus room where God only knew what was happening to Vincent and indicated a plain leatherette armchair.

"I'll put the kettle on." Mike busied himself at the sink while his colleague clattered around with mugs and a stainless-steel teapot. "You said his father had a heart attack?"

Jennie shuddered. It had never occurred to her, and probably not to Vincent either, that his father's early demise would have any implications for Vincent's own future health. To hear Vinnie Kelleher's death described as a *strong family history* instead of an untimely tragedy had been a great shock to Jennie when she'd heard the information she'd given being repeated to the hospital team by Taylor as soon as the trolley was out of the ambulance.

"Yes. He was around forty, I think. Vincent's mother had two children to bring up on her own." *What if I have to bring up Tim and Lucy without their father?*

"The fact that he's a non-smoker is definitely a positive for him." Mike handed her tea in a mug that said *Breast is Best*.

Jennie wondered if doing all the right things mattered at all but was still grateful for the fact that Mike thought there was something positive in all this.

"Is it definitely a heart attack?" She looked from Taylor to Mike for confirmation. She'd heard of people who were rushed to hospital with chest pains only to be told it was indigestion.

"Seems so. You'll know more once they've examined

him properly. I imagine he'll have to go to the Coronary Care Unit for a bit."

Taylor was trying to prepare her a little. She could tell and was grateful.

She sipped her tea, strong and overly sweet. She'd need to phone Elsie but not just yet – not until she could tell her that her youngest son was out of danger. Thank God for Maxine and Seán. They'd know what to do if Jennie didn't reappear before morning. Max had a key to the house and Jennie could visualise her friend rummaging for school uniforms and homework books before Tim and Lucy even woke. It would be business as usual for the kids, with any drama being diffused before it had a chance to develop into anxiety.

A silence developed in the small staff room and Jennie glanced at the large round clock that had obviously been donated by a company making osteoporosis medication. The logo *Which Would You Choose?* dominated the space between the hands. Two pieces of cheese, one a solid cheddar to denote a healthy bone and the other a Swiss one full of holes, reminiscent of a brittle bone, filled the space underneath. Jennie studied the clever advertising ploy as if her life depended on it.

It was ten minutes since she'd entered the room and still no sign of anyone coming to get her.

"Do you think I should go out and . . .?"

"I'll check." Taylor emptied his cup with a final gulp and headed for the door. Mike rinsed his and turned to Jennie.

"Come on, I'll find you a seat somewhere that they

can see you." His eyes were kind as he ushered her out into the busy corridor again.

Her eyes shot towards the door of the Resus room as it opened and Taylor emerged.

"All going well," he reported. "Someone will be out to you soon so don't go too far."

"We'll take off now, Jennie." Mike was gripping the trolley that he'd parked neatly in the corridor before their tea-break.

Again, it was like a loss and she understood how kidnapped people became attached to their captors. Taylor and Mike represented safety and she was terrified at the thought of them leaving.

"Thank you both so much." She knew it was inadequate to try to explain the gratitude she felt. Without them, Vincent would have had no chance at all.

"We'll keep an eye out for you if we're passing the CCU, Jennie. You take care."

"Yeah – take care, Jennie," Taylor echoed.

Jennie, all of a sudden, was alone. The bleakness was unbelievable and she closed her eyes to shut out the thoughts that were racing through her brain. Tim getting his confirmation. Lucy getting her First Holy Communion. Starting secondary school. Lucy's first boyfriend. Herself growing old as a widow.

"Mrs Kelleher?" She jumped again as a new voice bit into her reverie.

"Vincent . . .?" The question hung on her lips but the thin, fair-haired young man with the white face placed a hand on her arm to silence the rush of questions.

"I'm Derek Lonergan, Vincent's doctor. Please come with me for a moment."

"How is he? Is he still . . .?" She had to ask, yet couldn't formulate the words.

Gently, he guided her back into the small room where Taylor and Mike had made the tea.

"I'm sorry," he apologised and Jennie nearly got weak. Looking around the tiny, slightly messy staff room, he sighed. "Every other room is full."

Jennie had thought he was offering his condolences.

"It's fine. What happened? How is Vincent?"

"Doing well, considering that his initial ECG shows that he's had a heart attack."

Jennie, standing up to now, sat down abruptly. She'd known all along that this was what had happened but some part of her had still expected someone to tell her that she was wrong, that it was indigestion or a chest infection.

"But at his age? Are you sure?"

"Very sure. His ECG, as I said, indicates it and we've sent off a range of blood tests to confirm the level of damage. We'll have more information as the night goes on. Regarding his age, he *is* very young for this to happen. But considering the family history of heart disease and his own history of high blood pressure and raised cholesterol –"

"But Vincent has never had high blood pressure or cholesterol!" She'd *known* there was some mistake. The relief was intense to think they had it wrong.

Dr Lonergan's eyes locked with hers and he raised his eyebrows slightly. "For all emergency admissions, we check the laboratory files to ensure that there are no blood or test results that would contraindicate a particular medication. It was noted that your husband had a blood test taken by his GP earlier this year which showed a significantly raised cholesterol level."

"That can't be. Are you sure? He never said anything about it . . ." Jennie couldn't believe that Vincent would have something as big as this going on without telling her.

"Vincent confirmed this just now. And the fact that he's been taking medication for blood pressure for around three months. I'm very sorry to be telling you this – we were a little confused that you hadn't mentioned it to the paramedics."

"Oh my God – he's been sick all along. He was sweating every now and then. I didn't think . . ." She could hardly tell this pale young man with the sticking-up hair that she thought her husband's flushed face and damp hair had been the result of exciting sex and post-coital showers with an imaginary mistress. "I didn't realise," she finished lamely.

Dr Lonergan was obviously used to meeting all sorts in the course of his working day and didn't seem to be too surprised that something as big as this might not be discussed between a young, married couple. Jennie felt ashamed and embarrassed.

"Look, it's out in the open now and we're in a position to treat Vincent for the event that has occurred just now."

Jennie had almost forgotten that Vincent was still lying inside in the Resus room. "Tell me everything." She was still in shock but needed to know what had happened and if Vincent would recover from this.

"Thankfully, the time between your 999 call and the onset of treatment was extremely short. What happens with a heart attack is that one of the main blood vessels of the heart gets blocked and the blood is unable to flow through. The heart muscle is deprived of oxygen and can become permanently damaged. In Vincent's case, this was minimised by the fact that he received aspirin before admission."

"Taylor gave it to him in the ambulance." Jennie didn't know why she stated this. Maybe it was to reassure herself that everything had been done right, that she'd made the correct decision to phone the ambulance when she did.

The young doctor continued his explanation of events, calmly and without the rush that many people complained about after a visit to A&E. "He was admitted well within an hour of your 999 call and we gave him a stronger anti-clotting drug called Streptokinase straight away. In a man as young as your husband, this should have a very good effect in lessening the damage to the heart muscle. Ultimately, this is what will determine his recovery."

"Is he awake? Will I be able to see him?"

"We're hoping to transfer him to the Coronary Care Unit fairly soon but you can sit with him until then. He needs absolute rest right now so I'd encourage you to keep conversation to a minimum. Just sit with him really and let him sleep."

"Thank you so much for keeping him alive." For the first time, tears came and Jennie turned away from the young doctor and tried to wipe them away on her sleeve.

"This is an enormous shock, Mrs Kelleher. I understand you have two young children?"

"They're only five and eight. They'd never understand if Vincent . . ."

"It won't come to that, I hope. Your husband has been stabilised for now but there will be more tests and investigations over the coming days and weeks to see exactly what caused this and whether he will need any intervention to prevent it happening again."

He was meting it out gradually, Jennie saw. There was a long road ahead is what he was saying. It wasn't over yet. "Can I see him now?" She'd pulled herself together a little – the last thing Vincent needed to see was a tear-stained face that would frighten him into thinking he was on his last legs.

Dr Lonergan guided her towards the door of the Resus room. "Remember. Total rest."

The sight of Vincent laid straight out on the bed covered with a white sheet that exactly matched the colour of his face stunned her. He looked so vulnerable – not at all like the strong vigorous man who strode out the front door every morning to work, his briefcase in one hand and a wad of files under his arm. Quietly she went to him and took his hand.

"Vincent, I'm so glad . . ."

"Jen, I'm sorry I didn't tell you . . ." His face was a mask of anxiety but she silenced him gently by kissing his lips and then his forehead.

"Shhhh . . . we'll chat about all that later. You're fine now. Just rest, okay? I'll be here beside you."

"Tim and Lucy?" The worry was still there and she had to reassure him.

"They're having a ball with Sasha as we speak. I'll ring later and sort out the school things with Max. We'll tell them it's a tummy bug."

Gratefully, he closed his eyes at last. It was only then that Jennie took in her surroundings. The room was bare and clinical with a nurse, the same redhead that had been so efficient with her earlier, working quietly at a small desk. She glanced up now and smiled. Jennie smiled back and hoped that the nurse didn't think she was an hysterical wife with no sense after their small altercation earlier.

She could see a plethora of small wires peeping out from under the stiff sheet, the same type of ones that Taylor and Mike had used in the ambulance. Only for them . . . Jennie shuddered to think what might have happened otherwise. If they'd been delayed on another call, for instance.

An awkward-looking peg was attached to Vincent's index finger and she followed its lead to a machine high above the narrow trolley that he lay on. A read-out wavered between 96 per cent and 98 per cent and Jennie wondered if this was what the doctor had meant about damage to the heart. Perhaps it should have been reading 100 per cent. She made a mental note to ask someone but not just now when Vincent was resting. She saw the nurse approaching and stood up, thinking that she might want to monitor Vincent.

"I'll be here if you want to go and get a cup of coffee." She was speaking in a whisper so as not to disturb her patient. "I'm Laura Seymour, by the way. We won't be transferring until a bed becomes available in the CCU."

"But what if anything happens while I'm gone?" Now that she was back beside him, she was loath to leave.

"He'll be fine." She indicated all the monitors. "It might be another hour before the transfer so if you have calls to make or anything, now is the time."

Jennie could see that this Laura was making sense.

"I should phone his mother. And our neighbour has the children. I'll only be a minute."

"Maybe get a sandwich from the machine as well," Laura advised. "You might be here a while. And, in case people ask, you'll be the only one allowed into CCU for the moment."

Unwilling to wake him, she kissed Vincent quietly and left. It was only half nine and so much had happened. The two plates of pasta would still be on the table and the broken glass pushed into the corner by the back door. She'd have to warn Maxine about that.

First, though, she'd have to phone Elsie and tell her the bad news. Although to Elsie, the fact that her son had survived would be good news considering his father hadn't been so lucky.

Chapter 37

The whirlwind of the past month still amazed Emily when she looked around her very own sitting-room. Sandra reckoned that the accident was the best thing that had ever happened in terms of Harmony Cottage being put to rights.

If Emily had been in the full of her health, she would have been foothering around with all the painting herself. As it was, she'd had to get a painter in, as well as someone to sand and varnish the floors. Now it was all done so all she had to do was sit back and enjoy it. Tom had organised a plumber and a tiler to sort out the bathroom so the biggest job had been tackled almost immediately. Emily's spending too had been a little more free, now that she had a proper salary again. So much had happened in the past few months and yet things had finally come right. She imagined that Dermot from The Property People hadn't known what hit him when he'd re-introduced the sale of the cottage to her. Before he knew it, Tom had been on the doorstep with the deposit.

Thanks to Eamonn Harrington being in a rush for the sale to go through, Emily had been the proud owner of Harmony Cottage quicker than she'd ever imagined. She'd had all her plans made the last time so it was really only a matter of putting it into action.

Having Sandra to help her with the picking of colours had been fantastic. And because her own house would be coming on stream fairly shortly, Sandra was almost more enthusiastic than Emily in her search for paint, furniture and accessories.

Tiles had been mind-boggling but Emily eventually settled on a warm slate with rusty streaks running through it for the kitchen and dining-room. Getting just the right shade for the walls had been a bit of a nightmare too but between them they'd come up with Italian Terracotta, not too dark but giving a cosy glow to the open-plan back of the house.

The new back door looked out on a virtual wilderness but Emily didn't care. If she was feeling stronger later in the year she could tackle that but for now it was enough to just be living in the house. Her house-warming had consisted of Sandra and Dylan arriving with a Chinese take-away and two bottles of wine just when Tom and Niall had waved the carpet-fitter off and pulled the two squishy rose-coloured sofas back into the room.

The smell of new carpet and chicken satay would be mingled together in Emily's mind forever. It was one of the best days of her life and she'd been very lucky to be alive to share it with her family and friend. Niall had offered to stay that first night but she'd been insistent. He could stay as often as he wanted but first, Emily needed to feel that she was fit for independent living again. Her rehab period was over at last, even though she knew Jacinta would miss being able to mind her. Now though, she had a whole new house to fuss over.

It was a full week since she'd moved in and she still couldn't get over the novelty of it. Sandra would be over later for lunch, and Emily was planning to cook something delicious *and* low-fat for her as a "thank you" for all the help. It was almost a routine now, she'd joked, seeing as she'd been there for Emily's first Friday afternoon in the house as well.

It was like being back at college in Dublin with her friends calling around on Friday nights when they were short of money. When they were flush on foot of a new grant it would be a night on the town, but the end of term had meant an inevitable slowing-down in social activity.

She threw another log on the small fire that she'd made and put up the old-fashioned fireguard before making her way to the kitchen to start lunch. She knew it was a bit Irish to have a fire in mid-June but she just couldn't resist trying it out now that the chimney had been cleaned and the build-up of ancient bird's nests removed.

Thank God for Jamie Oliver, Emily mused as she laid out her ingredients on the hardwood worktop that had replaced the horrible brown formica one that Minnie and Ina had enjoyed. She knew Sandra would be starving after her morning in Curly Locks. They took a longer midday break on Fridays if there was a late evening of appointments planned and Emily had promised to be quick on the draw with the lunch.

The cream kitchen was a miracle as far as Emily was concerned. It had taken a full day to spray it but the results were nothing short of magnificent. New appliances had made a difference as well and she'd had the good sense to heed Sandra's advice and add a few new doors to integrate the fridge and dishwasher before the spray painters had arrived. Now, it was impossible to tell the old doors from the two new ones.

She started to rinse the vegetables now, unable to resist admiring the old Belfast sink that had been covered with stains until Sandra had got at it with a bottle of Milton. The cottage that she was renting from the council had a ceramic bath and Sandra had found out about the powers of Milton by accident when Dylan was still on bottles.

It was strange, Emily thought now, the way that she and Sandra had become such good friends. Especially the way it had come about with the accident and Paul's part in it.

A year ago, they'd have had nothing in common, with Emily living a very middle-class life in Dublin and Sandra a single mother in a council house. Their paths had hardly crossed since they'd left school, yet now it was like they'd been friends forever. Sandra was a great person and a fabulous mother to Dylan, although she sometimes thought of herself as a failure and a nuisance to her parents. Emily kept drumming it into her that she was a successful mother and that there was nothing more important. Paul had drained away almost every bit of her self-esteem but it was slowly coming back now that he was out of her life.

Emily just hoped that the court case, whenever it

happened, wouldn't set her back to square one again. Aggie Lenihan, to her credit, was an expert at keeping the whole Paul Delaney mystery alive and well in the village. She trawled the newspapers daily anyway in case there was anything of interest that she wasn't already privy to, but now Paul Delaney was her special mission and she persisted in checking off every unnamed drink-driving perpetrator that appeared in the paper. Too much *CSI*, Emily reckoned.

Emily put Aggie out of her mind and grinned as she turned on the electric oven. Their next step, according to Sandra, would be to find two fabulous men who deserved them. They'd both be career-girls with their own homes, after all. But as Emily kept reminding her, it looked like they'd have to go a bit farther than Rathmollin to find them.

Sandra rapped at the glass in the back door to get Emily's attention.

"Sorry, I got a bit of an urge for Led Zeppelin there! Did you ring the bell as well?"

"Did I what!" Sandra had pressed the brass bell several times but knew she wouldn't get a response. The whole of Rathmollin could probably hear the pounding rock music that emanated from the little cottage. "And what's with the Led Zeppelin thing?"

Emily giggled. "Before I moved in with Richard I was in an apartment in Christchurch with two of my friends. We had a bit of a thing for playing rock music when we were getting ready to go out. I found the CD just now and couldn't resist."

"Fair enough," Sandra laughed. She set down her bag of goodies and started to help with the lunch, already familiar with where everything was in the tidy kitchen. She couldn't wait to have a proper kitchen of her own instead of the old-fashioned one that she'd become so used to.

"What's this? The start of a diet?" Emily was rooting in the plastic bag that Sandra had plonked on the worktop. "I warned you to bring nothing!"

"Couldn't resist." She was so used to buying crisps and snacks to munch on when Dylan was gone to bed that she found it hard to pass them in the grocery – even though she wasn't actually going to eat them. "The Diet Coke is for me."

"And I'm supposed to eat a bucket of Maltesers and a king-size packet of crisps?" Emily held up the gigantic bag of Walkers Sweet Thai Chilli crisps incredulously. There was nothing else in the bag besides a Strawberry Cremoso with nought per cent fat.

"Something like that!"

"I suppose it'll keep Mam happy – if I don't die from heart disease first. I'd hardly get more saturated fat if I ate a pound of lard! Thanks though."

It was only then that Sandra remembered her conversation with Jack.

"Actually, speaking of heart disease – did you hear about Vincent Kelleher, Jennie's husband?" Emily might already have heard on the Rathmollin grapevine that had been so in tune with her own illness only a short while ago.

"No. What's the matter with him?" She paused what she was doing with the smoked salmon. Vincent was a little older than Jennie if she remembered rightly.

"I met Jack earlier in the grocery and he was telling me that Vincent had a heart attack. He's only thirty-six apparently."

"That's desperate. Poor Jennie! How is he? In CCU, I presume?"

Sandra nodded as she remembered that Emily's dad had had a heart bypass some years previously. "He's out of the woods now, I think. Jack says he'll be in hospital for at least a week."

Emily looked up sharply. "He seems to be in the thick of everything, Jack Rooney."

Sandra couldn't understand Emily's dislike of Jack. It was irrational considering the fact that he'd been brilliant the night of the accident, not to mention the fact that he'd been instrumental in her being able to finally secure the cottage. Jack was a decent bloke but every one seemed to know that except Emily.

"Seán Daly told him outside the school earlier. He and Maxine took Tim and Lucy last night. Emily . . . why is it that Jack annoys you so much?"

Emily snorted in response and continued spreading cream cheese on brown bread for her starter. "It's just that he seems to be stuck in everything."

"He knows Seán from the school and he does a lot of business with Vincent," Sandra explained patiently but Emily was obstinate.

"Buying up everything and then dropping things

when he feels like it." Emily stabbed at a tomato. "Going around yelling at people all over the place."

Sandra's newly plucked eyebrows shot up in disbelief. "Yelling at people?"

"Ages ago I was in a café in Academy Street and he ended up sitting at my table. I didn't actually *know* it was him – believe it or not, I didn't recognise him – but I nearly had indigestion in the end. He got some kind of business call and started shouting down the phone at whoever it was that rang. He's nothing but a big bully."

Sandra laughed out loud at this. "Jack? I can't believe you're saying that after the offer he's made to me about the house. He's really decent, Emily. He was actually upset about your accident and even blamed himself a bit because he gave Paul his job back a few days before it happened. Which is why the big eejit was down in The Stone's getting plastered that evening. Jack reckons he'd have been better off if he hadn't taken him back at all after the carry-on of him."

Emily was setting the table now while Sandra poured two glasses of sparkling water. "So why did he take him on again then?"

"Because I practically begged him to – and don't think I haven't regretted that as much as Jack does." Sandra had thought about this endlessly and wondered now why she'd been so bothered. Any normal person would just have kicked Paul out long before it got to that stage.

"Look, I know you like him but he's just . . . I don't know . . . just . . ." Emily was stuck for words to describe Jack.

"Just what?" It wasn't like Emily to be so vitriolic.

"The night of the accident, Sandra. He was there, wasn't he?"

"Yeah. And if it wasn't for him Paul would have scarpered and got away with it scot-free, I might remind you." Sandra bit into the delicious starter with a face grim at the memory of Jack and her effectively detaining Paul. "You knew all this, Emily."

"I know but . . ." She paused. "What was I like, Sandra?" Emily's forkful of salad leaves was suspended in mid-air and her face was flushed.

Sandra didn't know what she was asking. "What do you mean?"

"You know. My clothes. Were they all torn or what? Did they have to cut them off in front of everyone?" Emily spoke quietly but Sandra could see that her friend was depending on an honest answer.

"It wasn't like that, Emily. You were in between the wall and the taxi. I didn't even see you at first. It was only your feet really that were sticking out. The ambulance people put a blanket over you to keep you warm while the fire brigade were working on the cars. Paul's car went first, then they had to cut the taxi driver out and move that car to get at you." Emily's face was white now and Sandra realised that she didn't know these details already. "They got you onto the stretcher straight away after that. Your clothes must have been cut off in A&E." Perhaps Emily had an idea that she'd been lying there half-naked for all to see with the whole village staring at her inert body.

"And who else was there?"

"Well, Paul obviously, and your mam and dad. I came out – Dylan was just gone to sleep – and Aggie Lenihan, of course. Jack came after that, I think. He stayed with Paul until the guards came and then he brought your mam and dad to St Angela's. Aggie Lenihan tidied up and locked up for your parents." Sandra paused to take a sip of her water.

"And that was it until I got to hospital?"

Sandra thought about this for a moment. "More or less. You had a sort of oxygen mask on when you were going into the ambulance so I couldn't see your face. You had black high sandals on, that's all I could see from under the blanket."

The relief on Emily's face told Sandra that this was all her friend needed to hear.

"I thought maybe my skirt was up around my ears or that my top had to be cut off. Imagine everyone looking at me like that?"

Emily was only half joking. Sandra could understand this. It was bad enough looking at her own flabby tummy in the mirror with all its stretch marks but to have the whole of Rathmollin commenting on it would be a different story.

"It wasn't a bit like that so put it out of your head this minute. Now get on with that." She eyed Emily's food. "I'm dying to see what the main course is."

Looking better than she had since the conversation had started, Emily tucked in. "This is great isn't it, Sandra?" She glanced around her dining-room with a big grin on her face.

"It's brilliant. And thanks for all this. Apart from going

to Mam and Dad's, I don't know when the last time was that I had a break like this in the middle of the day. No wonder I was eating all the wrong things – I had no proper routine."

"I'm only storing up points for when you get your house!" Emily grinned at her.

"You've no idea how good it is to actually go somewhere on my own. Don't get me wrong – I love Dylan to bits – it's just that I missed out on all this when he was born. Like when you mentioned living in a flat earlier. I never did all that stuff when I should have so it's great to be able to have a bit of a life now."

It was true. There hadn't been time for friends and going out when Dylan was small and as time had gone on, there had been less and less money to waste on pubs and nights out.

"Well, I think you're great. Especially getting back to work and everything. Here, let's have a toast!"

"To . . .?" There was so much to toast these days that Sandra couldn't pinpoint one thing.

"To *us* . . .and our great futures," Emily announced finally.

"To us – and the future," Sandra echoed, clinking glasses with her. There really was a lot to look forward to.

Chapter 38

It was almost eight o'clock and Jennie was relieved to be nearing the CCU again. She'd left at half two so that she could pick the children up from school and it seemed as if she'd been away from Vincent for ages. It had been he who'd suggested she go home for a bit and she'd obeyed because she didn't want him worrying about Tim and Lucy.

Maxine had been brilliant but some level of normality would have to be restored, although they were into the weekend now so it'd be a bit harder for her to manage.

To her surprise, Vincent's mother had turned up trumps. She'd taken the news the previous night with shock and had taken on board the fact that she couldn't yet visit with equanimity. To date, Jennie's relationship with Elsie had been somewhat distant and her warmth and support had come as a bit of a surprise. At this very moment, she was at home in Rathmollin Woods with Tim and Lucy finishing the aborted jig-saw and would be staying for the weekend to allow Jennie as much time with Vincent as possible.

Thinking on it now as she stood at the lift waiting for it to open, it was quite incongruous that this was the first time that Vincent's mother had ever stayed a night in their home. Jennie knew now that it was her own insecurity that had kept Elsie at bay since she'd married her son. Granted, Elsie had been as protective as any mother who'd reared two teenage boys alone but Jennie had been intimidated by her from the beginning. Rather than risk losing Vincent in some sort of contest where she couldn't match up, Jennie had opted out instead. Elsie had been welcome to arrive for birthdays and every second Christmas but only on Jennie's terms. Christmas in Ballymore, Vincent's childhood home, had been a definite no-go area. She'd asserted her *own* position very well but it shamed her a little now when she realised the extent to which she'd excluded Elsie from their lives.

She seemed to be saying it almost every day now but things were going to be different from here on in. She was Vincent's wife, they had two children together. There was no reason to fear his mother. Jennie was no longer a gauche twenty-year-old arriving at Elsie's house with a big smile and an even bigger engagement ring.

Her mother-in-law had been through a lot and had been marvellous to put Vincent and Philip through school and college. Jennie wondered whether she herself would have had the same backbone. She resolved now to ask the night sister if Elsie could pop in later to see Vincent for a few minutes – he was her child, after all.

It was her own sense of inferiority that made her keep Elsie at a distance but now was the time for her to grow up and stand on her own two feet. She was an adult, a wife and mother. It was time to stop running away from things just because she was afraid to face them.

Jennie thought briefly of Ron Green and all the secrets that had lain stagnant between her and Vincent for such a long time. They still hadn't talked about his visits to the GP and the fact that he was on medication for high cholesterol and high blood pressure. There was so much to deal with, Jennie thought as she rang the bell outside the CCU. But she knew somehow that it would be fine now.

"Jennie Kelleher to see Vincent," she announced when the intercom was activated from inside. There was a very strict visiting policy in place here.

"Come on in." Deirdre, the day nurse, buzzed her in. So far, everyone that she'd met had been great, going to lengths to explain Vincent's condition and medication.

"Hi, babe," Jennie greeted, kissing Vincent on the lips.

"Hi, again," he grinned. He looked so much better now, a little pale and sunken around the eyes, but infinitely better than he had in the kitchen last evening. "Is it bedlam at home?"

"Only because they didn't get to see the imaginary flood in the kitchen. Maxine said Tim told everyone in the schoolyard about it yesterday morning. He was so wound up about it that he actually thinks he was there for it. Max said it sounded like a waterfall had come down into the kitchen."

"Better not let Jack hear that the plumbing he did was *that* bad!" Vincent gave a low laugh and sounded more like himself.

"How are you feeling now? No chest pain or anything?" Jennie sensed that he didn't like her asking but she'd decided that they'd both have to learn to open up a little.

"Nothing. The cardiac nurse came around and told me a bit about what happened, you know, the drugs they gave me and everything." He looked unsure, as if he didn't know whether she wanted to hear it or not.

"Was that a girl called Imelda?" When Vincent nodded, Jennie filled him in on what she knew already. "I met her this morning when you were asleep. She explained again about the aspirin you got in the ambulance to loosen any clots. And the other one that you got when you came in – Strepto-something?"

"Streptokinase," Vincent confirmed. "It thins the blood and breaks down clots that are blocking the arteries. Like the aspirin, only stronger. I'll have to stay on the aspirin for good, she said." Vincent looked dejected at this and Jennie squeezed his hand. She knew he hated this feeling of weakness and debilitation, which was probably why he hadn't told her everything in the first place.

"As long as it keeps you well, Vincent, it won't matter what you're on. Did she mention the blood-pressure tablets?"

"Yeah. I'm off the ones that Dr Lawlor had me on," he told her a little shamefaced. "I'm sorry about that, Jen. I didn't want to worry you and I felt such a crock . . ."

"You're not a crock. This isn't your *fault*, Vincent. It's

like anything – diabetes or having a sick child – we just have to get used to it." She wanted to say that as long as she knew what was going on they'd be able to cope with anything, but she thought of her own duplicity with Ron Green and couldn't bring herself to berate her husband even mildly.

"The new ones are called beta blockers," Vincent continued.

Jennie listened carefully. She needed to know all this stuff if they were going to face it together.

"Imelda is going to write it all down for me so that I know what everything's for. I'll have to go on a cholesterol tablet as well because my level is above 5. Dr Lawlor put me on a diet and she was going to check it again after three months to see if it had come down but this happened now and . . ." He closed his eyes and sighed again. "Jen, I'm sorry about all this . . . not telling you . . ."

Jennie rested her head on his chest and listened to his heart beating. She couldn't help thinking that, if things had been different, she might not be hearing it at all. She smelled the newness of the pyjamas that she'd bought in a nearby shopping centre at nine o'clock that morning and smiled.

"Remember the time I was on the phone and cooking at the same time and I dropped the Le Creuset pot on the tiles?"

Vincent smiled too. "I only remember having to pay for a whole box of tiles to come from Spain to replace the one that broke!"

Jennie remembered being newly married and in bits over the expense of it all, not to mention the hassle that ensued getting a tile to replace the one that had shattered under the weight of the cast-iron pot. "You told me there were to be no 'sorrys' now that we were married. Well, it's still the same – no sorrys, okay?"

"Okay." Vincent stroked her hair and they were silent for a while.

"It's actually 6.5," he said quietly. "The cholesterol, I mean."

Jennie was shocked. Imelda had mentioned that 5 was the magic number as regards cholesterol but that nearer to 3.5 or 4 was better. "No more croissants then," she smiled. If Vincent needed to do this then it was up to her to support him.

"I went to the doctor after the party at Bob and Noeleen's. The anniversary thing? I felt awful that night," he admitted.

Jennie remembered only too well how flushed he'd been and how he'd been so anxious to get home. She listened now as he began to explain.

"I got a tightness in my chest after the meal and I just put it down to eating too much. I went off and got a glass of water in the kitchen but I started sweating and I felt I couldn't breathe. One of the caterers brought me out into the garden and I started to feel better with the fresh air. I went to Dr Lawlor on the Monday."

One of the caterers. This was the part of the story that riveted Jennie. The woman in the dark dress with the severe French roll hadn't been his mistress – she'd been a Good Samaritan who'd been helping Vincent when he obviously didn't feel comfortable enough to tell his wife that he was feeling unwell. What did that say about Jennie?

Vincent's voice broke in on her thoughts now, making her push the feelings of guilt away momentarily. "I have to go for an ultrasound in the morning, too."

"Is that the ECHO?" Jennie was surprised that she'd taken in so much of the specialist cardiac nurse's information.

"We'll be experts after all this. The consultant said he'd be around at ten in the morning if we want to talk to him." He looked at Jennie to see if she wanted to be there with him.

"I'll be in loads of time once the kids are up and dressed. Your mother's been great, Vincent – she's going to stay the weekend. I was thinking of asking the sister if she could come in for a few minutes later on." She looked at him for confirmation. "If you're able for it, I mean?"

"It'd be nice all right. She's probably in a state – with Dad and everything. In those days, nobody survived a heart attack." Jennie was glad that he was able to use the words "heart attack" as the cardiac nurse had warned her about things like depression and even denial. Some patients refused to use the words, preferring to call it an "episode" rather than admit to a heart attack.

"Will I go up to the desk and ask? I could go home to the kids and let her come in."

Vincent looked pleased at this and she wondered if he'd had a hard time over the years rationing out his time to allow his mother some attention. He never said anything but it had become a routine for him to bring Tim and Lucy over to their grandmother's house on Saturdays after the playground while Jennie went shopping or to have her hair done.

She let go of his hand now and approached the nurse's station,

"Hi, Jennie," Deirdre greeted her warmly. The people they'd met had been so non-judgemental about the fact that there seemed to be so little communication between husband and wife up to now. "Things are better this evening?"

Jennie smiled back. She must have looked such a state when Deirdre came on duty this morning. She stayed with Vincent all night and had dozed in the chair until lunch-time, only breaking to go to Dunnes Stores for pyjamas and toiletries until Deirdre had mooted the idea of her picking up the children from school and getting a shower and some lunch. Vincent had agreed strenuously.

"You were right about the shower and lunch earlier. What time is your shift over – you seem to have been here for hours?"

The young staff nurse laughed quietly. "That's because I was! I do 8 a.m. to 9 p.m. three times a week – it suits the kids. Vincent told me you have a boy and a girl?"

"Tim and Lucy. They think Vincent has a tummy bug. When will they be able to come in, do you think?"

"I asked the day sister that earlier because Vincent was talking about them so much. It might do him good to see them. What about tomorrow after lunch? Ring first, though, to make sure he's well enough."

"That'd be brilliant. And what about his mother? She's minding the kids at the moment but she'd love to see for herself that he's doing well."

"Well, it's only one at a time so you could do a swap with her. It'll be quiet here for the next hour or so if she wants to drop in for a few minutes."

"That'd be great, Deirdre. I'll tell her not to stay long. And Vincent will be thrilled – he lost his father very young, you see. So they're very close." Jennie wondered if she'd been thick not to have seen this before.

"So Vincent told me. He might have to have a few more tests on account of that, you know. Family history is very significant but Imelda will go through all that with you. It'll be a less stressful life from here on in, I imagine."

"You're telling me! No more late evenings and foreign trips. All in good time, though." Imelda had warned Jennie about making Vincent feel like an invalid when he was only thirty-six.

"I'll head away so," she told him now after relaying the news that Elsie would be able to come in as soon as she got home to take over. "And I'll see you first thing for Dr Mulligan, okay?"

"Thanks, Jen. I love you, you know that, don't you? Even if I did . . ."

"No sorrys, remember? I love you too. I'll text you before I go to bed."

Jennie didn't know if she'd ever be able to tell him about Ron Green, especially now that all this had happened. When Ron had opened her eyes about Vincent's blameless lifestyle, she'd thought she was being issued with a second chance. Now, it seemed, she'd been given yet another. Would it ruin every bit of trust between them if he knew she'd had a private detective trailing him for two weeks?

Jennie thought it might. It was a burden that she'd have to carry for the rest of her life but Ron Green would have to be one secret that would never be disclosed. She filed it away now, right at the back of her mind. Vincent was alive and well. And she was going to do nothing to jeopardise that ever again.

Chapter 39

The first Emily knew about a problem with the antique plumbing in Harmony Cottage was at nine o'clock on Saturday morning when she found herself standing by the sink with a waterfall raining down on her head. Her immediate thought was that her hair, straightened quickly by Sandra yesterday afternoon, would now be a ball of frizz.

It was like she'd been transformed into a pillar of salt at the exact moment that the ancient tap had flown off in the direction of the fridge. All she could do was stand and stare at the column of water being extruded and watch in fascination as it hit the ceiling with force and cascaded back down over her.

The staring in fascination bit lasted approximately one second, enough time to soak Emily to the skin through her cotton pyjamas and to flood the tiny kitchen.

"Shit, shit, shit!" was all she could muster by way of expletives as she tried in vain to plug the flow of water with both her hands. Realising the futility of this, although the gush was no longer hitting the ceiling, she abandoned her post momentarily to locate the missing tap, thinking that maybe it had just come loose from years of use. The plumber *had* mentioned to her about getting some new fittings but she'd been reluctant to diminish the quaint image of the ancient Belfast sink and had refused steadfastly to have the old-fashioned tap replaced. Now, it seemed, she was about to suffer for her romantic notions.

Dashing off in the direction that she thought the offending tap had flown, the next sensation she experienced was that of her slippered feet skidding along the tiles and her hip colliding heavily with the kitchen table. Scrabbling to steady herself, her hands slipped on the now sodden table and she suddenly found herself lying on the flooded slate tiles with her head between the legs of a chair. All she needed now was another head injury.

Spotting the antique tap-head wedged between the integrated fridge and the washing machine she scrambled towards it, finally seeing light at the end of a very wet tunnel. She'd just screw it back on and the water would stop.

Still yelling her expletives, only more vociferously by now, Emily attempted to jam the tap back onto its base. She was shivering now and her hands were shaking from the cold, as well as the shock of having Niagara Falls in her sunny little kitchen.

"Go on, will you!" she ordered, grunting with the exertion of it, valiantly shoving the tap as hard as she could.

To her horror, the base of the tap unit crumbled under the pressure, rendering it impossible to get it back on in any shape or form.

"Fuck, fuck, fuck!" she wailed, thinking of her mother and father on their day trip to Griffin's Garden Centre twenty miles away. Niall was even more useless to her. He'd left early that morning for an interview with one of the pharmaceutical companies in Little Island having decided to remain in Ireland for the moment. She didn't even have a phone book in the house to look for a plumber.

Drenched and still dazed from her skidding incident, it occurred to Emily that maybe there might be a plumber on the building site across the road from the cottage, a building site that she was all too familiar with considering the amount of times she'd pored over the brochures with Sandra for "ideas".

Pausing briefly to pull a sweatshirt over her head lest the builders thought she was straight out of a Miss Wet Tee-shirt competition, she fled the tsunami and raced out the front door and across the road, suddenly terrified of facing a group of hard men in her pyjamas and even more terrified of not being able to locate someone to help her.

She needn't have worried. As soon as she appeared at the site entrance, a row of yellow hats faced her from behind a low stone wall. It occurred to her briefly that at least Jack Rooney was putting a traditional finish to the houses he was building. Then it struck her that she was probably about to make an eejit out of herself in front of him again. Knowing her luck, he'd pop out from behind a machine or a building any minute.

"Y'all right, love?" one of the yellow hats questioned with obvious interest, his round face florid beneath the hard hat. Three others looked at her in awe. It wasn't often that a woman appeared, not to mind one in pyjamas.

"My tap flew off – the whole place is flooded."

"Where did it fly to, love?" The fellow with the round face was obviously the spokesman for all of them. The other three stood like nodding dogs behind the incomplete wall.

Agitated at his obtuseness, Emily was just about to begin explaining when she noticed the corners of his mouth starting to twitch. Galled that she wasn't exactly in a position where flouncing off with her dignity intact was an option, she stood her ground, hoping that one of the others would be less inclined to find her predicament funny.

"I don't know where to get a plumber and I've no one to ask. Would any of you know how to turn off the water? It's an emergency," she pleaded plaintively, her eyes anxious as she visualised the sea of tap-water that must surely be halfway up the kitchen cabinets by now.

"Ah go on so, seeing as it's an emergency. Stanislaus here will have a look at it."

"Oh that's brilliant, thanks a million," Emily gushed, delighted that the nightmare might be coming to an end. Her relief was short-lived however when one of the nodding dogs looked at the spokesman in disbelief and uttered a single syllable.

"Me?"

"Yeah, you. Give the girl a hand, can't you?"

"But . . ."

"Don't mind him," he reassured Emily, adding lewdly, "He'll soon have your stopcock sorted out."

Mortified, Emily muttered her thanks and swung around to head back across the road, hoping that Stanislaus was following her.

"I'm not plumber," she heard behind her, the eastern European accent unmistakable.

That's all I need, a man who admits to knowing nothing about plumbing just before I let him loose in a flooded kitchen, Emily thought.

She blanched when she saw the rivulets of water that were already making their way down the shallow front step, having negotiated the tiled hall floor successfully. God only knew what the bedroom and sitting-room would be like, carpeted as they were. The fact that there was a small step up into both of them might be the saving grace, she thought hopefully. For once, she began to think that the erratic levels inside the house might turn out to be a bonus.

"Anything – anything you do will help," Emily reassured him, thinking that he couldn't possibly make things worst than they were. "I'm Emily, by the way," she added, extending her hand.

He shook her hand firmly as they splashed their way quickly through the hall and into the narrow kitchen. "Okay, Emily, where is the stopcock?"

"I have no idea," she answered carefully, unsure if this was another suggestive comment or if he really was looking for something called a stopcock.

Despite the torrent of water still raining down, Stanislaus made his way towards the source and knelt to check the press under the sink.

"Not here – maybe outside," he said, jumping up and making for the back door.

Emily watched anxiously from inside as he hunkered down and tinkered with something near the outlet pipe. Suddenly, miraculously, the water stopped.

"Oh, thank God!" Emily exclaimed, although she was sure that she'd need another miracle in order to have the house liveable again. Now that the onslaught had stopped, the resulting silence was deafening, broken only by the soft trickling of the last of the water dribbling from the walls, ceiling and every surface in the kitchen. The place was a mess.

"This tap cannot be fixed," Stanislaus pointed out, showing her the crumbled remains of the tap unit that Emily herself had destroyed in her impatience earlier. "Maybe you can get a plumber to see it. If you have a brush I will help you to clean."

"A brush?" Emily's mind was reeling. Where was she going to get a plumber on a Saturday afternoon to put on a new tap? It was almost ten now and her father mightn't be home until well after all the hardware shops closed. And how was she going to manage without water until she did get one?

"This one?" Stanislaus, although a man of few words, was proving to have more initiative than she'd first given him credit for. The back door was still open and he had already commandeered Emily's sweeping brush. He now started sweeping large sheets of water out onto the small square of gravel that she called a backyard.

"It's all right – I can do that," she told him, although not too convincingly. Stanislaus was about six feet tall with enormous biceps and was clearing the water at a rate of knots.

"It is no problem."

"Stanislaus, is there any plumber working with you that might like to do some work on the weekend?"

Emily knew from dealing with people's finances on a daily basis that many of the eastern European workers who migrated to Ireland needed to do extra, tax-free work to contend with the high cost of living that they encountered on arrival in the country.

"My brother is plumber but he is working on another job today. I can ask him to come later, maybe two or maybe three o'clock?"

Emily smiled at his turn of phrase. "That'd be great. Are you sure he'll be able to?" Most building sites operated up to lunch-time on Saturdays but what if he was offered, or maybe forced into, overtime? She looked up from where she was wiping down the worktop, her anxiety evident.

Her new friend grinned at her. "Don't worry, I'll phone him later and tell him to bring new tap."

Stanislaus was still working away at the floor, his jeans and checked shirt wet through. His hands, she noticed, were as large as shovels and a wedding ring glowed solidly against the tanned skin. Emily wondered if he had a wife and children living in Ireland.

"Where are you from, Stanislaus?" Emily pulled the

mop and bucket out of the small cupboard by the door and started to soak up some of the remaining water.

"From Poland. I am in Ireland since two years."

"Do you like it here?" From her time in the Voluntary Budgeting Agency, Emily had become accustomed to dealing with migrant workers who needed assistance with their allowances and entitlements, often because unscrupulous employers were paying them below the minimum wage or weren't engaging in correct taxation procedures. She often wondered how it was that so many foreign workers actually stayed in Ireland at all.

"Very much. I would like to stay maybe ten years."

"Is your wife here as well?" They were working away companionably now and she didn't feel at all intrusive asking him about his family.

"Yes, only since six months ago. I have one son who is three years almost."

Emily couldn't imagine how difficult it must have been to leave his wife and young child to start again in a new country. At least Stanislaus had his brother here with him.

"What's his name?"

"My son? Mikey." His pride was evident in the way that he spoke about his wife and child, making Emily a little envious.

Her teeth were starting to chatter with the cold now that the drama was over. Her whole body was freezing from her wet pyjamas and she could feel her hair clinging to her back. Sandra would get a good laugh out of this one.

"It is not so bad," Stanislaus commented, standing to

survey the place, the bulk of the water now gone. At least the kitchen was starting to look presentable, she thought, dropping a sodden brown loaf into the flip-top bin that was itself half-full of water. It would take her the whole day to sort the place out but the fact that she'd had help to remedy the worst of it was a bonus.

"Thanks so much for helping me – I don't know what I would have done otherwise."

"It's no problem. I will ask Lucas to come later."

"I'm afraid I can't even offer you a cup of tea," Emily smiled wryly, indicating the sodden box of Barry's teabags she was now throwing in the bin. Maybe she could give Lucas some money later to give to his brother in thanks. Right now, her purse was sitting soaked on the worktop.

"Thank you anyway but I must go or my boss will think I lay no blocks today!"

Emily smiled back at him and wondered as he left whether the florid man, obviously the foreman, would be irritated that he'd been gone from the site for so long. She hoped not but, having listened to some of the clients' experiences at the VBA, she wasn't so sure at all. Or maybe it was Jack Rooney he was talking about when he referred to his boss. Sandra had told her he was well able to handle the men on site, if the carry-on with Paul was anything to go by.

She sighed now and looked around to survey the damage. Tentatively, she made her way into the hall to examine the sitting-room. Miraculously, her precious rug was bone dry, as was the sisal flooring in her own bedroom when she ventured in there.

First things first, she decided, still shivering from the freezing water that had cascaded over her. She stripped off her sodden pyjamas and dressed. Granted the teabags were gone but a cup of coffee would soon put the heat back into her bones. Then she'd start to put Harmony Cottage back to rights.

Chapter 40

Sandra was caught between a rock and a hard place, as usual, with Aggie Lenihan. She had to be polite and not cut across the customer, as per Chrissie's stringent rules on Conversation With Clients, as Emily had christened the imaginary list of rules. On the other hand, she couldn't be seen to have any hand, act or part in Gossip or Other People's Business, also on the list of conversational rules.

Aggie ran on and on about Vincent Kelleher and her theory that he'd been worked to the bone, poor fellow, to keep Miss Jennie in style. Not to mention the get-up of her kids in their designer gear.

At the mention of Tim and Lucy, Sandra found an opening at last. "They're all the same these days, Aggie. Dylan wouldn't look at a football boot if it didn't have the Nike logo on the side of it. Maxine Daly says the same for her young one – it's Barbie this and Barbie that!"

Sandra noted Chrissie's almost imperceptible nod of approval in the mirror. It didn't do to be talking about who was to blame for someone's heart attack, especially when the person being irrationally blamed had become a customer in recent weeks.

"She'll have a halt called to her gallop now, I can tell you," Aggie resumed, oblivious of Sandra's diversionary tactics. She'd always been a bit tetchy about Jennie and the fact that she'd landed on her feet in Rathmollin Woods with a big SUV under her.

Sandra eased the final knot out of Aggie's newly permed hair and tried again. "That's the new thing, you know, Aggie. They're all talking about this work-life balance. You have the bingo, at least."

At the mention of her weekly bingo outing, Aggie took off on a rant about people parking on the grass verge outside the Community Centre. "They should put up bollards, that's what I say. I'm going to get onto the council about it."

Sandra had often wondered who the poor unfortunate council representative for Rathmollin was. His head must be melted from Aggie ringing to complain.

Behind her, she could see the whisper of a grin forming on Chrissie's face. Sandra averted her eyes from the mirror lest she get a fit of the giggles – Chrissie was obviously on the same train of thought as herself about the poor council rep.

"There you are, Aggie. Eileen will be along to finish you off in a moment. Will you have a cup of tea?" Sandra was sure that she wasn't the only person who'd ever mentioned finishing Aggie off.

"Only if it's Barry's. I've an idea it was one of those

valu-pack teabags I got here last week." Aggie's head was nodding hard with disapproval and Sandra reassured her that it was definitely Barry's teabags that she'd be using before escaping to the kitchen to put the kettle on. As usual, the first thing she did was to check her phone for messages.

The first one, from Emily, made her groan out loud. A flooded kitchen and no water for the rest of the day by the looks of it. Her shift would be over at one – maybe she'd collect Dylan and call down to keep Emily company while the tap was being fixed. She mightn't be able to do much but at least she'd be a bit of support.

The second message was from her mother looking to see if Dylan could stay the night. There was a play on in the city and Dan had booked tickets for the three of them but it would be late-ish when they got home if they went to Burger King afterwards. Sandra smiled at that – it was Dan and Rose who'd be looking to go to Burger King, not Dylan. She knew they loved spending time with Dylan and it was great, considering the way that things had turned out with Paul, that her son had at least one reliable father-figure in his life.

She texted her mother to say that Dylan could have a sleep-over and that she'd drop his things down later. Then she texted Emily to say that she had a baby-sitter and asked if she'd like to go down to The Stone's Throw later for a drink. It wasn't much in the way of a night out now that she was saving for her new house but at least it'd be sociable. And it was time to start showing her face again after all the racket that Paul had caused.

The kettle popped at the same time as Emily's text came back, simply saying *"Game on!"* Sandra took that as a yes and popped a Barry's Gold Blend into a china mug for Aggie. She'd already heard from Jacinta Gordon that Aggie had been complaining down in Connolly's butcher shop about Chrissie's arty-farty mugs with the ridiculous handles that you couldn't get a proper grip on. Sandra actually loved the trendy black and white set but who was she to argue with Aggie's good taste?

Chrissie called her discreetly as soon as she'd placed the elegant china mug in front of Aggie. "It's almost eleven and I think you deserve a tea-break!"

Sandra smiled. Life was good, especially now that she had a night out ahead of her. And now that her boss seemed to trust and respect her despite everything that had gone on before, things were even better.

"Thanks, Chrissie," she smiled. "See you in ten."

Aggie, sipping suspiciously on her Gold Blend, wasn't one bit pleased at all this bonhomie.

Chapter 41

"My apologies for being so late – I'm afraid I can never legislate for a proper schedule in this profession!"

The cardiologist shook hands with Jennie and Vincent and removed his stethoscope from around his neck. "I'll have a quick listen, Vincent . . ." He placed the head of the instrument at points around the chest, his face thoughtful. "All well from this vantage point," he commented, glancing quickly at the ECG readings above their heads. "How are you feeling generally?"

"Brilliant, to be honest. A bit weak but just glad to be here."

Jennie smiled – not once had she heard him complain since he'd arrived at St Angela's.

"No chest pain?" The consultant gazed at the monitors that were still getting read-outs from the leads attached to Vincent's chest.

"No, thank God – I couldn't go through that again."

"And what about you? It's Jennie, isn't it?"

Jennie was impressed that he'd taken the time to find out her name, considering that she hadn't actually met him before. She'd missed him the previous day when she'd left to pick up Tim and Lucy.

"*I'm* fine," she assured him. "I got a bit of a shock naturally but that's a minor detail."

"Well, you did the right thing on Thursday night, I'll say that much. I've looked at all the blood results and it seems that the damage to your heart, Vincent, was minimal, probably on account of getting in here so quickly." He looked at Jennie then. "So many people wait to see if the pain will improve or they try to get the person into bed to rest before they make a 999 call."

Jennie was embarrassed at his praise and Vincent squeezed her hand, smiling proudly. Jennie, to cover her confusion, spoke up. "What happens next?"

"Well, the good news, as I say, is that the damage to the heart muscle seems to be limited. We can tell that from your blood results because damaged heart muscle releases proteins called Treponins which can be measured in the bloodstream. In your case, Vincent, the Treponin levels are relatively low. The ECHO that you had this morning shows fairly good results as well and the fact that you've had no chest pain at all since admission is good news."

Vincent grinned. "It's great to hear good news for a change!"

"I know you've talked to Imelda on the cardiac team about future lifestyle plans and medication. But the seriousness of this can't be underestimated." Mr Mulligan's voice was grave now as he looked from Jennie to Vincent.

"You're only thirty-six, Vincent. It's not a matter of just taking tablets to prevent another heart attack. It's going to mean a re-think of everything, particularly your job, if it's as stressful as Imelda tells me it is."

Vincent looked at Jennie and took a deep breath. "I've had plenty of time to think about this since yesterday. I'll be cutting back in a big way and probably doing a certain amount from home. My business partner is close enough to retirement so I think we'll have to take on a partner to deal with the overseas business."

Jennie was stunned at how quickly he'd come around to this way of thinking. When the consultant was gone, she was going to spell out her intentions of taking over from Melissa as his PA. Then at least she'd be there to support him properly.

"You'll be starting to mobilise again today, just out to the bathroom first and building up gradually from there. You'll get an exercise programme from the Cardiac Rehab unit as soon as you're well enough and one of the rehab nurses will be visiting you at home in the first week after discharge."

This was the first time that home had been mentioned and Vincent caught on to it straight away. "When do you think I'll be able for home?"

"Well, it's only day 2 today so probably day 8, all going well. You'll be going home on your beta blocker as well as the aspirin and the statin – that's the drug for lowering your cholesterol. Once you've made an initial recovery, I may have to consider a surgical procedure to look at your coronary arteries." He paused to see if both of them were up to speed.

Jennie hadn't heard anything about surgery but Vincent seemed to be well tuned in. "An angiogram?"

It was typical of Vincent to get to the bottom of a problem. Jennie was amazed that he'd been able to take so much in at all.

"That's right. Sometimes we'll find that one or more of the arteries are blocked and in that case it might be beneficial to put a small device in place to keep the artery open."

"That's called a stent," Vincent said to Jennie, adding "Imelda mentioned it," for Mr Mulligan's benefit.

"I'll be seeing you over the next few days so we can talk again if you have questions that need to be answered." He stood up from the padded armchair and prepared to leave.

"Thank you for everything," Jennie said, injecting as much gratitude as she could into the simple words. "Everybody's been marvellous."

"All part of the service," the consultant smiled. "And we need the successes to keep us at it, Vincent."

As soon as the consultant had moved over to the nurse's station with Vincent's chart in his hand, Jennie laughed quietly.

"There you are – a success story!"

"And here I was thinking I was fecked!"

"On that note, I'll go down to the canteen and see if Tim and Lucy have wrecked the place yet. Elsie's probably having a nervous breakdown!" She'd left the three of them in the canteen while she went to the CCU for the ten o'clock appointment but it had been after eleven when

Mr Mulligan had arrived. Now it was half past and Jennie knew the attention span of Tim and Lucy in a confined space.

"It was great that she was able to come in last night, Jen. I think she didn't believe I was alive until she actually saw me."

"Well, I can imagine – especially when you think of her last experience with a heart attack. She's going to talk to Philip about it, you know, about getting checked out by a cardiologist." Vincent's brother lived in San Francisco with his wife and three children and Elsie would be going over for a holiday soon.

Jennie and Elsie had talked last night once the children were asleep and the older woman had expressed her guilt at not protecting her sons better. She just hadn't known enough about it, Jennie had reassured her. Now, they'd all had an education, unlike years ago when Elsie had seen her husband die as she'd waited for the local GP to arrive. They hadn't even had a phone in the house and she'd had to run to the local Garda Station to make the call, leaving her husband dying on the sofa. Thankfully, the boys had been in school that day and hadn't witnessed the terrible sight of their father being taken away by the undertakers.

"I think that's a good idea," Vincent said now. "There's no need for him to find out the hard way too. You've been great, Jen, with Mam as well the kids and all this." He looked around the CCU with all its monitors and accoutrements, not to mention the other five patients, each with their own set of problems.

"Vincent . . ." Jennie didn't need thanks, she was just

grateful that she wasn't going to face the life that his mother had had.

"I mean it, Jennie. We'll make a new start after this. And no more secrets, I promise."

If only he knew how much she understood that. "No more secrets," she echoed, kissing him one more time before she left.

Chapter 42

The idea of a night out with Sandra gave added impetus to Emily's overhaul of the kitchen. The wheelie bin was now full and there wasn't so much as a crumb left in the cupboards. If it hadn't been for the Tupperware container of her mother's that she stored the porridge oats in, she probably wouldn't even have had her breakfast considering that the cereal boxes had collapsed in a soggy mess after their unexpected cold shower.

As soon as Lucas came with her tap, and hopefully he would, she'd have to go out and do a massive shop to replenish her cupboards. If Lucas *didn't* come, then she'd have to debunk to her parents' house for the rest of the weekend and let her father sort the tap out on Monday.

The doorbell rang, its slightly musical tone breaking in on her thoughts. Emily hopped down off the worktop and thanked God that she'd wiped the last of the water streaks off the paintwork. So long as Lucas didn't let the whole thing explode again.

Instead of the Polish plumber, she found Sandra on the doorstep laden down with two paper cups and one of the brown paper bags that Connolly's Grocery wrapped their sandwiches in.

"Lunchtime," she announced brightly before a frown appeared across her face. "You haven't eaten already?" It was almost two o'clock.

"Eaten? There's nothing left only what's in the fridge. And I've been swinging a mop and dish-cloth since nine o'clock!" Emily knew she looked a sight in her tracksuit bottoms and an old pyjama top. The knees were wet and baggy from kneeling on the floor to get at the crevices between the kitchen unit and her hair was like a whin bush around her head.

Sandra was all business. "Quit now for a few minutes and eat something." She handed Emily one of the cups and followed her into the now-spotless kitchen.

"Only for the Polish fellow I don't know what I would have done. His brother is supposed to be coming over in a while to see if he can fix it."

They both examined the spot where the tap had sat proudly for almost a century.

Sandra, having lived in a decrepit cottage for the last six years, had no value on anything old or dysfunctional. "Best to be rid of it."

Emily wasn't sure what kind of a tap unit Lucas would bring but she imagined something modern and contemporary that wouldn't fit in with her kitchen one bit but resigned herself to accepting that it'd be better than no tap at all.

"I've been promising myself this all week – fecking gorgeous!" Sandra was uncovering a chicken tikka wrap, its creamy sauce staining the paper in which it was wrapped. "Same for you, if that's all right?"

Emily slid hers onto a newly washed Stephen Pearse plate and shoved a second plate in Sandra's direction. "Manna from heaven."

They sipped their coffees in silence for a moment, both of them concentrating on their food. "I'll straighten your hair again before we go out, if you like," Sandra commented eventually.

"It's like one of the wonders of the modern world," Emily giggled. She hadn't put in her usual dose of Frizz-Ease earlier and her curls were standing out about a foot from her head all round.

"I'll give you a ring as soon as I'm ready and you can have it washed by the time I get over. It'll be great to get out for a drink."

Emily hadn't been out at all since before the accident and hadn't been in The Stone's Throw in years. When she'd moved back to Rathmollin, she'd hated the thought of everyone commenting on the split with Richard and asking her questions so what little socialising she'd done had been in Cork with the VBA gang instead.

"What are you going to wear?" she asked. The last night she'd dressed up had been the fateful night that Paul Delaney had done his magic and she wasn't sure what she had in her wardrobe after the move from her parents' house.

Sandra's face lit up. "It's mad but I found these jeans that I had before Dylan was born – expensive ones that I blew a whole week's wages on – and they fit me again. So I think I'll wear them with that pink shirt." She'd been dying for an excuse to wear the pale cotton shirt that no longer gaped now that she'd lost a bit of weight off her bust.

"I'll have to think of something to go with jeans as well. The Stone's is hardly the kind of place to get glammed up for."

"You'd be surprised!"

"I'd say I would," Emily retorted cynically. The likelihood of meeting the men of their dreams in Danny Stone's was miniscule.

"I haven't been in there since the crash," Sandra said now and Emily could hear the uncertainty in her voice.

"Stop thinking about it," Emily ordered emphatically, knowing exactly what her friend meant. She still thought that people held her responsible for the chaos that Paul Delaney had caused.

"I know but . . ."

"No buts – it wasn't your fault. Paul was well able to paddle his own canoe and you didn't even know the half of it. People will forget about it, you know, if you just get on with it."

Sandra sighed. "I know. But when you have Aggie Lenihan giving you a dig about it every Friday morning . . ."

"Do you really think Aggie's opinion is a good representation of what everyone in the village thinks?" Emily was really annoyed that Sandra was still putting up with the small-mindedness of her next-door-neighbour. She'd have to tell her mother to put her straight the next time she landed for one of her griping sessions. Jacinta was worn out already from Aggie arriving at every hand's turn to report on something she'd heard about Paul Delaney.

Sandra smiled at last. "I suppose not. There should be a penalty for Inciting Gossip or something that she could get locked up for." They were laughing when the doorbell chimed again.

"Start a novena. I'll crack up if it isn't Stan's brother." Emily raced to the door to see.

The man facing her when she opened it could only have been Stan's brother. The same enormous build and the same dark blue eyes. Even their hair was the same, tightly cut and blond, although Lucas was slightly better-looking in his dark blue jeans and navy T-shirt. Emily didn't care if he looked like Brad Pitt so long as he sorted out her tap. With some relief, she noted that he was carrying a large case that looked like a toolbox and a solid paper bag that she hoped was full of plumbing paraphernalia.

"Lucas? Come in." She extended her hand when he'd acknowledged that he was indeed Lucas and stepped into the hall. "I'm Emily."

"Lucas," he repeated, shaking it firmly. Like his brother, his hands were large and capable looking. In contrast, his voice was surprisingly gentle, almost quiet.

"You're so good to come. Have you come straight from work?" He followed her down the hall, his enormous size almost blocking out the light in the confined space.

"It's no problem," he reassured her. "Stan told me you have a big problem this morning." He smiled when Emily looked over her shoulder and laughed.

"It was like Niagara Falls! This is my friend, Sandra."

"Hello, Sandra." Lucas stuck his hand out as Sandra turned around from where she was wiping down the worktop after their lunch. She'd already stowed the two plates in the temporarily defunct dishwasher.

"Nice to meet you." Sandra's voice was a little higher than usual as she took in the man standing before her and Emily could see her pulling in her tummy automatically, despite the fact that she no longer needed to. It occurred to Emily that Lucas hadn't stood grinning self-consciously at *her* when she'd opened the door to him just now.

"Well," she said, breaking the small silence that seemed to have developed.

"This tap?"

Sandra almost jumped away from the sink when Lucas moved to examine the denuded base of the tap unit.

"The very one," Emily confirmed, unable to stop herself grinning at Sandra behind his back. Sandra glared crossly at her and started folding the tea-towel that had already been folded perfectly on the worktop.

"This must go," Lucas announced after a few moments' consideration.

Emily peered around him to see that he was pointing at the shattered base that Emily had ruined earlier. Sandra hovered behind her.

"I have brought two choices to look at." He turned around suddenly to reach for the paper bag that he'd left on the table and both of the girls stepped back to give him space. The kitchen seemed smaller with him in it and Emily caught Sandra's eye again.

Lucas produced two different tap units from the bag

and, to Emily's surprise, neither of them were the modern horrors that she'd expected.

"A little more money," Lucas explained, holding up the nicer of the two. "Better for this old house, I think." Emily loved his turn of phrase and noticed that Sandra was hanging on his every word. She also noticed that his left hand wasn't sporting the same solid wedding band that his brother's had, although that mightn't count for anything when he was working with his hands all day.

Both of his choices were good, Emily thought, as she considered the two period-type tap units. It was obvious that Stan had explained exactly what kind of house the tap would be going into. Lucas was right about the more expensive one – it was almost a replica of the original.

"You're right," Sandra told him, then looked at Emily. "It *is* better."

"That's great, Lucas. Will it be a big job to install it?" Emily hoped he wasn't going to tell her that he'd come back next week.

"No problem. A few hours maybe because I must change the fittings. I think I must also look at the rest of the plumbing, if you want. This is very old."

Emily thought of the surveyor who'd assured her that the plumbing was in excellent condition and the fact that his expert opinion had landed her in the morning's calamity. The last thing she wanted was a flood in the bathroom or anywhere else in the house.

"Would you mind? I'd hate it to happen again."

"No problem, Emily." Lucas smiled his easy-going smile and opened the navy toolbox. "I will get started."

"Have you had lunch already or would you like me to get something?" Emily was conscious of the fact that he'd come straight from work and even though the cupboards were bare she'd be able to go up to Gleeson's Grocery for a sandwich for him. She had to go out to use the ATM anyway so that she could pay him later.

"No problem." This was obviously Lucas's favourite English-language phrase. "I have eaten in the canteen before I came here, thank you."

"Okay so. I have to go out for a bit but I should be back in an hour or two. I've left the coffee and sugar out and the milk is in the fridge."

He nodded in thanks and smiled at Sandra who was filling the kettle industriously. Emily held herself back from grinning at the obvious attraction between them.

As soon as they'd bid Lucas goodbye, Emily and Sandra closed the kitchen door and left him to his own devices.

"He's like something out of a Diet Coke ad," Sandra hissed as soon as they'd reached the security of Emily's bedroom.

Emily laughed at Sandra's reaction as she pulled off her work clothes and changed quickly into jeans and a fitted black T-shirt with a gold star on the front.

"He's a bit of a Fine Thing all right," she agreed.

"A bit? Did you see the muscles on him?" Sandra threw herself face-down on the bed like a teenager and propped herself up on her elbows.

Emily was rubbing a light skim of foundation on but she grinned at her friend's reflection in the mirror.

"You're very bad over him. Do you want to come to

Tesco with me or would you rather stay here and look after Lucas?"

"I know which I'd *rather* do but I suppose I'd be better off doing a proper shop and saving a few quid." Because she had no car, she had to do most of her shopping in Gleeson's and it was costing her a fortune. Sometimes she managed to get to Tesco if her mother was going but now that she was back at work it wasn't fitting in as well as it used to. "I've no bags though so I'll have to drop in home first."

"I've loads, we'll be grand." Emily finished her make-up and studied herself in the mirror. "I'm definitely less wishy-washy now."

Sandra knew that she didn't just mean the make-up and her appearance. She was less wishy-washy than she had been before she'd found Richard in bed with that Lorena one is what Emily really meant.

"You're gorgeous," Sandra giggled. "So don't go next or near Lucas in case he takes a shine to you."

"Right so – we'll just sneak out like two criminals."

Sandra jumped off the bed and smoothed the plain cream duvet cover again. Emily's room was so serene with the hessian curtains and the sisal carpet. The cherrywood wardrobe and dressing-table were shining, unlike the furniture in Sandra's house that had Dylan's sticky handprints all over it despite her best efforts with the Mr Sheen every chance she got.

"You're so neat," Sandra commented. There wasn't a bit of clutter around the place. Emily's make-up was stowed tidily in a little Burberry case and her chains and necklaces were hanging on one of those miniature Victorian dressmaker's dummies that had five or six different wire hangers extending from the top.

"The place is tiny! If I even leave my clothes on the chair at night there isn't room to move in the morning. The more space I have the messier I get." She followed Sandra out into the hall, closing the bedroom door behind her. It was a bit strange having a man that she didn't know from the back of a bus in her house.

She grinned when Sandra called out a cheery "Byeee . . ." to Lucas before they closed the front door behind them. She definitely had it bad.

It was half four before Emily pulled up outside Harmony Cottage again, having dropped Sandra off first with a clutter of Tesco bags. Aggie Lenihan had been out like a shot to see who it was that was dropping her neighbour off, no doubt hoping to see Sandra with a man in tow. Emily had expected Aggie to be disappointed that it was only poor Emily Gordon's car that the "unmarried mother" was alighting from but she, as usual, hadn't bargained for Aggie's bizarre train of thought.

"Emily?" Aggie's eyebrows had almost disappeared into her hairline with feigned surprise. "It's great to see the pair of you friendly again."

Emily did a double-take. "Friendly *again?*" She hoped she was being pointed enough for the gossipy old bat.

"Well, with everything . . ." Aggie trailed off as the two girls stared at her as if they were still waiting for an explanation. "Anyway, it's finished with now . . . with you being well again and everything, Emily. Just as well, *I* say."

Emily could see that Sandra was looking a little uncomfortable and now appreciated what she had to put up with from Aggie, especially in the hair salon where there would be an audience.

"It *is* just as well, Aggie, that I'm well again. We haven't had a night out in ages with all the hospital business, have we, Sandra?"

Aggie was looking from one to the other, hoping there was more to be said that she could store away and relate to someone else later. "Oh," was all she could come up with for now.

"So," Emily continued firmly, "we're going to have a good night out tonight. I'll be putting it all behind me so I won't want to hear another word about it."

"Well . . ." Aggie was shell-shocked at this new directness out of Emily.

"Now, Sandra, that's the lot." Emily landed the last of Sandra's shopping out onto the footpath and checked her watch. "Give me a bell later and I'll have the hair washed and ready." With the smallest of winks she hopped nimbly into the car and sped off with a final wave to Aggie.

"I'd better put these away," Sandra said perkily. She gathered up her bags and left Aggie open-mouthed at her garden gate.

Emily was delighted at the way she'd handled Aggie Lenihan. The old wagon would shut up as soon as something new came along anyway, but to imply that she and Sandra had fallen out over the carry-on with Paul Delaney – well, that was one rumour that Emily was scuppering right now.

Incensed on Sandra's behalf, she hauled her Tesco bags out of the boot and placed them one by one on the doorstep. Lucas's pick-up truck was still there, a fact that she was glad of considering that she wouldn't know where to find him in order to pay him if he'd left before she got home. The last thing she wanted to do was approach him on the building site across the road in case he got into bother for doing nixers outside of work. She knew from her time at the VBA that most employers, although it was none of their business, frowned on this and she didn't imagine that Jack Rooney would be any different.

The first thing she noticed when she opened the front door was the fact that the door into her bedroom was open. Glancing in, she saw that the trap door in the ceiling was open too and that Lucas had placed her small two-step ladder beneath it to access the attic. She hoped that he hadn't found anything too sinister that would cost her a bomb to fix.

Lugging the first of the grocery bags into the kitchen, she called out to let him know she was back before landing the bags onto the table so that she could examine the tap. To her delight, the new one was in place, a little shinier but overall looking as if it had been there forever.

"Brilliant," she crowed to herself, thanking her lucky stars that it had been Stan that the foreman had directed to her aid this morning. So long as there was nothing too alarming wrong with the rest of the plumbing, she'd be sorted before her father even knew there was a problem. He'd done enough for her recently and she hated to give him extra work if she could manage independently.

As soon as the last of the bags was unpacked and the things put away in their rightful places, Emily gathered up the bottles of shampoo, conditioner and shower gel that she'd placed on the counter, deciding to drop them on the dressing-table in the bedroom and see if Lucas wanted another coffee. He'd already had one, she figured, having noticed the empty mug on the worktop.

Her arms full, she entered her bedroom just as a pair of heavy-duty work boots emerged from the attic.

"Good timing, Lucas, I was just going to make coffee." She waited as his legs and body lowered from the trap door, his feet searching in mid-air for the top rung of the small step-ladder. Lucas's T-shirt had ridden up, exposing a very toned and very tanned midriff that Emily's eyes couldn't help but be drawn to. Sandra was right – it *was* like having the Diet Coke man in the house. Especially with the way his jeans rested so low on his hips and the fact that his exit from the attic seemed to be happening in slow motion.

The fact Lucas had been wearing a navy T-shirt when she and Sandra left the house and that the one emerging from her attic was actually *white* registered with Emily at the exact same moment as her eyes met Jack Rooney's. Emily just stood and stared at him, utterly shocked to find him here in her bedroom, his face looking as stunned as her own must be.

Her first though was one of mortification that he

might have noticed her unconscious study of his exposed abdomen when he was looking down to locate the ladder beneath him. Her heart seemed to have stopped but it suddenly started to beat again erratically. He was in her bedroom. Her eyes tore wildly around the room as the same feeling that she'd had after the accident, one of being totally exposed, overwhelmed her.

She'd left nothing out of place yet still she felt vulnerable, a bit like the way she'd felt the day he'd visited her in the hospital when she'd been so shaky after seeing Richard again.

Her voice had deserted her and it was Jack who spoke first, his voice steady and reasonable like it had been that day in the ward.

"Lucas had to go over to the site to sort out a pipe that got damaged – he asked me if I'd finish up here." His explanation was rushed, almost as if he'd been caught burgling the place and had to justify the fact that he was there at all.

Emily knew it was her own mad reaction that was making him feel like a criminal.

"He's done the tap," Jack continued, "and everything else seems to be fine. I'll just close this." He reached up to close the hatch, causing his top to ride up again. This time she looked away.

"Thanks," Emily said faintly, her voice barely audible. So much for announcing to Sandra earlier that she was no longer wishy-washy.

"No problem," Jack told her as he folded the ladder and propped it against the wall. "Sorry about just landing in but Lucas didn't have your phone number and he didn't want to leave the house unlocked. I'll send him back over as soon as he's finished."

"Thanks," Emily said again, this time a bit more stoutly. She'd have to pull herself together or he'd think the fractured skull had affected her permanently. What had she expected him to find in her private space? And somehow she didn't think he was the type to go snooping in her drawers. "I really appreciate all the help – the place was a total mess this morning."

Jack grinned suddenly and Emily could see why Sandra was always going on about him being some sort of god. "You should have picked a state-of-the-art semi-d." He nodded towards the development across the road and Emily had to smile.

"Over-priced," she shot back cheekily, more comfortable now that she'd put his being in her bedroom into perspective. "I was just putting the kettle on. Do you . . ."

"Hello?" Lucas's voice cut across her impromptu invitation as his massive frame appeared in the doorway. "Sorry I had to go, Emily. I hope everything is fine?" He looked at Jack for confirmation.

"All's well upstairs. I'll leave you to it, so." Jack, blocked inside the small room by Lucas, made to leave and somehow Emily was reluctant for him to go. On the other hand, she needed to pay Lucas and she felt that he would prefer his boss to be out of the way.

"I will get my things," Lucas announced and went off towards the kitchen, allowing Jack leeway to leave.

"Thanks again for coming over. I really appreciate it."

"No problem," Jack said, the words leaving Emily in no doubt as to whom Lucas and Stan had got their catchphrase from.

Jack's smile lit up his face, making her catch her breath. Then she thought of the day she'd sat opposite him in the coffee shop on Academy Street all those months ago and remembered him barking into the phone at someone. She'd had her share of devastating smiles in the form of Richard and cautioned herself against getting caught again. Her life was just getting back onto an even keel and she didn't need Jack Rooney's charm to throw her off kilter.

She heard the door close after him and made her way to the kitchen to sort Lucas out. She was glad that she hadn't got a chance to offer him coffee – he was gone now and her tap was fixed. She wouldn't be needing him again.

Chapter 43

Jennie watched Elsie as she carefully turned the sausages, concentrating all the while on Tim's stream of questions about America. Despite the fact that she'd only ever been to San Francisco to visit Philip, she had something to tell him about everything from the Grand Canyon to the Statue of Liberty.

"Can you *really* go all the way up along her body on the inside and come out at her head?" Lucy was sceptical about all the wonders that her grandmother was divulging to Tim and was annoyed that it wasn't she who'd commenced this line of questioning.

"Something like that," Elsie told her. "Now, come on and sit in for your tea."

It was six o'clock and Jennie was hovering over the boiled rice that she and her mother-in-law were going to have with a chicken tikka that had been cobbled together from the remains of yesterday's roast chicken.

"I'll definitely have to do a shop tomorrow or we'll be like stick insects by Monday morning," Jennie laughed.

Elsie had kept up with milk and bread but the supplies of everything else were running low. She drained the rice and ladled the creamy chicken onto two plates while Tim and Lucy buttered bread and made sausage sandwiches.

Elsie took a small forkful of her tikka. "This is gorgeous – I only ever make soup from the leftovers. I'll hold the fort in the morning if you need to go to Tesco."

"That'd be brilliant." Jennie still couldn't believe that she'd had Vincent's mother down as such a trial and tribulation. She'd been fantastic, slotting in seamlessly to the household routine as if she'd been doing it forever. Jennie had always had an idea that Elsie would be a typical interfering mother-in-law if she gave her an inch at all but she could now see that this had all been in her head. Elsie was only sixty and from the conversations that she and Jennie had had over the past few days, led an active life that included hill-walking and her writing group as well as her Saturday mornings with Tim, Lucy and Vincent.

"What will happen next, do you think?"

Jennie knew that Elsie was talking about Vincent's recovery and filled her in properly on Mr Mulligan's plans for his patient. "I know it'll be a while but he'll definitely want to go back to work. Bob was thinking of cutting back on all the travelling anyway so they're going to take on a few new people. Vincent says he might work from home a bit more as well, which I think would be great."

Elsie nodded her agreement. "Life's too short for it to be all about work."

"You're telling me! Vincent was working very hard and I'm not sure that I was keeping a good enough eye on him." Jennie sighed, still feeling a bit guilty that she'd thought all Vincent's symptoms were the signs of an affair.

"He may have been working hard, Jennie, but you were doing everything here. It's not easy with two children – I should know!"

Jennie grinned self-consciously, warmed by Elsie's understanding. She'd always imagined that her mother-in-law must think she was a glorified lady of leisure, another reason that she'd avoided too much contact with her. "It was a bit harder for you though," she acknowledged.

"In some ways. Although some things are more demanding now. I didn't have a mortgage, for instance."

"I'm thinking about going back to work," Jennie blurted out now. "Part-time, in Vincent's office. Melissa's going on leave soon so there's a gap there that I could fill."

"That's great, Jennie. Vincent did say that all the temps were stressing them out." She sat back thoughtfully, her plate now cleared. "Imagine, that was only last Saturday."

"I wish I'd seen it coming," Jennie mused regretfully.

Elsie's hand covered hers for a moment. "Don't think like that. I didn't notice either and you'd think that *I'd* have had some idea when I've seen it before."

"Thank God he's okay. I'll feel better if I'm in the office a bit, though. I know we can't treat him like a baby – he'd hate that – but I might be able to support him a bit more."

"I think you're right. How will you manage the little pair?" Tim and Lucy had by now disappeared into the playroom to have another go at Buckaroo.

"I was thinking I could do a few mornings and they could go to Maxine's after school if I have to do a full day." Elsie had met Maxine the previous day when she'd arrived across the green bearing the cooked chicken and a Pyrex dish of gratin potatoes.

"Don't forget that I could help as well for an afternoon or two," Elsie said, a little shyly almost.

"I couldn't ask you to give up your classes." Elsie was doing a computer course in the local VEC.

"That's only in the mornings and the writing group isn't until half eight on the Wednesdays so I'd be free in the afternoons if it's any good. Tim would keep my brain active with all the questions!"

"That'd be great, even for two days a week. But I don't want you to be tied down. If you had anything on they could go to Maxine's."

"That sounds good. But think about it, Jennie. I don't want to upset your arrangements with Maxine, either. It's fine if you've already booked them in or whatever."

Jennie could see that Elsie didn't want to foist herself on them and she was ashamed that this was the tone that she herself had set for their relationship. "I haven't said anything definite to her yet. And I'd *much* rather they were with you, even though they'd love the idea of going along with the rest of the gang now and again."

Elsie beamed. "That's settled then. And it doesn't matter to me what days it works out at."

"Vincent won't know what's hit him when he gets out," Jennie laughed as she collected the plates and opened the dishwasher. Somehow though, she suspected that this new easier relationship between his wife and his mother would mean a lot to him.

"Espresso?" Jennie and Vincent always had one after dinner and Elsie had tried one the previous evening. She glanced at the clock now, obviously wondering if it was early enough in the evening to have the caffeine hit wear off before bedtime.

"I will so. I might even buy an espresso-maker myself so that I can get a kick-start in the mornings."

Jennie grinned and resolved to buy one for her as a "thank you" for all the support that she'd given her over the past few days. And, she admitted to herself, as a demarcation line for yet another new start in her life.

Chapter 44

"Good Lord – I can't believe the change in this place since the last time I was here." Emily looked around The Stone's in amazement, its exposed stone walls and myriad secluded nooks and crannies a far cry from the barn-like structure it had been for years. Even the wobbly formica-topped tables with their equally wobbly stools were gone.

"I know. They did a major revamp last year. It's great, isn't it?"

"It was a bit more than a revamp," Emily exclaimed as she pushed her way to the already crowded bar. "They've completely gutted the place."

"Emily – you have perfect house now?" It was Stan looming over her, his open, friendly face smiling down at her.

She grinned up at him and wondered briefly what height his wife was. "Hi, Stan. It's brilliant – your brother did a fabulous job." Lucas, she noticed, was approaching from across the room.

"Would you like a drink, Emily? I am just about to order."

"Absolutely not, Stan," she insisted. "I'll get this round." Stan protested but Emily was having none of it. "You've both been so good to me today. What's Lucas having?"

Stan glanced over at his brother who had already spotted Sandra and was towering over her with an enormous smile on his face. Sandra was lapping it up.

"Beamish, if you insist, Emily," Stan was saying.

"For you as well?" she queried as she caught Danny Stone's eye and gestured that she was ready to order. Stan nodded and Emily called the two pints as well as Sandra's Bacardi and Coke and a glass of red wine for herself.

They waited together companionably for the drinks to arrive. "So everything is good, Emily? No more problems?"

"No more problems, thank God. It was such a mess this morning. It took me all day to sort the place out. Lucas had the tap fixed in no time."

"I am glad. Thank you," he said politely as she handed him the two pints of Beamish that Danny passed across the bar.

Stan turned to give one to Lucas while Emily waited for her change. Danny handed her the notes and, to her surprise, welcomed her back to the pub.

"It's great to see you out and about again after everything. You're back to work, I hear?"

Emily hadn't been in The Stone's in God only knew how long and she was touched at the proprietor's kindness. Maybe people weren't talking about her as if she was a side-show. Maybe they were actually just interested and supportive.

"I am, Danny. It's great to be back to normal."

"Well, mind yourself now, girl." He winked and moved on to the next customer, leaving Emily feeling more at home than she'd felt in years. Rathmollin *was* home now and she resolved to become much more a part of things in the future as she collected the rest of the drinks and joined Sandra, now chatting animatedly to Lucas and Stan.

"This is great," Sandra said quietly as Emily handed her the Bacardi.

"It is," Emily agreed. "The pink looks great on you."

She really did look great in the fitted jeans and delicate pink shirt. Emily felt great as well in her dark blue jeans and a jade green chiffon top that she hadn't worn since her Dublin days. The spindly sandals that she'd been wearing the night of the accident she'd found lurking at the back of the wardrobe and had had no compunction about wearing them again, even if they did remind her of that last awful night.

She turned to address Stan then so that Sandra could concentrate properly on Lucas.

"Is your wife coming out later, Stan? Or is she baby-sitting?"

"Her mother has come from Poland for one month so she will come when Mikey is asleep."

"That's great. How does your mother-in-law like Rathmollin?"

"Very wet here," he laughed. "Even in the summer. But she likes to see Mikey."

"And you – do you like working here?" Emily knew

that many of the immigrants were simply here for the money and had very little interest in Ireland in itself. The fact that Stan and Lucas were out for a drink in Rathmollin told her that maybe they were a little more settled here than most.

"Very much. We are very lucky to work for Jack. Some of our friends in Cork are not so lucky."

"Really?" Emily wasn't at all surprised that some of Stan's compatriots had been taken advantage of. It was a pleasant surprise to hear that Jack was a reasonable employer.

"Yes – we have very good facilities here, even our accommodation. And overtime pay is extra. We had a fire once in the house, you know, and I feared we would have to go but Jack fixed everything."

"A fire? Was anyone injured?" Emily had heard stories like this before about substandard housing that didn't come within an ass's roar of meeting fire regulations.

"Not badly. My little Mikey went to hospital but did not stay. We live in the city near the Quays. There are two apartments in the house and one of the women looks after the children while the other women work. She was cooking and the fire happened. My son, Mikey, was there when the fire started but the fireman saved him."

Emily was fascinated, as well as being horrified at what might have happened if the fire service hadn't been so successful. "How many children were in there, Stan?"

"Eight children with Monika Malisa. She also went to hospital."

"That's terrible, Stan. Where did everyone stay after that?" She could just imagine the distress of something like this happening, especially when many of those involved might have had a language barrier to deal with as well.

"Jack was very near so he came and organised all of this. He ran to the fire actually," Stan said proudly. "Lucas and one other friend went to Jack's house. Some went to other friends. But the house was fixed very quickly. Jack is a very good man, Emily."

From the significant way that Stan said this, it made her think that Lucas had reported to him about her and Jack talking in her bedroom earlier in the day. She immediately dismissed this as paranoia of the highest order. But something else struck her just then and she had to ask. "Stan, when exactly was this fire, did you say?"

"April the first. When the foreman called Jack on the phone, he thought he was making a joke. But it was no joke, Emily. It was very serious indeed."

Stan was frowning at the memory of his son's fortuitous escape. Emily too was frowning as she remembered the incident where she'd sat opposite Jack Rooney in the coffee shop on Academy Street. He'd been yelling into his phone that day, shouting about getting people out. With a sense of horror, she realised that he'd probably been trying to make himself heard over the chaos at the scene of the fire and she'd utterly misjudged him. And Stan, it was clear, idolised him.

"That must have been a nightmare," she said finally. "And very expensive," she added carefully.

"It was terrible, Emily. Everyone shouting and people coming to look. All the ambulances. Terrible. But only the baby getting full of smoke and no person dead – that was good. And everything else was fixed by Jack in one week."

"A week only?" Emily was beginning to think that maybe Jack Rooney *was* some sort of latter-day saint as Sandra kept telling her.

"It was over-time pay for all the workers and everything was fine again after that."

He'd even paid the workers overtime rates to repair a house that had probably been damaged through no fault of his, by the look of it.

"That's amazing, Stan. I'm so glad no one was badly injured." Emily looked over at Sandra to see how she was getting on with Lucas. She hoped for Sandra's sake that he was actually single. As if he'd read her mind, Stan nodded at the other pair and grinned.

"Perhaps my brother will find a lovely wife in Ireland?"

"He's not married?" Emily had to find out once and for all. The last thing her friend needed was a man with baggage.

"No, I'm afraid. Look, here is Sibile, my wife." Stan was smiling broadly at the approach of one of the smallest women that Emily had ever seen. Dressed in tight white jeans and a fitted fuchsia top, she wasn't even halfway up to her husband's shoulder.

"Sibile, this is Emily with the broken tap."

His introduction amused Emily and she smiled as she shook hands with the other woman and explained that it was now fixed thanks to Stan and Lucas.

"What would you like to drink, Sibile?" Emily had

again caught Danny Stone's eye with view to ordering another round. Lucas had insisted on taking only half of the money that she'd been trying to give him earlier in the day so she was determined to repay him and Stan properly now that she had the opportunity.

"White wine would be nice, thank you, Emily." Sibile had beautiful English and Emily recognised how beneficial this would be for little Mikey if he was to start school here in Ireland eventually.

"The same again, please, Danny, plus a white wine!" she called over the bar. The place was buzzing, something that Emily would never have suspected when she thought of how dingy The Stone's Throw had been not so long ago.

As soon as Danny had the two pints of Beamish settling on the counter, he served up the two bottles of wine and Sandra's Bacardi and Coke. Emily passed him a €50 note and gathered some of the bottles and glasses together. She swung around to hand them to Stan to distribute but found herself bumping unceremoniously into someone who was calling over her head to Danny for a pint of Murphy's. White wine sloshed over her hand, splattering the front of a pale blue shirt in the process. Emily was horrified at the mess she'd made.

"Oh God . . . I'm sorry . . . I didn't see you there . . ." The white wine was already spreading across the front of the shirt and Emily glanced up in dismay, her eyes meeting those of Jack Rooney at the same time as her brain registered the scent of the aftershave he'd been wearing earlier in her bedroom. A fleeting vision of his exposed midriff popped up from somewhere in her memory bank and Emily felt the blush starting at her collar-bones.

"It's grand – at least it wasn't the red!" Jack was smiling down at her as if the whole front of his shirt wasn't actually soaked through. "It'll dry out in a few minutes," he insisted.

Still attempting valiantly to suppress the colour that was insisting on rising up her neck and into her cheeks, Emily put on her coolest voice and decided that distraction was the best course of action. "Murphy's, was it?" She felt as if an enormous hollow had just opened up inside her and her heart had suddenly plummeted into it.

"It's okay. I'll get these, Emily . . ."

"No, really – I've started so I'll finish," she grinned and turned back to the bar, hoping that the colour in her face would subside sometime soon. "A Murphy's as well, Danny," she added as soon as he arrived back to top up the two pints of Beamish.

Emily busied herself with handing out the rest of the drinks while Sandra giggled and rolled her eyes discreetly at her. What was it about Jack that made her behave like a complete eejit, she wondered as she waited for the Murphy's to settle.

She'd gone to school with him, for one thing, so it wasn't as if there was any great mystery about him. Yet she couldn't help wondering if he had a girlfriend or partner, although she was sure that Sandra would have mentioned it if there was someone in his life.

Hearing Stan speak about him earlier had made her view him in a different light. For some reason, she'd been thinking of him as some kind of aggressive shark with a playboy lifestyle but looking at him now, he was starting to seem like a normal person. And gorgeous, she had to admit as she handed him the pint of Murphy's at last.

"There you go." She grimaced at the sight of his shirt. "And sorry about the mess."

"It'll be fine, Emily," he said, his smile hitting her like a ton of bricks. "Cheers."

Their eyes met then and suddenly Emily felt as if everyone else in the pub had just melted into the background, the way it happened in films and books.

"Cheers," she responded, knowing full well that all her resolutions about charming men had just gone up in a puff of smoke.

Jack tried to stop himself from staring down at Emily's face as she smiled and clinked her glass against his. She was so delicate and serene, yet every time they encountered each other he seemed to be invading her space and upsetting her. He could feel the coolness of the white wine soaking into his skin through the front of his shirt and couldn't believe that he'd done it again. He hadn't realised that it was Emily that he was leaning over when he'd beckoned to Danny Stone for his usual pint of Murphy's. At least not until she'd tried to turn around and found him blocking her like the big hulk that he seemed to become every time he came within an Irish mile of her. He could tell that she'd been mortified when he caused her to spill the drinks. She clearly hated to cause a fuss or draw attention to herself. The day that he'd upset her in the hospital, he'd noticed that she was gritting her teeth to stop herself from crying, even though she'd had perfectly good reason for doing so.

It galled Jack that Paul Delaney was walking around Mallow, as free as a bird by all accounts, while Emily had had her life interrupted and just had to get on with it. Just a few days ago, Jack had opened his post to find a request for a character reference for Paul, the headed paper indicating the firm of solicitors who had the poisoned chalice of representing him. Before he could even stop himself, he'd swiftly replied stating that he would be unable to give a favourable reference. He'd done enough harm to Emily by giving Paul Delaney back his job when he should have sent him packing – he certainly wasn't going to compound it now by setting him up as the next Padre Pio in a glowing reference.

The court case would come up soon enough, Jack suspected – another ordeal for Emily to go through. According to Sandra, she was tougher than she looked and had put Paul Delaney to the back of her mind. Not to mention the fellow she'd been engaged to. He didn't know exactly what had happened with that but it was beyond Jack's comprehension that anyone could be engaged to Emily and not think they were the luckiest man alive.

He watched her now as she chatted to Sibile, her face alive and interested, and wished for a moment that it was him making her laugh out loud instead of Stan's petite, charming wife. Jack knew that he'd overstepped the mark earlier by the way that she'd looked at him when she'd landed into her own bedroom to find him appearing out of the attic. He'd thought he was actually doing her a favour but from the shocked look on her face, it was clear that the last thing she expected was someone to invade her space without excuse or invitation.

The thought of Emily's bedroom, serene and ordered, made Jack close his eyes briefly. He took a large gulp from the pint glass, forcing himself to divert from any thoughts of actually being there again with her.

"Perhaps she might like to go on a date, Jack?"

Stan's voice broke in on his thoughts and Jack sensed that he'd been studying Emily a little more obviously than he'd imagined. His comment was definitely more a question than a statement.

"Who?" Obtuseness was definitely a better option than getting into a discussion with Stan about his status with Emily.

Stan just grinned and turned towards the bar. "Another Murphy's maybe would help?"

Jack couldn't help smiling at Stan's optimism. Asking Emily out would probably make her run a mile. He'd done enough already to alienate her. What he needed to do now was back off a little.

Despite Danny Stone calling time on at least six occasions from eleven o'clock onwards, it was half twelve by the time the pub began to clear properly. Sibile, anxious to get home before Mikey woke for his night feed, eventually herded her husband and brother-in-law towards the door, leaving Jack, Emily and Sandra to drain the last of their drinks and protect their ankles from Danny as he swiped a sweeping brush around the floor by way of evicting the last of the stragglers.

"That's our cue to leave – the next thing will be the bright lights switched on and we *have* to be out before that," Sandra giggled and grinned at Emily, who nodded her agreement vehemently.

Jack looked perplexed. "What's the big rush about the lights going on?"

"Easy known you've never worn mascara!" Emily informed him. "We'll be like two pandas when you get a proper look at us!"

Jack laughed. "Right – I'll take your word for it! Come on so and I'll drop the two of you home. On foot, if that's all right?"

"It'll take hours to get me home," Sandra joked, making her way towards the door. The cottage was only minutes away, whereas Harmony Cottage was at the far end of the village. Emily followed her closely, hoping that Sandra might be able to tell her discreetly if she'd be meeting Lucas again. They'd spent most of the evening talking and laughing together and Emily thought it would be a fantastic boost to her confidence if Lucas did ask her out. Especially now that they'd ascertained that he was free and single.

"There's no need to walk me, Jack – it's only a few minutes," Emily insisted as they crossed the street to Sandra's place. Jack lived at the opposite end of Rathmollin, about a hundred yards beyond The Stone's Throw in the big old two-storey that he'd inherited from his parents. Emily wondered what it was like inside and whether he'd modernised it at all, considering the line of business he was in. She'd passed it on her walks and had been impressed by the freshly painted pale cream dashing and the solid green front door. Solid like Jack, she thought, then berated herself for being fanciful and maybe a little tipsy.

"You can't walk off on your own. I know it's only Rathmollin but anything could happen to you."

"You're probably right, Jack," she laughed, the irony of his words not lost on her. "I lived safely in Dublin for years but I was knocked down in Rathmollin after a mere few months!"

Sandra smiled and gave her shoulder a quick squeeze, glad that Emily was able to make light of her ordeal.

Jack looked mortified. "Jesus, Emily, I'm sorry – I didn't mean that . . ."

They were at Sandra's gate now. "You're grand, Jack." She winked at Sandra. "Talk to you tomorrow, okay?"

"First thing," Sandra grinned, meaning that she'd be on the blower with news post haste.

"Okay so." The moment Sandra disappeared in her front door, Emily felt self-conscious. It was strange being on her own with Jack, even though *he* seemed to be his usual calm self.

"Sorry about earlier," Jack said suddenly. "I didn't mean to drag up the crash again."

It didn't bother Emily in the least and she told him so. "I've talked about it so much at this stage that it seems ages ago. I was really lucky, you know."

She could feel him smiling in the dark as they walked along. "That's what I call optimism!"

"You know what I mean – I'm back to work, I've bought the house, I'm as healthy as I was before. Probably healthier because of all the exercise I had to do!"

"You're not sorry you moved back here?" Jack's voice was quiet and there was a moment's silence as she considered this. Despite the fact that things had been a bit hairy since she'd left Dublin, Emily was still convinced that she'd made the right move in getting away from Richard and the circle of people that she'd thought of as friends.

"No, I'm delighted I did. The accident could have happened anywhere – there are asses like Paul Delaney everywhere." She tucked her arms around herself as a slight breeze lifted her top, the summer air fanning her back. "And it's a hell of a lot easier to get to work when you don't have two hours of grid-lock to face."

"True." They walked along in silence for a bit.

"What about you? Did you find it quiet here after being away for so long?" Emily didn't know how long he'd lived in the States but she imagined he must have found Rathmollin a bit dull when he'd returned.

"I always knew I'd come back at some stage – I just didn't think it'd be the best part of eight years before I did. But I settled in straight away again."

"I think it's good to get away," Emily said thoughtfully, remembering how keen she'd been to go to college in Dublin rather than Cork. And if it hadn't been for Richard's shenanigans, she'd probably still be away. It seemed like another life now, all the going out to smart restaurants with people they hardly knew and the big deal about having people over for ever more complicated dinner parties. It all seemed so false compared to the life she led now. "But I'm glad to be back."

"You kept the same name," Jack remarked as they arrived at her gate.

She studied the small wrought-iron name plate over the red door with its polished brasses. "I figured it'd be a shame to get rid of it in case all the harmony went as well." She opened the door and turned to face him, suddenly reluctant for him to leave. "I was going to ask you if you wanted coffee earlier today," she began hesitantly, "but Lucas arrived and . . ." She trailed off, conscious that Jack was looking down at his feet. He was probably dying to get home.

He looked up then, his voice barely a whisper. "I'd love coffee." He cleared his throat. "That'd be good." He was looking at her strangely and Emily knew there and then that she wanted to kiss him. Everything about him was right, she thought.

Jack stood stock still, terrified that he was going to put his foot in it again and frighten her away. He badly wanted to touch her face and see how her skin would feel under his fingertips, how her hair would feel in his hands.

Emily's eyes searched Jack's face. There was the briefest moment where she wondered if kissing him would be the wrong thing to do. In that split second she remembered telling Sandra that she was no longer going to be the old wishy-washy Emily Gordon.

Then she reached up to touch Jack's face, her thumb caressing the side of his mouth. She watched as his eyes closed and felt his fingers pushing gently into her hair. She knew then that there would be no coffee until much, much later.

New Year's Eve

Aggie rinsed and dried her willow-patterned cereal bowl and placed it next to Joe's on the sideboard, ready for the following morning's breakfast. She had a busy day ahead of her by all accounts. For a start, it was New Year's Eve and the Gala Bingo would be starting at nine o'clock. Aggie had narrowly missed out on the grand prize of €5000 last year and she planned to mark at least three books this year instead of her usual two.

Meantime, there was her hair to be done, seeing as it was Friday, and the whole mystery of the party to get to the bottom of. Sandra Coyne, for a start, would surely know something, although Aggie found her to be a touch reticent with news these days on account of her being so closely watched by Chrissie in the salon. Anyway, there would certainly be no harm in asking.

First though, she should ring Jacinta Gordon – straight to the horse's mouth, so to speak.

"Who are you ringing now?" Joe was always on at her

about the phone bill but as far as Aggie was concerned, it was the only bit of comfort she had, that and bingo.

"I want to have a word with Jacinta about this party. I'm surprised she didn't say anything about it yesterday in Connolly's."

Aggie had indeed been surprised, especially when she'd specifically asked Jacinta if she and Tom had anything exciting planned for New Year's Eve. Jacinta had only told her that they'd be staying in with a cup of tea and whatever was on the television, adding that they had a lot to be thankful for after all that had happened during the year. Not a word about Miss Emily and her party.

"Sure the party's only for young ones," Joe reasoned. "I can't see Tom Gordon jitterbugging all night to loud music."

"All the same," Aggie sniffed, very put out. You'd think it would at least have been mentioned, even if she had to refuse on account of the bingo. She continued dialling the Gordons' number, oblivious to her husband's exasperated look.

"It's Aggie here." She listened to Jacinta's greeting, anticipating at least a reference to the big night ahead in Emily's house. Jacinta, however, only asked after Joe and commented on the weather. "I'm only ringing to remind you of the big prize tonight," Aggie went on, "in case you wanted to come to bingo with me." Jacinta went occasionally and Aggie had forgotten to mention it in Connolly's yesterday, as she was on red alert for information on the party.

"Thanks, Aggie, but I think I'll stay put. Tom hasn't a bit of interest in bingo and I don't want to leave him here on his own on New Year's Eve. It's €5000 tonight, I hear."

Aggie nodded vigorously, forgetting that Jacinta couldn't actually see her. "I still have my doubts about Sadie Kilduff last year. She was only marking one book, you know. Kitty Cassidy was marking four and she didn't come within an ass's roar of a full house." Aggie was the queen of the conspiracy theory and this wasn't the first time that Jacinta had listened on as she questioned the veracity of a big win.

"Teddy Long would be keeping an eye on all that, surely?"

Aggie was disgusted. Since the time that she'd – quite rightly – instigated an investigation after Kitty Cassidy won the Snowball three weeks in a row, there had been a Commissioner of Oaths engaged to oversee proceedings. Kitty's win had been upheld, of course, despite Aggie's ongoing protest.

"Teddy's asleep half the time," she said disparagingly. "Well, that's it for now, Jacinta. I'd better get going or I'll miss my appointment and Chrissie will be like a dog about it." She could see Joe eyeing her from the corner of the sitting-room, wondering, no doubt, if she'd dare to ask about the party. "I suppose it'll be a quiet night in for Emily too after the year she's had?"

Jacinta laughed. "She's had enough excitement for one year, Aggie, but she doesn't let it get her down. She's having a few friends over to the house and a few drinks, I think. It'll do her the world of good."

There it was. Just like that. Not a word about invitations or who was going or anything.

"A party? In the cottage?"

That was what Aggie had heard the Polish fellow saying to Jack Rooney in the grocery, after all. Stocking up for Emily's party, he'd said, when Jack commented on the two bottles of vodka he'd had under his arm. Aggie wondered if it was possible that Jacinta didn't actually know about the party. Which might be the case if it was going to be full of drunk Polish fellows and maybe even Emily's old friends down from Dublin snorting cocaine up their noses.

"It'll be a sort of house-warming for her as well," Jacinta seemed to be agreeing. "She's after getting a patio heater so that anyone who smokes can go outside."

"Well . . ." Aggie didn't know how to answer this. It was clear that Jacinta *did* know about this party but she didn't seem one bit perturbed to be left sitting by the fire with Tom while the whole country, Poles and all, were living it up in Harmony Cottage. And the patio itself was another thing, come to think of it. Despite a wide and varied line of questioning, Aggie didn't seem to be able to get any definitive answer on the subject of Emily and Jack Rooney. Which was why she'd been hoping to see the evidence for herself in some shape or form. "Is the patio finished then, Jacinta?"

"Well, insofar as it can be done in the winter. It'll be great for her next year when she gets a few pots and containers going."

Aggie had noted Jack Rooney carrying in what looked like patio slabs through the small gate at the side of Emily's house a few Saturdays ago and his pick-up truck had been there on and off ever since, piled up with bags of cement and shovels. It baffled her, if anything. Not so long ago, Jack was trying to swipe the house out from under Emily while she was in her sick-bed and now here he was all about her, laying patio slabs. The autumn had gone by without her getting to the bottom of this new companionship between the two of them but Aggie knew there was more to it.

"It's hard going for a young one like her, Jacinta. And Tom isn't much use to her for heavy work after his bypass operation."

"Ah, she has plenty of help, Aggie," Jacinta said mildly. "There are plenty of builders around the place wanting to make a few bob of an evening."

So Emily was paying Jack.

"Especially those nice Polish fellows," Jacinta continued. "They're great workers."

Fast workers, more like! Aggie had heard on the grapevine that there was a great big hulk of a fellow stepping around with Sandra Coyne – indeed anyone with a pair of eyes in their head could see him coming and going from the house at all hours of the day and night. Not that Rose and Dan would admit much the day she called with an apple tart.

"I suppose they'll be all invited to the party?" It looked like the oldies were to be excluded but at the very least she might be told who *would* be there.

"I imagine so. Those two brothers were a great help to Emily the day the plumbing broke down. Did I tell you that, Aggie?"

Aggie, bored with hearing about how wonderful and

helpful the two foreigners were, decided that she'd had enough of Jacinta Gordon's evasiveness. "Well, goodbye for now," she said firmly. There was more to be gained from whoever she might meet in Curly Locks.

"Well?" Joe quizzed as soon as she'd put the phone down. "Are you any better off after that?"

If it was left to him they wouldn't know what day of the week it was, thought his wife.

"I'm off now to get my hair done. Don't forget to peel the potatoes, sure you won't?"

"I won't," he answered wearily.

Joe Lenihan had been listening to the non-details of Emily Gordon's party for three days now and badly needed a break from his wife. Peeling the potatoes would be therapy for him. It was getting harder these days to cope with his wife's obsession with other people's lives. Joe Lenihan was a man who liked a quiet life but, with Aggie, life wasn't quiet even for a moment.

Joe opened the press under the sink and pulled out the plastic bag of Roosters. An idea struck him then. Aggie wouldn't be back for at least a few hours. Potatoes were all very fine but maybe, if he put the skates on, he could slip away for an hour of *proper* therapy. Joe's eyes brightened and his pulse started to pace just a little faster. Even an hour would do him the world of good.

By the time Aggie reached Curly Locks, she'd spoken to three people, none of whom knew much about the party. She'd commented to Mac Gleeson as he polished the shop window that the grocery must be busy with all the Polish crowd buying more drink for the big party. Mac had shaken his head and said it was quiet so far this morning, hence his opportunity to clean the window. Then she'd bumped into young Niall Gordon getting out of his car. He said that he'd probably go to The Stone's for a few drinks and maybe drop down to Emily's place to ring in the New Year if the pub was quiet. *As if!* Finally, she'd met Sandra Coyne tearing along the street in a pair of suede knee boots and cropped black trousers. Disappointed that she might be on a day off, Aggie had decided to tackle her there and then in case she didn't get an opportunity later.

"You're in a rush, I suppose, getting ready for this party?"

"I'll be going nowhere if I don't get a move on, Aggie," Sandra grinned. "We're out of plain biscuits so I'm just nipping to the grocery. I'll see you inside in a few minutes."

That was that, Aggie thought to herself. Sandra would be like a nun in an enclosed order once she got back into Chrissie's domain.

It was Eileen who guided Aggie to the sink, seeing as Sandra was still over at the shop.

"Going anywhere nice tonight, Aggie?" Eileen, as always, took a polite interest.

"The Bingo, I suppose. Joe said he'd come too – there's €5000 in the pot tonight. What about you, Eileen?"

"A few drinks in The Stone's, I imagine. Danny has a band in tonight."

"I suppose Sandra will be knocking off early on account of Emily Gordon's party?" This was Aggie's usual trick. If she announced something in a tone that suggested the topic was common knowledge, then people were more likely to be forthcoming.

"We're all in till six. We'll have plenty of time to gear up for the night. Now, Aggie, you can sit up there to the mirror and I'll be with you in a minute. Ah, there's Sandra back. Will you have a cuppa?"

"I will but not in one of those triangle mugs. They're impossible to get a grip on."

"And it's just milk, Aggie, isn't it? No sugar?"

"That's it, Eileen."

She saw Sandra scuttling off into the back to put the kettle on. If she hadn't been so silly with that Delaney fellow, she'd have had her time finished long ago and a few bob saved to buy a house. It disgusted Aggie that the County Council had bought up the house adjoining her own and allocated it to an "unmarried mother" like Sandra. It lowered the tone of her own pristine home, although Joe was always saying that it was great to give a young girl like Sandra a chance to get back on her feet after her "mishap" as he called it.

"Now, Aggie, just a set, is it? The colour is perfect." Eileen was studying her hair as she combed it through, not half as roughly as Chrissie was wont to do, Aggie noted. Just then the door opened and Jennie Kelleher arrived in, dolled up to the nines for a Friday morning in tight black jeans with shiny leather knee boots and a short swing coat with a luxurious fur collar. Her hair, for one arriving in a hair salon, was already immaculate. It was fine for her, having her hair done day in and day out now that she was a career-woman. The same one hadn't done a hand's turn since the day she got married yet as soon as her husband got sick she couldn't stay at home to see after him. It amazed Aggie that more people didn't see through her.

"Morning, Jennie," Eileen called. "Take a seat and Sandra will be with you."

"Thanks, Eileen. Hello, Aggie." Jennie, as ever, was all politeness. Aggie nodded back at her in the mirror, sorry that she was out of her line of vision when she went to sit on one of the leather sofas by the door.

"There you go, Aggie." Sandra placed the china mug in front of her, accompanied by two biscuits on a Christmassy napkin. "Hi, Jennie, you can come straight over. You're looking great."

"Thanks, Sandra – it's all the running around after the pair of terrors at home."

Aggie watched as Sandra guided Jennie to the basin. The mirror next to Aggie was free at the moment and there was always the possibility that Jennie would be placed there as soon as her hair was washed. Aggie sat back and sipped her tea as Eileen applied the setting lotion and started on her rollers. Surely Sandra and Jennie would make some mention of the party?

As luck would have it, Jennie was indeed placed next to her a few minutes later. Aggie sat back with her eyes closed and concentrated on eavesdropping over the low hum of her hooded dryer as soon as Eileen set the timer and disappeared.

"I suppose we could," Jennie was saying. "Vincent's mother is staying the night and she was on at us to use the opportunity to have a night out. Maybe we could call in for an hour or so and be back home to ring in the New Year with Elsie."

"Do," Sandra was insisting. "It'll be a bit of crack and Emily's dying to show off the house. I'm heading over around eight to calm her down. Come anytime after that."

"I will so, Sandra." Jennie sounded pleased.

Aggie was more than surprised that she and the great Vincent Kelleher would be hanging around Rathmollin for their New Year celebrations. As far as she knew, there was some sort of New Year's Eve Ball on at the Mount Vernon that was all over the papers. Normally, the Kellehers would be pictured on the social pages of *The Echo* at such an event, snapped in all their glory next to the ever-glamorous columnist Martina O'Donoghue, doyenne of the Cork social circuit. It was a big comedown indeed to be traipsing down to Ina Harrington's old cottage for an hour.

"Great," Sandra continued, running a wide-toothed comb through Jennie's silky hair in preparation for the blow-dry. "Emily will be delighted." With that she switched on the hair-dryer, drowning out, from Aggie's perspective, any chance of further news.

Jennie, Aggie noted, was glowing. Going back to work was obviously suiting her, something that was a surprise to Aggie as she'd never appeared to be too fond of work before. Of course she was working for her husband and would therefore be suiting herself as regards time off and not getting involved in anything too difficult, Aggie imagined. You wouldn't see Jennie Kelleher going out to work in the real world like everyone else! And it wasn't as if she needed the money. Or maybe she did if it was a thing that Vincent's earning-power had collapsed as a result of his poor health. There was a turnaround! Jennie having to earn a living.

Aggie pondered on this as her head warmed up under the gentle blow of the hooded dryer and the heat seeped through to her scalp. It was amazing, she thought as she dozed off, the way things ebbed and flowed in a small village.

Jennie was delighted when she noticed Aggie dozing off under the overhead dryer. She'd been watching Jennie with barely concealed interest, especially when Sandra had commented on how well she was looking. It wasn't beyond the bounds of possibility that Aggie would have her news sussed before she'd had time to announce it herself.

It wasn't as if they'd planned anything like this. But now that it had happened, Jennie and Vincent were delighted. They'd talked about another baby in the early days but had decided fairly quickly that two children were enough, especially with the business taking off and Jennie being busy enough already with Tim and Lucy. What if it was twins maybe, they'd joked at the time, a risk that neither of them had really wanted to take. So Jennie had just taken her pill on autopilot every morning, a routine that was as second nature to her now as brushing her teeth or putting on her make-up.

Vincent being ill had disrupted everything, of course.

And sex had been the last thing on either of their agendas so it hadn't bothered her too much when her six-month prescription lapsed. Normally she'd have been down to the surgery well in advance to have her blood pressure checked before her script was written out by Dr Lawlor. But starting the refresher course had put paid to all the time she used to have to herself and renewing her prescription had been well down the list of priorities.

Vincent had been thrilled when she'd told him tentatively that her period was a week late. She'd spent the whole morning worrying that it might be too much for him but had decided that their new "honesty and openness" policy was paramount. He'd sat on the bed while she did the test in the en suite bathroom and had cried when the faint blue line became a strong, solid one.

"I'm so lucky," he'd whispered, his arms tight around her.

Jennie, mesmerised at this little miracle that was happening before their eyes, had reminded him that she too was lucky. A new baby, when only a few months ago she'd thought her life was an empty sham.

"I blame Mr Mulligan!" Vincent had said eventually and Jennie too had had to laugh. They'd gone together to the out-patients department for Vincent's follow-up appointment a few months earlier and out of the blue the cardiologist had asked delicately if they had "returned to intercourse" yet.

Jennie had been mortified. She'd thought about it, of course, but had been reluctant to bring up the subject with Vincent in case he saw it as a complaint about being denied her marital rights. It hadn't been long, after all, and she figured that Vincent would know himself when he was ready.

Vincent, to his credit, had answered the cardiologist with equanimity, saying that he hadn't wanted to do anything that would necessitate Jennie having to call an ambulance again.

"Well, there is no reason not to start again, if you both feel comfortable with that. As a rule of thumb, Vincent, you're ready as soon as you can do two flights of stairs without getting chest pain or breathlessness. So I'll leave it to the pair of you to work out."

"I think we're safe enough," Vincent had told her in the car on the way home. "Lucy had me up and down the stairs *three* times this morning looking for her Bratz bobbins when I was getting them ready for school. So that's the Rule of Thumb sorted out!"

Jennie grinned to herself now at the memory of that night and the wonderful surprise that she was now keeping to herself. They would wait, both of them agreed, until after the New Year to broadcast their surprise pregnancy – the likes of Aggie had had enough ammunition on their account so far this year. Sandra knew, of course, and Emily. Jennie had told them the news a few weeks earlier at one of the Saturday lunches that they'd started having lately.

Things *did* work in mysterious ways, Jennie thought now. If it hadn't been for her madness in thinking that Vincent was having an affair, she'd never have been forced into straightening her life out. It was like her life had become complete somehow, with her new friends and the close bond that she'd developed with Elsie. The baby would be the icing on the cake. They'd be a proper family, that was the main thing, especially now that Elsie had become a very real and important part of it.

She closed her eyes and enjoyed the sensation of Sandra ministering to her hair. It would be a wonderful New Year for them, she knew.

Aggie woke with a jolt when the timer on the dryer clicked off twenty minutes later.

Jennie Kelleher, to her disgust, was gone. Sandra, having noted the click of the dryer, arrived to remove Aggie's rollers and finish the job that Eileen had started.

"Will it be the Bingo tonight, Aggie? Mam says its €5000 for the Jackpot." Rose Coyne went to Bingo the odd Saturday night.

"It is," Aggie agreed, delighted with this opening about nights out. "You'll be going down to Emily's, I suppose? Jacinta said there was a bit of a hooley going on."

"Maybe not exactly a hooley, Aggie," Sandra smiled. "More of a get-together. Harmony Cottage wasn't exactly built for a big crowd!"

"I suppose not," Aggie sniffed, glad to be getting somewhere at last. Chrissie, she noted, had disappeared from the salon while she was dozing. "I saw that nice Polish fellow in the grocery – the one that helped Emily with the tap that time – getting ready for the party. Jacinta said he was a great help, him and the brother." They were so alike that Aggie couldn't actually pinpoint which one Sandra was consorting with.

"Mmmmm ..." Sandra reddened a little and continued teasing out the rollers carefully. Chrissie definitely wouldn't like to hear her discussing details of her personal life with a customer, even if Aggie had been the one to bring the subject up.

"It's hard luck on them, really, this down-turn in the economy," Aggie went on. "They say a lot of the foreigners will have to go back to their own countries as soon as the work dries up." She looked at Sandra to see if a reaction was forthcoming. She'd want to be careful, Aggie thought, or she'd be left with another child. And Chrissie mightn't be as understanding a second time around.

"Hopefully it'll level out a bit," Sandra answered non-committally. "There you go, Aggie. Eileen will be with you in a few minutes." She had collected the rollers into a plastic bowl and now laid out a series of round brushes for Eileen. "Have a good time later – you never know, you might sweep the jackpot!"

Sandra retreated to the back room with the rollers and let out a sigh of relief. Aggie was something else, implying that Lucas would be disappearing off the face of the earth at any minute. No doubt she was expecting another surprise pregnancy out of her any minute, considering how much she'd had to say to all and sundry the time Dylan was born.

There *was* a bit of a down-turn in the economy as Aggie had put it but hopefully it wouldn't be affecting Lucas, if he had anything to do with it. They'd talked about this, what would happen if the building trade slackened off and Sandra had been surprised to hear that Lucas had already applied for a teaching job in the plumbing department of the Institute of Trades and Technology.

He hadn't wanted to tell her until he had a definite date for an interview but he was determined to stay in Ireland, especially now that he'd met Sandra and Dylan. He'd said that – "you and Dylan". He saw them as a package and as a permanent part of his life, he'd told her in English that was now full of Dylan's buzz words. He was so open about it, the getting of a permanent job so that there would be no question of him moving from Rathmollin. It had taken her a while to get used to his straightforward, honest manner after all the shenanigans she'd endured with Paul.

"And then we will get a mortgage maybe, Sandra? And perhaps you would like to get married to me if you are happy and Dylan is happy?"

Sandra had been flabbergasted at what looked to be a proposal. She knew that Lucas loved her – he told her often enough and showed her in so many ways, but to hear him talk of marriage as if it were the most natural progression in the world was magical. "But we will wait until January 11th for my interview first," he'd continued. "I would like a good job before all this will happen."

Sandra, at this point, hadn't even mentioned the house that she and Dylan would be getting in the new development, terrified that it might somehow fall through and that she'd look a fool. She'd lost her confidence with Paul and it would take a lot to bring that back to rights.

Once she'd explained the situation to Lucas, he'd been marvellous.

"I have a lot of savings now. Perhaps later, if I get this job, I can help to pay for this house?"

Sandra hadn't thought for a moment when she'd discussed her finances with the bank manager that there would be two wage cheques helping to pay her mortgage. But now it looked like this would be the case. Lucas had been so good to her already, helping her around the house and cutting the grass – the kind of things that normal boyfriends did.

She wondered now how she'd ever been taken in by Paul Delaney. He'd never paid for a thing around the house whereas Lucas was always arriving with a bag of groceries or paying for their Friday night take-away. He automatically stood to clear the table after a meal, insisting that Sandra sat down to rest if she'd done the cooking. But it was his attitude towards Dylan that really showed Sandra the kind of man that Lucas was. He treated him with so much respect, asking his opinion on things like grammar if he heard a new English word and never undermining Dylan's position as the number one person in Sandra's life. Lucas was comfortable in his own skin and seemed to have no understanding of deceit or subterfuge. He'd showed her his credit union book only the previous evening and explained to her that he sent a small amount of his wages to his parents each month. She'd never known what Paul was earning or where his money went to other than what went across the bar to Danny Stone.

Sandra sorted the fresh towels now in the back room of Curly Locks while she waited for the next customer to arrive. Her life had changed dramatically and she was beginning to agree with Emily when she said that it had taken the car accident to let her really see Paul for what he was. Things happened for a reason, Emily said, although Sandra sometimes wondered how she could be so philosophical after all that she'd been through.

It was all over now, thanks to Nuala Crawford and her good sense. It was unbelievable to Sandra that the intimidating solicitor, of whom she'd always been a little bit terrified, had turned out to be a blessing in disguise. If it hadn't been for Sandra sticking up for Rufus against the bullies that day in the schoolyard, Emily might never have been the beneficiary of Nuala's expert advice, and for free at that.

Sandra had always felt a little bit sorry for Rufus the way he was deposited outside the school while his parents swizzed off to their high-powered jobs. It was only recently that Sandra had become aware of the reasons. Never in a million years would she have imagined that the Crawfords had been living on almost as tight a budget as she herself was. Well, maybe not quite – but almost. Nuala had thanked her outside the school for the change that she'd wrought in Rufus now that the resident bullies were kowtowing to him and confided that she didn't spend as much time with her son as she would like to. They'd bought the house in Rathmollin Woods at a time when Nuala was about to be made a partner in her firm, something that would have included a substantial pay increase. It hadn't come to pass, however, as a nephew of the senior partner had been elevated instead, leaving the Crawfords with a hefty mortgage that they really couldn't afford. It killed her, she told Sandra, that children like Dylan were lucky enough to have their mothers' time and attention while poor Rufus was nearly ready for bed by the time he was collected from Maxine Daly's Busy Kidz. To think that Nuala thought Dylan better off than Rufus astounded Sandra, considering that *she* spent the whole time regretting the things that she couldn't provide for him.

It had been Nuala who'd put Emily straight on what was the right thing to do. Yes, Paul deserved all the punishment that could be meted out to him but did Dylan deserve the indignity of having his father in jail? Would it be a stigma that would shadow him into his teenage years?

Sandra grinned to herself as the sound of Aggie giving out about how easy it would be to rig the Bingo. If the old busybody knew the half of what was going on in Sandra's life she'd be apoplectic. Paul Delaney's conviction done and dusted and Sandra Coyne on the brink of an engagement to the up-and-coming Lucas Kovaciwycz? She'd wear the tyres off her bicycle trying to deliver the news to the people of Rathmollin.

Aggie was grumpy as Eileen put the finishing touches to her hair. She'd managed to squeeze bugger-all in the line of news out of Sandra, who used to be such a chatty girl until she'd started hanging around with Emily Gordon and even Jennie Kelleher. It seemed to Aggie that neither of them had wanted to know Sandra when she was a struggling single mother with an undesirable boyfriend in tow. Now that she was back in the work force dressed to the nines, they were all about her. Aggie sat back and waited for Eileen to return with the hairspray that she'd gone to fetch. She'd have to ask her what band it was that Danny Stone had booked for later and maybe she and Joe could pop in for an hour after the Bingo. After all, it was New Year's Eve – there was bound to be someone doing something daft.

As soon as she was sprayed and had her hair-net in place, Aggie left the salon and mounted her bicycle. She needed to go to the butcher's to get a roast for New Year's Day as well as picking up a few bits in the grocery for Paddy Gallagher who was home from hospital after breaking his hip. Angela, his daughter, was a GP but there wasn't much sign of her as far as Aggie could see.

It was a lovely fresh day with bright winter sunshine and clear crisp air – the kind of day that the village was at its best, as far as Aggie was concerned. People were queuing up to have their cars washed at Dooley's Statoil, although there were more 4x4's than cars these days, she observed. She'd nip over to Paddy's first to get a list of what he wanted from the shops, she decided, pushing off outside Curly Locks. There was a car outside Jack Rooney's house, she noted, slowing down to see who it was. It was Vincent Kelleher re-arranging his boot and sure enough, Jack arrived out with a set of golf clubs as she passed.

"Morning, Aggie," Vincent greeted.

He looked to be in full health, making her wonder about the seriousness of his heart attack, if that's what he'd had at all. He couldn't be too bad if he was going off to play golf. It was a great little country – Jennie out at the hairdresser all morning, her husband off to the golf course and two small children at home with God only knew who looking after them. She'd heard Jennie saying to Sandra that her mother-in-law was staying. Maybe she'd been left to baby-sit while the other two were doing their own thing.

"Morning, Vincent, Jack – Happy New Year."

Aggie was on speaking terms with everyone in the village, something she enjoyed to the full. She pedalled on, her mind already plotting how to ask Paddy Gallagher more about Elsie Kelleher, to whom he was distantly related. The last she'd heard, Elsie and Miss Jennie didn't exactly hit it off. There was nothing in particular but whatever it was, it seemed to have thawed a bit.

Jack threw his golf bag and trolley into the boot and grinned at Vincent.

"She'll probably tell the whole village we're having an affair," he quipped, nodding at Aggie's retreating back.

"Better than telling them all that I'm on my last legs," Vincent retorted. "I'd say she has me ready for a heart transplant at the very least."

It was great to be heading out onto the golf course again, even if it was only nine holes to begin with. He'd felt comfortable clearing this with Jack, who was only too glad to take it easy after a hectic Christmas.

Somehow, things were starting to come back to normal. At first, Vincent had been tentative about even the slightest bit of exercise, terrified of causing a repeat of the horrendous evening that he'd had the heart attack. Gradually though, he started doing a little, extending it bit by bit until he felt comfortable. Jennie's idea of a walk with Tim and Lucy every Sunday had been inspired. The kids dawdled enough to prevent the pace from getting too hectic and they stopped to explore something or other every few minutes, allowing him to rest without too much fuss.

The baby was the icing on the cake, even though it was early days yet and they'd decided to keep their news to themselves for another few weeks. Jennie was in great form – not a bit sick – and was looking forward to the party at Emily's house later.

"Jennie and I are going to drop down to Emily's for a bit later," he told Jack now. "Mam says she'll baby-sit but we'll probably try to get home to ring in the New Year with her. Is there a big crowd coming?" Vincent was worried about Jennie being pushed and shoved if there was going to be a big gang of revellers squashed into the tiny cottage.

"If Niall has anything to do with it the whole parish will be there. Emily's trying to make him contain his enthusiasm in case she runs out of food, although she seems to be planning to feed a small army."

Vincent could see the way Jack's face lit up when he spoke about Emily. He'd met several of his friend's girlfriends over the years but none of them seemed to have had this effect on him.

"You're getting on well then?" Vincent was only

teasing – he already knew that Jack was hooked on Emily Gordon.

"Grand," Jack grinned and Vincent had never seen him looking so happy.

"So what's the plan?"

Jack was the type to keep his cards fairly close to his chest but Vincent couldn't help wondering exactly how serious it was. He'd been so lucky to have met Jennie – they'd hit it off straight away and, despite the hours he'd had to put in over the years to get the business off the ground and the shock of the heart attack, they'd never been closer.

Jack glanced over at him now, almost sheepish-looking. "*I* have plenty of plans – I'm just not sure that Emily's ready to hear them just yet," he said, his tone wry.

"Have you talked to her?" Vincent had learned the hard way that talking things through saved a lot of stress in the long run.

"Not exactly – I mean, she knows how I feel about her. But marriage. That Richard fellow . . ." Jack's voice trailed off and his face displayed an uncharacteristic anxiety.

"Is it that you think she's not ready yet?" Dithering was usually low on Jack's list of personal traits. "Not like you to dither."

"It's not that I'm dithering, Vincent," he said heatedly as they passed through the natural stone pillars of Glenconner Lodge. "I just don't want to rush her – especially after the year she's had."

"Jack, after the year that Emily's put down I imagine she'd be thrilled to make a new start." He pulled in neatly next to an Audi TT and killed the engine.

"Do you think?" Jack was looking at him so hopefully that Vincent had to laugh.

"I *do* think, actually. Don't sit around wasting time, Jack – I've learned the hard way that there mightn't be as many tomorrows as we expect. I'm sure Emily will think the same – not to mention the fact that she thinks you're a God, according to Jennie and Sandra!"

"And they'd know, would they?" Jack was smiling at last, the anxiety gone from his face. Vincent was right – there was no point in wasting precious time. Not where being with Emily was concerned.

To Aggie's surprise, Angela Gallagher-Brennan, as she liked to call herself, was tucking into a plate of sausages, rashers and Clonakilty black pudding with her father when Aggie arrived into Paddy's neat bungalow, situated just beyond Jack Rooney's two-storey at the edge of the village.

"Hi, Aggie," Angela greeted. "Cup of tea?"

Paddy wished her a Happy New Year and beckoned towards the chair next to him. "I'm delighted you came, Aggie. Angela here was just going to drop up to you with a Christmas box. I got a bit behind this year with the old hip giving up."

Aggie was totally taken aback. "There's no need, Paddy. Isn't it great you're on the mend?"

Angela placed a cup of tea in front of her, accompanied by a generous slice of Christmas cake.

"I'm off to Bandon with Angela now for a few weeks. She's after getting a locum in."

Angela, in jeans and a cotton sweater, didn't look a bit like a GP with a double-barrel name this morning.

"Are you now, Paddy? Isn't that great?" Aggie thought it was high time Angela pitched in. Paddy was home from hospital three days as it was.

"Sure there's not a bother on me, really, only they're all fussing." Paddy grinned at his daughter. "Damien stayed the past few nights to make sure I was all right – I have a stone weight put on, Aggie, to tell you the truth."

"Damien's going back to London later today," Angela told her. Damien Gallagher was a lecturer in some big university, Aggie knew. "It was desperate trying to get a locum this time of year," Angela went on, "but the fellow I got will do a full three weeks starting tomorrow."

Paddy started to laugh. "It'll be like a physio department, Aggie. She's going to make sure I do my exercises and all that to get me going again." Paddy tucked into the grill in front of him. "And I suppose I'll have to watch my cholesterol as well."

"You'll be in the right place for it, Dad," Angela said, then held out the teapot. "A hot drop, Aggie?"

"No, thanks, Angela – I only dropped in to see how Paddy was getting on and if he wanted anything from the shops."

She got up, the wind taken out of her sails at the fact that Angela Gallagher-Brennan seemed to have everything under control. And she couldn't exactly bring up the subject of Jennie Kelleher and her mother-in-law for no good reason in front of Angela.

"I'll see you in a few weeks so, Paddy. Let me know

when you're coming and I'll put the heat on in advance." Aggie had a key to nearly every house in Rathmollin.

Soon she was on her way again, a wrapped box from Paddy in the basket of her bike. Emily Gordon was pulled up outside her parents' house, her back bent as she rooted in the boot of her car.

"Hi there, Emily!" Aggie shouted, wondering whether to stop for a chat or not. She decided against it, not wanting Jacinta to think she was looking for news when she'd already phoned the house that morning. She wouldn't give her the soot of it.

Emily unloaded a pair of Tesco bags from her boot and straightened to greet Aggie as she pedalled by. Aggie wondered why she was doing Jacinta's shopping for her. Perhaps Tom wasn't well again – maybe that was the reason the elder Gordons were staying in this New Year's Eve.

Emily grinned at Aggie' retreating back and landed the first two Tesco bags on the doorstep. She had thought for a moment that she was going to stop and question her as to why she was bringing groceries into her mother's house. It wouldn't be beyond Aggie's capabilities. She'd known as soon as she'd left the checkout that she'd never fit everything in her own fridge so some of it would have to be left with Jacinta to be collected later. Glancing at her watch, she realised that time was moving on – it might be the thing to do some of the food here and Tom might be persuaded to bring it over in the evening.

A year ago, in the aftermath of Richard's deception,

Emily had sworn that she was never again buying into the superficial lifestyle that she'd been part of in Dublin. Pretentious cocktail parties where she stood around entertaining Richard's colleagues, performing to within an inch of her life. Looking back now, she wondered how she hadn't been able to see through it all.

Entertaining in their rented apartment had been a nightmare. How much of everything to buy in. Who was allergic to shellfish and who was on a diet. Which canapés were passé and *so* last year – just when she'd mastered the making of them. Pastry was out. Fish was in – unless someone had an allergy and could go into a convulsion even from it being in the same room. It had been nerve-wracking stuff but she'd managed to carry it off on so many occasions that she'd eventually been able to do it in her sleep.

Richard was always saying that as soon as their own house was ready, they'd be able to hold proper dinner parties, something that Emily was now glad had never come to pass.

Nonetheless, her knowledge of party food was about to stand her in good stead for her first proper get-together in Harmony Cottage. She had everything planned and, regardless of the limited space in the cottage, she'd invited practically everyone she knew. Gina and Cora from the VBA were coming, as well as some of the gang from the social work department at St Angela's.

Niall was meeting his friends in The Stone's first and as soon as they were all rounded up they'd be landing for food and drink. Sandra would be there with Lucas, as well as Stan and Sibile. And now it seemed that Jennie and

Vincent were going to drop in as soon as the kids were settled.

"Are you sure you'll have enough?" Jacinta joked as she continued ferrying bags from the doorstep to the kitchen counter.

"You know what Niall's gang are like. They'll be like those big scavenger birds that you see on the National Geographic channel – nothing but carcasses left. Where is he anyway?"

Jacinta rolled her eyes. "Jack rang him earlier and he took off to Cork – something about a keg."

"They're getting a bit carried away! Will I do some of the food here and put it in the fridge?"

"Do, so, and your dad can drop the plates down after the news." Jacinta started unpacking one of the bags, laying out pâté and smoked salmon in neat piles on the worktop.

"Are you sure you won't come down – even for ringing in the New Year?"

Jacinta laughed. "You're as bad as Aggie! She's been like a hen on a hot griddle since she got wind of a party. If she knew the oldies were invited she'd be in on top of you like a shot. Anyway, your father and I are happy to watch the telly in peace and quiet like we always do." She laid a hand on Emily's arm. "And you should be concentrating on enjoying yourself with Jack and the rest of them. There was a time we thought we'd never see you dressing up to go out again."

Jacinta gave a watery smile and started to pack stuff into the fridge. She didn't need any party to celebrate the way the year had ended for her daughter.

Emily knew her mother was thinking not only of the terrible aftermath of the accident, but about Richard and the wreck that Emily had been when she'd returned to Rathmollin after the trauma of last New Year. Jacinta and Tom were mad about Jack. And it wasn't just the fact that he lived in Rathmollin and that they knew exactly who he was, unlike Richard. They trusted and respected him, she could see that in the way they spoke about him so easily. He and Niall got on like a house on fire, a major bonus in Emily's eyes.

All of this was wonderful, of course it was, but none of it would have been any good if Emily herself hadn't felt the way she did about Jack. It didn't matter what her parents or Niall thought – nothing could stop her from loving Jack the way she did. It was all just so *right,* as if there had never been a time when they hadn't been together.

She thought about Jack now as she rolled out filo pastry with her mother's rolling pin. He'd sat there listening quietly as she told him about Richard and the kind of life they'd led in Dublin, the life that had ended when she'd had the good fortune to walk in on him wrapped around a naked Lorena Stockard on an opulent guest bed in someone else's house a year ago.

What would have happened if she hadn't found out like that? Would they be married now? Would Emily Gordon be living in blissful ignorance in a wealthy Dublin suburb with no clue of what her husband was really like? She'd asked these questions out loud to herself, and to Jack who'd listened with incredulity. He'd been genuinely outraged that *anyone* could behave the way Richard had, especially when Emily told him about her ex-fiancé's trip to St Angela's to visit her.

"What was it that he wanted from you?" Jack's eyebrows had risen into his hair in disbelief. "Don't tell me – forgiveness?"

Emily had been able to smile at this. "I suppose so. No point in both me *and* him feeling upset and bothered over the incident! He even suggested I forget all about it and return to Dublin to continue where we left off – his boss liked me, apparently!"

"Why wouldn't he?" Jack said indignantly. "Tell me you sent him away with a flea in his ear?"

"Did I what! No wonder I was in a state when you arrived in – I'd just decided to write off the male species as a bad job. You got the brunt of it that day!"

"Not permanently, I hope?"

Jack had been smiling but she'd sensed his anxiety. Jack really did want to be with her.

And if anyone had told Emily a year ago that she'd be happily fantasising about a happy-ever-after with Jack Rooney, she'd have told them that they were raving. That she was finished with men and their duplicitous ways. That she wouldn't ever be able to find it within herself to trust anyone ever again.

But here she was, getting ready for a party that would take place in her own house, Jack by her side in every way. She had her friends in Sandra and Jennie, real friends that she trusted and who cared about her – not false, superficial acquaintances like the ones she called friends in her old life.

Yes, there had been ups and downs but nothing that hadn't come full circle. Despite having to leave the job she loved in Dublin, she was back to square one with her job at St Angela's and was enjoying every day of it. The accident had been something else that had devastated her, yet she was as healthy now as she'd ever been. And since Paul Delaney and the spectre of what would become of him was no longer hanging over her, she felt she was free to put it all behind her.

It had been Nuala Crawford who'd put it all into perspective.

The Gardaí had been in contact with Emily to see if she'd give some sort of victim impact statement in their case against Paul, even though they were aware that she wouldn't be taking a case against him herself – her loss of earnings would be covered by Paul's insurance and, for Emily, that was enough. The last thing she needed was to rehash the whole thing in a protracted court case that could last years. In the case of the Gardaí, it was imperative that they get some sort of conviction, especially as Paul had been known to them before regarding a drink-driving offence.

It had been Jennie and Sandra who'd suggested that Emily talk to Nuala Crawford, Jennie's neighbour in Rathmollin Woods.

"I know she comes across as a bit of a wagon but she's her own worst enemy," Jennie had insisted. "We're having a coffee morning on Saturday and she's supposed to be coming around twelve – why don't you drop over and you can talk to her about it informally? I'll make sure to put you next to her."

"She's not a bad sort," Sandra had agreed. "She's supposed to be a real hot-shot in her job. It'd be great to have her opinion." Sandra and Nuala had become friendly after Sandra had put the fear of God into some of the bullies who'd been plaguing poor Rufus for ages. Rufus had eventually told his mother about the incident in the yard and Nuala had been like a new woman since.

The lunch at Jennie's house had proved to be an excellent environment for Emily to discuss the court case. Poor Nuala had been so delighted to be included and to see Rufus outside on the trampoline with the rest of the children that she'd been only too delighted to offer Emily her advice. She appreciated that Emily had a difficulty with giving the kind of emotional victim impact statement that could send Dylan's dad to jail, yet she reminded her of her civic responsibility to ensure that no other citizen endured what she had at the hands of Paul Delaney.

It was an onerous burden, she'd warned Emily, one that carried considerable power for better or for worse. Emily shuddered now even thinking about the way Nuala's words had made her feel. It would have been cowardly to walk away from it all and perhaps allow Paul to continue his trail of destruction.

It was Nuala who'd suggested gently that perhaps a long stint of community service might be of benefit to Paul Delaney, coupled with a stipulation that he attend counselling for his alcohol abuse - which is what the taxi driver and his solicitor had settled on. If Emily felt comfortable with it, Nuala would be only too delighted to help her prepare her statement and to coach her through it. Nuala, to whom Sandra had been so kind, had no desire to see Dylan's young life tainted with a jail-bird father unless it was absolutely necessary. *One chance*, Emily could stress in her statement. After that, it would be up to the courts.

The biggest surprise had been Paul's solicitor announcing that her client had brought a sum of money to the court to compensate his victim for the distress he had caused her. It might, the solicitor reasoned, prevent Miss Gordon having to endure the stress of a further legal action to recoup the costs that had been incurred as a result of the accident. Emily knew well that Sandra would snort cynically about his mother stumping up for him yet again.

Emily hadn't wanted money – if that was the case, she told the judge, she would already have commenced proceedings. Nonetheless, it was offered as a goodwill gesture and the judge had encouraged her to accept it. Paul, shamefaced next to his mother, had formally apologised and vowed to perform his community service to the best of his ability. He'd already joined Alcoholics Anonymous, he revealed, and was intent on regaining his good character with view to re-establishing a meaningful relationship with his son.

She'd wondered at the time what Sandra would have thought of that idea. Despite her insistence that it was entirely up to Emily to express her anger at the hand she'd been dealt, Emily knew she was relieved not to have to explain the concept of jail to Dylan.

Emily had travelled to Cork alone that day, despite everyone's entreaties that she needed support. Her parents and Niall had tried valiantly to be allowed to come but she'd needed to complete the journey to wellness on her own steam.

Nuala had been there, of course, silently urging her on when her voice had faltered and smiling her encouragement when Emily got to the part about bearing no malice towards Paul. She wanted something positive to come out of this, she told the court – perhaps a means of Paul Delaney getting another chance to prove himself. The judge had commended her integrity as Nuala had predicted, imposing the community service and a return to the courts with a probation report in six months.

For Emily, the €10,000 was something she hadn't factored into the equation at all. Nuala had encouraged her to do something special – a holiday maybe. Sandra, of course, thought she should use it to complete all the plans she had for Harmony Cottage. Her parents, needless to say, had urged her to look on the money as security – her Rainy Day fund.

It was Jack who'd suggested the party. It would be a marker, he reasoned, the end of a traumatic year and the beginning of a new and exciting one. Emily had agreed whole-heartedly. She wasn't ready to say it out loud then but the New Year was one that she vehemently hoped *he'd* be a part of. She'd blow a serious wedge of money on her housewarming, she'd promised him, to usher in her future.

Now she stood, surrounded by her expensive

ingredients, a feeling of peace surrounding her. Things *did* happen for a reason – her father was always saying that. And even though there were times that she found it hard to believe him, in the bleak January and February months when she sat on her bed and cried for all that she'd lost, she knew now that she was better for having lost Richard and her life in Dublin.

Yes, she could have done without the accident but then maybe her childhood friendship with Sandra and Jennie might not have been reignited. And maybe Jack would have gone ahead with his plans for the cottage and she'd have bought a boxed-in apartment in the city and hated him forever.

She grinned now to herself at this thought as she chopped the cooking apples finely for her mini apple strudels. She'd never have been able to hate Jack – not once she'd come to know him properly.

"Good God, Aggie is like a one-man Neighbourhood Watch these days," Jacinta laughed as she returned from stowing Emily's bottles of champagne in the front room.

"What's she up to now?" If there was one thing that Emily *didn't* appreciate about her new-found inner peace in Rathmollin, it was Aggie Lenihan. "She's already bombarded poor Sandra with questions about the party – Sandra texted me to be forewarned! And you know what Chrissie's like about blathering in the salon."

"Give over!" Jacinta exclaimed, rolling her eyes at Emily. "She went past the front window like a bullet out of a gun, whatever is up with her. She rang at the crack of dawn to see what we were all doing for the evening. I pretended I knew feck-all about the party – just for boldness. I don't know why I do it but I can't seem to help myself where Aggie is concerned. She definitely brings out the worst in me."

That was the thing about Aggie. Everyone knew she was so eager for gossip that they purposely withheld things that might be of interest to her. She often ended up going to outlandish lengths to find out things that were no big deal in the first place.

"Imagine if she knew about the court case? She'd wet herself with excitement!" Emily had been delighted that Paul Delaney's case had been listed for the very last day before the courts closed for the Christmas. There had been nothing else especially big listed for the same day so the court-room had been blessedly devoid of the gaggle of reporters that Nuala had warned her about. To date, there had been nothing mentioned about Paul Delaney in either *The Examiner* or *The Echo.*

"How has Joe put up with her all the years, I wonder?" Emily couldn't imagine how the mild-mannered Joe Lenihan had ever fallen in love with Aggie.

"I often wonder that myself. Maybe if she'd had children she might have had less time on her hands for gabbing. I suppose he just got used to her over the years, tunes out or something."

Emily smiled to herself and wondered what Aggie would think of the airline tickets secreted in her handbag that she planned to present Jack with tonight. A dirty weekend for two in a plush hotel in Vienna! Aggie would love the telling of that – Emily Gordon heading off with a fellow she barely knew when the mark of her engagement ring had barely left her finger!

A new year, a new me, Emily had decided, and she was going to make the very most of it. She just had to see now whether Jack could make himself available to join her.

Aggie cycled on towards Connolly's Master Butcher shop. She'd soon find out what the big cloak of secrecy around Emily Gordon's party was about. And maybe even whether Tom Gordon's heart was at him again. She'd have to ring Rose Coyne again to see whether there had been any update on that Paul Delaney – on the way back from Paddy Gallagher's house she'd stopped to chat to Declan Morrissey and *he'd* mentioned something about Tom Gordon being able to relax now that the whole racket was over and Emily could put it all behind her. What was over? Aggie went through both *The Examiner* and *The Echo* with a fine-tooth comb every single day and there had been no mention of anything about a court case. There was so much going on around the place, she mused – it was just a pity that people wouldn't spell things out instead of keeping everything under wraps. No wonder she could barely keep track of it all these days.

Joe Lenihan opened his eyes slowly and took in all the little details around him. He felt young again, more like the man he'd been before his wife had slowly drained the life out of him.

Aubergine, it seemed the new colour on the walls was called. The latest in fashionable décor, apparently. And this whole minimalist thing seemed to be very "in". Joe didn't know exactly what minimalist meant but he did know that he liked it better than the fussy, flowers-in-various-tones-of-dusty-pink that were everywhere at home.

It was the calmness the whole place exuded that seemed to do something for Joe, the sense of peace and quiet that he got as soon as he came through the door here.

Oh yes, everything else was a bonus, of course it was. But it was the fact of being listened to as well, of having an actual conversation about something instead of just sitting there like a nodding dog in a car window while Aggie ranted on about what other people were doing. People with lives, now that he thought about it.

Joe could talk about anything here. Things like expressing his thoughts on the government, if he wanted to. Or why people bought gimmicky things out of Lidl that they'd never use. He could ask things as well without being told he was an eejit, something that Aggie told him a lot. One day he asked what the difference was between Crème Fraiche and Fromage Frais, simply because he could. He kept seeing cartons of both next to the yogurts in the supermarket and had been interested for some time.

Joe had been interested in lots of things when he was younger but after years of being told it was all foolishness, he gave up what people called the Art of Conversation and just let Aggie do the talking for both of them. At least here he could be himself.

He shifted now to make himself more comfortable and felt the snug softness of the expensive down duvet envelop him. A little snooze wouldn't take up too much time and everything was ready for the dinner.

He'd had the car washed on the way to Vera's – his excuse for being gone if Aggie did happen to get back before him. It had happened a few times but he was always careful to have an alibi. Vera always laughed when she heard him talking about alibis – she said it made him sound like a criminal instead of a man who needed a little break from his routine.

It was great that there was only him now. Over the years, many of Vera's special clients had "phased out", as she put it. Some, Joe imagined, had got caught but others had probably become too long in the tooth to be bothered. There was only Joe now and Vera considered herself to be in semi-retirement, even though she was still a young and vibrant woman, full of interest and ideas about everything.

For Joe, the monthly trip to Vera wasn't about sex, it was about hearing what she had to say about things, what her plans were for the house or for her annual holiday. On the other hand, there was more to Joe Lenihan than just chatting. Vera always admired his performance, something that gratified him immensely.

He looked at the ornate crystal clock on the bedside locker now and realised that time was getting on. Soon it would be lunch-time and Aggie would be expecting him. Maybe a snooze was the last thing he needed – he could doze beside the fire later when Aggie went out for her afternoon spin on the bike. Joe stirred again, this time hoping that he *would* actually disturb Vera. Slowly, he ran his hand over her bottom and up over her hip. She was rounder and softer than she had been when he first started calling twenty years ago but she was still the same Vera.

She chuckled as his hand made its way along her side towards her breast. "Honestly, Joe, it's no wonder they've started me on blood-pressure tablets . . ."

Joe sighed as Vera's arms snaked around his back the way he liked it. To hell with Aggie and the dinner and the ear-bashing he would receive for being late home. It would be well worth it.

The End

If you enjoyed *Where the Heart is*
by Mairead O'Driscoll
why not try *Absolute Beginners*
also published by Poolbeg

Here's a sneak preview of
Chapters One and Two

MAIREAD O'DRISCOLL

Absolute Beginners

POOLBEG

Chapter 1

Rosa twisted slightly to get a better view of the back of the skinny jeans that she'd arrived home with earlier. Satisfied that they sat just right, she wriggled out of them and tossed them to one side while she tried on the floaty chiffon dress that she'd picked up in Razzmatazz on Patrick Street.

Swirling like a little girl with the gauzy material floating around her legs, Rosa stared critically at her reflection before kicking off the Jimmy Choos that she'd got on her last trip to London and slipping into a pair of peep-toes.

"That's better," she said out loud, pleased at the effect the shoes had on her slender legs. Wondering if the dress's blue and white check made her look like Dorothy of Yellow Brick Road fame, she pulled it off and picked up her other purchase, a black sheath dress that she'd spotted upstairs in Brown Thomas on one of her coffee breaks earlier in the week.

"Too formal," she announced to herself, glancing back

at the chiffon dress that lay in a pile on the bed. The tiny check was barely visible, certainly not too in-your-face. Trying it on once again she struck a few poses in front of the mirror, wondering if she looked ethereal and interesting or plain childish, like an overgrown ten-year-old at a birthday party.

Perhaps if my hair was up I might look like an adult, she thought, holding her riotous blonde curls back from her face to see if it made any difference.

Before she knew it the doorbell was pealing, a sure sign that her parents had already beeped the horn to let her know they were waiting outside.

As usual, Rosa threw open the upstairs window and held up five fingers to indicate that she'd be ready sometime in the next five minutes. Her parents were well aware by now that this signal generally meant ten. They sat patiently below in their gleaming Mercedes while their only daughter put the finishing touches to her make-up, knowing full well that if they went inside at all they'd be delayed even longer. Many a time they'd had to phone a restaurant to excuse their lateness on account of a crisis with a hair-do or an outfit on Rosa's part.

Inside, Rosa dragged a comb through her curls and scrunched a handful of them together at the nape of her neck with an ornate clip that she'd got from her mother at Christmas. Convincing herself that she didn't look like child, she touched up her make-up and dashed down the stairs, practically stripping the oriental runner from the treads in her haste, acutely aware of her parents waiting outside.

Maurice and Bernadette had bought the house in Bramwell Court the previous year, ostensibly as an investment property, and had offered it to their daughter to caretake until such a time as they decided what to do with it. Rosa suspected that they wanted her to gain her independence in an environment that was under their direct control and had been irritated at their habitual protectiveness until she'd realised that she couldn't afford any of the prices that the estate agents were mentioning, even for a one-bedroom apartment in the middle of nowhere.

A year on, she actually appreciated the fact that she had the spacious, elegantly decorated house to herself. She'd gradually moved all her things from her parents' house in Douglas and felt completely settled in the leafy cul-de-sac. Admittedly, it wasn't the sort of place that generated an exciting social life, with most of the other houses appearing to be occupied by staid couples in their fifties.

Anyway, she promised herself, things were about to change for the better. She only had to persuade her mother to get her onto the introductory course at The Gourmet Rooms and her life would be on track at last. If she discovered she had a flair for cooking, then it would simply be a matter of time before she embarked on a more extensive course that would lead, finally, to her own restaurant.

Rosa had a vision of the kind of discreet, darkened dining-room that would encourage elegantly understated guests to park their expensive cars along the tree-lined street outside her home and partake of the exquisite fare on offer at Number 3.

The house was perfect for such a venture, with its airy

well-proportioned kitchen running the full width of the house at the back. To the front, two large reception rooms opened off the hall, one of which extended into a substantial sun room, almost doubling its size. Rosa envisaged the room to the right of the hall as a reception room where guests could enjoy an aperitif as they perused the menu. Plush upholstered armchairs, intimately grouped, would also encourage the clientele to linger in a relaxed environment at the end of their dining experience. The larger room, to the left of the entrance hall, would make a perfect dining-room, with the conservatory area opened on the weekends to accommodate the larger guest list. If everything came to pass the way she planned she'd break a door through to the dining-room from the kitchen so that food wouldn't have to be transported via the hall.

In the spacious entrance hall, she took a final glance at herself in the ornate gilt-framed mirror that graced the wall above an antique mahogany escritoire her father had inherited from her Great-aunt Hilda – destined to be an unobtrusive reception desk, ideal for taking bookings and processing bills while maintaining a graceful ambience.

First things first, she cautioned herself as she slammed her front door, uncharacteristically suppressing the bubbles of excited anticipation that were forming in her head at the thought of opening the doors of Number 3 to the public. Once she'd succeeded in persuading her mother to exert her not inconsiderable influence on the formidable Mrs Carter, Rosa was certain that one of the coveted places on the heavily booked cookery course at The Gourmet Rooms would be hers.

Bounding down the limestone steps, she was heartened to see her parents smiling indulgently at her through the windscreen. Surely they'd see that this latest idea would herald the beginning of a new life for her? Surely they'd agree to help her?

Chapter 2

As soon as she opened her eyes, Kate Lewis remembered what day it was. He or she, although Kate always believed it would have been a girl, would be thirteen today.

When she'd been a teenager, Kate and her friends had spent endless hours spinning their Claddagh rings around on their necklaces to ascertain whether they'd have boys or girls and how many of each. No matter how many times they did Kate's, the result was always the same – one child, a girl.

In those days, she'd had a very definite plan to call her baby Ellen and somehow the name had stuck. Little Ellen would have been a fully-fledged teenager today, she mused, probably bickering with her parents about going out in clothes that were so small that they couldn't properly be classed as clothes at all. Or hiding at the back of the school so she wouldn't be caught smoking – something that Kate herself had done with enthusiasm but which she most likely wouldn't have tolerated if her daughter was at it.

She lay in the warm cocoon of the duvet for twenty minutes, fantasising about the imagined trials of parenthood until the snooze button activated again and broke in on her thoughts.

Timmy would have been thrilled to have an almost-grown-up daughter.

Don't start again! She steeled herself, pressing her eyes tight to stave off the tears that threatened. The piercing beep-beep-beep of the alarm brought her sharply back to reality. The thought of having to open the shop and put on a face for the regulars seemed like an insurmountable hurdle but Kate knew that there was nothing like a frantic morning in Good For You to chase away the bleak hollow in the pit of her stomach. Temporarily, at least.

She'd spent the previous day under a black cloud that had refused to lift until she fell into a fitful sleep at five in the morning. But the luxury of throwing herself on the sofa and weeping for hours on end was fine on a Sunday. Right now, she'd just have to pull herself together and face the Monday morning routine.

Knowing that she couldn't arrive at work looking like the wreck of the *Hesperus*, Kate riffled through her stock of Bach flower essences to see if there was anything that would lift her spirits. White Chestnut definitely, she decided, plucking the small glass bottle from among its companions. Expertly squeezing the tiny dropper she felt the familiar brandy-like taste on her tongue and tried to visualise the remedy chasing away the never-ending thoughts that had been racing around her mind for the past twenty-four hours.

Standing under the soothing needles of warmth in the shower, Kate did her best to empty her mind and focus instead on the list of orders she had to get out before lunch-time.

Angela Rowan usually arrived before ten so she'd start with getting together the selection of soya milk and yoghurts and whatever lactose-free foods were on the list for her son. Freddie had been diagnosed with galactosaemia shortly after birth and had to adhere to a strict diet. Angela was one of Kate's best customers and was confident that even if something new came on the market that would fit in with Freddie's diet, it would be ordered for her before she'd even mentioned it to the proprietor of the health shop.

Anja Hoening, another of her regulars, would be along to pick up the monthly supply of eco-nappies for her twins. Kate made a mental note to sellotape two sample tubes of a new calendula cream that had just come in onto the packs of nappies for Anja to try out, knowing that the earthy Finn would rather use a natural product on her babies' skin than a mixture of synthetic chemicals.

Mrs Carter would be in at one o'clock on the dot. The detailed list – handwritten in a neat, precise script that could only belong to the neat, precise proprietor of The Gourmet Rooms – was always handed in on a Friday afternoon and the order collected by the lady herself on Mondays.

In the early days, Mrs Carter had checked each item before leaving the shop but after a few months of receiving the quality products exactly as she required, Kate was heartened to notice that one day she just picked up the neat cardboard box and left after a few minutes' general conversation.

Kate always prepared the box for The Gourmet Rooms with care and gave a sizeable discount to acknowledge the substantial amount of business that the cookery school provided. A container of choice porcini mushrooms and authentic tahini paste were on today's order as well as the usual organic grains and fresh yeast for Mrs Carter's famous breads.

Now that her mind was occupied with the morning's business, Kate began to feel normal again. Dressed in white linen trousers and a matching tunic that came down below her hips, she added a string of large turquoise beads that her sister had brought from Thailand the previous summer.

This morning she knew she needed the light foundation and lipstick to make her look presentable, although her eyes didn't look too puffy considering the day and night she'd put in.

She stared at herself in the mirror for a few moments, taking in the neat chestnut bob that swung in around her small heart-shaped face. Her brown eyes looked despondent. Making yet another conscious effort to shake herself up, she abandoned her self-study and made her way downstairs, her resolve strengthening as soon as she entered the oasis of calm below.

Even before pulling up the blinds and letting the morning sun streak across the polished timber floor, Kate could find her way around the little shop. The contents of all its nooks and crannies were as familiar to her as the features of her own face and she rarely changed the position of the items on the shelves. Most of the regulars tended to wander around the shop picking out the products they wanted, happy that Kate was in the background for assistance if they needed it.

The silence of the little shop was comforting to her as she lit a tea light and added a few drops of lemongrass oil to the aromatherapy burner, always the first task of the day. Soon the fresh, vigorous scent would permeate the space around her, hopefully stimulating her sluggish brain into action.

Most of the customers had at some stage commented on the delightful aromas that filled Good For You and Kate always marvelled at the advertising power of the small act of choosing an essential oil to suit her own mood every morning. On several occasions, people had admired a scent and then gone on to buy the particular oil when Kate told them which it was.

The doorbell chimed as she began to reorganise the small selection of books at the back of the shop. Surprisingly, Mrs Carter strode purposefully in. Kate was immediately glad that she'd prepared the box for The Gourmet Rooms on Saturday afternoon, leaving space at the top for the fresh items she was expecting this morning, knowing that Mrs Carter was the type of woman who wouldn't tolerate inefficiency.

"I know I'm a bit early, Kate, but I'm afraid one of the staff is out sick today," Mrs Carter said pleasantly, allaying Kate's immediate fear that last week's order hadn't been up to scratch. "I hope I'm not *too* early?"

Kate prided herself on providing a good quality service

and would be annoyed with herself if something had been unsatisfactory for as solid a customer as Mrs Carter.

"Not at all. The order is almost ready. Except for the buttermilk but Declan should be along any minute with that."

"As I'm here, I wonder if you have any cherry juice – a concentrated one if possible?"

"There's an organic one that's very nice. I'll just get it down for you."

Kate pulled over the little set of steps that she used for getting the least frequently used items from the higher shelves and reached for a bottle of the luscious cherry juice that was so valuable to the many gout sufferers she supplied. The tall slim bottle, just above her reach, wobbled as she touched it and toppled to the floor, its contents spreading in a crimson pool around the feet of her most valued customer.

"Oh, my goodness, I'm so sorry! Your shoes are ruined!" she exclaimed, horrified, as she alighted to inspect the damage. Thank God Mrs Carter was the only customer in the shop!

"They're absolutely fine. Will I move this bag?" Mrs Carter indicated a large hessian bag full of dried beans near the counter, in the path of the advancing pool of cherry juice.

"Thank you, I'll do it," Kate insisted, shifting the bag immediately and darting to the store cupboard for the mop. "Would you like to sit in one of the armchairs while I sort this out? Declan should be here with the buttermilk soon."

Her hands were jittery as she ran the mop over the

floor, praying that Mrs Carter, who was now rolling a leaflet stand to one side for her, wouldn't skid on the wet floor and injure herself.

"You've no idea how many times a week this happens during the cookery classes."

Disarmed by her understanding and still emotional from her thoughts of Timmy and her baby, tears sprang to Kate's eyes. Swiftly she shoved the mop out into the small hallway that housed the stairs to the flat and turned to wash her hands, hoping that Mrs Carter wouldn't notice and think she was a complete wreck.

"Are you all right this morning, Kate?"

Her voice was kinder than Kate would have expected from such a brisk woman and caused two tears to trickle down her cheeks unbidden.

"God, I'm sorry," she sniffed, pressing her fingers to her eyes to stop herself breaking down completely. "Bad night's sleep."

"Are you sure that's all? Would you like me to hold the fort for a few minutes?"

Of all the things that Kate would ever have expected, the idea of Mrs Carter behind the counter in Good For You wouldn't have come to mind.

"Thank you, really – but I'm fine. Better off working to be honest." Then, seeing the look of understanding that passed over the other woman's face, she said quietly, "I had a miscarriage years ago – the baby would have been thirteen today. I'm a bit shaky, that's all."

"It's a loss that most people underestimate. I too lost a baby in the past."

Before Kate could get to say anything in response, Mrs Carter's face became closed as if she had said too much.

"Tell me, do you have any interest in cooking?"

Startled by the question, Kate was about to say that her own dashed-off recipes would hardly be up to Mrs Carter's standards but thought better of it, not wanting to seem like a boor who didn't appreciate the value of good food.

"I've lost interest over the last few years," she admitted instead, starting to feel a bit better now that the conversation had taken a more normal turn. "Cooking for one can be a bit unrewarding."

A woman of few words, Mrs Carter nodded sympathetically before proceeding to the point. "I've been meaning to ask you for a while if you'd like to join in on one of the courses, complimentary of course. I do value the service that you provide us and you've been more than competitive with prices over the years." Then she added gently, "And cooking can be very therapeutic."

"Well, thank you." Praise from Mrs Carter was praise indeed and Kate felt like a schoolgirl getting a medal. Building up a solid client base had been hard work but lately it seemed to be paying dividends at last. "And I'd love to go on one of the courses – I could certainly do with a bit of motivation in the culinary department."

"Good. Would you consider yourself a beginner or would you prefer to try the Intermediate or even the Advanced course?"

"The beginner's course would be marvellous," Kate enthused, interrupted by the doorbell as Declan Gleeson burst in bearing a boxful of organic goat's milk and her supply of buttermilk. "Morning, Declan, just in time," she greeted the florid dairy farmer.

Kate plucked out the cartons of buttermilk that would complete the order for the cookery school and added them to the box.

"That's everything," she confirmed, "and thanks again, Mrs Carter – I'll really look forward to the course."

"Pamela," the older woman insisted with a smile as she left. "I'll let you know what dates are available when I'm in next week."

"Fine-looking woman," Declan commented almost as soon as the door had closed behind Mrs Carter. "And single," he added longingly.

Declan was a bachelor farmer in his mid-fifties who'd made several efforts to get himself married, always to no avail. When he'd first started delivering to Good For You and discovered that Kate was 'available', he'd made a few attempts to strike up a romance but had been headed off time and again. His limited experience with members of the opposite sex had somehow led him to believe that any woman who was currently unattached was available, but Kate thought that Mrs Carter in particular wasn't the available type.

Attractive in a grave sort of way, Kate often wondered what Mrs Carter looked like at night when she unwound the roll of silver hair that was always pinned neatly at the nape of her neck. Her clothes too were somewhat severe, almost a uniform of neutral-coloured dresses with neat collars and toning lightweight cardigans.

"Does she come in here much?" Declan was asking now, his eyes gleaming fanatically.

Kate had nightmarish visions of her most valued customer being wedged ignominiously up against the herbal-remedies counter as Declan enthusiastically tried out a few of his best chat-up lines. She knew this was entirely possible as she'd been that soldier on more than one occasion until Declan had finally taken no for an answer.

"Hardly ever," she lied brazenly. "Usually sends one of her minions."

The sudden drooping of the farmer's jowls indicated that he believed her and Kate silently heaved a sigh of relief. At least she would be spared the sight of Declan pacing the floor every Monday, hankering in vain after the unobtainable Mrs Carter.

After Declan's forlorn departure, a steady trickle of customers kept Kate occupied until lunch-time. Because she was the only member of staff, she had to close the shop then, something she was considering remedying in the near future. Now that the business was established, it was time to get an assistant who'd be able to take over at lunch-times, weekends and holidays, which she'd had to forego for several years.

Maybe that would be her next step – that and the cookery course. Perhaps it was time to think about getting on with her life instead of hiding behind her little shop, she mused as she filled a pitta pocket with chicken and salad. Kate's mother was always reminding her that she was only thirty-eight, young enough to pick up the pieces and start again.

Guilt overcame her suddenly as she thought of Timmy, little unborn Ellen and the poor blameless farmer who'd thought he was on his way home from the mart. What about all the things that they would never get the opportunity to enjoy? And here she was moping about having no life.

Further resources

Hilton, Tessa with Messenger, Maire (1997) *The Great Ormond Street New Baby and Childcare Book: The essential guide for parents of children aged 0–5* Vermilion.

Leach, Penelope (1997) *Your Baby and Child: The essential guide for every parent* Penguin.

Progress check

1 Explain why it is important to support women in breast feeding their babies.

2 Give three examples of suitable early foods for babies who are being weaned onto a mixed diet.

3 Give three examples of how you could make a care routine with a baby a personal and communicative time.

4 Explain four ways to reduce the risk of cot death for babies.

5 Give three examples of warning signs that a baby may be seriously ill.

7

Supporting children's personal and social development

After reading this chapter you should be able to:

- understand the importance of very early attachment for babies and children
- recognise and promote children's personal development as individuals
- support children's social development and the formation of friendships from an early age
- recognise and support the social skills that children need to develop within play.

Introduction

In this chapter you will learn about the importance of children's emotional and social development. Children need the sense of security that develops from close attachments within their family and with other key adults in their life. Children develop as individuals with personal interests, talents and concerns. They develop friendships with other children from their earliest years and social contact is crucial for their learning. Chapter 8 covers children's emotional development and how adults can support children.

Links to early years qualifications

This chapter especially supports the following units:

Diploma in Child Care and Education: 4

National Vocational Qualification in Early Years Care and Education

Level 2: C4, E1

Level 3: C5

BTEC National Early Years Diploma: 4, 8, 9, 12

Early attachment and later relationships

Experiences in early childhood matter a great deal because they shape children's emotional development, their sense of security and how they think about their social world. There is more than one route to a happy and healthy childhood and different family patterns. But overall very young children need to have been able to build a base of emotional security as well as physical well being.

How much does early experience matter?

Patterns of experience, either positive or negative, are usually more significant for children than single events, although a badly handled and distressing event can leave a child very fragile psychologically. Over the decades, opinion in psychological theory and research has swung from one extreme to another in judgements about how far it is possible to compensate later for a very damaging early experience.

Supporters of Freudian psychoanalytic theory (see page 15) proposed that children's personalities and therefore their later reactions were fixed by the age of five years. Later theorists thoroughly challenged this viewpoint and there was considerable optimism in the 1970s that children could overcome, with help, even a very deprived early childhood.

In the last decade of the twentieth century, research established more clearly how neural connections are made within the immature brains of very young children. It seems likely now that grossly depriving experiences in the early years mean that vital connections relating to emotional and social development are never made. High quality care and support can make up some of children's development but they may always have great difficulty and confusion over relationships. This cautious outlook is supported by anecdotal evidence from adoptive families who took children from some of the Eastern European orphanages, for instance in Romania.

The importance of attachment

Children need to form attachments. Most babies are ready to be social – to make links of affection with their close family and regular carers. They need to form the important initial attachments within their family and then to make warm relationships with familiar carers and other children. If babies are not enabled to make a close attachment to their carers, usually their birth parents, then their continued well being can be at serious risk.

Attachment is a positive emotional link between people: adults and children. You can observe children's sense of attachment to someone through their reactions, whether their closeness is within the family or to very close friends.

- Babies and young children are pleased to see their parent (or other important individuals like siblings) after a brief separation.
- Young children often protest at being separated, even for a short period, from parents or carers to whom they are close.
- Young children usually want to be close to parents or other key, familiar carers. They especially want to be physically close, and not just in sight, when they are in unfamiliar or stressful situations.

Key term

Attachment
a positive emotional link between babies, young children and their parents or other key carers

Figure 7.1

Children can enjoy their time in your setting and still be delighted to see their parents again

Activity

Part of settling very young children into an early years setting is enabling them to feel secure and to separate from their parents, most likely their mother. Good practice in settling children involves partnership with parents (see page 629).

- Watch at least two babies or toddlers over the days that they settle into your early years setting.
- Track when and for how long they are willing to move away from their parents to explore the room. Keep a simple time count over the days.
- How do they react when their parent leaves the room for the first time?
- In what ways do the room team work to support both the baby or toddler and the parent?
- In what ways do the two babies or toddlers differ in their pattern of settling and separating?
- Write up your observations and make a short presentation to colleagues.
- Compare your observations with colleagues and discuss good practice in early years settings to support children and their parents.

Key skills links: N2.2 C2/3.3 C3.1a C3.1b

The development of early attachment

Attachment is a two-way process: within healthy psychological development, babies become attached to their birth parents but also parents become attached to their babies. These are two equally important sides to the same coin.

Discussion about attachment used to focus almost entirely on the earliest days of a baby's life and the word **bonding** was used to describe the closeness that ideally developed then between a baby and its mother. The impression was often given that bonding happened, or did not happen, within the first few days and that only the mother was really important. Closer observation and understanding of early social development has led to the concept of a process of attachment, lasting over weeks and months and involving both parents and other close family members.

Key term

Bonding
the term often used to mean the very earliest attachment soon after birth

- A first and important bond with a baby can be established in the period immediately after birth, so long as the mother and father are able to have this very early contact. Sometimes this is not possible or easy and supportive professionals need to let parents know that attachment is not a win-or-lose single opportunity.
- A growing attachment between parents and baby develops from time spent together over the early weeks and months of a baby's life. Both mother and father can get to know this baby as an individual. Strong attachments can be formed through care giving routines, early communication and play.

The development of attachment in childhood

The emotional and social development of children starts with their close attachment to their family as a baby.

- Most babies are born social beings. It is a cause for concern if babies do not seem to be socially responsive. Babies make contact through crying, looking, touching and later smiling.
- Such very early social skills come to be used deliberately to gain the attention of parents and older siblings.
- Babies and toddlers need familiar, trusted people as a safe base from which to explore their world. They turn to key carers for comfort when they are upset, uneasy or ill. They look to them for a check when they are uncertain, as if to ask, 'Is this alright?' or 'Should I be worried?'
- In supportive and healthy development, babies come to know familiar faces and voices and are reassured by their presence. The consequence is that by about 8 months old, babies can distinguish familiar from unfamiliar faces.
- They then tend to be wary or distressed by over close contact with people they do not know. This change is often called 'fear of strangers'. But the reaction is more often wariness, especially if unknown adults are wise and do not insist on invading a baby's personal space.
- At this age, most babies are visibly distressed if they are separated from their most familiar and favourite adult. In western culture mothers tend to undertake most of the primary care, so this most familiar adult is often a baby's mother. However, with changes in how family life is run, it is not unusual that babies are equally, or sometimes more, upset if they are separated from their father.
- Babies and very young children can also develop strong attachments to other family members: often to their father but also to siblings and other relatives like grandparents who are involved in their care. Older babies are well able to distinguish the different familiar people in their life and often show that they anticipate and enjoy different styles in care and games.
- Normal family life has some changes and mild disruptions. Babies and young children can tolerate some variety but healthy emotional development can

be threatened if there are too many changes and carers. Under these circumstances, babies and toddlers cannot begin to predict their lives and they cannot learn to relax and trust.

To think about

Babies and toddlers in families become close to parents, siblings and other relatives like grandparents. Sometimes they may be most closely attached to their mothers, especially when very young.

- For what reasons might babies be most close to their mothers? Discuss with your colleagues.
- Under what family circumstances might they be equally close to other family members?
- Look at this section as you consider your answers and discuss with colleagues. Look also at the section on page 5 about different kinds of families in current UK society.

Key skills link: C3.1a

When attachment is difficult

Circumstances can interfere with the development of attachment between a baby and its parents. Possible problems arise mainly from characteristics of the baby or from problems experienced by the parent(s). Family and professional support can be important in helping parents through these difficulties. For example:

- Parents can find it exhausting to care for a baby who cries a considerable amount. Even patient and caring parents can begin to feel unloved themselves.
- Very premature babies can be unable to respond socially like full term babies and fragile health may mean that babies are in intensive care. Premature baby unit teams work hard to enable and encourage parents to spend time with and, if at all possible, to touch their babies (see page 157).
- Babies with disabilities may not respond to parents' communication by looks and sounds and it may take some time before parents and professionals realise that something is amiss. Babies with visual loss tend to smile less than sighted babies and do not hold a mutual gaze. Hearing impaired babies may not respond until their parent enters the line of vision.
- Parents may have great difficulty in responding to the social signals that babies send to them. There can be many different reasons for this block: a deprived childhood which left the adults with no ideas about how to make affectionate contact, parents who demand that the baby meets their needs or convenience. Depression or overwhelming family stress can take all a parent's energies, as can addictions through abuse of alcohol or drugs.

The development of children as individuals

Personal development

Over the early years of childhood, young children develop a sense of themselves and this can be described in a number of ways:

- Children develop a **personal identity**, an understanding of who they are as an individual and how they fit into the social groups around them.
- Children have a **self image**, a feeling of what they are like as a person and the balance of positives and negatives within this.
- Children develop a sense of **self esteem** and this term is used to describe a child's evaluation of their own worth. Children, and adults, experience a level of self esteem that is created by a comparison between what they feel themselves to be and what they feel they ought to be. Children have a low level of self esteem when they believe there is a wide gap between what they are and what they should be.

Key terms

Personal identity children's perception of what makes them an individual uniquely different from other people

Self image children's view of themselves, as a mix of positive and possibly negative characteristics

Self esteem children's evaluation of their own self worth, including the relationship between what they feel they are and can do, and what they ought to be as a person and be able to do

A sense of personal identity

All children are dealing with a growing sense of their own self and coming to terms with any difficulties that arise.

- Babies need first to develop a sense of themselves as separate individuals. First of all babies act as if there is no difference between 'me' and 'not me'. They literally have to find and experience the physical boundaries of where their body ends and somebody or something else begins.
- By about 12 months babies not only have a clear sense of their own physical boundaries and their name, but that other familiar adults and children have their own ways of behaving.
- Toddlers show that they see themselves as someone who has a relationship with other familiar people and they see themselves a great deal through how they are treated. They need reassurance that they are loved, perhaps despite what they have just done.
- By three years most children are clear about themselves and others in terms of who is a boy and who is a girl. But they continue to learn what it means to be one sex rather than another and the expectations that are built around gender roles.
- By three and four years, children can also start to develop a sense of what it means for them to belong to a given culture, religion or nationality. Obviously the way in which they develop this aspect of their identity depends on their family and neighbourhood.
- Some children have to deal with clashes within the family or resolve conflict between family expectations and those of school or friends.
- Many of the experiences shaping identity will impinge upon individuals from the outside. For disabled children, their disability or ill health is part of life for them, but they are unlikely to wish to be seen through that exclusive filter.
- Young children are developing a sense of themselves as a worthwhile person, or as a child who is dismissed or apparently disliked by others. Some children's experiences make them very uncertain of their own worth, because of their personal group identity.

Figure 7.2

Sources of possible identity for children as they develop

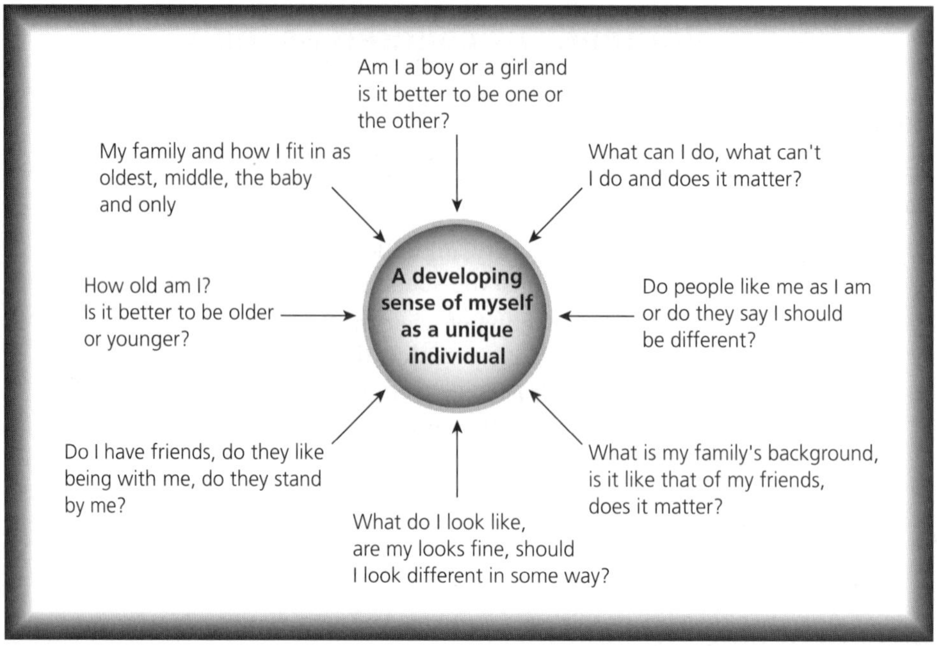

- Particular experiences as well as the resilience of different individuals affect their level of self esteem. Some individuals will be continuing to deal with the prejudiced reactions of others to some aspect of their personal identity.

Sources of personal identity

By the time that children are four or five years of age, they will have built, and be continuing to build, their sense of personal identity from any of the following sources and by understanding or finding the answer to a whole series of personal questions:

- *Family*: do I live with both my parents or one of them? Do I have brothers and sisters and where do I come in the order? What are my parents like, do they have jobs and does that matter if they do not? How large is my family and who else plays a part in my life?
- *Sex*: am I a boy or a girl and does that mean I look and behave differently? Is it better to be a boy or a girl?
- *Age*: how old am I now and is it better to be older or younger?
- *Competencies*: what can I do and what can I not manage? Am I good at some things and useless at others?
- *Friends*: do I have friends and who are they? Do they like me and will they help me if I need them? Who does not like me and does this create trouble for me?
- *Likes and dislikes*: what do I like and dislike? Do my friends feel the same way as I do, does it matter if friends do not agree sometimes?
- *Pre-school and school*: where do I go on a regular basis and who is in my group? What year and class am I in at school?
- *Ethnic group and culture*: what do I and my family look like and are there other people locally who look like us? Am I supposed to dislike some people because of how they look; do some people dislike me? Do we share

the same language as other people, do we talk in the same way and does this matter?

- *Faith*: is my family religious, what do we believe in and how does that affect our life? Do we share a faith with other local people and does this matter? Am I supposed to dislike some people because they do not share our faith; do some people dislike me?

Activity

- Listen in to the questions that children of five or six years ask each other on first or very early meetings. What questions do they ask and what seems to matter? What information do children volunteer to their peers: name, age, what school they attend?
- You could listen discreetly in a local park or in out of school care if you work in this kind of setting.
- Make brief notes of your observations and ideally discuss them with a colleague who has also undertaken this activity.

Key skills links: C2/3.2 C2/3.1a

Children learn about culture and faith

All children learn something about the cultural and linguistic background of their own family and therefore about themselves. In a neighbourhood with ethnic diversity, children's understanding can be grounded in the observation that not everyone is the same, so their own identity is built from similarities as well as differences. In a neighbourhood where there is very little obvious ethnic group or faith diversity, then children not surprisingly regard the ethnic or faith identity that they know as the only one, it is 'normal'. Broader experience will eventually tell them that everyone does not share the same background at all.

Culture can be seen as a distinctive way of life that is shared within one group and makes a clear distinction between this group and another. The details of culture may include:

- Ways of behaving, including use of communication and body language, expectations about the expression of feelings or certain kinds of emotions.
- Within a given group some skills may be valued above others.
- Cultural identity can include a blend of ethnic background, nationality and sometimes also religious faith.
- Children acquire the cultural patterns of behaviour, skills, knowledge, values from their immediate family and other members of the same community.
- Everybody has a culture and a cultural background.

In an early years setting your responsibility is to support all the children in their own cultural identity. Partnership with parents is crucial for you to understand family patterns in diet (see page 92), religious faith if that is important to this family (page 627) and language (see page 312). It is the responsibility of families to raise children in the way that is usual within their own culture. Whatever your own background, you have an important part to play in showing respect for cultures different from your own. But of course there is considerable variety in

Key term

Culture
a distinctive way of life that is shared within one group and makes a clear distinction between this group and others

any culture and families who share your own cultural background, faith and language will still be different from you in many ways.

How do you support children's identity?

Your most important contribution is to treat children genuinely as individuals and learn about them through partnership with parents and communication with the children themselves.

The importance of names

A child's name is part of him or her and you show respect by learning and using children's names properly.

- If you have any doubts, then do ensure that you pronounce a child's name correctly and get the spelling correct.
- Do not make a fuss about names that are less familiar to you. A child's name is not 'difficult'; you are finding it difficult to say or get right without some practice.
- You should never change or shorten a child's name because it is unfamiliar or initially hard for you to pronounce. Such a step is disrespectful of the child and the family.
- You can courteously ask the child or parents for help and honestly say, 'I'm finding it hard to pronounce Bhadrakumar. I'd be grateful if you can help me get it right.'
- If you really cannot get your mouth around some of the sounds (or if a child or parent has a continuing struggle with your name), then you can reach an agreed compromise.
- Identical twins can be difficult, almost impossible, to distinguish, even when you know them well. Ask their parents for some help; they will be able to point out small individual differences or perhaps come to some helpful arrangement with badges. Definitely do not call out to children as 'twins'.
- For the majority of the time in a group setting, you should call children by their names and not by the name that you have given to their nursery room. It is fine sometimes out in the garden to call in scattered children with, 'Everyone in "Dolphins", it's time for our lunch', because you can then smile and greet children as they come towards you. Avoid the bad habit of regularly referring to children as 'middle room' or 'reception children'.

To think about

- Names matter to children and it can feel very discourteous if adults make a fuss about a name being 'difficult' or if they insist on altering the way a child would rather be addressed.
- It is not for adults either to shorten children's names if they want them in full, nor to insist that they will use their 'proper' names when children prefer the shortened version.
- Do you or your colleagues have childhood memories about the names or nicknames you were called or what happened to your friends?

Key skills links: C2/3.1a

Tips for practice

- The positive development of children's identity cannot be promoted by an outlook that claims 'I treat them all the same' because children are not the same.
- Three or four years year olds will be clear that they are a boy or a girl so your approach needs to recognise their gender, just as much as cultural identity.
- Look at the activities that are on offer and check that they reflect different skills and interests. Are you as enthusiastic about the boys' interest in diggers as the girls' curiosity about animals?
- Be aware of your use of words, like ' I'd like two strong boys to help me with the climbing frame' rather than 'the ladders are heavy, I'd like some help'.
- Boys' pretend play themes may be on average more lively and perhaps higher volume. Be wary that you do not assume that the play is less rich. Energetic games may need some negotiation about where they are played rather than an outright ban (see page 124).

Supporting children's self esteem

The term **self esteem** is used to mean an overall evaluation of our own worth that is reached by the difference between what we believe ourselves to be and what we feel we should be.

- If we feel the gap between 'are' and 'should be' is relatively narrow, then we have high self esteem and feel secure in ourselves and our abilities.
- If the gap is wide, then our self esteem can be low and we feel less positive about ourselves and our ability to cope. Adults and teenagers have a level of self esteem as do older children.

Figure 7.3

Caring adults support children's sense of self worth

The development of self esteem

Children's experiences move towards a view of themselves that provide an internal judgement of their own self worth, so that by about seven years of age it is possible to talk about children's level of self esteem. In the early years, children's experiences in their family and early years settings work to build up their view of themselves and what is important. Their experiences can build a strong foundation for self esteem or make it likely that a child's view of herself is already fragile.

Children take on the standards of those around them, about what matters and is really important in how you judge yourself. So children vary, for instance a child in a very musical family may feel incompetent if she struggles to play an instrument when her parents and siblings seem to have such talent. In a non-musical family, her struggles would be far less significant. You can imagine similar situations for families, or schools who value sporting prowess very highly.

Children seem to develop their level of self esteem from five main sources of information through their experience:

- *Feelings of competence or lack of ability*: what can I do, what do I find difficult and does this matter?
- *Confidence in physical skills and abilities*: not just sports, feelings of physical competence are important in many areas of learning (see page 239)
- *Social acceptance and the support of friends*: am I liked, do I have friends to play with, am I chosen in games?
- *Acceptability based on behaviour*: do people like what I do, do I get into trouble with adults and does that matter, do people praise or criticise me?
- *Physical appearance*: how do I look, do I look attractive and what is important for that?

Children who develop a secure and high level of self esteem are not self centred or full of pride: an occasional misunderstanding of the term. On the contrary, children who have high self esteem can recognise that they find something difficult or are not highly talented in one area. But they feel confident that their struggles do not make them less worthy as a person; they are somebody who needs some help and cannot be 'brilliant' at everything.

Children who develop low self esteem can be at risk in a number of different ways because they may develop:

- a sense of self dislike, because they have few feelings of self worth
- better strategies for avoiding difficult situations (learning or social) than for boosting their competence
- a front of apparent confidence, even bravado that covers up their fragile self esteem
- difficulties in relationships or building links with children who are equally uncertain.

As an early years or out of school practitioner you can help by looking below the surface for children who have found disruptive ways to deal with low self esteem. You help all children by forming warm relationships with them and supporting their friendships. The most effective support is to boost children's positive disposition to learn (see page 393) and to take a positive approach to their behaviour (see Chapter 17).

Scenario

Michael attends Greenholt Pre-school. He is four years old and the pre-school staff feel that he pushes out the limits at most opportunities. Michael seems unable to stop himself, but he seems almost relieved when an adult steps in with a firm 'No' sometimes and re-directs him. Michael's way of getting attention is to shout, ever louder, until someone takes notice and then he does not ask for anything in particular. He just seems to want reassurance that he can get an adult's attention. The pre-school staff have noticed that Michael's parents seem to focus far more on what he does wrong than the boy's skills or interests. Michael is regularly compared unfavourably with his younger sister and an older cousin in the extended family.

Questions

1. How could the Greenholt team positively support Michael's confidence in himself in the pre-school? Suggest two steps they could take in the near future.
2. Discuss with colleagues a possible short-term plan for the pre-school.
3. How could the team talk with Michael's parents about their son's outlook and what his behaviour may show about his feelings?
4. Work with a colleague to role play what you could say and in what way.

Key skills links: PS3.1 PS3.2

Scenario

Becky is six years old and very quiet in comparison with the other children in St Jude's after school club. She seems uncertain of her welcome anywhere and very concerned about making a mistake of any kind. She is quick to say that she 'can't do' something or calls herself 'stupid'. Compliments, such as admiration of her drawings, are met with a surprised look and Becky often whispers that 'it's not really very good'. Sometimes she tears up her drawings. Becky seems keen to help within the daily routine but appears to be very worried about doing things wrong. Much more than the other children, she asks, 'Is this alright?' or 'Have I done it wrong?'

Questions

1. In what way could Becky's behaviour indicate that she has low self esteem?
2. Devise a short-term plan for ways that the after school club could boost her confidence and help her feel surer of her abilities.
3. Suggest ways that the club team might talk with Becky's parents in a constructive way, drawing on their observations in the club.
4. Role play the conversation with a colleague.

Key skills link: PS3.1 PS3.2

Temperament

Even a small amount of observation of children will tell you that they do not all behave the same way when they face what look like very similar happy, confusing or annoying circumstances. Furthermore, if you have the opportunity to observe the same children later on in their childhood, it is very likely, although not certain, that you will notice some continuities in how these same, now slightly older children, behave.

Perhaps Geeta is still more likely to be the group leader than Janie. Dan is still more likely to be hovering on the sidelines than not, although he seems to have conquered some of his anxious feelings when faced with a new situation. Of course children can learn to extend their options in how they face and tackle life. But they probably do not change dramatically in terms of the individual person that you came to know when they were younger.

Variety in temperament

Key term

Temperament inborn tendencies for individual children that shape their reactions and behaviour towards a more established adult personality

The word **temperament** is usually applied to mean in-built tendencies for individual children that shape their reactions and behaviour towards a more established adult personality. Children are still affected by experiences but their temperament works as a filter. The main sources of variation include:

- *Active–passive*: some children are more physically vigorous than their peers. Some are more likely to go out and find interest, whereas others may wait in a more passive way for experiences to be presented to them.
- *Sociability*: children vary in their predominant style of how they relate to new people and social experiences or objects. Some children are more keen than others to initiate social contact and others may be more cautious, less outgoing.
- *Wariness*: another dimension suggested from observation is that some children have a greater tendency to be anxious or frightened when faced with new experiences.
- *Negative emotions*: children have to deal with frustrating experiences within daily life but some react swiftly with annoyance, so that even minor frustrations (from the perspective of another child) lead to strong reactions of upset or anger.
- *Effort and persistence*: even allowing for the developmental progress in attention control, some children seem to find it that much harder to focus and persevere through distractions.

Tips for practice

An awareness of temperament, possibly inborn, should not make you overlook the impact of how children are treated and their experiences. But temperament can be a useful source of ideas and reflection on how you handle children's behaviour.

- There can be a match or mismatch between the temperament of children and their main carer. You and a child may find it easy to get along or constantly rub each other up the wrong way. It is an adult's responsibility to take a mental step back and find a way through the prickly relationship.
- Watch out for gender assumptions about temperament. For example, some adults are concerned about a boy who is very wary, thinking he should have more courage. Yet it is more acceptable for a girl to be seen as sensitive or cautious.

Activity

Take a fresh look at how your setting is organised and run.

- Will certain temperaments be a better fit?
- Perhaps you require that children are fairly passive and accept the day as you have planned it.
- In that case, children who want a more active part, especially physically, may be labelled as 'demanding' or 'unable to concentrate'.
- Discuss possible adjustments in your practice, even minor ones, that could be more flexible to children as individuals.

Key skills links: LP2/3.1–3 WO2/3.1–3

Social skills and friendships

Children's social and emotional development progresses hand in hand with the rest of their development. Their communication abilities support the friendships they develop and their reasoning abilities help them to consider and sometimes resolve interpersonal problems. Social contact and friendships are very important to children. Consultation projects that have asked children what they like about nursery or school regularly find that children emphasise the importance of friends. They want to be able to play and chat with their friends. Children explain that in the school playground it is very distressing and lonely if a child does not have friends or is rejected from a group.

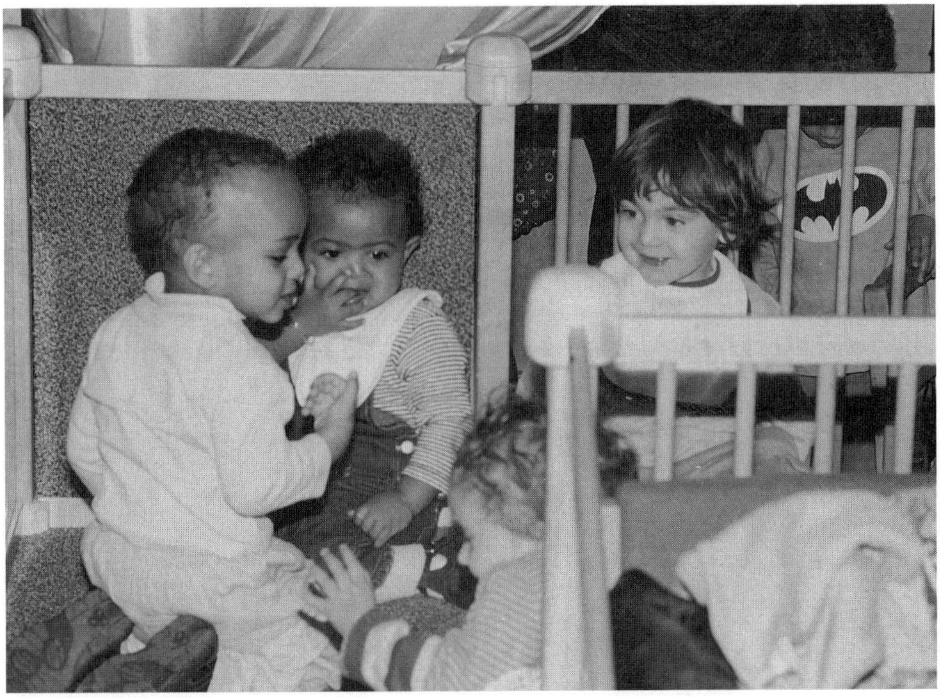

Figure 7.4
Very young children make friends too

Children's social development

Children's social world is of importance to them and can be a major source of self esteem, or a drain on their feelings of confidence.

- If you watch and listen, you will observe that even older babies and toddlers make social moves towards each other, develop shared games and are pleased to see each other.
- Very young children form friendships with each other and show a preference for playing with or being together with particular children. Friendships formed by four and five year olds can have their ups and downs but some close friendships last for many years, some into adulthood.
- Friends become increasingly central to children. They spend more time together and friends influence each other's opinions. Family remains important for children, even when relationships become fraught over disagreements.
- Children become more able to consider the perspectives of others and are willing, at least sometimes, to use their skills of communication and reasoning to problem solve when relationships have become difficult.
- In middle childhood, boys and girls start to face possible conflicting expectations from different friends or between friends and parents or teachers.

Tips for practice

You can help when you:

- Respect the friendships that children have made and support the development of social skills that enable children to deal with minor blips in social relations.
- Take adult responsibility to run home or nursery life in such a way that children can relax and make warm relationships with each other. If children have to compete for adult attention, in a family home or a poorly run early years setting, then they have limited emotional energy to make contact with each other.
- Help children with social troubles. Supportive friendships can be a strong source of self esteem to children, whereas unresolved troubles can be a drain, especially if key adults fail to take children's distress or worries with any seriousness.
- Listen to children who are struggling with being bullied. Continued bullying, verbal or physical, can be a direct attack on a child's self esteem, whatever the apparent focus of the bullying. Children who are unable to gain support against the bullies can seriously doubt their own worth.

To think about

- There will always be a balance in childcare provision between the needs of working parents (or students) and their children.
- Highly flexible patterns of attendance at nursery or pre-school are not always very positive for children, who may as a result not meet the same children on a predictable basis.
- Complex childcare arrangements, including what is called wrap around care, may also put young children in a position where they are required to find friends in more than one setting each day.
- In what ways do you think adults could resolve some of the social problems created for children by arrangements that are suitable for adult needs?
- Discuss some ideas with your colleagues, including how many changes are probably too many, from the child's point of view.

Keys skills links: C3.1a PS3.1

Social contact across the age groups

Practice in early years settings is usually to organise children into age related groups. If you work in a day nursery or centre, you will probably have three groups with age bands something like: babies younger than about 18 months, toddlers up to three years and then the 'pre-school' group aged from three to five years. There are some advantages of giving children a daily base and playtime with their peers and the physical care needs of the very youngest children require equipment that will be not be necessary for the over threes. However, there are serious disadvantages for children if they are kept separate throughout the day in a nursery.

- Contact between the ages is part of normal family life and of links between local families. Children benefit from regular friendly contact with both older and younger children.
- Older children enjoy and are often very adept at communicating with babies and toddlers and making them laugh. If you watch carefully, you notice that three and four year olds adjust their communication for babies; they understand that a different way of talking and showing is necessary.
- In their turn much younger children watch with interest, listen and anticipate a favourite game with a familiar older child or sibling.
- If you bring children together, at some parts of the day or in the garden, affectionate relationships develop across the age bands. Over threes are good at playing the repetitive 'do it again' games that toddlers adore and older children can be shown how to be gentle if necessary.
- Toddlers often love to share a book with an older child or sibling. Four and five years olds are, in their turn, proud to be the 'big' boy or girl who knows the story and so can 'read' it to the little one.
- The babies and toddlers learn from the older children and the latter get a boost to their confidence with the realisation that they have learned so much in contrast to the babies.

- Older children are pleased to show their physical and thinking skills as they share in the care of younger children. Of course adults remain responsible, but there are plenty of safe possibilities that support the learning of both the older and the younger child.

To think about

Nursery and centre teams, who are alert to what all the children can learn, have been exploring ways to bring the age groups together.

- What does your setting do to support contact across the ages?
- Discuss the different possibilities with colleagues from other settings.
- If possible, arrange a visit to another setting that has worked to bring the age groups together.

Write up the different practices you have heard about or seen and present them to the group. For instance, do nurseries:

- encourage visits between the rooms, for siblings or other children?
- use the beginning and ends of a nursery day as a useful time to have mixed age groups?
- mix age groups for local outings?

Key skills links: C2/3.1 C3.1a

Scenario

Joe is five years old and joined St Jude's Primary School and the after school club this term. Joe seems to find it very hard to trust anyone, taking the view that people make you promises and then break them. He seems uncertain about the predictability of even very ordinary daily events. Compared with other children in the club, he seems very reserved and does not exert himself to make friends. Joe has now attended the club for nearly a month and only yesterday exchanged more than a few words with any adult. This afternoon he had a short conversation with Pam, but he talked with feeling about two children he liked in a playgroup that 'I went to before Mum and I had to move on'.

Questions

1. Consider what the key issues are for the after school club in the near future.
2. What might they be able to offer Joe in the club and through the daily routines? Suggest some plans.
3. Should they try to find out a bit more about Joe's background and recent experience? If so, how should they start?

Key skills links: PS2/3.1–2

Social skills

Children need the **social skills** that they can learn over childhood with the support of observant adults who realise that such skills do not simply appear. If you watch children's play with an open mind, you will recognise the social complexities of playing together and the need for children to learn how to negotiate differences of opinion and interests.

Social skills cover a range of behaviours that enable children to become more attuned to others and to smooth social interaction. It is easy for unobservant adults to underestimate the social skills needed for children in the group life of nursery, playgroup or primary school. Even young children of two and three years start to tackle, or want your support in the following ordinary situations:

- How to approach an existing group of playing children and join them in a way that does not bring rejection by words or actions. Sometimes there is no way to join a closed friendship group and children on the outside need adult help to find playmates.
- Ways to be active in a group, finding a middle way between being told what to do and being too 'bossy'.
- How can you leave a group because you want to move onto something else, play with somebody else or you just want to be on your own for a while?
- Children bring their experience into your setting and some will have learned more acceptable strategies than others. For instance, some ways to make contact are more likely to start conflict than shared play. Pushing into the other child's personal space, or seizing play materials, do not usually go down well.
- Children also find difficulties in coping with children who want to play with them more often than is reciprocated.

Key term

Social skills
ways of behaving that enable children to get along in groups, to play and interact with other children

Figure 7.5
Working together

Activity (observation)

Choose two children, one who seems socially comfortable and another whom you feel often stands on the outside of play or is rejected. What happens?

- In what ways does the socially more adept child join a group or start a game?
- Does the less comfortable child have strategies and how do these work?
- In what ways could you help the less socially adept child?
- Are there more general points to note about how your setting operates to promote social skills?
- Share your ideas with colleagues, while being careful to maintain confidentiality about individual children.

Key skills link: C3.1a,b

Helping children to manage socially

Social skills are part of prosocial behaviour (see page 488). Early years practitioners can help by using their observation skills to identify regular conflict points within the day. There may be times and places where children get irritated easily. A positive approach is to avoid assuming that children's behaviour must be at fault and consider whether changes in the routine could help children to manage. Two examples explored by some early years settings revolve around times when children have to wait or queue:

- Self registration works to avoid the people jam that occurs as children are marked in or a lengthy sit down registration time. Children's names are on laminated card and they find their name, with their parent's help, as they arrive and then place it in a special container or hang it on a hook on a registration display board. Apart from reducing waiting time, this activity helps children to recognise their name and often the names of their friends as well as feeling pleased that they can achieve this task.
- Self service snacks and milk can solve the waiting time for this break and the fact than some children need a drink earlier than others. Self service milk and snack tables avoid irritation and promote relaxed conversation, because children chose when to take their snack break, often taking it with a friend. Children can show that they have had a drink or snack by moving their name label into a box or display hanger.

Social skills as part of play

Children learn the social rules of play and subtle communication cues. Most children manage to learn these skills by four or five years of age and it can seem automatic until you observe a child who has not learned them. Children who have had minimal contact with other children can find it hard to adjust when they join a nursery or playgroup and children who have an autistic spectrum disorder (see page 518) are very confused by social interactions that seem normal to their peers.

Children learn social skills in three related areas: how to behave in social interaction, ways of communication and imagination in play. For instance:

- Young babies of nine or ten months show that they recognise the play experience of joint attention with an adult as both focus on an object of interest. An open, alert expression on the baby's face, combined with deliberate looking at the adult, or older sibling, communicates 'we are doing this together'.
- Two, three and four year olds usually show through their play that they have expectations of how different people they know are likely to behave. They can then work this understanding into their play themes and pretend sequences.
- Happy playful exchanges between children depend on their ability to pick up subtle social cues. Is what my friend just said a serious comment, is it a joke or a telling off? Three and four year olds have gained enough understanding of communication to grasp the difference most of the time, especially with children who are familiar playmates.

Tips for practice

You may spend time with children who find these social skills hard, perhaps because they have been isolated or their family life has been unpredictable. You can help when you recognise that these children need support to learn. They are confused and do not recognise the social rules; they are not being deliberately awkward. You can help when you:

- give children enjoyable practice in doing something together with you and show how you can look or take simple turns
- try some games of imitation of actions and follow my leader
- play alongside a child who finds it impossible to play with other children – be friendly and comment on what you are doing, without requiring the child to reply
- talk through what you are doing in simple routines, so the child gets a clearer idea of, 'first we do this … then we …'

Courtesy, apologies and reparations

One aspect of social skills in interaction is to handle when matters go wrong. There are different ways of saying and showing 'sorry' and it is unwise for early years practitioners to insist that there is only one way, perhaps claiming the word is evidence of genuine regret. The opposite can be the case when children are pressured to say 'sorry'; they may well throw out the word in order to stop adults nagging and to get back to their play.

Activity

Consider and discuss with colleagues the different ways that a child could communicate that they are 'sorry', not only saying the words.

If it helps, imagine some everyday situations such as:

- A three year old pinches another three year old for no reason that you can see or hear.
- A two year old knocks over another child's carefully constructed brick tower.

- Three children of about four years old are absorbed in an exploration of the garden. They tell another child that she cannot join in, that she is not wanted.

Discuss issues such as does it matter whether children have a 'good' reason? Do remember that there may be a reason that you have missed. There is also the issue that 'good' reason or not, you may still want to re-direct a child's actions. (See the section on skills of conflict resolution below and the discussion about feelings and behaviour on page 480.)

Develop a presentation or display that can show different ways of communicating 'sorry'.

Key skills links: C3.1a C3.1b

The same balance can be true of expressing appreciation and thanks. There are more ways to communicate 'thank you' than saying those two words.

To think about

- It is important that unreflective adults do not end up supposedly promoting courtesy in children through being discourteous as adults.
- Demanding phrases from adults do not help, such as, 'Say "thank you" then!', 'I'm waiting!' or 'What's the magic word!'
- Furthermore, getting into power battles that children must say or do the right thing rarely work to create genuine courtesy, regret or

Learning skills of conflict resolution

Part of childhood (and adolescence and adulthood for that matter) is being able to handle situations in which all does not go well. In early childhood children have to negotiate many situations of minor or more major conflict, for instance:

- More than one child wants the favourite bike, to go first up the ladder of the climbing frame or to have longer at the painting easel.
- Children may have angry exchanges over how a play theme should be worked out or who should be involved.

Adults sometimes sort out children's conflicts for them or decide who is most in the wrong but there is more scope for learning if early years practitioners share skills of **conflict resolution**. If you are not familiar with these skills then you need to practise and become confident yourself.

Key term

Conflict resolution the skills to address and to try to resolve disagreements without verbal or physical argument

The practical steps in conflict resolution with children are:

- *Step 1*: Approach swiftly and calmly. Stop any hurtful behaviour between the children, using gentle touch if they have started to fight. However, you need to be calm as an adult and not raise your voice.
- *Step 2*: Acknowledge children's feelings by making simple statements like, 'You look cross' or 'Yes, I hear that you want the bike'.
- *Step 3*: Gather information from the children by asking, 'what has

happened?' or 'what's the problem here?' Listen, be fair and impartial and let children feel confident that they are heard.

- *Step 4*: Restate the problem, using the children's words but help them with the communication exchange. Ease the interaction between the children.
- *Step 5*: Ask for solutions with, 'What can we do here to solve this problem?' Listen to what children suggest and avoid filling a silence with your ideas. Give some time and help the children to find a way out of this situation without a loser. Sometimes, you may need to help, because the result is perhaps that one child really does not want to play with this other child at the moment. So the one who wants company may need you.
- *Step 6*: Be prepared to give follow up support and be pleased when children have resolved the situation.

In using these steps, you also draw on good quality communication skills. Generally, you should remain close to the children, on the child's eye level and use touch as appropriate. Supporting conflict resolution with children cannot be done from across the other side of the room. Your aim is to help children with the immediate problem. But, equally important, you aim to support them as they steadily learn the general skills of resolving conflicts and problems.

Activity

- Look for opportunities to use the skills of conflict resolution and to show a good model to the children.
- Write up examples and discuss them with your colleagues.
- In what ways could you improve your own practice?

Key skills links: C3.3 C3.1a LP3.1–3 WO3.1–3

Finding out more

An explanation and practical visual demonstration is available in the video from High/Scope *Supporting children in resolving conflicts*, available from High/Scope UK tel: 020 8676 0220 website: *www.highscope.org*

Supporting diversity in friendships

It is appropriate that early years practitioners support friendships across any social, ethnic or religious groups but children also need the freedom to choose their friends. Some practical issues may guide anti-discriminatory practice.

- Friendships are sometimes made between boys and girls, or children from different ethnic backgrounds, when this opportunity is available. But sometimes girls play with girls and children of a similar background gravitate towards each other.
- You need to be alert and use observation skills to ensure that children are neither chosen nor rejected only or mainly because of their sex, ethnic group or disability.

Figure 7.6
Boys and girls sometimes come together in play or conversation

- If children find one another's ways unfamiliar, then you may be able to help them find common ground. Children do play successfully together even when at the outset they do not share the same language. See also page 314 about supporting children whose fluent language is not shared by many, or any, of their peers in an early years setting.
- Children get cross with each other sometimes but it is fair and realistic to have group rules that children are not offensive about other children's social or ethnic group, their sex or any disability (see page 500).

Further resources

Hartley-Brewer, Elizabeth (1994) *Positive Parenting: Raising children with self-esteem* Cedar.

Lindon, Jennie (1998) *Understanding Child Development: Knowledge, theory and practice* Thomson Learning (especially Chapter 2).

Roberts, Rosemary (2002) *Self-esteem and Early Learning* Paul Chapman Publishing

Progress check

1. Describe three ways in which babies could show that they are closely attached to family members.
2. Describe four circumstances that could make early attachments difficult.
3. Describe the possible sources of personal identity for a child of four or five years of age.
4. Describe two social skills that children need in order to manage in group life and explain how early years practitioners could support children as they learn each of these skills.

8

Children in a social world: emotions, thinking and actions

After reading this chapter you should be able to:

- understand and appreciate children's emotional development
- support children as they learn emotional literacy
- identify ways to support children in distress or who are experiencing family upheaval
- recognise how children develop moral ideas and reasoning
- appreciate and support children's spiritual development.

Introduction

In this chapter you will learn about the importance of children's emotional development and that adults appreciate what and how children learn in this area. With sensitive adult support, children can develop in emotional literacy, growing in an understanding of their own feelings and those of others. Children's understanding of moral or spiritual ideas are a combination of feelings, thinking about the issues and making choices for action. Supportive adults acknowledge the complexity of what children are learning and are as attentive to their own adult behaviour and conversation as that of the children.

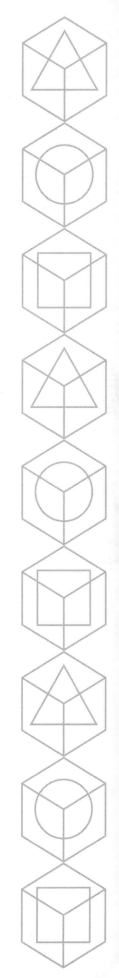

Links to early years qualifications

This chapter especially supports the following units:

Diploma in Child Care and Education: 2, 4, 10

National Vocational Qualification in Early Years Care and Education

Level 2: C4

Level 3: C5

BTEC National Early Years Diploma: 8

Figure 8.1
Children also learn about feelings through social interactions

Understanding the development of emotions

Part of children's personal development is about their emotions: what they feel, how they express and handle their feelings and the extent to which they understand that other people have feelings as well.

How children learn about emotions

Throughout the early years, children are learning about their own and others' feelings:

- Toddlers and very young children may be confused about their feelings and even unnerved by the strength of emotions like anger or fear. They need the support of adults who accept the feelings that children express, although the adults may direct children towards different expressions of feeling, if others are being hurt.
- Two and three years old especially can move swiftly from happiness and excitement to distress or frustration. They express their feelings in different ways: facial and body expression, actions, words and sounds and in communicating with adults that they want help or support.
- Strong feelings like anger and frustration may be expressed in what adults call temper tantrums. When adults take a positive approach to this kind of behaviour they address the feelings as well as the actions, which sometimes need to be re-directed.
- With support, three and four year olds learn to recognise their different feelings, to give an emotion a descriptive name like 'happy', 'sad' or 'cross'. In an affectionate environment children may also start to be able to link events with feelings, such as, 'I'm cross with him because he took my bricks!'
- Three to five year olds start to understand that other children also have feelings, some of them very strong. They are not aware or sensitive all the time to their peers or younger children and it would be unrealistic to expect children to be this way.
- Children also learn about social expectations, from adults and later from their peers, in how you deal with and express feelings. See the activity (observation) box.

Activity (observation)

By three or four years of age, children will sometimes hold back their feelings because of the messages they have been given about how they should behave. For example:

1. Perhaps children hold back feelings of distress, because they do not want to cry in front of other people. Perhaps children have been told that crying is silly or for babies. Boys may have been told that 'big boys don't cry'.
2. Perhaps children hold back their excitement or enthusiasm because important adults or older siblings have scorned their interests or told them not to get 'over excited'.

- Watch out for evidence that children have taken on these kinds of messages about 'good' and 'bad' feelings and emotional expression. They may tell each other or you may see a child struggling with an emotion.
- Gather any comments you hear from practitioners or parents that direct children's emotions.
- Discuss and share the observations you have made with colleagues. Maintain confidentiality about the children and families.

Key skills link: C3.1a

Adult feelings are involved too!

In dealing honestly with children's emotions, reflective adults can become more aware of their own feelings.

- Adults need to be aware that they may be directing girls and boys differently in awareness and expression of feelings.
- There is some growing concern that adults' behaviour in western society towards young boys pushes them towards stereotyped views of male toughness and makes it harder for them to recognise and deal with their emotional inner world.
- Young children of three or four start to appreciate that adults, including their parents, have feelings too. They can be confused sometimes, partly because the adult world is different from the social world of children, but also because adults are sometimes confused.
- For instance, an adult who is scared because a child has nearly walked into the road may shout at the child, who hears the anger and cannot read the adult's mind to understand, 'I was scared you might hurt yourself'.
- Five and six years olds become more adept at reading verbal and non-verbal clues from familiar figures. Their understanding can be muddled when adults are less than open about their feelings, for instance in a family crisis or bereavement (see page 219).

Promoting emotional literacy

The idea of literacy in children's development has so far usually been associated with reading and writing. However, the valuable idea has developed of how adults can support children's learning of **emotional literacy**. This term is used to mean the ability to recognise and understand our own emotions and those of others. Children can be supported as they:

- become clearer about their own feelings
- are more able to name those feelings and talk about them
- recognise the possible source of strong feelings, felt by themselves or others
- find ways to express feelings in non-disruptive and in assertive rather than aggressive ways.

Undoubtedly, adults need to be open-minded in how the ideas of emotional literacy are put into practice and that it does not become culture specific, but

Key terms

Emotional literacy the ability to recognise and understand our own emotions and those of others there are many options. Perhaps one of the most important points for an aware adult is to recognise that our own feelings are involved as well as the child's.

Through an approach of **emotion coaching**, John Gottman observed that some parents were supporting their children in three important areas of their emotional development and self esteem:

Key terms

Emotion coaching supportive adult conversation and behaviour that helps children towards learning emotional literacy

- understanding their own feelings
- having empathy with others
- being able to control their own impulses.

He described five steps within emotion coaching that parents, or other key adults, need to follow. None are technically difficult; all depend on respect for children. The steps are to:

1 Become aware of a child's emotion.
2 Recognise children's expression of these feelings as a time of potential learning and of closeness between adult and child.
3 Listen with empathy and affirm the child's feelings.
4 Help the child to find words to name the emotion.
5 Set limits while exploring strategies to solve the current problem.

The approach of emotion coaching is a direct attempt to help children to develop self esteem as they grow to understand feelings. Adults are more honest about their own emotions and perhaps share their feelings, in a simple and appropriate way.

The approach needs to be developmentally appropriate and the aim is certainly not that adults spend ages talking with children about their emotions. You will lose young children very quickly if you try this. Often a simple acknowledgement may be key: 'I can see that you're cross about ...', 'You look sad today ...' 'I can see that you want ...' or 'You don't like that, do you. Is it that it makes you frightened?' The approach is grounded in good communication skills with children and valuing their emotional life.

Understanding the feelings of others

Children can develop in prosocial behaviour, part of which is empathy, the ability and willingness to tune into the feelings of others. Prosocial behaviour (see page 488) is shaped by children's experience and is not an automatic development. You can help to promote children's understanding and supportive reactions to other people's feelings in different ways:

- The tell–show–do approach described on page 116 that builds on children's direct experiences and your setting a good example to them.
- Supportive conversation can be built around the stories in books or story telling (see page 222).
- Guided role play and use of puppets or dolls can add to children's ability to tune into the perspective of others.
- Discussions within circle time (see page 221) can be one way to raise and talk about feelings.

Any of these approaches can work positively so long as you stay realistic about what children are likely to understand at different ages and you keep any exploration or conversation simple, practical and a two-way process: children can contribute as well as listen to adults.

Figure 8.2

Children need sources of comfort

Using Persona Dolls

Babette Brown and Carol Smith have promoted the use of Persona Dolls as part of a well-rounded anti-discriminatory approach in the early years. The dolls build on young children's willingness to imagine their way into the world of one doll that is given a name, character and life story. The children talk about the doll and sometimes take her or him home for a stay overnight. Careful use of the doll by an early years practitioner gently extends children's ability to empathise with others, apparently unlike themselves. Sometimes the experience of the doll is chosen to reflect the troubles of a child in the group but never in any way that identifies that child.

The conversation and play around the doll can be one way to help children to be reflective about their attitudes and to see individuals rather than broad categories for children and adults who do not seem to be like them at the outset.

Books and stories

Stories and illustrations can be a useful way to approach feelings and encourage children to be more aware of their own and other people's feelings. You will find more books on page 222 about feelings in times of stress but there are a number of more general books to explore emotions:

- Kathy Henderson and Caroline Binch *New Born* (Frances Lincoln 1999) – an illustrated book about the sensations of a very new baby.
- Penny Dale *Big Brother Little Brother* (Walker Books 1997) – a simple story about family life, feelings and relations between siblings.
- Lindsay Leghorn *Proud of our Feelings* (Imagination Press 1995) – a story about the narrator's friends, their feelings and an invitation to children listening to or reading the book to explore 'how do you feel when …' or 'what makes you feel happy (or other emotions)?'

- Some stories raise the topic of feelings when the characters or main character is less than happy. *Something Else* by Kathryn Cave (Puffin 2000) – explores the experience of not being wanted through the story of a little creature called Something Else who does not seem to fit in with or be like any of the other creatures.

Activity

- Explore one of the books or the use of stories woven around dolls for supporting children's emotional development.
- Plan what you could do with a book or story involving a doll character.
- Create the opportunity for children to explore this activity, while leaving them plenty of choice as to whether to become involved or not.
- Write up the activity after it is complete:
  - In what ways did the children react to the story?
  - How did they choose to comment?
  - What did you learn about the children's views and feelings?
- Share what you learned with your colleagues.

Key skills link: C3.3

Promoting a sense of security

Children need to feel that they belong and to understand enough about how their family or an early years setting is organised so that they can predict the usual events and reactions. Children can feel very uneasy if they cannot get a sense of what is likely to happen and how adults are likely to behave. Children's uneasiness may arise from their own past experiences, that make it hard for them to settle or perhaps they bring disruptive expectations or habits into your setting.

Figure 8.3
There are different ways to help children feel they belong

However, children are sometimes made insecure as a result of the inconsistent or unkind behaviour of adults.

You can support children to feel at ease in your setting by:

- helping them to deal with change and transitions – when they join you and when they leave
- organising a day that has enough predictability that young children can look ahead a little and get to know the rhythms of the day, but not such a rigid routine that children feel harassed (see also Chapter 2 about care and care routines)
- noticing when children look ill at ease or worried and supporting them with words, body language and affectionate contact
- creating an especially secure environment for children who are having trouble coping in an ordinary group with their peers.

Look at page 629 about settling children into your setting and partnership with parents.

When children need extra support

Nurture groups

Sometimes children cannot cope in a group, such as a primary school classroom. Reception classes require children to be reasonably self directed and to manage with an adult–child ratio that delivers limited adult attention, even with a careful and experienced class team. Children who find it hard to cope with this situation may develop behaviour that disrupts the class but they may also remain uncommunicative and separate from the group.

In the 1970s Marjorie Boxall developed her idea of **nurture groups** to meet the emotional and intellectual needs of children whose early experiences had not prepared them for the demands of school. The approach has been successful in supporting children to become able to rejoin their mainstream school class after some months in the nurture group. The main characteristics of the nurture group are a reminder of what children need in order to feel secure:

Key term

Nurture group carefully planned small group experience for children who are struggling with the emotional demands of primary school life

- The adult–child ratio of 12 children to two adults allows children to relate to a manageable number of other children and to get to know the adults well.
- There is a focus on personal attention, plenty of encouragement and a blend of care and learning. Activities are drawn from an early years curriculum of play and exploration as well as addressing those parts of the reception or year one curriculum that children can manage.
- The day is organised with some choice, but not so much that children feel overwhelmed. Routine is kept predictable to that they can feel secure. Children are pre-warned about any changes and are given an active part in helping with the routine.
- The nurture group team are careful to communicate with and involve parents. The partnership can ensure that parents see the group as an experience that will help their child back into the mainstream; there is no sense of blaming the child or the family.

In many ways the nurture groups draw on good early years practice and are a useful reminder of how much children need this quality of early experience.

Activity

What can you learn from the practice of nurture groups?

- Look at the ideas in this section and make links to good practice with children younger than school age.
- What kinds of positive experiences can you give children in your setting that mean that they are ready to manage the demands of school?
- The nurture group work is a good reminder that children need emotional and social skills for school; it is not all about intellectual development.
- How do you put into practice some of the important themes in a nurture group day? For example, how do you communicate with children about what will happen in their day? How do you let children know about any changes, and how do you avoid the interruptions of unexpected visitors?
- Develop your ideas into a short presentation and share it with your colleagues.
- In what ways could you improve your own practice?

Key skills link: C/3.1b LP3.1–3 WO3.1–3

Helping children in distress

Even for a mainly happy and secure child, life does not unfold without some troubles. Some of these ups and downs will pass swiftly, especially if an adult is supportive. Some sources of distress are more entrenched and will need more extensive support for children, in partnership with their parents, and sometimes with additional help from other professionals.

Everyday events

Children can be distressed at the events of the day, for example that:

- They have had nobody to play with in the playground and when they try to join games, they are told 'we've got enough people' or 'no, you can't play with us'.
- Their best friend has taken up with another child.
- The pottery jug that they made with such care has been smashed to bits when another child picked it up to look at it and dropped it on the floor.

To think about

Events that distress children can look insignificant to adults, but only if those adults neither listen nor look at the child's distress. It is important and also respectful to a child when adults make the effort to the child's experience into something equivalent in their own life.

- For instance, a thoughtless adult might be tempted to say to the child, 'It's only a jug. You can make another one tomorrow'.

- Think about it, how would you feel if somebody had destroyed, even by accident, a dress or a complicated cake, that you had spent hours making?
- Or what is the adult equivalent of having no friends in the playground?
- Imagine going to a large social gathering where everyone else seems to be having a grand time and you cannot break into any of the social groups. Perhaps even people who you thought liked your company, edge closer so you cannot join in the conversation. How do you feel in your imagination?
- Discuss your ideas with colleagues.

Key skills links: C3.1a

Family crises

Within the years of childhood, there will also be some events that children find disruptive or confusing.

- These may include changes that are normal for many families, such as the arrival of a new baby or moving home. But these 'normal' events have substantially changed what has been the child's normal life so far.
- Many children, even young children, now experience the separation of their parents and a new family set up.
- Families may experience financial pressure from unemployment or a slump in the family business.
- Young children may experience bereavement in the family or a close family friend or neighbour.
- For some families there will be disruption when one parent is absent for a considerable time, perhaps because of serious ill health and hospitalisation or through being sent to prison.
- Children from refugee families and asylum seekers may have experienced a massive disruption to life as they knew it, as well as genuinely frightening events.

Young children are aware of atmosphere and notice much more than adults often think or want to believe. It is a mistake to assume that young children do not notice family or neighbourhood upheavals and therefore adults think that children's feelings and views can be discounted.

Children feel more secure if they feel they have someone to turn to who will take their concerns seriously. Some children of primary school age complain that adults do not listen properly, belittle their playground problems or offer clichés that show the adults do not understand the complexity of what they face. A positive experience of support and empathy from an adult helps a child with the current problem, but children can also learn general strategies about how to face and resolve problems. By six or seven years of age, some children already understand that even caring adults cannot solve everything but that talking about a problem can help you to feel more confident and it is good just to have someone listen.

Listening and supportive conversation

All these events are different and, of course, children are individuals and react in varied ways to an apparently similar experience. You will help best by drawing on good communication skills with the children and their parents.

- Listen to what children want to tell you. Pay close attention and show that you would like to understand their feelings.
- If a child is not speaking out, you could invite (but not insist) her to speak with, 'You look sad, is anything the matter' or 'You are very quiet today, is anything on your mind?'
- Avoid rushing in with a solution that sounds right to you. Consider with a child, 'What could we do about this?' or 'What could make this better for you?'
- Some troubles, perhaps of bullying from another child, will need your direct help but even then, it is better to discuss the possibility with the child rather than insist on operating on their behalf.
- Answer a child's questions if you can, but be honest if you do not know the answer ('why did my Daddy have to go to prison?'). Acknowledge the parents' preferred response to this question: 'does everyone go to heaven when they die?' But don't say you agree if you don't.
- You should give a child the same respect of confidentiality that you would give to a colleague but this does not mean that you keep absolute secrets. What children tell you should never become fuel for gossip among staff. It would, however, be appropriate to say to a child, 'I'd like to tell your Mummy about our conversation and what you would like to do.'
- If a child's problem is from her life outside your setting, then you do need to talk with her parents.

Circle time for general conversation

Children often want a personal conversation when they are concerned or confused but there are also opportunities to raise some issues in a more general way in a group.

Figure 8.4

Some conversations will happen in small group times

The idea of **circle time** developed for children in primary school but with sensitive adjustment for younger children, it can work as a way to introduce topics that are of relevance to three to five year olds and to pick up on issues that have arisen within the day.

Circle time can work so long as you plan carefully and are sensitive to what happens in circle time. A positive circle time experience for children does not happen just because you sit them in a circle or call a regular group slot by this name! Some useful guidelines include:

- Keep the discussion open and suitable for three to five year olds. Think about what they are likely to understand and how they will approach topics.
- Vary the content of circle time and ensure that it is not always very heavy emotionally.
- Pay attention to the children: listen to what they say and how they say it. Circle time will not work if adults overload the time with their talking or telling children.
- Enable all the children to take part at some time and in a way that they wish.
- Be sensitive to the feedback from children's words, expression and behaviour.
- Have a forward plan of what you may cover in circle time but be flexible. If a child announces that, 'My Mummy's going to have a baby', this may be a good time to explore babies, new and old.
- Be aware that if children feel comfortable and trust you, they may sometimes talk in the circle about very personal family issues. You need to be ready to show you have heard and gently bring an end to the topic if the matter is sensitive. Other children will repeat what is said in circle time and it would be inappropriate to try to establish this session as a closed confidential time with children.

Key term

Circle time
a carefully planned small group time to explore issues and ideas with children in a supportive way

Support children's behaviour

When children are under stress because of family changes and crises, you need to draw on a friendly working relationship in partnership with parents. If they trust you as another adult, you are more likely to hear that, for instance, the family has been disrupted because Dad has been made redundant or everyone is distressed because they have lost a baby cousin through cot death.

- You may be able to offer a friendly ear and comfort to parents and liaise with them about supporting the child.
- Children often react to family changes by some level of developmental regression, a backward step in what they can manage.
- Children may find it harder than usual to say goodbye to their parents or may actually say they are worried that 'Mummy is alright' during the day.
- You need to be sensitive to a child's stress, but hold to usual boundaries for behaviour if the child is expressing her distress by hurting others, by words or actions.
- Children's concerns will often emerge through their play or drawings. So long as the play does not impose on other children then it can help for children to play out their feelings and re-run events. If the content of a child's play or their drawings worry you, then it will be important to talk with your manager and the child's parents.

Tips for practice

- You may be able to explain to parents the importance of talking with children. A child whose mother is expecting another baby may be worried that she is sick all the time and needs to know that Mummy is not 'ill' in the usual way.
- Parents need to decide what to discuss and how they speak with their children but you may be able to put the important perspective that children are aware when something is wrong.
- If there is no other explanation, children often assume that they are at fault for the sadness or short temper of their parents.
- Part of the problem, for instance in family breakdown or bereavement, can be that nobody has explained to the child what has happened or is about to happen.

Using books and stories

Stories about other people, or playing out stories with dolls and puppets can be a support for children, alongside a chance to talk and be heard. Books do not substitute for emotional support work from caring adults but they can be a good supplement and may sometimes help a more reticent child to speak. Books can also be a source of information, given through words and pictures.

There are some excellent books about babies and where babies come from. Some are more explicit than others and in an early years setting it is probably better to go for the more low-key books. You need to select books with sketches or photos that you will be comfortable to share with the children. If you work as a nanny, you should also be guided by parents' preferences, but they will probably be pleased for some suggestions.

A story book with illustrations can bring in the children who may relate to the idea that 'Your Mummy brought you home all tiny like that too'.

Some possibilities include:

- Ann Kubler *Waiting for Baby* and *My New Baby* (Child's Play International 2000) – simple picture board books.
- Debbie MacKinnon and Anthea Sieveking *All about Me* (Frances Lincoln 1994) – suitable for three or four year olds with photos.
- Rosemary Stones *Where do Babies Come From* (Puffin 1989) – a very simple presentation.
- *Why is Mummy's Tummy so Big* (no author given, Dorling Kindersley 1997).
- Alastair Smith *How are Babies Made?* (Usborne 1997).

Activity

In a large, high street book shop, look for books for children about life events, such as described in this section.

- Make notes about possible books and the age of children for which you feel they are suitable.
- Are some books, perhaps about how are babies made, more appropriate for use by parents in their own family?

- Describe one book and how you feel that reading and talking about this story or the illustrations could support a child going through this experience.
- Write up your findings and discuss with or present to colleagues.

Key skills links: C2.1b C2.3

There are a range of books that cover family changes and loss. Books can be chosen that are suitable for different age groups and they offer a story that may give children a perspective or a way to express their own feelings. Some books are designed as 'talk about' books through the illustrations or suggestions for the adults to open up a general conversation.

- Rosemary Stones *Children don't Divorce* (Happy Cat Paperbacks 1991) – a title in the *Talking it Through* series.
- Jillian Powell *What do we Think about – Family Break-up* (Hodder Wayland 1998) – a simple story with some explanatory text and illustrations suitable for five year olds and older. The series has other titles by the same author, including *Death*, *Disability* and *Adoption*.
- Julia Cole *How do I Feel about my Parents' Divorce* (Watts 1997) – probably more for seven or eight year olds and older.
- Sarah Levete *How do I Feel about – When People Die?* (2001) is one title in the *How do I Feel about?* series published by Aladdin Books. These books are suitable for four, five year olds and older and have mini 'case studies' in which children talk about experiences.

You will also find series that offer a range of books covering different topics, for instance, *Let's talk about* (Franklin Watts), *Facing up* (Happy Books), *First Experience* (Usborne) or *Events* (Hamish Hamilton). You do not need to have all the books in your setting. If you make regular trips with children to the local library you can find books together that will fit what children want or might want to explore at the time.

Activity

In your support of parents you are not expected to undertake specialist work. You will be helpful as you share the care of their child and in partnership with parents, discuss what will best help a child who is confused or concerned. You can also support parents by having information to offer about other sources of help, advice or support, if parents ask.

It is well worth building up your own file of useful organisations, both local and national. Here are some to start your file. Check out local branches and contact one or two organisations to explore helpful leaflets. Start with the website, where possible, and then contact the organisation with some clear questions in your mind.

- Relate offers support for people with problems in relationships. Check out your closest office in your local telephone directory.

- Parentline Plus is an organisation specialising in support for parents and families and it incorporates Stepfamily. They have a free helpline 0808 800 2222 and you can find information on their website: *www.parentlineplus.org.uk*
- Cruse Bereavement Care, Cruse House, 126 Sheen Road, Richmond, Surrey TW9 1UR tel: 020 8940 4818 (general), helpline 0870 167 1677 website: *www.crusebereavementcare.org.uk*
- The Child Bereavement Trust, Aston House, High Street, High Wycombe, Bucks HP14 3AG tel: 01494 446648 website: *www.childbereavement.org.uk*
- Federation of Prisoners' families support groups c/o SCF, Cambridge House, Cambridge Grove, London W6 0LE tel: 020 8741 4578 website: *www.fpfsg.org.uk*

Key skills links: IT2/3.1 C3.1b

National and international events

Significant events that reach the news affect children as well as adults. Yet the feelings and fears of the children can be overlooked, especially when the adults are themselves confused, distressed or frightened.

The foot and mouth crisis in 2001 seriously affected the lives of families in parts of England, either because their own livestock were slaughtered or because normal life was disrupted in the whole neighbourhood. Children in rural areas were sometimes isolated, unable to reach their usual nursery or school. The children were aware of family stress and anger over what was happening and sometimes witnessed animals being killed.

Where children were able to reach their early years setting or school, aware teams worked hard to support the children, to explain and listen. Early years practitioners can be a very important source of comfort, especially when parents may be so hard pressed, it is hard to give emotional support to their children.

The events of 11 September 2001 and the aftermath has affected everyone's life in one way or another and adults have agonised over what to say to children. The same general guidelines have applied, even to such a distressing and frightening event. Bear in mind the following important points:

- Children's questions should be answered with simple but honest replies.
- Children should be reassured that this event happened a long distance away.
- It is inappropriate to tell children that, 'nothing bad will ever happen here'. You cannot make such a broad-ranging promise; there will be accidents and bereavements in any neighbourhood.
- Children must be helped to understand, especially given the news coverage and words used, that there are terrorists and people who use violence in many cultures and world faiths. Muslim families in the UK, and in the same neighbourhood as some children, are not all terrorists. Any more than all Christian families applaud the violence in Northern Ireland that is considerably closer to home.

Long-term effects of stress on children

Early experiences affect children in ways that can be seen through their development but also in the way they behave. Sometimes you will find that persistent worries or fears weigh on a child and are not lifting despite your sympathetic communication and attention. Bear in mind that young children can get depressed; this condition is not limited to adolescents or adults.

When children are weighed down

You should never overlook the seriousness of the situation when children continue to express feelings of hopelessness and helplessness. Children need help if they make comments about life being not worth living or that they wish they were dead. Heartfelt comments of this kind are not 'just a phase', nor are any events when children threaten, or carry out threats, to harm themselves. If you are responsible for a child who is behaving in these worrying ways you should definitely speak with your manager, the child's parent(s) and recommend that the family seek professional help.

Some confidences that a child offers you might raise concerns about child protection – see Chapter 19 for a full discussion of this topic.

Neighbourhood and domestic violence

Children live in a social world that is broader than your setting and events outside the nursery or pre-school affect children's behaviour. A positive approach to individual children within any early years setting has to start with the experiences that children bring with them into your setting.

Some children may have seen violence in their own homes, even if they have not themselves been on the receiving end of an aggressive attack. An accurate definition of **domestic violence** is that of verbal and physical aggression, threats or attacks made by family members within the home. Some commentators insist that domestic violence is only perpetrated by men on women, but this is not true. Although the majority of the reported attacks in the home are by men, a sizeable minority are by women and are likely to be under-reported. Some children in your early years settings may have violent or highly aggressive mothers.

> **Key terms**
>
> **Domestic violence** verbal and physical aggression, threats or attacks made by family members of either sex within the home

The experience of domestic violence may mean that children themselves are more likely to deal with even minor upsets with an aggressive attack. Fighting back with words or fists will be what they have known, so it seems the obvious option. Of course, you do not tolerate such behaviour but you cannot help a child to change unless you first recognise that she or he does not know that this reaction is unacceptable. To that child, it is a new idea that 'we don't hit each other here' or 'we don't use that word in the nursery'.

In some parts of the UK children will experience violence in their local neighbourhood. Adults who live and work in stressful neighbourhoods can hope that children somehow do not notice what is happening on the streets. But of course children are aware, can be very frightened and they learn negative attitudes at a very young age in line with local divisions, whatever those are.

More than one generation of children has now been raised in Northern Ireland during what this community calls the Troubles. As much as adults would often prefer to believe otherwise, young children have been affected by the disruptions and deaths. Children also understand the importance of symbols that relate to Catholic and Protestant groups in the Province and, without active adult support to the contrary, take on attitudes of bigotry – along religious lines. The application of equal opportunities and anti-discriminatory practice in Northern Ireland has meant anti-sectarianism: an active attempt to challenge religious discrimination and bigotry and to build positive connections between the communities and their children.

To think about

One difficulty for adults to recognise is that aggression and war can seem very exciting. Peaceful conditions often get described in terms of the absence of war, rather than positive characteristics of peace.

When you work with children, especially those who are slightly older and in school, you may well need to identify how to bring some excitement and challenge into the children's world that does not depend on conflict and win–lose scenarios.

Children in refugee families

Increasingly, early years settings in different parts of the UK are admitting children who have reached the neighbourhood because of serious disruptions and fighting in their country of origin. Many children will have significant adjustments to make to an unknown culture and language. Unlike families who have migrated out of choice, these children will also bring what may be very distressing experiences with them.

Even young children may have seen vicious fighting, witnessed the injury or murder of members of their family and experienced a terrifying flight out of danger. The children may have been part of experiences that you have only seen on the television news or in newspaper photographs.

Settling distressed and disturbed children can be hard work and any early years setting with refugee children ideally needs to have specialist support. However, such support may not be available locally and in any case nurseries and pre-schools may still be doing much of the supportive work. In terms of behaviour you need to be aware that:

- Children's experiences may make them very vulnerable to what seem to the outsider to be over-reactions to potentially aggressive situations. Children may be very easily distressed or hit out in self protection. You may well need to offer emotional support and understanding as well as guiding children towards more appropriate reactions in a safe place.
- Like their peers, refugee children are likely to play out their experiences: with dolls and small world figures, through pretend play themes and in drawings or stories. (See the scenario in the box.)
- Some children may wish to talk about their memories or continuing worries and some may have realistic fears for family or close friends left behind in a war zone or refugee camps.
- You need to allow for some of your early years routines being unfamiliar to these children.
- Good partnership with parents will help you to find out and understand what may be familiar and what may not be – it will depend a great deal on the family's country of origin.
- If you do not share a fluent language with the parent(s), then you will need to use the help of the local interpreting service.

Activity

- Save the Children Centre for Young Children's Rights has some supportive material for early years practitioners who work with refugee children, including a video pack called *In safe hands*.
- Contact them at 356 Holloway Road London N7 6PA tel: 020 7700 8127 email: cycr@scfuk.org.uk website: *www.savethechildren.org.uk*
- Gather some information and write up some practical plans for good practice with children from refugee families.

Key skills links: C3.3 IT2.1–3

Scenario

Over the last couple of years, children from refugee families have attended the Baker Street Children and Family Centre. Some of the children have witnessed very distressing events.

The centre team has so far worked to discourage any kind of pretend play involving weapons and fighting. They were close to reviewing the ban, since they were aware of its possible limiting effect on the boys. However, the arrival of Adok and Angelo from Somalia led to a thorough re-think of the centre approach.

The boys took many opportunities to play games built around the use of weapons and used some of the small world figures in fighting scenarios. The centre team, in careful conversation with the parents, realised that the boys' play was far from imaginary; they were playing out what they had actually seen. Sally, who was the boys' key worker, undertook some observation of their games that involved weapons and fights. The games were fairly contained and the boys became less agitated once staff stopped trying to discourage the games. Both Adok and Angelo were interested in other play opportunities and in beginning to make social contact with other children. However, they really needed to have the chance to play out their frightening experiences in the safety of the centre.

Over a matter of several months, the boys' weapon and war play became rare and they established broad interests in the centre.

Questions

1. What might have been the consequences if the centre team had stopped the boys working through their experiences in play?
2. In what ways have you noticed that some children in your own setting play out distressing experiences in their play? Write up your observations with care and attention to confidentiality.
3. In what ways can supportive adults help and under what kind of circumstances might you need to re-direct the play? Suggest such plans appropriate to your kind of setting.

Key skills links: C3.3 PS3.1–2

Children's moral development

Babies are born morally neutral but naturally social. Moral development in childhood has no meaning without social relationships (see Chapter 7). Moral values are relevant to how we treat other people, or how we expect to be treated in our turn. So children's moral development has to be just as much about learning as any other aspect of their development.

Children's understanding of moral issues and dilemmas

There are three main strands to what children learn and how they are able to think about this area: moral behaviour, understanding and judgement.

Moral behaviour

Young children learn about acceptable and unacceptable ways of behaving in different settings. Children may behave in ways that meet adult approval, by taking turns or being gentle with the rabbit. Young children may not yet fully understand concepts of 'sharing' or the hurt that can be experienced by others, even rabbits.

Moral understanding

Children learn ideas about what is acceptable or unacceptable, the words that adults use and their reasons for being pleased or disapproving. It takes time and consistent experience for children to grasp the moral concepts that underpin adult approval of 'kind' or 'courteous' behaviour and disapproval of 'rough' or 'rude' behaviour. Even more abstract concepts like ideas of right and wrong can be harder.

Moral judgement

Children learn to make decisions about how somebody should behave faced with a particular situation. Four and five year olds can start to show a grasp of moral judgement – what should or should not happen – so long as the situation is immediate and makes direct sense to them. Talking about imaginary 'what if …' scenarios is harder until they are about seven or eight years old.

Understanding ground rules and consequences

Children's grasp of moral issues tends to start with the rules that adults make about behaviour and their understanding grows in response to what they experience. There is further discussion of behaviour and positive response by adults in Chapter 17.

Under twos

- Babies do not have the knowledge required to break any rules; they do not yet know that rules exist. They cannot possibly be 'naughty' any more than they can be 'good'.
- Mobile toddlers are physically able to uncover some of the 'don'ts' in their family or nursery environment. They start to recognise that adults do not want them to follow through some actions. But they cannot yet understand that their actions have consequences, nor why some results are dangerous, messy or unkind to others.

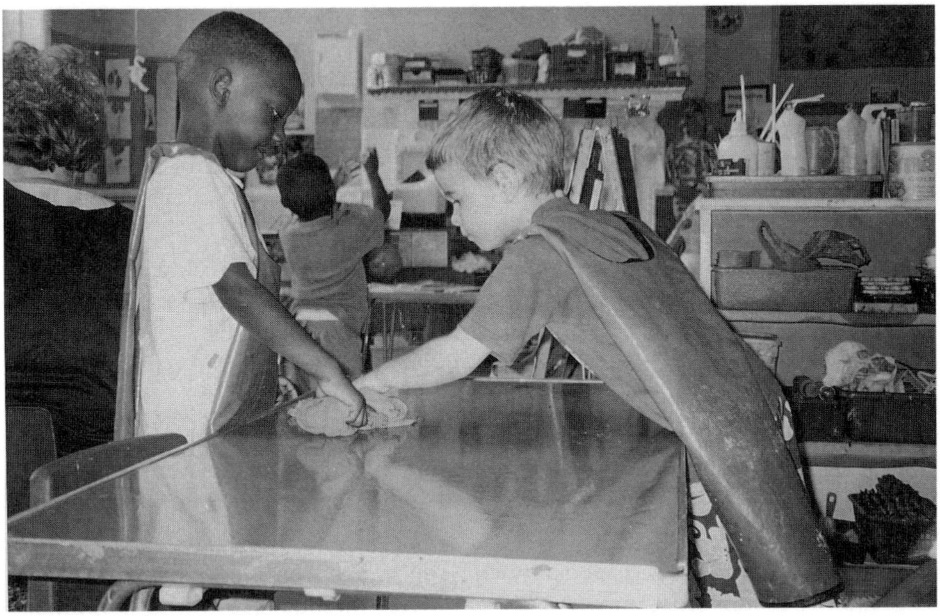

Figure 8.5

Children learn to be working members of your setting

Two and three year olds

- Such young children may follow a ground rule about how to behave in a supportive family home or early years setting. Two and three year olds do not understand the reasons or values underlying a rule, but they are happy often to cooperate. They are in the process of learning what you want.
- Toddlers and very young children observe and think, as well as act. Their moral behaviour will reflect what they have learned. For instance, children get to know familiar adults and realise that one person really means 'no' and another can be nagged into 'yes'.
- Very young children tend to judge the 'badness' of an act by the level of mess or how badly somebody has been hurt. But adult reactions probably increase this tendency – see the Think about box.

To think about

- When young children make judgements about actions, they tend to focus on the consequences of those actions and not on the intentions. But if you observe many adult–child interactions when something has gone wrong, adults often make much more fuss when the mess or damage is greater.
- It takes patience and a willingness to check what has actually happened to prevent this often unfair adult reaction. The moral judgements of young children may be less about the limits to their thinking power and more about their powers of observation.
- Discuss these ideas with your colleagues and consider any changes you could make in how you behave towards young children when something goes wrong.

Key skills links: C3.1a LP3.1–3 WO3.1–3

Three, four and five year olds

- Children of this age tend to believe that rules are fixed and unchanging, and that everyone will follow the same rules or codes of behaviour.
- Bit by bit, experience tells children that not all adults set the same rules nor the same consequences for rule-breaking. They notice that not all families are like their own and that even the same adult is not always consistent over rules.
- As children gain experience, and their intellectual skills develop, they grasp the subtleties that some rules may be more flexible than others. Their more complex thinking ability allows for some level of 'it depends ...'. They can be confused by adults who, for instance, say it is right to tell the truth and are then heard telling 'courtesy lies'.
- Children of this age still tend to judge how 'bad' actions are by the seriousness of the consequences. They may now make some allowance for the other person's intentions in their judgements of behaviour, but the link has to be very obvious.
- From about four years, especially with adult encouragement, children steadily become more able to allow for what someone else, perhaps another child, intends and that people sometimes make mistakes ('It was an accident', 'she didn't mean to knock over your bricks').
- From about four years of age, or even younger, children have learned the word 'fair', the criticism of 'that's not fair' and a working concept of fairness.
- Children from this age onwards can feel very strongly about fairness and justice in their social world. They lose respect for and will criticise adults who fail to follow their own rules or show unfair behaviour such as inconsistency or favouritism.
- From about four or five years of age, children can have a clearer idea of how and why rules for behaviour can work. They will also often agree that some rules are a good idea, so that a nursery or reception class can run in a way that is fair for everyone.
- Children of this age can take part in a supported group discussion, for instance in circle time, to develop or review sensible rules for their group.

Five, six and seven year olds

- Children are alert observers and will now often judge adults against the agreed rules for a school, out of school club or family home.
- Children do not respect adults (parents, early years practitioners, teachers or any carers) who disregard their own courtesy guidelines like 'don't interrupt' or safety rules like 'we walk in the corridor, we don't run'.
- By seven or eight years of age many children are aware that rules are not always straightforward to follow; it can be hard to do the right thing sometimes. They are more able to explain the moral uncertainties if adults will listen.
- Children lose patience and willingness to cooperate with adults who insist that the situation is simple. For instance, the reality in a primary school playground is that the school rule of 'telling' about verbal or physical bullying can force children to go against another rule, that children do not 'grass' on their peers.
- Children learn within the social context set by adults. Research with children of primary school age shows that they can usually make longer lists

of what is regarded as anti-social behaviour in school than prosocial options. Children are often clearer about what adults do not want them to do and have more words to describe the unacceptable behaviour than what the adults do want. Why do you think this happens?

- Throughout childhood there is not a perfect match between children's moral judgements (what they may say is the right choice) and their actual behaviour, when faced with this situation. This mismatch should surprise nobody; it is equally true for adults that what they say they would do in a theoretical situation is not an exact prediction of what they actually do.

Scenario

Over the last year Alastair, the head of St Jude's Primary School, has tried to build a more coherent team to include everyone from the nursery, reception, years 1–6, the playground supervisory staff and breakfast and after school club. Discussions have slowly revealed that differences in approach by adults have sometimes put children in a very awkward position. One recent example led to a lively discussion:

- The nursery, reception and after school club practitioners have been consistent in encouraging children to express their opinions, including courteous ways to disagree with adults.
- They are concerned that comments that are acceptable from children in the nursery and after school club have been criticised by some teachers and playground supervisors on the grounds that children are being 'cheeky' and 'rude'.
- This part of the team feel that they have supported children to be assertive and courteous. The children are not being rude and the situation is very confusing to them.

Questions

1. How might the children be thinking in this situation? What could be the thinking of those staff who regard the children as 'cheeky'?
2. What might be a way forward here?
3. What examples have you encountered where children have to negotiate very different adult expectations and what the children have learned to be 'right' in one setting is 'wrong' in another?
4. Share examples with your colleagues and consider whether there are some applications to your own practice.

Key skills links: C3.1a LP3.1–3 WO3.1–3

Supportive adults

The many points and examples in this section are a strong reminder to you that adults often choose to see only one aspect to children's development at a time. You will be a helpful adult when you take a well rounded approach to children's moral development. Children's feeling, thinking and behaving intermingle in daily life.

- Their thinking powers are not only applied to how to build a brick tower that does not fall down or to an early understanding of number. The same thinking brain is also trying to make sense of puzzling social situations and to anticipate, at least a bit, how familiar adults and children will act.
- You have to bring children's social behaviour together with their powers of thinking and reasoning. This area of children's development is called **social cognition**.
- Observation of children has shown that they have an impressive ability to learn prosocial behaviour and to support each other so long as adults take an active and positive approach to handling behaviour (see Chapter 17 for more on this topic).
- Young children think about other people: what they do, might do or should do. They also think to an extent about how other people feel or should feel (see page 214).
- Some four or five year olds are undoubtedly more reflective or curious than others and this wish to understand is shown in the questions they ask you.
- You can build on and encourage children's powers of social cognition by how you use stories, role play or puppets and simple drama.
- Some three year olds, and four or five year olds can enjoy the exploration in a story or picture about, 'I wonder what he's thinking' or 'Do you think she meant that to happen?' The ability to tune into the feelings of others is also explored from page 489.

Key term

Social cognition children's ability and learning to merge their understanding of social behaviour with their powers of thinking and reasoning

Children's spiritual development

It is hard to know where to place spiritual development in a book of this kind since it relates to different areas of children's development.

- Children's spiritual development includes knowledge and ideas. But all world faiths include acceptance of some beliefs that cannot be judged by rational means: you just believe or you do not.
- Religious faith is also closely linked to feelings of belonging and creates one source of personal and family identity.
- Children can also develop a sense of spirituality, which may be linked with their family faith, but can develop independently.
- For some adults clear moral beliefs and actions are strongly linked to a religious faith or philosophical stance. Children raised in these families will also link the moral with the spiritual.
- But children can learn moral values and behaviour without a faith framework.

It is appropriate for early years practitioners to support children's moral and spiritual development. Good practice means that you need to understand how children learn in this area, as well as show active respect for parents and the children's family background. In order to make sense of children's moral and spiritual development, you need to make connections to the rest of their development. Figure 8.6 shows one way to explore how children's learning connects within daily life and their learning over time. This section explores some of these ideas and issues.

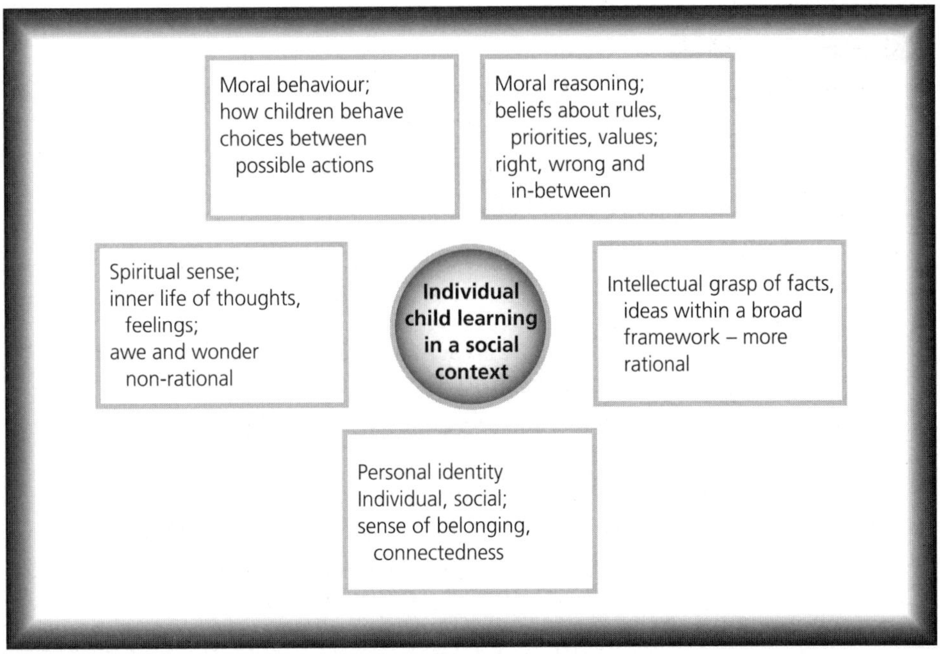

Figure 8.6

Learning within moral and spiritual development

Source: Jennie Lindon Understanding World Religions in Early Years Practice, 1999 Hodder & Stoughton

Children and religious faith

There is almost no research to guide early years practice on how children develop an understanding of and commitment to religious beliefs and practices. On the basis of the rest of their development, it seems very likely that:

- Young children, certainly up to about five or six years of age, will simply believe what familiar adults, especially their parents, tell them to be true.
- This process of learning operates for other information in their life. So there seems to be no reason why it would not also work for religious instruction within the family or in the community.
- At some point children become aware that not all families share the same beliefs and they may start to ask searching questions.
- In neighbourhoods with ethnic diversity, children younger than school age will be aware of different faiths from their contact with other children and their families.
- Young children also notice and may comment upon differences in dress that reflect different faiths as they show in cultural traditions.
- In some neighbourhoods, children of four and five years are aware of conflict between people of different faiths or different versions of the same faith, for instance between Protestant and Catholic Christians in Northern Ireland.
- Five and six year olds increasingly try to make sense of any ideas that are expressed to them and some children are more articulate in their questions or more inquiring than their peers.
- As the years of childhood pass into teenage, some young people will actively commit to their family faith and others will drift away.

To think about

Individual practitioners and teams need to be aware that religious faith is not the same as cultural background. There is great variety:

- People who follow each of the main world faiths come from very different ethnic and cultural backgrounds.
- Every faith has extended beyond its point of origin and been taken into different cultures, often with changes and the development of different sects to the faith.
- There are often several faiths represented in any country or cultural group, some may be in the minority for that country.
- Some adults may no longer actively practise a faith but feel more comfortable following at least some of the traditions in which they were raised, such as those relating to food.
- A faith can also form the backdrop to national and cultural identity, such that people who have never followed the faith still want to opt in to some of the rituals. In the UK this pattern is shown by adults who are not practising Christians, but who wish to have a church wedding or to have their baby christened, because it seems like the right thing to do.

Good practice in the early years

It is good practice that you show respect for the faith or more general philosophical beliefs of a family since these are part of a child's identity. You may not share those beliefs but you can acknowledge that they are important to children and their parents. You show respect in different parts of your practice:

- Good communication with parents about food or care needs (see pages 95 and 60) helps children to settle into your setting and shows appropriate respect for family ways.
- You can introduce children with care to a range of religious beliefs and celebrations – see the tips for practice box.
- Children will often want to share significant events with you or the whole group at circle time. You can enable children to describe what happened at the christening of their new baby or their elder brother's bar mitzvah. The other children will often be interested at these glimpses into the family life of other people.
- Good practice will also be to explore at some other time the different ways (not just christening) that families welcome new babies or celebrate important family events like the move from childhood into young adulthood.
- Children will draw on their family beliefs to explain serious life changes such as death or serious illness. You need to respect what children repeat of their family faith, such as 'Grandad has gone to heaven' or that he will return in the cycle of life because this family believes in reincarnation.

Tips for practice

Celebrations and festivals can be a positive contribution to anti-discriminatory practice and open children's horizons beyond their own back yard. You and your colleagues need to:

- Set a good example by showing respect and making an effort to understand what will sometimes be unfamiliar customs to you.
- Make some choices because you cannot celebrate all possible festivals. A practical plan is to celebrate the key festivals of families whose children attend your setting. Then add one or two festivals to your long term plan that will be new for everyone.
- Involve parents and the local community in any celebration and be ready to learn from them.
- Respect parents' wishes if they feel strongly that they do not wish their child to be involved in a given celebration. Partnership with parents will need to be balanced against the values of your setting. Much will depend on the parents' reasons for their reluctance.
- Take a distinctive approach to each festival. Definitely do not explain one celebration in terms of the beliefs or events of a religion more familiar to you.
- Show equal respect to all celebrations, both in the amount of time you devote and how you talk about artefacts or stories.
- Challenge any suggestion that 'other people have colourful festivals and myths, that are just a bit of fun' but 'we have serious religious events underpinned by stories that are true'.
- Be careful about activities that you undertake with the children. They should not feel compelled to make a card or other artefact. Equally important, celebrations should be respected in their own right and not just used as source material to support early learning goals or targets.

Anti-discriminatory practice

Children's personal identity can be strongly supported by a sense of belonging to a faith community; it is part of family life and group identity. However, some sensitive issues can arise from the personal and family commitment.

- Early years practitioners, and even more so practitioners in school and out of school care need to be aware that for some children, a sense of clear identity (religious or otherwise) goes hand in hand with rejection of children who are different. This pattern can be shown in any of the major world faiths.
- Some children may bring their family's convictions into your setting that their faith, or the sect to which they belong, is the one and only correct faith. Children, especially in the later years of primary school, may have serious arguments on such issues or inform their distressed peers that they are headed for some version of eternal damnation.
- On the other hand, some children experience verbal or physical harassment because of the outward signs of their religious faith, through clothes or hair (see page 61). Children may be subject to name calling or bullying in ways that are close to racial harassment.

Good early years and school practice has to be even-handed and clear about the ground rules of the group on anti-discriminatory practice. You need to address negative and rejecting attitudes, regardless of their source and direction. It is no more acceptable for children from Muslim or Hindu families to be verbally rejecting of other children on the basis of faith than you should tolerate children in Christian or nominally Christian families showing such an attitude towards any other faith.

Firm remarks from any children about the plight of 'non-believers' need to be courteously fielded with comments that acknowledge, 'Yes I know that you and your family believe that ... but not everyone agrees. I would like you to stop saying (particular remark) to Wendy, because you are making her very upset.'

Learning within spiritual development

There has been very little research on children's spiritual development and this gap is probably related to the lack of agreement between adults on what the word 'spiritual' means. The same confusion can make early years practitioners uneasy about how best to support children in this area of development. Extreme positions do not help to develop practice:

- People who have a personal religious faith may insist that 'spiritual' can have no meaning without a religious context. For people with faith, the two may well be intertwined, but an experience of spirituality can exist without religion.
- The opposite position is no more acceptable for early years or school practice. Some people claim that spirituality does not, and should not, have anything to do with religious belief. Yet for some children and families the two are definitely linked. So this extreme position is equally disrespectful.

My working definition of spirituality is that it is an awareness of and connectedness to that part of human experience that does not have to answer to rational

Figure 8.7
Young children can be intrigued and enchanted by many events

analysis. So, for children you can promote the spiritual side of their development by supporting their inner life of feelings and responsiveness to events. Children are ready to be thrilled or intrigued by sights, especially in the natural world. They can feel enchanted by the sight of a rainbow, appreciate a peaceful time sitting in the local park, feeling the breeze and watching the baby ducks. They can delight in seeing the moon and stars on a dark winter afternoon.

Support children in a sense of wonder

You can support children's spiritual development by the same personal attention that is good practice overall:

- Relax with the children and enjoy experiences with them. If they are keen to watch a spider making a web, what is the advantage in telling them to come and do something else?
- Do not feel you always have to ask questions or make comments. Supportive adults need to join in the delight and not rush to give scientific explanations. Children welcome knowledge but not if adult information undermines the 'what' of an interesting event to press on to the 'why' or 'how'.
- Watch with a child and share their absorption. Supportive adults are observant and respect when a child is peacefully absorbed, perhaps watching the ripples on a pond or how the sycamore leaves flutter down like helicopters.
- Avoid any cynical adult reaction along the lines of 'what's so interesting about that?' Children can rekindle in adults the kind of joy in discovery that you perhaps left behind in childhood.
- Sometimes you let children know by reminiscence that you enjoyed that experience and have not forgotten 'when we saw the baby chicks'.

Activity (observation)

- Watch out for and note those experiences that capture children's attention, the quality of 'Look, look!' or the 'Ooh' reaction.
- Apparently, in the Reggio Emilia nurseries in Italy, the practitioners draw in children with the question, 'Have you wondered about anything today?'
- What experiences can you gather over a few weeks? Share them with colleagues.

Key skills link: C3.1a

Further resources

Boxall, Marjorie (2002) *Nurture in School: Principles and Practice* Paul Chapman Publishing

Brown, Babette (2001) *Combating Discrimination: Persona Dolls in action* Trentham Books.

Gottman, John (1997) *The Heart of Parenting: How to raise an emotionally intelligent child* Bloomsbury.

Lindon, Jennie (1999) *Understanding World Religions in Early Years Practice* Hodder and Stoughton.

Mosley, Jenny and Sonnet, Helen (2001) *Here we go Round: Quality circle time for 3–5 year olds* Positive Press.

Progress check

1 In what ways are adult feelings important if you are to support children in their emotional literacy?

2 Describe two possible family crises and how the experience might affect a child of three or four years of age.

3 Describe briefly the three main strands to children's moral development.

4 Suggest two ways you could show respect for the religious faith of a child's family.

5 Give three ways you could support children's sense of wonder and enchantment.

9

Physical development and skills

After reading this chapter you should be able to:

- understand the importance of physical skills and activity for children's learning and well being
- recognise and support the ways in which children develop physically during the early years.

Introduction

Within this chapter you will learn about the ways in which babies and young children progress in their physical skills. Babies and toddlers are keen to use all the abilities they currently possess and are enthusiastic about getting on the move. You need to keep young children safe but within an environment where they can practise and use their physical abilities. Physical activity is important for children's health and physical strength but it is also the vehicle for much of their learning. Chapter 10 describes activities to support children's physical development.

Physical development and well being

It is useful for you to contrast a mental picture of a newborn baby with a mobile and active seven or eight year old. There have been many changes over these years.

Links to early years qualifications

This chapter especially supports the following units:

Diploma in Child Care and Education: 2, 3, 10

National Vocational Qualification in Early Years Care and Education

Level 2: C1

Level 3: C3, C14

BTEC National Early Years Diploma: 8, 24

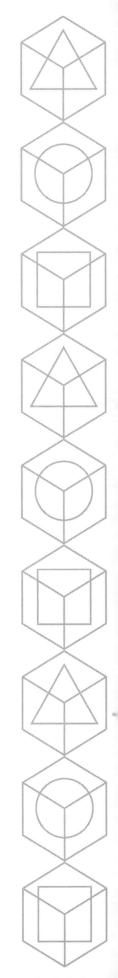

Newborn babies are almost helpless. They are physically unable to take care of themselves and they need their early communication skills of crying to call for help. They have reflex actions with which they are born (see page 153), but they are scarcely able to make deliberate physical actions. If all has gone well, a child of seven or eight is physically coordinated, able to chose from a wide range of large physical movements and fine skills to achieve different purposes. It is an impressive achievement and children's physical development underpins many of the other learning tasks that they face.

The importance of physical activity

Children's physical development is equally as important as other areas of their learning. This point needs to be stressed since some approaches to a child's day within early years settings, and some interpretations of the early years curriculum, have downgraded physical development in favour of intellectual. The strange idea has also developed that children can only be learning if they are sitting still and probably indoors (see page 279). A more rounded understanding of child development challenges this view and there are serious concerns about the consequences for children if their physical skills are undervalued and blocked.

Physical health

Children need to be active because enjoyable physical activity, through play and happy involvement in daily routines, supports children's overall health.

- Physically active children burn up their calories in an enjoyable way, work up a genuine appetite and enjoy their food. A positive circle is established.
- Exercise makes the heart and lungs work efficiently. This workout is important for all children, but can be crucial for the growing number of children who have respiratory difficulties like asthma.

Figure 9.1
Children can really enjoy physical activity

- Physical activity helps children to build up strong muscles and keeps their body and joints supple. Strength in the trunk of our body and flexibility of muscles seem to be important to reduce the risk of injury and back pain in later life. Physical exercise also builds bone density.
- Children who have enough physical exercise tend to enjoy better overall health. Of course they catch some illnesses, but active children tend to catch fewer infections and be more robust.
- Getting enjoyably tired promotes rest in much the same way as getting enjoyably hungry promotes eating. Physical exercise helps children to rest and sleep more soundly.

The risks of inactivity

There are concerns in our society now about under-active toddlers and children who risk becoming too passive because adults have limited their physical play, often because of over-concern about safety.

- Of course some young children simply find their way around restrictive adults and create physical activity from whatever they can. Very active children may then be inappropriately seen as having a behaviour problem (see page 285).
- Children who cooperate with the restrictions may lose the motivation to play lively physical games. They will probably turn to more passive activities like television and computer games, with the limits to learning that over-use of these resources can bring. There is a place for television and computers (see page 383) but not to dominate the time of young children.
- Lack of physical activity can also be linked with an unbalanced diet through snacking and the risk of obesity (see page 89).
- In extreme cases, the lack of activity combined with an unbalanced diet can make children and teenagers vulnerable to health problems usually associated with adults from middle age onwards. There are some very daunting signs from the United States, and to a much lesser extent in the UK, about the early occurrence of type 2 diabetes (see page 90), that usually affects adults from their 40s and 50s, and of osteoporosis (bones that fracture easily).

Tips for practice

- Children who are allowed to be physically active through play will be healthy.
- Children do not usually have to be persuaded to be active nor threatened with future back pain or diabetes! The range of activities described in this chapter are welcomed by children.
- A flexible choice of physically energetic games is far better than a schedule of highly organised and directed activities.
- Some parents and carers have responded to the need for physical activity by imposing a weekly round of gym clubs and highly structured sessions.
- Many children enjoy some time in a dance club or activities like Tumble Tots®. But they do not benefit from inflexible routines, nor from being over-supervised and over-organised.

Activity

When children's physical play is curtailed over a long period, they may become lethargic and no longer bother to be physically energetic. Through no fault of their own the children are well on the way to becoming 'couch potatoes'. As Marjorie Ouvry says when she promotes outdoor play, you want instead to encourage children to be 'runner beans'.

Plan and make a display to show the importance of letting children be active. Use photographs and children's own drawings to illustrate what they enjoy doing and how the activities can promote development as 'runner beans'.

Key skills link: C3.1b

Mental and emotional fitness

Observation of children has also highlighted that physical activity and movement is linked with mental alertness and emotional well being.

Increased physical activity actually increases the blood flow to the brain. This change, coupled with learning tasks (the sort of activities described in this chapter and others), promotes neural connections in the brain. Making children sit still and be quiet causes them to be more sluggish and less able to learn.

The idea that children must sit still to concentrate is actually counter-productive for younger children; it makes it harder and not easier for them to learn. Some primary schools have found that giving children a short burst of movement makes concentration easier rather than disrupting it. Staff have experimented with breaks for everyone, such as a brisk walk around the playground. The Active Primary Schools Project in Scotland stresses the importance of daily physical activity for children.

In summer 2001 a project called 'Fit to Succeed' was completed in Exeter, England. Staff encouraged children in seven middle schools (that is children of about eight to eleven years) to take more physical exercise. Scores in the SATs tests were highest in the children who reported exercising at least three times a week. Physical activity does not boost test scores as such. More active children are more mentally alert, because activity primes the metabolism and then children can do their best, achieving their potential.

There are also some indications that activity helps to reduce depression and anxiety in children. Of course physical activity does not remove the cause of a child's distress or worry; you need to offer support (see page 219). But enjoyable games and physical play with friends give children an alternative focus.

To think about

- Adults find it hard to concentrate after long periods of sitting and restrictions on movement. You will have direct experience of how your own mind can go woolly if you have been physically inactive for too long. Children have an even greater need to move.
- Discuss with colleagues whether you do risk believing that children only learn when they are still, or sitting down. What has led you to this conviction?

Key skills link: C3.1a

Learning through hands-on experience

Technological advances have made it possible to show that babies' brains are operating before birth. The neurons (brain cells) seem to be firing most in the part of the brain that will deal with vision and sound. This discovery explains how newborns sometimes seem to recognise sounds they have heard before birth, such as a parent's voice or the song they were sung. At birth, a baby's brain is poised to go; it is neither fully set up nor an empty gap. Most of the neurons are in place – a staggering 100 billion neurons – but a newborn's brain has yet to make many connections.

Babies' brains develop because connections are made between the neurons. All these new brain connections are literally made through babies' experiences from day one of their life. When you understand how babies' brains develop, then it is possible to see the importance of all your ordinary, everyday actions with babies (see also Chapter 5).

- All the babies' efforts with movement, making physical contact and early communication develop the possible neural networks within their immature brains.
- All their activities, from a broad, happy smile for a familiar face to an enthusiastic crawl across the room, support the development of the synapses in their young brain that shape how babies and toddlers continue to relate to the world.

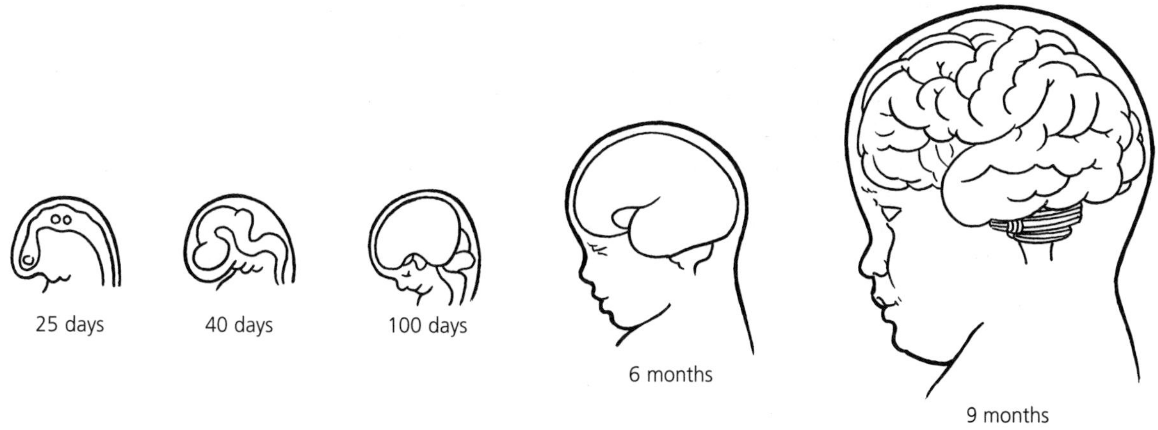

Figure 9.2 The development of the brain before birth. The majority of the development happens in the last trimester

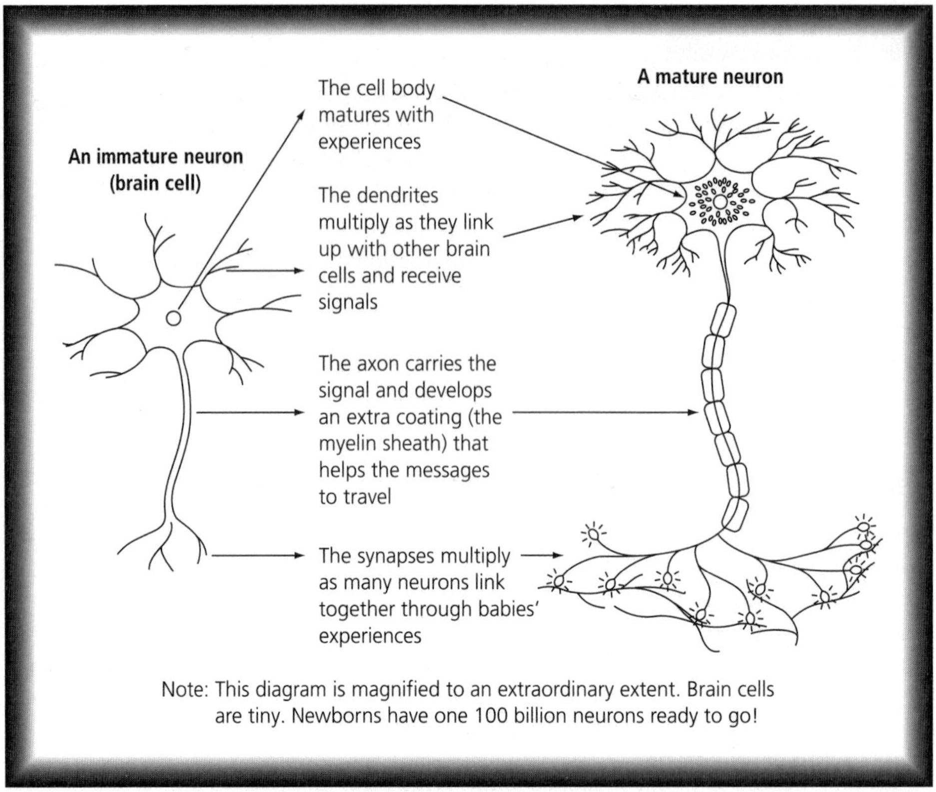
A mature neuron
The cell body matures with experiences
An immature neuron (brain cell)
The dendrites multiply as they link up with other brain cells and receive signals
The axon carries the signal and develops an extra coating (the myelin sheath) that helps the messages to travel
The synapses multiply as many neurons link together through babies' experiences
Note: This diagram is magnified to an extraordinary extent. Brain cells are tiny. Newborns have one 100 billion neurons ready to go!

Figure 9.3
Experience and activity builds babies' brains

- Continued experience in any area of development firms up those connections until they are permanent and creates the complex neural pathways on which babies then build more learning.
- Those connections that are not strengthened by repeated experience are less strong and may fade away.
- Babies need a wealth of opportunities to repeat experiences, and in many subtle different ways and they need to practise, to do it again and again.

The research into brain development in very early childhood has confirmed good practice in early years because babies and toddlers learn through physical doing. The enjoyable practice of crawling, grasping and handling objects builds vital neural connections in young brains. Babies and toddlers have a very strong drive to use their bodies and to apply their current muscle control to the utmost. They only require that caring adults keep them safe and let them explore.

Very young children want to make things happen and to work out how their world works. They use all their senses and apply their current physical skills to objects of interest. Their learning grows from the simple physical explorations of being able to get hold of objects and to experiment with actions. This learning is physically laid down through the neural connections in the brain.

Physical development supports intellectual

Sally Goddard Blythe has highlighted the importance of large physical movements for later development in areas such as reading and writing. She points out that these areas of child development are closely linked and adults can block children's learning by rushing them. Her main points are that:

- Attention, balance and coordination are the crucial ABC of later learning.
- The actions of crawling help babies and toddlers to synchronise their sense of balance. The enjoyable practise of this movement brings together the physical sensations and what toddlers can see.
- Crawling and then walking enable a child to recognise what it feels like to be in balance or about to lose their balance.
- Young walkers have to keep moving in order to keep their balance. Watch them and you will see that toddlers wobble when they come to a stop and plump down on their bottoms. It is only after plenty of practice that confident walkers are able to stand still.
- The necessary coordination of moving hands and vision in crawling is undertaken at the same distance that children will use some years later in reading and writing.
- Crawling and crawling games are enjoyable now. But they also form a strong basis for future learning, because young children strengthen their limbs and practise coordination of movement and vision.
- Children need to move in order to understand the messages from their body. This physical feedback about touch, grasp and balance is called **proprioception** and can only be gained by practice.

Key term

Proprioception the ability to recognise and use the physical sensations from the body that give feedback on balance and the position of our limbs

Activity (observation)

Watch a child who is in the early stages of walking and see how they begin to understand balance.

- Watch their face – can you tell when toddlers feel secure and when they sense they are about to topple?
- How do they stand and move to maintain balance?
- What changes can you observe in how toddlers get up to standing, move around and lower themselves to sitting as they become physically more confident?

Write up your notes and perhaps share observations with colleagues.
Another possibility is to take photos, with the permission of the child's parents and add a visual dimension to your notes.

Key skills link: C2/3.1 b C2/3.3

Physical development from baby to child

Babies have a great deal of growing to accomplish. Part of this development is putting on weight (see page 183) but they also change steadily in bodily proportions and internal development.

- Babies still have bones to develop. For instance, at his first birthday a baby has only three bones in each wrist and hand but by adulthood he will have twenty-eight.
- Babies' bones and the ligaments around the joints are relatively soft and that is why babies can seem to be so bendy. Bones harden and grow in length over the months.

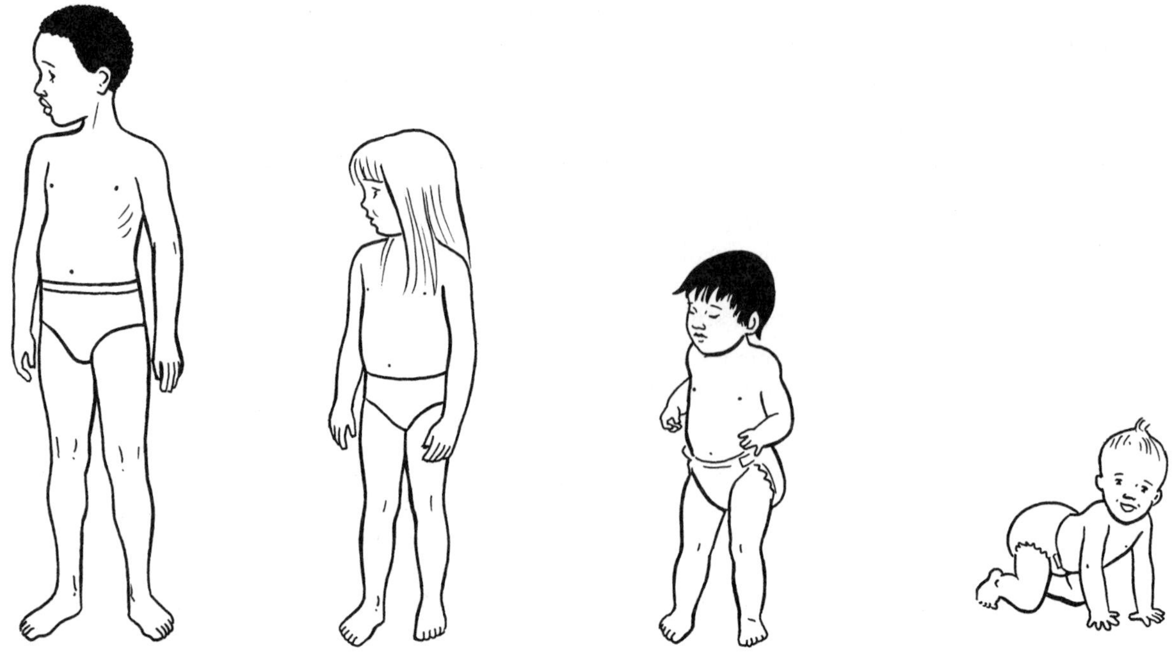

Figure 9.4 The changing shape of childhood

- Babies are born with several head bones joined only by soft cartilage or openings called fontanelles. These allow the baby's head to be moulded and squeezed during birth. The top of a baby's head feels soft and the bones do not completely harden and close over until abut two years of age.
- Babies are born with all the muscles they need. But their muscle tone is poor until their physical movements gain them control over their head, shoulders and limbs. They seem a bit floppy and uncoordinated at the outset.

Early childhood is a period of immense change in all areas of development and the physical changes are very visible. Babies and toddlers change in overall body shape and the relative proportions of their body (see Figure 9.4) and their increased mobility requires a lot of adjustment from carers. The next time for an equivalent burst of physical growth and visible change is the onset of puberty. This development will start for the early developers at about 10 or 11 years, but will not happen for most children until they reach adolescence.

The physical changes need to be fuelled by healthy diet (see Chapter 3) and exercise in all the ways that babies, toddlers and young children are able to use their physical skills.

The development of physical skills

Children's physical development progresses in several broad areas:

- The development of bodily control and physical awareness for babies and young children.
- Large movements that enable children to gain mobility. The large scale physical movements like crawling or walking are sometimes called gross motor development (motor simply means movement).

- Use of movement helps children to gain confident balance and to be sensitive to the messages that their body sends through movement.
- Fine physical skills require delicate, deliberate movements and the coordination of senses like sight and hearing with the movement of limbs like hands.

In this section you will find some details of how children's abilities develop over time. As with any other developmental information in this book, you need to take any ages as a guide only. Children vary considerably in when they manage certain skills and the ease with which they put them into daily practice.

A perspective on developmental milestones

Major achievements for children, like learning to walk or the first recognisable words, are called **developmental milestones**. Developmental records in a nursery or centre will track these events. But it is important not to overlook what happens in between the visible markers, nor to rush children. There is no advantage, and many disadvantages in trying to make very young children achieve a physical skill like walking before they are ready. Of course, you need to keep an eye on a child who is much later than average, in case there is any physical problem. Otherwise, children who are given space and encouragement to move will gain new skills when they are ready.

Key term

Developmental milestones observable achievements for children in the different areas of their development throughout childhood

Parents and other carers are of course excited when a child achieves a significant new skill. But it is important to share the likely perspective of children themselves. Toddlers are probably excited about their first steps, partly because the adults and perhaps older siblings clap and look pleased. But from the toddler's point of view, many of the interim stages towards learning to walk are just as interesting.

- Before children can walk they practise cruising along using hand holds on the furniture and practise negotiating narrow gaps that they can lean across.
- A firm hold on a table may enable an older baby to dance in time to some music and this experience may be just as thrilling as the first steps to him or her.

Figure 9.5

Toddlers are keen to apply their skills

Babies and toddlers are also very interested in applying skills. So, again, the adult developmental milestone is not the end but a beginning.

- A baby who has learned to crawl, or to walk at the same time as holding on to something (impossible to start with), is now keen to try out variations and to apply the skill.
- The crawling baby develops a surprising turn of speed as she triumphantly gets herself to an interesting corner of the room.
- Climbing skills are applied enthusiastically to reach items of interest.
- If you watch babies, toddlers and young children, you will also notice that they use their physical skills simply for the pleasure of the experience. A keen crawler does not always have to have some destination; the crawling is enjoyable in itself.

Activity (observation)

The interest for children and adults is in what can be done with physical skills and the pattern for any young child will reflect their interests and the opportunities in the setting where they spend most of their time. Even apparently simple physical actions from toddlers will also show you how they are thinking.

For example, when my own daughter was 16 months old, she used her skills of hand–eye coordination in many different ways. She used to:

- bring her outdoor shoes to show me in order to indicate that she wanted to go out for a local walk (she followed this with bringing my outdoor shoes as well, if I was slow to respond!)
- hand us items of clothing to put in the washing machine
- wield the dustpan and brush to help sweep crumbs up off the floor
- play with stacking toys, construction bricks and simple jigsaws
- select a book, pull it out of the shelf and carry it to us to be read.

Observe a toddler of 15–16 months and note the physical skills and movements that she or he can manage. But also describe how the toddler applies the skills, what does she or he do and with what purpose? Write up your findings and share with the child's parent(s).

Present or discuss your findings with colleagues and compare how similar fine skills are applied and practised differently by individual toddlers.

Key skills links: C2/3.3 C2/3.1b C2/3.1a

Babies up to one year old

Human babies are very vulnerable and they need the attentive care that is described in Chapter 6. They are dependent on adults like yourself to keep them safe and healthy but do not let this persuade you that the babies are somehow not doing very much at all.

All five senses

The senses of newborns have already been working in the womb and they are ready to take in the sights outside.

Newborn babies cannot move independently or reach out accurately, but they have *sight* unless a disability affects this sense. They direct their eyes towards anything that interests them, such as faces. It has been calculated that by four months of age, babies have already made over three million eye movements. They are taking in considerable amounts of information.

The newborn baby can see well at a distance of about 25 centimetres and this is the distance between babies' eyes and the parent's face when they are held to be fed. Young babies have difficulty coordinating their eye movements but the intention is definitely there.

Babies have the sense of *hearing*. Inside the womb babies have come to know the rhythmic pulse of their mother's heart beat and this familiarity is why they can sometimes be calmed by being held close to the chest of mother, father or a familiar carer. They can be startled by sudden noises.

New babies have already learned to recognise their mother's voice and newborns are responsive to the rhythm of speech from other people whom they now get to know. They soon begin to copy the movements of a speaker's mouth, open their own and put their tongue forward in imitation.

Even babies of a few days old can distinguish between some *tastes* and prefer sweet to bitter flavours. Newborn babies have a good sense of *smell* and learn to recognise the smell of their mother's body and her milk. Babies feel and are responsive to a gentle *touch* and stroking.

Activity (observation)

Newborn and very young babies are particularly attracted to faces and face shapes and they can follow a shape that interests them. Research has also shown that very young babies prefer patterns to solid colours and stripes or angles to circular designs.

- Experiment with making some basic shapes and patterns in plain colours and some face shapes (very simple).
- Show them to a young baby and note how long she or he stares at each one.
- Can you see any preferences in how the baby stares and for how long?
- Write up your observations and discuss with colleagues.

Key skills links: C2/3.1b C2/3.3

Physical control

The development of physical control for babies is a major issue. Babies and young children are designed to be mobile. Watch even young babies and you will see how they work hard to use all the physical skills currently within their power. They repeat and practise what they can do, even when, to an outsider, they look hopelessly unco-ordinated. Babies' ability to control their own body develops in two directions:

- from the top of the head downwards
- from the midline of the body outwards.

Babies are unable to control their head and neck and they seem almost surprised when their own hands and fingers come into view. They are learning steadily to control their body and realise that it all belongs to them.

Activity (observation)

Spend some time with two or three young babies, no more than about three months of age. Watch them when they are awake and content. Note what they do and any individual differences that you can identify even at this young age:

- Do they move their arms and legs with equal vigour?
- How do they like to be held? Have the babies already shown preferences for how they are cuddled or carried around?
- What seems to hold their visual attention? Do the babies look at different objects or items of interest?
- Write up and present or discuss with colleagues.

Key skills links: C2/3.1b C2/3.3

Up to three months

- The movements of very young babies are limited to reflex movements such as sucking (see page 153) and their physical movements tend to look jerky.
- They have a surprisingly strong grip if you place your finger in their palm.
- Held securely, for instance in their baby bath, even young babies have a vigorous kick.
- Because babies gain control over their own bodies from the head downwards, initially they need careful support along the length of their body.
- Within the first couple of months, you will see babies' efforts to hold up their relatively heavy head and increasingly vigorous arm and leg movements.
- Physical movements are accompanied by early visual skills. Babies of even a few weeks old spread and flex their fingers and sometimes stare at them in a rather perplexed manner. They gaze intently at an adult's face when they are cuddled or fed.

Three to twelve months – large movements

- By three or four months, babies have become more able to support their upper body. So they can hold up their head and their back is straighter when they sit on your lap.
- They are able to turn their head to track interesting sights or the source of sounds.
- By about six months, babies enjoy more control of their lower body to their waist and their explorations look more purposeful.
- Between six to nine months, babies will learn to sit. They need support to start with because of their tendency to lean off balance. Once babies can sit securely, their hands are free to explore playthings.
- Babies no longer stay still. If they are put on a rug on the floor, they are likely to be able to roll from back to front and soon to make a little distance.
- Once they can manage the position of all fours, they start to try to crawl.

This movement is trickier than it looks, since the baby's top half of the body is still stronger than the lower half. So vigorous rocking and attempts to move often result initially in going backwards rather than forwards.

- Most babies go through a stage of crawling in the second half of their first year. However, some babies never crawl. Either they go straight to walking or they favour mobility by bottom-shuffling.
- By their first birthday, babies are likely to be mobile through crawling and moving themselves along by hand holds on furniture. Some may already be walking, although this is early.

Three to twelve months – fine movements

Young children want to make things happen and to work out how their world works. They use all their senses and apply their current physical skills to objects of interest. Their learning grows from the simple physical explorations of being able to get hold of objects and to experiment with actions.

- Babies have to learn to coordinate the evidence of their senses with physical control of their hands and fingers. They watch with a steady stare but it is not until about five to six months that they are able to reach and grasp an object with confidence.
- To start with, babies get hold of objects in a whole hand scoop and then close their hands around the item. They also learn how to hold on before they learn the coordination needed to unclasp and let go.
- Once babies have got hold of something, like a rattle, they may shake it but without being able to control the action. It is fairly usual that babies manage to hit themselves with an energetically waved rattle.
- Once babies have managed to coordinate a deliberate grasp, then they bring objects to their mouth to suck and chew if they have any teeth. Babies use their mouths to explore because the nerve endings are most sensitive here. You should allow them to mouth objects, otherwise they cannot learn. Just ensure that anything they can get to their mouth is safe and clean.
- Mobile babies and toddlers learn through a fair amount of repetition and by using similar actions on different materials. In the first year of life, babies learn ways to explore objects as their physical skills extend.
- Holding and mouthing are the first methods of exploration. But once babies manage a secure hold, they stare and inspect something of interest.
- With better physical coordination and vision, they explore by hitting or tapping, shaking, poking, tearing, rubbing, dropping and throwing.
- All babies do not use every method and some are more enthusiastic for one method than others. Some actions like dropping or throwing develop into a shared game with an adult or older child.

Activity (observation)

Watch three or four babies in the second half of their first year and observe how they explore their world.

- If they are given an object of interest or reach out for it, what physical skills of exploration do they apply?
- Do they hold and turn the object? Do they stare and for how long?

- Have these babies become interested in tapping, hitting or shaking an object?
- Do they drop it and do they then look expectant as if you should pick it up?
- Do they now use a combination of ways of exploring?
- Write up and present or discuss with colleagues.

Key skills links: C2/3.1b C2/3.3

Activity (observation)

Watch at least two babies who are coming up to their first birthday.

- How does each baby move around: crawling, bottom shuffling, walking already?
- How quickly can they move across a room? (Obviously you must ensure that they are safe as well as timing them!)

Babies in a day nursery are in an environment that has already been modified for their age group. But babies at home are in an environment that also has to be suitable for older children and adults.

- Talk with the baby's parents to understand the modifications that they have made to keep the baby safe.
- Write up and present or discuss with colleagues.

Key skills links: C2/3.1b C2/3.3

Toddlers from one to two years

Large movements

- In their second year, toddlers become confidently mobile as they coordinate their limbs to manage the balance of getting up to their feet, walking, stopping and moving into other positions like sitting.
- Watch toddlers and you will realise that physical tasks that have become automatic to us require some serious concentration as a toddler.
- Walking toddlers still enjoy crawling for sheer fun and for a while they may alternate between a rather wobbly walk and a speedy crawling.
- Confident walkers move to a more child-like stance rather than the wide legged walk of a toddler who still does not feel safely in balance.
- By about 18 months many toddlers are able to add other actions to their walking. So they can carry a teddy or a book at the same time, using their skills of mobility to head across a room, fetch something and come back again.
- By the end of the second year confident walkers can show a striking turn of speed as they move into being able to run.

- Toddlers learn how to move simple push bikes or handle push-along trolleys. They often enjoy wheeled toys that can be pulled along.
- Toddlers are able to use their skills of large movement to further their explorations and play actively with other children and adults.
- Toddlers become able to climb up stairs, at first by a version of crawling and then by climbing one step at a time. Coming downstairs is more tricky and is usually managed first of all by turning around to face the stairs and doing a semi-crawl or slide.
- Even in a safe setting toddlers have accidents: colliding with people or furniture and falling.

Fine movements

- In the second year of life, toddlers have far more control of their fingers and thumb so it becomes possible to look at and move in on objects. They practise picking up, exploring and poking large and small objects.
- They explore possibilities by putting small objects into larger containers – often many times. They enjoy this game with ordinary household materials like saucepans, stacking toys and containers in water and sand play.
- They are able to play with materials like wooden bricks or Duplo™ that can be manipulated by toddler fingers. They start to be able to put one brick onto another to make a small tower and then the fun is usually to knock it down.
- Jigsaws with big pieces and holding pegs are a possibility but some toddlers are more interested in jigsaws than others.
- Toddlers who have been introduced to the enjoyment of books are now able to look at a book sometimes on their own. Thick board pages enable them to turn one page at a time, although soon their fingers will be able to manage paper pages.
- Their ability to coordinate looking and movement means that simple arts and crafts activities become possible and enjoyable. Toddlers can wield thick crayons, chalks and paint brushes.
- They can use their vision and improving physical skills to play with materials like play dough or containers in water play.

Toddlers' fine physical skills are directly applied in ways that support other aspects of their development:

- Within this year toddlers develop a range of gestures that they use to support their growing communication skills. Spoken expression develops over this time (see page 296) but so does a deliberate use of non-verbal gestures.
- Toddlers often learn to hold up their hands towards an adult to show that they want to be picked up.
- They learn the immensely useful gesture of pointing. This action can be used with two broad purposes. Toddlers can indicate that they would like something, for instance another piece of apple. They can use pointing to bring an adult into their area of interest to communicate 'Look at that!'
- Fine physical skills are also important for developing self reliance. Toddlers improve, with adult patience and encouragement, in some parts of dressing and feeding themselves. Toddlers also like to apply their skills to helping out in daily routines (see page 52).

Tips for practice

- Once they are independently mobile, older babies and toddlers engage in a great deal of physical play and sheer joy in using their skills. They need space to move about and hone their skills: to crawl, walk, balance, climb, bounce, jump and chase.
- The sheer practice of physical skills firms up those vital connections in the brain. Children need to be able to move in comfort, with pleasure and to be safe enough.
- They do not need to be hurried or bullied into sitting 'nicely', being 'quiet' and stopping 'fidgeting'.
- Babies and toddlers need plenty of opportunities to use their physical abilities and to apply their ideas.
- The clear preference of very young children for 'do it again!' is ideal for their learning.

Young children from two to five years

Large movements

Children within this age span can learn, practise and become very confident in a range of physical skills. But you will see a great deal of variety between individual children, because they vary in temperament and experience, including whether they have been given encouragement to be energetically physical.

- Young children become adept at running and three and four year olds are usually able to adjust their speed and direction most of the time.
- Three year olds are usually able to stand on tip toe (harder than it looks!) and maybe walk a few teetering steps before dropping back to full feet

Figure 9.6
Children relish outdoors activities and exploration

walking. Once they have managed this skill, children sometimes enjoy tip toeing around in play or as a game for moving very quietly.

- With practice children become able to jump up in the air, although you will watch two year olds struggling initially with how to launch off with both feet.
- They like to jump from low steps or walls, first of all with an adult hand or welcoming arms and soon without this safety net. It is useful if you show young children how to bend their knees when they land, otherwise they tend to jump stiff legged.
- Children apply their skills of running, jumping and climbing in play with friends, sometimes within pretend play games and often for the sheer satisfaction and enjoyment of vigorous movement. Jumping skills are applied with equipment like a simple trampoline.
- Three and four year olds can become confident with riding three wheeled bikes. It takes some practice to manage to work the pedals in a steady forward action and also to work out how to steer. Young bike riders tend to achieve forward motion before they are confident in stopping or steering round people or obstacle courses.
- Toddlers' enjoyment in push-along wheeled toys has often developed into confident use of wheeled trolleys or wheelbarrows for simple trundling or moving objects from place to place.
- Children use their physical skills and props to develop pretend play games that can be fairly contained or require open space for movement. Four and five year olds will often return to a game with friends and simply pick up from where the play theme was left yesterday.
- Some toddlers really like to dance but young children's ability to direct their movements enables them to explore different forms of dance, music and movement.

The large physical movements that you can observe over this age span require other related skills and bodily awareness. It can be easy for adults to underestimate the complexity of some physical sequences and how much children need to experience enjoyable practice.

Activity (observation)

- Observe a child of three or four years and note down their physical skills, watching out for some of the skills described in each section.
- Then draw a diagram for three of the observed skills to show how this physical ability links with other aspects of the child's development (look at page 12 for a reminder of different areas).
- For instance, does this skill support the child's growing self reliance, does the expression on the child's face suggest to you that her physical competence helps her to feel positive about herself (emotional development) or to make contact with other children (social and communicative)?
- Share your findings with your colleagues and explain the connections you have shown in the diagram.

Key skills links: C2/3.1b C2/3.3

Fine movements

- Children are able to coordinate the handling, moving and lining up of large scale play equipment like ladders in a nursery, often by working together with another child or adult. Although these may look like large physical movements, they actually require delicate adjustments and bodily awareness.
- Children enjoy playing games with equipment like bats or balls. Such play combines careful looking, judgement of timing and aiming, as well as the physical actions of hitting, throwing or kicking. Learning to hit or kick a ball takes coordination and plenty of enjoyable practice.
- With experience of the appropriate materials, two to five year olds learn to work with a wide range of constructional play materials and their skills to build are supported by the mental skills of planning, recall and cooperative working with their friends.
- Children learn to use tools like scissors, craft and woodwork equipment. Physical skills combine with communication skills of understanding so that children can learn good and safe techniques with tools.
- In a range of arts and crafts children can apply fine movements to all different kinds of painting, drawing, collage and printing. As they practise and explore, children's drawings develop in detail and become more recognisable as people, buildings or animals.
- Their improved coordination shows in children's self care. Within this age span children learn to take on the remaining skills for dressing and undressing, going to the toilet, cutting up their food or pouring drinks. They are also able and willing to help out in daily routines.
- At some point over this time period, it will most likely be clear whether children are right or left handed. Some remain somewhat flexible or have a different hand preference for different activities. Adults must respect the child's preference; there is no good reason and plenty of disadvantages if adults try to enforce a choice.

Children from five to eight years

Large movements

- So long as they are not confined for space, older children use their physical skills in spontaneous games that they create. The pretend play of younger children can be very complex with roles and scripts that are negotiated by the children.
- The physical skills of this age group become more varied. They use their earlier skills of running, chasing and climbing. But they may now be able to manage the more complex movements involved in skipping, hopping games or high speed catch.
- In open spaces or on the pavements some children show how skilled they have become with bikes or roller skates. Five or six years olds are more likely to be able to learn to ride a two wheeled bike (without stabilisers) but it takes practice and a deep breath to gain the balance needed. Often the most difficult part, as children learn, is to move from stationary to motion.
- Children now have more confident physical control and visual coordination. They are more accurate throwers and kickers and can handle a wider range of games equipment.

Figure 9.7

Balance requires concentration

- Children's physical skills combine with their greater social skills so that organised games with simple rules are possible. They may play football or simple cricket in informal groups or a wide range of team games organised by adults.
- Compared with older children and teenagers, the majority of six and seven year olds can still look 'clumsy' when they handle a bat or racquet or try to throw a ball with accuracy.
- Children need an adult coach (formal or informal) who makes the games easy and non-competitive. Games of hitting or throwing need to be organised so that it is easier for children to connect with the ball and not made difficult (the aim if you play competitively with teenagers or adults).
- A great deal now depends on what is available for children to learn. Five and six year olds can learn new skills of swimming, horse riding, ice skating or judo. Children of this age in mountainous areas can learn to ski. But of course all such activities are not available for every child.

A great deal also depends on the available play spaces for children and on whether they are encouraged to take physical exercise. Children who have access to adventure playground facilities can be very adept at this age in climbing, balancing, swinging on ropes and negotiating how best to move between different parts of large playground structures. By this age, you can also often see the impact of adult influence or peer pressure as some children decide that particular games or more active physical daring are better for one sex rather than the other.

Scenario

St Jude's Primary School has a large and rather bleak playground area. The nursery has a play area of its own that is fenced around. The nursery team has been aware of children who move into reception and look longingly back at the nursery play area. Pam works in the nursery and the after school club and is aware of growing complaints from the children that playground supervision staff 'stop all our good games, so it's boring'. On the other hand, the staff are aware of complaints from colleagues that 'children don't know how to play any more'.

The nursery, reception and after school staff are sure that, with space and supportive adults, the school age children will play a wide range of physical, pretend and social games in the playground. Difficulties seem to have arisen because the playground staff have become more focused on control and stopping games than promoting play.

Questions

1. What could be happening in St Jude's school and the playground and what could be more positive steps forward? You may also want to look at the scenario on page 23.
2. How might the children be involved in plans about equipment, games they would like to play and creating areas in the playground?
3. Visit some local primary schools and gather information on how they have organised their school grounds and how they promote play.
4. Present or discuss your findings with your colleagues.

Key skills link: PS2/3.1 C2/3.1b C2/3.3

Tips for practice

If you work in school, then you may find a more or less favourable attitude towards children's playtime. You can contribute when you:

- Value children's play rather than seeing it as wasted time from real learning.
- Wait and observe before deciding that a game should be banned or that children are not doing anything and therefore should be directed into an activity.
- Negotiate how and where a lively game can be played so as not to impose on other children, rather than bluntly telling this group to stop.
- Be ready to help in play and to join in. Good skipping games need an adult at either end of the rope and some chasing games need an adult to mark 'home'.
- Friendly adults can provide a welcoming place in the playground for a child who is temporarily without playmates.
- Consider with your colleagues ways to provide basic equipment like hoops, bean bags, balls and skipping ropes.
- Explain how to play games with children if they know very few or appear confused.

Fine movements

- Children in this age range are likely to be confident in the skills that need fine physical coordination and close attention. They can gain immense satisfaction from projects in art, craft and design. Children can have learned to handle materials and tools and they have greater patience to complete projects that last more than one session.
- Fine physical skills are supported by communication and intellectual skills so that children can organise projects, plan the steps and make choices. Their physical skills are working together with their increased ability to look ahead and consider what they want or need to make.
- Fine skills enable children to manage the physical coordination needed for forming letters in their writing (see also page 339). They need to move from a whole hand grasp to the finer fingers and thumb hold and some children find this harder than others.
- Children of this age can usually manage the skills of self care, although fastenings like shoe laces can be a struggle and need practice.
- Children also show their fine physical skills when they are given a safe role within domestic routines, at home or in out of school care. Five to eight years olds can be adept at food preparation, simple cooking, organising a setting, decorating and basic DIY and gardening.

Physical skills, exploration and learning

Gaining balance

Children's balance improves so that three and four year olds can be steady in walking along a low wall or a line on the ground. To become confident, children need plenty of practice in which they feel what it is like to be in balance, to begin to lose your balance and sometimes regain it after a wobble and that sometimes balance is gone and over you go.

Figure 9.8

We should be impressed by the skills children manage

Judging physical movements

Young children become adept at clambering on chairs or other furniture and at climbing on apparatus. Some children are more cautious than others and need to take their time. Most children judge how high they can climb safely, although the more intrepid climbers may sometimes want some help in coming back down again.

Children are usually safe at judging what they can manage in physical skills. Problems tend to arise if they are distracted or cannot maintain their balance. Children's learning can also blocked if adults are over-concerned about very minor risks and either stop physical activities or make children anxious by constant cries of 'be careful, you'll fall'.

Bodily awareness

Babies and young toddlers have limited awareness of their own body, although their movements are much more deliberate. Young children have gained enough control, of large and fine movements, that they become more aware of the physical messages of their body when they make different movements. This awareness of physical feedback is called proprioception (see page 245).

- So, for instance, two to five year olds often like twirling around, even to the point of feeling so dizzy that they fall over. It is fun to make something physical happen in a deliberate way.
- Many young children like to hang upside down, to experience the strange sensations that follow and then to right themselves deliberately.

Through their physical activity, children in this age range learn directly about concepts that later make sense in terms of words (see also page 275):

- Spatial awareness makes sense by closeness or distance and closing distance when children run towards each other.

- Temporal awareness develops through children's ability to vary their speed from very fast to medium to very slow. Movement gives children an understanding of 'how fast' they can get from one place to another.
- Directional awareness develops as they experiment with different movements forwards, sideways, backwards, round and round in circles, up and down the garden and with negotiating sudden turns.

Activity (observation)

- Watch and listen for examples of children using their physical skills deliberately to experience a physical sensation or explore what it feels like to move in a certain way.
- Write up your observation notes, with photographs, so long as children are happy for you to take photographs.
- Discuss your findings with colleagues or make a display.

Key skills links: C2/3.3 C2/3.1a

Young children can manage a range of basic physical skills. But they apply their skills in different ways, depending on the opportunities they are offered and the choices that they make. 'Do I want to?' becomes as important as 'Can I?' So you will not see all two to five year olds necessarily engaged in energetic play. If children have been very confined or required to be very quiet, then they may not be confident in these skills. Sometimes girls may have taken on the view that lively physical play is only for boys.

The idea of schemas

Key term

Schemas
patterns of behaviour, mainly ways of physical exploration, in which young children learn about their environment

Chris Athey developed Jean Piaget's idea of **schemas**: patterns of behaviour in which young children learn about their environment. The schema shows itself through children's physical exploration but you can also see strong hints of how a young child is thinking about the familiar world.

For instance:

- A two year old may explore the idea and physical experience of 'enveloping' as she experiments with different ways to cover or wrap herself or objects.
- A young child interested in 'rotation' may turn objects around or use his skills of movement to look at familiar sights from unusual angles. A child may rotate or spin herself.
- A toddler involved in a 'transporting' schema may be especially absorbed in moving objects from place to place in the nursery or family home.
- Some young children become interested in 'connection', how things are or could be joined together, as well as how they can become disconnected and separated.

Making sense of a child's way of thinking through schemas can be a very positive approach when adults feel that young children do not really do much in their play or just make a mess.

Activity (observation)

- Watch out for schemas in action in the play of young children in your setting.
- Look for examples, such as in this section, that show through different aspects of an individual child's play. Of course not all of a child's activity and interests link with their current schema, but much will.
- Make notes and compare your observations with colleagues.

Key skills links: C3.3 C3.1b C3.1a

Right or left handed?

It should be clear now whether children are right or left handed. Some children's preference is not finally clear until seven or eight years of age.

Most people are right handed and this bias can make life difficult for the left handed minority – about one in nine children and more boys than girls. Left handed children can have some difficulties with writing (see page 348) and the hand–eye coordinations in skills like cutting can be difficult with ordinary scissors (those designed for right handed people). When cutting along a curve or spiral, it is usually easier for a left handed child to cut in a clockwise direction, whereas right handed children are better cutting anticlockwise.

Some special tools as well as patience from right handed adults can make a big difference (see the activity box). It is also the case that many people (adults as well as children) do not work with an absolute preference for right or left.

Figure 9.9

Children will take time to develop a right or left preference

Activity

Most readers will be right handed, so you may need to take steps to understand what it is like to be a left handed child. Try the following exercise.

- As a right hander, when you cut along a line, you are able to line up the scissors using your right eye on the upper blade. Now shut your right eye and try to cut along a line on a piece of paper using your left hand. This is the problem for the left handed child.
- Ask any colleagues who are left handed about their childhood experiences. What was difficult? In what ways were they helped or what help would they have liked as children?
- Left handed children can have difficulty in orienting themselves for writing and in manipulating tools made for the right handed majority. The organisation Anything Lefthanded has experience in support of left handed children and a catalogue of useful tools. Contact them at 18 Avenue Road, Belmont, Surrey SM2 6JD tel: 020 8770 3722 website: *www.lefthand-education.co.uk*
- Use information from the organisation and their website to make a short presentation to colleagues about support for left handed children.

Key skills links: C2/3.1a C2/3.1b IT2/3.1

The impact of disability and ill health

Disability can affect physical development in different ways and you will find more detail in Chapter 11. This section summarises some main points in brief:

- Some children have disabilities that directly affect their ability to move and control their limbs. Children may be frustrated and need support, require extra space and some specialised equipment.
- Learning disabilities may mean that children's physical skills are not yet supported by their understanding of how to keep safe and assess risk. Children may need your watchful eye and guidance when their peers are safe to make independent choices.
- Children with continuing health conditions may need enough care to keep them healthy, without making them feel miserable that they cannot play as energetically as their friends.

Activity

The world is a very different place for a child who is partially sighted or who has almost complete loss of vision. It is hard for sighted adults to appreciate the experience unless they spend some time in a play environment without their sight.

Organise with colleagues or fellow students to spend time in an early years play environment in which you take turns having your eyes covered effectively so that you can see nothing. Ideally this should be a playroom or nursery that you do not know well. Your sighted colleagues are responsible for your safety. But it is also their task to understand what you need in order to be as independent as possible and able to access materials, drinks or food.

Discuss the experience in detail afterwards and write up the main issues. For instance:

- What was it like to have to negotiate an environment in which you did not know where everything was kept?
- In what ways did colleagues use language to support and guide you?
- What was unhelpful to you when you had to operate without sight?
- As an adult you had experience and ideas to help make some sense of the play environment. Try to imagine what it can be like for a young child for whom everything is new.

Key skills links: C3.1a C3.3

Dyspraxia

Some children experience difficulties in their physical movement and skills but their disability is not that obvious in early childhood. The condition is known as *dyspraxia* or Developmental Coordination Disorder (DCD). The word dyspraxia is made of two Greek words: dys meaning 'bad' and praxis meaning 'movement'. The prefix dys is used to describe disabilities where there is a problem with a skill. So, dyslexia is a problem with lexical (Greek word meaning relating to words) skills, that is with reading (see page 350).

Developmental dyspraxia is a possible explanation when children approach five or six years of age and they have not gained physical confidence and competence like their peers. Young children are still learning about physical control and it is normal for them to look relatively uncoordinated. By school, children's difficulties will be more obvious and tend to include:

- Physical movements that continue to look less fluent than their peers. Children may be called 'clumsy' or 'uncoordinated'.
- Children have difficulties with fine physical skills that show up when they struggle with the skills of self reliance such as dressing or feeding themselves neatly. They may regularly be the last one to finish this type of task.
- Learning to write, other fine pencil work and craft activities are hard for the children.
- Planning physical movements is difficult and many tasks in school as well as early years settings require children to be able to follow a remembered step by step sequence.
- Children seem not to read the messages from their own body, whereas their peers have much greater bodily awareness by now.

Children need support and an appreciation of their difficulties. They will not be helped by adult irritation or labelling them as 'clumsy'. Children need careful observation, strategies to help them follow physical sequences and useful equipment such as triangular pencils to help them grip. Children with dyspraxia can also have trouble in writing because they find it so difficult to judge how hard they are pressing with the pencil. Practical experience can be given with a set of paper, carbon and another sheet of paper. Children can directly see the results on the bottom paper of increased or decreased pressure on the pencil.

Tips for practice

- Ensure that children's sitting position is stable and then they can put their feet on the floor to create a firm base.
- Give instructions one at a time rather than requiring the child to manage several steps at one go.
- Use colour coding, pictures and friendly reminders to help them recall and manage a sequence of physical movements.
- Be patient and give children longer to complete fine physical skills or self reliance and be encouraging of perseverance.
- Provide chunky pencils or paint brushes and make any paper firmly fixed.
- Give plenty of practice with larger scale items like bigger size bricks or larger threading beads.
- Have enjoyable physical activity for all the children and ensure that children with dyspraxia are brought in fully.

To think about

- When you observe a child with developmental dyspraxia it can be a timely reminder of just how much other children have learned.
- This child's difficulties highlight that his peers can now manage, for instance, to do up their buttons without looking, because they can guide the movement of their limbs from feel.
- In a similar way the struggles of a child with autistic spectrum disorder to grasp social skills and subtleties of communication show you how much other children have understood (see page 518).

Finding out more

The Dyspraxia Foundation, 8 West Alley, Hitchin, Herts SG5 1EG tel: 01462 455016 helpline 01462 454986 website: *www.dsypraxiafoundation.org.uk*

Further resources

Chris Athey (1991) *Extending Thought in Young Children* Paul Chapman.

Blythe, Sally Goddard (2000) *'Mind and Body'* (*Nursery World* 15 June).

Healy, Jane (1994) *Your Child's Growing Mind: a Guide to Learning and Brain Development From Birth to Adolescence* Doubleday.

Similar articles from the Institute for Neuro-Physiological Psychology, Chester, tel: 01244 311414.

Ripley, Kate (2001) *Inclusion for Children with Dyspraxia/DCD: A handbook for teachers* David Fulton.

Progress check

1 Describe the main risks to physical and emotional health if children's physical activity is seriously restricted.
2 Describe four ways in which babies and toddlers may use their fine physical skills to explore objects of interest.
3 In what ways might five year olds use their large physical movements in play or with equipment?
4 Suggest two ways in which the physical action of children might highlight their thinking for attentive adults.
5 Describe two signs that might alert you to the condition of dyspraxia in a child.

10

Learning opportunities through physical activities

After reading this chapter you should be able to:

- understand the importance of physical skills and activity for children's learning and well being
- provide a wide range of learning opportunities for physical development
- recognise the importance of outdoor play and use the opportunities of an outdoor curriculum
- appreciate how children's attention control develops and what may be genuine problems in this area.

Introduction

Chapter 9 describes the ways in which babies and young children progress in their physical skills. In this chapter you will explore the many possibilities for babies and toddlers to use their physical abilities within an environment that is interesting and safe enough. Children can apply their skills through indoor and outdoor play and as part of their involvement in the daily routines. Children steadily learn to apply their skills of attention in all of their daily activities. Some children have genuine problems of attention and hyperactivity. But adults need to make sense of children's behaviour in light of their age and their learning environment.

Links to early years qualifications

This chapter especially supports the following units:

Diploma in Child Care and Education: 2, 6

National Vocational Qualification in Early Years Care and Education

Level 2: C1, C8

Level 3: C3, C10, C14

BTEC National Early Years Diploma: 9, 24

Learning within physical development

There is a wide range of activities that support children's physical development and, of course, enjoyable physical activities promote other aspects of their development as well. Learning opportunities exist outdoors as well as indoors and a full awareness of the potential of outdoor play can create a full day for children.

Babies, toddlers and young children need to be kept safe from harm and preventable accidents, but other than responsible caution from adults, they need to move and use their physical skills. In a well maintained early years setting (see page 109 on health and safety) children should simply be able to access enjoyable play with adults who keep a friendly eye and join in with the children.

Tips for practice

You can support children's physical development throughout early childhood so long as you:

- value physical activity as a genuine source of learning (as well as health) not as the poor relation to intellectual development
- keep children safe enough, free from preventable accidents and then let them enjoy play
- give them the space, equipment in the broadest sense and opportunity to practise
- observe and recognise the learning that can happen when children are on the move
- value the outdoors as well as the indoors
- enjoy physical play and using skills with the children, play games with them sometimes.

Activities with under threes

Babies, toddlers and very young children need plenty of varied materials that they can explore in different ways. So they benefit from a wide range of simple play materials, not all commercially produced, with which they can experiment.

Play materials for babies

Your choice of play materials needs to be linked to babies' development and their individual interests of the day and the moment. Babies only have to be persuaded if an adult is trying to push play materials or an experience that does not currently interest the baby. Otherwise, babies are only too ready to be intrigued and experience their world with all the skills at their disposal. When babies are not interested and are very passive, then it can be a source of concern to parents and practitioners.

Babies have no sense of danger and cannot foresee the consequences of their actions. They simply do not have the knowledge of the world to manage such thinking skills. Toddlers have learned a great deal but they can still predict only a little within their familiar world.

Babies, and to a lesser extent, toddlers, explore a great deal by putting objects in their mouths. They do this because their mouth is the most sensitive part of their body and gives them information about an object as well as being a source of comfort. It is a hopeless task to try to stop babies putting objects in their mouth. You will upset them and prevent them learning. The task of a supportive adult is to ensure that babies cannot get access to anything that would be dangerous if put in their mouths. So the main issues are:

- Size of objects – no plaything should be so small that the baby could swallow it. Soft toys need to be of a good quality so that neither the parts nor bits of fur come off and into a baby's mouth. The same concern remains an issue with older disabled children whose development is more like that of a younger child.
- Cleanliness of objects – playthings need to be clean enough to go in the baby's mouth. Most items do not need to be sterilised, and some will be ruined if you try. Most playthings need to be wiped with a clean cloth or washed in hot soapy water, rinsed and left to drip dry.
- Good quality in bought toys – well made playthings for babies and children are properly finished off, with no sharp edges or raised screws that hold the toy together. They are made without PVC, that can release chemicals when toys are put in the mouth. They are free of stickers that can be peeled off by keen little fingers.
- Toys made by reputable manufacturers will meet safety standards. The risks tend to come when a setting or family home has a tight budget and second hand toys are used or toys are bought from unreliable sources like market stalls or car boot sales.

Playing with babies

Caring adults are an ideal item of play equipment for babies, as are older children whose play is guided by an adult. Babies are social, they like to make

Figure 10.1

Babies like climbing too

contact with other people, who conveniently come equipped with a voice, the five senses and limbs and hair for easy grabbing.

- In the very early months, babies like human faces and voices. The distance at which you hold a baby is perfect for her to focus her eyes.
- They like movement – both being carried around in your arms and looking at objects that move, such as mobiles.
- As babies become able to control their legs, they like to use you as a baby gym, bouncing on their legs and holding onto you, confident that you will keep them safe.
- Cuddling, talking, laughing and being together are all appropriate play and learning activities for babies.
- Babies like songs and rhymes and by three or four months they will show that they recognise a familiar song.
- Play simple peek a boo and chasing crawling once they are mobile.
- Making funny faces and sounds to each other or in a mirror.

Scenario

The team of the Dale Parent and Toddler drop-in group have become aware that some of the parents are highly anxious about 'catching the window of opportunity' in early learning. The parents' concern has focused on the need to buy play materials that claim to enable babies and toddlers to achieve their potential. Annie, the group leader of the drop-in, does not wish to discourage parents' commitment to their toddlers' early learning. But she wants to find ways with her team to show that adult attention and simple materials will be most developmentally appropriate.

Questions

Parents can become anxious, especially with some of the aggressive marketing used to sell play materials and kits to families.

1. How could the Dale team show early learning in action through the kinds of activities described in this section?
2. Consider and discuss with your colleagues ways that they could demonstrate that an interesting and involved adult is an essential item of play equipment.

Key skills links: PS3.1 C3.1a

Play for all the senses

- Babies like something to watch, so mobiles are of interest as are other babies and activity going on around them.
- As they gain control over their bodies, hands and fingers, babies like to use their skills, so give them rattles and soft balls that they can grab, hold and let go of, when they are able.
- Objects to chew – babies like the comfort of sucking and chewing, and they may find chewing a relief when they are cutting teeth.

- Soft toys are enjoyable to cuddle but do not give so many that babies feel overwhelmed.
- Mirrors, either hand held or fixed to the wall, are a joy to babies and toddlers who like to look, make faces and press their noses to the glass.
- Babies like objects to stack and drop, to put in containers and take out of containers. Many ordinary objects are of great interest to them, they do not need all commercially bought toys.
- Babies like books because they can be looked at, touched and enjoyed with an adult or an interested older child. Sharing books with babies works when it is part of a warm, social exchange. The brain connections are as much, if not more, emotional as they are intellectual (see page 243).

Activity

By their first birthday and within the following year, older babies will show what are their favourite soft toys or other cuddlies. These will be the most important ones or one, that must never be lost and will have to be kept clean and mended as best you can.

- Talk with parents and other early years practitioners to gather information from many families about the favourite cuddly toy of their baby or toddler.
- Describe the range that you discover and suggest reasons why these particular cuddlies became so important for the child. How did it happen?

Key skills links: C2/3.1a

Space to move

The research into early brain development has shown that babies and toddlers need to move. The actual practice of crawling, handling, looking and communicating by gestures builds the neural connections in young brains.

- They need safe space for moving around without undue restrictions and often the best area will be on a comfortable floor.
- You need to be accessible, on the floor too for much of the time.
- You can watch, enjoy and be ready to join in the play.
- Let children crawl all over you and provide the facility of a human gym as they hold on and bounce.
- Play peep boo around furniture or with scarves and cloths.
- Toddlers love crawling–chasing, but you will need a comfortable flooring for this activity.
- Chase and catch and hide and seek become possible, so long as adults adjust to moving slowly and pretending they cannot see young children who believe they are invisible if their head is hidden.

Toddlers' use of wheeled toys is a handy reminder of how play equipment can support so many different kinds of learning and how usage changes over the months. For instance:

- a wheeled trolley is useful to a toddler as a balance for walking
- confident walkers then use the trolley to carry around teddies, bricks or push other small children
- later the same young child will sit in the trolley imagining it is a car or a bus. She or he is the driver, perhaps with an imaginary driving wheel.

Activity (observation)

Explore varied use of the same play materials, like the example of wheeled toys on this page.

- Gather observations of the same child over a matter of months or of different children spanning the ages of 12–36 months.
- Follow the same child's use of similar materials and/or gather observations of children of different ages in their use of the same item.
- Take photos, if possible, with parents' permission.
- Present your findings to your colleagues.

Key skills links: C2/3.3 C2/3.1b

What is 'early learning'

The marketing of some electronic consoles and activity centres claims to introduce babies and toddlers to numbers, letters, colours, talking – in fact everything that is jammed on to the toy. Such consoles tend to have a few letters, often in upper case (capitals like ABC), a few numbers (that mean nothing in isolation), some sound making buttons to press, bright colours and sometimes a facility that claims to 'teach early words'.

These marketing claims are nonsense.

- Toddlers can practise physical coordination and may enjoy the sound-making option of these toys, but that is the limit.
- They may enjoy one activity centre but there is no point in having half a dozen in the baby room. Babies will learn the same skills more effectively if you offer a range of separate sound makers that can be picked up and made to work.
- They learn all the other skills through communication and experience of a wide choice of different materials (see for instance the sections on pages 272 and 298).
- Babies and toddlers learn to talk through interaction with real people, not by pressing buttons on an electronic console.

Babies and toddlers do not need computers and toys that claim to introduce them to early computer skills. There is no evidence that a very early introduction to computers is positive for learning and there are strong indications that it can be negative. The main problem with early screen use is that young children need to use their physical skills and senses to make any sense of the concepts. See page 383 for more about sensible use of computers in the early years.

To think about

On a personal note, I admit to having a dislike of the terms 'stimulation' and 'stimulating' applied to babies' and children's learning. The words create a feel that babies need to be pushed and persuaded into being interested in their social world. Such a perspective is inaccurate and has grown with a misrepresentation of the research on early brain development.

Babies do not need to be 'stimulated'; they develop their own brains through the kinds of activities described in this chapter and others in the book. Nor do they need to be 'given a headstart' or 'jump started' – two very unpleasant terms in the marketing that accompanies some of the 'build a better baby' products from the United States.

- Take claims on packaging or catalogues with a pinch of salt. Some bought materials are excellent but ask yourself if claims to promote early learning seem likely from your knowledge of child development.
- Discuss these issues with your colleagues, perhaps taking opposite sides in analysing the likely value of a commercial toy or a pack promoted in a catalogue.

Key skills links: C3.1a

Exploratory play

Plastic toys can be easy to keep clean and many commercially produced baby toys are in strong plastic. But there are limits to plastic and babies need the chance to experience other textures, smells and the malleability of non-plastic play materials. Babies like a wide range of objects and ideally ones that they can get hold of and explore. Babies and toddlers in a family home have always been interested in saucepans and a wooden spoon and other safe access to objects that are of great interest because adults use them as well.

Elinor Goldschmied developed two kinds of play resource to promote relaxed exploratory play that enabled under twos to discover for themselves. The **treasure basket** and **heuristic play** sessions promote use of ordinary and recycled materials for babies and toddlers. (The term heuristic play is from the Greek word *eurisko*, meaning 'serves to discover' or 'gain an understanding of'.) Goldschmied was concerned about over-reliance in homes and nurseries on commercially made playthings. She stressed the importance of materials that support all of children's five senses: hearing, vision, touch, smell and taste. She also identified a 'sixth sense' in children's sensitivity to their own bodily movement and recognition of what physical skills feel like when they are used. This idea is very similar to that of proprioception (see page 245).

Key terms

Treasure basket
a play resource developed by Elinor Goldschmied for babies who can sit unassisted. The low basket contains a range of safe and interesting objects that are not conventional toys

Heuristic play
an exploratory play resource for toddlers and young children, developed by Elinor Goldschmied and using a wide range of ordinary objects and recycled materials for children to play with as they choose

Learning with the treasure basket

The treasure basket is an open, low container with a range of materials that can be explored by babies who are able to sit up comfortably on the floor, either without any help or with a support for their back. The basket can be made available to one or two babies, with an adult sitting quietly nearby. The idea is that you let the baby or babies explore as they wish. You do not suggest particular materials nor intervene, unless a baby were pushing something into his throat or hitting another baby. Toddlers often still enjoy playing with the treasure basket and this activity extends naturally into discovery or heuristic play.

The exact contents of the treasure basket can vary but the aim is to gather a range of materials and bring the resource out from time to time.

- You can collect ordinary, safe objects like small containers, large cotton reels, a wooden spoon or spatula, large wooden curtain rings, a bath sponge, a small scoop or pastry cutters and the larger type of wooden clothes peg.
- Other possibilities are fir cones (watch out for bits), woolly balls, a firm fruit like a lemon, a smooth shell – anything that is safe and interesting.
- Make a collection that varies in look, texture, shape and smell so that babies can explore in any way they wish.
- Make sure that no object is so small that a baby could swallow it.
- The resource can be valuable for older children with learning disabilities. In that case, you need to check the items carefully, since the children may still put objects in their mouths and their mouths will be bigger than a baby's.

Activity (observation)

Make several observations of babies enjoying the treasure basket on different occasions.

- Note down what items the babies selected and what they did with the item. For instance, they may look at it, stroke it, put it in their mouth or put one item into another.
- Do the babies return to some items? Do they look at each other if you have two babies sitting at the basket? Do they offer each other anything? Do they invite you to play in any way?
- Organise your notes into a short presentation to colleagues or fellow students. What have you observed about very early learning?

Key skills links: C2/3.3 C2/3.1b

Learning with heuristic play

Goldschmied further developed the treasure basket into the heuristic play sessions that she introduced into day nurseries.

- A rich resource of materials are kept in containers like large cloth bags and brought out perhaps once or twice a week.
- There is a similar emphasis as with the treasure basket on a wide range of natural materials and no commercially made or plastic toys.
- There should be enough materials that turn taking is not an issue.
- The idea is that toddlers play as they wish and adults watch with interest. They help if asked but do not direct children's play by actions or words.
- Materials can include cardboard and transparent tubes, a wide range of small and larger containers, large wooden clothes pegs, lengths of metal chain and other safe recycled materials.

Activity (observation)

Watch young children exploring heuristic play materials.

- Note what materials they choose and how they explore them.
- In what ways do these young children show absorption and concentration?
- Do children watch each other or play at handing each other items?
- Describe what and how children are learning in these sessions.

Key skills links: C2/3.3 C2/3.1b

Finding out more

If you do not have contact with an early years setting that offers a treasure basket or heuristic play sessions, then two videos show how this form of exploratory play can work so well.

Infants at work: babies of 6–9 months exploring everyday objects by Elinor Goldsmied and *Heuristic play with objects: children of 12–20 months exploring everyday objects* by Elinor Goldsmied and Anita Hughes can be purchased from the National Children's Bureau tel: 020 7843 6000 website: *www.ncb-books.org.uk*.

Over threes with physical play and activity

There is no firm boundary between what is appropriate for children younger and older than three years. Some ideas have been given in the previous section, because it is useful to adjust to what younger children can manage in large and fine movements. In this section many of the activities are appropriate for an age range from two or three years onwards.

Figure 10.2
Children need space for activities

Space to move and explore

Children practise large and fine movements. They relish opportunities to climb, run and jump within open space, climbing frames and with organised obstacle courses for crawling or negotiating with bikes.

Activity

An enjoyable obstacle course can happen indoors as well as outside.

In your early years setting look at the indoor possibilities. Plan and organise an obstacle course with the help of the children.

- What can you create with large floor cushions, a line of large wooden bricks, hoops that you can step in and out of, a table that you wriggle under?
- You could have a finishing area on a rug for children to stop and get their breath before another round.
- Observe the children as they use the course. What kind of movements are they using? What words could you naturally introduce to describe what they are doing?

Write up the activity and make a short presentation to your colleagues.

Key skills links: C2/3.3 C2/3.1b

You can look for appropriate opportunities to use vocabulary about movement and physical actions.

- The aim is to introduce words about speed, height or direction as part of the play. You do not want to overdo it or impose on children's activity.
- Look for natural opportunities to use words like up, down, through or under.
- Movements can be described as fast and slow but also as sliding, creeping or rushing.
- You will also find natural opportunities to help children to become more aware of their own bodies. Perhaps everyone is out of breath after a speed walk around the garden. Hanging by your arms from the climbing frame feels like a stretch. Jumping down feels exciting and the sensation of landing on the ground is felt in the feet.

To think about

Jigsaws are a useful kind of play material. When children enjoy doing them, they can practise looking, experimenting and the physical handling of pieces. However, not all children are enthused by jigsaws and there is nothing to gain in trying to make them play with materials they do not enjoy.

- Consider and list the skills that jigsaws can promote. You could do a diagram similar to that on page 278.
- Then describe other play materials or games that could support the same skills if children do not particularly want to complete jigsaws.

- Discuss your ideas with colleagues. Do you sometimes feel that a play resource is essential, when in fact the same skills can be learned and practised from different play materials and opportunities?

Key skills links: C2/3.3 C2/3.1a

Music and dance

Babies, toddlers and children enjoy different kinds of music and dance sessions:

- Babies are often calmed by some familiar music, not always quiet. Within the first year of life they show that they recognise some songs and pieces of music.
- Once they are mobile or able to stand resting on a low table, they will often move in time to music and will enjoy being danced around in your arms.
- Sometimes you can put on lively music for dancing together. Younger children like to be helped and held as you dance to the rhythm.
- Experiment with music that has changes of pace from fast to slower and to very slow.
- Build in imaginary themes with the movement, like 'we're tiptoeing through the forest' or 'we're on a roller coaster'.
- Four and five year olds can have enough coordination to try joint activities like simple line dancing. With you as a guide children can manage sequences like stepping from side to side, adding a clap and small jumps forward with both feet. Adding an energetic whoop finishes off the pattern.

Activity

- Collect examples of the kinds of music that young children like and recognise. It can include classical pieces of music as well as recent and older popular music.
- Compare notes with colleagues. What is the range of musical taste?
- Try introducing a type of music that has been well received by children in another setting.

Key skills links: C2/3.3 C2/3.1a

Constructional play

Children can build indoors with materials that range from the smaller scale lego™, a good supply of wooden bricks and recycled materials such as containers and egg boxes. Outdoor projects can be larger scale, perhaps involving large cardboard boxes, milk crates, bubble wrap and lengths of cloth. Children may make dens or work out ways to transport water with a series of crates and guttering.

Children practise their physical skills in constructional play but they are also learning in other areas of their development:

- Children think as they plan what they will do, recall previous works and communicate with other children who are involved in the same construction.

- Children can gain immense satisfaction as they plan, build and revise their constructions. A complex construction takes time and it is important that children's projects are not demolished prematurely because adults are following an inflexible schedule of activities.
- Children may return to an interesting construction over a day or several days. They may also like to use a camera to take photos of their work in progress as well as the final impressive construction.

There are many different kinds of constructional sets sold commercially. But children do not need lots of different types that have a relatively small number of items in each. Their physical skills are better supported, as well as the scope for planning, when settings have a small number of constructional sets but there are plenty of pieces. You will notice children's frustrations when they run out of pieces for a construction or they have to share a limited supply with other children so that nobody has sufficient. It is up to adults to help children manage turn taking over a period of time so that all children have the opportunity to work with constructional materials.

Helping out in the daily routine

Physical skills are used, practised and placed in a meaningful context when children are part of the daily routines of your setting. They may help with or take full responsibility for:

- watering the plants
- choosing and putting out equipment
- sweeping or tidying up
- laying the table for snack or meal time
- taking responsibility for their own organisation through self registration or a self service snack and drinks table.

Activity

There are more ideas about learning through the daily routine in Chapter 2, especially from page 52.

- Look at those suggestions and link them to the physical skills described in this chapter.
- Take one or two aspects of the daily routine and make a diagram to show the potential learning, especially of children's large and fine physical skills.
- Share your ideas with colleagues.

Key skills links: C2/3.3 C2/3.1a

Arts and crafts

Toddlers and very young children like and can benefit from hands-on arts and crafts activities:

- they work with materials such as play dough to shape, squeeze, press and increasingly make shapes that they say are a sausage or an animal

Figure 10.3
Potential learning from play with an obstacle course

You could create a similar diagram to show a breadth of learning from other activities described in this chapter, for instance constructional play, music and dance or handling natural materials such as sand or water.

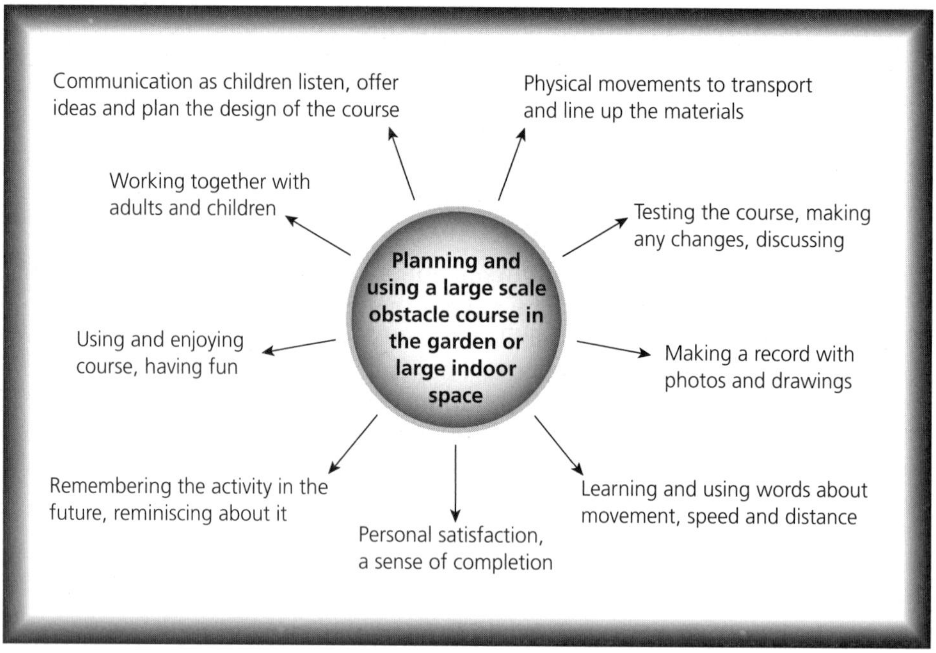

- toddlers and very young children like simple sticking and cutting
- with thick crayons and brushes they practise skills in drawing and painting
- different art materials enable them to explore printing with thick sponges, foot, hand and finger painting.

These art and craft activities support children's physical dexterity but the enjoyment also promotes imagination and ability to plan ahead a little. Under threes do not necessarily want or need to produce an art or craft product at the end. They benefit from experimenting and most of the value of the activity is lost if adults direct children's actions to ensure a neat painting or print that can be sent home or become part of a wall display.

One way forward is to use photos that you take of large scale art activity, dough models and of very young children having fun exploring materials.

- You can make a wall display of the photos, with short written explanations as one form of communication with parents.
- Some photos can also go into a child's individual portfolio as a record of what they have enjoyed and explored.
- The photos will be a pleasure for the family and children themselves when they look at them as they get older.

Scenario

Erin, the manager of Sunningdale Day Nursery has become aware that one or two team members in the baby and toddler rooms have become over directive in their use of arts and crafts with under threes. When Erin raises the issue of developmentally appropriate 'baby art' in a team meeting, it becomes clear that some practitioners are putting pressure on toddlers because of a few remarks from parents about 'hasn't she done anything today?'

Some team members had questioned the point of getting babies and toddlers to make neat Easter cards, and similar productions, just because the older children were involved in this activity. Erin diplomatically supports these team members and starts the process of ways to get round something for children to show for their day.

Questions

1 What do you think the Sunningdale team could do to enable the under threes to enjoy arts and crafts?

2 List some more appropriate craft activities than getting babies and toddlers to make neat cards.

3 Share your ideas with colleagues.

Key skills links: PS3.1 C3.1a

A wide range of arts and crafts can support children's creative development as well as their physical skills. Children learn from these activities so long as they are allowed to make choices about materials and the end product.

- Drawing and painting can be undertaken with crayons, chalks and paint. The materials can be applied with brushes, but also fingers, sponges, rollers or cut vegetables.
- It is possible for children to exercise their imagination in the use of materials, colour and texture.
- Printing can be on paper, cloth or on to shapes and containers.
- Woodwork offers a context for learning about tools as well as the pleasure of making something. You can help children to use tools when they need or appreciate some advice. A good technique will also help children to keep safe.

The importance of outdoor play

The first nursery schools in the UK, such as those pioneered by Margaret McMillan (see page 400), placed a great value on outdoor experience and play for young children. From the 1970s early education came to be much more focused on children's intellectual development and the unbalanced view grew that the most valuable learning occurred indoors, with activities more directed by adults.

Not every early years setting followed this route, but many began to see children's outdoor and physical play as less valuable and as 'just letting off steam'. Access by children to outdoor space was often restricted to scheduled times in the day, with the result that children were very wound up by the time the doors opened. They rushed around the garden, trying to pack in all their games and adults felt this confirmed their view that outdoor play was over-energetic and gave rise to too many accidents.

During the 1990s a more balanced view has returned, led by people like Marjorie Ouvry and Helen Bilton. They have promoted the value of outdoor play and described how flexible use of outdoor space can support every aspect of children's learning.

Figure 10.4
The woodwork table offers great potential for learning

- Physical play is valuable for itself, and gaining confidence in physical skills supports skills like literacy that are so often associated with the pressure to get children to 'sit down and concentrate'.

- Outdoor play between children can be the vehicle for social interaction and communication.
- When children are enthusiastic about outdoor projects, they talk together, plan, discuss ideas and solve some problem, especially if adult support is available.
- Children develop such skills precisely because they are on the move and enabled to make choices, carry out and then admire large scale projects.
- Outdoor space usually allows larger scale projects than are possible inside. Children can create a den, transport material about the garden and spread out with a project.
- Energetic pretend play where the imaginary themes need space for expansion can flourish in the outdoors. Awareness of boys' lively pretend play has raised concern that their learning is blocked if their play is forever curtailed or even banned because it is 'too noisy'.

Ideas for using the outdoors

Settings vary in the scope of their outdoor area but with some minor adjustments it is possible to consider any of the following.

- In the outdoor area children can move about easily with wheeled vehicles, trolleys and wheelbarrows. They enjoy the sheer movement and also use the equipment to transport materials around to serve their play.
- They can practise balance with versatile materials like crates, tyres, logs, planks. All of these can be moved about by the children and made to serve different purposes.
- Natural materials like sand, earth and water can easily be handled outside and do not necessarily have to be in a conventional wheeled tray.
- Children benefit from access to areas for digging and earth works. They can be cleaned up or help with their own cleaning later.
- Children enjoy permanent and temporary shelters, dens or the material to make a den and large cardboard boxes.
- Outdoor areas can provide treasure trails and obstacle courses, some of which the children can help in designing.
- A pavement or asphalt surface will allow chalk markings that can be for a roadway or to enable balancing games along a line or wiggly route.
- Children will develop many of their games themselves but they also appreciate adults with ideas for outdoor games and equipment like ropes, hoops, bats and balls. You can show that you enjoy playing with them.
- Garden projects and helping out with garden maintenance can be undertaken and enjoyed, even by young children. This activity supports physical skills but also gives rich opportunities for learning about the natural world and early science.
- Children are also very proud of gardening projects they have undertaken and have good ideas about making the most of the shared outdoor area, when they are consulted.

To think about

Helen Bilton (1998) reports her observations of the changes in children's behaviour when access to the outdoors was changed.

In the nursery a short fifteen minute timetabled outdoor session was altered so that children could move as they chose between indoors and the garden. The 'mad dash' to the outside stopped when children realised there was no time limit. The outdoor play calmed down and was more sustained when children were no longer trying to pack all their favourites into a scant quarter of an hour.

Helen Bilton, and the nursery team with whom she worked, realised that the restricted outdoor period had been a self fulfilling prophecy. With firm limits to their play, the children had rushed around and 'let off steam'.

Questions

1 Consider why some (not all) early years settings undervalue outdoor learning and greatly restrict children's access to the outdoor area.

2 How does access work in settings you know?

3 How do children use the garden if their time is very limited?

Key skills links: C3.1a

Scenario

Dresden Road Nursery School has taken the garden and use of the outdoors as a key theme in their long-term plan for the current school year. The team has explored several broad issues and implemented changes after discussion and some visits to other local settings, as well as an email link up with several nurseries in different parts of the country. The Dresden Road team is part way through an ambitious plan that involves children and parents as much as staff.

- Throughout the warmer weather, the nursery has explored all the possibilities of taking indoor activities into the garden.
- They now have tables that go outside with an office area and a regular outdoor resource of drawing and writing materials.
- Cushions and a blanket create a comfortable book and story area.
- The staff are part way through working with the children to create a discovery box for use in the garden with magnifying glasses, binoculars, bug boxes and paper and clipboards.
- The children have become enthusiastic gardeners and have almost completed what they call their 'smelly garden' with herbs and scented plants.

The team is aware that the less warm and dry weather will soon be upon them and they are keen not to lose the impetus of their work.

Questions

1 What activities could the Dresden Road team continue throughout the autumn and winter?

2 What could they do that especially draws on the possibilities of winter weather?

3 Discuss your ideas with colleagues.

Key skills links: PS3.1 C3.1a

Weather and the outdoors

It is important that the weather is not used as an excuse to restrict children's outdoor play, because it is too cold, too hot, too wet, too windy and so on. Enthusiasts for outdoor activities (for adults as well as children) do say that there is no such thing as unsuitable weather, only unsuitable clothing. There may be some limits to this claim but children are able to go out in varied weather.

- They can learn about the weather by watching, choosing appropriate clothing and experiencing different temperatures and weather conditions.
- Children (and adults too) need sun protection in hot weather (see page 58) but can enjoy the outdoors so long as there is some shade.
- Well wrapped up, they can still play in cold weather and rain can be enjoyed so long as they have wellington boots, coats and hats.

Figure 10.5

Taking activities outdoors gives children flexibility

Activity and attention

It is usual for young children to want to move about and for toddlers to go through a phase of 'being into everything'. They are curious and they learn through direct physical contact with their world. Young children can be inattentive, impulsive and boisterous but this is normal behaviour for early childhood.

A serious problem arises for children when adult expectations become shifted so that three and four year olds are expected to sit still for long amounts of time and physical activity is seen as an optional extra. Sally Goddard Blythe (see page 244) has pointed out that the most advanced level of movement for a child is to stay still. Young children often need to move in order to concentrate. They should not be told off for 'fidgeting', these involuntary movements are because they cannot yet stay completely still.

There is also a widespread misunderstanding that concentration can only happen when children are still or even sitting up to a table. If you observe children, it is very clear that they pay close attention as they ride their bikes or walk around the garden spotting flowers or small creatures.

Activity (observation)

- Watch children who are on the move, who are not still or not for very long. In what ways can you observe that they are looking and listening. Describe examples and suggest ways that you could appropriately join in their play and be observant with the children.
- Make a short presentation to your colleagues to promote the theme of 'attention on the move'.

Key skills links: C2/3.3 C2/3.1b

The development of attention

Children steadily develop the ability to attend: to use their skills of looking and listening. You will help children when you have realistic expectations and understand that learning to attend, or concentrate, is more than how long a child can stay focused. There is development in the kind of attention a child can manage, as well as the length of attention span.

Under one year: easily distracted

Babies are naturally very easily distracted; their attention is caught by any new sight and sound. Their interest in new experiences and shifting focus is useful as babies have so much to take in and learn. Supportive adults go with the flow of a baby's interest and move on physically or mentally with the baby.

One to two years: more fixed attention

Within the second year of life toddlers usually move on from being frequently distracted and may in contrast look fixed and inflexible. Toddlers will often concentrate hard on an action or object that has engaged their curiosity. Their attention may look rigid but their learning is supported by an inclination to gain every gram of possible interest from this collection of stones or the interesting ridges on the soles of their shoes. Anything can be intriguing and deserve their full attention.

Toddlers and young children are not being rude or uncooperative if they ignore your request that they stop now and look, instead, at this object. They can only focus on one thing at a time and find it hard to shift attention. So they may well not have realised you were talking to them, especially if you did not use their name or gain their attention by gentle touch.

Two to four years: more flexibility in attention

Between two and about four years children manage a gradual development of their ability to attend, but they can still only manage one focus of attention at a time.

- Over the months children become more able to stop what they are doing in order to listen to another child or an adult.
- But two and three year olds can have difficulty getting back into an activity from an interruption. They may wander off, not because they had finished their painting but because another child broke their concentration. They need help to settle back.
- Three and four year olds are learning that adults in nurseries or playgroups sometimes address a whole group but this realisation takes time. Children of this age may still need to be addressed as individuals.

Four years and older: double focus attention

Between four and five years old children become able sometimes to attend to more than one demand for their attention at the same time.

- Four and five year olds are more able to chat with a friend as they are absorbed in their building or drawing.

Figure 10.6
Children can show concentration on many different activities

- They are far more able to get themselves back to an activity once they have stopped to look or listen, even if this other focus is nothing to do with their current project.
- On the other hand, children return to single focus attention when they are coping with a difficult task or a new skill. The same is true of us as adults if we are tackling a new skill. We may say, 'Just let me finish this and then I can talk with you.'
- Following experience in the group life of early years settings, children of this age can also understand that adults sometimes give instructions or explanations to the whole group and each individual needs to attend.

Tips for practice

- Hold realistic expectations for children's age and previous experience.
- Create an environment that is sometimes peaceful as well as sometimes lively.
- Ensure that you have gained children's attention before you start speaking. Use their name at the beginning of your sentence rather than the end. Use touch to gain attention.
- Help children to get back to an activity if their attention has been disrupted.
- Manage children's expectations about shifts in the daily routine, so that they are not required to stop suddenly.
- Recognise that children can concentrate on the move. Be creative about different ways for children to learn and avoid the mistake of claiming children 'can't concentrate' just because they do not appreciate highly structured table top activities.
- Ensure that children get plenty of breaks from more concentrated intellectual tasks.
- Model good concentration yourself and avoid interrupting children's focus.

Attention deficit disorder

Young children learn the skills of attention control and organising themselves. An excessive focus by adults on sitting still and paper and pencil work can make it appear that children have problems when they do not. However, some children reach primary school age unable to concentrate on even simple tasks and they struggle to behave well in a group where their peers can focus.

Children who continue to have such problems may have one of two conditions that undermines their ability to concentrate and learn.

- Children with Attention Deficit Disorder (ADD) find it hard to focus on an activity and see it through, even a game they choose and enjoy. They are easily distracted but, because the children may simply go quiet or wander off, they can be missed in a busy nursery or pre-school.
- On the other hand, you will not miss those children who have Attention Deficit with Hyperactivity Disorder (ADHD). They not only move continuously from one activity to another, they also demand adult attention with loud behaviour and may disrupt other children's games. Their non-stop activity can also stretch into the night and their parents are exhausted.

Experts do not agree on the causes of ADD or ADHD but possibilities include a chemical imbalance, an inherited condition and the impact of diet.

- The human brain uses a chemical called a neuro-transmitter to send messages along the nerves. The amount of this chemical increases with children's age and, with appropriate play experience, they learn to attend and to remember. The theory is that children with ADD do not have enough of this chemical and that children with ADHD have too much.
- There seems to be a genetic link, since over a third of children with diagnosed attention problems have a least one other member of the family with similar difficulties.
- Diet, especially food additives, has been linked to hyperactivity in children. It seems most likely that food allergies or intolerance make an existing condition worse for some children, but are probably not the original cause.
- Some families have found that tracking and then adjusting their child's diet and overall nutrition has made a difference.

Children with ADD and ADHD need help, as do their families. However, there is concern in the UK, given what has happened in the United States, that the condition can be too enthusiastically diagnosed in children who just need normal adult attention and guidance, with lively and enjoyable play.

Proper support for children with ADD or ADHD includes structured help for them to learn to attend and to handle their energetic impulses. The amphetamine-type drug Ritalin can be part of the help for some children. But there is serious concern that it should not be prescribed just because children are a 'handful' or will not cooperate within early years or school settings. This concern about medicating normal exuberance in early childhood has been heightened with the shift in some early years settings to an inappropriate level of structure and adult control. In recent years, over-formal approaches have sometimes been developed by adults who are anxious to meet and gather evidence for learning targets.

Figure 10.7

Easy access to the outdoors supports children's learning

Tips for practice

It is very unhelpful to label young children as 'hyperactive'. Early years practitioners and parents need to hold on to a realistic understanding of what is within the normal range for young children.

- Young children do not play quietly or 'properly' all the time. They are naturally very curious and the normal state of toddlers is 'to be into everything' and to throw at least a few tantrums.
- Children are in the process of learning about boundaries to behaviour and social skills like sharing and cooperation. This does not happen overnight.
- Lively children, often the boys, may find a very formal nursery, pre-school or reception class heavy going. They can only be quiet and attentive for just so long and they will become uncooperative if adults stop all their more lively pretend games.

Finding out more

Hyperactive Children's Support Group, 71 Whyke Lane, Chichester, West Sussex PO19 2LD, telephone helpline weekdays 10am–1pm 01903 725182, fax: 01903 734726 website: *www.hacsg.org*.

ADD/ADHD Family Support Group UK, 1a High Street, Dilton Marsh, near Westbury, Wiltshire BA13 4DL telephone helpline weekdays 9am–5pm 01373 826045. Send a large s.a.e for their information pack.

Other causes of attention difficulties

You need to use your skills of observation with care, because not all children who have genuine struggles with attention have ADHD.

- Some children who have problems with attention have some difficulties with their hearing or vision. Severe loss of sight or hearing can be easier to observe than less severe visual loss or intermittent hearing loss (see page 319). It is worth working with parents to have children's hearing or vision checked, if they have difficulty in responding to positive strategies to help attention.
- Children with epilepsy can have seizures in which they go blank for a very short period of time. They can seem to be an inattentive or daydreaming child (see page 521).
- Children with an autistic spectrum disorder can appear inattentive and behave like a much young child in that they are highly focused on a narrow range of interests and very hard to re-direct (see page 518).
- Children with severe emotional problems and depression may seem to be in a world of their own.

Any concerns about children whose attention control does not meet realistic expectations for their age should be handled through the special needs steps in an early years or school setting (see page 528). Careful observation, strategies to help and further assessment if necessary will help to identify what is happening.

Further resources

Bilton, Helen (1998) *Outdoor Play in the Early Years: Management and innovation* David Fulton.

Cousins, Jacqui (1999) *Listening to Four Year Olds: How they can help us plan their education and care* National Early Years Network.

Green, Christopher and Chee, Kit (1997, 2nd edn) *Understanding A.D.H.D.: A parent's guide to Attention Deficit Hyperactivity Disorder in children* Vermilion.

Lindon, Jennie (2001) *Understanding Children's Play* Nelson Thornes.

Ouvry, Marjorie (2000) *Exercising Muscles and Minds: Outdoor play and the early years curriculum* National Early Years Network.

Titman, Wendy (1994) *Special Places, Special People: The hidden curriculum of school grounds* WWF/Learning through Landscapes.

Progress check

1 Describe a range of suitable materials for physical play that are not conventional 'toys'.

2 Suggest three activities that could be suitable for children younger than two years of age.

3 Describe three ways in which children's learning (other than their physical development) can be promoted through outdoor play.

4 Explain three ways in which the attention control of a four year old is likely to be different from that of a two year old.

5 Describe two signs that might make you concerned that a child had problems with attention control.

11

The development of communication and spoken language

After reading this chapter you should be able to:

- understand and explain the development of children's communication and spoken language
- use a wide range of strategies to support the development of communication for babies, toddlers and children
- recognise and support children who experience difficulties within language development.

Introduction

From the earliest sounds and gestures, babies strive to make social contact through communication. Their abilities to understand and to express themselves extend until they can use their spoken language in a wide range of ways. Some children become bilingual within early childhood. Supportive and attentive adults can help children with the skills of communication and broad use of spoken language. Reliable information also enables you to address delays or problems in language development.

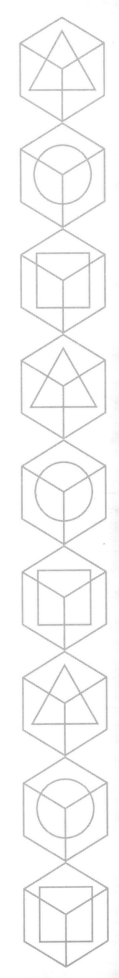

Links to early years qualifications

This chapter especially supports the following units:

Diploma in Child Care and Education: 2, 4, 6, 10

National Vocational Qualification in Early Years Care and Education

Level 2: C9

Level 3: C11, C14

BTEC National Early Years Diploma: 4, 7, 8, 9, 12

The development of communication

Spoken language is a very important part of human interaction and learning, but communication is much broader than spoken language.

Non-verbal communication

As well as spoken language, children and adults communicate in addition to and sometimes without the words. **Non-verbal communication** is possible through using **body language**:

- Facial expression, especially by the mouth and eyes. We have a considerable number of muscles in our face that can be used to produce a wide range of expressions.
- Gestures of the hands and arms or whole body; gestures communicate unspoken messages and mood.

Non-verbal communication is also made through the qualities of how something is said:

- The tone, volume, fluency and pace of what is said all add a message to the actual words of spoken language.

Before they can talk, babies and toddlers communicate a great deal by gestures and the variety of their sound making. They are also very dependent on non-verbal communication to make sense of their world. But of course non-verbal communication does not stop because the verbal expression starts. As adults we all send non-verbal messages and we receive them, although we may not be very aware of what we have noticed. The messages of body language may be positive and very supportive. On the other hand the messages may be negative and undermining. Body language can be confusing when this source of communication does not fit the words. Perhaps the words say, 'I'm pleased to see you' but the facial expression and tone say, 'No I'm not'.

Children continue to be alert not only to what is said but to how it is expressed. It is easy to underestimate how much young children notice of the messages sent non-verbally. Adults may assume that, because nothing is said, perhaps about a worrying or unhappy home situation, then children will be unaware. On the contrary, children know their parents and other familiar carers very well and are alert to different moods. They are very likely to be sure something is the matter, because a familiar adult's body language and general behaviour has changed. Children may not be able easily to put their understanding into words. They are also, unfortunately, likely to think they have done something wrong if there does not seem to be any other explanation. See page 218 for approaches to supporting children who are worried or distressed.

Key terms

Non-verbal communication ways of communicating without words by using body language and also the qualities of how something is said, such as tone, volume, fluency and pace

Body language ways of communicating that use gestures, facial expression and body posture

Activity

In pairs, explore how clear messages can be sent without words. For instance, use your face, gestures and whole body posture to:

- show to your partner that you are puzzled
- indicate frustration or annoyance

- communicate that you are pleased to see your partner.

As adults we will usually communicate with words as well as body language.

- Look for examples through observation of young children who have few if any words.
- How do they show the emotions that you have communicated in the pairs activity?
- Discuss your findings with colleagues.

Key skills links: C2/3.1a

Cultural differences

Children learn the social rules for non-verbal communication, including body language, and subtle use of spoken language. There are some cultural differences in the meaning of gestures and how spoken language is used. Your own use of non-verbal communication will have been learned within your own culture and will seem normal to you. When you meet and work with children and adults raised within another culture, unfamiliar to you, the differences may become clearer. You cannot anticipate every difference and, of course, there is a great deal of variation within cultures, as well as between them.

Gestures can vary in meaning. For instance, in the United States you might beckon somebody towards you by extending your hand and curling your index finger back and forth. In the UK you would probably use this gesture only to a child. Families of Indonesian origin would be unhappy even about this use, since in their culture such a gesture would only be used to an animal. It would be considered rude to use to a person.

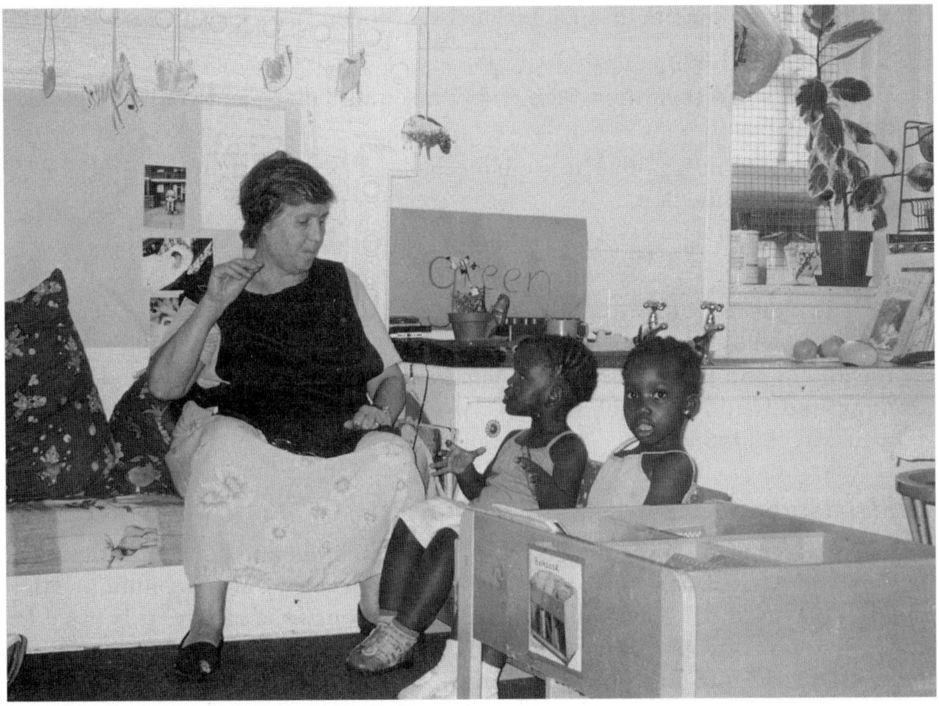

Figure 11.1
You will notice young children using gestures as well as words

There are cultural differences, as well as individual preferences, about personal space: how close you stand or sit to another person. Europeans tend to stand about one arm's length apart, unless the relationship is affectionate. People of Japanese origin tend to prefer a wider distance and people from the Middle East and some South American countries prefer to stand closer, perhaps almost touching.

Eye contact is another source of variation and individual difference. Children of UK origin tend to be raised to look directly at an adult. This body language is encouraged and directed with words like, 'Look at me when I'm talking to you'. Lack of eye contact in UK culture is often interpreted as lack of concentration or guilt about misbehaviour. Yet children in families of Middle Eastern or Caribbean origin are likely to have been taught the opposite. Looking directly at adults is likely to be interpreted as disrespectful and impolite.

To think about

- Collect ideas within your team or student group on the phrases and sayings that you recall from childhood.
- Many of these still guide us as adults in our body language. For example you may recall, 'It's rude to point' or 'Sit up straight – don't be so lazy'.
- Compare the examples that emerge from different people. You will find variations even if you all share very similar cultural backgrounds.

Key skills links: C2/3.1a

Spoken language

Children's development in spoken language covers two broad areas that are equally important:

- The sounds and then the words and phrase that babies and young children themselves use.
- Their understanding of what is communicated to them, by words and non-verbal communication.

Key terms

Speech or **expressive language** what children themselves say in words and later in phrases and sentences

Comprehension or **receptive language** children's understanding of what is said to them. Young children show through their behaviour that they have grasped words, in context, that they do not yet say

Speech

Children's **speech** or **expressive language** develops from the sound making and babbling of babies into recognisable words said to people. Children learn to speak in the accent and the version of a language spoken by the adults and older children around them. Some children learn more than one language and become bilingual in childhood.

Understanding

Young children also show through their communication and behaviour that they understand what is said to them. This aspect of their growing communication abilities may also be called **comprehension** or **receptive language**. It is usual for toddlers and very young children to show that they understand more words and phrases in a meaningful context than they actually say themselves.

Making meaning

It is possible to analyse the development of children's spoken language in terms of vocabulary and grammar. This more technical approach explores the words that young children use and how many in total they have at any given time. It is also possible and interesting to look at how a child's speech shows their grasp of grammatical structures in language, such as how to form a past tense or what is the more normal sentence order.

Yet children are very active in their learning and they are doing much more than passively absorbing words or grammatical forms. They are making meaning of their world and using the symbols of words to do so. Young children use words and put them together in phrases that are unique to them as individuals. Their mistakes in the words they use to describe their world show that they are thinking as well as speaking (see page 297).

Communication as social interaction

Children learn a very great deal in terms of words and phrases but they also learn the subtleties of communication.

- They use communication as a way to initiate social contact with others from the earliest months of babyhood. Communication is part of building close relationships.
- They learn social skills linked to language and gesture. Children also develop in terms of being able to listen, to take turns in a conversation and in learning social courtesies like not interrupting.
- They learn a range of uses for spoken language, depending on their everyday experiences. They can learn about using words to describe, to explain, to express an opinion or argue.
- Communication is part of social learning. Consequently girls and boys sometimes learn different patterns in using communication skills because these have been subtly used by the adults in their lives.
- Communication also links closely with children's intellectual development: how they are able to express their thoughts, use questions to explore and put words to abstract ideas (see page 361).

How do children learn language?

The vast majority of young children learn to speak and many around the world learn more than one language in their early years. There is no question that very young children manage to decode the language system and learn to communicate in meaningful words and gestures. However, there is no single theory about language acquisition that is able to explain fully how the young of our species manage this exciting task. The possible explanations include the following ideas.

Imitation

Learning theory (see page 15) attempts to explain children's acquisition of language through the principles of reward for imitation. The keen ability of babies and toddlers to imitate explains how babies' sound making moves towards the language that they hear rather than any other world language and that children develop an accent similar to the one they hear from adult speakers.

Learning through imitation will not work as a complete explanation, because toddlers soon produce word combinations that they have not heard from adults and other carers. Their creative, personal phrases and logical mistakes in grammar are a source of endearing anecdotes and show that toddlers and young children are thinking and not only copying.

Reward

Another idea that works as a partial explanation is that very young children learn to speak because parents and other carers are enthusiastic about correct versions of the language. Toddlers definitely flourish with positive feedback and attention for their early attempts at language. However, supportive adults are more flexible than a reward–no reward schedule would predict. Parents and carers are enthusiastic about toddlers' early and inaccurate versions of words and their pronunciation. Indeed, when adults highlight most of children's mistakes or insist on correct versions, this pattern tends to inhibit children in communication rather than encourage them.

A rich experience of language

In order to talk, young children definitely need to hear spoken language and have opportunities to use what they learn. There have been cases of children whose childhood has been severely deprived, with very limited social contact and care. These children have not learned to speak in isolation.

Children need to hear plenty of language and to experience adults who are responsive to their early communication, because language is grounded in social interaction. Babies who experience infant-directed speech (see page 306) seem to develop some aspects of their language slightly faster. But infant directed speech is not found in every culture and children still learn to speak those languages.

Children's rate of language learning and their use of language both appear to be influenced by the communication behaviour of their parents, or other important carers. It matters how we communicate with children, and there are many practical suggestions in this chapter. But neither language theory nor research identifies an exact pattern of how adults should behave, so long as they are communicative, attentive and responsive with children.

An innate readiness for language

Language development is not completely explained through the details of children's experience. Several decades ago some theorists proposed that babies must be born with an innate biological readiness to learn language.

The idea of an inborn language system was supported initially by research that suggested that the pattern of language learning is very similar between the languages of the world. The innate language system theory was shaken when it became clear that language learning patterns were very different. However, more recently research into early brain development (see page 243) has supported this idea that babies' brains are pre-programmed to be sensitive to human language and to sounds. They have a readiness that is in no way ready-wired to any specific language.

Language and thinking

Theorists such as Jean Piaget and Lev Vygotsky approached language as it is linked with children's capacity to think and make meaning from their social world. There is certainly no complete agreement on how early language connects to children's understanding of what they experience through their senses. But young children use direct experience to link sounds with objects and people. Young children's use of speech seems to start as a means to guide themselves as the words accompany their actions or are a means to direct the interest and actions of their carers. For some time children and adults may use the same or similar words, but there is good reason to assume that different meanings are assigned.

In conclusion

It seems very likely that several theoretical explanations are needed for early language development. There does seem to be an innate predisposition for babies to be ready to learn spoken language. However, children's learning is also shaped by their experience of language, especially from the key adults in their environment. But it is equally important what children do with this experience; they are active linguists, just as they are active thinkers.

Communication of babies and toddlers

Early sound making

Communication starts from the early weeks and develops in complexity long before the first spoken words.

- Newborn babies' main form of communication is to cry but they also stare and make eye contact with the carer who holds them close to cuddle or feed.
- Parents and other familiar carers learn to recognise and distinguish cries of distress from calls for attention, and contented sounds from firm complaints.
- Over the first six months, babies' attempts at sound making become more deliberate and playful.
- By three to four months they may have a 'conversational exchange' with an adult who responds to the baby's sounds or smiles and then leaves space for the baby to reply.
- From six to twelve months, babies increasingly use sound and gesture to gain attention and to express feelings of pleasure, interest or complaint.

Babies from six to twelve months show a range of deliberate patterns of vocalisation. For instance:

- sounds when the baby is annoyed are different from when she is contented
- vocalisations that accompany simple actions, like giving
- calls for attention or help
- patterns of sound linked with a familiar game like 'peep bo'

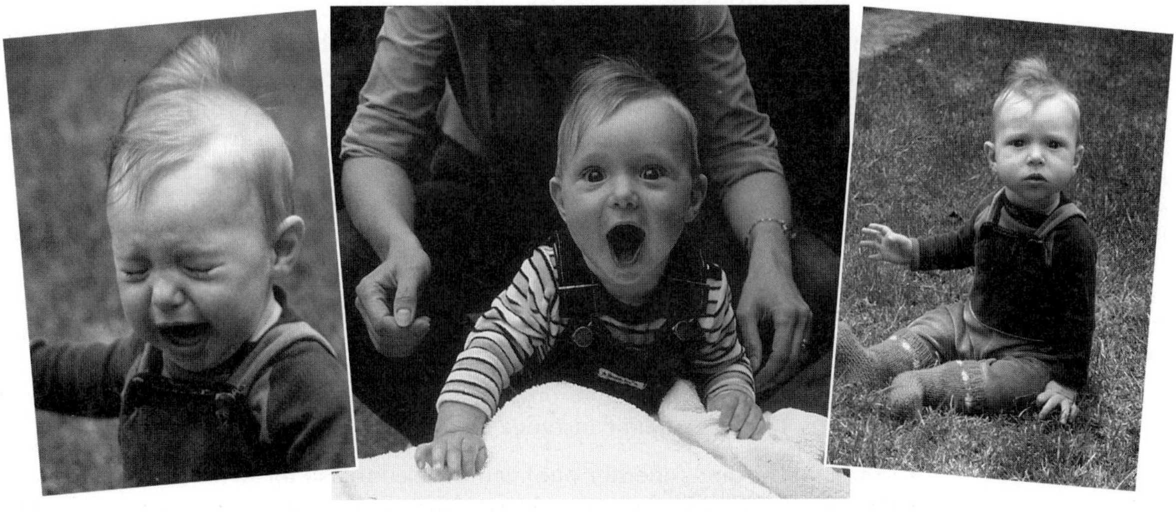

Figure 11.2 Babies will show you how they feel long before they have words

- copying sounds that an adult or older sibling makes to the baby in playful communication.

Gestures of communication

Sounds are accompanied by meaningful gestures as babies communicate:

- requests to be given something
- reluctance or full refusal to cooperate
- a wish for social contact
- directing attention with pointing
- holding the attention of an adult or older child with sounds that amuse like blowing raspberries.

From sound making to words

During the period from six months to about a year of age, babies experiment with a lot of deliberate **babbling** of sounds and sequences of sounds. They also respond to the enthusiasm of adults and older children by repeating sounds close to real words. Many, but not all, babies develop expressive jargon around the time of their first birthday. **Jargon** is the term used to describe a string of word-like sounds, expressed with the intonation of speech. There are no 'real' words yet, but it sounds as if there should be.

Key terms

Babbling
the early sound making, often very tuneful, of babies who are stringing together a series of sounds in a deliberate way

Jargon
the very expressive flow of word-like sounds that many babies make around about their first birthday

The first words

The first recognisable words emerge on average any time from twelve to nineteen months. Before the actual words appear, you will often hear young children use the same sound combination to refer to people or objects.

The first single words are likely to be drawn from a young child's familiar environment and from experiences that hold his interest. So, all children do not produce the same first words (or later an identical pattern of phrases). But they may produce the same kinds of words, such as:

- names of people or family pets
- familiar objects that are of importance to a child, like a cup or spoon
- animal noises ('woof-woof' to mean dog) or sounds associated with an object of interest like a car.

Single words are used very flexibly by young children, so that one word, supported by tone of voice and gestures can convey potentially several different messages. These single words, heavy with meaning, are called **holophrases**. So, for example, a toddler who has the word 'dolly' may say this word in very different ways, accompanied by varied gestures and facial expressions. In this way an eighteen month old toddler can be very capable of using one word to indicate the message of 'where's my dolly?', 'she's taken my dolly!' or 'I'm happy to have my dolly back'.

Key term

Holophrases
single words used flexibly by very young children, supported by tone and gesture to convey different meanings

It is very usual for young children to need time and practice to say words correctly. Toddlers and young children often say a word without the beginning sound ('poon' instead of spoon) or the end sound ('ca' instead of 'cat').

As well as words that name objects and people, young children learn words that are useful to them. For instance:

- 'More' or 'Na'one' (another one) can be used to ask for more food, the repeat of an enjoyable play action or be a comment on a similarity.
- 'Gone' or 'no more' can be a simple statement that something has gone, a

Figure 11.3
Toddlers enjoy your full attention

request for help in finding something, a description that the toddler has made something disappear and other possibilities.

- Following the social gestures, toddlers often also learn social words such as 'T'ank you' or 'Ta', 'hello', 'hiya' and other greetings.

Words combined into short phrases

With encouragement from adults or older siblings, toddlers add many more words so that by 20–24 months, sometimes younger, the first word combinations appear.

- The earliest short phrases tend to be communicated as if they are one word: 'here'y'are', 'nomorenow' or 'allgonenow'.
- One word may be used as if it is a movable prefix: 'moremilk', 'nomorebikky' or 'nobyebye'.
- Toddlers often make mistakes about words for objects or their short phrase. But such errors are usually logical and make sense if you know the child.

Activity (observation)

Gather examples of words and phrases from young children under two years of age. Focus on the mistakes that they make and see what sense you can make of this error in the light of this child's experience. For instance:

- Young children often use a word in a sensible way but too broadly. Perhaps anything with wheels is a 'car' or everything that is furry and has four legs is a 'cat'.
- They hear a phrase from an adult and pick the wrong word to use as a naming word: they hear 'look at the lovely flowers' and then call flowers 'lovelies'.

Discuss the examples you gather with your colleagues or fellow students. How do the logical mistakes highlight how much children have learned?

Key skills links: C2/3.3 C2/3.1a

Many of the early two word combinations only make sense in context and to a familiar adult. Even then you have to pay attention to how a child is saying the words, using tone and non-verbal clues was well as the words. The first combinations are not a random putting together of words; children show the beginnings of a grasp of basic grammar for the language they are learning. So, the early combinations are not the same structure in every language.

In English, the first combinations are often:

- one noun (naming words) and a second noun – 'Mummy ball' – which might mean 'please get me the ball' or 'Mummy's got the ball now' and so on
- noun plus a verb (doing or action words) – 'car gone'
- verb plus noun – 'give drink'.

These are combinations that support the child's desire to create meaning and to act on her environment.

Understanding of spoken language by babies and toddlers

Young babies are attuned to human speech, even before they are born.

- They turn to look towards the sound of a familiar voice.
- In the second half of the first year, older babies start to move their glance between people as the conversation shifts from one person to another.
- Babies and toddlers are alert to non-verbal clues of gesture, facial expression and following the gaze or the point from an adult.
- From six to twelve months they show signs of understanding very simple messages from carers about familiar routines.
- They show that they recognise a few names of everyday objects in context.

Towards the end of the first year and increasingly within the second year, babies and toddlers show that they understand a number of verbal and non-verbal requests so long as the context is familiar and the talker is known. They:

- are likely to come when called by their own name
- hand over a familiar object on request when an adult makes a 'give me' gesture with the hand and says something like, 'Can I have the cup?'
- can reply by gesture if they want a biscuit or drink
- understand negatives like 'No' and 'Don't touch', although they do not always comply.

Toddlers learn the routines, what usually happens, in familiar settings such as home or a day nursery. So, very young children only need to recognise one or two words and they grasp the remaining meaning from the familiar context. For example:

- 'Put your tissue in the bin': used tissues always go in the waste bin.
- 'Let's tidy up now': it is routine in the day care centre that children put their plates and cups on the trolley when everyone has finished a meal.
- 'No, don't touch the video': a young child knows from experience that this is not allowed.
- As toddlers start to control their own behaviour, they often use the same intonation and phrasing that has been said to them.

Throughout their second year of life, toddlers show an ever increasing ability to understand requests to fetch, show, give or find. They use their understanding of words but also the non-verbal communication from adults and older siblings.

- Initially toddlers' understanding is limited to the real object. They can point or look when asked, 'Where's Teddy?' or 'Where are your feet?'
- Then later they accept that pictures stand for objects or people and can point out familiar things by request in an illustration in a book or on a wall poster.
- By close to their second birthday, toddlers can often run very simple messages, for instance, to request something from an adult.
- They can fetch familiar objects from other rooms, which shows the operation of their short-term memory.
- Two and three year olds have gathered enough language experience that they are able to respond more to the words and are less dependent on context and non-verbal clues.

Activity (observation)

Organise yourself to undertake a series of observations of the communication development of a toddler. For instance, you could observe the same very young child at 12, 16, 20 and 24 months. Make a list on each occasion of this child's abilities of communication, using this section to guide you:

- What does she or he understand of what is said in a familiar context? Describe some examples each time.
- What meaningful sounds, early almost-words and recognisable words does the toddler use at each age when you observe?
- Share your observations with colleagues and discuss the variations between individual toddlers in the first words that they are motivated to learn and use and how they use their skills of communication.

Key skills link: C2/3.3 C3.1b

Communication skills of two to five year olds

Using different types of words

From two to three years it should be an increasingly tough job to list a child's vocabulary and examples of the phrases they use. Three year olds can have a working vocabulary of several hundred words, perhaps as many as 500. They add new words, create their own short phrases and ask questions. But the development of a two year old's language is more than how many words they say in total.

- A child's first set of words will be names of people and objects. By about two years of age, if the child has started talking by about 18 months, the words will start to include action words that describe what people are doing or what the child wants to have happen.
- Two year olds have usually started to use words to communicate very simple ideas. They show that they are ready to describe characteristics of the world around them, that mean something to a child.
- So the first ideas words are less likely to be about colour or shape than about hot, broken, tasty or nice (see page 368 about the development of abstract ideas and thinking.)

- Two and three year olds start to understand how objects relate together so that they may use words like 'in' or 'on' that describe simple connections between objects.
- Three and four year olds often develop interests that mean they learn a special vocabulary to reflect, for example, their interest in diggers, dinosaurs or different kinds of flowers.

Two to five year olds extend their applications of language to serve their play.

- Children use their language to think out loud and direct their own play. They need to speak their thoughts and find it very hard to keep quiet if something has interested or intrigued them.
- Self directing speech becomes a quiet mutter that older children, and even adults, tend to use when they are tackling a new or difficult task. Otherwise this type of language goes silent as **internal speech**.

Key term

Internal speech when children's talking to guide their actions or think goes silent or almost silent

To think about

Supportive early years practitioners need to recall that, for young children, there is a very short gap between an interesting thought and wanting to say it out loud. Children work on and process their thoughts by speaking. If adults place too much emphasis on 'sitting quietly' and 'not calling out in a group', they may squash the thinking and communication skills that they want to encourage. See also the discussion on page 311.

- If you listen in to the pretend play of this age group, you will hear them discussing and negotiating play themes: who will be which character and how the plot will unfold. Their language is serving a social purpose in guiding their play.

Figure 11.4
When you are close you can see what children are talking about in their play

- Children continue to learn new words and now know enough to ask the meanings of words or speculate on fine differences, such as 'what's the difference between a wood and a forest?'
- Two, three and four year olds show that they enjoy using their communication skills to show and entertain. Young children may enjoy singing or saying rhymes, even in front of a group.
- But children vary in their level of confidence and this can be most noticeable when they are in unusual or more formal situations.
- Some children are successfully learning two or more languages (see page 312).

Activity (observation)

Listen to the spoken language of a child who has not long passed his or her second birthday. Make a list of all the words that he or she uses spontaneously and then divide them into three broad groups:

- words that name people or objects (nouns) like nose, dog or Mummy
- words that refer to action (verbs) like jump, eat or sing
- words that describe an object (adjective) or action (adverb) like big, cold, messy or fast.

Look at your own observation and compare observations that colleagues have also made.

- What is the relative size of your three groups?
- What kind of describing words make sense to just two year olds, what have they learned and now use?
- How do these observations guide you in supporting children's early spoken language? Make a short presentation about tips for practice. For instance, there is no point in your pushing descriptive words about colour or shape when this child only has a small number of action words and no chosen describing words. He or she is not ready yet.
- Relate these ideas to your practice and plan any improvements. See also page 368.

Key skills links: C3.1a C3.1b LP2/3.1–3

Understanding of grammar

Young children learn new words at a fast rate between the ages of 20 to 30 months and they combine these in simple sentences.

- From about two and a half years of age, when young children have a sizeable vocabulary, they start to learn and use a very wide variety of grammatical structures and inflections that are particular to their language.
- Children learn both the regular and irregular grammatical forms by listening to what is said in their hearing. Adults can help by saying the correct form without pressing children to 'say it right'.
- Many of children's logical mistakes are now about generalising a regular grammatical rule to constructions that do not obey the usual rule. For example, children may say 'badder' rather than 'worse' or 'I eated' rather than 'I ate'. You see the evidence of their logical thinking.

- Children, of course, learn the grammatical forms that they hear. Different versions of English, including dialects, often use variations in the basic grammar ('we was' rather than 'we were' or 'me' instead of 'I').

Use of language

Children use their substantial vocabulary in many ways.

- Even two and three year olds start to adjust their language depending on the listener. Young children talk in a different way among themselves, in contrast to their words and intonation with an adult.
- Two years old have usually grasped the pattern of asking questions as well as replying to them. They use question words and the questioning tone in their voice to ask 'What?' questions and later 'Where?', 'When?' and often a regular 'Why?'
- Three and four year olds often show that they can simplify what they say when talking to a much younger child. Their adjustment shows a sophisticated understanding about the abilities of babies or toddlers.
- Three and four year olds can be capable of forming sentences that serve different purposes: to describe, question or argue, to create negatives ('I didn't make that mess!') or to speculate and wonder.
- They use their communication skills to seek information and their skills of listening to gather new knowledge.
- The spoken language skills of three year olds and older reflect their thinking and how they identify what they do not know or understand. Their questions can become challenging to answer, such as 'How does the light come on when you switch it?' or 'Why did my Grandad have to die?'

Activity (observation)

Collect some examples (by writing notes or tape recording) of the spoken language of three and four year olds. Look especially for the ways in which they use their language. For instance to:

- describe what is happening in front of them
- recount something that has happened from the recent past
- request you or another child to do something
- ask questions, sometimes tough ones
- create a story or retell a familiar one
- explain, justify or argue
- speculate and wonder about how or why.

Use your observations for the following tasks.

- Consider with colleagues the richness of the language that you have gathered from some children.
- Share your findings with the parents of individual children.
- Discuss with colleagues how you might help children with limited uses of their language to extend somewhat.

Key skills links: C3.1a C3.1b C3.3 LP2/3.1–3

Understanding of language and ideas

As well as a complex spoken language, most children also show a broad understanding of what is said to them. Their communicative behaviour shows that they understand a considerable range of ideas.

- Two and three year olds still show that they understand in context more words than they actually use themselves. Sometimes, in a long adult sentence, children still pick out the key words.
- The gap tends to close between what the child says and what they understand. Four and five year olds tend to use the words that they fully understand from the speech of others. If they feel confident, they probably ask, 'What does that mean?' if they recognise an unfamiliar word.
- Three year olds become able to use language as a tool in itself. If you ask young two year olds the question, 'What is a ball?', they will look for an actual ball or a picture of one and show you. When you ask a three or four year old the same question, they are far more likely to understand that this is a request for an explanation in words. The child may say, 'It's for playing' or 'It bounces'.
- Within the same age children grow in understanding of everyday objects and what we do with them. Older two year olds may and three year olds will probably be able to pick out a picture of a bed or a doll's house size version when asked, 'Which one do we sleep in?'
- By their own words and reactions to adult questions, three and four year olds show that they have understood, or nearly understood, a wider range of abstract concepts, ideas about how the world can be described. Children's language reflects their thinking and this area is further discussed from page 361.
- For instance their words allow them to talk about what has happened in the recent past or what may happen in the future. A four year old's understanding is partly a grasp of the grammar that enables them to say, 'I went to my Gran's at the weekend' or 'Tomorrow can we go to the park again?' But if you think about it, these words are also a sign that the child understands the concept of time beyond the immediate present.

Understanding social communication

Children are also learning the 'rules' about communication, including listening to others and holding a conversation.

- Children's general communicative behaviour is shaped by their experience – for instance, whether adults have listened to them or have interrupted.
- Children, who have had very little experience of enjoyable conversations, do not learn the skills or the pleasure of chatting together.
- Three and four year olds who have experienced turn taking in communication are able to start, sustain and end a conversation with peers and with an adult. They show a wish to explain, tell and share items of interest and a willingness to listen to others, at least some of the time.

Children from five to eight years

Older children continue to extend their vocabulary: what they use themselves and what they understand.

- These slightly older children comprehend some of the subtleties of spoken language. Six and seven year olds begin to learn that there are different versions of spoken language. They may be able to distinguish between ways of talking in a presentation in circle time or school assembly, realising that this form is different from informal conversation.
- Children learn best when the differences between versions of English are made explicit and their preferred spoken language is respected, rather than simply criticised as wrong.
- Five and six year olds are more able to control and direct the volume of their spoken language, whereas younger children find it hard to speak quietly.
- Five and six year olds usually understand how intonation patterns in speech can be shifted to change the meaning. The aspect of language is called **prosody** (see the box for an example). Children with speech and language difficulties linked with dyspraxia (see page 263) may have difficulties understanding how the meaning shifts with a different emphasis on the words.
- Children have extended into an understanding of written communication: writing and reading (see from page 342).
- They are beginning to grasp that some written language conventions are different from spoken and that writing can be used to different purposes.

Key term

Prosody
the ability to use intonation patterns and emphasis to shift the meaning of a sentence with the same words

Activity

- In order to understand the language skill of communicating meaning by intonation, take a simple sentence such as, 'I didn't say that she took my book'.
- Now say the sentence to a partner, but each time with an emphasis on a different word in the sentence. This list will help you; emphasise in turn the word that is in bold.
  - **I** didn't say that she took my book
  - I **didn't** say that she took my book
  - I didn't **say** that she took my book
  - I didn't say that **she** took my book
  - I didn't say that she **took** my book
  - I didn't say that she took **my** book
  - I didn't say that she took my **book**
- What does this do to the meaning? How does it sound to the speaker and to the listener in your pair?
- What does this activity tell you about the subtle learning in communication?

Key skills links: C3.1a

The phonological system

Children who learn to talk have worked hard to hear and then say the sounds that make up the language. The phonological system in the language is the pattern of sounds that are combined to make words. Young children have to learn not only single sounds such as 's', 'c' or 'r' but also the combination that is created by all three at the beginning of the word 'scream' or 'scrunchy'.

Many enjoyable play and early literacy activities described in this chapter support children to develop **phonological awareness**, that is the understanding that spoken words are made up of syllables ('snowman' breaks up into 'snow' and 'man') and individual sounds (dog is made up of d-o-g). Children do not usually manage to split the individual sounds until they are about five years old, but they do tune into the separate syllables and manage to hear the beginning and end sounds of words.

In order to master the sound system, children need to be able to hear the words clearly and have plenty of practice in speaking, without being pressured to say words correctly. Help and encouragement means that most seven year olds will have mastered all the sounds they need. Even when children are five or six years of age, a few problems are not unusual, although early years practitioners and parents should not wait too long to see if your support will solve the difficulty. Languages often have some more difficult sounds or combinations. In English, the tough groups tend to include sounds made with the letters 's', 'f' and 'th' or 'r', 'l', 'w' and 'y'.

Key term

Phonological awareness the understanding that spoken words are composed of separate syllables and sounds

Supporting the development of children's communication

In this section you will find many specific suggestions on how to help children's communication at different ages and through a variety of activities and opportunities. However, there are some practical guidelines that apply across every situation and these relate to how you behave as a communicative and interested adult.

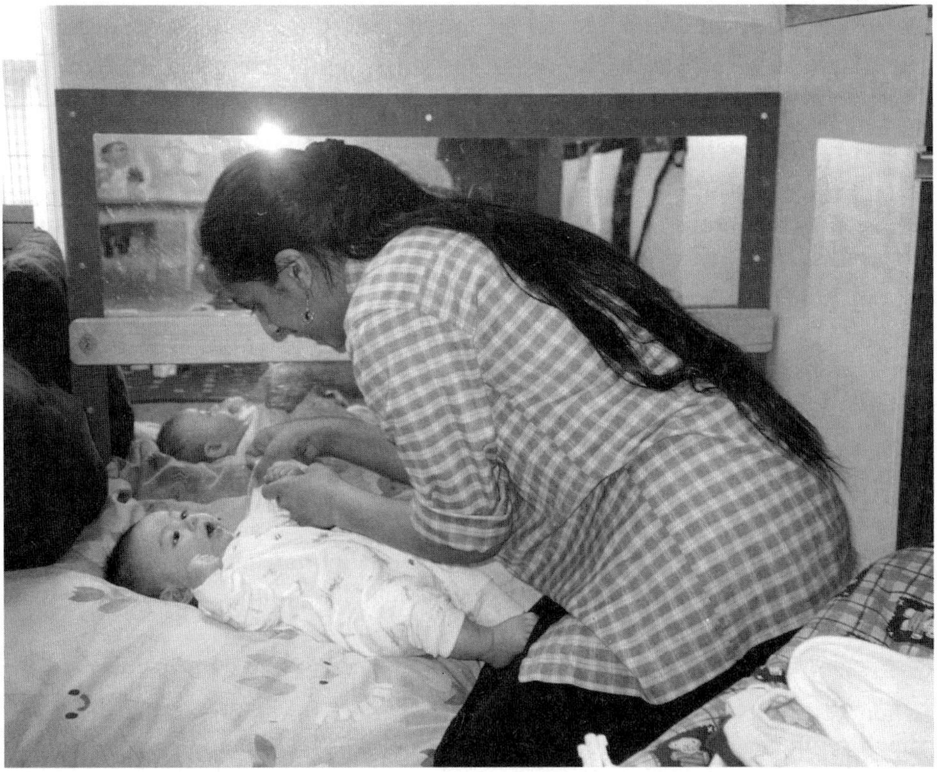

Figure 11.5 Warm communication with babies is so important

Tips for practice

- Be close to babies and children and at their eye level. Show your interest and pay attention. Children will then believe that you are genuinely interested and will imitate your attentive behaviour.
- Create an environment in which it is easy to attend: listening and looking. Sometimes enjoyable activities will be higher volume but children cannot communicate if noise levels are always high. Everybody just learns to shout.
- Avoid continuous background noise of any kind. Children can enjoy and learn from music and selected tapes or television that are a clear cut activity. Children are not 'stimulated' by non-stop background music, radio or television. It turns into sound wallpaper and is no longer distinctive as a pattern of interesting sounds.
- Set a good example in communication. Children learn to listen because they have experienced adults, and other children, who have listened to them. They learn to hold genuine conversations because adults have shown an interest.
- Be even handed in your communication with boys and girls. Boys may show less interest in conversation if adults rarely talk about what interests the boys.
- If you are not yourself bilingual, then recognise that learning more than one language in childhood is normal for many children around the world. Children benefit from help but being bilingual is *not* a 'problem'.

Very early communication with babies and toddlers

Babies are ready for social interaction and basic communication exchanges with their carers from the earliest weeks and months. They look and listen and are keen to take part in the give and take that can become a very early 'conversation'.

Use infant directed speech

Key term

Infant directed speech
the adjusted form of language used by adults and some older children to communicate with babies

Babies respond well to **infant directed speech**, a form of communication that is adjusted to the interest and hearing of babies. You communicate through infant directed speech when you:

- Speak slightly higher pitched than your normal speaking voice. You just pitch up a bit – not so much as to sound like a cartoon character!
- Go at a slightly slower pace than conversation with older children and certainly more slowly than with adults.
- Make pauses in which you look expectantly at the baby as if to say, 'Your turn now'.
- Keep what you say simple and say it in short phrases.
- Talk with simple repetitions and a circling quality to what you say, for instance, 'Well, how are you? You've just woken up. You've woken up from a nice sleep. Did you have a good doze then?'
- Speak with extra expressiveness, compared with normal conversation.

When you watch somebody who is at ease with babies, you will observe how they use infant directed speech and how much babies like and respond to this affectionate communication. Adults, and older siblings, who adjust their speech patterns for babies and toddlers in this way are also paying close attention to the younger ones. This behaviour creates a warm relationship within which babies can feel secure and will learn.

This adjusted form of communication was initially called 'motherese', because the researchers who identified the pattern only observed mother and baby pairs in their research project. The term is inaccurate since infant directed speech is not only used by mothers. Both men and women, and also older children, are capable of this kind of sensitivity to the needs of babies.

Activity

- Practise using infant directed speech with a baby of between 3 and 6 months.
- Follow the ideas in this section to engage the baby's attention.
- It does not matter what you say, babies are interested in any 'topic'. The key point is to have a happy turn taking exchange.
- Present your ideas to colleagues.

Key skills links: C2/3.1a

Listening and talking with children

Young children need to hear words used clearly in a relevant context so that they can:

- understand the word and link it to familiar events, people and situations
- imitate the word, with understanding
- spontaneously use the word in context.

In this way, new words and phrases become part of the active vocabulary of young children.

Unless children are delayed in their language development, you would not set out to help them learn a list of words. You simply use all the opportunities in daily routines and play. Of course, you should not deluge children with so much of your talk that they cannot get a word in edgewise. Be wise, listen and look and use those opportunities that arise. You can:

- Name what you are doing or giving a child, for instance, 'Here's your shoes' or 'Are you ready for more apple?'
- Comment naturally on the choices of a toddler that are shown by gesture or very early words. For example, 'Yes! Here comes Mummy' or 'Do you want the book? You'd like Spot again?'
- Keep your words simple and closely related to what is in front of you and a young child. Use gestures to support your words.
- Respond positively to the toddler's own version of words but there is no need for you to use 'baby' versions like 'gee-gee' for 'horse'. Respond to the child's own words but do not introduce bikky for biscuit on the grounds that it will be easier to say – it may not be.
- Expand appropriately on what a young child says. For example, a child's comment of 'Paul coat' can be expanded with, 'Yes, that's Paul's coat'.

As young children learn words and phrases you can build on what they know already:

- Make communication a two-way experience, even with the youngest child. You need to talk with children but you need to listen just as much. Children who are 'talked at' do not learn to communicate so easily.
- Use child-focused timing and go at the child's own pace. Look expectant as you wait for a child's reply in gesture and words.
- Talk with young children as individuals and use their name. Under threes do not learn well by being treated mainly as a group member rather than an individual.
- Talk directly with children and listen to their views about topics that interest them. Young children are focused on the here and now.

Children will make many mistakes in pronunciation and usage of words. It does not help to correct them in a critical way but children learn from accurate language feedback.

- If children have their own way of saying a word, then do not imply that they are wrong. Say the word clearly and correctly as you reply.
- So, if a child hands you a spoon and says, ''poon' then you can say, 'Yes, it's a spoon. Thank you.' If a child calls a train a choo-choo, then reply with, 'Yes, it's a train, it goes choo-choo' and maybe do the movements.
- You can suggest or give children words if they are struggling ('Is it the ... that you want?')

Figure 11.6
Young children simply enjoy a chat

Sensible use of questions

Questions have a place in communication: from the child to you and from you to the child. But you do not want your use of questions to unbalance communication. Questions come in two broad types:

- Closed questions to which there is really only one answer, such as 'Do you want some more mashed potato?' or 'What shape is this?'
- Open-ended questions to which there could be a number of possible answers, such as 'you know a lot about sharks, how did you find out so much?' or 'how are we going to catch that rabbit?'

There are times in the day and daily routine when you need to ask sensible closed questions about food preferences, choice of stories or songs or the practical questions such as, 'Do you remember where we keep the rolling pins?' Sometimes early years practitioners are tempted to use many closed questions to check a child's learning or to extend play in directions that make sense to an adult. Children feel under pressure if they are asked many of these testing questions, such as, 'What colour is this car?' or 'how many bricks have you got?' Children do not mind a few of such questions but they soon shut down their attention if they cannot play anywhere without having an adult question them.

Over use of questions usually arises when early years practitioners are keen to extend children's learning and not relaxed enough to go with the flow of what emerges from a routine or play activity.

To think about

You can make comments and share ideas as well as ask questions. But do not overdo the commentary. Bernadette Duffy tells a valuable story against herself in her book on creativity. She tells how five year old Shayma brought a drawing but held it behind her back. The exchange went as follows:

Shayma:	I want to show you something
BD:	Oh let me see, show me.
Shayma:	*But* only show you if you promise not to ask me to tell you about it
BD:	What do you mean?
Shayma:	Every time I show you something you say, 'Oh it's lovely, do tell me about it!' Sometimes I just want to show you my drawings, not tell you about them, sometimes they're for looking at.

What could you learn from the cautionary tale that Bernadette Duffy has shared?

Source: Bernadette Duffy (1998) *Supporting Creativity and Imagination in the Early Years* Open University Press (p. 100).

- Ensure that your use of language is not biased to question asking. Look at page 302 on children's use of language. Are you using all these ways to communicate?
- Ask questions to which you do not know the answer and where you would like to know that answer. For instance, you might ask, 'how did you manage to get that lovely swirly pattern?', 'which route shall we take to the market today?' or 'I wonder why Flopsy keeps running away today'.

- Be sparing with any testing questions because children do not learn faster, or at all easily, by being asked many questions by adults who want to check whether a child knows something. A good guide can be to consider whether you would ask an adult this question.

Promoting children's conversations

The skills needed for a conversation include talking, listening, linking what you say to what the other person has just said and being patient to wait your turn. Children can learn these skills and you can help:

- Have quiet time and quiet areas indoors and outside where children and adults can just chat together.
- Model good social skills yourself by listening, taking turns and showing a genuine interest in what a child wants to introduce into the conversation.
- Go with the flow of a conversation rather than directing it for adult ends.
- Be willing to contribute personally yourself if a child asks you questions like, 'Did you have a nice weekend?' (a question we often ask of children).
- Help children to take turns in a conversation when they find it hard. You can gently say, 'Hold on a moment. Theo hasn't finished yet ... now you're on, Jessica.'

Conversations flourish in an interesting early years environment. Children enjoy talking about real events, solving real problems in the setting, exchanging views and experiences and reminiscing about happy shared past experiences. Sometimes children will want to explore sensitive experiences with you through a conversation. Supportive communication can help children who face distress or major changes in their lives and this area is covered on page 220.

Communication in a group

Early years settings often have a time of the day when children are brought together in a group for stories, songs or guided conversation about issues – see the discussion about circle time that follows. A group time can work for children but it requires some thought by adults, including a realistic perspective on what the experience is like for the children.

- Under threes and certainly under twos cannot make sense of group time. Their communication skills are geared to enjoyable one-to-one talking and listening and they cannot manage the waiting time involved in even a small group.
- Three, four and five year olds can enjoy a group time, so long as the group is not more than 8–10 children maximum with an adult. If you are trying to run larger groups it is better to divide and assign an adult to each small group.
- Larger groups (see the example in the scenario) are too distracting for physical reasons: children are often squashed together on a mat, with somebody's elbow in their back. Discomfort does not promote enjoyable communication.
- The problem with large groups is also that children have to tolerate a very low level of interaction with the adult. Children need to have opportunities to express their thoughts in spoken words (see page 302) and in a large group calling out and not waiting becomes 'disruptive behaviour' rather than an expression of interest.

Scenario

The team of Greenholt Pre-school has been re-thinking the group time that has been part of the routine in the setting.

It has been usual that all the children, sometimes as many as 25, are brought together on a large mat for a story and discussion at the end of the session. There are some very articulate children in the current group and Marjorie has become concerned that group time has become too much 'crowd control'. Furthermore some children are being seen as 'demanding' and 'disruptive' because they are so keen to express views and share personal experiences. In a team meeting, Trisha also points out that none of the adults would feel able to concentrate if they were sitting so much on top of each other and were told off for speaking out of turn. Stephanie also suggests that they should stop calling this part of the day 'circle time' unless they are able to run the activity properly.

The team experiment with creating three groups and taking one group each, rather than all sitting together. They plan ahead to cover similar, although not identical discussion topics in the smaller group time, but allowing children to choose different books for a story. The smaller groups soon work much better. The children have more scope for contribution and any waiting time to express opinions and thoughts is much reduced. Marjorie, Stephanie and Trisha find they now enjoy the group time much more; it feels like enjoyable interaction rather than control.

Questions

1. How large a group do you and your colleagues try to run? If you spend a lot of time telling children to be quiet or wait, then the group is probably too large.
2. Step back and try to look at group time with a fresh perspective. Would you be able to concentrate under the group time conditions for the children?
3. Discuss and plan some possible changes with your colleagues.

Key skills links: C2/3.1a

Using circle time to promote communication

Circle time is a set time in the day when you sit comfortably with the children in a small group to talk about or show something of interest. Circle time works when practitioners in early years settings or schools have a plan of what they will do in this time over the days and weeks. Children then need to be allowed to influence the actual flow of conversation each day.

There are many good ideas for themes and activities in circle time (see the information box below), but these only work through the ground rules of considerate communication. Three and four year olds can begin to understand and practise good communication skills of:

- listening to each other: using their ears and waiting their turn
- looking at each other with their eyes – because we learn by looking as well as listening

- speaking to express ideas, views and feelings
- thinking with their minds and then expressing those thoughts
- concentrating by looking and listening to the adult and to friends.

Positive communication skills are the foundation for an enjoyable circle time and you need to set a good example through your own behaviour. For instance:

- Help children to take a turn in speaking by passing a talking stick or establishing a rule that all speakers – adults too – need to have teddy on their lap.
- Affirm children as they use good skills, including, 'Dorcas, thank you for waiting' or 'Maria, that's a good idea. I can hear that you've been thinking hard'.
- If children find it hard to speak up, they may be able to talk through a puppet of a happy/sad paper plate face.
- Take suitable opportunities to express your feelings and opinions, without of course tipping the balance away from children's communication. You might want to use circle time to thank children for their kindness to you when you broke your arm.

It is very important that circle time is run in a courteous way that models good communication. Certainly circle time should not be used to tell children off in front of their peers. Even when children go against the communication ground rules, you need to alert them in a considerate way. For instance, if two children are whispering to each other and not listening, then you need to restate the rule positively, with a comment like, 'Whispering stops us hearing what each person is saying. Let's try that again'. Circle time can also be used to promote positive behaviour (see page 496).

Find out more

You can find a wide range of useful materials about circle time from these publishers:

1 Lucky Duck Publishing Ltd tel: 0117 9732881 website: *www.luckyduck.co.uk*

2 Jenny Mosley Consultancies tel: 01225 719204 website: *www.circle-time.co.uk*

- Both sites give information about publications to buy.
- The Jenny Mosley Consultancies website has some material you can download. Access some items and plan how you could use the ideas in your own practice.

Key skills links: IT2/3.1–3

Key terms

Bilingual children children who are able to, or are in the process, of learning two or more languages

Simultaneous bilingual learning when children learn two languages at the same time from a very young age

Bilingual children

Bilingualism has a long history in the UK with speakers of Welsh, Scottish and Irish Gaelic. More bilingual families arrived as a result of migration to the UK from other parts of the world during the second half of the twentieth century. Depending on their family experience, children learn to be bilingual in one of two ways:

- **Simultaneous bilingual learning**: children learn two languages most likely within their family from a very young age.

- **Successive bilingual learning**: children, who have a good grasp of their family language, then learn a second language when they join an early years setting or go into school.

Diversity of languages is a reality in many urban areas of the UK. Some cities have primary schools where 90 per cent of the children are bilingual. In London it is estimated that more than 300 different languages are spoken across the city and some schools have 40–50 languages represented in the families whose children attend.

Key term

Successive bilingual learning
when children who have a good grasp of their family language, then learn a second language

To think about

A living language is part of cultural identity. A generation ago the future of Welsh looked precarious, since it was spoken only in limited areas of the country. However, a commitment to promote the language, backed by government finance, has made Welsh one of the most successful of Europe's regional languages, spoken by more than half a million of the country's three million inhabitants. The commitment was reflected in making Welsh prominent in the national curriculum for Wales and a system of dual language on road signs and official documents.

Tips for practice

You may be asked for advice by a parent in a bilingual family about the best approach for a very young child. The general guidelines are that:

- Young children are clearly capable of learning two languages and bilingualism has only been seen as a 'problem' by adult monolingual speakers.
- Children who are becoming bilingual sometimes go through a period where they muddle words or grammar between the two languages. But bilingual children soon reach the same level of language ability as their monolingual peers.
- Children need to have the languages clearly distinguished. It helps if one parent or another relative is consistently the person who speaks one language to the child. The second language is consistently spoken by another member of the family.
- It is best if adults speak their most fluent language to the child.
- Children also benefit from time spent with child speakers of the language as well as adults. Children use any language in different ways from adult speakers.

Helping children to learn an additional language

Many children learn English as an additional language (EAL) in an early years setting or on entry to school. Children have an immense capacity to learn but they do not just 'pick up' a second language, or in some cases their third language, without some help.

Children will feel reassured when early years practitioners take the trouble to learn some words of greeting and comfort in the child's first language. Some settings will be fortunate and have a fluent speaker of the family language on the team. But often, especially in urban areas with great ethnic diversity, there will be many languages that no team member speaks. A range of mail order companies offer useful resources to support your work, including dual language books for adults that provide useful words and phrases for you to learn and use, when you do not know the child's home language, multi-language signs, wall friezes and posters. See page 672 for a list of organisations.

Confidence in English as a shared language will open up real possibilities for children and the process can respect and acknowledge the family language(s). You can help in all these ways:

- Remember that a three or four year old learning a second language is in a very different position to a one year old learning the first. Look at the section on two to five year olds (page 299) and remind yourself that the potentially bilingual child has these ideas and abilities in his or her first language. The challenge is to express ideas, wishes and feelings in a new language.
- Children will assume that the words they hear are directly relevant to what they see in front of them. You can help by ensuring that you talk about the objects, events and activities that children can see and hear at this moment.
- Use your non-verbal communication of looking, pointing and gestures to support what you say.
- Keep your language simple and sentences short. You need to speak appropriately for the age of the child but communicate small amounts at a time. Speak at normal volume and avoid 'broken English'; the aim is to be clear and simple.
- Do not press children to talk in English. It is usual for children to spend time, perhaps a long time, listening before they speak. Encourage them by involving them by words, smiles and gestures. You will observe their interest and attention. Children who are listening and looking will take in language information and start talking when they are ready.
- At that point, you need to encourage children to talk and not worry too much about correct formats. Accept what they say and rephrase it if necessary as you make your next contribution to the conversation. Let children hear clear and correct language from you and they will self correct themselves, so long as they feel secure in your setting.
- Children who are becoming bilingual often imitate useful phrases that are common in an early years setting, such as, 'good morning', 'well done', 'let's have a look at ...'. When you listen to young bilingual children you will hear your most used phrases. The rhythm and repetition of songs and chants will also help the children.
- Children need to play happily with other children. They will sometimes gravitate towards speakers of their family language and it would be wrong to discourage chosen friendships. But try to look as well for ways to promote friendships across the languages.

Activity (observation)

Young children in play use non-verbal clues to follow play and their friends can then help them. But what are the most useful phrases for a child to learn in order to support play?

- In your setting, listen in to exchanges between three and four year olds who share a language.
- Make a note of any common phrases – they might be 'Can I have ...?', 'Do you want to ...?' or 'I've got a ...'.
- Share your observations with colleagues.

Key skills links: C2/3.3 C2/3.1a

Scenario

Dresden Road Nursery School has just admitted four year old Nur whose family has recently moved from Turkey. Nur's father is bilingual Turkish–English and her mother has some English but is far less fluent. Nur has one or two words of English and according to her father is very articulate and communicative in Turkish.

None of the Dresden Road team speak any Turkish and they wish to have a plan to support Nur as she settles into the nursery. The team have a list of questions to address:

- How can we welcome Nur and her family? They wonder about Turkish phrases they could learn – which would be the most useful?
- Are there ways to give a welcome and make Nur feel included by our displays, range of play materials, books and dual language signs in the setting?
- How can we encourage Nur to make social contact with her peers or younger children if she wishes? What activities could be least dependent on a shared fluent language?
- What could be the first useful English phrases for Nur to ease her social interaction?

Questions

1. Consider two or more of the issues that the Dresden Road team want to address. Draw up a list of suggestions for practical steps.
2. Discuss your ideas with colleagues.

Key skills links: PS3.1 C3.1a

Figure 11.7
Adult attention supports children's communication in different contexts

Difficulties in language development

Children vary considerably in when they show new skills in their language development and how they use their broad communication skills.

- Some children are quiet or reticent by temperament. Apparent 'limited language' may be more an issue about making sure that they have enough peace and adult attention to speak up with their comments or opinions.
- Some children's limited use of their language may relate to their limited conversational experience. You should be able to build this through a range of activities and attention to the children on their growing interests.
- You need a developmentally appropriate balance so you do not worry too soon but also do not miss difficulties that need some help.
- Some children are later starters on language than others but you need to ensure that you, and a child's parents, do not continue to think, 'he'll come along soon' when the months are rolling by.
- It is hard for unfamiliar adults to understand a two year old they do not know. But once children are past their third birthday, they should be understandable to an adult who speaks the same language with a similar accent, perhaps with a little bit of tuning, in time but not much.
- Young children do struggle with some sounds in the early years, especially those that sound similar, like *f* and s. With practice and adult patience and support, five and six year olds should be able to manage the sound range. Problems that persist with **articulation** and a wide range of struggles at a younger age need some specialist help.

Key term

Articulation
how children say the sound system that makes up the words in their language

Tips for practice

You should be ready to discuss any worries that you have about a child's broad communication abilities.

- First of all talk with your colleagues in an early years or school setting and your manager.
- You may decide that a detailed observation of the child would give you more information and perhaps put your concerns to rest.
- You also need to talk with the child's parent(s) in a relaxed conversation that brings in the parent's experience of their own child.
- In some situations, you will all have enough concern that another professional opinion, or help, will be appropriate. But it is the parents' choice to agree to a consultation or referral to a speech and language therapist. See Chapter 18 about the process of working with children with special needs.

Children who choose not to talk

Some children choose not to talk, although they are able to communicate. Children who make this choice are described as being elective (or selective) mutes: choosing to remain silent. You cannot make a child talk, nor should you try to put pressure on a child, however frustrating it may feel. One practical way forward includes:

- Talk with the child's parent and find out what the child is like at home. In some cases a child is communicative at home and even enthusiastic about the setting in which she or he resolutely refuses to talk.
- This information can put your mind at rest, although you may never know why the child chooses to be silent with you. Sometimes children feel ill at ease in an early years setting or simply would rather be at home.
- Try to relax and avoid getting irritated with the child. Continue to involve and invite her. Ignore the fact that she is not talking, but do not ignore her as a child. Welcome and include the child with words and gestures.
- If the child finally chooses to talk, take this change quietly and avoid any drama or questions of the child.
- Seek for any links with home through partnership with the parents. Perhaps the child would like to bring in something to show when there is a sharing in circle time. She could then show but not do any telling.

Stammering

When young children are learning to talk, their speech does not run smoothly all the time. Some three and four years noticeably stop to think of a word or start at the beginning of their thought once more. Temporary problems with **fluency** can get worse if children are put under pressure by impatient adults, but mainly children gain in confidence and language skills.

The British Stammering Association estimates that about 5 per cent of children under five years have difficulties with fluency that are severe enough to call a stammer. The difficulty is about four times more common with boys than girls. Most children emerge with adult patience and support and become more fluent in their speech, but about 25 per cent do not stop stammering and need some specific help from a speech and language therapist.

Key term

Fluency
how easily a child's speech flows. Some problems of fluency are a normal part of early language development

Stammering shows in different kinds of difficulty with fluency in a child's speech.

- Children may have trouble starting what they wish to say. Sometimes you see the silent struggle for several seconds before the first words come out in a rush.
- Children may develop a kind of non-verbal stammering as they struggle for words, for instance, facial tics, gasps or blinking.
- Their speech may emerge in a jerky way or they get out part of what they want to tell you and then stop.
- Words or sounds are repeated – like the first sound of a word (t-t-t-teddy) – or stretched out like verbal elastic (sssstory).

Stammering can become more than a speech difficulty, since the problem of fluency can undermine a child's confidence. Stammering sometimes runs in families and is found in many different languages and cultures.

Tips for practice

- Reassure parents about the importance of a patient approach, while acknowledging that the child does have fluency difficulties.
- Give the child time, show that you are listening, are not about to rush away and are interested.
- Slow your rate of speech to create a relaxed feel to your exchange.
- Avoid putting pressure on the child by your words, asking lots of questions or impatient body language.
- If the child raises the issue, then acknowledge that he or she is having some difficulties but show confidence that you will help the child.

You would not assume that all children with fluency difficulties would develop stammering. Giving children time, attention and patience will usually work well. Children should be referred to a speech therapist sooner rather than later for help if:

- there is a family history of stammering
- the child is having more general problems in learning to talk
- the child is distressed by his difficulties, showing severe struggles to get his words out or a great deal of non-verbal stammering
- he is learning a second language and is already stammering in his first.

Activity

- Find out more about children who stammer and how you can help.
- Write up a plan for practical activities, including positive adult behaviour towards children.
- You can contact:
  - The British Stammering Association, who offer advice and practical leaflets. You can reach the BSA at 15 Old Ford Road, London E2 9PJ tel: 020 8983 1003 helpline 0845 603 2001 website: *www.stammering.org*
  - The Michael Palin Centre for Stammering Children, Finsbury Health Centre, Pine Street, London EC1R 0LP tel: 020 7530 4238 *www.stammeringcentre.org*

Key skills links: IT2/3.1–3

Disabilities that affect speech

Children who are deaf

The National Deaf Children's Society uses the word *deaf* to cover all types of hearing loss, including temporary loss such as from glue ear.

Children need to be able to hear in order to learn to speak with ease. It is not at all easy to be sure whether a baby or toddler has some level of hearing loss because they may be adept at following non-verbal clues by gesture. Adults may reasonably assume for some time in the second year of life that this toddler is just a bit slower than average in learning to talk. It can also seem hard to get the attention of a very absorbed toddler, so it may be some months before it becomes clear that the child is unaware that someone has spoken to them.

If a child is deaf, then the sooner you are aware the sooner it is possible to start other forms of communication including learning signing systems such as Makaton. About 840 children are born each year in the UK with profound hearing loss and currently about 400, close to half of these children, do not have their hearing loss detected until they are more than a year old and a further 200 until about three years old. The distraction test used so far at the 8–9 month developmental check has been unreliable in picking up more than a proportion of babies with hearing loss. From 2001 the Universal Neonatal Hearing Screening test will be phased in for newborns and this test is far more accurate.

Ear infections and variable hearing loss

Children sometimes experience variable hearing rather than permanent hearing loss or a measurable percentage of loss. Variable hearing is a problem to children because adults may view them as inattentive or lazy. Yet the children do not know what the matter is; they cannot judge that they have variable hearing.

Ear infections should always be taken seriously because persistent infection can cause perforations (burst eardrums), which, although they heal, can leave scarring. Scar tissue is less sensitive to sound vibrations and reduces the quality of hearing. Recurrent middle ear infections can cause a condition called glue ear in which the eustachian tubes in the ear become blocked with fluid that has not drained. If the fluid needs to be drained by a doctor, they will often advise that grommets are fitted at the same time. These tiny hollow tubes of plastic allow the fluid to drain if it builds up again.

Finding out more

The NDCS (National Deaf Children's Society) has a wide range of leaflets to guide adults in how to help children who are deaf. Contact them at 15 Dufferin Street, London EC1Y 8PD Information and helpline: 0808 800 8880 website: *www.ndcs.org.uk*

Tips for practice

Some good practice that will specifically help deaf children:

- Use your skills of observation to explore any signs that a child may not be able to hear or that attention seems to vary from day to day.
- Gather information and discuss the situation with your manager and the child's parents.
- In partnership with parents, make contact with the Special Needs Coordinator (SENCO) for your setting or from the advisory team for your area.

Other good practice will have much in common with helping all children to attend and be able to communicate:

- Be patient with a child and ensure you have his attention by words, touch and gesture before you continue.
- Show, as well as tell, by gesture and words.
- Face a child on his eye level, speak clearly and a bit slower than normal speed. But otherwise speak normally.
- Speak at normal volume. Avoid raising your voice and definitely do not shout. Such changes make it more difficult for a deaf child to understand you, not any easier.
- Take your time and ensure that the child understands what you have communicated. Equally, make sure that you understand what a child has communicated to you. It is unhelpful to any child to believe adults have understood when they have not.
- Learn a form of **sign language**, such as the Makaton system that is mainly used with younger children. Continue to talk as well as sign. The child may be able to form words and your double communication serves to include other children.
- Encourage and help other children to learn to sign so that they can communicate with their peer.
- In group activities such as circle time, it can help a deaf child if everyone puts up their hand to signal when they are about to speak.

Key term

Sign language
a form of communication that uses agreed signs, made with fingers and hands, to convey words and concepts

Finding out more

The Makaton Vocabulary Development Project is a good source of information and runs courses on learning the Makaton sign system. Contact them at 31 Firwood Drive, Camberley, Surrey GU15 3QD tel: 01276 61390 website: *www.makaton.org*

Physical difficulties

Some children can understand perfectly and they want to speak, but physical difficulties are getting in their way. Children need to be able to coordinate the movements of jaws, lips and tongue to make different sounds.

Activity

- Experiment with saying different sounds and combinations of sounds to experience directly what happens with your mouth.
- For instance, what has to work with your tongue, lips and roof of your mouth to say, 'cat', 'ready', 'yesterday' or other words.
- It is useful to appreciate the combination of movements that are necessary.

Children with cleft palate may need therapy to help them to pronounce certain sounds. Children with cerebral palsy may need similar help because their condition affects their ability to direct movements and muscles (see Chapter 18). A speech and language therapist will help the child and should share ideas with the child's parent and with you so that practical help can be continued through the child's ordinary day.

Sight and communication

Children who are blind have to experience the world through touch, whatever sight they have, and the efforts of helpful adults to make direct links between what is said and what children can experience through their other senses. You should get practical advice from the SENCO of your setting or local advisory team about helping children who have total or partial visual loss. Some basic ideas are given in the tips for practice box.

Tips for practice

- Get the child's attention by using her name and other words before you move to any instructions or play. You have to keep recalling that the child has no visual information or the world is very blurry to her.
- Use simple commentary to tell a child what is happening as you help her with physical care, playing or moving around your setting. Your words and touch have to substitute for visual information.
- It is hard for a child to work out the naming of familiar objects when there is a confusing mix of real size and play size. Try to have real cups and plates until a child is able to understand about little and big versions.
- Help a child to feel safe moving around, because the lack of visual feedback and ability to check can make a child feel uncertain.
- Look at your environment and organise it so that a child with limited vision can learn the feeling landmarks and move around.
- Young children may need a lot of encouragement to reach out for toys or objects of interest. Help them move their hand out to feel.
- Visually impaired children need the information from their hands and the centre of the hand is the most sensitive.
- Help children to practise listening. Visually impaired children may fidget with their hands, so you may need to say, 'Katie, listen' and hold her hands.

Finding out more

The RNIB is a valuable source of information on supporting children who are blind or have some level of visual loss. Contact them at 224 Great Portland Street, London W1N 6AA tel: 020 7388 1266 website: *www.rnib.org.uk*

Non-specific language disabilities

Sometimes there is no obvious reason why a child is struggling with language development. Your observational skills and records kept in an early years setting will be important to identify children who may understand what is said to them but are not progressing in their own expressive communication through speech. Some children start to talk but do not manage longer sentences, persist in putting words in the wrong order at an age when their peers can manage or struggle to use words to express ideas. When such problems persist the child will need specific help and you and the child's parents will need some specialised input.

Finding out more

AFASIC is an organisation that supports children to overcome speech and language disorders: 69–85 Old Street, London EC1V 9HX tel: 020 7841 8900 website: *www.afasic.org.uk*

Further resources

Acredolo, Linda and Goodwyn, Susan (1997) *Baby Signs* Hodder and Stoughton.

Arnberg, Leonie (1987) *Raising Children Bilingually: The pre-school years* Avon: Multilingual Matters.

Murray, Lynne and Andrews, Liz (2000) *The Social Baby: Understanding babies' communication from birth*, The Children's Project.

Quilliam, Susan (1994) *Child Watching: A parent's guide to children's body language* Ward Lock.

Progress check

1 Describe three ways in which children and adults could communicate through body language.

2 Give four examples of how young children may make logical mistakes in their words or simple grammar.

3 Explain briefly what is infant directed speech and why it is important to communicate with babies in this way.

4 Suggest three practical ways in which you could help a four year old who was learning English as an additional language.

5 Describe three ways in which a child's disability could affect communication.

12

Supporting children's development of literacy

After reading this chapter you should be able to:

- understand the range of skills that children need in preparation for reading and writing
- encourage very young children towards an enthusiasm for books and stories
- work within realistic expectations for literacy learning
- support children in the early stages of literacy
- recognise problems in this area of development and support children.

Introduction

As well as grasping all the details of spoken communication, children also have to understand and use the written form of their language(s). The foundations for later literacy can start with babies and toddlers and their interest in books, stories and early mark making. With support, children can develop their interests and skills of literacy, both recognising the written word and producing writing themselves. This chapter will help you to gain a full understanding of this area of learning and to support literacy learning, without putting undue pressure on young children.

Links to early years qualifications

This chapter especially supports the following units:

Diploma in Child Care and Education: 2, 4, 5, 10

National Vocational Qualification in Early Years Care and Education

Level 2: C9

Level 3: C11, C24

BTEC National Early Years Diploma: 7, 9, 22

The development of literacy

Children who have become confident in the spoken word have another major task ahead of them, that of learning to cope with the written word: recognising and reading words and writing actual words themselves. Supportive adults need to acknowledge that this is a challenging task for children and to understand the many different skills that support literacy.

When will children become literate?

Obviously, part of your support is to remain realistic about the age at which children are likely to become confident in reading and writing. Some of the pressures in the English early years curriculum have raised the expectation that four year olds should be reading. A few early and enthusiastic readers do emerge at four years, but for the majority of children this expectation is definitely too early.

- With the kind of activities described in this section, four and five year olds can have grasped what writing looks like and be enthusiastic about learning to read.
- They can be interested in making meaningful marks and tell you that the marks say something in particular, and they may be able to write their own name.
- However, managing to read and write with confidence and fluency is a challenging task that most children will not start to manage until closer to six years of age. English is also a particularly difficult language in terms of spelling and grammar (see page 339).
- You will see children's skills and understanding improving over this period. Seven and eight year olds should be able to read and write, although some will be finding this easier or more enjoyable than others.
- Some children will be struggling, despite plenty of help. In this case, it is time for careful assessment of the source of their difficulties and planning of appropriate help, since the child may have a specific disability affecting literacy, such as dyslexia (see page 350).

Figure 12.1
Enjoyable mark making in the children's 'office'

A positive focus on early literacy

Views have changed over time about how children learn to read and write and what are the best methods to support them in this substantial task.

In previous decades reading and writing skills were seen as separate from the developments of early childhood. It was believed that children did not start on literacy until they were developmentally ready. This view is still appropriate, but not with the previously linked belief that no relevant literacy skills emerged until school age. The introduction of reading and writing was previously seen as a skilled adult task, undertaken only by school teachers. Parents and early years practitioners were actively discouraged from being involved in any way.

This exclusive approach was challenged effectively over the 1970s and 1980s. A focus on appropriate **early literacy skills** now highlights all the ways in which children steadily build the skills that they need for actual reading and writing:

- an interest in and enthusiasm for all kinds of books, stories and story telling
- understanding about how the written word is organised
- a sharp ear for sounds and rhymes, for the ways in which words are put together
- recognition of the everyday uses of the written word, that there is a practical point to literacy
- understanding that there are two written systems: letters and numbers
- enthusiasm for marking marks as communication with meaning
- physical practice with eye movements and hand–eye coordination.

Key term

Early literacy skills a blend of fine physical skills, understanding and a positive outlook that supports children towards being able to read and write

Tips for practice

- Parents and family are equally as important as early years settings and the child's primary school.
- Children's range of experiences will be individual and some may have a narrower range within their family, perhaps because parents feel that books are an expert task.
- As well as offering a suitable choice of activities in your own setting, good practice is to link with children's home experiences and to offer parents opportunities to become involved in children's early literacy learning, especially if they are not initially feeling part of the process.
- Children who learn to read more easily have had a well-rounded experience of language, both spoken and written.
- It is important to talk with and listen to children so that they hear and use language from an early age.
- Conversations support their learning of words and boost their motivation to make themselves understood and express ideas (see page 310). Conversations are also a valuable way of helping children to make connections between different experiences and to encourage them to explore further with books.

This section describes enjoyable experiences and opportunities that have all been shown to support children's later literacy.

Enthusiasm for books and stories

Appropriate early literacy involves enjoying books with and reading to children from a young age, from as early as babyhood. Sharing books engages children's attention and their interest. Children join in favourite stories and they choose their own books. Children learn to talk about the books they like and why and to discuss characters and plots in a simple way.

Books for babies and toddlers

Sharing books with babies and toddlers supports their future development in literacy. But you are definitely not pushing young children to be early readers – you need to be clear about this focus for yourself and in communication with parents. Relaxed enjoyment with stories and an interest in the book illustrations helps young children to feel enthusiastic about books. This feeling links with practical experience built up over time of how books work in terms of the same story line for the same book, turning the pages and talking about the illustrations.

In a nursery it is as important to consider how and where you share books with very young children as it is to think about what books you buy.

- Make looking at books and hearing a story a personal experience for babies and toddlers.
- Be physically close and enjoy a book with just one or two young children so they can be on your lap or right by you.
- Take your time and let babies and young toddlers touch the pages. If you have books with strong cardboard pages, they will take tougher handling. Many well known stories are available in board book as well as paper versions.
- Relax with a simple book and let children ponder the words as well as look at the illustrations. Avoid any temptation to rush a story just because it has few words.

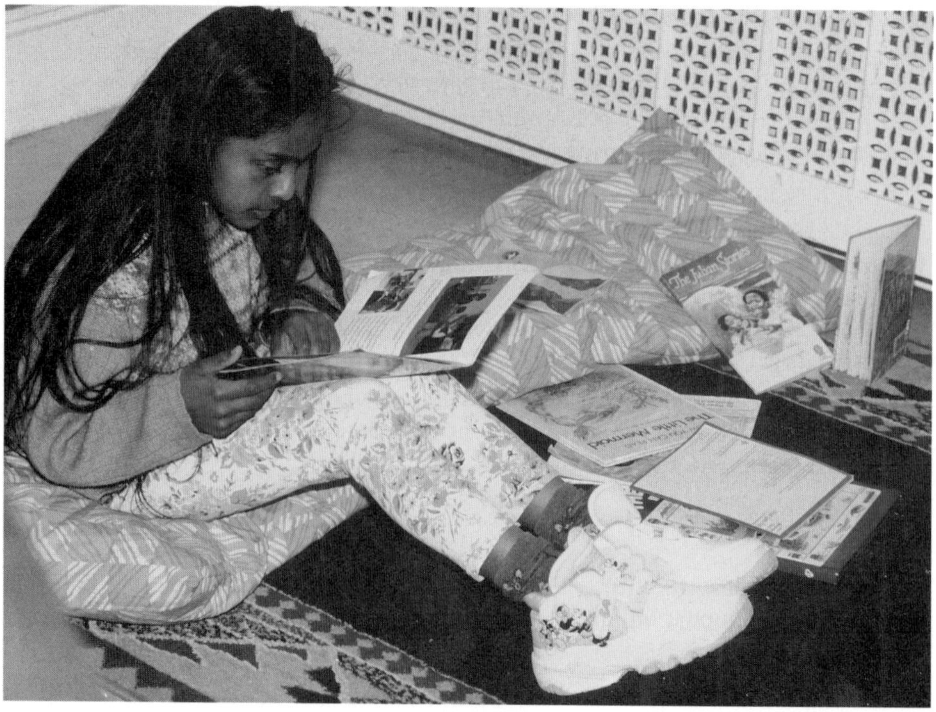

Figure 12.2
Your aim is that children become enthusiastic readers who enjoy books out of choice

- Toddlers, especially as they approach their second birthday often like spotting games with familiar illustrations. You can ask questions like, 'Where is the little girl?' or 'Where's that cat this time?'

Activity

- Find out more about Book Trust, the national charity that aims to promote enjoyment of books to people of all ages. Within the organisation, the Young Book Trust offers a service to support children and their experience with books. The Book Start project has promoted books for babies.
- Their leaflets are especially useful if parents in your nursery are dubious about the point of sharing books with babies and toddlers.
- Contact them at Book House, 45 East Hill, London SW18 2QZ tel 020 8516 2977 website: *www.booktrust.org.uk*
- Write up some key points about sharing book with babies, in your own setting and also ways to encourage parents, who may not consider books for very young children.

Key skills links: IT2/3.1–3 C2/3.1b C2/3.2

Activity (observation)

Robin Campbell tracked his granddaughter's absorption in books, stories and writing over her first five years (in *Literacy from Home to School: Reading with Alice* Trentham Books 1999). You will not be able to observe over such a long period, but try for regular observations of a child for six months or a year.

Select a toddler or young child with whom you will have contact, either through your work or personal and family life. Make sure that you have the parent's permission to make the observations and share what you have gathered at the end of the observation time.

Make regular observations of the child, say every month, and note down:

- The books that the child chooses and seems to like – what do they look at themselves or bring to an adult requesting the story?
- How many times does the child like to have a immediate repeat of the story?
- What kinds of books does the child like the best?
- How does the child handle books: choosing, looking, turning the pages?
- Does the child join in a story, perhaps with a repeating phrase or tell parts of the story to him or herself?

Compare the changes over time.

- What can you learn about the child's interests and how they change?
- What applications can you see for good practice in early years settings and working as a nanny or childminder in a family home?
- Share your main findings with your colleagues.

Key skills links: C3.3 C3.1b

Choosing a range of books

There is a rich selection of books for children throughout early childhood. An early years setting needs a good range and visits to the local library can ring the changes for a setting or a nanny or childminder working in a family home.

- You need story books with a range of different characters, for instance children and adults, animals and maybe some friendly monsters.
- Make sure that the illustrations reflect the diversity in families and your local neighbourhood, as well as showing people and places that are less familiar (see the activity).
- Books do not always need to have an actual written story. Toddlers and young children like books with a sequence of photographs or illustrations. The children will like you to tell a story to go with the pictures and will require that you tell it the same way each subsequent time.
- Young children like a simple story line that they can come to know by heart. Repeating phrases that recur in the story are enjoyable because the children can chime in with the phrase.
- Many stories are now available in the Big Book format. The larger text and illustrations are useful for groups, because all the children can see the pictures and the print. Big Books have often been associated with the literacy hour but they are valuable for any group story time.
- Children need plenty of books about topics, not all stories. They enjoy looking at pictures and photos of transport, animals, dinosaurs, sharks – almost anything from the world around them or imagination.
- Books can be about life events, either in story format or simple non-fiction to inform and interest children. You will find examples of such books in other chapters, for instance pages 222 and 223.

Figure 12.3

Children enjoy intimate story times

Activity

There are now plenty of books published that feature children from different ethnic backgrounds, strong female as well as male characters and children with disabilities. However, the rich choice is often not reflected in high street book stores.

- Explore your local facilities, book stores as well as your library, and find out how easily you can obtain books that feature:
  - children and families from a range of ethnic backgrounds, especially those that are present locally
  - strong female characters as well as male
  - children or adults who have a disability or health condition (fiction books, not books about the disability).
- Obtain the catalogues for one of these two mail order organisations that specialise in a wide range of books:
  - Letterbox Library, 71 Allen Road, London N16 8RY tel: 020 7503 4801 email: *info@letterboxlibrary.com* website: *www.letterboxlibrary.com*
  - Tamarind Ltd, PO Box 52, Northwood, Middlesex HA6 1UN tel: 020 8866 8808 email: *info@tamarindbooks.co.uk* website: *www.tamarindbooks.co.uk*
- Identify books that they offer – did you find any of these locally?
- Write up your findings and present to your colleagues.

Key skills links: IT2/3.1–3 C3.1b

A flexible 'story time'

Young children become enthusiastic about books because adults have made story time and use of books an enjoyable experience.

- Babies and toddlers cannot wait for a timed story time. They will learn to love books because you read and enjoy a book with them at the time that they pick a favourite book and bring it to you.
- Read the text expressively, using words and facial expression. You can use dramatic pauses like, 'And what happened then was ...' or wait a moment before you turn the page.
- Be ready to read young children's favourites again and again if they ask. You can add a new book from time to time but do not insist on all new.
- The repetition of familiar books is perfect for young children's learning: they exercise choice and the repetition helps them to remember. You will hear some toddlers begin to tell themselves the simple story to a favourite book.
- Younger children need stories that can be read in one sitting, often allowing several books in a story time.
- Children of five or six years can manage stories read in episodes day by day. Some of the books for early readers are suitable, for instance some of the simpler Roald Dahl stories. Children can support you as you start each day and recall together, 'Where did we get to in the story yesterday?'

Story telling

Good story telling is a bridge between speaking and reading and can be a source of listening and talking for children. You can explore story telling in different ways.

- You will know some books well enough to tell the story by heart. Try it.
- Story telling works well if you use a steady pace with pauses and use expressive gestures and facial expressions which hold the children's attention.
- Some stories lend themselves to audience participation in a question and answer format, such as what will happen next or who's hiding behind the hedge.
- Sometimes it will be appropriate to use a puppet or soft toy to tell part of the story. You may also like a prop if you are still building your own confidence as a story teller.

Key term

Storysacks large bags that include the props to support a particular story book and so to encourage interest and story telling for and with children

Neil Griffiths developed the idea of **storysacks** as a way to promote story telling and an active interest in books. A storysack is a large cloth bag with not only the book in it but also three-dimensional objects that appear in the story page by page. So you may have an animal or puppet figure and everyday items that appear in the story. You tell the story from the book and bring out the props as they feature. Storysacks can be purchased but Neil Griffiths' aim was that early year settings with parents and children would make their own storysacks for favourite books.

Activity

- Pick a book that you know the children like and look for items that appear in the pages. What can you collect or make with the children that could then be props to support the story?
- Create either a storysack or a storyboard and use it with the children.
- Explore possibilities using puppets from Puppets by Post, PO Box 106, Welwyn Garden City, Hertfordshire AL6 0ZS tel: 01438 714009 website: *www.puppetsbypost.com*
- Find out more about storysacks from Storysack Ltd, Resource House, Kay Street, Bury BL9 6BU tel: 0161 763 6232 email *storysack@cs.com* website: *www.storysack.co.uk*
- Find out more about storyboards from Dickory Dock Designs, Bridgemills, Huddersfield Road, Holmfirth, West Yorkshire HD9 3TW tel: 01484 689619

Key skills links: LP2/3.1–3

You can also enliven a told story or the narrative of a book with a storyboard. A storyboard is made with a piece of board large enough for all the children to see and to take a range of characters and illustrations. You cover the board with a textured cloth, like felt, and then make some of the characters and props from the book in cloth. If you can slightly fill some of them, it gives a more three dimensional image. Fix a piece of velcro to the back of each item. You then tell the story and add (or a child helper adds) each item as you reach that point in the tale.

Story through rhyme

Some books have a poetic pattern to the story and the rhythm helps children to tune into the words and to learn such stories themselves. Children also love poems, although when they are young, adults tend to call the poems nursery rhymes.

Saying and singing rhymes is not only enjoyable as far as children are concerned, it also supports their awareness of sounds and the sound system. Nursery rhymes encourage children to tune into the beginnings and endings of words and to hear similar and different sounds. The steady rhythm helps them to learn as they tune into the word patterns, and they develop phonological awareness that will support them later to learn to read and write.

Alice Sharp has developed the idea of **poetry pockets** to support the telling and enjoying of rhymes. Familiar rhymes like Incey Wincey Spider or Hey Diddle Diddle can be supported by props that appear in the rhyme. Children can be responsible for the props and making them do the actions of the rhyme; it does not have to be you who does all the actions.

Key term

Poetry pockets containers with all the props to support a poem or rhyme, in order to encourage the interest and involvement of children in poetry

Finding out more

Alice Sharp's Poetry Pockets may be available for purchase at some point in the future. At the moment you can read about the idea in her article *'Bags of fun'*, in *Nursery World* 26 July 2001.

Tips for practice

There are many ways to encourage children to feel enthusiastic about books:

- Ensure that any story time is enjoyable for children and make sure that they are comfortable. Have two smaller groups if one large group leads to distractions and interruptions.
- Be responsive to requests from children to read a story of their choice at times other than group story time. Settings can plan at least sometimes to have an adult available in the book corner. See how quickly a few children will gather!
- Read a story at a steady pace and be expressive in your voice and face.
- Be ready to use your dramatic skills to hold children's attention. Consider using props, storysacks and poetry pockets to promote greater involvement.
- Make sure that children all have chances over the week to choose which books and rhymes you will do today.
- Be willing to have repeats of stories, poems and rhymes that children enjoy.
- Take the children to the local library so that they can get the book borrowing habit and see an even wider range of books than your setting or home will be able to provide.
- Look at ways to make your book corner welcoming and to involve the children in keeping it easy to access and the books in good condition.

- Avoid using your book corner as a place to send children to 'be quiet' or 'calm down'. If you use this tactic, there is a high risk that children will associate the book corner, and books, with a feeling of constraint and being told off by adults.
- Be creative over ways that children can express their views on the different books (see the scenario).

Figure 12.4
Adults can make small group story time engaging

Scenario

Baker Street Children and Family Centre have been exploring different approaches to developmentally appropriate early literacy. The families who attend the centre are diverse in terms of ethnic group and social background. Some parents are very encouraging of their children's early literacy and some are keen but uncertain what to do. The Baker Street team have looked at activities that will engage the children but that also have the potential to involve parents who wish. They have several projects underway:

- Kayleigh has taken on the responsibility of running the 'Baker Street Library'. Children are welcome to take a book home each week and they have helped to make a simple card system in which they and their parents write or mark that they have borrowed this book. Several children are keen now that they make a special bag in which they can carry their book of the week.
- The team look for the opportunity to make scrapbooks with children of activities or local outings. The children have just completed 'our story

of the ducks' that arose from regular visits to the local park watching the ducklings grow up.

- The current project is to explore 'early literacy criticism' with the children, encouraging them to express views about the story line of books, their preferences for illustrations and the overall quality of books. So far the opinions are expressed in words, that the children dictate, and by putting books into one of three boxes: with a smiley face, a straight face and a downturned face to indicate judgements.
- The team have some dual language books and would like to promote the family languages of the children. Sian is able to tell stories in Welsh as well as English, but none of her colleagues are bilingual.

Questions

1. Consider the activities underway in the centre. In what ways can you see that these could support early literacy?
2. Make some plans for your own setting.
3. In what ways could parents be involved in each activity, if they choose?
4. Share ideas with your colleagues of ideas that have worked in settings you know or have visited.

Key skills links: LP2/3.1–3 C3.1b

Get some books out of the book corner

Ideas about the spread of books throughout an early years setting have tended to arise because of concern about boys and literacy. However, a creative approach to books as a resource benefits all the children.

Figure 12.5
The outdoor 'book corner'

Children need to see books as a source of information, to be consulted when they need ideas or to check something. Books can be useful in many ways in addition to being a source of enjoyable stories. You could put appropriate books in different parts of an early years setting as well as having a book corner. For example:

- Construction, design and technology areas: books about buildings and transport, with plenty of illustrations, ideas about projects to build and simple 'exploded' diagrams. Perhaps stories about building and constructing.
- Home corner: books to support pretend cooking, stories to read to dolls and teddies as they are put to bed, written material that would be in a home like a telephone directory or mail order catalogue.
- Office area: directories and material that supports the office area as it is currently used. For instance brochures for a travel agency as well as the equipment of phones and keyboard.
- Art and craft area: books with inspirational pictures and ideas to adapt, art magazines or books.
- Early science area: books about different aspects of science and basic experiments. Books with illustrations to support current displays like a wormery, caterpillars or a display of materials found on a trip to the local park.
- Maths area and around the setting: books to support counting, puzzle and pattern books, resource books about mathematical concepts like time or quantity. Any stories that raise these themes.
- When the weather is dry and warm enough, create an outdoor story corner with cushions, a range of books and perhaps some storysacks and/or storyboards that children can use to tell their own stories.

Activity

- Look at the possibilities for bringing books out of the book corner in your own early years setting. Or use a visit to a nursery or school to provoke your ideas.
- Prepare a short presentation, with photos if possible, and share what you have found with colleagues.

Key skills links: C2/3.1b LP2/3.1–3

Making books

Children enjoy making their own books and this experience offers opportunities for them to practise a range of skills in addition to the early literacy. Children use their creativity, apply skills of planning and discussion and use their physical skills of coordination.

- Books can be on paper, card or see-through plastic envelopes that are built into a ring binder. Stories can be told through a large wall display on strong paper or cloth.
- Children can compile a scrap book or visual record of outings, activities or interesting local trips. Illustrations can be laid out, with written explanations

that children dictate, partly write or completely write, depending on their age and abilities.

- They can create their own fictional story or an adventure for a character in a book they like.
- Some simple paper folding techniques can help children make pop-up, lift the flap or other multi-media books. Look at some of these books available commercially and choose some of the simpler techniques.

Beverley Michael (*Nursery World* 24 February 2000) offered creative ideas such as:

- A zig-zag book created by folding a long strip of card or stiff paper in even folds. The story is told with words and illustrations fold by fold and the whole story or poem is hung up.
- Scroll books can be created when you divide a long stretch of paper into even sections (by pencil lines). Children create the story section by section. Then you tape the top of the story to a piece of thick dowelling stick and roll up the story. It is pulled out to read by a tab fixed to the bottom of the sheet.
- Pocket books are created by having a series of paper pockets, or envelopes on each page of the book and something relevant to the story or poem is placed in each pocket.
- Box book mobiles are created by folding a long piece of card into four equal sections. Each section has one part of the four part story. Children can do illustrations, with or without a few words. Then the card is fixed into a box shape and string run from each corner to enable it to be hung up.

Dual language books

It is important for bilingual children to experience books in their family language as well as English. Another positive aspect is that all the children in your setting gain an understanding that some of their peers are able to speak more than one language. The over fours will have some recognition of the written form of their language and in some cases this will be a different alphabet and script from English.

Your local library should have a resource of children's books in different languages, especially if you live in a diverse neighbourhood. You can also use several mail order firms (see page 672).

To think about

Even very young children are ready to enjoy books, stories and rhymes. If children you encounter are resistant or unenthusiastic, then it is very likely that their experience of books has either been very limited (so they do not know how to use and enjoy books) or actually unpleasant. Children's experience of books is emotional as well as intellectual.

Perhaps children have experienced books only through uncomfortable large group story times or adults have cross questioned them about books or early reading. You then need to be creative about the use of books and stories in your setting so that you build enthusiasm.

Figure 12.6
Enjoying music

Music, singing and rhymes

Children enjoy music making, dancing to music and rhymes with hand movements. This playful activity supports children's physical skills including balance, attention and hearing. Children also exercise their memory for words, musical sequences and actions. Even young children are soon able to recognise a familiar piece of classical or popular music and the opening notes of their favourite dance song or nursery chant.

You can have sound makers and simple instruments on an open shelf for children to explore whenever they choose. An alternative for younger children, or to try if children do not seem to be interested in open choice, is to place the sound makers in a large container with a lid. Gather a small group around the container and open the lid with, 'Let's see what we've got in here!' Let the children look and choose their own sound maker, while you comment briefly on what they have chosen. Then move into a sound and music making activity.

Research has shown that an enjoyable experience of nursery rhymes and chants directly supports children's early literacy skills:

- The familiar sequence of words and hand movements helps children's communication and memory.
- The repetitive nature of rhymes, as well as repeating phrases in a favourite story, helps children to tune into the opening sounds of a word and to say the pattern of sounds clearly.
- They get practice in hearing words that start with a similar sound and words that rhyme in terms of their end sounds.

To think about

Some adults lack confidence in using music and singing activities with children. Adults may be at ease with art and craft activities, yet feel that you have to have a 'good singing voice' or be able to play an instrument to do music with children. Of course, you do not have to be a talented singer or musician, any more than you need to be a talented artist to do arts and crafts with children. Children are uncritical and simply enjoy the fact that you sing, do rhymes and story songs with them.

Discuss these ideas with your colleagues. If some of you feel uncertain about music, in what ways could you resolve your feelings? Chrys Blanchard (of the Natural Voice Practitioners' Network website: *www.naturalvoice.net*) suggests you could:

- Sing without any accompaniment (cassette or something on the piano), then you are not concerned about being in time with other music.
- Stay with a couple of songs you know well and sing them several times – children like repetitions anyway.
- Sing as a puppet or teddy bear that you hold on your lap.

Key skills links: C2/3.1a LP2.1–3

Tips for practice

You can use music and singing in different ways to help communication and support children's understanding of rhythm.

- Use music to reflect mood, so find some quieter pieces of music for times of the day when children rest or do quiet, thoughtful activities.
- Try out singing a welcome to each other on some mornings.
- Sing some simple instructions to help children focus on, 'This is the way we tidy books ...'.
- Music and movement activities can help children to attend: watching and listening.
- Making music with sound makers can help children practise patterns of sound, deliberate variations in sound and turn taking.

Learning about reading and writing

In order to cope with the move into written language, children need knowledge of the sound and the structure of their language. Two specific areas of knowledge are especially significant:

- Children's ability to recognise individual letters and to distinguish them one from another.
- Their awareness that spoken and written words are composed of individual sounds that make words when they are placed together in a deliberate way. This understanding is called **phonemic awareness**.

Phonemes are individual sounds. Children now have to learn what familiar sounds look like written down, and grasp that these do not have a one-to-one correspondence with actual letters.

Most four and five year olds have a large vocabulary for talking and understanding (see page 301). Their potential frustration as they start to read and write is that they do not have a clue how the words are written. That frustration can be significantly reduced when children have full experience of suitable early literacy activities. When children start to write they have to recall how a word is written in terms of letters and spelling. When they read, they can recognise the word on the page or on a notice. Children of four, five and six years of age can often read words correctly that they struggle to write from memory.

Key terms

Phonemic awareness
learning that spoken and written words are composed of individual sounds

Phonemes
the individual sounds that comprise a spoken language and that are written with combinations of letters from the alphabet

The tasks of learning to read and write

With time and experience, children have to grasp the important features of written material. These may seem obvious to you but that is only because reading and writing have been part of your life for so long. You will be a more helpful adult if you recognise the scope of the task that children face.

Understanding about written symbols

You need to home in on individual children's current understanding and help them on from that point. Recognise that the children are learning all of the following:

- The letters of the alphabet are symbols that stand for the sounds that children already know from spoken language.

- There is also a written system for numbers as the number itself (2) and the word (two) and children have to unravel that number symbols are different from sound symbols written as letters.
- Letters are put together to form words that build into sentences and which communicate meaning in books and other forms of written material.
- Words carry meaning and may support the pictures in a book, but it is the words that are read for the story.
- Print follows rules of format and layout and is made up of letters, words, punctuation and spaces.
- There is an order to how you print and read any language. English is read from the front of the book to the back, from the top of the page to bottom of the page and from left to right. But not all languages follow the same rules and bilingual children may already have some experience of different systems.
- There is a spoken language associated with using books – terms such as page, word, letter and front of the book.

Activity

- Look at the array of symbols in Figure 12.7.
- What do these mean? What are they?
- Make some notes yourself or use the activity with colleagues or fellow students.
- Now go ahead to page 342 where you will find a commentary on this activity.

Figure 12.7
Different kinds of written symbols

The physical skills of writing

Children also need plenty of practice in the physical skills that they will need for writing. These include fine physical skills, of course, but the large physical movements and children's confidence in their hand movements and overall motor control are all crucial (see page 256).

There is no advantage, and many drawbacks, for children when adults make them do 'proper' writing practice too young. Children tense up when they are made to do many worksheets, they develop an inappropriate writing posture and they find it harder when it comes to learn the flow of joined-up writing.

Supporting children

Learning to read and write successfully is key for children's later learning and achievement in schools. The most positive approach to teaching reading combines an equal emphasis on

- helping children to learn phonics: the complex relationships between the sound and letter system of language, and
- enabling children to gain plenty of experience in the patterns of letters that make up actual words on the page: that children recognise the letters and can form them through writing.

Activity

- English is a difficult written language to grasp (see also the Think about box) and helpful adults need to recall this fact.
- For instance, the words 'cat', 'circle' and 'church' all start with the letter 'c', but how are they pronounced? Say them out loud.
- The word 'fat' and 'phone' start with the same sound and 'rough' finishes with this sound. But look at the letters in each word and how two letters are put together to make a single sound in some cases.
- We should not be surprised that children get confused sometimes!

As children learn to read, they need some books graded for reading difficulty and a wide range of reading material, not all fiction, for personal choice and browsing. Children need plenty of practice, kind encouragement from adults and focused advice when they are struggling. Learning to read takes time and effort.

To think about

English is not an easy language to learn to read or write. For every rule about spelling, or grammar, there is almost always an exception. English has developed historically by drawing on many other languages for its vocabulary, and the relationship between sounds and letter combinations is complicated.

- In English we have 26 letters of the alphabet and these are the building blocks for writing words.
- But we have over 40 phonemes, which are the separate sounds that are required in total to be able to pronounce all the words in the language.

(The fact that I have encountered different estimates of the total of phonemes, from 40–44, says something about our language!)

- In English there are 1120 different combinations of letters used to spell these different sounds in the full vocabulary of the language.
- In contrast, Italian has 25 phonemes and only 33 combinations of letters are used in the written language to cover all these sounds. It is perhaps not surprising that the diagnosed level of dyslexia in Italy is barely half that of the United States or the UK.
- I am also told that Polish is a more straightforward language because it is written largely how it is said.

Realistic expectations

It is very important that adult expectations are appropriate for children over the major task of learning to read. Some of the early learning goals (ELGs) for communication, language and literacy in the curriculum guidance for England have created unrealistic adult expectations in the area of reading and writing. The ELGs are for the end of what is now called the foundation stage and some children are young five year olds at this point. The curriculum documents for Scotland, Wales and Northern Ireland include more developmentally realistic goals for this area of learning (see page 407).

It is not realistic to expect that most five year olds should be able to read and write a considerable number of words, even complex ones. Nor is it developmentally realistic that most five year olds should be able to form most letters correctly and use punctuation. Obviously, it depends on quite how these ELGs are interpreted in practice in English settings, but a more appropriate

Figure 12.8
Making marks and shapes in soft sand

expectation is that children are part way along steps towards these skills. Elizabeth Wood (reader in Early Childhood Education from the University of Exeter) undertook research into literacy teaching and commented in autumn 2000 that what was expected of seven year olds ten years ago was now being demanded of five year olds. Such a shift is particularly damaging for children when English is known to be a tough language to learn to read and write (see the To think about box on page 339).

The Literacy Hour

Since 1998 the national literacy strategy in England has required a structured literacy hour each day for children in school. The main features of this development are:

- Teachers are expected to provide reading and writing experiences for children at the level of single words, sentences and texts for a daily minimum of one hour.
- These experiences are offered in three broad ways: shared whole group writing and reading activities, guided work for small groups of children whose skills are at a similar level and independent work for individual children.

The hour is divided into four closely related slots:

- In the first 15 minutes the whole class works on a shared text.
- Then the class works for 15 minutes on individual words.
- The next 20 minutes is for small group work in which children either spend time with an adult on guided reading or work independently.
- The last 10 minutes are for the whole class to reflect and review what they have done.

There has been some confusion about how this method should be introduced, with some early years settings trying to introduce sit-down whole group sessions with three and four year olds. Such methods do not work with young children and carry a high risk of making them dislike literacy activities. Good practice with children up to five years of age is as follows:

- Use all the ideas given in this chapter to help children learn and enjoy early literacy activities. Keep those activities varied, meaningful for children and as natural extensions of their play and interests.
- Avoid lengthy sit-down sessions with young children. The most sensible goal is to build up slowly so that, *at the very earliest*, children at the end of the Foundation Stage (the last term in Reception in England) experience the full literacy hour.

There are sound reasons to question a literacy hour in Reception at all and some early years professionals (myself among them) advocate that the literacy hour approach should not start until Year One. As an early years practitioner in schools, you will need to work within the framework set by that school. Some reception class teachers have held fast to an appropriate early years curriculum on literacy, supported by the Foundation Stage guidance in England.

When the literacy hour is used with children of six years from Year One, then it should be feasible to build on children's broad experience to give regular practice in all the skills for reading and writing. Learning to read and write does require focused practice and children will not pick it up without adult help.

Activity

Here is the commentary on the illustration and the activity from page 338.

The point of this activity is to help you have empathy with young children, as they tackle the whole area of symbols. You know so much about the written language, so it is your job as a supportive early years practitioner to grasp what it is like for children not to know what is obvious to you.

- There are three kinds of symbol systems in the illustration: writing, numbers and musical notation. You will have worked this out, but to young children, they are all different kinds of squiggles.
- Children have to work out that there is a system of written numbers as well as letters. You will have looked at the number line, identified three numbers, know that they are different from the symbols for = and + and realised furthermore that the answer to the sum is wrong!
- If you can read musical notation, you will realise these are the opening notes to 'Humpty Dumpty sat on the wall'. If, like me, you cannot read music, you will have said 'It looks like musical notes' and have to take on trust that it is for Humpty Dumpty.
- You may have said that the English writing is the 'same'. The two versions give an identical message but the capitals, or upper case, version has many different shapes from the lower case. Children need to learn that R and r stand for the same letter of the alphabet, although they look completely different.
- There are two kinds of writing that share the English alphabet. The second example in the list is Welsh and gives the message of 'Wishing you a Happy Christmas'. I took this phrase from a bilingual Christmas card. If you had seen the card, you would have guessed that the Welsh phrase said much the same as the English, because you understand that is how dual language materials work. Out of context, non-Welsh speakers have no clues to help them guess the meaning.
- The last example in the list is Finnish and probably was not understood by many readers. This term describes a kind of childminding in Finland in which several childminders rotate around their different family homes. This word is also a reminder that some languages have accents on letters, but English does not.
- The writing in an alphabet different to English is Bengali and says 'Welcome', except that, as a childminder kindly told me, I have got one letter wrong. I have left the mistake because it is a good example of the task that children face. I neither speak nor write Bengali. I copied this phrase carefully. But I did not know what was important, or even whether I was copying the Bengali equivalent of scribble writing or of ornate italic script.

What insights can you learn from this activity to help you to tune into the task that children face? Think about and discuss your ideas with your colleagues, or share some ideas with parents.

Key skills: C1–3/1

Reasons for writing

Figure 12.9

Early years settings can demonstrate reasons for writing

Children benefit from shared everyday activities and conversation that alerts them to writing as a useful system. You want them to have plenty of reasons to learn to write and to read.

Writing is all around them and of practical use. You can help children over time, there is no rush, to notice and recognise everyday writing that will make sense to them in their lives. They will recognise the overall shape of a word that has meaning to them before they have worked out all the letters. For instance, some three year olds and many four year olds start to be interested in:

- their own name and the letter that starts their name
- writing on familiar food packets and over shop fronts
- road signs and other writing on directions
- menus in cafes and restaurants
- writing that adults do: hand written notes, 'to do' lists and the informal observations that you make in an early years setting
- writing that adults receive: letters, postcards, celebration cards of different kinds, bills and emails.

Meaningful writing practice

You can build on children's interests so that they become motivated to do their own early mark making and gain the everyday experience that helps them to distinguish the word and number systems and to tell them apart. You can use opportunities that arise naturally for children to see you use writing, and think about what you write and for them to do their own mark making that will become writing. For example:

- Make a list with the children before you go out to the local market, to get seeds in the gardening centre or of books that you want to look for in a library visit.
- Involve the children in drafting the wording, any writing they can do and illustrations for letters that will go to all parents, perhaps asking for help with a project or theme.
- Let children carry messages in your setting: a written note as well as the words said to them.
- Involve the children in drafting and laying our plans for activities, 'we must remember' lists about what will be needed next week or making a menu or weather board that will last.
- See if you can link up with an early years setting in another part of the country, or even in a non-UK setting. The children can exchange letters and drawings. If your setting has an email facility then you could organise to communicate electronically.
- Go on a local print spotting expedition and invite parents to come along as well. Make a list of signs and written notices, or even better take some photographs and have copies done, so that children accompanied by adults can walk around and spot the various examples of print.

Activity

- Choose two or three of the ideas in this section about meaningful use of the written word.
- Plan what you will do with the children.
- Write up the activity, with the children's cooperation and include any samples of emergent writing or illustrations of an activity that they would like to contribute.
- Throughout this process look for opportunities to give children constructive feedback (see page 396).
- Make a short presentation to your colleagues.

Key skills links: LP2/3.1–3 C2/3.1a C2/3.1b

Tips for practice

- Let children see you think about what you write, perhaps speak your thoughts out loud.
- Sometimes write down ideas when you ask children for their contributions – perhaps for where you will go on your local trip tomorrow or requests to the cook for puddings that you all really like.
- Be encouraging of children's efforts and do not rush to correct their letter shapes. Give constructive feedback as children wish and make clearly written versions easily available.
- Help children to look carefully at familiar words and to recognise the whole word as well as recognising letters that are familiar.
- Children will often be interested in the first letter of a word or letters they know from their own name. Help them to build meaningful connections.

Your writing and spelling matter!

You need to be a good role model for the children, so it matters that anything you write is well drafted and correct, even when you are working with very young children.

- Make sure that the spelling of any displays, public notices or letters home to parents is always correct, along with any punctuation. You have the opportunity to set a good example.
- Some early years practitioners are uncertain about their spelling or punctuation and perhaps you were not well taught in your own school years. But you are working with young children; they will not criticise you.
- Use a simple dictionary; it is positive for children to observe that you check your spelling. You can say to children, 'I'm making sure that I have the letters correct in (name the word)'.
- Use a simple punctuation and grammar reminder and let children see you using it. Either make your own or try *The Ladybird Book of Spelling and Grammar*.

You will find some more practical ideas on page 465 in the discussion about report writing.

Mark making and emergent writing

Key term

Emergent writing children's first attempts to make meaningful marks that they relate to the writing they see around them

Long before children write recognisable words, they are interested in making marks with crayons and pencils. They will tell you that a set of deliberately made marks is their shopping list or a letter to Grandma. You can help in many ways that encourage children to extend the skills they have and take satisfaction in what they produce.

- Show that you take the children's early mark making seriously by keeping their examples safe, perhaps in a portfolio.
- Use individual examples, chosen with children's agreement, to create a wall display of several children's mark making. Use brief written labels and explanations to communicate with parents the many ways in which their children are on the way towards 'proper writing'.
- Children are often enthusiastic about nice stationery materials. Offer as wide a range of materials as you are able. Parents will often be happy to contribute notepads, post it notes, sticky labels or receipt books.
- Make sure that you have supplies of card and marker pens for when children want to make signs for their outdoor bus depot or display cards for the natural history museum they have created.
- You will make writing materials available on a graphics table but also anywhere else that makes sense in your setting. A clipboard and pencils could be left in the garage or office role play area, a notepad by the telephone or a shopping list in the home corner or an order pad for the waiter or waitress in the pretend café.
- Respond to requests from the children if they ask for writing materials like your own, for instance a notepad on which you make informal observations of their play.
- If you have the opportunities provided by a diverse group of families, then be sure to use examples of writing from the different home languages. Children and parents will feel more involved and children who are monolingual English will have a greater understanding of their peers who are learning more than one kind of writing.

Figure 12.10
Enthusiastic mark makers do not need to be persuaded to practice

Activity

- Try two or three of the ideas in this section about meaningful writing practice.
- Plan what you will do with the children.
- Write up the activity, with the children's cooperation and include any samples of emergent writing and mark making that they would like to contribute.
- Throughout this process look for opportunities to give children constructive feedback (see page 397).
- Make a short presentation to your colleagues.

Key skills links: LP2/3.1–3 C2/3.1a C2/3.1b

Tips for practice

- Look at children's early mark making with the same positive outlook that you should bring to babies' early sound making (see page 295).
- As Penny Tassoni has pointed out, children's first attempts at letters and the shape of what looks like writing is a kind of written babbling and cooing.
- It would be a foolish adult who told babies to 'Talk properly!' Yet children sometimes hear very discouraging remarks from adults who dismiss their emergent writing as 'scribble' or criticise young children along the lines of, 'You don't make a "d" like that!'
- If adults correct every early spoken utterance of babies and toddlers, those very young children become discouraged. You let them hear the correct version (see page 308) and treat their early spoken language with respect.
- We need to behave in the same way with children's early attempts at their written language.

Scenario

The team at Dresden Road Nursery School has looked at ways for children to be involved in any written activity that is relevant to them.

Recently, an information and request sheet needed to be done for all the parents. The children were interested in setting up a hospital in the role play area and needed 'medical' materials, leaflets and posters. Jessica worked with three children to draft a flier explaining to parents about the project and asking for help with materials. The children agreed the wording and the design of the A4 sheet. Jessica then wrote the words and the children added drawings. With Jessica's help, the children then worked out how many copies they would need, used the photocopier and handed out the flier at going home time.

Question

1 What range of skills have the children explored and practised on this project?

Suggested activity for you

1 Think of two or three similar planning and writing projects in which children could be closely involved in your own setting or one that you know.
2 Write up a more detailed outline plan for one of your ideas, explaining what the adult might need to do, what help could be offered to the children and the parts of the project for which children could take responsibility.
3 Present your ideas and the more detailed plan to your colleagues.

Key skills links: LP2/3.1–3 C3.1b

Young writers and readers

Supportive activities for children encourage them to use the skills they have and extend a little, without feeling under pressure to perform.

- When children are happy to have a go at writing their name, you can use 'sign up sheets' for some activities. These sheets have a simple layout with a heading that you read out to the children as well as write down clearly. It might be 'Who wants to do cooking today?' and children sign up for this activity.
- Equally this kind of activity can be done with name recognition, so that children move their name cards into a container.
- A system of self registration can support children's recognition of their names and maybe their friends' as well. Have each child's name on a laminated card. You can add visual information to help, perhaps the picture logo that marks a child's coat peg or a photo. Children, supported by their parents find their card and move it from a table to a simple container. Some settings have made attractive registration displays with the children, for instance, a child's name on a bee shape that is 'flown' across to be fixed to the beehive.
- All the experience of story telling (page 330) can be extended into story planning and writing. Children who are ready can begin to write down their own stories, fitting the writing into any of the creative book formats (see page 334).

If you work with children who can recognise some letters and words, you can create flexible activities that let them work with written materials:

- If you have a magnetic surface, then use a set of magnetic letters.
- You can set up simple messages yourself and encourage children to compose their own names or those of their friends.
- Sometimes have a letter scramble in which the letters of a child's name or well known words are moved about and children need to put them back in the right order.

- Have some ready done words and basic spelling. You can use post it notes on a flat white board. Alternatively, make words on card with velcro on the back and use a cloth board (similar to the storyboard base).
- Again you can put up messages and so can the children.
- You can also start with a clearly written short message with appropriate basic punctuation like a full stop or a question mark. Let the children see the correct version and then scramble it. The children can sort it out at their leisure.

Activity

- Try out two or three of the ideas in this section about practice for children who are learning to write.
- Plan what you will do with the children.
- Write up the activity, with the children's cooperation and include any samples of writing that they would like to contribute.
- Throughout this process look for opportunities to give children constructive feedback (see page 397).
- Make a short presentation to your colleagues.

Key skills links: LP2/3.1–3 C2/3.1a C2/3.1b

Children who can write will like a full array of stationery for different kinds of writing (see page 345). You can also offer hand held white boards for writing practice and having a go at words. Five, six and seven year olds often like the boards because they can wipe out their word and practise until they get it correct. The boards can be used as well as paper and pencil writing.

Children who are learning to write need plenty of practice as outlined in this section. Do recall that some children will now show a left handed preference. The potential frustration for a left handed writer of English is that their writing hand covers, and may smudge, what they have just written. Children have to lift their writing hand to check what they have done so far. See page 262 for an organisation that offers advice and some useful materials.

Helping the boys

Some children are not enthusiastic about reading because their experience of books has been limited or not an enjoyable experience. Positive early literacy experiences, like those described in this chapter, are vital for all children. However, it is becoming clear that such experiences can be especially important for boys, some of whom may decide that books, reading and study are all 'girly' activities and to be avoided. You can help in many practical ways:

- Ensure that you have and encourage the use of a wide range of books and written material. You want the children to understand that reading, and writing, are valuable skills for life in general. You do not just learn to read to stop adults nagging you!
- Boys, and some girls, can be more enthusiastic about information books (non-fiction) than stories. Make sure you have books that tap into the

children's interests (and borrow from the local library). See also the suggestions on page 333 about getting books out of the book corner.

- Be observant of which books the boys choose to hear, or to read themselves when they are able. If you offer to photo each child with one or two of their favourite books, what are the titles that boys choose? (See also other ideas on page 333 for encouraging children to express views.)
- Be encouraging about any reading matter that a child is motivated to tackle. Boys may be keen to read magazines about computing, computer games or sports. Makes sure that you are not 'snobbish' about reading matter and show a genuine interest in what the boys, and reluctant girl readers, want to read.

Teams in early years settings, and primary schools, are overwhelmingly female, so it is important to be creative about bringing in some male role models for the boys, and the girls as well.

- When you have a male team member, he should of course cover the full range of tasks, but it will be especially important that he is seen to enjoy reading and to use information books to find out about topics.
- Male childcare students or teenagers on work placement can be very good role models. Teenagers may also be up to date with characters from television or film that appear in books and would hold the attention of less enthusiastic listeners or beginning readers.
- Invite and welcome fathers, grandfathers and uncles into your setting and encourage them to be in the book corner as well as mend the bikes.
- Older brothers or older boys in primary school are sometimes pleased to read with and to the younger children.
- Watch out for story telling sessions or the appearance of authors at your local library, especially if there is a male story teller or author.

Figure 12.11
You want children to become enthused by books about topics

Activity

- Identify and plan ways that you could give children positive experiences that literacy is for boys too. Write up possible plans.
- Put one plan into action and make a visual record, probably using photos that could form a display. Consider carefully what you write as explanatory captions to any display.
- Discuss your ideas and show any display to colleagues.

Key skills links: PS3.1–3 LP3.1–3 C3.1b

Finding out more

You will find a good source of leaflets and posters about boys and reading from Save the Children publications, 17 Grove Road, London SE5 8RD tel: 020 7703 5400 website: *www.savethechildren.org*

Helping children with dyslexia

Some children have more difficulty than necessary with reading and writing because their early experience has not helped them in the ways described earlier. However, some five, six and seven year olds have had positive experiences and plenty of help and are still struggling. In this situation the children may be dyslexic. It is estimated that about 4 per cent of the population of the UK is severely dyslexic and the figure rises to 15 per cent if mild versions are included. The condition is three or four times more common for boys than girls and probably affects about 10 per cent of schoolchildren in the UK.

The word *dyslexia* comes from Greek and means 'difficulty with words or language'. However, many dyslexic children do not only have difficulty with the tasks of reading and writing. Children with dyslexia have a broad problem with information processing. They can experience any of the following difficulties and, like many learning disabilities, dyslexia can be anything from mild to very severe.

- The problems that flag up a serious difficulty will focus on reading, writing and spelling. There will be an obvious gap between what children can manage in tasks that require written communication and those which draw on the child's other skills.
- Children who are finally diagnosed with dyslexia may have broader difficulties in communication, perhaps they were slower than average in learning to talk.
- Children may have related attention difficulties because the tasks are hard for them, but they may also find it difficult to stay still and focus on what they are doing.
- Children with dyslexia often find it hard to organise themselves, plan ahead and sort out a sensible sequence in actions. So they need broad help in study skills.
- Some children have related problems with physical coordination, including being muddled between left and right.
- Some dyslexic children also have difficulties with mathematics, but certainly not all of them.

Dyslexia is a learning disability; it cannot be 'cured'. However, early identification and appropriate adult help can allow children to learn to cope and to manage written communication to the best of their abilities. A supportive adult response can help to protect children's self esteem and confidence, which can otherwise can take a serious downturn.

It is important that you take notice of parents' concerns about a five or six year old whom they feel is struggling with the written word. This concern will arise from their knowledge of their own child and should not be dismissed as parents being 'pushy' or 'over ambitious' for their children. This anxiety is very different from parents asking why their three or four year old cannot yet read or spell properly.

Tips for practice

- Be observant for indications that children have more trouble when the written word is involved or clear anxiety from the child about facing the tasks of reading or writing.
- Notice when five, six and seven year olds write their letters or numbers back to front and their peers make few such mistakes. Likewise when children still confuse the order of letters in words for which they have had plenty of practice.
- Talk with parents about their observations of their son or daughter.
- Show patience with the child and ensure that they are able to pay attention. Avoid any assumption or labelling that the child is 'lazy' or 'won't listen'.
- Keep your instructions simple and one step at a time, to avoid memory overload for a struggling child.
- As well as encouraging a child to persevere with efforts at hand writing, look for the possibilities of using a word processing package on the computer. The keyboard does not solve all the difficulties faced by a child who is dyslexic but it does overcome the step of having to form the actual letters.
- Be ready to get some specialist help before children's self esteem is rock bottom.

Activity

Find out more about dyslexia and how you can help by contacting these organisations. Ideally look first at their websites.

- The Dyslexia Institute, 133 Gresham Road, Staines, TW18 2AJ tel: 01784 463851 website: *www.dyslexia-inst.org.uk*
- British Dyslexia Association, 98 London Road, Reading, Berkshire RG1 5AU tel: 0118 966 2677 website: *www.bda-dyslexia.org.uk*

Summarise the key ideas and practical applications for your setting and make a short presentation to your colleagues.

Key skills links: IT2/3.1–3

Further resources

Arnold, Cath (1999) *Georgia's Story* Paul Chapman.

Hughes, Anne and Ellis, Sue (1998) *Writing it Right? Children writing 3–8* Scottish Consultative Council on the Curriculum

Ostler, Christine (1991) *Dyslexia: A parents' survival guide* Ammonite Books.

Riley, Jeni (1997) *The Teaching of Reading: The development of literacy in the early years* Paul Chapman.

Riley, Jeni and Reedy, David (2000) *Developing Writing for Different Purposes: Teaching about genre in the early years* Paul Chapman Publishing.

Whitehead, Marian (1999) *Supporting Language and Literacy Development in the Early Years* Open University Press.

Progress check

1. Describe three ways to help babies and toddlers develop an enthusiasm for books and stories.
2. Explain four ways to help three and four year olds to explore meaningful mark making.
3. Suggest three ways to promote books and written materials in order to encourage boys as well as girls.
4. Describe three ways that you could help children become alert to written language around them.
5. Suggest three ways that children could practise fine physical skills to support learning to write.
6. Explain the possible consequences for children's learning if adults expect them to be able to read and write at an unrealistically early age.
7. Explain briefly the signs that could indicate that a child has specific difficulties with the written word.

13

Thinking and intellectual development

After reading this chapter you should be able to:

- describe ways in which children learn to think from early childhood
- recognise and help children as they learn abstract ideas and ways of thinking
- support children's development in early mathematical understanding
- use information and communication technology appropriately with children.

Introduction

Children develop impressive powers of thinking through early childhood. It is important in all areas of development that adults tune into children's current way of learning and their understanding. This perspective seems to be especially difficult for adults when approaching children's intellectual development. It is too easy to assume that the child knows what we know or that a particular idea or application of knowledge is obvious, because it seems so clear to us. Early years practitioners need a thorough understanding of how children's thinking unfolds and a willingness to see the world through a child's eyes.

Links to early years qualifications

This chapter especially supports the following units:

Diploma in Child Care and Education: 2, 4, 6, 10

National Vocational Qualification in Early Years Care and Education

Level 2: C8

Level 3: C10, C25

BTEC National Early Years Diploma: 7, 8, 9, 12, 18, 23

Learning to think in early childhood

Key term

Cognitive development the area of children's learning that focuses on their ability to think, gain knowledge, develop ideas and reason in a logical way

The area of children's development that focuses on their ability to think, gain knowledge, develop ideas and reason is called **cognitive development**. There are several strands to children's thinking:

- The skills that support thinking, such as memory through recognition and recall of people, objects, events and routines.
- The ability to make connections between experiences and therefore to link up more than one strand of thought.
- Using ideas to reason about 'why', 'how' and sometimes, 'That can't be right, because …'.
- Understanding a wide range of abstract ideas that describe the world around them, experiences and events, and intangibles like emotions.
- Building up knowledge in the broadest sense and a framework in which to make sense of the information.

Tips for practice

From our adult perspective it can be difficult to tune into the intellectual understanding of a child, especially a very young child.

- Part of our difficulty is to put to one side what we know and understand as adults. You need to come afresh to the point that this child has reached.
- You need to imagine what it is like not to know or understand what is now very obvious to you.
- Children do not have your knowledge or grasp of ideas. What you know is not at all obvious to this child or this group of children.
- As a helpful adult, you need to think as well as observe the results of the children's thinking!

How do children think?

Theories about child development, in combination with the study of children, have tried to explain what is happening and how. This section gives a brief explanation of the more influential approaches and the resources at the end of the chapter will help you to find out more.

The ideas of Jean Piaget have been influential for early years practice in the UK. But it is important to realise that researchers into child development have challenged many of his proposals, especially about children younger than five or six years old.

- The exciting part of Piaget's view of children was that he saw them as active learners, making sense of what was around them and exploring in a deliberate way.
- The drawback to his approach was that Piaget tended to describe younger children in terms of what they could not yet do, rather than what they could manage. If you look at the examples given from page 358, you can see how much young children are thinking, so long as you value where they are at the moment.

Figure 13.1

Young children are thinkers and explorers

- **Egocentricism** was a key description in much of Piaget's approach to younger children. However, further study, as well as daily observation, has shown that young children are not as egocentric as Piaget claimed and are able sometimes to grasp the mental or emotional perspective of other people at a far younger age than he claimed.

Lev Vygotsky worked in Russia through the 1920s and 1930s and he made strong links between children's social development, their use of language and their thinking. Vygotsky felt that play led children's development because play enabled them mentally to step outside the restrictions of real life and to use their imagination. Piaget's ideas have tended to be used to suggest adults should avoid involvement in children's play since they could interfere. In contrast, Vygotsky was sure that appropriate adult help could support children to extend, so long as it recognised their current point of learning.

Vygotsky developed the idea of the **zone of proximal development** (see Figure 13.2) to explain how adults, or other children, could support a child's learning. The zone of proximal development is the area of possibilities that lies between what individual children can manage on their own – their level of actual development – and what they could achieve or understand with some appropriate help – their level of potential development.

Key terms

Egocentricism
the quality that Piaget claimed was typical of younger children, that they were unable to envisage a situation from the perspective of other people, what the other person could see or what they felt

Zone of proximal development
the area of possibilities between what individual children can manage on their own and what they could achieve with appropriate help

Activity (observation)

Use the ideas of the zone of proximal development to observe and then plan a simple way you can support an individual child to extend in an area of learning, not necessarily intellectual. What interests and motivates this child at the moment: buttoning up her coat without help? being able to read her name? climbing four more rungs up the climbing frame?

- Focus on what the child can do at the moment, her level of actual development in this skill or idea.
- What might be possible with some well chosen help from you? Plan what you will do and how, and carry out your plans.

- Vygotsky also noted that children can help each other. Look out for and make brief notes of times when one child helps another in play or a daily routine, such that the younger or less sure child learns something new.
- Share your activities and observations with colleagues. (You will find another application of this idea on page 000.)

Key skills links: C3.1a C3.1b

Jerome Bruner extended Vygotsky's ideas into the concept of the spiral curriculum. Bruner explained, and you can observe, how children over time return to the same materials or ideas but use them in a different way. For example, children from toddlers to school age often enjoy building bricks, but what they do with them extends in variety as they learn.

Key term

Schemas
patterns of behaviour, mainly ways of physical exploration, in which young children learn about their environment

Chris Athey developed Piaget's idea of **schemas**. These were the patterns of behaviour that showed how young children were exploring and learning at a given time. You will find a description of Chris Athey's ideas on page 260. The approach can be very useful to help early years practitioners observe the thinking of very young children through their play behaviour. The approach is used in some nurseries and centres to help practitioners and parents move away from the perspective that under threes are not doing much or not 'playing properly'.

Margaret Donaldson and her team approached the study of children's thinking from the perspective that children worked to make sense of a situation and that

Figure 13.2
Vygotsky's zone of proximal development – for an individual child at a given point in time

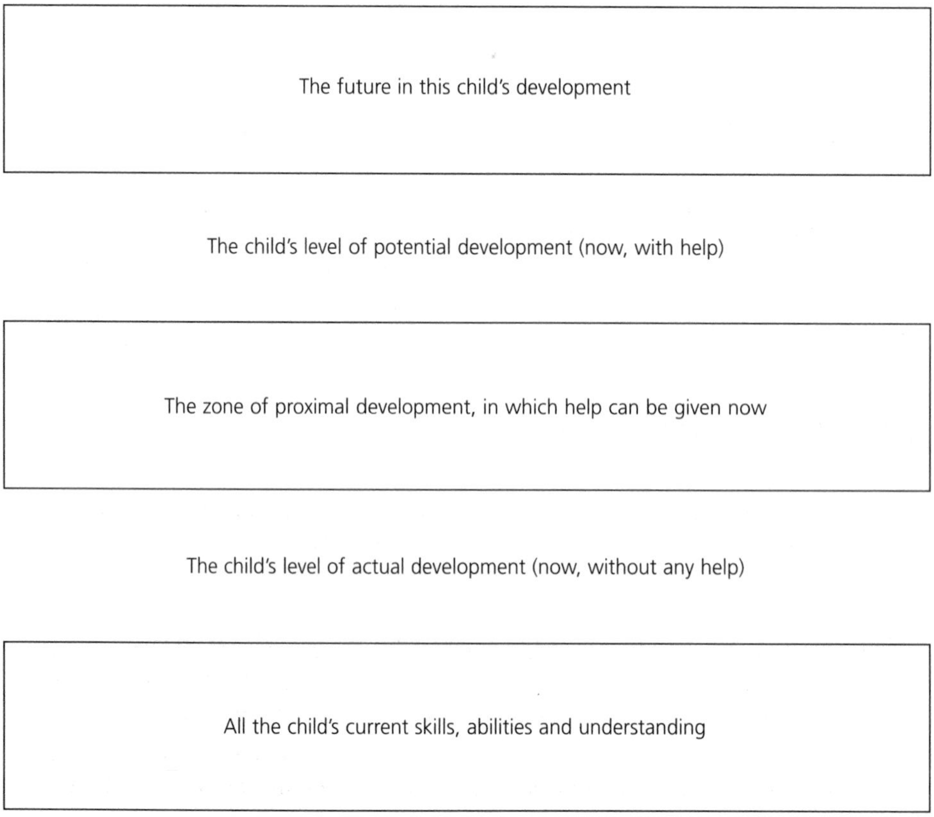

sometimes adults failed to grasp what a child had understood from that adult's questions. Margaret Donaldson has taken a very child-centred approach to the study of thinking. Her ideas highlight not only how young children think but also how adults can help:

- Children work to make sense of what they hear and observe and, in research studies as well as daily life, are sometimes confused about what exactly an adult is asking this time.
- The sense that children make of adult questions is not always the same meaning as that intended by the adult. For instance children asked to put a family of dolls in order do not necessarily do it by height. Sometimes they organise the family in a safe way for an outing, that is children are put close to an adult.
- Children are increasingly asked to manage what Margaret Donaldson called **disembedded thinking**, that is to handle ideas without a clear or familiar context. But children need to make connections to the knowledge and ideas that understand so far. Children can become very anxious and confused if their early years or school experience does not connect easily.

Key term

Disembedded thinking
when children are required to deal with ideas without a clear or familiar context with which to connect

Observation of children thinking

You can watch how the physical skills of a baby and toddler unfold, but how do you observe how they think? You have several choices:

- You watch what children do, how they react to situations. You have to be careful not to leap to conclusions; there is always an element of 'maybe', especially with younger children.
- You watch how they approach familiar and new situations and how they handle and explore play materials. Your alert observation will give you some strong hints about how children think their world works and the cutting edge of their learning at the moment.
- You listen to what children say and how they say it. Their comments and questions are a window on to how they think at the moment. Their nod of agreement or puzzled look will add information for the observant adult.
- You listen with care to children's answers and reaction to your questions, as well as taking care not to overload communication with adult questions.

Do babies and toddlers think?

If you use your skills of observation, you will see that very young children show evidence of thinking. Long before they put their thoughts into spoken words, babies show signs of making some sense of their world.

Babies and their social world

- Babies as young as 3–4 months show evidence that they recall familiar daily routines. They react to care routines and show pleasure if they enjoy, for instance, bath time or a familiar song at nappy changing time.
- Babies also show that they recall and understand the simple dynamics of playful early communication (see page 295). It would not be possible to

enjoy the turn taking exchanges of sound and expression with babies unless they were primed and able to learn these routines. With experience, babies show that they anticipate a response.

- In some ways the world is a puzzling place for babies and it is not until about 8–9 months that they work out that it is worth searching for objects that have been hidden, even in front of their eyes.

Cause and effect

- The development of communication and thinking are closely linked. Look again at some of the developments described from page 296. For example, the use of gesture by older babies and toddlers shows an understanding of basic cause and effect: 'I point my arm and hand and people follow the direction and look'.
- By twelve months, most babies have learned to work on simple cause and effect: a loud shout brings attention, blowing raspberries makes people laugh and dropping or throwing a toy usually encourages an adult or older sibling to pick it up and start a game.
- You will see evidence that toddlers have grasped further examples of the principles of cause and effect. Under twos are capable of repeating an action or set of nonsense sounds that makes an adult or other children laugh.
- They are also able to wind up other children, especially older siblings by tried and tested actions that they have learned will tease. Such actions tend to lead to trouble that adults then have to resolve, but you should not lose sight of the thinking power in evidence here.

Memory

- Mobile older babies and toddlers can clearly remember. For example, they recall the location of their books or play materials, within their own home and other familiar settings, such as their grandparents' home or their nursery.
- At home, toddlers can be very persistent in searching out objects they are not supposed to touch. Adults tend to view this behaviour in terms of a problem. But it does of course show memory, as well as intelligent planning by waiting until an adult's back is turned!
- Toddlers are able to recall and tell you that personal objects like a handbag or a watch belong to a particular person. Their behaviour demonstrates this understanding when they take the watch to their father or point to the handbag and say 'Nana'.
- When they are out on familiar local trips, older babies and toddlers in a buggy often show that they recognise landmarks. Perhaps they kick their legs gleefully when they recognise the last part of the walk to their grandparents' home. Maybe they look excited and start pointing when you are near the baker's where you usually buy a bread roll for instant eating.
- Under twos show evidence of recall and planning. They may show this in their ability to take a part in daily routines such as tidying up.
- Toddlers also return actively to an enjoyable peek-a-boo game or one of 'you build up the bricks and I'll knock them down'. Their actions and expressions show they understand how to start and request the game, rather than waiting for an adult or older sibling to initiate the play.

Let's pretend

- The development of young children's pretend play shows a leap in their thinking because they have understood enough about how their world works to pretend that it is otherwise (see page 366).
- Babies and young toddlers understand the world through real objects and they learn the names for those objects. From about 18 months onwards, toddlers show by their use of words that they have a basic understanding of symbolism. They use the same words for the picture of an object. So they become able to play, and often enjoy, spotting games with books or wall posters.
- Around about the same time young children also work out that objects can be represented by miniature versions such as dolls' house size furniture. The toddler understands that they cannot sit on this chair, it is for a little doll, but it is still a chair.

To think about

Very young children think around what they know and this pattern will be different depending on their daily experience.

Look at the photograph on page 360 of the toddler staring intently at the adult (Figure 13.3). She is looking at the practitioner's identity card for their nursery. This toddler was intrigued by the card and the practitioner patiently let her look and shared her interest. After I took that photograph, the little girl came and sat by me. She gently took hold of the visitor's identity card that hung on a chain around my neck. She looked intently at the card, then up at my face and then pointed at the card itself, with a puzzled expression on her face. She said no words but her actions said very loudly, 'And where is your photo?' because, unlike the practitioner, there was no photograph of me on the card.

Questions

1. Identity cards were meaningful to this toddler because they form part of the security system for her nursery. She noticed and questioned (by her body language) details that were a mis-match from her experience.
2. Can you recall (or collect) examples from very young children you know, where they show their understanding of familiar events or objects and notice when something is 'not quite right'?
3. Share your ideas with colleagues.

Key skills links: C3.1a

Figure 13.3
A very interested toddler

Activity (observation)

Collect brief observations of children younger than two years of age, looking for examples that suggest strongly that this child:

- has remembered something, for instance, the pattern of a daily routine, the gestures that accompany a song, a playful exchange or a local route or landmark
- is puzzled because something is unfamiliar, out of place or in some way does not 'fit'
- has made a connection between events or objects and so is bringing thinking power to bear and doing something completely original in play or actions
- write up your observations and present the main ideas to your colleagues.

Key skills links: C3.3 C3.1b

To think about

Careful research with young children has established that they are capable of taking the perspective of another person far younger than some developmental theories, for instance that of Jean Piaget, have claimed. This example is one of the intriguing studies reported in *How Babies Think* by Alison Gopnik and her colleagues (see page 391).

Toddlers in the study were aged 14–18 months old and, given a choice between eating raw broccoli and savoury crackers, they all chose the crackers. An adult then showed her own food preference through a pantomime of facial expression and saying 'yum' or 'yuk'. She then put out her hand and asked the toddlers, 'Could you give me some'. When she indicated her favourite was crackers just like the toddlers, she was given crackers. The difference came when she indicated a preference for the raw broccoli. The 14 month olds still gave her the crackers, their own favourite. But the 18 month olds gave her the broccoli, although this was a silly food choice as far as they were concerned. Conventional wisdom about toddlers' thinking would say that they could not have taken a perspective other than their own, but they did.

Figure 13.4
'Under' or 'through' make sense at first by actually doing it

Thinking skills of two to five year olds

Increasingly, children's use of language will show you directly what they have thought or are puzzling about. Children cannot easily grasp abstract ideas until their understanding has extended to take in ideas. For most children, this shift will be observable through their use of language. Look at, or look again, at the description on page 301 of how children's language extends from naming words, to doing words and then only to words that describe ideas.

Understanding ideas

Increasingly, young children begin to understand and show that they understand abstract ideas, the ways of describing people, objects and situations. There are many ideas to understand in the end and children learn from a range of experiences and from adults who take the trouble to grasp what a child understands, or does not yet understand. The pattern of learning is an individual sequence and you will find some very general indicators in this section. Suggestions for how to help are from page 369.

- From two to five years, children are working on many ideas. Few will be understood in one conversation or play exploration – learning tends to build up step by step. Children need to be able to home in on the difference that is described by a word before they can make sense of the concept. They need, for instance, to have felt differences in texture of 'soft' and 'rough', heard the difference between 'loud', 'quiet' and 'silent' and seen the difference that is 'red' or 'green'.
- Three and four year olds usually have some grasp of shape, number, size or colour and some of the words to accompany these ideas.
- They have basic ideas of temperature, weight, height and speed but do not understand the complexities of how these differences are measured. Young

children gain some idea of gradations in these ideas through using simple language such as 'very fast', 'a bit cold' or 'too heavy' (for me to lift) or 'too high' (for me to reach).

- It takes time for children to grasp opposites for those ideas where there is a flipside. Three and four year olds will usually get one idea, such as 'hot', 'heavy' or 'fast' and they learn the idea that makes most sense within their daily experience. Later they will learn or be told that the opposite of 'hot' is 'cold' and the opposite of 'fast' is 'slow'.
- Four and five year olds can have developed special interests on which they are very knowledgeable and have the relevant vocabulary and related ideas. For instance, some children may know more than you do about sharks, motorbikes or dinosaurs and understand the different groupings in these topic areas.
- Understanding time is much more difficult than some of the other ideas that four year olds can manage. It is not unusual for children of seven and eight years to still be struggling with telling the time with clocks and watches. Three and four year olds often grasp the first ideas of time as that of time passing and sequences in familiar daily routines.

Knowledge and understanding social issues

Children are often very curious and they extend their knowledge of facts. But they also need help, usually from attentive adults, to build a framework in which to make sense of information.

- Some children show great interest in human issues, such as why people behave the way they do, feelings and the basics of where babies come from or why people die. Children's understanding of these ideas is dependent on clear and honest explanations from adults (see page 222). There is also great variety between children and the questions they ask.
- Four year olds for instance usually have a clear idea that they are a boy or girl and the sex of their friends. They may still be confused, however, about what happens later in life: that boys grow into men and can become fathers, whereas girls grow into women and may become mothers.
- They notice and comment on differences in skin colour and patterns of dress that reflect different ethnic and cultural groups. They can begin to understand that not everyone's family runs like their own.
- For young children 'different' does not necessarily mean better or worse. Children develop attitudes about gender, ethnic groups and disability, as well other social issues and their outlook can be positive with adult guidance.

Activity (observation)

When children are able to ask questions, you can hear directly what is of interest to them and you get a hint of what they understand so far. Helpful adults take note of children's questions because they are keen to learn in those areas. Three, four and five year olds can ask you very searching questions and you may not know the answers to some. It is not unusual for children to ask, 'Where does the rain come from?', 'Why does my Mum give money to the pre-school?' or 'Can rabbits talk?'

Over a period of several weeks, collect questions from children that make you pause to think before you reply. Note down your reply as well.

Look back over your notes.

- What kinds of questions were asked? What do you feel you have learned about children's thinking and their current knowledge?
- Did some children ask very few questions at all? What ideas do you have for encouraging more enquiry from them?
- Were there some questions that you found it hard to answer? What made those questions difficult: because you did not know the answer, because there was an emotional content (perhaps 'why did my granny have to die?')

Compare your observations with colleagues and work together on drafting 6–10 points of good practice through which you can support and meet children's curiosity through questions.

Key skills links: C3.3 C3.1a LP3.1–3 WO3.1–3

Five, six and seven year olds

During this age range, children consolidate many of the ideas that have been developing in early childhood.

- Existing confusions in some ideas are overcome and the more challenging ideas, such as time, danger and risk level and the concept of left and right become clearer, sometimes with specific adult help.
- Children show an increasing grasp of symbols, such as those involved in mathematical understanding (see page 375).
- Children also develop concepts related to moral issues, reasoning and behaviour (see page 228).
- Children in this age range are even more able to consider ideas inside their heads. They weigh up possibilities or explanations not tied to their immediate experience. Some abstract thinking can be used alongside direct observation.

To think about

Working out left and right is a useful concept for adults to consider because you can often recall your own struggles and the memory can give you some empathy with children.

For instance, I can still recall clearly my confusion over left and right. I can now put into words that my difficulties revolved around, 'My right hand is always my right hand' but 'If I face my friend then her right hand is on the other side'. Since we did country dancing in my primary school, it was also rather important to be able to follow an instruction of 'turn left', otherwise the teacher shouted at us!

- When did you work out right from left? How did you manage it?
- Compare notes with your colleagues.
- Allow for the fact that some adults continue to have difficulty with telling right from left. It is associated sometimes with dyslexia.

Key skills links: C3.1a

What changes and what does not?

As well as extending their existing understanding of concepts, children are also working to grasp what changes and what does not. For instance, three and four years olds tend to say there are 'more' cars in a row when those cars are spread out than when they are bunched together. Children hold to their ideas of 'more' even if you count the cars with them. A similar situation arises with different shaped glasses and pouring out drink. Even if you use a standard measuring jug, children still tend to say there is 'more' drink in the taller glasses.

Jean Piaget took these observations as proof that younger children could not understand the concept of **conservation**, that the number or volume stayed the same despite reorganisation of the actual materials. It seems likely that children are slightly confused about the ideas. However, studies by Margaret Donaldson and her colleagues showed the possibility that children are also thinking about what the adult wants who asks the questions. They found that children were far more likely to say that two rows of the same number of toys were still the same when a soft toy, 'naughty teddy', had pushed one row up tighter, than when the adult researcher had brought about the same change.

Key term

Conservation the idea that objects continue to have the same quality such as number or volume even when they are moved to look different

A likely explanation is that children have social expectations about adult behaviour. When an adult makes a change and then asks a question about whether 'It's still the same', children are misdirected into thinking that something must have happened. Otherwise why would an adult ask that kind of question? If you find this explanation unlikely, then recall that asking the same question several times is a ploy used in law courts to trap adult witnesses into changing their answer. When a prestigious adult repeats a question, some otherwise confident adults find themselves thinking that there must have been something wrong with their first answer and they change it or appear doubtful.

Using logical thinking

Children build 'theories' based on what they have experienced. Children up to the early teenage years mainly use **inductive reasoning**. This method means that they work from what they have directly observed to form a more general principle. Because younger children lack information, some of their theories turn out to be wrong or simply too narrow, and they revise them. For example:

Key term

Inductive reasoning a process of thinking logically from direct observations and experience to reach a general principle

- A bad experience with his grandma's very fierce cat leads a four year old child to form a view that all cats scratch and should be avoided.
- A positive experience of taking turns in nursery has led a child to develop a general principle about fairness: that it is worth aiming for fairness and ways to behave in a fair way.
- A seven year old has never known anybody to die who was not in his terms 'very old'. He therefore concludes that only old people die. Now his best friend's family has lost a baby through cot death and he is very confused.
- A six year old has three friends who are Jehovah's Witnesses. His friends also happen to be black. So he concludes that all Jehovah's Witnesses are black, until further experience tells him that this pattern was just chance.
- A five year old is made to eat tinned spaghetti in tomato sauce that she dislikes very much. She says she does not like any spaghetti and generalises this refusal to any kind of pasta when she hears that spaghetti is a kind of pasta.

Activity (observation)

- Build up a collection of logical thinking from children. You will probably have examples where children's logic takes them in the correct direction and where their reasoning is sound, but they lack information.
- Consider the examples and how they help you to understand children and tune into their world view of the moment.
- Share your findings with colleagues, maintaining confidentiality about individual children.

Key skills links: LP3.1–3 C3.1a

Inductive reasoning moves from the particular to the general. So the accuracy of the principles that children develop depends on their experiences. Children can revise their theories with further experience and in conversation with supportive adults who listen and reply to questions.

Teenagers become more able to use **deductive reasoning**. In contrast, this logical approach moves from a general rule or principle to predict a particular event. In secondary school, students use this kind of thinking to handle scientific concepts. Younger children cannot handle this kind of reasoning unless they are dealing with very familiar ideas based on plenty of experience.

For instance, in the example earlier about turn taking, children who have experienced consistent and supportive adults may develop a general principle about fairness. Children in the early years of primary school may well say that rules like 'we walk in the corridor; we don't run' apply to everyone including teachers. So it would be unfair for teachers to run in the corridor.

Key term

Deductive reasoning a process of thinking logically from a general rule or principle to predict a particular event

Figure 13.5 Imagining and thinking

It is worth bearing in mind that some attempts to teach children road safety go directly against their thinking and reasoning abilities in the early years. Road safety campaigns for children often focus on a general principle like, 'find a safe place to cross' when children have no idea of what this rule means. But children learn about road safety through direct experience at the side of careful adults and then they understand through actions what a 'safe place' looks like and why it is safe.

Imagination and the power of thought

Another way to understand and observe the development of young children's thinking is to track how their pretend play develops. Toddlers in the second year of life often show the beginning of imagination that will steadily develop into the complex pretend play of a three or four year old.

The development of pretend play

Very young children take what they know of familiar life and routines and then play around with it.

- The very first pretend play actions are often fleeting. Perhaps a toddler uses a toy spoon to pretend to feed himself or a brush and pretends to brush his hair, scarcely touching his head. You can miss these swift actions but once you notice, then you realise that this very young child is thinking.
- Pretend play is at first directed by toddlers at themselves, but soon they pretend with someone or something else. They pretend to offer you a drink or to feed Teddy.
- They start to pretend an object is something else, for example, a brick is a car or a plastic bowl is a hat.
- Perhaps the whole action is pretend; there is not only no drink, the drinking action is made without a cup. Toddlers look at you as if to say, 'You know that I know that you know that this is all just pretend'.
- Two and three year olds show ever more complex pretend play. They may develop longer sequences as dolly is put to bed or the toy animals have a tea party.
- Doll's house size figures and small world play with animals become possible, because the children now understand that these little figures can stand in for the full size version.
- Three and four year olds dress up and begin to play pretend with friends, perhaps monsters or chase and rescue. They cook pretend meals and play with a pretend shop or garage.
- Three, four year olds and older children often show complex and rich pretend play sequences that they direct themselves and return to over a period of time. They decide on characters, negotiate the 'scripts' and plan out the action to a certain extent.

Activity (observation)

- Keep track over a period of weeks of the pretend play themes that occur in your setting.
- Given a choice (that is not confined to an adult-organised role play area) how do the children show their imagination, and thinking, through their play themes.

- Children draw from what they know in everyday life to feed their pretend play.
- What do you see and hear that they have built in from experience in family life, what they saw on a local trip or recall from a favourite television programme?
- Keep brief notes of the themes and discuss your findings with colleagues.

Key skills links: C3.3 C3.1a

The impact of learning disabilities

Some children will have disabilities that affect their intellectual development. You will find much more information about disability in Chapter 18 and this section briefly covers some of the main issues:

- Children with learning disabilities such as Down's syndrome (see page 518) will be delayed to some extent in their development but the patterns are very varied. Children's understanding of ideas or their ability to reason will be more like that of a younger child. But you have to get to know and observe an individual child to make sense of the gap between her chronological age in years and months and her developmental age.
- A child's language development and play, especially pretend play will be a help in building an accurate picture of her abilities. When you are responsible for a child with learning disabilities, it is important that you select activities, including any of the ideas in this chapter, in line with her current ability and support her onwards from that point.
- Children with disabilities that affect their powers of communication (see page 321) may have plenty of ideas in their head but be frustrated in ways to tell you. The children need your support through patience, watching what they show you through their behaviour as well as actual words and using any supports for communication that help this child.
- Children with autistic spectrum disorder have difficulties in making sense of their social world, communication and use of symbolic thinking as in imaginative play. You need to remember that these children are not being awkward. They are genuinely baffled, and sometimes made very anxious, by events or questions that their peers take in their stride (see page 518).

Helping children to think

Understanding and using ideas

Ideas can seem very obvious to adults but that is only because you have become so familiar with concepts of time, number or shape. Such ideas are not at all obvious to young children. An important point for adults to realise is that colour, size or texture (and all the other abstract concepts) are ways of describing the world. These concepts do not exist in their own right. Consider the points in the think about box:

To think about

- A child can see and touch a 'car'; she cannot see or touch a 'red'. She can see a 'red car' but she has to work out what the idea of 'redness' means.
- A child can lift a big wooden block but cannot find and pick up a 'heavy'. But through his actions he can directly experience a sense of 'heavy'.
- Children cannot do a 'fast' or a 'slow' but they can run, walk or crawl in a 'fast' or 'slow' style.

So, of course, children can only learn about all these ideas through direct experience and they need your patience and understanding. Time spent with children is also much more interesting for adults, when you are ready to observe and track the development of ideas, rather than take a blunt line of 'does she know her colours yet?' or even 'why doesn't he understand shapes!'

What are the first ideas?

Children of two to two and a half years of age often show that they have some abstract ideas already. You need to observe young children and especially listen to the words they use. Young children learn through personal experience and their current interests, so the pattern of first ideas is likely to be different between individual two year olds. For example:

- Young children, who are keen builders and like moving materials around your setting, may show a basic understanding of weight and relative weight. They directly experience this concept because they and their friends are busy lifting, pushing and manipulating materials of different weights.
- Keen climbers may soon grasp the concept of height of a climbing frame or walking along a wall. They may want to climb 'up high' or decide that a location is 'too high' to climb. Height in terms of people and 'tall' or 'short' may not be linked until later.
- Speed may intrigue young children, probably in terms of 'fast' rather than 'slow' at the outset. Young children may call out that you should watch how 'fast' they can run or ride the bike. They may be aware on local trips that a vehicle was going 'very fast'.
- Young children probably get their first idea of temperature when adults warn them about 'hot', especially at home where a parent or other carer may say, 'Let me move my coffee, it's hot'.
- Texture may become interesting to children through their pleasure in touch. They feel the contrast between 'soft' textures that are pleasant to stroke or rub and 'rough' surfaces that can scratch.
- Children who like their food may have concepts of 'tasty' or foods that are 'crunchy'.
- Sound may make sense in terms of 'loud' or 'too loud' for voice volume or the television.
- Because of the normal accidents of life, some children grasp the idea of 'broken'. Their knowledge extends to understand that some things can be mended but some are broken for ever.

How do you help?

You will help by being an observant and sensitive adult, who homes in on the children's current understanding. Use your observation skills to become aware of the ideas that children already have, or partly understand. Start with the child's interests, rather than insist that they learn about colour or shape, perhaps because that is a focus for three and four year olds in a group setting. Look at the scenario on page 371 and try some of the suggestions.

To think about

Anne Fine is a very successful author of books for children. In an interview in the summer of 2000 she was asked to pinpoint how she manages to write so well. She said her motto was:

> Never overestimate children's knowledge; never underestimate their intelligence.

I think this is wise guidance for all adults who work with young children.

Hands-on play activities

When you provide a wide range of play opportunities and learning through involvement in the daily routines, then children will gain the appropriate hands-on experience.

- Children will feel the differences in textures in various materials in your setting and by playing with treasure bags that have different textures to feel first and then bring out to look at.
- Use of construction materials, transporting materials around the garden and helping with tidying up all give direct experience of different weights and shapes.
- Children can see the difference between 'light on' and 'light off' or the 'dark' of a winter afternoon.
- Young children learn steadily through seeing and feeling the dimensions of same and different. They need to be able to match and sort different basic colours visually before the word has any meaning. Posting and sorting three dimensional shapes has meaning before shapes on a flat piece of paper.

Introduce the words

You can help children to learn the words for ideas by confirming their own use of language and adding a word to a natural conversation. For instance:

- You could provide the words for texture when you accept the invitation to stroke a child's jumper, 'Oh, it's so lovely and soft'. The crash of a cymbal in a music activity is met with, 'what a loud noise, that made me jump'.
- You can comment naturally on what you are doing with children, 'I think we need to make this sand more wet. Our sandcastles keep collapsing' or 'Have you seen my blue pen? It's blue, like this brick.'
- You can help children to notice by showing them direct comparisons to help them notice the relevant visual difference. You might say, 'I think we need another square shape now. We need another one like this' (showing the child).

- You can also help a child extend their language without in any sense suggesting their word is wrong. You might reply to a child, 'Yes, your uncle Ken is big isn't he? He is really tall. I think he's even taller than Jason from the pre-school room. Shall we ask them to measure against each other?'

Figure 13.6a
Different ways of learning about the chicks – a book

Figure 13.6b
Different ways of learning about the chicks – close observation

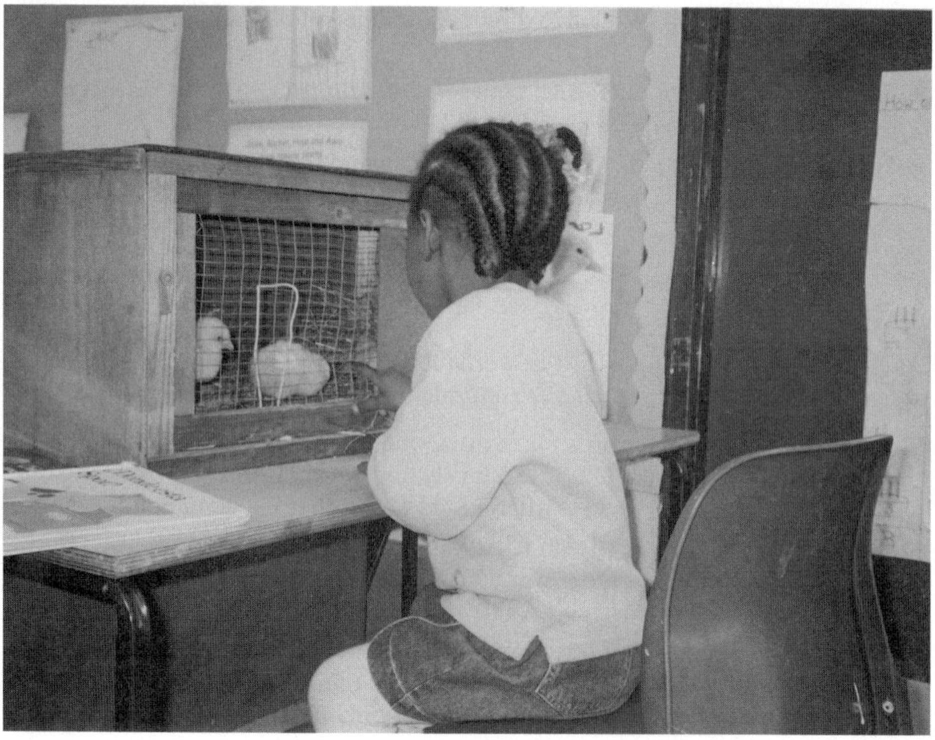

In this way children will learn the words and the context in which to apply them and their confusion will be much reduced. Children often use the word 'big' to mean 'large', 'tall' or 'older', as in 'when I'm a big boy, I'll go to school'. If you listen, you will hear that adults tend to use 'big' in these ways. So we can help children to learn by being more accurate with our own words.

Ask helpful questions

You can use different patterns of open-ended questions that leave children choice, but will highlight for you what they understand. Here are some examples.

- 'I wonder if we have any … or some more … (round shapes, blue cups, larger bricks, soft toys for the baby)?'
- 'Shall we count up how many … (children we have for tea, spiders we can see on our walk)?'
- 'Can you help me find … (another round shape like this one, something heavy to hold the door open, a dry tea towel)?' Other phrases might be, 'I need another …', 'Where did I put …?' or 'I'm looking for …'
- 'Shall we sort out … (the blue cars from the red ones, the large bricks from the small ones, the animals from the people in our farm set)?'

Avoid asking children lots of very directive questions, especially those designed to test or drill young children.

- Children younger than three years old often do not understand questions like 'what colour is this car?' or 'how many bricks have we got?'
- They may look confused, do not reply or give what sounds like a nonsense answer to your adult ear.
- Use confusing answers from children as a message to you that they need plenty more hands-on experience. Children need ways to see the difference in colour or make sense of numbers before they can answer such tough questions.
- Too many questions from adults can unbalance your communication with children (see page 309) and testing questions make children feel put on the spot to be correct.

Scenario

The team of Greenholt Pre-school decided to use observations to help them focus on the ideas understood already by the youngest children in their setting, the two and half to just three year olds. The team had become aware that they were planning as if colour, shape and number were the only concepts. They found themselves talking about the youngest children as if they had no grasp of concepts because they sometimes seemed to be confused about these three areas.

The team explained to parents about the observations and invited any anecdotes from home. A rich array of ideas was gathered and part way through the project the team started to use photos to record the context in which children had shown their understanding. A few examples include:

- The two and a half year to three year olds use words like 'hot', 'warm' and 'cold'. The church hall in which the pre-school runs has metal protectors on the radiators and one child points to those and explains, 'That's 'cos it's hot'.

- One snack time was devoted to raw fruit and vegetable tasting. Children used words like 'yummy' and 'tasty' for food they liked. Carrots were 'very crunchy' to one child. Marjorie, the pre-school leader, laughed as she ate into an orange and the juice ran down her chin. She said, 'it's so juicy' and the children took up and repeated the word.
- Some of the children are aware that Lottie cannot have any food with cow's milk in it. Her friend says dramatically, 'No cheese for Lottie. It makes her very, very sick!'
- The team has realised that their own adult concern about noise levels has been observed by the children. Some of the young three year olds are heard to say, 'that is far too noisy, we have to be quiet, like little mouses'.
- Anecdotes contributed by parents include several two year olds' awareness of 'light' and 'dark' in the late winter afternoons. One boy has become interested in the whole idea of visual similarity and shares his observations with phrases like, 'Fox – that's like a cat'. A child whose clothes are passed on to his younger sibling has the idea of 'old' and 'new' coat or trousers.
- And, yes, some children do have a grasp of basic colour and an interest to discover more but there is evidence of many more ideas.

Questions

1. What abstract concepts are shown through the examples gathered by the pre-school?
2. Collect similar examples from your own setting from two and young three year olds whom you know. Involve parents in this activity if they wish.
3. Early years practitioners are often tempted to home in on colour and shape, but these concepts will not necessarily be the first ideas to be linked with words. What is likely to interest very young children, what will catch their attention in their personal world?

- Present your findings.
- Consider possible improvements in your own practice in the light of what you have observed.

Key skills links: C3.1b LP3.1–3 WO3.1–3

You will help children when you understand the steps of learning in ideas that seem very familiar to you. There are more ideas on page 375 about early mathematical concepts and from page 230 about moral ideas. Some other common examples are given here.

Learning about colour

Many three year olds are well on the way to being able to distinguish and name the main colours. Four years olds are usually confident about colour. There may be some discussion around the shades, like when does blue become green or orange become red. But adults do not always agree about the subtleties. Learning colours is a process that involves observation as well as the words:

- First a child has to notice those differences in the world that you describe by colour. They have to recognise by sight the difference between red, blue, green or yellow.
- Part of seeing and noticing is also that children need to pick out the colour feature from any other characteristic of an object. For instance, their trousers may be 'blue' but they are also perhaps 'soft', stripey' and 'brand new'.
- When a child has realised that colour is a feature shared by different objects, they can pick out the colour and ignore other features. For instance, they can see the blueness of the car, their friend's hat and the water in the tray today.
- Children need to be confident about spotting same and different in colour before they are ready to identify a colour with questions like, 'Can you find me something red?' or 'Who's wearing something green today?'

You can help by enabling children to get plenty of enjoyable practice at the matching stage of learning. They can:

- sort out collections by colour and you help them by visually matching, 'I need another blue brick, just like this one' and holding it up or giving it to the child to match directly
- be involved in search-and-find activities for anything that is yellow or purple and then make a display
- play board games or use sorting apparatus where colour matching is the key to sorting out items
- hear you say the word for this colour, closely linked with the play resource or item of clothing. Use your words to confirm the concepts and resist asking testing questions such as 'What colour is this?'

If five year olds have had plenty of appropriate play experience and they are still confused about colour, there is the possibility that they have some degree of colour blindness. This condition is more common with boys than girls and does not mean that children, or adults, see the world in shades of grey. Some people who are colour blind have trouble with just one part of the colour spectrum, for instance not being able to tell red from green.

Activity

- This pattern of helping children to have plenty of hands-on and visual experience works well with other concepts such as size, shape, weight or height.
- Gather ideas for activities that could give children direct experience of any of the ideas given above.
- Present to your colleagues and consider possible improvements in your practice.

Key skills links: C3.1b LP3.1–3 WO3.1–3

Helping children to develop their thinking powers

Adults need to be careful about the balance of their communication with children and certainly too many questions can unbalance the exchange. However, there is a place for sensible adult questions that will help a child to think around a situation, rather than an adult telling a child what to do with a problem. For instance:

- If a child cannot reach a shelf or get to the taps to fill a container, you might say, 'How could you get up higher?' rather than just saying, 'I'll do it for you'.
- Perhaps children want your help because their project has gone awry. You could start with, 'You're right, your den is very wobbly. I wonder what would make it more secure. What do you think?' If children have few ideas, then you can suggest. But the aim is to encourage them to think around the problem a bit.
- You can invite children to help each other. For instance, one child may say, 'How do I put the books away? They keep falling out'. You could reply, 'Allan showed me yesterday a good system with the books. Shall we ask him to show you?'

There are also further ideas on page 208 for helping children to develop skills of problem solving and of resolving conflicts.

Scenario

Inspired by the changes in their garden (see page 281), the team at Dresden Road Nursery School have experimented this half term with a rather unusual topic, that of 'What can we do about it? Problem solving power in Dresden Road!'

In consultation with the children, the team has looked for problems they would all like to address. Some problems are local issues, like the children's concern about the 'horrible litter and dog mess in our park – what can we do?' and some are about nursery life with 'how can we get water from the tap to our pretend garage?'

The focus on 'what can we do about it?' has encouraged children to discuss everyday problems in their play. Adults help with questions to support ideas but not to tell children what to do. The children have also become very enthusiastic about recording some of their projects.

The task of getting the water from the outdoor tap was documented by the children, using a camera, and covering the ideas that did not work as well as the final version that did work. With the adults' support, the photos were made into a display with written explanations and drawings.

Questions

1 In what ways do you support children's thinking power in your own setting? Suggest some changes, even minor improvements to practice.

2 Suggest some ways in which three and four year olds in Dresden Road could be enabled to tackle the problem of the mess in their local park. How might they document the situation with the help of the nursery staff or parents? What might they do with their findings?

Key skills links: PS3.1 LP3.1–3 WO3.1–3

Helping children to remember

Children are learning a considerable amount of information and ideas over their early years. They also need to make sense of everything. Part of their task is to register and remember what they have previously experienced. Children will forget some things, just like us, but supportive adults can help them to sharpen up their memory skills.

Children cannot remember something to which they did not attend in the first place. So you can help memory skills by supporting children's ability to attend: to listen and look. See page 284 for a discussion about the development of attention in childhood.

- Make it easy for children to listen. Say their name first and ensure you have their attention before you say more.
- Be close to a child and at eye contact level.
- Keep your comments, suggestions or instructions as simple as a child needs. Under threes, and especially under twos will tend to forget the first thing you said when you give several instructions at a time.
- Sometimes encourage a child or small group to say back to you what they have just heard or been shown. You can invite them with, 'So, what you're going to do is ...?'

Tips for practice

You can use the normal activities of the day to help recall.

- Children need to practise in order to remember, so let them have enjoyable opportunities to become familiar with a rhyme or story, how to use a particular tool at the woodwork table or how to crack an egg.
- Use simple review sessions with three, four and five year olds to reflect back on the session or day. 'What was the best part of today?' or 'Who remembers what we learned about ...?
- Be ready to reminisce in conversation or to respond to their memories – 'Do you remember when ...?'
- Use simple games like picture pairs, round games like 'I went to the shop and I bought ...' or the memory game of objects on a tray that children see, you cover and remove one object and then uncover with 'What has gone?'
- Use visual supports to help children remember. For instance, make a recipe book with photos of the steps that children take to make gingerbread biscuits.
- Use your own times of forgetfulness with, 'What story did we agree to have today?' or 'Please remind me, whose turn is it to hand out the snacks?'

How children understand mathematical ideas

As well as all the other abstract ideas that children are learning, they are also working to understand a range of mathematical ideas. These include:

- an understanding of number as an abstract idea, a practical way of dealing with daily routines and as a written system

- ways of dealing with numbers and measurement and the basic mathematical operations of addition, subtraction, multiplication and division
- the idea of measurement: how and what you measure
- ways of describing the world in basic mathematical terms: size, shape, weight, height and volume
- all the ideas about money: how coins and paper money represent a value (big coins are not necessarily worth more than little coins), how money works in our society and how you do calculations involving money
- the concept of time, time passing and how to measure and tell the time
- ideas such as speed and distance, both small and large scale.

Children have a very great deal to learn and much like other abstract ideas described in this chapter, helpful adults need to tune into children's current thinking. You need to observe what children understand at the moment and help them on from that point. What is obvious to you, perhaps about counting, is not at all obvious to the children.

Tips for practice

- Offer plenty of hands-on activities. Number and other mathematical ideas start to make sense to children because they apply the ideas in a practical context.
- Show what you do with your mathematical abilities. It often helps children if you speak your thoughts out loud and explain clearly why you count or measure.
- Counting and mathematical operations like addition or subtraction make sense to children when they are experienced many times in ordinary daily routines.
- Practical play and routine activities help children to understand the point of weighing or measuring – why we do it as well as how we do it.
- Children need plenty of practice with mathematical ideas in a meaningful context so that they can make sensible connections. The abstract ideas need to come alive.

Helping under threes

Very young children need to build up plenty of hands-on experience and practical knowledge of how their world works. They begin to learn about number, much as they experience appropriate early literacy, through direct experience. Under threes are not ready to learn about written number, any more than written letters; it is too abstract for them. But they are keen, with your help, to build a strong foundation of understanding what will become early mathematics.

Experiencing shape and size

- Babies and toddlers are intrigued to stare at shapes and patterns, either two dimensional or the three dimensions in a mobile. They gain experience in how a pattern or shape starts and where it ends.
- Older babies and toddlers use their hands to feel shapes and what will fit into something else. Resources such as the treasure basket or exploratory play sessions (see page 272) enable children to learn through vision and touch about shape, texture and edges.

- Play materials that can fit and stack offer children plenty of experience in experimenting with what will fit and what will not.
- A range of containers can be used to explore relative size and wheeled transport like trolleys or wheelbarrows offer practical experience of what can be fitted into a given space.
- Young children who become interested in jigsaws or other play materials that fit together, get enjoyable practice in looking carefully at shape and matching what will fit.

Tips for practice

Numbers have to make sense to very young children so you need to use number words as a natural part of daily conversation, especially with under threes.

- You can comment during mealtimes, 'Do you want more potatoes? Here we go, one potato, two potatoes. Is that enough?'
- Helping children with personal care can be a chance for simple numbers. You could say, 'Show me how you wash your hands. One hand, two hands – well done' or 'Now where are your shoes? You've got one, two feet. So we need one, two shoes'.
- Simple physical games provide a meaningful context for use of number. You might remind children, 'one at a time on the slide', say 'there's time for one more turn, then it's lunch'.
- Enjoyable physical games can be accompanied by 'One, two, three – up you come!' or 'One, two, three – go!'
- Young children like spotting games, either from the pictures in a child's favourite book or on local trips. You can comment with, 'Yes, there's one cat. Now where's the other one? Yes, well done! Two cats'. On a local trip you might spot, 'There's a squirrel and another one. Two squirrels!'
- Young children enjoy all kinds of songs and rhymes. Some of these will include numbers and counting on the fingers.
- Early ideas of liquid quantity make sense at drink time and in water play. You can add the words 'a little bit more', 'just enough' and maybe 'Oh no! Too much, it's spilled over!'
- Young children want to be helpful and their enjoyable involvement in daily routines helps them to grasp numbers in action. They like to look for 'one more spoon' or finding the two missing pieces of jigsaw. Increasingly rising threes are also able to join in the practical counting as part of routines.

Helping three, four and five year olds

Appropriate early mathematical activities for the over threes are a natural extension of the ideas that work for younger children. It is equally important that you keep activities very practical so that the ideas have meaning for children.

Counting 'how many?'

Numbers are hard to fathom and children need plenty of practice:

- They need the practice of number order. You count up and back in the same pattern each time. So six follows five each time when you are counting higher numbers.

- But children also need plenty of experience that, when you want four plates, you stop counting at four, rather than going on and on.
- Counting by finger pointing or physically moving the plates, pieces of cheese or pencils all help children to understand how number works.

There are many opportunities for meaningful number work when children are involved in daily routines.

- Meal and snack times naturally lend themselves to 'How many children have we got for tea?' You can count by saying the names and showing the numbers on your fingers. 'That's 5 of us. So we need 5 plates ... Let's count them as we lay the table ... Now we need 5 spoons, one for each plate.'
- You can sometimes make a deliberate mistake such as, 'Who hasn't got a plate? I haven't, we didn't count me!'
- Hanging out washing needs discussion about how many pegs in total and for each item. Perhaps the children have had a good time washing the dolls clothes and now it time to hang them up to dry. (Dry washing also feels less heavy than wet washing – another mathematical idea.)
- Cutting up and sharing a large cake or an apple gives practical experience of dividing into equal shares or cutting into halves or quarters.

So long as you do not over-do the counting, children often like to use their counting skills in different kinds of play.

- Children like to count steps in the stairs, how many big buses you all see on a local trip or creepy crawlies under the stone you turn over in the garden.
- When the children want, you can make some displays out of 'what we saw' and 'what we counted'.
- The Children's House Nursery School in Edinburgh (reported in *Nursery World* 28 September 2000) developed number bags in a similar way to the storysacks (see page 330). Number songs such as 'One man went to mow' or 'Five speckled frogs' can be supported by number props as well as the characters. Everything related to the song is then kept in its own bag.

Figure 13.7
Daily routines can be excellent ways to learn practical application of numbers

When children have had plenty of meaningful practice for counting then they are able to look at five dots and know it is five without counting. Or they can start at five and know that you then go on to six, rather than having to count all the way up from one.

Simple ways to measure

You can be creative in finding ways to measure before children can make sense of centimetres and metres.

- Children like to count how many paces it takes to reach the door or cross the garden.
- Hand widths may be a good way to measure some distances or heights. (The height of horses is still measured in hands.)
- Children can explore relative size and volume through how many cups of water it takes to fill the big jug or how many buckets of earth we dug out for our hole in the garden.
- Indoor and outdoor gardening projects can be a good source of measuring and looking at change over time. If children are not yet ready to use a rule or tape measure, then use a length of string to check how tall the tomato plants have grown or other seedlings. Keep a record with the children.

There are many songs and rhymes that include number. These counting up and back rhymes can support children's understanding.

- Young children will join in the words and actions of songs that show number: 'buns in the bakers' shop', 'sausages in a pan go pop', 'ten green bottles' and 'there were ten in the bed'.
- Children become familiar with the order of numbers and practise adding on and taking away.

Cooking activities are a rich source of early mathematical ideas (see page 102).

- Children learn to measure and why it is important to be accurate.
- You can work together to calculate cooking times and when the cakes will be ready.
- Decoration helps with number matching because you need, for instance, a cherry to decorate each cake or two currants for the eyes of each gingerbread person.

Written number

Children need plenty of experience to make sense of numbers that are written. You can help in the following ways.

- Look for appropriate use of written number in your setting. You might have numbered 'parking bays' for the bikes and trolleys in the garden. Some areas of your setting might have a maximum number of children at any one time, so a reminder notice may say that there are to be no more than four children at the water tray.
- You could use a self registration system with some learning areas in your setting. For instance, perhaps the computer area has a display with numbered places for children to put their name card over the day or session. As each child leaves their card it becomes obvious how many children have used this area in total. A movable display could lead to a discussion at the end of the day or session about how many children used this area today.

- Display number books and wall friezes that link the written number to the same number of objects, cats or any other item that children can see.
- Birthday charts can link number to age and how the passing of a birthday means that a child is one year older.
- Simple board games give experience in looking at the numbers on dice and counting on the same number of spaces. Four and five year olds need plenty of help and practice to get the hang of this use of counting.
- Try to provide other games such as card pairs, or picture dominoes, where the written number is given as well as the correct number of objects.

Children need to understand that numbers have a practical use, just as you want them to understand that writing is useful.

- Try a number walk to find all the examples of number that you can: on house and shop fronts, bus route numbers and timetables, the prices in shops and the local market and many more.
- Or go out to spot the numbers in the local neighbourhood shown in a set of photos that you took earlier.

When children are interested in writing numbers, then encourage them to do their practice in a meaningful context. It is counterproductive to rush children into this task and far less meaningful to children if you do it mainly through worksheets. Four and five year olds will often be ready to have a go at writing numbers less than ten. Children of six and seven years of age start to understand the meaning of numbers beyond ten. They have to understand that the 1 in 12 stands for a value of 10 and not for 1.

- Children may like to write up the numbers for the kind of activities described in this section. If they are involved in counting up, they may initially use a tally of marks that are converted into an actual number.
- They may like to do the writing of numbers when they and you set up a pretend market, a café with a price list or a post box in the pretend post office with the timing of the mail pick up on the outside.

Activity

- Take three ideas from this section of the chapter and plan how you will use them in your own practice.
- Carry out your ideas and write up the activity, including any opinions expressed by the children.

Key skills links: C2/3.3 LP3.1–3

Different kinds of size

Children learn about size and relative size by plenty of hands-on practice.

- Initially children can be confused about the different aspects to a broad concept of size: height, weight and volume. You can help by being precise about the words you use. See page 371 for a reminder that adults often use the all-purpose word 'big' to cover these ideas as well as getting older as a child.

- Make height charts with children to explore 'big' in terms of how tall and relative size.
- You can talk about the height of children's constructions with bricks or cardboard boxes. Children will like to record with photos the height and other features of especially impressive constructions.
- You can explore weight, relative weight and ways to measure weight that do not initially depend on understanding grams and kilograms. Children can work out which is heavier when they compare play materials or use a balance to try to make the two sides the same.
- Look at different materials in your setting with a view to helping children experience different features. For instance, a balloon may be 'big' when it is blown up, but is much 'lighter' than an apple.

Shape

Children learn about the different kinds of shape by plenty of hands-on practice and seeing what is meant by word names such as 'square', 'triangle' or 'circle'. In a similar way to learning about colour (see page 367), children need to see and notice the visual, and sometimes touch, features of different shapes and then be able to apply the words to the right shape. Children also experience shape in two dimensions when it is drawn on a piece of paper, and in three dimensions with bricks or other sets of sorting shapes.

- Children can experience different shapes by sorting bricks and other three dimensional shapes into different types.
- Construction activities and some jigsaws encourage the search for a particular shape that will fit.
- Children can make different shapes with craft materials like play dough or clay.
- Craft activities such as material patchwork and paper collage offer the opportunity to find and fit different shapes.

Figure 13.8
Pretend play can be a rich source of thinking and communication

- Children can match shapes in a shape lotto or shape dominoes game.
- You can have I-spy hunts to find different shapes and document them by drawing or taking photos. Children will find shapes in the natural world as well as part of the indoor environment in patterns on lino or woodblock flooring.

Understanding time

Young children do not understand clock time and it is not unusual for six or seven year olds to be confused over telling the time. But an understanding of time is much more than clock time and you can support young children as they understand this concept.

- Children learn through familiar routines about a sequence in the day or a session as time passes. They learn the vocabulary of times of the day such as morning and afternoon and time indicators like 'soon', 'later' and 'afterwards'.
- A friendly routine with some flexibility helps children to predict what will happen next and to understand about 'snack time' or 'tidy up time'.
- Some predictability about what happens on days of the week is how children make sense of the fact that Monday comes before Tuesday and that Friday is the day before the weekend.
- Time measures like five minutes or half an hour do not mean anything to three, four or five year olds. They can make sense of 'you have time for one more painting' or 'one last run around the park and then we need to go back to nursery for our lunch'.
- Use simple time measuring devices such as large sand timers. Children are able to operate these and they like the fairness it brings to turn taking on bikes and other shared play materials.

Telling the time in terms of clocks is not easy. The division of time into 60 minutes in an hour and 24 hours in the day is an arbitrary system. Children need to have grasped the number system and to understand that, with the exception of 24 hour clocks, the 12 hour system is repeated in a day.

- When six and seven year olds struggle with telling the time, remember that children nowadays have to negotiate understanding time from clocks with moving hands and the many digital timepieces that give only numbers (in a 12 or 24 hour system).
- Clocks and watches with moving hands have to be understood on a 'big hand'–'little hand' basis. Then there is the confusing business of quarter past, half past and quarter to the hour. If you tune into the task for children, you will recall that telling the time takes lots of practice.

Activity

- Take three ideas from this section of the chapter and plan how you will use them in your own practice.
- Carry out your ideas and write up the activity, including any opinions expressed by the children.

Key skills links: C2/3.3 LP3.1–3

The Numeracy Hour

In England the National Numeracy Strategy was introduced along with the National Literacy Strategy (see page 341) to support standards. The usual approach to early numeracy has been less structured than some of the approaches to literacy.

The methods of supporting children's understanding described in this section are consistent with the expectations for children in the Reception class. The numeracy hour itself has usually been interpreted as a total that is met by activities for children that spread throughout the day.

Using information and communication technology

Information and computer technology, known as ICT for short, covers all the tools and techniques related to the use of computers. In practice, this area tends to include the use of technology to support learning for children younger than eight years. The broad objectives are that children:

- become familiar with all the ways in which they can use computers and the related technology
- learn how to use the mouse and the keyboard and the general ways in which information is organised
- are able to use programmable toys and simple robots as part of their play and exploration
- feel confident in the use of the technology in daily life, including calculators, cameras, remote controls, video and tape recorders.

Tips for practice

There is a bewildering array of hardware and software for computer usage. If you are involved in choosing and buying equipment or programs it is wise to get some impartial advice.

- The magazine *Nursery World* has regular reviews of software and an annual supplement *Nursery Computing*.
- Talk with other early years practitioners to find out how well equipment and programs work in practice.
- If you can, visit other settings to see different types of technology in action and children using them.

Computers for under threes?

Babies, toddlers and very young children learn best by direct involvement with play materials and safe access to explore ordinary objects (see page 270). There are no sound developmental reasons to give under threes regular access to computers.

You will encounter commercial interests who are very keen to sell computer software for toddlers, with the message that earlier must be better. But young children have plenty of time to become computer literate and they do not yet have the understanding of their social world to make sense of screen images. Computers are part of ordinary life now, so there is no need to keep under threes

Figure 13.9

Computers have a place in early years settings, but should not dominate

away from them. But there is also no advantage in pushing computers as a significant part of daily life for very young children. The rest of this section is written with over threes in mind.

Uses of computer technology

Children need to gain experience and confidence in the different uses of computers, and certainly not only about games. Children who have access to computers at home probably mainly, or only, use them for games. However, the range of options includes:

- software for drawing and design
- word processing packages for writing and experimenting with layout and style of text
- searching and finding information from a CD ROM
- simple handling of numbers and layout in spreadsheets
- using a scanner to integrate hand-drawn illustrations or pictures from magazines into a document
- use of images from a digital camera
- email options for sending communications.

You will not necessarily have all these options in your setting and some uses, such as data handling, will be more appropriate for school age children.

Tips for practice

- Ensure that you are familiar with how the computer works and the software packages that are loaded.
- Be ready to show and tell a child how to work the equipment and find their way in and out of a program.
- Then you can be enthusiastic when children can show you what they have discovered. You might say, 'That's an unusual drawing. How did you create it?' or 'I didn't know the program would do that. Can you show me please?'
- Be ready to help whenever children would like you to. Computers will go wrong and paper will jam. So it is important that your timely intervention reduces frustration for the children.
- Explain out loud your own problem solving strategies when it is not immediately obvious how to use a program or achieve a particular effect or function.
- Use the correct terms for computer usage such as 'keyboard', 'mouse', 'save', 'print' or 'menu'.
- Use the appropriate phrase to say out loud what you are doing or to confirm what the children are doing. You might say, 'I'm double clicking on this picture', 'Have you put in the CD ROM?', 'Do you know how to click and drag what you want?' or 'We could cut this paragraph and paste it in here. What do you think?'

Activity

- Take two or three ideas from the tips for practice box in this section.
- Consider especially how you can set a good example in problem solving strategies.
- Plan how you will use them in your own practice to support ICT.
- Carry out your ideas and write up the activity, including any opinions expressed by the children.

Key skills links: C2/3.3 LP3.1–3

A welcoming computer area

You need to take as much trouble over your computer area as any other learning area in your setting. You want children to develop good habits of computer use as well as familiarity with the technology.

- Children need good lighting to see, but not direct sunlight.
- They need enough space to sit comfortably and move their hands with ease.
- Ensure that the seating and layout of any computer area enables children to learn good habits of posture when working at the computer.
- They should hold their hands above the keyboard, keeping their hands in line with their wrists.

- Adjust the chairs, if necessary, so that children either look straight at the screen or slightly down, not up at the screen.
- Children should sit with their back straight. Provide a cushion for the small of their back if necessary.

You can help children to become familiar with the different parts of the computer:

- You can show and tell as children learn.
- You can also have written labels that say 'printer', 'CD ROM box' and 'paper'.
- A large drawing of the computer on the wall can label clearly the different parts, such as monitor, keyboard and mouse.
- Alternatively have a three dimensional junk model that shows the different parts of a computer. Making this model could be a creative project for the oldest children in your setting or for children in Reception or Year One to do for the nursery in a school.
- If your mouse has two or more buttons, then put a smiley sticker on the left hand button, which children will mainly use. Very few children in early years settings will be able to tell left from right yet.

Another source of practical writing will be a short list of ground rules for the computer area. You can write them up with the involvement of the children, who could add drawings. Like any other rules, keep these short and phrased in a positive way. You could include:

- our hands are clean (no sand!)
- two children at one time
- one child on the mouse or keyboard at a time
- we tidy up afterwards.

Children can understand that tidying up the computer area and putting everything away is as important as tidying other areas of your setting. Any CD ROMs need to go back in their containers, paper is tidied back into the box, the equipment is switched off and covers put over each item.

Activity

- Take two or three ideas from this section.
- Consider especially how you can involve children in the activity, like rules for the computer area.
- Carry out your ideas and write up the activity, including any opinions expressed by the children and illustrations of what you have all done.

Key skills links: C2/3.3 LP3.1–3

Monitor computer usage

Children should not spend too long at the computer, neither at one sitting, nor over the day or session, so that they ignore other sources of learning. Computer and other ICT usage should complement all the other learning opportunities and not supplant them. It may help to have some kind of self registration for this area (see page 379) as well as keeping a friendly eye yourself on who is at the computer and for how long. A self registration system can also help you identify children who rarely if ever use the computer.

There is no need to push children into using the computer area, especially if they are younger than four or five years and busy learning from other resources in your setting. However, it is useful to observe and see if lack of confidence may be stopping a child or perhaps the belief that computers are all about boring games. You can help by encouraging a child to explore what the computer will do and showing that you also use the possibilities of the technology.

It is possible that boys may dominate the computer area, although this is not the inevitable pattern. If you do observe an uneven gender division then look at how to encourage girls to use the technology. You could show, by your own actions, the different ways that computers can be a resource for other projects: to write, to draw and to search for information.

You can encourage use of the potential of computers linked with other resources in your setting, so that technology complements direct experience. For example:

- Images could be found or scanned into the computer and then printed out as part of a project to make books, cards, a wall frieze or any other creative project. The computer is used to extend the search for images and then these are used in hands-on design and creation.
- A project about gardening could involve direct work in the outdoor area, a visit to look for items and buy in the local gardening centre and searches with a CD ROM to discover information about plants and what they need in order to grow.

Tips for practice

- Be ready to show and explain to parents how children use and learn about ICT in your setting.
- If parents do not use computers much themselves, they may believe that children will do nothing but play computer games.
- Involve the children in making a display of how they have used different programs on the computer with 'we wrote about…' 'we drew …' and 'we found out all about …'
- Invite parents in for special afternoon or evening sessions to explore what can be done with ICT.

Scenario

Baker Street Children and Family Centre has explored how to introduce children to communicating through email. The computer in the office has an internet link and the centre has built up contact with settings in other parts of the UK and is now working on links in other countries.

Children are encouraged to make contact with the other settings, whose location is shown on a large map of the UK. Children plan what they want to say and dictate the email. Staff and children are learning together how to attach other files and will soon explore how to send photos from the digital camera. Some material is also sent between the settings by conventional post.

A recent team discussion has been about whether to set up an email link with 'Father Christmas'. Sian brought in a suggested project outline that would involve children in emailing to an address, perhaps that of one of the parents and then the parent emailing back as Father Christmas. Tyrone and Natalie are very dubious about this project. They argue that Father Christmas does not exist and surely this use of the technology undermines the existing communication with genuine people and places. Sian and Asha counter that it is just a bit of fun and part of other Father Christmas activities.

Questions

1 In what ways could the centre continue to link up with the other settings? Think of some possible joint projects and apply them to your own setting.

2 Should the centre use the technology to email 'Father Christmas'?

3 Consider the possible advantages and disadvantages of such a project. Discuss your conclusion with your colleagues.

Key skills links: PS3.1 WO3.1–3

Children with special needs

Computer technology can be of equal use for children with special needs and sometimes the possibilities open up a child's world.

- It is possible to get a larger scale mouse or overlays for the keyboard for some software programs. Then children can still be involved who have more difficulty than their peers in the physical movements that are required.
- It can be possible to record short phrases, such as refrains from a song, so that a child with communication difficulties may be able to press a button to add a contribution to songs and rhymes.
- Once children start to write, using the keyboard can ease the task for children. Some will have more difficulty with the physical coordination of writing than their peers and children who have dyslexia can be helped by keyboard use.

Finding out more

Inclusive Technology is an organisation specialising in making computers accessible to children with special needs. Contact them on tel: 01457 819790 website: *www.inclusive.co.uk*

Technology and play

Computers and other related technology are part of everyday life for children now. You can familiarise children with the equipment through other activities.

Role play areas

You can provide non-functioning computers or keyboards for role play areas, such as an office. An old keyboard can be very useful for younger and more vigorous children who cannot resist banging the keys and switching the buttons.

A technology table

Children are intrigued by how appliances work.

- A technology table can be provided with tools and old items of technology that children can take apart.
- Children can be part of drafting letters to parents requesting unwanted appliances.
- Remove any batteries and explain to children why old batteries need to be treated with care.
- Children need basic tools that work. One star-headed and one ordinary screwdriver plus a pair of pliers with wire cutting jaws will be sufficient.

Children are fascinated by what is inside old tape recorders, ordinary telephones and mobile phones. You can show your own interest and some children may want to document through photos and a display what they have discovered. Three, four and five year olds can understand that these items are for dismantling and looking at. Their valuable curiosity will then not be applied to working examples.

Local technology

You can explore with children through local trips how you can spot examples of technology in the neighbourhood. If you and the children explain your interest then it is likely that some people will give you time to show how equipment works and what it will do. Some possibilities include:

- use of a computer to store information for local businesses, such as an estate agent
- the bar code scanner at the supermarket
- the database for books at the library or the system for registering that books have been taken out or brought back
- video security systems in shops or train stations.

Figure 13.10
Children are interested in and can learn about a range of technology

Using cameras

Children learn how to be careful with cameras when adults take the trouble to show them how to be responsible. An increasing number of early years settings and schools now use cameras as a regular part of the children's day.

- You can use a camera to record activities as a supplement to other observations you make as an adult.
- But children also like to record projects, both the work in progress and the final end product of their hard work.
- A store of photos can be built up over time and made into a display, for example, of the exciting new building going up on the high street or the changes in trees and flowers in the local park.
- Children can use cameras and their later choice of photos to record their views about a setting: favourite places and activities, important parts of the setting and fun moments that nobody wishes to forget.
- Use the photos you take and those of the children to explore good technique, such as keeping your fingers out of shot, holding the camera steady and what is too close and too far away for a good photo.

Most settings will have an ordinary camera but some have invested in a digital camera, which costs more at the outset but then you do your own printing. Children of four, five years and older can become adept at handling the images on the screen, making adjustments and printing. If your system is linked with a website for your setting then you need to have good security systems for access, including passwords.

If necessary, discuss some ground rules with the children about what is photographed and how.

- You should of course follow your own guidelines. It is a good rule of thumb never to take a photo of a child that you would not take of an adult colleague, for instance in the toilet or in a state of undress.
- When you take the camera out on local trips, ask permission before you take photos of people.
- It may be very important to some families that photos of their children do not leave the setting. Some parents may have fled domestic violence and it is crucial that the violent partner does not know the current location of this parent and the children.

Activity

- Take two or three ideas from this section.
- Consider especially how you can involve children in the activity and avoid being an over-directive adult.
- Carry out your ideas and write up the activity, including any opinions expressed by the children and illustrations of what you have all done.

Key skills links: C2/3.3 LP3.1–3

Further resources

Caddell, Dorothy (1998) *Number Counts* Scottish Consultative Council on the Curriculum.

Donaldson, Margaret (1978) *Children's Minds* Fontana.

Healy, Jane (1998) *Failure to Connect: How computers affect our children's minds and what we can do about it* Touchstone.

Gopnik, Alison, Meltzoff, Andrew and Kuhl, Patricia (1999) *How Babies Think: The science of childhood* Weidenfeld and Nicholson.

Lindon, Jennie (1998) *Understanding Child Development: Knowledge, theory and practice* Thomson Learning.

Progress check

1 Describe two ways in which you could observe the results of children's thinking when they do not say much.

2 Give four examples of abstract ideas that three or four year olds might understand, other than colour or shape.

3 Explain why young children are not usually helped when adults ask closed and testing questions.

4 Describe four activities that could help children practice counting.

5 Suggest three reasons why you should monitor use of your computing area.

14

Supporting children's learning within the curriculum

After reading this chapter you should be able to:

- explain ways to support children towards a positive disposition to learn
- understand and explain different approaches to an early years curriculum
- consider positive ways to support children's learning in early years settings and school
- understand and promote flexible approaches to learning that give children choices.

Introduction

The overall objective of any early years setting and of early years practitioners has to be that children are supported positively in their learning. Children need not only to extend their learning through the years of childhood but to build an image of themselves as individuals who can learn. Early years practitioners support children through their own positive behaviour and through constructive planning within the curriculum. This chapter considers the broad approaches to children's learning and Chapter 15 then looks at ways to plan within early years settings.

Links to early years qualifications

This chapter especially supports the following units:

Diploma in Child Care and Education: 2, 6

National Vocational Qualification in Early Years Care and Education

Level 2: C8, E1

Level 3: M7, M8

BTEC National Early Years Diploma: 3, 7, 9

Developing a positive disposition to learn

Part of healthy personal development for young children is a growing sense that they are competent individuals. By three or four years of age, and certainly within the early years of school, it dawns on children that they have a very great deal to learn and much that they do not currently understand or know. If children are not to feel overwhelmed by this prospect, they need a positive outlook on themselves as learners and the process of learning. Supportive adults can make a very great difference to children's experiences.

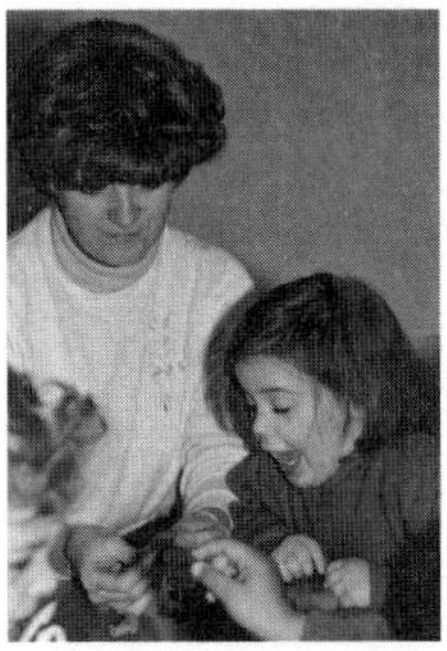

Figure 14.1
Your aim is that the children are enthusiastic about learning

To think about

- In Chapter 15 you will find different ways of planning ahead to give children a full range of activities and to support their learning.
- It cannot be emphasised too much that none of this planning will genuinely support children unless you are willing to tune into how children learn.
- Planning and curriculum paper plans or charts, no matter how well drafted and discussed, cannot do the work for you with the children day by day.

Supporting a positive disposition to learn

Learning is not all intellectual or rational; feelings are just as much involved. It is important that children develop a confidence that they can learn. Knowledge about child development will help you to be realistic about what is possible for children at different ages. You need to avoid putting unrealistic pressure on children and to focus on being pleased with them for what they manage now. Children's emotional well being supports them in all their learning.

Children's **positive disposition to learn** includes all of the following:

- curiosity and the wish to find out and explore
- a desire to become competent, to be able to do or say something
- a motivation to keep trying, even if something is neither easy nor obvious at the outset
- a sense of satisfaction for children when they practise, improve and realise that they have managed a new skill or idea.

This positive outlook can develop over time with adult support. Alternatively children may learn from negative experiences that they are incompetent, that adults think they keep making mistakes and that there is no point in trying.

Key term

Positive disposition to learn
an enthusiasm felt by children about learning, supported by a positive self-image and sense of 'I can'

Activity (observation)

Take any of the general points about a positive disposition to learn and look for examples of what this could mean for children of different ages.

For instance, collect some examples of what curiosity looks like in

- toddlers, younger than two years
- a four year old
- a six or seven year old
- perhaps an adult like yourself.

Look at your brief observations and consider in your own setting:

- What could be done to support children in curiosity and the wish to explore?
- What is likely to undermine children – from adult behaviour or the way that an early years setting or family home is organised?
- Then collect some observations relevant to another point.
- Discuss your findings with colleagues.

Key skills links: LP3.1–3 WO3.1–3 C3.1a

What is learning like for children?

Children are not only learning specific skills or gathering factual knowledge; they are also developing an outlook on learning. Adults, practitioners or parents, can help to encourage positive attitudes towards learning and support children's sense of self esteem and confidence.

You can help if you make the effort to look through children's eyes and observe the world from their perspective. Children will not use these exact words but they do wonder about:

- Can learning be satisfying? Can it be enjoyable? When is it fun? Learning is not fun for children all the time!
- Am I someone who can learn? Have I learned in the past? Children are not always aware of what they have learned so far, because they focus on the here and now.
- Are mistakes a disaster or can I really learn from what goes wrong?
- Can I get help and is it alright to ask for help?
- What can I do with what I've learned? Is it useful?
- Is newness a source of opportunity and interest? Or is it more a threat to be avoided?

Adults can often forget that children's experiences include a great deal of newness, sometimes with little time to feel confident in one area before another new skill or area of knowledge is introduced. Children in primary school regularly experience this sense of being moved on, so you need to avoid creating a sense of pressure earlier in childhood!

Studies of learning, by children or adults, has highlighted four general stages in awareness:

1 *Unconscious incompetence* – when you are unaware of your lack of

knowledge or skill in a particular area. You do not know that you do not know – blissful ignorance.

2 *Conscious incompetence* – when you are only too aware that you do not know something, do not understand or cannot manage a skill. This can be a very uncomfortable stage.

3 *Conscious competence* – when you are able to use knowledge or manage a skill, but you have to concentrate with care.

4 *Unconscious competence* – when you understand and have practised enough that this area comes automatically to you and you no longer have to concentrate on each step.

Activity

As an adult now, you have a great deal of learning experience behind you. Ideas or skills that seem obvious to you are not at all obvious to children. It can help you to tune into their feelings and struggles if you consider an area of learning that you tackled relatively recently.

For instance, perhaps the experience of learning to drive a car is fairly fresh in your mind or of becoming competent in using the internet. You will have gone through the four stages.

- What did it feel like, perhaps in learning to drive, when you did not seem to have enough hands and feet to manage all the movements?
- What was helpful behaviour from other people when you were struggling with the internet, or with becoming computer literate in the first place?
- What was not at all helpful? What made you feel incompetent and reluctant to ask for help?
- Now take a step across in your mind. How can you use those memories to tune into children's struggles and to be a helpful adult now?
- Discuss the experiences and issues with your colleagues.

Key skills links: C3.1a

It is far too easy for adults to forget that an area of knowledge or a skill, that seems so obvious now, was something that they learned.

- Effective help for children frequently depends on an adult willingness to take a task or skill apart and help a child through the various stages. See the example about self help skills on page 50.
- Part of this help is that adults make an effort to observe and understand how far a child's learning has progressed, where they are at the moment, whether they are stuck, and how they can be helped to move forward.
- Otherwise it is possible for adults to be impatient or assume that children are being awkward, when they do not understand.
- You will find examples throughout other chapters but a particularly useful area for tuning into children is when they are learning about abstract ideas (see page 368).

How you can support learning

In order to help children to learn day by day from the experience you offer, you also need to remain aware of their more general experiences of learning. How are they enabled to learn in your setting, your home as a childminder or their own home if you work as a nanny?

Perseverance, practice and making connections

Children need opportunities to practise and encouragement to persevere through the times when something does not come easily.

- An excessive emphasis that learning 'must be fun' is unhelpful for children, if this means that adults fail to help children to persevere through difficulties.
- You can then share in the delight when that perseverance brings success and satisfaction.
- Children need to learn that some skills take time and that they will understand an idea in the end, even when it does not come easily at the start.
- Without adult help in explaining simply how learning evolves, some children become trapped by their belief that you are either 'good at' something or you are not. By the early years of school, some children have already decided they are 'no good at maths' or 'clumsy at games'.
- Children will have some special talents and interests and helpful adults highlight those. But children will be able to learn in other areas with effort and adult support.
- Adults can help children to make connections between one skill and another or between apparently separate areas of knowledge. Adult comments can guide with 'Do you remember what we did with ... Perhaps that will help here'.

Informative encouragement

So long as adults help, children can learn from mistakes and frustrations.

- Some children need a great deal of reassurance along the lines of 'I can see your painting hasn't gone how you wanted. Let's see what happened' or 'I can hear you're having trouble with the scissors. Show me how you're doing it.'
- Knowing a child well can help adults to boost children's confidence, to encourage them to recognise their abilities in one area and not dismiss themselves as 'stupid' or 'no good at ...'.
- Perhaps you can remind a child how 'you told me you'd never ever be able to do up your buttons. And look at you now. Don't worry, we'll work out this problem together.'

Constructive feedback from adults can help children to focus on what has gone well, not just on what has gone wrong. Children are more likely to accept suggestions and helpful hints from adults who are generally supportive rather than critical. Some children, especially, need to be supported in accepting compliments and recognising their achievements. Good communication skills to support children have much in common with similar skills used in good working relationships with adults (see page 605).

- Adults have to acknowledge children's difficulties and current frustrations. It is unhelpful to pretend everything is fine when it clearly is not for this child.

- You can affirm a child's self worth, acknowledge problems and encourage them forward.
- Useful phrases can be, 'You don't understand this at the moment' or 'You can't do this yet …' or 'I can see that you're finding this tough. Let's see how I can help' or 'Now I see that's where you're getting stuck, let me show you …'.
- Adults also need to celebrate successes with children, to help them to register what they have managed before moving onto something else that is new and perhaps difficult.
- Moving on from positives ('You can manage this very well. You know, I think you're ready for …') is just as important as dealing constructively with negatives.

Tips for practice

Useful and constructive feedback for children addresses feelings as well as facts:

- Positive feelings can be expressed in words of encouragement to children along with positive body language and smiles.
- Negative feelings should be avoided in expressions by adults, since they will emerge to the child as blunt criticisms.
- Concerns should be expressed factually. Adults should, however, acknowledge and deal sympathetically with children's negative feelings about their abilities.
- Positive factual feedback is useful for children: what has gone well and why or how a child's perseverance has paid off.
- What could be negative factual feedback can be valuable if given in a constructive way. Focus on what has gone well as well as what has gone awry, and offer genuine help to children to learn from mistakes.

A focus on continuing learning

Adults help children and young people when they focus on the future as well as the present and the past. Lev Vygotsky's idea of the zone of proximal development is a useful way to consider the learning of any individual child at a given time. Look back at the explanation and the diagram on page 356.

The zone represents the area of possibilities that lies between what children can manage on their own at the moment and what they could achieve or understand with some appropriate help. The size of the zone is not fixed; some children may have a larger zone of proximal development than others. Your help (or that of an interested older child) builds on the young child's existing ability, understanding or skill, and helps her or him to move to a potential level of development through the short distance covered by the zone of proximal development. As children learn, their levels of actual and potential development continue to change.

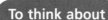

To think about

When my son was five years old, a close friend of his moved house and we were invited to tea at Piya's new home. I drove us most of the way and then pulled in to check my London A–Z. Drew and I then had a conversation that went like this:

Drew: How do you know where Piya lives?
Jennie: His Mum gave me their new address. I know it's round here somewhere. I'm just not sure of the last bit.
D: So how can we find it if you don't know?
J: I've got the map. I'm going to find it in the A to Z.
D: (looking at the map) But how can you find it on there?
J: It's okay. I know the name of the road.
D: But there's no houses or anything on it (the map). How can you find Piya's house on that?
J: Ah, right. The map doesn't show houses and things. But it shows me the roads. Look. We're here now and Piya's road is there. The map tells me we have to turn right, go straight on a bit and then turn left.
D: But what about his house?
J: That'll be alright because I know the number. We get onto Piya's road and then we look out for number fourteen. The houses will have numbers on the doors.

Questions

1 From this short exchange what can you learn about what Drew understood so far and what was confusing him about how maps worked?
2 Look out for situations with children you know when they are slightly confused. In what ways can you explain in words or show in actions so that you help them to extend their understanding?
3 Write up these examples as short case studies.
4 Discuss what you observed and what you did with colleagues.

Source: This example is taken from Jennie Lindon *Understanding Child Development: Knowledge, theory and practice* (Thomson Learning 1998).

Key skills links: C3.3 C3.1a

Key terms

Curriculum
a framework for supporting learning that specifies broad areas of learning and approaches to promote children's learning of knowledge and skills. A curriculum may describe precise content and methods to support learning

Early years curriculum
content and methods to support learning that are directly appropriate to children younger than 5–6 years of age

Learning within a curriculum

In general use, the word **curriculum** has tended to mean a course of study. You are following a curriculum in your studies as an early years practitioner. However, when the word is applied to the learning of younger children, curriculum carries a broader meaning.

What is a curriculum?

The phrase **early years curriculum** means the sum of all the experiences, opportunities and activities that you offer in your setting.

- Used appropriately, an early years curriculum is not restricted to particular kinds of learning or ways that children can learn.

Figure 14.2
Children's learning is supported through different types of play

- Young children are curious and flexible and they learn positively through many different routes so long as they have time, space and encouragement to learn.
- In the early years, good practice in the UK has been that children are enabled to learn through play and not by very adult dominated activities and formal teaching.
- A play-based curriculum is flexible and recognises that children's interests are broad and their view of play and playful activities extends beyond the boundaries that adults may draw around play.

The whole idea of a curriculum may seem more relevant if you are working with children in a group setting. Yet you still need a well-rounded approach to children's learning when you work as a nanny or a childminder. You may not talk in terms of a curriculum and will not plan ahead in the same way as an early years team. But the children will benefit from your taking a full view of what they could be learning and in what way.

Curriculum frameworks

Any curriculum needs a framework into which the details are then fitted. A curriculum framework is likely to define some or all of the following:

- The broad philosophy that underpins this approach to curriculum.
- The boundaries to what will be covered for children's learning – the broad areas in which their learning will progress.
- How children will be enabled to learn – the different methods that supportive adults will use. This aspect of a curriculum needs to tackle how adults will behave.

- The ways in which children's learning will be different after completion of this particular curriculum. Some curriculum frameworks are worded in terms of targets, goals or outcomes.
- Perhaps the ways in which the learning goals or targets will be observed and assessed.

The innovation of an early years curriculum

The ideas of a curriculum framework for children younger than school age developed from the eighteenth century onwards. Educational innovators developed approaches for young children that diverged from the repetitive drills and harsh discipline that were usual in schools and for children taught at home by a governess or tutor.

The innovators described in this section are all different and some ideas have continued to develop over time. They share a focus on early childhood as a time to be valued and the view that ways to support early learning need to allow children scope to explore, choose and practise, often through the medium of play. The different approaches also share a focus on broad areas of learning rather than narrowly defined school subjects.

Robert Owen (1771–1858)

Owen is often forgotten in discussions about educational innovators. Yet his work was much admired at the time and many visitors came from other parts of the UK and Europe. In 1819 Owen opened the first infant school in Britain for the children of his mill workers in New Lanark in Scotland. Owen was convinced that the early years of childhood were a vital time to develop health and a positive character in children. He insisted that children in the school be allowed to play and not to have to spend all their time with books. His view was extraordinary at the time, because prevailing Christian doctrine claimed that children were naturally sinful and needed uncompromising discipline in school life.

Friedrich Froebel (1782–1852)

Froebel built on the ideas of Johann Pestalozzi (1746–1827). Both men were concerned to develop a more kindly approach to children than the very strict rote-led learning normal in schools at the time. They emphasised children's capacity to explore and learn through playful activities. Froebel pioneered educational settings for children younger than school age that he called Kindergarten (German for children's garden). Froebel emphasised children's involvement in daily activities and learning through a wide range of structured play activities (called occupations), play materials (called gifts) and songs. Some of these materials, for instance the sets of wooden blocks, still delight children. Again, this approach may not seem very radical to the modern reader. So it is worth knowing that Froebel's approach caused such a stir that, at one time, the German authorities closed down all the Kindergarten.

Margaret McMillan (1860–1931)

McMillan was especially interested in how children could learn in an outdoor environment and concerned to improve the poor health of many city children. She developed nursery practice with a strong focus on being outside in the fresh air and exploration through the potential of a garden and working with real tools. Children worked on outdoor projects in which they exercised a great deal of choice. The open air nursery still exists as the Rachel McMillan Nursery School in south London.

In her approach and development of equipment, McMillan was very influenced by the French medical physiologist Edouard Seguin (1812–80). Seguin studied children with learning difficulties and promoted the idea, unusual for his time, that children's bodies and minds were linked, not separate. He developed an educational method for work with disabled children that aimed to train the muscular system through exercises and activities. Seguin's approach then led children from education of their senses to development of thinking and ideas.

Rudolf Steiner (1861–1925)

Steiner developed an approach to early education that focuses on how learning can be supported through the rhythm of daily routines. There is a strong focus on letting children, not adults, guide play and a value placed on the senses and physical movement. The curriculum followed in Steiner Waldorf nurseries and schools is based in the conviction that intellectual learning, especially the start to reading and writing, should not be rushed. The view is that children are not ready for this task until they are close to seven years. Steiner nurseries are concerned to offer a fully rounded curriculum and avoid the imbalance towards intellectual development and pressure from adults on children's choices and pace of learning.

Maria Montessori (1870–1952)

Based in Italy, Maria Montessori developed her approach from work with disabled children and those from very disadvantaged backgrounds. Montessori was also very influenced by the ideas of Seguin. She developed his materials into what is now known as the Montessori method, using specific educational equipment to help children manage skills through exploration and self motivated practice.

Montessori believed it was possible to provoke children's interest appropriately at different stages of development and to support their skills of self care, hand coordination and early literacy. The learning materials were designed to encourage individual rather than cooperative effort. However, group working was actively promoted with shared domestic responsibilities within settings such as her *casa dei bambini* (Italian for children's house). Her aim was to support children, especially socially deprived and disabled children, to be able to cope in later life and gain important skills of self reliance through exploration.

Susan Isaacs (1885–1948)

Isaacs was part of a therapeutic rather than an educational tradition. Her development of the Malting House School was very influenced by the ideas of Anna Freud and Melanie Klein, developed in the psychoanalytic tradition (see page 15). However, Susan Isaacs did not see education as a vehicle to analyse deep meanings in children's behaviour. She placed a high value on children's play because it gave such scope for imagination and thinking. Isaacs believed that play could help children work through emotional problems, but that it also helped children to develop social skills and was effectively children's 'work'.

High/Scope

The High/Scope approach developed in the mid-twentieth century in the United States as part of an intervention programme in Ypsilanti, Michigan to support children from disadvantaged neighbourhoods. This approach to curriculum has developed for general application in early years settings.

The High/Scope curriculum is based on two key principles: that children make sense of their world through interaction with people, materials and events and that adults need to support children's active learning. A consistent daily routine and easy accessibility of materials supports children's learning through a broad range of key experiences. The High/Scope approach places a strong emphasis on attentive observation by adults, since they need to respond to children's current interests. The approach also emphasises children's active choices and full involvement in the curriculum through the plan–do–review cycle.

Te Whāriki

During the 1990s educators developed a bilingual early years national curriculum for New Zealand that aimed to take a genuinely bicultural (English–Maori) approach to learning in early years setting. The Maori word whāriki means a woven mat for all to stand upon. The curriculum is built around key guiding principles, for example that children learn through responsive relationships. Broad goals for learning are built around the framework of five key aims: well being, belonging, contribution, communication and exploration.

The approach described in Te Whāriki has influenced some local authority curriculum frameworks in the UK through *Quality and Diversity in Education*, the report published in 1998 by the Early Education Forum based at the National Children's Bureau.

National curriculum frameworks

You may work in an early years setting that follows a curriculum developed from the ideas of the innovators described above. Otherwise you are likely to work within an example of the current national curriculum frameworks:

- If you work with children younger than school age then you are very likely to follow one of the national frameworks for early education for children older than three years of age (see page 403).

Figure 14.3
Young children need freedom to move and explore

- Settings that work with children younger than three years of age have to consider what will be a suitable curriculum framework for very young children and babies (see page 407). There are no national curriculum frameworks as yet for these very young children, although some local authorities have developed their own guidelines.
- Children who attend school will follow the educational national curriculum for their part of the UK (see page 407).

Guidance on an early years curriculum

During the 1990s, national guidance on early years curriculum was developed in England, Wales, Scotland and Northern Ireland. The national documents vary in the details, although the curriculum frameworks have much in common in terms of the areas of learning covered and the principles underlying the guidance. All the frameworks also suggest appropriate expectations for what children will most likely have learned in each of the broad areas of learning before they start school.

England

From autumn 2000 a new framework was established for children's pre-primary early education. The period from when children are three years old until the end of their Reception year was called the Foundation Stage. So this stage stretches into primary school, until children are five or six years of age, depending on their birthday.

The Foundation Stage has not changed legal requirements about education. In England, Wales and Scotland children have to start their education in the term after they reach five years of age. Children start school at four years of age in Northern Ireland.

The guidance for the Foundation Stage describes an early years curriculum built around helping young children to work towards early learning goals (ELGs). The ELGs represent achievements that it is expected most children will have gained by the end of their Reception year. A range of early learning goals are described for each of six broad areas:

- personal, social and emotional development
- communication, language and literacy
- mathematical development
- knowledge and understanding of the world
- physical development
- creative development.

The guidance indicates that children should be supported to learn in a way guided by their own interests and through the opportunities of play and involvement in daily routines. Approaches to support three to five year olds in any early years settings and Reception class are expected to be suitable to their age and understanding. In principle, the early learning goals are not supposed to be met through very formal activities or by making children sit still for long periods of time. In practice, some settings have felt a pressure to become more structured, especially when practitioners have been anxious to show evidence that children have made progress.

Wales

The *Desirable Outcomes for Children's Learning before Compulsory School Age* describes six areas of learning:

- language, literacy and communication skills
- personal and social development
- mathematical development
- knowledge and understanding of the world
- physical development
- creative development.

Like all the documents for Wales, *Desirable Outcomes* is written in English and in Welsh. The outcomes are worded in terms of 'By the time they are five, the experiences that children had had should enable them to ...' and the outcomes are flexibly expressed with phrases like 'begin to understand ...' and 'begin to appreciate ...'.

A review is being undertaken of this guidance as part of the planning for early educational places for three year olds. It looks as if a play-based early years curriculum in Wales will be extended into the first years of school for five and six year olds, along with the removal of SATs (Standard Assessment Tasks) at seven years of age.

Scotland

The document *A Curriculum Framework for Children 3 to 5* is built around five 'key aspects of children's development and learning':

- emotional, personal and social development
- communication and language
- knowledge and understanding of the world
- expressive and aesthetic development
- physical development and movement.

The guidance does not specify mathematical development as a separate area of learning; it appears in knowledge and understanding of the world. Each area has a section of 'children should learn to ...' with a list of broad developmental achievements by the end of the early educational phase. The guidance is also illustrated with 'examples from practice' for each area, with points to consider.

Northern Ireland

The *Curricular Guidance for Pre-School Education* describes seven broad learning areas:

- personal, social and emotional development
- physical development
- creative/aesthetic development
- language development
- early mathematical experiences
- early experiences in science and technology
- knowledge and appreciation of the environment.

The guidance emphasises the importance of observation, planning and record keeping. Each learning area has a box at the end on 'Progress in Learning' which is introduced as 'a general description of the characteristics and skills that the majority of children who have experienced appropriate pre-school education will display'. The sentences given in the paragraphs have much in common with other early years documents. In Northern Ireland, children whose birthday falls before June will start school at four years. Younger children will wait another year.

Activity

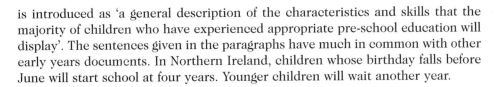

- If you work in an early years setting, it should be easy for you to consult your national guidance on the early years curriculum. If you have difficulty in obtaining a copy, then go direct to the relevant national body (see page 417 for contact details).
- Look at the guidance in terms of the main features (use the bullet points on page 403). Write up and discuss with your colleagues.

Key skills links: C3.1a C3.2

Learning through play

Young children learn a very great deal though their play and playful interactions. Every curriculum framework and any adult planning has to ensure that the content and approaches within any early years curriculum take serious account of children's play rather than a bias towards high levels of structure, adult-chosen and adult-led activities.

Children have many years of formal schooling to experience. There is no advantage, and many disadvantages, to pushing formal teaching methods down the age range. The power of learning through play is that:

- Children can make choices in their play and explore the directions that intrigue them at the moment.
- Children can take experiences and rework them or extend them through their play on their own or with friends.
- In play, children can mentally and emotionally step beyond the real limits of their life, especially in their use of pretend play.
- Play enables children to make connections between their own personal areas of learning and to push out the boundaries of what they can do and understand.
- Play and playful interactions can be a positive vehicle for learning from the earliest months of life.
- Play enables children to enjoy life and have a relaxed childhood – a perfectly reasonable objective in itself !

Play is a rich medium for learning but children do not only learn through play, especially if adults define play in a narrow way. Children learn a great deal through relaxed and happy conversation with adults who listen as well as talk (see page 310). Children can also learn a great deal from their natural involvement, in how your setting is run and from having a safe role to take in daily routines.

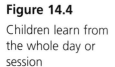

Tips for practice

Children will be able to learn through play when:

- They have plenty of choice in how they play and with what materials.
- They are able to use all the opportunities of a setting or family home, especially that they have easy access to the possibilities of outdoor as well as indoor play.
- Helpful adults plan ahead in a broad way for opportunities and then encourage and allow children to choose between what is available.
- Adults respect their play and deal courteously with any issues about behaviour within play.
- Adults value and observe how children are learning through their play.

Children are less likely to be able to learn through play if:

- Their choices are severely limited to what adults say is on offer today.
- Adults have been tempted to over-plan and over-supervise children's play and play interactions.
- Children are directed towards what adults feel are more valuable activities, that seem to have a better purpose from the adult point of view.
- Children's play is stopped or re-directed by adults with limited discussion or consultation, because the adults believe the play is unsafe, unacceptable or pointless.
- Children are interrupted in their play to do an activity, such as filling in worksheets, because adults feel this is more valuable or an easier way to produce evidence that children have learned something.

Figure 14.4

Children learn from the whole day or session

Children's development is also supported when they feel part of the routines that make each day run smoothly (see page 51).

- Young children experience a personal satisfaction in being a helper to adults and other children. They appreciate thanks in words and a smile and to be able to say, 'I did that' or ' I helped'.
- Ordinary routines can support children's all round learning and development. For example, when children are part of tidying up, they learn about simple time management, putting objects back into their right place and working together with other children.
- Their involvement in mealtimes can give practice in numbers for laying the table and physical skills with visual coordination are needed to help a friend to another helping of vegetables.
- Young children often chat when they are part of a shared domestic activity with an adult or perhaps one other child.

Young children learn better when they feel they have a trusted role to play within the daily routines. There may be some routines that you do yourself for safety reasons, but there are many in which children can be involved. Your adult contribution is to value this activity as a source of learning and allow enough time so that children can practise their skills and gain in confidence.

A very early years curriculum – under threes?

Currently there is no national framework in any of the four nations of the UK about good practice with children under three years. However, some local authorities have developed and published their own guidance for early years settings with babies, toddlers and very young children.

Over 2001–2 Lesley Abbott is leading a project in England to look at ways to develop a framework for effective practice with very young children. The aim is to cover principles, suitable experiences for babies and under threes and to shape suitable guidance to support practitioners. Lesley Abbott's team talks of a 'framework' and not of a 'curriculum' and their approach is likely to be consistent with the ideas described from page 418. Colwyn Trevarthen is leading an equivalent project in Scotland.

A national school curriculum

Since the 1980s there has been a national curriculum in the UK that determines the content, methods and assessment for education in state primary and secondary schools. Each nation in the UK is able to decide on the final shape of their state education and consequently there are some differences. In each country the school curriculum is organised more on a subject basis, although some have an explicit cross-curricular approach. The approach through areas of learning for the early years curriculum has been a statement that the subject approach is inappropriate for young children.

The legal requirement in the UK is that children receive an education from five years of age (four years in Northern Ireland). It is not the law that children have to go to school, although state or independent school is how most families met their obligations. A minority of families educate their children themselves, sometimes called home schooling.

England

Established in 1989 and revised in 2000, the national curriculum covers children from Year 1, when they are five or six years old until the end of statutory schooling at 16 years. Children's education is sub-divided into four stages, the first two in primary and the second two in secondary school:

- Key Stage 1 – school years 1 and 2, for five to seven year olds
- Key Stage 2 – school years 3, 4, 5 and 6, for seven to eleven year olds
- Key Stage 3 – school years 7, 8 and 9, for eleven to fourteen year olds
- Key Stage 4 – school years 10 and 11, for fourteen to sixteen year olds

In Key Stages 1 and 2 children are taught English, Mathematics, Science, Design and Technology, Information and Communication Technology, History, Geography, Art and Design, Music, Physical Education and Religious Education. There are required programmes of study for each subject and a national literacy and numeracy strategy. Achievement levels are described for every subject except Religious Education. There are non-statutory guidelines for personal, social and health education (PSHE) and citizenship and modern foreign languages at Key Stage 2.

Assessment of children takes place at the end of each Key Stage, by SATs for stages 1, 2 and 3 and GCSEs at the end of Key Stage 4.

Wales

The national curriculum established in Wales in 1989 was very similar to that in England, with the exception that Welsh can be a main language instead of English. However, since that time devolution (see page 26) has meant that Wales has increasingly made their own national decisions about educational content and methods. Wales for instance did not choose to have the literacy and numeracy hours that were introduced in England.

Scotland

The national curriculum in Scotland was introduced in 1991 and revised in 2000. The requirements cover seven years of primary school and four years of secondary school up to the age of sixteen when young people can choose to leave. The years are named from P1–P7 in primary school and S1–S4 in secondary. The required curriculum is described up to fourteen years of age at which point students then take options within specialised and vocational education that lead to the Scottish Qualification Certificate.

There are five main curriculum areas covered in Scottish schools:

- English Language, Gaelic where appropriate and another modern language no later than P6
- Mathematics
- Environmental studies: society, science and technology
- Expressive arts and physical education
- Religious and moral education with personal and social development and health education.

There are also five cross-curricular aspects to education:

- personal and social development
- education for work
- education for citizenship
- the culture of Scotland
- information and communications technology.

The curriculum specifies levels of attainment and teachers use national tests to assess children at the time when they are ready to move from one level to another in English and Mathematics. The timing is left to the judgement of the schools and there is no national assessment programme at particular ages in Scotland.

Northern Ireland

The Northern Ireland Curriculum was introduced on a phased basis from 1990. Children start school at four years of age, so the pattern is:

- Key Stage 1 – school years 1, 2, 3 and 4, for four to eight year olds
- Key Stage 2 – school years 5, 6 and 7, for eight to eleven year olds
- Key Stage 3 – school years 8, 9 and 10, for eleven to fourteen year olds
- Key stage 4 – school years 11 and 12, for fourteen to sixteen year olds

In Key Stages 1 and 2 children are taught:

- Religious Education
- English
- Mathematics
- Science and Technology
- History and Geography (known as the Environment and Society Area of Study)
- Art and Design, Music, Physical Education (known as the Creative and Expressive Area of Study)
- Irish in areas where Gaelic is the first language.

There are also four educational cross-curricular themes: Education for Mutual Understanding, Cultural Heritage, Health Education and Information Technology. These themes are not separate subjects but are expected to be woven through the main subjects of the curriculum.

Each subject is defined through programmes of study and attainment targets. The targets are described in terms of Level Descriptions and these form the basis for making judgements about children's attainments at the end of each stage.

Flexibility for learning: a curriculum in practice

Learning spaces in your setting

The aim in any plan for children's learning should be to leave plenty of scope for children to make choices and to extend an activity in the way that they wish. A positive way to promote such flexibility is to have a number of learning areas within an early years setting as semi-permanent spaces. There can be a slight confusion over wording, because 'learning areas' is also used to describe the six or seven areas of development and learning in the early years curriculum documents. Dedicated spaces for certain kinds of materials are not tightly linked to specific developmental learning areas.

Many nurseries and pre-schools have a book corner and a home corner, but other than that activities have often been laid out on tables or the floor in line with the adult plan. If your space belongs to the setting, then it can work well to have more learning areas than these two traditional ones.

You can make labels and illustrations with the children, so that it is clear what is available in this space. Life may be less flexible if you share the space, for instance, pre-schools which run in church halls where nothing can be left out between sessions. But it is still well worth looking at ways to move as far as possible from adult-determined activities on tables.

For example:

- An art area can be equipped with all the materials that children may use for different art activities. Books about art and pictures can be a semi-permanent part of the area – changed from time to time. Materials can be on accessible shelves or containers and ideally a sink is nearby so that cleaning up is an integral part of using this learning area.
- A construction area can have a good supply of flexible building materials and the space to lay out and sometimes display what children have made. A board could be made available for photos that children have taken of recent constructions.
- A graphics area could offer a good writing surface, plenty of writing materials and different kinds of stationery and a board for children to fix up any of their work or work in progress.
- A role play area, perhaps in addition to the ever-popular home corner, could have the flexibility to become a doctor's clinic, a travel agency or a train station, depending on children's interests and perhaps a project that has enthused a group of children.

Tips for practice

Learning spaces will work well when:

- Adults keep flexible about potential learning and the different areas. A construction area should not mean that all building has to happen in that space. Children will feel nagged if they are told that dressing up clothes should stay in the role play area. Why should they?
- Use of materials is allowed to be flexible. If children are enthused by writing and mark making materials they can access in the graphics area, they may well want to take their whiteboard or clip sheet to another part of the setting. The fact that the children see mark making as a transferable skill is very encouraging.
- Adults are observant and ready to adjust the focus and space of a learning area in response to children's play. Perhaps a group of children has become very enthusiastic about small world play and they need a larger space and some reorganisation of materials.
- Children are involved in discussion about new learning areas and re-organising existing spaces.
- It is also valuable to look at ways to enable children to tidy away as easily as possible in each learning space. Storage can be made accessible for children with low shelves and well labelled and illustrated containers. A tool outline board helps children to put the woodwork equipment back correctly and safely. Clear sketches or photos can be fixed up to show how the blocks are tidied back on the shelf.

Adults can use planning to look ahead and consider how they will discretely ring the changes in some of the areas and be available to help if children want, for instance with different kinds of craft activities. You can also be attentive and observant to look and listen to children's play so that you can offer an extension in a way that allows children to accept or decline.

Scenario

Greenholt Pre-school has only a limited ability to leave activities out in the church hall during the week. Discussion with the church warden and committee has established more flexibility through conversations that enabled the committee to understand better what children learn in the pre-school. The team also wanted to get away from the over-planned approach that had guided the pre-school so far (see scenario on page 484).

The home corner was allowed to become a more general role play area and the children's interest in a travel agency has opened the door to some early 'geography' through knowledge and understanding of the world. Trisha brought in a feature from *Nursery World* (26 October 2000) on the 'travelling teddies'. At first the team was uncertain since few of the current families have spare income for proper holidays. But travel could be anywhere that the children go away from home, even within a day.

The pre-school has three soft toys of which the children are very fond: a large bee, a floppy-eared dog and a purple dinosaur. The team explain to the children, and the parents, that the toys need to get out more and would like to travel with the children when they go somewhere interesting at the weekend.

- Over several weeks Buzy Bee, Floppy and Dino get to visit relatives, ride on a double decker bus, go walking in a nearby country park, visit hospital to see one mother and brand new baby and other local trips of significance to the children.
- The Greenholt practitioners follow the children's interest and realise that they are ready to do some very simple map making of the local area.
- A graphics table with flexible materials and a small world area become regular learning spaces in the pre-school.
- A few children also become concerned about the 'fairness' of trips and want to track where each toy has been. With help from Trisha, they draft a chart with written labels, photos when these have been taken and a simple count.
- Michael scans the chart with care and says, 'Buzy Bee is the only one who hasn't been to the garden centre. And it's very nice, with gnomes and a little fountain.' A discussion starts as to who will fill in the gap in Buzy Bee's local experiences.

There is great excitement when Dino is trusted to go off on a trip of several weeks with one of the traveller families whose children attend the pre-school when they are in the area. Dino and the family send postcards from several other locations and the children track him and the family on a map that encompasses several counties. Dino is returned safely with the child, whose family is also pleased that their travelling life style has been respected.

Questions

1 Any good idea, like the travelling teddies, can be adjusted for the conditions of a particular setting. How might you use this idea in the setting you know best?

2 If you do not use learning spaces in your setting, consider how you could set up semi-permanent spaces and equip them in a flexible way.

3 Make a short presentation of how you could, for instance, start with an idea you have heard from another local nursery or read in a magazine like *Nursery World*. Consider how you would develop the idea to fit your setting.

4 Discuss your ideas with colleagues, in your setting or on your course.

Key skills links: LP3.1–3 WO3.1–3 C3.1a

Creative development – an example of flexible learning

Each of the national curriculum documents includes children's learning within creative or expressive development. It is well worth thinking as a team about what is included in this area of learning and how you can support and encourage children's creativity rather than stifle its expression.

So what is creativity for children or for adults? Creativity develops when children are enabled to:

- Produce their own image and not reproduce somebody else's image – whether in the form of a picture, a story or a problem-solving idea.
- Learn through doing and exploring, rather than be required to follow a set pattern determined by adults.

Figure 14.5
Children are often pleased to see their work carefully displayed

- Focus at least as much on process as product. Sometimes there is nothing to show at the end of a genuinely creative activity except happy faces, feelings of satisfaction and a good memory.
- Learn useful techniques, because children should not be left to struggle, but then they can apply those techniques or use of tools in a way that makes sense to them.

Activities to promote creativity

A range of activities could potentially support children's creativity. So any planning needs to be open and creative in itself, not taking an unduly narrow view of what are creative activities and what are not. Children can develop in a creative way through:

- using a wide range of arts materials, exploring different textures, use of colours, techniques and styles
- exploring crafts like printing, collage, patchwork, needlework and woodworking
- all the different kinds of music, music making, singing and dance
- drama and role play – either of their own making or guided drama and story telling suitable for young children
- construction and building, especially with a wide range of materials, including recycled materials that leave plenty of scope for children to determine the nature of their project
- creative problem solving using imagination as well as more logical techniques.

But how you plan and then offer activities can make all the difference between whether the experience really does support children's creative development or not. You need to think creatively yourself. Look around, keep your eyes open for good ideas or techniques that children could manage and explore.

- Keep any type of project open. So for instance, you might put to the children that 'we need a shelter in the garden against the sun now it is so hot'. But do not immediately tell them what kind of shelter and how you are all going to build one 'just like this picture'. A creative project, and one that lets children explore the technology side, needs to be flexible.
- Get out and about yourself, and with the children. Bring examples of different painting or music styles into your setting.
- Look and listen with the children and explore the different ways to 'make a picture' or to 'create a tune'.
- Think beyond your own cultural background, whatever that may be. Art forms, dance and music, as well as cooking can seem unusual or exotic to you at first.
- Draw on experience and expertise that parents and other family members may be able to bring to your setting.
- You will help the children to think creatively if you do as well. Think big: projects can happen outdoors as well as indoors, on the walls as well as sheets of paper. Think creatively about how you can record and keep a memory of a good project.
- Look at any possibilities of getting out with the children to see an artist in residence, a dance or theatre group designed for children or a story teller.

Will anyone come to your own setting or close by so that several settings can enjoy the experience?

- In your own adult mind, keep a balance between the creative process and any end product. Avoid rushing children, some projects like woodwork take time and effort. Children cannot develop creatively if they are rushed because 'everybody has to do their hand print before going home time'.
- Introduce the idea of 'work in progress' and have safe places for unfinished projects so children can return to them. You can also be creative about how to 'hold on' to an end product – photos may be the best option with large projects or very fragile ones.

Tips for practice

- Support children to feel they 'can'. Children may very swiftly decide that they 'can't draw' or are 'no good at story telling'. Your adult approach may be too directive if you have many four year olds saying this to you, because at this age they are usually much more robust.
- Avoid following very directive topic books that prescribe very closely what has to happen with 'ask the children to make …' or 'tell the children to draw or cut …'.
- Showing and introducing different techniques is a positive and good use of adult knowledge – butterfly paintings, wax crayon rubbings, different ways to print. But then let children use and practise the technique to make what they wish and to experiment with the basic technique.
- You want the children to learn to look closely. Perhaps to consider a flower or leaf in all its details. But it is not a creative activity if children then have to paint the flower in the same way.
- Let children experiment if they wish and avoid the approach that everyone now has to do a painting like Monet, some Celtic knotwork or a representation of Mount Fuji.
- Arts and crafts are no longer creative when they are highly organised, either because sheets are pre-printed or because everyone has to make something very similar – an Easter card, a picture like the one on the wall, etc.
- Children should be able to make something or to solve a problem creatively because they find satisfaction, not to fill up a blank wall or have something neat to send home.

Activity

Under threes can relish many arts and crafts activities but in different ways from the older children. Adults often need to adjust how they view an activity in order to make it more suitable and enjoyable for very young children. But thinking about how best to offer creative activities to very young children can often help to focus your mind on what is the best way for adults to plan and behave in creative activities for the over threes.

In your own mind, or in discussion with colleagues:

- Focus on one activity, for example, painting or working with play dough, and gather ideas on the ways that you can adjust for the younger children, even for toddlers.

- For instance, do you modify how you lay out the materials or use of tools? Do you take a different approach to whether children produce something at the end?
- In your experience, how do toddlers want to use the materials?
- How can you best handle any sense of pressure about having something to show to parents or put on display from very young children?
- Write up and discuss your ideas with colleagues.

Key skills links: PS3.1–3 C3.1a C3.3

Early science – an example

Some practical thoughts about early science can help early years practitioners to appreciate how much children can understand when potentially complicated topics are presented through familiar routines and materials. Children's early understanding of science is described within the early years curriculum by areas such as 'Knowledge and understanding of the world' (English guidance) or 'Early experiences in science and technology' and 'Knowledge and appreciation of the environment' (Northern Ireland guidance). But it soon emerges that the topic area has connections to all the areas of early learning in childhood.

The enquiring mind

There is a 'scientific' outlook that is as much a part of early science as particular knowledge or skills. In an interesting and flexible early years setting, children can develop a scientific outlook appropriate to their years. They develop:

- curiosity and wanting to learn, to find out about how things work and why
- the language and behaviour of 'I wonder how, when, whether'..., 'Why does that/doesn't that happen ...' and 'What'll happen if I ...?'

Figure 14.6
Adult interest supports children's curiosity

- the skills of experimentation – safe and simple with 'let's see what happens if we ...'
- the skills of close observation and an interest in looking and listening
- the perspective of taking time, coming back to see what has happened now
- an interest in and techniques of recording and recalling – in any way children wish and are able
- the ability to make connections between experiences and simple explorations.

Ways into science 'subjects'

Obviously, the aim with young children, as well as older ones in primary schooling, is to avoid rigid divisions into the separate sciences. But it can be useful for us as adults to track back a little from the big three of physics, chemistry and biology. Young children are ready and able to learn in all these areas; they have already started.

They explore physics and the phenomena of the physical world through:

- what makes what happen – all kinds of cause and effect
- properties of objects such as floating and sinking
- the weather, how it changes, can we see the changes coming, the seasons; how the weather is linked with what else we see, like plants or how animals, wild or more domesticated, behave
- differences of light and dark, the sky, the moon and the stars.

Chemistry is part of everyday experiences:

- cooking is a practical and basic chemistry – mixes, the magic of yeast or making yoghurt, the impact of heat or cold, what works and what does not work
- what makes things happen when you mix them, natural mixes and safe mixing that children can do with sand, water, earth, paint
- what mixes can be reversed and which are now something new and irreversible
- natural chemistry and chemical reactions in the world around us – leaves into leaf mould, a compost heap for the garden, what grows on bread or other foods if you leave them (a link back into biology)
- interested children are keen to use information books about chemical and physical reactions in our environment – volcanoes, mud pools, earthquakes.

Biology is part of many of the ordinary indoor and outdoor activities for children:

- interest in living things of all kinds from the littlest mini beasts to huge mammals
- what we can see around us and watch over the seasons, understanding patterns of growth and change
- the interest of information books about animals, insects, plants, different environments
- plants and trees that we see, watch over time as they flower, fruit or produce conkers
- growing plants, fruit or vegetables ourselves – what do they need, what helps them grow and what makes it more difficult, what is growing without any help from us.

Activity

- Track 4–5 ideas from the section on 'early science' in your setting.
- Consider some ways to communicate this learning to parents.
- Write up and discuss with colleagues.

Key skills links: C3.1b C3.3

Further resources

Duffy, Bernadette (1998) *Supporting Creativity and Imagination in the Early Years* Open University Press.

Lindon, Jennie (2001) *Understanding Children's Play* Nelson Thornes.

Perkins, Sam (1998) *Seeing, Making, Doing: Creative development in early years settings* National Early Years Network.

Guidance on the early years curriculum

England: The *Curriculum Guidance for the Foundation Stage* and *Planning for Learning in the Foundation Stage* are available from QCA publications, P O Box 99, Sudbury, Suffolk CO10 6SN tel: 01787 884444 website: *www.qca.org.uk* or the Department for Education and Skills website: *www.dfes.gov.uk*

Wales: The *Desirable Outcomes for Children's Learning before Compulsory School Age* is available from ACCAC, Castle Buildings, Womanby Street, Cardiff CF10 9SX tel: 029 2037 5400, publications purchased from 07071 223647 website: *www.accac.org.uk*

Scotland: The *Curriculum Framework for Children 3–5* is available from Learning and Teaching Scotland, Gardyne Road, Broughty Ferry, Dundee DD5 1NY tel: 01382 443600 or the website: *www.ltscotland.com* or the Scottish Consultative Council on the Curriculum website: *www.scc.ac.uk*

Northern Ireland: *The Curricular Guidance for Pre-School Education* is available from CCEA, 29 Clarendon Road, Belfast BT1 3BQ tel: 028 9026 1200 or download from the website: *www.ccea.org.uk*

Progress check

1. Explain briefly why it is so important that children develop a positive disposition to learn.
2. Identify the main learning areas in the curriculum guidance in your part of the UK.
3. Give three reasons why any early years curriculum should promote learning through play.
4. Suggest two reasons why learning spaces in a setting can give children more scope for learning than activities laid out each day by adults.
5. Explain the difference between process and product in creative activities.

15

Planning for children's learning

After reading this chapter you should be able to:

- understand the role of planning to support the learning of young children
- plan appropriately for days with babies and very young children
- understand and use different time scales in a planning approach to support the learning of children from three years of age.

Introduction

An early years curriculum covers the content of what children can learn over early childhood and also the approaches to supporting their learning. In Chapter 14 you have explored ways to support children in a positive disposition to learn. Good practice is for practitioners to plan ahead to provide a well rounded curriculum in terms of children's experiences. This chapter suggests ways to plan that are developmentally appropriate for very young children and for children of three years and older.

Planning for children's learning – under threes

The national early years curriculum guidance documents (see page 403) are not designed for use with children younger than three years and the goals or targets certainly cannot be 'watered down' to use with babies and toddlers. Very young

Links to early years qualifications

This chapter especially supports the following units:

Diploma in Child Care and Education: 2

National Vocational Qualification in Early Years Care and Education

Level 2: E1, M1

Level 3: M7, M8

BTEC National Early Years Diploma: 7, 9

children need to be approached from their current developmental stage and they are in no way 'pre-foundation'. If the curriculum for over threes is used, there is a high risk that practitioners will be tempted to hurry younger children along and to find them always lacking, because they appear to have achieved so little.

Tips for practice

- The early years curriculum documents were not designed for use with under threes and nor was the topic approach (see page 435).
- It is inappropriate to try to plan around topics or themes for very young children.
- Sometimes there may be one or two activities within the topic being covered for the over threes that are genuinely suitable for younger children: perhaps a trip or an enjoyable game.
- But practitioners need to approach any activity from the perspective of younger children and make developmentally appropriate adjustments.
- It is inappropriate to make babies and toddlers complete activities like making a Mother's Day card just because the four year olds are doing this craft activity.
- Two year olds can enjoy simple mixing and cooking activities but their learning will not be supported if they are required to make neat gingerbread people as part of the topic.

Planning for the younger ones has some aspects in common with a curriculum for older children. But there are also unique features to under threes as they learn. Babies and very young children are primed to learn. But it is important to tune into the flow of their curiosity and current abilities.

- Very young children learn best at their own pace and by following their absorbing current interests. There is time for them to explore, find out, practise and learn.

Figure 15.1
In order to make choices toddlers need accessible materials

- Trying to make young children learn something earlier and quicker does not help them to learn better and can actually disrupt their confidence and flow of learning.
- Babies and toddlers learn through doing and need plenty of opportunities to use their physical abilities and to apply their ideas. The clear preference of very young children for 'do it again!' is ideal for their learning since it firms up their brain connections (see page 243).

Young children need plenty of play materials, but under threes are prepared to be interested in almost anything. There are some excellent play resources on the market, but children do not need all commercially produced toys. They learn best from flexible play materials that can be used in many different ways. You need to think creatively about activities and get well away from any sense of 'this toy will promote this kind of learning'. You will find many examples in other chapters but see especially pages 413 and 13.

Positive attitudes towards the under threes

Planning for under threes needs to be built around a full understanding of what is important in their day:

- Babies and toddlers are social beings. They are primed to learn and communicate. They need plenty of opportunities for early communication including close physical contact and touch (see also page 43).
- They need to develop affectionate social relationships because they learn through the security of a safe base and a predictable, familiar daily life.
- All their activities, from a broad, happy smile for a familiar face to an enthusiastic crawl across the room, support actual connections in their young brain that shape how babies and toddlers continue to relate to the world.

Developmentally appropriate care of very young children depends a great deal on your positive attitudes shown through how you handle the details of daily practice.

Babies and toddlers are interesting in their own right

You need to focus on very young children as they are now: what they can manage, what they find fascinating and the ways in which they relate to the world. What they are learning is important for itself and not just for what will happen later. For instance, the pre-verbal communication skills of very young children (see page 295) are all valuable and exciting – not just as steps towards being able to talk.

Caring adults count more than equipment

Think of yourselves as the most vital items of play equipment in your nursery. If adults relate fully and appropriately with babies and toddlers, then the children will learn through that relationship. Young children will also be able to take advantage of the play materials and activities that you offer. On the other hand, if adults are emotionally distanced from babies and toddlers, then good play equipment cannot make up that loss.

The whole day matters

Babies and toddlers do not split up their lives into different sections, so neither should their adult carers. Look ahead to see how you can use all the learning opportunities for the very young. You need to look at a baby's or toddler's day as a whole and not as a list of separate activities. It is useful to have plans for each day and young children like some sense of routine. But watch out that nobody in the team is making the assumption that some parts of the day are less valuable than others.

Physical care is important

The care that you provide and give, and that you increasingly share with a young child, is central to a well-rounded day with children under three years. Through affectionate and respectful touch you show children that, 'I care about you as well as care for you'. The view that 'care' is the poor relation compared with 'education' has been a long-standing block to addressing quality in work with babies and toddlers.

The daily routines of care are not something to hurry through in order to move on to other activities that are seen as early learning. Physical care *is* an ideal vehicle for a great deal of learning and warm communication between child and adult. Toddlers who feel relaxed, who have not been hustled through care routines, will be far more ready to enjoy everything else that is on offer in your setting (see pages 42 and 48).

Once a team has positive attitudes towards care, it is also possible to see and share with parents how children can learn through the care routines, that this time is definitely not 'wasted' time. See Figure 15.2.

Activity

- Look through this section and choose four key points that you can see are equally relevant to planning a good day or week with children over three years.
- Write up briefly the points you have noticed and how you would apply the ideas.
- Make a short presentation to your colleagues.

Key skills links: C3.3. C3.1b

Planning for under threes

In a group setting it will be necessary to have a broad daily routine and even in a family home, as a nanny or childminder, it may be easier to have a flexible working plan to ensure that overall you offer a well rounded week to children. Your plan will cover:

- some timed activities within each day
- some materials that are always accessible to children
- some special activities that you plan for some days.

By using these three broad ways of planning, you can have a flexible forward plan that still needs to be responsive to the interests of under threes on the day.

Some timed activities within each day

A broad timed routine is appropriate for children older than about 18 months. You may well have definite mealtimes and nap times. Babies and younger toddlers need to follow their own feeding and rest schedule especially when they

Figure 15.2

Ways that young children can learn through the care routines of the day

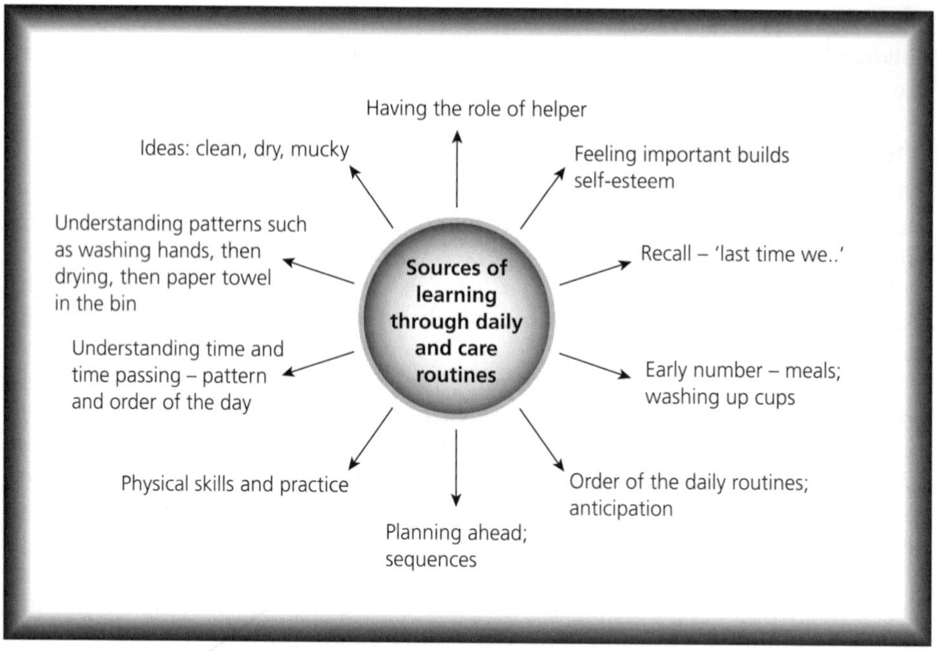

join your setting from home. Older toddlers and young children still need the flexibility to rest and have lunch later if they need to.

Care routines like nappy changing and toileting should not be firmly time tabled (see page 45). It is also important that any planning and discussion about the activities of the day should communicate a clear valuing of all the care routines and enabling children to share in their own care.

You may need to time some activities, especially in some group settings:

- Perhaps you do need to have a timed outdoor play period.
- You may have parts of the day when you bring different ages together in a setting.
- You may schedule some 'together time' for young children: singing, story telling, selected television programmes or video. Children can of course have a story or a song at other times as well.
- You may use soft background music at transition times to signal that 'we are moving into quiet time after lunch'.

Accessible play materials every day

Children can learn better, and young children are no exception, if they can access play materials easily themselves. There should be a wide range of materials always available to young children:

- Make it easy for young children to access materials themselves by low shelving, open containers and accessible browser boxes.
- Consideration of space and use of furniture can be important to enable young children to move around with ease.
- Mobile toddlers should be able to get to the water or sand tray and make some choices about what equipment they want to add to this key resource.
- Dressing up clothes and materials for pretend play. Some small world materials might be used from time to time to ensure novelty, but some pretend play materials should be easily accessible each day.

- Constructional materials suitable for this age group. Open containers of different kinds of bricks should be a regular activity that can be chosen.
- Adults are available all the time as play companions and as interested observers.

Special non-daily activities

Over a week or fortnight, you could plan a range of activities that do not each happen every day.

- A time for treasure basket and exploratory heuristic play (see page 272) can be made a regular but not a daily happening. Some play activities will not feel so special to children if they happen every day.
- Unless the weather is really grim, children need to get outside each day. Often this will be in the garden but simple, local outings should be a regular occurrence – if not every day, then several times a week.
- You can schedule a range of arts and crafts activities and plan ahead so that, over a couple of weeks, you ring the changes in terms of the materials that are available for young children to explore.
- Other possibilities are activities for music making and dance, when you might ensure that there is a regular dancing session, although children who dance can enjoy this fun at any time.
- Some special construction activities could be scheduled across a two week span, for instance, large cardboard boxes or major sticky activity involving recycled cardboard tubes and egg boxes.

Observation is key

Flexible planning only works for very young children because practitioners then relax during the day and are ready to be involved in whatever way absorbed

Figure 15.3
Go with the interests that young children show today

babies, toddlers and very young children require. Some early years settings build relaxed observation into how they work. For instance:

- some settings use the idea of schemas (see page 273) to support the team to notice what very young children do and in what way
- the High/Scope approach to children, under threes as well, emphasises the importance of adults being attentive to strands of learning.

Settings that use either of these approaches also emphasise the importance of choice for children. Very young children cannot show you what interests them unless materials are accessible to them. If toddlers are restricted to a small number of toys that are put out as part of a plan, but these play materials are uninspiring, then their only choice is to look and sound bored and distressed.

Planning for children's learning – over threes

The division between under- and over-threes is not a firm distinction and certainly there is no dramatic change over the third birthday. Services in the UK have traditionally been divided in this way (see page 20) and the early years curriculum documents are designed for over threes. Some early years settings have two and a half year olds as their youngest children. In this case, teams need to be sensitive to the needs and interests of these very young children as well as the less mature three year olds in a setting.

Why do you plan?

For planning to be part of good early years practice, you need to keep clear in your mind the reasons why you plan.

- the overall aim in planning is not that you have a plan
- the aim is that what happens day by day, guided by your plan, supports children's learning, their enthusiasm and developing disposition to learn
- you plan ahead to offer opportunities to children; you do not plan in detail exactly what children will do within a given day or session.

You should not be trying to plan all the activities for children. Some materials will always be available, such as sand or water. Some learning areas will always be available for children to use as they wish, for example a role play area, that may change over time but not every week, or a ready-set up art and craft area.

Tips for practice

If the plan, and following the plan, become more important than the children and their enthusiasm, then priorities have gone badly awry. The key issues are that you, and your colleagues, keep flexible:

- Do not forget the key point in the text of this section. You plan ahead to offer opportunities to children; you do not plan in detail exactly what the children will or have to do. This distinction is important; discuss what it means for your setting with your colleagues.
- Good plans are working documents; they are not carved in stone and the day or session should be open to taking a direction that enthuses children, whether or not it is 'in the plan'.

- Planning for learning needs to focus on potential, on what you hope children will be able to learn from the opportunities offered by materials, activities and outings. Only the day or session itself will show what children are most likely to have learned.
- Useful plans have to be grounded in adult understanding that children can learn the same skills or ideas through many different ways (see page 416). Furthermore, the same activity or item of equipment has the potential to support different kinds of learning (see page 379).

Child-initiated and adult-initiated

Useful plans offer a positive balance between activities that are mainly **child-initiated** and those which are **adult-initiated**.

- Adults have an important role in making materials available, perhaps through learning spaces (see page 409), but then children make free choices about how they use those materials.
- Some activities may be to all intents and purposes fully child-initiated and any adult involvement is fully responsive to what the children want.
- Adult initiated activities can be started by adults and offered to children. An interesting activity, offered by an enthusiastic adult, will attract children.
- The activity still has to be offered and run in such a way that children can opt in or out and have a significant input to the activity. Adult-initiated activities should not slide into being totally adult-led and controlled.
- Some plans use the idea of **extension activities** to a main activity plan. Extensions should be seen as possibilities and not run with any sense of compulsion. If the children are interested, then an extension activity is something that practitioners have 'up their sleeve'.

Key terms

Child-initiated activities
those experiences suggested or started by children themselves

Adult-initiated activities
those experiences offered by adults which can then be shaped by children's interest and choices

Extension activities
possible additional activities in a plan that can be offered to children, if they wish to continue

Figure 15.4

You can plan an activity, but it is then the children's choice how to explore it

Scenario

The team at Dresden Road Nursery School has been working hard to inject flexibility into their curriculum plans. When Hannah became head teacher, she found a rigid method of planning that left the existing team feeling that they had to follow the plan, even if the children were obviously bored. The plans had become more important than the learning they were supposed to promote.

Hannah is still working hard with one or two team members who were more comfortable with following a detailed plan with no deviations. The value of local trips has been an issue, with some staff agreeing to go out but then being inflexible about responding to children's interests. If the trip was to see the ducks as part of the topic on baby creatures, then there was no deviation to look at the interesting earth moving equipment on the high road.

Hannah has made a great deal of progress through explanation and encouragement and most of the team now understand the priorities. Over the recent few weeks, the staff and children have gathered materials from their local trips and built them into a large wall display to show the parents. Children have been able to show how they have learned about:

- looking and listening to the sounds of the neighbourhood: traffic, quiet areas, sounds of the park
- sharpening our memory with remembering what we saw last time, different routes, changes since last time we came this way
- favourite routes and landmarks and how we can draw and show these
- keeping a record of what we have done and seen – collecting and displaying, drawing, taking photos
- talking about what we did and planning what we want to do next
- counting up anything of interest like post boxes and the wall with all the snails.

Questions

1. Local trips can work in many different ways to support children's learning. Look at the description above and explain the different areas of an early years curriculum that have been addressed through the activity of local trips.
2. Note the possibilities of local trips from your own early years setting or one you have known well. Make a short presentation to colleagues.
3. Discuss the possibilities and what will make local trips interesting for children, or boring.

Key skills links: C3.3 C3.1b LP3.1–3 WO3.1–3

In this section you will find a number of approaches to planning for children's learning. There is no one right way, although a flexible outlook by practitioners and a willingness to review any approach is always important. See from page 409 in Chapter 14.

Time spans for curriculum planning

Curriculum planning for young children in early years settings usually follows three time scales: long-term, medium-term and short-term. There are no absolute 'rules' about the time span and you would need to check the details in any setting where you work.

- Long-term planning is usually for about a year ahead. This time scale sets a broad framework to help everyone in an early years team to consider the full span of children's potential learning across the day or session that they spend with you. Long-term planning can be useful in helping practitioners to open up on possibilities, as well as to lay a guiding structure for the following months.
- Medium-term planning looks in more detail at 2–3 months into the future. Settings that work on a termly basis would usually have a medium-term plan that covered a term or half term.
- Short-term planning is usually for next week and details what will happen each day, but in a flexible way.

The longer time-scales in planning come alive because of your more detailed planning that occurs close to the time. However, your weekly plans have meaning and can contribute to children's learning, because they are part of a larger framework. Your long- and medium-term plans have ensured that overall your team addresses all the areas of children's learning in an even handed way.

Several key principles run through each of the different time scales of planning.

- A focus on children's learning: what they will be enabled to learn and in what way. Possible plans for activities and experiences follow on from a clear vision of the learning.
- Children's learning crosses any adult definitions of learning areas, experiences or subjects. Young children need to be enabled to make connections and a rich array of applications of what they are learning.
- Teams need to avoid any narrow perspective that makes some times of the day or areas within your setting seem more important for 'real learning'.
- Daily routines and care need to be valued. Children learn from happy involvement in daily routines and relaxed conversation, just as much as narrowly defined 'educational' activities.
- Children can and do learn on the move as well as sitting down at a table. They learn outdoors as well as inside – see the discussion on the 'outdoor curriculum' on page 279.
- The curriculum framework and the supporting planning needs to reflect in a developmentally appropriate way the key principles and policies within any setting, such as equal opportunities.

Long-term curriculum planning

The objective of long-term planning for a team is that you work together to create the broad boundaries for the next twelve months.

Focus on children's learning

It is important in planning to start with children's learning and then explore how experiences and activities you currently offer can contribute to children's learning. Otherwise it is too easy to list activities with the assumption that 'of course' they will promote certain kinds of learning.

- Consider what you are hoping children will learn – in the broad sense, not named individual children at this point.
- You can however discuss questions such as, 'Are we allowing for the situation that some children might have hearing loss?' or 'Are we making the assumption that the group will continue to be a very similar ethnic mix as we have at the moment?'
- You cannot predict the future, but you can check on any assumptions that might make your long-term plan slightly restricted.
- Identify a rich array of connections between the different broad learning areas in your early curriculum guidance. The areas should not be separate in practice.
- Bring into your long-term plan what you have learned from the children who have been with you over the previous year. If you do not know what they think, then discuss how you could find out.

The learning environment, activities and experiences

A long-term plan can be the way that a team reflects on how you might develop what you now offer or reorganise as appropriate. Are there some needs for change and development?

- Perhaps you need to plan ahead for improvements in the outdoor area (see the scenario on page 281).
- Your team may need to step back to consider how to integrate literacy resources across different activity areas. The books do not all have to stay in the book corner, for instance, books on health could go in the pretend clinic role play space.
- You need to focus not only on activities and events but on your own constructive adult behaviour: listening, watching, talking, setting a good example to the children. Are there some general ways in which you could all work towards better support for children's learning?
- For instance, do you need to address more flexibility in how you use your plans? Are you all ready to make the most of children's current interests, do you respond to the unplanned moments?

Drafting the long-term plan

There are different possible ways to lay out and discuss a long-term plan. A possibility is to draft out a large piece of flip chart paper with the curriculum areas of learning along the top. Then take a selection of activities and experiences and work across, discussing how these can support children's learning.

- If you have tended so far to put out activities for children, can you move towards learning spaces (see page 409)? If your setting is organised into indoor and outdoor spaces for children, in what ways could there be change over the next years?
- In what ways can these areas and activities support children's learning across the early curriculum? Take a few examples and discuss in more detail in your team what will this learning look like. How will you notice changes in the children and are there some targets or goals that need to be discussed?
- Are you being as flexible as possible? For instance are you using the full potential of your outdoor area or the local neighbourhood. Has planning so far been too rigid about activities that are 'indoors' and 'outdoors'?

- Have you fully appreciated the value of children's involvement in your daily routines, their part in making choices and planning ahead? Or are you seeing this as lost time or an adult activity, because it is easier and quicker? Have you overlooked the potential of this source of learning?

This is one possible layout for a long-term plan. There are different ways of long-term planning in a team that are equally effective.

Broad areas of learning from your early years curriculum		
January 2002	**Personal, social and emotional development** →	**Communication, language and literacy** → **Other learning areas**
Priorities for children's learning (2–3 points) That we:	Promote their self confidence Encourage them to express and name feelings Support them to ask for help and to be helpful	Promote skills of conversation Help children express opinions Encourage understanding of how books and stories work
Indoor activities	Regular small group activities Books and stories about feelings Range of art and craft	Circle time A chart/display of favourite food or activities or books Different ways to make books
Outdoor activities	Large scale cooperative building – recycled materials Gardening project	Role play suitable story in garden Create seating areas for 'chatting'
Local trips	Involve children in choice and planning of trips Scrapbook or display of our outings	Check on special library sessions Tour of gardens and parks – children express views
Involvement in daily routines	Find more effective way to run 'tidy-up' time Find ways for children to support each other	Project about food, preferences, 'constructive feedback' to nursery cook – think about it! Make a book about the nursery rabbit or similar
Priorities for adult behaviour (2–3 points)	Observe children who seem to lack confidence Notice children's skills and improvements Talk appropriately about our adult feelings	Listen to children Set good example in holding conversations Model courteous ways to express opinions & disagree

Figure 15.5 Example of long-term planning

- Definitely give some discussion time to what the team needs to offer as individuals. Are you all clear within your team about the ways that you can improve your communication with children or how you show them your willingness. For each learning area within the curriculum, you could identify three or four points about what adults will do and how.

In a long-term plan, you need enough detail that the plan fully covers the main areas of learning and kinds of activities and experiences. But if you have too much detail, a team can feel overwhelmed. The long-term plan is a step along the way for supporting children's learning, not the end of your route. You can also use the long-term plan to look ahead constructively as a team to plan for changes in your practice and use of the setting's resources (see the scenario).

Figure 15.6 Find out possibilities in your neighbourhood – children are ready to be interested in many sights

Scenario

St Jude's after school club has children ranging from four years to ten or eleven years. The club has been inspected by social services because children younger than eight years attend. Their last inspection report was positive, although the inspector suggested that the club could make more of the opportunities for outdoor play. The after school club team want to address this area as part of a long-term plan and to be ready with changes under way, when they are inspected under the new system by the Early Years Directorate.

The after school club team have tended to see outdoor play as an opportunity for the children to run off steam after a day at school. Also, many of the children live in flats in the surrounding estate and do not have easy access to open space at home. The team have tended to keep an eye when children are in the outdoor area but not get closely involved, unless children are in dispute over equipment or take a tumble. However, the team are also very aware that play is an issue that needs addressing in St Jude's as a whole (see the scenario on page 257).

A preliminary meeting identified some key themes and an enthusiasm for taking a long-term focus on outdoor play and the outdoor space for the club and the holiday playschemes for half term and the school holidays. Suggestions include:

- Perhaps they could do some observations to get a clear idea of how the children use the outdoor space. The team's impression is that some children play more than others and some seem to stand around a great deal. Can they find out what the children think?
- The club keeps informal records of children's learning and interests and wonder if they could develop these to reflect outdoor play more fully and show that they value physical skills and developing confidence.
- A problem in the primary school has been that of 'policing' the playground, rather than promoting children's learning.
- A regular area of difficulty has been how to deal with a physically very active game developed by the boys and based on a popular cartoon television programme. The playground supervisors have favoured an outright ban on the game. The after school club team want to allow the game but lessen the disruption to other children's play. But there could be trouble if there is inconsistency between what children are allowed to do in school time and after school club time.

The school grounds have an asphalt and a grassed area, although children are usually kept off the grass in the winter time. There is limited seating and a small covered area. Two trees are relatively accessible: the children are not supposed to climb them, although some do. Birds often nest in these trees. Part of the garden has small shrubs and flowers which are tended by the school caretaker.

Questions

1. In your opinion, what are the main issues faced by the after school club team?
2. What could the children be learning through their outdoor play if the school grounds and its resources were used more effectively?

3 Discuss some realistic long-term plans for this team in changing how they currently use and approach the outdoor area. You could consider:
   - What would you do in their position?
   - What would be your priorities and why?
4 Write up and discuss your ideas with colleagues.

Key skills links: C3.3 C3.1a

Medium-term curriculum planning

The objective of the medium-term curriculum plan is to focus in more detail on what you hope children will learn over a few months, half term or term. You cannot detail every aspect of every learning goal or outcome; a plan becomes utterly unwieldy. So a team needs to home in on some detail in each curriculum area and to ensure that over time you give some attention across the whole span.

A possible medium-term plan could follow this outline

This is one possible layout for a medium-term plan. It is not the only way for a team to plan.

Area of learning: (cover each area in turn from your early years curriculum guidance) **May & June 2002**
Knowledge and understanding of the world (Knowledge and appreciation of the environment in Northern Ireland)

Overall children will learn	**Specific skills**	**Positive outlooks**
About their local neighbourhood: – location of market, post office fire station, nearest park – how to get there – change over time, simple local history	Close observation (of routes, changes between trips) Conversation and questions during trips	Curiosity and interest Wanting to know more and to find out (questions, using books etc.)

Activities and experiences	**Resources needed**	**Adult role in activity**	**Focus of observation**
Regular local trips Visit to post office and try to have our postman visit nursery Have children choose and 'navigate' routes Make record of trips – camera, scrapbook Use local library for recent history, invite grandparents in	Organise to get out Camera and film Scrapbook or display board	Make contact with postal service Check on local library – history Show interest and curiosity ourselves Contact local older residents	Listen and talk with children – what interests them? – what do they understand? Adjust trips for events of interest What is children's grasp of 'long ago'?

This plan is a guide and is then finalised week by week

Figure 15.7 Example of medium-term planning

The main features of a good medium-term plan are:

- A clear focus on what you hope the children will learn and how you will recognise that learning when it occurs. Ask yourselves the question, 'What will it look like?'
- A wide range of activities and experiences chosen deliberately to support that learning.
- Consideration of how the activities will be organised, including some thought about how adults will be involved and behave as people to support children's learning.

Scenario

The team of the Baker Street Children and Family Centre are very aware of the diverse population that they serve. Within the last medium-term plan the team planned a project to highlight the different backgrounds of many of the families and the fact that some had travelled considerable distances from their country of origin. In the current medium-term plan the aim is to have a very local focus but with a historical dimension. Some families have been in the area for two or more generations.

The team start to plan a local history project that will interest the children and ideally intrigue parents so that some will get involved. The first ideas include:

- A lively open discussion about how such a project could support every area of learning in the curriculum in one way or another.
- How to find out about local resources: people and places. What does the local museum have and are they friendly to children?
- What are the possibilities about setting up a 'museum display' in the centre? Do parents or grandparents have household items or artefacts that they would be happy to lend?
- In what ways can the children be 'history detectives' with some support? Can they contact older local residents or open discussions with the local library? How can the children and adults find out about how the neighbourhood used to look?

Questions

1. Think creatively about a local history project. The idea may initially sound as if it belongs in only one curriculum area. But look for the connections, ideally with colleagues, to the other areas.
2. In what ways might such a project benefit from medium-term planning, what might take some time and organisation?
3. Discuss your ideas with colleagues, including how such a project might be developed in your neighbourhood.

Key skills links: WO3.1–3

Once you have a clear focus on what you would potentially like children to learn, then you can plan the range of experiences and activities you will offer. A team needs to think and talk in a flexible way.

- For instance, a focus within creative development that enables children to explore texture, shape, form and space can happen through different kinds of activities, not just art. Shape can be explored through indoor and outdoor activities, sit down and on the move opportunities.

Plans definitely need a balance between adult-initiated and genuinely child-initiated activities (see page 425).

- For example, one part of a medium-term plan linked with promoting physical skills might be to plan for large scale works in the garden. The adult responsibility might be to organise a trip to the scrap bank or other local facility. However, when the materials are made available, practitioners are present as observers unless children invite them to join.
- On the other hand, adults might need to offer close involvement for a tie-dying activity linked with helping children to explore choices about pattern, colour and an understanding of bringing about change by printing. Children would still have great scope for choice but adults would help with the technique.
- In a medium-term plan you could plan ahead for some experiences that would be offered to the whole group, to smaller groups or to children whose needs are more specific, perhaps special needs.
- You would not usually name individual children in the medium-term plan for a setting. But a team could well plan some activities to support conversational skills or physical confidence, knowing that some children will especially benefit.
- A medium-term plan allows a large enough time scale to make contacts outside the setting, for visits into the local neighbourhood or to invite someone to visit the setting.
- The plan should build in clear awareness of the potential for children to learn within daily routines and enjoyable conversation between children and adults. No medium-term plan should risk setting up an over-planned future in which a team will feel unable to seize the moment.

A team with a medium-term plan in front of them needs to check that the setting has sufficient resources for what is planned.

Figure 15.8a Pretend play can be supported by bought materials …

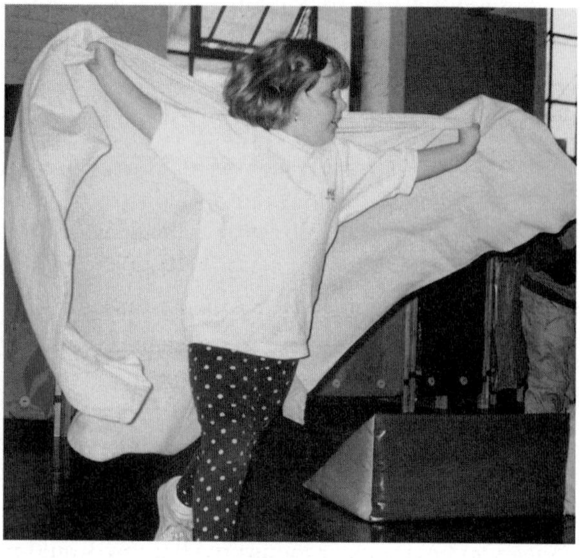

Figure 15.8b … but sometimes pretend play only needs the simplest of props

- Do you need to get any more supplies, find specific resources or check out local possibilities?
- In what ways can the children be involved in any of these 'planning ahead' activities?
- Be clear about who will do what by when. You want to avoid the situation summed up on the notice often seen in offices: 'Everybody thought that Somebody would do this, but Nobody did.'

Linking records with planning

Chapter 16 covers ways of observing and good practice in keeping records on children's development and behaviour. Often you will focus on records in terms of individual children. It is also possible that exploration with colleagues in a team or group discussion can help you all use the good quality information from your records on individual children in order to support long- and medium-term planning for the whole group.

A careful and honest look at the individual records might provide important links to planning for your group. If you are working with three to five year olds within your national early years curriculum guidance:

- You may realise from individual records that many children in the group need additional support in a particular area of learning, perhaps in using their language broadly in communication and conversation. A constructive focus on the children's conversational skills can help you to reflect on the opportunities you offer, or do not offer, for relaxed conversation (see page 310).
- You might also realise that learning in and through physical development is a real strength in your setting. Perhaps your records show how children are learning a wide range of skills, how even the less physically confident children feel safe to try and how children help each other. Be pleased with yourselves as well as with the children's competence and enthusiasm.
- You might realise from an overall consideration of records that there is one area of the children's learning about which you have noticed very little. Perhaps your team has not really explored children's sense of self respect and there is confusion about how children may develop a positive racial and cultural identity.
- On the other hand, the information from individual records may confirm that the team's efforts over the last couple of months to develop activities within science and technology have made a real and observable impact on children's learning and curiosity in this area.

Do you organise around topics?

Many settings plan in the medium term around a theme or topic. Teams often find this method useful, especially since there are many resources from magazines or booklets that revolve around different topics. You need to consider what will make such an approach work and what could undermine children's learning. Used in a non-reflective way, topics can be more of a convenience for adults than a genuine support to children's learning.

A topic approach can work so long as:

- You build your medium-term plan from a clear focus on the learning and interests of the children in your group rather than just taking the details from an attractive topic booklet without any fine tuning.

Figure 15.9

Some topic work will lead to a display

- If your team uses bought topic materials, then do not depend on a statement in a booklet or topic sheet that says, for instance, that an activity 'will promote cooperative working between children'. The activity will not achieve this goal on its own; your team needs to address 'how could we organise and offer our own adult involvement to help children to cooperate within this activity?'
- You need to offer creativity and variety over time, for yourself as well as the children. You really need to do some thinking and discussing when there is a general groan from the team that, 'Oh no, we've got to do that "season's" topic again'. If the children are with you for a while and the plans are repetitive, they may speak up and complain, 'But we did "castles" last year. I remember.'
- Everyone in the team fully understands that children's learning over this period will also happen 'outside' your chosen topic. It is unrealistic and can end up being very boring, when teams try to filter every single experience through the current topic.
- You all need to think creatively about suitable topics for the current group and children's social world outside the setting. Children may enjoy topics such as 'exploring weather' or 'our neighbourhood'. But you can consider a relevant practical theme such as 'our garden project' that involves children and their parents in every step on the way to developing your setting's outdoor space.

Scenario

Sunningdale Day Nursery developed a plan around setting up a greengrocers' shop for the children. Part way through work with the children to organise the shop area, Ian speaks up and asks, 'But does it have to be vegetables? Because, you know vegetables are a bit boring.' Penny replies that it can be any kind of shop they would like. Ian replies, 'Well, you know Jackie? Her Mummy and Daddy have a shop and it's got big, big things of material. Me and my Mum go in there and she lets me pick out the buttons.'

Penny listens as the other children add their comments and it becomes clear that they are keen to have a shop just like Jackie's. All the potential learning that Penny and her colleagues had planned can just as easily happen within the context of a materials and haberdashery shop. The project unfolds and parents, including Jackie's family, are pleased to contribute resource materials.

In Sunningdale, the team look at any topic or theme for developmentally appropriate activities for the under threes. In this case, these younger children are delighted with the feel of materials and ribbons. The four year olds set about making a feely book for the babies and a mobile with ribbons and zips.

The older children are also enthusiastic about games with long ribbons out in the garden. They make large circling movements and create shapes in the air. The children enjoy the game, but it is also excellent practice for their physical skills, balance and sensitivity to feedback from movement.

Questions

1 Consider a project like the materials and haberdashery shop. What activities could be developed from this focus?

2 Draw a diagram and make some notes in which the broad areas of learning in your curriculum guidance are linked to the shop activities.

3 Present your ideas to colleagues.

Key skills links: C3.3 C3.1b

Short-term curriculum planning

Your short-term plan is basically for 'next week' and is your opportunity to finalise the details of activities and experiences that will be made available this coming week. Your medium-term planning supports you to be clear about what you hope the children will learn from the planned activities.

- What ideas, information or experiences are you introducing over the week?
- You identify some areas of learning for most of the children.
- But now is also the point to identify specific learning that you wish to support for named individual children.
- These individual plans should not be so detailed that a child's week is unbalanced. It can be as straightforward as helping a child to have a go at doing up her buttons or stay for two songs or stories before he wanders off.

Possible short-term plan outline

This is one possible layout for a short-term plan. It is not the only way for a team to plan ahead for the week, but any plan has to be responsive to the children's interests of the day.

Week beginning: (date) 1 July 2002			
Area of learning	**Activity**	**Adult role**	**Observations**
Physical development – skills of climbing – balance – going 'under', 'on top of', 'through'	Outdoor obstacle course – large boxes Fixed climbing equipment	Encourage children to choose items and build Use appropriate words for position etc.	Children who are confident – notice and celebrate Children who are uncertain – offer help, celebrate progress
Creative/expressive – planning and choosing – pleasure in making an end product	Large scale collage with twigs, leaves etc collected from park	Encourage children to plan the collage and work together	Children who are full of ideas and those who hold back. Children who need help with fine skills
Early mathematics – recognition of numbers – simple counting	Local 'number walk' – spotting any numbers Measure rooms and garden by pacing	Organise local walk Help, support and say numbers Help with counting	Children who are clear about numbers and recognise Children who confuse numbers and letters
Even this short-term plan needs to be flexible to children's interests. Activities continue and are redirected in response to the children's wishes and enthusiasm.			

Figure 15.10 Example of short-term planning

Your short-term plan details the activities and experiences that are available this week and how they are organised. The plan should give answers to questions such as the following.

- What have you decided to extend or offer again from last week. Your decision may be as a result of your observation and reflection as a team. Alternatively, the final form of a short-term plan should be responsive to requests and ideas from the children.
- What activities, experiences, local outings or events are specifically planned for this week? And are any details that are needed in place?
- Flexibility remains important for the short-term plan. Everyone needs to be able to make choices and not feel tyrannised by the plan. Perhaps the children have plenty of scope left in their outdoor construction, so of course

they can continue. Or, after a very depressing run of weather, the sun is out, so an impromptu local trip is arranged.

In the short-term plan you make some decisions.

- Ways that you may group some children for some activities. Perhaps it will not be possible for everyone to do cooking at the same time.
- So, how many children will be invited and do you have the flexibility to extend or repeat a very popular activity? Are there some children whom you would definitely like to encourage to join a particular activity?
- How will your team be deployed around your setting? Some activities or areas may benefit from having an adult to help and support. Children at the needlework table may appreciate help with technique or some adult support may be needed as children tackle how you plant tomatoes and not have them fall over.
- There should still be plenty of scope for observing, admiring and responding to invitations from children to become involved.

The short-term plan also includes on-going assessment of learning:

- Without getting bogged down in too much recording (see page 440), in what ways are you documenting what the children are learning this week? The short-term plan can usefully identify a small number of named children who will be closely observed this week. The plan does not mean that you ignore the others, of course.
- In what ways do children have plenty of opportunities to record their own activity today or a longer work in progress?
- What do the children want to tell and show you about what worked, what was enjoyable, confusing, frustrating or annoying? Alert and attentive adults can pick up on the moments by watching and listening.

Figure 15.11

Children will be the experts on what they find interesting and absorbing

What have you learned as adults?

All planning benefits from time for reflection and review. The details of the plans as you work ahead focus on what you hope the children will learn. Reflection and discussion also has to highlight what the adults have learned. You can remain alert throughout the week for:

- How is this adult-led activity going? Are the children less or more absorbed than we anticipated?
- Is it time to call a halt or would the children like an extension? Are they keen to take this activity into another direction and will that choice slightly change the plan for tomorrow?
- What happened in an open-ended, child-led activity? How have the children used the office materials that were added to the hospital role play area? What have they done with them and does the activity seem to have more possibilities in the children's view?
- What were you hoping that the children would learn and what do you think they probably have learned? What is your basis for suggesting this? What have the children done or said?
- What has happened in an informal and unplanned way? Perhaps consider in what ways the children have been involved in the daily routines and events of the setting? Have you tried some new ways for children to be involved in tidying up and how have they gone?
- What kind of conversations have children had with each other or with interested adults?
- What have you learned as adults this week? What implications does it have for finalising your plan for next week?

Focus on learning: Support interest in books and promote concentration in a small group session for children who interrupt a lot in story time

In the week of (date) 20 May 2002

Adult Role: (Mina) Create a small group book time with named children	**Children:** Maximum 4 Definitely include Neil and Simone

Activity: At mid-morning I invited Neil and Simone, along with Jamal who was also interested, to choose a book each. Simone looked enthusiastic and said, 'Just us? With you?' Jamal and Simone chose story books. Neil wanted the large illustrated book about diggers and lorries.

We spent 15 minutes reading the stories, one of them twice ('Mr Bear') and talked about the book on diggers. Jamal is very keen on stories and knows favourites by heart. Neil is very knowledgeable about big trucks and transport. Simone was the one who found it hardest to remain still, but she managed far better than in large story time. She gets easily distracted.

Review of the activity: I suggest we make this a regular event. This small group time worked well. It seems to me that Neil and Simone interrupt main story time for different reasons. Neil has so much he wants to say and share. But Simone seems to find it genuinely hard to concentrate. She needs help to look at the details of a picture and to listen.

Figure 15.12 Planned activity to support named children

Tips for practice

You can learn from reflecting back on a plan or an individual activity – either through a team or group room discussion, or your own thoughts and notes. It is important to be constructive with yourself.

- Be pleased about what has gone well, even perhaps with unexpected success and enthusiasm.
- Do not spend all or most of your discussion and thinking time on what did not go so well.
- What can you learn from the successful activities, outings or new ways that you approached a daily routine with the children?
- If some parts of your flexible plan did not go so well, what can you learn? It is not necessarily anybody's fault; you cannot foresee everything. How can you make it better next time?
- You tell the children 'we learn through our mistakes'. So be kind to yourself and your colleagues and let yourselves learn!
- If your discussion and thinking has highlighted a problem area of any kind, then do not rush into a quick solution. Be clear now about the nature of the problem and then take a bit of time to think and consider a range of options. Consult the children if at all possible.

Further resources

Lindon, Jennie (2000) *Helping Babies and Toddlers Learn: A Guide to Good Practice with Under Threes* National Early Years Network.

Lindon, Jennie, Kelman, Kevin and Sharp, Alice (2001) *Play and Learning for the Under Threes* Nursery World/TSL Education.

It is useful to build up resources for planning ahead with young children. You will gather many ideas of your own but will also find a rich source in magazines like *Nursery World*, *Practical Pre-school* and *Nursery Education*. Contact details are on page 666.

Progress check

1. Give two reasons why care and care routines need to be a valued part of the day for young children.
2. Describe three ways that children's ideas and preferences could influence the plans of an early years setting.
3. Explain briefly the differences between long-term, medium-term and short-term plans for an early year setting.
4. Give three examples of a child-initiated and an adult-initiated activity.
5. Suggest two ways in which a team could learn by reviewing plans and the planning process in a setting.

16

Observation, record keeping and assessment

After reading this chapter you should be able to:

- understand the importance of observation and use different techniques for observing children
- use different ways of recording information about children
- recognise and follow good practice in making observations and keeping records within any early years setting
- understand different approaches to assessment within early years settings.

Introduction

In this chapter you will learn about different techniques for observing children. You may first use these techniques as a student but you certainly do not leave your skills of observation behind once you have completed an early years qualification. Good practice for all early years practitioners is to be able to use appropriate techniques of observation to supplement a good habit of being observant and attentive to the children.

Responsible practitioners consider why and how they observe. They follow good practice in how they write up observations of children and share appropriately with parents and the children themselves. You will continue to understand

Links to early years qualifications

This chapter especially supports the following units:

Diploma in Child Care and Education: 1

National Vocational Qualification in Early Years Care and Education

Level 2: no specific units but observation skills are needed to provide evidence for many of the units

Level 3: C16

BTEC National Early Years Diploma: 7, 8

good practice in how you write about and talk about children's development and behaviour. More organised assessment is now part of many early years settings and within the transition on to school. The possible ways that you may be involved in assessment are discussed along with most appropriate practice.

Good practice in observation

If you are currently completing an early years qualification then you will be asked by your tutor to undertake a number of observations to support your learning about children's development and behaviour. However, the skills and techniques of observation continue to be highly relevant once you are in a job as an early years practitioner.

The value of observation

Observation skills are important for the following reasons.

- You can learn about individual children and their interests and current capabilities.
- Careful observation and interpretation will help you to identify the cutting edge of children's learning: what they are ready to learn and where they would appreciate some help. (See page 356 about the zone of proximal development.)
- You will also be more able to give children encouragement and informative feedback (page 396).
- You will be able to see how children use the opportunities of your setting. It is possible to observe a learning space (see page 409) in your setting or to pay close attention to how children handle particular routines and times of the day.

Figure 16.1
Conversation with children supports observation

- Observation can support a positive approach to children's behaviour. You have the opportunity to gain a perspective on a child whose behaviour concerns you in some way.
- Careful observation is crucial if children are set targets for learning or changes in their behaviour. Adults have a serious responsibility to observe with accuracy and not make guesses about the child.
- Experience of using different techniques in observation can help you to develop good habits of being observant. You will become more generally attentive to what the children are doing and in what ways.

Scenario

Since Erin took over Sunningdale Day Nursery she has worked hard to convince her team that continued informal observation of the children is part of good practice. A few team members clearly felt that they should always look busy and that observing was a form of laziness.

Erin has encouraged those team members who were keen to watch and listen and has invited their views on what they have learned about individual children. She has also modelled the behaviour she wants from other team members by asking individuals to sit and observe with her in a relaxed way. Erin then comments on some aspect of a child's interests, behaviour or ways in which the child might appreciate some adult input.

Questions

1 Some early years practitioners gain the idea that they should look busy. How do you think that idea develops?
2 What kind of support do practitioners need if they are to feel confident about looking and listening to what is going on in a setting or family home?
3 How might the problems of 'we must look busy' be resolved?
4 Discuss your ideas with colleagues.

Key skills links: C3.1a PS3.1–3

Preparing to observe

There are differences between being generally observant as a practitioner and making a particular observation.

- You need to make some preparation for an observation, even relatively brief ones.
- You need to decide on your focus and purpose. What do you want to learn about?
- When you are clear what you would like to be able to do with your observation, you have a basis for deciding on a method of observation.
- Choose a method that is appropriate to what you wish to observe. Or understand the possible uses of a method that you are asked to use as a student.

- During your observation you attend selectively, in the way appropriate to this technique. You will make notes at the time and keep a note of the broader context in which an observation is made: where, when, who was present.
- When your observation is complete you need to consider what the observation tells you. What have you learned and what are fair conclusions?
- It is useful to reflect on your interpretations and if possible to discuss ideas with your colleagues.
- After you have observed, you will have some kind of outcome. You might write up brief notes, complete a developmental profile or a short report or contribute to a larger report on a child or group.

Courtesy and cooperation

Good practice in observation means that you explain what you will be doing in your observations and as appropriate you obtain the **informed consent** of anyone involved: your colleagues, the children and the children's parents.

Key term

Informed consent that adults and children are given sufficient information for them to make a decision about whether to agree to or decline involvement in an event or experience

With colleagues

It is sensible and courteous to discuss any plans about observations with your colleagues.

- It will help if your colleagues can know the range of observations you wish or need to undertake as a student.
- You can all then work cooperatively to plan a schedule so that you can complete different observations.
- A team needs to discuss the pattern of observations that are part of weekly practice in a setting.

Figure 16.2
You can observe while keeping children company

With parents

Make sure you are clear about the guidelines for this setting when talking with parents about observations.

- The setting may have a general agreement with families that students on placement will undertake observations and that observation is part of good practice to support children's learning.
- It is still courteous to talk with parents if you are undertaking a detailed observation on their child. Parents know their children, they can contribute to your observation from their experience of their child in the home setting.
- It is also parents' right to refuse consent for observations that are not part of usual practice in the setting, for instance, if the setting is participating in an external research project.
- Parents can also ask questions, show an interest in your observation and have their views respected if, for instance, they do not want photos or videos taken of their children.
- It is fair for parents to want to know what will happen to your notes, especially as a student, since you will leave the setting, and to any audio or video tapes, if you use this technology.

Parents can only give their informed consent when you, your colleagues or other professionals are completely honest about what you will observe, why and what you plan to do with the observations. Parents cannot give informed consent if they are only told half the story and they will probably be irritated if they later feel misled.

With children

The children are also often interested in what you are doing in an observation.

- Be ready with a simple explanation that is honest and does not break confidences about another child, for instance over behaviour or struggles in learning.
- Children often take little notice since they are familiar with adults doing odd things. But they may be interested in your notepad or anything unusual like a stop watch. You can explain simply.
- Look for ways that children could contribute their views and ideas in different types of observation.

Activity

- Find out the guideline in your setting for asking permission of parents to make observations.
- Do they give a general permission to practice in the setting?
- In what ways are parents' views invited and included in observations and record keeping in your setting?
- Compare guidelines with colleagues who have experience of other settings.

Key skills links: C2/3.1a

Tips for practice

You need to consider good practice and issues of confidentiality for any kind of observations and records. Consideration is especially important when you use photographs, video or audio recording:

- Always ask for parents' informed consent for this kind of recording.
- Parents should be fully informed if photos or tapes will be used by students to present to their course group or make displays, even if these will not go outside the college or assessment centre.
- Respect their wishes if the answer is 'no'.
- Parents do not have to give a reason. But family conflict is often the concern if parents do not want photos or video footage of their child to leave the setting.
- Tapes or photos should not be copied and used outside the agreed boundaries. For instance they should not become part of general teaching materials unless parents have given their informed consent.
- Be respectful of children's dignity. For instance it is a good rule of thumb never to take a photo or video of children in a situation that you would not use for adults. It would be inappropriate to take a photo of toddlers on the pot or to video a group as they changed into swimming costumes for a paddling pool session.

Approaches to observation of children

Your aim as an observer is to behave as unobtrusively as possible. It will help if you have everything you need to hand. What you need will vary slightly depending on the technique of observation that you use.

It is not possible simply to decide that you will watch whatever is interesting in a setting. Such a task is overwhelming and you will end up with incomprehensible notes. However, you can observe in a relatively flexible way, so long as you narrow your scope of observation in terms of how many children, over what period of time or with a focus on which learning space. This section describes some different observation techniques.

Tips for practice

There are some useful guidelines that apply to all the techniques of observation:

- Every observation will need a date and time or timings.
- You need a clear note of the child or children observed and a key if you use any shorthand versions, such as the first letter of a child's or adult's name.
- You also need a key if you plan to use pre-coded categories (see page 449).
- Observations as a practitioner in a setting would give the child's full name. As a student you are likely to keep to the first letter, in order to maintain confidentiality, since your observations will leave the setting with you and form part of your portfolio.

Tips for practice

- Lay out an observations sheet, as much as makes sense for the technique you plan to use. It is waste of time when you are actually observing children to be writing in headings or drawing columns that you could have done in advance.
- Record legibly at the time. It will be pointless to write at speed and then not be able to read your own notes later!
- After completion, take time to consider what your observations show (see page 456). You need to show objectivity in how you make sense of what you have observed.
- Use a range of techniques to summarise what you have found: written reports, simple counts, graphs or pie charts.

Time sampling

It is impractical to watch children continuously and make accurate notes at the same time. You would only manage this task if very little indeed were happening in a setting. You could cope if, for instance, children were sitting around a table and staring into space. But it should be a cause for concern if you did observe such a passive situation. So, usually you have to pace yourself for watching and noting. **Time sampling** enables you to make your observations in an organised rather than a random way.

Key term

Time sampling
a technique in which observations are made on a regular rather than continuous basis

Scenario

The team at Dresden Road Nursery School have used time sampling in different ways to build their understanding of what and how the children are learning within the nursery. Recently two team members have made observations that have then been shared with the team:

- Jessica decided to explore how the computing area was being used by children. Team discussions had raised a concern that some children were dominating the computer so that others could not get a turn. But the team realised that they were not sure and the assumption that the boys were taking over the area needed to be properly checked.
- Maria agreed to make an observation of Owen and Sachin, who have a clear preference for outdoor activities. There has been some concern that the children's play is very repetitive and they are 'not really doing much at all'.

The team agrees to organise so that Jessica and Maria can assign one hour for observation during two mornings in one week and two in the following week. Rosemary, the deputy, is freed up to be in the main nursery at those times.

At each agreed time Jessica sits close enough to see and hear activity within the computer area. She had laid out her paper in preparation for a plan to make notes once every five minutes (timed accurately with a stop-watch). For one minute she observes and then has four minutes to complete her notes. Her reminder list directed her to note down the names of the children at the computer table (there is room for two) and whether any are waiting. She also notes the programme on the screen and what the children said and did. On completion of the observations, Jessica creates a chart to show the children who most use the computer and the programmes that are used. Some children are more prominent, but not only the boys. The problem seems to be that some children are not aware of the potential in computer usage, rather than that they are excluded.

Maria uses a similar time sampling pattern to track Owen and Sachin in their outdoor play and shadows them in the garden. She is able to show that the children have a rich pretend game ongoing that involves finding and capturing pretend wild animals. The boys communicate a great deal with each other and invite Maria to join in their search for the 'gobbledegook'. Something that the boys say makes Maria think that their game has been developed from a story Sachin has been read at home.

Questions

1 How might the two observations be followed up by the Dresden Road team within the nursery?

2 In what ways might parents be involved, for instance by asking whether some children have access to computers at home or finding out about the story that Sachin was read?

3 Write up your ideas and discuss your ideas with colleagues.

Key skills links: C3.1a C3.3

Pre-coded categories

Sometimes you might be interested in a particular area of development or children's behaviour. You may then have a short list of **pre-coded categories** to help you note down the different types of observation that you might make. You will still need to make decisions about when, where, who and for how long you make your observations.

Any categories need to make sense to you, and any colleagues who will undertake similar observations. For instance if you were interested in children's use of language (see page 302), you might have a short list of categories to include: asks question, answers question, makes suggestion, guesses/speculates, describes, explains and argues. You would then lay out your observation sheet with the categories down one side and then you only need to mark the occurrence and ideally note down some actual examples of what children said.

Key term

Pre-coded categories
a set of short descriptions, decided in advance for organising observation of types of behaviour or events

In the scenario of Dresden Road, Rosemary used time sampling to observe the computer corner, so she made notes about any children in that learning space. Another use of time sampling is to make observations of children's spontaneous play over a period of time in your day or session.

Using time sampling you can probably watch three or four children at the same time, so long as they are in the same room or space. Lay out your paper ready and have an accurate watch or time piece at your side. Your observation might look something like the following. The observer has started at 9.45 and written down what Josie is doing, then Jake and then Saima. Then the observer returns to Josie at 9.55. The notes are brief but if you observe for 45–60 minutes you will gain a good idea of what the children do, their interests, play companions and whether adults could support their learning and interests in different ways.

Date: Monday 17 June 2002
Observation of: Josie, Jake & Saima
Observation made by: Teresa
Location: Main playroom

	Josie	Jake	Saima
9.45	Playing in sand with Mikey Making shapes	Watching boys at the water tray	Looking at book – sitting on floor Turns pages
9.55	Sand Laughs with Mikey Gestures to staff to come and see	Watching water tray Moves closer Tim says something J. steps back	Chooses another book Joined by Marie who looks over book S. pulls book closer
10.00	Explaining to staff about sand shapes says something to M.	Watching water tray Moves off to window Looking out	Looking at book M. sitting close S. gets up
10.05	J & M are flinging sand Staff calls over to stop – asks them to brush up	Sitting by window Looking at book corner	In home corner Watching play
10.10	M. fetches dustpan and brush J. watches M. brush	Staff comes to J. J. looks up Sits close to staff, touches hand	Joins staff and J. at window seat

Figure 16.3 Example of observation by time sampling

Scenario

The team at the Dale Parent and Toddler drop-in group are interested in tracking examples of early pro-social behaviour (see page 488). The aim of Annie and her colleagues is partly to help parents towards realistic expectations of their children, many of whom are not much older than two or two and a half years old.

Annie, Vicky and Liz discuss some simple categories to ensure that they all agree on the meaning – they are all going to take turns to observe and there is a risk that they will not be consistent. They agree to note examples of named children and their behaviour in six codes, with a shorthand key:

- C – Comforts: one child offers comfort to another child in any way
- I – Indicates need: one child calls an adult's attention to the distress of another child
- MB – Makes better: one child tries to put things right for another child
- H – Helps: a child voluntarily offers help of any kind to a child or adult
- T – Takes turns: a child is willing to wait to take a turn
- G – Gives: a child voluntarily lets another child have an item

The team use the categories in observations made by each of them in turn over a period of two weeks in the drop-in. They then pool their observations, make a simple count of the categories and names of children and discuss what they have found.

- In practice it has been hard to tell the difference between 'comforts' and 'makes better', so they add these codes together.
- Some children's names appear regularly. For instance, Bola has many mentions against 'gives'. So many in fact that the team wonder if Bola needs to understand that she can say, 'No' or 'When I've finished'. Bola's mother is very keen that she behaves well in the drop-in and it is possible that the consequence is interrupted play for the child.
- About half of children's offers to help adults are declined, usually by parents but sometimes by the drop-in team. Vicky suggests that they need to reflect on how to avoid a situation in which children become discouraged because adults want something done 'quickly' or 'properly'.
- There are plenty of examples of prosocial behaviour appropriate to the age of the children. The team are able to identify specific examples to describe to each parent about their own child.

Questions

1 In what ways could you use a similar format in your setting?

2 Plan and undertake a short observation and then write a brief report about what you have learned about the children and the adults.

3 Share your ideas with colleagues on your course, being careful to maintain confidentiality about children and adults.

Key skills links: LP3.1–3 C3.1b

Observations of children's behaviour

Key term

Event sampling a technique in which observations are made of specific events or types of behaviour, defined in advance of the observation

Sometimes you can use the **event sampling** approach to select events or a specific kind of behaviour. In order to observe children's behaviour in an accurate way, you need to have a clear focus of interest.

This technique is useful if you need an accurate view of how a child is behaving. Observation can help you and your colleagues gain a perspective on a child whose behaviour you find hard to handle. You need to observe at least over several days, to get a sense of patterns for this child.

In this observation, Ruth's behaviour is of concern because she bites other children. Another child might be seen as 'aggressive' or 'disruptive'. In that case, the first step has to be that the team gets beyond the negative label and is clear about what behaviour needs to be observed. So long as the team are clear about the behaviour to be observed, then more than one person can contribute to the observation sheet.

Later the observation has to be discussed in an open and flexible way, with the approach of 'what have we learned?' and 'what can we do now?' There should never be any sense of an observation 'proving' that a child is very difficult and that is the end of the matter.

Dates: 13–17 May 2002
Observation of: Ruth
Observation made by: David
Behaviour observed: Biting other children and any other unprovoked physical attacks

Days	Event	Comment
Monday	**1** Bit Marina – quarrel over dressing-up clothes **2** Nearly bit Marina again – responded to 'No biting!' from staff **3** Bit Nelson – unclear why	Marina seemed very wound up today Spoke with her father – family worries high at the moment – they are trying the 'No biting!' approach too
Tuesday	—	
Wednesday	**1** Pushed Nelson hard – response to pinching from N. **2** Nearly bit Jason – distracted by staff	Said 'no pushing' to Ruth but also 'no pinching' to Nelson. Ruth seemed pleased N. told off as well
And so on ...		

Figure 16.4 Example of observation by event sampling

Tips for practice

- If you set out to collect examples of 'sociable' or 'challenging' behaviour, you should work out, ideally in discussion with colleagues, what kind of behaviour you mean by the words. Otherwise your observations could gather in some very different actions.
- A clear agreement about words is also crucial if colleagues are to share in making observations around the same theme.
- Keep your focus as positive as possible. For instance, an observation may be undertaken because the team finds a child's behaviour hard to handle.
- Then it is important that an observation is not approached as a way to 'prove' that this child is so impossible.
- One option is to observe for the flipside of behaviour: look out for cooperative behaviour from Morag who is frequently spotted being uncooperative.

You can prepare your sheet of notes with a few key headings, including the behaviour you wish to observe, and also time of day, name of child(ren), name of adults involved and space for a brief description of what happened. It can be possible to make these kinds of notes and still remain responsible for the children.

Developmental profiles or checklists

Many early years settings have a prepared **developmental profile** for tracking children's learning. The profile will provide a selection of skills in all the areas of development or learning areas within an early years curriculum. A profile can work well to support you in exploring a child's level of skill or overall development. One advantage is that this technique guides you through observation of a wide range of skills, ensuring that you take a well-rounded look at individual children. Reservations about using **checklists** often refer to the risk of building a fixed picture of a child and perhaps one that focuses too much on what a child cannot do. Profiles or checklists have potential disadvantages, but appropriate use of them can produce a positive record of children and a sense that they will continue to learn.

Key terms

Developmental profile
record sheet for tracking children's progress in development and behaviour

Checklist or **tick list**
record layout in which it is possible to check or tick individual items relevant to children's development or behaviour

Tips for practice

For good practice in the use of profiles, it is important that you follow some guidelines.

- Approach a child with respect and plan carefully how you will explore the different kinds of items in a profile.
- Some items will be in the form of questions and it will matter how you ask these – see page 454.
- A profile in the form of a checklist needs space for you to add examples and explanatory notes.
- If a child does not manage a particular item, there is good reason to make a note that the child partly managed to complete a task. You might also make a supported comment about where the difficulty seems to lie at the moment. Checklists should definitely not be used like a pass/fail test technique.

- Nevertheless it is important to be honest and not to boost a child's achievements because you like the child or her parents. Inaccurate information will be unhelpful for the child in the long run.
- Keep a balance of children's strengths as well as difficulties as you write up an observation based on using a checklist.
- Spend time on what the child can manage, what he can nearly manage as well as those areas that are currently outside his capability.

The difference between assessment and helping a child

Early years practitioners spend a great deal of time looking for ways to help children to learn. In your everyday interaction with young children you will look for opportunities to give useful prompts and hints. You will be willing to show children how to do something. However, **assessment** is a special situation and, during the time that you are completing an assessment, you have to hold back on your usual inclination to help.

Key term

Assessment
a rounded approach to determine what children can manage in defined areas of development

The point of an assessment is to identify what children can do unaided. You may need to say to a child, 'Just for the moment, let's see what you can do on your own.' The point of your support to children's learning is that they learn to do it without prompting in the end. So assessment and helping need to be kept separate but, of course, a good assessment will give you ideas for how to help individual children on another occasion.

Consistency between practitioners

An effective assessment needs to be organised and run in a consistent way between different practitioners and on different occasions. All the team in any early years setting or school need to have discussions about how to assess the children.

- There needs to be a shared agreement about when children will be assessed and how long any assessment will take.
- The value of a focused assessment is that you gain an accurate snapshot of a child at a point in time. This value is lost if you spend weeks on gathering information.
- A focused assessment can work well alongside a continuous record of children to which you add on a regular basis. But remember that the two methods are different.
- Generally speaking, practitioners should not change items in a development record sheet, vary the wording or their own actions.
- Such changes can sometimes change the nature of what you are asking a child and perhaps make a task more difficult. For instance, copying a shape that a child can see is less challenging than being asked to draw a circle with no example on the table.
- Different practitioners need a shared understanding of what is meant by an item such as ' the child can describe a picture' or 'the child is able to share'.
- Sometimes you will need to create a situation for assessment, perhaps by encouraging a child to look at some relevant materials. Yet sometimes you will be able to observe and assess through children's spontaneous play.
- When you are assessing children's physical skills, it is fine to show them with 'Can you hop like this?' You are assessing their physical ability, not their understanding of the words.

- However, you do have to be careful not to give unintentional prompts with assessment of intellectual and communication development.

Creating an opportunity to observe

Sometimes you will observe children in an early years setting or family home and you can learn by watching their spontaneous behaviour.

- Sometimes, an observation may require you to intervene in one way or another but this involvement does not have to be intrusive.
- You might wish to create a situation to check and explore what a child can do.
- Perhaps you put out particular equipment or deliberately use a certain book, because you want to observe children's reactions.
- You might invite a child, or a series of children, to join you in an activity, ask them questions or invite their opinions.
- If children do not want to join you then it is unwise to insist. Children will not give their best when they feel harassed.

Tips for practice

It is very important that early years assessments should avoid any sense of pass or fail. This concern about performance may come from the children, their parents or your own team.

- Be ready to explain to the children, if they ask, what you are doing and why.
- If need be, reassure them, if they are having difficulties, that this activity will help you to help them later on. ('Now I understand better where you get stuck on this' and other encouraging remarks.)
- Profiles should never be laid out in a way that implies blunt success or failure.
- There should be scope to show progress over time. Profiles need options to note that the child can complete an item with confidence, is nearly there, appreciates some help or is unable to manage yet (and does this matter given the child's age?).

Figure 16.5
Children themselves often want you to 'look at me'

Making sense of your observations

As soon as we hear or see something, we start to make some sense of our observation and to link it to our existing knowledge and experience. To an extent, this making sense is inevitable because that is the way that our brains work. But it is important for good practice in observation that you hold back as much as possible from letting assumptions shape your observations as you write them.

Any interpretations, final conclusions or practical suggestions from your observations or use of a developmental profile must be supported. The key word is 'because ...' – whether you write it, say it or think it.

- Your notes or a summary report should avoid vague words like a 'good' child just as much as general criticisms like 'poorly behaved'.
- Focus on what you have observed and bring out the descriptive information. If you believe that Stevie is 'good at hand–eye coordination', then explain why. Give some examples of what you have observed of Stevie. If you judge his skills are striking for his age, then refer to some developmental material that backs your opinion.
- If you believe there is some reason why a child behaves in a particular way or shows particular interests, then support your view. Remain tentative along the lines of 'my observations suggest that ...'.
- Develop the habit of writing down what you see or hear and not your guesses about what children are feeling or what they meant to happen.
- It might mean the difference between writing, 'May frowns. She is staring at the book' rather than an interpretation that 'May is confused'. The closest you should get to this interpretation is that, 'May looks as if she may be confused'.
- You cannot read minds, so it is important not to imply that you have insight into a child's motivations or intentions. You can observe and write up that Rasheed watched Kelly fill the dump truck with dirt and then told a practitioner that 'Kelly has been naughty'. You cannot conclude from this single incident that 'Rasheed wanted to get Kelly into trouble' or that 'Rasheed must be taught not to tell tales'.
- When you look at completed observations, it is equally important that you check any assumptions and interpretations you make. Cultural bias has been known to creep into some observations of children's self care skills. For instance, eating with a knife and fork is not a universal method at mealtimes.
- Unreflective practitioners have sometimes written that a child has 'no language' or 'very limited language'. But the accurate situation has been that the child is in the process of learning English as an additional language and the practitioner has no idea about the child's ability in her first language.
- Keep within the context that you know this child. Perhaps Julie is 'a quiet child' in nursery and you can describe how Julie rarely speaks without being asked, looks on from the sidelines and other examples. But you cannot be sure, without checking with her parents, whether she is equally quiet at home. You cannot conclude that Julie is 'a quiet child' everywhere.

Scenario

The Wessex childminding network has been exploring ways to sharpen up everyone's skills in distinguishing a range of possible interpretations of an observation. Today they consider the following example provided by one of the group:

The observation was of Donnie, aged 18 months, over a period of fifteen minutes yesterday on the kitchen floor of his childminder. Donnie emptied out the contents of the vegetable rack and played with the vegetables one by one. Some of the separate notes describe how 'Donnie looks at the rack intently. He walks over and pulls the rack onto the floor. Donnie sorts out the potatoes' and so on.

But adults will rarely stop with a blow-by-blow of what Donnie has done; we are keen to make sense of what we see to interpret for meaning. The group has come up with four broad interpretations:

- Donnie is fascinated by what objects will do. He is experimenting and has learned that some potatoes roll, that raw carrots are good to eat and that a lot of sprouts can be fitted into his childminder's winter boots.
- Donnie shows evidence of learning from experience. He has worked out how to hook the vegetable rack off its bracket and what initially took him ten minutes of hard work is now completed in three minutes.
- Donnie is a naughty boy who has been allowed to get away with things. His childminder is too permissive and should give Donnie boundaries for his behaviour. He has to learn that vegetables are not toys.
- Donnie is a real boy, he is 'into everything' and has shown the impressive physical skills that are usual for little boys.

Questions

Consider on your own, or ideally with colleagues:

1. The four interpretations show different interests and perspectives – what are these?
2. What might lead practitioners to one interpretation rather than another?
3. Which interpretations are more accurate and positive?
4. Take an observation that has been done in your setting and consider different interpretations.

Key skills links: C3.3 C3.1b C3.3

Figure 16.6

The same event can be interpreted differently – a toddler artist to be encouraged or getting 'too messy'!

Tips for practice

You can help yourself to reflect on assumptions or interpretations with a series of questions. Within a team, colleagues can help each other:

- What is the basis for the sense I make of my observation? What is my evidence?
- What leads me to the conclusion that this child is 'distressed' or 'frustrated'? What have I seen or heard?
- What are other possible interpretations of what I have observed?
- Do I have to reach a firm conclusion? Perhaps I do not really understand what was happening in this observation. Can I ask the children or their parents? Perhaps I can just make a note that I am uncertain.

Recording information about children

Early years settings will keep some kind of written records of children and their learning but written formats are not the only way to gather and keep useful information:

- Settings often need to find practical ways to build informal notes into a more permanent record for a child. See the scenario for one option.
- A portfolio or folder for children can include their own choice of drawings, pieces of work they have been happy to do, early writing, photos of constructions or important outings to this child.
- Scrapbooks or photo albums can be important for individual children and for the current group. Children often enjoy poring over records of this kind that have real meaning for them and encourage recall and conversation.

- A diary can travel between a setting and home. This form of record can be one way to communicate with parents, especially if there is genuinely very limited time. A few notes about a child's interests or new skills can be written in a format that invites parents to add their own family perspective.
- Sometimes it may be possible to make audio or video recordings of activities or events. Only do this if you will have time to look at the recording. Children and parents can enjoy watching a video about the setting. Bear in mind the tips for practice on page 447.

Activity

- Look at the options for recording in this section.
- Consider and discuss which of them are suitable for a nanny or childminder and why.
- Write up a brief plan of how a nanny or childminder could keep appropriate records for this working role.

Key skills links: C3.3 C3.1a

Scenario

The team at St Jude's nursery and reception class have experimented with different ways of noting informal observations and then transferring them to the main record of a child.

Jessie first suggested a system of post-it notes that had worked well in her previous school. But they needed a main board to put the notes against each child's name before going into the main record. The only location was really too public. The notes were made with care but still needed to be more confidential than was possible with this board.

Pam brought in an alternative idea that she had heard during a training workshop. A local pre-school had used a notepad that could hang around the practitioner's neck or clip onto a waistband. Notes could be made of interactions or events during the day, then transferred into a child's record.

The team tried out this idea and it suited the nursery and reception as a way to supplement other forms of record keeping. A positive consequence was the great interest shown by some children in the 'special little note-books'. Several children wanted to make a notebook of their own and were encouraged and helped to undertake this activity. The notebooks have become part of some children's pretend play and have offered a positive route to show reasons to write.

Questions

1. In what way does your own setting deal with making informal notes?
2. Compare ideas with colleagues on your course. What could be the pros and cons of different methods?
3. Try out a new method for a few weeks and write up the activity.

Key skills links: C3.1a LP3.1–3 WO3.1–3

Figure 16.7

Any observations need to cover outdoors as well as indoors

Sharing records with children

Parents should have access to the records of their own children (see page 461) but communication with children is also important and often overlooked. Children can be involved in several ways:

- Children are often interested in what adults are doing when they notice you making observations. Be ready to explain simply what interests you and why.
- You can even explain what you have learned from observations of a child's behaviour, so long as you express yourself positively. You might say, 'Sometimes you look a little bit lost in playgroup. So I've been trying to work out how I could help.'
- Children usually like to collect and choose material for their portfolios. The range may include some of their artwork, early mark making and photos that document what they like doing as well as projects that are far too big to go into a portfolio except as a photograph.
- Children may like to dictate or partly write some of the explanatory notes in their records.
- Children can and should be involved in setting their learning targets. This discussion might be about 'what you're ready to manage next' in an open way or part of an Individual Education Plan for a child with special needs (see page 529).

Activity

It is well worth considering ways to involve and consult children on different kinds of record keeping. You want after all to support their view of themselves as learners and promote a positive disposition to learn (see page 393).

- Find out the ways that children are involved in your own setting.
- If there is limited involvement and consultation for children, then draft one or two ideas of what could be developed.
- Share ideas with your colleagues in the setting and exchange ideas with colleagues who are fellow students.

Key skills links: C3.1a LP3.1–3 WO3.1–3

Confidentiality and access

Parents should feel confident that personal information about themselves or their children is kept confidential. Records should not be simply left lying around a setting nor should they be left visible on a computer screen. Nor should details of families be the subject of gossip, either across a large setting or outside a setting.

However, parents should have straightforward access to the records of their own children. Apart from good practice in partnership with parents, people have a legal right to see records about themselves or your children, unless there are extenuating circumstances, for instance, a child protection case.

Figure 16.8

Children enjoy a photographic record of their activities

Tips for practice

- Practitioners within the setting, and especially the key worker, should have easy access.
- Anyone else should have only access on a clear need-to-know basis.
- Certainly, children and family records should not be made available to students, researchers or other professionals without the clear agreement of the parents.
- Parents should know the centre's policy on records, because you should have told them early on in the relationship and a clear statement about records should be part of written material on the centre.
- Parents should not have to make a song and dance about getting access; it should be simple. Good records also have sections to which parents can add their own comments.
- Some settings have specific procedures to follow when access is requested but these should not lengthy.
- It has sometimes been usual practice to remove any third party information in a file, that is any letters or reports that have been written by people outside your own setting. However, many local authorities and organisations now follow a policy that material goes on open file unless the other person specifically refuses.

When you write records it is important to remind yourself that parents will be able to read what you are writing. Early years practitioners sometimes find this realisation daunting. However, if you follow good practice in writing records and reports then the material should support communication with parents rather than annoy them. You will find more suggestions about good communication with parents from page 638.

Good practice in writing records

Good practice when completing any written record is to be clear about:

- *what* you need to record and how much is realistic, given your setting
- the reasons *why* you are recording this information, including the ways in which you hope it will be useful later

- good practice in *how* you record
- the related issues of confidentiality of reports and of appropriate access to them.

Scenario

The team of Greenholt Pre-school have reviewed their approach to record keeping to adjust to the different attendance patterns of the children. Although some children attend every day, others come for only one or two sessions a week. The team wishes to offer this flexibility to local families and feel that some younger children are not ready for full week attendance. However, the team has been trying to complete the same developmental profile on all the children to cover all the learning goals in the foundation stage. This approach has led to impossible pressure on the children who attend one or two sessions.

By the end of a rather anxious team meeting, Marjorie and her colleagues agree a much less ambitious profile for the children who attend for one or two sessions. The more flexible profile has headings for the six learning areas but leaves space for observations of what interests this child.

Questions

1. Why do you think that the team has set themselves such a tough observation task?
2. What adjustments could make sense when a team is keeping records of children who attend for less than a full week?
3. Discuss your ideas with colleagues.

Key skills links: C3.1a

Be factual

Good, and useful, written records or summary reports are honest and factual. Your supported opinions are important, see below, but it should be easy to distinguish facts, opinions and any suggestions or conclusions on the basis of these.

Support your opinions

It is not possible to avoid giving opinions as an early years practitioner. Your experience and knowledge make it possible to give opinions about the behaviour or development of a child that are built on your observations. The two key points of good practice are that:

- it is easy to distinguish the facts of what you have observed from your opinion and
- you support your opinion; there is a sense of 'because ...'.

Activity

Read through the following draft report. Ideally take a photocopy, so that you can write on the report itself. The report needs work, but what kind of changes could improve this first draft?

First draft of summary report on Joanna Yates

Date of report: 26 November 2001
Age of child: 2 years and 7 months
Date of admission to centre: 20 September 2001

Joanna comes to the centre three days a week. She started to attend because her health visitor was worried the child only had a few words and was too quiet. Mum isn't worried and keeps saying that Jo-Jo (her name for Joanna) is a very good child and was a good baby. Mum is only a teenager herself and doesn't have much idea what to do with Joanna.

Joanna settled in quickly and she didn't seem unhappy at all. She is usually quiet and doesn't join in much. She is a self-sufficient child and looks at the other children but hasn't shown much interest in the kind of activities we would expect her to like. She says 'No' and 'Mine' and follows instructions like going to the bathroom. But she might just be following the other children. When she is asked something directly, Joanna sometimes makes a silly, blank expression. Quite often she does not answer to her name.

Joanna eats well and is nearly toilet trained. She sleeps for up to an hour after lunch. Her clothes are odd but at least her mother keeps them clean. Once or twice lately Joanna wasn't wearing a coat when she arrived in the morning. Joanna seems fairly healthy, although she has a cold at the moment. She was off for a week in October with what her mother said was flu.

Joanna is no trouble to have in the group because she never gets cross with any of the other children, but she doesn't really play properly either. Her concentration seems alright since she will sit at a table activity for as long as it is out. Mainly she sits at the sand tray but I have seen her in the book corner as well.

The main worry is that Joanna says so little and that her mother won't accept that there is any problem. Mum is expecting yet another baby in April.

Questions

Please read through the draft then:

1. Mark up your copy with any points you would like to make about the actual wording that has been used in the written report. Be ready to explain your reasons for wanting changes.
2. What changes in organisation could improve the draft and why are these important?
3. Do you think there is any cause for concern about this child? If so, then what kind of observations would you make? What kind of conversation would you have with the child's mother?
4. Discuss your ideas with colleagues, including how you could advise the draft writers about necessary changes in a constructive way (see page 465). You will find some suggestions about improvement on page 466.

Key skills links: C3.3 C3.1a

To think about

It is valuable for you get practice in distinguishing between facts and opinions, in order to develop good practice habits of supporting your opinions. Early years practitioners will have valuable opinions and there is no way that you can restrict your written or spoken communication to matters of fact. Good practice is to be able to support your opinions and to express them in a positive way.

Look at the following comments and consider:

- Which comments are factual and which are opinions?
- Which comments need some changes to how they are expressed?
- Do some comments need further support: if spoken? If written down?
- Discuss your ideas with colleagues. You will find suggested answers on page 467.

1 Amy lacks confidence on the climbing frame.
2 Daniel hit Fiona this afternoon.
3 Lesley was crying for no reason.
4 Mrs Richie said she was worried that Teresa is not talking yet.
5 Anneka is only four years old and she can already read very well.
6 Mr Martinelli is an anxious father.
7 Billy is very aggressive and the other children are frightened of him.
8 Mrs Warwick claims that Lewis caused the bruises on his sister's arm.
9 Winston is sometimes very difficult to control and does not listen.
10 Nathan has a lot of colds and awful catarrh.
11 Mr Kwok asked if we were going to celebrate Chinese New Year.
12 Sara is a bright little girl with very good language.
13 Lee has been enthusiastic about the new storysack.
14 George is a bit of a bully.
15 Rafat only plays in parallel with other children.
16 Davie has asked me to help him with writing his letters.

Key skills links: C3.1a

Good quality in writing

It is important to write up any observations promptly because otherwise you will forget details or merge one event with another in your memory. Prompt recording is especially important if you are concerned about a child, perhaps with possible child protection issues (see Chapter 19).

Any records need to be written in a clear and concise style:

- Some records will be hand written. So you need to ensure that your writing is legible.
- Check the spelling of words if you have any doubt. If you work on a word processor, then make sure that you use the spell-check function.
- You will often have a layout with headings under which you write

observations or a summary report of a child. Let these headings help you plan what you write.

- You may be asked to write some reports without a layout to guide you. In that case, work out some sensible headings and ask your senior to help you.
- You will write a more useful report if you take a bit of time to consider, 'What are the areas I need to cover? and 'What do I want people to know or understand once they have read my report?'
- Make it easy for anyone to follow the flow of your report. Ensure that any narrative about a child or family goes in the right order, with dates given as appropriate.
- If at all possible, read a draft report out loud to yourself or somebody else. This strategy is the best way to pick up on repeated words, very long sentences and confused content.

Tips for practice

- Spelling matters – use a dictionary or spell checker on the word processor. Keep a personal note of words that you use regularly and you know you often confuse.
- But even on the computer, you will need a dictionary to tell you what a word means and whether you are using the word you intend.
- Use punctuation correctly. Many reports will not need any more sophisticated punctuation than the correct use of commas and full stops.
- Many people are confused about the use of the apostrophe and some people who write public notices make the mistake of thinking it is always used in front of the letter 's'.
- The first use of an apostrophe is to show that something is missing from a word, for example in 'don't' because this word is a shortened version of 'do not'. However, you would usually write such words in full because these abbreviations are mainly for spoken communication.
- The second use of an apostrophe is to show possession as in Gemma's coat or Asha's idea.
- Use clear and simple sentences and break your report into paragraphs. Generally you need a new paragraph for each new idea.
- Write clearly and avoid early years specialist language (see page 638).
- Avoid confusing sentence constructions like the double negative or it not being clear who has done what. For instance, in the sentence 'Andy's father did not say he could not go on the trip' who said what about whom?

Everyone needs to practise in order to improve their writing style and to become familiar with the range of written material that is required in your current role or setting.

- You will become more confident with practice but you also need constructive and encouraging feedback from more experienced or senior colleagues.
- You will not be helped if colleagues simply criticise your first drafts with words like 'muddled' or 'vague'.
- It is worth asking for specific suggestions on 'how can I improve?' and 'I found this section really tough, can you suggest how I can organise it?'

If you are dyslexic

Dyslexia is discussed on page 350 in relation to children's learning. But of course this learning disability stays with you for life. If you are dyslexic, then you will need extra support as a student and from your colleagues when you are in post.

- If your education has been helpful, then you may have some strategies that work for you in dealing with the written word.
- You need to explain the situation to colleagues in the team, so that they understand in what ways you would appreciate help and that you are not simply trying to dodge out of writing any reports.
- It is possible that you could think about and tape record your main points from an observation and similarly work them into a summary report. You could then draft a written version, without losing any of your thoughts in the stress of writing.
- Ask a colleague to look at your draft and give you constructive feedback. It may sometimes help if your colleague reads it aloud. You can then identify where the words are wrong, because you are far clearer in the spoken language about what you want to transfer into the written format.

Suggestions

Here are some comments on the draft report from the activity on page 463. You may have generated more or different comments in discussion with your colleagues. There is no single set of 'right' answers here.

- The report needs a clear structure to cover different areas of Joanna's development. At the moment the draft is very confusing. It also needs the name of the person who has written the report.
- Patronising to Joanna's mother, for instance 'only a teenager herself' and 'expecting yet another baby'. A good example of remarks that will be embarrassing when the parent asks to look at her daughter's file.
- Unacceptable offhand remarks: 'her clothes are odd', 'what her mother said was flu'.
- A negative feel to the few comments about Joanna's development: 'doesn't join in much', 'a silly, blank expression', 'doesn't really play properly'. There needs to be a better balance between what Joanna can do and what she cannot manage, as well as a better quality of description overall.
- Of course, the child may not reply because she is used to being called Jo-Jo and not Joanna!
- The report lacks a sense that the writer has any clear expectations about the abilities of a child who is just over two and a half. Sitting for a long time at the sand tray is not necessarily evidence of good concentration.
- A decent structure to the report, with headings for different areas of development, would require more information from the writer.
- As the report stands, it is hard to judge whether there are reasons to be concerned about the child, although the patchy description raises the possibility that Joanna may not yet be comfortable in this setting.

Suggestions

Here are some comments about the To think about box from page 464. You may come up with other points in discussion with colleagues. In each example of a child it would be necessary of course to know the child's age and whether he or she had any disabilities that could affect the sense you make of the situation and what the next steps might be, if any.

1 *Amy lacks confidence on the climbing frame.*

An opinion and needs some more information through descriptive examples. What makes the adult feel that Amy 'lacks confidence'?

2 *Daniel hit Fiona this afternoon.*

Factual, but more of an entry in a daily diary and should include some sense of what led up to the incident and how it was handled (ABC – see page 502).

3 *Lesley was crying for no reason.*

Opinion of an adult and inappropriate. Children always cry for a reason; it is just that adults sometime judge the reason is 'not good enough'. Needs more description and observation for patterns.

4 *Mrs Richie said she was worried that Teresa is not talking yet.*

Factual reporting of parent's concern. The follow up will depend on Teresa's age and abilities.

5 *Anneka is only four years old and she can already read very well.*

Factual for age and opinion about reading, needs to be supported with observation of Anneka, for instance that she does actually read rather than know favourite stories by heart.

6 *Mr Martinelli is an anxious father.*

Opinion and inappropriate as written. Mr Martinelli will have expressed anxiety about some situation(s); that does not necessarily make him an anxious person.

7 *Billy is very aggressive and the other children are frightened of him.*

Opinion that needs to be expressed differently and supported. The comment needs some description of Billy's behaviour and not just a label, as well as some support for the opinion that the other children are frightened.

8 *Mrs Warwick claims that Lewis caused the bruises on his sister's arm.*

Factual as a report of what Mrs Warwick said. It may not be possible for the early years team to assess whether the statement is true or not.

9 *Winston is sometimes very difficult to control and does not listen.*

Opinion that needs more description of what Winston does and under what circumstances.

10 *Nathan has a lot of colds and awful catarrh.*

Semi-factual but poorly expressed. How many colds does Nathan have and his catarrh could be described as 'serious' rather than 'awful'.

11 *Mr Kwok asked if we were going to celebrate Chinese New Year.*

Factual and could lead to the team re-considering their plans if the answer is 'no'.

12 *Sara is a bright little girl with very good language.*

Opinion and unhelpful as it stands, despite the positive feel. What does Sara do that makes the writer/speaker judge her to be 'bright'? Needs examples of her language to support the claim.

13 *Lee has been enthusiastic about the new storysack.*

Opinion that could be supported with more description of how Lee reacted.

14 *George is a bit of a bully.*

Opinion and poorly expressed as a negative label of the child. Needs rewording and description of George's behaviour.

15 *Rafat only plays in parallel with other children.*

Semi-factual or could be an opinion – hard to tell without knowing how far the comment is based on good observation of Rafat.

16 *Davie has asked me to help him with writing his letters.*

Factual reporting of a child's request.

Assessment of children's learning

The introduction of an early years curriculum in the UK has given a new focus for the observation and recording of children's learning. In England, the early learning goals within the foundation stage have been especially associated with the need to track children's learning in some detail. In some settings, the need to record and assess has been experienced as a great pressure.

Yet, good practice in observation, assessment and written records has been central to early years practice for a long time. It is important to recognise existing good practice as well as consider new applications and to deal with unhelpful pressure on how much and in what way to record children's learning.

What does assessment mean?

Different ideas and terms can become confused in discussions about the assessment of young children:

- *Gathering information*: useful work with children depends on good quality information, which you might gather through talking with children's parents, observations of children and talking with colleagues or other professionals who know this individual child.
- *Observation*: the skills of observation need an active use of the senses of sight and hearing. You are watching and listening to a purpose, although there can be many different purposes.
- *Recording*: good practice includes a written report of observations and the careful assessment of a child's abilities drafted in a positive way.

The gathering of information leads to an assessment, which has some element of judgement. What is happening with a given group of children? What can a child do, nearly do or not yet do? What sense can you make of a child's development or behaviour against the backdrop of her age, experience and any special needs (which may or may not be disabilities).

Why assess?

Any useful and sensible assessment of children has to be linked to a clear purpose. You need to be able to answer the questions 'Why are we doing this?' or 'What do we hope to gain from assessment?' In general, the functions of careful observation followed by an assessment are to:

- Provide information, a rounded picture rather than just what chances to catch an adult's attention.
- Inform future planning for this child – in the short-, medium- and longer-term future.
- Identify and diagnose problems, which may be minor or more serious.
- Support full communication with parents about their child. Good practice in assessment involves parents and gives scope for their unique knowledge of their child.
- Support communication with children so that they can understand, in a way appropriate to their age, how their learning has progressed.
- At some points in childhood, assessment is a tool to communicate information about a child with the next setting to which she or he is moving on. Such communication should be in full partnership with the child's parents.

Assessments are made of individual children but what you learn can also inform your future planning for the whole group. You might review the curriculum and approaches taken in the group and consider the balance for all children, given what has emerged from individual assessments (see page 456).

Figure 16.9

You will want an accurate idea of how children's skills are progressing

Tips for practice

- A key issue to bear in mind will always be that record keeping should clearly support your main goal of enabling children's learning.
- Your goal is not to have extensive records; the records should do a job.
- At least some early years settings may need to decide how much is enough in terms of written records and evidence gathering. This part of the job should not overwhelm time and attention given to the children, who are the priority.

Approaches to assessment

A range of different kinds of observation and record keeping can contribute to assessment. You might undertake any of the following or some combination:

- Continuous assessment through keeping notes of children's progress and development. Regular observation may be used to notice what children are doing in their spontaneous play, complemented by talking with children, colleagues and parents.
- A portfolio of work may be gathered, ideally selected by the child as well as an adult. Some settings are now using cameras with the children to document activities, events and work in progress.
- Regular notes may be made under descriptive headings that cover the main areas of children's development and behaviour.
- Settings may complete developmental record sheets on a regular basis and these offer a 'snapshot' of a child at a particular time. This kind of observation and assessment attempts to cover a wide range of skills and knowledge, not all of which children will show through spontaneous play.
- Focused observations may home in on particular developmental skills, children's behaviour, times of the day or session or use of particular items of equipment or learning spaces. Careful use of techniques of time sampling or event sampling can produce a fair observation that supports an assessment (see page 448).

Assessment of individual development and behaviour

There are two main approaches to assessing individual children:

1. Comparing a child with him- or herself at a previous point in time (ipsative). This approach gives a direct assessment of how much this child has changed.
2. Comparing a child with developmental norms for her age (normative) or against expectations for all children, such as the early learning goals in the English curriculum.

Key terms

Ipsative approach to assessment comparing a child with him/herself at a previous point in time

Normative approach to assessment comparing a child with developmental norms for her age or against expectations for all children, such as the early learning goals in the English curriculum

Both approaches are needed for a sensitive balance in assessment.

The **ipsative** approach will show how this individual child is or is not progressing over time. A focus on individual children is crucial if you are to encourage and value children from the point of view of where they are at the moment, rather than where they 'should' be. But a responsible approach to children also requires a **normative** perspective. Without this approach, you will not be able to make full sense of what you have observed. Perhaps Anya has made noticeable progress, but adults have to recognise that she is still very delayed in her language development. Perhaps Darren was strikingly ahead of his peers six months ago but seems scarcely to have changed in that time. Perhaps he is bored and needs more challenge?

The normative side to assessment has to be used in a flexible way and well grounded in general knowledge about child development:

- There can be significant variation between children in terms of the age at which they manage a skill. Children may be some months different from their peers and there still be no cause for concern. However, responsible practitioners would, of course, keep alert to the point at which there is reason to worry (see page 11).
- Children are not identical and their development does not progress in an even way for all aspects of their learning. Children have time to learn and any kind of assessment needs to take an overall look at their development, not imply that some aspects are more valuable than others.
- Disabled children may learn to a different time scale and their pattern of development may be very different from their peers, depending on the nature and extent of their disability.
- Care has also to be taken over observation and assessment of bilingual children, especially when the child is being asked to use her least fluent language to answer your questions.

Some important practical issues arise when you are using any kind of focused assessment technique, such as a developmental record sheet. This assessment is always selective to some extent. You cannot possibly observe and assess everything that a child can do or nearly do, without seriously unbalancing your work in an early years setting or school (see page 453 about using developmental profiles or checklists).

Making assessment work well

The potential value of good quality assessment is that:

- You know better what is happening with individual children.
- You can be pleased with children and their parents about what they have learned and can nearly manage. You can help children to see themselves as learners.
- You can spot, and plan to work with difficulties, delays or misunderstandings. You should be able to make a difference to a child.
- You are more likely to be able to identify imbalances in how you approach this child, what you have overlooked.
- A consideration of assessments of all the children should help you to reflect on your overall approach to the whole group. But your early years curriculum should be much broader than focused assessment tasks.

A positive atmosphere

Any kind of assessment of children needs to be undertaken in a calm way without rushing children and with a supportive approach to their efforts. Any assessment scheme can only be as good as the people who use it, their behaviour as they assess children and the ways in which they communicate with parents and with children after the assessment.

Tips for practice

To work well, assessment has to be a part of general good practice in your setting:

- Observations and assessments are an integral part of your work, not extras that you feel you have to do. Assessments lead to new insights, practical plans and actual work with children (not to piles of paper in the cupboard).
- Practitioners keep assessment clearly different from helping children to learn. The goal of assessment is usually to judge through observation what a child can manage without prompting (see page 454).
- Assessment is always undertaken and discussed with parents in a positive frame. Plans start with what a child 'can do' or ' can nearly do'. Written records and conversations are never a list of problems and 'can't do'.
- Progress and learning is celebrated and never dismissed as 'something she ought to be doing anyway'.
- Difficulties and developmental delays are acknowledged and this recognition leads directly into positive action.
- Children are never labelled, whether positively or negatively. Written records and conversations with parents are based on descriptions of what children do.
- Any kind of focused observation is also discussed in the context of everyone's knowledge of this child and of child development in general.
- A balance between subjectivity and objectivity. Early years practitioners, and parents, are personally involved with children and this personal perspective is important. However, it must be balanced with more objective methods of observation and an even-handed approach to assessment that depend on more than one person's opinion.

Feelings are also involved

Assessment is not just an intellectual task; feelings are also involved.

- Adults may experience mixed emotions about assessment. Early years practitioners and teachers can feel that they are being judged as much as the children. In a sense this perspective is partly true.
- Parents may feel that they are being judged, but it depends a great deal on the quality of communication from the early years practitioners. Without effective and genuine partnership, then parents and practitioners may try to assign blame for a child's difficulties.
- Children's feelings will also be involved, but the nature of those feelings will depend a great deal on the quality of work from the adults. Assessment does not in itself label children or discourage them. The communication from adults can send negative messages, or alternatively use the assessment experience to boost a child's confidence.

Baseline assessment

From 2002 there are likely to be changes in baseline assessment and other national equivalents across the four countries of the UK.

England

Until recently, children in England completed one of the over 90 accredited local baseline assessment schemes within the first half term of their start in the Reception class. Changes are underway at the time of writing so that:

- There will be one Foundation Stage Profile, from September 2002 that will be used at the end of the Reception year, so that it is consistent with the end of the Foundation Stage.
- The aim is to have a profile assessment scheme that is far more grounded in ongoing observation and assessment of children's progress. It is planned that the scheme will cover the six learning areas of the early years curriculum (see page 407).

Wales

Wales has used a baseline assessment system with 12 accredited schemes. The chosen scheme is used to assess children within seven weeks of starting in Reception or Year 1. There may be further changes in the Welsh system but it is not clear currently what those might be.

Scotland

So far local authorities have used their own systems of recording to pass information from early years to primary schools. Most systems draw on observations by early years practitioners and nursery teachers. There are plans to move to a more consistent national system but still within the framework of observation rather than testing. A few schools have opted to test children in Primary One, but the Scottish Executive is not in favour of this route.

Northern Ireland

Baseline assessment was planned for introduction in the province for September 2001. But plans were shelved because of a major curriculum review that is being undertaken to cover the period from early years to Key Stage 4. Children currently start school at four years of age in Northern Ireland and one proposal being discussed is to postpone formal education until six or seven years, as is the case in many other European countries.

Specialist assessments

Some children may be involved in other kinds of assessment to which your setting contributes. One possibility is the process of assessment for special educational needs (see page 526). Other professionals who may be involved in assessment are described on page 17. You might again contribute to an assessment or else be informed by parents of the details of a specialist assessment that could usefully shape how you approach a child's development or behaviour.

Further resources

Griffin, Sue (1994) *Keeping and Writing Records: A step-by-step guide for early years practitioners* Starting Points 17, National Early Years Network.

Hancock, Juliet and Dale, Barbara (1999) *Looking, Listening and Learning; Quality Interaction with Children* Scottish Consultative Council on the Curriculum.

Lindon, Jennie (1994) *Child Development from Birth to Eight: A practical focus* National Children's Bureau.

Lindon, Jennie (1998) *Understanding Child Development: Knowledge, theory and practice* Thomson Learning – especially Chapter 8.

Lindon, Jennie (1997) *Working with Young Children* 3rd edn, Hodder and Stoughton – especially Chapters 1–3.

Progress check

1 Describe three broad ways in which observation can support good practice.
2 Suggest two general examples of how you might use time sampling to observe a child's learning.
3 Explain briefly why it is important that you distinguish fact and opinion and that you are able to support your opinions from an observation.
4 Outline two ways to use a developmental profile so that children can experience success and not feel they have failed a test.
5 Suggest two ways in which practitioners might need to be aware of their own cultural background when making sense of observations.
6 Explain why parents should have easy access to the records of their child.
7 Describe two ways in which you should check your actual writing in a report on a child.

17

A positive approach to children's behaviour

After reading this chapter you should be able you to:

- describe ways in which children learn patterns of behaviour
- identify the elements in a positive approach to guiding children's behaviour
- promote the development of children's prosocial behaviour
- apply positive ways to deal with unwanted behaviour from children
- recognise and avoid unacceptable approaches to dealing with behaviour.

Introduction

Children's behaviour in any given situation will be the result of their individuality, the experience they bring to this setting and the genuine options they face at the time. Children have their own temperament and they are not born with fixed ways of reacting to what happens in their life. Children learn from their experiences, including how adults treat them and the possibilities for different courses of action. A positive approach to children's behaviour focuses at least as much on wanted behaviour as on unwanted. It also has to include adult alertness to their own behaviour; the children are not the only people present and they need the adults in their life to work well together.

Links to early years qualifications

This chapter especially supports the following units:

Diploma in Child Care and Education: 4, 10

National Vocational Qualification in Early Years Care and Education

Level 2: C4

Level 3: C7

BTEC National Early Years Diploma: 6, 12

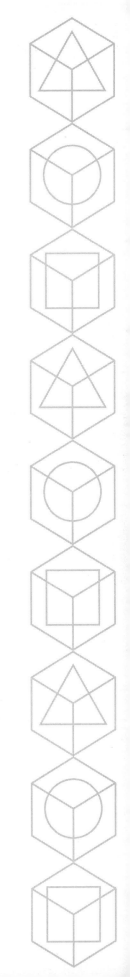

Children learn ways of behaving

Children's behaviour at any one time in your setting will be affected by their individual temperament as well as the experience and expectations they bring to your setting. They will have learned some ground rules about behaviour. Yet children who are settling in need to learn perhaps that your way is different from adults they have known so far. Children feel as well as act, so the pressures of the moment and the strength of emotions aroused can lead them to behave in ways that they know are not quite right. We need to acknowledge that it can sometimes be hard for children to do the right thing. We are also unfair if we require higher standards from children than we could meet ourselves in equivalent adult situations (see the To think about box).

Reasons are not always obvious

It is important that adults do not require simple explanations of children's behaviour. Even brief consideration of adult behaviour shows you that there are many factors that influence the outcome in any given situation. Children are much younger than we are, but they are alert and we do them no favours by wanting there to be simple answers to 'why?' Children are learning all the time and are responsive to the nuances of any situation they face. It would be most unlikely if adults could identify a neat cause-and-effect explanation for every action that children take.

To think about

For instance, how would you behave in response to the following scenarios? And what reasons underlie your choice?

- You have bought a jacket in a shop. As you leave the till, you realise you have been undercharged. Are you honest, do you speak up?
- You are late for work and driving along a road with a 30 mile limit. Do you let your speed creep towards 35 or 40 mph or do you obey the rule?
- A friend whom you know to be careless with possessions asks to borrow some of your CDs for her birthday celebration party. Do you share?
- A close friend has lent you a novel that she says is wonderful. You have struggled to read the novel and found it very boring. Your friend asks enthusiastically what you thought of the book. Do you tell the truth?
- You are in a training workshop all morning, your chair is uncomfortable and your attention is drifting. Do you sit still and concentrate? Or do you fidget, doodle on your notepad and let your mind drift off?
- At home you are desperate for a biscuit. There is only one left in the packet and you know your partner/flatmate is equally keen on these biscuits. Do you eat the biscuit? Do you hide the empty packet?

Questions

Discuss some of your reactions with colleagues:

- Consider your different reactions and reasons for your likely behaviour. Could you give a logical answer to 'why did you do that?'

- Make the link to children's behaviour and discuss whether adults (including you) demand unrealistically simple reasons from children.
- These examples are the adult equivalent of what we often ask of children: do the right thing, obey the rule, be nice and share. Can you think of other links into adult life for what we ask of children?
- Make some practical applications to your own practice.

Key skills links: C3.1a LP3.1–3 WO3.1–3

The impact of children's experience

All the main developmental theories (see page 10) are helpful to an extent in guiding adults towards sensible and supportive adult behaviour but it is helpful to take an overview that blends these ideas.

Behaviour is mostly learned, not inborn

Observation of children and knowledge of the patterns of child development show that children's experiences shape how they see and react to the world. Children learn ways of behaving from how they have been treated in their early years. Similar experiences do not have an identical impact on different children and so their temperament is almost certainly part of how they react (see page 200).

Temperament probably has some genetic component (it is inherited) so behaviour is not 100 per cent nurture, but a considerable amount of variation can be traced to experience. So, the practical conclusion for early years practitioners is that a positive approach by adults to children's behaviour can make a difference.

Figure 17.1
An early years group setting requires new social skills from children

Behaviour is part of social development

Children are very social; they learn from what they can observe. They learn through imitation of familiar adults, siblings, friends and sometimes characters from television or video. This imitation may be positive as well as negative – an important point to recall if your attention is most taken with imitation you would rather discourage.

Children's ability to learn from experience is also shaped by their age. It is up to adults to hold realistic expectations of what very young children can understand and the extent to which they can manage their own behaviour, especially with limited help from adults.

Behaviour is also linked to thinking

Cognitive theorists such as Jean Piaget or Lev Vygotsky (see page 15) have been more interested in the development of children's ideas and communication skills than their general behaviour. An awareness of children's powers to think, interpret and predict is important in any approach to behaviour. The adult perspective on a situation is not the only one that matters.

Children do not just act, they also watch, listen and think. For instance:

- Children may well observe that adults tell them to take turns, but do not help when they are shoved away after waiting patiently.
- Children are ready to be helpful to others, but the early years setting or school has a poor atmosphere and everyone feels ill-tempered and self centred.
- Children make their choices of action from the options that are genuinely open to them in their situation. It is no good, for instance, being annoyed with children who are reluctant to share if their nursery or family home is such a competitive environment that the only survival strategy is to hold fast to what you have.

Children are also shaped by their experience: what they have found works and what seem to be the various options.

- Young children's thinking is grounded in what they know so far. They can find it hard to imagine a situation with ground rules or social relations other than what they have experienced.
- You will work with some children who have never had the opportunity to learn different ways of handling everyday conflict. Perhaps they have only ever seen an impatient or angry approach and the children have no idea of what else they might do.
- An alternative scenario is that some children enter the hurly-burly of a primary school playground with the expectation from their family life that people stop doing something if you say 'that upsets me'. Children who have learned the habit of consideration can be shocked to realise that some of their peers do not care about causing upset and may actually be pleased.

Key terms

Behaviourism
a theoretical approach that emphasises how human behaviour responds to patterns of reward and punishment. The approach is also called **learning theory**. Social learning theory recognises the importance of feelings and thinking on actions

Learning through reinforcement

Behaviourism or **learning theory** emerged from experimental study of how animals learned. Early versions of behaviourism were too simple to describe the complexity of children's behaviour. However, the social learning theory of Albert Bandura gives a more recognisable explanation of how children think as well as act.

Within behaviourist theory there are two basic propositions to explain how patterns of behaviour are established (in childhood or adulthood). These are that:

1 behaviour is strengthened by **reinforcement**
2 behaviour that is reinforced on a partial schedule (that is not every time) is stronger, more resistant to stopping altogether, than behaviour that has been reinforced every single time.

Bandura's social learning approach added two more important propositions, that:

3 children learn new behaviours mainly through the process of modelling, that is, through observing adults or other children and imitating their actions
4 as well as actual behaviours, children also learn ideas, expectations and develop internal standards about choices in behaviour.

Behaviourism proposes that an experience of reinforcement increases the likelihood that a given behaviour will be repeated under similar circumstances in the future. Behaviour may be strengthened by positive or negative reinforcement.

- *Positive reinforcement* is an agreeable experience of something pleasant that follows behaviour. There are many possibilities. Reinforcement can be tangible rewards, like giving children sweets, some kind of treat, privilege or symbolic prize. However, it can just as easily be a smile, hug and words of admiration and encouragement.
- *Negative reinforcement* is the removal of something unpleasant or unwanted from the situation. Again this kind of reinforcement increases the likelihood that the behaviour will be repeated in the future. For example, perhaps children have learned that one carer will give in and stop saying 'No' if the children continue to nag.
- *Partial reinforcement* is a pattern in which behaviour is not reinforced (positively or negatively) every single time. Ordinary life for children tends to follow this pattern, since even adults who try to be positively consistent do not manage this all the time. Likewise a child may persist in nagging for sweets or a later bedtime because it works sometimes and adults give in and say 'Alright'.

Reinforcement strengthens a pattern of behaviour, the experience increases the likelihood. On the other hand, punishment may weaken the pattern.

- **Punishment** is the removal of something pleasant from the situation, for instance, withdrawal of friendly attention, cancelling treats or removal of privileges. Or else punishment is the addition of something unpleasant to this situation as a result of the behaviour, for instance, making children sit on a 'naughty chair', critical or rude remarks from adults or physical punishment such as hitting.

So, punishment is different from negative reinforcement (read the two explanations once more if you are confused). The impact of punishment can be unpredictable.

The result of patterns of reinforcement and punishment can be that a particular behaviour effectively disappears.

- **Extinction** is the term describing the complete removal of a pattern of behaviour; the child has stopped behaving this way in response to this situation.

For example, perhaps a child tries moaning and crying in order to be bought sweets at the supermarket checkout. Their parent or carer deals with the situation calmly and does not reinforce the behaviour with attention or giving in to the demands. After a few times, the child stops bothering to whine because she

Key term

Reinforcement
an experience that increases the likelihood that an action will be repeated in the future

Key term

Punishment
an experience that decreases the likelihood that an action will be repeated in the future

Key term

Extinction
when an action or pattern of actions ceases altogether

has learned there is no point. On the other hand, a child may also give up attempts at friendly interaction with adults, if their efforts are consistently met with serious unpleasantness and being told to 'Shut up!'

Observation in everyday practice

Interactions between children and adults in everyday life are complex and the skills of early years practitioners are needed to observe what exactly is going on in the situation. For instance, a child's view of what is rewarding may differ from the adult perspective – see page 486 or the example on page 505. Adults are part of the whole situation as well, so any consideration of patterns of reinforcement has to allow for adult behaviour.

Behaviourism or learning theory has many practical applications within daily life with children and an understanding of the principles can nevertheless be compatible with a friendly and social day. A more organised use of the principles of behaviourism is used in the techniques of behaviour modification. Specific rewards are offered by adults for target behaviours from children in a planned way. These ideas have sometimes been very useful in programmes designed for use with disabled children, for learning and for dealing with challenging behaviour.

Emotional needs and behaviour

Alfred Adler developed a strong social emphasis for child development, especially from children's experiences within family life. He believed that children's behaviour was shaped by the sense they made of social interactions with other people. So children's thoughts and interpretations were as relevant as their emotions. Rudolf Dreikurs extended these ideas and explored the dynamics of how children interact with their social environment. Dreikurs described what he called the four mistaken goals of behaviour. These were that children behaved so as to:

- gain attention
- show superiority or power
- get even or seek revenge
- avoid defeat by appearing inadequate and hopeless.

The practical application of these ideas is that:

- Supportive adults try to recognise the likely goals or purposes behind children's behaviour. Acceptable emotions can lie beneath what emerges as unacceptable behaviour.
- Adults can help a child seek and gain attention through non-disruptive means. Or they can address a young child's fear of failure, creating a situation in which he or she no longer needs to cope by appearing inadequate.
- Dreikurs and his colleagues also raised the important issue of adult feelings; children were not the only ones feeling strong emotions in some tense situations. They pointed out that an alert adult can often gain a sense of children's mistaken goals by the feelings they successfully arouse in adults (see the Scenario box for examples).
- Caring adults are sensitive to children's feelings and help children to redirect them into acceptable and constructive ways of behaving.

Rudolf Dreikurs and others in the Adlerian tradition also developed very practical ideas about the use of consequences in shaping behaviour (page 505) and the importance of encouragement, rather than reward or praise (page 485).

Scenario

In Dresden Road Nursery School the team have worked hard to address children's feelings as distinct from their behaviour and they use many of the ideas developed by Rudolf Dreikurs. The practitioners try to recognise the possible emotional needs underlying a child's behaviour, even when the way of expressing those needs has disruptive results for the group. On some occasions they find that honesty about their own feelings has been a window on the child's likely emotional needs.

Owen

The team initially found four year old Owen hard to handle. In the early weeks, practitioners found themselves in regular conflict with Owen, frequently telling him off and insisting he complete tasks or apologise for cheeky remarks. The team exchanged how they felt about Owen and admitted to having thoughts like, 'He's not going to get away with this!' They had been drawn into a power battle on issues that often did not matter that much. A consistent team approach would be required and it was decided that adults would:

- actively look for ways to give Owen a sense of position and responsibility in the group
- resist replying to Owen's backchat and loud whispers to other children
- decide on those issues where Owen needs to follow instructions and resist the pull into a power battle on unimportant issues.

Ramona

In a different kind of way, the team in another room needed to bring their ideas together to work more positively with four year old Ramona, whose helplessness was making the adults feel irritated and inadequate, because their usual approaches seemed to make little difference. A team discussion brought together what had been learned about Ramona's background and how she behaves in the nursery. Ramona seems to be so unnerved by the possibility of making a mistake that it is preferable that adults, and some of the other children, become irritated with her. The team agree that they:

- have to find further reserves of patience with Ramona
- identify even small successes and encourage the child forward
- recognise that success and approval is actually rather scary for Ramona. She has learned from her family that doing something well just means she is expected to do even better later.

Questions

- What mistaken goals are probably reflected in these children's patterns of behaviour?
- Consider similar steps that you could plan for children that you know.
- Discuss your ideas with colleagues, including how you could involve parents as well. In what ways could you improve your own practice?

Key skills links: C3.1a LP3.1–3 WO3.1–3

Positive ways to guide children's behaviour

All children are individuals and there are some different ways to operate as a supportive and positive adult. However, there are some broad guidelines established through research into family life and early years settings that identify the important features in a positive approach to children's behaviour.

Working together in an early years setting

A positive approach to behaviour is a joint effort. The adults in children's lives need to work in partnership and this means conversation and where necessary problem solving between those adults.

- If you have concerns about a child's behaviour, these should be raised sooner rather than later with the child's parent(s) and they should be part of any broad discussion about the best approaches to help their child.
- Parents will also want opportunities to discuss issues or incidents with you and to have any concerns they express treated with courtesy.
- Some parents will agree with your approach to behaviour, but some may have very different ideas about suitable 'discipline' for children. You need to be honest about what approaches you do take, as well as what you do not do in your setting.
- Early years practitioners need to work cooperatively as a team, so that children can experience consistency and fairness. You will find more on this topic in Chapter 20, including the contribution of a behaviour policy.
- And do not forget that you can work in collaboration with children on many aspects of behaviour. They can be involved in discussions and problem solving and you can still remain the adult with overall responsibility.

Create a positive adult role

One way of describing the role taken by adults in relationships with children is to look at the relative balance between the control that adults exercise and the warmth they show to children. Children flourish best with adults who express warmth towards them and who exercise a reasonable, but not excessive level of control, as a responsible adult.

This approach has been called an **authoritative role** and it is characterised by being firm yet fair with children. It is adults' responsibility to create boundaries and children do not benefit from adults who are unduly permissive or who are unpredictable over when they say 'enough' or on what.

In practice, of course, thoughtful adults need to check on the balance they achieve and adults who work together need to talk about what they are doing and why. Helpful adults realise that they are part of the situation; it is not only the children's behaviour that matters.

Key term

Authoritative role a pattern of behaviour from adults that combines emotional warmth with responsible boundary setting

To think about

Good practice is to be a reflective practitioner (see page 32), an adult who is willing to look at your own expectations, assumptions and action in your time with the children. Be honest and consider the following. If you want to answer 'yes' to any point, then note down a recent example to support your reply.

- To what extent are you willing to reflect on what you bring to your time with children, that your behaviour and outlook are part of the whole situation?
- Do you think thoroughly about what you want the children to do and not just what you want them to stop doing?
- Do you set a good example? Do you create an environment in which it is possible for children to behave in a cooperative or patient way?
- Do you make the effort to look through children's eyes? Do you mentally stand back from the scene and consider what is actually happening?
- Do you take the time to observe what is happening, rather than assuming you know?
- Discuss your ideas with colleagues.

Key skills links: C3.3 C3.1a LP3.1–3 WO3.1–3

Set a good example

There is a strong focus in this section on the behaviour of adults. This approach does not overlook the fact that the behaviour of children can sometimes be exhausting to handle. It takes physical, intellectual and emotional energy to deal with the normal ups and downs of life with young children, let alone the special difficulties that some children may bring into your setting with their past experience. The point is that:

- Adults' behaviour matters. It is definitely one of the ingredients in the whole situation. Little progress will be made if most discussion about children's behaviour focuses on what the children should not be doing.

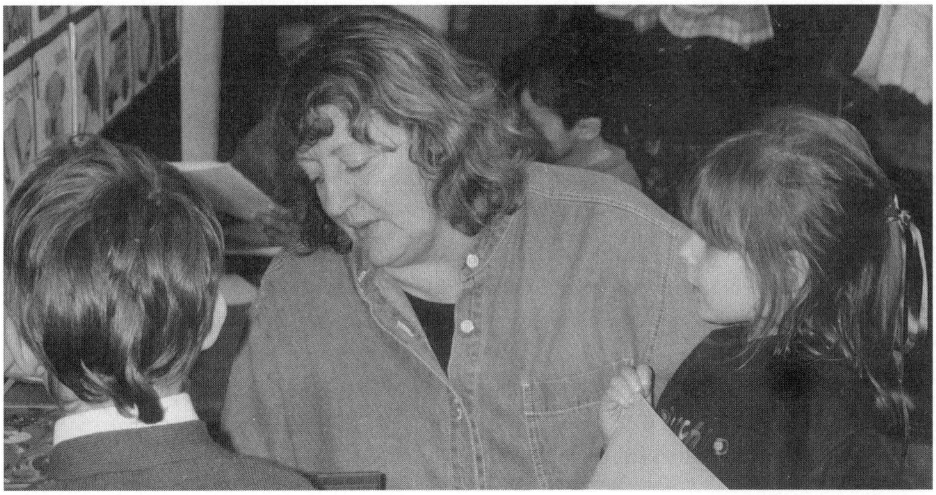

Figure 17.2
Children learn about listening or waiting because you set a good example

- Adults are the older ones in an interaction, supposedly the more mature people. You are the grown-up here, so you have a responsibility to make the first move, to be willing to look at your own actions, to consider the child's perspective and listen to what children feel and believe.
- Never forget that children are still learning even when you are not setting out deliberately to show them something. They are well aware of those adults who are inconsistent and can be nagged, or those who do not keep to their own rules.

Hold realistic expectations

Any positive approach to behaviour needs to be grounded in realistic expectations for the age of the children. Otherwise, it is far too easy for unreflective adults to create problems by the way they insist on organising and running the early years setting, out-of-school care or early years of primary school. Other chapters of this book highlight appropriate expectations in terms of children's development, so these are brief reminders:

- You cannot expect young children, especially under twos, to follow verbal instructions without active guidance. They need to be shown as well as asked.
- Children in early years settings cannot tolerate excessive amounts of time being required to sit still or sit neatly up to the table. They need room to move and choose and they need plenty of physical activity (see Chapter 10).
- If children are too constrained – physically or emotionally – then adults create problems that would not have been there otherwise. The same concern applies to children in the early years of primary school.
- It is up to adults to look at possibilities of changing the environment and the daily routines. See the Scenario box for some examples.

Scenario

The team at Greenholt Pre-school have become increasingly concerned that they seem to tell the children off a great deal for minor misbehaviour: fidgeting, being in the 'wrong' part of the pre-school and minor arguing amongst the children. The atmosphere in the pre-school is unhappy and fractious. The team decides to undertake some observations to identify the main sources of irritation. After two weeks they discuss the findings in a team meeting:

- The pre-school runs in a church hall and to keep the noise and movement down, the team developed a tight plan by which children have to follow a schedule and move from table to table. The aim was that children then experience all the learning opportunities within a session.
- But some children are resistant to following the schedule and are told off as a consequence. Practitioners 'waste' time trying to bring the wanderers back to 'their' table and moving children on who do not want to leave their project.
- As a result of the observation, some team members also express concern about the children who fall in with the schedule – are they being persuaded to be too passive?

- Registration and mid-morning drinks are chaotic times, with children milling around, along with parents at registration. The team discusses whether these times need more, or different, organisation and the play needs less structuring.

Questions

1. What could be a possible way forward for the Greenholt team? Describe some practical plans.
2. What are the disadvantages of over planning children's play (see page 424) and how might the team create a more positive atmosphere?
3. How might they introduce some form of self registration or a self service drink time (see page 98 for ideas).
4. Consider any applications to how you could improve your own practice.

Key skills links: PS3.1 C3.1a LP3.1–3

Use positives to guide children

In general, it is most effective to focus on being positive about the behaviour you would like children to show. Of course, you do need to deal with unacceptable behaviour (see page 501), but the most positive approach to children's behaviour is weighted towards helping children to feel pleased that they have behaved well.

The effectiveness of encouragement

Although the words 'praise', 'reward' and 'encouragement' are sometimes used as if they are the same, this is not the case in practice.

Rudolf Dreikurs and other writers within the Adlerian tradition stressed the difference between spoken praise (and tangible reward) and encouragement:

- **Praise** or **rewards** (or treats) focus mainly on the end result of what children have done, whereas encouragement by word and body language is freely given for effort and improvement.
- Praise or rewards risk stressing a fixed quality about children, that they are 'good' or 'clever'. In contrast, **encouragement** can focus on the here and now: what a child has managed this time ('Well done for working that out' rather than 'Good boy').
- Encouragement can focus helpfully on feelings rather than completed actions: adults express their feelings of appreciation that a child has waited for her turn. Children can be supported to acknowledge their frustration with their inability to complete the jigsaw and also feel satisfaction for how much they have managed.
- A pattern of adult encouragement can boost children's feelings of satisfaction and their strengths, with a sense of continued progress.
- Adult dependence on spoken praise and tangible reward can appear unforgiving of mistakes or days when children do not feel like being 'a good child ' or 'my little helper'.

When a positive approach to children's behaviour is led through encouragement, then the occasional praise or reward systems can have their place.

Key terms

Praise
positive feedback in words, usually for what has been done or achieved

Reward
giving tangible items or special experiences as a result of behaviour or achievement

Encouragement
positive feedback by words and expression, as much for effort as for achievement

- An effective approach to children's behaviour is to increase the positives in your own behaviour. Many people can double or treble their positive verbal and non-verbal comments.
- You can offer spoken encouragement to children through sincere compliments, saying 'thank you' to a child and showing appreciation of their efforts. Non-verbal encouragement is communicated through smiles, nods and friendly touch.
- Encouragement can be low key and operate on the principle of 'little and often' because children do not have to be especially 'good' to receive encouragement.
- The advantage of verbal and non-verbal encouragement is that it is an immediate and clear message to children. The best approach is to give it as close to the behaviour as possible, as part of natural communication with children. It is less effective if you save up comments for a group time at the end of a day or session. Circle time can be helpful (see page 496) in other ways.
- Consider the strategy that you 'catch children out being good'. You need to acknowledge the cooperative behaviour of a child who is not usually cooperative. But definitely avoid any sour undertone of 'why can't you always be like this?'; be pleased for today.
- You should also acknowledge the behaviour of a child who is usually well behaved, do not just let it pass because this is normal. Adults need to be thoughtful and avoid the kickback of not letting a 'good' child have an off day. Normally well behaved children are sometimes subjected to adult comments along the lines of, 'Now that's not like you, is it?'. Such remarks are very discouraging and impertinent from adults.

Careful use of rewards and incentives

Key term

Incentives
a promise of a reward in the future, as a result of particular behaviour or achievement

Tangible rewards and treats have a place in an early years setting. **Incentives** are also useful and these have a future promise of 'if … then'. However, rewards and incentives both need to be used with discretion. If you overuse either of them, then children are less likely to develop a sense of personal satisfaction about their choices in behaviour. Rewards can undoubtedly backfire on adults, and in ways that illustrate how sensible adults have to consider what children are probably thinking, the sense that they make of the situation.

If children are regularly rewarded, with treats or prizes for certain kinds of behaviour, such as tidying up, then the likelihood of this behaviour may increase, but not necessarily. Some early years professionals have therefore claimed that 'reward doesn't work' or that 'it doesn't have a long-term effect'. A more accurate view, taking into account the perspective of children as well as adults, is that the reward system clearly has had an effect. The children's behaviour has changed; they are choosing not to help with tidying up any more. Unfortunately this effect was unwanted.

One possibility is that over use of tangible rewards has influenced children's expectations and the way they think about this part of the routine. Instead of developing a sense of internal satisfaction ('I tidy up with my friends because I enjoy helping'), some children view the activity as linked to the reward. So if they do not want the reward, they choose not to do the activity, thinking, 'I only do this if I want to get a prize' or in a family home perhaps that, 'I ought to be paid to tidy my room'.

To think about

- People sometimes say, 'You can never give a child too much praise' but unfortunately this is not true.
- Material reported from the United States identifies the negative consequences when adults give indiscriminate praise to anything and everything a child does.
- This unwise approach is doubly foolish if it is combined with hardly any constructive feedback (see page 494) or boundaries to children's behaviour.
- The results are that children no longer value praise that is given regardless of their efforts or achievements. Without some constructive feedback, children also become intolerant of any adult guidance to their actions.
- Most people can double and treble the amount of warm encouragement they give to children but, like many positive things in a child's life, it is possible to overdo the positives if you really set your mind to it!

Symbolic rewards

When children are slightly older, about four years of age, children can be motivated by **symbolic rewards** such as stickers, certificates and having their name written in a book for specific positive behaviour or good quality work.

Key term

Symbolic rewards giving something that represents praise for behaviour or other achievements, such as stickers or certificates

Tips for practice

Symbolic rewards can be positive so long as:

- The system works flexibly so that even those children who find it very hard to meet adult expectations will get their sticker for something.
- Symbols or stickers are never taken away from a child. Unwise adults usually do this as a punishment for later unacceptable behaviour. This reaction is very unfair and undermines the whole system.
- Adults remain sensitive to what an older child experiences as a positive incentive. Some children do not like being the centre of attention and are deeply uncomfortable about public recognition, say in a certificate given in school assembly.
- Some children – this is probably more likely to be the boys – may be embarrassed by 'most well behaved child of the week' awards. Adults need to find other ways to acknowledge such behaviour.

Activity

Gather ideas of the use of symbolic rewards for older nursery children or those in primary school.

- What do the children think about the reward scheme? Do they understand how it works?
- You could ask open-ended questions such as, 'What do children have to do to get a smiley sticker?' or 'How do you feel when you get a good work certificate?'
- Compare your findings with colleagues, keeping the details of children confidential.

Key skills links: C3.3 C3.1a

Promoting the development of prosocial behaviour

A great deal of the positive behaviour that early years practitioners like to see from children falls within the area of prosocial behaviour. Adults in early years settings often make requests that children 'share', 'think of other people', 'cooperate together' or just generally be 'nice' to each other.

Within the early years curriculum frameworks for the four countries of the UK (see page 403) the goals or outcomes for children's personal, social and emotional development frequently include aspects of prosocial behaviour. So it is valuable for early years practitioners to understand how this area of development appears to unfold. Then it is more possible for adults to develop realistic expectations of children and understand how you can best promote the development of prosocial behaviour.

Responsiveness to the feelings of others

The term **prosocial behaviour** involves children's feelings and thoughts as well as their actions. A prosocial orientation arises when children have learned empathy and altruism.

- **Empathy** is the ability and willingness to tune into the feelings of other people – children or adults.
- **Altruism** means acting with a selfless concern for the well being of others.

When children show prosocial behaviour, they have made intentional, voluntary actions in the light of what they feel will be supportive to somebody else. Young children can and do develop prosocial behaviour as a result of their early experiences, but it is not an inevitable step in the development of all children. So how can prosocial behaviour develop and how can caring adults support this direction?

Steps towards empathy and altruism

Jean Piaget, in his theory of children's cognitive development, took the view that children younger than four or five years of age could not really grasp the perspectives and emotions of other people. Piaget described younger children as egocentric, grounded in their own world view, but observation of young children

Key terms

Prosocial behaviour
a blend of actions and feelings that can be observed when children have learned empathy and altruism

Empathy
the ability and willingness to tune into the feelings of other people

Altruism
a pattern of behaviour that shows a selfless concern for the well being of others

challenges his claims. Children younger than three years of age do sometimes show awareness of the feelings of others.

- If you observe babies, you will notice that they tend to join in the emotions around them: they often laugh along with others and sometimes their faces crumple and they cry when they see other babies crying.
- Yet, over the period from about one to three years, toddlers and young children behave in a way that shows they can tell the difference between a small range of strong feelings expressed by others and that they react differently, depending on that emotion.
- For example, in families where there is stress between parents, children as young as one or two years are visibly distressed when they witness arguments. Sometimes very young children will try to comfort one parent or shout and hit out at the parent they feel is in the wrong.
- From about 18 months onwards, you can observe behaviour from toddlers that shows they have an understanding that other children are separate individuals. Sometimes they clearly notice the distress of other very young children.
- Toddlers tend initially to offer another distressed child their own comfort object – an act of great generosity in itself. But soon, young children who know each other well (in the same family or early years setting) will offer the other child's favourite blanket or teddy.
- Very young children, as young as two years old, also show a deliberate wish to bring support to other distressed children when they get your attention as an adult, and point out that another child is crying or hurt.

It is important to recall, especially on difficult days with children, that of course they do not behave in a way that shows empathy and altruism all the time. Very few adults would pass such a tough test! Sometimes it is appropriate that young children have their own needs to the fore. Sometimes, unfortunately, they will use their personal knowledge of peers or siblings to wind them up and annoy them. Helpful adults have to intervene in order to deal with the consequences. But do try to notice the evidence of understanding, planning and thinking as well as the less attractive aspect to such teasing behaviour.

Activity (observation)

Look at the section that describes examples of prosocial behaviour, even in children younger than three years. Watch out for and briefly write up examples of children who show concern for other children or familiar adults. You may notice children in your setting or outside who behave in a comforting or helpful way. Perhaps children are pleased to follow a request that they make a new child welcome – what do they do?

- Look at your observations and discuss them with your colleagues.
- What can you learn about individual children? Of course you have to be cautious about any conclusions.
- But perhaps you feel that Saira is able to comfort her friend who is distressed because Saira herself feels loved and secure. Whereas Danny is so desperate for reassurance that he is liked that he has nothing left to give to other children. How can you help him?

Key skills links: LP3.1–3 WO3.1–3

Supportive adults

The lessons of developmental research into prosocial behaviour provide some practical guidelines for early years practitioners, and parents with their own children. Prosocial behaviour does not develop automatically in children; a great deal depends on their experiences and these are shaped by adults.

Early years settings are undoubtedly happier places for everyone if children behave in a more prosocial way, so how can you help?

- Create an affectionate and warm environment for children from the youngest ages. Children, who feel they have to compete with peers for the attention and affection of the adults, have little emotional energy left to give to each other.
- Be clear about your own rules for considerate or helpful behaviour (see page 494) and be ready to give children simple explanations why you would rather they behaved in this way.
- Just telling a child, 'you mustn't hit people' is less effective than alerting him to the consequences, for example, 'when you bit Sam, you really hurt him and made him cry'.
- Create opportunities for even very young children to do something helpful and then acknowledge what they have done. Again, this means that adults need to run a relaxed day in which children have time and choice to opt into helping. It is also important that adults do not require exacting standards to be met in tasks.
- Recognise helpful or considerate behaviour but avoid trying to make children feel guilty if today they feel less than helpful. Children (much like adults) do not respond positively to being criticised with, 'A nice child would share her bricks', or the pointless, unreal question of 'Don't you think that was a nasty thing to do?' (Is there any right answer to this question: think about it!)
- Probably the most important step for adults is to behave in line with what you would like children to do: model thoughtful and generous behaviour yourself. Telling children that they 'ought' to do this or 'shouldn't' do that is much less effective than being a good role model for what you would like.

Activity

People sometimes say that 'good' behaviour is 'caught and not taught'. This cliché has some useful truth when people appreciate that children learn better from being shown and encouraged than told they ought or must behave in a certain way. Adults need to work together, in a family home as much as an early years setting or school, to ensure that the 'good' behaviour is shown by adults and is therefore observable to be 'caught'.

With colleagues, please explore the following perspectives through discussion.

1 What do you want young children to do in your setting?
   - What kinds of helpful behaviour do you want to encourage from children? Be as specific as you can. If this is a hard question to answer, then possibly you are all too focused on what the children should stop doing and on 'bad' behaviour.

- If you use a word like 'kind' or 'patient', then discuss some examples of what kindness or patience looks like in practice from children within the age range with whom you work.
- Are your expectations realistic given the age of the children and how frequently you expect the 'good' behaviour from them? Nobody is 'kind' or 'patient' all the time!

2 What approaches are you all using to help children to behave in positive ways?

- What ways do you use to direct and guide children's behaviour? Look through this chapter for ideas if it helps.
- In your opinions, what works best to encourage the children?
- How do you ensure that you all keep alert to your own adult behaviour and that the team is consistent?

Key skills links: C3.1a WO3.1–3

To think about

- Young children, who feel secure and liked, want to be helpful. You do not have to persuade and cajole them.
- Even toddlers enjoy the satisfaction of the role of helper, especially since it tends to bring close contact with a friendly adult.
- If children are showing very little helpful behaviour in your setting, there is a real possibility that you are not making it easy for them to be helpful and you may even be discouraging their attempts.
- Do you tend to think, 'It's quicker if I do it' or the schedule has been set up that children have a story with one adult while another adult does the tidying up?
- Adults create the circumstances for children to learn to be helpful.
- Admittedly, children bring their expectations from past experience into your setting, but you have the chance to give them another perspective.
- A continued lack of helpful behaviour cannot simply be explained away by saying there is something the matter with the children.

Looking at your own setting

It is often easier to be detailed in discussion as an early years team about what you do not want. Perhaps you find it straightforward to list all the different kinds of aggressive behaviour that are unacceptable from children. But are you clear in just as much detail about what it means to 'share' from the children's point of view. Sharing is a social skill that needs to be understood and learned, yet adults are often quick to say it is obvious what is wanted, so you just tell children that they ought to share.

Sharing is an excellent example of what adults call 'acceptable behaviour', but where understanding the child's perspective is crucial if adults are to be fair (and

Figure 17.3

A generous supply of play materials makes sharing easier

empathic!) in their dealings with children (see the box). For instance, does a ground rule of 'sharing' mean that children have to hand over a toy or get off the bike as soon as another child asks? Surely not, or else cooperative children could be very disrupted in their play.

To think about

Children benefit from caring adults who are willing to look through children's eyes and demonstrate the meaning of 'sharing' in daily example of what is needed.

When I first started to work with nurseries, I heard children told to 'share' on a regular basis. I also heard the same instruction a great deal from parents to their children. Undoubtedly, family and nursery life is much happier with a large dose of what adults call 'sharing', but we use the same word to cover three distinct situations.

1 In their own home, children are asked to 'share' their toys when other children come to play or to 'share' with their siblings. The toys or books belong to the first child, so the rule should be that anything is returned to the owner. So adults are really asking here that children 'lend' and 'borrow'. It is worth noting that children are sometimes required to 'share' very precious or newly received possessions. It is questionable whether adults are fair to demand this action. They probably would not hand over something of equivalent value and importance from their own possessions.
2 In a group, children are asked to 'share' play materials that belong to the nursery or playgroup. But the bikes, bricks or swing do not belong to any one child, so children are being asked here to 'take turns'.

3 A third situation is when adults say, 'Share your crisps with the other children'. Crisps, or sweets, are a one-time possession and are not returned, so children are here being asked to 'give'.

Questions

Discuss these options with your colleagues:

1 What are the reasons why it matters for adults to understand what they are asking of children?
2 What may happen in the relationship between children and adults if the latter will not look through the children's eyes?
3 Do you have any childhood memories that can help here? Perhaps you were required to 'share' your new birthday presents with children who attended your party. How did you feel about that?

Key skills links: C3.1a

Helpful adults need to look at a positive approach to directing children away from aggressive ways of handling everyday conflict towards more cooperative strategies. Children are supported best when early years practitioners understand that they need to coach young children in social skills. So adults need to understand the options, for instance that:

- Sharing should not mean in practice that children simply have to say 'yes' if another child asks for something.
- It is also acceptable to say, 'I just want to finish playing with this hat, then you can have a go'.
- Children can also offer trades with, 'I need all these bricks to build my castle, but you can have those shapes'.
- With adult help, children can also use and appreciate simple technology to support turn taking, such as a large sand timer for turns on the bikes.

In any early years setting, school or out of school care, it has to be the adults who take responsibility for creating the kind of environment and daily routine where it is easier for children to behave in prosocial ways. Children cannot make this happen, but they can be active contributors in a happy and consistent setting. It is also an adult responsibility to ensure that more cooperative children do not lose out by following the ground rules. As children themselves would say, it is 'not fair!' if the less cooperative children get away with this behaviour because it makes for a quieter life for adults.

Activity

- Take two ideas from this section and work them into a plan of action for your own setting.
- Apply the ideas and write up the work, including any opinions that children express.

Key skills links: LP3.1–3 C3.3

Working cooperatively with the children

Adults do not have to do all the work about creating a positive atmosphere and approach to behaviour. The children can be part of your efforts when you offer ways that support their learning and are developmentally appropriate.

Be clear what you want from children

It may seem very easy to list all the behaviour that you want children to stop. But they can learn much more effectively if you are clear, and clear with them, about what you would like to have happen, both in general and when children are faced with situations that they experience as difficult.

Activity (observation)

In your setting, gather a list of examples of unwanted behaviour, actions for which children are stopped, told off or experience sanctions as a result. You could observe over a few days and also add any examples of children who are regularly discussed by you and your colleagues.

Now take each example and consider the following points either on your own or in discussion with colleagues.

- You are probably very clear about what you want the child to stop doing. But now consider what do you want them to do, how will they handle the situations that provoke this behaviour?
- For every 'stop doing', you need to come up with a 'start doing' and for every 'don't' you need to find a 'do'.
- For example, when you discuss 'we'd like Matthew to stop hitting other children', you need to reach something along the lines of 'we'd like Matthew to use words instead of his fists'.
- You are the adults in the situation. It is too hard for young children on their own to create enough emotional and intellectual distance to consider, 'I could handle this situation differently'.
- You can help them if you use your skills of observation to identify what is happening and then your skills of encouragement and explanation to direct a child towards a non-disruptive alternative.

Key skills links: LP3.1–3 WO3.1–3

Have some ground rules

Children like to know where they are in any setting and they often have some clear opinions about what is important to make a nursery or family home a happy place for everyone. Children can be involved in developing a small number of ground rules that apply to children and adults alike. Ground rules in an early years setting or after school club work best if:

- The rules are developed with the involvement and consultation of the children themselves. What do they think is important? What makes life nicer here and what makes a day less happy?
- You ask whether there are there some rules that the children want on the list, because of adult behaviour that is less than acceptable. You can explore this in a sensitive way and children will say, so long as you listen and do not interrupt or disagree.

- Adults recognise that sometimes it is very hard for children to do the right thing. They need adults to appreciate the real dilemmas in the action of some rules. What if telling the truth could get your best friend into trouble?
- Adults need to act to support the rules – in general and specific rules that they themselves clearly need to follow.

When children are younger than four or five, it will probably be an adult responsibility to draft the ground rules, but children can be involved in any appropriate conversation about how the rules can work for everyone's benefit. So, there may be a general ground rule about taking turns but children need to be involved in discussions about, 'how shall we help people to take turns on the computer?'

Scenario

The Wessex childminding network has been exploring possible ground rules that could work with children in a family home and in the childminders' drop-in group. The group has reached five possible ground rules and has ensured that the wording is positive – phrased as a 'do' and not as a 'don't'. The ideas have come from the childminders themselves, conversations with children older than about three or four years in their care and adult discussion of situations that most often lead to problems in the drop-in. The draft rules are:

- We treat other people with consideration and safety
- We take care of the play resources
- We take turns when there is not enough for everyone
- We listen to each other and work to find ways around problems
- We walk around when we are at the drop-in, we run outside.

The network now wants to try out the ground rules in family homes. They also wish to find ways to illustrate a poster that could be made for the drop-in.

Questions

1 Make some suggestions for the kind of illustrations or photos that could show the meaning of these ground rules in a visual form.
2 In what ways may ground rules like turn taking need to operate differently in the childminder's home (or a family home as a nanny) in comparison with a drop-in?
3 Write up your thoughts, with practical application to your own setting.
4 Compare your ideas with those of your colleagues

Key skills links: C3.1b C3.1a LP3.1–3 WO3.1–3

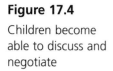

Tips for practice

If some kinds of behaviour are important enough to be made into a ground rule, they are certainly worthy of acknowledgement when children follow the rule.

- Look for opportunities to say simply to a child, 'Thank you for waiting your turn' or 'well done, you looked out for Nathan before you jumped off the bench'.
- Your comment can as simple as, 'Good listening!' or 'Good idea, I can hear you've been thinking about what we could do.'
- Even if a child's efforts go awry, you can recognise what they were trying to do with, 'Thank you, Jon. I could see you were trying to help Marcie. I think she wants to do it herself and that's why she got cross with you.'

Circle time and golden rules

The idea of circle time is described in Chapter 11 as a way to promote children's communication skills. Well-run circle time can also support a positive approach to behaviour, so long as:

- The communication ground rules (see page 311) are followed by adults as well as children.
- No children feel spotlighted for their misbehaviour. Incidents with individual children should be handled at the time. Circle time can be an opportunity to explore more general themes about how 'we show consideration' or 'ways to show our feelings'.
- Any patterns for highlighting positive behaviour work in an even-handed way, so that every child is mentioned for something over time. You need to avoid a situation in which some children never get their names on the 'kindness tree'.
- Circle time is not used to tell children they 'ought to be nice' to each other or 'everybody must share!' Children will feel nagged and not enjoy this time.

Figure 17.4
Children become able to discuss and negotiate

Activity

Vivian Paley has written about what she learned by observing and listening to the children over the years she worked as a nursery teacher in America. At the outset Vivian Paley saw circle time as a way for her to raise issues as an adult that seemed important for the nursery group. She tape recorded these sessions and then noticed that the children were most enthusiastic to discuss what had happened in their play.

- Read one of her books or ideally several colleagues or students could read different books (suggestions below).
- Write up the main points from this narrative and compare ideas with your colleagues.
- Consider some changes to your own practice.

Vivian Paley (sometimes given as Vivian Gussin Paley) has written several books. You could try *White Teacher* (Harvard University Press 1979), *Boys and Girls: Superheroes in the doll corner* (University of Chicago Press 1984), *The Boy Who would be a Helicopter: The uses of story telling in the classroom* (Harvard University Press 1990) and *You Can't Say You Can't Play* (Harvard University Press 1992).

Key skills links: C3.2 C3.1a LP3.1–3 WO3.1–3

Scenario

Sunningdale Day Nursery has introduced circle time with the four year olds as part of developing their practice in personal, social and emotional learning for children. Penny has taken responsibility for this time and has gradually introduced the ground rules for considerate communication.

Today several children speak up confidently and say it is not fair that Ian and Damian keep taking over the block area and will not let anyone else join their game. Penny listens to the children who wish to complain and then invites Ian and Damian to put their perspective. The two children explain clearly about their special game, what they are building and why they need all the blocks. Penny acknowledges with the group that this is a problem to be resolved and invites ideas from everyone.

Questions

1. Penny could just have told Ian and Damian they must let other children share in the block area. Why do you believe she resisted that option?
2. What are the advantages for all the children of a problem solving approach (see also page 124)?
3. Share your ideas with colleagues and make some practical applications for your own practice.

Key skills links: C3.1a LP3.1–3 WO3.1–3

Jenny Mosley suggests the following golden rules that can be introduced through circle time for children in school. She suggests that the last three can come later if children need time to understand what the rules really mean:

- Do be gentle, don't hurt anybody
- Do be kind and helpful, don't hurt people's feelings
- Do be honest, don't cover up the truth
- Do work hard, don't waste time
- Do look after property, don't waste or damage things
- Do listen to people, don't interrupt.

Activity

Look at Jenny Mosley's golden rules in this section and consider children in the early years of primary school.

- Children like to see that adults obey their own rules. Take any three of these rules and discuss in what ways teachers, nursery nurses and specialist teacher assistants could be good role models to show the rule in action.
- Try hard to consider the perspective of young primary school children. Are there any rules that, as a child, you might want to say, 'sometimes that's not so easy to do'?
- Apply to your own practice if you work with children older than four or five years of age.

Key skills links: C3.1a LP3.1–3 WO3.1–3

Using conversation

Children can learn about ways of behaving and extend their ability to direct themselves and make choices. You can help them through conversation in an even-handed exchange (nobody learns much of positive value when they are being told off). Guided discussions in circle time can also be supportive, so long as they are handled with sensitivity.

In conversation with individual children about behaviour:

- You need to talk with them and not at them. If children do not want to talk about the situation, then do not press them.
- Over particular incidents, you will get further with open-ended questions like, 'What happened here?' or 'What has made you both so cross?' Questions like, 'Why are you hitting each other?' tend to get self-justifying replies along the lines of 'she started it!'
- You need to listen to the children, whether for single incidents or more persistent problems between them. If children cannot get their views heard and you highjack the opportunity in order to tell them off, they will not cooperate in the future.
- Check that you have understood and help each child to hear the other one.
- If the situation needs resolving, then invite ideas from the children. Treat this as a problem that needs to be resolved by everyone.

- Try for a solution and agreement to which all the children will commit and help them to put this into action if they need support.

In any setting, however calm and supportive the atmosphere, children will sometimes get into minor or major conflicts – it is part of social life. You can make a difference by how you approach a trouble spot when you hear the shouting or see the shoving. You can also take the opportunity to help children to learn some social skills of problem solving (see page 208).

Books and stories

So long as children feel supported (and do not think they are being nagged!) books and stories can be one effective way to help three and four year olds, and older, to reflect on choices in behaviour. Good books are valuable because children can talk about the characters and what they face and feel. This discussion avoids the sensitive issues that arise when you talk about real children and their behaviour in the setting.

Some good books include:

- Claire Llewellyn and Mike Gordon *Why Should I Share?* and *Why Should I Help?* (Hodder Wayland 2000).
- Sam McBratney *I'm Sorry* (Collins 2000).
- Brian Moses and Mike Gordon's books in the Values series (Hodder Wayland 1997). Titles include *'It Wasn't Me!' Learning about honesty*, *'Excuse Me' Learning about politeness*, *'I Don't Care!' Learning about respect* and *'I'll Do It!' Taking responsibility.*

Anti-discriminatory practice and children's behaviour

Sometimes you will need to address behaviour from the children that shows they have learned unacceptable attitudes about particular social, cultural, faith or ethnic groups or negative attitudes related to gender or disability. These attitudes have then emerged through cruel words or rejecting behaviour.

You need to tackle such incidents because ignoring them leaves children with the impression that you feel the behaviour is acceptable. However, you are working with children and their attitudes and habits of behaviour are in the process of developing. General good practice guidelines for behaviour still apply when children's words or actions appear to be linked to prejudiced attitudes of any kind.

You need to find ways that make it more likely that children will:

- understand your reasons for finding the behaviour unacceptable
- be willing to change their habits of behaviour, at least in your setting
- be open to hearing information that could help them to think, feel and act differently because they choose to make this change.

None of these positive changes are likely if children are immediately labelled as 'racist' or 'sexist'. This adult action gives them limited manoeuvring room in the same way as negative labels like 'spiteful' or 'attention seeking'. The objective is that you help children to change their habits. So you need to give them the chance to change rather than feeling nagged or even oppressed by adult criticism.

Activity (observation)

It is poor adult practice to label children as 'racist', 'sexist' or any other uncompromising criticism. So, what words will make sense in a child's world? What words will link to ideas that they already have or that you are developing through play and conversation?

Children use words like 'unkind', 'unfair', 'untrue' and 'hurtful'. Perhaps you can think of some more. Here are some examples in action:

- 'It is unkind to call Charlie an "idiot". Charlie has Down's syndrome, as I explained, and he takes longer to think things out than you.'
- 'It is unfair to lump all girls together in that way. I know that Jessie was rude about your painting and we'll talk with her about that. But it's not true that "all girls are liars".'
- 'It is hurtful and untrue for you to shout that Teja is talking "nonsense". She is talking in Hindi; it's just that you don't understand her words.'

Questions

1. Over a few weeks, collect any similar examples from your own early years setting or school.
2. It takes practice to develop a positive approach to this area of children's behaviour. So do not be concerned if, with hindsight, you feel you could have expressed yourself better.
3. Make notes and learn from your observation and reflection on it.
4. Share your ideas with colleagues and plan improvements to your practice.

Key skills links: C3.1a LP3.1–3 WO3.1–3

Tips for practice

Children who have been on the receiving end of a hurtful or offensive remark deserve a considerate approach from you.

- Your comfort, given with consideration for their feelings by words or friendly touch.
- Acknowledgement that the remark was 'unfair', 'untrue', 'cruel' or other appropriate words.
- A clear message now, and as appropriate at other times, that you feel positive about their source of identity that has been undermined.
- Without too long a conversation, reassurance to this child that nobody has to put up with name calling in this setting and that it is not a joke when somebody's feelings are hurt.

Children who have given hurt or offence need to understand certain ideas.

- You say that the remark was unacceptable, with a brief explanation why, if the child seems confused about the fuss. Say briefly, 'That's a rude word to call somebody and we don't use it in this nursery'.
- Show that you disapprove of children's words or actions but do not confuse them as a person with their behaviour. You can say, ' I think

that was unkind not to let Aaron join your game' rather than, 'You are such an unkind child!'

- Still listen to the child who has behaved unacceptably. Children from all kinds of minority groups can still be 'the one who started it!' The child who used an unacceptable word is far more likely to change in the future if you show that, having said, 'We don't use that word here', you are helpful about the conflict that led to the insults. You ask 'What happened here?'
- Add information to the situation if, once you have listened you can understand some of the confusion. Perhaps you explain that 'Jason has cerebral palsy, he can't control his legs as easily as you and he didn't mean to knock your cars over'.

Dealing with unwanted behaviour

Caring adults can make a difference to children by a clear focus on what behaviour is welcomed and on generous use of encouragement. Of course, adults also need some strategies for dealing with and re-directing behaviour that you do not want from children. Several broad themes underpin a more positive approach to all children.

Focus on the behaviour rather than negative labels

You should avoid simple labels and aim for a description of what a child is doing. You will be more likely to develop an effective approach to individual children if you progress beyond the shorthand of 'aggressive' or 'disruptive'. It is also a matter of courtesy and fairness to children.

Separate children's behaviour from them as individuals. Your affection for them should not change from moment to moment, depending on how they behave. They are not defined by their behaviour: 'bad' or 'good'. You need to communicate clearly that, 'I like you, Donna. I don't like it when you say cruel things to Rosa.'

If appropriate, use some simple techniques of observation to help make some sense of what is happening (see page 452). A possibility is the ABC observational approach: antecedent (what happened before the incident), behaviour (what the child did) and consequence (what happened afterwards, including the adults' reaction).

Scenario

Six year old Freddie attends the reception class and after school club of St Jude's Primary School. The reception class team, Jessie and Maryam, have relieved their feelings by talking about Freddie's daily confrontations in the staff room. But after a term the two practitioners became uncomfortably aware that Freddie was gaining a negative reputation that would travel with him up the school. They decided to step back and, in consultation with the after school club, try to get a positive way through to Freddie.

Discussions with the after school club team revealed that they had experienced some early confrontations with Freddie. Matters had improved when they recognised that the boy had very few strategies to use if he got stuck on an activity. In the after school club Freddie could move on to something else, although the club team now aimed to help him persevere and learn some problem solving skills. In the reception class, Freddie was not allowed simply to give up on his work, so he seemed to use other tactics to solve his dilemma.

Jessie and Maryam decided to use a simple observational technique to understand what was happening for Freddie in class. They used the ABC technique, although sometimes in the hurly-burly of the class, they had to be swift to recall and note down what had happened first. Less than a fortnight after starting their observations, it became clear that the most common pattern for Freddie was:

- *Antecedent:* Freddie has difficulty with a piece of work or he is distracted by another child and cannot settle back. He starts to fidget or leave the table. He is told to stay still and finish his work.
- *Behaviour:* Freddie may try to settle back but not for long. He then behaves in ways that ensure he is removed from the table. One observed example was that he leaned back on his chair so that he fell over and everyone laughed. Another time Freddie stretched out his arms so that he pushed other children's work askew and they complained bitterly.
- *Consequence:* Freddie is removed from his work and told off. He has successfully escaped a task he found too difficult.

Jessie and Maryam talked over the pattern they had observed and decided that they needed a more constructive approach:

- They needed to gain a clearer idea of what Freddie found straightforward and what he found more difficult.
- They decide to make an effort to move towards Freddie and ask, 'Are you stuck?' or 'would you like some help?', rather than telling him to get on with his work.
- They will look for opportunities to encourage Freddie to ask for help and to be pleased with him for effort and perseverance.

The reception class is very busy but this approach begins to pay off and after a week Freddie calls for help with, 'Mrs Chandler, I'm a bit stuck on this'. Jessie overlooks the fact that the request is shouted and goes across to help.

Questions

1. What could have happened if the staff had only focused on Freddie's 'bad' behaviour? Discuss your ideas with colleagues.
2. Apply some of these ideas to a child whom you know at the moment. Make some practical plans for positive action.

Key skills links: C3.1a PS3.1 LP3.1–3.

Re-direct children

There are a number of tactics you can use in a positive way:

- Look for the opportunity to catch children before they misbehave. A warning look may be enough sometimes. You can use distraction, re-direction and selective ignoring.

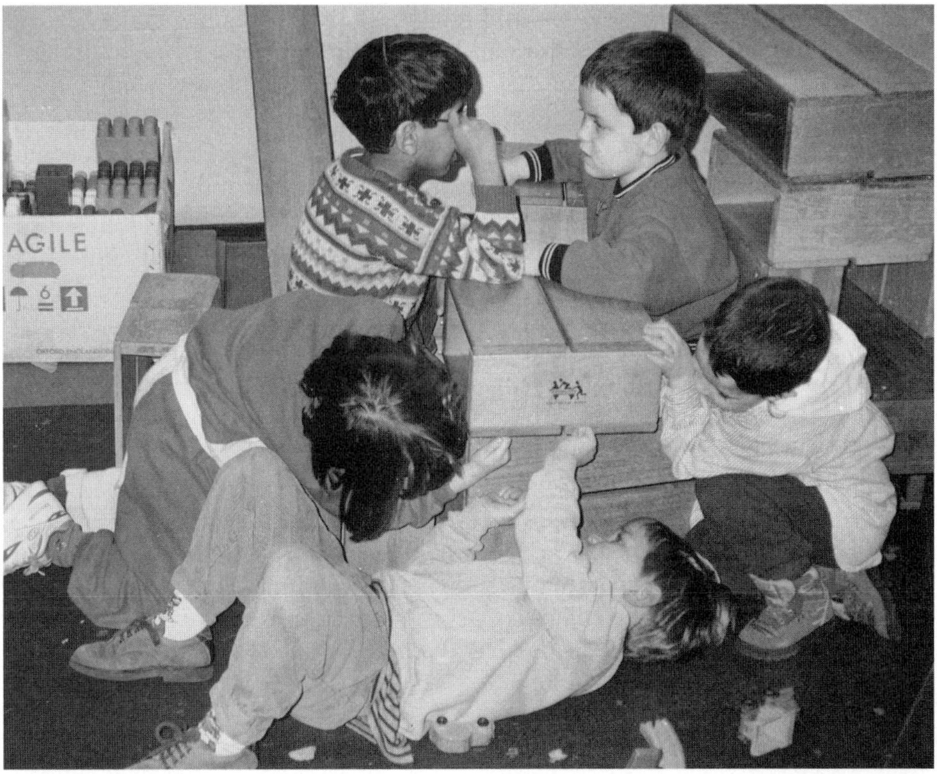

Figure 17.5
Sometimes children will sort matters out themselves

- You give children a chance to re-direct themselves, perhaps with a reminder of a ground rule, like, 'we keep the sand in the sand tray' or 'we ask "can I borrow that", we don't just take it'.
- Sometimes it will feel appropriate to thank children when they re-direct themselves. It would be mean spirited of adults to take the line of 'they should have done what I said the first time'.
- Be prepared to repeat requests or to guide a child, especially important for younger children.
- Notice the cooperative behaviour of a child close to one who is not cooperating. This approach may alert the child to what she should be doing or help her to get back on task. But do not embarrass the child who is behaving well by using her as a prop or 'teacher's pet'.

Intervene calmly

If children are unable to re-direct themselves or keep on with the behaviour, you have some other options to undertake calmly and consistently.

- *Removals:* you may remove a child from the immediate situation or remove the play materials or other items from the child. This adult action needs to be as calm as possible.
- *Calm down time:* some children need a calm down time. This option can work so long as the adult remains calm (no shouting), the time is brief (a few minutes only) and the child is helped to get back into the day's action. It is better not to have a 'naughty corner or chair' since this labels children. Some are distressed and others may like the notoriety and time in the 'naughty chair' increases their bravado level.

- *Making reparations:* a suitable consequence is that a child is offered the chance to make reparations. Perhaps Lenny helps to rebuild the section of the obstacle course that he shoved over or Maria is encouraged to comfort the child to whom she was unkind.
- *It is unwise for adults to insist:* children need to have a genuine choice and that adults also recognise there are many ways to say or show 'sorry' other than that actual word. Adult insistence on saying 'sorry' or tidying up risks moving into bullying the child or creating a power battle with children for whom winning means a great deal.
- *Keeping children safe:* sometimes children go beyond being able to stop themselves in angry words or actions. A responsible adult then offers gentle but firm physical containment by body language and holding children if necessary. Alternatively, sometimes you can get between two squabbling children and use gesture, touch and words to take responsible adult control.
- *Calm discussion:* so long as children do not feel they are being nagged, they may well (from three or four years of age) be able to take part in a conversation about an incident or recurring problems with a child or area of the setting. Adults need to set a friendly and communicative atmosphere with open questions like 'what's going on?' 'what can we do about it?' and 'what is going to help you deal with … better?'

Activity

Imagine different versions of a common scene in a nursery or pre-school. Three year old Harry gets very energetic at the sand tray. Once he is excited he flings sand in the air and over the other children close by.

- Version one: an adult sees what is happening and moves in close to Harry. She touches his arm to get his attention and says, 'Harry, enough now. You remember the rule, "We keep the sand in the sand tray".' Harry nods and manages to resist more throwing. The adult stays close and, when Harry is about to move away from the tray, asks, 'Would you sweep up the spare sand for me?' If Harry agrees, he gets a genuine 'thank you' and if he resists, 'Another time then. I bet you're a good sweeper'.
- Version two: an adult sees Harry, but calls from across the room, 'Harry, remember the rule, "we keep the sand in the sand tray". But without an adult close by, Harry cannot resist. The adult calls again, 'Harry, I told you to stop'. Harry keeps going and the adult now has to come across the room, her voice shows irritation and Harry is removed promptly from the tray, 'because you can't play properly'. He is left to find something else to do. Thirty minutes later, at tidy up time, Harry is told he has to clear up the sand, 'because you made the mess'.

Questions

1 Think about, and discuss with colleagues if possible, how Harry might experience these slightly different versions.

2 What is he likely to learn if his experience in this setting is usually version one or usually version two?

Key skills links: C3.1a

To think about

It is possible for adults to think they are punishing a child's behaviour when they are unintentionally rewarding that child. For example:

- Some children may increase their disruptive behaviour although they are told off at length or sent outside the room in school.
- The adult believes this action is punishment and it might be for some children. But perhaps this child enjoys having the full attention of an adult, having a row with the audience of other children or escaping from a schoolroom task that they cannot manage.
- As far as this child is concerned, the behaviour has been reinforced, it has worked.

Use the consequences of children's behaviour

In behaviourism, the prediction is that punishment will reduce behaviour, but in practice the results are unpredictable as children are complex individuals.

- As described in the think about box, what an adult believes to be a punishment may actually feel like reward to a child who relishes any kind of attention or who likes a power battle.
- Also, in ordinary life with real children, punishment may appear to stop a given behaviour, but sometimes children simply become more secretive and do not let you see them.
- The difficulty in practice is also that punishment is all about 'don't' and can fail to direct children towards how you would rather they behaved (see page 494).

The Adlerian approach to guiding children's behaviour offers a useful way of side-stepping the difficulties raised by the word 'punishment'. Rudolf Dreikurs developed the idea of using the consequences of children's behaviour. He distinguished between **using natural** and **logical consequences** as a way to deal with misbehaviour, to encourage children to take on the responsibility for their own actions and to exercise their own self discipline.

Behaviour that you want to stop or re-direct can be guided by ensuring that children experience the consequences of their actions.

- **Natural consequences** follow on as part of the child's behaviour. Adults can sometimes let a child experience the natural result. For instance, leaving toys on the floor at home may mean that they are trodden on and broken.
- **Logical consequences** are adult-determined but relevant to the behaviour. For instance, squabbling children whose problems cannot be resolved are split up or a book is taken away from a child who keeps tearing the pages.

A great deal depends on how adults behave because an apparently similar action can be punishing or a calm use of consequences. Adults have to:

- Ideally pre-warn that a given consequence will follow if a child continues in this way. For instance, a positive use of 'time out' aims to have children view it as a 'fair cop'.
- The adult remains calm: no shouting, threats or name-calling. Give children the chance to change direction themselves and save face.

Key terms

Using consequences an alternative to punishment in guiding children's behaviour

Natural consequences follow on as a highly likely result of a child's behaviour

Logical consequences are adult-determined but relevant to the behaviour

- Consequences are consistently applied, even when the adult is tired.
- Behaviour is dealt with at the time and then the child is allowed a fresh start. There is no nagging, no harking back.
- Children are given chances in the future – to play carefully or to be trusted. Children receive plenty of positive attention and appreciation when they are behaving well.

Tips for practice

- A strong message running through positive approaches is to look through the children's eyes and consider their feelings.
- What are they likely to take away from different ways of being treated?
- Consider also, would you like to be treated in the negative ways. How do you feel about verbal ridicule or nothing but criticism?
- On the other hand, how might you feel about regular encouragement and being given alternatives?
- Children need to feel they have been forgiven and now have a clean slate. If other children hark back to what a child has done, then say kindly but firmly, 'Please don't go on at Gerry. He and I sorted that out. It's done now.'

Adults whose behaviour has moved towards the positive can shift the whole atmosphere of a home or early years setting. The consequences are that:

- Children feel appreciated for what they have done well, rather than nagged and punished for misbehaviour and perceived failings.
- Their self esteem is boosted rather than undermined. They may also have learned some skills of problem solving and negotiation, helped by careful adult communication and intervention.
- They feel more able to exercise some positive control themselves. They have some choices and will begin to learn some self-discipline.
- They will learn to treat each other in encouraging and courteous ways.
- Time spent together is more enjoyable for adults and children.

Activity (observation)

Asking children 'Why?' they have done something is frequently a dead-end question, because adults usually ask this question about unacceptable behaviour. When children feel criticised and under pressure to justify their actions, they are far less likely to come up with coherent explanations (and nor would you under similar circumstances).

- Keep a simple log over two or three weeks of times you hear yourself, or another adult, asking 'why?' of children about their behaviour.

Then consider, and discuss with your colleagues

- How many of the instances are about unwanted, compared with wanted behaviour from children? Do a simple count.
- Do you have any examples of adults who ask children 'why?' they have done something about which the adult is pleased?

- Are there any examples when it seems to have been constructive to ask a child 'why?'
- What are your feelings as an adult if you are asked 'why?' over something you should not really have done?

Key skills links: C3.1a N2.2

Challenging behaviour from children

Some children have had very negative experiences that affect their emotional stability and ability to cope with life in nursery, pre-school or school. Some children have specific learning disabilities or a condition like autistic spectrum disorder that shapes their behaviour in some ways. You will find out more about children with disabilities in Chapter 18.

Changes to the Special Educational Needs (SEN) Code of Practice mean that all early years teams need to be aware of good practice with children with special needs and that includes **challenging behaviour**. If your positive approaches to a child's challenging behaviour do not make a noticeable difference, then you would use the stages of Early Action and Early Action Plus (see page 528).

Children with disabilities will not necessarily behave in more challenging ways than their peers, so long as you have realistic expectations of the children in the light of their disability. However, some children's disability may increase the likelihood of challenging behaviour. A friendly working relationship with parents will enable you to understand more about a child's disability and situations that she perhaps finds hard to tolerate or handle. An early years or school team may need to decide on areas of compromise that allow a child to cope with the demands of the normal day. You can make such allowances, often by explaining simply to the other children, without presenting an inconsistent front to the group.

Good practice will include the following:

- When children find it hard to cope with the setting, it is especially important to be encouraging of what they have managed and to communicate the positive to parents.
- If a child's behaviour becomes more challenging, then follow the good practice described in this chapter. In communication with parents be honest about the child's behaviour, but in a way that describes rather than labels. Explain how you have handled matters so far and invite comments and ideas from the parent(s).
- If a child's behaviour becomes seriously hard to handle, and your usual positive strategies have made little impact, then definitely have a detailed conversation with parents sooner rather than later.
- If children's behaviour is very challenging and they seem to have strong emotional reactions to your efforts to guide them, it is time to arrange a proper discussion meeting.
- The key person (worker), the child's parents and your setting's Special Educational Needs coordinator (SENCO) need to talk in detail about the child and his or her behaviour.
- You all need to agree a workable plan, written up as an individual education or play plan (IEP or IPP as some areas call it), that will enable this child to cope.
- Early years practitioners should consult with parents before seeking professional advice outside the setting. If you have an informal opportunity to gain advice, then discuss what you have been told with the parent(s).

Key term

Challenging behaviour a pattern of behaviour from a child that is especially hard to handle and does not initially respond to the usual positive strategies

- It is definitely the choice of parents to agree to any referral. You can advise and share information, but it is not your role to tell parents they ought to take a particular course of action.

Other professionals who can help

You can be supportive of parents by sharing information about other sources of help for the situation you are all facing. The available services may vary from one area to another (so try the activity in the box) but in general the options will be:

- early years advisors or specialist support teachers
- an area SENCO or Children with Disabilities Team
- an educational psychologist.

Look also at page 17 for a description of the different types of services and other professionals who can be a support in your work.

Activity

- Gather information for a file on local resources and professionals who could advise especially on challenging behaviour and children with special needs. Some local authorities have useful guidelines or a booklet.
- A good starting point will be your local Early Years Development and Childcare Partnership (Pre-School Advisory Group if you work in Northern Ireland). The partnership or group will have a coordinator or support officer, who will be able to alert you to what is available locally.
- If possible, make contact by email with practitioners in other parts of the country or students in colleges. Compare what you have found in this activity about resources local to the different areas.
- Present your findings and discuss with colleagues.

Key skills links: C3.1b C3.1a

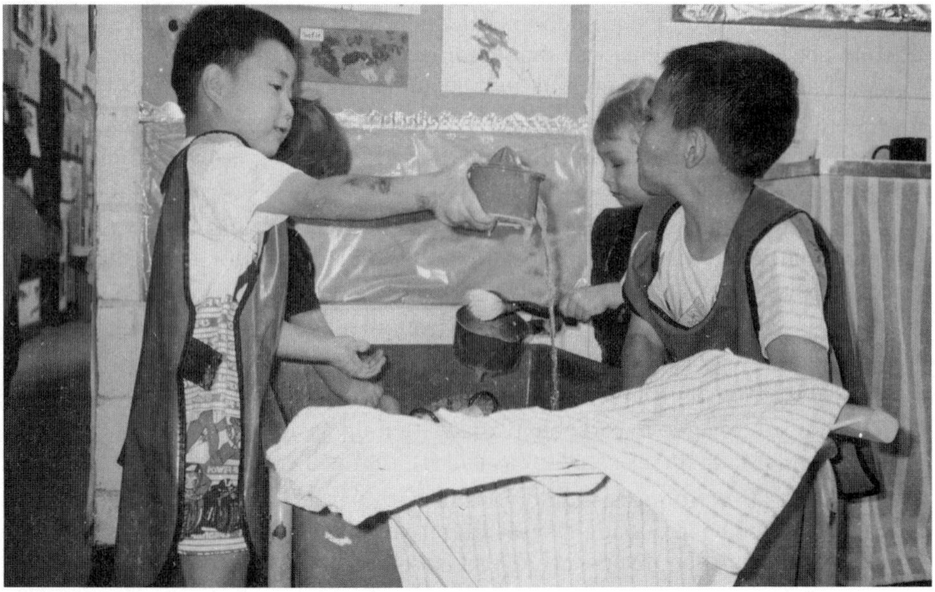

Figure 17.6
It is very important that we notice children's cooperative behaviour – and not only notice problems

Tactics that adults should not use

Harsh and unkind treatment affects children

Early years professionals have been concerned that young children are deeply affected by harsh treatment and unpredictable daily lives. The impact shows in how the children behave towards their peers, adults and to everyday situations. The discoveries of research into early brain development have explained much of how experience forms connections in the brain (see page 243) for positive learning, but it has also been possible to show how some of the negative patterns affect children.

What seems to happen is that repeated experience of harshness and unpredictable adult behaviour (not the odd 'off day') creates elevated levels of the chemical cortisol in the brains of young children. Cortisol is a steroid hormone that is important in the biochemistry of the brain. It is present in saliva and so changes in its level can be measured with a simple saliva test. Our brains need cortisol but too great a level, caused by stress, can actually destroy brain cells and reduce the density of the synapses, those crucial connections between the cells.

High levels of cortisol block children's ability to learn in positive ways. But, equally important, their brains make other connections that show through their behaviour, including uncertain, anxious or aggressive actions. These young children have become hard wired for trouble and are swift to interpret the actions of others as a potential threat.

In contrast, babies and young children who have experienced warm and consistent nurturing, have lower levels of cortisol than those babies whose daily lives have been highly stressful or traumatic. The other significant difference is that, when the nurtured infants experience stress, the natural elevation of cortisol reduces more rapidly. The brain connections of secure infants are telling them that this is a blip or a bad day, rather than further proof that life is dire and people are not to be trusted.

Bad adult habits

Adults can develop bad habits as individuals or within a team and feeling very tired or stressed does not help. Responsible adults need to take hold of their bad habits and work to turn them around. You owe it to the children to avoid unhelpful responses:

- Some adults' approach to children's behaviour is almost entirely negative, including cross words, nagging or a long stream of 'don't' and 'stop it'.
- It is also very rude to tell children they are 'silly', 'stupid' or 'bad'. They are none of these absolute descriptions, although what they have just done may have been dangerous, foolish or unwise.
- You would not like to be called these names and it does not help children learn new ways of behaving.
- It is usually no more effective to say something six times to a child than once. Children who taken no notice the first time may not have heard and, if they have, then they clearly need more guidance than blunt repetition.
- Make sure you have their attention, use the child's name and guide or show them as well as tell.
- Sometimes, adults deal negatively with dislike of an individual child or insist on getting into a power struggle on the grounds that no child can be allowed to 'get away with it'.

- You will not like all children equally and some will rub you up the wrong way. Responsible adults work hard to find something to like in every child.
- Perhaps for every feeling you have that, 'I am so irritated when Ian wipes his nose on his sleeve' you need to find a balance of, 'I am impressed with the way Ian is so gentle with the rabbit.'

The serious disadvantage of any negative approach is that the message is so limited, 'don't' rather than 'do'. Children are left to work out what they are supposed to do – an unnecessary detective job for them.

Tips for practice

Shouting is an unwise adult habit and, since you will tell children not to shout, you undermine your message if you do not set a good example.

- There are few occasions when it is right to shout. If children are doing something dangerous, you will need to warn them, but in early years settings there is rarely any justification for shouting.
- Shouting as a regular habit has the disadvantage of nagging. The children stop listening to you.
- Practise making your voice carry without raising the volume. It is possible if you pitch your voice a bit lower, especially if you are female.
- Avoid shouting at children who raise their voices to you. Children have limited volume control in any case. If you speak more quietly, they will probably follow your example.
- Use an agreed signal with children for 'Quiet now' or use two loud handclaps.

Unacceptable tactics

Adults are sometimes very forthcoming about unacceptable behaviour from children but, of course, some tactics by adults are unacceptable in any early years setting, school or out of school facility. It is important for everyone in a team to understand the reasons. But you may also have conversations with some parents about discipline that start with, 'Why don't you just …?'

The guiding rule is that responsible adults, who are committed to helping children learn, do not use any tactics to control children's behaviour that would be unacceptable if the children behaved in this way.

- You will not hit, shove or shake children because this is a misuse of your adult strength and is utterly contrary to your ground rules for the children's behaviour. You will keep children safe, if they endanger themselves or others but this is careful containment.
- You will take care of children and not physically manhandle or drag them, even if they need to be removed. Angry removals frighten children and say much more about the inequality of power between adults and children than about 'how we should all behave'.
- You will not use verbal humiliation, sarcasm or insults towards children. This approach undermines children's self esteem, it is a misuse of adult knowledge and sets a very bad example to all the children.

You will not do any of the above even in retaliation, such as being cruel to a child who has been deeply unpleasant to another child – in order to 'show him how it feels'. You are then behaving as unacceptably as the child and setting the unhelpful precedent that adults are allowed to break the ground rules of the setting if they feel like it. Children will think you are unfair and unkind and they will not respect you.

Why it is wrong to hit children

Adults who support physical punishment like to call the action 'smacking'. But even-handed observation on the high street will show you that what some adults do to children, often for very minor misbehaviours, would be called 'hitting' if they did it to a fellow adult.

The legal situation

In the UK there is a bizarre and illogical situation regarding children and physical punishment. Unlike some other European countries, the UK does not offer children the same legal protection against assault as is enjoyed by adults. However, a series of laws have restricted the use of physical punishment on children.

Since 1986 there has been no caning or other forms of hitting children in state schools. In 1998 this protection was extended to independent schools and to any early years settings that received funding for free early education places for three and four year olds. However, the legal loophole remains that parents, or people who have taken parental responsibility, can exercise what is called 'reasonable chastisement'. This option was established by a legal case as long ago as 1860. At that time the judge wanted to make it clear that killing children through physical punishment was beyond 'reasonable', since a boy had died as a result of his punishment at school!

In autumn 2001 the government reported on a consultation undertaken in 2000 for England and Wales about possible legal reform over hitting children. The result has been no change to the law regarding parents. In England, despite considerable pressure from early years professionals, the government has also insisted on building the right to hit children into the standards for childminders (so long as they have the written permission of parents). Wales and Scotland have not followed that unacceptable line. It is possible that the exception will be removed in England.

Scotland looks set to introduce legislation that would prevent the physical punishment of children younger than three years of age and limit the kind of physical punishment that was legally acceptable by parents. Northern Ireland is undertaking a consultation that will be complete in 2002.

The good practice arguments

It is important that you understand the compelling arguments against hitting children, since some parents may be perplexed or even irritated that you will not use this option.

- It is unacceptable to use physical violence on anybody. In our society it is not acceptable to hit, shove or shake adults because they have annoyed you or are uncooperative. So it certainly is not acceptable to use such tactics on children who are younger, smaller and have considerably more to learn.
- Hitting children gives the message that this is an acceptable way to deal with annoyance or conflict. Adults tell children not to hit each other. So it sets a very bad example when adults resort to this option.
- Physical punishment can get seriously out of hand. What happens if the first blow does not stop the child? Should an adult then feel justified in hitting harder and longer?

- A habit of hitting often reflects an adult's mood, tiredness or embarrassment because there is an audience. Apart from any other reason, the inconsistency confuses any message to the child.
- Hitting hurts children, physically and emotionally. The hurt again gets in the way of any possible learning. Adults who say, 'this hurts me more than it hurts you' are lying.
- Hitting is unreliable in the long run; it carries all the disadvantages of a focus on punishment and is an entirely negative message. Children who are hit do sometimes stop what they are doing, if only because they are too busy being shocked or distressed. They can see that adults are angry but are often confused about exactly why.
- Adults who claim that 'smacking never did me any harm' fail to come up with evidence that it did them any positive good, especially when there are other ways to guide children's behaviour.

Activity

Imagine the scene and how you will deal with the following:

- Four year old Stefan wrenches other children off his favourite bike and deals with any argument by hitting. Yesterday you heard his mother tell Stefan to 'hit him back' when there was a scuffle with another child at going home time. Somebody needs to talk with Stefan's mother and explain that nobody – child or adult – is allowed to hit other people in your setting.

Role play the exchange with a colleague or fellow student in your course group.

- You are the practitioner and you need to explain why you do not allow hitting to resolve disputes.
- Your role play partner should challenge you as Stefan's mother to explain, 'how do you discipline them here if you don't smack them?' and 'I can't have my son growing up a wimp. He's got to learn to defend himself!'
- Discuss the outcome with the rest of the group.

Key skills links: C3.1a PS3.1

Further resources

Department for Education and Skills (2001) *Promoting Children's Mental Health within Early Years and School Settings* The Stationery Office.

Finch, Sue (1998) *An Eye for an Eye Leaves everyone Blind: Teaching young children to settle conflicts without violence* National Early Years Network and Save the Children.

Leach, Penelope (1997) *Getting Positive about Discipline: A guide to today's parents* and *Why Speak out about Smacking: Questions and answers from the physical punishment debate* Barnardos.

Mosley, Jenny (2001) *Working Towards a Whole School Policy on Self Esteem and Positive Behaviour* Positive Press.

Mosley, Jenny and Sonnet, Helen (2001) *Here We go Round: Quality circle time for 3–5 year olds* Positive Press.

Mukherji, Penny (2001) *Understanding Children's Challenging Behaviour* Nelson Thornes.

Stacey, Hilary and Robinson, Pat (1997) *Let's Mediate: A teacher's guide to peer support and conflict resolution skills for all ages* Lucky Duck Publishing.

Booklets on a positive approach, including the use of encouragement and consequences are available from Adlerian Workshops and Publications, 216 Tring Road, Aylesbury, Bucks HP20 1JS.

Progress check

This chapter will help you to answer the following questions. Look back through the contents if you need to check.

1 Describe two ways in which children's early experiences could shape their behaviour later.
2 Explain the difference between positive and negative reinforcement and how it can shape children's behaviour.
3 Outline four ways in which you could use encouragement of children in your setting.
4 Describe three ways in which you can promote children's prosocial behaviour.
5 Outline three acceptable ways to deal with unwanted behaviour from children.
6 Give three reasons why adults should not use physical punishment on children.

18

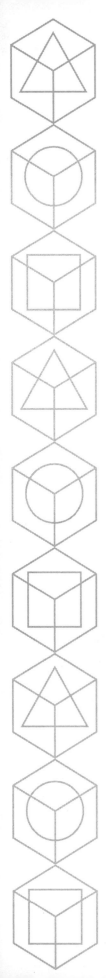

Children with disabilities and continuing health conditions

After reading this chapter you should be able to:

- understand the different types of disability or ill health and their impact on children's development
- identify the responsibilities of early years practitioners in working with disabled children and their families
- contribute to the inclusion of disabled children in your setting through support for their learning
- support children and their families through ill health and periods in hospital.

Introduction

This chapter is relevant to all readers and not only to those who work, or intend to work, in specialist units or schools. The revised SEN Code of Practice for England, and the likely revisions elsewhere in the UK, mean there will be a greater emphasis on inclusion for young disabled children.

You are increasingly likely to have disabled children, or children with a continuing health condition, who attend your early years setting, primary school or out of school care. It is important to develop an understanding about the impact of disability and how you can positively support children and families. This chapter will help you to understand your role, provide ideas about what you

Links to early years qualifications

This chapter especially supports the following units:

Diploma in Child Care and Education: 5, 10, 11

National Vocational Qualification in Early Years Care and Education

Level 2: P1

Level 3: C17, C18, P2

BTEC National Early Years Diploma: 10, 22

can do and give you a sound basis for finding out more information when you need it.

Many disabilities and health conditions are mentioned in this chapter and it would be impossible to give significant information about each. So you will see more *Finding out more* boxes here than in other chapters. Please access this information as and when you need it, but do bear in mind the guidelines given on page 667 about contacting organisations, especially in the context of a student project.

Different types of disability and health conditions

Different phrases are used to describe children who are affected by some level of disability: disabled children, children with disabilities, children with special needs. You may hear some strong views expressed about why one phrase is more acceptable than another phrase.

I most often use 'disabled children' because it tends to be the preferred term among disabled adults who have shared their views about past and current experiences. Older disabled children often say that they do not want to be seen as 'special' in the way that the term 'special needs' is used. But there is nothing like 100 per cent agreement about terminology and it would be surprising if there were. So long as you show respect to children and strive towards good practice, how you behave towards disabled children is in the end far more important than the phrase you choose to use.

The focus on children rather than their disability

Into the 1980s, most professionals treated disabled children as medical cases. Diagnosis, treatment and management of the condition were a greater priority than behaving towards children as individuals with interests, preferences and concerns. Strong criticism of this **medical model of disability** was launched by disabled adults on the basis of their childhood memories and by parents of disabled children. An alternative **social model** of disability focuses on the child as an individual and highlights social restrictions that can that mean a child is disabled by social circumstances. This approach does not reject useful programmes or medical treatment but stresses that children should never be seen only as their disability label.

Key terms

Medical model of disability
an approach to disabled children that focuses exclusively on diagnosis and medical management of the condition

Social model of disability
an approach that focuses on disabled children as individuals and ways they can be disabled by social circumstances and attitudes

The wide range of disability

The first step in understanding disability is to recognise that:

- There are very many different kinds of disability and continuing health conditions.
- There is great variety within any given diagnosed condition. Different children may have mild through to very severe versions of the same condition.
- Children remain individuals and disability does not stop them having their own temperament, interests and mischievous inclinations.

Tips for practice

- Even experienced practitioners do not know everything about every kind of disability or health condition.
- In an early years setting or school, you will not encounter every kind of disability and some conditions are rare.
- Good practice is to be very willing to learn and remain open-minded about what may be possible or best for any individual child and family.
- You are not expected to know everything but it is reasonable to expect you to have good ideas about how to find out.
- This chapter offers many useful suggestions for information searches that you may need to do, or support a parent in undertaking, at a later stage in your career.

Physical disabilities

Some children are physically disabled and the effect may be anything from mild to very severe. Some physical disabilities also have associated learning difficulties.

Children with *cerebral palsy* share a condition in which their brain fails to send the appropriate signals to their limbs. Some children experience only mild difficulties in hand control, yet others can have great difficulty in standing and making deliberate movements with their limbs. The brain damage that has led to the cerebral palsy may not only have affected the parts of the brain that control movement. Some children may be deaf, blind and experience severe learning disabilities.

Finding out more

Scope, 6 Market Road, London N7 9PW tel: 020 7619 7100 or try *www.scope.org.uk*

An organisation concerned with all aspects of life with cerebral palsy.

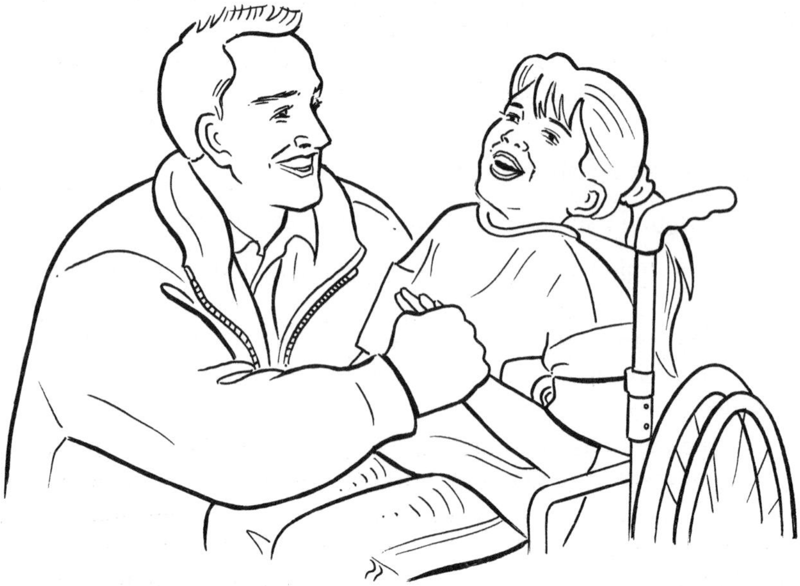

Figure 18.1
Disabled children can have fun – but they will be unhappy sometimes, like any child

Some children are born with disabilities that affect their level of vision or hearing. When children are *deaf* or *blind*, this physical disability affects the ways in which children can learn in a society that assumes children can see and hear. Children do not always have total loss of these senses and partial loss can sometimes be harder to detect in very early childhood.

Finding out more

NDCS (National Deaf Children's Society), 15 Dufferin Street, London EC1Y 8PD tel: 020 7250 0123 email: *helpline@NDCS.org.uk* website: *www.ndcs.org.uk*

RNIB, 224 Great Portland Street, London W1N 6AA tel: 020 7388 1266 website: *www.rnib.org.uk*
Advice and information on all aspects of blindness.

Children with *spina bifida* are born with some of the bones in their spine not properly joined together ('bifid' is from the Latin meaning 'split'). Some children have no more than a slight swelling on their back but if the split is more severe, then the consequences can include physical disability, incontinence and learning disabilities.

Finding out more

ASBAH (Association for spina bifida and hydrocephalus), Asbah House, 42 Park Road, Peterborough, PE1 2UQ tel: 01733 555988 email: *postmaster@asbah.org* website: *www.asbah.org*

Muscular dystrophy is a progressive disease in which the muscles in a child's body waste away. The most common type in early childhood is called Duchenne and only boys are affected. The condition is usually diagnosed because a young boy is late in learning to walk and has serious difficulties in physical coordination. The increasing muscle weakness leads to poor posture that makes the boys vulnerable to chest infections. The boys may not survive childhood.

Finding out more

Muscular Dystrophy Group, Nattrass House, 7–11 Prescott Place, London SW4 6BS tel: 020 7720 8055 website: *www.muscular-dystrophy.org*

Learning and social disabilities

Some children's disability mainly affects their ability to learn in the broadest sense. It may be that children find difficulty learning the skills of communication, both understanding and expression (see page 295), so that it is hard for them to learn about their world. Children's intellectual capacity may be affected in a way that learning will take longer for them and they will need help through the fine steps of grasping an idea or skill that you scarcely notice with their peers.

Finding out more

MENCAP provides information and advice on a wide range of learning disabilities. Contact them at 123 Golden Lane, London EC1Y 0RT tel: 020 7454 0454 (general) email: *info@mencap.org.uk* website: *www.mencap.org.uk*

The British Institute of Learning Disabilities (BILD) offers a range of publications and reading lists and would be a useful contact if you decided in the future to specialise in this area. Contact them at Wolverhampton Road (no number is needed), Kidderminster, Worcestershire DY10 3PP website: *www.bild.org.uk*

Down's syndrome is an inherited condition that affects about one child in every 1000. Some children have relatively mild learning disabilities and manage well in mainstream nursery and school, especially with some support at later levels. Other children may need carefully structured support from a young age. Many children are relatively healthy, although the syndrome is associated with an increased risk of frequent infections, difficulties with hearing or vision and sometimes problems in the functioning of children's heart that can require surgery.

Finding out more

Down's Syndrome Association, 155 Mitcham Road, London SW17 9PG tel: 020 8682 4001 website: *www.downs-syndrome.org.uk*

To think about

- Part of good practice in working with disabled children has to be putting to one side any inaccurate assumptions and stereotypes about the children and their condition.
- For instance, the myth has built up that all children with Down's syndrome have a sunny disposition and are easy to manage.
- In fact they vary just as much as any other children. Some children are of an amenable temperament, but some will definitely keep you on your toes.

Some children have what is now called an *autistic spectrum disorder*. This phrase is used to describe children (and also young people or adults) who share a condition that affects their ability to:

- understand and use verbal and non-verbal skills of communication
- make sense of social behaviour so this disability in turn affects children's ability to interact and play with their peers and adults

- think and behave in a flexible way, such as understanding how to adjust their behaviour to certain situations
- deal with pretend and the use of the imagination. It is hard for these children to think about a situation being other than it actually is.

Children with autistic spectrum disorder vary considerably but in general they have a developmental disability that affects their brain functioning. Some children will have immense difficulty in learning to speak and may never use spoken language. Other children will be able to use language but remain confused about the subtleties that are communicated by exactly how something is said or the social conventions that their peers have managed. The ordinary routine of a nursery or playgroup can seem unpredictable and scary. Children may develop what look like rigid routines of their own in order to cope.

An awareness of the struggles of children with autistic spectrum disorder can help you appreciate also the complexity of what their peers have learned. For instance, four year olds have usually understood that the English phrase, 'Can you help me tidy up the bricks?' actually means 'Please do it' and not 'Are you capable of it?' Children with an autistic spectrum disorder may find it impossible to grasp this nuance. They also have difficulties in understanding non-verbal clues in play, what is a joke and what is serious and the social skills involved in pretend play.

Finding out more

National Autistic Society, 393 City Road London EC1V 1NE tel: 020 7833 2299 website: *www.oneworld.org/autism_uk*

All about Autistic Spectrum Disorders is a free booklet from the Foundation for People with Learning Disabilities, part of Mental Health Foundation tel: 020 7535 7429 or download it from the website: *www.learningdisabilities.org.uk* or *www.mentalhealth.org.uk*

Continuing health conditions

All children become ill at some time and some so-called childhood illnesses can be very unpleasant indeed. Chapter 4 covers illnesses that children may catch in the early years but will subsequently recover from. Some children are less robust in health because of health consequences of their disability or they have a specific continuing health condition that affects their daily life. Such conditions can be managed to an extent but are not curable.

Cystic fibrosis is a life-threatening condition that affects children's lungs and their digestive system. The condition means that the mucus in children's lungs is too thick and blocks the bronchial tubes. Children with cystic fibrosis have a persistent cough, difficulties in breathing and are very vulnerable to chest infections.

Finding out more

Cystic Fibrosis Research Trust, Alexandra House, 5 Blyth Road, Bromley, Kent BR1 3RS tel: 020 8464 7211 website: *www.cftrust.org.uk*

Asthma is the most common chronic medical disorder in childhood, affecting an estimated one child in every ten. Some children experience mild attacks of breathlessness but about half of the group have more serious attacks with bad coughing fits and an inability to get their breath. Asthma can be very serious and result in young children having regular times in hospital. Although most children and adults manage their asthma, severe attacks can lead to death.

Finding out more

National Asthma Campaign, Providence House, Providence Place, London N1 0NT tel: 020 7226 2260 website: *www.asthma.org.uk*

Sickle cell disease is a blood disorder and the most common and severe form is sickle cell anaemia. Sickle cell disease is inherited and most common in families who originated from Africa or the Caribbean. But the condition also occurs in families from the Eastern Mediterranean, the Middle East, India and Pakistan. Children and adults with sickle cell anaemia are not ill all the time but experience bouts of illness, called crises, in which severe anaemia and pain require urgent hospital treatment. Children are vulnerable to infections.

Finding out more

Sickle Cell Society, 54 Station Road, London NW10 4UA tel: 020 8961 7795 website: *www.sicklecellsociety.org*

Diabetes is also an inherited condition and it is usually in the form of early onset diabetes (type 1) when it occurs in childhood. The condition means that the pancreas fails to produce enough insulin, or any at all. Glucose formed by the breakdown of sugars and starch through digestion cannot be absorbed as normal. The person then cannot use sugar and starch for energy and glucose accumulates in the kidneys. Children with diabetes usually need insulin injections, given by parents until the child is able to take over this task. The potential complications of diabetes mean that children need great care with their diet and their general health.

In recent years in the United States, and to an extent in the UK, doctors have seen an increase in children and adolescents of the type of diabetes that previously only affected adults from middle age (late onset or type 2 diabetes). The cause seems to be a serious lack of physical activity and poor eating habits, leading to obesity for some children. The unhealthy life style of some children creates the conditions that usually only affect adults. Type 2 diabetes can have serious health implications if not well managed.

Finding out more

Diabetes UK, 10 Queen Anne Street, London W1M 0BD tel: 020 7323 1531 website: *www.diabetes.org.uk*

Epilepsy results from a problem in the brain's communication system. The tiny electrical signals from one group of nerve cells become stronger than normal and overwhelm nearby parts of the brain. This sudden, excessive electrical discharge is what brings on an epileptic seizure. About 1 in 200 children has epilepsy but not all of them have a severe version. However, for some children and young adults the condition is very serious and a seizure may be fatal.

Children with epilepsy can have different types of seizure and the main types are:

- Tonic clonic seizures (that used to be called grand mal) are a generalised seizure in which the child may stay unconscious for a few minutes. The pattern is that the child's muscles contract, force the air out of the lungs, causing the body to stiffen (the tonic phase) and possibly also jerk uncontrollably (the clonic phase).
- Absence seizures (that used to be called petit mal) is a momentary lapse of awareness when the child may simply look blank for a short while then carries on with what she was doing. This type of seizure may occur many times in a day and, without careful observation, adults may explain the event as problems of attention or a child who is inclined to be vague.

There is no cure for epilepsy but anti-convulsant medication can help to control the condition.

Finding out more

Epilepsy Action, New Anstey House, Gate Way Drive, Yeadon, Leeds LS19 7XY tel: 0113 210 8800 freephone helpline on 0808 800 5050 website: *www.epilepsy.org.uk*

Activity

- Take one disability or health condition that is covered in this section.
- Use the resource suggested to build your understanding of the condition. Write up your findings to support practical help for the child and family in an early years setting or family home.
- Make a presentation to your colleagues.

Key skills links: C3.1b IT2/31–3

What causes disability or chronic ill health?

There is no single cause for the different kinds of disability or health conditions. Sometimes there is no obvious cause at all for a child's disability and possibly no clear-cut diagnosis either.

Genetic causes

Sometimes either the sperm or the egg that combine in fertilisation contain genetic material that carries the information leading to a disability. The condition is then said to be **genetic** or inherited through the genes. Some inherited

Key term

Genetic causes of disability
when a child inherits a condition from the genes of their parent(s)

conditions include Down's Syndrome, cystic fibrosis, sickle cell anaemia and muscular dystrophy.

Congenital conditions

Key terms

Congenital causes of disability
pre-birth conditions lead to a disability or health condition, so that the baby is born with this condition

Trauma (birth)
unexpected events during childbirth that can create high risk to the future well being of the unborn baby, such as being deprived of oxygen

Congenital means that the baby is born with a disability or health condition. Inherited conditions are therefore congenital, but not all congenital conditions are inherited. The human fetus is mainly very safe in the womb, but some events can cause lasting damage. If the mother is infected with rubella (German Measles) during the first three months of pregnancy, then there is permanent damage to the organs developing at that time, with resulting blindness, deafness or cerebral palsy. Excessive use of alcohol crosses the placenta and causes fetal alcohol syndrome, which can include learning disabilities. Use of addictive drugs like heroin also affects the fetus and she or he is born drug-dependent.

Trauma during birth

If a baby is deprived of oxygen at birth, the consequence can be brain damage. The pattern of disabilities will depend on the severity of brain damage and what parts of the brain are affected. Very premature babies are at risk of later disability, because their organs are so immature.

Illness and accidents after birth

Very serious illnesses can cause permanent disabilities even though children survive. Meningitis can leave children with hearing difficulties and, less often, with brain injury or epilepsy. Rheumatic fever can damage the heart, leading to the formation of scar tissue, which in turn prevents the valves from operating properly.

Some children's physical or learning disabilities result from injuries, especially damage to the head, and therefore to the brain. Children are involved in traffic accidents or have serious falls at home or at play. Serious head injuries can lead to the development of cerebral palsy.

Multiple possible causes or unknown

There is sometimes no clear pattern of cause and effect. For example, epilepsy can result from brain injury at birth or from a serious accident. Some seizures may be caused by a faulty gene and so the condition is inherited for this child. But for about 6 out of every 10 people who have epilepsy there is no obvious cause.

The role of the early years practitioner

Working well with disabled children depends on all the skills that you will learn and apply within general good practice. There are additional skills and knowledge to gain but these build on the firm foundation of good practice in giving attention to children as individuals. You need to work as always in partnership with parents and to work cooperatively with other involved professionals. Furthermore, effective use of your skills of observation, record keeping and planning are equally important in this area of your work. You also need a practical understanding of the legal framework for good practice with disabled children and their families and the Code of Practice.

Partnership with parents

Good practice in early years is always to build a good working partnership with parents or other important carers who share responsibility for the child. This partnership is vital when children are disabled or have a continuing health condition.

- Parents will often know a great deal about their child's disability or health condition. Even more important, they have unique experience about what the disability means for this child and they know their child as a person.
- When you make the time to have a conversation, you will learn from parents but also they feel welcome and able to learn from you.
- Some parents and other carers have managed with hardly any support before their child attends nursery or pre-school. They will not necessarily know about the local support that is available or a helpful national support organisation for their child's condition.

Settling a child with a disability or health condition

Much of what you will do in you first contact will be a normal part of your process of welcoming and settling children and parents into your setting. If you have a friendly and effective settling in process (see page 630), then you will not need to do anything significantly extra for this family. Some of the issues you cover may be slightly different, for instance:

- Do you need to do some preparations before the child arrives? Will it be sensible to prepare the existing group for the child's arrival?

Scenario

Marcella is joining Sunningdale Day Nursery within the coming week. She is four and half years old and has Down's syndrome. Her understanding and behaviour is more like a young three year old and this is the first time she has attended any kind of early years setting.

This will be the first time that Sunningdale has welcomed a child with learning disabilities. Simon, who is about to move onto school, has serious hearing loss and, with hindsight, the team wish they had prepared more for his arrival. Marcella has been assigned Penny as her key worker and Penny has already done a home visit, meeting Marcella, her parents and her older brother. In a team meeting, Penny leads an open discussion about how best to prepare for Marcella's arrival.

- In what way, if at all, should the other children be given some idea of what to expect from Marcella?
- Are there any adjustments that should be made in the routine or play opportunities for Marcella?
- What kind of questions might the other children or parents ask and what would be suitable answers?

Questions

1 Think about the questions above and gather your own thoughts on what would be good practice.

2 You might like to make some preliminary notes now and then come back to this scenario when you have read the whole chapter.
3 Discuss your answers with colleagues.
4 Plan a short presentation to explain what you feel would be appropriate and your reasons.

Key skills links: C3.1a C3.1b

- You need to hear some personal details about this child's needs, even if you have previously worked with children with the same condition. For instance, health conditions like diabetes or epilepsy do not affect all children in the same way. You may have worked previously with a child who has dyspraxia (see also page 263). But this disability affects physical coordination and sequencing in different ways and to different levels of severity.
- When you speak with parents, it makes a difference if you take a positive line. Of course you do not pretend that the fact that Matthew is in a wheelchair will make no difference. You cannot treat him 'just the same' as all the other children, but you can avoid a conversation with his parents that focuses on 'difficulties' and 'I suppose there'll be problems about ...'.
- When you welcome a disabled child into your setting, you are not agreeing to meet all his needs. Other professionals will be involved and you will become part of the network supporting this family. You may also in time be able to help parents make contact with other support services.

Figure 18.2
Easing access in your environment can benefit all the children

Tips for practice

You are starting to learn about this child and her condition.

- Do not feel embarrassed about admitting that you do not know something or that you would appreciate it if the parent explained one more time.
- Be clear about any particular health issues to which you need to be alert for this child. You do not want to be too anxious or over-protective, but some children will be especially vulnerable to infections.
- You definitely need to understand warning signs for some children, for instance about an asthma attack and what to do in an emergency.
- Do ensure that all relevant information becomes known to the full team. This sharing is the responsibility of the early years setting or school; parents should not have to track down every person who could have contact with their child.
- For example, Tim who has epilepsy could be at risk if only his key worker is able to deal calmly with a seizure. Suppose Tim has a seizure when out with a small group on a local trip and staff panic because they are uncertain what to do.

Policy and practice on medication

Every setting should have a policy about medication. The policy in your setting may usually be to say that, if children are ill enough to need medicine, then they should be at home. However, children with a disability or health condition may need regular medication as part of their normal day. An inflexible medication policy may mean that a child with epilepsy or asthma cannot attend your setting. This exclusion is unlikely to be acceptable nowadays. Early years settings, schools and out of school care need a realistic medication policy. Your employers' insurance policies must cover practitioners who support children with health conditions that require medication.

You need to talk with parents to understand their child's needs and whether you can meet them in your setting. No setting should immediately refuse without discussion.

- You need to be clear about what is needed and get the final details in writing through discussion with the parent.
- You need to know if there are any possible side effects of the medication for the child.
- All the relevant details should be recorded in a medication or drugs book, with the full name of the child, name of drug, dosage and timing when the medication needs to be given or supervised.
- You will need parents to give you medication that travels between home and setting. It should never be left in a child's bag or on a table.
- The medication should then be stored in a safe place. An exception will be the inhaler for a child with asthma that should travel with the child. Talk with parents about a suitable container.
- You may give the medication to a younger child, but if you work with school age children, your role may be to remind them to take their medicine in whatever format they need.

- For instance a child with asthma may take regular preventative doses through an inhaler operating as a reliever of the condition. Some children need controlled doses of insulin for diabetes or adrenaline for serious allergic reactions and these may be delivered by pen-like syringes.

Activity

Find out about the policy for medication in your setting.

- What are the main issues that are covered?
- In what ways do the team keep records of medication?
- Does the policy cover the eventualities that are discussed in this section – what if anything has possibly been overlooked?
- Write up your findings.
- Share what you have learned with your colleagues.

Key skills links: C2.3 C2.1a

Continued communication with parents

The discussion so far has assumed that when parents and children join your setting it is already known that the child has a disability. This situation will not always be the case and a child's difficulties may only become clear after the family has joined your setting. The SEN code of practice (see page 528) describes the steps to take when a child is not progressing as well as his or her peers.

Whatever the timing of a diagnosis or assessment, families with a disabled child often appreciate support and a friendly ear. Parents may be trying to balance advice, sometimes incompatible, from different sources. Disabled children and their families are sometimes required to liase with many different agencies and professionals, some of whom do not really try to understand the competing priorities within a family.

Tips for practice

- Some parents will be very well informed and may already have made contact with an appropriate organisation. But do not hold back on information that you have on the grounds that, 'I'm sure parents will know about that'.
- You can share information, details of useful leaflets and contact details for organisations in a friendly way along the lines of 'I was wondering if you had already heard about ...'.
- Open a file on useful contacts, both local and national, and organise the details in a way that is easy to access and show to parents.
- You also need to gain an insight into the experiences of families with disabled children. You will learn through communication with individual parents but a broader base is useful.
- For instance, the Foundation for People with Learning Disabilities (see page 519 for details) has produced a booklet on *Learning Disabilities and the Family: The young child with a learning disability*. You can obtain the booklet from the Foundation or download it from the website: *www.learningdisabilities.org.uk*

Legislation and good practice

There have been a number of laws that affect services and provision for disabled children and their families. Similar legal requirements apply across the UK. The exact practice varies between England, Wales, Scotland and Northern Ireland because educational and social services are organised rather differently.

Disabled children were specifically defined as being 'in need' by the Children Act 1989 (for England and Wales), the Children (Scotland) Act 1995 and the Children (Northern Ireland) Order 1995. Local authorities have to offer services to children 'in need' but the details will vary. In some case suitable provision is seen to be an early years place for children.

A series of laws have shaped good practice on equality for disabled children and adults and educational provision for children. The main strands are:

- a policy of inclusion for disabled children
- an agreed process for assessment of special educational needs
- a code of practice for working with disabled children and their families.

The Special Educational Needs (SEN) and Disability Bill 2001 has placed significant responsibilities on schools in England, Wales and Scotland to ensure that disabled children are able to access mainstream education and are not placed at a serious disadvantage compared with their peers. Similar legislation is likely in Northern Ireland.

Inclusion

Until about the last quarter of the twentieth century, services for disabled children kept them almost completely separate from their peers. Parents were often told to send their children away to special, residential schools and there were often very limited alternatives. Programmes for disabled children often ran with very low expectations for what children could manage and specialist units sometimes brought together children with very different disabilities and ability level.

The situation has now changed significantly. Parents have the legal right to seek mainstream provision, including schooling for their disabled child, supported by additional services appropriate to the child. Of course any family, and professionals who offer advice, can only work with the services that are actually available locally. Some parts of the UK are better served than others.

Children with a wide range of physical or learning disabilities can and do manage in mainstream school. Their special needs are met with appropriate educational support, and sometimes a designated support assistant. An **inclusive approach** is a commitment to enabling children to be part of mainstream early years or school provision and the approach values the benefits of contact for both disabled children and their peers:

- Inclusion prevents the segregation that used to be the norm for all disabled children.
- Children, whose disabilities are physical, need the intellectual challenge that comes from mixing with their peers. Children with learning disabilities can partake in much of the daily nursery or school life and have specialist support as appropriate.
- For generations, disabled or very sick children were effectively invisible. Young children can be very straightforward about difference and early contact with disabled friends and acquaintances can contribute to changing attitudes in society as a whole.

Key term

Inclusive approach a commitment to enable disabled children to join mainstream early years or school provision as far as possible and with necessary support

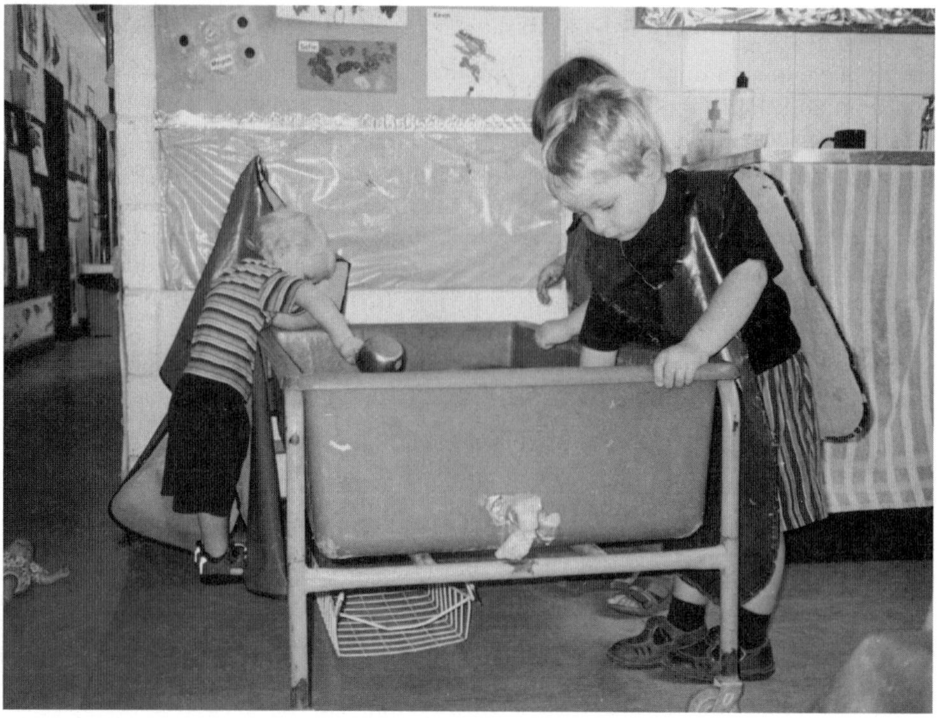

Figure 18.3

Mainstream early years play will be suitable for many disabled children – perhaps with some extra help

An inclusive approach should not mean the closure of special units or schools, where this service is in the best interests of children. If you have a disabled child in your early years setting, the result of careful support and partnership between the team and parents may be that this child needs and will benefit from a more specialised environment. Going on to mainstream primary school is not the best choice for every child.

Finding out more

The Centre for Studies on Inclusive Education, Room S203, S Block, Frenchay Campus, Coldharbour Lane, Redland, Bristol BS16 1QU tel: 0117 923 8450 website: *www.inclusion.org.uk*

Support in the early years

In England and Wales the revised SEN Code of Practice now specifically includes early years services and similar changes are also likely in other parts of the UK. The new Code of Practice outlines a two stage approach for children with disabilities and other special needs in early years settings called **Early Years Action** and **Early Years Action Plus**. The approach allows for the fact that it is not immediately obvious with all children that they will need additional help.

In England, every early years setting (that offers free early educational places) should have a member of staff with special responsibility for implementing the **SEN Code of Practice** on the Identification and Assessment of Special Education Needs (SEN). This person is known as the Special Educational Needs Co-ordinator (**SENCO**). The SENCO for the early years setting has special responsibility for liaison between the setting, parents and any outside agencies. The aim is to

Key terms

Early Years Action and **Early Years Action Plus**
two stages of special support for children with disabilities in early years settings

SEN Code of Practice
the clear guidelines describing good practice for disabled children in early years and school settings

SENCO
the Special Educational Needs Co-ordinator responsible for liaison between the setting, parents and any outside agencies

ensure that all information is brought together in a workable way and that parents are aware of local advice and support services.

It will take time before every setting has a designated SENCO. If your setting does not have one, you can contact your local Early Years Development and Childcare Partnership who will tell you the name of the area SENCO.

Early Years Action is set in motion when any of the following situations occur.

- Despite appropriate help and support, children are still struggling, compared with their peers in some, or most, of their areas of learning.
- Children's behaviour or emotional reactions are hard to handle, even though you have persevered with positive strategies (see page 507).
- Your observation, and the knowledge of parents, shows you that the child has specific difficulties in physical skills, communication, use of the senses or social interaction.
- Some children may enter your setting with a known primary cause of SEN, for example, it is already known that a child has visual loss or there is good reason to support that the child has autism. Without a definite diagnosis, then learning difficulties will most likely come to your attention at this stage.

Tips for practice

- Be alert to parents' feelings when you raise the issue that their child is not progressing or is showing challenging behaviour.
- Use your communication skills of listening and careful explanation. Check you understand what parents say and feel and be willing to have more than one conversation (see page 531).
- Some parents may not be surprised by what you share. Perhaps they have been anxious about their child's development or behaviour and have been reassured that the child will 'catch up', 'grow out of it'. In this case, parents may feel relief that you understand and agree with their concern. They may be keen to get going in order to help their child.
- But some parents may be distressed or unwilling to accept that all is not well with their child and that some special help is really needed.
- You need to work in partnership whatever the parents' reaction.

You should then:

- Discuss with the child's parents the need to involve your setting's SENCO. This conversation should be part of a continuing communication between a child's key worker and parents.
- The key worker, parents and SENCO should then work to bring together all the useful information and observations on the child. You and the parents could make further observations and ensure that all aspects of the child's development, health and behaviour have been considered.
- Together you all then develop an **individual education plan (IEP)** for the child. The IEP can cover appropriate areas for this child and needs to be manageable. Focus on no more than three or four targets that are special for this child, in addition to the play opportunities she or he shares with the other children.
- Decide when you will get together to discuss progress – probably no more than a couple of months ahead. If at any point the IEP does not seem to be

Key term

IEP
Individual Education Plan for children whose disabilities require special support and planning in early years or school settings

working, and you have all given the targets your full attention, then be ready to adjust it.

- Parents should be able to be fully involved in this process. If parents lack confidence or feel they do not want to have much say in the detail, then ensure that they are informed in straightforward language.
- The same guidelines on good practice about written material and files on children apply in this instance as in all other parts of your work (see page 461).

The revised Code of Practice emphasised the importance of involving children. Early years practitioners are expected to look for ways to involve the children themselves in any part of the IEP: the targets, the activities and opportunities that can help the child to reach targets and the ways of recording success step by step.

Appropriate work with a child will be enough support for some children. The next stage of Early Years Action Plus is set in motion if, despite well planned and delivered extra help, the child is still struggling in any of the identified areas or the setting is still having difficulty in dealing with challenging behaviour.

- At this point, it is important to involve agencies outside the early years setting, but of course in partnership with the parents.
- A review meeting should be held with the SENCO, key worker and child's parents.
- You would consider what you have learned from all the information and observations of this child: progress as well as continued difficulties.
- The external specialist will need to understand what has been learned about the child so far. Then he or she can be part of a revised IEP, targets and any new strategies.
- The new IEP needs to be reviewed every two or three months (termly if you work on terms). Parents and children need to feel and be an integral part of the work.

Activity

- Ensure that you understand the steps in Early Years Action and Early Years Action Plus.
- Explore how the process works in your setting or make arrangements to visit a local setting.
- Make brief notes to support a presentation to colleagues.

Key skills links: C3.3 C3.1b

Extra help and support for a child

The Code of Practice is flexible about the kind of extra or different provision that an early years setting makes for a child. It might include:

- Extra time to observe a child so you can build on his strengths and fine tune a strategy.
- Individual adult support for a child, either for parts of a day or for most of his time with you.

- Agreement within the team about how everyone will support a child with special learning needs or allow more flexibility for a child who has trouble coping with routine.
- Provision of some special equipment or play materials suitable for this child, or flexible access to specialist resources in a large setting.
- Organisation so that a child can be in smaller groups for some or part of the day.
- Perhaps a flexible pattern of attendance with a shorter day or even a temporary break and re-start when the child has matured enough to cope with help.

It is possible that some strategies will enable a child to cope and not need further special support. However, some children will continue to need specialist help and will move into the process of statementing in school (see page 532). The observations, records and plans made in the early years setting will be very helpful at this later stage. You should follow the same good practice as with any kind of records. So, parents should be a full part of an agreement to pass on records or a summary of a large portfolio.

Scenario

Baker Street Family and Children's Centre have developed IEPs for two children in recent months.

Winston

Winston, who is nearly four years old now, has been diagnosed with autistic spectrum disorder. Winston's key worker Kayleigh had been concerned for some time that Winston's communication, social skills and play were not within normal developmental range. It took some time before Winston's parents were willing to consider that there was a greater problem than delayed language. Kayleigh remained patient and supportive, while undertaking observations that she shared with Winston's parents in a positive way. Over time she was able to help his parents to recognise that their son needed special language support and that in play he showed a limited range of interests, as well as having difficulty in playing with his peers. Winston's parents agreed to an external assessment that confirmed autistic spectrum disorder and they are now actively involved in his IEP. A recent target in the plan is to enable Winston to join small groups of children for a story, supported by Kayleigh. She is also starting short play sessions with Winston to help him to learn basic play social skills. First of all, she is working with Winston on very simple turn taking games and imitation.

Joanne

Joanne, two years old, has severe visual loss, and has only recently joined the centre. Tyrone is her key worker and he is at the stage of bringing together information from Joanne's family and his own observations of her in the centre. The first target has been to enable Joanne to feel confident in moving around the room and out into the garden. Discussion around this target has helped to focus the centre team on how everyone can help Joanne by talking simply about where she is in the centre, enabling her to touch and showing the other children how to communicate with Joanne without alarming her. Tyrone is close to developing a short play programme to support Joanne's language development. Joanne is a very decided child and as likely to say 'No!' as to join in play. Tyrone wants to discuss some strategies with her parents – what might encourage Joanne and what does she enjoy the most in play and other daily routines?

Questions

1 Describe briefly the themes of good practice in the examples of Winston and Joanne.
2 Draft a possible IEP with two appropriate targets for each child.
3 Discuss with your colleagues.

Key skills links: C3.3 C3.1a

Support of special educational needs in school

In order to receive appropriate support, disabled children need to be assessed. Generally this procedure of assessment, followed by a statement of special educational needs, has taken place when a child is in school. However, even before the recent changes it was possible to start the process of special assessment for a child as young as two years of age.

The new Code of Practice has changed the pattern in schools in England and Wales from what was usually a five stage process to two broad stages called **School Action** and **School Action Plus**. This change means that stages one and two are part of School Action and stages three, four and five are School Action Plus. It is possible, although not certain that Scotland and Northern Ireland may move towards a similar system. In case they continue with a four- or five-stage approach, these are given in brackets below. The new Code has stressed the great importance of partnership with parents. The Code has also strengthened the view that good practice means involving children as much as possible in conversations about their learning and setting realistic targets to which children can feel committed.

Key terms

School Action and **School Action Plus** two stages of special support for children with disabilities in school settings

The process of support and assessment will continue to reflect differences around the UK in the organisation of services. For instance, in England the local educational authority (LEA) would be involved but in Northern Ireland it would be the Education and Library Board. Each school should still have a named member of staff who is the SENCO.

School Action

In the stage of School Action a child's teacher would record any concerns about children's ability to learn and access the curriculum. The information gathered should include parents' knowledge of their child at home and in other settings (previous stage one). When children have attended an early years setting, then there can be valuable information from that experience (see page 531) and the school should be willing to draw on this expertise. Careful discussion involving the parents and child can sometimes identify how to help a child to overcome a difficulty.

If a child continues to struggle then the teacher should draw up an individual education plan (IEP) with other teachers and the child's parents (previous stage two). The plan will set appropriate targets for the child, with suggestions about how to support him or her and a date for review. The school SENCO should also be involved. Sometimes, extra support helps the child to cope but, if not, then the process moves on to the next stage.

School Action Plus

The school looks for external specialist advice or help, for instance a speech and language therapist or psychologist (see page 17 for a discussion of services). The SENCO will be involved in drawing up a new IEP with any outside specialist who has been consulted and with the involvement of parents (previous stage three).

If the child is not progressing, then anyone involved can request a formal assessment (previous stage four). The head teacher of the school will consult with the teacher, SENCO, parent and external specialist to decide whether the child needs to be formally assessed. This statutory assessment should include the opinions of educational, medical or psychological services, and take account of parents' views. This assessment leads to a written **statement of special educational needs**. Any individual statement should cover:

1 The details of this child's learning difficulties: strengths as well as weaknesses.
2 The specific learning needs of the child, described to show the kind of additional help that will be appropriate.
3 Details of special facilities or equipment that should be made available to this child.
4 The statement leads to the further development of the IEP for this child.

The statement of special educational needs is a legal document that sets out what this individual child needs and commits the local authority to supply the extra support or facilities. The requirements of the statement have to be put into practice (previous stage five). The child, with this help, may still continue in mainstream school. In some cases, it may be judged that the child's needs could be better met in a specialist school or unit.

Key term

Statement of special educational needs
description for an individual child of his/her difficulties and needs for support in school

Activity

- Ensure that you understand the steps in School Action and School Action Plus.
- Explore how the process works in your setting or make arrangements to visit a local setting.
- Make brief notes to support a presentation to colleagues.

Key skills links: C3.3 C3.1b

Supporting children's learning and behaviour

This section describes general good practice in working with children who have disabilities. The most important point to bear in mind is to see the child and not primarily the disability or continuing health condition. All the ideas and good practice in the rest of this book also apply to disabled children.

Tips for practice

- You treat disabled or very sick children as individuals. You get to know them and they get to know you.
- In supporting their learning, you look for a disabled child's interests and work on from what they can do and can understand – just as you would with any child.
- A sensitive approach to disabled children means that you work to understand and observe in what ways the disability affects what and how the child can learn.
- You make suitable adjustments to your expectations of a child. But you still have expectations and aim to help the child progress.
- You adjust your communication or suggestions about play materials and ensure that the early years environment does not disable the child by unnecessary restrictions.
- Disabled children will often have a special learning programme but this plan must never be more important than the child. Disabled children need choice, they need sometimes to be able to say or communicate, 'no', 'I've had enough' or 'I'm bored with this'.
- They need friendships, fun, challenge and to be allowed to get messy and make mistakes like everyone else.

Activity

Choose a particular disability or health condition that is mentioned in this chapter. Imagine that a child, with this disability or health condition, is going to join your setting.

- Gather some general information about the condition. You can start your research with contacting the relevant specialist organisation given within this chapter. Start with their website.
- Now consider five or six important points that should guide your good practice with this child.
- Now imagine this child in your setting. Of course you do not know the child as an individual, but would a child with this disability or health condition be able to relate personally to your range of books, posters or play materials?
- Share your main ideas with colleagues through a short presentation.

Key skills links: IT2/3.1–3

Access and welcome within the setting

Contact with disabled children or parents can make you look at your setting afresh. Some issues will be about ease of access for children, or disabled adults, who use a wheelchair or mobility aids. Other issues may be about different ways of communication and an awareness of the play materials and illustrations in your setting.

To think about

- Since the 1980s there has been an obligation for public services and facilities to offer easier access for physically disabled adults.
- I have heard complaints about the cost of making changes for 'only a few people'. But many improvements for disabled people are inclusive; they are facilities that can be used by anyone.
- Speaking as a parent who was pushing a buggy, single and double, in the first half of the 1980s, I can attest that sloped entrances rather than steps, wide aisles in supermarkets and more spacious toilets are an immense help to all those adults who are temporarily pushing wheels!

Perhaps the arrival of a child with cerebral palsy makes you look at how easy it is for anyone to move around in your nursery or pre-school. Creating more space for movement or ease of reaching play materials may improve the environment for everyone.

Tips for practice

You need to build a warm and personal relationship with a disabled or sick child, just as you would with any child. Knowledge about the disability or health condition has to be put into daily practice as part of getting to know this child as an individual.

- Adults can have empathy for a child's frustrations, but ensure that you and your colleagues avoid showing a patronising attitude or pity.
- Children do not benefit from sad looks and whispered comments along the lines of 'poor little …'.
- A positive attitude is shown by avoiding phrases like, 'Marlon suffers from sickle cell anaemia'. You can support Marlon when he feels very ill but he does not 'suffer' all the time, nor he is a 'victim of sickle cell disease' and this image is not helpful.
- Children should never be described by their disability or health condition, as if it were a personal label. Courtesy is shown by the difference between 'Katie has Down's syndrome' rather than 'Katie is our little Down's' or 'Tim is the epileptic'.

Different channels of communication

Physically disabled children (as well as young people and adults) still experience discourteous and thoughtless people who blithely assume that visible physical disability means someone cannot communicate or hear. Some children will have disabilities that affect communication (see page 319) and some adjustments will be needed and appreciated. All the guidelines for courteous communication with children (see page 305) apply to interaction with disabled children.

- Children who have hearing loss need other people to face them, so that it is easier to see that they are being addressed, and can see any signs and lip read, if possible. Children with slight hearing loss or variable hearing (for example, from glue ear) benefit from the same attention.

Figure 18.4

Supported special play sessions can be a personal time

- Awareness of the needs of a child with hearing loss can alert a setting to noise levels in general and perhaps bad habits in adult communication (see page 356) that can be improved.
- Some children have physical difficulties in forming their words and making themselves understood. Apart from any specialist support, helpful adults are patient and attentive, since pressure to speak usually makes matters harder.
- Children with learning disabilities may need simpler language and shorter sentences spoken to them than their peers, and patience as they understand and reply.
- Adults should talk at a normal volume. Raising your voice or shouting do not make words any clearer and can distort them.
- Some children may use, or be learning to use, sign language. You are most likely to encounter Makaton, a system developed from British Sign Language (BSL) to focus on naming words and concepts most relevant to young children. Makaton is carefully structured so that children first learn the signs for basic needs and more complex ideas are introduced step by step. You sign and talk with a child, so other children in your setting or the family are involved.
- Other children are often ready to learn about communication with their disabled peers. Hearing children can be enthusiastic to learn to sign to a peer who is deaf. Sighted children can soon learn that they need to say their name to Susie who has visual loss until she can recognise everyone's voice. Children will then be pleased to announce, 'Susie knows me already!'

Activity (observation)

Children with physical or learning disabilities that affect spoken language communicate in different ways: gestures, facial and whole body expressions as well as learning to sign.

- Explain to the child's parents what you are doing and ask for their permission and experience of their child.
- Ask the child's permission, unless he or she is very young.
- Build up a record of notes and photographs of how a disabled child communicates without words.

You can observe any of the following:

- How does this child use sounds, perhaps a few words, facial expression or gestures to communicate feelings of happiness, puzzlement or frustration?
- When the child is playing with you or a friend how does he or she indicate 'my turn', 'do it again!' or 'enough now!'?
- How does this child get your attention when she or he wants to express wishes or indicate a question?
- Show parents the final project and if at all possible give them a copy.
- Share your findings and ideas about practice with your colleagues.

Key skills links: C3.3 C3.1b

Tips for practice

Many of the main features of good care of disabled children are identical to that for any child. Some additional issues arise for individual children but these do not change the whole pattern.

- At meal and snack times, communicate directly with children and ask them what they would like as you would for any child. Avoid talking about them as if they are invisible and redirect anyone who ignores the child with, 'Does Eric want carrots?'. Depending on the child, you might say, 'You can ask Eric himself' or show how you ask.
- Disabled children will tell you, in different ways, about the kind of help they would appreciate and which actions are not actually helpful from their point of view.
- If you attend and listen, you will be far more able to offer physical care and assistance that is courteous and enables the child to be as self reliant as possible.
- Good practice is to ask and indicate 'How would you like me to help?' rather than insisting on helping a child. Disabled children may be able to manage with more time, guidance if they want and perhaps some specialised equipment.
- Disabled children may still need help with personal care when their peers can manage in the toilet or feed themselves. A physical disability may mean that a child has greater difficulty becoming toilet trained, or may always have problems with continence. Older children will want privacy and a respectful approach offered by a key worker.

- Disabled children are put at risk of possible abuse if they are given the impression that many different people will attend to their physical needs and with scant attention to them as a person with feelings.
- Children with learning disabilities may take longer to manage skills and need that you break those down into finer stages. You can all be encouraging about what a child has managed, rather than what she cannot yet do.
- Finally, early years practitioners need to be careful to protect their back when lifting or helping some children to move. Sometimes you will need a colleague to help you support the weight of an older child.

Helping all children learn about illness and disability

You can help children understand that not everything is 'catching'. You will want to encourage children in healthy behaviour and some of this guidance will highlight that coughs and colds can be passed on to other people. Children sometimes assume, not surprisingly, that health conditions can all be passed on to other people and they may also wonder about disabilities.

You need to take those opportunities that arise to explain that children are born with, or later develop, some health conditions and there is no way that these can be passed on. For instance, conversations with some children who have eczema have highlighted how their unhappiness has been worsened because other children are convinced eczema is some kind of 'lurgy' that passes with contact.

You encourage children to ask questions when they are curious but adults sometimes become uneasy when those questions are about serious illness or disability.

Tips for practice

- It is not fair to make a curious child feel awkward with 'Ssh' or saying, 'It's rude to stare'. Adults often make these comments because they feel uncomfortable, but children are not necessarily being rude.
- You can redirect a blunt question or comment like, 'What's wrong with her?' or 'He's dribbling like a baby!'. Reply with a factual explanation like, 'Angelica is having trouble breathing, so she's using her inhaler' or 'David finds it hard to swallow; he's not a baby. He has cerebral palsy'.
- You can ask parents, or an older child themselves about ways they would prefer you to name and explain a condition. It is not true to say, 'David is just like you' when he clearly is not.
- Work on simple but honest explanations like, 'The part of David's brain that sends messages to his muscles doesn't work properly. That's why he finds it hard to move where he wants.'
- You will often find useful ideas for explanation in free leaflets from the relevant specialist organisation, many of which are listed in this chapter.

Activity (observation)

Young children are learning; they do not know everything and they may believe that a condition like eczema or epilepsy can be passed on by touch. After all, you probably take care to show children how to use a tissue and not cough or sneeze in people's faces because of germs. Children need to learn that some conditions can be caught and some absolutely cannot be passed on to other people.

Open a file and take your time in gathering any comments or actions from children that show how they think of or understand illness and disability. Children in your setting, who have a disability or continuing health condition, may also contribute spontaneous comments that give you an insight into how they are treated. Consider the range of examples and write up:

- What you have learned about how children think at this age. You can make some links to material in other chapters of this book.
- The possible applications to daily practice with children. How might you extend their understanding through conversation, information books and stories and imaginative use of materials like the Persona Dolls (see page 215).

Share your ideas with colleagues through a short presentation of what you have learned, with special attention to the insights provided by the children themselves. Look together for applications to your daily practice.

Key skills links: C3.3 C3.1b LP3.1–3 WO3.1–3

Books, stories and illustrations

Two kinds of books are valuable as you help children to learn. These are:

- information books about specific disabilities or health conditions
- stories that have disabled or sick children (or young people and adults) as main characters in the story.

Information books are a good source of straightforward information and illustrations. Possibilities include:

- Nigel Snell's books in the Events series, published by Hamish Hamilton.
- The One World series, published by Franklin Watts, with a long list of titles, each beginning with '*I have …*' and covering a wide range of disabilities and illness.
- Claire Llewellyn series '*The facts about …*', with the topics arthritis, asthma, diabetes and epilepsy, published by Belitha Press.
- Some books for older children can be read in episodes with children who cannot yet read the book themselves. For example, Helen Young's story about living with epilepsy *What Difference does it Make Danny?* published by Fontana Young Lions.
- If you are unsuccessful in finding a book about a particular condition, then try the relevant specialist organisation. For example, the Down's Syndrome Association has a list of books suitable for explaining the condition to young children. Or try some of the mail order firms listed on page 672.

You can use information books as part of an explanation to children and some you will find give a sound base of information to you. However, you also need books that offer a story in which disabled or sick children are simply getting on with lives, being happy, bored or mischievous. Some possibilities include:

- Emily Hearn's series about Franny who is in a wheelchair. Some titles are published by Magi and some by the Women's Press.
- Sue Brearley's *Adventure Holiday* (A & C Black).
- Berniece Rabe *Where's Chimpy* (Albert Whitman 1988) – a book in which the main character has Down's Syndrome.
- *Boots for a Bridesmaid* and *Are we there yet?* by Verna Wilkins in which the child's parent is disabled (Tamarind tel: 020 8866 8808).

Finding out more

You will find more ideas as well as reviews of books in Kathy Saunders (2000) *Happy ever Afters: A storybook guide to teaching children about disability* (Trentham Books). Kathy Saunders also offers some ideas about possible discussion that might follow a reading of the different story books to children.

Activity

Early years settings will have a wide range of illustrations in books or on your wall as well as the play materials. All children need to be able to see themselves in some of these illustrations, otherwise they are given the impression that they are effectively invisible. Look around your setting:

- Could disabled or sick children see themselves in any the illustrations or story books?
- If they can see children or adults like themselves, are they in everyday situations and not only specialist settings?
- Disabled children are certainly not always 'heroic' and 'brave'. Are there images of children who are happy, excited, serious, absorbed, perhaps sometimes sad or thoughtful and sometimes in a mess and up to mischief?
- Write up your findings.
- Share your impressions and ideas with colleagues. Explain any improvement you feel could be made to practice.

Key skills links: C3.3 LP3.1–3 WO3.1–3

Play materials and games

Disabled children do not all need specialist play materials or equipment and those who will benefit from additional play materials do not want these instead of everything else.

Figure 18.5

Materials designed originally for disabled children are inclusive play resources

A range of activities

A very great deal of ordinary play activities and equipment are completely suitable for disabled children.

- Some children may need some support to access materials, for instance to get a child's wheelchair or standing frame close enough.
- Children may need some guidance if they have learning disabilities and perhaps your awareness that they do not yet have the understanding about risk that their peers have gained.
- Otherwise disabled children enjoy painting, sand and water play, books and dressing up just as much as their peers.
- Some modifications are minor, like providing materials on tables of different heights suitable for children or having some materials on the floor rather than a table top. Many young children prefer to work on the floor.
- Quiet areas in the garden and sensory areas are enjoyable for all children.
- Visual props to a story help a child who needs different forms of communication but the use of puppets, large gestures and suitable props enhance the story for everyone.
- Flexible ball and throwing games can allow a physically disabled child to join in, perhaps because everyone sits on the floor, but this adjustment still includes the other children.

Many of the materials marketed for disabled children are truly inclusive. Soft play items or mats, soft construction pieces, large foam wedges and shapes and ball pools were developed for disabled children. But you will soon see that all the children enjoy these materials. Disabled children have a more enjoyable time when they can play with other children. It can be very boring to be restricted to 'special' equipment and older disabled children will be insulted if they are limited to play materials designed for younger children, perhaps on the grounds that these are safer or easier to handle.

Special programmes

Some children will have supportive programmes for their disability or health condition, for instance: speech therapy, physiotherapy and directed physical exercises or a graded learning programme. Some children in your setting may have an Individual Education Plan (see page 530). Special programmes need to be a happy part of the rest of a child's day and not feel like a chore or be something that restricts choice and interrupts their conversations with friends. It is a question of balance and keeping activities as enjoyable as possible with the companionship of the adult who is undertaking the special work.

Certainly disabled children will not benefit from an over-organised and serious day. They should never feel like the object of a special educational or physical programme. Children need enjoyable times, the company of other children and opportunities just to mess about without feeling oppressed by targets. If you use your observational skills, then you will be able to notice and write up as disabled children learn and practise, just as you can with any child.

Children who are ill or in hospital

This section covers the general issues in good practice with children and families when the child has chronic ill health or a condition that requires special attention or care. The facts and suggestions here will provide a sound basis for care and working in an inclusive way with children in your setting. It will then be your responsibility as an early years practitioner to seek further information and advice at such time as you work with an individual child who has any of these conditions.

Awareness of health needs

Disabled children may have related health needs that you need to understand, some of which have been mentioned within this chapter.

- Children with continuing health conditions may be especially vulnerable to infection. In partnership with their parents, you need to understand what kind of care and attention the children need.
- Such knowledge will help you to keep children as healthy as possible without over-protecting them and reducing their enjoyment of childhood.
- This balance can be difficult to maintain sometimes and regular communication with parents, colleagues and any other involved professionals is essential.
- It is equally important to listen to what the children themselves tell you about how they feel.

Medication

Some children may be on regular medication (see page 525). Some children may have medication or a health aid like an inhaler, that must be easily available in an emergency. A child's inhaler will be no use locked safely in a cupboard if she has an asthma attack at the other end of the building in a large primary school.

Physiotherapy

Some children may need regular physiotherapy to work their muscles. Children with cystic fibrosis need this help to keep their lungs clear. Your role may be to welcome a physiotherapist who visits the child in your setting. But often it is possible for early years practitioners, like parents, to learn the appropriate exercises for a child.

Vulnerable children

Some children may be generally prone to particular kinds of infection or you need to monitor their condition. Children with sickle cell anaemia can get very sick from ordinary infections and they need to be kept warm, especially in cold, damp weather. Children who have diabetes need a carefully balanced diet and regular meals. It will be their family who handles the need for insulin injections but you need to monitor food in a discreet way.

In partnership with parents you need to understand serious warning signs for this child as well as what to do in an emergency. What does a sickle cell crisis look like for Marlon? Is there any warning just before Angelica has an asthma attack or Tim fits? Under what circumstances should you call parents to the setting?

Time in hospital

Some children will have to spend time in hospital and this experience is not only unpleasant at the time but it disrupts a normal childhood. You can help in your setting when you have empathy for the child; try to understand the experience through her eyes.

- It is unpleasant to feel ill and some children are very sick indeed. Their medication and medical procedures may cause them further distress, discomfort or pain.
- Children stuck in hospital or ill at home can also become bored and fed up. Talk with parents and make contact with the hospital play staff where the child stays. Together you can promote continuity in a child's life and reassure him that he is not forgotten when he spends time elsewhere.

Activity

- Hospital play staff are invaluable in helping children to be more happily occupied and continue to learn. They are also experienced in using play to support children through unpleasant procedures or operations.
- Make contact with your nearest hospital and arrange to visit the play staff. Write up a brief report on what you learn covering:
  - The range of play activities and events that the play team use with children.
  - Different ways that they support children who are in bed and those able to move around.
  - What play techniques the team use to help children prepare for medical procedures or support them in anxieties about what will happen.
  - Appropriate ways that you can apply what you have learned in your own setting.

Key skills links: C3.3 LP3.1–3 WO3.1–3

- Being ill at home or repeated periods in hospital has a disruptive effect on children's friendships. It may be hard to make close friends in the first place or pick up where they left off before this bout of illness. An early years team can help, in partnership with parents, by organising continued contact between friends: messages and drawings, telephone calls and emails if possible.
- Illness interrupts the continuity of children's learning and their education when they start school. Again you can work with families to minimise the disruption as far as possible. Children who are extremely sick will have no energy left for play and learning activities. But there will be a point when they become bored but are not yet well enough to return to your setting. In partnership with parents, you could let the family know what projects are ongoing and the child may be able to do some exploration at home.

Finding out more

Action for Sick Children is a source of publications, information and advice for families whose children are spending time in hospital. Contact them at 300 Kingston Road, Wimbledon Chase, London SW20 8LX tel: 020 8542 4848 email: *enquiries@actionforsickchildren.org* website: *www.actionfor-sickchildren.org*

For information about the work of hospital play specialists send a large sae to the National Association of Hospital Play Staff, Fladgate, Forty Green, Beaconsfield, Buckinghamshire HP9 1XS or access the website: *www.nahps.org.uk*

Tips for practice

Children need emotional support as well as your attention to their physical care. They need to see themselves as children rather than through the lense of their illness and this perspective can be hard.

You can help in the following ways, all of which should be in partnership with the child's parent(s):

- Children may feel embarrassed about their symptoms or their need for special medication.
- Or they may not, of course, especially if their parents have managed to keep a positive outlook and enable their son or daughter to play and have as normal a childhood as possible.
- You can talk and play with the child with the aim of helping her to see herself as separate from her illness. This outlook is summed up by the attitude of, 'I'm Saima and I have diabetes' rather than 'I am a diabetic'.
- Give some thought to how you welcome and introduce a child to the group. Is the child's condition such that it would make sense to say something in advance?
- Consider what you tell and explain to the other children or whether you wait for their questions. Talk over with parents, and the child herself if possible, how they would like you to explain.

- Other children in the group will be curious and they are not being rude if they ask direct questions. Your approach needs to be honest and straightforward. You can show them by your behaviour how to ask questions politely and address them to the child herself.
- If they are given information and helped to look through another child's eyes, young children can be suitably matter of fact about another child with a continuing health condition or a disability.

Specific support for health and safety of children

Some children will need very specific support, either on a daily basis or in the event of an emergency. This section gives basic information for some conditions and in all cases you would need to talk with parents about their child, liase with other involved professionals and be ready to learn more as necessary.

Cystic fibrosis

Children with cystic fibrosis vary considerably: some can manage more physical exercise than others and some need intensive, daily physiotherapy. Cystic fibrosis disrupts digestion because it blocks the pancreatic gland whose task is to help absorb fats and starch. Consequently, these nutrients pass straight through a child's body and he or she can fail to thrive. Children need to take medication that substitutes for the pancreatic gland and some need careful monitoring of their diet.

Epileptic seizures

Parents should tell you if their child has seizures and how you should handle these. You need to know if there is any pattern to an individual child's seizure, including how long they usually last. What follows is very general advice.

Children do sometimes drift off in their mind and seem inattentive but you should share with a parent if your observations suggest that a child goes vague on a regular basis. It is possible that she is experiencing absence seizures. If the parent has also noticed this pattern or is willing to accept your concern, then the family should consult their GP.

If a child has a tonic clonic seizure, your calm support is crucial for her safety and the anxiety of the other children.

- You cannot stop a seizure or shorten it.
- Remain calm and loosen any tight clothing around a child's neck.
- Do not move a child unless her location puts her in danger, for instance, she has collapsed in the middle of a road.
- Ensure the child cannot hurt herself or others. Move objects out of her way or cover sharp edges with padding like a blanket.
- You can aid breathing by putting the child on her side if she has fallen. Definitely do not put your fingers in her mouth or try to force anything between her jaws.
- Stay with the child and keep her safe.
- When she has emerged from the seizure, make sure she is comfortable and keep her company.
- Children sometimes lose bladder or bowel control during a seizure and a child who is toilet trained may be distressed by the accident. Be sensitive

and help children to deal with the consequences when they are fully recovered.

- Call her parents to let them know what has happened and to come to take the child home.

There is no need to call a doctor or ambulance if the seizure follows the pattern that is normal for this child. It becomes an emergency if:

- this is the child's first seizure
- a tonic clonic seizure lasts more than about three minutes
- a child starts another seizure a few minutes after the first
- the child is badly injured during the seizure
- the child does not come properly awake after about fifteen minutes.

Asthma

Asthma is the most common chronic medical disorder of childhood. Some children have only mild attacks but such experiences can still be distressing for them.

You need a conversation with the child's parents to understand fully how asthma affects this child:

- What are the signs that he is about to have an asthma attack?
- The severity of symptoms vary but tend to include coughing or wheezing, increased difficulty in breathing, feeling that the chest is tight and loss of colour compared with how the child usually looks.
- Are there some circumstances that make an attack more likely? Some children are more at risk after physical exercise or at night.
- Some children have an allergic reaction to some foods which then brings on an asthma attack. Parents might explain that they have learned to keep eggs or chocolate out of their child's diet.

Asthma is not curable but medication can help children and adults to cope with the condition. An inhaler is used to send appropriate drugs directly into the lungs and these can be used as a preventative or to relieve the symptoms of an attack. If children need to take medication in a preventative way then you need to understand what they do, or you do for them, and when during the day.

Understand what you should you do if children have an asthma attack.

- The most useful adult behaviour will be to keep calm and reassure the child. The last thing a frightened child needs is an adult in a panic.
- Children will have an inhaler, but you will have to help a young child in their use. Ensure that parents have shown you what to do.
- Help a child to sit in the best position to breathe: this will be upright and probably leaning forward slightly. Lying down is less safe.
- Loosen any tight clothing.
- Stay close to the child but do not put an arm around her since this can feel constricting.
- Encourage the child to use her inhaler and to take slow and calm breaths.

If the attack is relatively minor then there may be no need to contact the child's parent, although you should of course say what happened when you hand over responsibility later. A child who has been worn out by a serious attack in an early years setting may be better at home, so you should then contact the parent(s).

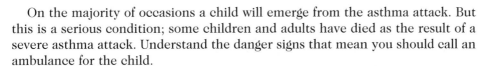

On the majority of occasions a child will emerge from the asthma attack. But this is a serious condition; some children and adults have died as the result of a severe asthma attack. Understand the danger signs that mean you should call an ambulance for the child.

- The inhaler should work in about 5–10 minutes. Call an ambulance if the inhaler does not seem to bring relief. Encourage the child to continue to use the inhaler while you wait for medical help.
- Get help if the child is very distressed or unable to talk, or is exhausted.

Sickle cell disease

Parents should tell you if their child has sickle cell anaemia and explain how you recognise the signs of a crisis in their child. Children will be more vulnerable to minor infections and fevers, so it is important that you tell the parents swiftly about any infection sweeping through your setting. It is, of course, important that children with sickle cell anaemia are enabled to play and be with their friends. However, they will need extra care to keep them warm and should probably avoid playing out in cold and damp weather. They need to drink plenty, since dehydration or vigorous exercise may trigger a crisis.

Tips for practice

Useful notes are very practical. For instance, the notes of Marlon who has sickle cell disease may remind the team that:

- Marlon needs to be given an indoor activity when the weather is cold or damp.
- He needs to be encouraged to drink, especially if he has been running about.
- It is crucial to call Mr or Mrs Gray immediately if Marlon complains of abdominal or chest pain, headache or stiffness in his neck and if he gets drowsy.

Activity

One

- In your setting, look at the personal notes of a child who has a specific health condition.
- In what ways do the records help his or her carers to attend to the special needs of this child?

Two

If possible, ask to be part of the home visit or first meeting with a family whose child will join your setting and who has a disability or health condition.

- With the permission of the parent, make notes of the questions that are helpful for practitioners to ask.
- What kinds of information do parents think it important to communicate?

- And what does the child want to add, if he or she is old enough to join the conversation?

Write up your work and share with colleagues, paying attention to confidentiality.

Key skills links: C3.3 LP3.1–3 WO3.1–3

Serious illness and bereavement

Some conditions are life threatening and you may experience the loss of a child who has attended your setting. You can of course experience bereavement as the result of an unexpected serious illness or a fatal accident involving a child.

As hard as you may find the experience, it is better to be honest with the other children in your setting. Children become upset and very confused when adults avoid talking about the death of someone familiar, or if adults actually lie.

- Tell the children what has happened and speak with them in a group at a quiet time. Explain simply and answer any questions they want to ask now or later.
- Children may need reassurance that all disabled children do not die and that children and adults can recover from serious illness or accidents.
- Share your sadness at the loss of a child and let children express their feelings if they wish.
- There is no need to tidy up everything belonging to or made by the child who has died. Why not leave her paintings on display until her parents would like them or be ready to look at the child in photographs on the display board.
- Look carefully for ways to support children to understand loss with books or puppet play as well as supported conversation.
- See if the children would like to send a message in words or pictures to the child's family.

Activity

Your own emotions are involved in the loss of a child whom you know. It can be hard to think straight at the time along with what you will feel and supporting the other children in your group. Take the opportunity to build a resource of material now. You can gather together within one folder:

- Useful addresses and contact details. This chapter will give you a good start.
- Informative books or leaflets for adults who are supporting children as well as dealing with their own sense of loss.
- Books specifically for children about serious illness, the death of a friend or relative.

Prepare a short presentation that you can give to colleagues or fellow students. What are the main good practice themes for a caring and honest approach to children?

Key skills links: C3.3 C3.1b

Activity

Find out more to support your work with children and families under times of distress or bereavement. You can contact these organisations.

1 ACT, Orchard House, Orchard Lane, Bristol BS1 5DT tel: 0117 922 1556 email: *info@ act.org.uk* website: *www.act.org.uk* (ACT stands for Association for Children with Life-threatening or Terminal Conditions and their families.)

2 Cruse Bereavement Care, 126 Sheen Road, Richmond, Surrey TW9 1UR tel: 020 8940 4818 (general), helpline 0870 167 1677 website: *www.crusebereavementcare.org.uk*

- Use the website first and organise your questions or requests.
- Write up your findings and present to colleagues, with the aim of identifying how you can all learn and improve practice in this sensitive area.

Key skills links: IT3.1–3

Further resources

Dickins, Mary and Denziloe, Judy (1998) *All Together: How to create inclusive services for disabled children and their families* National Early Years Network.

Drifte, Collette (2001) *Special Needs in Early Years Settings: A guide for practitioners* David Fulton Publishers.

Jeffree, Dorothy and Cheseldine, Sally (1984) *Let's Join In* Souvenir Press.

Jeffree, Dorothy and McConkey, Roy (1993) *Let Me Play* Souvenir Press.

Lansdown, Richard (1996) *Children in Hospital: A guide for families and carers* Oxford University Press.

Lindon, Jennie (1998) *Equal Opportunities in Practice* Hodder and Stoughton.

Mason, Micheline (1993) *Inclusion, the Way Forward: A guide to integration for young disabled children* National Early Years Network.

Finding out more

It would be unrealistic for you to aim to know about every possible health condition or disability that you might encounter within your entire career. Furthermore, new research as well as reviews of practice can often mean that the information and advice of ten or even five years ago is overtaken.

You cannot know everything, but you should understand how to find out about a health condition or disability when you need this information, for yourself or to support a parent. There are several ways to be a good detective in your role as an early years practitioner:

- You have the details of many organisations given in this chapter. There are many more since there is a support and information organisation for just about every health condition or disability, even those that are rare.

- Open a file and keep carefully any information that you gain from advice lines, leaflets or that you download from websites.
- If you have a specific search, then some of the more general organisations working in the area of disability and continuing health conditions may be able to direct your search. Some examples follow.

Action for Sick Children, 300 Kingston Road, Wimbledon Chase, London SW20 8LX tel: 020 8542 4848 email: *enquiries@actionforsickchildren.org* website: *www.actionforsickchildren.org*

British Institute of Learning Disabilities, Wolverhampton Road (no number is needed), Kidderminster, Worcestershire DY10 3PP website: *www.bild.org.uk*

Council for Disabled Children, 8 Wakley Street, London EC1V 7QE tel: 020 7843 6061 email: *cdc@ncb.org.uk* website: *www.ncb.org.uk/cdc.htm*

MENCAP, 123 Golden Lane, London EC1Y 0RT tel: 020 7454 0454 or 020 7696 5593/5584 (information department) email: *info@mencap.org.uk* website: *www.mencap.org.uk* Mencap have copies of inventories of information and can direct your search in useful directions. For instance they hold the Contact-a-Family material and may be able to identify a support group for even rare syndromes.

These organisations are committed to promoting enjoyable play and leisure for disabled children and young people.

Action for Leisure, c/o Warwickshire College, Moreton Morrell Centre, Moreton Morrell, Warwickshire CV32 9BL tel: 01926 650195 email: *john@actionforleisure.org.uk* website: *www.actionforleisure.org.uk*

Kidsactive has a focus on adventure play: Pryor's Bank, Bishop's Park, London SW6 3LA tel: 020 7731 1435 email: *KTIS@kidsactive.org.uk* website: *www.kidsactive.org.uk*

Progress check

1. Give one example each of a physical disability, a learning disability, a condition that would affect a child's social interaction and a continuing health condition.
2. Explain three broad causes of disability in early childhood.
3. Give three reasons for the importance of partnership with parents of a child with a disability.
4. Explain briefly the advantages of an inclusive approach for children with a disability and for their fully-abled peers.
5. Suggest three general ways in which you could support a child who has difficulties in social interaction and play with peers.
6. Describe three ways in which fully-abled children can support and understand peers who are disabled.
7. Suggest three ways in which early years practitioners can be supportive of children who spend time in hospital.

19

Child protection in the early years

After reading this chapter you should be able to:

- understand what is meant by child protection and the legal requirements that underpin good practice
- explain and follow an appropriate role in child protection for an early years practitioner
- recognise signs in children's development or behaviour that should concern you and could indicate possible abuse
- offer appropriate support to children and families.

Introduction

This chapter covers the details of what you need to know in order to fulfil your role as an early years practitioner supporting child protection. You will find an explanation of the child protection system as a whole and the legislation that underpins it. Your role is to work with other professionals within the local child protection network, understanding your valuable contribution and understanding the role of others. A section then explains how you need to be aware of different types of abuse and what could be possible signs that a child is at risk from or is experiencing abusive treatment. The final section of the chapter explains how you can support children and families within your role.

Links to early years qualifications

This chapter especially supports the following units:

Diploma in Child Care and Education: 9, 10, 11

National Vocational Qualification in Early Years Care and Education

Level 2: E2

Level 3: C15, P2, M6

BTEC National Early Years Diploma: 4

Understanding child protection

The current approach to child protection in the UK has developed over several decades and has several equally important strands. The following points have been established.

- Legislation and guidance for good practice is required because children need to be protected; child abuse is more than a few isolated incidents.
- Children could be abused, and fail to be protected, in different ways: through physical abuse, neglect of their care and well being, emotional abuse and sexual abuse.
- Adults, parents or other carers, are responsible and can be held accountable for how they treat children and young people. There are limits to family privacy or professional judgement about what is an appropriate way to treat children.

Key term

Child abuse
a pattern of ill-treatment of a child or persistent failure to provide appropriate protection and care for children

In broad terms, **child abuse** means:

- Doing something to a child that should not be done, actions that will injure them physically, distress them deeply emotionally or seriously disrupt their natural development.
- Failing as a responsible adult to do something for a child that should be done, for the sake of the child's well being, safety or continued positive development.

Who are the abusers?

Legislation and guidance is needed because children are most likely to be abused by people who are well known to them.

What about strangers?

Key term

Child protection
preventative systems and direct action to ensure the well being of children and young people and to take direct action to ensure their future health and development

The idea that 'stranger danger' is a major issue in **child protection** has arisen from media attention to a very small number of cases of child abduction.

Sarah Payne was abducted in July 2000 and her murderer convicted in December 2001. Both events had massive media coverage and there is no doubt that her family deserve heartfelt sympathy for their loss. But families as a whole are not helped by the media message that predatory strangers are on the increase and pose the greatest threat to children's well being. Between June and November 2000 about 50 children in the UK were murdered or died under suspicious circumstances, mainly involving their family or close circle. Few of those children gained more than a brief mention in the media, perhaps only in their local newspapers.

The number of children killed deliberately by total strangers in the UK has rarely risen above double figures (10) annually over the last couple of decades. The vast majority of strangers who kill or seriously injure children are driving a vehicle. Children are most likely to be deliberately hurt, and can only be neglected, by adults or young people who are family, friends or in a position of trust and professional responsibility for a child.

Abusers come from all parts of society

You need to be fully aware that women abuse children as much as men do. Some discussion of child protection has suggested that men are more likely abusers, but this is wrong and unjust. The only exception has been that sexual abuse of children has more often been perpetrated by men. However, women have also been known to abuse children sexually. Women are as likely as men to perpetrate other forms of abuse and neglect. So, any assumption that children will be fully protected by restricting their contact with men is sadly misplaced (see page 599).

The more likely abuser is an adult, but young people (under 18s) have abused children who are known to them or for whom they are temporarily responsible. Actions between children, that would be viewed as abusive if done by an adult, will be handled through behaviour and anti-bullying policies in a school or early years setting.

A greater awareness of child abuse has demonstrated that individual abusers can be found in every social class, ethnic, cultural and religious groups. As well as relatives or friends, child abusers have been identified in professions who have contact with children, such as youth workers, social workers in residential homes, day care and educational staff, clergy and other religious leaders from different faiths and people who coach children in sports activities.

Activity

Everyone has some assumptions about abuse of children, likely abusers and abusive situations. Unless you air and discuss these beliefs, they cannot be checked and challenged.

Consider the following statements, either on your own, or preferably with colleagues. For each statement, please think and talk around:

- Is this statement true or false – can you really say either way?
- How do you think this idea has arisen? What could make people convinced it is true (or perhaps untrue)?

1. Child neglect happens in inner city areas with lots of problems; you wouldn't find it in a nice neighbourhood like ours.
2. Lone parents are more likely to abuse their children; two parent families don't have the same level of stress.
3. Men shouldn't work with young children; it's right to be suspicious of anyone who wants to do that kind of job.
4. You can be confident about people with religious faith, like nuns or priests; they couldn't abuse children.
5. Disabled children are safe; nobody would ever be so cruel as to abuse them.
6. Bullying has always been part of children's lives; they just have to learn to live with it. Children are naturally cruel to each other.
7. Sexual abuse doesn't hurt children; it's not like being beaten up.
8. You really have to go with what the adults say. Children can't tell the difference between facts and fantasy and they tell lies very easily.
9. A mother would always know when her child is being abused by her own partner.
10. Abused children would certainly want to leave their family. So if they want to stay, then they can't be abused, can they?

Key skills links: C3.1a

To think about

Assumptions and beliefs about child abuse are built by what you hear locally or on television and read in the newspapers.

- In the nature of 'news', you will hear about less likely events and what is considered newsworthy.
- So stranger danger gets more coverage than children hurt by people they know.
- Child protection cases that go badly wrong get more coverage than the successful work of protecting children. Of course, successful child protection remains confidential, whereas seriously bad practice becomes public.

How common is child abuse?

It is important that you keep child abuse in proportion. Good practice is that you should be aware and understand your role in the local child protection system. However, most children are not abused.

One way of getting a sense of proportion is to look at the numbers of children who are on the child protection register. Now, not all children who are at risk of abuse will be on the register (see page 557) if it is judged that family support will protect children and improve the situation. Over the year 1999–2000 there were 30,300 children on the child protection register in England. This figure represents 0.27 per cent of the child population younger than 18 years of age. The proportions are similar for Scotland, Wales and Northern Ireland, whose total child populations are lower.

Legislation to protect children

During the 1990s new legislation was passed in the UK to provide a more effective framework for the care and protection of children. The relevant laws are:

- the Children Act 1989; applies to England and Wales
- the Children (Scotland) Act 1995
- the Children (Northern Ireland) Order 1996.

Each of these laws are primary legislation (see page 26) so they do not explain how child protection works in daily practice. The laws are supported by guidance issued by national government departments. Local area child protection committees, who bring together key professionals, are expected to draft specific local guidance documents.

These laws have similar content and guiding principles (see page 27), but they operate within the different national systems of law and social services. Child protection procedures are very similar across the UK, including the key role of social workers, the use of case conferences and the operation of the child protection register. All countries in the UK also have a system of police checks on anyone who applies to work with children and a register of named people whose behaviour has made them unsuitable to be in close contact with children.

Activity

The local child protection guidelines are a public document and you should know what they look like. Your options are:

- If you are currently working in an early years setting or on placement, then ask if the setting has a copy.
- Otherwise contact your local Early Years Development and Childcare Partnership, or the Pre-School Advisory Group if you work in Northern Ireland, and enlist their help to find the local guidelines.
- Take a good look through the guidelines so that you get a sense of what is covered.
- To what extent are early years settings are mentioned? Some local guidelines are better than others at recognising the importance of early years practitioners in a fully rounded approach to child protection.
- Make notes and present to your colleagues.

Key skills links: C3.2 C3.1b C3.3

Child protection procedures

Figure 19.1 outlines the necessary pattern of steps in child protection in the UK. The exact detail of your local procedures may look slightly different but the process has been laid down in the legislation.

Step 1: Initial concern and referral

The child protection process is started when someone expresses concern about the welfare and well being of a child. This concern may be raised by a professional, including an early years practitioner like yourself, by a relative or neighbour or because a social worker is already involved with the family.

A concern that raises possible child abuse might be made by contacting the local social services department, the police child protection unit or the local NSPCC. You need to be clear as an early years practitioner to whom you should first speak in your setting (see page 560).

Step 2: Initial inquiries and strategy

The aim in child protection is that concerns are checked carefully and that any action is sufficient but not excessive. Despite the fears of some parents and practitioners, the first step in child protection is rarely to take children away from their family.

The strategy meeting involves professionals who know the family and the group weighs up the information to decide whether to go further in the child protection process. There are three main possibilities at this stage:

1. On the basis of the information available, it is decided that there are no child protection concerns. It may be suggested that the family would benefit from support and this option can be taken at any point (see Figure 19.1).
2. There are child protection concerns and detailed plans are made for an investigation and assessment of the child and family.
3. The child or children in a family are judged to be at serious risk and emergency legal steps will be taken to protect them.

Step 1
Concern about a child
Does this raise possible abuse?
YES NO → Other work with child or family
↓
Referral to social services, NSPCC or police child protection unit
↓
Step 2
Initial inquiries and strategy meeting
Is there possible abuse?
YES NO → Other services for child or family
↓
Is the child at risk of immediate and significant harm?
YES NO
↓
Emergency action
↓
Plan for investigation
↓
Step 3
Investigation and assessment
↓
Step 4
The child protection conference
Place the child's name on the child protection register?
YES NO → Further work with child and family
↓
Form a core group
Name the key worker
↓
Step 5
Meetings of the core group
Develop an individual child protection plan
Implement the plan
Comprehensive assessment of child and family
↓
Step 6
Child protection reviews
Should the child remain on the register?
YES NO → Further work with child and family
↓
Continued protection work with child and family

Note: This chart is modified from the one in Lindon *Child Protection and Early Years Work*, Hodder and Stoughton, 1998.

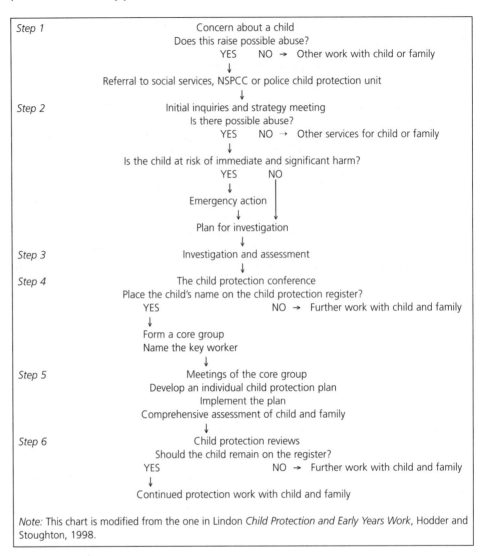

Figure 19.1 Steps in the process of child protection

The police are concerned with evidence and possible prosecution, so their role is different from other professionals. The police cease to be involved in a child protection case for two reasons.

- There is no crime involved, for instance emotional abuse, however severe, is not a crime.
- There is insufficient evidence to ensure prosecution.

It is important to understand that considerable work can be done in child protection without there being any possibility of prosecuting an alleged abuser.

Step 3: Investigation and assessment

A full investigation is now undertaken to gather all the facts of the situation and to identify whether there are grounds to consider that the child is likely to suffer significant harm and from what sources.

Good practice is that any investigation must be child-centred and any interviews or examinations undertaken with the child's feelings to the fore. Parents also have to be involved and informed, although if parents are uncooperative it is possible to take action to insist on an assessment of the child.

Step 4: The child protection conference

This conference is led by a social worker and brings together any professionals with relevant information to share and the family itself. As an involved early years practitioner your information and observations could be valuable at this point.

The point of the conference is to decide whether to place the child's name on the local child protection register. Children can only be placed on the register if the evidence shows that the child has been abused, or there is good reason to suppose the child has been at risk of abuse, and the risk still exists. When a child's name is added to the register, then the risk to them must be categorised under one, or more, of the four types: neglect, physical abuse, sexual abuse or emotional abuse.

After the child's name is placed on the register, then a core group must be formed and a key worker identified. A child protection plan must be developed specifically for this child and a more detailed assessment will now be organised. Part of the plan then has to be decisions about how to protect the child and support the family.

Step 5: Meetings of the core group

The core group will meet regularly to bring together a small number of professionals directly involved with the family. The parents should also be involved.

The core group has to ensure that the child protection plan, including any developmental or medical assessment of the child, is now undertaken.

Step 6: Reviews

Children do not just remain on the child protection register for ever. Every six months there must be a review, the aim of which is to assess whether the child's name should remain on the register.

If the review decides that the child's name will be taken off the register, work can continue with the child and family, involving whichever professionals are appropriate. The child and family may still need help, but the child is judged no longer to be at risk.

The role of early years practitioners

You need to understand the bigger picture of how the child protection system works as a whole, in order to grasp your role as an early years practitioner.

The importance of early years practitioners

Early years settings can have a very important part to play in child protection:

- You see children on a regular basis and your setting will keep records that help you to track progress but also any significant changes in a child.
- You get to know the children as individuals and you develop a friendly working relationship with the child's parent(s) and sometimes also other members of the family.
- Your growing experience and knowledge of child development will help you to make sense of a child's communication, play and general behaviour.

Of course, your role is within a broader network of child protection and it is other professionals, notably social workers, who would lead any child protection investigation. But never underestimate the potential importance of your contribution.

Child protection is supported by your skills

It may at first seem daunting to contemplate your role within child protection. It is a serious matter, but your contribution is fully supported by all the other skills you learn and your knowledge as an early years practitioner.

The good practice you learn and continue to develop in all the other aspects of your work are precisely what is needed to support your role in child protection. These related skill areas include the following.

- Good general practice in communication with children, a habit of attentiveness to their interests and concerns (see page 305).
- A respectful approach to the care needs of young children and disabled children who continue to need this support (see page 45).
- Good communication between the adults, within the team in an early years setting (see page 600).
- Descriptive written records of all children that can track progress and changes in behaviour, combined with your skills of observation, both informal and more structured (see page 461).
- Your skills of observation are important because child abuse often shows up in patterns of a child's experiences, behaviour or injuries. Some single events can be very significant, but patterns are more often what catch your attention and arouse concern.
- Partnership with parents that establishes as far as possible a friendly working relationship that can make raising the tougher issues possible (see page 621).
- A willingness to make links with other local professionals, understanding what they do and how their work relates to your own, but retaining self respect for your own professional skills (see page 612).

Tips for practice

You will continue to learn and extend your skills relating to child protection. Part of your developing good practice is to put to one side any misleading or unrealistic assumptions about abuse or abusers.

- There are no simple predictions about who is likely or unlikely to abuse children.
- Some parents in 'nice' homes and 'nice' areas sometimes attack or neglect their children. Some parents in 'rough' estates and under serious stress still manage to take very good care of their children.
- Most abusers are *not* men any more than most men are abusers. It is an unjust assumption that a male practitioner, or a father as primary carer, should be more carefully watched. Such an approach could also put children at risk if practitioners refuse to believe that a female practitioner or mother could abuse.

Clear policy and procedures

All early years settings should have a clear policy on child protection that explains what you should do if you are concerned. Figure 19.1 offers some guidance of the general steps and you would need to discuss appropriate action with your manager.

In the same ways as any other policy and set of procedures, the guidance on child protection in your setting should be drafted so that it is easily consulted by all the team. Your policy and the obligations of the setting should also be communicated in a courteous way to parents when they join the setting. The procedures should be seen to work both ways: that parents can express concerns to you about their child's experience in your setting as well as your awareness of their child's continued well being.

The child protection procedures in your early years or school setting should lay out clearly:

- The responsibility of all the team to protect children through their own good practice and early response to any concerns.
- The importance of consulting within the team, especially with your senior. Nobody, however experienced, should act on their own in child protection.
- The importance of speaking with parents (see page 579). There would have to be very compelling reasons not to talk with parents if you have a concern.
- The ways in which an early years practitioner might be involved and contribute to a child protection investigation and how you will be supported by the team in this work.
- Good practice in supporting a child, and parent, who is involved in the child protection process.
- The duties of the setting for child protection, including the professional balance between confidentiality and the obligation to pass on concerns.
- Clear guidance with details of who should be consulted locally when you have a child protection concern (names and contact details).
- A child protection policy should also cover how you ensure appropriate security in your setting and checks on new staff and volunteers.
- There should also be clear procedures for dealing with concerns about team members, expressed by parents or colleagues.

Procedures can support your work in child protection but there are no simple answers in this area of work. Even experienced professionals in child protection still have to make careful judgements and weigh up the information. A very experienced social worker will not know the child as well as you do and will need the input of the setting and your knowledge of child development and behaviour.

Activity

- Ask to read the child protection policy and procedures of your setting.
- Take some of the practical points raised in this section. Can you follow how you would be expected to behave in your setting? Note down any questions and discuss uncertain areas with your senior.
- Share what you have learned with your colleagues in a student group, including any significant differences between the procedures you have read for different individual settings or types of early years setting.

Key skills links: C3.1a

Ways you may be involved in child protection

Early years practitioners have an important role in child protection.

- You or your colleagues might be the first to raise concerns about a child through awareness of the normal range of development and behaviour.
- A child, parent or other carer might disclose to you information relevant to child protection.
- You might be contacted by a social worker because concerns have been raised elsewhere about a child for whom you are responsible.
- You will contribute valuable observations but no early years practitioner, however senior, will undertake an investigation, that is the social worker's role.
- When a child is on the local child protection register then your setting may be asked to monitor this child's attendance and development.
- A child's key worker could present reports at a case conference or later review of the case.
- Support work with the child in an early years setting may be part of the child protection plan. Unless you have additional experience, your support of the child would be through the daily opportunities of play and friendly communication.

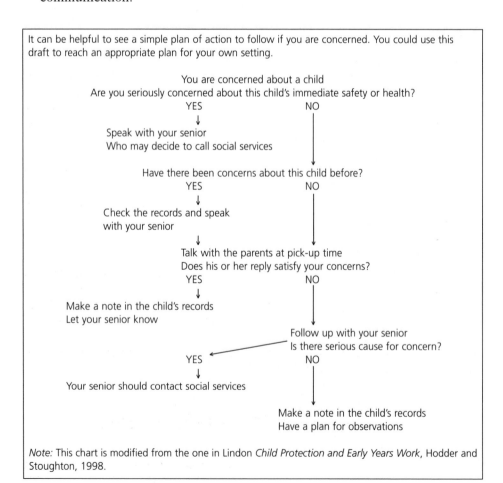

It can be helpful to see a simple plan of action to follow if you are concerned. You could use this draft to reach an appropriate plan for your own setting.

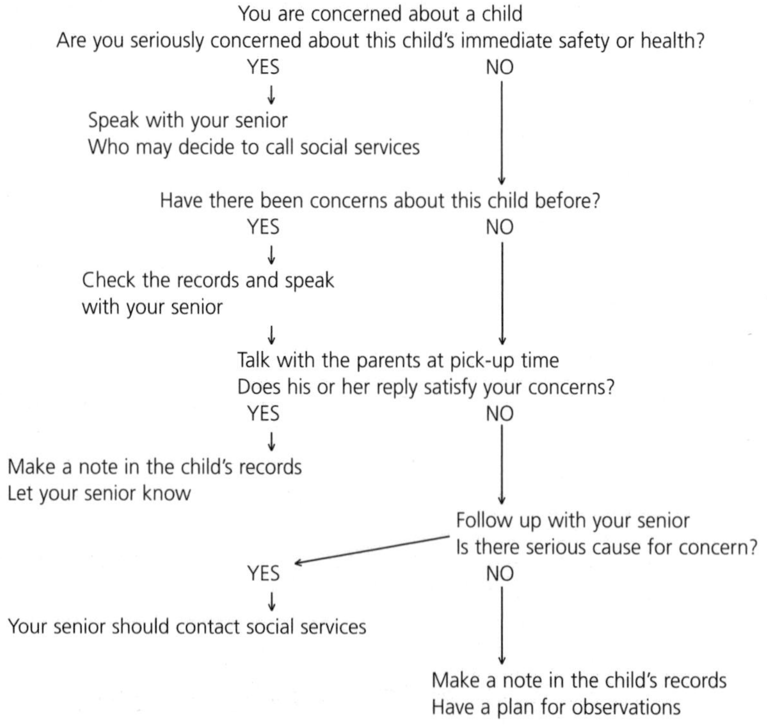
You are concerned about a child
Are you seriously concerned about this child's immediate safety or health?
YES
NO
Speak with your senior
Who may decide to call social services
Have there been concerns about this child before?
YES
NO
Check the records and speak
with your senior
Talk with the parents at pick-up time
Does his or her reply satisfy your concerns?
YES
NO
Make a note in the child's records
Let your senior know
Follow up with your senior
Is there serious cause for concern?
YES
NO
Your senior should contact social services
Make a note in the child's records
Have a plan for observations

Note: This chart is modified from the one in Lindon *Child Protection and Early Years Work*, Hodder and Stoughton, 1998.

Figure 19.2 Possible procedure map for an early years setting

When you work on your own

Working as a nanny

Many early years practitioners spend some part of their career working with families as a nanny. Without a doubt, you are in a different position regarding child protection if you work on your own. You will not have colleagues or a senior with whom to discuss your concerns. Unless you are very certain of professional confidentiality, it will not be appropriate to talk with another nanny, a friend or your partner.

Obviously much will depend on the nature of your concerns:

- In the same way as you would in an early years setting, you need to draw on your skills as a practitioner. Observe the child or children and make sense of what you see and hear against normal range child development.
- It may feel easier to raise the issue with the parent(s), if your concerns are aroused about someone outside the family, perhaps a neighbour or the person who runs the gym club to which you take the children.
- If your concerns are about immediate members of the family, you may want to talk first with an uninvolved professional. Try your local early years department (different areas use varied names) or look for a local NSPCC helpline. Some duty social workers may be willing to have a conversation to help; it will depend a lot on their work load.
- Your responsibility for the children will mean that talking with the parent(s) will become essential soon. Look at page 579 for some of the opening remarks that are suggested.

Much will then depend on the parent's reaction. So try not to anticipate what this may be, at the time or after he or she has had chance to reflect. When parents are able to place their child's welfare to the fore, they may be able to deal with the fact that you brought the situation to their notice. Your supportive relationship may offer very welcome support, if you are relating to the non-abusing parent or relative in a family abuse case, or if the abuser came from outside the family.

Unfortunately, it is very possible that your job will become untenable, if the parent cannot emotionally divide you from what you have had to reveal. If you have to leave your job and you are convinced the child protection concerns have not been resolved, then you should make contact with your local child protection system (see page 560).

Working as a childminder

If you run a business as a childminder, in your own home, you will work alone a great deal but you will have some connections with the local authority through the process of becoming a childminder. Your first step would still usually be to talk with a child's parents. However, if you are uncertain or very uneasy then you can contact the local early years department or local NSPCC helpline in the same way as suggested for nannies. If you are part of a childminding network then you can contact your network coordinator.

Causes for concern about children

You need to build your experience to recognise signs in children's development or behaviour that should concern you and could indicate possible abuse. This section explains the different kinds of child abuse and the possible signs.

There are four broad types of abusive experience for children and these have to be reflected in all local child protection systems:

- physical abuse
- neglect
- emotional abuse
- sexual abuse.

Tips for practice

- You will sometimes see brief checklists that claim to list the warning signs of child abuse.
- Such checklists are unhelpful since there are too many 'if's' and 'maybe's' in the identification and assessment of child abuse.
- Many signs should concern you, but there are few that on their own would firmly point towards abuse.
- Any professional, however experienced in the child protection field, needs to draw on a sound knowledge of child development as well as gathering information about this individual child and family.

General signs that should concern you

Your awareness in relation to child protection should be an extension of your normal, good practice alertness to children: their communication, well being, overall health and behaviour. You do not need to develop a whole new skill area of observing for signs of abuse.

Your skills of observation and communication and your knowledge of child development are the very best foundation. Sometimes, you will observe children and be right to feel concern. A small amount of checking will reassure you, and your head of centre, that child protection is not an issue, but the child and family may need and appreciate help in other ways.

Situations that you should never ignore include the following:

- Unlikely accidents or patterns of injury – unlikely given the age, understanding and ability of the child.
- Unexplained developmental delay or regression in a child's skills or behaviour. Children may be distressed by events, but are not necessarily being abused.
- Unexplained and persistent illness or faltering growth in children (see page 569).
- Normally friendly children who seem very resistant to spending time with a particular adult, either in the setting or when someone in particular collects them at the end of the day or session.
- Behaviour patterns that are unusual for this age of child. Of course you can only make sense of such observations from a basis of knowledge of child development and the usual variations.
- Physical self-harm by children, persistent negative remarks about themselves or obsessive rituals such as hand washing.
- Children who are persistently cruel to animals. Younger children need to understand that animals can be hurt and they learn to be kind. Children who are abused may take out their pain and frustration in ill-treatment of vulnerable animals.

Children will sometimes communicate, by words and actions, that they are distressed, frightened or have come to believe that certain experiences are normal when an outside would judge them to be abusive. Disclosure by children of an abusive experience is covered on page 576.

To think about

- Warning signs are *not* a two-way street and some simple checklists are seriously misleading (hence no lists in this chapter!).
- For instance, some children who have been physically abused are enmeshed in family secrecy and are reluctant to remove layers of clothing. Yet, such reluctance to undress should never be seen as likely 'evidence' of abuse.
- Experience with children will give several alternative reasons, for instance that the child has eczema and is self conscious about his skin or that a young girl is from a family whose religious beliefs value modesty.
- In a similar way, bed wetting is sometimes on brief lists of signs of abuse. Children who are abused do sometimes respond by regressing in development, including bed wetting. But most children who wet the bed either have continued problems getting dry at night, or are reacting to emotional distress, but not abuse.

Physical abuse of children

Physical abuse is defined as the actual or likely physical injury to a child. Children can be physically abused through direct attack from their carer. However, it is also regarded as physical abuse when a child is put in danger or injured as a result of an adult's deliberate failure to protect them from injury or suffering. Concerned adults would make sense of an incident in the light of an individual child's age, understanding and any disabilities.

Children have been physically ill treated in different ways. Hearing or reading about what some carers do to children can be distressing.

- It is regarded as physical abuse if adults attack children physically. Children have been hit, kicked, shoved or shaken hard. (See page 511 for the legal situation in the UK about hitting children.)
- Sometimes children fall, or are pushed, and sustain even greater damage as a result.
- Children have been bitten and deliberately burned or scalded.
- It is dangerous to shake any child, but babies are especially at risk because they have limited muscle control and a relatively heavy head compared with their body (see Figure 19.3).
- Sometimes children are not directly attacked but are deliberately poisoned with common household substances, alcohol, drugs or inappropriate medicines.

Key term

Physical abuse non-accidental physical injury to a child or young person, caused either by direct attack or irresponsible actions highly likely to put a child in danger of injury

Signs that should concern you

The most likely warning signs of physical abuse are:

- injuries such as bruises, marks, scrapes and abrasions, especially when they appear on a regular basis or children are injured on a part of their body where it is less likely for someone to sustain an accidental injury

Figure 19.3

It is dangerous to shake babies

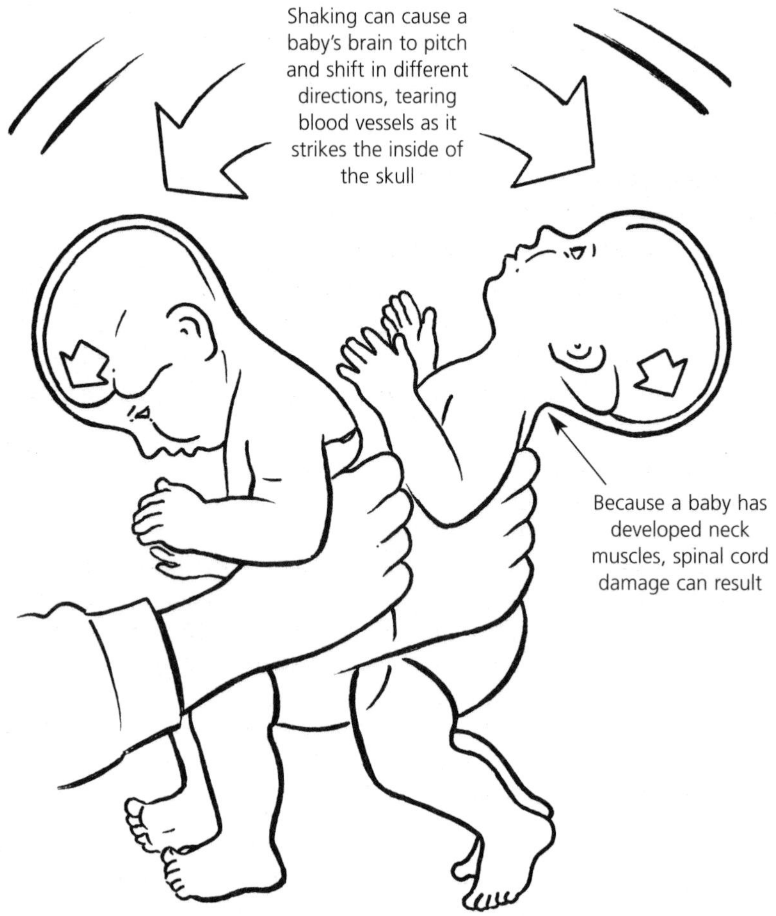
Shaking can cause a baby's brain to pitch and shift in different directions, tearing blood vessels as it strikes the inside of the skull
Because a baby has developed neck muscles, spinal cord damage can result

- when children continue to have perplexing illnesses or symptoms of illness
- a continuing pattern of accidents to a child for which the responsible adult(s) give no believable explanation.

Generally speaking, patterns are more concerning than single events. But your role as an early years practitioner will be to ask about unexplained bruises or illness, as indeed you should respond positively if parents ask you similar questions.

Scenario

The team at St Jude's Primary School recently had a day workshop on child protection led by a social worker and police officer. Some of the teachers came away with the strong impression that, if they suspected abuse, then their first step should be to call social services rather than speak with the parents.

But members of the team who work in the nursery and after school club are deeply uneasy about any guideline that cuts out communication with parents. Pam who works in both the nursery and the after school club describes several recent examples where children experienced minor injuries in play that were definitely accidental. One child had not mentioned to staff that she had fallen off the bike and her father came in the next day to say, 'Becky's got this dramatic bruise. What happened?'

Pam comments, 'How would we have felt if Becky's Dad had phoned social services rather than talking with us?'

Questions

1 Any setting or individual practitioner needs to be wary of procedures that you would find disrespectful if turned on you and your colleagues.

2 Check on the details of procedures in your setting.

3 Discuss with your colleagues why it may seem easier to practitioners to avoid talking with parents. What could be the consequences of going straight to social services?

4 You can also look at page 579 for ideas about talking with parents.

Key skills links: C3.a

In the case of possible physical abuse, the key question is often 'was this an accident?' It will not be your role to make a final assessment of whether an injury was genuinely an accident. Yet, your knowledge of the individual child, and of children in general, will be valuable to ensure that a real accident and normal bumps and scrapes are not turned inappropriately into a child protection investigation. Equally so, you need to ensure that neither you, nor other members of your early years team, are too accepting of a string of unlikely explanations from a parent, nor for that matter from a colleague or volunteer in the setting.

Activity

Patterns of accidental and non-accidental injury are not always easy to predict.

- With a group of colleagues, look at the front and back body outline that is given in Figure 19.6 on page 583. Copy this or draw similar outlines on a large sheet of paper.
- Now mark up the sites of accidental injuries you have known, either because you injured yourself in that way during your own childhood or because you observed an accident with a child. Maintain confidentiality about the details of any accident involving a child other than yourself.
- Look at the patterns that have emerged. It is very likely that many sites of accidental injury will be the more predictable places. However, in a group you will have reliable anecdotes that illustrate how a child manages to sustain accidental injury in unlikely sites.
- Discuss how this activity emphasises the importance of observation and avoiding assumptions or neat lists.

Key skills links: C3.1a

A consideration of possible physical abuse has to be *both* the visible injury to the child *and* the explanation, from adult and/or the child, of how this injury was caused. A regular pattern of accidents, even if each had a credible explanation, should make you wonder if this child is being adequately supervised.

Figure 19.4

Sites of more likely accidental injury to a child

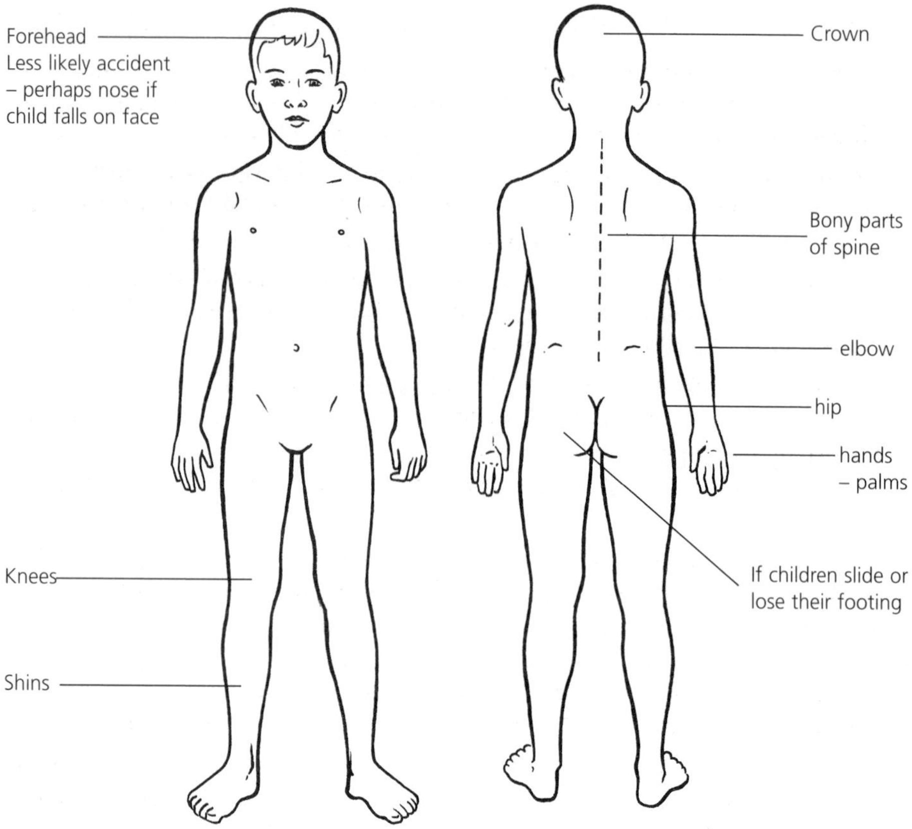

Figure 19.5

Sites of more likely non-accidental injury to a child

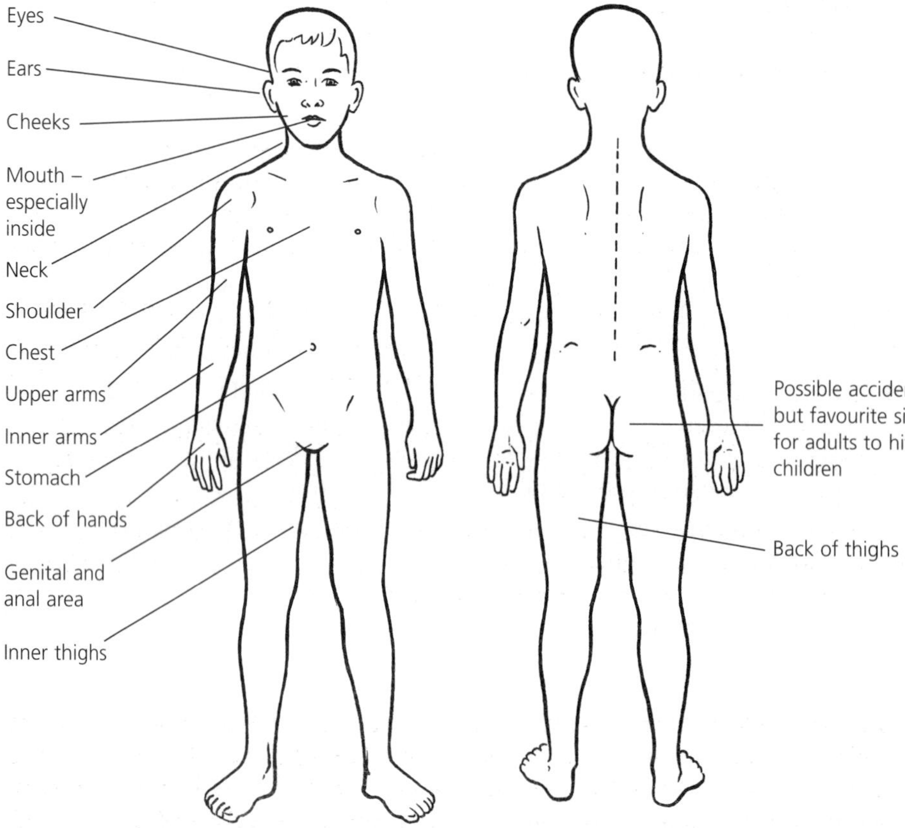

Important note:
These diagrams are only a guide, not a definite prediction about injury. Always consider your knowledge of the child, age, ability or disability as well as the pattern of any accidents over a period of time.

Here are some basic guidelines to likely accidental and non-accidental injury:

- Accidents that occur during normal play or boisterous activities tend to lead to a small number of bruises to the bony parts of children's bodies, such as elbows and knees, because they stick out and are likely to be hit in a fall.
- Children usually, although not always, fall forwards so are likely to hit themselves on the forehead or other parts of the front of the body. They may also injure their hands as they automatically put them out to break their fall.
- Bruising to the softer and less accessible parts of a child's body, such as upper arms, thighs and cheeks, are more likely to result from deliberate pinching, biting or beating children.
- Some areas of the body, such as the genital or anal area or under the arm, are very unlikely (although not completely impossible) places for a child to damage by accident.
- Children, especially babies, do not usually manage to bruise inside their mouths.
- Symmetrical bruising is unlikely to be accidental since children tend to hurt themselves naturally in one place, and children in pain do not return to get themselves a 'pair'.
- Some patterns of bruising should arouse suspicions, for instance, 3–4 small bruises on each side of a child's face could be finger marks and outline bruising, rather than solid bruises, may be the mark of a belt or hand.
- Young children do sometimes bite each other, but an oval or crescent shape more than 3 centimetres across will have been made by an adult or older child with permanent teeth.
- It can be hard to distinguish between non-accidental and accidental burns or scalds. Accidental scalds are more likely to have an uneven outline. Explanations should also make sense in terms of any care routine and the age and mobility of the child.

Of course, an apparently non-accidental injury should trigger your concern, but suspicious signs do not tell you who may have made that injury. Children sometimes deliberately hurt each other and very distressed children sometimes engage in self-harm. Either of these patterns should be taken seriously and may bring further child protection issues.

Some child protection books are written as if all children were pale skinned and of course this is not the case. Genuine bruising may be harder to observe on dark skinned children, although some differences in coloration may show and children will experience pain in a bruised area.

One more note of caution: many children have slight differences of coloration in their skin. However, this variation can look like bruising on dark skinned children, especially those of Afro-Caribbean, Mediterranean and Asian origin. These naturally occurring patches are called Mongolian blue spots. They have a defined edge and are a consistent slate blue in colour, unlike genuine bruising that tends to vary in shade and changes over a period of days.

Neglect of children

Neglect is the failure to care adequately for a child so as to ensure their health and well being. Neglect by responsible adults is a continuing pattern in the treatment of a child and may be linked with physical abuse as well. Persistent neglect is very dangerous. Some children have died as the direct consequence of neglect, and

Key term

Neglect
the failure to care adequately for children or young people in order to ensure their continuing health and well being

others have been in a very poor state of health by the time the neglect has been discovered and stopped. Malnutrition in early childhood can have serious consequences of growth and long-term health, some of which can never be reversed.

Types of neglect

It is the responsibility of parents and other carers to ensure the well being of the children in their care. Some families have serious financial problems and child protection professionals should always consider whether family support is the most important step in helping a child. However, children have been seriously neglected when there is enough money and where other members of the family, adults and sometimes other children, are cared for adequately.

Persistent and severe neglect includes different kinds of failure to care properly for a child.

- Neglected children have sometimes been given such inadequate food that they have been starving when found. Babies, toddlers and disabled older children may be fed in an inappropriate way so that they cannot swallow food or vomit it back again.
- Some children become very ill because neither their clothes nor their bedding are warm enough for the winter months.
- Some parents or other carers grossly neglect the basic physical needs of very young or disabled children. The babies or children are not offered basic hygiene so that they are dirty or become sore from unchanged nappies. Ordinary infections get worse because of lack of simple medical attention.
- It would be regarded as neglectful to leave a young or disabled child alone or with another carer who could not be properly responsible, for instance because he or she is young themselves.

Signs that should concern you

Children who are abused through persistent neglect will show the consequences of their poor care, for instance:

- Children may be thin and records show that they fail to put on weight. Some children will always be on the lighter side and slim parents tend to have slim children. So you have to use weight charts with care.
- When children have been malnourished, they lack energy and may seem passive or lethargic.
- Children may eat large amounts of food when it is available and some will take and hide food. In a daily setting you may find that the children are most hungry after the weekend.
- Children may be chilled in winter time because they are not wearing enough warm clothes. Children who are cold on a regular basis can develop chapped hands, chilblains or unnaturally reddened skin in a white child.
- It takes a while for children to smell, since they have not yet developed the body odour of teenagers and adults. Neglectful adults fail to pay attention to body and hair washing and have probably put dirty clothes back on the children.
- No children are healthy all the time, but neglectful parents and carers allow avoidable illness and conditions like nappy rash or infections get worse.
- You may consider neglect when children have a considerable number of accidents, especially given their age and mobility. The possibility arises that

adults do not watch over them properly or leave them with an inappropriate carer.

- It is important to realise that sometimes all the children within a family are equally neglected. However, some parents have singled out one child and treated him or her badly or significantly worse than siblings.

Tips for practice

Children who are neglected sometimes have a condition called **faltering growth**, sometimes still described as 'failure to thrive'. This term is used to describe when babies or children do not put on weight, may also appear in poor health and there is no obvious medical reason.

You would of course be aware of a baby, toddler or child who seemed unduly thin or regularly tired. However, this is an area in which different aspects of your knowledge and practice need to be merged. Any concerns about possible faltering growth need to be supported by a careful assessment, over a period of time and with the cooperation of the parents. Key issues include that:

- Growth charts give variations around the average because some babies and children will always be on the 'light' side, just as some are on the 'heavy' side. Small parents are likely to produce children who are smaller and lighter than the average.
- Some babies and children have digestion or allergy problems that affect their ability to keep food down or to digest it properly (see page 95).
- Some children develop problems about eating a range of foods or enough in total. Their parents' understandable anxiety can worsen rather than improve the situation. The family may appreciate advice and support, but they are not neglecting their children (see page 91).

Key term

Faltering growth when babies and children do not put on weight and may also appear in poor health, for no obvious reason. The condition used to be called failure to thrive

Emotional abuse of children

Emotional abuse is a persistent pattern of deliberate, uncaring or emotionally cruel treatment of a child or young person. From the child's perspective, all abuse and neglect has an element of emotional abuse. Children's feelings are involved and their sense of security is undermined. Abuse and neglect make children doubt that they are worthy of care.

Not all children experience physical attack or actual neglect. Some children experience a regular verbal battering against their sense of well being and of themselves as likeable. Even when nobody lays a hand on them, children can be so deeply affected by emotional abuse that they are in poor physical as well as psychological health and the damage lasts into adulthood.

Key term

Emotional abuse a persistent pattern of verbal cruelty to children or young people such that they feel unworthy and unloved

Types of emotional abuse

Even the best-intentioned adults have off days and children who mainly experience kindness will take the odd cross remark, and the apology that follows, in a forgiving way. In contrast, emotionally abusive treatment is unrelenting.

- Emotionally abused children are told in words or clear facial expressions from adults that they are 'stupid' or 'hopeless'. Their achievements are never enough or are compared unfavourably with a sibling or other relative.
- Children may be criticised for their looks or blamed for the fact they were born and 'ruined my life!'

- The behaviour of their adult carers makes the child uncertain of their worth, since approval is made dependent on the child's behaviour. Affection is given in an inconsistent way, so that the child cannot easily predict what will make the adults withdraw their warmth.
- When there is family conflict, children may be made to feel inappropriately guilty about troubles between parents or forced to take sides in a conflict of loyalties.
- An excessively protective attitude towards a child can verge towards emotional abuse. The parent or carer may make a strong case that this child needs extra care. However, adults outside the family have to consider the consequences for children and whether their well being and learning is being blocked.

Signs that should concern you

Children vary considerably as individuals and some will always be more cautious or reserved. You should be concerned about any of the following patterns of behaviour, but would need to discuss your observations with colleagues and carefully with the child's parents.

- All children have down days. But children who are happy in their life do not frequently communicate that they feel worthless, someone who is always making stupid mistakes or is ugly.
- Be aware of children who persistently blame themselves or seem to expect that you will criticise and punish them.
- You should always take notice of children who harm themselves, whether by persistent hair pulling, picking their skin or head banging.
- Children who have compulsive rituals such as very regular and lengthy hand washing may have been made to feel dirty.
- Some children appear very wary of adults and seem to expect unpredictable or unpleasant behaviour.
- Or the other hand, it is important to notice those children who attach themselves indiscriminately to any halfway kind adult.

To think about

- Look at the first four bullet points in signs of possible emotional abuse.
- You will see that this behaviour from children is likely to arise from persistent ill treatment, but you cannot easily know who is ill treating the child.
- If you work in a school or after school club, the children will be old enough that you should consider possible patterns of bullying between the children.
- You would take any of these signs with seriousness, but it will be good practice to keep an open mind about the exact source of a child's troubles.

Key term

Sexual abuse
actual or likely sexual exploitation of a child or young person who has neither the age nor understanding to give their informed consent

Sexual abuse

Sexual abuse is the sexual exploitation of a child or young person who has not reached an age or maturity when he or she can give informed consent to sexual activities with another person. Some children experience sexual abuse for a brief period of time, but for some children the abuse extends over years of their childhood.

Most sexual abusers, whose activities come to light, have been male. But females have been known to sexually abuse children – either on their own or in collaboration with male abusers. It would be very risky to assume that dubious behaviour from a female could not be sexually abusive.

Sexual abusers claim that their actions are not harmful, that the child agreed or was in some way sexually provocative. However, sexual abusers operate in a moral vacuum. It is the responsibility of caring adults to help children learn appropriate boundaries for expressing affection and touch. Sexual abusers deliberately distort the very boundaries they should be helping children to understand.

Types of sexual abuse

Adults, who abuse children sexually, seek to involve them in some kind of adult sexual activity, but the abusive actions can vary.

- Adults (or young people) who sexually abuse children sometimes have full sexual intercourse with them. Children or young people may also be forced into oral or anal sex.
- It is regarded as abusive to involve children in any sexual practices even if these stop short of actual penetration. It is unacceptable for children to be touched in an intimate way or for them to be induced to engage in sexual fondling of others.
- It is also abusive to induce children to watch sexual activity, even if they are not touched themselves.
- Some abusers take video footage or photos as part of the abuse. Child pornography is integral to the use made of the internet by paedophiles.

Children are harmed by sexual abuse:

- They may be at risk physically since sexual practices can cause children physical injury, sometimes serious, and lead to infection, including sexually transmitted diseases.
- Even if the abuse has not caused visible physical damage, children are psychologically damaged by the experience. Adults have abused children's trust and have often used threats to ensure children's compliance and secrecy.
- Depending partly on how long the abuse has lasted, children can be very confused about the expression of affection and of their ability to form close relationships.
- When sexual abuse is uncovered, the trauma in the family or other group can be serious. Without careful support, children can feel even less protected and weighed with feelings of guilt.

Signs that should concern you

Some physical and behavioural signs would make you deeply uneasy about the possibility of sexual abuse, but other signs could have alternative explanations. In this area of abuse you still need to make sense of children's behaviour and play within the context of usual child development.

Disabled children may show different patterns of development as a result of their disability and learning disabled children may behave more like a younger child in some ways. However, adults can put disabled children at risk if they assume that unusual behaviour must arise from the child's disability. If this behaviour would concern you in a child with no identified disabilities, then you have to ask yourself, and your colleagues, why are we not concerned about this child? Some people assume that disabled children will be less at risk from sexual or other abuse, but unfortunately the reverse is the case (see page 573).

Your concerns might be aroused by any of the following:

- Children like to be close and they are in the process of learning about respect for other people's bodies and private areas. Yet, it is not within normal range development for children to keep on trying to touch the private parts of other children or adults, despite a firm 'No'.
- Some children are more reserved than others, but you may notice that a child seems excessively wary about physical closeness.
- As a nanny, you might notice a child's distress related to a normal routine such as bath time or being read a bedtime story. There is a possibility that the child has been abused as part of this routine (not necessarily by the parents).
- Children often like to express their daily experiences through play with dolls or small figures. So it is possible that children, who have been sexually abused, will make the dolls perform sexual acts that should be outside the normal experience of childhood. Children may also produce paintings or drawings which are sexually very explicit.
- You need to recall that young children often fiddle with their private parts or take off their clothes. So your observations need to weigh up whether a child seems to be masturbating a great deal more than intermittent fiddling. Or does the child look rather exhibitionist about going naked?
- Young children are often interested in bottoms, willies and poo. But their giggly talk tends to revolve around toilets, which they understand, rather than the sexual connotations of private parts.
- Again, careful observation needs to assess in a developmental context whether the children's words or actions suggest a sexual knowledge or curiosity unlikely for their age.

Activity

- Collect some examples of children's natural curiosity about bodies, babies and bodily functions.
- Write up your examples with care and attention to confidentiality.
- Share with your colleagues and discuss the backdrop of normal childhood interests and behaviour against which you need to make sense of behaviour that is out of the ordinary.

Key skills links: C3.3 C3.1a

Some physical symptoms should always concern you and lead to a conversation with parents about the need to visit their GP.

- Pain, itching or redness in the genital or anal area needs medical attention. But do recall that these symptoms can arise from thrush, threadworms or persistent constipation. Broken skin can result from vigorous scratching and the strain of constipation can even lead to anal fissures and bleeding (see pages 134 and 72).

- Any bruising or bleeding in the genital or anal area needs a medical check, as does any child's clear discomfort in walking or sitting down. They could have fallen and hurt themselves, but these are unusual sites for accidental injury.
- A vaginal discharge or apparent infection in a girl or persistent urinary infections and pain in passing urine for either sex should always be checked.
- Pregnancy in an under-age girl and evidence of a sexually transmitted disease in either sex will indicate either sexual abuse or risky sexual activity in older children – in itself a cause for concern.

Combined abusive experiences

For simplicity, each category of abuse has been discussed separately in this chapter but, for some children, their experiences cross the boundaries between physical abuse, neglect, emotional abuse and sexual abuse.

It is the responsibility of adults to care for and comfort children. Abusive adults draw on their knowledge of what will distress children in order to abuse them. For instance:

- Some children have been terrified by adults who shut them in cupboards or other confined, dark spaces as a punishment. Sexually abusive adults have sometimes used such techniques to make the children more compliant.
- Neglectful adults fail to meet the basic physical needs of children, but the same adults may also justify such neglect by disdainful attitudes towards the child that are emotionally abusive.
- Uncaring adults may fail to provide a minimum level of emotional and intellectual stimulation to support children's normal development and learning.
- Or harsh adults may make their approval utterly dependent on strict standards of intellectual achievement. Some textbooks refer to this treatment as 'intellectual abuse', but this term is misleading since there is no such category within the child protection system.

The risks for children with disabilities

A sentimental view of disabled children has sometimes led people to believe that surely they must be less at risk of abuse. Unfortunately, there are several factors that can combine to put disabled children at even greater risk. You need to be aware of these issues, since it is more likely nowadays that disabled children will join early years and mainstream school settings. The main issues are:

- Children with physical and severe learning disabilities may need a high level of personal care well into later childhood and perhaps will always need help. Poor practice in care routines can leave disabled children vulnerable to abuse or neglect as well as lacking an important sense of personal dignity, that they should be treated with respect. See also the discussion about physical care on page 46.
- Disabled children can sometimes have a high numbers of carers or attend a range of settings. If nobody is keeping a close eye on the children's experience, they can be vulnerable to abusive behaviour.
- A problem can also arise that children consider it normal for people they scarcely know to undertake intimate care or intrusive medical procedures.

- Physically disabled children may have less capacity to resist an abuser. Children whose disabilities affect communication may find it hard to express what is happening to them. A related problem is that lack of respect for disabled children may mean that their disclosure is not taken seriously.

Activity

- Draw out four or five practical points from the section on support for disabled children.
- Describe how you could support and improve good practice in your setting.
- Share your ideas with colleagues.

Key skills links: C3.3 C3.1a LP3.1–3 WO3.1–3

Supporting families and children

You need to understand possible patterns and signs of child abuse, in order to support children and families within your role. You also need to have a grasp of the different reasons for how child abuse may arise.

Why do adults abuse children?

There is no neat pattern to predict who is likely to abuse children. Adults who have been found to abuse or neglect children have come from all possible social, ethnic and religious groups, from prosperous as well as economically deprived areas, from professional people – including childcare practitioners – as well as non-professionals. Most adults do not abuse or neglect and some families who are under great strain can be helped away from a high risk situation by support.

Good practice is that early years practitioners have an understanding of what may lead parents and other carers into abusive patterns with children. You can try to understand what has happened without in any way excusing the abusive consequences for the children.

Family stress

Families that are under immense stress may have difficulty in finding time and patience for their children.

- Some families on the edge of coping may be tipped by harder than average childcare, for instance, a baby who is very wakeful, cries a great deal or is difficult to feed.
- In homes with domestic violence the children may be caught in the crossfire, as well as deliberately threatened and targeted.
- Parents with severe problems of addiction – to drink, drugs or gambling – have little energy or commitment left to give to their children.
- Young, very lonely or unsupported parents may feel overwhelmed. Sometimes they may be ignorant of the high risks of their action, for instance, believing that it is better to shake a baby than to hit.

Philosophical, cultural or religious beliefs

Family beliefs may lead to what outsiders regard as an unacceptable risk to children or abusive treatment.

- Some parents who are accused of physical abuse continue to maintain that they were only exerting their right to discipline. Some will quote religious beliefs as justification.
- Extreme views on diet applied to babies and children may lead to severe ill health and malnutrition.
- Some families refuse medical treatment for children on religious grounds. Such cases may go to court and a legal decision can be made to overrule parental choice in these circumstances.
- Female genital mutilation (FGM), also sometimes called female circumcision, is against the law in the UK because of the physical damage caused to young girls. FGM is a cultural practice within some North African communities originating from Somalia and the Sudan, some Middle Eastern countries such as the Yemen and in parts of Indonesia.

Good practice in child protection, as in other aspects of early years work, is to show respect for family cultural and religious beliefs. However, such respect cannot overrule an assessment of the well being of a child (see page 581).

Personal experience of adults

The personal history of some adults may incline them more to potential abuse.

- Some adults, who feel without power and weak in their adult lives, relish wielding power over young and vulnerable children, either their own sons and daughters or those for whom they are responsible.
- It may be easier to blame a child for personal inadequacies than address what the adult has failed to achieve in life. Twisted logic may say that everything would be fine if it were not for this son or daughter's behaviour, demands or even their unwanted birth.
- Sometimes carers bring their own childhood into how they treat children. Adults may excuse harsh words and hitting children as the right way to teach respect and discipline, with the justification that, 'It didn't do me any harm'.
- Without support to consider alternatives, parents and carers may not even contemplate other ways of treating children.

Emotional imbalance and deviant behaviour

Some abusive adults bring children into their own mental and emotional imbalance.

- It is rare, but some parents (more often mothers) have deliberately injured their children as a way of seeking attention for themselves. This pattern is called Munchausen Syndrome by Proxy and sometimes Illness Induction Syndrome.
- Adults who sexually abuse children exploit the unequal power relations in order to satisfy their adult sexual desires. Some sexual abusers are able to sustain adult relationships, but appear to turn to children when they feel under stress or rejected.
- Paedophiles are specifically attracted to children rather than adults. Part of their sexual excitement arises through the process of targeting and preparing a child for abuse, known as grooming. Paedophiles may target only one sex but some attempt to abuse both boys and girls.

Responding to disclosures from children

Sometimes concerns will first be raised because of your own observations of a child or young person. Alternatively, a colleague, another professional or the child's parent may alert you to events or problems of which you are unaware. Sometimes, however, children will choose to disclose their experience or feelings directly to you. A **disclosure** is a communication by words or actions when children choose to share an experience of abuse or neglect, or fears that relate to potential abuse.

Key term

Disclosure
communication by children's words or actions when they share an experience of abuse or neglect, or their fears that relate to potential abuse

Different ways of communicating

It is important to realise that a disclosure is not always a 'big' or obvious event. Sometimes, it may only be on reflection, or confidential discussion with a colleague, that you realise a child has made a disclosure.

- Younger children may make a brief, almost throwaway remark in conversation or their play.
- Some children may take the opportunity for a long conversation in which many details emerge, but this is by no means always the pattern.
- Children may approach a disclosure through an apparently unrelated comment: they may ask you a question or invite your opinion. What the child says makes you concerned.
- Be aware, however, that children who have experienced lengthy abuse or neglect may not be able to imagine life any other way. Sadly, they may simply be informing you about another part of their life and are not actually asking for help.
- Children may take the opportunity to speak out, when you ask sympathetically about how they got a bump, bruise or cut.
- Some children will not use words but will effectively 'tell' you through their behaviour and body language, perhaps their obvious unhappiness or fear to follow a request or routine.
- Children express themselves through play, so they may weave unhappy as well as happy experiences into pretend games, drawing or story telling.

When disability affects disclosure

Bear in mind that children with communication or severe learning disabilities may not disclose with words, or may have limited spoken communication. Your concerns could be aroused because of their behaviour, in the light of your knowledge of this child and more general knowledge of development.

Give time and listen

You can draw on your existing skills of communication when a child discloses to you. You do not need a whole new set of specialist skills, although there are some sound guidelines given the nature of this communication.

- The first and most important guideline is to listen to children and give them your calm and supportive attention. Listen with your ears and watch with your eyes for their body language and how they say something.
- Be calm for the child. Even if you feel anxious or distressed about what you have just been told, then do your level best not to show that emotion and disturb the child.

- Take what they say seriously. Do not leap in with calming reassurance like, 'I'm sure it's not so bad' or 'You may be mistaken'.
- Be guided by the children themselves; the conversation ends when they wish it. You can offer to listen again, but that is all for the time being.

With children, you should ideally listen now, because this time is when they are ready to communicate.

- If this moment really is impossible, perhaps because the situation is very public, then support the child by saying, 'I have heard/noticed you. Can we talk in private when we get back to nursery/home?' Do not put the child off speaking just because this moment is inconvenient to you; it is clearly right for her.
- The child has chosen to communicate with you, so it is inappropriate to stop the child and ask him or her to speak with someone more senior. You will have to talk with someone else about the disclosure later, but the child has chosen and trusted you.

Use open ended questions

It is very important that you do not cross-question a child. Such adult behaviour can put a child under uncomfortable pressure. It may also direct children into saying what they think you want to hear.

- Keep any questions open ended: 'How do/did you feel?' rather than 'Do you feel frightened?' ask 'What happened next?' rather than 'Did he ask you to keep this secret?'
- You can also use the technique of reflective listening in which you gently repeat back what the child says but with a questioning tone in your voice. If the child says, 'Uncle Jon does dirty things to me' you can reflect back, 'You say your uncle does dirty things to you?'
- You can also simply encourage a child by your open and attentive expression and simple questions like 'Yes?' or 'Anything else you want to tell me?'

Support and reassure

You show positive support and commitment to children by the fact that you give time and listen.

- If it feels right, given your relationship with the child, you can offer a hug or a gentle touch.
- Take appropriate opportunities to show, through words or smiles, that you care about the child. He or she may even ask, 'Do you still like me?'
- Avoid making promises that you cannot keep. You cannot, for instance, make a commitment that 'this will just stay between us'.
- You have a professional responsibility to pass on child protection concerns. You can reassure the child that you will only tell the few people who need to know, 'so that we can keep you safe'.

A supportive conversation for children is one in which the adult follows their lead and stops when the child wishes. You then need to write up the conversation you have had with the child or the incident that you have observed. These careful notes should be made as soon as possible and certainly within the same day (see page 582).

Activity

Early years practitioners are sometimes very concerned that they may 'do the wrong thing' when a child makes a disclosure. However, you need to feel confident that good quality communication skills are what are needed.

- Draw out four or five practical points from the section on communication when children disclose.
- Write them up in your own words to guide practice in your setting.
- Discuss and share your ideas with colleagues.

Key skills links: C3.3 C3.1a LP3.1–3 WO3.1–3

Scenario

Members of the Wessex childminding network have been discussing the appropriate balance in taking what children say seriously, rather than dismissing it on the grounds that it cannot be true. The network members have taken on board the positive shift in child protection to take full account of what children say, rather than to assume that children are prone to lie or fantasise. However, some network members have read material on child protection that seems to direct adults to believe everything that a child says when child protection concerns are aroused.

Laura, the network coordinator takes an everyday example of conflict between young children to highlight the difference. She asks the group to imagine this situation in a family home or an early years setting and they talk through the possibilities:

- Four year old Nina comes up to you and says, 'Peter hit me and I hadn't done anything!'
- It would be unjust if you immediately took Nina's word as the full truth of what had happened. A fair approach would be to listen to what Nina has to say and show that you take her feelings seriously.
- Then you would find out from Peter his side of the event and perhaps any other child who had been present.
- You would come to a conclusion on the basis of information and then take the best way forward for both children.
- So you are taking what Nina said seriously but you do not accept her version of events as the full truth without checking.

The childminders are well aware that concerns about child protection raise anxieties in a way that conflict between children does not usually do. However, the balance is very similar.

Questions

1. Discuss the example with your own colleagues.
2. Consider for your own setting how to address the balance between taking what children say seriously while still leaving opportunities to find out more.

Key skills links: C3.1.a

Talking with parents

You may be wary about broaching a concern with the parent and it is fine to ask a more experienced colleague for advice prior to that conversation. But you need to build the confidence to speak up in a friendly yet honest way.

There is no doubt that this conversation will be easier when you have developed a friendly working relationship with parents (see page 625). They know you share exciting events in the child's day, tell them if the child has taken a tumble and genuinely share the care of their son or daughter. You are then coming from a positive basis to ask about the marks on Sandy's inner thighs or to explain how you handled Malcolm's strident announcement in the market about 'ladies' furry bits'.

It is tempting to find reasons not to talk with parents but such reluctance could put children at risk. Failure to have a conversation could also leave you worried, when there is a perfectly safe explanation that a parent can give you. It makes sense that the key worker speaks with a parent. If necessary, a colleague or senior staff should rearrange their time so you can talk without interruption and enough privacy with the parent.

If you have limited experience, then it may help to try some forms of words in advance with a colleague but avoid trying to find a neat formula. You need to sound authentic and there is no perfect form of words. In general, you need to be clear in your own mind what you want to tell or ask a parent (or other relevant carer like a grandparent):

- What exactly is puzzling you about what the child said or did?
- What and where are the bruises, cuts or other marks?
- What patterns of behaviour from the child have concerned you, what is happening or not happening?
- What are your feelings that are relevant and could appropriately be voiced?

Here are some possible ways in to the conversation after saying that you would like to talk with a parent and before you go into more detail:

- 'I noticed a large bruise on Sandy's thigh and she seems uncertain how she got it. Do you have any ideas?'
- 'I'm uneasy about the games Barmila tries to play with two other children.'
- 'I'm confused about what Saima said today. She said that ... Does it make any sense to you?'
- 'From watching and listening to (name of child) I feel that she/he is frightened by ... unusually upset by ... doesn't seem to notice that ...'.
- 'I want to talk about (name of child)'s nappy rash ... the pain from the decay in her teeth ... the fact that he is so very hungry after the weekend ... that her shoes and socks are far too small for her feet ...'.
- 'I feel I need to tell you that Allison seems very upset on the days when your au pair/childminder/stepson picks her up. She is like a different little girl from the days that you or your husband does the pick up. I don't know what's going on, but you need to know that it's a consistent pattern.'

Do not expect that a parent's response will necessarily be negative. He or she may have a credible explanation for a child's bruise or odd remark. Some parents may be relieved you have spoken because they share your concern, without knowing what has happened to their child. They want help and would welcome support. Depending on the situation, you may be able to help or may need to consider involving your manager or a senior team member.

You will not always be able to give considerable time to parents and complicated adult problems need expert help. If parents want to talk with someone else in confidence, you could tell them about *Parentline Plus*. This organisation has brought together several parent and family support organisations (for general support, not specifically child protection). They can be contacted at 520 Highgate Studios, 53–79 Highgate Road, London NW5 1TL tel: 020 7284 5500, helpline: 0808 800 2222 website: *www.parentlineplus.org.uk*

Tips for practice

If you have a concern, then you need to be ready for when the parent, or other carer, arrives to pick up the child:

- Find a way to talk with parents courteously and in some degree of privacy.
- If the parent wants to rush off, be prepared to emphasise, 'I appreciate you're in a hurry. But I think this is too important to wait until tomorrow/next week.'
- Share your concern with honesty but without pre-judging what may have happened.
- Listen to the parent's reply. If necessary, wait through a short silence.
- Be ready to repeat your question or comment if the parent seems not to have listened or understood.
- Remain calm if the parent or carer becomes distressed or angry.
- Have a conversation that opens up the topic and be ready to make an arrangement to talk further with the parent in the very near future, if this seems appropriate.
- When appropriate, be clear about limits to confidentiality and honest about the next steps if concerns persist.
- Listen with equal attention when parents wish to raise concerns with you about other team members, volunteers or regular visitors.

Activity

Bear in mind also that sometimes a parent will want to raise a concern with you. You really need to set a good example for such an exchange, since your reaction will travel through the local parent grapevine.

Imagine a parent starts a conversation with you along the lines of these examples:

- 'My child has this huge scrape down the back of her leg. What happened yesterday?'
- 'When are you going to do something about (name of team member)? She shouts at the children all the time. My daughter says she was called "a little cow" yesterday.'
- 'My daughter was forced to eat all her lunch yesterday and she was sick. I think this is abusive treatment.'
- 'I don't think that (name of male staff member) should be changing nappies. It doesn't seem right to me.'

- 'Your son (of childminder or nanny who is allowed to bring child to work) said a very odd thing to my child last week.'

Discuss with colleagues how you could start a positive response, as well perhaps as thinking about what would be poor practice in your reply.

Key skills links: C3.1a

After the conversation

You may talk with parents or other carers and they give a plausible explanation for what concerned or puzzled you. Good practice would still be to make a note in the child's record of the conversation. Bear in mind that a child's records will be open to their parents, so consider how you write (see page 582).

Another option is that the conversation does not relieve your concern and perhaps adds to it. Alternatively, the parent is pleased you have opened the subject and makes a disclosure about themselves or someone else involved with the family. The same guidelines for good communication apply, including that you cannot keep secret an adult disclosure about possible abuse. Tell parents what you will be doing next and when you will speak with them again. You need to follow the procedures of your setting (see page 560).

Anti-discriminatory practice

Early years practitioners can feel uneasy about child protection issues when they do not share the same ethnic or cultural background as the parents or carers. Nobody wishes to be accused of racist attitudes and behaviour, but you cannot avoid concerns for this reason. Good practice in child protection will be supported by more general good anti-discriminatory practice within the team, as well as partnership with all parents.

In any setting or group discussion, such as a childminding network, you need to:

- Courteously challenge assumptions that there is one 'normal' or 'right way' to raise children, or that some people as a whole group do not care about their children.
- The challenge needs to be made whoever is making these statements. It is no more acceptable for an African colleague to make disparaging remarks about a family of Caribbean origin than it would for a white European colleague.
- Focus clearly on the child's well being and behaviour. No tradition in child rearing from any culture should be permitted to damage children.
- Avoid blunt accusations of racism directed at colleagues. This kind of attack does not help to improve practice and can seriously undermine people's motivation to learn and change, not only within child protection.
- Strive for open communication within a setting or network so that you can extend your understanding and knowledge of cultures and faiths that are unfamiliar to you, whatever your own background.
- But be cautious about being certain you know 'all about' a faith or cultural background just from acquaintance with a few families.

Keeping records

Your notes should include specific details of the conversation with a child or parent and of any incident that concerns you. If this is your first experience of disclosure, then ask for support from a more senior colleague. It will help to talk matters through before you write down the details.

All your skills of good practice in writing records and reports (see page 561) are equally relevant now. You may find it helpful to guide your record of a conversation with a child by answering the following questions abut the disclosure:

- When and where did the child talk with you?
- What did the child say to you? Note it down as accurately as you can recall and in the child's own words. Add any necessary explanations if the child uses personal words, for instance, for parts of the body.
- How did the child behave and, from your knowledge of him or her as an individual, what else does that add?
- Support any opinions with your reasons. For instance, that the child was showing a pattern of behaviour that you have seen before when he has been anxious or distressed.
- Avoid any guesses or speculations. You need to take the child seriously; it is not your role to work out exactly where the truth lies in the events.

Continuing records of a child will need to follow good practice as described in more general terms on page 462. When child protection is an issue, it is even more important that you keep high standards in what and how you record:

- Be careful to keep to the facts, what you have observed and when.
- Describe in factual detail any concerns about a child's behaviour, health, development or injuries.
- Support any appropriate opinions that arise because of your knowledge of child development in general and this child as an individual.
- Otherwise avoid any guesses or speculation – your own or those of other people.
- Be specific over concerns raised about the family. For instance avoid comments like, 'Gaby's parents take poor care of her' and be specific about what you have observed, such as, 'Each day this week Gaby was dressed in a thin summer frock when the morning temperature was close to freezing'.
- If a child has injuries, then make an accurate record of the nature and extent of the bruises, cuts or other marks. You could use a simple outline figure of a child, front and back versions, to sketch the location of any injuries (see Figure 19.6). Do not guess about the possible cause of any injury.

Working with child protection

General support for children

Much of your general good practice will support children regarding child protection:

- Respectful physical care of all children helps them understand how responsible adults should behave.
- When you listen to children's interests and concerns, you make it more likely that they will confide in you if something serious is worrying them.
- Physical closeness (see page 43) and showing affection to children, helps them to feel secure and to experience appropriate touch and boundaries.

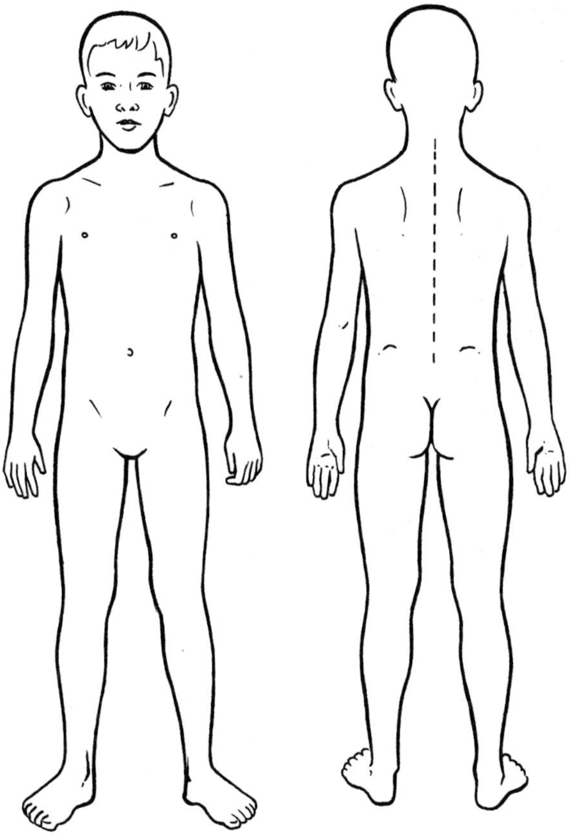

Figure 19.6

Body outline: a way to record patterns of injury in a child

- Your positive approach to dealing with behaviour (see Chapter 17) gives children direct experience of adults who behave well and do not use negative physical or emotional tactics.
- You can help children learn to keep themselves safe without making them feel inappropriately responsible (see page 116).

Tips for practice

If children have been abused or neglected, they need your good practice in all aspects of their care:

- Support children's feelings and listen to them if they wish to talk.
- Otherwise treat children as normally as possible. Definitely avoid showing pity, making 'poor little soul' remarks or sad and meaningful glances between adults.
- You may make some allowances for children but mainly they need the same positive approach to their behaviour as their peers.
- Children who have experienced abuse still need boundaries. They should not simply be allowed to vent their feelings on to other children and they need you to ensure that they still have friends.
- Some children may receive specialist help, perhaps through play therapy. It will help if you can understand the kind of work being undertaken. Play therapy is a specialised task but you can support by low-key involvement in children's play.

Working with other professionals

If you become involved in a child protection investigation, then you will work with other professionals. These will include:

- a social worker
- possibly the police (but see page 556)
- the designated teacher responsible for child protection in a school
- professionals who are already involved with the family, such as the family health visitor or GP
- professionals who become involved in order to assess the child, such as a medical officer or clinical psychologist.

It is important that you show your own professionalism and that of your setting.

- Be clear in your explanations about procedures and clear policy.
- Demonstrate good practice in your records and summary reports.
- Show a professional approach in how you discuss families or children.
- Prepare well for and contribute to meetings. If necessary, speak up to say that you wish to contribute the knowledge of the nursery or playgroup about this child or family.

Support for practitioners

Dealing with child protection issues can be emotionally draining and it is appropriate that you should be able to talk in confidence about how you handle each stage of the work and how you feel. In an early years setting it should be possible to discuss your work with a senior colleague or the manager in a supervision time. Even experienced practitioners need to talk about this child and this family. A professional approach includes the awareness that you have feelings about the child, the family and what has happened.

It is also possible that dealing with child protection will stir practitioners' own memories of childhood abuse, either that they experienced or knew happened to a friend. It is important to talk about these feelings in confidence, although if you are very distressed it will be wise to seek professional help outside your workplace. As with any other deeply felt personal experience, you need to be able to acknowledge and put your feelings temporarily to one side. If you were abused as a child, you can still help children now that you are an adult. But you need to focus on this child now and in no way re-run your own experience through them.

Allegations against early years practitioners

Children are most usually at risk from people they know. Although the risk will often come from within the family, children have also been harmed by adults who are in a professional relationship with them. Procedures for an early years setting or school have to include a response to concerns about or accusations of staff.

Any setting, led by the manager, has to be seen to take seriously any allegations, by parents, children or colleagues, about the behaviour of paid practitioners, volunteers or visitors to the setting. Good practice is similar to what has been described elsewhere in this chapter.

- Other policies in the setting should make it very clear how adults should act, for instance in response to children's challenging behaviour. Some tactics are unacceptable in a setting (see page 510).

- Practitioners should listen carefully when a parent or child expresses concerns about a colleague. You should be able to express concerns yourself in confidence to a senior colleague.
- Concerns should then be checked and information gathered in a way that does not leap to conclusions in either direction.
- Equal opportunities should be seen to apply to all staff. Certainly male practitioners should not be more easily accused or suspected than their female colleagues.

Often there will be an acceptable explanation in response to the concerns raised.

- This explanation needs to be communicated clearly so that no doubts are left.
- Sometimes the possibility of child abuse is resolved but a practitioner's behaviour does not meet good practice and needs to be addressed firmly. In the example on page 580, perhaps a practitioner is unacceptably rude to children and does bully them into eating a dinner they dislike.
- Sometimes a parent's concern might highlight lax practice. Perhaps the team is not careful enough about telling parents of minor accidents children have in play.
- Or the team realises that teenagers come on work placement without any proper introduction and discussion with the children. This lax approach gives children the impression that strangers can appear and play with you, and nobody tells you about them.

A small minority of early years settings and schools will experience a time when the team includes an adult who has abused children in one or more of the four broad ways described on page 562. Depending on the circumstances, the setting may be involved in a child protection investigation or the incident(s) may be dealt with through disciplinary action.

- When children have been ill-treated by practitioners or volunteers it is important that their experience is acknowledged.
- They need explanations suitable for their age including the fact that what the adult did was wrong.
- It is important to talk with parents, individually or in a group meeting. Reliable information needs to be given and questions answered.

Scenarios

A slightly different approach has been taken to scenarios in this chapter. Child protection is a complex area of practice and examples often do not fall neatly into one of the categories of abuse. Please consider the following examples, ideally with colleagues and discuss one or more examples guided by the following questions:

- Would this incident concern you?
- If yes, then on what basis?
- If no, then explain your reasons for feeling that child protection is not an issue here. If you would have other concerns, then explain those.
- If you faced such a situation, what other information might you need?
- What should the people do who are involved in this situation?

1 James and Marilyn are jointly registered as childminders in the Wessex network. They are concerned to observe the behaviour of a local childminder, not part of the network, at a drop-in. The childminder is responsible for a physically disabled four year old and she talks about him as if he were not present. It also sounds as if she leaves the child in his wheelchair in front of the television for long periods in the day.

2 Kimberley is part of a nanny share with two families. One family has recently had a premature baby (see the scenario on page 158). The baby's three year old sister, Claire, has started to wet herself and be very distressed if Kimberley does not promptly give her attention when she calls. Kimberley was given a checklist during a child protection workshop and this list states that wetting and attention seeking are signs of abuse.

3 A boy and a girl, aged four years old who attend Sunningdale Day Nursery have developed a game of mummies and daddies in the garden. Today they were found with their pants down, looking at each other's private parts.

4 Two fathers in Dresden Road Nursery School have insisted that their sons should be allowed to hit or bite back if squabbles turn physical. One of the children seems doubtful when challenged by a practitioner but says, 'My Daddy says a good smack never hurt anyone'.

5 A mature student on placement in Baker Street Children and Family Centre is uncompromising about the right way to treat young children. A parent mentions to Ciaran, the manager, that her two year old daughter appears to have been left in soiled knickers for most of yesterday afternoon, because she refused to use the pot.

6 There is some disagreement currently in Greenholt Pre-school. A four year old has joined whose parents follow a vegan diet. The pre-school team has been happy to take advice from the family to offer a balanced lunch. However, a parent helper has been scathing about 'parents who impose their views on little children' and she brought in today a newspaper cutting about parents who were prosecuted for causing severe malnutrition in their toddler.

Key skills links: C3.1a

Further resources

Hewlett, Sylvia Ann (1993) *Child Neglect in Rich Nations* UNICEF.

Leach, Penelope (1992) *Young Children under Stress* National Early Years Network – Starting Points No. 6.

Lindon, Jennie (1998) *Child Protection and Early Years Work* Hodder and Stoughton.

Lindon, Jennie and Lance (1997) *Working Together for Young Children: A guide for managers and staff* Thomson Learning.

NCH Action for Children publishes factsheets, summaries and reports that provide useful information in a concise format. Contact them at 85 Highbury Park, London N5 1UD tel: 020 7226 2033 website: *www.nch.org.uk*

The NSPCC publishes booklets useful for early years practitioners or to make available for parents and older children. Contact them at 42 Curtain Road, London EC2A 3NH tel: 020 7825 2500 website: *www.nspcc.org.uk*

Progress check

1 Describe two misleading assumptions about child abuse and abusers.

2 Explain three broad ways in which an early years practitioner could be involved in a child protection case.

3 Describe briefly the four main types of child abuse.

4 Suggest two sites on a child's body that are unusual for accidental injury.

5 Explain two signs that could raise concerns that a child was being neglected.

6 Describe two behaviours from a child that could indicate emotional abuse.

7 Describe two behaviours from a child that could indicate sexual abuse.

8 Give three possible reasons why parents or other carers might neglect or abuse children in some way.

9 Explain in brief how you would use good communications skills if a child disclosed abuse to you.

20

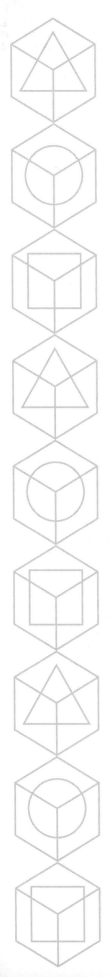

Developing good practice as an early years practitioner

After reading this chapter you should be able to:

- understand how to work in a professional way as an early years practitioner
- work as a member of a team and appreciate the importance of teamwork
- understand and apply the skills of communication and problem solving
- understand the importance of policies and their application in practice.

Introduction

Early years practitioners need to develop a professional outlook and to work well with other people. Teamwork is crucial if you work in any early years setting, school or out of school care. Cooperation and support within a team is built through good communication and a willingness to address and resolve issues rather than work against one another, for whatever reason. Good communication and a cooperative approach are equally important when you work mainly on your own, as a nanny or childminder. These practitioners need to work closely with the children's parents, form good working relationships with other members of a childminding network or with local early years professionals.

Links to early years qualifications

This chapter especially supports the following units:

Diploma in Child Care and Education: 8, 10

National Vocational Qualification in Early Years Care and Education

Level 2: M3, CU10

Level 3: M6, MC1/C4

BTEC National Early Years Diploma: 1, 2, 3, 21

Working in a professional manner

There are different aspects to your professional life. You need to apply for and obtain a job, became familiar with what is required in your current post, work in a **professional** manner and continue to develop your skills and knowledge. In all of these areas your employers have responsibilities as well as you.

Key term

Professional
a description of behaviour and outlook appropriate to the responsibilities in a job or a work placement as a student

Seeking a new job

You will most likely approach a possible new job through applying to an advertisement and then attending an interview. You are likely to have a proper interview, even if you obtain a post in a setting where you are already known from a work placement as a student.

An early years setting has a legal obligation to follow a consistent process in seeking new staff that addresses equal opportunities. Legal requirements mean that an early years setting cannot decide they only want female practitioners, wish to employ only certain ethnic groups or will not have anyone with even minor disabilities. However, a setting can advertise for a new team member with specific experience skills, ethnic background or language skills, so long as they can show that this background or knowledge is essential for the post.

Your application

It is your task to present yourself in a positive and honest light, through written and spoken communication and your behaviour during an interview.

- Some jobs will have an application form and you will then need to complete those details.
- It is also valuable to prepare a written **curriculum vitae (CV)** and be ready to update it as you gain experience.
- Where requested, you would send a copy of your CV with a covering letter. Otherwise, take a copy with you to an interview.
- Ensure that any covering letter is well written, checked for spelling and says something appropriate to this job. You will not create a positive impression by general letters that could just as easily be for a job in the Parks department as working with young children.

Key term

Curriculum vitae (CV)
summary of your qualifications, experience and professional career

The same points apply if you write to potential employers without replying to an advertisement. You might, for example, write a prospective letter to a large nursery chain that you know has nurseries in different towns. Or you might very much want to gain experience in working with an early excellence centre.

- This approach is fine, but it is essential to consider what you write. An impersonal 'Dear Sir or Madam' beginning to an all-purpose letter and a general CV will not gain anyone's attention.
- Contact the main office of a chain to ask for the name and title of the person to whom you should write. Or phone a centre and ask for the name of the manager.
- Draft your letter to say something specific and sensible about what attracts you to a job with this nursery chain or why you feel you are suited to working in this kind of centre. Then enclose a copy of your CV.

Tips for practice

- Take care in drafting your CV. It will create the first impression of you for most prospective employers.
- Lay your CV out clearly, spell it correctly and write or type it on good quality paper. If you have more than one page, then use a second sheet, rather than writing on the back.
- There are great advantages to using a word processor and saving your CV in a file. A printed CV looks more professional than a hand written one and you can update it more easily.
- You can also save slightly different versions of a CV if your professional experience means you are suitable for different types of jobs.
- Your CV should include basic personal information, your education and qualifications, relevant experience and any jobs – all with dates. You could add a couple of sentences about your leisure interests.
- Include the names and contact details of at least one, preferably two people who could give you a reference. Ask their permission first. Suitable references would be from a previous employer or your college tutor, if this is your first job.

The job interview

If you are successful, your job application will lead to an interview. If there are considerably more candidates than posts, then settings, or a family seeking to employ a nanny, will make a short list rather than interviewing everyone. This is one more reason why your application and CV, as well as any telephone conversation you have, needs to promote a positive image.

Tips for practice

- Prepare yourself for an interview with a clear understanding of where you need to be and by when.
- Take original copies of your certificates in case the interviewers wish to see these.
- Dress in a smart style. The actual work with children does not require very formal clothes. But you show serious purpose in an interview when you arrive with well pressed clothes, clean shoes and tidy hair.
- Go with a few questions that you would like to ask. You may have some specific queries that could affect whether you would want the job.
- But some sensible questions will show the interviewers or family that you can communicate and have thought about this post.
- It is reasonable for you to ask a setting in advance about the interviewing procedure. For instance, will you be shown around the setting? Will you face a panel of people or just the manager?

No interview is the same and being interviewed for a nanny post is likely to be less formal, although no less serious, than an interview with an early years setting.

- You may be interviewed by one person or more than one, even a small panel in some settings.

- The interviewer(s) will have prepared questions to ask. You should answer honestly and in reasonable detail but not at great length.
- If you face a panel, then speak to the person who asked you the question, but try to include the others in your eye contact.
- You are likely to be asked some questions specific to your experience so far. Be ready to show, for example, how your experience of traveller families will be an asset to this setting. Even if this will be your first job, you could speak positively, perhaps about your voluntary work with children with learning disabilities.
- If you know there are gaps in your CV, then have some sensible replies to what you were doing in the 'empty' six months or why you had three jobs in very quick succession.
- You could well be asked a couple of 'What if …?' questions to explore how you would approach common dilemmas in work with children or parents. You might be asked, 'How would you handle the situation if a three year old swore in your group?' or 'What should you do if a parent asked you confidential information about another family?'
- Any post should allow that you will continue to learn within this job so you can show enthusiasm for continued professional development. You do not have to know everything.
- You may also be asked what has attracted you to this job. You need to make a professional response linked to the work as you understand it. Interviewers will not be impressed by a reply that it is an easy bus route from your home.

Starting a job

If you are successful in the interview then a final job offer, in a setting or with a family, will usually depend on checking your references. So long as that stage is positive, you will be offered a job. You then want, and need, written confirmation of your terms of employment. If you work with a family, the contract may be short but a formal agreement is still wise to ensure that both you and the family are clear about the conditions.

Conditions of the job

Written agreements manage everyone's expectations of the job. At the most basic you need:

- A contract that provides your conditions of employment, including salary, hours of work and holidays, notice period and any sickness and maternity rights associated with the job.
- In a setting you should have a job description that outlines the main responsibilities of your post.
- If you work as a nanny, then a contract plus a detailed conversation should lead to clarity on the boundaries to your job.

A written contract and job description should allow you to see broadly what is expected of you and then conversations can reasonably fill in the details as you need. In an early years setting, the policies should also help you to understand what exactly is meant by 'use positive strategies to guide children's behaviour' or 'promote equal opportunities'.

Support in your job

In a job with a family, you would use conversation as a means to explore further how the job can develop and resolve any different perspectives. If you work in a setting then it is reasonable to expect a pattern of support from the manager and more experienced colleagues:

- Support and guidance in the early weeks and months of your post. You should not be left to discover what is expected because you make avoidable mistakes.
- Colleagues should be ready to explain and show you the different responsibilities within your work. You need, in your turn, to be ready to ask for guidance.
- Some settings have an organised induction period or offer a named, more experienced colleague who can act as your mentor.
- It is good practice that settings offer supervision to all the team, however experienced. Your supervision sessions, with the manager or deputy, will be an opportunity to ask questions and raise issues.

Continued professional development

Key terms

Continued professional development active efforts to extend and update your own knowledge and skills in your area of work

Constructive feedback positive approaches to communication in order to enable others to learn from their actions, choice of approach and decisions

Good practice in early years is to be ready to extend your learning, known as **continued professional development**. You will be able to develop your skills in different ways:

- Learning from colleagues who are more experienced than you overall or in some areas. Be ready to ask as well as express appreciation for guidance from colleagues. You will soon offer ideas and experience in return.
- Flexible roles within a setting can ensure that team members add to their skills because no one is fixed in the same pattern.
- You can learn through individual study: reading or using other resources such as video. This approach will probably be more valuable if you can then exchange ideas with colleagues.
- You can attend short or longer courses. Again, you will gain more when team members share key ideas and perspectives on their return to the setting.

You will sometimes make mistakes and a supportive team and manager should help you learn from any error or confusion. The principles of **constructive feedback** are important to create a positive exchange (see page 605).

Figure 20.1

Early years practitioners build experience by involvement in all activities

Tips for practice

- Everyone needs to be willing to continue to learn. Only stale, irresponsible practitioners take an approach of 'I've done my training, so that's it.'
- You need to be willing to reflect on your practice. Realising that you could improve in an area of practice is not the same as saying you have done it all wrong up to now.
- You need to build the confidence to ask for feedback on your current practice from a supervisor or colleagues.
- It is then fair to expect constructive remarks, designed to help you improve and not blunt criticism.

Some errors may be more significant and any manager will take seriously a pattern of persistent poor practice, especially once a practitioner has received support and clear guidance about what is expected. Serious mistakes that led to potential or actual risk to a child would almost certainly have to be written up as a report. Errors of judgement that affected families have to be documented, in case parents wish to lodge a formal complaint (see page 618).

The development of teamwork

There needs to be a sense of community within any early years setting, so that everyone can depend on support through good working relationships.

Building a team

The development of **teamwork** depends on trust, which grows from direct experience of how other people behave. Teams within an early years setting, or any other workplace, learn to trust each other because daily experience tells them that their colleagues are:

- *Reliable*: people do what they promise to do. Being reliable does not mean you have to be perfect. Reliable team members speak up if there is any difficulty or confusion.
- *Consistent*: you need to trust that your colleagues will show good practice every day. Behaviour should not depend on their mood or whether they like a colleague, a child or parent.
- *Honest*: people will tell you, courteously, what they feel and what is happening, rather than leaving you to guess or to carry on with a misunderstanding.

The manager of a setting has a responsibility to promote teamwork and to address any circumstances that disrupt good team working and open communication. It is, however, the individual responsibility of each early years practitioner in a team to behave professionally and to raise any issues in a balanced and honest way if team working has become difficult.

Key terms

Teamwork
actions and an outlook that enable individuals to work in a way that is consistent and supportive of each other and the values of the setting

To think about

- Saying that a team has to build up trust in each other is not the same as suggesting colleagues are deceitful or untrustworthy characters. If teams have a low level of trust, it usually means that colleagues lack confidence in each other.
- Perhaps you check up on each other too much. Or some team members may have brought their uneasiness into this team because in a previous job they really did have to keep chasing, 'Have you done that report yet?' or 'You haven't forgotten you were going to get the museum tickets?'
- This kind of chasing feels like being nagged and can create irritated exchanges. Colleagues need to discuss what is happening and the feelings experienced by both parties. More general problems of trusting each other may need to be expressed at a team meeting, supported by your manager.

As an early years practitioner you need to recognise that you are part of a team. In any early years setting you do not all have the same responsibilities and some of your work may leave you scope for initiative about exactly how you run a day or session. Any team will benefit from the skills and talents of individuals. But those individual practitioners are interdependent; they depend one each other. **Interdependence** means that:

Key term

Interdependence when the actions of one person have direct consequences for others in a team situation

- What one individual does in his or her work will affect other team members, for instance, an offhand approach to parents by one person can sour relations in the whole setting. On a daily basis in early years settings, you need to discuss plans. For instance, your wish to take a group to the local library may have consequences for colleagues' potential choices.
- You all need to follow policies and procedures on key aspects of your practice such as health and safety or child protection. Again, one team member cannot decide to opt out.
- Good practice for the children requires a consistent approach on issues such as a positive approach to behaviour. Children recognise that adults are individuals, but they should not have to deal with significant differences in what practitioners will allow (see page 482).

Working well as a team member

You need to understand how your setting is organised and that different early years and out of school care settings can vary.

- Your broad working role should be clear from your job description. However, you and your colleagues will need to discuss the details of who does what within each day or session.
- Flexible working can ensure that work with children is more interesting and that you can extend your skills. Perhaps you have a talent for printing and can take the craft group today. Or perhaps you would like to improve your story telling skills, so would like to work alongside a colleague who is currently more confident in this area than you feel.
- Teamwork and open communication needs to support all your colleagues and to address any problems of restricting anyone in their role.

- For instance, it is important that male colleagues in a mixed team do not end up with all the football and none of the nose wiping. Or none of the football, because the team has become confused about anti-discriminatory practice and believes that challenge to gender stereotypes should be continuous.
- Teamwork also means that you need to be clear when you would need to involve a more senior colleague in a situation, for instance in some aspects of child protection (page 560) or if a parent became highly argumentative.

The key person system

Quality in work with babies and young children can only be delivered through a caring, personal relationship between baby or child and an individual practitioner. It is not possible to meet this good practice without a **key person** (key worker or primary worker) system. This way of organising a team in a nursery applies across the age range, but is especially important in good practice with babies and toddlers.

If it is to work well, the main features of the key person system are:

- The same practitioner is responsible for the physical needs of a very small number of individual babies and toddlers. Very young children need to be able to recognise the face of the person who changes them, feeds them or to whom they wake from a nap.
- The key person can respond sensitively to individual babies and toddlers, know their preferences and develop personal rituals of songs, smiles and enjoyable 'jokes'.
- The key person can develop a friendly relationship with the child's parent, sharing ideas about the young child and communicating important information about the day or the baby's state of health.
- The key person will also be the one who keeps a baby or young child's records, to track her learning and to observe.
- The key person system does not create exclusive relationships; there should be no possessive sense of 'my children' as opposed to 'your children'. You would relate warmly to other children and parents.

Key term

Key person
a named team member who has special responsibilities for working with a small number of named children and building a relationship with their parent(s). Also sometimes called key worker or primary worker

Activity

- How does the key person system work in your setting?
- Compare usual practice with the description in this section.
- Be pleased about good practice and make suggestions about any improvements.

Key skills links: C3.3 WO3.1–3

Diversity in teams

There will always be some diversity within a team; practitioners are all individuals. But sometimes the diversity may seem more obvious or needs to be discussed in an open way because practice issues have arisen.

Figure 20.2

In many settings, adults will include practitioners and parents, also perhaps volunteers and students

The multi-disciplinary team

In some early years settings the team will not all share the same qualifications and sometimes there may be a mix of colleagues who have experience but no formal qualifications as yet. A multi-disciplinary team is more usual in family centres or combined settings such as early excellence centres. It is also usual that schools have a mix of staff with early years and childcare qualifications, teacher training and classroom support assistant training and/or experience.

Tips for practice

Good teamwork requires that everyone shows respect for the experience and qualifications of colleagues.

- You can show actively that you value colleagues' different skills by being willing to consult and learn from them.
- There must be no sense of 'I'm qualified so you do what I tell you' to an unqualified colleague.
- It is equally important that you show confidence and are prepared to be assertive, if you work in a setting where your qualifications and experience are not appreciated.
- Partly your approach needs to avoid unnecessary apology; there is nothing to be gained by comments that start, 'I know I'm only a …'.
- But then you need to show your good practice and professionalism in work such as report writing, responsible discussion about the children or being able to problem solve rather than argue.

Activity

All teams include some diversity in personal background, skills and interests. Check first with your manager to explain what you are doing. Then undertake a simple 'skills and experience audit' of your own setting.

- Ask your colleagues to describe their particular talents and interests.
- What are the areas of knowledge within the team?
- Do emphasise, if need be, that you are not requiring immense expertise. Many adults are very quick to say, 'I'm not very good at …'.
- Have colleagues travelled and do they have additional languages?
- What range of social, cultural or faith backgrounds are represented in the team?
- Do not forget your own contribution; what do you have to offer?
- Write up your notes and make a short presentation to your colleagues on the course, being careful to maintain confidentiality about your setting colleagues.
- Discuss what you have found in different settings.

Key skills links: C3.1a C3.1b

Scenarios

These settings have faced some issues and uncertain decisions about appropriate and inappropriate use of the diversity in their teams. Please consider, and ideally discuss with colleagues, each example and decide:

- Is this an appropriate use of this practitioner's individual background or skills?
- If you feel the situation is inappropriate, then briefly explain your reasons. How might it be made more appropriate, if necessary?
- Discuss with your colleagues and make links across to similar situations you have faced in your setting.

1 *Greenholt Pre-school* has 15 year old Justin on work placement from the local secondary school. The boys in the pre-school have been thrilled to have a 'big boy' coming every morning. They hang on Justin's arm and want him to play monsters with them. Marjorie, the pre-school leader has suggested that Justin also try some quieter activities with the children, especially books and songs, but Justin does not seem comfortable with either reading or singing.

2 *Dresden Road* Nursery School serves an ethnically diverse area that has more variety than the team itself. Rosemary, the deputy, is of mixed heritage, Jamaican and Irish. Some of the less experienced team members seem to lack confidence in talking with African-Caribbean parents and are keen for Rosemary to take these conversations.

3 Within the *Wessex childminding network* James is the only male childminder. In group meetings of the network he feels that he is asked

to speak far too much as a male childminder rather than a childminder who happens to be a man and a father. Laura, the network coordinator, listens, but suggests that if they ignore that James is male then they are losing a valuable perspective.

4 In the *Dale Parent and Toddler drop-in group* Liz has experience from another job of using sign language. It has become clear that two year old Kitty in the group may be deaf and is certainly having difficulty in her language development. Kitty's parents are keen for Liz to use her sign language with Kitty and to teach them as well.

5 *St Jude's Reception class* is run by Jessie and Maryam. They are currently organising a festivals topic for next term. Maryam was raised a Muslim but she would not count herself as practising. Jessie wants Maryam to gather the information on Id–ul–Fitr and organise the visit to the local mosque. Maryam is unsure why this work should be delegated to her.

6 *Kimberley* works as a nanny with two families. The parents of one family recently discovered that Kimberley is relatively fluent in Spanish. They have asked her to introduce the children to this language through books and songs. The family is not bilingual but the parents have read that young children are open to learning a second language.

Key skills links: C3.1a

Male early years practitioners

Most of you reading this book are going to be women, because the vast majority of early years practitioners are female. In 2001 less than 1 per cent of trained nursery nurses were men, about 1.5 per cent of playgroup leaders were male, 0.5 per cent of childminders, 3.3 per cent of classroom assistants and 3 per cent of nursery teachers and still only 17 per cent of primary school teachers. In terms of daily contact in early years settings, the teams are overwhelmingly female.

Figure 20.3

Teenagers on placement can be a positive addition to a setting

A male early years practitioner will be in the minority, usually a minority of one. So it is important that:

- Teams welcome a male colleague and are ready to talk around what he brings as a male grown-up for the children as well as an individual member of the team.
- Of course a male colleague has responsibilities to work well with the team, but everyone needs to acknowledge that he will stand out visually as a minority, at least in the beginning.
- Some parents may be wary and feel that care of young children is more appropriately a woman's task. It is a team responsibility to promote that men can be competent carers of babies and young children.
- A male practitioner can show a good role model of a caring male to all the children, some of whom may not have good experiences of responsible men.
- But it is an appropriate use of his skills that a male colleague also takes a visible role in promoting intellectual learning, especially important for boys and early literacy.
- A misunderstanding of child protection has fuelled unease about male practitioners (see page 553). Your setting should have effective checks on new staff and an atmosphere that enables concerns to be raised about any colleague. It is discriminatory to assume a male colleague is more likely to abuse than a female and therefore to restrict his duties in care.

Diversity in ethnic and cultural background

Some teams will have the opportunities that arise from having colleagues from a range of ethnic backgrounds and perhaps with two or more languages at their disposal. Any use of team members' knowledge or experience needs to be against a backdrop of responsibilities to the children and parents that are shared by everyone. For example:

- It would be inappropriate to say that a Greek Cypriot colleague would always be the key worker for the Cypriot children in your setting, not least because some families may be Turkish Cypriot. But it may be very helpful that your colleague is bilingual in Greek and English for those parents and children who are at an early stage of learning English as an additional language.
- A colleague who follows the Hindu faith may be a good initial source of knowledge in building up the resources of your setting. But it would be unwise to depend upon one person for an understanding of any world faith. All the world religions have different sects and a project exploring celebrations or faith artefacts can be a learning experience for adults too – both for those who are within as well as outside that faith.

Colleagues with disabilities

The larger early years settings (those with more than 15 staff) are required like any other organisation to make reasonable adjustments to allow disabled employees to work effectively. However, equally so, a setting is not required to employ a disabled person if there would be an unacceptable risk to children or anyone else.

So, it is possible that your team could include some colleagues with disabilities or you yourself could have a disability or continuing health condition.

- Teams need to see, and discuss when necessary, the opportunities and need for support that may arise. Practitioners who have disabilities need to be colleagues first and disabled second (see also the approach to disabled children in Chapter 18).

- A colleague with some level of hearing loss might be able to offer children direct experience of communication when one partner is deaf.
- Some team members may have dyslexia and need support over written material. This disability should not mean that a practitioner opts out of this part of the job, but that he or she will need some practical help (see page 466).
- Disabilities that affect mobility may help a team to consider the use of space and furniture in a way that could open up the environment for everyone.

If you are on your own

Some early years practitioners do not work within a team. Childminders may have a local advisor or a network coordinator who could be consulted in confidence. Nannies are likely to work very much on their own. In both these working roles it can be even more important that you are able to talk with and raise issues with children's parents. Nannies and childminders will still sometimes need to work cooperatively with other professionals in childcare, education or health.

Skills of communication and problem solving

At the most basic level of good practice, good communication means that you take the time to talk with and listen to your colleagues in an even-handed and fair way. You have the right to expect that your views and concerns get a hearing, but you need to offer the same level of attention and respect in return.

Exchange of information

Colleagues in an early years setting need to keep each other up to date with children's progress and with any events in a family. Practitioners who work together will usually pass on information as they carry out the tasks of the day. But conversation between adults should never become more important than paying attention to the children and, of course, you would not discuss confidential family matters in front of the children. You will often have to brief senior or other colleagues responsible for a child or family. A system of written reminders, a diary or notebook, can help.

Activity

Teamwork requires good communication and part of your role is to understand clearly what kinds of information need to be passed on and to whom in your setting. Look at the following examples and check that you are clear on the following points.

- Should you tell or ask someone else about this matter?
- Who should you tell or ask?

1 You notice a plant in the garden that looks like deadly nightshade.
2 You and your room colleague would like to take the children to a story telling session in the local library.

3 A parent explains the advice she has been given to support the communication and play of her son who has autistic spectrum disorder. She would like the suggestions followed in your setting.
4 A father telephones to say that his daughter is in hospital with suspected meningitis.
5 You notice threadworms in the pot after one toddler has gone to the toilet.
6 A mother explains her tears to you by confiding that she had a miscarriage last week.
7 A parent tells you that she has heard loud arguments and screaming coming from the home of a family whose children also attend your setting.

Discuss your answers and any guidance from your setting with your colleagues on the course.

Key skills link: C3.1a

Active listening and understanding

Genuine listening is hard work because your attention has to be on what the other person is saying, and meaning, rather than on what you wish to say. Colleagues who work together need to listen to each other so that their work with children and parents can be safe and effective. You also need to listen as well as talk in meetings (see page 604), so that all ideas can be gathered and problems effectively resolved.

You need to combine attentive listening with other communication skills to check that you understand. All these skills are generally valuable; in slightly different ways you can also apply them in communication with parents and the children.

Reflecting back

You can reflect back in your own words what you believe your colleague meant. You will not always need to use reflecting back, but it can be useful to confirm that you have understood and to avoid misunderstandings. For instance: 'So, you'd like me to keep Sharon occupied while you have a chat with her Mum. That's fine with me.' Or 'You're not happy about the way we've been organising tea time. Let's talk about it then.'

Summarising

Sometimes it is useful to sum up what you have discussed with a colleague. Your brief summary gives the other person the opportunity to confirm, clarify or expand on what has just been covered. For instance: 'I'll do the first draft of the reports on Melanie and Damian. You'll do Sammi and Alric. Then we'll get together Tuesday afternoon and work on the final versions.'

Using questions

Sometimes these will be closed questions, which need only one-word answers. For instance: 'Did you say that Ella and her daughter were starting next Monday?' On other occasions, the use of open-ended questions invites fuller answers and will lead to more information. For instance: 'What issues would you like me to raise with Selena's health visitor?' It is far better to ask questions than to risk making wrong assumptions.

You can use your own communication skills to set a positive tone in working well with colleagues. If they do not appear to listen to you, then you may need to address the situation in a courteous way. Perhaps you could say, 'Is that fine with you? What I've just said about writing the reports?' or 'I find it hard to believe you're listening if you don't look at me'.

Tips for practice

Some people are probably better natural listeners than others, but everyone can improve their listening skills. You need to:

- Plan how to listen well in your own working situation and draw on those communication skills that you already have.
- Pay attention to what seems to distract you from listening well and work to improve those areas within your control.
- Focus on what is being said rather than your next question or immediate concerns about what you have heard.
- Good listeners do not rush to interrupt or make their own points.
- Establish a comfortable personal space between you and the other person.
- Maintain friendly eye contact through regularly looking at the other person, holding the gaze for a while and breaking the gaze, usually by looking down briefly.
- Keep your body language open and gestures simple. Try to avoid both a very closed posture and gestures that are so expressive as to be distracting.

Misunderstandings

However well you communicate, it is inevitable that sometimes there will be misunderstandings. People can draw very different conclusions from the same conversation. This can even happen when communication is at its most straightforward – between two people, sharing the same language, face-to-face and with no interruptions. The potential for misunderstanding can arise for different reasons:

- There is a gap between what someone is thinking about saying and what is actually said. The comment or request does not come out as you or they intended. This situation is the one where one person says, 'But didn't I say …?' and the other person honestly answers, 'No you didn't.'
- If one person is not speaking in their most fluent language, then they may not be easily understood in everything they say. Team members need to support each other and be ready to ask, 'Can you say that again, please' or 'I'm not sure if I follow. Is it that you want me to …?'
- There are subtleties in every language that may only come to light when you have a mixed staff team. For instance, in English the phrase 'Would you like to lay the table' is often used as a request and not a question. A colleague whose English is an additional language, as well as some children, may react as if this is a question and say, 'No'.

- Everybody approaches communication with some assumptions – about the person speaking and what she or he is likely to mean. These assumptions shape the sense that is made of any conversation and can lead to a gap, sometimes wide, between what was heard and what was actually received.
- Non-verbal communication carries more meaning than the spoken words. Gestures, tone of voice and the facial expression of the speaker give additional messages which may not be intended, although they may be an honest reflection of what is felt.

In a setting with a good working atmosphere, it should be possible for misunderstandings to be resolved before matters become serious. Senior practitioners may need to intervene as a third party if misunderstandings have created a bad atmosphere that is not being resolved.

Honest expression of views

Good communication within an early years team depends on an assertive approach from each individual. **Assertiveness** is frequently confused with an **aggressive approach**, so it is important to distinguish between the two.

When you behave in an assertive way then you are:

- standing up for your own rights, but in such a way that you do not dismiss or ignore the rights of other people
- expressing your wants, opinions, feelings and beliefs in a direct and honest way and allowing space for the ideas and experience contributed by others.

Assertive communication in a team means that opinions or concerns are far more likely to be expressed honestly and in a timely fashion, but also with a sensitivity to the feelings and perspective of colleagues.

The alternative to an assertive approach is not always one of aggression. It is equally unhelpful if team members take a **passive** or **submissive approach**. When you or your colleagues behave in a submissive way, then opinions do not get expressed, or else they are lost in too much apology or, 'I'm sure this really isn't important …'.

Of course your manager has a major responsibility to run meetings and other informal exchanges in a way that makes it easier for everyone to speak up and be heard. But the responsibility for assertive communication is shared within the team. Managers can only give so much help if a team member chooses to remain silent but moans later, 'I had a good idea but of course nobody bothered to ask me!'

Key terms

Assertiveness confident expression of your own views and preferences and allowing space for the views and choices of others

Aggressive approach using fierce words and/or actions to insist on your own views or preferences and to minimise those of others

Passive or **submissive approach** reluctance to be honest about your own opinions or preferences and allowing others to make the choice

Activity

Look at the comments that follow and decide which of them show an assertive approach. Discuss your ideas with colleagues, especially:

- What might be the consequences in an early years team of the non-assertive comments?
- How could you re-phrase the aggressive or submissive comments to make them assertive?

(You will find the answers on page 610.)

1 'The problem with you is that you always think you're right. Just because you've worked in a school, you think you can lord it over the rest of us. We're qualified too, you know!'

2 'I expect this isn't really important. Probably it's because I'm not a physiotherapist. But isn't Dolan's therapy actually making her worse?'

3 'I'm concerned. I think the parents who help us in the pre-school aren't getting enough explanation before they start. So they're making mistakes that could be avoided if they knew better what we wanted.'

4 'Maybe I've got the wrong impression about this trip. I know I'm new here and I suppose you know best. But shouldn't we have a few more adults in the group?'

5 'Jerry, we've spoken before about how you criticise the children's behaviour in their hearing. I believe it's disrespectful towards them. If you keep doing this, I'll have to talk with Olivia (the manager).'

6 'That just won't work with this kind of family. If you'd worked with children for twenty years like I have, then you'd understand.'

7 'Tony, I would really like your observations of Kathy to add to our report by Tuesday at the latest. Can you do that?'

8 'I'm terribly sorry; I know this is short notice and I guess it's because I'm so disorganised. But would you mind very much if I left the keys for you to lock up tonight?'

9 'I don't know how you can stand there and ask me to listen out for the phone. Can't you see how busy I am?'

10 'I would prefer not to change shifts with Sandy. I'm taking my daughter to an orthodontic appointment that afternoon. I don't want to cancel it because it'll be months before they give me another date.'

11 'I appreciate that you're very busy Saira, but welcoming the parents is part of our job in this room.'

Source: This exercise is modified slightly from Jennie and Lance Lindon *Working Together for Young Children: A guide for managers and staff* (Thomson Learning 1997).

Key skills links: C3.1a

Communication in meetings

Figure 20.4

Team discussion can mean consistency in the approach to activities

A great deal of valuable communication in early years settings will happen informally through conversation. But you will experience some communication within meetings, either whole staff or room meetings and possibly some meetings to which other professionals are invited. It is likely that a meeting will be led and chaired by your manager or a senior colleague. This person will be responsible for ensuring an effective meeting but it will be your responsibility to:

- Speak up and express your views in a courteous and assertive way, as described earlier within this section.
- Listen to colleagues and ask questions if you do not understand or completely follow what they have said or suggested.
- Share the responsibility in any meeting to speak up if you are not clear about, 'exactly what we are going to do about …' or who is going to do what and by when.
- Be ready to fulfil your own commitments to a team meeting, such as give a short report on how the children have reacted to the new role play area. Or

you might present the information you promised to track about opening times and costs for a visit to the new wetlands centre and bird sanctuary.

Tips for practice

Some early years practitioners feel more comfortable in meetings than others. You need to get to know how you react and improve your skills from that point.

- Listen properly to others and build your contribution onto what has already been said.
- You can also courteously point out gaps in the discussion by comments like, 'I think we may be overlooking ...' or 'Can we go back to ...'.
- If you know you lack confidence in speaking up, then prepare yourself rather than sit there fuming, 'Why doesn't anybody ask me!'
- You might make yourself a few notes or ask for a specific slot on the agenda. Practise non-apologetic ways of starting your contribution.
- On the other hand, you may realise that you tend to dominate meetings – be honest with yourself.
- Practise making your contribution and stopping. Listen to others and ensure you understand what they are saying before you start.
- You may need to tolerate silences rather than rushing to fill them.

Constructive feedback

Communication within a team and in other working relationships is much more effective if everyone understands and follows the principles of constructive feedback. In this chapter the focus is on communication in the team but these ideas can also be useful for your partnership with parents.

Giving constructive feedback is a communication technique in the sense that there are basic ground rules to follow, but these are not complicated. Learning to give feedback well requires serious consideration of two key points:

- What is the basis for what I am saying?
- How can I make what I say as useful as possible to the other person?

Tips for practice

In working life, or personal for that matter, your feedback will be most useful if you give it in such a way that the person on the receiving end is able to:

- understand the content of the feedback
- accept the feedback
- able to do something as a result of the feedback.

Be specific

When you are giving feedback, you need to focus on what has happened and on your reactions – positive or negative.

- Vague feedback is not useful in helping others to do better, nor to appreciate what has been very well done.

- Being told 'you did well this morning' is pleasant, but the words do not tell you much about your practice. It will be more useful if you hear, 'I think you've really got the idea now of when to speak up in the parents' group and when to listen.'
- Vague negative comments, especially if they are from a more senior practitioner, may make staff feel that they should change – but in what way?

Describe what you have observed

Useful feedback focuses on *what* someone has done or not done: how exactly this person behaved.

- The emphasis on description rather than judgement makes the feedback more useful, as well as easier to accept.
- Words such as 'never' or 'always' are best avoided in feedback, since they are rarely true and tend to make the person on the receiving end feel defensive or hostile.
- It is unhelpful to use labels of someone's personality or style. Negative labelling (for instance, 'you're insensitive') is likely to place other people on the defensive because they have no manoeuvring room.
- Positive labels can restrict workers as well. For instance, a worker who is told 'you're always so capable' may feel unwilling to admit to having any difficulty with anything.
- It is more helpful if you give a recent example of what you mean, whether the message is a compliment or criticism.

What and not why

Useful feedback is restricted to what you have observed and an honest expression of your viewpoint.

- Sometimes people offer an explanation of someone else's behaviour because it seems to soften the criticism, but this is rarely helpful because it is based on assumptions like, 'I'm sure what you meant was …'.
- Undoubtedly, a person's reasons behind a particular action, or inaction, can be an important part of the conversation that develops from good feedback.
- If you feel you need to explore possible reasons with a colleague, then open-ended questions will do the job much better than guesses. For instance, you could ask, 'What were your concerns about …?' or 'How were you hoping that the conversation would go …?'

Be honest about opinions

When you work alongside someone or have observed their practice, you will have opinions.

- These views can be very useful but only if they are honestly communicated, with evidence, as your opinion and not as if they are absolute facts.
- A personal opinion should be expressed honestly as 'I think' or 'I feel'. You should follow with 'because …' or 'Here's the way that I've been looking at this incident … Let me explain'.

Scenario

Ciaran, the manager of Baker Street Children and Family Centre, is in a rush this morning and has spoken without thinking. He has said 'Sian, you've got yourself in a state about anything to do with parents, all because Joanne's Dad came charging in over the business of the trip money.'

Ciaran thinks during the morning and goes back to Sian to say, 'I'm sorry. I wasn't very helpful earlier today', and he takes a more constructive approach now with, 'I'd like to talk with you about what happened with Joanne's Dad. I'm concerned that incident has shaken your confidence about facing the more argumentative parents.'

Questions

1. What makes Ciaran's first remark less helpful to Sian?
2. Discuss with your colleague any recent examples when members of your own team, or you yourself, have expressed an opinion as if it were a fact that needed no further support. (Keep any details about team members confidential.)
3. How were people encouraged to support their opinion or could they have been helped to be more constructive in what they said?
4. Possibly role play one or more examples in a positive way.

Key skills links: WO3.2 C3.1a

Balance positives and negatives

A brief conversation may focus on a single part of someone's work or on a particular event. If the working relationship between two colleagues has been constructive so far, then there will be no need to add a positive comment to the current constructive criticism. The previous experience of the practitioner receiving the feedback tells him or her that the colleague does not simply pick on what has gone less well in the work. Within your whole working relationship with colleagues, children and parents it is important to balance up positives and negatives.

Tips for practice

Feedback will not always be welcome, however carefully you express yourself.

- You can never be certain that people to whom you are giving feedback will not become defensive. You can only increase the chance that they will listen and consider what you are saying.
- Sometimes, other people's feelings about your feedback will be strong enough to make it hard for them to listen.
- In this case, there is little point in repeating yourself. Focus on the other person's feelings and try to understand why the emotions are running high.
- Team members' reactions will be influenced by their previous experiences of feedback. It takes time to build everyone's confidence that the feedback is being shared from a genuine desire to improve the quality of work and to develop everyone's skills.
- Managers and senior team members have a special responsibility to encourage a positive working atmosphere and to model good practice in giving and receiving feedback.

Receiving feedback

There is a shared responsibility over feedback since good working relationships also depend on how people react to what is said to them. These are positive guidelines for when you are on the receiving end of feedback.

Look and listen

This is a very simple guideline and is the one that is probably most often broken.

- You cannot possibly understand what is being said to you, nor come to decide whether it is useful or fair, unless you keep quiet and listen.
- Allow the other person to finish. Resist the temptation to interrupt and try to quieten your inner thoughts.
- But when you have listened, it is fair that you can comment in a positive way on what you have heard.

Make the effort to understand the feedback

- Suspend, for the moment, any attempts to come to a conclusion over whether the feedback is right or justified.
- Concentrate on making sure that you understand what is being said to you. Use the communication skills of reflecting back and summarising to check (see page 601).
- Asking questions can help you to gain more information or clarification but will not help if you use questions in a confronting way.
- For instance, you will not learn anything much of use if you claim, 'How can you possibly say my records are "messy". I'm a very neat person!'
- As an alternative, you might say, 'I don't like being called "messy". But, perhaps it's just the word. Can you explain it to me another way?'
- If the feedback is vague, then ask for a recent example of what your colleague or manager means.

Scenario

Stephanie has spent a great deal of time drafting a new brochure for Greenholt Pre-school. She presents her draft at the team meeting, along with some illustrations and two estimates of costs from local printers. She finds the reaction from her colleagues disheartening, since it all sounds critical.

Marjorie asks, 'Why haven't you included children's drawings?' and 'Why did you only get two estimates?' Trisha comments, 'I'm really not sure about this paragraph on equal opportunities'. Despite feeling daunted Stephanie says, 'These are all good suggestions and I'll think about them. But isn't there anything you liked about my draft?'

Her colleagues look surprised at Stephanie's tone. Marjorie replies, 'Oh, yes, the cartoons are lovely; I just meant we could have some drawings too' and Trisha says, 'Oh, I thought most of it was fine, I was just pointing to what could be a bit better.'

Questions

Unless a team has slid into very negative relationships, a specific request to 'tell me something good about my idea' will usually encourage people to voice the positive reactions that they are not bothering to express.

1 Why do you think people are often swifter with criticisms than positive comments?

2 What tends to be the reaction to 'Why?' questions (as in the example)?

3 Imagine an alternative version to the scenario in which Marjorie and Trisha's comments were very positive. But Stephanie had replied with, 'Do you really think so? I'm still not happy with the wording.' Or 'I'm not sure the cartoons work'. How might her colleagues have felt?

4 Look over the guidelines on giving and receiving feedback. Note three ways that feedback could be improved in your setting.

Key skills links: WO3.2

Think about the feedback received

Listening carefully to feedback can provide some useful thinking time, so long as you are thinking about the feedback details, and not how you intend to argue about it. Further thinking time often occurs afterwards.

- You may especially need to think if the feedback has raised new issues about how you work, or is making you re-evaluate, perhaps uncomfortably, something about which you had previously felt so sure.
- Even if feedback was not put very constructively, there may still be value in what was said. Think over *what* was said more than *how* it was expressed and perhaps consult one or two colleagues.
- Seeking other opinions needs to be done positively, such as 'I'd like to hear your view on …' or 'I'm trying to understand …'.
- It is not helpful to force colleagues to take sides, as in, 'What Ted said in the meeting was rubbish, wasn't it? I'm always polite to parents.'

Accepting compliments

Workers are usually most concerned about how criticism will be taken. Yet, some people respond to positive feedback in such a dismissive way that others no longer bother to give them compliments. If this is the pattern in a setting, the result can be discouraging for everyone. It will be the responsibility of senior practitioners to change the team's approach. It is also possible that practitioners who cannot deal with positive feedback may be failing to offer enough encouragement to children or parents.

- An appropriate reaction to a compliment is simply to say 'Thanks' or 'Thank you for telling me'.
- You might follow this with something specific like, 'I'm glad you think I handled Michael's tantrum calmly.'
- Being pleased is not the same as being boastful. Modesty may lay behind comments such as 'It wasn't that impressive' or 'I thought I could have done better'.
- However, another view is that these replies openly disagree with the person who has made the effort to point out what was done well. Dismissing the compliment then actually appears rude.

Figure 20.5 The whole team needs to be committed to shared values – such as the importance of outdoor play

Ask for feedback

You do not have to wait for a colleague to offer you feedback on some part of your work; you can ask. Use all the guidelines to make the feedback as useful as possible to you.

Dealing with disagreement in a team

Practitioners who have experienced a pattern of positive communication with constructive feedback are more likely to be able to handle differences of opinion and even outright disagreement. A team, led by their manager, needs a reasonable balance:

- Most people would rather have less argument than more. But the lack of any disagreement in a team is not always a positive sign. There are likely to be some differences of opinion and they will still affect practice, even if they are never voiced out loud.
- You can of course have too high a level of disagreement in a team or a negative way of handling differences, so that everyone is forced to take sides. Apart from an unpleasant working atmosphere, good ideas can be lost in the hurly-burly of argument.

Answers to Activity box on page 603

- Assertive comments: 3, 5, 7, 10, 11
- Submissive comments: 2, 4, 8
- Aggressive comments: 1, 6, 9

Tips for practice

- Your manager should encourage good communication as well as set a good example to the whole team.
- Everyone should listen as well as want time to express their own views.
- Problems need to be described in terms of examples of 'what' and 'when'.
- Avoid sweeping statements such as 'you never listen to me' or 'you're always going on about …'.
- Try very hard to see disagreement as something to be discussed and resolved, rather than as a personal attack on you.
- Everyone needs to let incidents go and not hark back once the issues are resolved. You need to start afresh, much as you encourage the children to do after an argument.

Activity

Several scenarios in other chapters could be used to explore problem solving techniques and dealing positively with disagreement.

You can explore by asking:

- What are the more constructive ways out of this difference of opinions?
- What might make matters worse?
- You could role play an incident with colleagues.
- Make links to your own practice.

You can use any of the following scenarios:

1. The Dale Parent and Toddler drop-in in Chapter 3, on page 105 about the use of food as play materials.
2. St Jude's Primary School in Chapter 8 on page 231 about whether children are being 'assertive' or 'cheeky'.
3. Sunningdale Day Nursery in Chapter 10 on page 278, about suitable baby arts and crafts.
4. Baker Street Children and Family Centre in Chapter 13 on page 387 about the Father Christmas email project.
5. Greenholt Pre-school in Chapter 17 on page 484 about over-planning of activities.
6. St Jude's Primary School in Chapter 21 on page 643 about children being made to apologise for something they did not do.

Key skills links: LP3.103 WOI3.1–3

It is important that your manager or a senior colleague runs meetings so that everyone has a chance to speak and more than one side is heard for an issue. Sometimes difficulties in the team will need to be resolved in face-to-face conversation.

An assertive approach can help to defuse a problem situation between colleagues. You need to focus on what is happening, rather than on personal criticisms. For instance, assertive communication about a problem follows this kind of pattern:

- A brief description of the event or the problem area – for example, 'When I was speaking with Stefan's father you interrupted me and started to explain about our policy on equal opportunities …'.
- Your feelings, expressed honestly – 'I felt angry and embarrassed …'.
- Brief explanation – 'because I felt it made me look as if I didn't understand …'.
- What you would rather have happen – 'I don't mind you listening or even joining a conversation, but please wait to see what I'm going to say.'

This kind of approach has more chance of being a constructive conversation between colleagues than an approach such as: 'Why don't you trust me?' or 'You're always interrupting and undermining me with the parents!'

Ideally colleagues resolve problems in an informal way. But if daily communication does not resolve conflict between you and a colleague, it is your responsibility to ask your manager or a senior to facilitate a discussion in which she or he ensures that both of you get to speak and listen.

Working with other professionals

You will work most closely with the other team members in your setting but you will have contact with other professionals who work with children and families. Look at page 17 for a description of the range of services and professions with whom you may have contact.

Good practice in your working relationship with other professionals will have a great deal in common with teamwork with your colleagues and partnership with parents. Good communication skills and approaches to resolving problems or disagreements are consistent across working relationships with any other adults. It will also be important that you develop a positive and confident professional identity yourself. In society there tends to be a hierarchy of professions and people who work with the very youngest children have often not been fully respected.

Figure 20.6
You may need to explain the value of play to some outside professionals

Tips for practice

- Working together with other professionals means showing confidence in your own skills as well as respecting those of others.
- If other professionals seem to doubt your skills, then show what you can do through your behaviour. Demonstration will be more effective than saying, 'I am a professional too, you know'.
- Share your ideas, perspectives and knowledge without always waiting to be asked. Be courteous, yet assertive and show that you expect a two-way exchange of professional knowledge.
- Be clear about the priorities in your work as well as the boundaries.
- If in doubt, then check with your manager about appropriate practice, for instance if an external professional asks to consult a family's file.
- It is professional to admit that you do not know something or that you would like further explanation. Of course, it is also professional that you ensure you have information at your finger tips that you should know.
- Keep the commitments you offer and avoid making promises or setting time scales which you cannot honour.
- Be ready to follow up courteously on other people's commitments when you are working together.

Policies and practice in a setting

Your responsibilities as an early years practitioner include following the policies and procedures of your setting. The difference is usually that:

- *policies* lay out key principles that inform and guide work
- *procedures* give the details of the steps that must be followed.

The law will sometimes shape policy, for instance over equal opportunities in employment or requirements for health and safety. But policies are also a form of clear communication for a team and parents about values and priorities in the work. Policies need not be very long but should be clearly written, ideally in the main languages spoken by families who attend your setting. Polices should also be open to discussion and review.

Most settings will have written policies on the following issues:

- the application of equal opportunities in the work of the setting
- admissions to the centre, including how any waiting list is operated
- positive handling of children's behaviour and your approach to discipline
- partnership with parents and what this means for this setting
- the details of the early years curriculum in work with the children
- health and safety for workers, children, parents and any visitors
- personnel policy for workers and volunteers.

Of course no policy, however well written, does all the work for a team. Your health and safety policy does not in itself keep children and staff healthy and safe. This goal is achieved because you put the policy into practice day by day. A behaviour policy (see page 614) will contribute to good practice when everyone on the staff team is involved, parents are consulted and of course children are asked for their opinion.

Tips for practice

- You need to know the details of any policies that affect the work in your setting.
- Be ready to look at the details and to ask constructive questions about how the policy comes alive through practice.
- It is important that you behave in line with the policy but you cannot work for good practice if you are unclear what some details of the policy mean.
- Using principles of good communication and feedback, be ready to ask, 'Does this mean that I should ...?' or 'Can you please explain the consequence here if I face ...'.

Developing a policy on behaviour – an example

Children need and deserve consistency from the key adults in their lives as well as an overall positive approach. Early years practitioners have a responsibility to talk and plan positively about the children. You need to work together consistently for the sake for the children.

- Try to notice children's cooperative behaviour at least as often as problems and preferably much more often.
- You should avoid using tales of 'bad' behaviour as coffee time drama. Teams can slip into this bad habit without realising and it creates a negative work atmosphere for dealing with children.
- Be clear and talk in your team about how would you like the children to resolve everyday conflicts. Of course you do not want them to hit each other or grab toys. So how can a young child be enabled to deal with frustration?
- Are you all making sure that difficult times of the day and areas of your setting are made easier? What changes can you make as a responsible adult?
- Are you all consistent between each other on the main approaches to supporting children's behaviour? Do you all follow your own ground rules?

To think about

Some practitioners and parents are very resistant to the positive approach. Within your team, or in communication with parents, you may need to talk through one or more of the following beliefs, well grounded in British cultural traditions of child rearing.

Some common blocks are described, with suggested ways to counter argue.

Belief
Children should just do what they are told. They should not argue, nor expect explanations. Respect is something that children owe adults.

Counter argument
This approach will not work in our current society unless adults bully children and that is unacceptable. But it can be hard for adults to learn that respect can work both ways.

Belief
You have to tell children what they are doing wrong, or else they will not learn. If you do not punish children, they think they can get away with misbehaviour. You need to make children feel guilty about their actions and motives.

Counter argument
This approach just creates unhappy children, anxious about their mistakes; it does not promote learning.

Belief
Too much praise makes children big-headed and spoils them. Offering incentives is the same as bribery.

Counter argument
Encouragement, well used, does not spoil children and is different from the mistake of rewarding them with sweets or treats. Children who experience encouragement generously given, soon show they can give in return, often to their peers or siblings.

Some adults, because they have experienced very limited encouragement within their own childhood or even now as adults, feel uncomfortable initially about being very positive with children. It takes practice and commitment.

- Discuss in your team.

Key skills links: PS3.1 C3.1a

A clear behaviour policy may help a team to develop and maintain a positive approach to children and such a policy is part of communication in partnership with parents.

A behaviour policy is a public statement about your team's commitment to support children's learning in terms of their behaviour. No policy should be too long, probably two or three pages is enough and your policy should communicate three important areas of your practice:

1 The key values that inform your team's overall approach to children's behaviour – similar to those laid out in Chapter 17.
2 Your expectations for everyone's behaviour in the setting: a constructive policy is as much about the behaviour of adults as that of the children.
3 The strategies you will use to guide children's behaviour: your policy should give a flavour of how you help children to behave within the boundaries that are set.

Your behaviour policy can show the vital links between how you handle children's behaviour and how you support their development and learning. The details of your policy could show that the choices made about how to guide children's behaviour are because you want to support their all round development. Such links are very positive because your behaviour policy then shows that this aspect of your good practice is completely linked with how you support children's learning. You could, for instance, explain briefly in the setting's policy, and by conversation with parents, that you all act to support children's:

- self respect and their growing sense of self esteem

- potential for prosocial behaviour
- ability to guide their own behaviour with encouragement and friendly support
- competence in useful social skills such as negotiation with other children and simple problem solving.

Activity

Look carefully at the behaviour policy of your setting and try to read it as someone new to the setting.

- What are the values that underpin the policy? What does it say really matters in a positive approach to children's behaviour?
- Is there a balance between wanted behaviour from children and unwanted?
- Is there a clear commitment to partnership with parents?

If possible, ask for the opinions of some parents:

- Have they seen the policy?
- Do they understand and agree with it?
- Are there parts of the policy that are unclear to them or with which they disagree?

If you work in a primary school or after school club, take the opportunity to invite the children's opinions of the behaviour policy in action.

- What do the children think works well?
- What do they feel needs re-thinking or perhaps would allow for the experience of children in common playground situations?
- Listen to what the children tell you and try to understand their point of view.
- Resist arguing with them; they probably have valid points to make.

If your setting does not have a behaviour policy, then make contact with another local early years setting or school and ask if you could have a copy of theirs. Explain why you would like to read it.

- Discuss the issues with your team and make a draft policy for consideration.

Key skills links: WO3.1–3

To think about

Adults generally spend a great deal more time talking about children whose behaviour troubles them or that is disruptive in the group. You probably do not spend anything like as much time discussing children's cooperative behaviour, thoughtful actions and pleasant periods spent getting along together. Why do you think there is this gap and does it matter? The imbalance matters for several reasons:

- As helpful adults you could probably learn from some discussion about children whose behaviour makes you pleased. Perhaps you behave differently towards them, although not intentionally.
- Excessive discussion about problems can make a team think that all the children are 'difficult'. It can also lead to a situation in which parents are only told when there is a problem. If a child is behaving well then little is said. Such an imbalance does not promote partnership and it is also unfair towards the children.

Policies to deal with poor practice

Poor practice and unacceptable standards in a setting are dealt with through three procedures:

1 *Disciplinary procedures* are started when a worker has failed to comply with codes of conduct in the setting or has behaved unprofessionally.
2 *Grievance procedures* are available for paid staff or voluntary workers when ordinary communication has failed to resolve serious issues such as their conditions of service, lack of management support or unacceptable behaviour towards this practitioner.
3 The *complaints procedure* is for service users, that will be parents in the case of early years settings, although in theory an older child could also act as an aggrieved service user.

Each of these procedures should be easily available in written form to be consulted in any setting. The aim would always be to try to resolve problems through conversation and discussion in the first instance and not to take the more serious and formal steps unless other forms of communication had failed.

Disciplinary procedures

These procedures should never be started lightly, nor should the prospect be held as a threat against a practitioner. But it is a serious matter if practitioners neglect the welfare of children or behave contrary to the policies of a setting, for instance over anti-discriminatory practice.

Disciplinary procedures should include clear steps to be followed if a practitioner's behaviour falls below acceptable standards and that would include a disciplinary interview. Any practitioner should be able to expect fair treatment and the opportunity to speak as well as listen.

The disciplinary interview should be run by the manager in a way that is business-like and formal, including the taking of objective notes. The aims of this interview are to:

- Check the facts of the situation. A manager should explain clearly the gap between what is expected from this practitioner and what is happening in practice.

Key term

Disciplinary procedure
steps to deal with unacceptable behaviour from a member of the team in a setting

- Explore the reasons for this gap. The manager should ask open-ended questions and *listen* to what you, the practitioner, have to say.
- Agree a plan of action to close the gap. The manager should get commitment from the practitioner about changes in her or his practice and explain the consequences if these commitments are not kept. Under some circumstances the manager may also agree to offer special support.

If the practice does not improve then a practitioner should be given formal warnings, at least one in writing. The manager will keep written records and a case will be made for dismissal.

Grievance and complaints procedures

It will be the choice of practitioner to initiate **grievance procedures**, as it is the option of parents or other users of the centre to make a formal complaint through the **complaints procedure**. The manager should neither encourage nor dissuade anyone from starting the process. It is the manager's role to give any necessary paperwork and explain the steps of the procedure. Managers will not handle any of these procedures alone but will inform and consult with their own line management and with the management committee or board of governors as appropriate.

If disciplinary procedures have arisen because of a formal complaint from a parent, then the two processes have to be keep separate. Both are handled in line with the correct procedures and must be seen to be resolved one way or another. The complaint from the parent will become part of the information that has to be considered in the disciplinary process.

Key terms

Grievance procedure
process for a team member to lodge a complaint that she or he has been treated in an unacceptable way

Complaints procedure
process for parents and other users of the setting to lodge a formal complaint about any aspect of the setting and the actions of the team

Activity

Ask to read the procedures in your setting for grievance, disciplinary action and complaints from parents.

- Are the steps in the process clearly explained in the document?
- If there is any confusion about the details, ask questions so that you understand.
- Is it clear what kind of behaviour from practitioners could lead to a disciplinary interview? Again, ask questions if the circumstances are vague.
- Write up a short report on what you have found.
- Compare what you have found with colleagues on your course.

Key skills links: C3.2 C3.3

Figure 20.7

A staff board gives clear communication to staff and visitors

Further resources

Back, Ken and Kate (1991) *Assertiveness at Work – A practical guide to handling awkward situations* McGraw Hill.

Hyder, Tina and Kenway, Penny (1995) *An Equal Future: A guide to anti-sexist practice in the early years* National Early Years Network.

Lane, Jane (1999) *Action for Racial Equality in the Early Years* National Early Years Network.

Lindon, Jennie and Lance (1997) *Working Together for Young Children* Thomson Learning, especially Chapters 3 and 4.

Whalley, Margy (1994) *Learning to be Strong: Setting up a neighbourhood service for under-fives and their families* Hodder and Stoughton.

Progress check

1 Describe three ways to make a positive impression at a job interview as an early years practitioner.

2 Explain briefly why teamwork matters in an early years setting.

3 Describe two ways in which trust can be built in a team.

4 Suggest two ways that early years practitioners can improve their listening skills.

5 Describe two ways that can improve constructive feedback between colleagues.

6 Explain two reasons why settings need clear policies.

7 What is the difference between disciplinary and grievance procedures?

21

Partnership with parents

After reading this chapter you should be able to:

- explain the importance of partnership with parents
- understand ways to build a friendly working relationship with parents
- use skills of communication appropriately with parents
- offer different ways for parents to be involved in your setting.

Introduction

As an early years practitioner, your involvement with a child can be very positive, but in terms of their childhood, you will be temporary. Parents will create the continuity in children's lives and they continue to be important throughout the time that you are involved with the child and family. It is therefore very important that you work in partnership with parents and show respect for their relationship with their child. Parents should be informed about how you work as an individual practitioner or the approach of your setting. They have the right to be consulted about their own children and involved as appropriate, and to the extent that they wish in your setting. This chapter explains good practice in a working relationship with parents as fellow adults.

Links to early years qualifications

This chapter especially supports the following units:

Diploma in Child Care and Education: 7, 10, 11

National Vocational Qualification in Early Years Care and Education

Level 2: P1, P9, C13

Level 3: M7, P5, P8, C14

BTEC National Early Years Diploma: 3, 21, 22

The importance of partnership with parents

Partnership with parents has been raised throughout this book and has been part of some examples. The aim of this chapter is to bring together some of the most important themes and to discuss some of the issues and possible dilemmas that can arise.

Key term

Partnership with parents
the value and practice of working together with parents for the care and learning of their children, acknowledging the continuing importance of parents in the lives of their children

Why is partnership part of good practice?

Partnership with parents is an integral part of good early years practice; it is not an optional extra:

- Parents are the continuity in their own children's lives. They know them as individuals and are emotionally involved in a different way to the most committed practitioner.
- You have expertise and experience but so do parents and your support for children will be that much more effective because you work well with parents.
- Parents have the right to be involved in decisions about their children and to be fully involved in any discussion or specialist assessment.
- You should ask parents for their permission about significant changes in the day that you have agreed for their children or for trips outside the usual schedule.
- Parents and other family members can be a rich source of expertise and experience and are often pleased to help a setting or become involved in different ways that respect and acknowledge their other commitments.

Figure 21.1
All settings need to relate to parents as well as children

Diversity in family life

Through friendly communication in partnership with parents you will understand some details of a child's home circumstances that help you to settle children and to make both the child and parent(s) welcome. Part of your responsibility as an early years practitioner is to be open-minded about different family styles and to be ready to learn about cultural backgrounds that are less familiar to you.

Scenario

Marsha has recently joined St Jude's reception class. After a slightly confused conversation, it has become clear that the person who staff thought was Marsha's mother is in fact her foster carer. Mrs Chance had been reticent because they had encountered negative attitudes in Marsha's pre-school to children who were looked after in foster care.

Jessie and Maryam in the reception class are concerned to reassure Mrs Chance and to establish a good working relationship with her. They suggest an informal meeting in which they:

- Reassure Mrs Chance that they behave in a professional way and that Marsha's personal circumstances will be kept confidential.
- Talk with Mrs Chance about names: how does Marsha refer to her foster carers and their own children, what other names might crop up in conversation?
- Explain that they are sensitive to family issues of all the children, for instance in activities such as making Mother's Day cards or themes in some stories.
- Would welcome guidance about whether Marsha's experiences might affect her development or behaviour. Mrs Chance is then able to explain that Marsha's birth family became violent and that she is easily distressed or frightened by loud noises or arguments.
- Check whether Marsha's birth parents are likely to come to the school and whether that situation could pose a risk to the child.

Questions

The supportive conversation that you have with a foster carer is very similar to friendly openness that you should show to all parents, with sensitivity to the variety in family patterns and background.

1. What could be the consequences if you do not realise that a child lives with a foster family?
2. Consider ways that you might support children if they are questioned about their family circumstances. Bear in mind that you can raise this issue in advance with a foster carer and that you should also be guided by how the child wants to handle the situation.
3. Write up your ideas and discuss with colleagues.

Key skills links: C3.3 C3.1a

You will have your own experience as a child and some readers may be raising their own families now as adults. It is important that neither you nor your colleagues allow unchecked assumptions to shape your work, because families come in many forms (see page 5).

- Some children are being raised by two parents and some by lone parents. Some families will go through changes while you share responsibility for the children and may divide or form new homes as stepfamilies.
- Some children will be cared for within a family, but not by their parents. Other relatives, such as grandparents, may have primary responsibility. Or children may be in the short- or long-term care of a foster family.
- Adults can become parents at different times of their life. In your setting, or work as a childminder or nanny, you may relate to parents who are very young, perhaps still in their teens and some who are into middle age. It is important that you relate to everyone as a parent without assumptions.
- Older parents are not necessarily more confident about parenting than a teenage parent. You may also need to deal with any feelings you have, if you are very different in age from the parents with whom you relate.
- Parents may or may not share your own cultural background or faith. It is important that, whatever your own background, you make the effort to understand this family.
- But you will not necessarily warm more easily to people with whom you share a social or cultural background. Every social or ethnic group includes a great deal of variation within the group.
- Some families are travellers and although some may remain in the same area for a long period of time, others will move around following seasonal work. Traveller families (some prefer to be called gypsies) are as varied as any other social and cultural group, so it is important not to make assumptions. It is appropriate for you to learn about traveller life and how children's experiences can be respected and used appropriately in your setting.

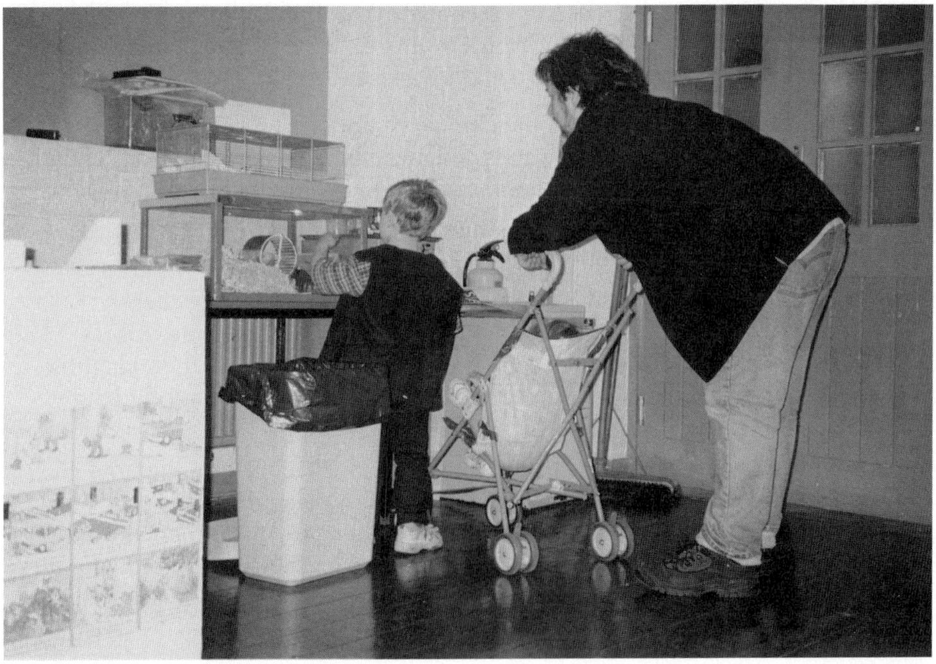

Figure 21.2
Children like to show their parents what goes on in their setting

- Some parents will have disabilities and it is important that you avoid assumptions about what the disability means to them as parents in your setting. Be ready to talk, listen and make adjustments when appropriate. But avoid thinking of 'disabled parents' as a group who must be similar to each other, any more than applying this assumption about 'black parents' or 'teenage parents'.

The adults whom you think of as 'the parents' have many other roles in their life. You and they get to know each other because they are the parents of the children for whom you are temporarily responsible. You need to develop a friendly working relationship (see page 625) because of the professional link, but do not forget that parents are individuals and a fellow adult like you.

Tips for practice

- Early years settings can be very female environments, so men may feel more comfortable initially if you invite them to become involved in a more 'male' activity, like building or games. But men vary, of course, so do not assume this.
- But offer variety as soon as possible and certainly enable children, especially the little boys, to see that 'real men' read, tell stories and do cooking (see page 598).
- If you are female, do not expect your male colleague(s) to take on all the partnership with fathers or other male carers, any more than a black practitioner should work exclusively with black families. It is a team responsibility.

Activity

The team at the Dale Parent and Toddler Drop-in is aware that, although they are keen to use the word 'parents', they often assume 'mothers' in practice. A couple of fathers have recently arrived with their toddlers, but only one has become a regular. Annie wants to ensure a welcome without over-reacting. Several issues have already arisen:

- A couple of regular mothers have made remarks, not unkind but thoughtless, about why Donovan is looking after his daughter Olivia. There is the assumption that it is temporary or Donovan must be out of work.
- When there were two fathers in the group, one of the regular attenders made a remark about 'all these men coming to our group'.
- Conversation in the drop-in, because it has been all female, has sometimes veered into complaints about men. The first time this happens with Donovan in the group, there is a pause and then laughter with, 'But we don't mean you'. Annie and Vicky are not entirely happy about this way of handling the situation.
- Donovan is entirely competent with Olivia and seems well able to deal with any surprise about his skills. He is also honest about the frustrations. For instance the health clinic has only just stopped asking when Olivia's mother will come to an appointment and despite making a persuasive case he still cannot get entrance to the local mothers and babies' swim session.

Questions

1 Consider what the Dale team might do to make Donovan welcome and deal with any issues courteously.

2 Discuss for your own setting what will help fathers (or uncles or grandfathers) to feel welcome.

3 For instance, are there pictures on the wall of men playing with and caring for children? Suggest some plans for improvement in practice.

Key skills links: C31a WO3.1–3

A friendly working relationship with parents

Good practice in early years is to aim for a friendly working relationship with parents. You have come together because you share the care of the children and not because you have chosen each other as friends.

It is your responsibility to be equally responsive to all the parents and not to spend more time talking and listening to those to whom you find it easier to warm. It does not matter how well you get along with individual parents, you cannot guarantee to behave to them in the way that a friend would react. For instance, a friend might drop all other obligations to help out or would promise to keep all confidences secret. But you have responsibilities to other families that cannot be pushed aside. Furthermore, you are obliged to report some confidences, particularly those that imply possible risk to the child.

Dilemmas can arise if the boundaries between your work and personal life have become unclear: perhaps you work in the same neighbourhood as your home or you went to school with some of the parents whose children now attend the setting where you work. You have a right to a private, personal life, but some circumstances may undermine your professional objectivity. Your manager or a senior colleague should be ready to listen to you and offer support and advice if a complicated situation has arisen.

Scenario

Please look at each of the following examples. Ideally discuss your views with colleagues and together reach some ideas on what should happen in the situation. You could consider these general questions for each example:

- Is the example an appropriate form of partnership with parents and involvement with families?
- Briefly explain your reasons for concluding 'yes' or 'no'.
- If you feel 'no', then how should the situation be handled – by this practitioner or by a manager or senior, if appropriate?

1 Christopher lives close to Sunningdale Day Nursery where he works. Last week he met one parent with her child very close to the nursery and, since she was in a hurry, took responsibility for the child at that point. This morning the same parent knocked on his front door and asked Christopher to take her child now, since she had an early

meeting at work. He refused courteously but the parent was not pleased.

2 Several children who now attend Baker Street Children and Family Centre have severe disabilities. One team member, Asha, agreed to do some evening sitting for one family, knowing that they had great difficulty getting a sitter. Another family has now asked Asha and when she said she was already committed for that evening, asked Kayleigh to help. Kayleigh refused but felt uncomfortable and has now questioned whether Asha should have agreed.

3 A six year old boy who attended St Jude's Primary School and after school club was recently killed in a road accident. His mother has written to the head of St Jude's with details of the funeral, inviting the staff who knew the child to attend the service.

4 The Dale Parent and Toddler drop-in has had some successful social events over the last year. Two parents have now invited Annie and her team to parties at their home. Annie and Vicky do not really want to go, feeling that this will blur the boundaries between their work and private life. Their colleague Liz feels it will be rude to refuse.

5 Nancy has experienced friendly relations with both the parents in the family with whom she has worked as a nanny for two years. She has felt recently that the parents' marriage may be under some strain. This afternoon the mother came home early from work and started to talk with Nancy about her worries that her husband is having an affair.

6 Sophie is a childminder who takes care of Alison. The child has gone into hospital to have her appendix removed. Sophie has made plans to visit Alison in hospital, taking some books and also her own son who has spent a lot of time with Alison.

7 Hannah is the head teacher of Dresden Road Nursery School. This morning she overheard part of a conversation that makes her think one of her staff was seen at a local restaurant over the weekend with the father of a child who attends the nursery.

8 Marjorie is the leader of Greenholt Pre-school and she attends the church that owns the hall in which the pre-school takes place. Marjorie knows a number of the parents because of church attendance and their conversations in the centre sometimes include church business.

The beginning of the partnership

Your relationship with parents starts when they contact or visit your centre to decide whether they want their child to attend.

- First impressions matter, so courteous communication is important from the first meetings. You also set a pattern for an equal relationship and honesty.
- Be clear about any information that you need to communicate to parents and be ready with a written leaflet or brochure about your setting.
- At some point, you will need to explain any procedures about admissions and details of how you work with the children. But partnership is a personal process and parents will want to talk with you, not only look at written material.

Once the family decides to take up a place for their child, you will need to ask a number of questions and to answer further questions from parents.

- It is important that you approach each family afresh. You should not look as if this is the umpteenth time you have explained about the setting's positive approach to behaviour or why you need an emergency contact number.
- The way that you ask questions can show a family that it matters to you and your colleagues to treat a child and the family in an individual way. It is important to check on matters such as religious faith and diet and not make assumptions from broad guesses about cultural background.
- Explain carefully safety issues, such as why you need to know who will pick up children. You cannot release them to someone you do not know, even if the child recognises her grandma or his teenage cousin. You need to explain what has to happen if there is a real emergency and parents cannot pick up their child.

Tips for practice

Part of your first conversation with parents will be to explore details of family life that it is your business to understand. You need to know about family diet and the individual care of this child. But you also need to be correct about names.

- You need to ensure that you say and spell the child's name correctly and that of the parent(s).
- Many early settings are informal and work on first name terms between adults. If a parent or grandparent would rather be known as Mrs or Mr, then it is courteous to follow their preference.
- Adults often do not mind being referred to as 'Paula's Dad' or 'Finn's Gran', so long as their proper name is used sometimes and you do not call them 'Gran' or 'Mum'.
- You also need to know if children prefer to be known by a shortened version of their name. You should not shorten nor change a child's name because you choose or find the name hard to pronounce.
- Some children will not share the surname of the parent whom you meet, so it is important to check rather than assume.
- The European naming system is that the personal name(s) come first, followed by a family surname. All cultures do *not* follow this pattern, so a good rule of thumb is, if in any doubt, ask.

Agreements between a setting and parents

Partnership will always include clear communication about the service that your setting offers, or a clear agreement between a family and nanny or childminder about the boundaries to your professional role. It is now more usual for early years settings to have a written agreement with parents. The Schools Standards and Framework Act 1998 has required that schools have a written **home–school agreement** in England.

Key term

Home–school (or **home–setting**) **agreement**

a written description of the obligations and expectations of the school (or early years) team and parents. A representative of the setting and parent(s) would sign a copy

Tips for practice

- A written agreement between any setting and parents should be used to ensure a shared understanding of the service – what the providers of the service offer and what parents and their children can expect.
- Written agreements do not work like legal contracts and will only support genuine partnership if you and the parents develop good channels of ordinary spoken communication.
- Signing an agreement will not force an uncooperative parent to become more amenable.
- Agreements can however undermine the friendliness of cooperative parents if the requirements seem uneven or practitioners fail to keep their promises!
- Agreements need to be written, discussed and used in an even-handed way. They do not work, and parents become irritated and disillusioned, if an agreement is a long list of what parents must do, yet the commitments from practitioners seem to boil down to 'we'll do our best'.

An agreement should not become a long document, since parents can consult the full length policies of your setting. An agreement between any setting and parents would usually include:

- The aims of your setting and key values, expressed briefly.
- What the setting and the team commit to provide for children and parents.
- The responsibilities of parents in return and, as appropriate for their age, the children's own responsibilities.
- The details of the place offered to the child(ren): the number of sessions or days and any payment that is due within an early years setting.
- An agreement might explain the conditions for ending a place and a period of notice, especially for settings that offer childcare.
- No agreement can impose conditions that are either unlawful or unreasonable. For instance, state schools can invite a financial contribution from parents but cannot insist. Nor can there be a required uniform that a child could not wear for religious or cultural reasons.
- An agreement may make clear that the setting does not look after children when they are sick and would expect parents to fetch them in the event of illness or accident.
- Parents would usually give a general permission for local trips that are part of the usual day or session. More extensive outings would require specific permission from parents.

An agreement should be signed and dated both by the parent(s) and a senior practitioner representing the setting, since the commitment is two-way. Although these agreements are sometimes called 'contracts', they are not legal documents. Nor can practitioners, even in schools, insist that parents have to sign.

Activity

- Look at the agreement used by your setting.
- What does it contain and how even-handed are the requirements made of parents and offered by the setting team?
- Ask the views of some parents and listen carefully.
- Suggest some improvements for your setting.

Key skills links: C3.1a WO3.1–3

Settling in

Helping children to settle into your setting is a joint activity with their parents or other carers. Settling in is a process for both children and parents and is not only about the very first day. You will support children's emotional well being when you:

- Value the time that is given to making a relationship with a child and parent.
- Use home visits and familiarisation visits to the setting as a gentle introduction for everyone.
- Encourage the family to provide links from home, such as a photo or drawing to go on a child's peg or drawer.
- Give time and attention to developing a relationship of partnership with parents or other key carers in a child's life.
- Gather individual information about children, such as their personal interests, what comforts them, special words they use that you might not understand, what may concern them and their past experiences of being away from the family.

Figure 21.3
Parents and children can take part in self-registration

Children benefit from a positive approach to their arrival and making sense of the setting.

- They need a real welcome on the first and subsequent days.
- A settling in period for the child: helping her or him to understand and follow the routine, help them make social contact.
- Preparation of the group for a new child is important so that the existing group know that a child is coming and can perhaps greet her or him by name. If children are disabled, there can sometimes be good reason to prepare the group (see page 523).
- Be ready to remind children of names of staff and other children. You can tell and use the names in appropriate phrases like, 'Here comes Tony' or 'I can see Marie over there, would you like to join her?'
- Encourage but do not press a child to join in the daily routines.
- However careful you are in settling a child, some children will find it hard to feel 'at home' with you. It is important that you persevere in supporting a child and do not allow your frustration to tempt you into labelling a distressed child as 'clingy' or 'attention seeking'.

You need to communicate with and reassure parents as well as the children.

- Allow for the mixed feelings that parents could be experiencing, especially if this is the first time they have been separated from their child.
- Enable parents to let go slowly. Perhaps they can call in by telephone to check that their child is reasonably happy and are able to talk about their child's day.
- Parents need to feel confident that you are getting to know their son or daughter as a person, that you value helping their child to get to know you, your setting and your routine.

Tips for practice

- Any setting should have a general policy on how children and families will be enabled to settle. But this cannot be rigid because children and their parents differ so much.
- Mothers will often be the person who settles a child but do not assume this. Sometimes fathers will be very involved, sometimes you may have more contact with another relative or other carer like a childminder or nanny.
- It can really help parents and other carers when you are clear about their role, for instance, making suggestions for ways that they can help in the setting to ease the separation from their children.
- In most early years settings, children will stay without their parent once they are settled. However, if you work in a drop-in facility or your setting offers this service, it will be understood that parents stay and remain responsible for their children.
- Children may settle into after school clubs or holiday schemes mainly without their parents. But some children will want their parent to be around for a while.
- Early years practitioners who work in out of school care still need to make friendly contact with parents and many of the issues in this chapter are equally important.

Activity

Find out the details of the settling in policy of your setting.

- What are the main steps? How well do they work? Ask experienced colleagues but also some parents who have recently settled in their children.
- How quickly do individual children settle? What does settling look like? How do you tell?
- Where can parents stay who are settling in their children, what do they do? Has the team considered what makes it easier for parents to feel at ease in a setting, as well as how to help children to feel comfortable?
- If you work with children of four and five years or older, then ask them for their views. What was it like for the children when they joined reception class or your after school club? What worked well and what could be improved?
- Write up your findings and discuss what you have found with colleagues who work in a different setting or on work placement.
- Look for any improvements that could be made to practice.

Key skills links: C3.1a C3.3 WO3.1–3

Special issues in the care of very young children

You are sharing the care of babies and very young children with their parent(s). It is especially important that you build a friendly working relationship with parents as well as a warm relationship with the baby or toddler. This three-way relationship is important for all shared care, but especially so when children are very young. You need good quality communication with parents and they need to feel reassured that you will take good care of their baby as an individual. You cannot develop this good practice without a key person (or key worker) system in early years settings (see page 595).

- A good working relationship with parents is essential because of the importance of continuity in the shared care of very young children. Partnership between parents and carers depends on open and regular communication that acknowledges the contribution of both parties and works hard to avoid any sense of competition.
- Regular, friendly communication is crucial to ensure continuity between parents at home and nursery over shared routines and timing any changes.
- Babies and toddlers manage some differences between carers but major differences will disrupt their day and make them uneasy.

Tips for practice

- Conversation is the best way to keep one another up to date with what a baby or toddler has learned or is nearly ready to do.
- Early years practitioners and parents need to exchange what they notice and to have a shared satisfaction in the baby or toddler's discoveries and interests.
- But be sensitive to parents' feelings that perhaps all the exciting events are happening in your setting.
- You can help by focusing on all the fine steps rather than the 'big' developmental milestones such as the first word or steps.
- You can also be sensitive in your approach by making comments like, 'She's very close to ... isn't she?', 'He's nearly walking; he'll do it for you soon' or 'Do you think she's talking? It sounds like it, but I wasn't sure.'

The dilemma of attachment

Early years practitioners are often concerned, or feel that parents are anxious, about young children becoming 'too attached' to staff. This area definitely has to be faced with children's needs kept central.

- Babies and toddlers need to form close attachments (see page 190). They cannot be 'too attached' to adults who are key in their daily lives and some young children spend many hours in out of home care. They need and deserve to develop attachments to their key person.
- Adults, practitioners and parents, need to resolve the mixed feelings that undoubtedly exist. Parents who work long hours may well be worried if their young child is clearly fond of her key person. But these understandable feelings need to be discussed between the adults and not 'solved' by making it hard for young children to form attachments in out of home care.

In communication with parents, you might need to consider all of the following issues.

- Let parents know when babies and toddlers missed them or were happy to see them come back in at the end of the day. It is a delicate balance between reassuring parents that they are not forgotten and avoiding worrying them that their baby cries for ages when they are gone.
- Share what babies and toddlers have done during the day: a trip out, a song or game that was especially enjoyed, a new step in the child's development. But make sure that you give parents plenty of space to share with you about what happens at home, and not just about problems.
- Talk with parents about how young children can care very much about more than one person. They are able to make different kinds of close relationships and they can have different special times with a small number of caring adults.
- Reassure parents that they will be the continuity in their child's life. You are pleased to be part of the child's time now, but parents will be there when the child has moved on from your nursery or care as a nanny or childminder.

When children move on

In an early years setting with a full age range, very young children may well have moves within the setting, from a baby or toddler room to the group for older children. Any setting will face the situation of children leaving finally, either because the family has moved them to a different early years setting or because it is time for the child to go to school.

When children face a move of any kind, you can help.

- Understand that the child is facing a transition from a familiar environment and people to somewhere new.
- Even within the same setting, it helps if children can visit the room they will soon join and spend some time becoming familiar with the new room, children and adults. In a flexible setting where groups mix, then these adults should already be familiar faces.
- It is appropriate to have a flexible approach to the age at which a child moves from one room to another, since some children will be ready at a younger age than others.

It will be parents' responsibility to organise their child's school place and to get to know that school and the staff. An early years setting can help in the following ways.

- Prepare children about the move: talking, exploring what it may be like and listening to any concerns that children express. Some children are rather daunted by the move to 'big school' but others are mainly excited and more than ready to move on.
- Organise a proper goodbye to children and parents. You may have a party, especially if a number of children are moving on to school at the same time. You celebrate the family's time with you as well as show that they will be in your memories.
- Gather children's drawings, photos and other materials into a file or portfolio for them to keep now.

It matters how children leave your setting but it is also important to recall that adults, parents and early years practitioners have feelings too.

- It is right that you form close relationships with children and some will be with your setting for a matter of years. It is fine to express to a child, 'I will miss you' and 'I won't forget you'. If you are very sad, then it is appropriate to share those feelings with colleagues.
- In some early years settings, parents may be very sad at the end of an era. An early years team may have been very supportive of a family and perhaps helped a parent to feel more confident. Even without family stresses, parents have shared the care of their child with you, so a relationship is ending for them as well.

Good practice in communication with parents

Communication with parents should draw on the same skills that you use with fellow adults. You are in a professional relationship, so some of the issues are different from communication with friends or in a social setting. The main issues include:

- A fair and even-handed approach to all parents and carers, so that you are not tempted to have longer or more honest conversations with the parents with whom you feel more comfortable.
- Both practitioners and parents need a clear understanding of confidentiality and the limits. Parents should feel assured that what they say does not fuel gossip within or outside the setting.

Figure 21.4 Visual and written communication supplements conversation

- However, you cannot commit to keep secret any information that could affect a child's safety (see Chapter 19 on child protection).
- Easy access for parents to information about their own child and to conversations with appropriate members of the team when they have concerns or questions.
- Respect for parents' family values and beliefs and clear communication from you that parents' requests will be followed, for instance on food, or when it will not possible and why.

Partnership with parents is a two-way process and they too have a responsibility to communicate with you. In an early years setting it is your job and that of colleagues to make that communication as easy as possible.

Tips for practice

Partnership with parents will have different applications in practice depending on the setting in which you work as an early years practitioner. However, the basics of good practice do not vary.

- Make friendly contact with all the parents of the children for whom you are responsible.
- Behave towards parents with courtesy and a respect for how important they are, and will continue to be, for their children.
- Offer ways to build continuity between parents' care of their children in the family and your contribution in your own setting or as part of family life, as a nanny or childminder.

A welcome for parents

Partnership is built on regular communication with parents. Your conversations will not always be about something very significant or problematic.

- Express a friendly welcome by a smile and wave to parents if it is not possible to speak. But ensure that you do have short conversations with all parents on a regular basis.
- It is your responsibility to make the first move, since parents may feel that the setting is your 'territory'. Some parents may feel uneasy in school settings, especially if they have less than happy childhood memories of school.
- Parents are disheartened if practitioners only create time to talk when there is a problem. You would feel this way too. So make the effort to say that Daniel has overcome his fear of the hamster or that Mairi made a magnificent dragon out of recycled materials.
- You don't always have to talk about the children. You might ask if a parent feels better from the flu or comment on the bright sunshine outside.
- If you want a longer conversation about a child, it can help to check whether this is convenient. Ask, 'I'd like to talk with you about how Tony is settling in. Is now a good time?' If the answer is 'No', then agree a day and time that will be fine.

Figure 21.5
Parents and carers need to feel welcome

Activity

- Note the conversations that you have over two or three weeks with parents.
- Write up the content in brief and note any differences between parents in the approximate length of conversations or the ease of chatting.
- Are there any parents with whom it is hard to find a few moments? What appear to be the reasons and what can you do to address the situation?

Key skills links: LP3.1–3

Part of the warm welcome for parents and children is that they see people like themselves reflected in your wall displays, books and play materials. All your materials should show a range of ethnic groups, male and female carers and some people with disabilities. If parents or children cannot see themselves, then the message is that they do not really matter or are effectively invisible. It is now possible to obtain a full range of play materials, wall friezes and books – from mail order if they are not available in your local high street (see page 672).

Tips for practice

Courteous communication with parents will follow much the same pattern as you yourself appreciate when you are on the receiving end of service.

- You respond as soon as possible to a parent's approach and apologise if you have to keep someone waiting.
- Give your full attention to what the parent is saying. If you have to break off to deal with a child then acknowledge the interruption with, 'I'm sorry, you were telling me about …'.
- Show that you are listening with regular eye contact, not staring. If your eyes are distracted, perhaps by what a child is doing, then apologise in the same way as if you need to interrupt to speak with someone else.
- Be alert to the comfortable speaking distance of the other person.
- Make brief comments of your own as appropriate to the conversation.
- Check you have understood a longer or complicated conversation by reflecting back your understanding with, 'Can I check that I have followed what you would like …' or 'I think I got confused around … can you please tell me again the bit about …'.

When communication is less straightforward

It is possible that you, a colleague or a parent has a disability that affects communication, for instance, deafness or a stutter. Communication with adults is not the same as with children but good practice in this area is very similar.

- If you are deaf, then it is important for parents to know, as well as the children, otherwise they may think you were inattentive or uninterested.
- Explain simply to parents how they can make communication easier for you. The ideas are the same as described below for parents who are deaf.

- If a parent is deaf then you need to face the person, talk at normal volume and speak clearly (see page 320).
- All team members need to know that a particular parent cannot, for instance, hear a call from a distance and will not respond unless she can see the message of a wave or a beckon.
- Some parents may have a stutter that interrupts the fluency of their speech. This difficulty is likely to become worse if they feel rushed. You can help by showing no signs of being in a hurry and do not rush to finish parents' sentences for them (see page 317).
- Perhaps a parent with a disability of hearing or speech will find communication easier through a hearing friend. If you are involved in this kind of three-way conversation, then it is important to share your attention between the parent and the friend. It would be very discourteous to look only at the speaking adult or to refer to the parent as 'she'.

Sometimes you will not share a fluent language with parents. In this case:

- Your spoken communication needs to be direct and simple. Use short sentences, communicating one point at a time.
- Support spoken communication with written material (brochures about the centre or letters to parents) in the family's language.
- In the same way as described for children on page 637, you can learn some phrases in the family's language such as greetings or thanks.

Talking about the children

In any setting or practitioner role you should have informal conversations with parents about their children. In many early years settings and schools you will also have regular discussions in which you sit down and talk with parents about their child's developmental progress and behaviour. Good practice in communication is very similar across these different conversations.

Figure 21.6
Early communication is important

Tips for practice

- Most professions have a shared language and early years is no exception. Some words or phrases will be familiar to you from training and conversations within your team. It is easy to forget that the rest of the adult world does not talk in this way.
- Be aware of specialist terms and replace them with ordinary language. Confident parents may ask, 'what do you mean by that?' but sometimes you will need to be alert to a puzzled expression.
- Most adults do not talk about 'motor development', and certainly not 'gross motor'. Parents talk about specific physical skills like walking or jumping.
- Parents do not usually use phrases like 'separation anxiety' or 'gender stereotyping'. So you need to talk (and write also) about 'Jane's concern about letting her Dad go out of sight' or that 'Declan has firm views about boys' games and those just for girls'.

Sharing children's development and behaviour

Your records should be open to parents, to look at the reports on their own child. Early years practitioners can feel uneasy about sharing some observations and assessments, but care taken over records that will be seen by parents usually improves practice (see page 462).

- Many parents will want to talk about their child, as well as read the report. Furthermore, some parents may have difficulty reading a report and want you to talk them through it.
- A conversation with parents, just like a written report, needs to be a rounded picture, in which you share details of what the child can do, as well as what she cannot yet manage.
- Since parents can become anxious, it is also important to communicate whether not being able to manage a particular skill is usual for this age or a cause for concern.
- You can share your observations about what a child can nearly do, the cutting edge of her learning, and how she has changed since the last assessment or written report.
- These perspectives give parents, as well as practitioners, a positive sense of a child who is continuing to learn.
- Neither written reports nor supporting conversations with parents should focus only on difficulties. You should have a decent length conversation with all parents. There should be no sense of 'Andy is doing fine. There are no problems' – with the implication that this is the end of the conversation.
- On the other hand, if you have observed any developmental delays or difficulties for this child, then these need to be placed in a positive, although honest, framework.
- Communicate with parents what you have observed, your reasons for being concerned and your thoughts about what can be done. Your words will help to communicate the facts of what you have heard or seen with the conclusion you draw for the moment.
- In the same way as described on page 464 about written reports, you need to communicate 'I am concerned about … because …' or 'I think we can be really pleased that …'.

- Ask for parents' opinions and, if they are quiet, then encourage them to contribute their knowledge of their child.

Parents may be unhappy of course to hear that there is cause for concern about their child's behaviour or struggles in some aspects of learning. But when you share how you have reached your professional opinion, rather than giving blunt pronouncements, then discussion is much more possible. It sounds and feels very different when you say to a parent, 'I find it challenging to handle Janice's temper tantrums' in contrast with, 'Your daughter has such a temper on her'. In the first approach, your words and body language can show that this is a problem you would like to resolve and you are not blaming anyone.

Early years practitioners are usually more edgy about parents' possible reaction to critical comments. You need to be aware, however, that unsupported positive remarks are not very useful in the long run. Parents may be pleased to hear, or read in a report, that 'Sally is a bright little girl' or 'Mark has good language'. Yet, without the supporting evidence of your observation, in the context of the child's age, then it is hard for parents to tell whether you are giving a well supported assessment of their child or an empty compliment.

Parents whose first language is not English may be fully fluent in written and spoken English but some will not be. Good practice will be to have a conversation that supplements any written reports and to seek an interpreter where possible (perhaps a bilingual colleague or a friend of the parent).

To think about

Confidentiality for families extends to what may seem like little things to you.

- Perhaps you are very clear that you would keep confidential that a child's parents were on the verge of splitting up or that Mark's mother has just been made redundant.
- But it is just as important that you keep confidential to the child's own parent that a child has had a bad day or was the one who did the biting this afternoon.
- It is also crucial never to forget that children have ears and you should not discuss parents or children's personal business in the hearing of other children.
- The address and phone number of families is also confidential, even if the request from another parent seems fine, like a birthday party invitation. But these are not details you should divulge. It is for parents to make contact personally themselves.
- A professional approach to confidentiality continues to apply when families or you have left an early years setting.
- Nannies have a serious responsibility since they are part of intimate family life. This commitment to confidentiality applies to any family and not only to nannies who work for 'celebrity' families.

When parents ask to talk with you

Real partnership between early years practitioners and parents (and other carers) is two-way. A good working relationship is not only about when you choose to share ideas with parents or want to find a way to express your concerns. You also need to be responsive to parents' concerns and their suggestions, even if these do not initially fit comfortably into your perspective.

Parents who ask, 'Can I have a quiet word?' may wish to raise a concern from a wide range of possibilities and these will certainly not always be complaints. It is very important that neither you, nor your colleagues, behave as if parents are more likely to be moaning than not. Parents may:

- be concerned that their child has been bitten, or is being bullied, and what you are doing to resolve this situation
- wish to raise their own concerns about their child's behaviour or development
- tell you in confidence about a family upheaval or bereavement that is very likely to affect their child's emotional well being
- want to understand the policy or approach of the setting on an important aspect of children's learning
- have a legitimate complaint because someone in the team has failed to act in a responsible way or to communicate with this parent or carer.

You do not have the time for lengthy conversations, but a useful exchange with parents will not take ages. Good communication skills with parents are very similar to those that you need to apply with colleagues and, in a different way, with children.

- Most important of all, listen to what a parent wishes to say to you. Hold back if you are tempted to plunge in with explanations, justifications or advice. Unless you listen, you do not know what is needed.
- Ask open ended questions, so that you can understand the issues for this parent. Useful questions tend to start with 'what?' or 'how?' For instance, 'what has happened that makes you feel Nina has been bullied?'
- You can use simple reflective listening that feeds back a parent's comment as a question to check that you understand. For instance: 'So, you think Marlon is very upset about his dog, but he's not talking about it?' or 'It would help you to know whether Dorcas gets so easily upset here?'

Once you have listened, you can make a sensible response to what the parent has told you.

- Sometimes it will be appropriate to say, 'I'm pleased you told me about Nina. I would like to check out what has been happening'. You should then keep any promise to 'find out about …' or 'get back to you later'.
- Some parents may need another, or a more detailed, explanation of the positive approach to behaviour in your setting of what early literacy really means for three year olds.
- If a number of parents raise similar issues, it could be a clear message that your team needs to consider a broader communication, perhaps through displays or a parents' evening.
- It will be for parents to choose what they do in their own home, but they may welcome advice from you. For instance, it will be better for Marlon to know that his dog has actually died. Since you have listened to the parent, you now realise that Marlon thinks the dog is still at the vet's, because his family cannot find a way to tell the child.

Tips for practice

Parents may sometimes ask you for advice about their child's development or behaviour. You can share your experience and knowledge as appropriate so long as you keep realistic.

- It may help to be able to reassure a parent that their four year old's development is normal for this age, perhaps that in language development it is not unusual for children to mis-pronounce some sounds.
- Good ideas for dealing positively with children's behaviour are not simple, one-try answers. Adults, practitioners and parents often need to persevere. So you can share how you deal with tantrums or lack of cooperation, but perhaps say, 'It works often enough that we feel it's worth trying'.
- Parents will have to put an idea into action and feel committed. So it is important that you talk about 'what we find works well' rather than imply this approach will definitely work for this family.
- Any good ideas have to allow for family circumstances and the final choice has to be made by parents. For instance, the approach to night waking that suggests parents let their child cry for short periods before going in may be impractical for families whose home has thin walls and complaining neighbours.

Sometimes you may need to get through the particular way in which this parent or carer expresses concerns.

- Some parents will be fairly confident in describing what concerns them and why. Then there will only be difficulties if you or your colleagues are over-sensitive and react as if the parent is complaining or making an excessive fuss.
- Less confident parents, or those whose personal style is louder, may find it hard to express a concern or to question you without higher volume and expansive body language. A calm approach from you and an obvious intention to listen will then shift most conversations in a more constructive direction.
- In some cases you need to be aware of parents' body language, the music behind the words you hear. Some parents may say, 'I'm not really that worried' but their face and posture tells you that they are or 'I'm sure there's a very good explanation for what happened …' and you need to hear the important, unspoken 'but …'.

To think about

- We are individuals with a personal style but we are all also influenced by our own cultural traditions.
- The style of communication in some cultures and social groups or classes can be very direct, with forthright spoken and body language and strong eye contact.
- This approach can feel threatening if your social and cultural background tells you this behaviour is aggressive or out of control.

- Equally some social and cultural traditions stress that disagreement and conflict is to be avoided. Individuals may then communicate differences of opinion by subtle words and body language.
- A practitioner of a different social or cultural background may not realise that a parent is seriously concerned or dissatisfied.

Tips for practice

- It is important that you do not swiftly assume a parent, or a colleague for that matter, is being aggressive when they are simply outspoken or passionate about what they want to say.
- Furthermore a dismissive attitude towards parents will show through the body language of a disrespectful practitioner.
- It is poor practice for any setting to develop a team attitude towards parents as 'difficult' or 'ungrateful'.
- It is also bad practice to generalise from a few parents who are hard to work with to talk about the parents as a whole group as 'aggressive' or 'demanding'.
- You would not like this unfair behaviour if it were directed at you.

Activity

- In most cases, parents will not want to make a formal complaint. But all settings should have a complaints procedure that is open to parents.
- Ask to read the procedure for your setting.
- Make sure you understand the steps and how you would need to behave if a parent first made the complaint to you.
- Write up your findings in a short report and discuss with colleagues.

Key skills links: C2.3 C3.1a

Dealing with aggression

You may sometimes face adults who are aggressive in word or action or whose behaviour makes you uneasy that they could become aggressive.

You will be able to defuse some incidents:

- Stay calm, speak quietly and show you are willing to listen. If you are calm, the other person may calm down, whereas this change is unlikely if you tell them to 'calm down!'
- If you answer angry words and gestures with your own anger, then the situation will worsen.
- Acknowledge that the other person has strong feelings. You might say, 'I can hear you're angry. Please tell me what has happened'.
- Listen and find out the reasons for this other person being angry, frustrated or whatever.
- Keep what you say simple and avoid getting defensive or arguing.

- If there is a swift and appropriate solution, then offer it. If apologies are due on behalf of your setting or you personally, then say 'sorry'.
- You should listen carefully to what a parent is saying but then you need to check on the facts before taking any action.
- You should not, for example, take the claims of a furious parent that named children have bullied her child or that a volunteer made her vegetarian child eat a sausage. You can use a phrase such as, 'That sounds serious, I would like to check out what happened and I will get back to you'.
- If a parent or any other fellow adult will not behave in a calmer way, then it is appropriate to be assertive yourself in setting boundaries to the situation. You might say, 'I understand that this situation is very frustrating for you. But I am not willing to listen to you swear at me'.
- You also have a responsibility for the children and may need to say, 'You are frightening the children. I want you to leave this room now'.

Scenario

A difficult situation has arisen recently in St Jude's Primary School. Last week Wayne's mother appeared to see the Year Two teacher, Rona. Mrs Kent demanded that 'something should be done about the children who bullied Wayne' about wetting himself. It turned out that Wayne had a toileting accident and Mrs Kent is now claiming that a number of children made fun of him. Rona finds Mrs Kent very intimidating and takes a list of the children said to have been cruel to Wayne, with the promise that they will be made to apologise properly.

Rona speaks with the children on the list, most of whom say definitely that they had not been horrible to Wayne. Rona feels that she has to go ahead with her commitment to Mrs Kent and tells the children that they must all write a letter of apology and bring it in the following day.

Pam hears about the incident from two children who attend the after school club who want her help with their letters. The children are adamant that they did not say what Mrs Kent is claiming but 'Miss' says they must do a letter. Pam feels the children should not write an apology under these circumstances and speaks with parents as they arrive.

The following day Pam brings the matter up in the staff room and it becomes clear that at least one parent has sent in a letter saying that her child is not going to apologise for something she has not done.

Questions

1 What are the issues in this dilemma? In what ways was Rona's reaction poor practice and for whom? What should happen now?

2 Discuss the situation with your colleagues. Consider whether you have, or could, make an unwise choice of action, because you felt intimated by a parent.

Key skills links: PS31–3 C3.1a

It is your choice whether to have a row within your personal life, but you have to take a professional approach in your job. It is, therefore, right that you should be able to expect support from your colleagues.

- A team should have an agreement that someone will come to support you if they hear raised voices.
- You may need a panic button system if your setting has many parents who abuse drink or drugs, since their behaviour could be very unpredictable.
- You should also be offered a supportive conversation after a distressing incident. Your manager or a senior should help you regain your composure as well as identify what you did well in the situation.

Involvement of parents in early years settings

Key term

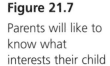

Parental involvement ways in which parents can be invited and choose to be directly involved in the activities or running of an early years setting or school

Parents can be involved in different ways within an early years settings. There is no single or right pattern for involvement because families vary and so does the service that different settings offer to parents. Therefore, there should never be any sense that parents have to become involved in the ways that are on offer. Good practice will be to explore what would interest parents as well as what is realistically possible for them. Parents who are unable, or do not wish, to become involved in activities in your setting will still want to be informed and consulted about their own child.

Different ways to be involved

Parents can be offered a role or encouraged to become involved in early years settings in all of the following ways.

Supporting their child

Parents are involved as part of the settling in process for children and families (see page 629) and also through:

- An open invitation to stay a while in the setting or to come to tea and be part of their child's day or session.

Figure 21.7
Parents will like to know what interests their child

- Regular meetings between practitioner and parents to discuss children's progress and look ahead to what they are now ready to learn. Such meetings need to be positive; they are certainly not just called when there are problems.
- Parents may be pleased to support their child's learning at home, either because the child wants to carry on with a project or because some work comes home with the child, for instance, reading practice or homework in primary school.
- Parents remain fully involved with their child's progress and any concerns. There should be a clear procedure to enable all parents to look at their own child's files (see page 461).
- Parents should be involved and fully consulted in any special work, for instance if it emerges that their child has special educational needs (see page 529).

Tips for practice

It helps to bear in mind how parents may feel if they are invited to a more formal meeting than just you and them over a cup of coffee. Some settings may have regular reviews or perhaps your service is linked with family support for parents under stress. You can help parents to feel prepared and to reduce anxiety.

- Talk with parents before the meeting or review and ensure that they understand the aims of this meeting, how it will be run, who will be there and what, if anything, will be decided.
- If you will give a report on the child's development or behaviour, you should have discussed the content with the parents, so there are no surprises.
- If somebody needs to take notes at this meeting, explain to the parent why and that they will get a copy.
- Ensure that parents are properly introduced to everyone at the meeting.
- Seat parents so that they feel part of the meeting and as comfortable as possible. They may appreciate sitting next to the practitioner they know best.
- Some thought beforehand about seating arrangements and furniture can reduce a daunting feel in some more formal meetings.

Information about early learning or other issues

Individual conversations are important and can be supplemented in a number of ways.

- Invitations to open days or evenings for parents. Parents can see their own child's work but some events can be to communicate the setting's general approach on aspects of children's learning.
- Information on offer through a parents' notice board, newsletter or informative wall displays of illustrations and simple written explanations.
- A file that you keep of useful material that is designed to explain what you do and why. For instance, *Nursery World* has published a series of Parent's

Guides within the magazine that can be directly copied and given to parents or used to help draft material that you develop within a setting.

- You can also download information for parents from government websites. For instance, *www.parents.dfes.gov.uk* has material written for parents about the literacy and numeracy strategies and the Foundation Stage.

Support for activities within the setting

Some parents with available time may be interested in becoming involved from time to time or on a regular basis:

- Parents might take or share responsibility for a project like sorting out the garden or a continuing activity such as running the toy library.
- Some parents may be pleased to be regular helpers within the daily activities of the setting and/or join the group on special outings.
- All parents will have some talent or interest and it is good practice to look for opportunities to invite parents to show a skill or share an experience with the children.
- Parents who cannot give regular time to the setting may be delighted to help out with projects because they can use their leisure time at home. Perhaps parents are pleased to look out some materials for the local history display or contribute to the contents of a storysack or poetry pocket (see page 330).
- Early years settings are very female, so do think around how you can encourage fathers and other male family members to feel welcome and at ease. Perhaps try a 'Dads' day' if the fathers seem reluctant.
- Some parents may be happy to operate as organisers or supporters of fund-raising events for the setting.

Figure 21.8

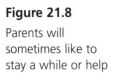

Parents will sometimes like to stay a while or help

Tips for practice

When you invite parents to be part of the regular day or session, it is good practice for a team to be clear about expectations and boundaries.

- Have an idea how parent helpers will be involved. Would you like this parent to support children at a particular activity? Perhaps you are especially keen that fathers spend some time in the book corner.
- Or has this parent a talent for story telling or woodwork that you really want shared with the children?
- Some parents will be quickly at ease in a group, others will appreciate your suggestions. For instance, 'The children have a big construction project in the garden. Can you keep them company and give any help they want?' or 'We're about to tidy up now. Could you be with the children who are sorting out the bikes? We have numbered parking bays and we encourage them to match the numbers.'
- Parent helpers, like any volunteers, need to behave consistently with policy in your setting, for instance, about how to handle a child's behaviour or that you aim for social, rather than silent, mealtimes. You need to anticipate any differences as far as you can and deal with them in a courteous way.
- Parent helpers will not complete children's records or access confidential material. Nor should they get involved in detailed conversations with other parents about the children; this is the role of practitioners.

Activity

Ask about guidelines for parent helpers in your setting.

- Has the team considered the practical issues raised in this section?
- In particular are there some tasks that parent helpers would not do?
- Write up brief notes and compare with colleagues on your course.
- Draft together a short policy to guide the involvement of parent helpers in an early years setting.

Key skills links: C3.2 WO3.1–3

Activities for parents themselves

Some settings offer involvement to parents directly for their own adult interests.

- There may be social events arranged for parents, either daytime drop-in coffee sessions or evening social events, perhaps as fund-raising activities.
- It is important that any events with food and drink are organised to cater for the needs of all families. Some parents will be vegetarian and a table full of nothing but sausage rolls and ham sandwiches will not feel welcome.
- There may be an ongoing parents' group, club or room for the exclusive use of parents and other carers.
- After consultation with parents, sessions could be offered that interest them, for instance, cooking, learning English as an additional language or early maths.

- Some parents' groups operate as a source of support and advice, perhaps in a very low key way and sometimes as an organised support group.

Tips for practice

Some regular events for parents will be through an organised group. Successful groups do not just happen; they take some planning and communication.

- Make sure that the expectations of parents and those of the team are similar. It is no use planning a group for parents that they do not really want or is not at a time that suits you.
- If parents choose not to support a group or an information meeting planned by the setting, it does not mean they are uninterested in their children. It is more likely to mean that they were not interested in this topic and would have said so, if you had asked them.
- One or two practitioners need to take responsibility, even for an informal group. This is partly because you need to be sure somebody will sort out the coffee and enough chairs.
- However, it is also a courtesy to parents that they can get to know the practitioner who leads or supports the group.
- Everyone needs to know when the group will meet, in what room, for how long each time and for how many meetings, if more than one. You also need to sort out practicalities like refreshments and no smoking in the setting.
- Review your pattern of meetings or groups from time to time. Are there some parents who rarely if ever attend?
- Is there a message perhaps that these activities are for mothers rather than fathers and how could you make the men more welcome?
- Are there some parents who do not share a fluent language with most other families? What could you do to make these parents more at ease?

A role in policy and decision making

Parents should of course have the necessary information and opportunity to participate in decisions about their own child. They may also be offered involvement in the broader running of a setting.

- Some nurseries or centres have parent representatives on management committees.
- Schools have some elected parent governors on the governing body.

Settings might offer less formal ways to influence decisions.

- A setting can give parents the opportunity to comment on the setting by a parents' board, newsletter or suggestions box.
- Open meetings for parents could allow them to express their views about the curriculum for the children or ways to create school grounds that are more child friendly.

These informal ways of communicating and exchanging views will only work if parents can see that their comments sometimes lead to change. No adults are pleased about giving their time and views if nothing comes of their contribution. Nor will it promote good relations if early years or school professionals meet parents' questions or constructive criticism with frosty and defensive replies.

Activity

- Find out the different ways in which parents can become involved in your setting if they choose.
- Talk with colleagues in your setting to understand whether the current pattern has changed over recent years.
- Write up brief notes and make a brief presentation to your colleagues on the course.
- Compare the different patterns of parent involvement that you have found in the different settings that you know.

Key skills link: C3.1b C3.3

Scenario

There can be different patterns of parent involvement that work well in different settings. These two settings offer a different type of service, although some the issues they face are similar.

Sunningdale Day Nursery is a private nursery, part of a small chain and offers a service to working parents who pay fees for their childcare. Currently the nursery offers the following kinds of involvement:

- Parents are closely involved in settling their children into the nursery.
- After children are settled the nursery has an open door policy and parents are very welcome to be part of the normal day. A few parents take this invitation up, but for most their work obligations do not allow this kind of involvement.
- Regular communication with parents is valued and practitioners aim to have at least short conversations with parents once a day. This objective is not achieved with all parents, especially those who dash in and out at speed.
- Regular meetings are offered every two to three months for parents to come in and talk about their child's progress.
- The nursery team monitors any issues raised by parents and plans informative displays and parents' evenings around any theme that seems to concern parents. The most recent evening and display was built around children's early mark marking and early writing, after several parents had expressed concern about, 'when is s/he going to start proper writing?'

St Jude's Primary School is a medium sized school with a nursery class and out of school care on the premises. Some different patterns of involvement have developed in the parts of the school:

- The primary school itself has a 'Friends of St Jude's' association that organises fund-raising activities and some social events. The most active parents in this association are likely to leave soon as their children move on to secondary school.

- Parents settle their children into the nursery and the out of school care. There is no agreed pattern to help children settle who start in the reception class without coming through the nursery.
- Parents are made welcome if they want to help out on a regular basis in the nursery or the school. There has been a particular drive recently to encourage fathers and other male relatives to join literacy activities to boost the boys' interest. The team has realised that they really need some clarity about what parent helpers do and what should be left to staff.
- The school has offered a programme of information evenings but the head has second thoughts about continuing after an argumentative meeting on assessment and SATs last month.

Questions

1 What main issues would determine a different pattern of possible involvement in these two settings?

2 Parents may not always agree with the approach of the setting over learning or behaviour. How might different forms of involvement address such issues?

3 Make links to your own practice.

Key skills links: WO3.1–3

Further resources

Ball, Mog (1997) *Consulting with Parents: Guidelines for good practice* National Early Years Network.

Caddell, Dorothy (2001) *Working with Parents* Learning and Teaching Scotland.

Hyder, Tina, Kenway, Penny and Roels, Clare (1997) *On Equal Terms: Ways to involve parents in early years settings* National Early Years Network and Save the Children.

Lindon, Jennie and Lance (1997) *Working Together for Young Children* Thomson Learning, Chapters 5 and 6 on partnership with parents.

Lindon, Jennie and Lance (2000) *Mastering Counselling Skills: Information, help and advice in the caring services* Macmillan, especially Chapter 2 on communication and Chapters 6, 7 and 8 if your setting offers broader support and help to parents and carers.

Progress check

1 Give two reasons why partnership with parents is part of good practice in early years settings and schools.

2 Explain briefly the difference between making friends and a friendly working relationship with parents.

3 Suggest three ways that you could help parents and children to settle into your setting.

4 Describe three ways in which good communication skills will support partnership with parents.

5 Give four examples to illustrate ways you could offer parent involvement in an early years setting or school.

Appendix 1

Working towards an early years qualification

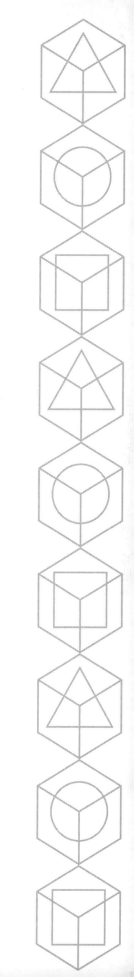

This appendix covers:

- links between this book and the main early years qualifications
- key/core skills
- building a portfolio of work as a student
- using a range of resources.

Links with different qualifications

In this section the full title of the units is given and then grids provide a cross reference to the different chapters in this book.

CACHE Diploma in Child Care and Education (DCE)

Units

1 Observation and assessment
2 Work with young children
3 Foundations to caring
4 The developing child
5 Health and community care
6 Play, curriculum and early learning
7 Work with babies in the first year of life
8 Preparation for employment
9 The provision of services and protection of children
10 Anti-discriminatory/anti-bias practice
11 Work with parents.

Units 1 and 11 are also covered in most chapters within activities, scenarios and short sections.

National Vocational Qualifications (NVQ) in Early Years Care and Education

Level 2 mandatory units

C1	Support children's physical development needs
C4	Support for children's social and emotional development
C8	Implement planned activities for sensory and intellectual development
C9	Implement planned activities for the development of language and communication skills
E1	Maintain an attractive, stimulating and reassuring environment for children
E2	Maintain the safety and security of children
M3	Contribute to the achievement of organisational requirements
P1	Relate to parents

Level 2 optional units

C12	Feed babies
C13	Provide for babies' physical development needs
CU10	Contribute to the effectiveness of work teams
M1	Monitor, store and prepare materials and equipment
P9	Work with parents in a group

Level 3 mandatory units

C2	Provide for children's physical needs
C3	Promote the physical development of children
C5	Promote children's social and emotional development
C7	Provide a framework for the management of behaviour
C10	Promote children's sensory and intellectual development
C11	Promote children's language and communication development
C15	Contribute to the protection of children from abuse
C16	Observe and assess the development and behaviour of children
E3	Plan and equip environments for children
M7	Plan, implement and evaluate learning activities and experiences
P2	Establish and maintain relationships with parents

Level 3 optional units

C14	Care for and promote the development of babies
C17	Promote the care and education of children with special needs
C18	Develop structured programmes for children with special needs
C24	Support the development of children's literacy skills
C25	Support the development of children's mathematical skills
M6	Work with other professionals
M8	Plan, implement and evaluate routines for children
P5	Involve parents in group activities
P8	Establish and maintain a child care and education service
MC1/C4	Create effective working relationships

This book does not attempt to cover the following optional units:

M2, M20, P4 P7, MC1/C1

BTEC National Early Years Diploma

Core units

1 Values and personal development
2 Communication and interpersonal skills
3 Professional practice
4 Protecting children
5 Safe environments
6 Child care practice
7 Learning in the early years
8 Human growth and development

Optional units

9 Play and learning activities
10 Child health

This book does not attempt to cover the remaining optional units 11–24 at the academic level required by the BTEC framework. However, the practice content is covered in part for the following units:

12 Developmental psychology
18 Design and technology
21 Managing the early years service
22 Special needs
23 Supporting literacy and numeracy skills
24 Physical activities

Table A1.1 Cross reference of DCE units to chapters of this book

	Units										
Chapters	**1**	**2**	**3**	**4**	**5**	**6**	**7**	**8**	**9**	**10**	**11**
1				*				*	*	*	*
2		*	*		*					*	
3			*							*	
4			*		*						
5							*				
6			*				*				*
7				*							
8		*		*						*	
9		*		*						*	
10		*				*					
11		*		*		*				*	
12		*		*		*				*	
13		*		*		*				*	
14		*				*					
15		*									
16	*										
17				*						*	
18					*					*	*
19									*	*	*
20								*		*	
21							*			*	*

Table A1.2 Cross reference of NVQ level 2 units to chapters of this book

	Units												
Chapters	**C1**	**C4**	**C8**	**C9**	**E1**	**E2**	**M3**	**P1**	**C12**	**C13**	**CU10**	**M1**	**P9**
1											*		
2	*				*	*		*		*			
3	*		*										
4	*					*						*	
5													
6									*	*			
7		*			*								
8		*											
9	*												
10	*		*										
11				*									
12				*									
13			*										
14			*		*							*	
15					*							*	
16													
17		*											
18								*					
19						*							
20							*				*		
21								*		*			*

Table A1.3 Cross reference of NVQ level 3 mandatory units to chapters

	Units										
Chapters	**C2**	**C3**	**C5**	**C7**	**C10**	**C11**	**C15**	**C16**	**E3**	**M7**	**P2**
1											
2	*								*		*
3	*										
4	*								*		
5											
6											
7			*								
8			*								
9		*									
10		*			*						
11						*					
12						*					
13					*						
14										*	
15										*	
16								*			
17				*							
18											*
19							*				*
20											
21											*

Table A1.4 Cross reference of NVQ level 3 optional units to chapters

	Units									
Chapters	**C14**	**C17**	**C18**	**C24**	**C25**	**M6**	**M8**	**P5**	**MC1/C4**	**P8**
1						*				
2							*			
3							*			
4	*						*			
5										
6	*									
7										
8										
9	*									
10	*									
11	*									
12				*						
13					*					
14							*			
15							*			
16										
17										
18		*	*			*				
19						*				
20						*			*	
21	*							*		*

Table A1.5 Cross reference of BTEC units to chapters of this book

	Units															
Chapters	**1**	**2**	**3**	**4**	**5**	**6**	**7**	**8**	**9**	**10**	**12**	**18**	**21**	**22**	**23**	**24**
1	*			*			*				*		*			
2			*		*	*										
3						*										
4			*		*	*				*						
5																
6						*		*								
7			*					*	*		*					
8								*								
9								*								*
10									*							*
11			*				*	*	*		*					
12							*		*						*	
13							*	*	*		*	*			*	
14			*				*		*							
15							*		*							
16							*	*								
17						*					*					
18										*				*		
19				*												
20	*	*	*										*			
21			*										*	*		

Key skills/core skills

The revised and accredited key skills (core skills in Scotland) relevant to this book include the areas given in this appendix. The patterns for levels 1, 2 and 3 are similar, although levels 2 and 3 require a more challenging standard. This appendix provides a full list of the skills that are referenced in the text by the short version, for example C2.1a.

Many of the activities within this book can support you in developing and practising these key skills, at a lesser or greater level of difficulty. The activities are cross-referenced within the chapters for both levels. It is up to you, and your college tutor or supervisor, to make the task more or less challenging. Your tutor or supervisor will also be responsible for guiding you towards appropriate sources of evidence to show that you have demonstrated the necessary skills.

All this material is available from QCA Publications, PO Box 99, Sudbury, Suffolk CO10 6SN tel: 01787 884444 or on the website: *www.qca.org.uk/keyskills*

Communication: level 1

C1.1: Take part in a one-to-one discussion and a group discussion about different, straightforward subjects.

C1.2: Read and obtain information from two different types of documents about straightforward subjects including at least one image.

C1.3: Write two different types of documents about straightforward subjects; include at least one image in one of the documents.

Communication: level 2

C2.1a: Contribute to a discussion about a straightforward subject.

C2.1b: Give a short talk about a straightforward subject, using an image.

C2.2: Read and summarise information from two extended documents about a straightforward subject. One of the documents should include at least one image.

C2.3. Write two different types of documents about straightforward subjects. One piece of writing should be an extended document and include at least one image.

Communication: level 3

C3.1a: Contribute to a group discussion about a complex subject.

C3.1b: Make a presentation about a complex subject, using at least one image to illustrate complex points.

C3.2: Read and synthesise information from two extended documents about a complex subject. One of the documents should include at least one image.

C3.3: Write two different types of documents about complex subjects. One piece of writing should be an extended document and include at least one image.

Application of number: level 1

N1.1: Interpret straightforward information from two different sources. At least one source should be a table, chart, diagram or line graph.

N1.2: Carry out straightforward calculations to do with (a) amounts and sizes, (b) scales and proportions and (c) handling statistics.

N1.3: Interpret the results of your calculations and present your findings. You must use one chart and one diagram.

Application of number: level 2

N2.1: Interpret information from two different sources, including material containing a graph.

N2.2: Carry out calculations to do with (a) amounts and sizes, (b) scales and proportions, (c) handling statistics and (d) using formulae.

N2.3: Interpret the results of your calculations and present your findings. You must use at least one graph, one chart and one diagram.

Application of number: level 3

N3.1: Plan and interpret information from two types of sources, including a large data set.

N3.2: Carry out multi-stage calculations to do with (a) amounts and sizes, (b) scales and proportions, (c) handling statistics and (d) rearranging and using formulae.

N3.3: Interpret the results of your calculations, present your findings and justify your methods. You must use at least one graph, one chart and one diagram.

Information Technology: level 1

IT1.1: Find, explore and develop information for two different purposes.

IT1.2: Present information for two different purposes. Your work must include at least one example of text, one example of images and one example of numbers.

Information Technology: level 2

IT2.1: Search for and select information for two different purposes.

IT2.2: Explore and develop information, and derive new information, for different purposes.

IT2.3: Present combined information for two different purposes. Your work must include at least one example of text, one example of images and one example of numbers.

Information Technology: level 3

IT3.1: Plan and use different sources to search for and select information required for two different purposes.

IT3.2: Explore, develop and exchange information and derive new information to meet two different purposes.

IT3.3: Present information from different sources for two different purposes and audiences. Your work must include at least one example of text, one example of images and one example of numbers.

Problem solving: level 1

PS1.1: Confirm your understanding of the given problem with an appropriate person and identify two options for solving it.

PS1.2: Plan and try out at least one option for solving the problem, using advice and support given by others.

PS1.3: Check if the problem has been solved by following given methods and describe the results, including ways to improve your approach to problem solving.

Problem solving: level 2

PS2.1: Identify a problem and come up with two options for solving it.

PS2.2: Plan and try out at least one option for solving the problem, obtaining support and making changes to your plan when needed.

PS2.3: Check if the problem has been solved by applying given methods, describe results and explain your approach to problem solving.

Problem solving: level 3

PS3.1: Explore a complex problem, come up with three options for solving it and justify the options selected for taking it forward.

PS3.2: Plan and try out at least one option for solving the problem, review progress and revise your approach as necessary.

PS3.3: Apply agreed methods to check if the problem has been solved, describe the results and review your approach to problem solving.

Improving own learning and performance: level 1

LP1.1: Confirm understanding of your short-term targets, and plan how these will be met, with the person setting them.

LP1.2: Follow your plan, using support given by others to help meet targets. Improve your performance by:

- studying a straightforward subject
- learning through a straightforward practical activity.

LP1.3: Review your progress and achievements in meeting targets with an appropriate person.

Improving own learning and performance: level 2

LP2.1: Help set short-term targets with an appropriate person and plan how these will be met.

LP2.2: Take responsibility for some decisions about your learning, using your plan and support form others to help meet targets. Improve your performance by:

- studying a straightforward subject
- learning through a straightforward practical activity.

LP2.3: Review progress with an appropriate person and provide evidence of your achievements, including how you have used learning from one task to meet the demands of a new task.

Improving own learning and performance: level 3

LP3.1: Agree targets and plan how these will be met over an extended period of time, using support from appropriate people.

LP3.2: Take responsibility for your learning by using your plan, and seeking feedback and support from relevant sources to help meet targets. Improve your performance by:

- studying a complex subject
- learning through a complex practical activity
- further study or practical activity that involves independent learning.

LP3.3: Review progress on two occasions and establish evidence of achievements, including how you have used learning from other tasks to meet new demands.

Working with others: level 1

WO1.1: Confirm what needs to be done to achieve given objectives, including your responsibilities and working arrangements.

WO1.2: Work with others towards achieving given objectives, carrying out tasks to meet your responsibilities.

WO1.3: Identify progress and suggest ways of improving work with others to help given objectives.

Working with others: level 2

WO2.1: Plan straightforward work with others, identifying objectives and clarifying responsibilities and confirm working arrangements.

WO2.2: Work cooperatively with others towards achieving identified objectives, organising tasks to meet your responsibilities.

WO2.3: Exchange information on progress and agree ways of improving work with others to help achieve objectives.

Working with others: level 3

WO3.1: Plan complex work with others, agreeing objectives, responsibilities and working arrangements.

WO3.2: Seek to establish and maintain cooperative working relationships over an extended period of time, agreeing changes to achieve agreed objectives.

WO3.3: Review work with others and agree ways of improving collaborative work in the future.

Building a portfolio

You will need to build up a portfolio of your work for many of the early years qualifications. This portfolio may be built from a number of specific assignments given to you by your tutor within given units or modules of a course.

Activities in the book will help you to develop evidence of what you have completed in your work and the key issues involved. A habit of keeping clear notes of events and experiences will help you to focus your learning and improve your practice.

Your programme assessor on a CACHE, BTEC or NVQ course should guide you over what should form your portfolio and how much material is needed for a full portfolio or within separate assignments of a course. However, there are some important practical issues to bear in mind for any early years qualification.

The portfolio or assignments matter

- Your portfolio is one way that you are assessed within the framework of these vocational qualifications. The assessor will also sometimes observe you at work but assessors cannot observe everything you can do or have learned.
- Your portfolio is part of the evidence of your competence in a specific unit and all its elements. The quality of your portfolio or separate assignments matters.

Organisation matters

- The contents of your portfolio need to be clearly linked to the relevant module or unit. Your assessor needs to be able to match your portfolio directly with the part of the qualification that it supports.
- For any material, you need yourself to be clear about, 'why am I putting this into my portfolio now?' and 'what does it demonstrate about my competence and understanding on this topic or skill area?'
- You need enough material in a portfolio to support a given assignment. But quantity is not all; everything has to be relevant and shown to be so. It will not work to copy masses of material and put it into the appendix of an assignment or your portfolio folder.
- Organise yourself and your material. You have some personal choice about how to sub-divide, present and order your material. But the best way will never be just a big carrier bag. Your tutor or assessor should have some suggestions that are practical and economical.

Links to your practice

- Equally important, the contents of your portfolio need to be clearly linked to your work with children and families. Your assessor needs to be able to see how you have applied knowledge or information searches directly to your work.
- The portfolio cannot stop at a collection of ideas and underpinning knowledge, as important as that is. Each contribution to your portfolio will need to make a clear link to what you do, and have done in the course of your work.

- Show how you have taken ideas and applied them your work role, or how you anticipate that you could in the future.
- You can build in personal examples of your practice and supported opinions. But they have to be linked into the main theme: why have you chosen this example, how does it highlight other ideas, what have you learned from this experience?

Different types of material

- Part of your whole portfolio may be a ring binder or hard back folder with sheets of paper, but that is unlikely to be all.
- Some units and modules may offer the potential for evidence in the form of photographs, audio or video tapes, maybe sometimes even pieces of work you have undertaken with the children.
- Some craft work or exciting play activities cannot be 'filed', so photographs and written accounts will be important.
- In some cases your portfolio will need authenticated accounts from colleagues, your manager, parents or even older children of what you all did.
- Get into the habit of collecting such evidence at the time and explaining, as appropriate, your reasons for asking the cooperation of other people.
- Date pieces of material and make notes promptly, before the freshness wears away.

Using a range of resources

Tips for using written material

In your work, you will consult some books and articles. It takes some practice to get into the swing of how you use written material, whether a chapter in a book, a magazine or journal article or material you download from a website. Your college tutor or supervisor will help you in the details but here are some guidelines that you will need to bear in mind whatever the nature of your current assignment or project.

Ways of reading and noting material

It helps sometimes to read a chapter or article at least twice:

- First of all take a quick skim to see what is included in the content. Books and chapters that have headings are a great help here.
- Then read in more detail and either highlight key points by underlining or using a highlighter pen (if you own the book or the copy of the article) or make notes.
- In your written notes it can help to use your own underlining or bullet some main points that stand out for you.
- Use your notes to link to your own examples and observations and ensure that an original idea you have had is marked clearly as your own in your notes.
- Always write down the full reference of the book or article as part of your note taking: title, author and date.

- It will be much easier if you get into the habit of making this note at the time. It is much harder, and very frustrating, to have to chase up a proper reference later, when you have read many other sources and have only a vague memory of where you obtained a particular example, quotation or ideas. The other important reason for making this note is to avoid plagiarism (see below).

Acknowledge original material

You are responsible for avoiding plagiarism, meaning the direct copying of the work of another person, either published writers or a fellow student. You might understand very well that copying a fellow student is a form of cheating. But inexperienced students can slip into plagiarism if they do not attend.

When you draw ideas from a published book or article, you must always acknowledge the source of those ideas. Plagiarism does not only involve copying word for word. It is also judged unacceptable and a form of written deceit if students, or any other writer, has taken ideas, a reasoned argument or examples from someone else and has changed them so little that they are recognisable. Perhaps you only change a word or two or simply re-order a list of points.

You can avoid this pitfall by observing the following tips:

- Ensure that you always clearly head any personal notes you make with a clear and full reference to what you are reading at the time.
- Sometimes you will have a good idea that emerges from what you have read. Then mark that up clearly in your notes. You certainly do not want to acknowledge someone else as the origin of your idea when it was a result of your own creativity!
- Give a clear reference when you quote from a written source of any kind or you paraphrase, that is you put ideas into your own words but the origins are still those of another writer.

It is acceptable to use quotations from books and articles but:

- You must fully reference the source of the quotation.
- Choose your quotations with care since they have to do a job in your work. Why have you chosen this section, what does it add to your assignment or this part of your portfolio? The answers to these questions should be clear from how you introduce the quotation or refer to it afterwards.

You should have a list at the end of your assignment of all the books or articles from which you have directly drawn ideas or given quotations within your work. This list should be properly organised and placed at the end of your written work, but before any appendices. You would not usually add books or articles that had not directly supported this assignment.

Proper references

There are correct ways to refer to books, writers and ideas within your assignments. There are some choices and your tutor or supervisor will help you on this decision. This course may have a handbook that explains these details or the college or assessment centre may have a general handbook to assist you in study and writing skills.

Useful magazines

You will often find practical articles in magazines written for early years practitioners. Many of the magazines listed below also have a news and information page and can be very helpful for keeping you up to date with national developments relevant to your profession.

I find the following publications especially helpful. You will find some of them in the early years settings where you work or are on placement. Others should be available in the library of a college or assessment centre. The magazine websites, where they are available, will tell you something about the publication and some make previous features available to subscribers using a personal number.

You will not want to buy all these out of your own funds. But if you find a magazine regularly useful, then it will be worth the money. You can keep articles and ideas in your own file rather than having to share them with colleagues. Not all the magazines are available over the counter at newsagents; some are only available on subscription whereby you receive each issue through the post. Some organisations offer a special student rate for subscriptions. Where you want to buy a weekly magazine, it is usually cheaper to take out a subscription than to buy each issue over the counter.

- *Nursery World* is a source of articles, topic booklets and news. They have regular supplements. *The Professional Nanny*, *Training*, *Nursery Chains*, *Nursery Equipment, Nursery Computing*. Available from newsagents or on subscription tel: 01454 642480 *www.nursery-world.com*
- *Nursery Education* had a wide range of practical features and inserts. Published by Scholastic, available from newsagents or on subscription tel: 01926 816250 *www.scholastic.co.uk*
- *Practical Pre-School* has news, features and a wide range of practice inserts that can be collected in a ring builder format. Published by Step Forward Publishing, available on subscription tel: 01926 420046 *www.practicalpreschool.com* Step Forward Publishing is also a good source of topic and information books and booklets.
- The National Early Years Network journal *Co-ordinate* is sent to NEYN members but should be available in libraries. If you are searching in vain for a particular issue or feature try the Network tel: 020 7607 9573.
- *TES Primary* is more geared to primary school than nursery but will be useful for readers on placement or working in a primary school. Tel: 020 7782 3000 *www.tesprimary.com*

Getting used to the internet

If you are not yet confident working with computers and especially in accessing the internet, now is the time to tackle this area of competence. Increasingly, many useful organisations and government departments have websites, some reports are available to print directly off the website and some of the more useful search engines can help you track information. Whenever I have suggested a source that is on the internet, I give precise addresses, so you have directions and are not being directed to lengthy searches.

The dedicated website for this book is
www.thomsonlearning.co.uk/childcare/lindon

Information searches and advice

There are a considerable number of useful organisations for the early years practitioner and some of the main groups are listed in Appendix 2. You will make the best use of the resources offered by these organisations if you allow a little advance thought and planning.

- Consider in advance what you want to know or check. Some organisations (including those listed in other parts of the book) have a very broad remit, but others have a definite focus.
- Read the explanations given with the name of the organisation and you are more likely to contact those organisations that can best help you on this occasion. You will avoid wasting your time and that of the organisation.
- If you are able to use the website information, then you can find out about an organisation in advance. The website will sometimes give you what you need to know and the more extensive websites allow you to download updates, information and sometimes copies of leaflets.

All these organisations will be ready and keen to help early years practitioners, but they cannot be expected to field very broad queries.

- If your query relates to a project or assignment, then make sure you have done some planning about the content before you start contacting organisations. It is your responsibility to organise your thoughts.
- Think a bit about what you want to know. Be ready with the query you want to ask over the telephone. Draft some definite questions or a reasonably narrow focus in a letter or email, or in your own notes before you pick up the telephone.
- The same guideline applies if you write to magazines or individuals (perhaps whom you met through a workshop).

Check out some practical details:

- Some organisations have library and information services where you can visit. Always call for an appointment, since most will have limited sitting space.
- Use of some library services is free, but not all. Ask before you arrive.
- Always check on the cost of any publications. Some will be free, but many will cost something.
- Some organisations will be happy to supply free leaflets but will appreciate your sending a stamped self-addressed envelope.

Continued professional development

Responsible early years practitioners, as in any profession, remain open to learning as part of their continued professional development. Children and families are poorly served by any sense of 'I've done my training now, so that's it' or 'I've got twenty years' experience, don't tell me what to do'. It is important that everyone remains open to new information, ideas and practice.

You are not expected to know everything, no matter how experienced you are. Indeed, one of the advantages of feeling more experienced can be that you feel more able to say, 'I'm not sure about the answer to that, but I know how to find out'. In many of the topics covered in this book you will find suggestions for further reading, useful organisations and information for website research.

There is a considerable amount of information and advice in this book. On any topic, I have given what is, to the best of my knowledge, the most up to date information or the contrasting views when there is no clear agreement. I am especially aware that on health and medical conditions, I have summarised relatively briefly areas of concern about which entire books can be written. It is your responsibility as an early years practitioner, early years advisor or college tutor to pursue some of the suggestions about further resources, particularly when a child's health and well being may be at risk.

Finding out more

Your college may have a study skills handbook. If so, read it in detail and take notice of what you are directed to do and how.

Two books may also be helpful for developing your study and organisational skills. The first book is more appropriate if you are at the beginning of your career or learning to be a student. The second book supports study at a more academic level:

- Mitchell, Alison (2001) *Study Skills for Early Years Students* Hodder and Stoughton.
- Cottrell, Sheila (1999) *The Study Skills Handbook* Palgrave Study Guides.

Appendix 2

Useful organisations

Some organisations are of relevance to the whole of the UK, whereas some are more applicable to one of the four countries that comprise the UK. The first set of organisations are of general interest.

Advisory Centre for Education (ACE), 1c Aberdeen Studios, 22–24 Highbury Grove, London N5 2DQ tel: general 020 7354 8321 advice line (2–5 p.m.) 0808 8005793 email: *ace-ed@easynet.co.uk* website: *www.ace-ed.org.uk*

Advice and information on the state education system and a range of publications suitable for parents and practitioners.

Children's Legal Centre, University of Essex, Wivenhoe Park, Colchester, Essex CO4 3SQ tel: 01206 873820 email: *clc@essex.ac.uk* website: *www.childrenslegalcentre.com*

Publications and information about the legal position of children on a wide range of issues. Good for the legal situation as it affects the UK as a whole and England in particular.

Children's Play Council, 8 Wakley Street, London EC1V 7QE tel: 020 7843 6016 email: *cpc@ncb.org.uk* website: *www.ncb.org.uk/cpc.htm*

Brings together national voluntary organisations who are working to promote children's play.

Children's Play Information Service (CPIS), 8 Wakley Street, London EC1V 7QE tel: 020 7843 6303 email: *CPIS@ncb.org.uk* website: *www.ncb.org.uk/info.htm*

The CPIS provides a library and information service on all aspects of play and playwork. You can visit the library by appointment or make enquiries about books or research by telephone, letter or email.

Daycare Trust, 21 St George's Road, London SE1 6ES tel: 020 7840 3350 email: *info@daycaretrust.org.uk* website: *www.daycaretrust.org.uk*

Provides information for practitioners and parents and a consultancy service for local authorities and organisations, promoting quality in child care services.

Early Years Trainers Anti-Racist Network (EYTARN), PO Box 28, Wallasey L45 9NP tel and fax: 0151 639 1778 email: *eytarn@lineone.net*

Produces booklets, some posters and other illustrations, and runs training workshops and conferences.

Early Education, 136 Cavell Street, London E1 2JA tel: 020 7539 5400 website: *www.early-education.org.uk*

An organisation concerned about all aspects of young children's learning, with a particular focus on early educational settings. Promotes good practice in early years work. Offers advice and information, publications, conferences and the journal *Early Education*.

Kids' Clubs Network, Bellerive House, 3 Muirfield Crescent, London E14 9SZ tel: 020 7512 2112 email: *info.office@kidsclubs.co.uk* website: *www.kidsclubs.com*

Promotes after school and holiday playschemes for children. Offers consultancy and advice on services for 5–15 year olds.

National Childminding Association (NCMA), 8 Masons Hill, Bromley, Kent BR2 9EY tel: 020 8464 6164 email: *info@ncma.org.uk* website: *www.ncma.org.uk*

Supports childminders in England and Wales and promotes the childminding service in the UK.

National Children's Bureau, 8 Wakley Street, London EC1V 7QE tel: 020 7843 6000 website: *www.ncb.org.uk*

The NCB publishes books, reading lists, the journal *Children UK* and the *Highlight* series. The valuable resource collection that used to be in the Early Childhood Unit is now in the main library. The website has pages dedicated to the individual units that form part of the NCB.

National Day Nurseries Association (NDNA), Oak House, Woodvale Road, Brighouse, West Yorkshire HD6 4AB tel: 01484 541641 email: *ndna@btinternet.com* website: *www.ndna.org.uk*

The NDNA provides a national organisation, support and advice for day nurseries and centres, most of which are private nurseries and chains, that are not funded by local authorities.

National Early Years Network, 77 Holloway Road, London N7 8JZ Tel: 020 7607 9573 email: *info@neyn.org.uk*

A wide range of publications about early years practice, the journal *Co-ordinate* and some posters.

NSPCC (National Society for the Prevention of Cruelty to Children), 42 Curtain Road, London EC2A 3NH tel: 020 7825 2500 email: *mbishop@nspcc.org.uk* website: *www.nspcc.org.uk*

A national organisation that works to protect children and promote their welfare. Local branches are likely to work closely with the local authority Child Protection Team.

Playgroup Network, PO Box 84, Middlesborough TS7 0XT tel: 0191 230 5520 website: *www.playgroup-network.org.uk*

Playgroup Network provides a national umbrella organisation to support local groups.

Pre-school Learning Alliance, National Centre, 69 Kings Cross Road, London WC1X 9LL tel: 020 7833 0991 email: *pre-school.mh@plas-tek.co.uk* website: *www.pre-school.org.uk*

Promotes quality care and education for under fives, with a focus on pre-schools. Publications and posters are available from PPA Promotion, 45–49 Union Road, Croydon CR0 2XU tel: 020 8684 9542.

Save the Children, 17 Grove Lane, London SE5 8RD tel: 020 7703 5400 email: *enquiries@savethechildren.org.uk* website: *www.savethechildren.org.uk*

A national organisation committed to children and their welfare. Supports a wide range of projects and other units. For instance, *Save the Children Centre for Young Children's Rights*, 365 Holloway Road, London N7 6PA tel: 020 7700 8127.

Working Group Against Racism in Children's Resources (WGARCR), Unit 63a Eurolink Business Centre, 49 Effra Road, London SW2 1BZ tel: 020 7501 9992 email: *wgarc.r@virgin.net*

If you work in Wales

Children in Wales (Plant yng Nghymru), 25 Windsor Place, Cardiff CF10 3BZ tel: 029 2034 2434 email: *ciw@globalnet.co.uk* website: *www.childreninwales.org.uk*

Works with organisations and professionals working with children and their families in Wales.

Wales Pre-School Playgroups Association, Ladywell House, Newtown, Powys SY16 1JB tel: 01686 624573.

Supports the playgroup movement in Wales.

If you work in Scotland

Children in Scotland (Clann An Alba), Princes House, 5 Shandwick Place, Edinburgh, EH2 4RG tel: 0131 228 8484 email: *info@childreninscotland.org.uk* website: *www.childreninscotland.org.uk*

Brings together statutory and voluntary organisations and professionals working with children and their families in Scotland.

Play Scotland, Cramond Campus, Edinburgh EH4 6JD tel: 0131 312 80880.

A focus on play and playwork in Scotland.

Scottish Childminding Association, Suite 3, 7 Melville Terrace, Stirling FK8 2ND tel: 01786 445377 email: *info@ childminding.org* website: *www.childminding.org*

Supports childminders in Scotland.

Scottish Independent Nurseries Association (SINA), Unit 3, West Building, Rosemont Workspace, 141–147 Charles Street, Glasgow G21 2QA tel: 0141 553 1099.

The organisation for independent nurseries in Scotland.

Scottish Out-of-School Care Network (SOSCN), Floor 6, Fleming House, 134 Renfrew Street, Glasgow G3 6ST tel: 0141 331 1301 website: *www.soscn.org*

Scottish Pre-School Play Association (SPPA), 14 Elliot Place, Glasgow G3 8EP tel: 0141 221 4148.

If you work in Northern Ireland

NIPPA – the Early Years Organisation, 6c Wildflower Way, Apollo Road, Belfast BT12 6TA Tel: 028 90 662825 email: *mail@nippa.org* website: *www.nippa.org*

NIPPA works with early years practitioners and services in Northern Ireland.

Northern Ireland Childminding Association, 16–18 Mill Street, Newtownards, Co Down BT23 4LU tel: 028 91 811015 website: *www.nicma.org*

Focus on childminding in Northern Ireland.

Finding a wide range of play resources and books

Even if you live in a well resourced urban area, you will not necessarily find that your local book or toy store is well equipped for the needs of early years practitioners. Even in ethnically very diverse areas, shelves of books and toys do not necessarily reflect the local neighbourhood, let alone society at large. So a good source of materials will often be through mail order firms.

The following organisations are useful for a wide range of materials, a good list of early years books, children's books or some combination of all of these. Most organisations will have a catalogue that they will be happy to send you, mostly without charge (but check).

Children's Bookshop, HMP Books Ltd, 29 Fortis Green Road, London N10 3HP tel: 020 8444 5500.

A wide range of good books for children of all ages. No catalogue, but they will suggest titles if you explain what kind of books you want.

Development Education Centre, 998 Bristol Road, Selly Oak, Birmingham B29 6LE tel: 0121 472 3255 email: *info@idec.org.uk*

Booklets and photo packs on different aspects of development education, families around the world and varied cultures.

Save the Children, 17 Grove Lane, London SE5 8RD tel: 020 7703 5400 email: *enquiries@savethechildren.org.uk* website: *www.savethechildren.org.uk*

Publications and research projects concerned with services for and policy for children. Booklets, photo packs and other visual materials.

Community Insight, The Pembroke Centre, Cheney Manor, Swindon SN2 2PQ tel: 01793 512612 email: *books@c-insight.demon.co.uk* website: *www.c-insight.demon.co.uk*

Mail order company specialising in publications about children and a range of books for children.

Galt Educational and Pre School, Culvert Street, Oldham, Lancashire OL4 2GE tel: 0870 2424477 email: *enquiries@galt-educational.co.uk* website: *www.galt-educational.co.uk*

A wide range of play materials and equipment.

Learning Design Ltd, Ground Floor South, Limehouse Court, 3–11 Dod Street, London E14 7EQ tel: 020 7093 4051 email: *info@learningdesign.biz* website: *www.learningdesign.biz*

Dual language books and information books about children from a range of cultural backgrounds.

Letterbox Library, 71 Allen Road, London N16 8RY tel: 020 7503 4801 email: *info@letterboxlibrary.com* website: *www.letterboxlibrary.com*

Mail order children's books, specialising in a non-sexist and multicultural list. Dual language books and posters.

Little Tiger Press, 1 The Coda Centre, 189 Munster Road, London SW6 6AW tel: 020 7385 6333 email: *info@littletiger.co.uk*

Publishes children's books in different languages and some dual language books.

Mantra Publishing, 5 Alexandra Grove, London N12 8NU tel: 020 8445 5123 website: *www.mantrapublishing.com*

A wide range of books in different languages, tape and story packs, song collections and posters.

Multilingual Matters, Frankfurt Lodge, Clevedon Hall, Victoria Street, Clevedon, Avon BS21 7SJ tel: 01275 876519 website: *www.multilingual-matters.com*

Books and journals about bilingualism and a newsletter for bilingual families.

NES Arnold, Findel House, Excelsior Road, Ashby Park, Ashby-de-la-Zouch, Leicestershire, LE65 1NG tel: 0845 120 4525 email: *enquiries@nesarnold.co.uk* website: *www.nesarnold.co.uk*

Dressing-up clothes, dolls reflecting different ethnic groups, dolls with visible disabilities, posters and display cards and other play materials.

Pre-school Learning Alliance through PPA Promotion, 45–49 Union Road, Croydon CR0 2XU tel: 020 8684 9542 email: *pre-school.mh@plas.tek.co.uk* website: *www.pre-school.org.uk*

For a wide range of publications and visual materials.

RDS, 8 Merton Road, London E17 9DE tel: 020 8521 6969 website: *www.rdsbooks.com*

Dual language storybooks, dictionaries and cassettes.

Step Forward Publishing, The Coach House, Cross Road, Leamington Spa CV32 5PB tel: 01926 420046 email: *enquiries@practicalpreschool.com* website: *practicalpreschool.com*

A wide range of practical books and booklets, also the magazine *Practical Pre-School*.

Tamarind Ltd, PO Box 52, Northwood, Middlesex HA6 1UN tel: 020 8866 8808 email: *info@tamarindbooks.co.uk* website: www. *tamarindbooks.co.uk*

A wide range of fiction, puzzles and posters that show children of different ethnic backgrounds, disabled children and books with non-sexist themes.

Glossary

This is an alphabetical list of all the key terms that are defined in the chapters of this book.

active birth movement: an approach emphasising that women in labour should be enabled to move and to take up different positions for managing contractions and the birth itself

adoption: a legal process through which one or two adults take full responsibility for children whose own families cannot care for them and who then commit to raise the children

adult-initiated activities: those experiences offered by adults which can then be shaped by children's interest and choices

aggressive approach: using fierce words and/or actions to insist on your own views or preferences and to minimise those of others

altruism: a pattern of behaviour that shows a selfless concern for the well being of others

anaphylaxis: a severe and sudden allergic reaction to foods or other substances, that can be fatal without a swift injection of adrenaline or other appropriate medication

anti-bias curriculum: a framework of activities, play materials and experiences that avoid stereotypes and actively promote understanding and knowledge of all the groups within society

anti-discriminatory practice: an active attempt to promote positive attitudes and behaviour and to challenge and change negative outlooks and actions, on the basis of any group identity

articulation: how children say the sound system that makes up the words in their language

assertiveness: confident expression of your own views and preferences while allowing space for the views and choices of others

assessment: a rounded approach to determine what children can manage in defined areas of development

attachment: a positive emotional link between babies, young children and their parents or other key carers

authoritative role: a pattern of behaviour from adults that combines emotional warmth with responsible boundary setting

babbling: the early sound making, often very tuneful, of babies who are stringing together a series of sounds in a deliberate way

baby blues: the term describing a temporary low state for mothers in the first few days after birth

behaviourism: a theoretical approach that emphasises how human behaviour responds to patterns of reward and punishment. The approach is also called *learning theory*. *Social learning theory* recognises the importance of feelings and thinking on actions

bilingual children: children who are able to, or are in the process, of learning two or more languages

biological approach: theories that focus on the importance of genetic programming to explain child development or adult behaviour

birth parents: the biological mother and father of a child

body language: ways of communicating that use gestures, facial expression and body posture

bonding: the term often used to mean the very earliest attachment soon after birth

challenging behaviour: a pattern of behaviour from a child that is especially hard to handle and does not instantly respond to the usual positive strategies

checklist or **tick list:** record layout in which it is possible to check or tick individual items relevant to children's development or behaviour

child abuse: a pattern of ill-treatment of a child or persistent failure to provide appropriate protection and care for children

child-centred (or **child-oriented**) **approach:** a perspective that aims to place children's interests and focus central to all aspects of childcare and learning

child-initiated activities: those experiences suggested or started by children themselves

child protection: preventative systems and direct action to ensure the well being of children and young people and to take direct action to ensure their future health and development

circle time: a carefully planned small group time to explore issues and ideas with children in a supportive way

cognitive development: the area of children's learning that focuses on their ability to think, gain knowledge, develop ideas and reason in a logical way

cognitive (or **cognitive developmental**) **theory:** theories that focus on how children think and make sense of their world

complaints procedure: process for parents and other users of the setting to lodge a formal complaint about any aspect of the setting and the actions of the team

comprehension or **receptive language:** children's understanding of what is said to them. Young children show through their behaviour that they have grasped words, in context, that they do not yet say

conflict resolution: the skills to address and try to resolve disagreements without verbal or physical argument

congenital causes of disability: pre-birth conditions lead to a disability or health condition, so that the baby is born with this condition

consequences: see *using consequences*

conservation: the idea that objects continue to have the same quality such as number or volume even when they are moved to look different

constructive feedback: positive approaches to communication in order to enable others to learn from their actions, choice of approach and decisions

continued professional development: active efforts to extend and update your own knowledge and skills in your area of work

culture: a distinctive way of life that is shared within one group and makes a clear distinction between this group and others

curriculum: a framework for supporting learning that specifies broad areas of learning and approaches to promote children's learning of knowledge and skills. A curriculum may describe precise content and methods to support learning

curriculum vitae (CV): summary of your qualifications, experience and professional career

deductive reasoning: a process of thinking logically from a general rule or principle to predict a particular event

developmental milestones: observable achievements for children in the different areas of their development throughout childhood

developmental profile: record sheet for tracking children's progress in development and behaviour

disciplinary procedure: steps to deal with unacceptable behaviour from a member of the team in a setting

disclosure: communication by children's words or actions when they share an experience of abuse or neglect, or their fears that relate to potential abuse

discrimination: when any kind of behaviour is more or less favourable to other people on the basis of their group identity. *Direct discrimination* is when somebody deliberately acts so as to favour or disadvantage members of given groups. *Indirect discrimination* occurs when the actions of a person or organisation result in more or less favourable treatment by group identity, even if this consequence was not deliberately intended

disembedded thinking: when children are required to deal with ideas without a clear or familiar context with which to connect

domestic violence: verbal and physical aggression, threats or attack made by family members of either sex within the home

early literacy skills: a blend of fine physical skills, understanding and a positive outlook that supports children towards being able to read and write

Early Years Action and **Early Years Action Plus:** two stages of special support for children with disabilities in early years settings

early years curriculum: content and methods to support learning that are directly appropriate to children younger than five or six years of age

ecological approach: theory that focuses on children's development within their social environment

egocentricism: the quality that Piaget claimed was typical of younger children, that they were unable to envisage a situation from the perspective of other people, what the other person could see or what they felt

embryo: the term used to describe a baby in the first eight weeks after conception

emergent writing: children's first attempts to make meaningful marks that they relate to the writing they see around them

emotion coaching: supportive adult conversation and behaviour that supports children towards learning emotional literacy

emotional abuse: a persistent pattern of verbal cruelty to children or young people such that they feel unworthy and unloved
emotional literacy: the ability to recognise and understand our own emotions and those of others
empathy: the ability and willingness to tune into the feelings of other people
encouragement: positive feedback by words and expression, as much for effort as for achievement
equal opportunities: the daily practice to ensure that all children are enabled to have positive experiences, to use the resources of a setting fully and see that action is taken if children's opportunities are blocked
event sampling: a technique in which observations are made of specific events or types of behaviour, defined in advance of the observation
expressive language: see *speech*
extended family: the relatives in a family beyond mother and father
extension activities: possible additional activities in a plan that can be offered to children, if they wish to continue
extinction: when an action or pattern of actions ceases altogether

faltering growth: when babies and children do not put on weight and may also appear in poor health, for no obvious reason. The condition used to be called failure to thrive
fetus: the term used to describe a baby from eight weeks after conception to birth
fluency: how easily a child's speech flows. Some problems of fluency are a normal part of early language development
food allergies: when a child or adult becomes ill after eating particular foods or ingredients. The consequences of a food allergy may be mild through to very severe
foster carers: people who take temporary responsibility for children when their own family is unable to care for them
full term babies: when babies are born close to the usual gestation period of about 40 weeks

genetic causes of disability: when a child inherits a condition from the genes of their parent(s)
gestation: the development of the embryo and fetus over the months of a pregnancy
grievance procedure: process for a team member to lodge a complaint that she or he has been treated in an unacceptable way
guidance: government guidelines that are issued to explain how the details of laws should work in practice

heuristic play: an exploratory play resource for toddlers and young children, developed by Elinor Goldschmied and using a wide range of ordinary objects and recycled materials for children to play with as they choose
holistic: see *whole child*
holophrase: single words used flexibly by very young children, supported by tone and gesture to convey different meanings
home–school (or **home–setting) agreement:** a written description of the obligations and expectations of the school (or early years) team and parents. A representative of the setting and parent(s) would sign a copy
home schooling: when families educate their children within the family for part or all of their childhood

IEP: Individual Education Plan for children whose disabilities require special support and planning in early years or school settings
incentives: a promise of a reward in the future, as a result of particular behaviour or achievement
inclusive approach: a commitment to enable disabled children to join mainstream early years or school provision as far as possible and with necessary support
independence: the move in childhood toward children's being able to take responsibility for their own care and decisions
indirect discrimination: see *discrimination*
inductive reasoning: a process of thinking logically from direct observations and experience to reach a general principle
infant directed speech: the adjusted form of language used by adults and some older children to communicate with babies
informed consent: that adults and children are given sufficient information for them to make a decision about whether to agree to or decline involvement in an event or experience
interdependence: when the actions of one person have direct consequences for others in a team situation
internal speech: when children's talking to guide their actions or think goes silent or almost silent
ipsative approach to assessment: comparing a child with him/herself at a previous point in time

jargon: the very expressive flow of word-like sounds that many babies make around about their first birthday

key person: a named team member who has special responsibilities for working with a small number of named children and building a relationship with their parent(s). Also sometimes called *key worker* or *primary worker*

learning theory: see *behaviourism*
logical consequnces: see *using consequences*
lone parents: mothers or fathers who are raising their children on their own
looked after children: a descriptive of the status of children and young people who have become the responsibility of the local authority because their own families cannot take care of them on a temporary or permanent basis. The local authority assumes parental responsibility

maturation: a biologically determined pattern for the sequence of development for babies and children
medical model of disability: an approach to disabled children that focuses exclusively on diagnosis and medical management of the condition
miscarriage: the loss of a fetus before 24 weeks gestation within the pregnancy
mixed feeding: see *weaning*

natural childbirth: labour without medical intervention in which women manage the process by breathing techniques and movement
natural consequences: see *using consequences*
nature: the part of children's development that is shaped by heredity, what is inherited through the child's genes
neglect: the failure to care adequately for children or young people in order to ensure their continuing health and well being
non-verbal communication: ways of communicating without words by using body language and also the qualities of how something is said, such as tone, volume, fluency and pace
normative approach to assessment: comparing a child with developmental norms for her age or against expectations for all children, such as the early learning goals in the English curriculum
nurture: everything that happens to influence child development after birth
nurture group: carefully planned small group experience for children who are struggling with the emotional demands of primary school life

parental involvement: ways in which parents can be invited and choose to be directly involved in the activities or running of an early years setting or school
partnership with parents: the value and practice of working together with parents for the care and learning of their children, acknowledging the continuing importance of parents in the lives of their children
passive or **submissive approach:** reluctance to be honest about your own opinions or preferences and allowing others to make the choice
personal identity: children's perception of what makes them an individual uniquely different from other people
phonemes: the individual sounds that comprise a spoken language and that are written with combinations of letters from the alphabet
phonemic awareness: learning that spoken and written words are composed of individual sounds
phonological awareness: the understanding that spoken words are composed of separate syllables and sounds
physical abuse: non-accidental physical injury to a child or young person, caused either by direct attack or irresponsible actions highly likely to put a child in danger of injury
poetry pockets: containers with all the props to support a poem or rhyme, in order to encourage interest and involvement of children in poetry
positive disposition to learn: an enthusiasm felt by children about learning, supported by a positive self-image and sense of 'I can'
postnatal depression: a more serious and longer lasting condition when women feel unable to cope with their baby, are highly anxious and sometimes reject the baby
praise: positive feedback in words, usually for what has been done or achieved
pre-coded categories: a set of short descriptions, decided in advance for organising observation of types of behaviour or events
premature babies: when babies are born earlier than the usual gestation period, usually less than 37 weeks
primary carer: the parent who undertakes most of the daily care and responsibility for children
primary legislation: laws that have been passed and have to be obeyed as a legal obligation
professional: a description of behaviour and outlook appropriate to the responsibilities in a job or a work placement as a student
projectile vomiting: when a baby brings up milk or food with force. A sign of possible serious digestive problems needing medical attention
proprioception: the ability to recognise and use the physical sensations from the body that give feedback on balance and the position of our limbs

prosocial behaviour: a blend of actions and feelings that can be observed when children have learned empathy and altruism

prosody: the ability to use intonation patterns and emphasis to shift the meaning of a sentence with the same words

psychoanalytic tradition: theories that focus on how early conflicts and unconscious thoughts shape personality

punishment: an experience that decreases the likelihood that an action will be repeated in the future

receptive language: see *comprehension*

reflective practitioner: an outlook for early years, and other professionals, in which you are ready to think as well as to act and to be open to new ideas and approaches

reflex reactions: physical movement of newborn babies that are inborn. The reflexes are instinctive reactions and are not learned

reinforcement: an experience that increases the likelihood that an action will be repeated in the future

respite care: a service offering temporary care of children to families in order to give the parents a break from stressful childcare

reward: giving tangible items or special experiences as a result of behaviour or achievement

risk assessment: the process of checking the likely risks involved in an activity or an outing and sensible ways to address the risks

schemas: patterns of behaviour, mainly ways of physical exploration, in which young children learn about their environment

School Action and **School Action Plus:** two stages of special support for children with disabilities in school settings

self esteem: children's evaluation of their own self worth, including the relationship between what they feel they are, and can do and what they ought to be as a person and be able to do

self image: children's view of themselves, as a mix of positive and possibly negative characteristics

self reliance: an area of children's skills in which they become more able to use their own resources and knowledge to undertake their own care and make choices

SEN Code of Practice: the clear guidelines describing good practice for disabled children in early years and school settings

SENCO: the Special Educational Needs Co-ordinator responsible for liaison between the setting, parents and any outside agencies

sexual abuse: actual or likely sexual exploitation of a child or young person who has neither the age nor understanding to give their informed consent

sign language: a form of communication that uses agreed signs, made with fingers and hands, to convey words and concepts

simultaneous bilingual learning: when children learn two languages at the same time from a very young age

social cognition: children's ability and learning to merge their understanding of social behaviour with their powers of thinking and reasoning

social constructivist approach: emphasises how children and adults make sense and meaning of situations

social model of disability: an approach that focuses on disabled children as individuals and ways they can be disabled by social circumstances and attitudes

social skills: ways of behaving that enable children to get along in groups, to play and interact with other children

speech or expressive language: what children themselves say in words and later in phrases and sentences

statement of special educational needs: description for an individual child of his/her difficulties and needs for support in school

stepfamilies: families formed when one or both adults bring their children from a previous relationship into the new relationship. Stepparents will not be the biological parent of all the children in the family

stereotypes: simple, strongly held beliefs (positive or negative) about the characteristics shared by individuals in an identified group

stillbirth: the loss of a fetus after 24 weeks of gestation within a pregnancy

storysacks: large bags that include the props to support a particular story book and so to encourage interest and story telling for and with children

submissive approach: see *passive* or *submissive approach*

successive bilingual learning: when children who have a good grasp of their family language, subsequently learn a second language

sudden infant death syndrome (SIDS): the term that describes the unexpected death of a baby, that cannot be easily explained by specific illness or accident. Also known as *cot death*

symbolic rewards: giving something that represents praise for behaviour or other achievements, such as stickers or certificates

teamwork: actions and an outlook that enable individuals to work in a way that is consistent and supportive of each other and the values of the setting

temperament: inborn tendencies for individual children that shape their reactions and behaviour towards a more established adult personality

theories of child development: attempts to explain how and why the events of child development unfold. People who propose a particular theory try to go beyond a description of what happens in child development to a prediction of what might happen under certain conditions

time sampling: a technique in which observations are made on a regular rather than continuous basis

trauma (birth): unexpected events during childbirth that can create high risk to the future well being of the unborn baby, such as being deprived of oxygen

treasure basket: a play resource developed by Elinor Goldschmied for babies who can sit unassisted. The low basket contains a range of safe and interesting objects that are not conventional toys

using consequences: an alternative to punishment in guiding children's behaviour – *natural consequences* follow on as a highly likely result of a child's behaviour; *logical consequences* are adult-determined but relevant to the behaviour

weaning: when babies are introduced to first foods in addition to their milk diet, also sometimes called *mixed feeding*

whole child or **holistic approach:** a perspective on children's development stressing that children should not be viewed from just one part of their development and learning; they should be treated as entire individuals

zone of proximal development: the area of possibilities between what individual children can manage on their own and what they could achieve with appropriate help

Index